THE ANALYSIS AND USE OF FINANCIAL STATEMENTS

Third Edition

Gerald I. White, CFA
Grace & White, Inc.

Ashwinpaul C. Sondhi, Ph.D.
A. C. Sondhi & Associates, LLC

Dov Fried, Ph.D.
Stern School of Business
New York University

WILEY

To Penny, Jean, Rachel, and Our Families and Friends

CFA® Examination questions are reprinted by permission of AIMR. Copyright 1986–2001.
Association for Investment Management and Research, Charlottesville, VA. All rights reserved.

First awarded in 1963, the CFA© charter has become known as the designation of professional excellence within the global investment community. Around the world, employers and investors recognize the CFA© designation as the definitive standard for measuring competence and integrity in the fields of portfolio management and investment analysis.

   For more information on the CFA© Program, administered by AIMR, you can visit *www.aimr.org/cfaprogram*.

Acquisitions Editor   Mark Bonadeo
Marketing Manager   Keari Bedford
Senior Production Editor   Patricia McFadden
Senior Designer   Dawn Stanley
Cover Photo © M. L. Sinibaldi/Corbis Stock Market

This book was set in 10/12 Times New Roman by UG / GGS Information Services, Inc. and printed and bound by Courier/Westford. The cover was printed by Lehigh Press.

This book is printed on acid free paper.   ∞

ISBN 0-471-37594-2

Printed in the United States of America

10 9 8 7 6 5 4 3

PREFACE

The objective of this book is the presentation of financial statement analysis from the point of view of the primary users of financial statements: equity and credit analysts. The analysis and use of financial statements is not restricted to analysts, however. Managers, auditors, educators, and regulators can also benefit from the insights and analytic techniques presented in this text.

Corporate managers, and those training to be managers, require an understanding of how financial statements provide information regarding an enterprise. This book is intended for use as a university level textbook for MBA and advanced undergraduate financial statement analysis courses. In addition, it should help equip businesspeople to prepare, audit, or interpret financial information. Finally, the text is designed to be a useful reference for both neophytes and informed readers.

WHO SHOULD READ THIS BOOK?

We believe that our work will be valuable to numerous audiences. First, it will benefit the working financial analyst. Some of the areas covered (off balance sheet financing and hedging techniques, for example) are rarely covered either in the professional literature or in accounting textbooks. While many analysts are familiar with some of the techniques in this book, we believe that even the most experienced analyst will find fresh insights on financial reporting issues.

Financial analysis, in some cases, is nothing more than journalism. Analysts accept the financial statements and what management tells them at face value. Good analysis is hampered by the inadequacies of published financial data. Many analysts examine the trend of reporting earnings but are unable to go "behind the numbers" or beyond them. The analysis taught in most textbooks starts and ends with reported financial statements or computerized databases.

Our view is that good financial analysis requires the analyst to understand how financial statements are generated in order to *separate the economic process that generates the numbers from the accounting process that (sometimes) obscures it*. Such analysis requires the use of assumptions and approximations, as reported financial data are often inadequate. We may dislike the need to make assumptions, but most financial analysis depends on them. Good analysis also requires the recasting of reported data into other formats when the latter yield superior insights.

However, we do not believe that there are always simple solutions to analytic problems. There is, for example, no precisely correct or "optimal" leverage ratio; there are many possible ratios, depending on the goals of the analysis and the judgement of the analyst. Our view is that asking the right questions is more than half the battle. This text asks many questions, and suggests some answers.

Previous financial analysis books have been written from an academic point of view, stressing either an accounting or an empirical (data analysis) approach. While both financial accounting and empirical analysis are present in this text, they are integrated with, and subordinated to, user oriented analysis. They are subjected to the test or relevance: how do they aid in the interpretation of financial statement data?

Most of the analysis presented is based on the financial statements of actual companies. While such analysis can be frustrating (due to inadequate data), we believe that financial analysis can be presented best in a real world setting. While "models" are sometimes required for exposition purposes (such as for the analysis of foreign operations), the principles learned are always applied to real company statements.

The end-of-chapter materials (all problems and solutions were written by the authors) are also largely based on real corporate data. Some problems are adapted from the Chartered Financial Analyst examination program. Readers and students need to apply the text material to actual financial statements and the problems are designed to test their ability to do so.

The past few years have seen a resurgence of interest in accounting and financial statement analysis. The bursting of the market bubble produced evidence that some preparers had used accounting methods that pushed the limits of acceptable financial reporting, and that many financial analysts used reported financial data to make valuation judgments despite evidence of those excesses.

We believe that the readers of the earlier editions of this text were better prepared to recognize the risks inherent in financial reporting and to make the analytical adjustments required to avoid many of the pitfalls resulting from overly aggressive accounting methods.[1] We have done our best to incorporate the lessons of the past few years in the third edition. However, both accounting and financial analysis continue to evolve and new issues will emerge. Our goal, therefore, is to encourage the analyst to think critically about reported data rather than blindly accepting them for valuation purposes.

ORGANIZATION AND CONTENT

A few comments on the organization and content of the book may be helpful to both reader and instructor. As already stated, we have integrated accounting, economic theory, and empirical research into a financial analysis framework. In doing so, we realize that some topics may be more important to some readers than to others. For that reason some advanced material (e.g., the Analysis of Oil and Gas Disclosures in Chapter 7) appears in appendices. Within chapters, we have organized some material into boxes that are available to interested readers without distracting those who are not.

As the globalization of financial markets continues apace, we include discussions and comparisons of relevant foreign and international (IASB) accounting standards throughout the text. Some of this material is in separate "international" sections but much of it is integrated. As the comparative analysis of companies using different accounting standards is an increasingly common concern, our goal is to help the user who must make an investment decision despite the lack of comparability. In some chapters, non-U.S. companies are used to illustrate international accounting differences. Non-U.S. companies are also used extensively in the cases and problem sections.

The first five chapters introduce the essential elements of financial statement analysis. Chapter 1 provides the framework, including discussions of data sources and the roles of preparers, auditors, and standard setters in the financial reporting process.

Chapter 2 describes the accrual method of accounting and its implications for financial reporting, leading to a discussion of the income statement and balance sheet. Chapter 3 describes the cash flow statement and cash flow analysis. Chapter 4 presents ratio analysis, suggesting both its advantages and its limits. Chapter 5 reviews empirical research, emphasizing its implications for financial analysis.

Chapters 6 to 15 focus on specific areas of analysis, ranging from inventories to multinational corporations. Throughout these chapters our goal is to show how differences in accounting methods and estimates affect reported financial condition, results of operations

---

[1] For example, Case 16-1 in the second edition used the 1995 financial statements of Enron to raise questions about their risk-management activities.

(including cash flows), and ratios. In many cases, analytic techniques are used to restore comparability, enhancing the decision usefulness of financial data. Each chapter includes a discussion of international accounting differences and relevant empirical research findings.

Chapter 6 considers the analysis of inventories, where differing methods have far-reaching effects on financial data. Chapter 7 (Long-Lived Assets) addresses the capitalization versus expensing decision, which has pervasive effects on reported financial statements. Chapter 8 considers differing methods of allocating capitalized costs to operations and the thorny topics of impairment and restructuring. Chapter 9 concerns income tax accounting, and focuses on the information content of income tax disclosures.

Chapter 10, the first of a series on long-term liabilities, provides an analysis of varying forms of debt. Chapter 11 turns to off-balance-sheet financing techniques, with particular emphasis on leases. Chapter 12 considers pension and other employee benefits (including stock options).

The next three chapters focus on problems resulting from the combination of more than one enterprise. Chapter 13 considers the cost, mark-to-market, equity method, and consolidation issues resulting form intercorporate investments, including joint ventures. Chapter 14 presents the alternative methods of accounting for business combinations, as well as the analysis of leveraged buyout firms (LBOs) and spinoffs. Chapter 15 describes the impact of changing exchange rates on multinational firms and suggests how available data can be used to separate exchange rate and accounting effects from operating results.

Chapter 16 examines risk management activities (including hedging), an area of inconsistent accounting standards and incomplete disclosures.

Chapters 17 through 19 pull together all previous text material. Chapter 17 shows how to use financial statement disclosures to prepare current cost balance sheets and to normalize reported income and cash flows. Such recast data, we believe, provide superior inputs for investment decisions. Chapter 18 demonstrates how financial data can be used to assess different forms of risk. Chapter 19 presents a variety of valuation models, and relates their use to the material covered earlier in the text. It also considers forecasting models for which financial data constitute the input. Chapter 19 concludes with a section on financial statement forecasts.

Changes in Third Edition

This edition has been substantially rewritten. There is also a major organizational change. The book is accompanied by a CD containing all appendices, cases, and the financial statements of eight companies used to illustrate the analysis. This material is also located at a Web site to which all who purchase the text will have access. The icon adjacent to this paragraph will be placed in the text when reference to the CD/Web site is required.

There were two reasons for this organizational change. First, we wanted to be able to use a larger number of companies in this edition. The eight firms chosen include four that are located outside the United States. Three of these companies use non–U.S. accounting principles (one IAS, one Swedish, one Japanese). Three of the eight firms are drug companies, and three are forest product companies.[2] The choices allow the text to compare firms within a single industry using different accounting methods and to illustrate a variety of accounting differences and analytical techniques.

The second reason follows from the first. The second edition exceeded 1200 pages (including the financial statements of three companies) and the expansion of our financial statement group to eight would have made the third edition impossibly large. Moving the ancillary material to a CD and Web site enabled us to greatly reduce the text size while expanding the number of financial statements.

The Web site will also be a means of communicating with our readers. We will post updates for new FASB and IASB standards on the Web site as well as errata.

---

[2] We had intended to include two technology companies within our corporate set, but those firms refused permission to reprint their financial statements. However, the text has many illustrations of technology company financial reporting and analysis.

The third edition also includes the following changes:

1. We have increased our focus on U.S. GAAP and IASB GAAP given the increasing use of International Standards and the expectation that they will gradually replace virtually all non-U.S. standards. In every chapter we explain both sets of standards and the most significant differences between them, providing illustrations when appropriate.

2. We have updated the text to reflect all FASB and IASB standards issued through June 2002, discussing proposed standards as well. New standards resulted in major revisions to Chapters 12 (pensions), 14 (mergers and acquisitions), and 16 (derivatives). Discussions of empirical research have also been updated for recent publications.

3. Chapter 2 contains additional material on revenue and expense recognition, using illustrations from technology and nontechnology firms.

4. Chapter 19 has a new section on financial statement forecasting.

5. We distinguish real companies used in examples and problems by placing the ticker symbol (primary market as reported on the Bloomberg© system) in brackets (e.g., [IBM]) following the name. This convention is not followed for the companies whose financial statements are on the CD/Website.

ACKNOWLEDGMENTS

We acknowledge the help of our many teachers, mentors, colleagues, and friends throughout our respective careers. In particular we thank the late Oliver R. Grace, as well as Professors Michael Schiff, George Sorter, Joshua Livnat, and Sanford C. Gunn, and Raj Malhotra.

The first and second editions were reviewed by a number of colleagues, friends, students, and outside reviewers. We appreciate their valuable insights, constructive criticisms, and encouragement. The contribution of Eric Press (Temple University), the main reviewer for the second edition, deserves special recognition.

We accept full responsibility for any errors. We welcome comments and corrections, which can be directed to us through the Wiley Web site.

GERALD I. WHITE
ASHWINPAUL C. SONDHI
DOV FRIED

August 2002

CONTENTS

Appendices and Cases are located in the Wiley web site (wiley.com) and on the CD.

1

FRAMEWORK FOR FINANCIAL STATEMENT ANALYSIS

CHAPTER OUTLINE

CHAPTER OBJECTIVES

The goals of this chapter are to:

1. Explain why financial statement analysis is needed.
2. Discuss the general principles of the financial reporting system.
3. Compare the roles of the Financial Accounting Standards Board and the Securities and Exchange Commission in setting U.S. GAAP.
4. Review the elements of the FASB's conceptual framework.
5. Discuss the progress in setting global accounting standards and the role of the International Accounting Standards Board.
6. Briefly describe the principal financial statements: Balance Sheet, Income Statement, Statement of

1

Comprehensive Income, Statement of Cash Flows, and Statement of Stockholders' Equity.

7. Discuss the usefulness of financial statement footnotes and supplementary data.

8. Describe the usefulness of the Management Discussion and Analysis and other sources of financial information.

9. Discuss the role of the independent auditor and information conveyed by the audit opinion.

INTRODUCTION

Why are financial statements useful? Because they help investors and creditors make better economic decisions. The goal of this book is to enhance financial statement users' understanding of financial reporting in order to facilitate improved decision making. We will examine the impact of the differential application of accounting methods and estimates on financial statements, with particular emphasis on the effect of accounting choices on reported earnings, stockholders' equity, cash flow, and various measures of corporate performance (including, but not limited to, financial ratios). We will also stress the use of cash flow analysis to evaluate the financial health of an enterprise.

Financial statements are, at best, only an approximation of economic reality because of the selective reporting of economic events by the accounting system, compounded by alternative accounting methods and estimates. The tendency to delay accounting recognition of some transactions and valuation changes means that financial statements tend to lag behind reality as well.

This chapter provides a framework for the study of financial statement analysis. This framework consists of the users being served, the information system available to them, and the institutional structure within which they interact.

NEED FOR FINANCIAL STATEMENT ANALYSIS

The United States has the most complex financial reporting system in the world. Detailed accounting principles are augmented by extensive disclosure requirements. The financial statements of large multinationals add up to dozens of pages, and many of these firms voluntarily publish additional "fact books" for dissemination to financial analysts and other interested users.

Financial reporting in other major developed countries and many emerging markets has also evolved substantially in recent years, with an increasing emphasis on providing information useful to both domestic and foreign creditors and equity investors. International Accounting Standards have become a credible rival to U.S. standards.

In an ideal world, the user of financial statements could focus only on the bottom lines of financial reporting: net income and stockholders' equity. If financial statements were comparable among companies (regardless of country), consistent over time, and always fully reflecting the economic position of the firm, financial statement analysis would be simple, and this text a very short one.

The financial reporting system is not perfect. Economic events and accounting entries do not correspond precisely; they diverge across the dimensions of timing, recognition, and measurement. Financial analysis and investment decisions are further complicated by variations in accounting treatment among countries in each of these dimensions.

Economic events and accounting recognition of those events frequently take place at different times. One example of this phenomenon is the recognition of capital gains and losses only upon sale in most cases. Appreciation of a real estate investment, which took place over a period of many years, for example, receives income statement recognition only in the period management chooses for its disposal.[1]

---

[1] However, in countries (such as the United Kingdom) where periodic asset revaluation is permitted, balance sheet recognition of market value changes may occur much sooner.

Similarly, long-lived assets are written down, most of the time, in the fiscal period of management's choice. The period of recognition may be neither the period in which the impairment took place nor the period of sale or disposal. Accounting for discontinued operations, in the same manner, results in recognition of a loss in a period different from when the loss occurred or the disposal is consummated.[2]

In addition, many economic events do not receive accounting recognition at all. Most contracts, for example, are not reflected in financial statements when entered into, despite significant effects on financial condition and operating and financial risk. Some contracts, such as leases and hedging activities, are recognized in the financial statements by some companies but disclosed only in footnotes by others. Disclosure requirements for derivatives and hedging activities are in place in many jurisdictions, but recognition and measurement is only recently required[3] in the United States.

Further, generally accepted accounting principles (GAAP) in the United States and elsewhere permit economic events that do receive accounting recognition to be recognized in different ways by different financial statement preparers. Inventory and depreciation of fixed assets are only two of the significant areas where comparability may be lacking.

Financial reports often contain supplementary data that, although not included in the statements themselves, help the financial statement user to interpret the statements or adjust measures of corporate performance (such as financial ratios) to make them more comparable, consistent over time, and more representative of economic reality. When making adjustments to financial statements, we will seek to discern substance from form and exploit the information contained in footnotes and supplementary schedules of data in the annual report and SEC filings. The analytic treatment of "off-balance-sheet" financing activities is a good example of this process. We also illustrate the use of reconciliations to U.S. GAAP in foreign registrants' Form 20-F filings.

Finally, information from outside the financial reporting process can be used to make financial data more useful. Estimating the effects of changing prices on corporate performance, for example, may require the use of price data from outside sources.

FOCUS ON INVESTMENT DECISIONS

This book is concerned with the concepts and techniques of financial analysis employed by users of financial statements who are external to the company. Principal emphasis is on the financial statements of companies whose securities are publicly traded. The techniques described are generally applicable to the analysis of financial statements prepared according to U.S. GAAP. However, we will also discuss the pronouncements of the International Accounting Standards Board (IASB) and standard setters in other countries, compare them to U.S. GAAP, and analyze financial statements prepared in accordance with these other reporting standards.

The common characteristic of external users is their general lack of authority to prescribe the information they want from an enterprise. They depend on general-purpose external financial reports provided by management. The Financial Accounting Standards Board (FASB) in its Statement of Financial Accounting Concepts (SFAC) 1, Objectives of Financial Reporting by Business Enterprises, aptly describes the objectives of these external users:

Information Useful in Investment and Credit Decisions

Financial reporting should provide information that is useful to present and potential investors and creditors and other users in making rational investment, credit, and similar decisions. The information should be comprehensible to those who have a reasonable understanding of business and economic activities and are willing to study the information with reasonable diligence.[4]

---

[2]In the United States, Statement of Financial Accounting Standards (SFAS) No. 121, Accounting for the Impairment of Long-Lived Assets and for Long-Lived Assets to Be Disposed of, as amended by SFAS No. 144, Accounting for the Impairment or Disposal of Long-Lived Assets, constrains but does not eliminate management control over the timing of recognition and the measurement of impairments. In most foreign countries there are few, if any, guidelines governing the accounting for impaired assets.

[3]SFAS 133, Accounting for Derivative Instruments and Hedging Activities, became effective in 2000 (Chapter 16).

[4]SFAC 1, para. 34.

Classes of Users

External users of financial information encompass a wide range of interests but can be classified into three general groups:

1. Credit and equity investors
2. Government (executive and legislative branches), regulatory bodies, and tax authorities
3. The general public and special interest groups, labor unions, and consumer groups

Each of these user groups has a particular objective in financial statement analysis, but, as the FASB stated, the *primary users are equity investors and creditors*. However, the information supplied to investors and creditors is likely to be generally useful to other user groups as well. Hence, financial accounting standards are geared to the purposes and perceptions of investors and creditors. That is the group for whom the analytical techniques in this book are intended.

The underlying objective of financial analysis is the comparative measurement of risk and return to make investment or credit decisions. These decisions require estimates of the future, be it a month, a year, or a decade. General-purpose financial statements, which describe the past, provide one basis for projecting future earnings and cash flows. Many of the techniques used in this analytical process are broadly applicable to all types of decisions, but there are also specialized techniques concerned with specific investment interests or, in other words, risks and returns specific to one class of investors or securities.

The equity investor is primarily interested in the long-term earning power of the company, its ability to grow, and, ultimately, its ability to pay dividends and increase in value. Since the equity investor bears the residual risk in an enterprise, the largest and most volatile risk, the required analysis is the most comprehensive of any user and encompasses techniques employed by all other external users.

Creditors need somewhat different analytical approaches. Short-term creditors, such as banks and trade creditors, place more emphasis on the immediate liquidity of the business because they seek an early payback of their investment. Long-term investors in bonds, such as insurance companies and pension funds, are primarily concerned with the long-term asset position and earning power of the company. They seek assurance of the payment of interest and the capability of retiring or refunding the obligation at maturity. Credit risks are usually smaller than equity risks and may be more easily quantifiable.

More subordinated or junior creditors, especially owners of "high-yield" debt, however, bear risks similar to those of equity investors and may find analytic techniques normally applied to equity investments more relevant than those employed by creditors.

Financial Information and Capital Markets

The usefulness of accounting information in the decision-making processes of investors and creditors has been the subject of much academic research over the last 35 years. That research has examined the interrelationship of accounting information and reporting standards in financial markets in great detail. At times, the research conclusions are highly critical of the accounting standard-setting process and of the utility of financial analysis. This criticism is based on research performed in a capital market setting. These findings do not negate the usefulness of financial analysis of individual securities that may be mispriced or of decisions made outside a capital market setting.[5]

Some researchers argue that financial data are useful to investors only for prediction of a firm's risk characteristics. To a great extent, this line of reasoning is influenced by the finance literature and the prevalent acceptance of the efficient market hypothesis. Others argue that the impact of accounting is not so much in its information content per se, but rather in the "economic consequences" to the firm resulting from contracts (implicit or explicit) that are based on or driven by accounting-determined variables.[6]

---

[5]Examples include acquisitions and credit decisions made by banks or other institutional lenders.

[6]Management compensation contracts and covenants contained in debt agreements are two examples of such contracts.

By and large, the early conclusions of the academic literature have proven to be somewhat premature. More recent research demonstrates that the interplay between markets and information is richer and more sophisticated than originally thought. In fact, the trend in research is now to incorporate techniques of fundamental analysis in model development and research design.

Various research trends and relevant economic considerations are discussed throughout the book, with varying emphasis from topic to topic. Chapter 5 is devoted entirely to a review of the major strands of empirical research in order to set the stage for discussions of other topics, where appropriate, in subsequent chapters. Throughout the text we focus on what the analyst can learn from the research and how its implications are relevant to analysis.

THE FINANCIAL REPORTING SYSTEM

An understanding of the conceptual bases of the financial reporting system and of the preparation of financial statements are essential prerequisites to financial analysis. Corporate management issues financial statements and is responsible for their form and content. It is management that selects accounting methods, compiles accounting data, and prepares the financial statements. For smaller companies, auditors may carry out portions of the preparation work.

The accounting process or financial reporting system, which generates financial information for external users, encompasses five principal financial statements:

1. Balance sheet (statement of financial position)
2. Income statement (statement of earnings)
3. Statement of comprehensive income
4. Statement of cash flows
5. Statement of stockholders' equity

These five financial statements, augmented by footnotes and supplementary data, are interrelated. Collectively, they are intended to provide relevant, reliable, and timely information essential to making investment, credit, and similar decisions, thus meeting the objectives of financial reporting. An example is the 1999 financial statements of Pfizer,[7] contained in the CD[8] accompanying the text.

General Principles and Measurement Rules

Financial statements provide information about the assets (resources), liabilities (obligations), income and cash flows, and stockholders' equity of the firm. The effects of transactions and other events are recorded in the appropriate financial statement(s). The income statement reports revenues, expenses, and gains and losses. The balance sheet shows assets, liabilities, and stockholders' equity; the statement of stockholders' equity reports capital transactions with owners. The statement of comprehensive income reports changes in certain balance sheet accounts[9] that bypass the income statement. The statement of cash flows includes operating, investing, and financing inflows and outflows. Many transactions are reflected in more than one statement so that the entire set is required to evaluate the firm.

The financial reporting system is based on data generated from *accounting events and selected economic events*. The financial statements recognize events and transactions

---

[7]The statement of comprehensive income may be combined with the income statement or balance sheet. Pfizer has chosen to integrate comprehensive income into its balance sheet.

[8]Financial statements for Pfizer and the other companies featured in the text are contained both on the accompanying CD and on the book's website. The icon shown in the margin will appear whenever the financial statements of one of these companies is referenced.

[9]Pfizer shows currency translation adjustments, changes in the market value of marketable securities, and a minimum pension liability. These items are discussed in Chapters 15, 13, and 12 respectively.

meeting certain criteria, primarily exchange transactions (the exchange of cash or another asset for a different asset or to create or settle a liability). Other events recognized in the financial reporting system include the passage of time (e.g., accrual of interest), the use of services (e.g., insurance) or assets (e.g., depreciation), estimates such as bad debts or accruals for warranties, and the impact of some contracts (e.g., capital leases). Selected external or economic events, including some market value changes, are also recognized. However, many contractual arrangements and market value changes are disclosed only in the footnotes or in supplementary schedules, if at all.

The emphasis on reporting exchange transactions does not mean that the exchange of cash is necessary for the recognition of revenue and expense events. Under *accrual accounting*, revenues are recognized when goods are delivered or services are performed and expenses are recorded as services are used, rather than when cash is collected or expenditures are incurred for these transactions. Accrual accounting rests on the *matching principle*, which says that performance can be measured only if the related revenues and costs are accounted for in the same period.

Financial statements are prepared using a monetary unit to quantify (measure) the operations of the firm. Transactions are generally measured at their *historical cost*, the amount of cash or other resources exchanged for the asset or liability; changes in value subsequent to acquisition are usually ignored. The advantage of historical cost is that it is objective and verifiable. Its utility declines as specific prices or the general price level changes; as a result, the SEC, FASB, and non-U.S. standard setters have added disclosure and accounting standards for financial instruments.

Financial reporting also relies on the *going concern assumption*, that the firm will continue in operation indefinitely. The alternative assumes liquidation or sale of the firm, which requires different measures of assets and liabilities. Only by assuming normal future operations is it possible, for example, to depreciate fixed assets over their useful life rather than valuing them at their estimated disposal value.

THE U.S. FINANCIAL REPORTING SYSTEM

In the United States, the Securities and Exchange Commission (SEC) through its regulation S-X governs the form and content of the financial statements of companies whose securities are publicly traded. Although the SEC has delegated much of this responsibility to the FASB, it frequently adds its own requirements. The SEC functions as a highly effective enforcement mechanism for standards promulgated in the private sector.

Securities and Exchange Commission

As stated above, while financial reporting standards are developed primarily in the private sector, the SEC often augments the FASB's work. For example, the SEC-mandated Management Discussion and Analysis (MD&A) provides helpful information regarding past operating results and current financial position. In such areas as segment data, leases, the effects of changing prices, and disclosure of oil and gas reserves, SEC-required disclosures preceded FASB action.

Audited financial statements, related footnotes, and supplementary data are presented in both annual reports sent to stockholders and those filed with the SEC. The SEC filings often contain other valuable information not presented in stockholder reports. Exhibit 1-1 contains a listing of SEC-required filings. Quarterly financial reports and SEC 10-Q filings, both of which contain abbreviated financial statements, may be reviewed by auditors but are rarely audited.

As the SEC reviews the financial statements of public companies, and those wishing to issue securities in the U.S. capital markets, its views on proper financial reporting carry great weight. It promulgates these views through Staff Accounting Bulletins (SAB) and through participation in the FASB's Emerging Issues Task Force (see next section) as well as through the review process and enforcement actions. SABs and EITFs are discussed where appropriate throughout this text.

EXHIBIT 1-1
Corporate Filings: Securities and Exchange Commission

10-K Annual Report

Contents (partial listing):
Business of Company
Properties
Legal Proceedings
Management Discussion and Analysis
Changes or Disagreements with Auditors
Financial Statements and Footnotes
Investee Financial Statements (where applicable)
Parent Company Financial Statements (where applicable)

Schedules:
I. Condensed Financial Information
II. Bad Debt and Other Valuation Accounts
III. Real Estate and Accumulated Depreciation
IV. Mortgage Loans on Real Estate
V. Supplementary Information Concerning Property-Casualty Insurance Operations

Due Date: 3 months following end of fiscal year.

10-Q Quarterly Report

Contents Financial Statements
Management Discussion and Analysis

Due Date: 45 days following end of fiscal quarter. Not required for fourth quarter of fiscal year.

8-K Current Reports

Contents (used to report important events):
Change in Control
Acquisitions and Divestitures
Bankruptcy
Change in Auditors
Resignation of Directors

Due Date: 15 days following event.

Source: Adapted from SEC Regulation S-X.

Financial Accounting Standards Board

The FASB is a nongovernmental body with seven full-time members. The board sets accounting standards for all companies issuing audited financial statements. Because of Rule 203 of the American Institute of Certified Public Accountants (AICPA), all FASB pronouncements are considered authoritative; new FASB statements immediately become part of GAAP. Prior to creation of the FASB in 1973, the Accounting Principles Board (APB), an AICPA committee, set accounting standards. Unless superseded, APB opinions remain part of GAAP.[10]

---

[10]FASB statements and interpretations, Accounting Principles Board (APB) opinions, and AICPA accounting research bulletins constitute the highest level of authority in the hierarchy of accounting principles. These are followed in descending order of authority by FASB technical bulletins, cleared AICPA industry audit guides, and AICPA statements of position at level B. ("Cleared" means that the FASB has not objected to the issuance of the guide or the statement of position.) Positions of the FASB Emerging Issues Task Force and cleared AcSec practice bulletins constitute level C, followed by AICPA accounting interpretations, question-and-answer guides published by the FASB staff, uncleared AICPA statements of position, and uncleared AICPA industry audit and accounting guides. The lowest authoritative level includes FASB concepts statements, APB statements, AICPA issues papers, and IASB statements.

Because the SEC recognizes FASB statements as authoritative (as it recognized APB opinions prior to 1973), there is only one body of GAAP applicable to the United States. There are a few instances (e.g., earnings per share) in which nonpublic companies are exempted from certain GAAP requirements. Generally speaking, however, all audited statements are prepared using the same financial reporting framework.

The FASB is an independent body whose members are required to sever all ties with previous employers. Although historically most board members have been former auditors, others have come from the corporate world, government service, and academia. The analyst community is currently represented on the board by Gary Schieneman; Frank Block, CFA, served from 1979 to 1985, and Anthony Cope, CFA, from 1993 to 2000.

Before issuing a new Statement of Financial Accounting Standards (SFAS), the FASB staff often works with a task force—composed of public accountants, representatives from industry, academics, regulators, and financial statement users—to develop a discussion memorandum. After public comments are received and hearings held, the staff prepares an exposure draft (a proposed standard) for public comment.[11] The FASB also collaborates with other standard-setting authorities. For example, recent standards on earnings per share and segment reporting were developed in conjunction with the IASB and the Canadian Accounting Standards Board.

The Board's due process rules necessitate extensive dissemination of its agenda. SEC rulemaking is also normally preceded by a request for comments on a proposed set of rules. Thus, it is possible to anticipate new accounting and disclosure standards well in advance of their issuance and implementation.

After new standards are issued, and in areas where standards are nonexistent or ambiguous, there may be a need for guidance as to proper accounting. The FASB staff sometimes issues such documents, especially after major new standards (such as the one on hedging). The Emerging Issues Task Force (EITF), with members from auditing firms, preparers, and the SEC (but under FASB purview) tries to achieve consensus on technical issues. Some projects, especially those that are industry specific, are handled by the AICPA's Accounting Standards Committee (AcSec); these Statements of Position (SOPs) must be cleared by the FASB to become effective.

FASB Conceptual Framework

The conceptual basis for U.S. GAAP stems from FASB concepts statements that create a "constitution" or conceptual framework used by the board to set standards. Many critics of the FASB view the conceptual framework as a failure.[12] They state that the definitions are unduly vague and that the board has repeatedly deferred difficult decisions (such as how to measure income). Others believe that the conceptual framework has helped the board set better standards.

For the analyst, the conceptual framework is an important building block in understanding the information provided by financial statements. The conceptual framework delineates the characteristics accounting information must possess to be useful in investment and other economic decisions.

We have already addressed Statement of Financial Accounting Concepts (SFAC) 1, which sets forth the objectives of financial reporting. SFAC 2 is concerned with the Qualitative Characteristics of Accounting Information. These characteristics are shown in Figure 1-1, which is reproduced from the statement. A brief discussion follows.

Qualitative Characteristics of Accounting Information. Analysts' concern with the qualitative characteristics of accounting information derives from the need for information that facilitates comparison of firms using alternative reporting methods and is useful for decision making. Although some of these characteristics are self-evident, others require some explanation. We start with relevance and reliability, key characteristics from the analyst point of view.

---

[11]The FASB sometimes issues an intermediate document, labeled *preliminary views or tentative conclusions*, to obtain comment on difficult issues.

[12]For example, see David Solomons, "The FASB's Conceptual Framework: An Evaluation," *Journal of Accountancy* (June 1986), pp. 114–124.

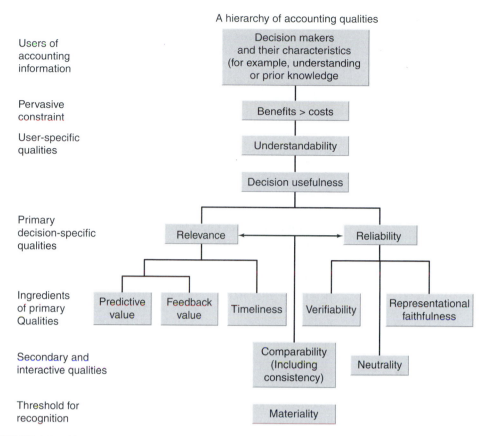

FIGURE 1-1 A hierarchy of accounting qualities. *Source*: Figure 1 of FASB Concepts Statement No. 2, *Qualitative Characteristics of Accounting Information*, copyright by Financial Accounting Standards Board, Norwalk, CT.

Relevance is defined as "the capacity of information to make a difference in a decision. . . ."[13] In practice, of course, the relevance of information depends on the decision maker. To a technical analyst (chartist), all financial data are irrelevant. For fundamental analysts, the relevance of information varies with the method of analysis (emphasis on income statement, cash flow, balance sheet, etc.).

Timeliness is an important aspect of relevance. Information loses value rapidly in the financial world. Market prices are predicated on estimates of the future; data on the past are helpful in making projections. But as time passes and the future becomes the present, past data become increasingly irrelevant.

Reliability encompasses *verifiability, representational faithfulness*, and *neutrality*. The first two elements (verifiability and representational faithfulness) are concerned with whether financial data have been measured accurately and whether they are what they purport to be. Data without these characteristics cannot be relied on in making investment decisions.

Neutrality is concerned with whether financial statement data are biased. FASB proposals are frequently the object of complaints that companies will be adversely affected by the new standard. The principle of neutrality states that the board should consider only the relevance and reliability of the data, not any possible economic impact.

Unfortunately, relevance and reliability tend to be opposing qualities. For example, the audit process improves the reliability of data, but at the cost of timeliness. For that reason, financial statement users have generally not supported the auditing of quarterly data, believing that the time delay does not compensate for any improved data quality.

[13]SFAC 2, Glossary.

Relevance and reliability also clash strongly in a number of accounting areas. Market value data are probably the best example. Information on the current market value of assets such as real estate and agricultural properties may be highly relevant but may be accurate (reliable) only to a limited extent. Yet historical cost, although highly reliable, may have little relevance. It is the old argument as to whether it is better to be "precisely wrong" or "approximately right."

Analysts have generally opted for approximately right. They have supported the disclosure of supplementary data in such areas as natural resources (SFAS 69, Chapter 7), off-balance-sheet financing (Chapter 11), and segment data (SFAS 131, Chapter 13). Auditors and preparers, more concerned with reliability (and legal liability), have often opposed the inclusion of less reliable data in the financial statements.

Consistency and *comparability* are also key characteristics of accounting information from the analyst perspective. Consistency refers to use of the same accounting principles over time. A broader term, comparability, refers to comparisons among companies.

Consistency is affected by new accounting standards and voluntary changes in accounting principles and estimates. Accounting changes hinder the comparison of operating results between periods when the accounting principles used to measure those results differ. As the transition provisions of new accounting standards vary, it is frequently difficult to obtain a consistent time series of earnings properly adjusted for such changes. For voluntary changes (such as depreciation methods and lives), the effect of the change is generally disclosed only for the year of the change.

Comparability is a pervasive problem in financial analysis. Companies are free to choose among different accounting methods and estimates in a variety of areas, making comparisons of different enterprises difficult or impossible. Although the FASB (and to some extent, the IASB) has narrowed these differences somewhat in recent years, new types of transactions (such as securitization of assets) create new sources of noncomparability. Even when accounting differences do not exist, however, comparability may be elusive because of real differences between the firms (e.g., one has foreign operations and the other does not).

Materiality is paradoxically the most elusive accounting quality and arguably the most important. As shown in Figure 1-1, materiality is the threshold for financial statement recognition. FASB statements routinely state that they do not apply to immaterial items.

We define information to be material when it would make a difference in the valuation of the firm. While some use quantitative measures of materiality (e.g., 5% of income), even very small items can affect valuation. For example:

- A firm makes sales (just prior to the end of the quarter) under unusually favorable conditions (to the buyer) to meet sales expectations for the quarter.
- A firm realizes capital gains on long-term investments to achieve projected earnings growth for the period.

In Staff Accounting Bulletin (SAB) 99,[14] the SEC provided additional guidance regarding materiality because of perceived abuses. The SEC stated that financial statement issuers and auditors must consider qualitative factors as well as quantitative rules of thumb. These qualitative factors include:

1. Obscuring changes in earnings trend
2. Hiding the failure to achieve analyst forecasts
3. Changing a reported loss to income or vice versa
4. Obscuring changes in significant business segments
5. Increasing management compensation
6. Affecting compliance with regulatory requirements, loan covenants, or other contracts
7. Concealing unlawful acts

Materiality is best defined in a firm context. The analyst should always be wary of firms that use "materiality" to hide significant data.

[14]August 12, 1999.

BOX 1-1
SFAC 7: Using Cash Flow Information and Present Value in Accounting Measurement

---

SFAC 7 (2000) deals only with measurement. It does not state when assets or liabilities must be measured using these principles. While present values are widely used in financial reporting (e.g., retirement plans), the FASB is expected to extend their use in the future. The statement says:

> The objective of using present value as an accounting measurement is to capture, to the extent possible, the economic difference between sets of future cash flows.*

Capturing the economic difference requires consideration of the following elements of the present value calculation:

1. Estimation of future cash flows
2. Expectations regarding the timing and amounts of those cash flows
3. Time value of money, measured by the risk-free interest rate
4. The effect of uncertainty on the required rate of return
5. Other factors, such as liquidity, that affect the required rate of return

In traditional present value calculations, factors 2 through 5 are rolled up into a single interest rate. SFAC 7, however, requires that each of these factors be considered separately, using the *expected cash flow* approach. We illustrate this method using the following example:†

Cash flow = $10,000 due in 10 years
Probability of collection = 80%
Risk-free rate (10 years) = 5%
Risk premium = $500

The initial step is to compute the expected cash flow:

$$(\$10,000 \times 80\% + \$0 \times 20\%) = \$8,000$$

Second, deduct the risk premium that a risk-averse investor would demand to assume the default risk:

$$\$8,000 - \$500 = \$7,500$$

Finally, discount by the risk-free rate:

Present value at 5% of $7,500 due in 10 years = $4,604

Under this approach, the carrying value would be $4,604. This works out to an effective interest rate of 8.065%, which can be broken down into the following components:‡

Risk-free rate	5.000%
Adjustment for expectations	2.370
Adjustment for risk	.695
Total	8.065%

After initial measurement, the asset (or liability) would increase (accrete) at that 8.065 interest rate. Thus, after one year (assuming annual compounding), the carrying amount would be:

$$\$4,604 (1 + .08065) = \$4,975$$

At the end of 10 years, the carrying amount would be $10,000. Depending on the amount actually paid, there would be a gain or loss recognized at that time.

The extent to which SFAC 7 is applied to more assets and liabilities in the future may depend on whether preparers, auditors, and users become convinced that the expected value method provides better information. Auditors are especially concerned that the SFAC 7 method is less auditable than the historical approach of applying a composite discount rate to management's best estimate.

---

*Para. 20.

†Asset D from Appendix 1 of SFAC 7; see that appendix for comparison with other variations.

‡This example ignores factor 5 (liquidity or other factors).

In addition to concept statements 1 and 2, which we have just reviewed, there are four others. SFAC 3, Elements of Financial Statements of Business Enterprises, has been superseded by SFAC 6, Elements of Financial Statements, which is discussed in subsequent sections of this chapter. The topics covered by SFAC 4, Objectives of Financial Reporting by Nonbusiness Organizations, are beyond the scope of this text. SFAC 5, Recognition and Measurement in Financial Statements of Business Enterprises, is referenced in Chapter 2. SFAC 7, Using Cash Flow Information and Present Value in Accounting Measurement, is discussed in Box 1-1.

INTERNATIONAL ACCOUNTING STANDARDS

Growing international trade, multinational industrial and financial enterprises, and increasingly global capital markets have significantly expanded investment opportunities. Creditors and equity investors need to analyze both domestic and foreign companies. Yet differences in accounting and reporting standards make it difficult to compare domestic companies with those in other countries. Furthermore, as accounting standards are established separately in each country, it is difficult to generalize about those differences.

Financial reporting requirements are a function of tax regulations, corporate law, the comparative significance of capital markets and financial institutions in industrial development, and cultural differences. However, as capital markets and international investments expand, the need for global accounting standards is obvious.

Two questions arise: Who should develop such standards, and who would enforce them?

This section provides a brief discussion of the International Organization of Securities Commissions (IOSCO), the International Accounting Standards Board (IASB), and European financial reporting standards; a review of SEC reporting requirements for foreign registrants follows. These discussions review the significant recent progress toward harmonization of international reporting requirements.

International Organization of Securities Commissions

IOSCO is an organization of securities regulators from more than 65 countries, including the SEC from the United States. IOSCO's Technical Committee investigates regulatory issues related to international securities transactions and is charged with developing solutions to problems in these areas.

IOSCO is also involved in standard setting through the Technical Committee's Working Party 1 on Multinational Disclosure and Accounting, which is charged with advocating financial reporting regulation that facilitates cross-border securities offerings and promotes effective and efficient international capital markets.

The Technical Committee's Working Party established a comprehensive core set of international accounting standards that could be recognized by IOSCO members for use in cross-border offerings and global multiple listings. However, each country's regulatory agency must approve these standards. It appears that enforcement would also remain a country-by-country matter.

International Accounting Standards Board

The IASB was established in 1973 to harmonize (conform) the accounting standards of different nations. In 2001, the IASB adopted a new structure, moving away from its "consensus" model[15] to one more like the FASB.

The new IASB structure provides for 19 trustees, headed by Paul Volcker, former chair of the U.S. Federal Reserve Board. The trustees, most of whom are not Americans, perform the functions of a corporate board of directors. The new IASB Board consists of 14 members; its chairman is David Tweedie, former head of the UK Accounting Standards Board. Anthony Cope, CFA, a former analyst and FASB member, is an IASB Board member. The IASB is maintaining its Standing Interpretations Committee (similar to the FASB's EITF), which deals with questions that arise after a new standard is adopted. There is a new Standards Advisory Council, which (like the similar FASB body) provides input from constituents.

As of December 31, 2001, the IASB has issued 41 international accounting standards (IAS) as well as a Framework for the Preparation and Presentation of Financial Statements, similar to the FASB conceptual framework, used to review existing standards and develop future IAS. This framework is also used to promote harmonization of regulations and standard setting by providing a basis for reducing the number of alternative accounting treatments permitted by the IASB.

The IASB has largely "caught up" with the FASB. In October 1993, IOSCO endorsed IAS 7, Cash Flow Statements, and published a list of core standards that would form the basis for a reasonably complete set of global standards. IASB completed work on these "core standards" and the SEC and other IOSCO members are evaluating their suitability for "global GAAP."

---

[15]The prior IASC had representatives from national accounting federations, stock exchanges, financial institutions, and other groups (including the International Coordinating Committee of Financial Analysts Associations). Because of a supermajority approval requirement, a broad consensus was required to adopt a new standard.

As capital markets become more international in scope, the need for global accounting standards and the demand for multiple listings grow. Discussion of financial reporting in Europe will be followed by an examination of the SEC's efforts to facilitate foreign listings.

European Financial Reporting Standards

Financial reporting requirements in Europe differ from those in the United States and other countries because of differences in their economies, relevance of local commercial law to the development of reporting standards, comparative importance of capital markets and banks as a source of financing, and the degree to which tax laws influence financial reporting.

Because of their desire to access other capital markets, a number of European multinational firms have adopted either U.S. standards (Daimler adopted U.S. GAAP even before it merged with Chrysler) or IASB GAAP. Despite occasional talk about "European GAAP," cultural differences and the existence of the IASB model suggest that large European companies will continue to gravitate toward either U.S. or IASB standards, depending on the outcome of the SEC decision concerning the acceptability of IASB standards for U.S. capital markets.

SEC REPORTING REQUIREMENTS FOR FOREIGN REGISTRANTS

Foreign issuers that wish to sell securities in the United States must register with the SEC and are subject to substantially the same reporting requirements as their domestic counterparts. Foreign issuers may elect to file the registration and reporting forms used by domestic issuers (see Exhibit 1-1). Alternatively, foreign filers may elect to file the generally less stringent Forms 20-F (similar to 10-K) and 6-K (similar to 8-K). Issuers of American Depositary Receipts (ADRs)[16] may register either Form F-6 or 20-F and are exempt from Form 8-K requirements.

Foreign issuers commonly use Form 20-F filings, thereby exempting them from requirements to file proxies and insider trading reports. Form 20-F annual reports are due six months after the fiscal year-end, quarterly reports are optional, and relatively little business and segment data disclosure is required.

Form 20-F filers must identify both the reporting principles used and the material variations from U.S. GAAP and reconcile reported income and stockholders' equity to U.S. GAAP. These reconciliations provide insights into the differences in reporting requirements across countries and the tasks involved in developing universal financial reporting standards. The data provided in Form 20-F reconciliations are used to illustrate accounting differences throughout the text.

Staff Accounting Bulletin 88 (August 1990) clarified the disclosures and quantitative reconciliations required by Item 17 of Form 20-F. The new guidance requires some additional disclosures regarding pension obligations (SFAS 87) and financial instruments (SFAS 105) in the MD&A. However, SAB 88 does not mandate those disclosures required by U.S. GAAP or the SEC but not required by the foreign issuer's local GAAP.[17]

The SEC no longer requires foreign issuers to reconcile to U.S. GAAP for differences stemming from the use of:

- IAS 7, Cash Flow Statements
- IAS 21, The Effects of Changes in Foreign Exchange Rates
- IAS 22, Business Combinations

These changes reflect two parallel developments. First, some IAS standards are considered equivalent to U.S. GAAP and are deemed acceptable for filings in the United States.

---

[16]ADRs are depositary shares representing a specified number of shares and are issued against the deposit of a foreign issuer's securities. ADRs must be registered on Form F-6 unless another registration form is more appropriate.

[17]See R. Dieter and J. A. Heyman, "Implications of SEC Staff Accounting Bulletin 88 for Foreign Registrants," *Journal of Accountancy* (August 1991), pp. 121–125.

Second, U.S. filing requirements for foreign registrants have affected requirements for U.S. entities. FRR 44 (December 13, 1994) eliminated the requirement for domestic issuers to file schedules with data on marketable securities, property, plant, and equipment, accumulated depreciation, and short-term borrowings. Although these amendments "leveled the field" for domestic and foreign filers, they also eliminated a significant amount of information useful in financial analysis.[18]

PRINCIPAL FINANCIAL STATEMENTS

The preceding sections described the general principles and measurement rules of the basic accounting process applicable to financial reporting in the United States. They also examined the role of international and domestic standard-setting bodies (the SEC and FASB) and the latter's conceptual framework that guides this process, along with the qualitative characteristics of accounting information. This section provides a detailed discussion of the output of this system: the different financial statements, footnotes, and supplementary data.[19]

The Balance Sheet

The balance sheet (statement of financial position) reports major classes and amounts of assets (resources owned or controlled by the firm), liabilities (external claims on those assets), and stockholders' equity (owners' capital contributions and other internally generated sources of capital) and their interrelationships at specific points in time.

Assets reported on the balance sheet are either purchased by the firm or generated through operations; they are, directly or indirectly, financed by the creditors and stockholders of the firm. This fundamental accounting relationship provides the basis for recording all transactions in financial reporting and is expressed as the balance sheet equation:

$$\text{Assets (A)} = \text{Liabilities (L)} + \text{Stockholders' Equity (E)}$$

In the United States, firms issue balance sheets at the end of each quarter and the end of the fiscal year. Annual or semiannual reporting is the norm in most other countries.

Elements of the Balance Sheet

SFAC 6 discusses the elements of financial statements. Although this statement also deals with nonprofit organizations, we restrict our comments to business enterprises.

Assets are defined in SFAC 6 as

> probable future economic benefits obtained or controlled by a particular entity as a result of past transactions or events. (para. 25)

This definition seems to be noncontroversial. Its weakness is its lack of reference to risk. It seems to us that an enterprise that retains the risks of ownership still "owns" the asset. This issue is important, for example, as it relates to the sale of assets (such as accounts receivable, loans, and mortgages; see Chapter 11) when the seller retains some risk of loss.

Liabilities are defined, similarly, as

> probable future sacrifices of economic benefits arising from present obligations of a particular entity to transfer assets or provide services to other entities in the future as a result of past transactions or events. (para. 35)

Again, the definition reads well. Yet it permits the nonrecognition of contractual obligations such as operating leases (see Chapter 11). The interpretation of "present obligation" and "result of past transactions or events" is key to accounting for all such contracts; some believe that only payments immediately due as a consequence of completed transactions cre-

---

[18]In 1999, the SEC proposed reinstating disclosure requirements relating to bad debt and other valuation reserves and property, plant, and equipment.

[19]The requirements of IAS standards are very similar; differences are discussed in Chapters 2 and 3.

ate liabilities.[20] Others believe that all long-term contracts should be recognized as long-term liabilities. Another important problem area is the derecognition of liabilities that have been prefunded but remain outstanding (see the discussion of defeasance in Chapter 10).[21]

As required by the fundamental accounting equation, *stockholders' equity* is therefore

> the residual interest in the net assets of an entity that remains after deducting its liabilities. (para. 49)

In practice, some financial instruments have characteristics of both liabilities and equities, making them difficult to categorize. Convertible debt and redeemable preferreds are two common examples examined in Chapter 10. That chapter also discusses the FASB Exposure Draft (ED) on recognition and measurement of instruments with equity and liability characteristics.

The Income Statement

The income statement (statement of earnings) reports on the performance of the firm, the result of its operating activities. It explains some but not all of the changes in the assets, liabilities, and equity of the firm between two consecutive balance sheet dates. Use of the accrual concept means that income and the balance sheet are interrelated.

The preparation of the income statement is governed by the matching principle, which states that performance can be measured only if revenues and related costs are accounted for during the same time period. This requires the recognition of expenses incurred to generate revenues in the same period as the related revenues. For example, the cost of a machine is recognized as an expense (it is depreciated) over its useful life (as it is used in production) rather than as an expense in the period it is purchased.[22]

Elements of the Income Statement

Revenues are defined in SFAC 6 as

> inflows . . . of an entity . . . from delivering or producing goods, rendering services, or other activities that constitute the entity's ongoing major or central operations. (para. 78)

Expenses are defined as

> outflows . . . from delivering or producing goods, rendering services, or carrying out other activities that constitute the entity's ongoing major or central operations. (para. 80)

These definitions explicitly exclude *gains (and losses)*, defined as

> increases (decreases) in equity (net assets) from peripheral or incidental transactions. . . . (para. 82)

Gains or losses are, therefore, nonoperating events. Examples would include gains and losses from asset sales, lawsuits, and changes in market values (including currency rates).

These definitions are, like the others in SFAC 6, easy to accept as stated. The difficulties come in practice. For example, investment activities may be "central" to a financial institution but "peripheral" to a manufacturing company. Similarly, sales of assets such as automobiles may be "incidental" to a retailer but "central" to a car rental firm. The writedown of inventories due to obsolescence is more difficult to characterize: Is this an operating expense or a loss? To some extent, the distinction between revenue and expense on the one hand and gains and losses on the other is a precursor of the controversies over the characterizations of

---

[20]The capitalization of all executory contracts was advocated in the AIMR position paper "Financial Reporting in the 1990s and Beyond" (1993).

[21]SFAS 125 (1996), Accounting for Transfers and Servicing of Financial Assets and Extinguishments of Liabilities, prohibits derecognition of liabilities using in-substance defeasance.

[22]Note that no depreciation would be recorded if the products manufactured were not sold in the period the machine was used; the cost of using the machine would be added to work-in-process or finished goods inventories and carried on the balance sheet as an asset until the goods were sold.

"recurring versus nonrecurring activities," "operating versus nonoperating activities," and "extraordinary items." From the analyst point of view, disclosure is more important than classification; analysts prefer to make their own distinctions between operating and nonoperating events in many instances. From the point of view of database users, however, the outcome of the debate is important.

Even more important is the decision on when to recognize revenues and expenses. The recognition decision can be a major determinant of reported income, especially for technology and other "new economy" enterprises. This issue is discussed in Chapter 2.

Statement of Comprehensive Income

Comprehensive income is defined as:

> the change in equity of a business enterprise during a period from transactions and other events and circumstances from nonowner sources. It includes *all changes in equity during a period except those resulting from investments by owners and distributions to owners.*[23]

Thus, comprehensive income includes both net income and direct-to-equity adjustments such as:

- Cumulative translation adjustments under SFAS 52 (Chapter 15)
- Minimum pension liability under SFAS 87 (Chapter 12)
- Unrealized gains and losses on available-for-sale securities under SFAS 115 (Chapter 13)
- Deferred gains and losses on cash flow hedges under SFAS 133 (Chapter 16)

These adjustments are collectively known as *other comprehensive income*. SFAS 130 (1997) requires that firms with items of other comprehensive income report:

- The closing balance of each such item. Their total is reported as a separate component of equity called *accumulated other comprehensive income*.
- The change (either pretax or after-tax) in each item; the change can be reported either gross (showing both additions and subtractions) or net.
- Reclassification adjustments to avoid double counting. For example, realized investment gains that include unrealized gains from prior years would be double counted unless those unrealized gains are deducted from other comprehensive income in the year of realization.[24]
- Total comprehensive income in condensed financial statements provided for interim periods.

Alternative displays are permitted. For example, firms can provide a separate statement of comprehensive income or can combine that statement with the income statement. Some data can be reported either on the statement face or in footnotes. IAS 1 (1997), with similar requirements, also permits alternative formats.[25]

Illustration: Pfizer. The shareholders' equity section of Pfizer's balance sheet has a line item: accumulated other comprehensive income. Note 5 shows the Statement of Comprehensive Income, with annual changes and balances for the currency translation adjustment, net unrealized gain on available-for-sale securities, and minimum pension liability.[26] All items are presented net of tax with the tax benefit shown as a single annual total. The individual items will be discussed in the appropriate chapters.

---

[23]SFAC 6 (1985), para. 70, emphasis added.

[24]Reclassification adjustments are not required for the minimum pension liability. Such adjustments for the cumulative translation adjustment are limited to translation gains and losses realized upon sale or liquidation of the investment in foreign subsidiaries. Reclassification adjustments in comparative statements provided for earlier periods are encouraged, but not required.

[25]IAS 1 does not use the term comprehensive income; its example is titled "Statement of Recognized Gains and Losses."

[26]These same amounts are shown in Pfizer's statement of shareholders' equity, which follows the balance sheet.

Statement of Cash Flows

The statement of cash flows reports cash receipts and payments in the period of their occurrence, classified as to operating, investing, and financing activities. It also provides supplementary disclosures about noncash investing and financing activities. Cash flow data also help explain changes in consecutive balance sheets and supplement the information provided by the income statement.

SFAS 95, Statement of Cash Flows (1987), defines investing cash flows as those resulting from:

- Acquisition or sale of property, plant, and equipment
- Acquisition or sale of a subsidiary or segment
- Purchase or sale of investments in other firms

Similarly, financing cash flows are those resulting from:

- Issuance or retirement of debt and equity securities
- Dividends paid to stockholders

The standard requires gross rather than net reporting of significant investing and financing activities, thereby providing improved disclosure. For example, cash flows for property acquisitions must be shown separately from those related to property sales.

Enterprises with foreign currency transactions or foreign operations must report the effect of exchange rate changes on cash and cash equivalents as a separate component of the reconciliation of cash and cash equivalents for the period.

Significant noncash investing and financing activities (such as capitalized leases) must be disclosed separately within the cash flow statement or in a footnote elsewhere in the financial statements. Complex investment and financing transactions sometimes involve combinations of cash, debt, and other resources—these diverse but related components must be reported separately.

Cash from Operations. This key performance measure includes the cash effects of all transactions that do not meet the definition of investing or financing. This measure, moreover, excludes the effect of changes in exchange rates. In effect, it includes the cash flow consequences of the revenue-producing activities of the firm. Cash from operations may be reported either directly, using major categories of gross cash receipts and payments, or indirectly by providing a reconciliation of net income to net cash flow from operating activities. Both methods require separate disclosure of the cash outflows for income taxes and interest within the statement or elsewhere in the financial statements.

Statement of Stockholders' Equity

This statement reports the amounts and sources of changes in equity from capital transactions with owners and may include the following components:

- Preferred shares
- Common shares (at par or stated value)
- Additional paid-in capital
- Retained earnings
- Treasury shares (repurchased equity)
- Employee Stock Ownership Plan (ESOP) adjustments

and as components of other comprehensive income:

- Minimum pension liability
- Unrealized gains and losses on available for sale securities.
- Cumulative translation adjustment (foreign operations)
- Unrealized gains and losses on cash flow hedges

Equity events and transactions are generally recognized as they occur, but capital market developments have created significant measurement and classification problems in transactions with owners.

The firm usually records the issuance of preferred and common stock at par (or stated) value and the amounts received in excess of par as additional paid-in capital. Repurchases or retirements of common stock may be reported as Treasury shares, a contra account, which reflects a reduction in common stock outstanding. Retained (reinvested) earnings, which increase with income and decline with dividend declarations, are also reported. Finally, this statement also includes adjustments related to ESOPs.

The minimum pension liability results when the accounting liability for pensions is less than the accumulated benefit obligation (Chapter 12). The unrealized gains and losses on available for sale securities and the cumulative foreign currency translation adjustment result from selective recognition of market value changes and exchange rate changes (Chapters 13 and 15, respectively). Unrealized gains and losses on cash flow hedges result from the provisions of SFAS 133.

Footnotes

Information provided in the financial statements is augmented by footnotes and other supplementary disclosures. Footnotes are an integral part of the financial statements and provide data on such subjects as business segments, the financial position of retirement plans, and off-balance-sheet obligations. These data are required by either GAAP (FASB standards) or regulatory authorities (the SEC). The financial statements and footnotes in the annual report and the SEC 10-K filings are audited.

Supplementary schedules, some required by the SEC in 10-K filings (see Exhibit 1-1), provide additional useful information. Some of these supplementary data are unaudited.

Footnotes provide information about the accounting methods, assumptions, and estimates used by management to develop the data reported in the financial statements. They are designed to allow users to improve assessments of the amounts, timing, and uncertainty of the estimates reported in the financial statements. Footnotes provide additional disclosure related to such areas as:

- Fixed assets
- Inventories
- Income taxes
- Pension and other postemployment benefit plans
- Debt (interest rates, maturity schedules, and contractual terms)
- Lawsuits and other loss contingencies
- Marketable securities and other investments
- Hedging and other risk management activities
- Business segments
- Significant customers, sales to related parties, and export sales

Contingencies

Footnotes often contain disclosures relating to contingent[27] losses. Firms are required to accrue a loss (recognize a balance sheet liability) when *both* of the following conditions are met:

1. It is probable that assets have been impaired or a liability has been incurred.
2. The amount of the loss can be reasonably estimated.

If the loss amount lies within a range, the most likely amount should be accrued. When no amount in the range is a better estimate, the firm may report the minimum amount in the range.[28]

---

[27]The FASB defines a contingency as an "existing condition, situation, or set of circumstances involving uncertainty as to possible gain or loss" (SFAS 5, para. 1).

[28]See FASB Interpretation 14, Reasonable Estimation of the Amount of a Loss.

SFAS 5 defines *probable* events as those "more likely than not" to occur, suggesting that a probability of more than 50% requires recognition of a loss. However, in practice, firms generally report contingencies as losses only when the probability of loss is significantly higher.

Footnote disclosure of (unrecognized) loss contingencies is required when it is *reasonably possible* (more than remote but less than probable) that a loss has been incurred or when it is probable that a loss has occurred but the amount cannot be reasonably estimated. The standard provides an extensive discussion of loss contingencies.

The recognition and measurement of loss contingencies are problematic because they involve judgment and are subjective at best. External analysis is hampered by the paucity of data, as disclosures are often vague. Footnote disclosures and the SEC-mandated MD&A are the best sources of information.

Significant problem areas include environmental remediation liabilities, litigation, expropriation, self-insurance, debt guarantees, repurchase agreements, take-or-pay contracts, and throughput arrangements. In later chapters we provide discussion of analytical techniques applicable to many of these contingencies and examples of losses recognized in the financial statements as well as others disclosed only in footnotes.

Pfizer's Note 18, Litigation, includes substantial disclosures regarding legal and governmental actions affecting the company. As the drug industry is heavily regulated and patents are important assets,[29] most of the note concerns these two areas. Although the note contains considerable uninformative "boilerplate," it does tell us that:

- Pfizer pleaded guilty to price fixing in 1999, and class action suits have been filed against the company.
- In 1999, a jury awarded $143 million in damages against Pfizer in the Trovan case.
- Pfizer is paying claims resulting from settlement of the Shiley lawsuits concerning defective heart valves.
- The company has been designated a "potentially responsible party" for certain waste sites and may be responsible for the cost of environmental remediation.
- A Pfizer subsidiary sold products containing asbestos, and many personal injury claims are pending against the company. The company expects the cost of such claims to be largely covered by insurance.

There is no indication, however, what provision Pfizer has made (if any) for losses from these suits. There are a couple of clues:

1. The Management Discussion and Analysis discloses (under Net Income) that 1998 includes $126 million "other" expense, mainly for legal settlements.
2. Note 8 shows provisions for the cost of antitrust litigation of $2 million and $57 million for 1999 and 1998, respectively.

Footnote and MD&A disclosures of contingencies should be read carefully, as they provide clues about possible future expense provisions and cash outflows.[30] While firms making acquisitions are generally careful to examine environmental and other risks of the acquired company, liability may emerge years later.[31] In extreme cases (asbestos, for example), environmental claims have driven firms into bankruptcy. Lawsuits and claims are, in addition, sometimes indicators of illegal acts or poor management practices.

Case 1-1 shows the effect on Bristol Myers, another drug company, of breast implant litigation that took a number of years to be fully reflected in its financial statements.

---

[29]Self-developed patents are not recognized in the financial statements, however. Chapter 7 discusses patents and other intangible assets.

[30]See M. E. Barth and M. F. McNichols, "Estimation and Valuation of Environmental Liabilities," *Journal of Accounting Research* (Supplement 1994), pp. 177–209.

[31]In 2000, Aventis (a large French chemicals and pharmaceutical firm) agreed to pay up to $916 million to clean up a defunct copper mine. The mine was owned by Stauffer Chemical, which was acquired by Rhone-Poulenc, which merged with Hoechst to form Aventis in 1999. (*New York Times*, October 22, 2000, p. 32.)

Risks and Uncertainties

In 1994, the AICPA issued Statement of Position (SOP) 94-6, Disclosure of Certain Significant Risks and Uncertainties.[32] Although most AICPA SOPs are narrow in scope, applying to only one industry or narrow category of transactions, SOP 94-6 has broad application. It requires that audited financial statements report the following information:

1. *Nature of operations.* Description of the firm's major business activities and markets.
2. *Use of estimates.* Statement that financial statements use estimates.
3. *Certain significant estimates.* When it is reasonably possible that an estimate used to prepare financial statements will change in the near term, and such change would have a material impact on those statements, then disclosures must be made regarding the nature of the uncertainty involved. Examples include the effect of technological obsolescence on operating assets, capitalized costs that might not be recoverable from operations, and contingent liabilities for environmental remediation or litigation.
4. *Current vulnerability due to certain concentrations.* Firms must disclose concentrations when it is reasonably possible that there could be a severe impact in the near term. Examples include concentrations in customers, suppliers, or markets.

For companies subject to SEC reporting requirements, the SOP has limited effect,[33] although it was intended to help firms (and their auditors) understand the application of SFAS 5 (Contingencies). The major effect of the SOP is on nonpublic companies, whose disclosures are not governed by the SEC; their disclosures were inadequate to analysts accustomed to reviewing the financial statements of public companies.

Supplementary Schedules

In some cases, additional information about the assets and liabilities of a firm is provided within the financial statement footnotes, or as supplementary data outside the financial statements. Examples include:

- Oil and gas companies provide additional data on their exploration activities, quantities and types of reserves, and the present value of cash flows expected from those reserves (Chapter 7).
- Supplemental disclosures of the impact of changing prices (Appendix 8-A).
- Disclosure of sales revenue, operating income, and other data for major business segments and by geographic areas (see Chapters 13 and 15). Firms also provide information about export sales.
- Disclosures related to financial instruments and hedging activities (Chapter 16).

OTHER SOURCES OF FINANCIAL INFORMATION

Stockholder reports often contain useful supplementary financial and statistical data as well as management comments. In some cases, the stockholder report is included ("incorporated by reference") in the SEC filing, or vice versa. The MD&A required by the SEC may appear in either reports to stockholders or SEC filings. A brief discussion of the contents of the MD&A is followed by a discussion of other sources of financial data.

Management Discussion and Analysis

Companies with publicly traded securities have been required since 1968 to provide a discussion of earnings in the MD&A section. The MD&A included in the financial statements of Pfizer is one example. In 1980, the SEC expanded the requirements to a comprehensive, broad-based discussion and analysis of the financial statements to encourage more meaningful disclosure.

---

[32]One of the authors of this text was a member of the task force that prepared the SOP.

[33]SFAS 14 (see Chapter 13) requires more detailed segment data. The SOP permits the use of imprecise language such as "approximately."

The MD&A is required to discuss:

- Results of operations, including discussion of trends in sales and categories of expense
- Capital resources and liquidity, including discussion of cash flow trends
- Outlook based on known trends

In 1989, the SEC issued an interpretive release providing additional guidance on compliance in the following areas:

1. Prospective information and required discussion of significant effects of currently known trends, events, and uncertainties; for example, decline in market share or impact of inventory obsolescence. Firms may voluntarily disclose forward-looking data that anticipate trends or events.

2. Liquidity and capital resources: Firms are expected to use cash flow statements to analyze liquidity; provide a balanced discussion of operating, financing, and investing cash flows; and discuss transactions or events with material current or expected long-term liquidity implications.

3. Discussion of discontinued operations, extraordinary items, and other "unusual or infrequent" events with current or expected material effects on financial condition or results of operations.

4. Extensive disclosures in interim financial statements in keeping with the obligation to periodically update MD&A disclosures.

5. Disclosure of a segment's disproportionate need for cash flows or contribution to revenues or profits. Also, disclosure of any restrictions on a free flow of funds between segments.

On January 22, 2002, the SEC issued a statement reinforcing its views on the importance of MD&A disclosures. The release reminds registrants that disclosure "must be both useful and understandable."

Topics addressed include:

1. Liquidity and capital resources, including the impact of off-balance-sheet arrangements on liquidity and capital resources,

2. Disclosures about contractual obligations and commercial commitments (that is, off-balance-sheet arrangements),

3. Disclosures about trading activities, including non-exchange traded contracts, and

4. The effects of transactions with related parties, including persons (such as former employees) that may fall outside of the technical definition of a related party.

Other Data Sources

Companies that issue securities to the public are required to publish a registration statement, including a prospectus. For large companies, the 10-K and other SEC filings are "incorporated by reference" and little new information is provided. For initial public offerings (IPOs) and smaller companies, however, the prospectus will contain a detailed discussion of the enterprise as well as full financial statements.

Proxy statements, issued in connection with shareholder meetings, contain information about board members and management, executive compensation, stock options, and major stockholders.

Many companies prepare periodic "fact books" containing additional financial and operational data. Corporate press releases also provide new information on a timely basis. Computerized services (e.g., the Dow Jones News Retrieval System) and various on-line services provide databases of corporate releases and other business news. In addition, many companies hold periodic meetings or conference telephone calls to keep the financial community apprised of recent developments regarding the company. In between or in lieu of such meetings, a company officer may be designated to answer questions and provide additional data to analysts following the company.

Industry data and other information about a company also may be obtained from sources outside the company. Trade publications, the general business press, computerized databases, investment research reports, and the publications of competitors are among the sources that may supplement company-originated financial data.

The growth of the Internet has greatly improved access to data relevant to investment decisions. Given the rapid change in Internet offerings, we have not attempted to compile a specific list. Examples include:

- Company home pages that contain financial, product, and other data
- EDGAR, which contains corporate filings with the SEC
- Market data from exchanges and private data providers
- Tax regulations
- Economic data
- Industry data

A comprehensive analysis of a company requires the use of all of these sources of information.

When reviewing corporate reports to stockholders and other publications, it is important to remember that management writes them. Management often views annual reports as public relations or sales materials, intended to impress customers, suppliers, and employees, as well as stockholders. As a result, these reports must be read with at least some degree of skepticism. Only the financial statements (including footnotes and other disclosures labeled "audited") are independently reviewed and attested to by outside auditors.

ROLE OF THE AUDITOR

The auditor (independent certified public accountant) is responsible for seeing that the financial statements issued conform with generally accepted accounting principles. Thus, the auditor must agree that management's choice of accounting principles is appropriate and any estimates are reasonable. The auditor also examines the company's accounting and internal control systems, confirms assets and liabilities, and generally tries to ensure that there are no material errors in the financial statements. The auditor will often review interim reports and "unaudited" portions of the annual report. Although hired by the company (often through the audit committee of the board of directors), the auditor is supposed to be independent of management and to serve the stockholders and other users of the financial statements.

Audited financial statements are always accompanied by the auditor's report, often referred to as an "opinion." Because of the boilerplate nature of these reports, there is a tendency to skip over them when reviewing financial statements. Failure to read this report, however, may cause the financial analyst to miss significant information.

Exhibit 1-2 is the independent auditor's report issued by Ernst & Young, LLP after its 1999 audit of Amerada Hess. The first three paragraphs of the report are standard and are required by Statement of Auditing Standards (SAS) 58, Reports on Audited Financial Statements,[34] which addresses the audit report in which auditors express their opinion on the financial statements developed by management. It clarifies the scope of the assurance provided by the auditors and briefly describes the audit work. The report tells us the following:

1. Although the financial statements are prepared by Amerada management and are the responsibility of management, the auditor has performed an independent review of the statements.
2. The audit has been conducted using generally accepted auditing standards (GAAS) that require the auditor to provide "reasonable assurance" that there are no material errors in the financial statements. The auditor does not guarantee that the statements are free from error or no fraud is present. The auditor has performed tests of the company's accounting system designed to ensure that the statements are accurate.

---

[34]Auditing Standards Board of the American Institute of Certified Public Accountants, 1989.

3. Amerada's financial statements are prepared in accordance with GAAP. The auditor is satisfied that the accounting principles chosen and the estimates employed are reasonable.

An auditor's report on GAAP-based financial statements will always include these three claims.

SAS 58 also requires the addition of an explanatory paragraph to the auditor's report when accounting methods have not been used consistently among periods. For Amerada, the final paragraph tells us that the company changed its method of accounting for inventories in 1999 (a change discussed in Chapter 6).

Reporting on Uncertainties

In some cases, the SAS requires the addition of an explanatory paragraph (following the "opinion" paragraph) that reports and describes material uncertainties affecting the financial statements, such as:

- Doubt concerning the "going concern" assumption that underlies the preparation of financial statements
- Uncertainty regarding the valuation or realization of assets or liabilities
- Uncertainty due to litigation

For the second and third cases, the opinion references the footnote(s) to the financial statements that further detail those uncertainties. The auditor's report on material uncertainties depends on

---

EXHIBIT 1-2
Audit Report: Amerada Hess

Report of Ernst & Young LLP, Independent Auditors

The Board of Directors and Stockholders
Amerada Hess Corporation

We have audited the accompanying consolidated balance sheet of Amerada Corporation and consolidated subsidiaries as of December 31, 1999 and 1998 and the related consolidated statements of income, retained earnings, cash flows, changes in common stock and capital in excess of par value and comprehensive income for each of the three years in the period ended December 31, 1999. These financial statements are the responsibility of the Corporation's management. Our responsibility is to express an opinion on these financial statements based on our audits.

We conducted our audits in accordance with auditing standards generally accepted in the United States. Those standards require that we plan and perform the audit to obtain reasonable assurance about whether the financial statements are free of material misstatement. An audit includes examining, on a test basis, evidence supporting the amounts and disclosures in the financial statements. An audit also includes assessing the accounting principles used and significant estimates made by management, as well as evaluating the overall financial statement presentation. We believe that our audits provide a reasonable basis for our opinion.

In our opinion, the financial statements referred to above present fairly, in all material respects, the consolidated financial position of Amerada Hess Corporation and consolidated subsidiaries at December 31, 1999 and 1998 and the consolidated results of their operations and their consolidated cash flows for each of the three years in the period ended December 31, 1999, in conformity with accounting principles generally accepted in the United States.

As discussed in Note 3 to the consolidated financial statements, in 1999 the Corporation adopted the last-in, first-out (LIFO) inventory method for valuing its refining and marketing inventories, and in 1998 the Corporation adopted AICPA Statement of Position 98-1, Accounting for the Costs of Computer Software Developed or Obtained for Internal Use.

/s/ Ernst & Young LLP

New York, NY
February 24, 2000

Source: Amerada Hess, 1999 Annual Report.

the probability of material loss due to uncertainty. If the probability of a loss is remote, the auditor issues a standard, unqualified opinion. When a material loss is probable and the amount of the loss cannot be reasonably estimated, an explanatory paragraph is required.

The first category is the most serious. A "going concern" qualification conveys doubt that the firm can continue in business. It may be that the firm requires financing due to losses or a lack of liquidity. This paragraph should be viewed as the equivalent of a flashing red light.[35]

Exhibit 1-3 contains the auditors' report on the financial statements of Read-Rite, a producer of magnetic recording heads for computer disk drives. It indicates that the company was not in compliance with financial covenants of its loan agreements and that "these

---

EXHIBIT 1-3
Audit Opinion: Read-Rite

Report of Ernst & Young LLP, Independent Auditors

The Board of Directors and Stockholders
Read-Rite Corporation

We have audited the accompanying consolidated balance sheets of Read-Rite Corporation as of September 30, 1999 and 1998, and the related consolidated statements of operations, cash flows and stockholders' equity for each of the three years in the period ended September 30, 1999. Our audits also included the financial statement schedule listed in the index at item 14(a). These financial statements and schedule are the responsibility of the Company's management. Our responsibility is to express an opinion on these financial statements and schedule based on our audits.

We conducted our audits in accordance with generally accepted auditing standards. Those standards require that we plan and perform the audit to obtain reasonable assurance about whether the financial statements are free of material misstatement. An audit includes examining, on a test basis, evidence supporting the amounts and disclosures in the financial statements. An audit also includes assessing the accounting principles used and significant estimates made by management, as well as evaluating the overall financial statement presentation. We believe that our audits provide a reasonable basis for our opinion.

In our opinion, the consolidated financial statements referred to above present fairly, in all material respects, the consolidated financial position of Read-Rite Corporation at September 30, 1999 and 1998, and the consolidated results of its operations and its cash flows for each of the three years in the period ended September 30, 1999, in conformity with generally accepted accounting principles. Also, in our opinion, the related financial statement schedule, when considered in relation to the basic financial statements taken as a whole, presents fairly in all material respects the information set forth therein.

The accompanying financial statements have been prepared assuming that Read-Rite Corporation will continue as a going concern. As more fully described in Note 1, the Company has incurred operating losses and is out of compliance with certain financial covenants of loan agreements with its lenders. These conditions raise substantial doubt about the Company's ability to continue as a going concern. Management's plans in regard to these matters are also described in Note 1. The financial statements do not include any adjustments to reflect the possible future effects on the recoverability and classification of assets or the amounts and classification of liabilities that may result from the outcome of this uncertainty.

/s/ Ernst & Young LLP

San Jose, California
October 22, 1999, except for the
sixth paragraph of Note 1, as to
which the date is December 29, 1999.

Source: Read-Rite Annual Report, September 30, 1999.

---

[35]Empirical studies [e.g., Carcello et al. (1995) and Rama et al. (1995)] have indicated that approximately 60% of bankrupt firms received a prior going-concern modified audit report and approximately 10% of firms receiving a first-time going-concern qualification entered into bankruptcy within one year of the date of the financial statements. Similarly, Holder-Webb and Wilkins (2000), with respect to SFAS 59, report evidence that resultant going-concern qualifications were useful in "warning" the market of imminent bankruptcies.

conditions raise substantial doubt about the Company's ability to continue as a going concern." The paragraph then references the paragraph in Note 1, which discusses the conditions that warranted the going concern qualification and management's plans to remedy them.[36]

The other two categories suggest problems that are significant, but may not threaten the firm's existence. In these cases, the analyst should examine the uncertainty and incorporate any concerns in the investment decision.

Whenever the auditor's report contains any of the three types of disclosures just listed, or the consistency exception, the financial statements should be examined closely. Note that "subject to" and "except for" disclosures no longer appear in auditors' reports; they were replaced in 1989 by the language (SAS 58) discussed above.

Other Auditor Services

The auditor also performs other services less visible to readers of financial statements. The auditor examines the internal control system of the company and reports any weaknesses to management or the audit committee of the board of directors. The report to the audit committee sometimes also contains information regarding significant audit adjustments, unusual transactions, disagreements with management, or serious audit difficulties. This report is generally not available to outside financial statement users. In 1989, the Auditing Standards Board (ASB) of the American Institute of Certified Public Accountants issued two standards dealing with these reports.

U.S. companies are required to report in their proxy statement the amount paid to the auditor for audit services and (separately) for other services (such as consulting).[37] The intent of this SEC requirement is to alert investors that the auditor's nonaudit fees may be material enough to affect the independence of the audit.

Changing Auditors

Changes in auditors have become more frequent in recent years. In many cases, changes are due to an effort to reduce audit costs or to personality issues. Some changes, however, result from disagreements regarding the application of accounting principles. When an auditor is willing to lose a client because of such a disagreement, the financial analyst should exercise extreme caution with respect to the financial statements of the company in question.

Auditing Outside of the United States

The role of the auditor is determined by auditing standards that vary, as do accounting standards, from one jurisdiction to another. Aracruz, while a Brazilian company, follows U.S. GAAP and its audit opinion is based on U.S. auditing standards.

Reviewing the Report of Group Auditors shown in Roche's annual report, we see that:

1. Roche financial statements are prepared in accordance with International Accounting Standards.
2. These statements also comply with Swiss law (Roche is a Swiss company).
3. The audit was conducted in accordance with International Standards on Auditing, issued by the International Federation of Accountants.

Reviewing Note 1 of Roche's financial statements, we see that the company adopted a number of new IAS standards in 2000. The auditor's opinion makes no reference to these changes. This is one example of how standards applied to the audit of non-U.S. companies

---

[36]In fact, Read-Rite did take steps to reduce its debt and, with the help of improved industry conditions, regained stability. It received a "clean" audit opinion at September 30, 2000. Case 10-1 is concerned with the restructuring of Read-Rite debt.

[37]In July, 2002 U.S. legislation restricted the non-audit services that auditors are permitted to perform for firms that they audit.

may differ from those that readers of U.S. GAAP financial statements are used to. Thus it is especially important to read the accounting principles note of the financial statements of non-U.S. companies to determine the accounting and auditing principles followed.

SUMMARY

Chapter 1 provided an informational background for the study of financial statement analysis. It examined the sources of financial data and the institutional framework in which accounting and disclosure standards are set. In addition, it provided a general guide to the contents of the financial statements and the roles played by statement preparers and auditors. In Chapters 2 and 3, we build on this informational framework by addressing the financial statements—the raw material of analysis.

Chapter 1

Problems

1. [Conceptual basis for accounting standards] Explain why accounting standards might be different if they were established by:

    (i) Short-term lenders such as banks

    (ii) Long-term equity investors

    (iii) Tax authorities

    (iv) Corporate managers

2. [Basic accounting concepts] Describe the relationship between the matching principle and the accrual method of accounting in the preparation of financial statements.

3. [Basic accounting concepts] Describe why the going concern assumption is important in the preparation of financial statements.

4. [Sources of information] Contrast investors in public companies with those in private companies with respect to access to financial and other information useful for investment decisions.

5. [Sources of information] Contrast investors in public companies in the United States with those in foreign countries with respect to access to financial and other information useful for investment decisions.

6. [Sources of accounting standards] Contrast the roles of the Financial Accounting Standards Board and the Securities and Exchange Commission in the setting of accounting standards for American companies.

7. [Basic accounting concepts] Explain why the definitions of assets and liabilities affect accounting standards and, therefore, the preparation of financial statements.

8. [Basic accounting concepts] Explain why the distinction between liabilities and equity is important to investors and creditors.

9. [Basic accounting concepts] Explain why the difference between historical cost and market value affects the relevance and reliability of financial statement data.

10. [Basic accounting concepts] Contrast the role of contra accounts and adjunct accounts in financial statements.

11. [Basic accounting concepts] Contrast gains and losses with revenues and expenses. Explain why the distinction is important for financial analysis.

12. [Basic accounting concepts] Define *comprehensive income* and explain how that concept makes financial statements more useful for financial analysis.

13. [Basic concepts] Explain why the distinction between recurring and nonrecurring income is important for financial analysis.

14. [Basic concepts] Explain why cash flows are classified into three categories. Discuss the usefulness of each category.

15. [Basic concepts] Differentiate between financial statement footnotes and supplementary schedules as sources of financial data.

16. [Basic concepts] Discuss the SEC requirement for MD&A and explain how MD&A disclosures can assist financial analysis.

17. [Global accounting standards] Discuss the advantages and disadvantages of having global accounting standards from the perspective of the financial analyst.

18. [Role of auditor] You are reviewing a company's financial statements. Its auditor has issued an unqualified opinion regarding the financial statements. Discuss what that opinion tells you about:

    (i) Possible changes in accounting principles

    (ii) Possible changes in accounting estimates

    (iii) The existence of significant risks regarding the future operations of the company

    (iv) The possibility that the financial statements are fraudulent

19. [Role of auditor; accounting changes] Review the 2000 auditor's report for Roche, discussed on page 25. Discuss:

a. Why knowledge of changes in accounting principles is important for analysis purposes

b. Whether such changes should be highlighted in the auditor's opinion

20. [Role of auditor] Compare the role of the auditor with that of the financial statement preparer (firm being audited) in preparation of the firm's financial statements.

21. [Sources of information] Discuss the importance to investors of the controversy over the conditions under which companies may issue securities in foreign jurisdictions.

22. [Contingencies; CFA© adapted] Bonnywill Auto produced 10,000 Fiery models. On December 31, 2002, company engineers discovered a possible fire hazard for this model. The probability of fire is estimated at 0.00009. If a fire occurs, the company's liability is estimated at $100,000 per occurrence, plus or minus $30,000. When answering the following questions, show any calculations.

a. Describe the most likely treatment of this contingency in Bonnywill's 2002 financial statements.

b. SFAC 7 (2000) provides a framework for using expected cash flows and present value to measure assets and liabilities. Suggest an alternative treatment using expected values that would portray the liability more accurately.

23. [Contingencies] Consider two firms that self-insure for workers' compensation losses. Assume that the annual probability of a claim is 1 in 1,000 for each firm and that each claim has an expected value of $10,000.

a. Firm A has 3 employees.

b. Firm B has 10,000 employees.

Discuss how each firm should account for its liability for workers' compensation benefits. If there is any difference in your answers, explain why.

24. [Contingencies] Roche made an income statement provision of CHF 2,426 million in 1999 for costs of antitrust cases involving vitamins. Review the references to that case in Roche's financial statements.

a. How much of the 1999 provision was included in cash flows from operating activities?

b. Where does the remaining provision appear on Roche's balance sheet?

c. When will the remaining provision affect cash flows from operating activities?

d. Discuss whether Roche shares should be valued including or excluding this provision.

e. Excluding the effect of the loss provision, should an investor's view of the attractiveness of Roche shares be affected by this loss?

2

ACCOUNTING INCOME AND ASSETS: THE ACCRUAL CONCEPT

CHAPTER OUTLINE

 CASE 2-1

CHAPTER OBJECTIVES

The objectives of this chapter are to:

1. Discuss the accrual principle of accounting.
2. Review the format and classification of the income statement.
3. List and discuss the components of the income statement.
4. Describe the criteria for revenue and expense recognition.
5. Discuss major issues in revenue and expense recognition, and how they affect reported earnings.
6. Compare the percentage-of-completion and completed contract methods of contract accounting.

7. Discuss the revenue recognition methods used for selected industries.
8. Review the types of nonrecurring items, including extraordinary items, discontinued operations, the cumulative effect of accounting changes, and prior period adjustments.
9. Discuss the significance of nonrecurring items to firm valuation.
10. Discuss the concept of earnings quality.
11. Review the format and components of the balance sheet
12. Describe the information contained in the statement of stockholders' equity.

INTRODUCTION

The primary objective of this book is to help users of financial statements develop the skills needed to analyze financial statement data and use these data when making rational investment, credit, and similar decisions. Such decisions require comparison of the risk and return characteristics of alternative investments. Risk and return projections depend on income and cash flow forecasts and assessments of firm assets and liabilities.

Financial statements are the starting point for analysis as they report data about income, cash flows, and assets and liabilities that users can tailor to their specific needs. To do so, they need to understand the information provided by financial statements and the shortcomings of those data. In addition, financial statement users must be able to rearrange the information provided in a manner consistent with their objectives.

The first question is, How should income and cash flow be defined and measured? Are they simply the amounts provided by financial statements or should reported amounts be adjusted? Reporting methods, measurement techniques, and the presentation of financial information can all be criticized in many cases; good analysis requires skepticism.

Comprehensive financial analysis, therefore, requires a thorough understanding of the financial reporting system and its output. Chapter 1 provided a general overview of the accounting process, the reporting system, and their product: the financial statements. We are now ready for the next step. This chapter deals with the income statement and balance sheet—products of the accrual system of accounting. Chapter 3 considers the statement of cash flows. For exposition purposes, we use Pfizer's financial statements.

INCOME, CASH FLOWS, AND ASSETS: DEFINITIONS AND RELATIONSHIPS

As background for the discussion of net income and cash flows in this and the following chapter, we first examine conceptual definitions of "income." We will then explore the relationship between these concepts of income and "accounting income" reported by the current financial reporting system. We use insights from this discussion to delve into the relationship among income, cash flows, and assets as the first stage of the development of our understanding of "return" in our study of comparative risk–return analyses. Later chapters will broaden our understanding of the analysis and use of financial statement information in the evaluation of different elements of risk and return.

This section introduces several conceptual definitions of income, measured in terms of cash flows and changes in the market values of assets.

In a world of certainty,[1] the interrelationship among income, cash flow, and assets is captured by the concept of *economic earnings*, defined as net cash flow plus the change in market value of the firm's net assets. The market value of the firm's assets in this certain world is equal to the present value of their future cash flows discounted at the (risk-free) rate r.

We illustrate this concept using a two-period model with the following assumptions:

- The entity has a single asset, an investment with zero liquidation value.
- The entity has no debt; the asset is 100% equity financed.
- The investment generates a return of $100 at the end of each of two years.
- The $100 received at the end of year 1 is distributed to the owners and not reinvested in the firm.
- The (risk-free) rate r equals 5%.

Because the cash received at the end of each period equals $100 and $r = 5\%$, the value of the firm's assets is

$$\text{Beginning of period 1} = \$100/(1.05) + \$100/(1.05)^2 = \$185.94$$

$$\text{Beginning of period 2} = \$100/(1.05) = \$95.24$$

---

[1]This would include perfect financial markets.

and economic earnings equals cash flow plus the change in net asset value:[2]

$$\text{Period 1: } \$100 + (\$95.24 - \$185.94) = \$9.30$$
$$\text{Period 2: } \$100 + (\$0 - \$95.24) = \$4.76$$

Note that economic income in each year is equal to the rate of return times the opening value of the assets:

$$\text{Period 1: } 0.05 \times \$185.94 = \$9.30$$
$$\text{Period 2: } 0.05 \times \$95.24 = \$4.76$$

Equivalently, the market value at the beginning of the period is equal to a (constant) multiple of earnings equal to $1/r$. In this example, the price/earnings multiple is 20 (1/0.05).

However, future cash flows and interest rates are uncertain in the real world, and the interrelationships are not as neat. Therefore, market prices of assets are also uncertain;[3] available prices may be difficult to relate to the present value of generally unknown, estimated future cash flows discounted at estimated interest rates. These estimates of future cash flows and interest rates and their interrelationships depend on the expectations of different decision makers.

Moreover, the market value of an asset may be measured with different levels of reliability using various (often inconsistent) methods, for example, at its replacement cost or liquidating value. *In this world of uncertainty, income (however measured) is, at best, only a proxy for economic income.* Thus, economists, analysts, and others have developed a number of analytic and practical definitions of earnings to serve as proxies for economic earnings.

Distributable earnings are defined as the amount of earnings that can be paid out as dividends without changing the value of the firm. This concept is derived from the Hicksian definition of income:

> The amount that a person can consume during a period of time and be as well off at the end of that time as at the beginning.[4]

A related measure, *sustainable income*, refers to the level of income that can be maintained in the future given the firm's stock of capital investment (e.g., fixed assets and inventory).

Another measure, *permanent earnings*,[5] used by analysts for valuation purposes is the amount that can be normally earned given the firm's assets and equals the market value of those assets times the firm's required rate of return. Similar to economic earnings, it is the base to which a multiple is applied to arrive at a "fair price."[6]

All these definitions are attempts to capture the concept of economic earnings. Box 2–1 provides a discussion of the difficulties associated with applying these concepts in practice due to measurement and asset valuation problems.

As a result of these difficulties, the financial reporting concept of income—*accounting income*—is often quite different. The analyst, therefore, needs to relate accounting income to the economic income concepts just discussed.

Accounting income is measured using the accrual concept and provides information about the ability of the enterprise to generate future cash flows. It is not, *a priori*, equivalent to any of the definitions discussed earlier.

---

[2]The change in net asset value in this example is often referred to as economic depreciation (see Chapter 8).

[3]Some assets are heavily traded on regulated markets (common stock of companies like Pfizer and Sears), others may be thinly traded (stocks of small companies), and still others have limited secondary markets from which verifiable prices can be obtained (most manufacturing equipment).

[4]J. R. Hicks, *Value and Capital*, 2nd ed. (Oxford: Chaundon Press, 1946), p. 176.

[5]Normalized earnings and earnings power are similar concepts.

[6]The price/earnings ratio used by analysts represents this conceptual relationship.

BOX 2-1
Elaboration of Conceptual Income, Cash Flow, and Asset Relationships

---

The following discussion assumes that all income is paid out as dividends, allowing us to avoid considering reinvestment of income in the firm.

Case A

Assume that a firm purchases an asset at the beginning of each period for $10 and sells it for $12 at the end of each period. Further, assume that this markup of 20% is equivalent to the interest (discount) rate.* Under these conditions, the market value of the firm at the beginning of the period equals the $10 paid for the asset.

The market value of $10 can be derived in a single- or muliperiod context. For a single period, the present value of the end-of-period cash flow is $12/1.20 = $10. If we use a multiperiod model, the firm will earn $2 ($12 sale price less $10 cost of asset). The present value of $2 per period earned for an infinite period equals $2/0.20 = $10.

The economic earnings of the firm equal the cash flow of $2 ($12 − $10), the expected level of earnings in the future; the market value of the firm is a constant $10. Based on this same calculation, the distributable income is also $2, since paying out $2 will not change the value of the firm. Similarly, sustainable income is also $2, as that amount can be distributed without altering the firm's level of operations (buying and selling one asset per period). Finally, since the value of the firm is $10, permanent earnings equal $2 (0.2 × $10). Thus, economic, distributable, sustainable, and permanent earnings are all identical in this simplified case.

However, introducing uncertainty and changing one assumption make the problem much more complex.

Case B

Now assume that the sale price of the asset suddenly increases to $13.20. Accordingly, the purchase price of the asset should also increase as its one-period present value is now $13.20/1.20 = $11.00. Thus, if the firm replaces the asset at the end of that period, economic earnings are the sum of the cash flow of $2.20 ($13.20 − $11.00) and an increase in the market value of the firm of $1.00 (from $10.00 to $11.00), for a total of $3.20.

What are the expected earnings of the firm, given the change in the value of the asset? The answer is clearly not $3.20. It depends on the assumption one makes as to the level of operations the firm maintains.

Maintenance of Physical Level of Assets

If the firm retains the original level of *physical* assets, now valued at $11.00, the expected earnings are $2.20 (20% of $11.00). Note that economic earnings now have two components: operating earnings of $2.20 and a *holding gain* of $1.00. The holding gain results from owning an asset while its market value increases. This "onetime" occurrence cannot be expected to recur. Expected earnings would be the operating earnings as this amount can be expected to continue into the future given the level of physical assets.[†]

Maintenance of Monetary Level of Assets

If we assume that the asset is divisible and the firm does not replace the entire asset but only maintains its *monetary* level of assets by purchasing $10.00 of the now more expensive asset, economic earnings for the current period will still be $3.20.

Net cash flow will be $3.20 ($13.20 sales proceeds − $10.00 reinvestment). Since the market value of assets remains $10.00, economic earnings are $3.20 as above. Expected earnings, however, differ. If the firm retains the original level of monetary assets of $10.00, expected earnings are $2.00 (20% of $10.00).

What happens to the other definitions of income under this scenario? Distributable income is $3.20, which maintains the initial wealth level of $10.00, equivalent to economic earnings. However, sustainable income, the achievable earnings level of the firm in the future, is only $2.00 (if we assume that $3.20 is distributed).

However, if the firm maintains the same physical level of assets and we consider the Hicksian definition of income in terms of the physical measure of assets, both distributable and sustainable income equal $2.20. Similarly, permanent earnings depend on whether the firm retains its original physical asset base (whose value is now $11.00), or whether it retains its original monetary asset base of $10.00. In the former case, permanent earnings are $2.20; in the latter, they will be $2.00.

Under real-world conditions, income measures become judgmental. The neat mappings from one definition to another no longer hold as they become situation specific.

---

*Under conditions of certainty, the rate of return earned on the asset (the 20% markup) equals the prevailing interest rate.
[†]See Box 19-2 for an elaboration of the differing market valuation of permanent and transitory earnings components.

THE ACCRUAL CONCEPT OF INCOME

Accounting and economic income both define income as the sum of cash flows and changes in net assets. However, in financial reporting, the determination of

- Which cash flows are included in income and when
- Which changes in asset and liability values are included in income
- How and when the selected changes in asset and liability values are measured

are based on accounting rules and principles that make up generally accepted accounting principles (GAAP). With a few exceptions, the accounting process only recognizes value changes arising from actual transactions.

Accounting income represents a *selective* recognition of both current period actual cash flows and changes in asset values. Reported income under the accrual concept provides a measure of current operating performance[7] that is not solely based on actual current period cash flows. Cash inflows and outflows (past, present, and future) are recognized in income in the "appropriate" accounting periods, that is, as goods and services are provided and used rather than as cash is collected and expenditures incurred. *The selected period "best" indicates the firm's present and continuing ability to generate future cash flows.*

The accrual concept of accounting income assumes that forecasts of future cash flows require more than historical cash flow data:

> Information about enterprise earnings based on accrual accounting generally provides a better indication of an enterprise's present and continuing ability to generate cash flows than information limited to the financial effects of cash receipts and payments.[8]

The accrual basis of accounting thus allocates (recognizes as revenue and expense) many transactions and events producing cash flows to time periods other than those in which the cash flows occur. Accrual accounting principles are, fundamentally, the decision rules that tell preparers of financial statements when to recognize the revenue and expense consequences of cash flows and other events.

The recognition of revenues and expenses in periods other than when cash is actually received or spent has a corollary effect on the balance sheet. *Under accrual accounting, both the recognition and measurement of certain assets and liabilities are results of the application of the accrual concept of income.* The differences between the income recognized and actual cash flows for the period are *accrued* as assets or liabilities.

In case A in Box 2–1, we assume that an item purchased for $10 at the beginning of period 1 is sold for $12 at the end of that period and replaced at the start of the next period at a cost of $10. If we further assume that the sale is made on credit and cash will be collected in the following period, the actual cash outflow in period 1 is $10, the cost of acquiring the asset at the beginning of period 1.

Under accrual accounting, revenue (expected future cash flow) is recognized at the time of sale, and is reported as an increase of $12 in the asset "accounts receivable." Income is measured as the change in assets plus actual cash flows:

Income = $12 Increase in accounts receivable − $10 Cash outflow = $2

Which is a better indicator of the earning power of the firm and its ability to generate future cash flows: the cash outflow of $10 or the income of $2? The accrual accounting concept reports income of $2, providing better forward-looking information than pure cash flow accounting.

The Matching Principle. Revenue and expense recognition are also governed by the *matching principle*, which states that operating performance can be measured only if related revenues and expenses are accounted for during the same time period. It is the matching principle that requires the expense (cost of goods sold) of inventory to be recognized in the same period in which the sale of that inventory is recorded. This facilitates measurement of the periodic income, that is, operating performance generated by selling inventories during the period regardless of when collections or expenditures occur. In the previous example, if we assume that the item also was purchased on credit in period 1 with payment expected in the following period, accrual accounting would still recognize income of $2 in period 1:

Income = $12 Increase in accounts receivable − $10 Increase in accounts payable = $2

Over the life of the firm, income and cash flows converge. They differ only as to timing of recognition. The recognition of revenues and expenses in "appropriate" accounting periods is both the strength and the weakness of the accrual method. It is a strength in that it results in more meaningful measurement of current operating performance (income statement) and is a better indicator of future operating performance and earnings power. If accrual ac-

---

[7]However, see the discussion of nonrecurring items later in this chapter.

[8]SFAC 1, Objectives of Financial Reporting by Business Enterprises (November 1978), p. ix.

BOX 2-2
Accrual Income versus Cash Flow: Some Empirical Evidence

A number of empirical studies have compared the benefits of accrual income with those of cash flows. Some of these studies asked whether one of the measures provided incremental information,* given the other measure. Those studies[†] offer consistent evidence that, given cash flows from operations (CFO), accruals give incremental information, and given accrual income, CFO provides incremental information.

Bernard and Stober (1989) noted that the variation in cash flow results found by some studies may be caused by using models that do not capture the specific implications of any particular company or situation. That is, in many cases the relative benefits of accruals versus cash flows may be firm-, industry-, and/or situation-specific; they suggest that "further progress in this line of research will require a better understanding of the economic context in which the implications of detailed earnings components are interpreted."[‡]

Livnat and Zarowin (1990) found that, although aggregate CFO did not provide additional informational content, individual components from both CFO and financing cash flows did add incremental information. This, however, does not mean that cash flow information is superior to accrual information as the relevant comparison would have to be with individual components of accrual income.

Dechow (1994) compared accrual income directly with CFO showing that accrual income more closely measured *firm performance as reflected in stock returns*. Moreover, she found that the "superiority" of accrual income as a predictor of stock returns was more likely to occur when cash flows have significant timing and matching problems. That is, accrual income performed better:

- The shorter the interval over which performance is measured
- The more volatile the working capital requirements and investment and financing activities
- The longer the operating cycle of the firm§

Dechow, Kothari, and Watts (1998) showed (consistent with our conjecture in the chapter) that accrual income is a *better predictor of future (operating) cash flows* than current (operating) cash flows (CFO) themselves. Barth, Cram, and Nelson (2001) extended Dechow et al.'s model and found that disaggregating accrual income into its major components** significantly enhanced the predictive ability of operating cash flows incremental to current cash flow itself and aggregate accrual earnings.

Sloan (1996), on the other hand, found that the CFO component of income was more "persistent" than the accrual component; that is, CFO levels achieved were more likely to carry into the future, whereas accruals were (relative to CFO) more transitory and likely to be reversed. Sloan noted that this finding supported financial analysts who compare CFO with reported net income to test the "quality of earnings." Interestingly, Sloan also found that the market seemed to ignore this distinction, lending credence to investing strategies that attempted to find mispriced securities by exploiting the differences between CFO and net income.

---

*In Chapter 5, we provide a more detailed look at and critique of the nature of the "information content" line of empirical research.

[†]See, for example, Judy Rayburn (1986), Wilson (1986), and Bowen, Burgstahler, and Dailey (1987).

[‡]Victor Bernard and Thomas Stober, "The Nature and Amount of Information in Cash Flows and Accruals," *Accounting Review* (October 1989), p. 648. Dechow (1994), Dechow et al. (1998), and Barth et al. (2001) also examined some of these factors.

§Similarly, Dechow et al. and Barth et al., using predictive ability of future CFO as the object of interest, also found their results to vary with the length of the operating cash cycle.

**The components they examined (in addition to cash from operations) were changes in accounts receivable, inventory, accounts payable, depreciation, amortization, and other accruals.

---

counting did not exist, financial analysts would have to invent it.[9] The weakness is that the amount and timing of accruals are subject to management discretion and are based on assumptions and estimates that can and do change over time. Analysts need to differentiate between real events and accruals stemming from management choice.

Overall, as the empirical evidence in Box 2–2 indicates, the accrual process does provide information and enhances the predictive ability of cash flows. However, as the evidence also indicates (and as we elaborate on in Chapter 3), it does not mean that cash flows are not relevant. They provide information as to the *quality* of accounting earnings and can be used to mitigate the weaknesses of the accrual process.

The determination of accounting earnings is also governed by:

- General principles and measurement rules underlying all accounting transactions and events
- Specific rules to determine revenue, expense, gain, and loss recognition

---

[9]This occasionally happens. Because of the deficiencies of (cash-based) regulatory accounting in the insurance industry, analysts developed methods of analysis in the 1960s that eventually were adopted as GAAP by the industry. More recently, German analysts developed their own method of adjusting tax-based income statements.

For example, the *historical cost-based* approach underlying GAAP results in rules that exclude from income *many* unrealized holding gains or losses (increases/decreases in the market value of certain assets and liabilities held by the firm). Recognition of these gains/losses must await the disposal of the assets and the retirement or settlement of the liabilities.

However, some nontransaction-related changes in asset values *can* affect reported income. For example,

- Current assets must be evaluated at each financial statement date and any estimated declines in asset values recognized as losses.
- SFAS 121, Accounting for the Impairment of Long-Lived Assets and for Long-Lived Assets to Be Disposed of, extended this requirement to most classes of fixed assets. The amount and timing of loss recognition remain substantively discretionary because these assets must be evaluated for declines only when certain impairment criteria are present.[10]
- Certain investments in securities are marked to market and changes in market value are reported as a component of income.[11]

Generally, although changes in market values of assets and liabilities may occur over a number of periods, they are recognized in income either in the period of sale or disposal or when certain impairment criteria are met. The result is current period income that may be distorted and may not be indicative of normal earning power. As an initial step, one needs to understand the components that make up the income statement.

Income Statement

Format and Classification

U.S. GAAP do not specify the format of the income statement. Actual formats vary across companies, especially in the reporting of the gain or loss on sale of assets, equity in earnings of affiliates, and other nonoperating income and expense. In some cases, income statement detail appears in financial statement footnotes. Consequently, the sample format presented below should be viewed in a generic sense rather than as a strict rendition of how an income statement is laid out:

Sample Income Statement Format

	Revenues from the sales of goods and services:
+	Other income and revenues
−	Operating expenses
−	Financing costs
+/−	Unusual or infrequent items
=	Pretax earnings from continuing operations
−	Income tax expense
=	Net income from continuing operations*
+/−	Income from discontinued operations (net of tax)*
+/−	Extraordinary items (net of tax)*
+/−	Cumulative effect of accounting changes (net of tax)*
=	Net income*

*Per share amounts are reported for each of these items.

---

[10]See Chapter 8 for a discussion of this standard.

[11]Other investments in securities also are reported at fair value with the unrealized gains and losses accumulated in "other comprehensive income"; these changes are moved to income when the investments are sold. See Chapter 13 for a discussion of the accounting for investments in securities.

IAS Presentation Requirements

IAS 1 (revised 1997) governs the presentation of financial statements prepared in accordance with IAS GAAP. The requirements are broadly similar to those under U.S. GAAP in that financial statement preparers are permitted considerable flexibility as to format as long as all required information is disclosed either on the face of the financial statements or in the financial statement notes. IAS 1 specifically allows for presentation of the income statement in either of two formats:

1. Classification of expenses by function (the format shown above).
2. Classification of expenses based on their nature. Under this alternative, the company reports expenditures using categories such as raw materials, employees, and changes in inventories.

Components of Net Income

The format typically found in actual statements may not be the most useful for analytical purposes. It is important for the analyst to be cognizant of the various categories or groupings into which the income statement components *can* be combined. These groupings do not necessarily coincide with the classifications presented in actual financial statements (or our sample income statement above). In our discussion of the income statement components, we shall follow the suggested groupings presented below. These groupings provide information about different aspects of a firm's operations:

Suggested Format

	Revenues from the sales of goods and services
−	Operating expenses
=	Operating income from continuing operations
+	Other income and revenues
=	Recurring income before interest and taxes from continuing operations
−	Financing costs
=	Recurring (pretax) income from continuing operations
+/−	Unusual or infrequent items
=	Pretax earnings from continuing operations
−	Income tax expense
=	Net income from continuing operations
+/−	Income from discontinued operations (net of tax)
+/−	Extraordinary items (net of tax)
+/−	Cumulative effect of accounting changes (net of tax)
=	Net income

The income statement reports revenues generated by the sales of goods and services from a firm's continuing operations. The costs and expenses incurred to generate these revenues follow. The costs of manufacturing or purchasing the goods sold are normally listed first since they are directly related to the period's revenues. Indirect costs of selling and administrative activities and expense categories such as research and development are reported next. The excess of revenues over these costs and expenses (excluding interest expense) measures the firm's *operating income from continuing operations*, which is independent of its capital structure.

In addition to its core business, a firm may have income (loss) from other activities, such as interest or dividends from investments, equity in (share of) the income of its unconsolidated affiliates, and gains or losses on sales or disposal of assets. *Recurring earnings before interest and taxes from continuing operations* usually include these items and are also independent of the firm's capital structure. Deducting financing costs (interest expense) results in *recurring (pretax) income from continuing operations*.

Unusual or infrequent items, such as pretax gains and losses from the sale or impairment of assets or investments,[12] are often shown as separate line items yielding *pretax income from continuing operations*. Income tax expense is usually the final deduction before arriving at *net income from continuing operations*.

The income statement effects of discontinued operations (discussed later in this chapter) are segregated and reported net of income tax to emphasize the fact that these operations will not contribute to future revenues and income. The net of tax effect of "extraordinary items" is also reported separately because they are incidental to the firm's operating activities, unusual in nature, and not expected to be a normal, recurring component of income and cash flows.

Finally, the income statement separately reports the cumulative effect of accounting changes adopted during the period since they are unrelated to the period's income or operating activities and rarely have any cash flow consequences.[13] Footnotes provide detailed information on both mandatory and voluntary changes in accounting methods, which must be analyzed to evaluate the impact on present and future reported earnings.

A more detailed description and discussion of an income statement and related footnotes, using Pfizer, Inc. as an example, are provided in Box 2–3.

Changes in Income Statement Presentation. Companies sometimes change their income statement presentation in order to obscure unfavorable trends. IBM provides an instructive example. Through 1999, the company listed revenues and various expenses in its income statement separately, showing gross profit, operating income, and net income. Using the 1999 format, the analyst could compute the following trends in operating income[14] and net income.

	Years Ended December 31		
	1997	1998	1999
Percentage change in operating income	5.84%	0.73%	30.15%
Percentage change in net income	12.23%	3.87%	21.87%

In 2000, IBM changed its income statement format to exclude the line item, "operating income," from its income statement. The company continued to report all other line items included in income statements in prior years. This permits us to extend the table through 2000:

	Years Ended December 31			
	1997	1998	1999	2000
Percentage change in operating income	5.84%	0.73%	30.15%	−2.46%
Percentage change in net income	12.23%	3.87%	21.87%	4.94%

Why did IBM change the income statement format? We assume that the company did not wish to highlight the decline in operating income. The lesson is that analysts should use their own formats, allowing them to see trends that management may wish to conceal. Using the same format for all companies within an industry also facilitates comparisons.

---

[12]The appropriate income statement classification of such items and their analytic significance are discussed later in this chapter.

[13]Actual cash flows are not affected by accounting changes unless the firm also changes the method used for income tax reporting (e.g., LIFO, discussed in Chapter 6). However, changes in accounting methods may affect the classification of cash flows, as discussed in Chapter 3.

[14]See Case 17-1 for a comprehensive analysis of IBM's income statement.

BOX 2-3. PFIZER, INC.
Income Statement Components

Pfizer's 1997–1999 income statements illustrate the format used by a manufacturing company. Comments on the individual line items are provided in this box. In addition, we provide below an index listing the chapters containing detailed discussions of selected components of the income statement:

Income Statement Component	Chapter
Net sales–revenue recognition	2
Alliance revenues	2
Costs and operating expenses, which include:	
Cost of sales (Note 1-C)	6
Employee benefits	12
Amortization of goodwill and other	
intangibles (Note 8)	14
Depreciation expense (Note 1-D)	8
Research and development	7
Other income (Note 8), which includes:	
Interest Income	2
Interest expense (net of capitalized interest)	7, 10
Asset impairments	8, 14
Restructuring charges	2
Gain (loss) on foreign currency transactions	15
Legal settlements	2
Other "nonrecurring" items	2
Minority interests	13
Income taxes	9
Discontinued operations	2
Earnings per share	4

Net sales include proceeds from human and animal pharmaceutical product sales. Pfizer also reports alliance revenues (generally, a percentage of partners' sales) from co-promoted products developed by other companies. Reported revenue may not be comparable across firms because it depends on management's choice of revenue recognition methods and significant estimates and assumptions.

Costs and operating (selling, informational, and administrative) expenses include the majority of the costs of producing the medical products that constitute Pfizer's operations. Cost of sales includes the cost of raw materials, supplies, and manufacturing outlays. Pfizer's 1999 cost of sales also includes a $310 million write-off of excess inventories of a suspended drug (Note 1-C) and a $6.6 million benefit of a change to the first-in, first-out (FIFO) inventory costing method (Note 6).

Depreciation expense reflects the allocation of past expenditures for property, plant, and equipment. Goodwill amortization (reported in the other deductions–net component) represents a systematic allocation of the excess purchase price (over fair value) of net assets acquired. Pfizer's expenditures for *research and development* are expensed in the period incurred as required by U.S. GAAP.

Selling, general, and administrative expenses* (SG&A) include operating expenses not reported as components of costs of goods sold. The division between costs of goods sold and SG&A depends on the company's accounting choices, and the breakdown may not be comparable among firms. SG&A expenses are not always directly related to sales levels as they contain fixed components. In Note 1-H, Pfizer separately reports its accounting policies and annual expense for advertising and promotional activities.

In *other deductions* (see Note 8) Pfizer reports interest income, interest expense (net of capitalized interest), and costs of legal settlements. The company also incurred a loss on foreign currency transactions.

Note 8 also shows that, in 1998, the company recorded $177 million of restructuring charges and $213 million in asset impairments for workforce reductions and plant and product lines rationalizations. These restructuring plans were substantially completed in 1999. In 1998, Pfizer recorded large expenses for co-promotion payments to Searle and for a contribution to the Pfizer Foundation.

Interest expense reflects financing charges net of capitalized interest. The recognition of minority interest in consolidated subsidiaries and a *provision for income taxes* completes the computation of income from continuing operations.

Note 2, Discontinued Operations, reports a 1999 payment of $20 million to settle antitrust charges concerning a business group divested in 1996. *Earnings per share* are reported separately for income from continuing operations, loss from discontinued operations, and net income. Note 15, earnings per common share, discloses and reconciles the number of shares used to compute both basic and diluted per-share amounts. The note also reports the effect of dilutive securities.

*Unlike most companies, Pfizer uses the term *selling, informational, and administrative (SI&A) expenses*.

Recurring versus Nonrecurring Items

Reported net income is only loosely related to the concept of *comprehensive income* discussed in Chapter 1. It contains income from operations as well as all realized (but only some unrealized) changes in the market value of assets and liabilities.

From an analyst's perspective, however, it may not be the most informative measure of the income and cash-generating ability of the firm. Generally, income from a firm's recurring operating activities is considered the best indicator of future income. The predictive ability of reported income is enhanced if it excludes the impact of transitory or random components, which are not directly related to operating activities and are generally more volatile. The economic concepts of income discussed earlier (and elaborated on in Box 2–1) tell us that transitory gains or losses should not be regarded as components of permanent or sustainable income. The concept of recurring income is similar to permanent or sustainable income in the sense that it is persistent; that is, its level or rate of growth is relatively predictable, and cash flows will eventually follow at the predicted levels and growth rates.

If we use the terminology above, *recurring income (pretax or post tax[15]) from continuing operations* should be the primary focus of analysis.

Segregation of the results of normal, recurring operations from the effects of nonrecurring items facilitates the forecasting of future earnings and cash flows. Financial reporting defines nonrecurring by the *type of transaction or event*. However, depending on the firm, the nature of the event, and to some extent management discretion, similar transactions may be included in operating income or reported below the line. Operational definitions of "operating," "nonrecurring," and "extraordinary" are elusive and both accounting standards setters and analysts have struggled with this issue for decades.

More recently, companies have increasingly provided early indications of their results for a period by announcing earnings in advance of scheduled annual or quarterly release dates. The nature of these early announcements has further blurred the distinctions between "operating," "nonrecurring," and "extraordinary" components of income. We elaborate on this issue elsewhere in this chapter.

For purposes of analysis, however, the important issue is whether each item classified by management as nonrecurring income or loss in a given year is a good predictor of future income or loss. For example, for some firms, a material gain or loss from the sale of fixed assets will be rare; the transaction reported has no predictive value. Other firms retire fixed assets each year and regularly report gains or losses (e.g., consider a car rental company that retires part of its fleet of cars annually). In the latter case, the analytic issue is whether this year's income or loss from the sale of retired property is higher or lower than the "normal" amount.

Ultimately, the analyst must evaluate the significance of nonrecurring items, regardless of whether they are reported in the extraordinary, unusual, or some other category, in the prediction of earnings power. The goal of analysis of the income statement is to derive an effective measure of future earnings and cash flows. Therefore, analysts often exclude components of reported income (regardless of their accounting labels) that may reduce its predictive ability.

Fairfield et al. (1996) examined whether the classification scheme used in financial statements can improve predictive ability. Their results indicated that the forecasting of one-year-ahead profitability, that is, return on equity (ROE), was improved by disaggregating previous year's ROE into the separate components discussed earlier. They found that extraordinary items and discontinued operations were not useful in predicting bottom-line ROE or ROE from continuing operations *although unusual and infrequent items were*. This latter result implies that unusual or infrequent items often contain a recurring element.

The predictive ability objective does not mean that financial analysis of the income (or other financial) statements is simply the extrapolation of previous trends. Rather, all financial statement information should be viewed as part of a database that provides limited information about future prospects and opportunities facing the firm. For example, an increase in the sale of semiconductors also provides useful information about the demand for equipment used for their manufacture.

Nonrecurring items can also provide such information, but in a different fashion. The implication of the sale of an operating asset, for example, depends on the utilization of the cash generated by the sale, and how its productive capacity will be replaced.

---

[15]Recurring income on a post-tax basis can be arrived at by either (1) adding back to net income from continuing operations the after-tax consequences of unusual or infrequent items, that is,

$$\text{Net income from recurring operations} =$$
$$\text{Net income from continuing operations} +/- [\text{unusual or infrequent items} \times (1 - \text{tax rate})]$$

or (2) adjusting recurring income from continuing operations directly for taxes:

$$\text{Net income from recurring operations} =$$
$$\text{Recurring income from continuing operations} \times (1 - \text{tax rate})$$

We return to nonrecurring items later in the chapter. First, however, we look at the revenue and expense recognition rules used to report a firm's recurring operations.

Accounting Income: Revenue and Expense Recognition

When accrual accounting is used to prepare financial statements, two revenue and expense recognition issues must be addressed:

1. *Timing*. When should revenue and expense be recognized?
2. *Measurement*. How much revenue and expense should be recognized?

The responses to these questions determine the amount and timing of periodic revenue and expense. In practice, there is considerable scope for management discretion with respect to both revenue and expense recognition. At this point, however, the focus of our discussion is revenue recognition and how the application of the *matching principle* relates expense recognition to revenue recognition.[16] Other issues of expense recognition are discussed, on an issue-by-issue basis, in the chapters that follow.

Statement of Financial Accounting Concepts (SFAC) 5, Recognition and Measurement in Financial Statements of Business Enterprises, specifies *two conditions that must be met for revenue recognition to take place.* These conditions are:

1. Completion of the earnings process
2. Assurance of payment

To satisfy the first condition, the firm must have provided all or virtually all the goods or services for which it is to be paid, and it must be possible to measure the total expected cost of providing the goods or services; that is, the seller must have no remaining significant contingent obligation. If the seller is obligated to provide future services, for example, warranty protection for equipment or upgrades and enhancements for software, but cannot estimate the cost of doing so, this condition is not satisfied.

Revenue recognition also requires a second condition: the quantification of cash or assets expected to be received for the goods or services provided. Reliable measurement encompasses the realizability (collectibility) of the proceeds of sale. If the seller cannot reasonably estimate the probability of nonpayment, realization is not reasonably assured, and the second condition is not satisfied.

The general rule for revenue recognition includes this concept of realizability: Revenue, measured as the amount expected to be collected, can be recognized when goods or services have been provided and their cost can be reliably determined.

The amount of revenue recognized at any given point in time is measured as

$$\frac{\textbf{Goods and services provided to date}}{\textbf{Total goods and services to be provided}} \times \textbf{Total expected revenue}$$

This equation measures the amount of revenue recognized *cumulatively* to date. Revenue reported for the current period is the *cumulative total less revenue recognized in prior periods.*

The most common case is revenue recognition at the time of sale. Goods or services have been provided, and the sale is for cash or to customers whose ability to pay is reasonably assured.[17]

---

[16]Direct costs, such as cost of goods sold, are recognized as related revenue as recognized under accrual accounting. Note that the cost of goods sold often includes depreciation expense or capitalized overhead. However, other expenses cannot be directly related to revenues and must be recognized using different principles. Some, called period costs (e.g., advertising costs), are expensed as incurred. Other costs are recognized as time passes, for example, interest costs. Finally, some costs may be based on other criteria, for example, taxes on income.

[17]In some cases, the buyer has a right to return unsold goods. If the risks or benefits (or both) of ownership are retained by the "seller," the transaction is, in economic substance, a consignment rather than a completed sale. SFAS 48, Revenue Recognition When Right of Return Exists, governs such sales. See also SFAS 49, Accounting for Product Financing Arrangements.

In some cases, payment is received prior to the delivery of goods or services. Examples include:

- Magazine publishers receive subscription payments in advance; the receipts represent an obligation to provide periodic delivery of the publication. Revenues are recognized in proportion to issues delivered.
- Credit card fees are recognized as advances from customers; revenue is recorded as the right to use the cards expires over time.
- Revenue from leased equipment is recognized as time passes or based on usage (copier rental is sometimes based on a per-copy charge).

These examples show that revenue recognition can be measured by cash expenditures, the passage of time, or the provision of service (measured in physical units) to the customer.

Departures from the Sales Basis of Revenue Recognition

Revenue may be recognized *prior* to sale or delivery when the earnings process is substantially complete and the proceeds of sale can be reasonably measured. For example, revenue is recognized at the completion of production in the case of commodities (such as oil or agricultural products) with highly organized and liquid markets or, in the case of long-term construction contracts, as production takes place.

Alternatively, revenues may not be recognized even at the time of sale if there is significant uncertainty regarding the seller's ability to collect the sales price or to estimate remaining costs. Either the installment method or the more extreme cost recovery method, both discussed shortly, must be used in such cases.

Percentage-of-Completion and Completed Contract Methods

The *percentage-of-completion* method recognizes revenues and costs in proportion to and as work is completed; production activity is considered the critical event in signaling the completion of the earnings process rather than delivery or cash collections. This method is used for long-term projects when there is a contract, and reliable estimates of production completed, revenues, and costs are possible.

The percentage-of-completion method measures progress toward completion using *either*:

- Engineering estimates (or physical milestones such as miles of road completed), or
- Ratios of costs incurred to expected total costs.

This method may overstate revenue and gross profit if expenditures made are recognized before they contribute to completed work, for example, when the costs of raw materials and advance payments to subcontractors are included in the determination of work completed.

When estimates of revenue or costs change, a catch-up effect is included in the earnings of the period in which the change in estimate is made. Earnings of prior periods are not restated because it is a change in accounting estimate. When a loss is expected on the contract, it must be recognized in the period the amount of the loss can be estimated.

The *completed contract method* recognizes revenues and expenses only at the end of the contract. It must be used when any one of the conditions required for the use of the percentage-of-completion method is not met, generally when no contract exists or estimates of the selling price or collectibility are not reliable. It must be used for short-term contracts.[18]

Comparison of Percentage-of-Completion and Completed Contract Methods

Exhibit 2–1 compares the percentage-of-completion and completed contract revenue recognition methods. Part A compares the revenues, expenses, and income reported under each method for each year. Computations for the percentage-of-completion method use the ratio

---

[18]SFAS 56 (1982) emphasizes that the percentage-of-completion and the completed contract method are not "intended to be free-choice alternatives under either Accounting Research Bulletin No. 45 (ARB 45) or AICPA SOP 81-1." ARB 45 states that the percentage-of-completion method is preferable when estimates of costs and degree of completion are reliable. SOP 81-1 reiterates this position.

EXHIBIT 2-1
Comparison of Percentage-of-Completion and Completed Contract
Revenue Recognition Methods

In 2001, Justin Corp. entered into a construction project with a total contract price of $6 million and expected costs to complete of $4.8 million resulting in expected profits of $1.2 million.

Actual production costs and cash flow information over the duration of the contract are provided as follows (in $thousands):

	2001	2002	2003
Costs incurred: Current year	$ 800	$2,800	$1,200
Cumulative	800	3,600	4,800
Estimated *remaining* costs to complete (as of December 31)	4,000	1,200	0
Amounts billed and cash received			
Current year	$1,300	$2,500	$2,200
Cumulative	1,300	3,800	6,000

A. Income Statement (in $ thousands)

	Percentage-of-Completion				Completed Contract			
	2001	2002	2003	Total	2001	2002	2003	Total
Revenue*	$1,000	$3,500	$1,500	$6,000	$0	$0	$6,000	$6,000
Expense	(800)	(2,800)	(1,200)	(4,800)	(0)	(0)	(4,800)	(4,800)
Income	$ 200	$ 700	$ 300	$1,200	$0	$0	$1,200	$1,200

$$*2001: \frac{\$800}{\$4,800} \times \$6,000 = \$1,000$$

$$2002: \frac{(\$800 + \$2,800)}{\$4,800} \times \$6,000 = \$4,500 - \$1,000 = \$3,500$$

$$2003: \frac{(\$800 + \$2,800 + \$1,200)}{\$4,800} \times \$6,000 = \$6,000 - \$4,500 = \$1,500$$

B. Balance Sheet (in $ thousands)

	Percentage-of-Completion			Completed Contract		
	2001	2002	2003	2001	2002	2003
Assets						
Cash	$500	$200	$1,200	$500	$200	$1,200
Construction in progress	0	700	0	0	0	0
Total assets	$500	$900	$1,200	$500	$200	$1,200
Liabilities and equity						
Advance billings	$300	$ 0	$ 0	$500	$200	$ 0
Retained earnings	200	900	1,200	0	0	1,200
Total liabilities and equity	$500	$900	$1,200	$500	$200	$1,200

Explanation:

Cash: Identical for both methods and equivalent to cumulative cash received less costs incurred.

Retained earnings: Cumulative earnings since inception of project.

(continued)

EXHIBIT 2-1 *(continued)*

Construction in progress and advance billings: *Net* amount of following table where advance billings represent cumulative cash received and construction in progress is based on cumulative costs incurred plus profit recognized:

	Percentage-of-Completion			Completed Contract		
	2001	2002	2003	2001	2002	2003
Costs incurred	$ 800	$3,600	$4,800	$800	$3,600	$4,800
Profit recognized	200	900	1,200	0	0	1,200
Construction in progress	**$1,000**	**$4,500**	**$6,000**	**$800**	**$3,600**	**$6,000**
Advance billings	**(1,300)**	**(3,800)**	**(6,000)**	**(1,300)**	**(3,800)**	**(6,000)**
Net asset (liability)	**$ (300)**	**$ 700**	**$ 0**	**$(500)**	**$ (200)**	**$ 0**

C. Change in Estimated Costs to Complete

On December 31, 2002, Justin Corp. determines that the total cost of the project will be $5,400, making remaining costs to complete $1,800, an increase of $600 from the original estimate. This changes *both* revenue and income for 2002 under the percentage-of-completion method. The adjustment is made on a cumulative basis; revenue and expense reported for previous years are *not* restated.

Cumulative revenue recognized is

$$\frac{\$3,600 \text{ (cumulative costs incurred}}{\$5,400 \text{ (revised total costs)}} \times \$6,000)$$

$$= \$4,000, \text{ of which } \$1,000 \text{ was recognized as revenue in 2001.}$$

Therefore, $3,000 ($4,000 − $1,000) is recognized as revenue for 2002.
Cumulative expense recognized is $3,600, the total incurred. Expense recognized for 2002 remains unchanged at $1,800. As a result, income recognized in 2002 is $3,000 − $2,800 = $200.

The revised income statements for percentage of completion are presented below in panel I. (For completed contract, the revision would all be reflected in year 2003.)

Panel II shows what percentage of completion income would have been had Justin known the actual costs at the beginning of the project.

Percentage-of-Completion

	I. Revised				*II. Foreknowledge of Actual Costs*			
	2001	2002	2003	Total	2001	2002	2003	Total
Revenue	$1,000	$3,000	$2,000	$6,000	$889	$3,111	$2,000	$6,000
Expense	(800)	(2,800)	(1,800)	(5,400)	(800)	(2,800)	(1,800)	(5,400)
Income	$ 200	$ 200	$ 200	$ 600	$ 89	$ 311	$ 200	$ 600

of costs (assumed to provide a reliable measure of actual work performed) incurred each period to expected total costs. In 2001, 16.67% of estimated costs are incurred, so that revenue recognized for that year equals 16.67% of the contract price. As a result, if we use the matching principle, the same percentage (16.67%) of expected total expenses and total income is recognized for 2001. This pattern is repeated as long as actual results closely mirror expectations.

Under the completed contract method, revenues, expenses, and income are recognized only at the end of the contract period; no revenue, expense, or income is reported during the first two years.

As a result, the two different revenue recognition methods produce different patterns of reported revenue, expense, and income, although total revenue, expense, and income over the life of the contract are identical under both methods.

The percentage-of-completion method provides both a better measure of operating activity and a more informative disclosure of the status of incomplete contracts. For a firm with constant revenues the two methods produce identical results.[19] However, since the business world is rarely in a steady state of equilibrium, *the percentage-of-completion method reports income earlier and is a better indicator of trends in earning power*. Although better disclosure of contracts in progress under the completed contract method would help analysts forecast future operating results and cash flows, the percentage-of-completion method is more informative.

The choice of method also affects the reported assets and liabilities on the balance sheet. Part B shows the balance sheet effects of the two methods.

Under the completed contract method, expenditures prior to completion are reported as inventory (*construction-in-progress*) and cash receipts as advances from customers.

Using the percentage-of-completion method,

- Costs incurred are also accumulated in an asset account titled *construction-in-progress*. However, *gross profit* (*income*) *for the period is also accumulated in the construction-in-progress account*. (Periodic gross profit is not recognized under the completed contract method.)

- Amounts billed to customers are recorded as a liability (*advance billings*) and an asset (accounts receivable). When cash is received, the receivable is reduced. The difference between cash received and billings is treated as accounts receivable.[20]

For financial reporting purposes, construction-in-progress and advance billings are netted. For example, at the end of 2001 (percentage of completion method), Justin's balance sheet will show (a liability of) $300 as "amounts billed in excess of contract costs." At the end of 2002 (percentage of completion method), Justin will report (an asset of) $700 as "contract costs in excess of amounts billed." For a company with many contracts in process, it is typical to find both net asset and net liability amounts on the balance sheet. The gross amounts will be reported in footnotes.

At the end of the contract period, under both methods, the construction-in-progress and advance billings accounts are eliminated. Thus, at contract completion under both methods, the only remaining balance sheet amounts are cash and retained earnings. Both amounts equal $1,200, which is the profit on the contract.

■ Example

Chicago Bridge & Iron is a global engineering and construction firm. Its 10-K report for the year ended December 31, 1999 lists, among significant accounting policies:

> REVENUE RECOGNITION: Revenues are recognized using the percentage of completion method. Contract revenues are accrued based generally on the percentage that costs-to-date bear to total estimated costs.

Footnote 3 contains the following table:

Contracts in Progress	1999	1998
Revenues recognized on contracts in progress	$808,312	$871,100
Billings on contracts in progress	(813,140)	(896,506)
Shown on balance sheet as:		
Contracts in progress with earned revenues exceeding related progress billings (asset)	$ 48,486	$ 51,953
Contracts in progress with progress billings exceeding related earned revenues (liability)	(53,314)	(77,359)
	$ (4,828)	$(25,406) ■

---

[19]This statement assumes that, with a large number of contracts, income recognized from contracts completed in each period would be equal to the income recognized from the partial completion of contracts in process.

[20]In our example, amounts billed and cash received were identical, leaving a zero receivables balance.

As can be seen from the above table, the netting process reduces very large activities to relatively small net amounts on the balance sheet. As Chicago Bridge had total assets of $337 million at December 31, 1999, reporting revenues and billings gross would have greatly increased total assets and liabilities.

Returning to part B of the Justin example, the only difference in the balance sheet effects of the two methods is that, under the percentage-of-completion method, there is an additional accrual of gross profit in construction-in-progress. When there is an excess of advance billings over costs (e.g., 2001), reported total assets are identical under both methods. When construction-in-progress exceeds billings (e.g., 2002), total assets will be higher under the percentage-of-completion method. For all years, liabilities are lower and retained earnings (equity) higher under the percentage-of-completion method, reflecting the higher level of construction-in-progress.

Generalizing these effects for a company with a continuing flow of profitable contracts, under the percentage-of-completion method:

- Total assets are higher, reflecting the accrual of gross profit during the contract period.
- Liabilities are lower as the higher level of construction-in-progress provides a larger offset.
- Stockholders' equity is higher due to the earlier accrual of gross profit.
- The ratio of liabilities to equity is lower, reflecting lower liabilities and higher equity.

Part C shows the impact of a change in estimate: The estimated cost to complete is increased at the end of the second year (2002). This increase is recognized in 2002, and that year's income reflects the income on work completed during the period offset by the impact of the change in estimate. Note that the cumulative income correctly reflects the degree of completion using the revised cost estimate.[21]

Installment Method of Revenue Recognition

Revenues should not be recognized at the time of sale or delivery when there is no reasonable basis to estimate collectibility of the sales proceeds. The installment method recognizes gross profit in proportion to cash collections, resulting in delayed recognition of revenues and expenses as compared with full recognition at the time of sale. This method is sometimes used to report income from sales of noncurrent assets and real estate transactions.

Cost Recovery Method

Revenue recognition on sale or delivery is also precluded when the costs to provide goods or services cannot be reasonably determined, for example, in the development of raw land. This occurs when completion of the sale is dependent on expenditures to be made in the future (e.g., road construction) and it is impossible to estimate the amount of those expenditures (which may depend on zoning or environmental factors).

In many cases, there is also substantial uncertainty about revenue realization since only small down payments may be required with nonrecourse financing provided by the seller. With both future costs and collection uncertain, the cost recovery method requires that all cash receipts be first accounted for as a recovery of costs. Only after all costs are recovered can profit be recognized under this method.[22]

---

[21]The firm has completed two-thirds ($3,600 of costs incurred to date out of total expected costs of $5,400) of the work on the project and at the end of the year will have recognized $400 or two-thirds of expected income of $600 ($200 in 2001 and $200 in 2002).

    Similarly, if the firm estimated the remaining cost to complete the project at $2,750 at the end of 2002 (rather than the original $1,200), the expected loss of $350 (on the entire contract) would be recognized in that year. The previously recognized earnings would be offset and the full contract loss would be recognized in 2002, the year in which it can be estimated, even though some of that loss will be incurred in 2003.

[22]When a company markets, sells, or leases software originally developed for internal use, SOP 98-1, Accounting for the Costs of Computer Software Developed for Internal Use, requires the application of the cost recovery method until all unamortized costs have been recovered.

The installment and cost recovery methods may be used to recognize franchise revenues[23] when revenue is collectible over an extended period and there is no reasonable basis to estimate that collectibility. These methods may also be used, under specific circumstances, in real estate sales and retail land sales.[24]

Issues in Revenue and Expense Recognition

While the theoretical basis for revenue and expense recognition appears to be straightforward, the application of these principles has been inconsistent in practice, especially in those areas where GAAP itself lacks definitive standards. Companies have strong incentives to accelerate the recognition of revenues and delay the recording of expense. The significant growth in (1) technology and (2) the use of revenue and gross margin to value companies without earnings have increased the incentives to use accounting methods that increase reported revenues. The result has been new guidelines (a series of consensuses from the Emerging Issues Task Force (EITF) and the U.S. Securities and Exchange Commission). SEC Staff Accounting Bulletin 101, Revenue Recognition in Financial Statements, and Frequently Asked Questions and Answers related to SAB 101[25] forced many companies (including many "old economy" firms) to change their reported revenue and expense.

The accounting issues can be categorized as follows:

1. Revenue recognition
2. Expense recognition
3. Classification

We discuss each of these in turn. The end-of-chapter problems illustrate the financial statement effects of some of these accounting methods. While some of these issues relate primarily to technology companies, virtually any company's income statement may be affected.

Revenue Recognition

Some accounting issues affect the amount and/or timing of revenue recognition. Examples include:

- Sales incentives (such as discounts or the granting of stock options to customers) to achieve revenue goals. Such incentives may become especially important when a company nears the end of a reporting period and wishes to meet its preannounced revenue goals. In extreme cases, companies may provide rights of return or other privileges that violate the realization principle (and may not be recorded or disclosed to auditors).
- Barter arrangements under which a firm provides goods or services to another in exchange for that firm's goods or services. Barter revenues may be recorded at "list prices" rather than the lower prices that would pertain to arm's-length transactions.
- Recording license fees or membership fees when an agreement is signed, rather than over the term of the agreement.
- Recording revenues based on estimated usage, even when bills have not been sent out.[26]
- Companies that act as agents (e.g., advertising agencies or sales intermediaries) record the gross amount billed as revenue rather than their commission income.
- Recognition of all revenue from a contract even when the customer has not yet agreed that the project is fully installed and operational.
- Reporting shipping and handling costs charged to customers as revenues.

---

[23] See SFAS 45, Accounting for Franchise Fee Revenue, para. 6 (FASB, 1981).

[24] See SFAS 66, Accounting for Sales of Real Estate (FASB, 1982).

[25] http://www.sec.gov/info/accountants/sab101faq.htm.

[26] Many utility companies report "unbilled revenues" as sales.

These and other practices vary among companies, making comparisons of revenue levels and growth difficult. When analysts use revenues to value company shares, the incentive to use accounting methods that maximize reported revenues is very high.

When companies are forced to change their revenue recognition policies, the consequences for shareholders can be dire. Consider the example of MicroStrategy [MSTR], a provider of business software, which was required to restate its operating results for 1997 through 1999. Exhibit 2–2 contains an extract from MSTR's 10-K report, showing the effect of the restatement and explaining the accounting changes. Note the significant changes in revenues (1998 and 1999), net income (all three years), accounts receivable, deferred revenues, and stockholders' equity.

EXHIBIT 2-2. MICROSTRATEGY
Restatement for Change in Revenue Recognition Policies

NOTES TO CONSOLIDATED FINANCIAL STATEMENTS
(3) Restatement of Financial Statements

Subsequent to the filing of a registration statement on Form S-3 with the SEC which included the Company's audited financial statements for the years ended December 31, 1999, 1998 and 1997 the Company became aware that the timing and amount of reported earned revenues from license transactions in 1999, 1998 and 1997 required revision.

These revisions primarily addressed the recognition of revenue for certain software arrangements which should be accounted for under the subscription method or the percentage of completion method, which spread the recognition of revenue over the entire contract period. For example, when fees are received in a transaction in which the Company is licensing software and also performing significant development, customization or consulting services, the fees should be recognized using the percentage of completion method and, therefore, product license and product support and other services revenue are recognized as work progresses. Revenue from arrangements where the Company provides hosting services is generally recognized over the hosting term, which is generally two to three years. The effect of these revisions is to defer the time in which revenue is recognized for large, complex contracts that combine both products and services. These revisions also resulted in a substantial increase in the amount of deferred revenue reflected on the Company's balance sheet at the end of 1999 and 1998. Additionally, these revisions include the effects of changes in the reporting periods when revenue from certain contracts are recognized. In the course of reviewing its revenue recognition on various transactions, the Company became aware that, in certain instances, the Company had recorded revenue on certain contracts in one reporting period where customer signature and delivery had been completed, but where the contract may not have been fully executed by the Company in that reporting period. The Company subsequently reviewed license agreements executed near the end of the years 1999, 1998 and 1997 and determined that revisions were necessary to ensure that all agreements for which the Company was recognizing revenue in a reporting period were executed by both parties no later than the end of the reporting period in which the revenue is recognized. The total effect of all revisions to revenue was to reduce revenues by $54.0 million, $10.9 million and $1.0 million for the years ended December 31, 1999, 1998 and 1997, respectively.

The Company also made certain revisions to our balance sheet as of December 31, 1999.

Accordingly, such financial statements have been restated as follows:

Statements of Operations Data	1999 Reported	1999 Restated	1998 Reported	1998 Restated	1997 Reported	1997 Restated
Revenues:						
Product licenses	$143,193	$85,797	$72,721	$61,635	$36,601	$35,478
Product support and other services	62,136	65,461	33,709	33,854	16,956	17,073
Income (loss) from operations	18,319	(34,533)	9	(2,549)	372	(634)
Provision for income taxes	7,735	1,246	3,442	—	—	—
Net income (loss)	12,620	(33,743)	6,178	(2,255)	121	(885)
Balance sheet data						
Accounts receivable, net	61,149	37,586	33,054	25,377	16,085	15,121
Deferred revenue and advance payments (current and noncurrent)	16,782	71,283	11,478	13,048	9,387	9,429
Retained earnings (deficit)	17,849	(37,953)	5,229	(4,210)	(634)	(1,640)

Source: MicroStrategy 10-K, December 31, 1999.

MicroStrategy shares, which reached a price of $333 on March 10, 2000 (ten days prior to announcement of the restatement) fell to less than $17 in late May. One year later the share price was below $4.

Expense Recognition

The following accounting issues affect the amount and/or timing of expense recognition:

- Deferral of marketing expenses and sales commissions
- Accrual or deferral of the cost of periodic major maintenance projects
- Bad debt expense
- Warranty expense

Deferral of Marketing Expenses and Sales Commissions. When marketing costs or sales commissions are deferred, reported income increases. While deferred expenses must be recognized sooner or later, the deferral of expenses by growth companies may exceed the recognition of previously deferred costs for extended time periods.

■ Example

Sears defers direct marketing expenses associated with catalog and other sales activities. Note 1 states that such capitalized costs rose from $131 million at January 2, 1999 to $180 million at January 1, 2000. If all costs had been expensed, Sears' pretax income would have been $49 million ($180 − $131) lower. ■

Expensing Periodic Major Maintenance Projects. Some fixed assets require periodic major overhauls. Firms can either accrue the costs in advance (and charge the actual expenditure against the accrued liability) or defer recognizing the expense until it is actually incurred. The latter method delays expense recognition, increasing reported earnings.[27] A third alternative is to capitalize the actual expenditure and amortize it against earnings in subsequent years (as will be discussed in Chapter 7).

■ Example

Airborne Freight [ABF] stated in its 2000 annual report:

> Effective January 1, 2000, the Company changed its method of accounting for major engine overhaul costs on DC-9 aircraft from the accrual method to the direct expense method where costs are expensed as incurred. Previously, these costs were accrued in advance of the next scheduled overhaul based upon engine usage and estimates of overhaul costs.

The change resulted in a cumulative effect (for prior periods) of $14.2 million and increased earnings for 2000 by $3.7 million. Adding the two components together, the change accounted for 63% of Airborne's total earnings for the year of $28.5 million. ■

Bad Debt Expense. Credit losses affect reported income only indirectly and not at the time they actually occur. The timing of the expense recognition for bad debts and the actual receivable write-off do not coincide. Each year a company makes a provision for bad debt expense reflecting its estimate of the proportion of its credit customers who will default. In making this estimate, the company sets up a reserve for bad debts (allowance for doubtful accounts). When an actual write-off occurs (i.e., it becomes certain that the customer will not pay), the charge is made to the reserve, not earnings.

---

[27]For example, a company anticipating a $3 million overhaul in three years would, under the accrual method, recognize an expense (and accrued liability of) $1 million in each of the three years in advance of the overhaul. At the time of the overhaul, the $3 million expenditure would reduce the liability. Recognizing the expense only when incurred would result in a $3 million expense in the year of the overhaul and no expense (or liability) in the years leading up to the overhaul.

The procedure is illustrated in the example below. The example also indicates that the estimation process for bad debts can be used to smooth earnings and/or delay the reporting of bad news. Analysts should watch the level of the reserve relative to receivables (considering economic conditions within the industry) as well as the provision against earnings.

■ Example: Lucent

The Lucent [LU] 1999 financial statements show the following data ($millions):

	September 30	
	1998	1999
Sales	$31,806	$38,303
Receivables (net of allowance)	7,405	10,438
Allowance for doubtful accounts	416	362
Add back the allowance to get gross receivables	$7,821	$10,800
Allowance as % of gross receivables	5.32%	3.35%

There are two red flags here. One is the decline in the allowance relative to gross receivables. The second is the 38% increase in gross receivables, compared with a 1999 sales increase of only 20%.

Lucent's 1999 10-K reveals the following additional data relating to the changes in its bad debt reserve:

	Years Ended September 30	
	1998	1999
Allowance for doubtful accounts (beginning balance)	363	416
Bad debt expense	132	68
Write-offs	(20)	(159)
Other changes	(59)	37
Allowance for doubtful accounts (ending balance)	416	362

As the above table indicates, the timing of the expense for bad debt and the actual write-off do not coincide. In 1998 Lucent recorded bad debt expense of $132 million, increasing the allowance for doubtful accounts. The actual accounts receivable written off as uncollectible was only $20 million. That amount was not expensed but charged against the reserve.[28] In 1999, the situation reversed, as the amount expensed ($68 million) was considerably less than the amount actually written off ($159 million).

Lucent reduced its provision for bad debts in 1999 although actual credit losses rose substantially from the 1998 level. Had Lucent made a provision sufficient to bring the allowance relative to gross receivables up to the fiscal 1998 level ($10,800 × .0532 = $575 million), its pretax income would have been ($575 − $362) $213 million (4%) lower.

It should be noted that in the years 2000 and 2001, Lucent wrote off approximately $1 billion of receivables, evidence that the 1999 year-end provision (of $362 million) was insufficient.

In September 1999, a Lucent subsidiary sold $625 million of accounts receivable to a nonconsolidated entity and the company itself transferred $700 million of accounts receivable as collateral to that entity. Thus, Lucent removed $1,325 million of receivables (but not the related allowance for doubtful accounts).[29] Without these transactions, on September 30, 1999, Lucent's receivables balance would have been $12,125 million

---

[28]Lucent's entries in 1998 were

| Bad debt expense $132 | | and | Allowance for doubtful accounts | $20 |
| Allowance for doubtful accounts $132 | | | Accounts receivable | $20 |

[29]See Chapter 11 for our discussion of the financial statement impact of sales of receivables.

(instead of the reported $10,800 million). The actual increase in receivables was 55%, much higher than the 20% increase in sales. The company would have needed an allowance for doubtful accounts balance of $645 million to reflect an allowance comparable to that reported in 1998 and its pretax income would have been ($645 − $362) $283 million (5.4%) lower. *During December 1999, Lucent repurchased $408 million of the $625 million receivables sold in September 1999.* ■

Warranty Expenses: Many firms provide warranties—guarantees to fix or replace defective products. Expense recognition is similar to that of bad debts. GAAP requires that firms estimate the cost of providing warranties, and deduct that expense from income at the time of sale. A corresponding reserve (liability) is set up on the balance sheet.[30] Such estimates are inherently difficult, especially for new products. The analyst should watch the trend in warranty reserves, as they can be used to smooth reported income.

■ **Example: AT Cross**

AT Cross [ATX] produces pens with a lifetime warranty. In 2000, the company's fourth successive loss year, it reduced its warranty reserve "reflecting lower cost trends among the several factors that impact the company's cost to service the warranty." The data follow ($thousands):

| | Years Ended December 31 | | |
	1998	1999	2000
Sales	$152,783	$126,994	$130,548
Warranty expense	881	720	(761)
% sales	0.6%	0.6%	−0.6%
Warranty reserve			
Opening balance	$5,821	$5,821	$5,821
Expense	881	720	(761)
Costs paid	(881)	(720)	(367)
Closing balance	$5,821	$5,821	$4,693

The accounting change increased operating profit margins by 1.2%. If Cross had recorded sufficient warranty expense to maintain its existing reserve (as in 1998 and 1999), the expense would have been $367,000; if it had accrued expense equal to .6% of sales, the expense would have been $783,000. Either amount would have increased the operating loss further. ■

Capitalizing current period expenditures can also reduce reported expenses. Chapter 7 discusses the capitalization of interest, research and development, and software development expense.

Classification Issues

Many analysts use gross margin (revenues less cost of goods sold) and gross margin percentage (gross margin as a % of sales) to evaluate companies, especially those that have negative earnings. Some reporting methods boost gross margins without affecting operating income:

- Including costs such as discounts and marketing costs as operating expense rather than cost of goods sold
- Recording shipping and handling costs (included in revenue) as operating expense rather than cost of goods sold

---

[30]The reserve is reduced when an actual warranty cost is incurred.

Classification issues and changes in classification may not be explicitly disclosed in financial statements. However, differences in classification for the same firm over time and among competing firms may distort analyses and comparisons of gross margin levels, percentages, and growth rates.

The analyst should question companies regarding their revenue and expense recognition practices, and the classification of revenues and expense. Intercompany comparisons may require adjustment for reporting differences.

Software Revenue Recognition

Transactions in the software industry range from the sale or license of a single software product to complex contractual arrangements that involve delivery, significant subsequent production, modification, or customization of the software. The latter complex arrangements generally must be accounted for in accordance with Accounting Research Bulletin (ARB) 45, Long-Term Construction-Type Contracts, and SOP 81-1, Accounting for the Performance of Construction-Type Contracts and Certain Production-Type Contracts.

SOP 97-2, Software Revenue Recognition, and SOP 98-9, Modification of SOP 97-2, Software Revenue Recognition, With Respect to Certain Transactions, apply to software transactions that do not require significant subsequent production, modification, or customization of the software. SOP 97-2 stipulates four criteria that must *all* be satisfied to recognize revenue for single- or multiple-element software transactions:

1. Persuasive evidence of an arrangement
2. Delivery
3. A fixed or determinable fee
4. Assurance of collectibility

SOP 97-2 requires that revenue be allocated among the components of a multiple-element arrangement based on fair values of the individual elements. In the absence of fair value data, all revenue must be deferred until completion of the project. However, vendor-specific objective evidence (VSOE)[31] of the fair value of the elements can be used to recognize revenue for individual elements.

SOP 98-9 amends SOP 97-2 to require the use of the "residual method" of revenue recognition when:

- VSOE of the fair values of all the undelivered elements is available,
- VSOE of one or more delivered elements is not available, and
- All other revenue recognition criteria of SOP 97-2 are met.

The residual method requires that the total fair value of the undelivered elements be deferred; only the excess of the total sales price over the amount deferred is recognized as revenue. SOP 97-2 applies to the subsequent revenue recognition for the undelivered elements.

Illustration. Assume that a software company agrees to sell a product for $950, including one year of customer support. The company separately sells customer support for $150 a year (providing VSOE for the price of customer support). If the company does not have VSOE for the software, customer support ($150) revenue would be deferred and recognized over the one-year term. Under SOP 98-9, the remaining $800 would be recognized when the software product is delivered (assuming all other requirements of SOP 97-2 are met).

However, absent VSOE for the customer support price, the entire $950 would be deferred and recognized over the one-year term. The deferral method would apply even if there were VSOE regarding the software product price. In other words, to recognize the revenue related to one or more elements of a multi-element sale, there must be VSOE to support the revenue allocated to the undelivered elements.

---

[31]VSOE means the price charged when the element is sold separately or the price established by the vendor for that element.

EXHIBIT 2-3. MICROSOFT CORPORATION

Years Ended June 30 (amounts in $millions)

	1995	1996	1997	1998	1999	2000
Revenues	$5,937	$8,671	$11,936	$15,262	$19,747	$22,956
Unearned revenue*	69	983	1,601	3,268	5,877	6,177
Recognition of prior period unearned revenue*	(54)	(477)	(743)	(1,798)	(4,526)	(5,600)
Change in accounts receivable		(58)	(341)	(480)	(785)	(1,005)
Cash collections	$5,952	$9,119	$12,453	$16,252	$20,313	$22,528
Cash collections growth rate (%)		53.21%	36.56%	30.51%	24.99%	10.90%
Unearned revenue (year-end balance sheet)	$54	$560	$1,418	$2,888	$4,239	$4,816
Prior period revenue as % of reported revenue		5.50%	6.22%	11.78%	22.92%	24.39%
Reported revenue growth rate (%)		46.05%	37.65%	27.87%	29.39%	16.25%

*From statement of cash flows.
Source: Microsoft *Annual Reports, 1996–2000*.

■ Example

Microsoft provides an instructive example of revenue recognition issues in the software industry.[32] Starting in 1996, Microsoft deferred increasing amounts of revenue (designated as unearned revenue), recognizing the deferred revenue in future time periods. The company adopted SOP 97-2 in the fourth quarter of fiscal 1999. Concurrently, Microsoft extended the life cycle of its principal product from two to three years. Maintenance and subscription revenue, based on the average sales prices of each element, are recognized ratably (straight-line basis) over the product's life cycle.

Exhibit 2–3 shows that the company has reported declining revenue growth rates since 1996. The growth rate of cash collections also steadily declined, from 53% in fiscal 1996 to less than 11% in fiscal 2000. However, Microsoft changes accounting methods and estimates as the products mature and as the undelivered components of the products are developed or delivered. Although Microsoft discloses the various components of unearned or deferred revenues, the disclosures do not enable the user to forecast the rate and amount of unearned revenues that will be recognized over the products' life cycles. ■

Other Issues

The software industry is not the only one that has particular revenue recognition issues. We have examined it at length given its richness and current relevance. Four examples of other industries and situations follow:

1. In the broadcast industry, television stations buy the rights to show a film for a given period of time. Should the revenue be recognized by the film's owner:
   - When the agreement is signed?
   - When the film is physically transferred to the television station?
   - Over time as the film is shown?
2. Mortgage issuers charge a fee, *origination points*, that is, in effect, interest paid in advance. Points are not refundable even if the mortgage is repaid before its due date. Should the fee be recognized as income:
   - Over time?
   - At the time of origination?

---

[32]See the footnote on revenue recognition under Accounting Policies in Microsoft's *Annual Report* for the year ended June 30, 2000.

3. An exercise club charges a refundable annual membership fee, payable quarterly. Should revenue be recognized:
   - When the membership is sold?
   - When payments are received?
   - Over one year?

   Should the answer change if payment is made when the contract is signed? What if it is nonrefundable?

4. A company offers price incentives or preferential access to goods to induce customers to purchase future period requirements in advance.[33] The result is an increase in current period revenues. Should all sales be recognized in the current period?

These are but a few examples of complex revenue recognition issues. Case 2–1 contains a comprehensive analysis of revenue and expense recognition issues. Other examples are provided in the problems at the end of this chapter. It should be clear, however, that the analyst must have a thorough understanding of the nature of the business and its relationship to revenue recognition. *When valuation is based on revenue or gross margin, pay careful attention to accounting methods that affect these measures, even when net income is unaffected.*

Summary of Revenue Recognition Methods

The preceding sections discuss the conceptual bases and financial statement effects of different revenue recognition methods. The analyst must be aware of the assumptions underlying these methods both for interfirm comparisons and because questionable revenue is a poor predictor of future cash flows.

Furthermore, revenue recognition abuses may also indicate more serious problems. Richard H. Walker, the SEC head of enforcement, stated that:

> . . . the most common type of accounting fraud has been improper recording of revenue. This can occur when a company books revenue for sales that never took place, accelerates or defers revenue to another quarter, or books sales before they are confirmed. . . . Investors have lost billions of dollars in the last few years when companies dropped in market value after restating earnings. . . .[34]

Although the United States has a rich (and growing) body of revenue and expense recognition rules, IAS standards and those of most foreign countries provide little or no guidance. For example, Sir David Tweedie, chairman of the UK Accounting Standards Board, acknowledged the deficiency in UK standards: "It seems ridiculous, we have no rules."[35]

Revenue and expense recognition rules will change as global standard setters respond to the need for improved guidelines. Whichever reporting method is used, the analyst needs to monitor the income statement and its relationship to the cash flow statement. As discussed in the next chapter, the statement of cash flows can warn the financial statement user when overly aggressive revenue recognition methods are being used.

NONRECURRING ITEMS

Nonrecurring items affect the analysis of the income- and cash-generating ability of most firms. As companies have increased their effort to explain earnings variations, they have made greater use of the "unusual" and "nonrecurring" labels, especially for items that reduce reported income. Many new economy firms have taken this practice to new depths.

---

[33]In 2002, Bristol-Myers [BMY] reported that it had offered sales incentives to wholesalers in 2000 and 2001 that resulted in approximately $1.5 billion of wholesaler inventory buildup. The required inventory workdown significantly reduced earnings in 2002 and 2003.

[34]Interview with Neil Roland of Bloomberg, February 27, 2001.

[35]Quoted in *The Financial Times* (London), December 1, 2000, p. 24. In January 2001, Tweedie became chairman of the reconstituted IASB.

These firms often announce *pro forma earnings* amounts that exclude goodwill amortization, stock compensation expense, and other selected accruals. We have previously noted that, when estimating a firm's earning power, analysts should exclude items that are unusual or nonrecurring in nature. However, this does not mean that everything management labels nonrecurring should be ignored. In this section, we discuss the extent to which such items provide useful information and how they should be treated in financial analysis.

Types of Nonrecurring Items

The income statement contains four categories of nonrecurring income:

1. Unusual or infrequent items
2. Extraordinary items
3. Discontinued operations
4. Accounting changes

Unusual or infrequent items are reported "above the line" as part of "income from continuing operations" and are presented on a pretax basis. The other three categories are "below the line," excluded from "income from continuing operations," and presented net of tax.[36] We first describe these classifications and then discuss their analytical implications.

Unusual or Infrequent Items

Transactions or events that are *either unusual in nature or infrequent in occurrence but not both* may be disclosed separately (as a single-line item) as a component of income from continuing operations. These items must be reported pretax in the income statement; the tax impact (or the net-of-tax amount) may be disclosed separately. Common examples are:

- Gains or losses from disposal of a portion of a business segment
- Gains or losses from sales of assets or investments in affiliates or subsidiaries
- Provisions for environmental remediation
- Impairments, write-offs, writedowns, and restructuring costs
- Expenses related to the integration of acquired companies

Texaco has reported several "special items" every year for the last several years. The 1999 Management Discussion and Analysis (MD&A) reported write-downs of assets in both domestic and international business segments and gains (losses) on major assets sales in each year, 1997 through 1999. These amounts were recorded as components of depreciation, depletion, and amortization expense. Texaco has also reported:

- Reorganizations, restructurings, and employee separation costs
- Inventory valuation adjustments
- Settlements of royalty valuation issues
- Environmental liabilities

The company provides extensive disclosures for the reorganizations, restructurings, and employee separation programs including the amount and location (in the income statement) of the expenses recorded each year, changes in provisions, cash payments made during the year, amounts transferred to long-term obligations, and the remaining obligations at the end of each year. Note that many of these charges should be considered normal operating charges for a company of the size and complexity of Texaco. While it may be helpful for near-term earnings projections for Texaco to disclose these items, we cannot assume that similar items will not appear in future years. In 2000, for example, Texaco again reported asset impairment

---

[36]The fact that some nonrecurring items are presented pretax (and included in income from continuing operations) but others are reported after tax (excluded from income from continuing operations) hampers analysis. Attention to detail and a little thought, however, can conquer the inconsistent presentation of nonrecurring items.

and employee separation costs. Thus, while such disclosures are useful adjuncts to the income statement, the analyst should carefully consider case-by-case whether valuation should be based on earnings that exclude "nonrecurring" items.

The Texaco example shows us that nonrecurring items are not always disclosed as separate line items in the income statement. They may be included in the catchall "other income" classification or may be buried in COGS or SG&A. Both footnote disclosures and the MD&A should be scrutinized for events and transactions that may have had a material impact on earnings, but that management has either chosen to treat as normal, recurring items or classified as nonrecurring transactions or events.

Extraordinary Items

APB 30 (1973) created the U.S. GAAP income statement format discussed earlier. It defines *extraordinary items* as transactions and events that are *unusual in nature and infrequent in occurrence and are material in amount*. Extraordinary items must be reported separately, net of income tax. Firms are also required to report per-share amounts for these items and encouraged to provide additional footnote disclosures. Extraordinary items are intended to be rare; based on APB 30, such events as losses due to a foreign government's expropriation of assets qualify as an extraordinary item, whereas gains or losses on the sale of noncurrent assets do not.

In the early 1970s, high interest rates and an economic recession led firms with depressed profits to refinance low coupon debt, whose market value was below the face amount, with high coupon debt, reporting an accounting gain.[37] SFAS 4 (1975) broadened the classification of extraordinary items by requiring that *gains or losses on qualifying early retirement of debt*[38] be classified as extraordinary.

In April 2002, SFAS 145 rescinded SFAS 4. As a result, gains or losses on the early retirement of debt are extraordinary items only when the requirements of APB 30 are met.

In recent years, firms have refinanced high coupon debt, whose market value exceeded face amount after sharp declines in interest rates, and these debt retirements have resulted in reported extraordinary losses. Of the sample of 600 companies in the 2000 *Accounting Trends and Techniques*, 61 companies reported 62 extraordinary items and 56 (10 at a gain and 45 at a loss) of these represented the early retirement of debt. The other items included casualty losses and gains from asset disposals.

Discontinued Operations

The discontinuation or sale of a component of a business may indicate that it:

- Has inadequate or uncertain markets or prospects
- Has an unsatisfactory contribution to earnings and cash flows
- Is no longer considered by management to be a strategic fit
- Can be sold at a significant profit

Operating income from discontinued operations and any gains or losses (net of taxes) from their sale are segregated in the income statement, since these activities will not contribute to future income and cash flows. As in the case of extraordinary items, this segregation makes the reported information more useful for analysis.

A component of business is defined by SFAS 144 (2001) as any business component with separately identifiable operations, assets, and cash flows that has been disposed of or is held for sale. Subsidiaries and investees also qualify as separate components.

To qualify for treatment as discontinued operations, the assets, results of operations, and investing and financing activities of a component must be separable from those of the firm. SFAS 144 states that the separation must be possible physically and operationally, and for financial reporting purposes.

---

[37]See Chapter 10 for a comparison of the accounting and economic consequences of refinancing.

[38]Gains and losses on early retirement of debt were considered extraordinary, except for those related to sinking fund requirements (SFAS 4, 1975).

Once management develops or adopts a formal plan for the sale or disposal of a component (the *measurement date*), the operating results of the component are segregated within the income statement. The income statement will report the income or loss from operations of the discontinued component only on a net-of-tax basis. A condensed income statement for the component is usually shown in a footnote. Prior-period income statements are restated as well.

In the period in which a component of an entity is classified as held for sale or has been disposed of, the results of operations of the component and any gain or loss recognized[39] must be reported as discontinued operations in the income statement for current and prior periods.

Pfizer (see Note 2 to 1999 annual report) sold four businesses in 1998, treating them as discontinued operations. The significant effects include:

- The 1997 balance sheet shows a single line item—net assets of discontinued operations.
- The revenues and expenses of the discontinued operations have been removed from the income statement. The operating earnings from these businesses are combined with the net gain on disposal as earnings from discontinued operations, reported separately on the income statement. Note 2 contains a summarized income statement for these operations.
- The operating cash flow from discontinued businesses is *not* shown separately.[40]

Accounting Changes

Accounting changes fall into two general categories: those undertaken voluntarily by the firm and those mandated by new accounting standards. Generally, accounting changes do not have direct cash flow consequences.

The change from one acceptable accounting method to another acceptable method is reported in the period of change. Any cumulative impact on *prior period* earnings is reported net of tax after extraordinary items and discontinued operations on the income statement.[41] Firms are required to provide footnote disclosure of the impact of the change on current period operations (and on each prior period, if restated) and their justification for the change. However, accounting changes also affect future operating results. That impact is rarely disclosed but can sometimes be estimated. Accounting changes are dealt with frequently in the remaining chapters of the text.

APB 20 (1971) identifies four exceptions to the general treatment of accounting changes. These are:

1. Change from LIFO to another inventory method (see Chapter 6)
2. Change to or from the full cost method (see Chapter 7)
3. Change to or from the percentage-of-completion method
4. Change in accounting methods prior to an initial public offering

These exceptions require retroactive restatement of all years presented.

■ Example

In 1999, Lucent changed its method for calculating the market-related value of pension plan assets (see Chapter 12 for a detailed discussion). The cumulative (net-of-tax) effect

---

[39]A component classified as held for sale must be reported at the lower of its carrying amount or fair value less cost to sell. A loss must be recognized for any initial or subsequent writedown to fair value less cost to sell. Subsequent gain recognition is limited to the cumulative loss recognized. Only a previously unrecognized gain or loss must be recognized on date of sale or disposal.

[40]Separate disclosure of the cash flows from discontinued operations is optional under U.S. GAAP. However, IAS 35 (1998) requires (para. 6) separate disclosure of "the net cash flows attributable to the operating, investing, and financing cash flows of the discontinuing operation."

[41]In most cases, prior period results are not restated. The cumulative impact is computed under the assumption that the new method had been used in all past periods and is therefore the difference between reported income and what income would have been if the new method had been applied.

In some cases, prior period results are restated; the portion of the cumulative impact applicable to periods preceding those for which an income statement is presented is shown as an adjustment to retained earnings.

of the accounting change was $1,308 million (net of income taxes of $842 million) or $0.42 per diluted share, shown as a separate line item in the income statement. Note 10, Employee Benefit Plans, also reports that the accounting change increased reported 1999 income by $260 million (net of taxes of $167) or $0.08 per diluted share. Lucent reported 1999 net income of $1.52 per diluted share of which nearly one-third ($0.50 per diluted share) came from this accounting change.   ∎

Prior Period Adjustments

A change from an incorrect to an acceptable accounting method is treated as an error, and its impact is reported as a *prior period adjustment*. On occasion, newly available information clarifies transactions that were accounted for in prior periods. In some cases, the appropriate adjustment is not reported as a component of current period income, but recorded directly to retained earnings. SFAS 16, Prior Period Adjustments, restricts this treatment to accounting errors. In most cases, however, these adjustments are included in reported income of the period in which the new information becomes available.

IAS Standards for Nonrecurring Items

IAS 8 (revised 1993) governs the treatment of nonrecurring items under IAS GAAP. While these standards are similar to U.S. GAAP, there are several significant differences:

- The IAS definition of extraordinary differs slightly from the U.S. definition, allowing for the possibility of different treatments of the same item.
- IAS 8 does not require the separate presentation of earnings from continuing operations, earnings from discontinued operations, and income before extraordinary items.
- For accounting changes, IAS 8 permits *either* the cumulative change method *or* the restatement of prior periods.[42]
- Errors can be corrected by *either* restating prior periods *or* including the item in current period results.

IAS 35 (1998), which provides standards for discontinued operations, also differs slightly from U.S. GAAP. The most important differences are:

- IAS GAAP requires the estimated losses from a discontinued unit to be reported as incurred, rather than accrued as under U.S. GAAP.
- Impairment losses associated with discontinued operations may be reported as part of the loss from continued operations under IAS GAAP, even if recognized prior to the announcement date.
- Under IAS 35, the "discontinuation" date may differ from that under SFAS 144.

∎ **Example**

In 1999, Roche announced plans to spin off its flavors and fragrances division, Givaudan (see Note 7 to Roche annual report). Yet the results of Givaudan are included in the Roche income statement for 1999 and its assets and liabilities remain on Roche's December 31, 1999 balance sheet. Givaudan's operating results and cash flows were included in those of Roche through the spinoff date (June 8, 2000).   ∎

Analysis of Nonrecurring Items

The preceding discussion of unusual items, extraordinary items, and discontinued operations illustrates the difficulty presented by nonrecurring items. Accounting standard setters cannot draw "bright lines" that are adequate to separate clearly unusual items. In practice, gains tend

---

[42]IAS standards do not require the restatement of prior period results in deference to the prohibition against restatement in the GAAP of many countries.

to be buried in continuing operations, whereas losses are often shown separately; disclosure is not always sufficient. In some cases, the MD&A provides more information about unusual items than the financial statements themselves.

When estimating a firm's "earning power," analysts normally exclude items that are unusual or nonrecurring in nature. Yet such events seem to recur, more so in some companies than others. Some companies seem to be "accident prone," although each "accident" is different. Nonrecurring items are not all alike. Although the sale of assets, divisions, or segments may not be part of continuing operations, such sales may recur, albeit sporadically. Recurring and nonrecurring are not two distinct categories but rather a continuum. The objective, therefore, is to place each item in its appropriate place on the spectrum. *When determining the earnings amount used for firm valuation, the analyst must classify income and expenses between operating and nonrecurring using the preceding discussion rather than relying on the classification provided by the company.*

Income Statement Impact of Nonrecurring Items

The current period income statement effect of nonrecurring items is generally clearly stated. However, such items also have implications for previously reported income and future earnings.

Some nonrecurring items are, in effect, a correction of prior period income. A common example is asset writedowns, frequently included in "restructuring" provisions. Such writedowns suggest that prior period depreciation or amortization changes were insufficient and reported income for these periods was overstated. The recognition of liabilities for environmental remediation is another indication that prior year earnings were overstated.

Asset impairment and "restructuring" charges result in increases in future reported income. To the extent that assets are written down, future depreciation and amortization expense will be lower than would otherwise have been the case. The accrual of future lease rental expense and employee severance costs also affects future earnings, which will no longer be saddled with these costs. The restructuring charges recorded by Texaco contain asset writedowns that reflect on both past and future reported earnings.

These implications for previous and future earnings must be carefully considered. *If nonrecurring charges are really prior year expenses taken too late or future expenses charged off early, then the practice of ignoring nonrecurring charges and focusing on recurring operating income results in an overestimation of the firm's earnings trend.*

Some commentators have criticized the ever-increasing spate of restructurings and special charges (e.g., Texaco reports several in each of the years 1997 to 2000) as being motivated by the desire to paint a better earnings picture:

> How can repeated write-offs be nonrecurring or extraordinary? *How can investors believe that reported earnings are real and won't be canceled by subsequent write-offs?* . . .
>
> Here's how this kind of charge can boost earnings. Say Company XYZ reports rising profits of $1 million in year 1 and $1.2 million in year 2; in year 3, XYZ takes a restructuring charge of $5 million for the cost of closing a few businesses. The charge turned year 3's net into a loss of $3.5 million—but XYZ says profit would have been $1.5 million before the charge. The next year, year 4, the upward trend resumes as XYZ reports profits of $1.8 million. But the results are helped because $2 million of the company's year 4 expenses—say, for severance payments and plant closings—can be counted against the charge already taken in year 3. . . .
>
> *The most obvious way restructuring charges make companies' earnings look better is if the companies can convince investors that operating earnings—before the charges—provide a more meaningful indication of trends.* . . .
>
> Wall Street analysts often use some version of operating earnings—not counting charges—to track a company's earnings trend. Thus, many analysts and research services that follow AT&T show a tidy growth track for the company: $3.13 a share for 1994, $3.45 for 1995, and $3.95 for 1996. But that doesn't include AT&T's 1995 charges of $5.4 billion, or $3.35 a share. . . .[43]

---

[43]Quotations are excerpted from "Are Companies Using Restructuring Costs to Fudge the Figures?: A Repeated Strategic Move Makes Future Earnings Seem Unrealistically Rosy," *Wall Street Journal* (January 30, 1996), emphasis added.

BOX 2-4
Pro Forma Earnings

An increasing number of companies are reporting pro forma earnings in press releases announcing their earnings before filing quarterly reports with the SEC. Companies use varying definitions of "pro forma earnings" and some companies report more than one category of such earnings. Unlike GAAP-based earnings, pro forma earnings *exclude one or more of the following* expenses and gains or losses:

- Goodwill amortization
- Other intangible-asset amortization
- Stock-compensation expense
- Writedowns of impaired assets
- Restructuring charges
- Severance pay and early or involuntary termination benefits
- Interest expense
- Marketing expenses
- Results of Internet operations (and other wholly or majority-owned subsidiaries, and equity-method investees)
- Gain or loss on sale of stock in subsidiaries, investees, or other affiliates

Companies have advanced several reasons to justify reporting pro forma earnings:

- Users of financial statements and analysts prefer "cash earnings" that exclude amortization of goodwill and other noncash charges.
- Management's breakdown of earnings and cash flows enhances the transparency of financial statements and is more informative.
- Restructuring charges, impairments, and other onetime or nonrecurring charges are not relevant as they are not expected to contribute to future earnings and cash flows.
- The results of operations of Internet operations and other subsidiaries or affiliates may not be relevant if the company plans to spin off the operations at some unspecified or uncertain future date.

The SEC has expressed concern about but has no authority to specify what companies say in press releases. Unfortunately, some analysts have acceded to management demands to forecast pro forma earnings rather than GAAP-based earnings.

In 2001, Financial Executives International (FEI) proposed guidelines for press releases intended to reflect best practices and reduce abusive practices.

■   **Example**

In a January 30, 2001 press release, Amazon.com announced its fourth quarter 2000 results, with the following headline:

Fourth-Quarter 2000 Pro Forma Operating Loss Improves from 26 Percent to 6 Percent of Net Sales

The release reported a pro forma operating loss for the fourth quarter of 2000 of $60 million, or 6% of net sales. The reported pro forma net loss was $90 million. Later in the press release the company reported that its fourth-quarter GAAP loss from operations was $322 million and the GAAP-based net loss was $545 million, including charges of $339 million for impairment of goodwill and equity investments. Stock-based compensation charges and equity in losses of equity-method investees were among the other items excluded from the pro forma operating loss.   ■

When a company has truly nonrecurring gains or losses, or has made a large acquisition or divestiture, data that remove the effects of these distortions may be very informative. However, in most cases, the reporting of pro forma operating results is an effort to persuade analysts to ignore certain expenses or categories of expense and thereby improve the valuation of the firm's securities. Thus it is important to cast a skeptical eye on such reports; the analyst should use reported GAAP data (after appropriate adjustments by the analyst) for valuation decisions.

We believe that the need to assess "nonrecurring" charges has increased since these words were written. Moreover, the increased use of pro forma earnings for valuation purposes (discussed in Box 2–4) has made these issues even more pressing.

Cash Flow and Valuation Impact

Nonrecurring items with cash flow consequences do affect the wealth of the firm. However, they should still be segregated because their valuation implications differ from those for recurring income. As outlined in Box 2–1 and discussed in greater detail in Chapter 19, (true) nonrecurring components of income have only a onetime dollar-for-dollar effect on valuation, whereas the multiple for changes in recurring income (the price-earnings multiple) is greater.

The analyst must distinguish among items that:

- Have no cash flow implications (e.g., asset writedowns)
- Affect current period cash flow only (e.g., employee severance costs)
- Have future cash flow effects (e.g., lease payments for closed facilities)

Careful attention must be paid to footnote disclosures to ascertain the cash flow effects of "restructuring" provisions in particular. In some cases, the cash drain from such provisions extends years into the future.

The 1995 pretax business restructuring charges of $2,467 million and asset impairment and other charges of $188 million reported by Lucent are a good example of the continuing income and cash flow consequences of such announcements. Its 1999 annual report shows deductions from business restructuring reserves, noncash charges, and cash payments continuing through fiscal 1999. In 1999, Lucent reversed $141 million of the business restructuring charges due to favorable experience in employee separation and lower costs of other restructuring projects announced in 1995.

Implications for Continuing Operations

Nonrecurring events, even those without cash flow effects, may also provide useful information about the firm. A plant closing and the write-off of its book value are one example. The actual cash outflows occurred in the past and are only now being expensed. The value implication of the gain or loss reported on the income statement may be nonexistent. The plant closing itself may, however, help forecast the firm's future sales, earnings, and cash flows. Similarly, Lucent's 1995 restructuring charge included employee severance costs. Future reported earnings should be higher than previously expected because its employment costs are reduced. The reduced number of employees also will affect benefit accruals (see Chapter 12).

Management Discretion and Earnings Manipulation

When estimating earnings trends, the analyst must also be wary of the discretionary nature of the income statement. Items requiring separate disclosure on the income statement may be discretionary with respect to the:

- Timing of the occurrence (e.g., the disposal of an asset or the discontinuation of a segment)
- Classification of the item (ordinary, unusual, or extraordinary)

In addition, changes in accounting methods can alter reported income statement trends. In many cases, there is no disclosure (except in the aggregate) of the effects of the accounting change on income reported in individual prior periods, making adjustment difficult.

The discretionary nature of income recognition permits an examination of the degree of management manipulation of earnings under one or more of the following guises:

- Classification of good news/bad news
- Income smoothing
- Big-bath behavior
- Accounting changes

Classification of Good News/Bad News. Management prefers to report good news "above the line" as part of continuing operations and bad news "below the line" as extraordinary or discontinued operations. For example, management determines whether the component of the firm sold meets the definition of a discontinued operation and hence is given below-the-line treatment as income from discontinued operations. As SFAS 131 notes, the

> management approach (to segmentation) is based on the way the management organizes the segments within the enterprise for making operating decisions and assessing performance.[44]

This discretion permits management to report unusual items most favorably.[45]

---

[44]SFAS 131, para. 4.

[45]Rapacciolli and Schiff (1991) show that in their sample of about 500 disposals, approximately 60% of the cases were accorded the more favorable treatment, with 61% of gains reported above the line and 57% of losses reported below the line.

Income Smoothing. Some firms reduce earnings in good years (defer gains or recognize losses) and inflate earnings in bad years (recognize gains or defer losses) in order to report stable earnings. Empirical evidence indicates that managements can and do engage in such behavior by engaging in two types of smoothing. *Intertemporal smoothing* refers to either:

- Timing expenditures such as research and development, repairs and maintenance, and asset disposals, or
- Choosing accounting methods (e.g., capitalization or expensing) that allocate the expenditure over time.

Classificatory smoothing is smoothing by choosing to classify an item as either income from continuing operations, or extraordinary income. The implicit assumption is that analysts focus on ordinary income and ignore nonrecurring/extraordinary items. Thus, by shifting items above or below the line, management can report a desired trend.

Asset sales are an example of a nonrecurring item that has been used as both an intertemporal and classificatory smoothing instrument. Bartov (1993) showed that such sales have been *timed* to smooth income. Furthermore, as there is discretion in how a segment is defined, the sale of a portion of a business can be classified as part of continuing operations or as a discontinued operation. Fried et al. (1996) showed that the *classification* choices made by their sample of firms were consistent with smoothing.

Ronen and Sadan (1981) have argued that smoothing is not necessarily bad. Rather, by engaging in smoothing, management may be aiding the predictive ability of reported earnings by conveying information about the future prospects of the firm. Moses (1987) made similar arguments. Possible incentives for earnings manipulation are varied [see the discussion in Bartov (1993) and the survey paper by Healy and Wahlen (1999)] and not necessarily limited to the desire to show stable earnings and/or aid predictive ability. A number of authors [e.g., Healy (1985), Holthausen et al. (1995), and Gaver et al. (1995)] examined executive bonus plans and showed that depending on the structure of such plans, management may be motivated to engage in discretionary accruals, manipulating earnings in an upward or downward direction. Jones (1991) showed that firms that would benefit from import relief (e.g., tariff increases and quota reductions) decrease income through earnings manipulation in order to influence the U.S. International Trade Commission. Bartov, on the other hand, demonstrated that firms attempt to manipulate earnings in an upward direction in order to escape possible restrictions imposed by their bond covenant agreements.

More recently, research has focused on earnings management geared to meet (or just beat) analysts' expectations. Burgstahler and Eames (1998) found that managers manage earnings upward to avoid missing analyst expectations.[46] In this spirit, Bradshaw, Moberg, and Sloan (2000) broaden the definition of earnings management to include "management of the 'perception' of earnings" and argue that managers have taken earnings management a step further by encouraging analysts to focus on (management defined) pro forma earnings (discussed in Box 2–4) rather than GAAP earnings.

Big-Bath Accounting. In contrast to income smoothing, the big-bath hypothesis suggests that management will report additional losses in bad years in the hope that, by taking all available losses at one time, they will "clear the decks" once and for all. The implicit assumption is that future reported profits will increase.

This hypothesis is more widely accepted in the financial press than in the academic literature. Francis, Hanna, and Vincent (1996) and Elliott and Shaw (1988) found that analyst forecasts following large write-offs are not consistent with the big-bath theory. Rather than increasing following a write-off, indicating a clearing of the deck, forecast earnings tended to decrease. Fried et al. (1989) reported that a firm taking an asset writedown in one year is likely to take another one soon after. This is inconsistent with big-bath behavior, which argues that firms would overestimate rather than underestimate the size and amounts of write-offs.[47]

---

[46]Similar evidence was found by Kaznick (1999) with respect to meeting management's own earnings forecasts.

[47]See the discussion of impairment in Chapter 8 for more details of these results.

Accounting Changes. Regardless of whether accounting changes are voluntary or mandatory, they typically have no direct cash flow consequences for a U.S. company.[48] Thus, such changes can be viewed as a form of earnings manipulation. Empirical research has studied accounting changes extensively, focusing on both managerial motivations and stock market reaction. We shall refer to many of these studies in later chapters.

Elliott and Philbrick (1990) examined the effects of accounting changes on earnings predictability. Not surprisingly, they found that analysts had difficulty forecasting earnings for the year of the change. That difficulty was more pronounced for mandatory changes, for which there was no prior information regarding the change. Moreover, they found that when analysts had no prior information about the change, the effect of the accounting change tended to be in the *opposite* direction of forecast revisions made by analysts in the latter part of the fiscal year (fourth quarter). For example, accounting changes that *increased* income were associated with *downward* forecast revisions; that is, when income was lower than originally expected (causing downward forecast revisions), accounting changes were adopted that raised reported income. This behavior, the authors concluded, was consistent with management's use of accounting changes to manipulate or smooth earnings.

Quality of Earnings

The term "quality of earnings" is used in two different senses. We use it to mean the use of accounting methods and assumptions that tend not to overstate reported revenues and earnings. The discussion of revenue and expense recognition earlier in this chapter should already have provided a sense of how accounting methods and assumptions can affect reported operating results.

However, some use the term to indicate consistency of reported earnings (lack of volatility). The two meanings are somewhat contradictory. Firms that report "consistent" earnings growth often do so by managing earnings in ways that the external analyst cannot see. Earnings management may include the use of aggressive accounting assumptions when required to meet analyst expectations. Companies that stretch the financial reporting system to meet unattainable expectations may also cross the line into financial fraud. Companies that use conservative methods are unlikely to commit fraud, as they can change accounting methods and assumptions first.

We return to the subject of quality of earnings in Chapter 17, as the discussion is more useful after all of the intervening chapters have been covered.

THE BALANCE SHEET

The balance sheet (statement of financial position) reports the categories and amounts of assets (firm resources), liabilities (claims on those resources), and stockholders' equity at specific points in time. In the United States, balance sheets are generally issued at the end of each quarter and the end of the fiscal year; outside of the United States, annual or semiannual reporting is the general rule.

Format and Classification

The definitions of assets, liabilities, and stockholders' equity are discussed in Chapter 1. We now discuss the format and classification prevalent in most companies. IAS standards are similar to those used by firms in the United States. Box 2–5 lists and discusses Pfizer's balance sheet components.

Assets and liabilities are classified according to liquidity, that is, their expected use in operations or conversion to cash in the case of assets and time to maturity for liabilities. Assets expected to be converted to cash or used within one year (or one operating cycle, if longer than one year) are classified as current assets. Current liabilities include obligations the firm expects to settle within one year (or one operating cycle, if longer).

Assets expected to provide benefits and services over periods exceeding one year and liabilities to be repaid after one year are classified as long-term assets and liabilities. Tangible

---

[48]The FIFO to LIFO change is the major exception in the United States (see Chapter 6).

BOX 2-5. PFIZER, INC.
Balance Sheet Components

Although every firm's financial statements are unique, we can use Pfizer's 1997–1999 balance sheets* to review the components of the balance sheet. These components are discussed in greater detail in various chapters as listed below:

Assets	Chapter
Cash and cash equivalents	3
Investments and loans	13
Accounts receivable	2, 4
Inventories	4, 6
Deferred income taxes	9
Prepaid expenses	2
Deferred taxes	9
Current assets	4
Net assets of discontinued operations	2
Fixed assets	7
(Accumulated depreciation)	8
Capital leases	11
Investments in affiliates	13, 15
Prepaid pension costs	12
Intangible assets†	7, 14

Liabilities	
Accounts payable	4
Income tax liability	9
Advance billings	2
Current liabilities	4, 10
Debt—short- and long-term	10
Capital leases	11
Pensions and other postretirement benefits	12
Deferred income tax	9
Minority interest	13
Stockholders' equity	2
Cumulative translation adjustment	15
Minimum pension liability	12
Unrealized gains and losses	13
Treasury stock	2

In the discussion that follows, all "Note" references are to the financial statement footnotes of Pfizer.

Assets

SFAS 95 defines *cash and cash equivalents* as risk-free assets with original maturities of 90 days or less. Examples include bank accounts, U.S. Treasury Bills, and similar assets. The net change in cash and cash equivalents for the period is reported in the statement of cash flows. Other investments (Note 4-A), which do not meet the criteria for reporting as cash equivalents, are shown separately (broken out into short-term and long-term components).

Accounts receivable may contain both trade receivables (which may include loans to customers) and notes receivable (e.g., from asset sales or loans to management). The distinction is important. Trade receivables are a result of credit sales of products and services and they are important indicators of liquidity and the sound-

ness of revenue recognition methods. The maturity and collectibility of notes receivable may have important implications for the future cash flow and the liquidity of the firm. As Pfizer shows loans separately, its accounts receivable may be trade-only.

The accounting method used for *inventories* (Notes 1-C and 6) can significantly affect the measurement of this important operating asset as well as the level and trend of reported income. As noted in Box 2-3, Pfizer wrote off $310 million of excess inventories of a suspended drug and it switched to the first-in, first-out inventory costing method in 1999, recording a pretax benefit of $6.6 million.

Deferred income taxes represent deferred tax debits. Note 9 provides details regarding the firm's income tax position. Prepaid expenses and taxes (some companies use the "other current assets" caption) may include prepaid expenses such as tax and insurance prepayments, items that will be reported as expenses in future income statements.

Total current assets include all of Pfizer's assets that are expected to generate cash (or reduce cash outflows) within one year or one operating cycle. However, most of these assets revolve; new receivables and inventories arise as old ones are used in the manufacturing process and turned into cash. Thus, current assets alone are not a forecast of future cash flow.

As required by U.S. GAAP, Pfizer shows the assets of discontinued operations net of liabilities.

Property, plant, and equipment (PPE) is the largest asset category for many industrial and manufacturing companies. The stated amount is a function of accounting policies regarding the capitalization, depreciation, and impairment. Note 7 contains a breakdown of Pfizer's fixed assets and Note 11 tells us that a small amount of operating properties have been leased. Assets under operating leases are not included in the PPE totals; Note 11 provides data on Pfizer's operating leases.

We assume that Pfizer has included prepaid pension cost (Note 10) in its "other assets, deferred taxes, and deferred charges" category. Pensions are discussed in Chapter 12. Pfizer reports *goodwill and other acquired intangibles* reflecting the excess of the purchase price over the fair value of identifiable net assets acquired in purchase method business acquisitions.

"Other assets, deferred taxes, and deferred charges" may contain long-term deferred tax debits, investments in securities, and intangible assets such as goodwill. Unlike some firms, Pfizer does not provide complete footnote disclosure of the components of this category, although Note 9 does report the location of all deferred tax accruals.

Liabilities

Total current liabilities include *accounts payable* (trade payables represent amounts owed to the suppliers of operating assets such as inventories), *payroll and benefit-related liabilities* (obligations to employees for services received), debt maturing within one year (amounts expected to be repaid during the next year; see Notes 4-B and C), and the relatively significant (15% of current liabilities) other current liabilities.

Note 10 provides necessary detail for *postretirement and benefit-related liabilities. Long-term debt* (Notes 4-C and 11 for operating leases) reflects amounts to be paid after one year. Note

9 lists the sources of *deferred income taxes—net*, and the poorly explained *other noncurrent liabilities* rounds out the long-term liabilities.

Stockholders' Equity

Pfizer has authorized but never issued *preferred stock*. When issued, preferred stock would represent a claim senior to that represented by the outstanding *common stock*. The *additional paid-in capital* and common stock in total represent the total amount received by the firm from issuance or other sales of stock. Pfizer reports adjustments to additional paid-in capital due to employee stock option and benefit trust transactions. Pfizer, as most companies, separately reports Treasury stock, representing expenditures incurred to repurchase common stock. Pfizer also reports shares held by its employee benefit trusts (Note 14).

Retained earnings report the accumulated earnings that were not paid as dividends to stockholders. For most companies, the distinction between these three components of capital is unimportant. In rare cases, however, a low level of (or absence of) retained earnings may affect the firm's ability to declare dividends or the tax treatment of those dividends. The *employee benefit trusts* reflects transactions with or commitments to those plans.

Accumulated other comprehensive income (loss) includes (Note 5):

- Foreign currency translation adjustment,
- Minimum pension liability, and
- Unrealized holding gains (or losses) on investments carried at market value.

---

*Pfizer reports three consecutive balance sheets, facilitating analysis. Most companies report only two years.

†Not shown in these years.

---

assets and liabilities are generally reported before intangibles and other assets and liabilities whose measurement is less certain.

This classification scheme can be used to develop ratios employed in financial analysis. The current–noncurrent distinction can be used to measure liquidity, for example. In recent years, however, that distinction has become somewhat arbitrary as differences between short-term and long-term investments and debt are sometimes difficult to discern.

The most liquid assets, cash and cash equivalents, precede marketable equity securities, receivables, inventories, and prepaid expenses in the current asset section of the balance sheet. Long-lived assets, including property, plant, and equipment, investments in affiliated companies, and intangible assets such as brand names, patents, copyrights, and goodwill, are reported as noncurrent assets.

Short-term bank and other debt, the current portion of long-term debt and capitalized leases, accounts payable to suppliers, accrued liabilities (amounts owed to employees and others), interest, and taxes payable are classified as current liabilities. Long-term debt, capitalized lease obligations, pension obligations, and other "liabilities" (such as deferred income taxes and minority interest in the net assets of consolidated affiliates) are commonly observed noncurrent liabilities.

Stockholders' equity (the residual interest in the firm) lists components in order of their priority in liquidation with any preference (preferred) stock listed before common stock, Treasury stock, and reinvested earnings. This section may also include the additional components shown in Box 2–5.

Measurement of Assets and Liabilities

Most components of the balance sheet are reported at historical cost, that is, the exchange price at their acquisition date. As noted earlier in this chapter, in the discussion of the accrual concept of income, the nature (and amount) of a recognized asset is a function of the firm's revenue recognition method.

In some cases (e.g., accounts receivable), valuation allowances (reserve for uncollectible receivables) adjust the originally recorded amount to an approximation of net realizable value. The reserve for uncollectibles is an estimate of bad debts, reported as a deduction from the gross receivables balance; this is called a *contra* account. (Accumulated depreciation is also a contra account since it reduces the carrying value of long-lived assets to reflect their use.)

Changes in some other assets or liabilities are accumulated in *adjunct* accounts, such as the premium on bonds payable that records the excess of the bond's issue price over its face value. These contra and adjunct accounts allow firms to report both the original, historical cost (e.g., gross plant assets) and the net carrying amount (plant assets net of accumulated depreciation). They also reflect management's estimate of realizable values of the underlying assets, for example, receivables net of the allowance for uncollectibles. However, these are accounting estimates of net realizable values and not market values.[49]

Lower of cost or market and impairment rules[50] may, however, require writedowns to fair or market values when they are below cost. In most cases, however, market values are not reflected in the balance sheet prior to realization, and recoveries (reversal of previous writedowns) to the original acquisition cost are not allowed under U.S. GAAP.[51] The exception to this rule is the accounting for investments in securities (see Chapter 13).[52]

Finally, the assets and liabilities of foreign affiliates or those denominated in other currencies are reported at amounts translated from other currencies at the exchange rate prevailing on the financial statement date or a combination of this current rate and specific historical rates for certain components.[53]

The balance sheet does not report all assets and liabilities of the firm, but reflects only those meeting specific recognition criteria.[54] Some assets and liabilities meet these criteria, but are not reported because they cannot be reliably measured (see the discussion of contingencies in Chapter 1).

Some intangible assets have extremely uncertain or hard-to-measure benefits, for example, customer lists or brand names, and they are recognized only when acquired in a purchase method acquisition. Others, such as research and development, are never recognized as assets under U.S. GAAP. Similarly, liabilities may exist as a result of legal action, but because they are not reliably measurable, only footnote disclosure may be required (see, e.g., Note 18 on litigation in Pfizer's 1999 financial statements).

Thus, a balance sheet does not report the market value of a firm's assets, liabilities, or equity, although the information provided can be useful when estimating the market value of the firm or its securities.

Uses of the Balance Sheet

The reported balance sheet is one starting point for the analysis of a firm. It provides information about a firm's resources (assets) and obligations (liabilities), including liquidity and solvency. For creditors, the balance sheet provides information about the nature of assets that the firm uses as debt collateral.

The balance sheet also reports on a firm's earnings-generating ability in two ways. First, assets are defined as economic resources that are expected to provide future benefits. Consistent with the long-run going concern perspective of the firm, these future benefits are not only cash flows but also the ability to generate earnings.

Receivables are forecasts of cash collections. Fixed assets and inventory, on the other hand, are assets that generate future sales. Increases and decreases in such assets assist forecasts of the firm's sales and profitability.

---

[49]The level and trend of the allowance for uncollectible receivables may, however, help assess the market value of receivables, as well as the firm's credit policies and revenue recognition method.

[50]See Chapter 8.

[51]Under IASB standards, however, writedowns of fixed and intangible assets can be written back up to the original carrying amount if conditions change (see Chapter 8).

[52]Companies also record acquired assets and liabilities at fair market value when the purchase method is used. See Chapter 14 for a comparison of the purchase and pooling methods.

[53]See Chapter 15 for a detailed discussion.

[54]SFAC 5, Recognition and Measurement in Financial Statements of Business Enterprises (FASB 1984), requires financial statement recognition when four basic criteria are met:

Definition. The item qualifies as an element (e.g., asset or liability) of financial statements.

Measurability. It can be reliably measured.

Relevance. The information provided by the item can make a difference in user decisions.

Reliability. The information is representationally faithful, verifiable, and neutral.

Recognition is subject to cost/benefit and materiality constraints.

Second, proper evaluation of a firm's profitability must consider the amount of resources, that is, the level of investment, required for a specified level of sales or profitability. The balance sheet provides such data and (together with the income statement) can be used to measure the efficiency of a firm's operations and its return on investment.

The balance sheet can also generate forecasts about a firm's future cash flow needs. The asset levels needed to generate certain operating levels as well as the age of the firm's assets are useful inputs in assessing when a firm may have to replace its assets.

Finally, the reported balance sheet is the starting point for the preparation of an adjusted balance sheet and book value using current cost data. In Chapter 17, we show how to prepare a current cost balance sheet, using adjustments discussed in many chapters along the way.

Limitations of the Balance Sheet. The usefulness of the balance sheet is limited by the following three factors:

1. *Selective reporting.* Important assets and liabilities may be omitted from the balance sheet because GAAP does not require their inclusion. One example is operating leases and other off-balance-sheet financing techniques (see Chapter 11). Some included assets may have no economic value (see the discussion of goodwill in Chapter 14).

2. *Measurement.* Some assets and liabilities are carried at historical cost, others at market value. Historical costs may bear little relationship to their real market value. Inventories (Chapter 6) and long-lived assets (Chapter 7) are good examples.

3. *Delayed recognition.* GAAP permits companies to delay recognition of value changes. An important example is employee benefit plans, discussed in Chapter 12.

Fortunately, footnote and supplementary data are often used by analysts to adjust reported balance sheets and thereby improve their usefulness. Starting with Chapter 6, we discuss the adjustments that can be made to prepare a current cost balance sheet that provides a better measure of a firm's resources and obligations. In Chapter 17, as already stated, we show how to prepare a current cost balance sheet.

STATEMENT OF STOCKHOLDERS' EQUITY

This statement reports components of stockholders' equity or the investment of the owners in the firm, the earnings reinvested in the business, and various accounting adjustments that reflect selected market value changes in certain investments in securities, any minimum pension liability, certain unrealized gains and losses on cash flow hedges, and the effect of exchange rate changes on certain foreign subsidiaries. U.S. and IAS GAAP have similar requirements for the presentation of stockholders' equity.

Format, Classification, and Use

Companies generally report components of stockholders' equity in order of preference upon liquidation. For each class of shares, firms report the number of shares authorized, issued, and outstanding at each balance sheet date.

Preferred (preference) stock has priority for liquidation and dividends. Common characteristics and related disclosure requirements include but are not limited to:

- Cumulative rights to dividends that may be:
  - Fixed.
  - Floating rate.
  - Tied to amounts declared for common stock.
- Callable by issuer; call price must be disclosed.
- Convertible into common stock at option of holder; specified prices must be disclosed.
- Mandatory conversion into common shares at a specified date or under certain conditions; terms must be disclosed.

These features must be evaluated to determine the treatment of different classes of preferred stock in the analysis of leverage, capital structure, and earnings per share.

Redeemable preferred stock is redeemable at the option of the holder or according to a fixed time schedule. Such issues must be excluded from stockholders' equity, and reported after liabilities but before the equity section of the balance sheet.[55] The liquidation preference or redemption price should be used in the computation of book value per share, leverage, and capital ratios.

Common stock represents the owners' residual interest in the firm after all other claims have been met. Firms may issue one or more classes of common stock. The balance sheet or related footnotes generally disclose the various rights (such as voting rights and dividends) of the different classes of common stock. The par (or stated) value of common stock is normally reported separately from any additional paid-in capital. The latter represents the cumulative difference between the par value of common and the amount received when issued.

Firms often purchase their own common stock on the open market when management thinks it is undervalued, for reissue, or to prevent hostile takeovers. Treasury stock is usually reported as a contra account within stockholders' equity.[56] Although such repurchases were largely a U.S. phenomenon, they have become increasingly common in other countries.

The statement of stockholders' equity also reconciles the beginning and ending balance of retained earnings reinvested in the firm. This reconciliation reports the net income for the period, preferred and common dividends declared during the year, and any adjustments for stock splits, stock dividends, and acquisitions or quasi-reorganizations.

The statement must also report changes in comprehensive income (see Chapter 1 for presentation and discussion). There may be changes in the:

- Minimum liability recognized for underfunded pension plans (see Chapter 12)
- Market values of noncurrent investments (see Chapter 13)
- Unrealized gains and losses on cash flow hedges (see Chapter 16)
- Cumulative effect of exchange rate changes (Chapter 15)
- Unearned shares issued to employee stock ownership plans (ESOPs)

However, these items are sometimes different under IAS standards than under U.S. GAAP.

The valuation allowance for changes in the carrying amount of investment securities and the cumulative translation adjustment are examples of reserves permitted by U.S. or IAS GAAP. For many foreign companies, the statement of stockholders' equity includes reserve accounts that are required or discretionary under financial reporting standards or tax rules. Some foreign firms appropriate some percentage of earnings to preserve liquidity by limiting earnings available for dividends. The use of conservative accounting rules can achieve the same goal.

Some foreign countries permit firms to account for selected transactions as direct charges to the additional paid-in capital account. These include debt and equity issue and repurchase costs (including premiums and discounts on debt) and organization costs. Finally, some countries allow the revaluation of assets with the resulting gain or loss reported in a revaluation reserve. UK GAAP (SSAP 6) requires a statement or a separate footnote on changes in reserves.

The growth of international capital markets has increased the transparency of reserves reported by foreign multinationals. Examples are provided and analyzed in various chapters in the text.

■ Example

Pfizer's 1999 Consolidated Balance Sheet and Statement of Shareholders' Equity report the:

1. Number of preferred shares authorized (none are outstanding).
2. Par value and number of common shares authorized and issued as of year-end.[57]

---

[55]Rule 5-02(28) of Regulation S-X requires the exclusion of mandatorily redeemable preferred stock from the equity section of the financial statements. Preferred stocks that are not redeemable or are redeemable only at the option of the issuer and common stock should be included in the equity section. Staff Accounting Bulletin 64 details the accounting treatment of redeemable preferred.

[56]Some companies report the difference between the purchase price of Treasury stock and the price at subsequent reissuance of that Treasury stock as a component of additional paid-in capital. Other firms reflect this difference as an adjustment to retained earnings.

[57]Note that the 1999 stock split increased par value by $138 million and reduced APIC by an equal amount.

3. Additional paid-in capital.

4. Retained earnings and changes due to net income and common dividends declared.

5. Accumulated other comprehensive income (expense) and changes in each of its after-tax components.

6. Deduction for shares held by employee benefit trusts, and the annual changes (see Note 14 for discussion).

7. Deduction for Treasury stock repurchased (see Note 12 for details). ■

When a company has preferred shares outstanding, careful attention should be paid to their terms. When shares are convertible into common, the analyst should consider treating them as common shares when conversion is highly likely. When computing book value per common share, preferred shares should be stated at their redemption value when higher than the par or stated *amount*.

Example

Hecla Mining reported the following in its annual report for the year ended December 31, 2000:

Shareholders' Equity

December 31 Amounts in $thousands	2000	1999
Preferred stock, $0.25 par value, authorized 5,000,000 shares; issued and outstanding—2,300,000 shares, liquidation preference $119,025	575	575
Common stock, $0.25 par value, authorized 100,000,000 shares; issued 2000—66,859,752 shares, issued 1999—66,844,575 shares	16,715	16,711
Capital surplus	400,236	400,205
Accumulated deficit	(366,523)	(278,533)
Accumulated other comprehensive loss	(4,858)	(4,871)
Less stock held by grantor trust; 2000—139,467 common shares, 1999—132,290 common shares	(514)	(500)
Less treasury stock, at cost; 2000—62,114 common shares, 1999—62,111 common shares	(886)	(886)
Total shareholders' equity	44,745	132,701

Note 11: Shareholders' Equity
Preferred Stock

Hecla has 2.3 million shares of Series B Cumulative Convertible Preferred Stock (the Preferred Shares) outstanding. Holders of the Preferred Shares are entitled to receive cumulative cash dividends at the annual rate of $3.50 per share payable quarterly, when and if declared by the Board of Directors. As of January 31, 2001, Hecla has failed to pay the equivalent of two quarterly dividends of $4.0 million.

The Preferred Shares are convertible, in whole or in part, at the option of the holders thereof, into shares of common stock at an initial conversion price of $15.55 per share of common stock. The Preferred Shares were not redeemable by Hecla prior to July 1, 1996. After such date, the shares are redeemable at the option of Hecla at any time, in whole or in part, initially at $52.45 per share and thereafter at prices declining ratably on each July 1 to $50.00 per share on or after July 1, 2003.

While the preferred shares are shown at their carrying amount (575,000) they should be valued at their liquidating preference of $119 million [(2.3 million shares × $50 per share) + $4 million of unpaid dividends].[58] Correctly valuing the preferred

---

[58]One can also argue for a liquidating value of $121.4 million [(2.3 million shares × $51.05 per share) + $4 million of unpaid dividends], where $51.05 is the redemption price at December 31, 2000.

shows that Hecla's common stockholders' equity was negative. As the market price of Hecla's common shares was $.50 at December 31, 2000, clearly the conversion feature had insignificant value at that date. ∎

SUMMARY

This chapter introduces the balance sheet, the income statement, and the accrual concept that links them together. Financial statements are interrelated and good financial analysis requires the use of all available information. Our introduction, therefore, is incomplete.

The next chapter discusses the use of the cash flow statement and cash flow data in the assessment of the firm. It begins with the cash flow statement and the information it contains, and then develops the relationship between cash flow and income. Chapter 3 concludes our introduction to a firm's financial statements—the raw material of analysis.

Chapter 2

Problems

1. [Revenue recognition criteria] Describe the conditions under which revenue would be recognized:

(i) At the time of production, but prior to sale

(ii) At the time of sale, but prior to cash collection

(iii) Only when cash collection has occurred

2. [Contract accounting; CFA© adapted] On December 31, 1999, LASl Construction entered into a major long-term construction with the following terms:

Total contract price $3,000,000

Total expected cost $2,400,000

Construction is expected to take three years. Production costs and cash flows are shown in the following table:

Projected Production Costs and Cash Flows

Year	Costs Incurred	Cash Received
2000	$ 900,000	$1,000,000
2001	800,000	1,000,000
2002	700,000	1,000,000
Totals	$2,400,000	$3,000,000

a. Show the revenue and pretax income for each year under *both* the percentage-of-completion and completed contract methods.

b. Show the balance sheet accounts at December 31, 2000 resulting from the contract under the

(i) Percentage-of-completion method

(ii) Completed contract method

c. Assume that total projected costs increase by $100,000 and the change in estimate is made at December 31, 2001. Compute the revenue and pretax income for 2001 under the revised assumption.

3. [SOP 97-2, Software Revenue Recognition Criteria; 2001 AlCPA Technical Practice Aids adapted] Jasmine Inc., a soft-ware vendor, delivers its product to a customer on January 30, 2001 pursuant to a licensing arrangement that permits the customer to use the software indefinitely. The contract calls for payment of $600,000 in 30 days and $400,000 due in 13 months.

a. Calculate the amount of revenue that Jasmine can recognize during each of the following periods. Justify each calculation.

(i) The fiscal year ending January 31, 2001.

(ii) The fiscal years ending January 31, 2002 and January 31, 2003.

(iii) The fiscal year ending January 31, 2001 if the licensing period begins on March 1, 2001.

b. Assuming that Jasmine is not involved with its customers' financing arrangements, explain how your answers to part a would change if the customer paid in advance of the scheduled payments.

c. Explain whether Jasmine's ability to recognize revenue would change if, on January 30, 2001, it transfers, without recourse, the rights to receive all payments to an unrelated third party.

d. Assuming that Jasmine participates in a customer's financing arrangements with an unrelated party and receives payments in advance of the contractual terms,

(i) Explain whether Jasmine can recognize revenue on receipt of payment.

(ii) Describe the income statement and balance sheet impact of the payments received.

4. [Timing of revenue recognition] Heilig-Meyers Company is one of the largest furniture retailers in the United States. Until March 1, 2000, like other major retailers, Heilig-Meyers recognized revenue upon determination of the availability of merchandise, establishment of delivery date, and (when applicable) approval of customer credit.

a. Critique the revenue recognition method used by Heilig-Meyers Company. Your response should include an evaluation of whether the method conforms to U.S. GAAP.

b. Effective March 1, 2000, the company (and other U.S. furniture retailers) changed its revenue recognition to record merchandise sales upon delivery. Describe the effects of the change in accounting method on the company's income statement, balance sheet, and statement of cash flows.

c. Concurrent with the change in accounting method, Heilig-Meyers stated that it would continue to report monthly sales based on orders written rather than on orders delivered. Discuss the advantages and disadvantages from the analyst perspective of reporting monthly orders rather than recognized sales.

5. [Earnings volatility—percentage-of-completion versus completed contract; CFA© adapted]

a. Compare the volatility of reported earnings over the life of a contract of both the completed contract and percentage-of-completion accounting methods.

b. Discuss the difference in volatility when a firm has many contracts.

c. Discuss how the volatility discussed in parts A and B impacts the usefulness of the information provided by the statement of cash flows.

6. [Percentage-of-completion versus completed contract method] Compare the effect during the contract period of the completed contract and percentage-of-completion methods of accounting on the level and trend of reported:

   (i) Revenues and cost of goods sold

   (ii) Earnings

   (iii) Operating cash flows

   (iv) Accounts receivable, total current assets, and total long-term assets

7. [Balance sheet effects of revenue recognition methods] Lucent's balance sheet shows the following accounts:

- Contracts in process (current assets)
- Advance billings (current liabilities)

a. Describe the nature of the two accounts listed above.

b. State the other accounts on the company's balance sheet to which these accounts are similar.

c. Determine the accounting method that Lucent uses to account for its long-term construction projects.

8. [Percentage-of-completion] On April 1, 2001, Pine Construction enters into a fixed-price contract to construct an apartment building for $6 million. Pine uses the percentage-of-completion method. Information related to the contract follows:

	December 31, 2001	December 31, 2002
Percentage-of-completion	20%	60%
Estimated total construction cost	$4,500,000	$4,800,000
Income recognized to date	$ 300,000	$ 720,000

a. Calculate the following for both 2001 and 2002:

   (i) Revenue recognized

   (ii) Costs incurred

b. Assume that during 2002, Pine purchases and pays for $0.3 million of products and services that will be used in construction during 2003.

Describe the impact of these expenditures on Pine's revenue recognition for 2002.

9. [Revenue recognition effects; CFA© adapted] Describe the effect of recognizing revenue earlier than justified by GAAP on each of the following:

   (i) Accounts receivable

   (ii) Inventories

   (iii) Revenues

   (iv) Operating profit

   (v) Stockholders' equity

10. [Revenue recognition methods; income and cash flow effects] The Able, Baker, Charlie, and David companies are identical in every respect except for their revenue recognition methods:

   (i) Able recognizes sales when an order is received.

   (ii) Baker recognizes sales at the time of production.

   (iii) Charlie recognizes sales at the time of shipment.

   (iv) David recognizes sales when cash is collected.

After the first year of operations, Charlie's closing inventory was $30,000 and accounts receivable was $50,000. Backorders, for which production had not yet started, were $10,000. Charlie recognized sales of $100,000 for the year.

a. Assuming that each company charges a markup of 100% over cost, complete the following table:

	Able	Baker	Charlie	David
Sales	___	___	$100,000	___
Cost of goods sold	___	___	___	___
Net income	___	___	___	___

b. Ignoring income taxes, state which company will have the largest cash balance at year-end.

c. State which company will report the largest cash from operations.

11. [Effect of revenue recognition methods on bonus] The Kwai Co. has obtained a contract to build a bridge over the Celluloid River. The bridge will take three years to construct and will require Kwai cash outflows of $1.0 million, $0.5 million, and $0.5 million in years 1, 2, and 3, respectively. Kwai will receive the $3 million contract price in three equal installments of $1 million. As manager of this project, you have three revenue recognition choices:

   (i) Completed contract

   (ii) Percentage-of-completion

   (iii) Installment basis

a. Assume that your objective is to maximize the present value (the discount rate is 12%) of your bonus. Bonus payments are made at the end of each year. State which accounting method you would choose if the bonus were based on:

   (i) 10% of annual income

   (ii) 10% of annual revenue

   (iii) 10% of cash flows from operations

For each case, justify your choice.

b. Assume that bonuses are calculated on an annual basis but paid only when the bridge is completed. Explain how your answers to part a would change.

(*Note*: This problem (parts a and b) can be solved without calculations. The answer can be deduced with some thought and by inspection of the data.)

12. [Revenue and expense recognition: pricing season tickets—the Toronto Raptors, courtesy of Professor I. Krinsky] The Toronto Raptors, a 1995 NBA expansion team, announced an elaborate season-ticket plan with a ticket price and vantage point to satisfy almost every need. Ticket prices range from $85 per game for 45 games—*plus a one-time license fee of $8,750*—for the best seats, to $10 per game—*plus a one-time license fee of $750*—for the cheapest seats; the team has eight ticket prices.

   The license fee, used for the first time by a sports team in Canada, entitles the holder to a de facto lease on the seat. The license holder retains the right to buy the accompanying ticket and may sell that right to anyone at a mutually agreed-on price.

a. Discuss how the Toronto Raptors should recognize revenue from ticket sales and the license fee under this system.

b. Discuss how a corporation that purchases Toronto Raptors tickets and gives them to its customers should recognize the license fee.

c. Discuss how, as an analyst, you would incorporate

   (i) The licensing fee

   (ii) Season-ticket sales

in your estimation of the Toronto Raptors' expected earnings.

13. [Effects of nonrecurring events, courtesy of Professor M. Schiff] Monsanto's *1994 Annual Report* stated that the Chairman and CEO, Richard J. Mahoney, would retire on March 31, 1995. Mahoney's cash compensation for 1994 consisted of:

Salary	$950,000
Annual incentive award (based primarily on achieving or exceeding a net income goal)	1,680,000
Total cash compensation	$2,630,000

   In addition, Mahoney participated in a long-term compensation plan that granted annual stock option awards if the return on stockholders' equity (ROE) exceeded 20%. Monsanto's reported ROE was

Net income = $622 million

Opening stockholders' equity = $2,855 million

Closing stockholders' equity = $2,948 million

ROE = Net income/average stockholders' equity = $622/$2,902 = 21.4%

EXHIBIT 2P-1. MONSANTO
Excerpts from *1994 Annual Report* (in $millions)

	1994	1993	1992
Net income (loss)	$622	$494	($88)
ROE	21.4%	16.9%	(2.6%)

Note: Restructurings and Other Actions

In December 1994, the board of directors approved a plan to eliminate redundant staff activities across the company and consolidate certain staff and administrative business functions. The plan will result in reductions in worldwide employment levels of approximately 500 people. In addition, the company will close or exit certain facilities and programs. These workforce reductions and closures will be substantially completed by the end of 1995. The pretax expense related to these actions was $89 million ($55 million after tax).

   In September 1994, Monsanto received $67 million from the U.S. Internal Revenue Service in settlement of certain tax matters related to the 1985 acquisition of Searle. This settlement included interest of $33 million ($21 million after tax), recorded as a one-time gain. Most of the remainder of the proceeds reduced the balance of unamortized goodwill related to the Searle acquisition. . . .

   . . . Restructuring expenses are recorded based on estimates prepared at the time the restructuring actions are approved by the board of directors. In the fourth quarter of 1994, the board approved the reversal of $49 million of pretax excess restructuring reserves from prior years. The excess was primarily due to higher than expected proceeds and lower exit costs from the sale and shutdown of nonstrategic businesses and facilities included in the 1993 and 1992 restructuring actions. The balance in restructuring reserves as of Dec. 31, 1994, was $254 million, and consisted primarily of workforce reduction costs under the 1994 actions and planned facility dismantling and site closure costs remaining under previous restructurings. Management believes that the balance of these reserves as of Dec. 31, 1994, is adequate for completion of those activities. . . .

Source: Monsanto, *1994 Annual Report*.

Given the reported ROE of 21.4%, Mahoney was granted options for 275,000 shares at $77.75 per share, the market price on the grant date. At the end of November 1995, the market price of Monsanto shares was $120 per share. If exercised and sold, the options would have gained about $11,600,000 ($42.25 × 275,000).

a. Using the information presented and Exhibit 2P-1, discuss whether Mahoney's stock options were deserved. Provide at least one argument for and one argument against the option award.

b. Discuss whether the nonrecurring events disclosed in Exhibit 2P-1 should be included in management performance measures such as ROE.

c. Using the information presented and Exhibit 2P-1, discuss the expected level of Monsanto's future income and ROE.

14. [Recurring and nonrecurring income, courtesy of Professor M. Schiff; revised] Many analysts focus on recurring income and ignore nonrecurring charges. Exhibit 2P-2, adapted from AT&T's *1997* and *2000 Annual Reports*, reports sales and operating income (earnings before interest and taxes) for the 10-year period 1991 to 2000. The exhibit also provides information about the company's restructuring charges and other writedowns.

a. Compute AT&T's operating income before nonrecurring charges.

b. Compare the trend in AT&T's reported operating income with the trends of sales and adjusted income computed in part a. (Graphical analysis may be useful.)

c. Discuss which set of operating income data is most relevant in analyzing AT&T and show how you might incorporate the nonrecurring charges in your analysis. State any other adjustments or data needed.

15. [Cost of sales and treatment of fulfillment costs; pro forma operating results] Amazon.com [AMZN] sells books, videos, music, and many other products online. For the years ended December 31, 1997 to 2000, Amazon reported the following data ($ millions):

	1997	1998	1999	2000
Net sales	$148	$610	$1,640	$2,762
Cost of sales	119	476	1,349	2,106
Gross margin	19.5%	21.9%	17.7%	23.7%
Fulfillment costs	$12	$65	$237	$415

In the footnotes to its financial statements, Amazon defines fulfillment costs as "costs of operating and staffing distribution and customer service centers, including costs attributable to receiving, inspecting, and warehousing inventories; picking, packaging and preparing customers' orders for shipment; credit card fees; and responding to inquiries from customers."

a. Evaluate Amazon's policy of excluding fulfillment costs from cost of sales.

b. Without prejudice to your response to part a, recalculate Amazon's gross margin percentage including fulfillment costs in cost of sales.

16. [Pro forma reporting] In its April 24, 2001 press release announcing its first quarter 2001 results, Amazon.com [AMZN] reported a "pro forma operating loss" of $49 million or 7% of net sales, compared with $99 million, or 17% of net sales in 2000. The pro forma operating loss excludes stock-based compensation costs, amortization of goodwill and other intangibles, and impairment-related and other costs. Discuss the relevance of pro forma operating loss as a percentage of net sales as an indicator of operating performance, profitability, and valuation.

17. [Deferred revenue] Microsoft defers a portion of the sales price of some products and services over the product life cycle.

Deferred revenue includes technical support, unspecified enhancements (such as service packs and Internet browser updates), maintenance, and other subscription contracts, including organization license agreements.

During the fourth quarter of 1999, Microsoft

- Adopted SOP 98–9, changing the method used to allocate fair value to undelivered elements, thereby increasing revenue recognized on shipment by $190 million,
- Extended the life cycle of Windows, decreasing reported revenue by $90 million, and
- Reduced estimated product returns by $250 million due to declining risk of product returns from distributors and resellers.

a. Using the data provided in Exhibit 2P-3 and any additional assumptions you need, calculate the revenue growth rate for each year based on:

  (i) Revenues as reported

  (ii) Revenues assuming no deferral

b. Discuss the effect of the 1999 accounting changes on reported revenue growth in:

  (i) 1999

  (ii) 2000

EXHIBIT 2P-2. AT&T
Revenues and Operating Income 1991–2000 (in $millions)

Year	Total Revenue	Operating Income (loss)	Special Charges*
1991	$41,842	$2,681	$(3,500)
1992	42,960	6,246	
1993	43,780	6,577	
1994	46,000	7,409	
1995	48,455	5,184	(3,000)
1996	50,546	8,763	
1997	51,319	6,968	
1998	53,223	7,487	(2,514)
1999	62,600	10,859	(1,506)
2000	65,981	4,277	(7,029)

*Restructuring and other charges, pretax.

Source: Adapted from AT&T's *1997* and *2000 Annual Reports*.

EXHIBIT 2P-3. MICROSOFT

	Years Ended June 30					
	1995	1996	1997	1998	1999	2000
	(in $millions)					
Revenues	$5,937	$8,671	$11,936	$15,262	$19,747	$22,956
Unearned revenue:						
opening balance	$ 39	$ 54	$ 560	$ 1,418	$ 2,888	$ 4,239
deferred during year	69	983	1,601	3,268	5,877	6,177
recognition of previously deferred revenue	(54)	(477)	(743)	(1,798)	(4,526)	(5,600)
closing balance	$ 54	$ 560	$ 1,418	$ 2,888	$ 4,239	$ 4,816

c. Discuss the advantage of measuring Microsoft's revenue growth using:

  (i) Revenues as reported

  (ii) Revenues assuming no deferral

18. [Revenue recognition for nonrefundable and refundable fee payments; adapted from Frequently Asked Questions and Answers: Staff Accounting Bulletin 101] Gigondas.com provides customers with nonexclusive access to proprietary databases on its website for a nonrefundable annual fee. The company provides customers an identification number and training in the use of the databases; post-training, the company incurs no incremental costs to provide services to its customers.

a. Discuss the amount, timing, and justification for revenue recognition by Gigondas. Consider recognition:

  (i) On completion of the initial setup, or

  (ii) Ratably over time as services are delivered.

b. Answer part a assuming that the unused portion of the membership fee is refundable.

19. [Revenue recognition for refundable fee payments and layaway transactions] Wal-Mart Stores [WMT] operates membership-only, cash-and-carry Sam's Clubs. The Company states that its analysis of historical membership fee refunds shows de minimis refunds. In fiscal 2000, the Company changed its method of accounting for Sam's Club membership fee revenues both domestically and internationally, from recognition on receipt to recording revenue ratably over the 12-month term of membership.

a. Describe the expected effect of the accounting change on WMT net income

  (i) In fiscal 2000

  (ii) In following years

b. Evaluate whether the new method better reflects revenues earned by the company.

c. Discuss whether Wal-Mart should record any reserves for membership fee refunds.

20. [Revenue recognition] Until the first quarter of 2001, Wal-Mart Stores [WMT] recognized revenues from layaway transactions [putting merchandise aside for customers who make partial payment] when the merchandise was placed on layaway. During the first quarter of 2001, the Company changed its accounting method to recognize revenues for layaway transactions when the customer has satisfied all payment obligations and takes possession of the merchandise.

a. Describe the expected effect of the accounting change on WMT net income

  (i) In fiscal 2001

  (ii) In following years

b. Discuss whether the new method better reflects the completion of the earnings process associated with layaway transactions.

21. [Provision for bad debts] Nucor [NUE], a large U.S. steel producer, reported the following (amounts in $millions):

	Years Ended December 31			
	1997	1998	1999	2000
Allowance for Doubtful Accounts				
Opening balance	$14.6	$18.0	$16.3	$21.1
Charged to earnings	4.2	(1.4)	5.3	
Write-offs (net of recoveries)	(0.8)	(0.3)	(0.5)	
Closing balance	$18.0	$16.3	$21.1	$27.6
Other Financial Data				
Accounts receivable (net)	$386.4	$299.2	$393.8	$350.2
Sales	4,184.5	4,151.2	4,009.3	4,586.1
Pretax income	460.2	415.3	379.2	478.3

a. Compute the following ratios (in %):

  (i) Ending balance of reserves to gross receivables for all years

  (ii) Accounts written off to revenues for 1997 to 1999

b. Assuming that Nucor had expensed accounts written off rather than accruing a reserve for bad debts, compute pretax income for 1997 through 2000.

c. Assuming that Nucor had maintained its bad debt reserve at the 1997 ratio of gross receivables, compute the effect on pretax income for 1998 through 2000.

d. Discuss two reasons that might explain the level of reserve accrual by Nucor for 1998 through 2000.

Nucor did not disclose the charge to earnings and writeoffs in 2000. Nucor's CFO told one of the authors that: "the amounts are clearly immaterial, bad debt writeoffs for the last six years averaged .02% of sales, and in no year were more than .03% of sales."

e. Evaluate the CFO's statement that the amounts are immaterial, stating one argument that supports his statement and one argument against it.

f. Explain why a chief financial officer would prefer not to disclose the charge to earnings and writeoffs.

g. Explain why a financial analyst would want those disclosures.

22. [Provision for bad debts] Boron LePore [BLPG} provides marketing and other services to major drug companies. The following data were obtained from the company's 10–K report for 2000 (amounts in $thousands):

Allowance for Doubtful Accounts and Credit Memo Reserve	*Years Ended December 31*		
	1998	1999	2000
Opening balance	$400	$535	$1,332
Charged to income	135	1,249	654
Deductions*	—	(452)	(700)
Ending balance	$535	$1,332	$1,286

*Charged to reserve for accounts written off and credits issued

Other financial data

Accounts receivable			
(net of allowance)	$44,394	$27,567	$42,402
Revenues	164,670	149,448	167,881
Pretax income	15,997	(973)	9,073

(Assume that credits issued equal addition to the credit memo reserve for both 1999 and 2000.)

a. Compute the ratios (in %) of:
   (i) Ending balance of reserve to gross receivables
   (ii) Accounts written off to revenues

b. Assuming that Boron had expensed accounts written off rather than accruing a reserve for bad debts, compute pretax income for 1999 and 2000.

c. Assuming that Boron had maintained its bad debt reserve at the 1998 ratio of gross receivables, compute the effect on pretax income for both 1999 and 2000.

d. Discuss two reasons that might explain the level of reserve accrual by Boron for 1999.

e. Explain why a financial analyst must examine the provision for bad debts. Your answer should draw on your responses to parts b through d.

23. [Trends in income and profitability] Rayna reported the following financial data:

$ in millions	Year 1	Year 2
Sales	$7,103	$7,047
Cost of goods sold	(4,295)	(4,122)
Selling and administrative expense	(1,712)	(1,724)
Depreciation	(235)	(260)
Interest expense	(146)	(149)
Gain on sale of business		127
Net income	$ 715	$ 919

(*Note*: Year 1 includes restructuring charges of $125 million ($103 million included in COGS and $22 million in S&A expense) relating to employee severance charges, relocation costs, and facilities consolidation and closing charges. Assume zero income taxes.)

Compare the trend in profitability over the two-year period with and without the nonrecurring items. Your comparison should include the preparation of a common size income statement. (*Note*: Problem 3–15 extends this problem to include cash flow as well as income analysis.)

3

ANALYSIS OF CASH FLOWS

CHAPTER OUTLINE

CHAPTER OBJECTIVES

Chapter 1 introduced the reader to the financial reporting process and Chapter 2 presented a detailed review of the accrual process, its role, and its impact on a firm's income statement and balance sheet. This chapter focuses on the statement of cash flows (SoCF) that recasts the financial statement data provided by the accrual process. It discusses the use and analysis of the information provided by the SoCF on its own and in conjunction with other financial statement data. As in the previous chapter, we use Pfizer's 1999 financial statements to illustrate many of the points raised.

The objectives of this chapter are to:

1. Describe the three components of a cash flow statement.

2. Distinguish between direct method and indirect method cash flow statements.

3. Show how to use the transactional analysis method to prepare a direct method cash flow statement using financial statement data.

4. Describe the effect of acquisitions and foreign currency exchange rate changes on the relationship between the cash flow statement and the balance sheet.

5. Recast an indirect statement of cash flows to a direct basis or to any format desired.

6. Understand how classification rules and accounting policies can affect the components of the cash flow statement.

7. Use the cash flow statement to examine a firm's liquidity position and the basic assumptions inherent in the accrual process.

8. Define the free cash flow measure used in valuation models.

9. Understand how cash flow statements can be used to derive information about a firm's acquisitions and how such activities distort reported operating cash flows.

10. Analyze trends in cash flow components.

11. Explain how cash flow statements prepared under IAS GAAP may differ from those prepared under U.S. GAAP and how to adjust for these differences.

STATEMENT OF CASH FLOWS

Cash flow data supplement the information provided by the income statement as both link consecutive balance sheets. The statement of cash flows reports all the cash inflows and outflows (classified among operating, investing, and financing activities) of the firm for a specified period. It also includes disclosures about that period's noncash investing and financing activities.

The classification of cash flows among operating, financing, and investing activities is essential to the analysis of cash flow data. Net cash flow (the change in cash and cash equivalents during the period) has little informational content by itself; it is the classification and individual components that are informative.

Cash flow from operating activities (cash from operations or CFO) measures the amount of cash generated or used by the firm as a result of its production and sales of goods and services. Although deficits or negative cash flows from operations are expected in some circumstances (e.g., rapid growth), for most firms positive operating cash flows are essential for long-run survival. Internally generated funds can be used to pay dividends or repurchase equity, repay loans, replace existing capacity, or invest in acquisitions and growth.

Investing cash flow (CFI) reports the amount of cash used to acquire assets such as plant and equipment as well as investments and entire businesses. These outlays are necessary to maintain a firm's current operating capacity and to provide capacity for future growth. CFI also includes cash received from the sale or disposal of assets or segments of the business.

Financing cash flow (CFF) contains the cash flow consequences of the firm's capital structure (debt and equity) decisions, including proceeds from the issuance of equity, returns to shareholders in the form of dividends and repurchase of equity, and the incurrence and repayment of debt.

Firms with significant foreign operations separately report a fourth category, *the effect of exchange rate changes on cash*, which accumulates the effects of changes in exchange rates on the translation of foreign currencies. This segregation is essential to accurately report the cash flow consequences of operating, investing, and financing decisions, unaffected by the impact of changes in exchange rates.

Direct and Indirect Method Cash Flow Statements

SFAS 95, Statement of Cash Flows (1987), and IAS 7 (1992) govern the preparation of cash flow statements under U.S. and IAS GAAP, respectively. Both standards permit firms to report cash from operations either *directly* by reporting major categories of gross cash receipts and payments, or *indirectly* by reconciling accrual-based net income to CFO.[1] Both investing and financing cash flows are usually computed identically under the two methods. However, there are reporting options under IAS 7 that can create noncomparability between cash flow statements prepared under the two standards.[2]

Exhibit 3-1 contrasts the direct and indirect cash flow statements of the WSF Company. These statements are generated from the company's balance sheet (Exhibit 3-2) and income statement (Exhibit 3-3).

Under the indirect method, CFO is computed by adjusting net income[3] for all:

1. Noncash revenues and expenses (for example, depreciation expense)
2. Nonoperating items included in net income (for example, gains from property sales)
3. Noncash changes in operating assets and liabilities (operating changes in receivables, payables, etc.)

---

[1]Para. 19 of IAS 7 encourages use of the direct method.

[2]See table in Cash Flow Statements: An International Perspective, later in this chapter.

[3]Income from continuing operations may be used when the cash flows from discontinued operations are shown separately. IAS 35 (1998) requires separate disclosure of cash flows from discontinued operations; SFAS 95 does not.

EXHIBIT 3-1. THE WSF COMPANY
Statement of Cash Flows for Year Ended December 31, 2001

A. Direct Method

Cash collections		$ 2,675,000
Less: Cash inputs	$(1,750,000)	
Cash expenses (rent, operating)	(430,000)	
Cash interest	(125,000)	(2,305,000)
Cash flow from operations		**$370,000**
Capital expenditures	(500,000)	
Investment in affiliate	(710,000)	
Cash flow from investing		**(1,210,000)**
Short-term borrowing	500,000	
Dividends paid	(35,000)	
Cash flow from financing		**465,000**
Net cash flow		**$ (375,000)**
Cash balance, as of December 31		
2001	$ 3,625,000	
2000	4,000,000	
Net change		**$ (375,000)**

B. Indirect Method

Net income		78,870
Add: Noncash expenses		
Depreciation expense		175,000
Changes in operating accounts		$ 253,870
(Increase) in receivables	(224,500)	
Decrease in inventories	425,000	
(Decrease) in accounts payable	(475,000)	
Increase in accrued liabilities	50,000	
Increase in interest payable	125,000	
Increase in taxes payable	40,630	
Increase in advances from customers	175,000	116,130
Cash flows from operations		**$ 370,000**

Note: Cash flow from investing and financing identical to that shown on direct method. The firm would also provide a separate footnote on cash payments for interest and taxes. The WSF Company paid $125,000 in interest, but it made no tax payments during the year ended December 31, 2001.

Enterprises using the direct method must also provide this reconciliation. Firms using either method must disclose the cash outflows for income taxes and interest within the statement or elsewhere in the financial statements (e.g., in the footnotes).[4]

Cash flow statements prepared using the indirect method have a significant drawback. Because the *indirect format reports the net cash flow from operations, it does not facilitate the comparison and analysis of operating cash inflows and outflows by function with the revenue and expense activities that generated them, as is possible from direct method cash flow statements*. In the absence of acquisitions, divestitures, and significant foreign operations, the indirect method simply recasts the income statement and the balance sheet, providing little new information on or insight into the specific components of a firm's cash-generating ability. As a majority of firms prepare the SoCF using the indirect method,[5] it is often necessary to convert an indirect statement into a direct one.

---

[4]Required by para. 29 of SFAS 95. The AICPA's 2000 *Accounting Trends and Techniques* reports that 33 of the 600 firms surveyed did not disclose interest payments and 22 firms did not disclose income tax payments.

[5]Of the 600 firms surveyed by the AICPA in the 2000 *Accounting Trends and Techniques*, only 7 report using the direct method.

EXHIBIT 3-2. THE WSF COMPANY
Balance Sheets at December 31, 2000 and 2001

	2000	2001
Assets		
Cash	$4,000,000	$3,625,000
Accounts receivable	0	224,500
Inventory	850,000	425,000
Current assets	$4,850,000	$4,274,500
Investment in affiliates	0	710,000
Buildings	3,500,000	4,000,000
Less: Accumulated depreciation	0	(175,000)
Long-term assets	$3,500,000	$4,535,000
Total assets	$8,350,000	$8,809,500
Liabilities		
Short-term debt	$0	$500,000
Advances from customers	0	175,000
Accounts payable	850,000	375,000
Accrued liabilities	0	50,000
Interest payable	0	125,000
Taxes payable	0	40,630
Dividends payable	0	35,000
Current liabilities	$ 850,000	$1,300,630
Bonds payable	2,500,000	2,500,000
Total liabilities	$3,350,000	$3,800,630
Common stock	1,000,000	1,000,000
Additional paid-in capital	4,000,000	4,000,000
Retained earnings	0	8,870
Stockholders' equity	$5,000,000	$5,008,870
Total liabilities and equities	$8,350,000	$8,809,500

EXHIBIT 3-3. THE WSF COMPANY
Income Statement for Year Ended December 31, 2001

Net sales		$ 2,724,500
Less: Cost of goods sold		(1,700,000)
Gross margin		$ 1,024,500
Less: Operating expense	$360,000	
Depreciation expense	175,000	
Rent expense	120,000	
Interest expense	250,000	(905,000)
Income before taxes		119,500
Tax expense		(40,630)
Net income		$ 78,870

Statement of Retained Earnings

Beginning balance, January 1, 2001		$ 0
Net income		78,870
Dividends declared		(70,000)
Ending balance, December 31, 2001		$ 8,870

Preparation of a Statement of Cash Flows

The cash flow statement combines cash flows for events that are reported on the balance sheet (e.g., purchases of inventories) and the income statement (e.g., the cost of goods sold). The process is complicated by timing differences between when cash flows occur and when they are recognized as revenues, expenses, assets, or liabilities. The next section discusses methods used to prepare direct and indirect method cash flow statements.

Transactional Analysis

Transactional analysis[6] is a technique that can be used to create a cash flow statement for firms that do not prepare such statements in accordance with SFAS 95 and IAS 7.[7] It can also be used to convert indirect method cash flow from operations to the direct method.

One objective of transactional analysis is to understand the relationship between the accruals of revenues, expenses, assets, and liabilities and their cash flow consequences. Another goal is to facilitate analysis by classifying gross cash flows between operating, financing, and investing activities.

The method reconciles line-item changes in the balance sheet with their related income statement components to derive the cash flow consequences of the reported transactions and events. These changes are grouped according to whether they are operating, investing, or financing in nature. The classification and cash flow description for a typical firm follow:

Changes in Balance Sheet Accounts	Income Statement Items	Cash Flow Description
Cash Flow from Operating Activities (CFO)		
Accounts receivable	Net sales	Cash received from customers
Advances from customers	Net sales	Cash received from customers
Inventories and accounts payable	COGS	Cash paid for inputs
Prepaid expenses	SG&A expense	Cash operating expenses
Rent payable	Rent expense	Cash operating expenses
Accrued expenses	SG&A expense	Cash operating expenses
Interest payable	Interest expense	Interest paid
Income tax payable and deferred income taxes	Income tax expense	Income tax paid
Cash Flow from Investing Activities (CFI)		
Property, plant, and equipment	Depreciation expense	Capital expenditures
Intangible assets	Amortization expense	Capital expenditures
Investment in affiliates	Equity in income of affiliates	Cash paid for and received from investments in affiliates
Short and long-term investments and gains (losses) on certain investments	Realized gains or losses on investments	Cash paid for and received from investments
Assets and liabilities resulting from acquisitions and divestitures		Cash paid for acquisitions or received from divestitures

[6]See Ashwinpaul C. Sondhi, George H. Sorter, and Gerald I. White, "Transactional Analysis," *Financial Analysts Journal* (September/October 1987), pp. 57–64. "Cash Flow Redefined: FAS 95 and Security Analysis," *Financial Analysts Journal* (November/December 1988), pp. 19–20 by the same authors links the transactional analysis method of preparing cash flow statements to those required by SFAS 95.

[7]The number of non-U.S. companies preparing statements of cash flows is on the increase. Firms using IAS 7 are not required to reconcile their cash flow statements to U.S. GAAP. Despite the increased use of IAS GAAP by non-U.S. firms, many foreign firms do not report any cash flow statement or report changes in funds (see "Cash Flow Statements: An International Perspective," near the end of this chapter).

Cash Flow from Financing Activities (CFF)

Dividends payable	Dividends paid
Notes payable	Increase or decrease in debt
Short-term debt	Increase or decrease in debt
Long-term debt	Increase or decrease in debt
Bonds payable	Increase or decrease in debt
Common stock and APIC	Increase or decrease in equity
Retained earnings	Dividends paid

The relationship between balance sheet changes and cash flows can be summarized as follows:

- Increases (decreases) in assets represent net cash outflows (inflows). If an asset increases, the firm must have paid cash in exchange.
- Increases (decreases) in liabilities represent net cash inflows (outflows). When a liability increases, the firm must have received cash in exchange.

While these points are simple (they ignore payments or receipts other than cash), they are useful in practice.

Two examples clarify the application of these points to transactional analysis:

1. When accounts receivable increase, the period's credit sales (revenues) must have exceeded cash collections. Thus, the increase in receivables must be deducted from the accrued sales revenue to derive the cash collected from customers during the period.

2. When interest payable increases, the firm has not paid all the interest expense accrued during the period. Hence, the increase in interest payable must be deducted from the interest expense to compute the amount of interest paid during the period.

Preparation of a Direct Method Statement of Cash Flows

Exhibit 3-4 illustrates the use of transactional analysis to prepare a direct method statement of cash flows for the WSF Company. We use the data from Exhibits 3-2 and 3-3 to explain the method without the complications present in most actual financial statements. A brief discussion of the most critical problems in the preparation of cash flow statements is provided later.

Cash Flows from Operations

Cash Collections. The principal component of CFO is the cash collections for the period. To derive this amount, we start with WSF net sales of $2,724,500 in 2001. The increase of $224,500 in the balance of accounts receivable means that cash has not yet been collected for all the sales recognized. In addition, the firm received cash advances ($175,000) for which revenue has not yet been recognized.

We modify net sales by deducting the increase in accounts receivable and adding the increase in advances, to arrive at cash collections. This is the amount of cash actually received during the period as a result of sales activities, regardless of when the related revenues are recognized.

Cash Outflows. The next stage involves the computation of operating cash outflows incurred to generate the cash collections. The first component is the cash outflow for inputs into the manufacturing or retailing process. The decrease in inventory balances[8] (cash outflow occurred in the prior period) is subtracted from, and the decrease in accounts payable (cash outflow in the current period for goods received in a prior period) is added to the cost of goods sold to determine the cash inputs or outflow for the manufacturing process.

---

[8]The cash outflow for inputs is not affected by the inventory valuation method used by the firm, facilitating comparison across firms.

EXHIBIT 3-4. THE WSF COMPANY
Transactional Analysis ($000)

	Income Statement	Balance Sheet 12/31/00	Balance Sheet 12/31/01	Change	Cash Effect	Cash	
Cash Collections							
Net sales	2,724.5				Increase	2,724.5	
Accounts receivable		—	224.5	224.5	(Decrease)	(224.5)	
Advances		—	175.0	175.0	Increase	175.0	**2,675.0**
Cash Inputs							
COGS	(1,700.0)				(Decrease)	(1,700.0)	
Inventory		850.0	425.0	(425.0)	Increase	425.0	
Accounts payable		850.0	375.0	(475.0)	(Decrease)	(475.0)	**(1,750.0)**
Cash Expenses							
Operating expense	(360.0)				(Decrease)	(360.0)	
Rent expense	(120.0)				(Decrease)	(120.0)	
Accrued liabilities		—	50.0	50.0	Increase	50.0	**(430.0)**
Cash Taxes Paid							
Tax expense	(40.63)				(Decrease)	(40.63)	
Taxes payable		0	40.63	40.63	Increase	40.63	—
Cash Interest paid							
Interest expense	(250.0)				(Decrease)	(250.0)	
Interest payable		0	125	125	Increase	125.0	**(125.0)**
Operating Cash Flow							**370.0**
Capital Expenditures							
Depreciation	(175.0)				(Decrease)	(175.0)	
Buildings—Net		3,500	3,825	325.0	(Decrease)	(325.0)	**(500.0)**
Cash Invested in Affiliates							
Investment in affiliates		—	710.0	710.0	(Decrease)		**(710.0)**
Investing Cash Flow							**(1,210.0)**
Cash from Borrowing							
Short-term debt		—	500.0	500.0	Increase	500.0	
Bonds payable		2,500	2,500	—		—	**500.0**
Equity Financing							
Common stock		1,000	1,000	—			
Additional paid-in capital		4,000	4,000	—			
Net income	78.87						
Dividends							
Dividends declared					(Decrease)	(70.0)	
Dividends payable		—	35.0		Increase	35.0	**(35.0)**
Financing Cash Flow							**465.0**
Change in cash							**(375.0)**

The remaining income statement accounts and their related balance sheet accounts are similarly modified to their cash analogs to determine the cash outflows for operating expenses, interest, and taxes. In each case, the goal is to link the income statement account with related balance sheet accounts. By related, we mean the balance sheet account that contains cash flows that either have been recognized in that income statement account (accruals and payables) or will be recognized in the future (prepayments).

In many cases, disclosures are inadequate to do this precisely. Educated guesses and approximations may be necessary. For example, we assume that accounts payable reported by WSF relate only to the purchase of inventory for operating purposes although they may also be related to other operating expenses.

A careful reading of footnote data is necessary to obtain additional information on aggregated balance sheet accounts, permitting finer breakdowns of assets and liabilities. For example, in addition to trade accounts receivable, the amounts reported on the balance sheet may include notes and loans receivable, which represent investment cash flows.

Additionally, balance sheet and income statement accounts may require reallocation of some components. For example, when depreciation expense is not reported separately in the income statement, we must reduce COGS by the amount of depreciation expense to accurately reflect cash inputs and create a "depreciation expense" account to correctly estimate cash invested in property. The depreciation expense may be disclosed separately in footnotes, or in the indirect cash flow statement.

Cash flows that are considered nonrecurring[9] or peripheral to the basic activities of the firm are combined in the miscellaneous category, which also includes the cash impact of transactions for which the financial statements and the footnotes do not provide information enabling more precise classification.

Investing Cash Flow

Capital expenditures for long-term assets such as plant and machinery are usually the primary component of investing cash flow. As depreciation changes (net) property, plant, and equipment, the calculation of capital expenditures requires the amount of depreciation, depletion, and amortization expense in addition to the changes in all related long-term asset accounts.[10]

Capital expenditures may be calculated net or gross of proceeds on the sales of these assets. The cash flows from such sales are considered investment cash flows, regardless of whether they are netted in capital expenditures. Trends in gross capital expenditures contain useful insights into management plans.

Other components of cash flows from investing activities include cash flows from investments in joint ventures and affiliates and long-term investments in securities.[11] The cash flow consequences of acquisitions and divestitures must also be reported in this category. Footnote disclosures (when available) should be used to segregate operating assets and liabilities obtained (relinquished) in acquisitions (divestitures). This analysis, as discussed below, may be necessary to calculate CFO.

Financing Cash Flow

Components of financing cash flow include inflows from additional borrowing and equity financing, and outflows for repayment of debt, dividend payments, and equity repurchases. Debt financing for the period is the sum of the changes in short- and long-term debt accounts.

---

[9]However, the transaction should be analyzed to determine whether it is best classified as operating, investing, or financing.

[10]The deduction for depreciation expense is not taken because depreciation represents a cash flow; rather, it is needed to calculate the cash capital expenditures.

[11]The nature of the relationship between parent and subsidiary or joint venture affiliate should be periodically reviewed to ensure proper classification; in some cases, affiliates may be more accurately considered part of operations. However, contractual arrangements may constrain the parent's control over or access to cash flows from affiliates. (See Chapter 13 for a detailed discussion of these issues.)

The calculation of equity financing cash flows requires analysis of the change in stockholders' equity, separating:

- Net income.
- Dividends declared.
- Shares issued or repurchased.
- Changes in valuation accounts included in equity (each of these may require reallocation to appropriate operating or investing cash flow categories[12]).

Once this is done, every change in the balance sheet has been included (net income is included by incorporating each of its components) except cash. The net cash flow must, by definition, be equal to the change in cash. This identity provides a check on computations.[13]

The last step is to summarize the cash flows from operations, financing, and investing activities. The result is a direct method statement of cash flows, as shown in Exhibit 3-1A.

Indirect Method

Exhibit 3-1B presents the indirect method statement of cash flows for the WSF Company. The reporting of investing and financing activities is identical to the direct method. *The reporting of cash flow from operations, however, is quite different.* Under the indirect method, the starting point is the period's net income. Two types of adjustments are then made to net income to arrive at the CFO:

1. All "noncash" expense (revenue) components of the income statement are added (subtracted).
2. Changes in operating accounts are added/subtracted as follows:
   - Increases (decreases) in the balances of operating asset accounts are subtracted (added).
   - Increases (decreases) in the balances of operating liability accounts are added (subtracted).

The second type of adjustment represents the same balance sheet changes that were used to derive individual components of cash from operations under the direct method. As these adjustments are provided by the reconciliation in the indirect cash flow method, they can be used to derive a direct method cash flow statement from an indirect one.

In Box 3-1, we demonstrate this process using Pfizer's indirect method statement of cash flows. As the discussion in the box indicates, careful analysis of footnote information is required to make the necessary adjustments.

Two important requirements of SFAS 95 must, however, be explained before proceeding to Box 3-1:

1. *Changes in operating accounts shown on Pfizer's statement of cash flows do not equal the balance sheet changes.* For example, in the 1999 cash flow statement, accounts receivable are reported to *increase by $978*; the balance sheet shows an *increase of $950*. What accounts for this and similar discrepancies in other operating assets and liabilities?
2. Pfizer's statement of cash flows contains the *effect of exchange rate changes on cash* (in addition to the three cash flow categories: operating, investing, and financing). The 1999 amount is $26 million. What does it represent?

We address both issues below.

---

[12]For example, the change in the unrealized gains (losses) on investments account must be reflected as a component of investment cash flows (see Chapter 13).

[13]As an additional check, make sure that the income statement components used in the transactional analysis add up to net income.

Reported versus Operating Changes in Assets and Liabilities

The discrepancies between the changes in accounts reported on the balance sheet and those reported in the cash flow statement are primarily due to two[14] factors:

- Acquisitions and divestitures
- Foreign subsidiaries

Acquisitions and Divestitures

Changes in reported balances of operating asset and liability accounts may include the effects of both operating activities and acquisitions or divestitures. For example, the inventory account may have increased as a result of:

1. Purchase of inventory from a supplier (an operating activity)
2. Acquisition of (merger with) another firm that has inventory as a component of its balance sheet (an investing activity)

SFAS 95 requires that CFO include only operating transactions and events. Thus, for firms that acquire the operating assets and liabilities of another company, the changes reported in the statement of cash flows as adjustments to income to arrive at CFO will not match the increase or decrease reported on the balance sheet.

The difference between the changes reported in the two statements provides useful information to the analyst. If the difference for any balance sheet account represents the amount of that component acquired through a merger, *the analyst can reconstruct the assets and liabilities obtained by the firm through an acquisition*.[15] This information is generally not provided anywhere else.

Although the reporting requirements accomplish the necessary segregation in the period of the acquisition (or divestiture), cash flows for subsequent periods may be distorted. For example, cash paid for the accounts receivable of an acquired firm is reported as an investment cash outflow. However, collection of the acquired receivable in a subsequent period will be reported as a component of operating cash flows. The result is overstated cash flows from operations, as the cost of acquiring the accounts receivable was never reflected in cash outflows for operations.[16] *Acquisitions, divestitures, and continuing corporate reorganizations can therefore distort trends in both cash flows from operations and investing cash flows*. These issues are examined in greater detail in Chapter 14.

Translation of Foreign Subsidiaries

The second difference between the changes reported on the cash flow statement and those reported on the balance sheet relates to foreign operations. The assets and liabilities of foreign subsidiaries must be translated into the reporting currency (i.e., U.S. dollars) upon preparation of consolidated financial statements. This process generates a U.S. dollar balance for each asset and liability account that includes both operating changes (representing real cash flow effects) and exchange rate effects that have no current cash flow consequences.

---

[14]As previously discussed, balance sheet accounts may include both operating and nonoperating (investing or financing) items. The cash flow statement must allocate balance sheet changes to the appropriate activity.

[15]This can be done if we assume that the confounding effect of exchange rate changes (discussed next) is not significant. Thus, ignoring that issue for the moment, one would estimate that Pfizer's accounts receivable increased by $978 million and the balance sheet change reflects a divestiture of $28 million ($978 − $950).

[16]Similarly, cash received for accounts receivable of a divested business is reflected as an investment cash inflow, whereas the cash outflow required to generate the receivable (purchase of inventory, selling costs) was previously reported as a component of CFO. However, the CFI characterization is correct since the divested business will no longer contribute to cash flows from continuing operations. Prior period receivables (and CFO) would also exclude balances related to the divested business.

BOX 3-1. PFIZER
Derivation of Direct Method CFO ($ in millions)

1999 Income Statement

Net sales	$14,133
Alliance revenue	2,071
Total revenues	$16,204

Costs and expenses:

Cost of sales	(2,528)
Selling, informational, and administrative expenses	(6,351)
Research and development expenses	(2,776)
Other deductions—net	(101)
Income from continuing operations before provision for taxes on income and minority interests	$ 4,448
Provision for taxes on income	(1,244)
Minority interests	(5)
Income from continuing operations	$ 3,199

Indirect CFO from SoCF

Income from continuing operations	$ 3,199

Adjustments:

Depreciation and amortization	542
Trovan inventory write-off	310
Deferred taxes and other	286

Changes in assets and liabilities:

Accounts receivable	(978)
Inventories	(240)
Prepaid and other assets	68
Accounts payable and accrued liabilities	61
Income taxes payable	(179)
Other deferred items	7
Net cash provided by operating activities	$ 3,076

Derivation of Direct Method CFO

Cash collections from customers		
Net sales (excluding alliance revenues)	$14,133	
Change in accounts receivable	(978)	**$13,155**
Cash from alliance revenues		**2,071**
Cash payments for inputs		
COGS	(2,528)	
Depreciation and amortization	542	
Trovan inventory write-off	310	
Change in inventories	(240)	
Change in accounts payable	61	**(1,855)**
Cash payments for SI&A		
Selling, informational, and administrative expenses	(6,351)	
Prepaid and other assets	68	**(6,283)**
Cash for research and development		**(2,776)**
Cash taxes paid		**(1,293)**
Cash interest paid		**(238)**
Miscellaneous cash flows (including minority interest)		**295**
Cash flow from operations		**$ 3,076**

(continued)

Discussion

The direct method CFO is derived from the income statement and indirect method CFO.* Unlike many other companies, Pfizer does not provide details for most balance sheet categories. A number of assumptions were used to develop the direct method cash flow statement.

Cash collections are derived by deducting the $978 million increase in accounts receivable [see the reported indirect method statement of cash flows (SoCF)] from reported net sales of $14,133 million.

Pfizer reported cost of sales of $2,528 million; depreciation and amortization expense of $542 and the $310 million inventory write-off are added back as they reflect noncash portions of COGS.† We also adjust for the changes in inventory and accounts payable. This latter adjustment requires the simplifying assumption that the accounts payable are related primarily to inventories.

To derive cash expenses, we add the $68 million of prepaid expenses to the reported selling, informational, and administrative expenses of $6,351 million. Research and development expenses are taken directly from the income statement. Pfizer discloses cash tax payments of $1,293 million and cash interest payments of $238 million.

The miscellaneous amount of $295 million is a"plug" amount used to arrive at the reported CFO of $3,076 million.

---

*Note that the CFI and CFF portions of the SoCF are identical under the direct and indirect methods. Thus we need only adjust the CFO portion.
†Many companies disclose depreciation as a separate item on the income statement. For those companies, depreciation on the SoCF equals the depreciation expense shown on the income statement. For companies that do not disclose depreciation separately, an assumption has to be made as to whether the depreciation is (primarily) included in COGS or SG&A. The rule of thumb is to assume COGS for manufacturing firms and SG&A for other firms.

For example, assume a firm has a foreign subsidiary that has an opening and closing accounts receivable balance of £10,000. Assume further that at the beginning of year 1, the pound is worth $1.00, but at the end of the year a pound is worth $1.10. Upon consolidation, the parent's balance sheet will include

Opening accounts receivable from foreign subsidiary (£10,000 × opening exchange rate of £1 = $1)	$10,000
Closing accounts receivable from foreign subsidiary (£10,000 × closing exchange rate of £1 = $1.1)	11,000
Increase	$ 1,000

This $1,000 increase is included in accounts receivable shown on the balance sheet. However, it will not appear as a component of cash collections for the period because it is not a change resulting from operations. Thus, CFO does not include the effects of the translation process.

Translation gains and losses resulting from exchange rate changes are excluded from cash flows from operating, investing, and financing activities.[17] The effect of these excluded gains and losses is reported as the effect of exchange rate changes on cash (see below). The $28 million discrepancy between the balance sheet increase in receivables ($950 million) and that reported in Pfizer's cash flow statement ($978 million) most likely reflects the impact of changes in exchange rates as the $U.S. appreciated during 1999, reducing the $U.S. equivalent of foreign currency receivables.

Effect of Exchange Rate Changes on Cash

An explanation of the *effect of exchange rate changes on cash* follows directly from our previous discussion. Suppose the foreign subsidiary in our previous example had a cash balance of £4,000 at the beginning and end of the year. Upon consolidation, the parent's reported cash balance includes $4,000 at the beginning of the year and $4,400 (£4,000 × 1.10) at the end of the year. This increase of $400 needs to be reported as it does not appear as an operating, investing, or financing activity.

In Pfizer's case, the $26 million reported as "effect of exchange rate on cash" reflects the effect of exchange rate changes on the firm's foreign currency cash holdings.

---

[17]These issues are discussed in greater detail in Chapter 15.

■ Example: Pfizer

We examine each component of Pfizer's cash flow statement, in turn, to demonstrate the use and analysis of cash flow statements.

Cash from Operations.   Pfizer reports cash flows using the *indirect method*. As a result, the company provides a reconciliation of the difference between income from continuing operations[18] and CFO. The reconciling adjustments fall into three categories:

1. Noncash expenses
2. Nonoperating cash flows
3. Changes in operating assets and liabilities

Noncash expenses consist mostly of the amortization of past investment outflows. Although the matching principle requires amortization when computing net income, it is not a current-period cash flow. Pfizer adds back depreciation and amortization expense. The company also adjusts the income from continuing operations for the noncash effect of the Trovan inventory write-off.[19]

Nonoperating cash flows relate to investment and financing activities. For example, gains and losses from the sales of investments result from investment activities (discussed below) and must be excluded from the CFO. Similarly, extraordinary losses relate to the early extinguishment of debt, a financing activity, and must also be excluded from the computation of the cash flows from operations.

Finally, cash from operations reports changes in balance sheet accounts that are operating in nature. Such accounts include inventories, accounts receivable and payable (excluding amounts relating to investing and financing activities), and accruals for such operating items as interest,[20] income taxes, and employee benefits.

The reconciliation uses only the changes due to operating activities and, as discussed in the preceding section, excludes two other sources of changes in operating assets and liabilities: acquisitions/divestitures and the impact of changes in exchange rates.

Investing Cash Flow.   Pfizer's net investment in property, plant, and equipment (PPE) grew steadily each year from $831 million (purchases of $878 million less disposal proceeds of $47 million) in 1997 to $1,490 million in 1999. Pfizer received cash inflows from the sale of businesses, most significantly proceeds of $3,059 million from the sale of the medical technology segment (see Note 2 for details). The company also reports significant transactions in short-term financial instruments, purchases of long-term investments, and other investing activities.

The separate disclosure of cash outflows for acquisitions is an important feature of the cash flow statement. These amounts reflect the assets purchased less liabilities assumed in acquisitions accounted for using the purchase method (see Chapter 14 for a full discussion). *The cash outflows for the acquisitions of operating assets and liabilities of the acquired firm are excluded from CFO but included in CFI.*

Pfizer's transactions in short-term investments require some discussion. These investments are not considered "cash equivalents" because they do not meet the SFAS 95 definition (risk-free with maturities of less than three months). Nonetheless, from a practical point of view, they may be little different. If their risk is low and liquidity high, they should be treated analytically as cash equivalents as they represent additional short-term liquidity. Note that changes in the level of these investments may be reported net, one of the exceptions to the "gross" reporting requirements of SFAS 95. Under that standard, changes in balance sheet assets and liabilities that turn over fre-

---

[18]Net cash used in (provided by) discontinued operations is separately reported for each year from 1997 to 1999. This distinction is important for the analysis of current CFO and future forecasts of CFO because the discontinued operations will no longer contribute to cash flows.

[19]Other examples of noncash expenses include the cumulative effect of adopting new accounting standards when those standards have no cash flow consequences.

[20]In a subsequent section of this chapter, we argue that cash flows for interest represent financing rather than operating activities.

quently (another example is credit card receivables) may be reported net. Investments that are long-term, less liquid, and riskier (e.g., stocks or long-term bonds) must be treated differently (such investments are discussed in Chapter 13).

Financing Cash Flow. This category contains cash flows between the firm and suppliers of its debt and equity capital. Pfizer reports a net increase in short-term debt and repayment of long-term debt. CFF also includes dividends paid to shareholders, purchases of common stock, cash effects of stock option transactions, and cash received from the sale of common stock.

Effect of Exchange Rate Changes on Cash. Pfizer has foreign subsidiaries and cash balances denominated in foreign currencies. Changes in exchange rates create translation gains and losses that are not cash flows, but must be reported for the cash flow statement to balance. The $26 million reported by Pfizer captures, in a single number, the effect of exchange rate changes on the firm's foreign cash holdings.

Change in Cash and Cash Equivalents. The net reconciling number is the period's change in the balance of cash and equivalents, equal to the sum of the three major cash flow components (CFO, CFI, and CFF) and any exchange rate effects. This number is necessarily equal to the difference between cash at the beginning of the year and the amount at the end of the year. However, although this number is easy to measure, it has no analytic value. Firms can influence the net change by accelerating or delaying payments, or by making use of short-term financing facilities. ■

ANALYSIS OF CASH FLOW INFORMATION

The cash flow statement is intended to help predict the firm's ability to sustain (and increase) cash from current operations. In doing so, the statement provides more objective information about:

- A firm's ability to generate cash flows from operations
- Trends in cash flow components and cash consequences of investing and financing decisions
- Management decisions regarding such critical areas as financial policy (leverage), dividend policy, and investment for growth

Neither the statement of cash flows nor the income statement alone contains sufficient information for decision making. (See Box 2-2 for some empirical evidence in this respect.) Income statement and balance sheet data must be combined with cash flows for insights into the firm's ability to turn its assets into cash inflows, repay its liabilities, and generate positive returns to shareholders. All three financial statements are needed to value the firm appropriately.

Free Cash Flows and Valuation

An important but elusive concept often used in cash flow analysis is *free cash flow* (FCF). It is intended to measure the cash available to the firm for discretionary uses after making all required cash outlays. The concept is widely used by analysts and in the finance literature as the basis for many valuation models (see Chapter 19). The basic elements required to calculate FCF are available from the cash flow statement. In practice, however, the definition of FCF varies widely, depending on how one defines required and discretionary uses.

The basic definition used by many analysts is cash from operations less the amount of capital expenditures required to maintain the firm's *present* productive capacity.[21] Discretionary uses include growth-oriented capital expenditures and acquisitions, debt reduction, and payments to stockholders (dividends and stock repurchase). The larger the firm's FCF, the healthier it is, because it has more cash available for growth, debt payment, and dividends.

The argument for this definition is similar to Hicks's argument regarding the computation of net income, discussed in the previous chapter. If historical cost depreciation provided

[21]IAS 7 recommends this disclosure.

a good measure of the use of productive capacity, then FCF would equal CFO less depreciation expense. However (as discussed in Chapter 8), historical cost depreciation is arbitrary and measures the cost to replace operating capacity only by coincidence.

The obvious alternative to depreciation is the amount of capital expenditures made to maintain current capacity, excluding capital expenditures for growth. In practice, however, it is difficult to separate capital expenditures into expansion and replacement components. Lacking better information, all capital expenditures are subtracted from CFO to obtain FCF.

Subtracting all capital expenditures from CFO to arrive at FCF brings the definition of FCF closer to the one used in finance valuation models. In these models, required outflows are defined as operating cash flows less capital expenditures to replace current operating capacity *as well as capital expenditures necessary to finance the firm's growth opportunities.* Growth opportunities are defined as those in which the firm can make "above-normal" returns. It is difficult to determine *a priori* the amount of capital expenditures required to maintain growth and the discretionary portion of these expenditures; pragmatically, FCF is generally measured as CFO less capital expenditures.

Valuation models do, however, differ as to whether FCF is measured as *FCF available to the firm* [i.e., *all providers of capital (debt and equity)*] or as *FCF available to equity shareholders.* In the former case, required payments *do not* include outlays for interest and debt. In the latter case, they do. Thus, for FCF to the firm, one cannot use reported CFO (less capital expenditures) because CFO includes outlays for interest expense. We return to this issue later in this chapter. In Chapter 19, we elaborate on the differing definitions of FCF and their implications for valuation models.

Relationship of Income and Cash Flows

When periodic financial statements are prepared, estimates of the revenues earned and expenses incurred during the reporting interval are required. As discussed in the previous chapter, these estimates require management judgment and are subject to modification as more information about the operating cycle becomes available. Accrual accounting can therefore be affected by management's choice of accounting policies and estimates. Furthermore, accrual accounting *by itself* fails to provide adequate information about the liquidity of the firm and long-term solvency. Some of these problems can be alleviated by the use of the cash flow statement in conjunction with the income statement.

Cash flow is relatively (but not completely) free of the drawbacks of the accrual concept. It is less likely to be affected by variations in accounting principles and estimates, making it more useful than reported income in assessing liquidity and solvency.

Figure 3-1 compares the level and trend of net income, cash from operations, and two measures of free cash flow for three different companies: Kmart, Westvaco, and Intel. Reported income and CFO were taken directly from the firms' financial statements. Two measures of free cash flow are used:

FCF1 equals CFO minus (net) capital expenditures.

FCF2 equals CFO minus CFI and thus includes expenditures (receipts) for acquisitions (divestitures) and other investments.

Note that CFO exceeds income for all three companies because CFO is not reduced by the cost of productive capacity.[22] Depreciation is usually the largest component of the adjustment from income to CFO. When the cost of productive capacity is included, as in FCF1, the relationship is company specific and varies from year to year.

Intel is a "growth" company; its income[23] and CFO (except 1998) show steady growth from 1997 to 2000. FCF1 is below income in each period (except 1999), reflecting capital

---

[22]This point is elaborated on further in the section entitled "Cash Flow Classification Issues."

[23]Although Intel reported increasing income, one source of that increase was gains on investments in new technology companies, which proved to be ephemeral. Net income was also increased by substantial interest income. Since management has considerable discretion over the amount and timing of realized gains on investments, and the measurement of unrealized gains, the analyst needs to be wary of income growth stemming from nonoperating sources.

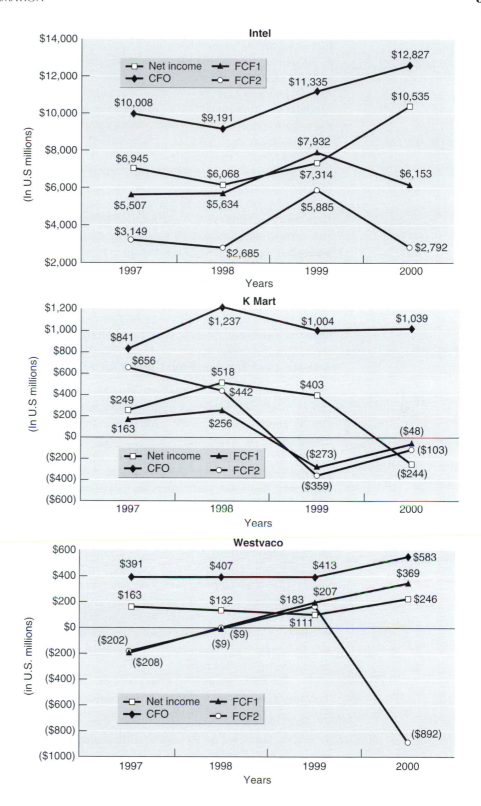

FIGURE 3–1 Comparison of patterns of income, CFO, and free cash flows.

expenditures for expansion as well as for replacement. FCF1 is positive in each year, a healthy sign given rapid growth. FCF2 is also positive each year. FCF patterns have to be monitored carefully for growth companies to ensure that they are not growing too fast, which can cause liquidity problems.

While the 1998 and 1999 increases in free cash flow (due to declines in Intel's CFI) are surprising for a growth company, the decrease may simply mean that Intel avoided overexpansion during those years. The 2000 declines in FCF1 and FCF2 are the result of increased capital expenditures and acquisitions.

Kmart reported increases in both income and cash flow from 1997 to 1998, lower CFO in 1999 and 2000, and a decline in income in 1999 and a loss in 2000. CFO remained positive despite a loss in 2000. Both FCF1 and FCF2 deteriorated over the four-year period as capital expenditures and CFI increased. Investments in operating assets, new businesses, and the acquisition of leases of other companies explain the difference between the income and cash flow measures.

Westvaco is an example of a cyclical company. Income declined from 1997–1999 with significant improvement in 2000. Debt and interest costs increased every year. After peaking in 1997, capital expenditures declined every year. Net operating assets declined as well until 2000. The result was high and increasing (relative to income) CFO every year from 1997 to 2000. FCF1 was positive in 1999 and 2000 but FCF2 was positive only in 1999. The 2000 decline in FCF2 reflects significant global acquisitions as the company expanded its packaging business.

The above discussion illustrates the use of cash flow statements together with information from the income statement, the balance sheet, and footnotes to assess the cash-generating ability of a firm. This assessment should consider the firm's liquidity, the viability of income as a predictor of future cash flows, and the effect of timing and recognition differences. We elaborate on these points in the next sections.

Income, Cash Flow, and the Going-Concern Assumption

As noted earlier, income statement amounts based on accrual accounting are generally presumed to be good predictors of future cash flows. That predictive ability is subject to a number of implicit assumptions, including the going-concern assumption. For example, the classification of inventories as assets rather than expenses implicitly assumes that they will be sold in the normal course of business. Similarly, the accrual of revenue from credit sales and the valuation of receivables assume that the firm will continue to operate normally; failing firms may find that customers are unwilling to pay.

When the going concern assumption is subject to doubt, revenue recognition and asset valuation can no longer be taken for granted. The value of inventory and receivables declines sharply when they must be quickly liquidated. Long-term assets (especially intangibles and other assets with little or no value in a nonoperating framework) also must be reexamined when the going-concern assumption is questioned. In this respect, *the statement of cash flows serves as a check on the assumptions inherent in the income statement.*

To find out why income can fail as a predictor of cash-generating ability (uncollected receivables or unsold inventories) requires a comparison of amounts recorded as sales and cost of goods sold on the income statement with the pattern of cash collections from customers and cash paid for inventories on the cash flow statement. A direct method cash flow statement is helpful in this regard.

Income, Cash Flow, and the Choice of Accounting Policies

Consider the income statements for the three hypothetical companies presented in Exhibit 3-5. They are based on the example illustrated in Exhibit 2-1. Their income patterns differ only because of the choice of accounting policy. The policies selected convey information about management expectations. In case A, income is positive each year as management expects to complete the project within budget. In case B, a more conservative management recognizes income only when the project is completed. The annual income statement reports no activities during the first two years. Finally, in case C, management assumes that the eventual collectibility of the revenues is uncertain and thus does not recognize profit until collections are sufficient to recover all costs.

The periodic net income differs because accounting methods and assumptions of managers differ, not because their economic activities differ. *The cash flow statement allows the analyst to distinguish between the actual events that have occurred and the accounting assumptions that have been used to report these events.* This is not to say that the assumptions

EXHIBIT 3-5
Derivation of Cash from Operations Under Alternative Accounting Methods

Indirect Method	Year			
	1	*2*	*3*	*Total*
Company A: Percentage of Completion				
Revenue	$1,000	$3,500	$1,500	$6,000
Expense	(800)	(2,800)	(1,200)	(4,800)
Net income	$ 200	$ 700	$ 300	$1,200
Add (deduct): Increase (decrease in advances)	300	(300)	—	—
Add (deduct): Decreases (increases) in construction in progress	—	(700)	700	—
Cash from operations	$ 500	$ (300)	$1,000	$1,200
Company B: Completed Contract				
Revenue	$ —	$ —	$6,000	$6,000
Expense	—	—	(4,800)	(4,800)
Net income	$ —	$ —	$1,200	$1,200
Add (deduct): Increase (decrease in advances)	500	(300)	(200)	—
Cash from operations	$ 500	$ (300)	$1,000	$1,200
Company C: Cost Recovery				
Revenue	$ 800	$2,800	$2,400	$6,000
Expense	(800)	(2,800)	(1,200)	(4,800)
Net income	$ —	$ —	$1,200	$1,200
Add (deduct): Increase (decrease in advances)	500	(300)	(200)	—
Cash from operations	$ 500	$ (300)	$1,000	$1,200
Direct Method: Identical for All Three Companies				
Cash collections	$ 1,300	$2,500	$2,200	$6,000
Cash disbursements	(800)	(2,800)	(1,200)	(4,800)
Cash from operations	$ 500	$ (300)	$1,000	$1,200

made by management are wrong. These assumptions may provide useful information. The user of financial statements needs to understand the interrelationship between these events and financial reporting choices.

The cash flow statement shows that the cash collected, cash disbursed, and the cash flow from operations is identical for all three companies because the economic activities of these companies are identical. The three companies differ only with respect to reported income, which is a function of different accounting assumptions and policies.

Income, Cash Flow, and Liquidity

Companies can grow too fast, resulting in liquidity problems. Although Intel, discussed above, does not suffer from liquidity problems, its cash flow pattern can be a prelude to such problems. Another fast-growing company, The Discovery Zone, an operator of children's indoor entertainment facilities, provides such an example. The company filed for bankruptcy reorganization under Chapter 11 in 1995. At that time, its CEO stated:

> A successful Chapter 11 reorganization will address the problems caused by the company's *rapid expansion* and put Discovery Zone on stronger financial footing.

Rapid growth is often accompanied by increases in capital expenditures and negative free cash flows. Moreover, growth companies may also report weak operating cash flows because they must finance growth in current operating assets. As firms usually pay for inventories before they are sold and collect sales proceeds subsequent to sale, there may be a long time lag between payments to suppliers and receipts from customers.

The cash flow statement provides information about the firm's liquidity and its ability to finance its growth from internally generated funds. It can highlight potential liquidity problems, such as an increasing need for operating capital or lagging cash collections.

However, reliance on the cash flow statement is insufficient for a complete assessment of the underlying strength of the company. Trends in sales and earnings must be evaluated from income statement data to determine whether there is a strong growth pattern that indicates a sustainable ability to generate cash flows in the future.

Analysis of Cash Flow Trends

The data contained in the statement of cash flows can be used to:

1. Review individual cash flow items for analytic significance.
2. Examine the trend of different cash flow components over time and their relationship to related income statement items.
3. Consider the interrelationship between cash flow components over time.

We examine each of these uses continuing with Pfizer as an example. A summary of Pfizer's cash flow statements for 1997–1999 is presented below:

Pfizer Statement of Cash Flows

	1997–1999 (in $millions)		
	1997	1998	1999
Cash from operations (CFO)	$1,580	$3,282	$3,076
Investing cash flow (CFI)	(963)	(335)	(2,768)
Financing cash flow (CFF)	(981)	(2,277)	(1,127)
Cash provided by (used in) discontinued operations	118	4	(20)
Effect of exchange rate changes	(27)	1	26
Change in cash and equivalents	$ (273)	$ 675	$ (813)

The CFI portion of Pfizer's cash flow statement shows a significant increase in investment[24] in property, plant, and equipment from $831 million in 1997 to $1,490 million in 1999. Pfizer's segment data (Note 19) tell us that more than 90% of the investment has been made in the pharmaceutical segment. The company derives most of its revenues and profits from that segment. Pfizer's merger with the Warner-Lambert Company indicates a continuing emphasis on pharmaceuticals. Revenues are nearly unchanged and profits have been erratic in the only other segment of operations, animal health.

The CFF component reports significant and increasing payments to stockholders; net repurchases of stock and dividend payments were $1,467, $2,888, and $3,586 million in 1997, 1998, and 1999 respectively. Pfizer's free cash flow (CFO—capital expenditures) was not sufficient to meet the demands of its capital structure choices in 1997 and 1999. The company borrowed (short-term debt) $2,083 million in 1999 and Note 4B tells us that weighted-average interest rate on those borrowings during that year was 4.3%. Note that the company reports significant investments in securities during these three years while it increased both Treasury stock and short-term debt. These actions raise the following questions:

- Why is the company borrowing and investing short-term?
- What do the share repurchases say about the company's investment opportunities?

For an example of the second type of analysis, we look at cash from operations. Because CFO is subject to random and cyclical influences, it should be analyzed over long periods

[24]The capital expenditures are calculated net of disposals. In 1997, for example, there were purchases of $878 million less disposal proceeds of $47 million.

(three to five years). In general, CFO should be positive and increase over time because it provides the resources to service debt, invest in growth, and reward shareholders.

Pfizer's CFO grew by $1,496 million or 95% from 1997–1999. Given the company's sales growth (47%) and increasing profitability (44%), higher CFO is a healthy sign. Significant growth often results in negative CFO for brief periods, as the required increase in working capital more than offsets growth in income. This is not the case for Pfizer, which reports improved CFO despite an increase in operating assets.[25]

In other cases, however, weak CFO may reflect operating problems such as unrealistic revenue recognition accounting policies or the inability to collect receivables. A comparison of revenue and expense trends with the pattern of cash collections from customers and cash payments should reveal the causes of lower CFO and suggest whether the trend is likely to reverse.

Direct method statements allow analysts to make such comparisons because they provide information better suited to trend analysis. Direct method statements reveal, for example, whether CFO is increasing because cash collections are increasing or payments to suppliers are decreasing. The discussion of Pfizer uses the 1999 data derived in Box 3-1, and 1997 and 1998 data derived using the same method.

First, we compute a "cash gross margin" percentage and compare it to one based on income:

Pfizer: Cash and Income-based Gross Margins

	1997 to 1999 (in $millions)		
	1997	1998	1999
Cash Flow Statement			
Cash collections	$10,262	$11,912	$13,155
Cash inputs	(2,189)	(1,905)	(1,855)
Cash gross margin	$8,073	$10,007	$11,300
Percent	78.7%	84.0%	85.9%
Income Statement			
Sales	$10,739	$12,677	$14,133
COGS	(1,776)	(2,094)	(2,528)
Gross margin	$ 8,963	$10,583	$11,605
Percent	83.5%	83.5%	82.1%
Other Ratios			
Cash collections/sales	95.6%	94.0%	93.1%
Cash inputs/COGS	123.3%	91.0%	73.4%

Pfizer's cash gross margin increased by $3,227 million (40%) over the 1997–1999 period, more than twice the $1,496 million improvement in CFO. Pfizer has reported increases in both cash expenses and research and development expenditures. Cash gross margin improved in both 1998 and 1999. The income statement–based gross margin held steady at 83.5% in 1997 and 1998, falling to 82.1% in 1999.[26] Future pricing pressures combined with required increases in expenditures may limit growth in Pfizer's CFO.

The cash collections/sales ratio has declined marginally as receivables have increased 74% while sales rose only 32% during this period. *The major improvement over time derives from cash inputs.* The cash for inputs/COGS ratio declined, as inputs declined despite rising COGS. Inventories have generally increased, with 1999 inventories declining partly because of the Trovan inventory write-off. The cash for inputs/COGS ratio would be 84% if we exclude the write-off from COGS.

---

[25]The ratio analysis of Pfizer in Chapter 4 provides further insight into this issue.
[26]Excluding the Trovan inventory write-off, this gross margin would have risen to 84.3%.

The third type of analysis of cash flow components looks at the relationship among those components over time. An example is provided by Pfizer's free cash flows defined here as CFO less capital expenditures.

Pfizer Free Cash Flows

	1997 to 1999 (in $millions)		
	1997	1998	1999
Cash from operations	$1,580	$3,282	$3,076
Capital expenditures	(831)	(1,119)	(1,490)
Free cash flow	$ 749	$2,163	$1,586
CFF	(981)	(2,277)	(1,127)

Pfizer's FCF increased significantly (by $837 million or nearly 112%) over the 1997–1999 period. This increase reflects the improvement in CFO despite higher capital expenditures. As noted in a preceding section, Pfizer did not generate sufficient free cash flow to fund its dividend and share repurchase programs. In 1999, the stockholder payments (share repurchases and dividend payments) were offset by a significant increase in short-term borrowing.

Trend analysis of cyclical companies requires more than the evaluation of data for individual years; aggregated data should be evaluated as well. In Box 3-2, we provide an analysis of A. M. Castle (a cyclical company) over the five-year period 1996 through 2000.

Cash Flow Classification Issues

Although the classification of cash flows into the three main categories is important, we must recognize that classification guidelines can be arbitrary. The resulting data may require selective adjustment before they are used to make investment decisions. The classification guidelines of SFAS 95 often create problems for users of the cash flow statement in the following areas:

- Cash flows involving property, plant, and equipment
- Differences due to some accounting methods
- Interest and dividends received
- Interest paid
- Noncash transactions

Some of these issues have been touched on earlier in the chapter. We discuss each in greater detail now.

Classification of Cash Flows for Property, Plant, and Equipment

Consider the components of cash flow from operations in the following simple example:

Net income	$30,000
Noncash expense: depreciation	5,000
	$35,000
Change in operating accounts: decrease in inventory	15,000
= Cash from operations	$50,000

The cash flow statement adds both depreciation expense (a noncash expense) and the decrease in inventory (change in an operating asset) to net income to arrive at cash from operations for the current period. Their differing classifications suggest that the reason for these addbacks is not identical. Both adjustments reflect prior-period cash outflows that are recognized in income in the current period. Depreciation allocates the cost of fixed assets to the period in which they are used. Similarly, the cost of goods sold allocates the cost of inventory to the period in which the inventory is actually sold.

BOX 3-2. A. M. CASTLE
Analysis of Cash Flows, 1996–2000 (in $thousands)

	1996	1997	1998	1999	2000	Total
Cash collections	$675,236	$742,275	$802,283	$710,024	$736,235	$3,666,053
Cash inputs	(479,343)	(555,006)	(617,401)	(431,424)	(537,847)	(2,621,021)
Cash expenses	(142,596)	(164,214)	(188,791)	(190,856)	(197,972)	(884,429)
Cash joint ventures and minority interest					(2,547)	(2,547)
Cash taxes	(15,268)	(13,729)	(10,134)	(3,302)	(5,402)	(47,835)
Cash interest	(2,997)	(4,209)	(7,987)	(11,353)	(10,992)	(37,538)
Miscellaneous	(117)	48	(1,498)	508	(81)	(1,140)
CFO	$ 34,915	$5,165	$(23,528)	$ 73,597	$(18,606)	$ 71,543
Capital expenditures	$ (22,544)	$(16,182)	$(30,236)	$(17,770)	$(13,231)	$ (99,963)
Proceeds from sales of PPE	2,521	2,470	9,640	7,399	8,264	30,294
Investments and acquisitions	(17,984)	(29,265)	(26,171)	(3,129)	(4,050)	(80,599)
CFI	**(38,007)**	**$(42,977)**	**$(46,767)**	**$(13,500)**	**$ (9,017)**	**$ (150,268)**
CFF	**4,230**	**38,782**	**70,474**	**(60,473)**	**27,124**	**80,137**
Change in cash	**$ 1,138**	**$ 970**	**$ 179**	**$ (376)**	**$ (499)**	**$ 1,412**
Beginning balance	667	1,805	2,775	2,954	2,578	10,779
Ending balance	$ 1,805	$ 2,775	$ 2,954	$ 2,578	$ 2,954	$ 13,066
Cash inputs/cash collections	70.99%	74.77%	76.96%	60.76%	73.05%	
CFO/cash collections	5.17%	0.70%	−2.93%	10.37%	−2.53%	
COGS/net sales*	71.58%	71.57%	70.52%	68.29%	70.23%	
Operating expense/net sales*	20.84%	21.81%	23.35%	26.73%	26.26%	

*These ratios are based on income statement data not shown.

Discussion

A direct method cash flow statement for A. M. Castle (Castle) for the five years from 1996 to 2000 is presented. These statements were derived from the reported indirect method statements using the methodology depicted in Box 3–1.

Castle is a metal wholesaler. Its revenues and earnings are heavily influenced by the business cycle. Because of the cyclicality, we start by reviewing cash flows over the entire five-year period.

Aggregate cash from operations was approximately $71.5 million, although CFO was negative for two of the five years. Net capital expenditures were nearly $70 million (capital expenditures of $100 million less proceeds from sales of $30 million). The company also reported investment and acquisition outflows of $80.5 million during the same period. Even if we assume that the capital expenditures reflect replacement of productive capac-

ity, free cash flow of $1.5 million would have been inadequate for expansion. Sales have risen from $672 million in 1996 to $745 million in 2000, peaking at $793 million in 1998.

Castle has paid its stockholders nearly $50 million in dividends over the five-year period and borrowed nearly $130 million to finance its investments and acquisitions. Total balance sheet debt has grown from $43 million in 1996 to $164.5 million in 2000 with the debt-to-equity ratio rising from about 36% in 1996 to 127% in 2000.

During this five-year period, cash for inputs (production costs) ranged from 61% in 1999 to as much as 77% in 1998 while the COGS as a percentage of net sales remained comparatively stable (68% to 71.6%). The difference is due to swings in inventory levels and prices.

Note that problem 3–6 extends this analysis into 2001.

The difference between the two adjustments is the classification of the initial cash outlays. In one sense, both initial outlays were for investments. In one case, the firm invested in fixed assets; in the other, it invested in inventories. The latter, however, is classified as an operating cash outflow,[27] deducted from CFO in the period of the initial outlay and added back to income when expensed to avoid double counting.

The original investment in fixed assets was reported as an investment cash outflow, and its allocation (depreciation expense) is added back to income and never classified as an operating flow, but always as an investment flow.[28]

[27]An exception occurs, as previously discussed, when inventory is acquired as part of an acquisition.

[28]As discussed later in this chapter, this applies to all expenditures that are capitalized and amortized rather than expensed.

The implications of this classification issue follow:

1. Cash from operations does not include a charge for use of the firm's operating capacity. Cash required to replace the productive capacity or physical plant used during operations is not included in CFO.

2. Firms reporting positive CFO may not thrive unless the CFO (generated and retained) is sufficient to replace the productive capacity used to generate the operating cash flow.

3. Identical firms with equal capital intensity will report different CFOs when one firm leases plant assets and the other owns its assets. The firm that leases reports lower CFO because lease rentals are operating expenditures (operating cash flows), whereas the other firm's expenditures are reported as investment cash flows.

4. Cash payments for operating assets and obligations to pay operating liabilities may also be excluded from CFO. For example, the cash paid for an acquired firm's inventories is included in investing cash flow. However, the proceeds from the sale of such "purchased" inventory in subsequent periods are included in CFO, distorting reported CFO because its purchase cost is never reported in CFO. Similarly, cash paid to settle acquired operating liabilities would be reported in CFO in subsequent periods.

5. An additional problem is that "investment" is not precisely defined. Two examples follow:

   • Hertz classifies its investment in rental cars as inventory, and purchases are included in CFO. In this case, CFO is understated relative to a firm that classifies its operating assets as property (see Problem 3-12).

   • Media companies consider programming purchases as long-term fixed assets. Although amortization impacts reported earnings, purchase costs are never reported in CFO. Yet financial markets seem to value such firms based on multiples of CFO per share rather than earnings per share!

Free cash flow, which deducts capital expenditures (however defined) from CFO, is generally free from the classification issue. However, the classification decision can have a significant impact on reported CFO.

Effect of Differences in Accounting Methods

We previously demonstrated that CFO is not affected by the timing differences generated by revenue and expense recognition methods. In that sense, CFO is less affected by differing accounting policies. However, *CFO is affected by reporting methods that alter the classification of cash flows among operating, investing, and financing categories.* If one accounting method results in the classification of a cash flow as investing and an alternative results in its classification as operating, then the reported CFOs will differ. Moreover, unlike revenue and expense differences in accounting policies that reverse over time, *the differences in CFO classification caused by reporting methods are permanent.*[29]

The capitalization of expenditures such as internal-use computer software leads to the classification of cash outflows as investing cash flows. However, they are reported as operating cash flows when expensed immediately.[30] Chapter 7 contains an extensive discussion of this issue. Lease classification (discussed in Chapter 11) also affects cash flow components for both lessors and lessees. We shall demonstrate other examples throughout the book.

■ Example

On July 1, 2000, Amazon.com, Inc. adopted the consensus of Emerging Issues Task Force Issue 00-2, Accounting for Web Site Development Costs. For the year ended December 31, 2000, the company capitalized costs of $3.0 million, reported as a

---

[29]The effects on the calculation of free cash flows must also be considered. If the classification difference is just between CFO and CFI, then Free Cash Flow = CFO − CFI will not be affected. However, if the classification difference results in a shift between CFO and CFF (as in the case of leasing), FCF is affected as well.

[30]This effect depends on the cash flow classification of the capitalized amount. Overhead capitalized in inventory, for example, will not change reported CFO because changes in inventory are also included in CFO. Overhead capitalized in fixed assets, however, will result in reclassification of the outflow from operating to investing cash flow.

component of fixed assets, and amortized over a period of two years. The company also capitalized the cost of internal-use software including the costs of operating the company's website. *None of these capitalized costs will ever be reported as components of CFO.*   ■

Interest and Dividends Received

Interest income and dividends received from investments in other firms are classified under SFAS 95 as operating cash flows. *As a result, the return on capital is separated from the return of capital.*[31] Combining these two returns to report cash flow to and from investees facilitates analysis. More important, the reclassification of after-tax dividend and interest from operating to investing cash flows has the advantage of reporting operating cash flows that reflect only the operating activities of the firm's core business.[32]

Interest Paid

Interest payments are classified as operating cash outflows under SFAS 95. Such payments are the result of capital structure and leverage decisions and they reflect financing rather than operating risk. The reported CFOs of two firms with different capital structures are not comparable because returns to creditors (interest) are included in CFO, whereas returns to stockholders (dividends) are reported as financing cash flows. For analytical purposes, therefore, interest payments (after tax to reflect the cash flow benefits of tax deductibility) should be reclassified as financing cash flows. The resulting operating cash flow is independent of the firm's capitalization, facilitating the comparison of firms with different capital structures.

The treatment of interest payments in cash flow statements has an important valuation impact. The telecommunications company Sprint has issued two tracking stocks. One is the wireless unit, Sprint PCS, and the other is Sprint FON, comprised of the local, long-distance, and data businesses. Sprint allocated $14 billion of debt to Sprint PCS and $4 billion to Sprint FON. Sprint PCS pays nearly 8% interest (2% more than the actual cost) on its debt. In its 10-Q filings, Sprint says that the difference between actual interest cost and the amount charged to Sprint PCS is reported as a deduction from Sprint FON's interest expense.

The August 6, 2001 issue of *Barron's* suggests a reason: Sprint PCS (as a start-up, without earnings) is valued on pretax cash flow before interest by the financial markets whereas Sprint FON is valued on after-tax earnings.

Noncash Transactions

Some investing and financing activities do not require direct outlays of cash. For example, a building may be acquired by assuming a mortgage. Under current disclosure rules, such transactions do not appear as cash from financing or investing activities but are given separate footnote disclosure as "significant noncash financing and investment activities."

For analytical purposes, however, this transaction is identical to the issuance of a bond to a third party, using the proceeds to acquire the building. *The "noncash" transaction reflects both a financing and investing activity and should be included in each category.* Knowledge of the firm's cash requirements for investing activities is as important as the method of financing. The latter provides information about future cash flow needs for interest and the repayment of principal.

The classification issues discussed in this section should provide the reader with an awareness that the cash flow statement is based on assumptions, definitions, and (somewhat arbitrary) accounting rules. Knowledge of these assumptions and rules allows the analyst to make informed adjustments that may be better suited for analytical purposes.

---

[31]Only the nominal (cash) return (dividend or interest received) is reported as an operating cash flow; the real (total) return (which includes capital gain or loss) is split between operating and investing cash flow.

[32]However, some investments and joint ventures are operating in nature. Such investments may assist in current and future operations, require significant financing commitments, and provide some control over the cash flows generated by the investee. See Chapter 13 for more discussion of these issues.

CASH FLOW STATEMENTS: AN INTERNATIONAL PERSPECTIVE

As discussed earlier in the chapter, the requirements of IAS 7 are quite similar to those of SFAS 95. The following table highlights the most significant differences:

Issue	US GAAP (SFAS 95)	IAS GAAP (IAS 7)
Bank overdrafts	Shown as liability; changes are shown in cash flow statement	May be shown as part of cash equivalents, in countries where it is customary to use overdrafts as part of cash management programs; changes *not* shown in cash flow statement
Interest and dividends received	Cash from operations (CFO)	May be shown as *either* CFO *or* cash from investing (CFI)
Interest paid	Cash from operations (CFO)	May be shown as *either* CFO *or* cash from financing (CFF)
Dividends paid	Cash from financing (CFF)	May be shown as *either* CFO *or* cash from financing (CFF)
Reconciliation from net income to CFO	Always required	Not required when direct method used

The cash flow classification differences are especially significant for companies using IAS GAAP that choose the alternative that differs from U.S. GAAP. For example, the cash flow statement in the 2000 annual report of Roche includes interest and dividends received in cash flows from investing activities and interest paid in financing activities.[33] Financial statement users must watch for such differences and adjust for them to make cash flow measures comparable.

 The International Organization of Securities Commissions (IOSCO) has endorsed IAS 7 in financial statements used in cross-border offerings; the U.S. SEC does not require reconciliation when foreign issuers prepare cash flow statements using IAS 7.

Although income statements and balance sheets are required as part of the periodic financial statements virtually around the world, there is no cash flow statement requirement in many countries. For example, Germany and The Netherlands have no requirement; in Japan, it is only required of listed companies as part of an unaudited schedule. Takeda includes a cash flow statement in its English language reports (as explained in Note 1) although Japanese GAAP do not require it. Holmen's cash flow statement uses a quite different format.[34] When no cash flow statement is provided, the analyst should use the transactional analysis method (Exhibit 3-4) to generate a direct method cash flow statement.

When cash flow statements are required, their format varies greatly across countries. Australian GAAP require the use of the direct method. In the United Kingdom, interest and dividends paid (returns to providers of capital) are grouped in a separate category, not included as part of either CFO or CFF. Although we believe this format is superior to the SFAS 95 format, reported cash flows are not comparable without adjustment.[35]

Cash flow analysis is an important tool for international comparisons because of significant accounting differences across countries. As noted, cash flows (CFO and FCF) are generally less susceptible than income to variations resulting from differences in accounting methods. However, differences in accounting methods do affect cash flow classifications. Thus, international comparisons may require the adjustment of reported cash flows.[36]

---

[33]Problem 3–8 requires adjustments for these differences.

[34]Problem 3–7 requires adjustment for this format difference.

[35]A few countries still present a statement of changes in funds (working capital). The focus on working capital ignores changes in operating accounts. Such statements do not add informational value to net income. Problem 3–13 requires adjustment of a statement of source and application of funds to a cash flow statement.

[36]See, for example, Kenneth S. Hackel and Joshua Livnat, "International Investments Based on Free Cash Flow: A Practical Approach," *Journal of Financial Statement Analysis* (Fall 1995), pp. 5–14, where such an approach is applied to a sample of firms. See also Chapter 10 of *Cash Flow and Security Analysis*, 2nd ed. (Irwin, 1995) by the same authors.

SUMMARY

This chapter completes our discussion of the basic framework for financial statement analysis. We have discussed financial statements that are the raw data of financial analysis and introduced users of financial statements to the interrelationship among them.

In the next chapter, we examine financial statement ratios, which are used as shorthand indicators of firm performance. Although some ratios use data from only one financial statement (debt/equity ratio), others use data from several statements (return on equity). Sound investment decisions, based on the comparative assessment of alternative investments, require the use and analysis of all three financial statements as well as footnote and supplementary disclosures.

In the following chapter, we review trends in empirical research to gain insight into the information content of financial data. Starting in Chapter 6, we examine areas of financial reporting more specifically, seeking to apply the general principles articulated in these first three chapters.

Chapter 3

Problems

1. [Cash flows; CFA © adapted] Cash flow data of Palomba Pizza Stores for the year ended December 31, 2000 follow:

Cash payment of dividends	$(35,000)
Acquisition of Naples' Pizza	(14,000)
Cash payments for interest	(10,000)
Cash payments for salaries	(45,000)
Sale of equipment	38,000
Retirement of common stock	(25,000)
Purchase of equipment	(30,000)
Cash payments to suppliers	(85,000)
Cash collections from customers	250,000
Cash at December 31, 1999	50,000

a. Prepare a statement of cash flows for Palomba for 2000. Classify cash flows as required by SFAS 95.

b. Discuss, from an analyst's viewpoint, the purpose of classifying cash flows into the three categories used in part a.

c. Discuss whether any of the cash flows should be classified differently.

d. Discuss the significance of the change in cash during 2000 as an indicator of Palomba's performance.

e. Calculate Palomba's *free cash flow*.

f. In your calculation of free cash flow, justify your treatment of cash payments for interest and cash paid for acquisitions.

2. [Revenue and expense recognition: cash flow analysis] The Stengel Company showed the following pattern of sales, bad debt expense, and net receivables for 1997 through 2001 (in $ millions):

	1997	1998	1999	2000	2001
Sales	$140	$150	$165	$175	$195
Bad debt expense	7	7	8	10	10
Net receivables*	40	50	60	75	95
Net receivables* at 1996 = 30					

*At year-end.

a. Calculate the cash collected from customers each year from 1997 to 2001.

b. For each year presented, calculate the following ratios:

(i) Bad debt expense/sales

(ii) Net receivables/sales

(iii) Cash collections/sales

c. Based on the patterns of sales, net receivables, and cash collections in part A and ratios calculated in part B, discuss the adequacy of the provision for bad debts.

3. [Cash flow: transactional analysis; CFA© adapted] The following financial statements are from the *2001 Annual Report* of the Niagara Company:

Income Statement for Year Ended December 31, 2001

Sales	$1,000
Cost of goods sold	(650)
Depreciation expense	(100)
Sales and general expense	(100)
Interest expense	(50)
Income tax expense	(40)
Net income	$ 60

Balance Sheets at December 31, 2000 and 2001

	2000	2001
Assets		
Cash	$ 50	$ 60
Accounts receivable	500	520
Inventory	750	770
Current assets	$1,300	$1,350
Fixed assets (net)	500	550
Total assets	$1,800	$1,900

Liabilities and Equity

Notes payable to banks	$ 100	$ 75
Accounts payable	590	615
Interest payable	10	20
Current liabilities	$ 700	$ 710
Long-term debt	300	350
Deferred income tax	300	310
Capital stock	400	400
Retained earnings	100	130
Total liabilities and equity	$1,800	$1,900

Use the direct method to prepare a statement of cash flows for the year ended December 31, 2001.

4. [Cash flow and income analysis] The financial statements of M Company and G Company for the years 1996–2000 are contained in Exhibit 3P-1.

a. Derive the 2000 income statement for G Company.

b. Derive the 2000 cash receipts and disbursements for M Company.

c. Convert the schedules of cash receipts and disbursements for the years 1996 through 2000 for both G Company and M Company to statements of cash flows segregating the cash from operations, financing, and investment. Use the direct method.

d. As a bank loan officer, state which company (M or G) you would prefer to lend to. Justify your answer.

EXHIBIT 3P-1. M COMPANY
Comparative Balance Sheets at December 31, 1996 to 2000 (in $thousands)

	1996	1997	1998	1999	2000
Cash	$ 34	$ 35	$ 50	$ 30	$ 46
Accounts receivable	365	420	477	545	599
Inventory	227	265	304	405	458
Current assets	$626	$720	$831	$ 980	$1,103
Property, plant, and equipment	120	137	174	204	237
Less: accumulated depreciation	(40)	(50)	(61)	(73)	(87)
Total assets	$706	$807	$944	$1,111	$1,253
Accounts payable	$104	$118	$125	$ 113	$ 104
Taxes payable	81	95	113	130	133
Short-term debt	181	246	238	391	453
Current liabilities	$366	$459	$476	$ 634	$ 690
Long-term debt	48	46	143	143	239
Total liabilities	$414	$505	$619	$ 777	$ 929
Common stock	81	72	80	73	76
Retained earnings	211	230	245	261	248
Total equity	$292	$302	$325	$ 334	$ 324
Total liabilities and equity	$706	$807	$944	$1,111	$1,253

M COMPANY
Income Statements for Years Ended December 31, 1996 to 2000 (in $thousands)

	1996	1997	1998	1999	2000
Sales	$1,220	$1,265	$1,384	$1,655	$1,861
Cost of goods sold	818	843	931	1,125	1,277
Operating expenses	298	320	363	434	504
Depreciation	9	10	11	12	14
Interest	15	19	16	21	51
Taxes	38	33	27	26	6
Total expenses	$1,178	$1,225	$1,348	$1,618	$1,852
Net income	$ 42	$ 40	$ 36	$ 37	$ 9

M COMPANY
Cash Receipts and Disbursements, 1996 to 2000 (in $thousands)

	1996	1997	1998	1999	2000
Cash Receipts from					
Customers	$1,165	$1,210	$1,327	$1,587	$?
Issue of stock	5	5	8	3	?

EXHIBIT 3P-1. (*continued*)
M COMPANY
Cash Receipts and Disbursements, 1996 to 2000 (in $thousands)

	1996	1997	1998	1999	2000
Short-term debt	64	65	—	153	?
Long-term debt	—	—	100	—	?
Total receipts	$1,234	$1,280	$1,435	$1,743	$?
Cash Disbursements for					
Cost of goods sold and operating expenses	1,130	1,187	1,326	1,672	?
Dividends	20	21	21	21	?
Taxes	23	19	9	9	?
Interest	15	19	16	21	?
Property, plant, and equipment purchase	14	17	37	30	?
Repurchase of stock	22	14	—	10	?
Repayment of long-term debt	2	2	3	—	?
Repayment of short-term debt	—	—	8	—	?
Total disbursements	$1,226	$1,279	$1,420	$1,763	$?
Change in cash	$ 8	$ 1	$ 15	$ (20)	$?

G COMPANY
Comparative Balance Sheets at December 31, 1996 to 2000 ($ in thousands)

	1996	1997	1998	1999	2000
Cash	$ 28	$ 32	$ 35	$ 54	$ 19
Accounts receivable	249	321	419	549	711
Inventory	303	391	510	672	873
Current assets	$580	$744	$ 964	$1,275	$1,603
Property, plant, and equipment	200	200	220	230	230
Less: Accumulated depreciation	(10)	(20)	(32)	(46)	(61)
Total assets	$770	$924	$1,152	$1,459	$1,772
Accounts payable	$102	$134	$ 177	$ 235	$ 309
Income tax payable	20	25	36	38	45
Short-term debt	138	190	281	284	344
Current liabilities	$260	$349	$ 494	$ 557	$ 258
Long-term debt	40	63	83	208	258
Total liabilities	$300	$412	$ 577	$ 765	$ 956
Common stock	440	440	445	490	520
Retained earnings	30	72	130	204	296
Total equity	$470	$512	$ 575	$ 694	$ 816
Total liabilities and equity	$770	$924	$1,152	$1,459	$1,772

G COMPANY
Income Statements for Years Ended December 31, 1996 to 2000 (in $thousands)

	1996	1997	1998	1999	2000
Sales	$1,339	$1,731	$2,261	$2,939	$?
Cost of goods sold	1,039	1,334	1,743	2,267	?
Operating expenses	243	312	398	524	?
Depreciation	10	10	12	14	?
Interest	11	13	23	29	?
Taxes	13	20	27	31	?
Total expenses	$1,316	$1,689	$2,203	$2,865	$?
Net income	$ 23	$ 42	$ 58	$ 74	$?

(*continued*)

EXHIBIT 3P-1. (*continued*)
G COMPANY
Cash Receipts and Disbursements, 1996 to 2000 (in $thousands)

	1996	1997	1998	1999	2000
Cash Receipts from					
Customers	$1,110	$1,659	$2,163	$2,809	$3,679
Issue of stock	10	—	5	45	30
Short-term debt	80	52	91	3	60
Long-term debt	40	23	20	125	50
Total receipts	$1,240	1,734	$2,279	$2,982	$3,819
Cash Disbursements for					
Cost of goods sold and operating expenses	1,214	1,702	2,217	2,895	3,778
Dividends	—	—	—	—	—
Taxes	13	15	16	29	35
Interest	11	13	23	29	41
Property, plant, and equipment purchase	—	—	20	10	—
Repurchase of common stock	—	—	—	—	—
Repayment of long-term debt	—	—	—	—	—
Repayment of short-term debt	—	—	—	—	—
Total disbursements	$1,238	$1,730	$2,276	$2,963	$3,854
Change in cash	$ 2	$ 4	$ 3	$ 19	$ (35)

EXHIBIT 3P-2. THE GREEN COMPANY
Balance Sheet and Income Statement

Balance Sheet			*Income Statement for the Year*	
As of December 31	2000	2001	**Ending December 31, 2001**	
Assets			Sales	$10,000
			Cost of goods sold	6,000
Cash	$ 1,000	$ 1,100	Depreciation	600
Accounts receivable	1,500	1,650	Selling, general, and	
Inventory	2,000	2,200	administrative expenses	1,000
Total current assets	$ 4,500	$ 4,950	Interest expense	600
Fixed assets—at cost*	11,000	12,150	Taxable income	$ 1,800
Accumulated depreciation	4,500	5,100	Taxes	720
Net fixed assets	6,500	7,050	Net income	$ 1,080
Total assets	$11,000	$12,000		
Liabilities and Equity				
Accrued liabilities	$ 800	$ 880		
Accounts payable	1,200	1,320		
Notes payable	5,500	6,050		
Total current liabilities	7,500	8,250		
Long-term debt	2,000	1,602		
Common stock	1,000	1,000		
Retained earnings	500	1,148		
Total liabilities and equity	$11,000	$12,000		

*No fixed assets were sold during 1996.

5. [Preparation of cash flow statement—direct and indirect methods; CFA© adapted] The balance sheet and income statement for the Green Company are presented in Exhibit 3P-2.

a. Based on the financial statements provided, prepare a statement of cash flows for 2001 using the

   (i) Indirect method

   (ii) Direct method

b. Calculate the company's free cash flow.

6. [Extension of Box 3-2; cash flow; conversion of indirect to direct method] Exhibit 3P-3 contains financial statement data for

A. M. Castle, a steel wholesaler. The statement of cash flows is prepared using the indirect method.

a. Using the data in Exhibit 3P-3, prepare a direct method statement of cash flow from operations for the six months ended June 30, 2001.

b. A. M. Castle reduced its common stock dividend from $.195 per quarter to $.12 per quarter after the first quarter of 2001 and to $.06 per quarter after the third quarter of 2001. Discuss how the cash flow statements in Box 3-2 and your answer to part a would have helped an analyst to forecast the dividend reductions.

EXHIBIT 3P-3. A. M. CASTLE
2001 Financial Data (in $thousands)

Condensed Balance Sheets

Assets	6/30/01	12/31/00
Cash	$ 2,603	$ 2,079
Accounts receivable, net	85,224	91,636
Inventories (principally on last-in, first-out basis)	158,451	163,206
Income tax receivable	2,889	4,116
Other current assets	1,843	1,426
Total current assets	$251,010	$262,463
Investment in joint ventures	9,591	9,714
Prepaid expenses and other assets	56,630	55,566
Fixed assets, net	90,966	91,108
Total assets	$408,197	$418,851

Liabilities and Stockholders' Equity		
Accounts payable	$ 72,678	$ 84,734
Accrued liabilities	16,299	17,854
Income taxes payable	2,383	1,130
Current portion of long-term debt	3,425	3,425
Total current liabilities	$ 94,785	$107,143
Long-term debt, less current portion	165,799	161,135
Deferred income taxes	18,574	18,096
Minority interest	1,187	971
Postretirement benefit obligations	2,130	2,265
Stockholders' equity	125,722	129,241
Total liabilities and stockholders' equity	$408,197	$418,851

Condensed Statements of Cash Flows

	Six Months Ended June 30	
Cash flows from operating activities:	2001	2000
Net income	$ 930	$ 6,602
Depreciation	4,732	4,924
Other	(521)	(6,886)
Cash provided from operating activities before working capital changes	$ 5,141	$ 4,640
(Increase) decrease in working capital	(743)	(15,720)
Net cash provided from (used by) operating activities	$ 4,398	$(11,080)
Cash flows from investing activities:		
Investments and acquisitions	—	(4,050)
Capital expenditures, net of sales proceeds	(4,089)	(5,889)
Net cash provided from (used by) investing activities	(4,089)	(9,939)

(continued)

EXHIBIT 3P-3. (*continued*)

Condensed Statements of Cash Flows

	Six Months Ended June 30	
Cash flows from financing activities:	2001	2000
Long-term borrowings, net	4,664	28,258
Dividends paid	(4,461)	(5,484)
Other	12	(316)
Net cash provided from (used by) financing activities	215	22,458
	$ 524	$ 1,439
Net increase (decrease) in cash:		
Cash—beginning of year	2,079	2,578
Cash—end of period	$ 2,603	$ 4,017
Supplemental cash disclosure—cash paid during the period:		
Interest	$ 5,303	$ 4,751
Income taxes	(2,127)	2,910

Comparative Statements of Income

	Six Months Ended June 30	
	2001	2000
Net sales	$342,215	$387,517
Cost of material sold	238,799	269,841
Gross profit on sales	$103,416	$117,676
Operating expenses	91,795	96,953
Depreciation and amortization expense	4,732	4,924
Interest expense, net	5,128	4,740
Income before taxes	$ 1,761	$ 11,059
Income tax expense	831	4,457
Net income	$ 930	$ 6,602

Source: A. M. Castle, *10-Q Report, June 30, 2001.*

7. [Differences between U.S. GAAP and Swedish GAAP—statement of cash flows] Holmen's consolidated cash flow statements are based on Swedish accounting standards.

a. Identify and discuss the major differences between the Swedish GAAP cash flow statement and the U.S. GAAP requirements (SFAS 95) for cash flow statements.

b. Convert Holmen's Swedish GAAP cash flow statement to a U.S. GAAP–based cash flow statement using Westvaco's statement of cash flows as a guide for the format.

c. Identify and discuss two significant advantages and two disadvantages of the Swedish GAAP approach to cash flow statements. Your answers should discuss the usefulness of the data provided for financial analysis.

8. [Differences between U.S. GAAP and International Accounting Standards—statement of cash flows] Roche provides cash flow statements based on International Accounting Standards.

a. Identify and discuss the major differences between the International Accounting Standards cash flow statement and the U.S. GAAP requirements (SFAS 95) for cash flow statements.

b. Convert Roche's International Accounting Standards–based cash flow statement to a U.S. GAAP–based cash flow statement using Pfizer's statement of cash flows as a guide.

c. Identify and discuss at least one significant advantage and one disadvantage of the International Accounting Standards approach to cash flow statements.

9. [Income statement and cash flow analysis, courtesy of Professor I. Krinsky] The income statement and statement of cash flows of the Radloc Company are presented in Exhibit 3P-4. This is a merchandising company that has been expanding rapidly. Assume that you are the credit manager of a bank and the company approached you for a loan in the first quarter of 1995. State whether you would grant the company a loan and justify your answer.

As part of your analysis, you should:

(i) Compute (to the extent possible) a direct cash flow statement.

(ii) Compare the trends in
  • Cash collections from customers
  • Cash payments to suppliers
  • Cash payments for expenses
    with their counterparts in the income statement.

(iii) Examine trends in income, CFO, and free cash flow.

10. [Cash flows; free cash flows; effect of acquisitions; CFA© adapted] In October 1988, Philip Morris announced an unsolicited cash tender offer for all the 124 million outstanding

EXHIBIT 3P-4. THE RADLOC COMPANY
(in $millions)

Income Statement	Years Ended December 31		
	1992	1993	1994
Net sales	$2,127,684	$2,414,124	**$2,748,634**
Cost of merchandise sold	1,527,731	1,742,276	**1,975,332**
Gross margin	$ 599,953	$ 671,848	**$ 773,302**
Selling, general, and administrative	458,804	520,685	**605,538**
Depreciation and amortization	34,954	40,501	**48,478**
Preopening expense	3,492	8,228	**8,624**
Facilities relocation expense			**3,786**
Interest expense	39,934	34,904	**34,948**
Earnings before taxes and extraordinary items	$ 62,769	$ 67,530	**$ 71,928**
Income tax provision	25,507	26,152	**27,569**
Earnings before extraordinary loss	$ 37,262	$ 41,378	**$ 44,359**
Extraordinary loss		(5,378)	
Cumulative effect of accounting changes	(2,812)	(2,768)	
Net income	$ 34,450	$ 33,232	**$ 44,359**

Statement of Cash Flows	1992	1993	1994
Net earnings	$ 34,450	$33,232	**$ 44,359**
Expenses not requiring the outlay of cash:			
Amortization of debt issuance costs	2,051	1,537	**1,000**
Depreciation and other amortization	34,954	40,501	**48,478**
Cumulative effect of accounting changes	2,812	4,500	
Deferred income taxes	4,090	501	**1,594**
Extraordinary loss—early retirement of debt		5,430	
Loss on disposal of property and equipment		650	**1,459**
Changes in working capital and other:			
Accounts receivable	(8,121)	6,837	**(4,475)**
Merchandise inventories	(28,401)	(60,893)	**(82,863)**
Prepaid expenses and other	1,317	(2,137)	**(3,358)**
Accounts payable	53,718	61,020	**(6,620)**
Accrued wages and benefits	4,038	(652)	**7,321**
Other accrued liabilities	(10,017)	5,293	**5,990**
Federal and state income tax payable	9,003	2,662	**17,567**
Other assets and long-term liabilities	246	254	**342**
Cash flows: operating activities	$ 100,140	$ 98,735	**$ 30,794**
Capital expenditures	(48,878)	(110,534)	**(90,009)**
Acquisition of leasehold interests	(36,602)	(21,894)	**(8,025)**
Cash flows: investing activities	$ (85,480)	$ (132,428)	**$ (98,034)**
Retirement of senior notes		(200,000)	
Borrowings under term loan		180,000	
Borrowings under revolving credit			**70,243**
Proceeds from long-term debt	(3,276)	(3,831)	**(19,432)**
Proceeds from sale of common stock		53,334	**34**
Proceeds from exercise of warrants and options	1,995	1,126	**1,016**
Cash flows: financing activities	$ (1,281)	$ 30,629	**$ 51,861**
(Decrease) increase in cash	13,379	(3,064)	**(15,379)**

shares of Kraft at $90 per share. Kraft subsequently accepted a $106 per-share all-cash offer from Philip Morris. Following the completion of the acquisition of Kraft, Philip Morris released its 1988 year-end financial statements.

a. Prepare a statement of cash flows for Philip Morris Companies, Inc. based on the format utilized in SFAS 95 using

only the actual 1988 financial data contained in Exhibit 3P-5.

(*Important Note*: The acquisition of Kraft requires that you remove the assets acquired and liabilities incurred as a result of that acquisition from the balance sheet changes used to prepare the statement of cash flows. Philip Morris paid

$11.383 billion for Kraft, net of cash required. A breakdown of the purchase is contained in Exhibit 3P-5.)

b. Based on your answer to part a, compute Philip Morris's free cash flow for 1988 and discuss how free cash flow may impact the company's future earnings and financial condition.

c. In the Philip Morris cash flow statement prepared in part a, the cost of Kraft's inventories and receivables acquired by Philip Morris was classified as cash from investment rather than cash from operations. Discuss how this classification may distort the trend in CFO, and state under what conditions this distortion will occur.

EXHIBIT 3P-5. PHILIP MORRIS COMPANIES, INC.
Balance Sheets at December 31, 1987–1988 (in $millions)

	1987	1988
Assets		
Cash and cash equivalents	$ 90	$ 168
Accounts receivable	2,065	2,222
Inventories	4,154	5,384
Current assets	$ 6,309	$ 7,774
Property, plant, and equipment (net)	6,582	8,648
Goodwill (net)	4,052	15,071
Investments	3,665	3,260
Total assets	$20,608	$34,753
Liabilities and Stockholders' Equity		
Short-term debt	$ 1,440	$ 1,259
Accounts payable	791	1,777
Accrued liabilities	2,277	3,848
Income taxes payable	727	1,089
Dividends payable	213	260
Current liabilities	$ 5,448	$ 8,233
Long-term debt	6,293	17,122
Deferred income taxes	2,044	1,719
Stockholders' equity	6,823	7,679
Total liabilities and stockholders' equity	$20,608	$34,753

PHILIP MORRIS COMPANIES, INC.
Income Statement for Year Ended December 31, 1988 (in $millions)

Sales	$31,742
Cost of goods sold	(12,156)
Selling and administrative expenses	(14,410)
Depreciation expense	(654)
Goodwill amortization	(125)
Interest expense	(670)
Pretax income	$ 3,727
Income tax expense	(1,390)
Net income	$ 2,337
Dividends declared $941 million	

PHILIP MORRIS PURCHASE OF KRAFT
Allocation of Purchase Price (in $millions)

Accounts receivable	$ 758
Inventories	1,232
Property, plant, and equipment	1,740
Goodwill	10,361
Short-term debt	(700)
Accounts payable	(578)
Accrued liabilities	(530)
Long-term debt	(900)
Purchase price (net of cash acquired)	$11,383

11. [Income statement and cash flow analysis—Westvaco]

a. Prepare a direct method cash flow statement for 1999. (Note H reports the changes in operating assets and liabilities, reconciles capital expenditures on a cash basis, and discloses other cash payments.)

b. Discuss the insights provided by the direct method cash flow statement.

c. Westvaco made acquisitions in fiscal 2000 for more than $1.3 billion. Discuss how Westvaco's cash flows for 1997—1999 positioned the company to make major acquisitions. (*Note*: Figure 3-1 and the related text provide cash flow measures and related discussion.)

12. [Cash flow from operations; free cash flows] Hertz is the world's largest provider of rental cars and trucks. Extracts from its statement of cash flows follow:

Cash Flow Data of Hertz Corp.

Amounts in $millions	*Years Ended December 31*		
	1989	1990	1991
Net income	$ 108	$ 89	$ 48
Depreciation of revenue equipment	475	530	497
Depreciation of property	57	69	75
Self-insurance and other accruals	100	85	122
Purchases of revenue equipment	(3,003)	(4,024)	(4,016)
Sales of revenue equipment	2,354	3,434	3,784
Changes in operating assets and liabilities (net)	(141)	13	(118)
Payment of self-insurance claims	(67)	(104)	(106)
Cash flow from operations	$ (117)	$ 92	$ 286
Cash flow for investing	(133)	(79)	(72)
Net change in debt	241	(4)	(84)
Dividends paid	(90)	(64)	(62)
Cash flow from financing	$ 151	$ (68)	$ (146)
Effect of foreign exchange rates	1	11	0
Net increase (decrease) in cash	$ (98)	$ (44)	$ 68

Source: Hertz Corp., *1991 Annual Report*

Note that Hertz includes the purchases and sales of revenue equipment (cars and trucks to be rented) in cash flow from operations.

a. Recompute cash flow from operations, classifying the purchases and sales of revenue equipment as investing cash flows.

b. Compare the trend of cash flow from operations as reported with the trend after reclassification.

c. Recompute cash flow for investing, classifying the purchases and sales of revenue equipment as investing cash flows.

d. Compare the trend of cash flow for investing as reported with the trend after reclassification.

e. State and justify which classification provides the better measure of cash flow from operations for Hertz. Define and compute a useful measure of free cash flow for Hertz. State your assumptions.

f. Assume that Hertz leases (rather than purchases) some of its rental cars and trucks. Discuss the impact of leasing (rather than buying) on cash flow from operations as reported by Hertz.

g. Discuss the impact of leasing on cash flow from operations, assuming that the purchases of revenue equipment are reported as cash flows from investing. (*Hint for parts f and g*: Think of leasing and buying as expensing and capitalizing, respectively.)

13. [Conversion of source and application of funds statement to statement of cash flows]. Repsol is a Spanish multinational oil producer that prepares its financial statements in accordance with Spanish GAAP. Following is a condensed statement of source and applications of funds taken from Repsol's 1999 annual report. (*Note*: As stated in chapter note 35, some non-U.S. companies use funds from operations rather than cash from operations as the cash flow statement focus.)

Repsol Statement of Source and Application of Funds

	(€millions)	
	Years Ended 12/31	
	1998	1999
Sources of Funds		
Funds from operations*	€2,150	€ 3,182
Shares issued		5,665
Subsidies and other revenues	92	74
Minority interests	11	25
Loans received	544	12,942
Other long-term debt	11	23
Disposal of property	111	767
Disposal of investments	116	152
Change in working capital	830	4,949
Total sources	€3,865	€27,779

(continued)

Repsol Statement of Source and Application of Funds
(*continued*)

	(€millions)	
	Years Ended 12/31	
	1998	1999
Applications of Funds		
Investments in property	1,723	2,630
Acquisitions	197	14,277
Other investments	297	804
Net assets from consolidation	16	520
Net effect of currency changes	(84)	714
Dividends paid	517	567
Debt repaid or reclassified	1,199	8,267
Total applications	€3,865	€27,779

*Net Income + noncash income and expense.

a. Using the data provided, prepare a statement of cash flows for 1998 and 1999 in accordance with SFAS 95. State any assumptions made.

b. Discuss the usefulness of the statement of cash flow relative to the statement of source and application of funds.

c. Discuss the additional data that would be needed to insure the accuracy of the statement of cash flow.

d. Compare the 1998–1999 change in cash from operations (from part b) to the change in total sources of funds from the table as a measure of liquidity.

e. Repsol reports the net effect of currency changes as an application of funds.

   (i) State how those changes are reported in the statement of cash flows.

   (ii) Discuss which treatment provides better information for investment decision making.

14. [Conversion of indirect to direct method cash flow statements; analysis of income and cash flow data; implications for valuation] Exhibit 3P-6 contains financial data for the Hampshire Company for 2000 and 2001. The following additional information is provided:

   • Hampshire is not subject to income tax.

   • Year 2000 includes a restructuring charge of $125, of which $100 is a noncash inventory writedown included in COGS and $25 is severance payments included in SG&A. The severance payments were made in 2001.

a. Convert the 2001 indirect method statement of operating cash flows to the direct method.

b. Prepare income statements for 2000 and 2001 excluding the effects of nonrecurring items

c. Compare the 2000–2001 change in each of the following income statement components with that of its cash analogue:

   (i) Sales

   (ii) COGS

   (iii) SG&A expense

(*Note*: Both the income statement and cash flow components should exclude nonrecurring items.)

EXHIBIT 3P-6. HAMPSHIRE COMPANY

Years Ended December 31			
2000		**2001**	
Income Statement		**Income Statement**	
Sales	$7,100	Sales	$8,000
COGS	(4,300)	COGS	(5,000)
SG&A	(1,700)	SG&A	(2,000)
Depreciation	(250)	Depreciation	(250)
Interest expense	(150)	Interest expense	(150)
		Gain on sale of division	400
Net income	**$ 700**	**Net income**	**$1,000**
Statement of Cash Flows		**Statement of Cash Flows**	
		Net income	**$1,000**
Collections from customers	$7,000	Depreciation	250
Payments to suppliers	(4,100)	Gain on sale of division	(400)
Payments for SG&A	(1,750)		$850
Payments for interest	(150)	*Changes in Working Capital*:	
Cash from operations (CFO)	**$1,000**	Accounts receivable	(150)
		Inventory	(165)
		Prepaid expenses	(25)
		Severance payments	(25)
		Accounts payable	215
		Cash from operations (CFO)	**$ 700**

EXHIBIT 3P-7. RAYNA COMPANY

Years Ended December 31

	2000		2001	

Income Statement

	2000		2001	
Sales	$7,103	Sales	$7,047
COGS	(4,295)	COGS	(4,122)
SG&A	(1,712)	SG&A	(1,724)
Depreciation	(235)	Depreciation	(260)
Interest expense	(146)	Interest expense	(149)
		Gain on sale of division	127
Net income	**$ 715**	**Net income**	**$ 919**

Statement of Cash Flows

	2000		2001
Net Income	715		
Depreciation	235	Collections from customers	7,182
Restructuring charge	125		
	$1,075	Payments to suppliers	(4,097)
Changes in Working Capital:		Payments to SG&A	(1,634)
Accounts receivable	(138)		
Inventory	(114)	Severance payments	(22)
Prepaid expenses	(47)	Interest paid	(149)
Accounts payable	15		
Cash from operations (CFO)	**$ 791**	**Cash from operations (CFO)**	**$1,280**

d. Show the effects of net income and changes in working capital on the decline in cash from operations from 2000 to 2001.

e. State and justify whether the effects of the nonrecurring charges should be used for valuation purposes.

15. [Conversion of indirect to direct method cash flow statements; analysis of income and cash flow data; and implications for valuation] Exhibit 3P-7 contains financial data for the Rayna Company for 2000 and 2001. The following additional information is provided:

- Rayna is not subject to income tax.
- Year 2000 includes a restructuring charge of $125, of which $103 is a noncash fixed asset writedown included in COGS and $22 is severance payments included in SG&A. The severance payments were made in 2001.

a. Convert the 2000 indirect method statement of operating cash flows to the direct method.

b. Prepare income statements for 2000 and 2001 excluding the effects of nonrecurring items.

c. Compare the 2000–2001 change in each of the following income statement components (from part b) with that of its cash analogue:

   (i) Sales

   (ii) COGS

   (iii) SG&A expense

(*Note*: Both the income statement and cash flow components should exclude nonrecurring items.)

d. Show the effects of net income and changes in working capital on the increase in cash from operations from 2000 to 2001.

e. State and justify whether the effects of the nonrecurring charges should be used for valuation purposes.

16. [Analysis of changes in cash flows] The income statement and cash flow data below are for years 1 and 2 of the same company. For year 1, the cash flow statement is provided using the direct method; for year 2, the indirect method is used.

	Year 1			Year 2	
Sales	$10,000		Sales		$12,000
COGS	6,000		COGS		7,100
SG&A expense	3,000		SG&A expense		3,700
Interest expense	300		Interest expense		300
Net income	$ 700		Net income		$ 900
Cash collected			Depreciation expense		1,000
from customers	9,800		Effect of changes in		
Cash paid:			Accounts receivable		(240)
Suppliers	(5,800)		Inventory		(200)
SG&A	(2,000)		Accounts payable		(240)
Interest	(275)		Accrued liabilities		(25)
Cash from					
operations	$ 1,725		Cash from operations		$ 1,195

a. Convert the company's indirect cash flow statement provided for year 2 to the direct method. (*Note*: Assume depreciation is included in SG&A expense.)

b. Compare the cash receipts and disbursements with the related income statement item.

c. Using your answers to parts a and b, explain why cash from operations declined from year 1 to year 2.

4

FOUNDATIONS OF RATIO AND FINANCIAL ANALYSIS

CHAPTER OUTLINE

INTRODUCTION
Purpose and Use of Ratio Analysis
Ratio Analysis: Cautionary Notes
Economic Assumptions
Benchmarks
Timing and Window Dressing
Negative Numbers
Accounting Methods

COMMON-SIZE STATEMENTS

DISCUSSION OF RATIOS BY CATEGORY
Activity Analysis
Short-Term (Operating) Activity Ratios
Long-Term (Investment) Activity Ratios
Liquidity Analysis
Length of Cash Cycle
Working Capital Ratios and Defensive Intervals
Long-Term Debt and Solvency Analysis
Debt Covenants
Capitalization Table and Debt Ratios
Interest Coverage Ratios
Capital Expenditure and CFO-to-Debt Ratios
Profitability Analysis
Return on Sales
Return on Investment
Profitability and Cash Flows
Operating and Financial Leverage
Operating Leverage
Financial Leverage

RATIOS: AN INTEGRATED ANALYSIS
Analysis of Firm Performance
Disaggregation of ROA

Disaggregation of ROE and Its Relationship to ROA
Trends in ROE and ROA
Economic Characteristics and Strategies
Competing Strategies
Product Life Cycle
Interindustry Economic Factors
Classification and Selection of Ratios

EARNINGS PER SHARE AND OTHER RATIOS USED IN VALUATION
Earnings per Share
Simple Capital Structure
Complex Capital Structure
Adjustments for Options and Warrants
Limitations of EPS Calculations
Cash Flow per Share
EBITDA per Share
Book Value per Share
Price-to-Earnings and Price-to-Book-Value Ratios
Dividend Payout Ratio

PATTERNS OF RATIO DISCLOSURE AND USE
Perceived Importance and Classification
Disclosure of Ratios and Motivation

SUMMARY

APPENDIX 4-A
APPENDIX 4-B
CASE 4-1

CHAPTER OBJECTIVES

This chapter introduces ratios, the basic tools of financial analysis. The objectives of Chapter 4 are to:

1. Examine the purpose and use of ratios and provide some cautionary notes.
2. Explain the use of common-size statements.
3. Discuss the construction and use of:

- Short-term and long-term activity (turnover) ratios that measure the efficiency with which the firm uses its resources.

- Liquidity ratios, including working capital ratios, the cash cycle, and the defensive interval, that assess the firm's ability to meet its near-term obligations.

- Solvency ratios that examine capital structure and the firm's ability to meet long-term obligations and capital needs.
- Profitability ratios that measure income relative to revenues and invested capital.

4. Define and compute measures of operating and financial leverage.

5. Show how the integrated analysis of ratios can be used to evaluate corporate performance.

6. Relate ratios to corporate strategy and the product life cycle.

7. Examine the computation and usefulness of earnings per share and other ratios used for valuation purposes.

INTRODUCTION

Financial ratios are used to compare the risk and return of different firms in order to help equity investors and creditors make intelligent investment and credit decisions. Such decisions require both an evaluation of changes in performance over time for a particular investment and a comparison among all firms within a single industry at a specific point in time.

The informational needs and appropriate analytical techniques used for these investment and credit decisions depend on the decision maker's time horizon. Short-term bank and trade creditors are primarily interested in the immediate liquidity of the firm. Longer-term creditors (e.g., bondholders) are interested in long-term solvency. Creditors seek to minimize risk and ensure that resources are available for the payment of interest and principal obligations.

Equity investors are primarily interested in the long-term earning power of the firm. As the equity investor bears the residual risk (which can be defined as the return from operations after all claims from suppliers and creditors have been satisfied), it requires a return commensurate to that risk. The residual risk is highly volatile and difficult to quantify, as is the equity investor's time horizon. Thus, analysis by the equity investor needs to be the most comprehensive, and it subsumes the analysis carried out by other users.

Purpose and Use of Ratio Analysis

A primary advantage of ratios is that they can be used to compare the risk and return relationships of firms of different sizes. *Ratios can also provide a profile of a firm, its economic characteristics and competitive strategies, and its unique operating, financial, and investment characteristics.*

This process of standardization may, however, be deceptive as it ignores differences among industries, the effect of varying capital structures, and differences in accounting and reporting methods (especially when comparisons are international in scope). Given these differences, changes (trends) in a ratio and variability over time may be more informative than the level of the ratio at any point in time.

Four broad ratio categories measure the different aspects of risk and return relationships:

1. *Activity analysis:* evaluates revenue and output generated by the firm's assets.
2. *Liquidity analysis:* measures the adequacy of a firm's cash resources to meet its near-term cash obligations.
3. *Long-term debt and solvency analysis:* examines the firm's capital structure, including the mix of its financing sources and the ability of the firm to satisfy its longer-term debt and investment obligations.
4. *Profitability analysis:* measures the income of the firm relative to its revenues and invested capital.

These categories are interrelated rather than independent. For example, profitability affects liquidity and solvency, and the efficiency with which assets are used (as measured by activity analysis) impacts profitability. Thus, financial analysis relies on an integrated use of many ratios, rather than a selected few.

Ratio Analysis: Cautionary Notes

Ratio analysis is essential to comprehensive financial analysis. However, ratios are based on implicit assumptions that do not always apply. Ratio computations and comparisons are further confounded by the lack or inappropriate use of benchmarks, the timing of transactions, negative numbers, and differences in reporting methods. This section presents some important caveats that must be considered when interpreting ratios.[1]

Economic Assumptions

Ratio analysis is designed to facilitate comparisons by eliminating size differences across firms and over time. Implicit in this process is the *proportionality assumption* that the economic relationship between numerator and denominator does not depend on size. This assumption ignores the existence of fixed costs. When there are fixed costs, changes in total costs (and thus profits) are not proportional to changes in sales.

Moreover, the implicit assumption of a linear relationship between numerator and denominator may be incorrect even in the absence of a fixed component. For example, the inventory turnover ratio, COGS/inventory, implies a constant relationship between the volume of sales and inventory levels. Management science theory, however, indicates that the optimum relationship is nonlinear and inventory levels may be proportional to the square root of demand.[2] Thus, a doubling in demand should increase inventory by only 40% (approximately) with a consequent 40% increase in the turnover ratio. *The inventory turnover ratio is clearly not size independent.*

Benchmarks

Ratio analysis often lacks appropriate benchmarks to indicate optimal levels. The evaluation of a ratio often depends on the point of view of the analyst. For example, for a short-term lender, a high liquidity ratio may be a positive indicator. However, from the perspective of an equity investor, it may indicate poor cash or working capital management.

Industry Norms as Benchmarks. One relevant benchmark is the industry norm[3] as empirical evidence[4] indicates that (1) industry classification is the primary factor in explaining ratio dispersion and (2) ratios of individual firms tend to converge toward the industrywide average.

Two differing explanations are offered:[5]

1. Industrywide economic characteristics operate on the firm to correct deviations from the industry norm.
2. Managers view the industry norms as targets and aim their ratios accordingly. This is done by the choice of accounting method, allocation of resources, or both.

Using an industry average as the benchmark may be useful for comparisons within an industry, but not for comparisons between companies in different industries. Even for intraindustry analysis, the benchmark may have limited usefulness if the whole industry or major firms in that industry are performing poorly.

---

[1] For explanatory purposes, this discussion uses specific ratios as examples; these ratios are defined later in the chapter.

[2] See Chapter 6 for a more detailed discussion of this issue.

[3] Industry norms may be calculated directly through the use of computerized databases such as Standard & Poor's Compustat database. Alternatively, industry profiles are available from sources such as Robert Morris Associates (RMA) and Dun & Bradstreet's (D&B) *Industrial Handbook*. These sources provide common-size balance sheet, income statements, and selected ratios on an industry basis.

[4] The industry factor was first documented by Horrigan (1965), and the tendency for ratios to converge to industry norms was documented by Lev (1969), Frecka and Lee (1983), Peles and Schneller (1989), and more recently Davis and Peles (1993).

[5] Davis and Peles (1993), extending earlier work by Peles and Schneller (1989), found that on average the management effect is faster than the industry one, although both contribute significantly to the total adjustment.

Timing and Window Dressing

Data used to compute ratios are available only at specific points in time when financial statements are issued. For annual reports, the fiscal year-end may correspond to the low point of a firm's operating cycle, when reported levels of assets and liabilities may not reflect the levels typical of normal operations. As a result, especially in the case of seasonal businesses, ratios may not reflect normal operating relationships. For example, inventories and accounts payable may be understated. Reference to interim statements is one way of alleviating this problem. However, most foreign countries either do not require interim statements or require them less frequently.[6] Moreover, foreign filings are generally less timely than U.S. reports.

The timing issue leads to another problem. Transactions at year-end can lead to manipulation of the ratios to show the firm in a more favorable light, often called *window dressing*. For example, a firm with a current ratio (current assets/current liabilities) of 1.5 ($300/$200) can increase it to 2.0 ($200/$100) by simply using cash of $100 to reduce accounts payable immediately prior to the period's end.

Generally, any ratio where a transaction affects the numerator and denominator equally can be manipulated as follows. If the ratio is greater than 1, it can be increased by a transaction that subtracts the same amount from both the numerator and denominator. If it is less than 1, it can be increased by a transaction that adds the same amount to both the numerator and denominator.[7]

Negative Numbers

Two examples illustrate the care that must be taken in ratio analysis when negative numbers occur.

■ **Example 1: Return on Equity = Income / Equity**

	Income	Equity	ROE
Company A	$10,000	$100,000	10%
Company B	(10,000)	(100,000)	10%

Ratio analysis without reference to the underlying data can lead to wrong conclusions as it appears that both companies earn identical returns on their (equity) investment. Because much financial and ratio analysis today is computer generated, the existence of negative numbers will be overlooked unless the program is well written. ■

■ **Example 2: Dividend Payout Ratio = Dividend / Income**

	Dividend	Income	Payout Ratio
Company A	$10,000	$50,000	20%
Company B	10,000	30,000	33%
Company C	10,000	(50,000)	(20%)

Ranking these firms by payout ratio (highest to lowest) would list them as B, A, and C. However, in reality, Company C has the highest payout ratio. The payment of dividends despite negative income indicates a high payout ratio; that ratio is intended to measure the extent to which income is paid to shareholders rather than retained in the business. For the same income, a higher dividend increases the proportion paid out (higher payout ratio). As income approaches zero, the payout ratio approaches infinity. ■

---

[6]Foreign firms using Form 20-F filings to sell securities in the United States are not required to provide interim statements if there is no home-country filing requirement.

[7]To decrease the ratio, for ratios greater (less) than 1, the same amount is added to (subtracted from) the numerator and denominator.

Accounting Methods

The choice of accounting methods and estimates can greatly affect reported financial statement amounts. In addition, as described in Chapter 3, even "pure" numbers such as cash flows from operations may be affected by accounting choices. Thus, ratios are not comparable between firms (with differing accounting methods) or for the same firm over time (when it changes accounting methods). To interpret such ratios, it may be necessary to convert from one accounting method to another. A strong understanding of accounting rules and a judicious eye for information contained in the notes to financial statements are required for this type of analysis. Subsequent chapters will detail the impact of specific accounting methods on affected ratios.

The balance of this chapter describes specific ratios, primarily in narrative form. We illustrate the calculation and interpretation of these ratios in Exhibits 4-4, 4-6, 4-8, 4-10, 4-12, and 4-14, using the financial statements of Pfizer, a leading firm in the pharmaceutical industry.[8]

The calculations in these exhibits are intended for illustrative purposes; in most cases, they are based on data taken directly from financial statements without any adjustments. The required adjustments will become clearer as we progress through the book. Ratios should not be viewed as an end unto themselves, but rather as a starting point for further analysis. Ratios highlight where further investigation and adjustment may be needed. In that sense, even ratios calculated with unadjusted data can serve a useful purpose.

COMMON-SIZE STATEMENTS

A pervasive problem when comparing a firm's performance over time is that the firm's size is always changing. Firms of different sizes are also difficult to compare. Common-size statements are used to standardize financial statement components by expressing them as a percentage of a relevant base. For example, balance sheet components can be shown as a percentage of total assets; revenues and expenses can be computed as a percentage of total sales, and in the direct method cash flow statement, the components of cash flow from operations can be related to cash collections.

Common-size statements should not, however, be viewed solely as a scaling factor for standardization. They provide the analyst with useful information as a first step *in developing insights into the economic characteristics of different industries and of different firms in the same industry*. For example, significant changes in net income over time may be traced to variations in cost of goods sold (COGS) as a percentage of sales. Changes in this ratio may indicate the efficacy of the firm's efforts to streamline its operations and/or a change in pricing strategies. Additionally, differences over time in a single firm or between firms due to operating, financing, and investing decisions made by management as well as external economic factors are often highlighted by common-size statements.

Exhibit 4-1 compares the 1999 balance sheets and income statements of three pharmaceutical companies: Pfizer, Takeda, and Roche. Both actual data and common-size statements are presented. Exhibit 4-2 presents common-size balance sheets and income statements for the pharmaceutical industry and selected other industries. The scaling factors are total assets for the balance sheets and sales for the income statements.

Cross-Sectional Comparisons. Comparison of the three companies based on actual reported data is fraught with problems because of the currency differentials as well as the disparity in size.[9] Comparisons of assets, working capital, and income cannot provide much insight unless the numbers are scaled.

---

[8]The CD and website accompanying the book contain the financial statements of Pfizer, Roche, and Takeda.

[9]The combination of the two also masks these relationships. Takeda is by far the smallest of the three companies, but that is not apparent from the raw data. Takeda provides "convenience" translations converting its yen financials into dollars on the basis of the yen–dollar relationship at the 1999 year-end. Total assets were approximately $11 billion, one-half that of Pfizer.

EXHIBIT 4-1
Comparative Balance Sheet and Income Statements (1999 data)

A. Comparative Balance Sheets

	As Reported			Common Size(%)		
	Pfizer (Millions of $)	Takeda (Millions of Yen)	Roche (Millions of CHF)	Pfizer	Takeda	Roche
Cash and cash equivalents	739	313,798	16,544	4	24	23
Short-term investments and loans	3,976	227,032	2,322	19	17	3
Accounts receivable	3,864	224,878	6,178	19	17	9
Inventories	1,654	107,767	6,546	8	8	9
Prepaid expenses and taxes	958	39,788	3,041	5	3	4
Current assets	11,191	913,263	34,631	54%	69%	49%
Long-term investments	1,721	123,822	2,271	8	9	3
Net property land and equipment	5,343	224,229	14,240	26	17	20
Net goodwill and other intangible assets	763		15,672	4	0	22
Other assets	1,556	65,685	3,617	8	5	5
Total assets	20,574	1,326,999	70,431	100%	100%	100%
Short-term debt	5,001	11,480	5,702	24	1	8
Accounts and notes payable	951	113,034	2,378	5	9	3
Income taxes payable	869	38,698	728	4	3	1
Other current liabilities	2,364	116,846	6,048	11	9	9
Current liabilities	9,185	280,058	14,856	45%	21%	21%
Long-term debt	525	9,858	15,962	3	1	23
Other noncurrent liabilities	1,676	99,847	5,717	8	8	8
Deferred income taxes	301	—	3,895	1	0	6
Total liabilities	11,687	389,763	40,430	57%	29%	57%
Minority interests		29,863	3,047	—	2	4
Common Stock and APIC	5,629	113,177	160	27	9	0
Retained earnings	13,396	779,946	26,669	65	59	38
Accumulated other comprehensive income	(399)	—	125	(2)	0	0
Reserves and trusts	(2,888)	14,250	—	(14)	1	0
Treasury stock	(6,851)	—	—	(33)	0	0
Total equity	8,887	937,236	30,001	43%	71%	43%
Total liabilities and equities	20,574	1,326,999	70,431	100%	100%	100%

Note: Common-size columns may not add due to rounding.

B. Comparative Income Statements

	As Reported			Common Size(%)		
	Pfizer (Millions of $)	Takeda (Millions of Yen)	Roche (Millions of CHF)	Pfizer	Takeda	Roche
Sales	16,204	844,643	27,567	100%	100%	100%
Cost of goods sold	2,528	435,787	8,874	16	52	32
Gross profit	13,676	408,856	18,693	84%	48%	68%
Selling, general, and administrative expenses	6,351	189,149	10,194	39	22	37
Research and development expenses	2,776	77,487	3,782	17	9	14
Other operating expenses (income)	(130)	—	(14)	(1)	0	0
Income from operations	4,679	142,220	4,731	29%	17%	17%
Other income (expense)	—	40,981	4,057	0	5	15
Income before interest and taxes	4,679	183,201	8,788	29	22	32
Interest expense	236	1,059	1,237	1	0	4
Income before taxes	4,443	182,142	7,551	27%	22%	27%
Provision for taxes	1,244	89,019	1,902	8	11	7
Income from continuing operations	3,199	93,123	5,649	20%	11%	20%

Source: Data from annual reports of Pfizer, Roche, and Takeda.

EXHIBIT 4-2
Industry Comparisons, 1999: Common-Size Balance Sheets and Income Statements

	Retailers		Manufacturers					
	Groceries	Department Stores	Fabricated Rubber Products	Paper Mills	Medicinal Chemicals	Industrial Organic Chemicals	Iron and Steel	Petroleum Refining
A. Comparative Balance Sheets(%)								
Cash and equivalents	11	9	7	5	9	9	7	9
Receivables	5	16	27	22	23	25	25	26
Inventories	28	41	22	17	28	18	26	19
Other	3	1	1	1	4	2	1	3
Current assets	46	67	58	45	63	53	59	56
Fixed assets (net)	41	24	31	49	26	32	33	36
Intangibles (net)	5	2	5	2	6	10	2	2
Other	8	8	6	5	5	5	7	5
Total assets	100	100	100	100	100	100	100	100
Notes payable	5	9	10	7	8	7	10	8
Current portion of long-term debt	5	2	5	5	3	3	5	2
Trade payables	18	12	14	14	16	14	13	21
Income taxes payable	0	0	0	0	0	0	0	1
Other	10	9	9	7	10	7	7	9
Current liabilities	37	31	38	34	37	32	35	41
Long-term debt	30	17	19	25	15	21	19	13
Deferred taxes	0	0	1	1	0	1	1	2
Other	4	3	6	4	4	3	7	7
Total liabilities	71	52	63	64	55	57	62	63
Equity	29	48	37	36	45	43	38	37
Total liabilities and equity	100	100	100	100	100	100	100	100
B. Comparative Income Statements(%)								
Sales	100	100	100	100	100	100	100	100
Cost of sales	75	65	69	72	57	64	74	80
Gross profit	25	35	31	29	43	36	27	21
Operating expenses	23	33	25	22	35	29	22	16
Operating profit	2	2	6	7	9	8	5	4
Other expenses (income)	(0)	(3)	1	1	0	1	1	1
Profit before tax	2	5	5	6	8	7	4	3

Source: Reprinted with permission, copyright Robert Morris Associates 1999. Data adapted from the ALL SIZES column appearing in 1999 *Annual Statement Studies*. RMA cautions that the studies be regarded only as a general guideline and not as an absolute industry norm. This is due to limited samples within categories, the categorization of companies by their primary Standard Industrial Classification (SIC) number only, and different methods of operations by companies within the same industry. For these reasons, RMA recommends that the figures be used only as general guidelines in addition to other methods of financial analysis.

Common-size balance sheets and income statements provide such insight. Looking at the common-size balance sheets in Exhibit 4-1, we immediately see that:

- Takeda is the strongest financially, as its cash and short-term investments (marketable securities) of 41% of assets exceed total liabilities at 29% of assets. Long- and short-term debt combined equal only 2% of assets compared with 27% and 31% for Pfizer and Roche, respectively. Takeda has cash and equivalents (net of all debt) equal to 39% of assets, Pfizer has debt (net of cash equivalents) of 4%, and Roche has net debt of 5% of assets.

- Takeda also has the highest ratio (71%) of equity to total assets. Comparing Pfizer and Roche, we find the former relies primarily on short-term debt whereas the latter's financing comes primarily from long-term debt.

- Pfizer and Takeda have much higher accounts receivable than Roche.

- Pfizer has the largest relative property investment, at 26% of total assets, followed by Roche (20%) and Takeda (17%). These differences may be due to either differences in depreciation methods or differences in the use of and the accounting for off-balance-sheet leasing.
- Roche has the highest proportion of goodwill and intangible assets, suggesting that it has been the most active of the three companies in acquiring other companies (directly or purchasing their patents). Takeda's lack of such assets may either reflect a lack of acquisition activity or be a reflection of Japanese GAAP concerning accounting for goodwill.
- Takeda has the highest ratio of accounts payable.
- Takeda has no deferred income taxes, reflecting the Japanese requirement for conformity between tax and financial reporting.

Turning to the income statement, we find that:

- Pfizer has the lowest ratio of cost of goods sold to sales at 16%, whereas Roche at 32% and Takeda at 52% are much higher.
- Pfizer and Roche have the highest ratios of selling expense to sales, with Takeda's ratio far lower.
- Pfizer reports the highest investment in research and development (17% of sales), followed by Roche and Takeda.
- Reflecting these differences, Pfizer has the highest income from operations (29% of sales), while Takeda and Roche each report 17%.
- Roche has the most significant "other income" (15% of sales), which in 1999 was due to Roche's sale of shares in Genentech. As a result, its pretax income margin of 27% equals that of Pfizer.
- As Takeda has a higher tax rate than both Pfizer and Roche, its net income margin is 11%, barely half that of its two competitors.

A number of factors can explain these differences in profitability components:

- Japan, to some extent, has price controls on its drug industry, limiting its profit margins.
- As shown in Exhibit 4-3, Pfizer's sales include "alliance revenues," which in effect are royalties and commissions that Pfizer earns from distributing and advertising competitors' products. Such revenues have no cost of goods sold associated with them, only selling, general, and administrative expenses.
- Finally, all three companies operate in areas other than pharmaceuticals. As the pharmaceutical sector is the most profitable, the relative concentration in that sector can explain the differences in profitability of the companies. As shown in the table below, almost all of Pfizer's sales and profits are derived from the pharmaceutical segment. Pfizer's lower COGS, higher operating profits, and high R&D are consistent with this higher pharmaceutical segment concentration. Only 70% of Roche's profits are related to pharmaceuticals. Takeda's operating profits are derived almost completely from the pharmaceutical segment. As 71% of sales come from pharmaceuticals, the other segments it operates in apparently have very low profit margins.

	% of Revenues from Pharmaceutical Segment	% of Operating Profit from Pharmaceutical Segment
Pfizer	92%	100%
Roche	60%	70%
Takeda	71%	94%

These variations in operating characteristics may explain some of these differences. Different accounting methods may also play some part. Common-size analysis has provided a starting point for analysis, however.

Industry Comparisons. As noted, some of the differences among the three firms may reflect differences in the industry segments in which they operate. Industry comparisons in Exhibit 4-2 show that balance sheet compositions differ widely. For example:

- The two retailer categories (groceries and department stores) show (as would be expected) the lowest levels of receivables and highest inventory balances. Customers

EXHIBIT 4-3. PFIZER INC. AND SUBSIDIARY COMPANIES
Common-Size Income Statements (1995–1999)

	Years Ended December 31				
	1995	1996	1997	1998	1999
As reported (in $millions)					
Net sales	10,021	9,864	10,739	12,677	14,133
Alliance revenues	—	—	316	867	2,071
Total sales	10,021	9,864	11,055	13,544	16,204
Cost of sales	2,164	1,695	1,776	2,094	2,528
Gross profit	7,857	8,169	9,279	11,450	13,676
Selling, informational, and administrative expenses	3,855	3,859	4,401	5,568	6,351
Research and development expenses	1,442	1,567	1,805	2,279	2,776
Other deductions (income), net	76	55	67	868	(130)
Operating income	2,484	2,688	3,006	2,735	4,679
Interest expense	192	166	149	143	236
Income before taxes	2,292	2,522	2,857	2,592	4,443
Provision for taxes	738	758	775	642	1,244
Income from continuing operations	1,554	1,764	2,082	1,950	3,199
As % of total sales					
Net sales	100	100	97	94	87
Alliance revenues	—	—	3	6	13
Total sales	**100**	**100**	**100**	**100**	**100**
Cost of sales	22	17	16	15	16
Gross profit	78	83	84	85	84
Selling, informational, and administrative expenses	38	39	40	41	39
Research and development expenses	14	16	16	17	17
Other deductions (income), net	1	1	1	6	(1)
Operating income	25	27	27	20	29
Interest expense	2	2	1	1	1
Income before taxes	23	26	26	19	27
Provision for taxes	7	8	7	5	8
Income from continuing operations	16	18	19	14	20
As % of 1995 level (selected items)					
Net sales	100	99	107	127	141
Total sales	100	98	110	135	162
Cost of sales	100	78	82	97	117
Gross profit	100	104	118	146	174
Selling, informational, and administrative expenses	100	100	114	144	165
Research and development expenses	100	109	125	158	192
Operating income	100	108	121	110	188
Interest expense	100	86	78	74	123
Income before taxes	100	110	125	113	194
Income from continuing operations	100	113	134	125	206

Source: Data from Pfizer annual reports.

generally pay for purchases with cash (or with credit cards), keeping receivables low. Inventories are relatively high, as customers demand a variety of goods.

- Paper mills report the highest fixed assets, reflecting large required investments in plants and natural resources.
- The medicinal chemicals sector (which includes pharmaceuticals) and the industrial chemicals sectors report the highest intangibles, probably due to patents and acquisition intangibles.

Common-size income statements also delineate some critical income statement differences. Groceries show low gross margins and drugs the highest, reflecting the economic characteristics and cost structures of these industries. Groceries have the lowest operating profit margin, typical of a low-margin, high-turnover business. Medicinal chemicals have the highest operating margins, reflecting their high-research, patent-protected position.

Comparisons Over Time. Common-size statements can also be used to compare the performance of a single company over time. Exhibit 4-3 shows actual and common-size income statements for Pfizer over the period 1995 to 1999. Sales in this exhibit are disaggregated between regular sales and alliance revenues described previously. Total sales increased 60% from $10 to $16 billion, with one-third of the increase coming from alliance revenues. Profits, on the other hand, increased 100% from $1.5 to over $3 billion. An examination of the components indicates that the increased profitability (relative to sales) is primarily due to efficiencies in cost of goods sold. As a percentage of sales, COGS decreased from 22% of sales in 1995 to 16% of sales in 1999, whereas all other line items maintained or increased their levels as a percentage of sales.

Exhibit 4-3 also illustrates the use of common-size statements for trend analysis. A base year is selected, 1995 in this case, and data for all subsequent years (1996–1999 for Pfizer) are shown as percentages of base-year data. This statement confirms our previous findings. Relative to 1995, COGS increased by only 17%, whereas net sales increased by 41% and total sales increased 60%. All other line items (except interest expense) grew at least as fast as sales.

Changes in balance sheet and cash flow statement components can also be analyzed over time. For common-size cash flow statements, cash collections is the appropriate scaling factor. The insights obtained from the analysis of common-size statements facilitate detailed analysis of the firm and comparative analysis of firms—issues discussed in the following sections.

DISCUSSION OF RATIOS BY CATEGORY

The ratios presented here and their modes of calculation are neither exhaustive nor uniquely "correct." The definition of many ratios is not standardized and may vary from analyst to analyst, textbook to textbook, and annual report to annual report. Not all such variations are logical or useful; we believe that the ratios presented in this book meet both of these criteria.[10]

The analyst's primary focus should be the relationships indicated by the ratios, not the details of their calculation. As we proceed through this book, we will suggest many adjustments to and modifications of these basic ratios.

Activity Analysis

A firm's operating activities require investments in both short-term (inventory and accounts receivable) and long-term (property, plant, and equipment) assets. Activity ratios describe the relationship between the firm's level of operations (usually defined as sales) and the assets needed to sustain operating activities.

---

[10]In this chapter, when one of the components of the ratio comes from the balance sheet and the other from the income or cash flow statement, the balance sheet component is an average of the beginning and ending balances. An exception is the cash flow from operations to debt ratio. In practice, some analysts use beginning or ending balances for such mixed ratios.

The higher the ratio, the more efficient the firm's operations, as relatively fewer assets are required to maintain a given level of operations (sales). Trends in these ratios over time and in comparison to other firms in the same industry can indicate potential deficiencies or opportunities. Furthermore, although these ratios do not measure profitability or liquidity directly, they are important factors affecting those performance indicators. For example, low inventory turnover results in high carrying costs that reduce profits and declining inventory turnover should also alert the analyst to an increased probability of falling demand.

Activity ratios can also be used to forecast a firm's capital requirements (both operating and long-term). Increases in sales will require investments in additional assets. Activity ratios enable the analyst to forecast these requirements and to assess the firm's ability to acquire the assets needed to sustain the forecasted growth.

Short-Term (Operating) Activity Ratios

The *inventory turnover ratio*, defined as

$$\text{Inventory Turnover} = \frac{\text{Cost of Goods Sold}}{\text{Average Inventory}}$$

measures the efficiency of the firm's inventory management. A higher ratio indicates that inventory does not remain in warehouses or on the shelves but rather turns over rapidly from the time of acquisition to sale. This ratio is affected by the choice of accounting method; an explanation and an adjusted ratio are discussed in Chapter 6.

The inverse of this ratio can be used to calculate the average number of days inventory is held until it is sold:[11]

$$\text{Average No. Days Inventory In Stock} = \frac{365}{\text{Inventory Turnover}}$$

The *receivables turnover ratio* and the *average number of days of receivables outstanding* can be calculated similarly as

$$\text{Receivables Turnover} = \frac{\text{Sales}}{\text{Average Trade Receivables}}$$

and

$$\text{Average No. Days Receivables Outstanding} = \frac{365}{\text{Receivables Turnover}}$$

The receivables turnover ratios:

- Measure the effectiveness of the firm's credit policies.
- Indicate the level of investment in receivables needed to maintain the firm's sales level.

Receivables turnover should be computed using only trade receivables in the numerator in order to evaluate operating performance. Receivables generated from financing (unless customer financing is provided as a normal component of sales activities) and investment activities (e.g., receivables from the sale of an investment) should be excluded, as they do not represent normal recurring operating transactions. Adjustments may also be necessary if the firm has sold receivables during the period.[12]

---

[11]For manufacturing firms, the computation is less straightforward. See the discussion in Box 4-1.

[12]See Chapter 11 for a discussion of this issue.

The *accounts payable turnover ratio* and *number of days payables are outstanding* can be computed in a similar fashion as

$$\text{Payables Turnover} = \frac{\text{Purchases}^{13}}{\text{Average Accounts Payable}}$$

and

$$\text{Average No. Days Payables Outstanding} = \frac{365}{\text{Payables Turnover}}$$

Although accounts payable are liabilities rather than assets, their trend is significant as they represent an important source of financing for operating activities. The time spread between when suppliers must be paid and when payment is received from customers is critical for wholesale and retail firms with their large inventory balances. The relationship among accounts payable, accounts receivable, and inventories will be seen shortly when we examine the operating and cash cycles.

The *working capital turnover ratio*, defined as

$$\text{Working Capital Turnover} = \frac{\text{Sales}}{\text{Average Working Capital}}$$

is a summary ratio that reflects the amount of operating capital needed to maintain a given level of sales. Only operating assets and liabilities should be used to compute this measure. Short-term debt, marketable securities, and excess cash should be excluded, as they are not required for operating activities.

In Chapter 1, we discussed the going-concern assumption, a basic tenet of accrual accounting. The deferral of inventory cost until the item is sold and recognition of revenues prior to cash collection assumed that the inventories will be sold and the receivables collected.

Similarly, the use of operating capital as a proxy for cash flow (and liquidity—see the next section) is contingent on this assumption. The level and trends of turnover ratios provide information as to the validity of this assumption. Declining turnover ratios, indicating longer shelf time for inventory and/or slower collection of receivables, could be indicators of reduced demand for a firm's products or of sales to customers whose ability to pay is less certain. This might signal one or more of the following:

- The firm's income may be overstated because reserves are required for obsolete inventory or uncollectible receivables.
- Future production cutbacks may be required.
- Potential liquidity problems may exist.

When activity ratios decline, the statement of cash flows helps assess whether income is overstated relative to cash collections. As will be discussed shortly, profitability and liquidity ratios can also improve our understanding of the cause(s) of lower turnover ratios.

Long-Term (Investment) Activity Ratios

The *fixed asset turnover ratio* measures the efficiency of (long-term) capital investment. The ratio, defined as

$$\text{Fixed Assets Turnover} = \frac{\text{Sales}}{\text{Average Fixed Assets}}$$

reflects the level of sales generated by investments in productive capacity.

The level and trend of this ratio are affected by characteristics of its components. First, sales growth is continuous, albeit at varying rates. Increases in capacity to meet that sales

---

[13]Purchases are computed as cost of good sold plus the change in inventory.

growth, however, are discrete, depending on the addition of new factories, warehouses, stores, and so forth. Compounding this issue is the fact that management often has discretion over the timing, form, and financial reporting of the acquisition of incremental capacity.

The combination of some of these factors, as Figure 4-1 shows, results in an erratic turnover ratio. The life cycle of a company or product includes a number of stages: startup, growth, maturity (steady state), and decline. Startup companies' initial turnover may be low, as their level of operations is below their productive capacity. As sales grow, however, turnover will continually improve until the limits of the firm's initial capacity are reached. Subsequent increases in capital investment decrease the turnover ratio until the firm's sales growth catches up to the increased capacity. This process continues until maturity when sales and capacity level off, only to reverse when the firm enters its decline stage.

Additional problems can result from the timing of a firm's asset purchases. Two firms with similar operating efficiencies, having the same productive capacity and the same level of sales, may show differing ratios depending on when their assets were acquired. The firm with older assets has the higher turnover ratio, as accumulated depreciation has reduced the

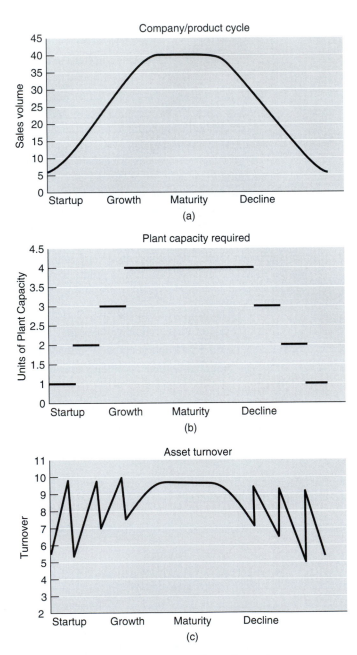

FIGURE 4–1 Asset turnover and capacity requirements.

carrying value of its assets. Over time, for any firm, the accumulation of depreciation expense improves the turnover ratio (faster for firms that use accelerated depreciation methods or short depreciable lives) without a corresponding improvement in actual efficiency. The use of gross (before depreciation) rather than net fixed assets alleviates this shortcoming. However, this is rarely done in practice.

An offsetting and complicating factor is that newer assets generally operate more efficiently due to improved technology. However, due to inflation, newer assets may be more expensive and thus decrease the turnover ratio. Using current or replacement cost rather than historical cost to compute the turnover ratio is one solution to this problem. Finally, it should be noted that methods of acquisition (lease versus purchase) and subsequent financial reporting choices (capitalization versus operating lease reporting) also affect turnover ratios for otherwise similar firms. See Chapter 11 for a discussion of these issues.

Total asset turnover is an overall activity measure relating sales to total assets:

$$\text{Total Asset Turnover} = \frac{\text{Sales}}{\text{Average Total Assets}}$$

This relationship provides a measure of overall investment efficiency by aggregating the joint impact of both short- and long-term assets. This comprehensive measure is a key component of the disaggregation of return on assets, presented in a later section of this chapter. The computation and analysis of turnover measures are illustrated, using Pfizer as an example, in Exhibit 4-4.

EXHIBIT 4-4. PFIZER INC. AND SUBSIDIARY COMPANIES
Activity Analysis

	Years Ended December 31,					
	1995	1996	1997	1998	1999	Average
Inventory turnover[a]	**1.63**	**1.30**	**1.32**	**1.27**	**1.45**	**1.40**
No. of days[b]	223	282	277	287	251	264
Accounts receivable turnover[c]	**5.43**	**5.01**	**5.35**	**5.28**	**4.78**	**5.17**
No. of days[d]	67	73	68	69	76	71
Fixed assets turnover[e]	**3.06**	**2.85**	**3.05**	**3.30**	**3.32**	**3.12**
Total assets turnover[f]	**0.84**	**0.73**	**0.76**	**0.81**	**0.83**	**0.80**

1999 Calculations:

[a]Inventory Turnover = COGS/Avg. inventory = {$2,528/[($1,828 + $1,654)/2]} = 1.45

[b]Avg. No. Days Inventory in Stock = 365/Inventory Turnover = 365/1.45 = 252

[c]Accounts Receivable Turnover = Total Revenue/Avg. AR(Trade) = {($14,133 + $2,071)/($2,914 + $3,864)/2} = 4.78

[d]Avg. No. Days Receivables Outstanding = 365/AR Turnover = 365/4.78 = 76

[e]Fixed Assets Turnover = Total Revenues/Avg. Fixed Assets = {$16,204/[($4,415 + $5,343)/2]} = 3.32

[f]Total Assets Turnover = Total Revenues/Avg. Total Assets = {$16,204/[($18,302 + $20,574)/2]} = 0.83

Comment: Pfizer's number of days inventory in stock (251) is relatively high (more than 8 months) both in absolute terms and compared to the norm for the industry. As Pfizer is a manufacturing company, one can, as discussed in Box 4-1, disaggregate the number of days (given the information available) into two components to see where the turnover is slow.

$$\begin{array}{l}\text{\# of days from purchase of} \\ \text{raw materials to end of} \\ \text{production cycle}\end{array} = 365 \times \frac{\text{Average (Work in process and raw material) inventory}}{\text{Cost of goods manufactured}}$$

$$= 365 \times \frac{\frac{1}{2}\,[(890 + 241) + (711 + 290)]}{2,481} = 157 \text{ days}$$

$$\begin{array}{l}\text{\# of days from completion of} \\ \text{production until sale}\end{array} = 365 \times \frac{\text{Average finished goods inventory}}{\text{Cost of goods sold}}$$

$$= 365 \times \frac{\frac{1}{2}(697 + 650)}{2,528} = 97 \text{ days}$$

The above indicates that Pfizer's production cycle exceeds five months and that finished goods spend more than three months in inventory.

Liquidity Analysis

Short-term lenders and creditors (such as suppliers) must assess the ability of a firm to meet its current obligations. That ability depends on the cash resources available as of the balance sheet date and the cash to be generated through the operating cycle of the firm.

Figure 4-2 is a schematic representation of the operating cycle of a firm. The firm purchases or manufactures inventory, requiring an outlay of cash and/or the creation of trade payables debt. The sale of inventory generates receivables that, when collected, are used to satisfy the payables, and the cycle begins again. The ability to repeat this cycle on a continuous basis depends on the firm's short-term liquidity and cash-generating ability.

Length of Cash Cycle

One indicator of short-term liquidity uses the activity ratios as a liquidity measure. The *operating cycle* of a merchandising firm is the sum of the number of days it takes to sell inventory and the number of days until the resulting receivables are converted to cash. The circumference of the circle in Figure 4-2 represents the length of this cycle. If a firm operates without credit, it also represents the total number of days cash is tied up in operating assets.

To the extent a firm uses credit, the length of the cash (operating) cycle is reduced. Subtracting the number of days of payables outstanding from the operating cycle results in the firm's *cash cycle*, the number of days a company's cash is tied up by its current operating cycle (the circumference of the shaded portion of the circle in Figure 4-2). The cash cycle[14] captures the interrelationship of sales, collections, and trade credit in a manner that the individual numbers may not. The shorter the cycle, the more efficient the firm's operations and cash management; longer cycles, on the other hand, may be indicative of cash shortfalls and increased financing costs.

These financing costs are often not minimal. Boer (1999), for example, estimates that for Dollar General, a retail chain, reducing its 101-day cash cycle by a single day would increase

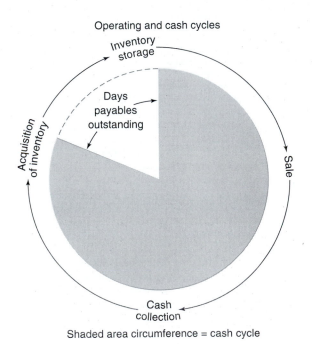

FIGURE 4–2 Operating and cash cycles.

---

[14]The inverse of the working capital turnover ratio (times 365) is sometimes used as a crude approximation of the cash cycle. [See Richards and Laughlin (1980) for an extended discussion.]

BOX 4-1

Estimating the Operating and Cash Cycle for a Manufacturing Firm

A merchandising firm holds only one type of inventory: finished goods inventory. Consequently, the inventory turnover ratio measures only one time stage: the time from inventory purchase until its sale. For a manufacturing firm, on the other hand, inventory is held through three stages:

1. As raw material, from purchase to beginning of production
2. As work in process, over the length of the production cycle
3. As finished goods, from completion of production until sale

Only the last stage (as finished goods) is comparable to a merchandising firm. The inventory turnover ratio, COGS/average finished goods inventory, computes the length of time from completion until sale.

The length of time inventory is in the production cycle (stage 2) can be calculated as

$$365 \times \frac{\text{Average work-in-process inventory}}{\text{Cost of goods manufactured}}$$

The length of time it takes for raw material to enter production is

$$365 \times \frac{\text{Average raw material inventory}}{\text{Raw materials used}}$$

The breakdown among finished goods, work in process, and raw materials inventory is often available in the notes to financial statements. Cost of goods manufactured can be calculated from financial statements as cost of goods sold + ending (finished goods) inventory − beginning (finished goods) inventory. However, the amount of material used in production is rarely available, making the calculation of the length of stage 1 infeasible. Some approximations are possible. The first involves calculating the combined length of stage 1 and 2 as

$$365 \times \frac{\text{Average (work-in-process and raw material) inventory}}{\text{Cost of goods manufactured}}$$

The accuracy of this approximation depends on the proportion of the various inventories and the degree to which the individual ratios differ. Another (less accurate but perhaps simpler) approximation ignores this whole discussion and uses the composite turnover ratio, thereby mirroring the merchandising firm:

$$365 \times \frac{\text{Average (total) inventory}}{\text{Cost of goods sold}}$$

---

pretax profit by almost half a million dollars. *Each day of the cash cycle costs the firm over $440,000!*[15]

To a great extent, industry factors may determine the length and components of the cash cycle. Department stores, for example, may have short or negligible accounts receivable collection periods but lengthy inventory days on hand. For a manufacturing firm, as discussed in Box 4-1, further refinements and approximations may be necessary to calculate the length of the operating and cash cycle.

Some firms may actually have negative cash cycles. One example is Dell Computers:

Cash Cycle for Dell Computers

	Fiscal Year Ended		
	2/1/98	1/29/99	1/28/00
Days of sales in accounts receivable	36	36	34
Days of supply in inventory	7	6	6
Days in accounts payable	(51)	(54)	(58)
Cash cycle	**(8)**	**(12)**	**(18)**

Source: Management's Discussion and Analysis, Dell Computers *2000 Annual Report.*

Dell manufactures and ships directly to its customers only after an order is received. Thus, its inventory days are minimal. Its customers pay on time (perhaps by credit card or on a COD basis), resulting in a low receivable collection period. On the other hand, Dell, itself

---

[15]The calculation is derived as follows. Dollar General has annual sales of $3.2 billion, or approximately $8.8 million average daily sales. Since cost of sales is approximately 72% of sales, the company has to finance $6.4 million for each day of its cash cycle. Since its cash cycle is 101 days, it will have to generate financing for $646.4 million of inventory. At a rate of 7%, the cost is $45.2 million annually, or (45.2/101) $448,000/day of the cash cycle.

EXHIBIT 4-5. AURORA FOODS
Analysis of Operating Cash Cycle

	1997	1998	1999
A. Turnover Ratios			
Inventory	11.3	7.6	4.2
Receivables	20.0	16.4	1.2
Payables	16.0	11.8	6.4
B. Average No. of Days			
Inventory in stock	32	48	86
Receivables outstanding	18	22	33
Length of operating cycle	**50**	**70**	**119**
Less payables outstanding	23	31	57
Length of cash cycle	**28**	**40**	**62**

Source: Data from Aurora Foods annual reports.

(given its market power) can take its time in paying its suppliers. The net result is a negative cash cycle.

Exhibit 4-5 presents the 1997 through 1999 operating and cash cycles for Aurora Foods Inc., a producer and marketer of branded food products across the United States. Aurora went public in June 1998 but its share price declined more than 80% over the following two years. The stock price decline was accompanied by management changes, the restatement of previously reported earnings, and lowered debt ratings.

As seen in Exhibit 4-5, inventory and receivables turnover both declined sharply over the period 1997 to 1999, resulting in a 133% increase in the operating cycle from 51 to 119 days. While the company cut back on its payments to suppliers, it could not compensate for the increase in the operating cycle, and the cash cycle increased from barely one month in duration to just over two months. This analysis illustrates the importance of examining the relationship among the cash cycle components. In the case of Aurora, the deterioration in the cash cycle preceded the poor performance of the company's shares.

Working Capital Ratios and Defensive Intervals

The concept of working (or operating) capital relies on the classification of assets and liabilities into "current" and "noncurrent" categories. *The traditional distinction between current assets and liabilities is based on a maturity of less than one year or (if longer) the operating cycle of the company.*

The typical balance sheet has five categories of current assets:

1. Cash and cash equivalents
2. Marketable securities
3. Accounts receivable
4. Inventories
5. Prepaid expenses

and three categories of current liabilities:

1. Short-term debt
2. Accounts payable
3. Accrued liabilities

By definition, each current asset and liability has a maturity (the expected date of conversion to cash for an asset; the expected date of liquidation for cash for a liability) of less than one year. However, in practice the line between current and noncurrent has blurred in recent years. Marketable securities and debt are particularly susceptible to arbitrary classification. For this reason, working capital ratios should be used with caution.

Short-term liquidity analysis compares the firm's cash resources with its cash obligations. Conceptually, the ratios differ in whether *levels* (amounts shown on the balance sheet) or *flows* (cash inflows and outflows) are used to gauge the relationship per the following table:

	Numerator Cash Resources	Denominator Cash Obligations
Level	Current assets	Current liabilities
Flow	Cash flow from operations	Cash outflows for operations

Three ratios compare levels of cash resources with current liabilities as the measure of cash obligations. The *current ratio* defines cash resources as all current assets:

$$\textbf{Current Ratio} = \frac{\textbf{Current Assets}}{\textbf{Current Liabilities}}$$

A more conservative measure of liquidity is the *quick ratio,*

$$\textbf{Quick Ratio} = \frac{\textbf{Cash + Marketable Securities + Accounts Receivable}}{\textbf{Current Liabilities}}$$

which excludes inventory and prepaid expenses from cash resources, recognizing that the conversion of inventory to cash is less certain both in terms of timing and amount,[16] and that prepaid expenses reflect past cash outflows rather than expected inflows. The included assets are "quick assets" because they can be quickly converted to cash.

Finally, the *cash ratio,* defined as

$$\textbf{Cash Ratio} = \frac{\textbf{Cash + Marketable Securities}}{\textbf{Current Liabilities}}$$

is the most conservative of these measures of cash resources, as only actual cash and securities easily convertible to cash are used to measure cash resources.

The use of either the current or quick ratio implicitly assumes that the current assets will be converted to cash. In reality, however, firms do not actually liquidate their current assets to pay their current liabilities. Minimum levels of inventories and receivables are always needed to maintain operations. If all current assets are liquidated, the firm has effectively ceased operations. As suggested earlier by Figure 4-2, the process of generating inventories, collecting receivables, and paying suppliers is ongoing. These ratios therefore measure the margin of safety provided by the cash resources relative to obligations rather than expected cash flows.

Liquidity analysis, moreover, is not independent of activity analysis. Poor receivables or inventory turnover limits the usefulness of the current and quick ratios. Obsolete inventory or uncollectible receivables are unlikely to be sources of cash. Thus, levels and changes in short-term liquidity ratios over time should be examined in conjunction with turnover ratios.

The *cash flow from operations ratio,*

$$\textbf{Cash Flow from Operations Ratio} = \frac{\textbf{Cash Flow from Operations}}{\textbf{Current Liabilities}}$$

---

[16]Inventory balances of actively traded commodities such as oil, metals, or wheat can be considered very liquid and should be included in the quick ratio.

EXHIBIT 4-6. PFIZER INC. AND SUBSIDIARY COMPANIES
Liquidity Analysis

| | *Years Ended December 31* | | | | | |
	1995	1996	1997	1998	1999	Average
Average no. of days inventory in stock[a]	223	282	277	287	251	264
(plus) Days of receivables outstanding[a]	67	73	68	69	76	71
Length of operating cycle	**291**	**355**	**345**	**356**	**328**	**335**
(minus) Payables outstanding[b]	99	178	132	121	149	136
Length of cash cycle	**191**	**177**	**213**	**235**	**179**	**199**
Current ratio[c]	**1.19**	**1.36**	**1.49**	**1.38**	**1.22**	**1.33**
Quick ratio[d]	0.68	0.67	0.76	0.95	0.90	0.79
Cash ratio[e]	**0.29**	**0.31**	**0.32**	**0.55**	**0.48**	**0.39**
Cash from operations ratio[f]	0.35	0.35	0.32	0.46	0.33	0.36
Defensive interval no. of days[g]	**182**	**192**	**184**	**264**	**273**	**219**

1999 Calculations:

[a] Average no. of days inventory stock and receivables outstanding computed in Exhibit 4-4

[b] Purchases = COGS + Change in Inventory = [$2,528 + ($1,654 − $1,828)] = $2,354

Average No. Days Payables Outstanding = 365*[Avg. AP(Trade)/Purchases] = {365*[(($971 + $951)/2)/$2,354]} = 149

[c] **Current Ratio = Current Assets/Current Liabilities = $11,191/$9,185 = 1.22**

[d] Quick Ratio = (Cash + Marketable Securities + AR)/Current Liabilities = ($739 + $3,703 + $3,864)/$9,185 = 0.90

[e] **Cash Ratio = (Cash + Marketable Securities)/Current Liabilities = ($734 + $3,703)/$9,185 = 0.48**

[f] Cash from Operations Ratio = CFO/Current Liabilities = $3,076/$9,185 = 0.33

[g] **Projected Expenditures = Cost of Goods Sold + Other Operating Expenses except Depreciation Expense = $2,528 + ($6,351 + $2,776 − $542) = $11,113**

Defensive Interval No. Days = 365*[(Cash + Marketable Securities + AR)/Projected Expenditure] = 365*[($734 + $3,703 + $3,864)/$11,113] = 273

Comments: The operating and cash cycles are relatively long (see comments in Exhibit 4-4). The operating cycle lengthened over the period, but improved in 1999 as inventory turnover declined. The cash cycle deteriorated through 1998, but then recovered in 1999. The payable cycle (especially in 1996 and 1999) is long and raises the question of whether Pfizer actually has five months to pay its suppliers or whether reported accounts payable include nonoperating payables (e.g., for equipment purchases) that distort the ratio.

The current, quick, and cash ratios as well as the defensive interval improved over the five-year period, whereas the CFO ratio remained relatively stable (other than 1998).

measures liquidity by comparing actual cash flows (instead of current and potential cash resources) with current liabilities. This ratio avoids the issues of actual convertibility to cash, turnover, and the need for minimum levels of working capital (cash) to maintain operations.

An important limitation of liquidity ratios is the absence of an economic or real-world interpretation of those measures. Unlike the cash cycle liquidity measure, which reflects the number of days cash is tied up in the firm's operating cycle, there is no intuitive meaning to a current ratio of 1.5. For some companies that ratio would be high, for others dangerously low.

The *defensive interval*, in contrast, does provide an intuitive "feel" for a firm's liquidity, albeit a most conservative one. It compares the currently available "quick" sources of cash (cash, marketable securities, and accounts receivable) with the estimated outflows needed to operate the firm: projected expenditures. There are different definitions of both cash resources and projected expenditures.[17] We present here only the basic form:

$$\text{Defensive Interval} = 365 \times \frac{\text{Cash + Marketable Securities + Accounts Receivable}}{\text{Projected Expenditures}}$$

The calculation of the defensive interval for Pfizer (Exhibit 4-6) uses current-year income statement data to estimate projected expenditures. The defensive interval represents a worst-case scenario indicating the number of days a firm could maintain the current level of operations with its present cash resources but without considering any additional revenues.

---

[17] See Sorter and Benston (1960). The most conservative variation, the "no credit" interval, measures the number of days the firm could survive if it loses all access to trade credit. In this version, accounts payable are subtracted from the numerator.

Cash Burn Ratio. Originally developed in the sixties, the defensive interval never caught on with the analyst community. Recently, however, it has enjoyed a belated popularity in the form of the *cash burn rate*. Applied for the most part to startup and rapidly growing technology companies, the cash burn rate measures how much cash the firm consumes over a given period of time and consequently estimates the number of days (defensive interval) the company can survive with the cash it has raised from its investors (private placement or IPO). For startup companies with no revenues, only cash expenditures matter. For such companies, the ratio, in effect, measures how much time the company has until it must have a working business model.

Exhibit 4-7, taken from *Business Week E.Biz* (September 18, 2000), provides examples of technology companies believed to be suffering severe cash crunches with defensive intervals ranging from one to three months. Part B updates the performance of these companies, three and one-half months later, when the defensive interval had passed. One of the companies had ceased operations, whereas another reported a going-concern qualification, and the

EXHIBIT 4-7
Defensive Interval and Cash Burn Rates for Startup Companies

A. Excerpt from "Net Worth" by Peter Elstrom, Business Week E.BIZ
(September 18, 2000); P. EB 114.

Cash Crunch

With capital harder to come by, many tech companies are running low on the cash needed to fund their businesses. Some notable examples:

COMPANY	Cash (in millions)	Cash used last quarter (in millions)	Days to depletion at current rate
En Pointe Technologies	2.0	7.4	24
This Los Angeles-based provider of e-commerce software has laid off employees and restructured to make its cash last.			
Acclaim Entertainment	29.0	45.6	57
The maker of software for Nintendo and other games is reducing expenses but still faces a cash crunch.			
Streamline.com	7.0	10.4	60
The Net grocer has hired an investment bank to raise money or sell the company.			
IdeaMall	3.8	5.4	64
This seller of computer products is revamping to focus on business customers.			
Wavo	4.8	4.9	87
Can this Net media company recover? Its stock is down to about 69¢ a share.			

Data: Standard & Poor's Compustat

B. Performance of Above Companies' Shares 3.5 Months Later (at end of defensive interval period)

Company	Stock Price 9/18/00	Stock Price 12/29/00	% Change	52-Week High	Comment
En Pointe	$ 8.00	$ 3.12	−60.9%	$ 55.00	
Acclaim	2.00	0.03	−98.4	6.63	11/29 report going-concern qualification
Streamline	0.69	0.00	−99.7	12.00	11/13 ceased operations
IdeaMall	3.56	1.12	−68.4	15.50	
Wavo	0.75	0.04	−95.2	8.63	10/29 auditor resigns
NASDAQ	3,726.52	2,470.52	−33.7		

auditor of a third had resigned. All the companies suffered declines in their stock price ranging from 60% to nearly 100%. The NASDAQ index fell by one-third during the same period, undoubtedly contributing to these declines but not fully explaining their severity.

Long-Term Debt and Solvency Analysis

The analysis of a firm's capital structure is essential to evaluate its long-term risk and return prospects. Leveraged firms accrue excess returns to their shareholders as long as the rate of return on the investments financed by debt is greater than the cost of debt. The benefits of financial leverage bring additional risks, however, in the form of fixed costs that adversely affect profitability (see the next section) if demand or profit margins decline. Moreover, the priority of interest and debt claims can have a severe negative impact on a firm when adversity strikes. The inability to meet these obligations can lead to default and possible bankruptcy.

Debt Covenants

To protect themselves, creditors often impose restrictions on the borrowing company's ability to incur additional debt and make dividend payments. These *debt covenants* are often based on working capital, cumulative profitability, and net worth. It is, therefore, important to monitor the firm to ensure that ratios comply with levels specified in the debt agreements. Violations of debt covenants are frequently an "event of default" under loan agreements, making the debt due immediately. When covenants are violated, therefore, borrowers must either repay the debt (not usually possible) or obtain waivers from lenders. Such waivers often require additional collateral, restrictions on firm operations, or higher interest rates.[18]

Capitalization Table and Debt Ratios

Long-term debt and solvency analysis evaluates the level of risk borne by a firm, changes over time, and risk relative to comparable investments. A higher proportion of debt relative to equity increases the riskiness of the firm. Exhibit 4-8 presents capitalization tables for Pfizer. Two important factors should be noted:

1. The relative debt levels themselves,
2. The trend over time in the proportion of debt to equity

Debt ratios are expressed either as

$$\text{Debt to Total Capital} = \frac{\text{Total Debt (Current + Long-Term)}}{\text{Total Capital (Debt + Equity)}}$$

or

$$\text{Debt to Equity} = \frac{\text{Total Debt}}{\text{Total Equity}}$$

The definition of short-term debt used in practice may include operating debt (accounts payable and accrued liabilities). The short-term debt shown in Exhibit 4-8 excludes operating debt because it is a function of the firm's operations and its essential business and contractual relationship to its suppliers rather than external lenders. However, many lenders define debt as equal to total liabilities.

As with other ratios, industry and economywide factors affect both the level of debt and the nature of the debt (maturities and variable or fixed rate). Capital-intensive industries tend to incur high levels of debt to finance their property, plant, and equipment. Such debt should be long-term to match the long time horizon of the assets acquired.

---

[18]The relationship between debt covenants and ratios is explored in greater detail in Chapter 10.

EXHIBIT 4-8. PFIZER INC. AND SUBSIDIARY COMPANIES
Long-Term Debt and Solvency Analysis (in $millions)

| | *Years Ended December 31* | | | | | |
	1995	1996	1997	1998	1999	Average
Short-term debt	2,036	2,204	2,251	2,729	5,001	2,844
Long-term debt	833	681	725	527	525	658
Total debt	**2,869**	**2,885**	**2,976**	**3,256**	**5,526**	**3,502**
Trade payables[a]	1,538	1,635	1,389	2,133	1,820	1,703
Total debt (including trade)	**4,406**	**4,520**	**4,365**	**5,389**	**7,346**	**5,205**
Total equity	**5,507**	**6,954**	**7,933**	**8,810**	**8,887**	**7,618**
Total capital	**8,375**	**9,839**	**10,909**	**12,066**	**14,413**	**11,120**
Total capital (including trade)	**9,913**	**11,474**	**12,298**	**14,199**	**16,233**	**12,823**
Debt						
To equity[b]	**0.52**	**0.41**	**0.38**	**0.37**	**0.62**	**0.46**
To capital[c]	0.34	0.29	0.27	0.27	0.38	0.31
Debt (including trade)						
To equity[d]	**0.80**	**0.65**	**0.55**	**0.61**	**0.83**	**0.69**
To capital[e]	0.44	0.39	0.35	0.38	0.45	0.41
Times interest earned[f]	**12.94**	**16.19**	**20.17**	**19.13**	**19.83**	**17.65**
Capital expenditure ratio[g]	2.62	3.09	1.90	2.93	2.06	2.52
CFO to debt[h]	**0.63**	**0.63**	**0.53**	**1.01**	**0.56**	**0.67**

1999 Calculations:
[a]Trade payables = AP + Income Taxes Payable = $951 + $869 = $1,820
[b]**Debt to Equity = Total Debt/Total Equity = $5,526/$8,887 = 0.62**
[c]Debt to Capital = Total Debt/Total Capital = $5,526/$14,413 = 0.38
[d]**Debt (including trade) to Equity = Total Debt (including trade)/Total Equity = $7,346/$8,887 = 0.83**
[e]Debt (including trade) to Capital = Total Debt (including trade)/Total Capital (including trade) = $7,346/$16,233 = 0.45
[f]**Times Interest Earned = EBIT/Interest Expense = $4,679/$236 = 19.83**
[g]Capital Expenditure Ratio = CFO/Capital Expenditures = $3,076/$1,490 = 2.06
[h]**CFO to Debt = CFO/Total Debt = $3,076/$5,526 = 0.56**
Comments: Leverage ratios increased over the period as debt almost doubled ($2.9 billion to $5.5 billion). The ratios increased less as equity also grew, reflecting the company's profitability. The times interest earned ratio improved despite the increase in debt, due to increased profitability and declining interest rates (Pfizer's debt is short-term).

An important measurement issue is whether to use book or market values to compute debt ratios. Valuation models in the finance literature that use leverage ratios as inputs are generally based on the market value of debt and equity. Market values of both debt and equity are available or can readily be estimated, and their use can make the ratio a more useful analytical tool.

The use of market values, however, may produce contradictory results. The debt of a firm whose credit rating declines may have a market value well below face amount. A debt ratio based on market values may show an "acceptable" level of leverage. A ratio that would control for this phenomenon and can be used in conjunction with book- or market-based debt ratios is one that compares debt measured at book value to equity measured at market:

$$\frac{\text{Total Debt at Book Value}}{\text{Equity at Market}}$$

If the market value of equity is higher than its book value, the above ratio will be lower than the debt-to-equity ratio using book value.[19] This indicates that market perceptions of the firm's earning power would permit the firm to raise additional capital at an attractive price. If this ratio, however, exceeds the book value debt-to-equity measure, it signals that the market is willing to supply additional capital only at a discount to book value.

[19]The analysis assumes that all debt has been included. See Chapter 11 for a discussion of off-balance-sheet financing techniques.

The measurement of debt and equity used to compute leverage ratios may require adjustments to reported data. Leases (whether capitalized or operating), other off-balance-sheet transactions such as contractual obligations not accorded accounting recognition, deferred taxes, financial instruments with debt and equity characteristics, and other innovative financing techniques must all be considered when making these calculations. These issues are discussed in later chapters.

Interest Coverage Ratios

Debt-to-equity ratios examine the firm's capital structure and, indirectly, its ability to meet current debt obligations. A more direct measure of the firm's ability to meet interest payments is

$$\text{Times Interest Earned} = \frac{\textbf{Earnings Before Interest and Taxes (EBIT)}}{\textbf{Interest Expense}}$$

This ratio, often referred to as the *interest coverage ratio*, measures the protection available to creditors as the extent to which earnings available for interest cover interest expense.[20] A more comprehensive measure, the *fixed charge coverage ratio*, includes all fixed charges,

$$\text{Fixed Charge Coverage} = \frac{\textbf{Earnings Before Fixed Charges and Taxes}}{\textbf{Fixed Charges}}$$

where fixed charges include contractually committed interest and principal payments on leases as well as funded debt.

This coverage ratio may also be computed using adjusted operating cash flows (cash from operations + fixed charges + tax payments) as the numerator:

$$\text{Times Interest Earned (Cash Basis)} = \frac{\textbf{Adjusted Operating Cash Flow}}{\textbf{Interest Expense}}$$

$$\text{Fixed Charge Coverage Ratio (Cash Basis)} = \frac{\textbf{Adjusted Operating Cash Flow}}{\textbf{Fixed Charges}}$$

Capital Expenditure and CFO-to-Debt Ratios

A firm's long-term solvency is a function of its ability to:

- Finance the replacement and expansion of its investment in productive capacity, as well as
- Generate cash for debt repayment.

Cash flows generated internally are needed for investment as well as debt service. The coverage ratios discussed do not take this into consideration. Cash flow from operations, as noted in Chapter 3, ignores the cost of additions to operating capacity. Net income, with its provision for depreciation, amortizes the original cost of existing fixed assets. However, given their relatively long service life, the replacement costs of these assets (even with minimal inflation) may be significantly higher, and historical cost depreciation cannot adequately provide for their replacement.[21] Neither net income nor cash from operations, of course, makes any provision for the capital required for growth.

The *capital expenditure ratio*

$$\text{Capital Expenditure Ratio} = \frac{\textbf{Cash from Operations (CFO)}}{\textbf{Capital Expenditures}}$$

---

[20]Because firms may capitalize some interest expense, using reported interest expense may overstate the coverage ratio. See Chapter 7 for a discussion of capitalized interest and adjustments to coverage ratios.

[21]See Chapter 8 for a discussion of these issues.

measures the relationship between the firm's cash-generating ability and its investment expenditures. To the extent the ratio exceeds 1, it indicates the firm has cash left for debt repayment or dividends after capital expenditures.

The *CFO-to-debt ratio*[22]

$$\text{CFO to Debt} = \frac{\text{CFO}}{\text{Total Debt}}$$

measures the coverage of principal repayment requirements by the current CFO. A low CFO-to-debt ratio could signal a long-term solvency problem, as the firm does not generate enough cash internally to repay its debt. Exhibit 4-8 shows the computation and interpretation of long-term debt and solvency measurements for Pfizer.

Profitability Analysis

Equity investors are concerned with the firm's ability to generate, sustain, and increase profits. Profitability can be measured in several differing but interrelated dimensions. First, there is the relationship of a firm's profits to sales, that is, the residual return to the firm per sales dollar. Another measure, return on investment (ROI), relates profits to the investment required to generate them. We briefly define these ratios and then elaborate on their use in financial statement analysis.

Return on Sales

One measure of profitability is the relationship between the firm's costs and its sales. The ability to control costs in relation to revenues enhances earnings power. A common-size income statement shows the ratio of each cost component to sales. In addition, six summary ratios measure the relationship between different measures of profitability and sales:

1. The *gross (profit) margin* captures the relationship between sales and manufacturing or merchandising costs:

$$\text{Gross Margin} = \frac{\text{Gross Profit}}{\text{Sales}}$$

2. The *operating margin*, calculated as

$$\text{Operating Margin} = \frac{\text{Operating Income}}{\text{Sales}}$$

   provides information about a firm's profitability from the operations of its core business, excluding the effects of:
   - Investments (income from affiliates or asset sales)
   - Financing (interest expense)
   - Tax position

3. A profit margin measure that is independent of both the firm's financing and tax position is the

$$\text{Margin Before Interest and Tax} = \frac{\text{EBIT}}{\text{Sales}}$$

4. The pretax margin is calculated after financing costs (interest) but prior to income taxes:

$$\text{Pretax Margin} = \frac{\text{Earnings Before Tax (EBT)}}{\text{Sales}}$$

---

[22]The definition of debt may depend on the objective of the analysis. It should include all short- and long-term debt and may include trade debt.

5. Finally, the overall profit margin is net of all expenses:

$$\text{Profit Margin} = \frac{\text{Net Income}}{\text{Sales}}$$

The five ratios listed above can be computed directly from a firm's financial statements.

6. Another useful profitability measure is the contribution margin ratio, defined as

$$\text{Contribution Margin} = \frac{\text{Contribution}}{\text{Sales}}$$

where Contribution = Sales − Variable costs.

The contribution margin ratio, however, cannot be computed directly from a firm's financial statements as the breakdown between fixed and variable costs is rarely provided.

Return on Investment

Return on investment (ROI) measures the relationship between profits and the investment required to generate them. Diverse measures of that investment result in different forms of ROI.

Return on Assets. The return on assets (ROA) compares income with total assets (equivalently, total liabilities and equity capital). It can be interpreted in two ways. First, it measures management's ability and efficiency in using the firm's assets to generate (operating) profits. Second, it reports the total return accruing to all providers of capital (debt and equity), independent of the source of capital.

The return is measured by net income prior to the cost of financing and is computed by adding back (after-tax) interest expense to net income:[23]

$$\text{ROA} = \frac{\text{Net Income} + \text{After-Tax Interest Cost}}{\text{Average Total Assets}}$$

ROA can also be computed on a pretax basis using EBIT as the return measure. This results in a ROI measure that is unaffected by differences in a firm's tax position as well as financial policy:

$$\text{ROA} = \frac{\text{Earnings Before Interest and Taxes (EBIT)}}{\text{Average Total Assets}}$$

In practice, however, the ROA measure is sometimes computed using either net income or EBT as the numerator. Such postinterest ROI ratios make leveraged firms appear less profitable by charging earnings for payments (interest) to some capital providers (lenders) but not others (stockholders). Preinterest ROI ratios, in contrast, facilitate the comparison of firms with different degrees of leverage. Therefore, *ROI ratios that use total assets in the denominator should always include total earnings before interest in the numerator. As interest is tax deductible, post-tax profit measures should add back net-of-tax interest payments.*

Return on Total Capital. One particularly useful ROI measure is the *return on total capital (ROTC)*. This ratio uses the sum of *external* debt and equity instead of total assets as the base against which the firm's return is measured. ROTC measures profitability relative to all (nontrade) capital providers.

---

[23]The after-tax interest cost is calculated by multiplying the interest cost by $(1 - t)$, where t is the firm's marginal tax rate.

Return can be measured either (pretax) by EBIT or (after tax) by net income plus after-tax interest:[24]

$$\text{ROTC} = \frac{\textbf{EBIT}}{\textbf{Average (Total Debt + Stockholders' Equity)}}$$

or

$$\text{ROTC} = \frac{\textbf{Net Income + After-Tax Interest Expense}}{\textbf{Average (Total Debt + Stockholders' Equity)}}$$

Return on Equity. The return on total stockholders' equity (ROE) excludes debt in the denominator and uses either pretax income (*after* interest costs) or net income:

$$\text{ROE} = \frac{\textbf{Pretax Income}}{\textbf{Average Stockholders' Equity}}$$

or

$$\text{ROE} = \frac{\textbf{Net Income}}{\textbf{Average Stockholders' Equity}}$$

For companies with preferred equity, another ROI measure focuses on the return accruing to the residual owners of the firm—common shareholders:

$$\text{Return on Common Equity (ROCE)} = \frac{\textbf{Net Income − Preferred Dividends}}{\textbf{Average Common Equity}}$$

The relationship between ROA and ROE reflects the firm's capital structure. As shown in Exhibit 4-9, creditors and shareholders provide the capital needed by the firm to acquire the assets used in the business. In return, they receive their share of the firm's profits.

ROA (and ROTC) measure returns to all providers of capital. ROE measures returns to the firm's shareholders and is calculated after deducting the returns paid to creditors (interest). The equity shareholder can earn higher returns by "leveraging" the investment provided by the debt holders as long as the returns earned by the company's assets (ROA) are greater than the cost of debt.

Profitability and Cash Flows

Profitability ratios traditionally use accrual-based income measures, as shown for Pfizer in Exhibit 4-10. Cash flow analogues for these ratios should also be calculated. Examples include cash gross margin (cash collections less cash paid for inputs) and ROI measures using CFO in the numerator (either before or after interest, depending on the denominator). A direct method cash flow statement is required for ratios such as cash gross margin and operating margin. There is empirical evidence that such cash-flow-based ratios have different properties from traditional profitability measures.[25]

Operating and Financial Leverage

Profitability ratios imply that profits are proportional to sales, which may misstate the true relationship among sales, costs, and profits. Generally, a doubling of sales would be expected to double income only if all expenses were variable. Conceptually, expenses can be classified

---

[24]As in the case of ROA, preinterest measures of profitability should be used to compute ROTC, as total capital includes debt obligations.

[25]See the discussion of Gombola and Ketz (1983) that follows.

EXHIBIT 4-9
Relationship of ROA and ROE to Providers of Investment Base—Effects of Leverage

Schematically, we can show the relationship as:

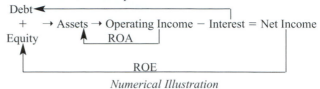

Numerical Illustration

Assume a company has assets of $600,000 financed by $400,000 of equity and $200,000 of debt. Also assume the following income statement:

Operating income	$100,000	*After-tax* operating income* (100,000 × .7)	$70,000
Interest	(20,000)	*After-tax* interest cost (20,000 × .7)	(14,000)
	$80,000	Net income	$56,000
Income tax @ 30%	(24,000)		
Net income	$56,000		

*Alternatively, net income + interest (1 − t) = $56,000 + 20,000 (.7) = $70,000.

That is, the $70,000 generated by the assets is distributed as follows:

- To the debt holder: $14,000
- To the equity shareholder: 56,000
                               $70,000

Returns on Investment

	Investment	Return[†]	%
Debt	$200,000	$14,000	7.00%
Equity	400,000	56,000	14.00%
Assets	$600,000	$70,000	11.67%

[†]Returns are after tax.

Effects on Leverage for Equityholder[‡]	Return on $400,000
• Invests $400,000, earns 11.67%.	$46,667/$400,000 = 11.67%
• On borrowed funds of $200,000 earns 11.67% but pays 7%. Therefore earns spread of 4.67% (or 11.67% − 7%) × $200,000 =	$ 9,333/$400,000 = 2.33%
• Total:	$56,000/$400,000 = 14.00%

[‡]This relationship can be expressed (see following section in text) as

$$ROE = ROA + (ROA - \text{Cost of debt}) \times D/E$$
$$14.00\% = 11.67\% + (11.67\% - 7\%) \times (200{,}000/400{,}000)$$

into variable (V) and fixed (F) components. Variable expenses tend to be operating in nature, whereas fixed costs are the result of operating, investing, and financing decisions.[26]

The mix of variable and fixed operating cost components in a firm's cost structure often reflects the industry in which the firm operates. Fixed investing and financing costs depend on the asset intensity of the firm's operations and (somewhat related) on the amount of debt financing used by the firm.

Leverage, which is the proportion of fixed costs in the firm's overall cost structure, can be subdivided into fixed operating costs that reflect *operating leverage* (the proportion of fixed operating costs to variable costs), and fixed financing costs or *financial leverage*.

---

[26]Financial markets sometimes create investing and financing transactions with variable payment streams such as lease payments tied to revenues (e.g., retailers) and adjustable rate loans. These payments may have both variable and fixed components.

EXHIBIT 4-10. PFIZER INC. AND SUBSIDIARY COMPANIES
Profitability Analysis

| | *Years Ended December 31* | | | | | |
	1995	1996	1997	1998	1999	Average
Gross margin pre Alliance revenue (%)[a]	78.41	82.82	83.46	83.48	82.11	82.06
Gross margin (%)[a]	78.41	82.82	83.93	84.54	84.40	82.82
Operating margin (%)[a]	**24.79**	**27.25**	**27.28**	**20.21**	**28.88**	**25.68**
Pretax margin (%)[a]	**22.87**	**25.57**	**25.93**	**19.15**	**27.42**	**24.19**
Profit margin (%)[a]	**15.51**	**17.88**	**18.92**	**14.41**	**19.74**	**17.29**
ROA (preinterest)						
After tax (%)[b]	**14.14**	**13.94**	**15.05**	**12.37**	**17.33**	**14.57**
Pretax (%)[c]	20.85	19.93	20.63	16.44	24.07	20.38
ROE						
After tax (%)[d]	**31.62**	**28.31**	**28.11**	**23.32**	**36.15**	**29.50**
Pretax (%)[e]	46.63	40.48	38.52	30.99	50.21	41.37
ROTC (preinterest)						
After tax (%)[f]	**21.70**	**20.64**	**21.21**	**17.93**	**25.45**	**21.39**
Pretax (%)[g]	32.01	29.52	29.07	23.83	35.34	29.95

Note: In this table we use income from continuing operations (i.e., before discontinued operations) as our measure of net income.
1999 Calculations:
[a]Return on sales and margins from Exhibit 4-3 except for calculation of
Gross margin pre Alliance revenue (%) = (Net Sales − Cost of Sales)/Net Sales = [($14,133 − $2,528)/$14,133] = 82.11
[b]After Tax (%) = {[Net Income + (Interest Expense × (1 − Effective Tax Rate))]/Avg. Assets}
= {[$3,199 + ($236(1 − 0.28)]/(($18,302 + $20,574)/2] = 17.33
[c]Pretax (%) = (EBIT/Avg. Assets) = [$4,679/(($18,302 + $20,574)/2)] = 24.07
[d]After Tax (%) = (Net Income/Avg. Equity) = [$3,199/(($8,887 + $8,810)/2)] = 36.15
[e]Pretax (%) = (EBT/Avg. Equity) = [$4,443/(($8,887 + $8,810)/2] = 50.21
[f]After Tax (%) = {[Net Income + (Interest Expense × (1 − Effective Tax Rate))]/Avg. Total Capital [Debt + Equity]}
= {$3,199 + ($236 (1 − 0.28))]/(($12,066 + $14,413)/2] = 25.45
[g]Pretax (%) = [EBIT/Avg. Total Capital (Debt + Equity)] = [$4,679/(($12,066 + $14,413)/2)] = 35.34
Comments: See the section on "Common-size Statements" for a discussion of trends in margins. Trends in ROA/ROE are discussed later with reference to Exhibits 4-12 and 4-14.

Leverage trades risk for return. Increases in fixed costs are risky because they must still be paid as demand declines, depressing the firm's income. At high levels of demand, fixed costs are spread over a larger base, enhancing profitability. These concepts are illustrated in Exhibit 4-11.

Operating Leverage

Part A of Exhibit 4-11 illustrates operating leverage. With sales of $100 (scenario B), Company V and Company F have the identical return on sales of 20% and ROA (= ROE) of 10%. The return on sales is constant for Company V, since its operating costs are completely variable. Changes in net income are directly proportional to changes in demand—a 50% increase in sales to $150 results in a 50% increase in income to $30. Company F's profitability, on the other hand, varies by more than changes in demand. A 50% change in demand changes net income by 150%. Because of fixed costs, the return on sales does not remain constant with volume.

The *contribution margin ratio* is a useful measure of the effects of operating leverage on the firm's profitability:

$$\text{Contribution Margin Ratio} = \frac{\text{Contribution}}{\text{Sales}} = 1 - \frac{\text{Variable Costs}}{\text{Sales}}$$

This ratio indicates the incremental profit resulting from a given dollar change in sales. For Company V this ratio is 20% (1 − 80%), and for Company F it is 60% (1 − 40%). Thus, a change of $50 in sales results in a change in operating income of

Company V: 20% × $50 = $10

Company F: 60% × $50 = $30

EXHIBIT 4-11
Illustration of Operating, Financial, and Total Leverage Effects

General Assumptions	Company V	Company F
Fixed costs	$ 0	$ 40
Variable costs/sales	80%	40%
Assets	$200	$200

A. Assume 0% Financing, Debt $0, Equity $200

	No Leverage Company V			Operating Leverage Company F		
Scenario	A	B	C	A	B	C
Sales	$50	$100	$150	$50	$100	$150
Variable cost	40	80	120	20	40	60
Contribution	$10	$ 20	$ 30	$30	$ 60	$ 90
Fixed cost	0	0	0	40	40	40
Operating income	$10	$ 20	$ 30	($10)	$ 20	$ 50
Return						
On sales	20%	20%	20%	(20%)	20%	33%
On assets	5%	10%	15%	(5%)	10%	25%
On equity	5%	10%	15%	(5%)	10%	25%

B. Assume 50% Financing, Debt 100, Equity 100, Interest Rate = 5%

	Financial Leverage Company V			Total Leverage Company F		
Scenario	A	B	C	A	B	C
Operating income	$10	$ 20	$ 30	($10)	$ 20	$ 50
Interest	5	5	5	5	5	5
Net income	$ 5	$ 15	$ 25	($15)	$ 15	$ 45
Return						
On assets	5%	10%	15%	(5%)	10%	25%
On equity	5%	15%	25%	(15%)	15%	45%

The *operating leverage effect (OLE)* is defined as

$$\text{OLE} = \frac{\textbf{Contribution Margin Ratio}}{\textbf{Return on Sales}} = \frac{\textbf{Contribution}}{\textbf{Operating Income}}$$

and is the ratio of the contribution margin to operating income. The OLE can be used to estimate the percentage change in income (and ROA) resulting from a given percentage change in sales volume:

% Change in Income = OLE × % Change in Sales

When OLE is greater than 1, operating leverage is present. However, this measure of operating leverage is not constant across all levels of activity.[27] *The OLE is a relative measure and varies with the level of sales.*

For Company V, the OLE is equal to 1, at all sales levels, because its costs are completely variable. Thus, for Company V, a given percentage change in sales results in equivalent percentage changes in income and ROA.

---

[27]Similarly, the financial leverage measure discussed shortly is also a function of the chosen starting point.

For Company F, however, the OLE varies: It is equal to 3 (60%/20%) for scenario B. A 50% change in sales (to scenario A or scenario C) will result in a threefold percentage change (3 × 50% = 150%) in income and ROA. Using scenario C as the base starting point, however, results in an OLE measure of 1.8 (60%/33%). A 33% drop in sales from scenario C to scenario B ($150 to $100) results in a 60% (1.8 × 33%) drop in income ($50 to $20) and ROA.[28]

Financial Leverage

The effects of financial leverage can also be quantified. From the point of view of common shareholders, financial leverage is, like operating leverage, a risk and return trade-off. The firm takes on the risk of fixed financing costs, anticipating that higher returns will accrue to the common shareholders at higher levels of demand.

In part B of Exhibit 4-11, we assume that each company is 50% financed by debt and interest costs = $5 (5% interest rate). For Company V (which has no operating leverage), changes in net income are now proportionally higher than changes in demand; changes of 50% in volume are accompanied by changes of 67% in profit and ROE. (Note that ROA, because it is computed before interest expense, is unaffected by financial leverage.)

The *financial leverage effect (FLE)* relates operating income to net income:

$$FLE = \frac{\text{Operating Income}}{\text{Net Income}}$$

The FLE for Company V is (at scenario B) $20/$15 = 1.333. Thus, a 50% change in sales (and operating income) results in a 67% (1.333 × 50%) shift in income (from $15 to $25) and ROE (from 15% to 25%).

For Company F, the changes in income relative to changes in demand are even higher. Here, the effects of *both* operating and financial leverage coincide, giving a *total leverage effect (TLE)* equal to the product of the individual leverage effects:

$$TLE = OLE \times FLE = \frac{\text{Contribution}}{\text{Net Income}}$$

$$TLE = 3 \times 1.333 = 4.00$$

A 50% decline in Company F's sales (from $100 to $50) results in a 200% (4 × 50%) decline in income (from $15 to $ − 15). This suggests that firms with high operating leverage take on high financial leverage only at their peril. Traditionally, high debt ratios have been considered acceptable only for firms with low operating leverage or with stable operations (such as public utilities), where the risk of combining operating and financial leverage was low. In recent years, however, financial leverage has been applied to companies with high operating leverage as well (airlines, for example), resulting in financial distress or even bankruptcy during periods of economic adversity.[29]

RATIOS: AN INTEGRATED ANALYSIS

The ratios surveyed in this chapter measure such diverse aspects of an enterprise's performance as its efficiency of operations (activity ratios), liquidity, solvency, and profitability. The discussion thus far has focused on the characteristics of individual ratios. Comprehensive financial analysis requires a review of three interrelationships among ratios:

1. *Economic relationships.* Interdependent changes in various components of the financial statements stem from underlying economic relationships. For example, higher sales are

---

[28]In all cases, the ROE is identical to ROA, as we have assumed no financing in part A.

[29]The growth in off-balance-sheet financing can be partly explained by the desire of firms to report lower levels of operating and financial leverage. The use of operating leases allows firms to avoid the recognition of debt and related financing costs. All leverage ratios should be adjusted for operating leases and other forms of off-balance-sheet financing. (See Chapter 11.)

generally associated with higher investment in working capital components such as receivables and inventory. Ratios comprising these elements should be correlated.

2. *Overlap of components.* The components of many ratios overlap due to the inclusion of an identical term in the numerator or denominator, or because a term in one ratio is a subset or component of another ratio.[30] Change in one of these identical terms will change a number of ratios in the same direction. Similarly, ratios that aggregate other ratios can be expected to follow patterns over time consistent with those of their components. For example, the total assets turnover ratio is essentially a (weighted) aggregation of the individual turnover ratios. Trends in this ratio will mirror those observed in the inventory, accounts receivable, and fixed asset turnover ratios.

3. *Ratios as composites of other ratios.* Some ratios are related to other ratios across categories. For example, the ROA ratio is a combination of profitability and turnover ratios:

$$\frac{\text{Income}}{\text{Assets}} = \frac{\text{Income}}{\text{Sales}} \times \frac{\text{Sales}}{\text{Assets}}$$

A change in either of the ratios on the right-hand side will change the return on assets as well.

The interrelationships among ratios have important implications for financial analysis. Disaggregation of a ratio into its component elements allows us to gain insight into factors affecting a firm's performance; for example, significant changes in ROA may be best understood through an analysis of its components. Further, ratio differences can highlight the economic characteristics and strategies of:

- The same firm over time
- Firms in the same industry
- Firms in different industries
- Firms in different countries

These relationships among ratios imply that one might be able to ignore some component ratios and use a composite or representative ratio to capture the information contained in other ratios. For example, in the ROA relationship described earlier, the effect of the two ratios on the right side of the equation may be captured by the ROA ratio. For certain analytical purposes, this composite ROA ratio may suffice.

Analysis of Firm Performance

This section will exploit some of these interrelationships to analyze a firm's performance by focusing on disaggregations of the overall profitability measures ROA and ROE.

Disaggregation of ROA

The ROA ratio can be disaggregated as follows:

$$\text{ROA} = \text{Total Asset Turnover} \times \text{Return on Sales}$$
$$= \frac{\text{Sales}}{\text{Assets}} \times \frac{\text{Operating Income}}{\text{Sales}}$$

The firm's overall profitability is the product of an activity ratio and a profitability ratio. A low ROA can result from low turnover, indicating poor asset management, low profit margins, or a combination of both factors.

Exhibit 4-12 (part A) presents an analysis of Pfizer's ROA for the period 1995 to 1999. Note that in our illustration, we use EBIT to measure profitability. The use of EBIT (rather

---

[30]An example of the first type is the use of sales in various activity and profitability ratios. Examples of the second category include cash as a component of quick assets, which in turn are a part of current assets.

EXHIBIT 4-12 PFIZER INC. AND SUBSIDIARY COMPANIES
Disaggregation of Pretax ROA and ROE

A. Return on Assets

	Preinterest and Tax Margin[a] EBIT/Sales (%)	×	Asset Turnover[b] Sales/Average Total Assets	=	Preinterest ROA[c] EBIT/Average Total Assets (%)	−	Interest on Assets[d] Interest Expense/Average Total Assets (%)	=	Postinterest ROA[e] EBT/Average Total Assets (%)
1995	24.79	×	0.84	=	20.85	−	1.61	=	19.24
1996	27.25	×	0.73	=	19.93	−	1.23	=	18.70
1997	27.28	×	0.76	=	20.63	−	1.02	=	19.61
1998	20.21	×	0.81	=	16.44	−	0.86	=	15.58
1999	28.88	×	0.83	=	24.07	−	1.21	=	22.86
Average	25.68		0.80		20.38		1.19		19.20

B. Return on Equity

	Postinterest ROA[e] EBT/Average Total Assets (%)	×	Leverage[f] Average Total Assets/Average Common Equity	=	Pretax ROE[g] EBT/Average Common Equity (%)
1995	19.24	×	2.42	=	46.63
1996	18.70	×	2.17	=	40.48
1997	19.61	×	1.96	=	38.52
1998	15.58	×	1.99	=	30.99
1999	22.86	×	2.20	=	50.21
Average	19.20		2.15		41.37

1999 calculations:

[a]Preinterest and Tax Margin (%) = (EBIT/Sales) = \$4,679/\$16,204 = 28.88

[b]Asset Turnover = Sales/Avg. Total Assets = [\$16,204/((\$20,574 + \$18,302)/2)] = 0.83

[c]Preinterest ROA (%) = Preinterest and Tax Margin × Asset Turnover = 28.88 × 0.83 = 24.07

[d]Interest on Assets (%) = (Interest Expense/Avg. Total Assets) = {\$236/[((\$20,574 + \$18,302)/2]} = 1.21

[e]Postinterest ROA = Preinterest ROA − Interest on Assets = 24.07 − 1.21 = 22.86

[f]Leverage = Avg. Total Assets/Avg. Common Equity = {[(\$20,574 + \$18,302)/2]/[(\$8,887 + \$8,810)/2]} = 2.20

[g]Pretax ROE = Postinterest ROA × Leverage = 22.86 × 2.20 = 50.21

EXHIBIT 4-13
Disaggregation of ROA into Basic Components

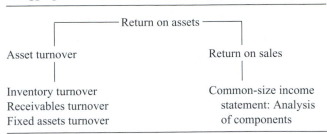

than after-tax operating income) has the advantage that it shows trends independent of the tax position as well as capital structure of the firm.

Comparing 1999 with 1995, we find that Pfizer's ROA increased by 20% (to 24.07%) and that increase was due to an increased profit margin. Asset turnover, on the other hand, showed little change. However, the increase in ROA only occurred in 1999. If we turn our attention to the changes in Pfizer's ROA on a year-to-year basis, our findings are somewhat different. In 1996 and 1997, increases in profitability (EBIT/sales) were more than offset by lower turnover, resulting in lower ROA. In 1998, the reverse occurred as profit margins dropped considerably, whereas turnover only inched up with the result being sharply lower ROA.

The analysis of changes in ROA can be refined further by examining individual turnover ratios (Exhibit 4-4) and the elements of profitability (Exhibit 4-10). Exhibit 4-13 provides an overall summary of this hierarchical analysis.

Disaggregation of ROE and Its Relationship to ROA

The next logical step is a detailed examination of ROE. Exhibit 4-9 illustrates the relationship between ROA and ROE. At low levels of volume when the ROA is equal to the 5% cost of debt, there are no benefits to Company V from financial leverage. As volume increases and the ROA is greater than the cost of debt, the excess return accrues to the common shareholders.

The relationship between ROE and ROA is a function of the proportion of debt used for financing and the relationship of the cost of that debt to ROA. This can be formally expressed as

$$\textbf{ROE} = \textbf{ROA} + \left[(\textbf{ROA} - \textbf{Cost of Debt}) \times \frac{\textbf{Debt}}{\textbf{Equity}} \right]$$

In effect, the benefit of financial leverage is the product of the excess returns earned on the firm's assets over the cost of debt[31] and the proportion of debt financing to equity financing. If there are no excess returns (i.e., ROA < cost of debt), then ROE will be lower than ROA.

The relationship between ROA and ROE may also be expressed as

$$\textbf{ROE} = \left(\textbf{ROA} - \frac{\textbf{Interest Cost}}{\textbf{Assets}} \right) \times \frac{\textbf{Assets}}{\textbf{Equity}}$$

Exhibit 4-12 illustrates the ROA and ROE relationship on a pretax basis using Pfizer. Part B extends the ROA calculation, deducting the interest component and multiplying by the assets/equity ratio.

The assets/equity ratio is a capital structure/financial leverage ratio indicating the degree to which assets are internally financed. A higher ratio indicates more outside financing. The ratio

---

[31]This relationship is, of course, just another manifestation of the financial leverage effect defined earlier as operating income/net income, where net income = operating income − interest costs.

equals 1 plus the debt/equity ratio, where debt is defined as total liabilities.[32] Thus, if we recall the components of ROA, ROE is a function of three of the four categories discussed.[33] That is,

$$\text{ROE} = \textbf{Profitability} \times \textbf{Activity} \times \textbf{Solvency}$$

$$= \frac{\textbf{Income}}{\textbf{Sales}} \times \frac{\textbf{Sales}}{\textbf{Assets}} \times \frac{\textbf{Assets}}{\textbf{Equity}}$$

Exhibit 4-14 (part A) disaggregates Pfizer's (after tax) ROE into these three components for the years 1995 to 1999. The analysis can be expanded by examining the individual components (from Exhibits 4-4, 4-8, and 4-9) making up these categories.

The analysis of the components of ROE, which is frequently known as the *duPont model*,[34] enables the analyst to discern the contribution of each factor to the change in ROE.

From Exhibit 4-12 we learn that, from 1995 to 1999, Pfizer's ROE increased from 46.6% to 50.2% (we ignore, for the moment, the lower returns in 1996 through 1998). This increase mirrors that of the change in ROA and is also due to increased profitability. Leverage decreased slightly as the ratio of average total assets to average common equity decreased from 2.42 (1995) to 2.20 (1999).

Exhibit 4-14, using post-tax data, shows similar results. ROE increased from 1995 to 1999 because of an increased after-tax profit margin. On a short-term (year-to-year) basis, variations in ROE were due primarily to increased profit margins being offset by lower turnover and leverage.

Although the three-component model shown is the standard duPont analysis, that model can be developed further. In many cases, it is worthwhile to look at the effect of interest payments or tax payments. To do so, we must disaggregate the profitability ratio further as follows;

$$\frac{\textbf{Net Income}}{\textbf{EBT}} \times \frac{\textbf{EBT}}{\textbf{EBIT}} \times \frac{\textbf{EBIT}}{\textbf{Sales}} = \frac{\textbf{Net Income}}{\textbf{Sales}}$$

yielding a five-way breakdown of ROE. This decomposition is presented in Exhibit 4-14 (part B); it allows the analyst to view the income tax burden (ratio one is 1 minus the tax rate) separately from the interest burden (ratio two, which shows the percentage of EBIT that is not paid to debtholders) and each separately from operating profitability (EBIT/sales).

For Pfizer, we find that overall increases in profitability were not only (as noted earlier) driven by operating profit (EBIT/sales). The firm's tax and interest burdens also declined over the period.

Trends in ROE and ROA

As the duPont model suggests, ROE is an important summary measure of a firm's profitability and return on investment. It captures many facets of a firm's operating, investing, and financing characteristics. In Chapter 19, ROE is used as a key input in an accounting-based valuation model.

---

[32]Recall that assets = liabilities (debt) + equity.

[33]Selling and Stickney (1990) disaggregate ROE as follows:

$$\text{ROE} = \text{ROA} \times \text{Assets/Equity} \times \text{Net Income/Operating Income}$$

The terms to the right of ROA are clearly measures of financial leverage. Because the assets/equity ratio (capital structure leverage) discussed earlier will always be greater than 1, its effect is to increase ROE relative to ROA. The ratio of net income to operating income (the common earnings leverage) is the inverse of the financial leverage and will always be less than 1, tending to drive ROE below ROA. Whether ROE is greater or less than ROA depends on whether the positive effects of capital structure leverage outweigh the negative effect of earnings leverage; do the returns on all assets that accrue to common shareholders (capital structure leverage effects) exceed the cost of external financing (common earnings leverage)?

[34]This model was originated by duPont. See C. A. Kline, Jr. and H. L. Hissler, "The duPont Chart System for Appraising Operating Performance," *NACA Bulletin* (August 1953).

EXHIBIT 4-14. PFIZER INC. AND SUBSIDIARY COMPANIES
Disaggregation of Return on Equity (After Tax)

A. Three-Component Disaggregation of ROE

	(Profitability	×	Turnover)			×	Solvency	=	ROE
	Net Income / Sales	×	Sales / Average Total Assets	=	Net Income / Average Total Assets	×	Average Total Assets / Average Common Equity	=	Net Income / Average Common Equity
1995	15.51%	×	0.84	=	13.05%	×	2.42	=	31.62%
1996	17.88%	×	0.73	=	13.08%	×	2.17	=	28.31%
1997	18.92%	×	0.76	=	14.31%	×	1.96	=	28.11%
1998	14.41%	×	0.81	=	11.73%	×	1.99	=	23.32%
1999	19.74%	×	0.83	=	16.46%	×	2.20	=	36.15%
Average	17.29%	×	0.80	=	13.72%	×	2.15	=	29.50%

B. Five-Component Disaggregation of ROE

				(Profitability	×	Turnover)			×	Solvency	=	ROE
Effects of:	Taxes		Financing	Operations								
	Net Income / EBT	×	EBT / EBIT	×	EBIT / Sales	=	Net Income / Sales	×	Sales / Average Total Assets	=	Net Income / Average Total Assets	×	Average Total Assets / Average Common Equity	=	Net Income / Average Common Equity
1995	0.68	×	0.92	×	24.79%	=	15.51%	×	0.84	=	13.05%	×	2.42	=	31.62%
1996	0.70	×	0.94	×	27.25%	=	17.88%	×	0.73	=	13.08%	×	2.17	=	28.31%
1997	0.73	×	0.95	×	27.28%	=	18.92%	×	0.76	=	14.31%	×	1.96	=	28.11%
1998	0.75	×	0.95	×	20.21%	=	14.41%	×	0.81	=	11.73%	×	1.99	=	23.32%
1999	0.72	×	0.95	×	28.88%	=	19.74%	×	0.83	=	16.46%	×	2.20	=	36.15%
Average	0.72	×	0.94	×	25.68%	=	17.29%	×	0.80	=	13.72%	×	2.15	=	29.50%

Given its importance, it is worthwhile asking whether current ROE can be used to forecast future ROE levels. A related question is whether abnormally high levels of profitability can be expected to continue into the future. Figure 4-3, from Penman (1991), provides some insight into these questions.[35] The following points are apparent from the graph:

1. In the short term, approximating five years (except for the extreme portfolios), current levels of ROE persist into the future.
2. Over the long term, ROEs tend to revert toward an average "economywide" ROE.
3. Although there is a trend toward the mean, the portfolio rankings persist. That is, the portfolios with higher (lower) ROE tend to have higher (lower) ROEs in the future; however, the differences between the portfolios narrow.

---

[35]Penman ranked firms (each year in the 1969–1985 period) by ROE and formed 20 equal-sized portfolios based on those rankings. He then remeasured the average ROE of those portfolios for the next 15 years. Figure 4-3 presents the trend in ROE for eight (the highest, lowest, and three others above and below the median ROE portfolio) of those portfolios.

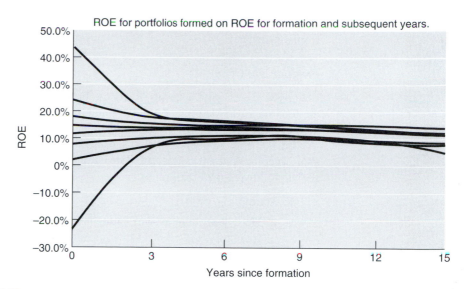

FIGURE 4-3 ROE for portfolios formed on ROE for formation and subsequent years. *Source*: Based on (eight) selected portfolios from Stephen H. Penman, "An Evaluation of Accounting Rate-of-Return," *Journal of Accounting, Auditing & Finance*, Spring 1991, pp. 233–256, Table 1, p. 238.

Similar results were reported by Nissim and Penman (1999) for a measure[36] of ROA. Over time, the ratio tended toward a mean level, but relative rankings persisted.

Looking at components of ROA, asset turnover, and profit margin, Nissim and Penman found that these also tended to rapidly converge toward a mean level (within three years). Interestingly, Fairfield and Yohn (1999) found that although *neither levels* of asset turnover nor profit margins could be used to forecast trends, *changes* in the asset turnover ratio were good predictors of future trends in turnover ratios as well as profit margins (and consequently measures of ROI).

Economic Characteristics and Strategies

Ratios are not randomly distributed among companies; management strategy, industry characteristics, and product life cycle all are reflected in a firm's ratios. In this section, we examine these influences.

Competing Strategies[37]

Firms (and industries) can often be differentiated by whether they employ a high-turnover/low-margin strategy or a low-turnover/high-margin strategy to generate profits. The high-turnover/low-margin firm sells large volumes at low prices and profit margins; to be successful, the firm must carefully control costs. The firm must also control investment to achieve an acceptable ROI. The supermarket industry generally follows this strategy.

The low-turnover/high-margin firm, in contrast, competes on the basis of attributes other than price (quality or product differentiation). If successful, the firm is able to charge a high price, generating higher profit margins. Cost control is less important when costs can be passed on to the customer through higher prices. Specialty (gourmet) food

[36]To be precise, they used RNOA (return on net operating assets), where net operating assets essentially equal operating assets (accounts receivable, inventory, prepaid expenses, property, plant, and equipment) less operating liabilities (trade payables and accrued operating expenses).

[37]Much of the discussion of economic characteristics and strategies is based on Thomas Selling and Clyde P. Stickney, "The Effects of Business Environment and Strategy on a Firm's Rate of Return on Assets," *Financial Analysts Journal* (January–February 1989), pp. 43–52.

shops would follow this strategy by offering goods and services not generally available from supermarkets.

Product Life Cycle

The *product life cycle* concept affects the firm's financial performance as it passes through the four stages in the cycle. Figure 4-1 and our discussion of asset turnover ratios is one example of such an analysis.

Savich and Thompson (1978) discuss the impact of product cycle stages on balance sheet, income statement, and cash flow components. Based on their discussion, we expect to see the following pattern of ratios:

1. Startup
   a. High short-term activity ratios but low liquidity ratios. Although seemingly contradictory, these reflect low inventory and receivable levels; the company is cash hungry and cannot build these elements of working capital.
   b. Profits and cash from operations are very low (or even negative). Thus, all ratios—profitability, solvency, and liquidity—with these components in the numerator will tend to be poor.
   c. Debt (both short- and long-term) will be high.

2. Growth
   a. Profits grow, but cash from operations lags; cash receipts are based on past sales levels, whereas disbursements are geared toward higher expected sales levels. Thus, ratios based on income tend to improve prior to those based on cash flows.
   b. Investment in capacity also rises, decreasing long-term activity (turnover) ratios. At the same time, expansion in productive capacity delays the full benefit of operating leverage; fixed costs remain high relative to sales. Profits and ROA, as a result, remain low. Debt ratios remain high. At later stages, these ratios will approach the pattern typical of the maturity stage.

3. Maturity

4. Decline (Harvest)
   a. The firm reaches its optimal operating levels, and ratios approach industry norms. Profit margins and turnover ratios are high. Debt declines relative to equity as retained earnings grow; funds are not needed for expansion. Liquidity is high, as CFO has caught up with profits.
   b. As the firm begins the decline (harvest) stage, cash flows resulting from past investments remain positive even when current profits decline. Moreover, with a reduced asset base, ROA peaks as the firm enters this last stage.

The product life cycle concept, although providing some useful insights, can be overrated. The concept is primarily product based. Successful firms build a portfolio of products, continually introducing new ones; at any one time, a firm will most likely have products at each stage of the cycle. The stage of the firm depends on the stage of the preponderance of its products. Figure 4-4, from the cover of Pfizer's *1990 Annual Report*, provides a good illustration of this concept.

It is instructive to review Pfizer's major products nine years later. In its 1999 annual report, Pfizer states that seven drugs exceeded sales of $1 billion: Norvasc, Cardura, Zithromax, Diflucan, Zoloft, Viagra, and Zyrtec. The first five of these are shown in Figure 4-4, and in 1990 all five were in the startup or pre-startup portion of the graph. Viagra was introduced in 1998 and Zyrtec licensed from another company.

Procardia XL, an important Pfizer product in the 1990s, was still in its growth phase in 1990. The 1999 10-K report states that:

> Sales of Procardia XL continued to decrease during 1999, due, at least in part, to the medical community's increasing emphasis on Norvasc.

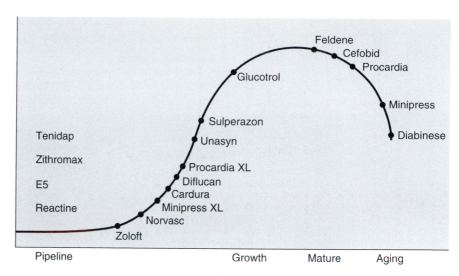

FIGURE 4–4 Illustration of product life cycle.

Interindustry Economic Factors

Our earlier discussion of common-size statements and Exhibit 4-2 demonstrate that *industry norm* ratios reflect industry characteristics. Gombola and Ketz (1983) compared the means of 58 ratios for two broad-based industry classifications: manufacturing and retail firms. Finding differences in ROA, activity ratios, and profit margins, they stated that

> All of the income measures expressed as a percentage of sales are much smaller for retail firms than manufacturing firms. All of the turnover ratios show much higher values for retail firms than for manufacturing firms. Retail firms also tend to show less cash and fewer receivables than manufacturing firms as well as somewhat more debt than manufacturing firms.[38]

Selling and Stickney examined ROAs for 22 industries over the period 1977 to 1986 as well as the components that make up ROA. Their results are plotted in Figure 4-5. They noted that the same overall ROA (represented by the lines in Figure 4-5) can result from an infinite number of different combinations of turnover and return on sales. For example, both the real estate and apparel industries have ROAs of 6.3%. The relative components (i.e., turnover ratios and profit margins), however, differ significantly. As indicated by their different locations along the turnover and profit margin axes, the real estate industry has high profit margins (12%) but low turnover (< 1.00), whereas the apparel industry has profit margins in the 3% range but higher turnover (> 2.00).

They explained these differences by distinguishing between capital-intensive and noncapital-intensive industries. Capital-intensive industries tend to have low asset turnover and higher fixed costs. As a result, profit margins can fluctuate greatly due to the effects of operating leverage.

Competitive Factors. The microeconomics literature classifies firms' operating environments as ranging from monopolistic at one extreme to pure competition at the other. Monopolistic industries are characterized by high barriers to entry, high capital intensity, and high profit margins. High capital intensity results in low turnover ratios and "monopoly" profits. In addition, barriers to entry, whether a result of regulation, technology, or capital requirements, also give rise to monopoly profits. Pure competition, on the other hand, is characterized by low barriers to entry, low levels of capital intensity, and correspondingly low profit margins. Products are commodity-like in nature and product differentiation is limited.

---

[38]Michael J. Gombola and J. Edward Ketz, "Financial Ratio Patterns in Retail and Manufacturing Organizations," *Financial Management* (Summer 1983), pp. 46–56.

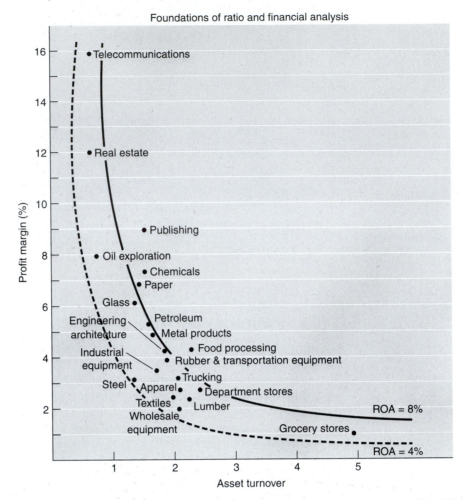

FIGURE 4-5 ROAs of sample firms, 1977–1986. *Source*: Thomas Selling and Clyde Stickney, "The Effects of Business Environment and Strategy on a Firm's Rate of Return on Assets," *Financial Analysts Journal* (January–February 1989), pp. 43–52, Fig. 1, p. 48.

Companies in highly competitive industries attempt to generate higher returns through increased efficiency and turnover.

Oligopolistic or multifirm industries have turnover ratios and profit margins at the midpoint of the continuum. Selling and Stickney summarize the argument with the following table:

Capital Intensity	Nature of Competition	Strategy
High	Monopoly	High profit margin
Medium	Oligopolistic	Combination of profit margin and turnover
Low	Pure competition	High turnover

Source: Thomas Selling and Clyde Stickney, "The Effects of Business Environment and Strategy on a Firm's Rate of Return on Assets," *Financial Analysts Journal* (January–February 1989), pp. 43–52, Table II on p. 47 (adapted).

Classification and Selection of Ratios

The ratios discussed in this chapter are by no means exhaustive, and a full list of the ratios available (and used) in our four categories would include nearly 100 different ratios. One possible reason for the proliferation of ratios is that ratio analysis is used not only in (external) financial analysis but also as a tool in internal management analysis and evaluation.

Ratios designed for managerial analysis may not add information to those already used for financial analysis, as the needs of these two types of users are not the same. Management needs detailed information to pinpoint and remedy specific problem areas. The financial analyst's needs, however, are more general and thus may be satisfied with a ratio that captures the effects of other ratios or is highly correlated with other ratios. Unfortunately, once a ratio is developed for one purpose, it tends to be used in ways never intended. Ratio analysis is an area where more is not necessarily better.

Much empirical work on ratios has been descriptive: to examine the properties of and correlations among the ratios available in an attempt to find a manageable set of ratios suitable for analytical purposes. The benefit of collinearity among ratios for financial analysis is a reduction in the number of ratios that must be computed and monitored. The reduced set can be used for decision making directly[39] or as a signal that more detailed analysis is required.

Using a small subset of ratios to represent the whole set requires choosing ratios that are both:

1. Highly correlated with those ratios excluded, and
2. Not correlated with the other ratios in the subset

Condition 1 ensures that any information available from excluded ratios is captured, whereas condition 2 ensures no overlap and hence maximum information provided by the ratios included.

Academic studies[40] have attempted to identify ratio subsets that meet these conditions. Multivariate statistical analysis tools such as factor analysis and principal components have been used to partition ratios into groups and to find representative ratios for each group that meet the two conditions listed above. Each of these partitions is assumed to be affected by an underlying factor, the nature of which is not specified by the statistical model. Rather, the researcher, after examining the ratios grouped in a given partition, attempts to find the unifying theme descriptive of the ratios in the group.

Interestingly, the results on the whole found that ratios grouped themselves along factors consistent (e.g., Return on Investment, Liquidity, Solvency, Short- and Long-term Activity) with classifications used in our earlier discussions. Thus, the analyst could choose one representative ratio from each grouping to convey the information available within that grouping, thereby reducing the ratios monitored from 100 to a more manageable seven or eight.

Moreover, researchers who included cash ratios in their pool of ratios also tended to find a cash flow and cash expenditure factor that did not group with the other classifications, suggesting that cash flow information is incremental to that provided by the other ratios. These results are consistent with our view that ratios based on income/expense flows should also be examined on a cash flow basis.

EARNINGS PER SHARE AND OTHER RATIOS USED IN VALUATION

Ratios are often used explicitly or implicitly for securities valuation. Equity valuation models use ratios such as earnings per share and book value per share. Fixed-income ratings and valuation techniques also lean heavily on ratios. This section introduces the ratios used in these models; their use in ratings and valuation models is discussed in Chapters 18 and 19.

Earnings per Share

Earnings per share (EPS) is probably the most widely available and commonly used corporate performance statistic for publicly traded firms. It is used to compare operating performance and for valuation purposes either directly or together with market prices in the

---

[39]A second empirical approach (described in Chapter 18) uses these results to identify ratios as inputs in specific predictive models of risk in the analysis of bankruptcy, bond ratings, and beta (equity risk).

[40]Unfortunately, interest in this line of research has waned over time and results available are based on studies carried out mostly in the 1970s and 1980s [e.g., Pinches et al. (1975), Johnson (1979), Chen and Shimerda (1981), and Gombola and Ketz (1983)]. Notwithstanding the above, the results would tend to be robust over various time periods.

familiar form of price/earnings (P/E) ratios. The EPS and P/E ratios are reported in the business section of many newspapers.

Unlike other ratios discussed in this chapter, however, the calculation of EPS is mandated by GAAP. SFAS 128 (1997) governs EPS reporting in the United States; the discussion below summarizes the important issues.[41] IAS 33 (1997) governs EPS reporting under international accounting standards. As the two standards were developed together, the computational requirements are identical. Appendix 4-B provides details on these reporting requirements.

Simple Capital Structure

For firms that have only common shares, the computation of EPS is relatively straightforward. In such cases, the computation is

$$\text{Basic EPS} = \frac{\textbf{Earnings Available for Common Shares}}{\textbf{Weighted-Average Common Shares Outstanding}}$$

or

$$\frac{\textbf{Net Income} - \textbf{Preferred Dividends}}{\textbf{Weighted Average Common Shares Outstanding}}$$

where the shares are usually weighted by the number of months those shares were outstanding.[42] The numerator used to calculate EPS must equal earnings available for distribution to common shareholders. Therefore, preferred stock dividends, whether declared or cumulative, must be deducted from net income. Contingent shares must be included once the conditions required for their issue have been met.[43]

Complex Capital Structure

Companies whose capital structures include options or convertible securities (preferred shares and debt) are said to have complex capital structures. *These firms must recognize the potential effect on EPS upon conversion of those securities if such a conversion will result in dilution (lowering) of EPS.* These firms must report two EPS numbers:

1. Basic EPS as calculated above
2. Diluted earnings per share (DEPS) to reflect the potential dilution due to options and convertible securities on the number of shares outstanding as well as income available for common shareholders

$$\text{DEPS} = \frac{\textbf{Adjusted Income Available for Common Shares}}{\textbf{Weighted-Average Common and Potential Common Shares Outstanding}}$$

The adjustments to the numerator reflect the fact that if the convertible securities were converted to common shares, interest and (preferred) dividend payments would no longer have

---

[41]SFAS 129 (1997) requires disclosures related to the EPS computation and capital structure, including:

1. Rights and provisions of all outstanding securities, including debt, common and preferred shares, options, and warrants
2. Number of shares issued during the period due to conversions, exercises, and contingent issuances
3. Liquidating value of preferred shares when significantly greater than par value or stated amount
4. Call and redemption provisions for preferred shares
5. Redemption requirements by year for the next five years
6. Dividend arrears for cumulative preferred shares

[42]EPS calculations may also be based on daily or weekly weighting.

[43]Contingent shares are sometimes issued to the previous owners of acquired companies when sales or profitability targets are met.

to be made to those security holders, increasing the amount available to common shareholders. Numerator adjustments therefore include

1. Dividends on convertible preferred shares
2. Interest (after-tax) on convertible debt
3. Effect of the change resulting from 1 and 2 on profit sharing or other expenses[44]

Adjustments for Options and Warrants

Options and warrants are also a source of potential dilution. For these instruments, assumptions must be made with respect to:

- Whether the conversion or exercise will actually take place, and
- How the proceeds of exercise will be used

To calculate the dilutive impact of options and warrants on EPS, the *Treasury stock method* is used. This method assumes that the proceeds from exercise are used by the firm to (re)purchase common shares on the open market at the average market price (MP). As long as MP is greater than the exercise price (EP), the effect will be dilutive and the options and warrants will affect DEPS calculations. *The denominator of the EPS ratio is adjusted by adding the incremental (I) shares equal to*

$$I = \frac{MP - EP}{MP} \times N$$

where N equals the number of shares issuable on exercise. No adjustment is made to the numerator.

Example of EPS Computation. An actual earnings per share computation is shown in Exhibit 4-15. Note that the effects of the options and convertible bonds enter the calculation of DEPS only. For the options, only the denominator is adjusted and the effect will always be dilutive. For the convertible bonds, adjustments are made to both the numerator and denominator and the effect may not always be dilutive. Only when it is dilutive, as in this case, are convertible securities included in the calculation.

Limitations of EPS Calculations

The following limitations of EPS as a measure of profitability should be considered before using that ratio for valuation or comparison purposes:

- The assumptions behind the Treasury stock method are unrealistic; they mirror the actual impact of exercise only in rare cases.
- EPS growth rates can be distorted by a firm's dividend and financing policies. Firms with lower dividend payout ratios will show higher EPS growth rates than firms with higher payout ratios (see Chapter 19 for further discussion of this point).

Cash Flow per Share

Cash flow per share is calculated using CFO as the numerator. Computed in this manner, it reports on the cash-generating ability of the firm. Like all summary measures, cash flow per share should be used with caution. CFO/share suffers from the following problems:

- Variability from year to year
- Dependence on accounting methods
- Does not reflect cash needed for required debt payments
- Does not reflect cash required for maintenance of productive capacity

---

[44]The reduction in interest expense from the assumed conversion of convertible debt increases income, and, therefore, might increase profit sharing, royalties, or other expenses based on income.

EXHIBIT 4-15
Computation of Earnings per Share

Assumptions

2000	Net income	$500,000
	Average common shares	100,000
	Tax rate	40%
Convertible bond, issued July 1, 2000:		
	Face amount	$1,000,000
	Coupon rate	8% (semiannual)
	Conversion terms	25 shares per $1,000 bond
Options on common stock, issued December 31, 1999:		
	Number of shares	25,000
	Exercise price	$25 per share
	Average price during 2000	$27.50 per share

Computations

$$\text{Basic EPS} = \frac{\$500,000}{100,000} = \$5.00$$

$$\text{Diluted EPS} = \frac{(\$500,000 + \$24,000^A)}{(100,000 + 12,500^B + 2,273^C)} = \$4.57$$

The adjustments are:

- Convertible bond (for six months):

^{A}interest (net of taxes) of $24,000.

^{B}$1,000,000/$1,000 × 25 = 25,000; 12,500 additional common shares for six months.

- Options:

$$^C\text{Incremental shares} = \frac{\text{MP}-\text{EP}}{\text{MP}} \times \text{N} = \frac{\$27.50 - \$25}{\$27.50} \times 25,000$$

$$= 2,273 \text{ additional common shares*†}$$

Diluted earnings per share are 8.6% below primary EPS.

*2,273 incremental shares are added to the denominator because SFAS 128 requires the use of the average market price in the application of the treasury stock method for options.

†For options issued under nonqualified plans, the exercise proceeds are increased by the tax benefits realized by the firm when options are exercised. Dilution is therefore reduced as more shares are deemed to be repurchased.

In the late 1990s the concept of "cash EPS" was promoted as a performance measure. Proponents argued that amortization of goodwill and other intangible assets, the write-off of purchased "in-process research and development," charges related to stock compensation plans, and other noncash charges should be added back to reported earnings. We view cash EPS as part of the effort to justify high price/earnings ratios and believe that it lacks any analytical basis.

EBITDA per Share

Earnings before interest, taxes, depreciation, and amortization (EBITDA) is computed by adding depreciation and amortization expense to earnings before interest and taxes (EBIT). It is often used as a measure of cash flow, but suffers from many limitations in that it ignores

- Variations in accounting methods
- Cash required for working capital
- Debt service and other fixed-charge requirements
- The need to maintain productive capacity

For these reasons, it should not be used blindly for valuation purposes.

Book Value per Share

This ratio represents the equity of the firm (common equity less preferred shares at liquidation value) on a per-share basis (number of shares outstanding at balance sheet date) and is sometimes used as a benchmark for comparisons with the market price per share. As discussed in Chapter 19, work by Ohlson (1995) has renewed interest in book value (and the price-to-book ratio) as an input in accounting-based valuation models.

Book value per share, however, has limitations as a valuation tool as it is subject to valuation measures based on GAAP

- That are bound by historical cost rather than current market value conditions, and
- Whose definition of what constitutes an asset or liability may not coincide with economic reality

Thus, the balance sheet may contain goodwill or other intangible assets of uncertain value; the market value of investments and fixed assets may differ markedly from the balance sheet valuation and there may be significant adjustments for off-balance-sheet activities. Adjustments to book value are considered in detail in Chapter 17.

Price-to-Earnings and Price-to-Book-Value Ratios

The P/E ratio measures the degree to which the market capitalizes a firm's earnings. The P/E ratio has been the subject of much scrutiny in the academic as well as the professional world. Its theoretical underpinnings, empirical behavior, and relationship to the price-to-book-value ratio are discussed in greater detail in Chapter 19.

Book value per share and its relationship to price in the form of the price-to-book (P/B) ratios has received recent attention in the finance and accounting literature. The Ohlson (1995) valuation model noted above is one reason. Additionally, Fama and French (1992) found that the P/B ratio (along with size) was the best predictor of future stock returns. Firms with low P/B ratios subsequently had consistently higher returns than firms with high P/B ratios. We discuss this research further in Chapters 18 and 19.

Dividend Payout Ratio

The dividend payout ratio equals the percentage of earnings paid out as dividends, that is,

$$\text{Dividend Payout} = \text{Dividends/Net Income}$$

Generally, growth firms have low dividend payout ratios as they retain most of their income to finance future expansion. More established, mature firms tend to have higher payout ratios.

PATTERNS OF RATIO DISCLOSURE AND USE

Before concluding this chapter, we remind the reader that the definitions and classifications of ratios we have presented are not set in stone. The proper definition of a ratio is not mandated, and there is wide diversity in practice regarding definition, relative importance, and even the categorization of particular ratios (do turnover ratios measure activity, liquidity, or profitability?). This section presents some evidence regarding

- How analysts classify and rank ratios
- Which ratios are most commonly disclosed by firms

Perceived Importance and Classification

Gibson (1987) asked 52 CFA© (Chartered Financial Analyst) charterholders to classify a set of 60 ratios in terms of whether they measure profitability, liquidity, or debt and to rank (on a scale of 0 to 9) their relative importance. The analysts agreed on the classification of very few ratios (net profit margin before and after tax and the current, cash, and quick ratios). They gave profitability ratios the highest significance rating of any classification category, followed by debt and then liquidity ratios.

Disclosure of Ratios and Motivation

Ratios are readily derived from financial statement information. There is rarely any explicit disclosure requirement. When firms do disclose ratios, the chosen ratios are consistent with those perceived to be most important by the analysts. That is, ROA, ROE, profit margins, and the debt-to-equity ratio are disclosed most often. However, Gibson (1982) documented the wide disparity in ratio definitions across a sample of 100 annual reports.

Williamson (1984) examined the 1978 annual reports of 141 Fortune 500 firms for voluntary disclosure of ratios. His purpose was to test whether firms engaged in selective disclosure; that is, were the ratio values of reporting companies significantly different from (better than) those of nonreporting companies?

Williamson found evidence of selective disclosure for the three ratios (ROE, current ratio, and return on sales) that had the highest frequency of voluntary disclosure. Williamson's results also provide indirect evidence that the industry norm is a relevant benchmark. His strongest results were consistent with the hypothesis that firms tend to disclose a ratio voluntarily when that ratio exceeds the industry norm.

SUMMARY

This chapter provides an overview of ratios most commonly used in the analysis of financial statements. These ratios, classified as activity, liquidity, solvency, and profitability indicators, are designed to measure different aspects of a firm's operating, investment, and financing activities. Ratios are used to standardize financial statements across firms and over time, facilitating comparative analysis. Ratios also provide insight into firm performance and economic relationships when evaluated in an integrated analysis.

Ratio analysis is not intended to provide all the answers about a firm, but rather to point to the relevant questions. Throughout the remainder of this book, we will address the questions raised by these ratios and show how an understanding of the accounting process facilitates their use.

Chapter 4

Problems

(*General Note*: For ratios that are generally calculated on average data, use year-end data when prior-year information is not available.)

1. [Transaction effects on ratios; CFA© adapted] A company's current ratio is 2.0. The company uses some of its cash to retire notes payable that are due within one year.

a. Describe the effect of this transaction on the company's

   (i) Current ratio

   (ii) Asset turnover ratio

   (iii) Cash burn ratio

   (iv) Debt-to-equity ratio

b. Redo part a assuming that the company's current ratio was 0.8 at the time of the transaction.

(Problems 4-2 and 4-3 are based on the financial statements of Walt Disney in Exhibit 4P-1.)

2. [Ratio calculations; CFA© adapted] Calculate the ratios below for Disney at September 30, 2000 (use ending balance sheet amounts). Briefly explain the use of each of these ratios in the evaluation of a company's operations:

   (i) Accounts receivable turnover

   (ii) Total asset turnover

   (iii) Current ratio

   (iv) CFO to current liabilities

   (v) Debt to equity

   (vi) Times interest earned

   (vii) Operating income to sales

EXHIBIT 4P-1. THE WALT DISNEY COMPANY
Selected Financial Statement and Other Data, Years Ending September 30 (in $millions)

	2000	1997
Income Statement		
Revenue	$25,402	$22,473
Operating expenses	(22,554)	(18,161)
Operating income	$ 2,848	$ 4,312
Other	236	(232)
Interest expense	(558)	(693)
Pretax income	$ 2,526	$ 3,387
Income tax expense	(1,606)	(1,421)
Net income	$ 920	$ 1,966
Balance Sheet		
Cash	$ 842	$ 317
Receivables	3,599	3,726
Inventories	702	942
Film and television costs	3,606	4,401
Other	1,258	
Current assets	$10,007	$ 9,386
Investments	2,270	1,897
Property, plant, and equipment	12,310	8,951
Other	20,440	17,542
Total assets	$45,027	$37,776
Current liabilities	$ 8,402	$ 7,744
Borrowings	6,959	11,068
Other liabilities	5,566	17,285
Stockholders' equity	24,100	1,679
Total liabilities and equity	$45,027	$37,776
Cash flow from operations	$ 6,434	$ 7,064

Source: Walt Disney annual reports, 1997 and 2000.

(viii) Return on sales

(ix) Return on assets

3. [duPont model; CFA© adapted]

a. Using the duPont method, identify and calculate the five primary components of Disney's return on equity for each of the two fiscal years ended September 30, 1997 and September 30, 2000. Using these components, calculate Disney's return on equity for each year.

b. Identify the components that contributed most to the observed change in Disney's return on equity from 1997 to 2000. State two reasons for the observed change in each of these components.

(Problems 4-4 to 4-6 are based on the financial statements of Brown Company; see Exhibit 4P-2).

4. [Ratio calculation; CFA© adapted] Calculate the following ratios for 2002:

a. Activity ratios

   (i) Inventory turnover

   (ii) Accounts receivable turnover

   (iii) Fixed asset turnover

   (iv) Total asset turnover

b. Liquidity ratios

   (i) Length of operating cycle

   (ii) Length of cash cycle

   (iii) Current ratio

   (iv) Quick ratio

   (v) Cash ratio

   (vi) Defensive interval

c. Solvency ratios

   (i) Debt to equity

   (ii) Debt to capital

   (iii) Times interest earned

d. Profitability ratios

   (i) Gross margin

   (ii) Operating income to sales

   (iii) Return on sales

   (iv) Return on assets

   (v) Return on equity

EXHIBIT 4P-2. BROWN COMPANY
Financial Data, 2001–2002

Income Statement *Year Ending December 31*			*Balance Sheet* *as of December 31*		
	2001	2002		2001	2002
Sales	$12,000	$19,000	*Assets*		
Cost of goods sold	7,200	12,000	Cash	$ 2,000	$ 2,200
Depreciation expense	1,200	1,500	Accounts receivable	3,000	3,500
SG&A expense	700	1,000	Inventory	4,000	4,200
Interest expense	1,300	1,200	Current assets	$ 9,000	$ 9,900
Income before taxes	$ 1,600	$ 3,300	Fixed assets at cost	22,000	24,300
Income tax expense	700	1,440	Accumulated depreciation	(9,000)	(10,500)
Net Income	$ 900	$ 1,860	Net fixed assets	$13,000	$ 13,800
			Total assets	$22,000	$ 23,700
			Liabilities and Equity		
			Accrued expenses	$ 1,600	$1,760
			Accounts payable	2,400	2,640
			Current liabilities	$ 4,000	$ 4,400
			Notes payable	11,000	11,800
			Long-term debt	4,000	3,204
			Common stock	2,000	2,300
			Retained earnings	1,000	1,996
			Total liabilities and equity	$22,000	$ 23,700

5. [Disaggregation of ROE] Disaggregate the 2002 return on equity of Brown Company using the three-component and five-component models.

6. [Operating and financial leverage; effects of growth]

a. Estimate Brown Company's fixed and variable costs.

b. Estimate Brown Company's operating, financial, and total leverage effects for 2001 and 2002.

c. Discuss how the company's rapid growth in 2002 may have distorted the estimates calculated in parts a and b.

(Problems 4-7 and 4-8 are based on the common-size statements presented in Exhibit 4P-3.)

7. [Common-size statements—ratios] Using the common-size statements of Company 1 in Exhibit 4P-3, calculate the following ratios:

  (i) Inventory turnover
  (ii) Receivable turnover
  (iii) Length of operating cycle
  (iv) Length of cash cycle
  (v) Fixed asset turnover ratio
  (vi) Cash ratio
  (vii) Quick ratio
  (viii) Current ratio
  (ix) Debt to equity
  (x) Interest coverage
  (xi) EBIT/sales
  (xii) Sales/assets
  (xiii) EBIT/assets
  (xiv) EBT/assets

  (xv) Assets/equity
  (xvi) EBT/equity

(*Hint:* Ratios for which one component is derived from the balance sheet and the other from the income statement can be calculated by making use of the asset turnover ratio, which is given in Exhibit 4P-3.)

8. [Ratio analysis—industry characteristics] The nine companies in Exhibit 4P-3 are drawn from the following nine industries:

  (i) Aerospace
  (ii) Airline
  (iii) Chemicals and drugs
  (iv) Computer software
  (v) Consumer foods
  (vi) Department stores
  (vii) Consumer finance
  (viii) Newspaper publishing
  (ix) Electric utility

a. Based on the common-size statements, match each company to its industry.

b. Briefly discuss the balance sheet and income statement characteristics that enabled you to identify the industry to which each company belonged.

9. [CFA© adapted] Discuss two uses of common-size financial statements for financial analysis.

10. [Ratio calculations] By calculating some ratios based on the average of opening and closing balances, we make the implicit

EXHIBIT 4P-3
Common-Size Balance Sheets

Company	1	2	3	4	5	6	7	8	9
Cash and short-term investments	2%	13%	37%	1%	1%	3%	1%	22%	6%
Receivables	17	8	22	28	23	5	11	16	8
Inventory	15	52	15	23	14	2	2	0	5
Other current assets	6	0	5	1	4	2	2	1	0
Current assets	40%	73%	79%	53%	42%	12%	16%	39%	19%
Gross property	86	40	26	44	63	112	65	1	106
Less: accumulated depreciation	(50)	(19)	(8)	(15)	(23)	(45)	(28)	(0)	(34)
Net property	36%	21%	18%	29%	40%	67%	37%	1%	72%
Investments	3	1	0	0	3	14	16	55	0
Intangibles and other	21	5	3	18	15	7	31	5	9
Total assets	100%	100%	100%	100%	100%	100%	100%	100%	100%
Trade payables	11	21	22	13	26	7	11	NA	20
Debt payable	4	0	3	6	4	6	2	46	4
Other current liabilities	9	43	0	0	1	4	1	16	8
Current liabilities	24%	64%	25%	19%	31%	17%	14%	62%	32%
Long-term debt	20	5	12	27	23	34	24	27	21
Other liabilities	16	0	1	21	16	12	13	5	12
Total liabilities	60%	69%	38%	67%	70%	63%	51%	94%	65%
Equity	40	31	62	33	30	37	49	6	35
Total liabilities and equity	100%	100%	100%	100%	100%	100%	100%	100%	100%

NA = Not available.

Common-Size Income Statements

Company	1	2	3	4	5	6	7	8	9
Revenues	100%	100%	100%	100%	100%	100%	100%	100%	100%
Cost of goods sold	58	81	58	63	52	0	59	0	0
Operating expenses	21	7	24	28	33	84	29	55	91
Research and development	7	5	9	0	1	NA	0	0	0
Advertising	3	0	3	2	5	NA	NA	0	2
Operating income	11%	7%	6%	7%	9%	16%	12%	45%	7%
Net interest expense (income)	1	(1)	0	2	2	6	3	41	1
Income from continuing operatings before tax	10%	8%	6%	5%	7%	10%	9%	4%	6%
Asset turnover ratio	0.96	1.12	0.94	1.38	1.82	0.45	0.96	0.15	0.96

NA = Not available.

assumption that changes in these accounts occurred uniformly throughout the year. Sometimes, however, the actual change occurs unevenly, perhaps due to an acquisition. In such cases, ratios based on averages will be distorted. Discuss how you would calculate the return on assets ratio if the growth in assets occurred:

(i) At the beginning of the year

(ii) At the end of the first quarter

(iii) At the end of the second quarter

(iv) At the end of the fourth quarter

11. [Financial and operating leverage; CFA© adapted] Company F's and Company O's financial and operating leverage differ. Explain how it is possible for the two companies to have the same total leverage. In your answer, be sure to define financial, operating, and total leverage.

12. [ROE components; CFA© adapted] Using the following financial ratios for the RAMI Company, calculate its return on equity:

- Net profit margin   5.5%
- Asset turnover   2.0
- Dividend payout ratio   31.8%
- Equity turnover (sales/equity) 4.2

13. [Liquidity and activity ratios—balance sheet forecasting] You have been asked to project next year's working capital requirements of the OB Company. The company's sales forecast for next year is $12 million. OB's target ratios are:

Gross profit margin	45%	Cash ratio	1.2 times
Inventory turnover	6 times	Cash cycle	45 days
Receivables turnover	12 times		

Use the sales forecast and target ratios to forecast each of the following elements of OB's balance sheet:

(i) Inventory

(ii) Accounts receivable

(iii) Accounts payable

(iv) Cash

(v) Current ratio

Assume that beginning and ending A/R, A/P, and inventory are equal. (The latter also implies COGS equals purchases.) Furthermore, assume A/P is the company's only current liability.

14. [Ratio calculations] You have been provided with the following ratios and other indicators of RSEF Inc.:

Asset turnover (sales/assets)	3.5
Return on equity	56.3%
Tax rate	20%
Net income/sales	10%
Accounts payable turnover	13.5
Accounts receivable turnover	6
Interest/sales	4%
Operating cycle	80 days

Using the data provided above, compute RSEF's:

(i) Inventory turnover

(ii) Cash cycle

(iii) Financial leverage (assets/equity)

(iv) Return on assets

(v) Interest coverage ratio

15. [Liquidity analysis] The working capital accounts of Queen Chana, a retailer, are as follows:

Year	2001	2002	2003
Cash	$1,000	$ 1,500	$ 2,000
Accounts receivable	2,000	4,000	6,000
Inventory	2,000	4,500	8,000
Current assets	$5,000	$10,000	$16,000
Accounts payable	2,000	3,500	4,500
Short-term debt	500	1,500	3,500
Current liabilities	$2,500	$ 5,000	$ 8,000

a. For years 2001 to 2003, calculate Queen Chana's:

(i) Current ratio

(ii) Quick ratio

(iii) Cash ratio

b. Describe the other useful indicators of the firm's liquidity that can be calculated from the data given.

c. Using the results of parts a and b, discuss the limitations of the current ratio as a measure of liquidity.

d. List other ratios that would be useful to confirm your analysis. State what you would expect these ratios to show.

16. [Cash cycle for e-commerce company] The following information was taken from Amazon's 1999–2000 annual reports. Like many e-commerce retailers, Amazon.com has had difficulty in generating profits and/or operating cash flows (all amounts in $millions):

Years Ended December 31

	1998	1999	2000
Inventory	$ 30	$ 221	$ 171
Accounts payable	113	463	485
Cost of goods sold		1,349	2,106

Note: Amazon.com has no accounts receivable.

a. Calculate purchases for the years 1999 and 2000.

b. Calculate the company's operating and cash cycles for the years 1999–2000.

c. Describe the effect of the company's operating and cash cycles on its cash from operations.

17. [Common-size statements; analysis of ROA; competitive strategies] Ann Taylor and The Limited compete in the market for apparel for the fashion-conscious professional woman. Ann Taylor targets the "better-price" and "upper-moderate price" categories whereas The Limited has a broader target audience. Financial data of the two companies is presented below in columns labeled Company 1 and Company 2. (*Note*: The amounts are in $millions for one column and $10 millions for the other.)

	Company 1	Company 2
Sales	$1,084	$977
Cost of goods sold	(536)	(644)
Gross margin	$ 548	$333
Operating expenses	(414)	(241)
Operating income	$ 134	$ 92
Total assets	$ 765	$413

a. Prepare common-size income statements for Company 1 and Company 2.

b. Calculate ROA for each company and disaggregate the ROA into profitability and activity components.

c. Using the information from parts a and b, identify which company is Ann Taylor and which is The Limited. Justify your choice.

d. Explain how the financial data computed in parts a and b reflect the companies' competitive strategies.

18. [Disaggregation of ROE; effects of operating leverage] The following data were taken from Texaco's 1997–1999 annual reports:

Selected Data for Texaco, 1997–1999

	($millions)		
	1997	1998	1999
Sales	$45,187	$30,910	$34,975
EBIT (earnings before interest and tax)	3,847	1,124	2,083
Pretax income	3,327	701	1,779
Net income	2,664	603	1,177
Assets	29,600	28,570	28,972
Equity	12,766	11,833	12,042

a. Calculate Texaco's ROE (return on equity) for 1997–1999.

b. Disaggregate Texaco's 1997–1999 ROE into its five-components and analyze the factor(s) responsible for the changes in ROE over the period.

c. Using 1997 as your base, estimate the operating leverage effect for
  (i) 1998
  (ii) 1999

d. Based on your answer to part c, discuss whether the activity component and the operating margin components are distinct or related.

19. [Solvency and liquidity analysis] The Warnaco Group Inc. declared bankruptcy in June 2001 soon after publishing its financial statements for its year ended December 31, 2000. Warnaco Group's financial data for 1997 through 1999 are presented in Exhibit 4P-4.

a. Discuss whether the information provided in the exhibit provides any warning of the company's eventual demise. Your answer should be based on an analysis of Warnaco's 1998–1999 activity, solvency, liquidity, and profitability ratios.

b. Briefly describe any anomalies or peculiarities in Warnaco's ratios and/or financial data.

c. Warnaco's fiscal year 2000 annual report included the following revisions and restatements of previous years' data:

- The allowance for doubtful accounts was revised to $90, $86, and $94 million for 1997–1999, respectively, from the previously recorded amounts (of $46, $37, and 33 million).
- COGS and SGA for 1999 were increased by $12.4 million and $5.3 million, respectively. (Net income was not affected as income tax was reduced by $17.7 million.)
- Previous years' equity was reduced by $26 million.

Discuss the relevance of these items to parts a and b.

EXHIBIT 4P-4. THE WARNACO GROUP INC.
Financial Data, 1997–1999

Balance Sheet ($millions) December 31				Income Statement ($millions) Years Ended December 31		
Assets	1997	1998	1999		1998	1999
Cash and marketable securities	$ 12	$ 10	$ 82	Net revenue	$1,950	$2,114
Accounts receivable*	297	199	315	COGS	1,413	1,413
Inventories	431	472	735	SGA expense	452	471
Prepaid expense and other	45	27	66	Operating income	$ 85	$ 230
Current assets	$ 785	$ 708	$1,198	Interest expense	63	81
Net property	130	224	326	Pretax income	$ 22	$ 149
Other assets	736	851	1,239	Tax expense	8	51
Total assets	$1,651	$1,783	$2,763	Net income	$ 14	$ 98

Liabilities and Equity	1997	1998	1999
Short-term debt**	$ 21	$ 30	$ 145
Accounts payable	289	504	600
Accrued liabilities	122	128	111
Taxes payable	—	17	24
Current liabilities	$ 432	$ 679	$ 880
Long-term debt	354	412	1,188
Other long-term liabilities	14	12	29
Total liabilities	$ 800	$1,103	$2,097
Redeemable preferred shares	101	102	103
Common equity	750	578	563
Total liabilities and equity	$1,651	$1,783	$2,763

*Accounts receivable are net of allowance for doubtful accounts of $46, $37, and 33 million for 1997–1999.
**Includes current portion of long-term debt of $9 and $11 million for 1998 and 1999.
Source: Warnaco annual reports 1998–2000.

20. [Comprehensive review of ratios, operating and financial leverage, and financial statements] Company C and Company L operate in the same industry and have equal market shares. Their operating and financing characteristics differ as Company C has adopted newer manufacturing practices: It operates highly automated plants and maintains tight control of inventories consistent with just-in-time inventory techniques. To achieve these inventory levels, close coordination with suppliers and customers is needed; collections and payments are relatively prompt.

Financial data for 2002 for Company C and Company L follow:

	Company C	Company L
Gross plant assets	$175,000	$65,000
Current ratio	9.475	3.592
Quick ratio	8.875	3.192
Return on equity	0.130	0.167
Cash from operations/ current liabilities	5.275	0.942
Decline in receivables	($3,000)	($4,500)
Decline in inventory	0	(6,000)
Decline in accounts payable	0	(5,000)
Cash from operations	52,750	28,250
Cash from financing: decline in short-term debt	(1,000)	(5,000)
Cash for investment	0	0

Common-size statements for Company C and Company L, prepared by your assistant, follow, but they are unidentified as to which company they belong to. Sales in 2002 for both companies were one-sixth less than in 2001.

Common-Size Statements

	Company ?		Company ?	
	2001	2002	2001	2002
Sales	100.00%	100.00%	100.00%	100.00%
COGS	63.89	66.67	58.33	66.67
Sales and administrative expenses	19.44	20.00	17.78	20.00
Interest	1.67	2.00	3.89	4.67
Taxes	3.75	2.83	5.00	2.17
Subtotal	88.75%	91.50%	85.00%	93.50%
Net income	11.25%	8.50%	15.00%	6.50%

Finally, your assistant also computed the ratios shown for 2002 (again unidentified as to company). In addition, the ratios are mixed up: Some in column 1 belong to Company C and some to Company L (similarly, the ratios in column 2 are a mixture of Company C and Company L):

	Column 1	Column 2
Inventory turnover	6.667	16.667
Receivable turnover	11.111	7.409
Payable turnover	25.000	4.444
Long-term debt to capital	0.195	0.429

(When answering the following questions, round all numbers to the nearest $50.)

a. Identify the common-size statements and each ratio with Company C or Company L. Briefly explain your reasoning.

b. Recreate the income statements for 2001 and 2002 for Company C and Company L.

c. Using the two years of data available, estimate for each company:

　(i) Level of fixed costs

　(ii) Variable costs (as a percentage of sales)

d. The recession is expected to continue with a 20% drop in sales in 2003. Forecast the 2003 income statements for each company.

e. Comment briefly on the impact of operating and financing leverage on the 2001 to 2003 financial performance of the two firms.

21. [Extension of Problem 4-20]

a. For Company C or L, recreate the balance sheet for 2001 and 2002. The balance sheet will have the following components:

Assets	Liabilities
Cash	Accounts payable
Accounts receivable	Short-term debt
Inventory	Long-term debt
Property, plant, and equipment	
Less accumulated depreciation	Shareholders' equity

b. For the same company selected, forecast the balance sheet and cash from operations for 2003. (*Hint*: Use the ratios to make the required assumptions regarding levels of inventories, payables, and receivables.)

c. Assess the strength of the cash position and cash flows of the company analyzed.

22. [Relationship of ROE, ROA, leverage, and cost of debt] The Vac Company has an ROA of 10%. The company has no debt (not even trade liabilities). Its total assets are $1 million and its tax rate is 20%. The company is considering borrowing some money and using the proceeds to buy back outstanding stock. The bank has stated that the interest rate charged will depend on the level of bank debt according to the following schedule:

Debt to Equity	Interest Rate
(1) 0.25	6%
(2) 0.50	8%
(3) 1.00	10%
(4) 1.50	12%
(5) 2.00	15%

a. Compute the company's current ROE.

b. Using the formula in the chapter that related ROE to ROA and interest costs, calculate the expected ROE for each level of debt.

c. Confirm your calculation of cases (1) and (5) by completing the following for each case:

　(i) Debt in dollars

　(ii) Equity in dollars

　(iii) Income before interest and taxes

(iv) Interest expense

(v) Tax expense

(vi) Net income

(vii) Return on equity

d. Discuss the implications of this table regarding "optimal" levels of debt and limits to the use of leverage.

23. [Relationship of ROE, ROA, leverage, and cost of debt] Redo problem 4-22, assuming that the company has trade payables of $200,000 and intends to maintain that level. Note that the debt-to-equity ratio in the schedule is calculated by excluding the trade payables; that is, debt is defined as bank debt only. (*Hint:* The formula used in part b will require adjustment of the interest cost as the trade payables carry a zero interest rate.)

24. [Analysis of liquidity, profitability, and cash flow—extension of problem 3-4] In Problem 3-4 in Chapter 3, you were asked to analyze the liquidity of the M and G companies based on income and cash flow trends.

a. State the ratios that can be used to support the conclusions reached in Problem 3-4. Justify your choices.

b. Calculate those ratios for the years 1996–2000, using the data in Exhibit 3P-1.

c. Discuss how the ratios computed in part b affect the conclusions reached in Problem 3-4.

25. [Profitability analysis] The financial statements of Harley Davidson, Inc. for the period 1985–1990 are presented in Exhibit 4P-5. Harley-Davidson was considered one of the success stories

EXHIBIT 4P-5. HARLEY-DAVIDSON INC.
Comparative Income Statements for Years Ended 1985 to 1990 (in $millions)

	1985	1986	1987	1988	1989	1990
Sales	$287.48	$295.32	$685.36	$757.38	$790.97	$864.60
Cost of goods sold	209.69	210.45	506.91	559.53	582.70	619.10
Selling, general, and administrative expense	57.34	60.06	104.14	111.91	127.61	144.27
Depreciation	7.53	8.72	14.86	15.73	14.23	16.45
Operating income after depreciation	$ 12.91	$ 16.10	$ 59.45	$ 70.20	$ 66.42	$ 84.78
Interest expense	(9.41)	(9.51)	(25.51)	(24.67)	(17.96)	(11.44)
Other income (expense)	(0.34)	0.75	0.52	4.38	4.54	(2.12)
Special items	0	0	(3.60)	(3.90)	0	(8.60)
Pretax income	$ 3.16	$ 7.33	$ 30.85	$ 46.01	$ 53.01	$ 62.62
Income tax expense	0.53	3.03	13.18	18.85	20.40	24.31
Income before extraordinary items	$ 2.64	$ 4.31	$ 17.67	$ 27.16	$ 32.61	$ 38.31
Extraordinary items and discontinued operations	7.32	0.56	3.54	(3.24)	0.33	(0.48)
Net income	$ 9.95	$ 4.87	$ 21.21	$ 23.91	$ 32.94	$ 37.83

HARLEY-DAVIDSON INC.
Condensed Comparative Balance Sheets, 1985 to 1990 (in $millions)

	1985	1986	1987	1988	1989	1990
Assets						
Current assets	$ 72.89	$148.76	$197.90	$211.29	$187.67	$196.68
Net property	38.73	90.93	100.43	110.79	115.70	136.05
Intangibles	—	82.11	74.16	70.21	66.19	63.08
Other assets	2.47	5.39	8.38	8.82	9.36	11.65
Total assets	$114.09	$327.19	$380.87	$401.11	$378.92	$407.46
Liabilities and Equity						
Current debt	$ 2.88	$ 18.09	$ 28.33	$ 33.23	$ 26.93	$ 23.86
Other current liabilities	53.77	90.73	105.35	103.16	109.43	122.67
Long-term debt	51.50	191.59	178.76	135.18	74.79	48.34
Other liabilities	1.32	0.62	5.52	7.89	11.52	13.82
Total liabilities	$109.47	$301.03	$317.96	$279.46	$222.67	$208.69
Stockholders' equity	4.62	26.16	62.91	121.65	156.25	198.77
Total liabilities and equity	$114.09	$327.19	$380.87	$401.11	$378.92	$407.46

of the 1980s, having introduced world-class management techniques to turn around the company. At the same time, however, an examination of the company's return on equity indicates that after initial growth, the ratio stabilized and then declined.

a. Using the five-component duPont model, disaggregate Harley's return on equity (ROE) for the period 1985–1990.

b. Discuss the contribution of each component to the change in ROE over the period.

26. [Earnings per share and book value per share; CFA© adapted] As an analyst you have gathered the following information about a company for the year ended December 31, 1999:

- Net income was $10.5 million.
- Stockholders' equity at December 31, 1999 was $100 million.
- Common stock dividends of $3.5 million were paid.
- 20 million shares of common stock were outstanding on January 1, 1999.
- The company issued 6 million new shares of common stock on April 1, 1999.
- Outstanding preferred shares:
  5 million shares, each convertible into 1.5 common shares
  Par value $1 per share; liquidating value $5 per share
  Annual dividend $4 per share

a. Compute the company's basic earnings per share for 1999.

b. Compute the company's diluted earnings per share for 1999.

c. Compute the company's book value per share at December 31, 1999.

d. Compute the company's book value per share at December 31, 1999, assuming conversion of the preferred shares into common shares.

e. Explain why the diluted calculations (parts b and d) provide per-share amounts that are more suitable for valuation than the amounts calculated in parts a and c.

27. [Earnings per share and book value per share with more complex capital structure] Isabelle Industries reported the following data at December 31, 2001:

2001 net income	$50 million
Tax rate	40%
Stockholders' equity	$500 million
Common shares outstanding at January 1, 2001	50.0 million
Common shares issued on June 30, 2001	20.0 million
Preferred shares issued on January 1, 2001	4.0 million
Par value	$5.00
Redemption value	$25.00
Dividend	$1.25
Conversion rate (common shares per preferred share)	2.0
Convertible debt issued on September 30, 2000	$100 million
Interest rate	6.5%
Conversion rate	$10 per share
Stock options outstanding for all of 2001	25.0 million
Exercise price	$9.60
Market price of common shares on December 31, 2001	$12.00

a. Compute Isabelle's basic earnings per share for 2001.

b. Compute Isabelle's diluted earnings per share for 2001.

c. Compute Isabelle's book value per share at December 31, 2001.

d. Compute Isabelle's book value per share at December 31, 2001, assuming conversion of the convertible debt and preferred shares into common shares, as well as exercise of all options.

e. Explain why the diluted calculations (parts b and d) provide per-share amounts that are most suitable for valuation than the amounts calculated in parts a and c.

5

EMPIRICAL RESEARCH: IMPLICATIONS FOR FINANCIAL STATEMENT ANALYSIS

CHAPTER OUTLINE

CHAPTER OBJECTIVES

The goals of this chapter are to:

1. Review the classical approach to accounting theory and the framework that still underlies most accounting standard-setting activities.
2. Survey market-based accounting research that examines the relationship between stock prices and financial reporting.
3. Explain "positive" accounting theory and its emphasis on the effect of financial reporting on management, creditor, and regulatory decision making.
4. Examine the current trend of accounting research.
5. Discuss the relevance of empirical research to financial statement analysis.

INTRODUCTION

The objectives, methodology, and underlying philosophies of accounting research have changed considerably over the past few decades. To a great extent, these changes mirrored (or, some would argue, merely followed) shifts in financial economic theory. Current trends in accounting research evolved from three major approaches to accounting theory and research. This chapter presents an overview of the research. We will not try to review all this research[1] here but rather:

- Characterize the nature of the research.
- Indicate the relevance of the research for financial analysts and where in the book it is discussed in further detail.
- Summarize important research findings without getting bogged down in detail.

The three approaches to accounting theory are represented schematically in Figure 5-1. The *classical approach* to accounting theory was prevalent prior to the mid-1960s and is still the framework underlying much of existing accounting regulation. This approach attempts, using a theoretical perspective, to develop an optimal or "most correct" accounting representation of some true (but unobservable) reality.

The second approach is commonly referred to as *market-based accounting research*. Criticizing the classical approach for its lack of testability, market-based research takes a more empirical, as well as user-oriented, perspective. Its primary focus is the market reaction to (or association with) reported accounting data. Market-based research uses observable relationships between reported earnings[2] and market returns to draw conclusions about the role of accounting information.

The *positive accounting theory* approach also focuses on observable reactions to accounting numbers, but this is not its primary focus. As Figure 5-1 indicates, it broadens the research perspective in two ways. First, in addition to financial markets, it includes other environments influenced by financial statements: management compensation plans, debt agreements with creditors, and the host of regulatory bodies interacting with the

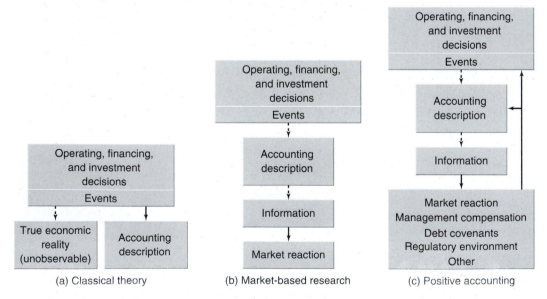

FIGURE 5-1 Schematic representation of three approaches to accounting theory and research.
Solid arrow indicates research focus

[1]The interested reader can find an excellent review of the literature in Kothari (2001).

[2]We use the term *earnings* here and throughout the chapter in a generic sense. It is not meant to preclude other measures of firm performance examined by researchers.

firm. More important, it recognizes that since financial statements impact these other environments, there are incentives for accounting systems to be used not only to measure the results of decisions but, in turn, to influence these decisions in the first place. This feedback interaction can influence both management's operating decisions and accounting choices.[3]

These competing approaches evolved over time in response to both research results and new developments in information economics and finance theory. Empirical research began in the 1960s with much fanfare and promise, only to be tempered over time both by the economic (in)significance of the results and by perplexing elements of reality, or what academics euphemistically call *anomalies*.

This sets the stage for the present direction of accounting research. This trend is characterized by a return to the examination of *a priori* linkages between financial statements, the analysis thereof, and security valuation. It grew out of extensions of market-based research on an empirical level and, on a theoretical level, a rediscovery of a valuation paradigm built on fundamental accounting variables and relationships. This underlying structural or fundamental analysis,[4] in some respects, combines the direction of the classical approach with the empiricism of market-based research.

Discussion of this research is intended to provide a context for the remainder of this book, in two respects. First, the financial reporting system has been shaped by accounting research (especially the classical approach), and users of that system must understand the factors that influence it. Second, accounting research provides valuable insights into the usefulness of financial statement data.

CLASSICAL APPROACH

Classical accounting theory approaches issues from a normative point of view. Writers such as Edwards and Bell (1961), Chambers (1966), and Sterling (1970) evaluate accounting methods and technologies in terms of how close reported information comes to some preconceived "true" picture of the firm. In this approach, the ideal picture is viewed as determinable within the accounting system itself. Concepts such as economic profit and its relationship to accounting income are a key focus of debate. Thus, much discussion (without consensus) ensues over topics such as current cost versus replacement cost versus historical cost accounting frameworks.

The classical approach is concerned with deducing correct accounting methods from a stated set of concepts, principles, and objectives. Implicit in this approach is the view that financial statement users accept (and react to) those statements at face value; thus, great importance is attached to ensuring that statements reflect the firm's true financial status.[5] Moreover, as the nature of users' reactions to financial information is deemed predictable, no explicit effort is made to examine, empirically or otherwise, the interrelationship between financial statements and users' motivations and/or reaction to the information contained in those statements.

Concurrent with the early development of this approach to accounting theory, the teachings of Graham and Dodd reigned supreme in the academic and professional finance communities. In their world, stocks have intrinsic value and investors could use ratios and other

---

[3]These three approaches view the underlying economic reality of a firm in different ways. In the classical approach, an underlying reality exists, and it is the role of accounting to best describe it. Market-based research, on the other hand, views reality as determined by market value—"what you see is what you get"—and accounting alternatives, *a priori*, really do not make any difference. The positive approach adds a new twist: Accounting alternatives (help) define and determine reality.

[4]Use of the term "structural" for modeling the *a priori* linkages can be traced to Ryan (1988). Using fundamental (or financial statement) analysis to classify the research can be attributed to empirical studies by Ou and Penman (1989), Ou (1990), and Penman (1991, 1992).

[5]This is equivalent to the concept of representational faithfulness discussed in Chapter 1.

financial analysis techniques based on financial statement data to develop filter rules that identify stocks as over- or undervalued.[6]

The classical approach fell out of favor in academic circles due to its lack of testability. It was argued that the usefulness of accounting information could be evaluated only by observing its effects on financial statement users. The research emphasis turned to empirical investigations of the decision relevance of the information contained in accounting reports.

Accounting regulators never *fully* embraced this new (empirical) approach to accounting theory.[7] Whether this was because they did not agree with it philosophically or because they felt that its results had no practical implications is a matter of debate. *It is important to note that existing accounting rules, which make up GAAP, are greatly influenced by and are still a product of the classical approach*; we return to this issue in the concluding section of this chapter.

MARKET-BASED RESEARCH

Advances in finance theory in the mid- and late 1960s were the primary catalyst for the shift in accounting research described in this section. The two major advances in finance literature that influenced accounting research in this period were the efficient market hypothesis and modern portfolio theory.

Efficient Market Theory

Underlying the new approach to accounting theory and research was the widespread interest in (and increasing acceptance of) the efficient market hypothesis (EMH) in the academic and professional finance community. The EMH, as defined by Fama (1970), states that a market is efficient if asset prices fully reflect the information available. "Fully reflecting" means that knowledge of that information does not allow anyone to profit from it, because prices already incorporate the information. Further, the information is impounded in the prices correctly and instantaneously as soon as it becomes known.

Information is classified into three sets, resulting in three forms of the EMH:

1. *The weak form.* The information set includes only information about past securities prices.
2. *The semistrong form.* The information set includes all publicly available information.
3. *The strong form.* The information set includes all information, including privately held (insider) information.

Empirical evidence in the accounting and finance literature during this period supported the weak and semistrong forms. The weak form implies that series of past security prices cannot be successfully used to predict future prices. Hence, charting techniques (head-and-shoulder patterns, double tops, etc.) and other types of technical analysis are deemed meaningless and unprofitable.

The information set assumed to be used by financial markets under the semistrong form includes all publicly available information, such as financial statements, government reports, industry reports, and analysis. Two key implications for accounting research, policy, and analysis flow from the semistrong form of the EMH.

First, financial statements are not the only source of information for making investment decisions. Second, and more important, *no trading advantages accrue to users of financial*

---

[6]Simultaneously (and, perhaps, paradoxically), it was argued that, although determining a company's true financial condition was a worthwhile objective, accounting rules did not actually mirror the underlying reality. Thus, financial statements were often seen as meaningless and of little use to investors. Canning (1929) was often quoted in support of this viewpoint:

> What is set out as a measure of net income can never be supposed to be a fact in any sense at all except that it is the figure that results when the accountant has finished applying the procedures which he adopts [John B. Canning, *The Economics of Accountancy* (New York: Ronald Press, 1929), p. 98].

[7]There are some exceptions. For example, the change in the current cost disclosures from mandatory to voluntary required by SFAS 33 (see Appendix 8-A) was partially a result of empirical evidence indicating that the market ignored the information.

statements because the information contained in them is instantaneously impounded in prices as soon as the information becomes public. This latter point was a direct attack on fundamental analysis—the mainstay of financial analysts who searched for stocks that were over- or undervalued relative to their intrinsic value.

The ironic part of the argument is that the very analysts engaged in fundamental analysis (looking for the bargains) ensure that there are no bargains to be found. Their research results in prices that fully reflect all available information:

> This error takes the form of asserting that accounting data have no value. . . . The efficient market in no way leads to such implications. It may very well be that the publishing of financial statements data is precisely what makes the market as efficient as it is.[8]

The EMH also had implications for the setting of accounting standards; no longer did such standards have to specifically protect the naïve investor. Sophisticated analysts and investors, who ensure that prices correctly and instantaneously reflect available information, protect the naïve investor. Any trades by such investors are made at fair prices.

Modern Portfolio Theory

The second trend in finance theory impacting accounting theory and research was modern portfolio theory (MPT), as embodied in the capital asset pricing model (CAPM). The CAPM characterizes the relationship between a common stock's expected return and risk as

$$E\,(R_i) = R_f + \beta_i\,[E(R_m) - R_f]$$

where

R_i = the rate of return on stock i
R_f = the risk-free rate of return
R_m = the rate of return on the market as a whole
β_i = the beta on firm i that measures the comovement of that firm's returns with those of the overall market
$E\,(*)$ = the symbol representing the expected value

The realized return on stock i is therefore [removing the expectation symbol $E\,(*)$]

$$R_i = R_f + \beta_i\,[R_m - R_f] + e_i$$

where *e is the unexpected or abnormal return.* In other words, e_i represents the portion of a stock's realized return that is different from its expected return (given existing market conditions).

Under MPT, higher risks are associated with higher (expected) returns, but the relationship holds only for that portion of risk that cannot be diversified away. Risk is classified as either systematic or unsystematic. Systematic risk is that portion of uncertainty faced by a firm that is due to common factors facing all firms,[9] the business cycle, interest rates, inflation, and so on. Its measure under CAPM is the *beta* of the firm, β_i.

Unsystematic risk is the uncertainty specific to a given firm. The unsystematic return is the return e_i accruing to the firm after accounting for the systematic effects. The unsystematic risk can be diversified away by investors holding well-diversified portfolios. Because this risk can be diversified away, there is no reward to investors (higher returns) for bearing this risk; the expected abnormal return is $E\,(e_i) = 0$. The systematic risk, on the other hand, which cannot be diversified away, must be rewarded by offering the investor a higher expected return.

MPT and CAPM shaped the development of accounting theory in a number of ways. First, it implied that *since the expected return for a given firm does not depend on risks that can be diversified away, information regarding the outlook for a specific firm was largely*

---

[8]William Beaver, "What Should Be the FASB's Objectives?," *Journal of Accountancy* (August 1973), pp. 49–56.
[9]The single-index model just defined provides for systematic risk only on an economywide basis. Multiindex models, however, can capture industrywide effects.

irrelevant. The only thing that mattered was the systematic risk of the firm and its relationship to the total portfolio.

The ability of accounting data to predict and provide measures of risk thus became an avenue of accounting research, with the evidence indicating that such data could be used to enhance the prediction of risk measures such as beta.[10] What is surprising is that this line of research, although promising, did not *originally* play a bigger role.

Recent empirical findings, however, have once again brought attention to the area of risk management. Contrary to the relationship predicted by the CAPM, Fama and French (1992) conclude that, during the period 1963 to 1990, beta was not related to average returns on stocks. On the other hand, measures such as company size, the market-to-book ratio, leverage, and the price-earnings ratio were found (by Fama and French as well as others) to be related to average returns. We return to the implications of these findings for risk measurement, the CAPM, and the issue of market inefficiency later in the chapter.

Second, the CAPM and MPT influenced accounting theory development by providing a model to measure the reaction of market returns and earnings. Deviations from expected earnings could be shown to influence the realized rate of return or, more specifically, the unexpected portion or abnormal return (e_i).

This led to market-based research studies that can be classified into the following categories:

1. Tests of the EMH versus the classical approach
2. Tests of the informational content of accounting alternatives
3. Tests of the earnings/return relationship

Tests of the EMH versus the Mechanistic Hypothesis

The mechanistic hypothesis, consistent with the classical approach to accounting theory, holds that users of financial statements accept the information provided at face value.[11] Implicit in this hypothesis is the assumption that users of financial statements do not access other sources of information nor do they adjust financial statements for the effects of alternative accounting methods. Clearly, the mechanistic hypothesis stands in opposition to the EMH, which holds that current prices reflect all information available.

The mechanistic hypothesis was tested by examining stock market reaction to changes in accounting methods that increase reported income but have no cash flow effect.[12] Since such changes increase reported income, the mechanistic hypothesis leads us to expect increases in stock prices. The EMH would argue that the market sees through the change and no stock price reaction should result.

Tests of the mechanistic hypothesis versus the EMH eventually became passé.[13] Although there was much disagreement as to the types of information markets reacted to, the general consensus[14] was in line with the EMH (i.e., the market does not follow reported earnings blindly and adjusts the information accordingly).[15]

---

[10]A detailed review of the research that relates accounting variables to risk is presented in Chapter 18, where overall risk and credit analysis is discussed.

[11]The mechanistic view is sometimes referred to as "functional fixation."

[12]For example, firms that changed their depreciation method for financial reporting (but not for tax) purposes from accelerated to straight line were examined by both Archibald (1972) and Kaplan and Roll (1972).

[13]In light of some of the anomalies associated with the EMH, however, the functional fixation hypothesis has returned in the form of the extended functional fixation hypothesis [see Hand (1990)]. Under this guise, it is argued that some unsophisticated investors on the margin can and do affect prices.

[14]The general consensus here refers to the academic accounting community and sizable portions of the professional community. However, some accountants and accounting policymakers continued to believe that investors needed to be protected from blindly following reported results.

[15]On the other hand, studies of changes in accounting method continued with other objectives in mind. Switches from first-in, first out (FIFO) to last-in, first-out (LIFO), which have real cash flow effects due to their tax consequences, were studied extensively; these results are discussed in greater detail in Chapter 6. In addition, positive accounting theory (discussed later) suggested motivations for accounting changes beyond those provided by market-based accounting research.

Beaver (1973) summarized the implications for accounting policy and disclosure:

> Report one method, with sufficient footnote disclosure to permit adjustment to the other and let the market interpret implications of the data for security prices. . . If there are no additional costs of disclosure to the firm, there is *prima facie* evidence that the item in question should be disclosed.[16]

The belief that the market does not blindly follow reported numbers led researchers to question how (if at all) markets react to accounting information. The methodology and philosophy underlying this mode of research can be understood best with an analysis of the seminal Ball and Brown (1968) study.

Ball and Brown Study

The goal of Ball and Brown was to document the association between the price (returns) of a firm's securities and the accounting earnings of the firm. To do so, they partitioned the firms in their sample into *good news/bad news* groupings. Based on a firm's reported earnings, a company was classified as reporting good (bad) news if the reported earnings were above (below) those predicted by a time-series forecasting model. Then, acting as if this knowledge was known as far back as March of the year in question, two portfolios were constructed on the basis of the good news/bad news partition.

Ball and Brown's main finding is reproduced in Figure 5-2, which compares the cumulative abnormal returns over the year for the good and bad news portfolios.[17] Good (bad) news firms enjoyed, on average, abnormally positive (negative) returns as measured by e_j. Ball and Brown demonstrated a clear (empirical) association between earnings and stock market reaction.

These results, although opening the door to future avenues of research, also raised many questions. As can be seen in Figure 5-2, the abnormal good/bad market reaction began one year prior to the announcement date. Further, there is little information content to the announcement itself. Ball and Brown estimated that 80% to 85% of the abnormal market performance occurred *prior* to the publication of the annual report. This suggests that although earnings are meaningful measures of a firm's financial performance, by the time they are published they are redundant and have little or no market impact.

The market anticipation of reported earnings raises questions about the *timeliness of annual reports* and is a reminder that the annual report is not the sole source of information available to the marketplace. Competing sources of information about the economy as a whole, the industry the firm operates in, and the firm itself are available from the media, government reports, industry associations, financial analyst reports, and management announcements, as well as the firm's own interim reports.

Ball and Brown triggered an explosion of empirical accounting research over the next two decades that can be roughly described as studies of either the information content of earnings or the overall relationship between stock returns and reported earnings.

Information Content Studies

Ball and Brown spurred a series of studies intended to examine the "information content" of accounting data, with information content measured by market reaction to the announced earnings and its deviation from expected earnings. The procedure generally involved calculating cumulative abnormal returns resulting from alternative measures of earnings.

For example, Beaver and Dukes (1972) compared the informational content of earnings with and without the deferral of income taxes. Others examined the information content of segment earnings, unusual items, capitalized leases, alternative accounting methods for oil and gas properties, and so on. These individual studies are discussed in the chapters where the related accounting principles are presented.

At first, researchers argued that, given a choice of accounting alternatives, the most desirable was the one that triggered the greatest market reaction (i.e., had the most information content). In this vein, researchers were led to draw standard-setting implications from their

---

[16]Beaver (1973), p. 51.

[17]The graph depicts one (EPS, naïve model) of the three variations of earnings examined by Ball and Brown.

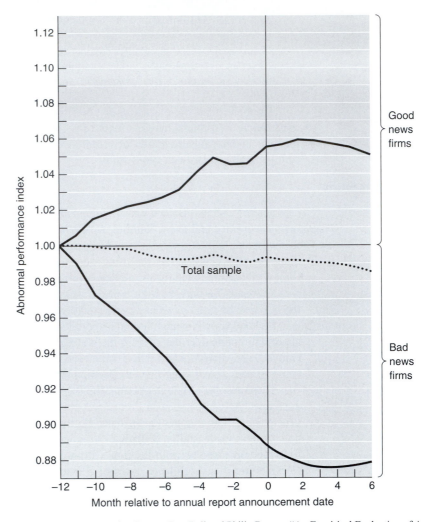

FIGURE 5-2 Ball and Brown results. *Source:* Ray Ball and Philip Brown, "An Empirical Evaluation of Accounting Income Numbers," *Journal of Accounting Research* (Autumn 1968), pp. 159–178, Figure 1, p. 169 (adapted), reprinted with permission.

findings.[18] This notion was soon challenged, not because earnings and market reaction were unrelated, but rather because any transactions (purchase/sale of shares) or change in market prices made some people better off than others. Thus, deciding the best alternative necessarily involved judgments affecting social consequence and the general welfare, which were deemed to be political in nature and beyond the realm of academic research.[19]

The reluctance to prescribe normative solutions did not diminish the quantity of research carried out in this area; it just shifted the emphasis. Recognition was now being given to the implicit cost/benefit trade-offs resulting from any disclosure requirement.

Relationship Between Earnings and Stock Returns

Studies of the earnings/return relationship were by far the most prevalent form of market-based research. Some research studies were broad in scope; others merely replicated previous studies, with an emphasis on methodological refinements. All in all, the research results were

---

[18]See Beaver (1972, p. 321) and Beaver and Dukes (1972).

[19]This view held that intrinsic value, even if it existed, was not necessarily a good standard to measure the choice of accounting alternatives since somebody may "suffer" if the "truth" were known. An extensive rationale for this argument can be found in Gonedes and Dopuch (1974). In response to this argument, Beaver (1973, p. 55) reversed his earlier view.

somewhat disappointing, with no major breakthroughs in terms of understanding the role of accounting earnings in the stock-return-generating process. *In addition, some of the research began to turn up evidence that contradicted the semistrong form of market efficiency.*

Organizing and classifying the nature of this research is best done by reference to Ball and Brown. Their study included the following interrelated categories:

1. Accounting variable
2. Market-based variable
3. Tests of the relationship between the good news/bad news parameter and abnormal returns

Accounting Variable

Choice of the Appropriate Accounting Variable. Ball and Brown used the sign of the forecast error of annual net income and earnings per share (EPS). Beaver et al. (1979) considered the magnitude of the error, weighting their portfolios by the size of the error.[20] Other researchers [e.g., Foster (1977); Bathe and Lorek (1984)] examined quarterly earnings and found that quarterly reports also possess information content.

However, a number of studies [see Ball (1978) and Joy and Jones (1979) for surveys] began to document postannouncement drift, whereby positive (negative) abnormal return patterns continued for some time after the announcement of good (bad) news quarterly earnings.[21] This phenomenon was contrary to the EMH assertion that information was *immediately* impounded by prices.

Gonedes (1975, 1978) and Ronen and Sadan (1981), among others, focused on the appropriate definition of income—operating income, income from continuing operations, or net income—by examining whether the inclusion of special, nonrecurring, or extraordinary items had any impact on security returns. The spate of restructuring charges and other write-offs in the 1980s rekindled research in this area.

In line with the focus on cash flows in accounting and finance, researchers examined the informational content of cash flows relative to net income. As discussed in Chapter 2, the results do not generally show that cash flow data provide information that is superior to that found in accrual-based earnings data.

In response to criticisms [such as Lev (1989), discussed shortly] that using a single number such as earnings to explain return behavior was too simplistic, some studies examined the relationship between returns and various components of earnings (Lipe, 1986) and between returns and cash flow components (Livnat and Zarowin, 1990). Finally, the required disclosure of comprehensive income led Dhaliwal, Subramanyam, and Trezevant (1999) to compare the performance of that measure with net income.

Expectations of Accounting Variables. An important byproduct of the earnings/return relationship research, which soon became a major area of research in its own right, lay in the development and construction of earnings-forecasting models. Simple and complex time-series models, using annual and/or quarterly data, were compared against one another and with those generated by financial analysts and management to examine two independent but closely related questions:

1. Which forecasting model or forecast has the best predictive ability?
2. Which forecasting model or forecast most closely mirrors the market's expectations?

The first issue is discussed in detail in Chapter 19, where various forecasting models are described and compared.

Research into the second issue (also discussed in Chapter 19) suggests that financial analysts' forecasts are a better surrogate for market expectations than models based solely on

---

[20]Others [Rendelman et al. (1982)] carried this a step further by weighting the forecast error by a measure of the overall variability of the earnings stream.

[21]Interestingly, Ball and Brown's original seminal article noted that their data exhibited postannouncement drift.

the historical time series of reported income.[22] *This superiority was attributed [Brown et al. (1987)] to the fact that analysts have both more timely information and a broader set of information on which to base forecasts.*

The fact that market expectations coincide with those of financial analysts led researchers to examine whether financial analysts in some sense lead the market and the market derives its expectations from analyst forecasts. Such studies found that there is indeed market reaction to changes in analysts' forecasts. Givoly and Lakonishok (1979), however, also indicated that abnormal returns could be earned by trading on revisions of analyst forecasts, again raising questions as to the efficiency of capital markets.

Market-based Variable

Measurement Period (Window) for Market Performance. Ball and Brown examined monthly returns over a full year. Other studies, depending on the issue examined, used weekly (or daily) returns in the periods immediately surrounding the announcement.[23] The trade-off between using narrow (short) versus wide (long) windows is that in the former case there is less risk that the market could be reacting to information other than that being tested. Wider windows have the advantage of allowing for the possibility of information leakage, thus implying earlier market reaction. In addition, and perhaps more important, the significance of a piece of information may not be known until a later date. Using too narrow a window would miss this reaction. The emergence of postannouncement drift, alluded to earlier,[24] increased the relevance of this issue.

Test of the Relationship Between the Good News/Bad News Parameter and Abnormal Returns

Early studies, as we have discussed, grouped firms into good news/bad news portfolios by the sign and/or magnitude of the earnings forecast error. There was no explicit theoretical consideration or measurement of the relationship between earnings and returns. Later studies explicitly related the response of stock returns to earnings by the introduction of the earnings response coefficient (ERC).[25]

ERC studies tested for differential reactions across firms and for differential reactions to various components of earnings. Moreover, the ERC permitted testing of explicit relationships between prices and earnings as implied by finance valuation models. Collins and Kothari (1989) show that, as predicted by such models, risk and growth variables explain some of the cross-sectional differences in ERCs.

ERCs were typically found to be much lower than expected. This finding led to interest in the "persistence" issue, namely which components of earnings were permanent and hence had implications for future valuation and market reaction, and which were transitory and thus had limited implications. Kormendi and Lipe (1987) and Easton and Zmijewski (1989), for example, found that the greater the persistence, the higher the ERC.[26]

The end of the 1980s triggered a number of "20-year" retrospectives of developments since Ball and Brown. The consensus was not complimentary. We shall return to these evaluations and research trends that evolved subsequently in the concluding section(s) of this chapter. First, however, we turn to a discussion of the third major stream in accounting research.

---

[22]O'Brien (1988), however, presents contradictory findings.

[23]Patell and Wolfson (1982, 1984) focused on the intraday measure of market reaction.

[24]See the subsequent discussion of market anomalies.

[25]The ERC is the coefficient b in the regression equation $R = a + b\Delta E$, where R and ΔE measure returns and earnings change (growth), respectively. The ERC has strong theoretical underpinnings as it reflects price/earnings capitalization, and *ceterus paribus*, the coefficient b should equal the firm's P/E ratio.

[26]Chapter 19 discusses the ERC, issues of persistence, and their relationship to the price/earnings (P/E) ratio in greater detail.

POSITIVE ACCOUNTING RESEARCH

The positive accounting approach is sometimes referred to as "contracting theory" or as the "economic consequences of accounting" literature. This approach assumes that accounting information is not merely a result of a firm's actions, but forms an integral part of the firm and its organizational structure. This information is the basis on which resources are allocated, management is compensated, debt restrictions are measured, and so on. Management, therefore, would be expected to take into consideration financial information effects in making

- Their operating, investing, and financing decisions
- Their choice of alternative accounting methods[27]

Impetus for this broader approach was once again led by changes in the finance and economics literature.

Disclosure and Regulatory Requirements

Economists examining regulation and its effects began to question the belief that all regulation was motivated by concern with the pubic good and regulation necessarily increased social welfare. Politicians and regulators were now viewed as motivated by their own self-interest and, hence, have private incentives to promulgate certain regulations.

Disclosure requirements were also viewed in this light. The benefits from increased disclosure requirements were not automatically assumed to outweigh the costs. Moreover, it was argued (further elaborated on shortly) that firms have private incentives to produce information so long as the cost of disseminating and producing the information does not outweigh its potential rewards. These cost/benefit trade-offs are believed to influence the choice of accounting alternatives. The motivations for accounting choices, however, still required explanation.

Agency Theory

The agency theory literature also took as a starting point the argument that people are motivated by their own self-interest. Thus, managers take steps to maximize the value of the firm only if that is consistent with their own best interests. If managers could, moreover, *in the absence of a monitoring device*, enhance their well being (1) by appropriating resources for themselves in addition to their agreed-on compensation or (2) by shirking their duties, equity or debt investors could be reluctant to provide financing to the firm.

Similarly, in the absence of a monitoring device, managers might engage in risk taking and other activities that would hurt the bondholder to the advantage of the equity holder. Thus, a monitoring device is needed to ensure that the agreements (contracts) among managers, shareholders, and creditors are adhered to. This discussion leads to viewing a firm not as an independent entity but rather as a "nexus of contracts"[28] (explicit or implicit) between parties, each motivated by its own self-interest. *The role of accounting in this scenario is to provide one of the monitoring devices enabling the contracting process to function.*

This approach to the accounting process views financial statements as the means by which contracting parties measure, monitor, and enforce the objectives of the various contracts.[29] Thus, as mentioned earlier, accounting data do not merely *describe* reality—they in effect *define* reality, as real economic consequences flow from the reported numbers.

---

[27]Although both types of research fall into this paradigm, research on the effects of accounting on management's operating decisions preceded the research on the choice of an accounting method. However, the "Rochester school," which popularized (and applied the label of) "positive accounting" [see Watts and Zimmerman (1986)], focused most of its attention on the second type.

[28]This term can be traced to Jensen and Meckling (1976).

[29]Under this view, the choice of accounting policy by management may not necessarily have sinister implications. The various parties view the accounting process as an efficient way to operate the firm. Otherwise, if there were no proper monitoring device, equity shareholders would be reluctant to hire managers (or they would pay them less). Thus, management has an incentive to have a "proper" monitoring system in place.

The specific hypotheses flowing from the positive theory approach to accounting that are most often tested are the:

- Bonus plan hypothesis
- Debt covenant or debt/equity hypothesis
- Political process hypothesis

Bonus Plan Hypothesis

The contract between management and shareholders concerns the performance expected from the manager and his or her level of compensation. Under the *bonus plan* hypothesis, managers are compensated for how well they manage the firm. The financial statements are used (often explicitly identified by the firm's executive compensation plan) as the benchmark for the firm's performance. Thus, it is in the best interest of the firm's management to choose "liberal" accounting policies to improve their own compensation.

The motivation for choosing liberal accounting policies under this view is not "fooling the market," with all the implications vis-á-vis the efficient market hypothesis. Rather, its driving force is simply the increased management compensation resulting from higher reported earnings.[30]

However, the implications of the bonus plan hypothesis may be more complex:

> A bonus plan does not always give managers incentives to increase earnings. If, in the absence of accounting changes, earnings are below the minimum level required for payment of a bonus, managers have incentives to reduce earnings this year because no bonuses are likely to be paid. Taking such an "earnings bath" increases expected bonuses and profits in future years.[31]

Similarly, when earnings exceed the maximum rewarded under the compensation plan, there is no incentive to increase earnings any further.

Healy (1985), for example, found that managers tend to change accounting policies because of bonus plan incentives and these changes are associated with the initial inception or modification of the plan. However, Healy also reports that managers do not seem to alter accounting policies if they are either below the minimum threshold or over the maximum ceiling for the current period.[32]

Debt Covenant Hypothesis

Bondholders and other creditors want to ensure repayment of their principal and interest. To protect themselves, they impose restrictions on the borrower as to payments of dividends, share repurchases, and issuance of additional debt. These restrictions often take the form of accounting measures and ratios. Typical covenants call for the maintenance of acceptable levels of working capital, interest coverage, net worth, and similar variables.

Accounting choices can greatly affect measures of these variables and consequently define whether a firm is in *technical default* of debt covenants. The debt covenant hypothesis states that managers are motivated to choose accounting methods that minimize the likelihood that covenants would be violated. Operationally, this is often expressed as the debt/equity hypothesis that asserts firms with higher debt/equity ratios tend to choose accounting policies that increase current income at the expense of future income. More recent research has refined this measure by incorporating explicit debt covenants and estimates of the cost of violation. A more elaborate description of the nature of bond covenants and research in this area is provided in Chapter 10.

---

[30]As footnote 29 points out, the management compensation hypothesis is also consistent with an efficiency point of view and not necessarily tied to opportunistic behavior on the part of managers.

[31]Watts and Zimmerman, "Positive Accounting Theory: A Ten Year Perspective," *The Accounting Review*, Jan. 1990, p. 139.

[32]More recent studies by Holthausen et al. (1995) and Gaver et al. (1995) further refined the interrelationships between bonus plans and accounting choices.

Political Cost Hypothesis

Our previous discussion of regulation implied that the political process imposes costs on the firm. When politicians and regulators can enhance their (or their constituents') interests at the expense of others, they will often do so. Financial data, and how they are perceived, play an important role in this process. If it is believed that a firm or an industry is taking advantage of the public and is making "obscene" profits, then reported earnings will be examined to see if profits are excessive. This may result in pressures from companies to reduce prices (drug industry) or for regulators to impose a "windfall profits" tax (oil industry).

Affected firms may be induced to choose accounting methods that reduce reported profits so as to lower their political risk. For example, in 1991 (when oil prices were high because of the Kuwait crisis) some oil companies reduced reported earnings by [see Han and Wang (1998)] "managing earnings downward" and making provisions for environmental costs or asset impairment.

Similarly, as Cloyd, Pratt, and Stock (1996) report, accounting methods that reduce income reported to shareholders can be motivated by the desire to use those same methods on tax returns. Even though alternative methods are permissible,[33] it is less "embarrassing" to be paying little or no taxes if financial statement income is also low.

The political cost hypothesis is often tested in the research literature as a size hypothesis. It is argued that large firms are most susceptible to political costs and pressures. The larger the firm, the more likely it would choose accounting methods that lower profits and hence lessen political pressures. One example is the oil industry. Large firms uniformly use the successful efforts method (see Chapter 7), which minimizes reported earnings; among smaller firms the full cost method is more common.

Summary of the Research

In addition to suggesting incentives for firms to choose income-increasing (or -decreasing) accounting methods, the bonus plan, debt covenant, and political cost hypotheses led to studies examining the effects of accounting data on management operating decisions. Thus, for example, the requirement that research and development costs be expensed rather than capitalized (SFAS 2) lowers reported earnings for many firms. This could induce a cutback in the amount of actual research and development work undertaken if managers felt that the lower earnings would hurt their compensation and/or imperil the status of the firm's bond covenants. A number of studies examining this issue are discussed in Chapter 7. Similarly, research dealing with the interaction of accounting methods and the incentives for mergers and acquisitions, pension plan terminations, and oil exploration is discussed in the chapters dealing with these topics.

Positive accounting theory also had implications for the debate (alluded to earlier) as to whether standard setters should use the results of information content studies in their deliberations. Proponents argued that using such results hinged on the assumption that the (sole) purpose of accounting data was valuation. However, if accounting data also acted as a monitoring device, it was not clear that the best measure(s) for valuation were the same as those required to optimize the monitoring function.[34]

Finally, positive accounting research expanded the focus of market-based studies that examined market reaction to mandated and voluntary accounting changes. Instead of just viewing returns as a function of earnings, it was now posited that return reaction may vary across firms as a function of a number of variables in addition to earnings, such as debt/equity, size, and management compensation. Changes that increase earnings, for example,

---

[33]In the United States, only in the case of LIFO (see Chapter 6) must firms use the same accounting method for financial reporting as for tax reporting. However, in many industrial countries, such as Germany and Japan, firms must use the same accounting methods for both purposes, strengthening the motivation to use "conservative" methods.

[34]For example, valuation requires forward-looking data in the form of expected earnings and cash flows. The monitoring function, in its stewardship role, on the other hand, is in some sense backward looking (i.e., "What have you done for me lately?"). See Holthausen and Watts (2001) and Barth, Beaver, and Landsman (2001) for a detailed discussion of these issues.

could result in positive market reaction for firms with high debt/equity ratios because the increased income would permit wealth transfers from the firm's existing bondholders to equity shareholders as additional debt could be taken on without affecting the reported debt/equity ratio. On the other hand, for large-sized firms, the increased income could increase the possibility of political costs, thus resulting in negative market reaction.

Empirical Research: A Mid-Course Evaluation

The late 1980s and early 1990s proved to be a turning point in the direction of empirical research in accounting. Lev[35] (1989) and Bernard[36] (1989), in separate papers, detailed many shortcomings and weaknesses of market-based research. In doing so, they voiced the growing concern among academics and practitioners as to the benefits of this research. Similar findings emanated from Watts and Zimmerman's (1990) ten-year retrospective of positive accounting research. Additionally, cracks began to appear in the efficient market hypothesis (and CAPM), the underpinnings of market-based research. This section reviews these two retrospective papers, followed by a summary of EMH anomalies that have important implications for financial statement analysis. This sets the stage for a discussion of current research trends.

Critical Evaluation of Research Findings

Both Lev and Bernard were critical of prior research and, as Exhibit 5-1 indicates, their views were consistent. They found that although some initial research findings were beneficial,[37] in general, the results contributed to neither:

- An understanding of how and to what extent earnings are used by investors, nor
- The deliberations of accounting policy makers

EXHIBIT 5-1
Summary of Bernard and Lev's Findings

Lev suggests a number of reasons for the failure of market-based research and directions for future research. Bernard echoes Lev's suggestions.

Baruch Lev, "On the Usefulness of Earnings and Earnings Research: Lessons and Directions from Two Decades of Empirical Research," *Journal of Accounting Research* (Supplement 1989), pp. 153–192.

1. Researchers used reported earnings and did not adjust for accounting manipulations by managers, year-to-year random occurrences, or the inherent arbitrariness of many accounting measurement and valuation techniques.

2. There is little or no knowledge as to how accounting information is disseminated in the marketplace; that is, what financial analysts do (adjust) with the information.

3. Lev argues for a research emphasis on the quality of earnings that incorporates effects of alternative GAAP measures on earnings and their relationship to valuation models.

Victor L. Bernard, "Capital Market Research During the 1980s: A Critical Review," in Thomas Frecka (ed.), *The State of Accounting Research as We Enter the 1990's* (Urbana-Champaign: University of Illinois, 1989), pp. 72–120.

1. "Progress will require that we end reliance on simple, naïve models. . . . An injection of knowledge about the accounting system and fundamental analysis is necessary . . . "

2. "It would frequently be useful to sacrifice large sample sizes and sophisticated statistics for the sake of achieving a deeper understanding of the relations among accounting variables, and between those variables and equity values. . . . "

3. "Further reliance on formal modeling would be fruitful."

---

[35]Baruch Lev, "On the Usefulness of Earnings and Earnings Research: Lessons and Directions from Two Decades of Empirical Research," *Journal of Accounting Research* (Supplement 1989), pp. 153–192.

[36]Victor L. Bernard, "Capital Market Research During the 1980's: A Critical Review," in Thomas Frecka (ed.), *The State of Accounting Research as We Enter the 1990's* (Urbana-Champaign; University of Illinois, 1989), pp. 72–120.

[37]As Bernard stated,

Imagine what our view of the role of accounting information might be if Ball and Brown had found, as many predicted they would, that accounting earnings were completely uncorrelated with the information used by investors! (Ibid., p. 5.)

To a great extent, they attributed this failure to a fixation on the part of the researchers on sophisticated statistical techniques at the expense of model building and specification of fundamental relationships. Studies focused on finding *statistical significance* even if the results had little or *no economic significance.*[38] The lack of model building further resulted in researchers focusing on one number—earnings—rather than on the richer information set available to investors.[39]

As a result of their criticisms, both Lev and Bernard suggested a research approach incorporating the following elements:

- More careful analysis of valuation models as they relate to accounting and earnings.
- Measuring earnings/returns relationships on an individual rather than portfolio basis (as analysts usually view firms).
- Averaging reported earnings over time[40] and examining longer time horizons as well as future year impacts rather than the immediate effect of a single period's earnings on stock prices.
- Earnings components used in research should incorporate all possible adjustments, not just one at a time, to arrive at a more comprehensive and meaningful analysis.

Watts and Zimmerman's review of the positive accounting literature led to findings and prescriptions similar to the reviews of market-based research. In reviewing the research, they contend that the results are generally consistent with the bonus plan and debt/equity hypotheses. With respect to the political cost hypothesis, however, results appear to hold only for the largest firms and are driven by the oil and gas industry. However, they noted that although results tend to be statistically significant, in many studies the explanatory power (R^2) or *economic significance of the models is low.*[41]

In their discussion of avenues for further research, Watts and Zimmerman note that most studies were concerned with incentives for management to behave opportunistically, as these tend to be the most observable (and hence testable) phenomena. However, they argue that greater effort is needed to *strengthen the relationship between theory and empirical testing* in determining whether management choices are purely opportunistic, or are motivated by efficiency considerations inherent in the firm's organizational structure and/or industrial dynamics.[42]

Market Anomalies

A number of anomalies have been found that question the validity of the EMH and the conclusions drawn from the research described previously. Some of these anomalies are related to the relationship between earnings and returns, whereas others seem to be purely market

---

[38]Lev, for example, noted that studies that examined the earnings/returns relationships tended to report low R^2 scores. (The R^2 measures the percentage of variation in returns explained by variations in earnings. A high R^2 implies a strong earnings/return association.) On average, earnings could explain no more than 5% of the variation in returns. Such results, while statistically significant, do not provide a meaningful explanation of the relationship between earnings and returns.

[39]These criticisms suggest an interesting irony of accounting research. Although researchers have argued that financial analysis is meaningless since the market is not fooled by reported data, they tested their arguments using the same data that the market supposedly adjusts. The rationale offered is that with large samples the noise resulting from nonadjustment would tend to be averaged away. This contention itself is subject to empirical verification, as it would depend on whether the errors cancel, or they are in some fashion systematically related. Subject to the evidence on this issue, it would seem that many researchers suffer from a form of functional fixation.

[40]To test for this, Lev examined the relationship of earnings and returns taken over a five-year period. He argued that over a longer period manipulations and smoothing tend to even out and earnings mirror cash flows. The R^2 over this longer period proved to be 35%—seven times the R^2 for the one-year data.

[41]Watts and Zimmerman, "Positive Accounting Theory: A Ten Year Perspective," p. 140.

[42]A more recent review of the literature on accounting choice by Fields, Lys, and Vincent (2001) concludes that Watts and Zimmerman's prescriptions were not successfully implemented.

> We conclude that research in the 1990s made limited progress in expanding our understanding of accounting choice because of limitations in research design and focus on replication rather than extension of current knowledge.

based. Additionally, some of the anomalies tend to overlap. For example, the Monday effect and post announcement drift are most pronounced for small-sized firms.

January Effect. Empirical evidence suggests that markets perform relatively well during the month of January. This would seem to be a violation of the weak form of the EMH, as knowledge of this pattern could lead to abnormal gains by buying shares at the end of December.

Monday Effect. After the weekend, market prices tend to open at lower levels, suggesting an advantageous strategy of selling short at the Friday close and covering the short position Monday morning.

Size Effect. Smaller firms (measured by total assets or total capitalization) tend to outperform the market even when returns are adjusted for risk. This suggests that investing in a portfolio of smaller-sized firms is a sound investment strategy.

Price-Earnings Ratio. Firms with low P/E ratios tend to outperform the market even when returns are adjusted for risk. This suggests that investing in a portfolio of firms with low P/E ratios is a sound investment strategy.

Book-to-Market Ratios. Fama and French (1992) found that the book-to-market ratio was a strong predictor of average returns. Figure 5-3 (based on Fama and French) shows that firms with higher book-to-market ratios had higher monthly returns than firms with lower ratios. This suggests investing in firms with high book-to-market ratios.

The Briloff Effect. Professor Abraham Briloff has periodically criticized the financial reporting practices of some firms in *Barron's*. The common stocks of these firms typically suffered large price drops [see Figure 5-4, from Foster (1979)] following publication. Since Briloff's analysis is based on publicly available information, it would seem that the market price prior to Briloff's analysis did not fully reflect all the available information.[43]

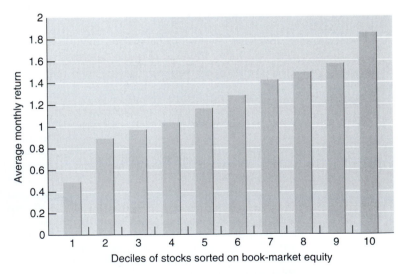

FIGURE 5-3 Evidence of book-market effect. Note that the ranking of book-market equity goes from the lowest (1) to the highest (10) decile. *Source:* Data based on E. F. Fama and K. R. French, "The Cross-Section of Expected Stock Returns," *Journal of Finance* (June 1992), Table 2, p. 436.

[43]We note that there is anecdotal evidence that Briloff's articles continue to have a negative effect on the stock price of companies he criticizes. A recent example is Cisco, whose stock fell approximately 12% in the week that Briloff's article, "Pooling and Fooling," appeared in the October 21, 2000 edition of *Barron's*.

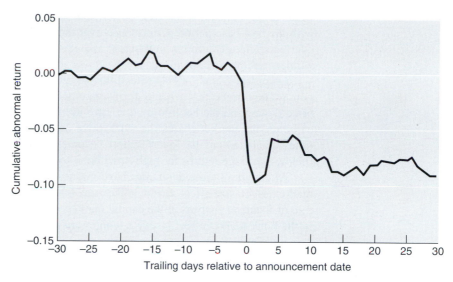

FIGURE 5-4 The Briloff effect: market reaction for 28 stocks. *Source:* George Foster, "Briloff and the Capital Market," *Journal of Accounting Research* (Spring 1979), pp. 262–274, Figure 1, p. 266, reprinted with permission.

Value Line. Figure 5-5 presents the performance of the stock groupings ranked by Value Line Investment Services. The continued and consistent performance of these groupings, relative to the market, implies that Value Line is able to beat the market.

Postannouncement Drift. The EMH holds that stock prices adjust instantaneously to new information. Empirical evidence, however, suggests that price changes persist for some time after the initial announcement.

Overreactive Markets: Contrarian Strategy. DeBondt and Thaler (1985) found that if stocks were ranked by their performance over a previous five-year period (the base period),

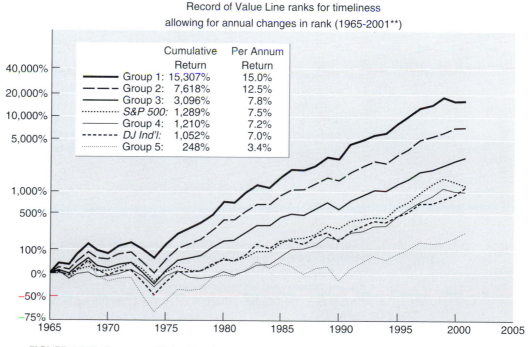

FIGURE 5-5 Performance of Value Line groups. Group 1 = highest performance; group 5 = lowest predicted performance. *Source:* Value Line Selection and Opinion, (July 27, 2001), p. 4129.

those firms with the worst base-period investment performance outperformed those firms with the best base-period performance over the next three years. This suggests that markets overreact and a contrarian investment strategy of buying recent losers and avoiding recent winners will be successful.

Lakonishok et al. (1994) extend this argument to explain the book-to-market phenomenon.[44] They argue that when a firm's earnings decline, the market overreacts, driving the price down (and the book-to-market ratio up) sharply. Similarly, when a firm reports good earnings, the market chases the stock price up (and the book-to-market ratio down). Over time, the extent of the overreaction becomes clear and prices reverse, yielding above- (below-) average returns for high (low) book-to-market firms.[45]

Although all these anomalies have implications for analysts, explanations of the book-market effect, size effect, Briloff effect, and the Value Line results relate most directly to the role of financial analysts in the capital markets. The results of Lakonishok et al. with respect to the book-market effect justify a (contrarian and) value approach to investments á la Graham and Dodd.[46] *Underpriced securities exist if the market overreacts.*

The size effect is often attributed to the fact that fewer analysts follow smaller firms than larger firms. Thus, not all information available about these firms is immediately incorporated in stock prices, leaving room for abnormal returns to be earned by those who trade on the information early enough. The excess returns on small-firm portfolios may also represent compensation for the cost and difficulty of analyzing underfollowed companies.

Some researchers have made similar arguments with respect to postannouncement drift. Bartov, Radhakrishnan, and Krinsky (2000) found the drift to be less pronounced for stocks having large institutional holdings.[47]

As a possible explanation of the Briloff effect, Foster noted that Briloff's superior accounting knowledge and analytical insights were in a sense nonpublic information, and hence capital market efficiency was not violated per se. This suggests that Briloff could earn a (competitive) return from using his superior skills. The so-called information market, rather than the capital market, is seen as the explanation for the research results.[48]

Value Line rankings are based on the performance of variables referred to as "earnings momentum" and "earnings surprise." The former relates to changes in quarterly earnings over time, whereas the latter relates to the deviation between actual and forecasted earnings. Whether this qualifies as statistical or fundamental analysis is open for debate. The results, however, indicate that superior analysis can lead to results that outperform the market.

In summing up the evidence on efficient markets, Bodie, Kane, and Marcus (1999) state:

> The lesson is clear. An overly doctrinaire belief in efficient markets can paralyze the investor and make it appear that no research effort can be justified. This extreme view is probably unwarranted. There are enough anomalies in the empirical evidence to justify the search for underpriced securities that clearly goes on. The bulk of the evidence, however, suggests that any supposedly superior strategy should be taken with many grains of salt. The market is competitive enough that only differentially superior information or insight will earn money; the easy pickings have been picked.[49]

---

[44]See also Zarowin (1989, 1990) who argues that the overreaction effect may just be another manifestation of the size effect.

[45]The interested reader is referred to Robert A. Haugen, *The New Finance: The Case Against Efficient Markets* (Englewood Cliffs, NJ: Prentice Hall, 1999).

[46]David Dreman ["Value Will Out," *Forbes* (June 17, 1996), p. 146] makes the point that the academic community has finally came around to recognizing the teachings of Graham and Dodd.

[47]Ali, Hwang, and Trombley (1999), however, found little relationship between investor sophistication and abnormal returns.

[48]George Foster, "Briloff and the Capital Market," *Journal of Accounting Research* (Spring 1979), pp. 262–274.

[49]Zvi Bodie, Alex Kane, and Alan J. Marcus, *Investments* (Homewood IL: Richard D. Irwin, 1999), p. 362.

DIRECTION OF CURRENT RESEARCH: BACK TO THE FUTURE?

Market-based and positive accounting research were originally fueled by parallel developments in economics and finance theory (e.g., efficient markets and agency theory) and the desire to find empirical results for testable hypotheses. The current state of accounting research is also driven by the above forces but with a twist. From a theory perspective, the EMH is no longer taken as a given but has itself become a legitimate area of research. Furthermore, as the survey papers indicated, there was dissatisfaction with the nature of the test designs and results emanating from the research.

Current research involves a return to principles of valuation, fundamental analysis, and as noted, tests of (the degree of) market efficiency. No longer are prices or returns taken as given and accounting data just tested to justify their usefulness. The emphasis is no longer on stock behavior in reaction to accounting information but rather on forecasting future *accounting* attributes (such as ROE and book values) and their relationship to a firm's *intrinsic or fundamental* value. Emphasis has shifted to the information derived from accounting data and its relationship to value. Furthermore, that value may or may not be the same as that reflected in market prices. This shift signals a return to the thinking inherent in the classical approach (i.e., accounting data could yield information about value), however, with a major difference. The relationships posited had to be justified empirically and doing so required building models with stronger theoretical underpinnings.

The current approach, thus, in some sense, synthesizes elements borrowed from both the classical and market-based approaches. Initially, the trend evolved from market-based research. However, it has been sustained to a great degree by the application of theoretical valuation models originally developed close to a half-century ago in the works of the classical writers.

Much of the empirical research was, at first, cast as a refinement of earlier information content studies. However, eventually a difference set in. Research on the diversity of the earnings response coefficient across firms led to a rethinking of basic price/earnings relationships. Evidence that prices could be used to forecast future earnings led to the (re)awareness (in research design) that prices react not only to changes in current earnings but also to changes in expected earnings. Consistent with these directions in the research were calls for a return to fundamental analysis. As Ou and Penman (1989) noted:

> There have been many claims of market efficiency with respect to "publicly available" information, but (astonishingly, when one considers the many tests of technical analysis) little research into the competing claim of fundamental anlaysis.[50]

Ball and Brown Revisited

Ou (1990) is indicative of the *initial* trend in this research. We describe this study in some detail because its research design contrasts with Ball and Brown, discussed earlier in the chapter.

Figure 5-6 captures Ou's salient results. Similar to Ball and Brown, Ou separates firms into good- and bad-news categories. The graphs marked E^+ and E^-, in fact, are replications of Ball and Brown's study and are based on whether a firm's reported earnings for the year were above (good news) or below (bad news) earnings predicted by a time-series forecasting model.

Ou then extended this analysis by partitioning the firms on the basis of both current-year earnings and a *forecast* of the next year's earnings. A model was designed to predict whether the next year's reported earnings would be above (F^+ = good news) or below

---

[50]Jane A. Ou and Stephen Penman, "Financial Statement Analysis and the Prediction of Stock Returns," *Journal of Accounting and Economics* (November 1989), pp. 295–329.

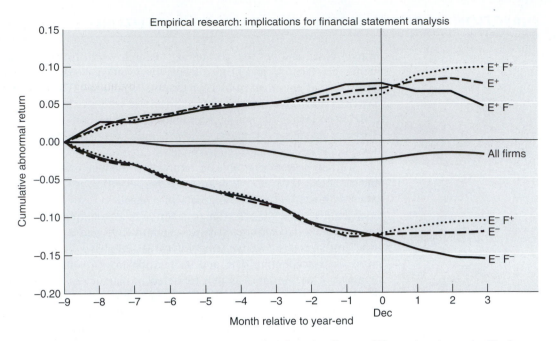

FIGURE 5-6 Ou's results. *Source:* Jane A. Ou, "The Information Content of Nonearnings Accounting Numbers as Earnings Predictors," *Journal of Accounting Research* (Spring 1990), pp. 144–162, Figure 1 on p. 158, reprinted with permission.

(F^- = bad news) the earnings forecast by a time-series model. This resulted in the formation of four portfolios:

Portfolio	Reported This Year	Predicted Next Year
E^+F^+	Good news	Good news
E^+F^-	Good news	Bad news
E^-F^+	Bad news	Good news
E^-F^-	Bad news	Bad news

The next-year forecast was in the form of a probability assessment (Pr) as to whether next year's earnings would be above or below those predicted by a (naïve) time-series model. The following eight variables were used in the forecasting model:[51]

1. Percentage growth in the ratio of inventory to total assets
2. Percentage growth in the total asset turnover (net sales/total assets)
3. Change in dividends per share relative to previous year
4. Percentage growth in depreciation expense
5. Percentage growth in the ratio of capital expenditures to total assets
6. Percentage growth in the previous year's ratio of capital expenditures to total assets
7. Return on equity
8. Change in return on equity relative to the previous year

As the graph indicates, all the E^+ portfolios and all the E^- portfolios moved together until year-end. Then, from January on, the F^+ portfolios (good-news forecasts) moved upward, whereas the F^- (bad-news forecasts) turned downward. The results indicate that the forecast model could be used successfully to predict (the direction of) future prices.

---

[51]These variables, culled from a list of 61 variables, are characteristic of those commonly used in financial statement analysis.

Ou's study is characterized by two attributes that differentiate it from previous market-based research. First, the analysis is not motivated to show whether accounting information is associated on an *ex post* basis with market prices, but rather whether the information can be used *ex ante* as a basis of valuation. Second and consistent with this *ex ante* approach, Ou broadens the set of accounting information by utilizing "tools of fundamental analysis" in her research design.

Subsequent papers by Ou and Penman (1989) and Holthausen and Larcker (1992) using similar tools of fundamental analysis examined whether financial ratios could be used in a successful trading strategy. Ou and Penman (1989) was an extension of Ou (1990). Their purpose was to see whether a trading strategy[52] based on earnings forecasts (Pr) would prove to be fruitful. It was; the average market-adjusted return was 14.5% per annum over a 24-month holding period.[53]

Holthausen and Larcker (1992) replicated Ou and Penman with some variation. They did not use ratios to forecast earnings first and then "trade" based on the expected earnings. Rather, they developed a model to forecast abnormal returns directly. Implementation of this model proved to be more successful in earning abnormal returns than Ou and Penman's strategy.

It is worth noting that we refer to these approaches *as utilizing tools of fundamental analysis rather than fundamental analysis itself*. All firms and variables were subjected to identical statistical analysis. The utilization of variables in these studies was done in a purely mechanical fashion.[54] *Fundamental analysis requires more in-depth analysis, the nature of which varies from firm to firm. Additionally, it needs theoretical underpinnings.* Both these attributes are missing from these studies.[55]

Contextual Approaches and Fundamental Analysis

Lev and Thiagarajan (1993) took a step in this direction. Rather than just allowing statistical models to select their predictive variables, they attempted to, *a priori*, select predictive variables claimed to be useful by financial analysts. The variables they examined are listed in Exhibit 5-2. Additionally, the authors allowed for the possibility that the effects of these variables might vary (contextual approach), depending on the state of the economy or industry. For example, the impact of changes in inventory levels may depend on whether the firm itself increases inventory levels, or the economy as a whole is expanding. They found that the variables were generally value-relevant and could be used to forecast abnormal returns. Moreover, varying economic and industry conditions had the desired effect. The interpretation of the financial variables, however, could be quite subtle and situation-specific.

---

[52]Specifically, they tested the following trading strategy. If the Pr was greater than 60% indicating at least a 60% probability that the earnings change would be positive, a long position in the firm's stock was taken. If the Pr was less than 40%, equivalent to a greater-than-60% probability that the earnings change will be negative, a short position in the firm's stock was taken.

[53]There is much debate [see Ball (1992)] as to whether Ou and Penman's results are an example of market inefficiency as the returns they garnered were abnormal, or whether their model allowed them to predict better than expected earnings relative to the CAPM. Others [Greig (1992) and Stober (1992)] argue that the abnormal returns merely compensate for risk. We do not intend to enter that debate. What is important is that under either premise, the variables proved to be valuation-relevant.

[54]If anything, this shortcoming may have biased the results downward; more promising results may be obtainable with more in-depth analyses.

[55]Ou and Penman (1995), in a subsequent paper, recognize this drawback and note that their approach "was an empirical analysis, without a guiding conceptual foundation" (p. 5). Similarly Holthausen and Larcker viewed their results as somewhat of a puzzle:

> We find it surprising that a statistical model, derived without any consideration of any economic foundations, can earn excess returns of the magnitude determined here. Had our trading strategy been based on some new economic insight . . . or if it had been based upon hours of diligent investigation of annual reports of the firm, its suppliers, customers, the industry, and/or government documents, we would be more convinced that the trading strategy was earning "true" excess returns. As such, we view the results of our paper as something of a puzzle. [R. W. Holthausen and D. F. Larcker, "The Prediction of Stock Returns Using Financial Statement Information," *Journal of Accounting and Economics,* (June/September 1992), p. 410.]

EXHIBIT 5-2
Fundamental Analysis Variables Used by Lev and Thiagarajan (1993)

1. Indications of future growth, for example:
   a. Levels of investment (capital expenditures and R&D)
   b. The percentage change in inventory and receivables relative to that of sales
2. Profitability measures, for example:
   a. Changes in the gross margin percentage
   b. The rate of change in SG&A expenses

3. Quality of earnings indicators, for example:
   a. LIFO versus FIFO earnings
   b. Audit qualification
4. Leading indicators, for example:
   a. Order backlog
   b. Change in labor force indicating changes in future costs

More recently, Abarbanell and Bushee (1997 and 1998) and Pitrowski (2000) also used *a priori* conceptual arguments in selecting the accounting variables and ratios they studied and found them to be useful in predicting future earnings as well as stock returns.

Other Areas of Research

The shift in emphasis in research paradigms suggested by the contextual approach also influenced other areas of research. The question of whether accrual income or cash flow is a better predictor of future cash flows and/or stock returns has long been a subject of considerable interest to researchers. Dechow (1994), Dechow et al. (1998), and Barth et al. (2001) showed that the relative performance of income versus cash flows could be better examined by taking into account differences caused by environments (industries) where cash flow would have significant timing and matching problems (e.g., shorter windows, volatility of working capital and investing requirements, and longer operating cycles).[56]

In Chapter 4, we noted that factors that affect a firm's (current and future) profitability include the stage of its life cycle, its competitive strategies, operating leverage, and the competitive environment it faced. Anthony and Ramesh (1992) used the first two factors and Ahmed (1994) the latter two to explain cross-sectional variation in ERCs. In a similar spirit, Teets and Wasley (1996) show that the low ERCs found in previous studies may be a result of using cross-sectional data (one size fits all). By using firm-specific time-series models they were able to estimate substantially larger ERCs.

On an industry level, a number of studies have also taken a contextual approach. Amir and Lev (1996) examined the wireless communication industry and showed that accounting information had relevance only once nonaccounting industry-specific variables were considered. A number of studies [e.g., Beatty et al. (1996), Collins, et al. (1996), and Bishop (1996)] have examined the banking industry. Eccher (1996) examined the computer software industry.

Although many of these latter studies are an improvement insofar as they are based on *a priori* relationships, they still lack a formal model relating firm value to accounting variables.

Coming Full Circle: From Edwards and Bell to Ohlson

Ohlson's residual income model filled this gap. With Ohlson (1995) and Feltham and Ohlson (1995), accounting research came full circle.[57] These papers rediscovered and expanded on valuation equations originally put forth by Edwards and Bell (1961) and Preinreich (1938).[58] Ou and Penman, referring to the valuation relationships emanating from the EBO (Edwards and Bell, and Ohlson) paradigm, note (p. 8) that the equations

"are presumably what traditional fundamental analysts had in mind when they talked of "buying (future) earnings."

---

[56]Box 2-2 in Chapter 2 discusses these papers in greater detail.

[57]These papers were originally completed in 1991 and 1992, respectively, and earlier versions were well-known in the academic community. As noted, it took some time until the work was accepted.

[58]Biddle, Bowen, and Wallace (1997), in fact, trace the idea of residual income valuation to Hamilton (1777) and Marshall (1890)!

Unlike valuation models in vogue in the finance literature that undo the accounting (accrual) process, using (free) cash flows to arrive at value, these (i.e., Ohlson's) models express value using basic accounting variables such as earnings, ROE, and book values.[59]

The efficacy of this model compared to other valuation models and the assumptions inherent in the model have come under close examination.[60] Although not all researchers have accepted the appropriateness (of all details) of the model, its introduction has had a major impact on accounting research as the model:

- Provides theoretical underpinnings for some market-based empirical research
- Supplies a framework for future research by directly connecting accounting variables and (intrinsic) value

In doing so, these models have become "hot" and have spawned a number of papers and research directions. For example, Easton et al. (1992) show that over long horizons, a pre-specified earnings model can explain price changes. The results of Ohlson (1989) provide insight as to whether ERCs should be defined in terms of earnings levels or earnings changes (or both). Penman (1996) analyzes which variables are relevant in differentiating price/book and price/earnings ratios.

Most importantly, from the perspective of financial statement analysis, Frankel and Lee (1998) and Dechow, Hutton, and Sloan (1999) used (variations of) the residual income model combined with analysts' earnings forecasts to determine stocks' *intrinsic value*. They then determined that abnormal returns could be earned by investing in mispriced securities (on the basis of their intrinsic value).

Market (In)efficiency and Accounting

Many of the studies listed above and their results implicitly reject market efficiency. They showed that abnormal returns could be earned using accounting data. At the very least, these studies reject the assumption that markets immediately reflect all available information, as it appears that prices take several years to fully reflect accounting information.

Other studies have gone a step further and examined whether firms use earnings management techniques to "fool the market." Rather than manipulate earnings solely (as suggested by the positive account literature) for contracting purposes, managers may do so [see Teoh, Welch, and Wong (1998a and b)] in order to inflate stock prices prior to (IPO as well as seasoned) equity offerings.[61]

Originally (in the 1970s and 1980s), market efficiency was a given and it was deemed futile for managers to engage in income manipulation of this kind unless another motivation could be found. Positive accounting and the implications for debt covenants and management compensation were offered as the answer. Obviously, we have come full circle.

IMPLICATIONS OF EMPIRICAL RESEARCH FOR FINANCIAL STATEMENT ANALYSIS

The empirical studies reviewed in this chapter put to rest a number of beliefs, some of which, with hindsight, may have been overly naïve in the first place. Financial markets are not simplistic and do not react in knee-jerk fashion to accounting information. On the contrary, the reactions seem to be complex enough that the vast methodological carpet-bombing of the last 30-plus years has not been able to uncover them.

The current state of academic research can be summarized with the following characteristics:

- Further *theoretical development* and *empirical validation* of models that relate accounting variables to firm valuation

---

[59]These models have their commercial equivalents (e.g., Stern Stewart's EVA℠ and McKinsey's Economic Profit Model).

[60]See Chapter 19 for a more detailed discussion of valuation models and research in this area.

[61]The technology bubble of the late 1990s and the accounting practices of these companies may be another example of this phenomenon. See Problem 5-14 for further discussion of this issue.

- Development of (forecasting) models that predict future values of those accounting variables deemed relevant by the theoretical models
- Analysis of *firm-specific* and/or *industry-specific* valuation models
- Tests of market efficiency with respect to accounting data

These characteristics indicate that research needs to focus on understanding the work of the financial analyst as well as the relationships between accounting variables and market prices. Analysts seem to be the driving force keeping the market intelligent, and there is evidence that they lead the market.[62] Moreover, it is acknowledged that "better" analysts can carve out worthwhile areas of expertise.

Positive theory has pointed out the important contractual considerations that cannot be ignored when examining accounting data. These other considerations need to be included when the foundations for contextual analysis are laid.

Classical theory, at the same time, cannot be discarded for two reasons. Even if one disagrees with the view that theory can dictate "correct" accounting standards, the fact remains that much of GAAP is based on the measurement of theoretical constructs. Thus, in analyzing financial statements, it is important to know the underlying principles that argue for a given treatment before interpreting or adjusting it to the analyst's own view. Second, empirical evidence shows that accounting data generated by the accrual process are value-relevant both *ex post* and *ex ante*.

At the same time, the analyst must be aware that the relationships governing accounting information involve complex interactions among investors, managers, and regulators and these interactions may have powerful implications for securities valuation.

In conclusion, accounting research has clearly not proven that financial analysis is a futile exercise. On the contrary, it is trying to get a better understanding of how financial analysis works. Although financial markets have become increasingly sophisticated in recent years, we believe that superior financial analysis is still rewarding. We advance three arguments for this belief:

1. The ability to understand the impact of alternative accounting methods places the investor at a competitive advantage in a world of increasingly complex transactions and sophisticated analytical techniques.

2. Market efficiency cannot be taken for granted, especially for smaller, less intensively researched companies.

3. Recent financial history provides, at least in retrospect, many cases where financial markets ignored warning signals. Those left holding the bag suffered significant financial losses. Investors in some technology companies and financial intermediaries are recent examples of this phenomenon.

At the same time, it would be foolish to ignore the lessons learned from the research and theory reviewed. Successful investing cannot simply focus on financial statements themselves. An awareness of the environment of the firm and its management is needed for proper analysis.

As Bernard stated:

There is much groundwork to be laid . . . moving to within-industry analyses, explicitly considering how the information conveyed by accounting numbers is conditioned on the accounting context, gaining a better understanding of the relations among accounting numbers before understanding price data, emphasizing economic interpretation more and statistics less—may be useful in laying that groundwork.[63]

We agree with that point of view and believe that this book can be useful in laying such groundwork. It is with this belief that we continue with the remaining chapters of this book.

---

[62]A more detailed discussion of analyst forecasts and other forecasting models is presented in Chapter 19.

[63]Bernard, p. 106.

Chapter 5

Problems

1. [Approaches to accounting standard setting] In Chapter 1 we discuss neutrality, one of the qualitative characteristics of accounting information:

> Neutrality is concerned with whether financial statement data are biased. FASB proposals are frequently the object of complaints that companies will be adversely affected by the new standard. The principle of neutrality states that the Board should consider only the relevance and reliability of the data, not any possible economic impact.

Contrast this approach to accounting standard setting with that taken:

(i) By academics in drawing conclusions from information content studies

(ii) By proponents of the positive approach to accounting theory

2. [Predictability, surprises, and information content] Suppose it were possible to evaluate the effects on stock prices of two information systems: Alpha and Gamma. Each produces two accounting reports. The second report of each system will be identical. Information system Alpha allows you to predict the second report more accurately than the Gamma system.

a. State which of the two systems you believe to be a better information system. Justify your choice.

b. State under which system the second report would show more information content. Justify your choice.

c. Discuss the implication of your replies to parts A and B on the factors that must be considered when evaluating the usefulness of financial reporting systems.

d. Ingberman and Sorter, in their paper, "The Role of Financial Statements in an Efficient Market," *Journal of Accounting, Auditing and Finance* (Fall 1978), pp. 58–62, suggest that

> financial statements are seldom the place in which significant firm-related events are initially reported. Instead, these statements help the investor to construct a forecasting model for future income and cash flows. During the period, firm-related events become known in various ways, and these are inserted into the forecasting model.

Relate this view to your reply to parts a through c and the approach used by information content studies.

3. [Efficient market hypothesis; CFA© adapted] The efficient market hypothesis (EMH) exists in three forms: *weak, semistrong,* and *strong*.

a. Briefly discuss the implications of each of these forms for investment policy as it applies to:

(i) Technical analysis (e.g., charting)

(ii) Fundamental analysis

b. *Assuming the EMH holds*, discuss two major roles or responsibilities of portfolio managers in an efficient market.

c. *Given the empirical evidence to date*, discuss the possible roles for investment managers.

4. [Implications of adjusting for general market conditions] Assume that new information arrived affecting all aspects of the economy.

a. Under standard research procedures, using a model such as the capital asset pricing model to test for market reaction, what would the results show?

b. What does this imply about the nature of conclusions that can be drawn from certain market studies?

c. Can you think of any (mandated) accounting standards that may have had pervasive effects across many sectors of the economy?

5. [Accounting standard setting] Describe how the proponents of the three approaches to accounting theory would respond to the following statements

> "Generally accepted accounting principles are anything but principled. How could they be? They are a product of a political process."

6. [Motivation for income manipulation] A *Business Week* (February 14, 1994, pp. 78–92) article entitled, "Did Pfizer Doctor Its Numbers," suggests that for the 1993 fiscal year, Pfizer, a pharmaceutical and chemical company, "managed down the numbers." Specifically, the article contends that:

> the company is spending heavily and delaying sales to deliberately dampen Pfizer's profit growth rates. . . . Pfizer pinched fourth-quarter sales while boosting expenses. . . . Pfizer also boosted R&D spending more than its rivals.

Suggest why Pfizer might have engaged in such actions.

7. [Implications for analysis] WSF Investment Services has a policy of completing a "company profile" for each new company whose financial statements it intends to analyze. You have been hired by WSF as an instructor in their training program. For each item on the checklist, explain to a trainee what the relevance might be for financial analysis:

(i) Terms of labor contract

(ii) Number of analysts following the company

(iii) Details of management compensation plans

(iv) Capitalization size

(v) The proportion of stock held by managers

(vi) Industry classification

(vii) Bond covenants

8. [Mandated accounting changes; economic consequences; market reaction] *Newsweek* (January 11, 1993, p. 59) reported that a survey

> found that two-thirds of major corporations have curtailed retiree health plans or intend to in 1993.

EXHIBIT 5P-1
Selected Indices and News Reports, February 24–25, 1993

February 24, 1993

	Close	Change	Percent
Overall Averages			
Dow Jones Industrial Average	3356.50	+33.23	1.0%
S&P 500	440.87	+6.07	1.4%
NASDAQ Composite	662.46	+10.90	1.7%
Technology (Dow Jones)	331.14	+6.81	2.1%
Industry Group Performance			
Biotechnology	669.27	+34.50	5.4%
Computers	275.35	+3.00	1.1%
Heavy machinery	167.73	+4.73	2.9%
Closing Prices			
Amgen	$46\frac{1}{4}$	$+2\frac{3}{4}$	6.3%
Dell Computers	$30\frac{1}{8}$	$-6\frac{1}{8}$	−16.9%
Deere	$50\frac{3}{4}$	$+2\frac{1}{2}$	5.2%

The following news items are from the *New York Times*, Feb. 25, 1993, p. D3.

Amgen Shares Plummet After Profit Forecast

Shares of Amgen, Inc., a biotechnology company, plunged in after-hours trading yesterday after the company said it expected its first-quarter earnings to come in well below Wall Street expectations. Amgen made the disclosure after regular trading hours, when its shares had closed on NASDAQ at $46.25, up $2.75. But in the half-hour of after-hour trading, shares plummeted $9, to $37.25.

Amgen's chief financial officer, Lowell Sears, said the company had anticipated that earnings per share for the first quarter would be 10 to 15 percent lower than Wall Street's average estimate of 60 cents a share. . . .

Dell's Stock Price Plunges After Forecast by Thomas C. Hayes

Dallas, Feb. 24—The stock of the Dell Computer Corporation plummeted nearly 17 percent today after analysts said an earnings projection for the current fiscal year raised worries that the fast-growing maker of personal computers had quietly reduced its long-term profit goal to below 5 percent of sales.

The projection of Dell's chief financial officer was part of the announcement that it had withdrawn an offering of four million new common shares because its stock price fell sharply recently and because declining interest rates made borrowing more attractive.

The earnings and revenue projections were interpreted as a sign of Dell's determination to expand in the months ahead a price war [sic] that has crimped its profitability and pushed smaller rivals into financial distress.

Dell's stock fell $6.125 today, to $30.125, on volume of more than 9.5 million shares—the heaviest in NASDAQ trading. The stock hit an all-time high of $49.875 only last month.

Deere Plans to Expand Production This Year

Deere & Company, the world's largest producer of agricultural machinery, told shareholders yesterday at its annual meeting in Moline, Ill., that it would expand production this year for the first time since 1990. Hans W. Becherer, chairman and chief executive, said output would grow 5 percent this year, thanks to sharp reductions in inventories at dealers, renewed buying from American farmers and the appeal of new products. Growth would be even stronger, he said, but for declines in the European market, where debates about the level of farm price and production supports have made farmers cautious about investing in new machinery.

The article attributes the curtailment of such benefits to

a change in the national accounting rules that, beginning this year, require companies to carry the cost of such benefits as liabilities on their balance sheets. Technically, the new rule is a hit only on paper. But critics say many companies are using it as an excuse to cut costs and renege on past promises to workers.

Evaluate the argument made in the *Newsweek* article in the context of the accounting theories discussed in the chapter. Consideration should be given to the following points:

- Whether the article is consistent with the efficient market and/or positive theory views of accounting
- The possibility that firms were not aware of the magnitude of the health costs until the new accounting rule came into effect
- The expected market reaction to the
  (i) New accounting rule
  (ii) Subsequent financial statement disclosures
  (iii) Results of the survey
- Whether curtailments of health plans around the time of the implementation of the new accounting rule necessarily show the economic consequences of accounting rules

9. [News releases, market reaction, and abnormal returns] Exhibit 5P-1 contains information as to:

- Closing prices and news items/releases of three companies
- The performance of various market indices on February 24, 1993

a. Ignoring the news items, state and justify which of the three stocks you believe exhibited abnormal returns. Describe how you would go about determining whether that was the case.

b. The Amgen news was disclosed after the market close. Thus, the closing price and price change do not reflect the news. Discuss whether the sharp market reaction to the news was an indication of market efficiency or whether the lack of anticipation of the news indicated inefficiency. Discuss whether this question could be asked with respect to the price change of Dell's shares in the last month.

c. The news items for Amgen and Dell imply that the price change was a reaction to the news reported. Although the same argument can be made in the case of Deere, the article does not do so. State and justify for which of these three companies there is the strongest argument that the market reaction is associated with the news release.

d. Discuss why, in the case of Dell, it is particularly difficult to determine the cause of the market reaction.

e. Most research studies would test for the market reaction to an announcement coming after the close of the market on the basis of the market reaction of the following day. In the case of Amgen, its shares on February 25, 1993, the following day, closed at 37, down 9.25 or 20%. The biotechnology index closed at 591.07, down 11.68%.

(i) Discuss why a research study might underestimate the effects of the earnings announcement under these circumstances.

(ii) The *Wall Street Journal* reported that the weakest stocks in the biotechnology group (on February 25, 1993) were Amgen, Chiron, and Centocor. Chiron stock fell by 1.02% and Centocor was unchanged. Discuss how this information affects your response to (i).

f. These news items are examples of the flow of information about a company during the year. Assuming the projections implied by these news items prove to be true, discuss the expected market reaction to the release of financial statements. Discuss whether these news items make financial statements irrelevant.

g. The Deere article does not deal with earnings, but rather with production. Discuss the relevance of financial statements in this case.

10. [News releases and market reaction] Avant! [AVNT] produces software for the semiconductor industry Figure 5P-1 presents the daily stock price graph of the company for the months

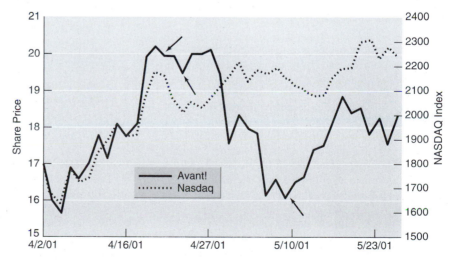

FIGURE 5-P1 Share price of Avant! April–May 2001. Arrows indicate price at 4/20, 4/24, and 5/09 respectively.

of April and May 2001. For comparison purposes, a graph of the NASDAQ index is also provided.

During the period, the following news emanated from the company:

- On April 20, 2001 Avant! Filed a Form 8-K stating that the company had dismissed KPMG LLP as the company's independent accountants.

- On April 24, 2001 an amended 8-K reported that KPMG stated in a letter to the Securities and Exchange Commission that

we have issued letters to the Audit Committee related to the audits of the Company's consolidated financial statements for the years ended December 31, 1999 and December 31, 2000 that noted certain matters involving internal control and its operation that we consider to be reportable conditions under standards established by the American Institute of Certified Public Accountants. For the year ended December 31, 1999 the reportable conditions related to incomplete and missing contract documentation, inadequate internal communications in connection with recording revenue on complex contracts, and the lack of timely and accurate account reconciliations in a number of areas including cash, unbilled accounts receivable, prepaid commissions, and investments in affiliates. For the year ended December 31, 2000, the reportable condition relates to the ineffectiveness of internal controls associated with recording revenue, which resulted in numerous errors through the year and post-closing journal entries to correct such errors.

- On May 9, Bloomberg reported the amended 8-K filing.

The above three dates are indicated by arrows in Figure 5P-1.

a. Describe the expected stock market reaction to the original and amended 8-K filings.

b. Describe the expected stock market reaction to the Bloomberg news story.

c. Discuss whether the actual stock market reactions were consistent with the expectations in your answers to parts a and b.

d. Discuss a possible explanation for the actual stock market reactions.

11. [Disclosure; need for regulation] In describing the financial reporting environment, William H. Beaver [*Financial Reporting: An Accounting Revolution* (Englewood Cliffs, NJ: Prentice Hall, 1998)] portrays an environment in which investors with (perhaps) limited access to or knowledge of financial information make use of financial intermediaries/analysts. These intermediaries provide information gathering as well as investment services and compete with each other in the information-processing function. Managers and firms compete for investors' capital by producing and disseminating information to investors and their intermediaries. The information provided is often more timely than the annual report or SEC filings.

In this environment, Beaver suggests that there exist incentives for firms to produce information on their own in the absence of any regulation. (*Note*: The interested reader is referred to Chapter 7 of Beaver's book.)

Given this argument, discuss the need for regulators such as the SEC and FASB to mandate the type and form of disclosure required.

12. [Regulatory accounting, market reaction, and economic consequences] Certain regulated industries such as utilities, banks, and insurance companies are subject to accounting rules, known as *Regulatory Accounting Principles (RAP)*. These RAP rules, which can differ from GAAP, are the basis by which, for example, the permitted rate of profit is calculated. Additionally, for many of these industries, certain minimum-net-worth requirements must be met. RAP governs how these requirements are measured.

The following article, by Greg Steinmetz, appeared in the *Wall Street Journal* on January 8, 1993:

> *Certain Life Insurers Plan Reserves for Real Estate Losses due to New Rule*
>
> Giant, policyholder-owned life insurance companies plan to set aside billions of dollars in coming months to cover potential losses from real estate holdings.
>
> The actions do not signify further deterioration in the companies' real estate holdings, nor will they seriously weaken the companies' financial strength. Rather, they stem from an accounting change that affects already identified problems. The change will bring the insurers' reserves up to the levels already established by publicly traded insurers. . . .
>
> The new rules, established by the National Association of Insurance Commissioners, require companies to build reserves to a level determined by a complicated formula. Insurers have several years to build the reserve to their minimum requirement.
>
> The new rules came in response to criticism that insurance accounting practices let insurers hide losses. The rules are also part of an effort to ward off federal regulation of insurance, which is now overseen by states.
>
> In anticipation of the new rules, some insurers began to voluntarily put up real estate reserves in 1991.

a. Notwithstanding the manner in which the first paragraph was written, no actual cash was set aside in these reserves. They were merely accounting entries. Discuss whether

  (i) Proponents of the efficient market hypothesis would view this accounting change as cosmetic.

  (ii) One should expect the market to react when it first heard about the accounting change.

  (iii) You could predict the nature of the market reaction.

b. Discuss any expected reaction around the time this article was published.

c. Discuss the similarities between the implications of changes in RAP and the positive accounting approach to GAAP.

13. [Market crashes and efficient markets] On October 19, 1987, the Dow Jones Industrial Average dropped by over 500 points. Overall market value on the New York Stock Exchange stocks fell by close to 25% on that day. Discuss the implications of the crash for the efficient market theory.

14. [Market bubbles and efficient markets] The late 1990s witnessed a technology stock bubble that burst in 2000–2001.

It has been suggested that the bubble was partly fueled by aggressive revenue and expense recognition policies (such as those discussed in Chapter 2) with management stock options providing enormous incentive for management to increase their share price. Compare how proponents of the efficient market and positive theories of accounting would view this phenomenon.

15. [Accounting theories and pro forma earnings] Chapter 2 discussed the increasing use of pro forma earnings measures in press releases. Such pro forma earnings numbers often adjust GAAP-based earnings measures for various revenue and expenses on items including, but not limited to, stock compensa-

tion, goodwill amortization, interest expense, losses in equity method investees, and writedowns of investments in equity-method investees.

a. Compare how proponents of the efficient market and positive theories of accounting would view this phenomenon.

b. *Assuming the EMH holds*, discuss the role of pro forma earnings measures in an efficient market.

c. Problem 5-2 cited an article by Ingberman and Sorter. Discuss their view of information provided by financial statements in the light of press releases containing pro forma earnings measures.

6

ANALYSIS OF INVENTORIES

CHAPTER OUTLINE

CHAPTER OBJECTIVES

The objectives of Chapter 6 are to:

1. Define and illustrate the alternative accounting methods used by companies to account for product inventory: LIFO, FIFO, and average cost.

2. Compare the usefulness of inventory and cost of goods sold data provided by these different accounting methods.

3. Describe the cash flow and working capital effects of the choice of inventory method.

4. Show how price increases and decreases affect reported income under different accounting methods.

5. Contrast the effect of different inventory methods on financial ratios.

6. Adjust the financial data of companies using different accounting methods to achieve comparability.

7. Adjust reported financial results to remove distortions caused by price changes.

8. Compare the two different signals transmitted by a decline in the LIFO reserve.

9. Discuss the motivation for adoption of the LIFO method and show the financial statement effects of that adoption.

10. Describe what research tells us about why firms choose to adopt (or not to adopt) the LIFO method.

11. Discuss the inventory methods used outside the United States.

INTRODUCTION

During 1999, the spot price of crude oil[1] rose from less than $10 per barrel to more than $25 per barrel, an increase of more than 150%. Crude oil continued to rise in early 2000, nearing $32 per barrel in March. Simultaneously, the price of gasoline sold at the pump increased dramatically in most countries. Consumers and politicians criticized oil companies for immediately raising the price of gasoline sold at the retail level. They argued that the gasoline being sold had been refined from oil purchased at a price of $10 per barrel and, hence, raising the price of this "old" gasoline resulted in windfall profits.

The oil companies countered that since the market price of oil had risen, replacing the old oil now cost more and thus raising the price of gasoline was justified by current market conditions.

The accounting choice of last-in, first-out (LIFO) versus first-in, first-out (FIFO) for inventory and cost of goods sold (COGS) mirrors this debate as to the more appropriate measure of income. The choice affects the firm's income statement, balance sheet, and related ratios. Perhaps more important, in contrast to most financial reporting choices, the choice of inventory method has real cash flow effects as it affects income taxes paid by the firm.

INVENTORY AND COST OF GOODS SOLD: BASIC RELATIONSHIPS

The inventory account is affected by two events: the purchase (or manufacture) of goods (P) and their subsequent sale (COGS). The relationship between these events and the balance of beginning inventory (BI) and ending inventory (EI) can be expressed as

$$(1)\ EI = BI + P - \text{COGS or}$$
$$(2)\ BI + P = \text{COGS} + EI$$

For any period, prior to the preparation of financial statements for the period, the left side of the second equation is known: the beginning inventory plus purchases (cost of goods acquired for sale during the period). Preparation of the income statement and balance sheet for

---

[1]Measured by the Brent Crude "near contract generic future" as reported on Bloomberg.

the period requires the allocation of these costs ($BI + P$) between COGS and ending inventory. This process is illustrated under two scenarios:

Beginning inventory: 200 units @ $10/unit = $2,000

		Scenario 1: Stable Prices		Scenario 2: Rising Prices	
Quarter	Purchases Units	Unit Cost	Purchases Dollars	Unit Cost	Purchases Dollars
1	100	$10	$1,000	$11	$1,100
2	150	10	1,500	12	1,800
3	150	10	1,500	13	1,950
4	100	10	1,000	14	1,400
Total	500		$5,000		$6,250
			$BI + P = $7,000$		$BI + P = $8,250$

Units sold: 100 units per quarter for a total of 400 units

Ending inventory: 300 units

Scenario 1: Stable Prices

Beginning inventory plus purchases equals $7,000. Since unit costs are constant at $10 per unit and 400 units were sold, the COGS equals $4,000 (400 × $10) and the cost of the 300 units in ending inventory equals $3,000 (300 × $10).

$$BI + P = COGS + EI$$
$$\$2,000 + \$5,000 = \$4,000 + \$3,000$$

However, perfectly stable prices are the exception rather than the norm. In addition to general inflationary pressures, costs and prices for specific goods are constantly changing. Accounting for inventory and COGS in such an environment, as a result, becomes more complex.

Scenario 2: Rising Prices

Beginning inventory plus purchases equals $8,250. Unlike the case of stable prices, the allocation between COGS and the cost of ending inventory requires an assumption as to the flow of costs. Essentially, three alternative assumptions are possible: *FIFO, LIFO, and weighted-average cost.*

FIFO accounting assumes that the costs of items *first purchased* are deemed to be the costs of items *first sold* and these costs enter COGS; ending inventory is made up of the cost of the most recent items purchased.

At the opposite extreme is LIFO accounting where items *last purchased* are assumed to be the ones *first sold* and the ending inventory is made up of the earliest costs incurred.

Finally, as its name implies, weighted-average cost accounting uses the (same) average cost for both the items sold and those remaining in closing inventory.

In our example, *the assumptions of rising prices and an increase in the inventory balance generate three alternative allocations of the cost of goods available for sale ($BI + P$),* on the income statement and balance sheet (the calculations are shown in Exhibit 6-1):

Method	BI	+	P	=	COGS	+	EI
FIFO	$2,000	+	$6,250	=	$4,300	+	$3,950
Weighted-average	2,000	+	6,250	=	4,714	+	3,536
LIFO	2,000	+	6,250	=	5,150	+	3,100

EXHIBIT 6-1
Allocation of Costs Under Different Inventory Methods, Scenario 2

A. FIFO

The 400 units sold (COGS) are assumed to carry the earliest costs incurred and the 300 units left in inventory carry the latest costs:

COGS	Ending Inventory
200 @ $10 = $2,000	100 @ $14 = $1,400
100 @ $11 = $1,100	150 @ $13 = $1,950
100 @ $12 = $1,200	50 @ $12 = $ 600
400 $4,300	300 $3,950

B. LIFO

The 400 units sold (COGS) are assumed to carry the latest costs incurred and the 300 units left in inventory carry the earliest costs:

COGS	Ending Inventory
100 @ $14 = $1,400	200 @ $10 = $2,000
150 @ $13 = $1,950	100 @ $11 = $1,100
150 @ $12 = $1,800	
400 $5,150	300 $3,100

C. Weighted-Average

The total costs for the 700 units = $8,250. On a per-unit basis, this results in a weighted-average unit cost of:

$$\frac{\$8,250}{700} = \$11.786$$
$$COGS = 400 \times \$11.786 = \$4,714$$
$$\text{Ending inventory} = 300 \times \$11.786 = \$3,536$$

COMPARISON OF INFORMATION PROVIDED BY ALTERNATIVE METHODS

This section compares the information provided by the three alternative accounting methods.

Balance Sheet Information: Inventory Account

The ending inventory consists of 300 units. At current replacement cost (i.e., the fourth-quarter unit cost of $14), the inventory would have a carrying value of $4,200. The FIFO inventory of $3,950 comes closest to this amount because FIFO allocates the earliest costs to COGS, leaving the most recent costs in ending inventory.

Conversely, the LIFO balance of $3,100 is furthest from the current cost as LIFO accounting allocates the earliest (outdated) costs to ending inventory. In fact, the cost of ending inventory for many companies using LIFO may be decades old[2] and virtually useless as an indicator of the current or replacement cost of inventories on hand.

From a balance sheet perspective, therefore, inventories based on FIFO are preferable to those presented under LIFO, as carrying values most closely reflect current cost. In other words, FIFO provides a measure of inventory that is closer to its current (economic) value.

The carrying amount of inventory can also be affected by changes in market value as discussed below.

---

[2]For example, Caterpillar has stated that the LIFO method "was first adopted for the major portion of inventories in 1950."

Inventory Valuation: Lower of Cost or Market

GAAP requires the use of the lower-of-cost-or-market valuation basis (LCM) for inventories, with market value defined as replacement cost.[3] The LCM valuation basis follows the principle of conservatism (on both the balance sheet and income statement) since it recognizes losses or declines in market value as they occur, whereas increases are reported only when inventory is sold. LCM can be used with LIFO for financial statement purposes. However, for tax purposes LIFO cannot be combined with LCM. Firms using LIFO cannot recognize (and obtain tax benefits from) writedowns and declines in market value for tax purposes.[4]

Income Statement Information: Costs of Goods Sold

Consider a situation where an item purchased for $6 is sold for $10 at a time when it costs $7 to replace it. Prior to replacement of the item, reported income is $4 ($10 − $6). However, if income is defined as the amount available for distribution to shareholders without impairing the firm's operations, then it can be argued that income is only $3, as $7 (not the original cost of $6) are needed to replace the item in inventory and continue operations. The $1 difference between the original cost of the item and the cost of replacement is referred to as a holding gain or inventory profit,[5] and it is debatable whether this amount should be considered income.[6]

In our hypothetical case, *only if the item were not replaced* would there be $10 to distribute to shareholders, indicating income of $4. Under a going-concern assumption, however, firms that sell their inventory need to replenish it constantly for sales in the future. Thus, income should be measured after providing for the replacement of inventory. In addition, the increase in inventory costs suggests that income of $3 is a better indicator of expected future income than $4.

In our example, the replacement cost of the items sold (using the unit cost for each quarter) is $5,000[7] [(100 × $11) + (100 × $12) + (100 × $13) + (100 × $14)]. As U.S. GAAP use a historical cost framework, however, replacement cost accounting is not permitted. LIFO allocates the most recent purchase prices to COGS. The reported LIFO COGS of $5,150 is, therefore, closest to the replacement cost, with the FIFO COGS of $4,300 furthest from this cost. *During periods of changing prices and stable or growing inventories, LIFO is the most informative accounting method for income statement purposes, in that it provides a better measure of current income and future profitability.* This leaves us in something of a quandary, since FIFO provides the best measure for the balance sheet.[8]

---

[3]However, replacement cost cannot exceed the net realizable value or be below the net realizable value less the normal profit margin.

[4]Otherwise, the firm could have the best of both worlds and obtain tax savings whether costs were rising or declining.

[5]If we use the terminology of Chapter 2, economic income equals $4. As the holding gain is $1, sustainable (future) income is $3. Jennings, Simko, and Thompson (1996) confirm that LIFO-based cost of goods sold is a more useful indicator of the firm's future resource outflows than ("as-if") non-LIFO cost of goods sold as LIFO-based income statements explained more of the variation in equity valuations than non-LIFO income statements. However, in contrast to our earlier argument, they did not find ("as-if") non-LIFO balance sheets to be more informative than LIFO-based balance sheets. See Appendix 6-B for a further discussion of this and related empirical findings.

[6]The situation is analogous to having purchased a home before a rapid increase in real estate prices and not being able to benefit from your good fortune because any replacement home would cost as much as the home you live in now.

[7]If the computation were done on an annual basis, the replacement cost would be $5,600 (400 × $14) using the most recent purchase price to measure replacement cost.

[8]The weighted-average method falls someplace in between the FIFO and LIFO methods both in terms of the balance sheet and income statement. It is seen by some as a compromise method. Alternatively, we can argue that it is the worst of the three choices: Unlike LIFO and FIFO, which provide good information on one financial statement, the weighted-average method does not do so for either statement. Practically speaking, however, the weighted-average method tends to be closer to FIFO than LIFO, especially with respect to inventory costs on the balance sheet.

The preceding discussion implied the use of a single method for all inventories of the firm. In practice, firms often use more than one inventory method. They may use different methods for their foreign operations since LIFO is rarely used outside the United States, or they may use different methods for particular business segments. This factor serves to disguise further the impact of reported inventory on the income statement and balance sheet.

Additionally, the LIFO measurements are based on assumptions and estimates that are complex in a multiproduct environment and are affected by management choice. These issues are detailed in Appendix 6-A.

Finally, the use of FIFO, LIFO, or weighted-average for the allocation of cost of goods available for sale is preceded by the measurement of costs included in inventory. In a manufacturing environment, as Box 6-1 illustrates, such measurement is also affected by management choice.

From an analyst's perspective the use of different methods is not so grim. Information is often available to permit restatement of financial statements from one method to the other.

BOX 6-1
Inventory Costing in a Manufacturing Environment

Accounting for inventories in a manufacturing environment adds another dimension to the problem of inventory costing. Unlike merchandising operations, which carry only finished goods inventory, manufacturing operations carry three types of inventory: (1) raw material, (2) work in process, and (3) finished goods.

Inventories include raw material costs as well as labor and overhead costs required to transform the raw materials into finished goods. Determining the amount of overhead (indirect) costs poses the most problems. Included in (factory) overhead are items such as: supervisors' salaries, depreciation/rent of factory plant and equipment, utilities, repairs and maintenance, and quality control costs.

Such costs are *joint costs* and, in a multiproduct environment, are difficult to allocate among products. As the inventory carrying amount of any one product line depends on the allocation procedure, that amount can be somewhat arbitrary and capable of manipulation. For example, a manufacturer can increase reported income by choosing an allocation method that charges more of the joint costs to slower moving items. These costs then remain in inventory longer, and products with higher turnover rates appear more profitable.

A second aspect of this problem is the fixed nature (in the short run) of items such as depreciation, rent, or supervisors' salaries. Allocating such costs to products involves an averaging process that is affected by changing levels of production. A simple example in a single-product environment will illustrate this effect.

Assume a company has factory rent of $12,000 and it sells 10,000 units. If it produces 10,000 units, the full $12,000 of factor rent will be expensed through COGS (at a rate of $1.20/unit). If production increases to 12,000 units, then factory rent is allocated to inventory at $1.00/unit. But if only 10,000 units are sold, then only $10,000 is expensed as part of COGS and $2,000 of unallocated (but incurred) rent remains in inventory. Income increases by changing production levels rather than increasing sales.

The income effect of changing production rates can be the result of either intentional management decision (manipulation) or the unintended result of sales levels that differ from expectation. In either case it is imperative for the analyst to recognize:

- The accounting policies used by different firms in the same industry
- The effects of fluctuations in production on COGS and reported income

Finally, which costs are charged to inventory (and expensed when sold) and which costs are expensed as incurred vary among firms. Schiff (1987) notes that, although it is commonly suggested in accounting textbooks that fixed overhead costs must be allocated to inventory, in practice, many companies* have (historically) charged certain overhead costs (e.g., depreciation, pension costs, and property taxes) directly to expense. For such companies, variations in production and inventory levels will not affect the amount expensed. However, for firms that allocate such costs to inventory, when inventory levels increase, the amount expensed will be less than the amount actually incurred, with the difference remaining in inventory. On the balance sheet, those firms that capitalize more indirect costs in inventory will have higher carrying values of inventory, working capital, and equity balances. Unfortunately, not all companies disclose their practices in this respect. This can make comparisons between companies difficult.†

---

*The steel industry is one example noted by Schiff.

†The matter is further complicated by the increased emphasis in recent years in improvements in manufacturing processes. As a result, many firms have adjusted their method of inventory costing. [Bartley and Chen (1992) also report tax-related motivations for firms to switch from expensing to capitalization of certain items.]

Such restatement is illustrated later in the chapter. Our discussion now, however, turns to the financial statement effects of the choice between LIFO and FIFO.

LIFO VERSUS FIFO: INCOME, CASH FLOW, AND WORKING CAPITAL EFFECTS

The above example illustrates that, in periods of rising prices and stable or increasing inventory quantities, the use of LIFO results in higher COGS expense and lower reported income. In the absence of income taxes, there would be no difference in cash flow. Cash flow would equal payments made for inventory purchases and be independent of the accounting method used.

When LIFO is a permitted method for income taxes, however, lower income translates into lower taxes and thus higher operating cash flows. In the United States, unlike other accounting policy choices that allow differing methods of accounting for financial statements and tax purposes, *IRS regulations require that the same method of inventory accounting used for tax purposes also be used for financial reporting.* From an economic perspective, given rising prices, LIFO is the better choice, as taxes will be lower and cash flows will be higher despite the lower reported income.[9]

In Chapter 4 (ratios), it was noted that working capital is used as a broad liquidity measure because it includes cash and near-cash assets. Inventory accounting can distort the working capital measure and lead to erroneous and contradictory conclusions. LIFO accounting results in higher cash flows, but it reports lower working capital because the inventory balances retain earlier (lower) costs and the cash saved is only a percentage (the marginal tax rate) of the difference in inventory values.

In periods of rising prices and stable or increasing inventory quantities, the impact of LIFO and FIFO on the financial statements can be summarized as

	LIFO	FIFO
COGS	Higher	Lower
Income before taxes	Lower	Higher
Income taxes	Lower	Higher
Net Income	Lower	Higher
Cash flow	**Higher**	**Lower**
Inventory balance	Lower	Higher
Working capital	Lower	Higher

Cash flow has been highlighted because it is the only amount with direct economic impact. The others are accounting constructs and their economic significance is indirect and informational.

Continuing with the previous numeric example and assuming that 400 units are sold for $10,000 (average price of $25) with a tax rate of 40%, we can illustrate the above differences as follows. The resulting income statements are

	FIFO	LIFO	LIFO Higher/(Lower) by
Sales	$10,000	$10,000	$ 0
COGS	(4,300)	(5,150)	850
Income before tax	$ 5,700	$ 4,850	$(850)
Income tax @ 40%	(2,280)	(1,940)	(340)
Net income	$ 3,420	$ 2,910	$(510)

[9]The question of why, given the foregoing, all firms do not use LIFO will be considered later in the chapter.

If we assume that sales are for cash and payments for purchases and taxes are made immediately, then cash flows are

	FIFO	LIFO	LIFO Higher/(Lower) by
Sales inflows	$10,000	$10,000	$ 0
Purchases	(6,250)	(6,250)	0
Inflows before tax	$ 3,750	$ 3,750	$ 0
Income tax paid	(2,280)	(1,940)	(340)
Operating cash flow	$ 1,470	$ 1,810	$340

Therefore, changes in balance sheet accounts are

Assets

	FIFO	LIFO	LIFO Higher/(Lower) by
Operating cash*	$1,470	$1,810	$340
Inventory†	1,950	1,100	(850)
Working capital	$3,420	$2,910	$(510)

Liabilities and Stockholders' Equity

	FIFO	LIFO	LIFO Higher/(Lower) by
Retained earnings‡	$3,420	$2,910	$(510)

*Net cash flow for period.
†Purchases less COGS.
‡ Net income for period.

The difference in net income of $510 and the difference in cash flows of $340 are related to the difference in COGS (equivalently the difference in inventory balances) of $850 as follows:

$$\text{Income Difference} = (1\text{-Tax Rate}) \times \text{COGS Difference}$$
$$\$510 = 0.6 \times \$850$$
$$\text{Cash Flow Difference} = \text{Tax Rate} \times \text{COGS Difference}$$
$$\$340 = 0.4 \times \$850$$

However, these differences are in *opposite directions*, with higher income for the FIFO firm and higher operating cash flows for the LIFO firm. The difference in working capital is the net of the difference in inventory balance and cash flow:

$$\$510 = \$850 - \$340$$

This results in misleading liquidity measures for the LIFO firm as its working capital is understated:[10] The increase in cash is more than offset by the understatement of inventory.

Our illustration shows that the choice of inventory method can greatly affect reported operating results. Moreover, depending on whether the focus is the balance sheet or income statement, differing methods may be preferred. Thus, the analyst needs to be able to adjust between LIFO and FIFO in order to:

- Eliminate differences between firms due to accounting methods so that any remaining differences reflect economic and operating variations.
- Obtain the measure(s) most relevant for their analytical purpose.

The next sections describe how such adjustments can be made.

---

[10]Johnson and Dhaliwal (1988) studied firms that abandoned LIFO in favor of FIFO. Their evidence suggests one possible motivation for the abandonment decision was to increase their reported working capital. Compared to firms that retained LIFO, the abandonment firms had tighter working capital constraints under their debt covenants.

ADJUSTMENT FROM LIFO TO FIFO

Adjustment of Inventory Balances

LIFO inventory balances generally contain older costs with little or no relationship to current costs. Because of this deficiency, firms are required to disclose the *LIFO reserve*. The LIFO reserve (usually shown in the financial statement footnotes, but sometimes on the face of the balance sheet) is the difference between the inventory balance shown on the balance sheet and the (approximately current or replacement cost) amount that would have been reported had the firm used FIFO.

To adjust inventory balances of firms using LIFO to current or FIFO cost, we must add the LIFO reserve to the LIFO inventory amount. We can express this as

$$\text{LIFO Reserve} = \text{Inventory}_F - \text{Inventory}_L$$

or

$$\text{Inventory}_F = \text{Inventory}_L + \text{LIFO Reserve}$$

(where the subscripts F and L represent the accounting methods FIFO and LIFO, respectively).

■ Example: *Sunoco*

Exhibit 6-2 contains details of inventory and portions of financial statement footnotes from the 1996–1999 annual reports of Sunoco, a large U.S. oil refiner. Sunoco uses the LIFO method to account for virtually all crude oil and refined product inventories.

Exhibit 6-3A shows the adjustment of inventory from LIFO to FIFO, adding the LIFO reserve to the LIFO inventory. Sunoco's LIFO reserve is large, indicating that the balance sheet carrying amount significantly understates inventories. This understatement is typical of firms whose products have risen in price and that have used LIFO for many years. In the case of Sunoco, the LIFO cost of inventories is only 30% of the FIFO cost in 1999. As the price

EXHIBIT 6-2. SUNOCO
Inventory Disclosures

Inventories of crude oil and refined products are valued at the lower of cost or market. The cost of such inventories is determined principally using LIFO.

	Inventories* at December 31 (in $millions)			
	1996	1997	1998	1999
Crude oil	$157	$150	$184	$158
Refined products	252	214	219	163
Inventories valued at LIFO	**$409**	**$364**	**$403**	**$321**

The current replacement cost of all inventories valued at LIFO exceeded their carrying cost by $780, $492, $205, and $763 million at December 31, 1996 through 1999, respectively.

	1996	1997	1998	1999
Cost of goods sold (in $millions)	$8,718	$7,610	$5,646	$7,365

*The above data only include inventories intended for resale. Sunoco also carries materials and supplies on its balance sheet as inventories.
Source: Sunoco, 1996–1999 annual reports.

EXHIBIT 6-3. SUNOCO
Adjustment from LIFO to FIFO, 1996–1999

A. Adjusting LIFO Inventory to FIFO (Current Cost)

	1996	1997	1998	1999
Inventories carried at LIFO	$ 409	$364	$403	$ 321
LIFO reserve	780	492	205	763
Inventories adjusted to FIFO	$1,189	$856	$608	$1,084

B. Adjusting LIFO COGS to FIFO COGS

	1996	1997	1998	1999
Cost of goods sold at LIFO (COGS$_L$)		$7,610	$5,646	$7,365
Less: LIFO effect*		(288)	(287)	558
Equals: cost of goods sold at FIFO (COGS$_F$)		$7,898	$5,933	$6,807

*Change in LIFO reserve from previous year-end.
Source: Data from Sunoco, 1996–1999 annual reports.

of oil is volatile, the difference between Inventory$_F$ and Inventory$_L$ is highly variable over the period shown in Exhibit 6-3. ■

Adjustment of Cost of Goods Sold

COGS can be derived using the opening and closing inventory balances and purchases for the period:

$$COGS = BI + P - EI$$

Thus, to arrive at FIFO cost of goods sold (COGS$_F$), these amounts must be restated from LIFO to FIFO. The adjustment of inventory balances was illustrated earlier. Purchases (which are not a function of the accounting method used) need not be adjusted and can be derived directly from the (opening and closing) inventory balances and COGS reported in the financial statements:

$$P = COGS_L + EI_L - BI_L$$

■ **Example: *Sunoco***

Sunoco's purchases for 1999 can be calculated (in $millions) as

$$P = \$7,365 \text{ million} + \$321 \text{ million} - \$403 \text{ million}$$
$$= \$7,283 \text{ million}$$

Using 1999 purchases, just calculated, and the FIFO inventory amounts derived in Exhibit 6-3A yields the 1999 COGS on a FIFO basis for Sunoco:

$$COGS_F = BI_F + P - EI_F$$
$$= \$608 \text{ million} + \$7,283 \text{ million} - \$1,084 \text{ million}$$
$$= \$6,807 \text{ million}$$

Thus COGS on a FIFO basis is lower than on a LIFO basis by $558 million ($7,365 million − $6,807 million). The astute reader will note that this amount equals the increase in the LIFO reserve during the year (from $205 to $763 million). This is no coincidence and the adjustment from LIFO to FIFO COGS can be made directly from the LIFO reserve accounts without going through the intermediate steps of calculating purchases and adjusting inventories. The direct adjustment (shown in Exhibit 6-3B) is [11]

$$COGS_F = COGS_L - \text{Change in LIFO Reserve}$$

or

$$COGS_F = COGS_L - (\text{LIFO Reserve}_E - \text{LIFO Reserve}_B)$$

$$\$6,807 \text{ million} = \$7,365 \text{ million} - (\$763 \text{ million} - \$205 \text{ million})$$

where the subscripts E and B refer to ending (inventory) and beginning (inventory), respectively. The change in LIFO reserve during the year, sometimes called the *LIFO effect* for the year, is thus the difference between the COGS computed under the two methods.

Before leaving this discussion, consider two questions. First, why does conversion to FIFO in 1996 to 1998 increase COGS (see Exhibit 6-3B) when we normally expect $COGS_F$ to be lower than $COGS_L$? Second, why did the LIFO reserve decrease in those years.

The answer to both questions is the same: Oil prices decreased. This decline reduced the difference between inventory cost on a LIFO basis and cost on a FIFO basis. The LIFO reserve, which represents this difference, is thus reduced. In both years, use of the LIFO method reduced COGS by almost $290 million, increasing pretax earnings by an equal amount. The lesson here should be clear: *When prices are declining, LIFO produces lower COGS and, therefore, higher earnings.*

In 1999, when prices (and the LIFO reserve) increased, the expected effect was obtained. $COGS_L$ was higher and pretax income was reduced by the amount of increase in the LIFO reserve. In industries such as oil and gas, based on volatile commodity prices, fluctuations in the LIFO reserve due to price changes are common. ∎

ADJUSTMENT OF INCOME TO CURRENT COST INCOME

This section discusses the adjustment of FIFO (and weighted-average) COGS to reflect current costs.[12] There are two reasons for making this adjustment. One is to estimate the impact of price changes on a firm's COGS and earnings; we wish to separate price effects from operating effects. The second reason is to compare the firm with other firms in the same industry using LIFO accounting.

Note that *only the adjustment of COGS to LIFO COGS is relevant*. Adjustments of inventory balances to LIFO serve no purpose, as LIFO inventory costs are outdated and almost meaningless.

Unlike the adjustment from LIFO to FIFO discussed in the previous section, information needed to adjust COGS to LIFO is not generally provided in the financial statements of firms using FIFO (or average cost). An approximate adjustment, however, is often possible.[13]

---

[11]For those with a more mathematical bent, this result can be proven as follows:

  Purchases ($P = COGS + EI - BI$) are identical for both accounting methods.

  Thus $COGS_F + EI_F - BI_F = COGS_L + EI_L - BI_L$.

  Rearranging terms yields $COGS_F = COGS_L - [(EI_F - EI_L) - (BI_F - BI_L)]$.

  or $COGS_F = COGS_L - [(\text{LIFO Reserve}_E - \text{LIFO Reserve}_B)]$.

[12]Although we use the terms LIFO and current cost COGS interchangeably, our objective is to estimate current cost COGS. Generally, as long as the firm does not deplete any of its opening inventory, these two are equivalent. When opening inventory quantities are reduced (known as a LIFO liquidation), LIFO COGS and income are both distorted, as old costs flow into the income statement and COGS no longer reflects the current cost of inventory sold. When a LIFO liquidation occurs, LIFO COGS does not equal current cost COGS; in a subsequent section of the chapter we illustrate how to adjust for this distortion.

[13]A more complex adjustment taking into consideration the firm's inventory turnover is possible. Falkenstein and Weil (1977) discuss the use of turnover, but note (p. 51 of their article) that estimates from the more basic procedure (used here) have always approximated the estimates from the more complex methods.

This adjustment requires multiplying the opening inventory by the (specific) inflation rate and adding the result to $COGS_F$ to arrive at $COGS_L$. More formally,

$$COGS_L = COGS_F + (BI_F \times r)$$

where r is the *specific inflation rate appropriate for the products in which the firm deals.*[14]

To the extent that a firm's inventory purchases are steady throughout the period, the above adjustment will approximate the actual FIFO-to-LIFO (current cost) adjustment.

Weighted-average COGS (with subscript w) can be similarly adjusted to current cost (LIFO); the adjustment to opening inventory can be appoximated[15] by one-half the (specific) inflation rate:

$$COGS_L = COGS_W + (BI_W \times r/2)$$

Obtaining r. The inflation rate needed for the adjustment is not a general producer or consumer price index, but rather should be the specific price index appropriate to the firm in question. (For a multiindustry firm, the calculation should be done on a segmented basis.) Many industry indices are readily available, published by government or private sources. For companies whose inputs are commodities (oil, coffee, steel scrap), the spot price for the commodity may be used.

Alternatively, the specific price level change, r, for a given FIFO (or weighted average) firm can be estimated from data of a competing (LIFO) firm (in the same industry) by making use of the following relationship:[16]

$$r = \frac{\Delta \text{LIFO reserve}}{BI_F}$$

---

[14]The appropriateness of the approximation can be illustrated by the following proof. Assume that a firm carries a *quantity Q* of inventory and this quantity is equal to three months of inventory. The inventory level Q is replenished every three months. Assume further that the inflation rate over the year is equal to r. Finally, let P be the unit cost at which the opening inventory Q_o was purchased at the end of the previous year. Thus, the unit cost of the inventory at the end of the current year will equal $P(1 + r)$. The following illustrates the actual flow of goods purchased throughout the year:

Beginning inventory $= Q_0 =$ Sales during 1st Quarter
End of 1st Quarter Purchase $= Q_1 =$ Sales during 2nd Quarter
End of 2nd Quarter Purchase $= Q_2 =$ Sales during 3rd Quarter
End of 3rd Quarter Purchase $= Q_3 =$ Sales during 4th Quarter
End of 4th Quarter Purchase $= Q_4 =$ Ending Inventory

Under FIFO, the cost of $Q_0, Q_1, Q_2,$ and Q_3 will appear in COGS. Under LIFO, the cost of $Q_1, Q_2, Q_3,$ and Q_4 will appear in COGS. Thus, the difference between the two methods lies in the difference between the cost of the beginning (Q_0) and ending (Q_4) inventory. Hence, the difference between LIFO and FIFO equals

$$Q_4 P(1 + r) - Q_0 P = Q_0 Pr$$

since the inventory quantity purchased each period is the same.

[15]When weighted-average cost is used, the inventory turnover rate affects the adjustment.

[16]This can be proven since

$$COGS_F = COGS_L - \Delta \text{LIFO reserve}$$

and

$$COGS_L = COGS_F + (r \times BI_F)$$

Therefore

$$(r \times BI_F) = \Delta \text{LIFO reserve}$$

and

$$r = \frac{\Delta \text{LIFO reserve}}{BI_F}$$

This procedure provides a reasonable approximation of r as long as the LIFO firm has not had a *significant* reduction of its inventory from year to year. The example that follows illustrates the adjustment procedure to LIFO.

■ **Example: *Caltex Australia***

Exhibit 6-4 part A contains relevant income statement and balance sheet information for Caltex Australia, a major oil producer and refiner in Australia. LIFO is not permitted under Australian GAAP and Caltex Australia uses the weighted-average cost method to account for inventory. Our objective is to demonstrate the adjustment of COGS and earnings to a current cost basis using the methodology described above.

One advantage of using Caltex Australia as our example is that the company discloses (Exhibit 6-4, part B) the estimated effects of inventory holding gains on its earnings. Thus, we can double-check our estimates with those provided by management. The company states that it provides this information because:

> As a general rule using the historic cost basis of accounting, rising crude prices will result in increased operating profit for Caltex, falling crude oil prices will result in decreased operating profit. This movement in operating profit, often referred to as an inventory gain or loss, can create large variations in Caltex's results as calculated by the historic cost method. *Consequently, in order to provide a better insight into the operating performance of the company, Caltex's Financial reporting now includes earnings on a replacement cost of sales basis*. Replacement cost of sales earnings exclude inventory gains and

EXHIBIT 6-4.   CALTEX AUSTRALIA
Selected Income, Balance Sheet and Replacement Cost Disclosures (in $AUS millions)

A. Income Statement and Balance Sheet Data

	1998	1999
Net revenue	$2,891	$3,153
Operating costs and expenses	(2,693)	(2,936)
Operating profit (before interest, income tax, and abnormal items)	$ 198	$ 217
Ending inventory	234.8	429.0

Caltex Australia uses the weighted-average method to account for its inventory.

B. Replacement Cost of Sales Basis of Accounting

• To assist in understanding the company's operating performance, the directors have provided additional disclosure of the company's results for the year on a replacement-cost-of-sales basis, which excludes net inventory gains and losses adjusted for foreign exchange.

• Operating profit before interest, income tax, and abnormal items on a replacement-cost-of-sales basis was $75.0 million, a reduction of $221.8 million over 1998.

	1995	1996	1997	1998	1999	Total
Historical cost operating profit before interest, income tax, and abnormal items	$263.7	$272.6	$200.6	$216.7	$198.2	$1,151.8
Add/(deduct) inventory losses/(gains)*	(15.5)	(27.9)	53.4	98.6	(141.7)	(33.1)
Replacement cost operating profit before interest, income tax, and abnormal items	$248.2	$244.7	$254.0	$296.8	$ 75.0	$1,118.7

*Historical cost results includes gross inventory gains or losses from the movement in crude prices, net of the related exchange impact. In 1999, historical cost result includes $141.7 million net inventory gain (1998: $98.6 million net inventory loss) from the increase in crude oil prices, made up of **$144.9** million in inventory gains (1998: $124.7 million in inventory losses) net of an unfavorable exchange impact of $3.2 million (1998: $26.1 million gain).
Source: Caltex Australia, *Annual Review 1999.*

losses and are calculated by restating cost of sale using the replacement cost of goods sold rather than the historic cost. (Caltex Australia's *1999 Annual Review*, emphasis added.)

The price of crude oil increased dramatically in 1999. In Australia, the price increased from $10.60/barrel at the beginning of the year to $23.85/barrel at year-end.[17] This implies a specific price index (r) of 125% for oil products.[18] The adjustment to Caltex Australia's weighted average COGS (the LIFO effect) is

$$(BI_w \times r / 2) = (\$AUS\ 235\ million \times 1.25/2) = \$AUS\ 147\ million$$

where the $AUS 235 million is the inventory balance at the beginning of 1999.

This $AUS 147 million is the holding gain included in income reported under the weighted-average method. Removing the holding gain from income (adding it to COGS) results in a better measure of reported income ($AUS in millions):

Operating income (reported)	$AUS 217
Adjustment for holding gain	(147)
Operating income (approximate current cost)	$AUS 70

Note that this approximation almost equals the estimated ($AUS 144.9 million) inventory holding gain provided by the firm itself in the footnote to part B of Exhibit 6-4.

An alternative approach to arrive at the specific price index appropriate for the oil refining industry would be to examine the financial statements of a competing firm in that industry using LIFO. The LIFO reserve information presented earlier in Exhibit 6-3 for Sunoco Company can be used to approximate the effect of inflation on Caltex Australia.

The 1999 increase in Sunoco's LIFO reserve of $558 million ($205 to $763 million) represents the increase in current costs during 1999. The specific inflation rate r was, therefore,

$$\$558\ million/\$608\ million = 92\%$$

where $608 million is Sunoco's Inventory$_F$ on December 31, 1998.

This estimated r of 92% is considerably smaller than the estimated r of 125% derived from the spot price of oil. However, from Exhibit 6-3, we see that Sunoco's *physical* inventory must have been reduced by approximately 20%. Inventory$_L$ decreased from $403 million to $321 million. As noted, the estimate of r is biased when inventory is reduced dramatically and the greater the change in the relevant price index, the greater the distortion.

We can eliminate the distortion by estimating r based on only 80% of the opening inventory:

Estimating r from Sunoco Data After Adjusting for Reduction in Inventory

	1999 Opening Inventory	80% of 1999 Opening Inventory	1999 Closing Inventory
Inventory$_L$	$403	$321	$321
LIFO reserve	205	164	763
Inventory$_F$	$608	$485	$1,084

---

[17]*Source*: U.S. Energy Information Administration, Department of Energy.

[18]This estimate of r reflects the price increase in U.S. dollars. To more accurately measure the effect on Caltex Australia, the analysis should be done with oil prices expressed in Australian dollars, thereby taking into account exchange rate effects as well. However, as the method demonstrated is only an approximation and the exchange rate effect is relatively small, for ease of exposition we have ignored this technicality. (Exhibit 6-4 indicates that the exchange rate effect was only $3.2 million of the total $142 million effect.)

Using the second and third columns, the change in the LIFO Reserve equals $599 ($763 − $164) and BI_F = $485. By using the price change (LIFO effect) only for those inventories that Sunoco retained the whole year, our estimate of r becomes 123.5%($599/$485). This estimate is virtually identical to the 125% estimate using the alternative methodology and, as we showed earlier, is consistent with Caltex Australia's estimate of 1999 inventory holding gains.

Before proceeding to the next section it is worthwhile to explore further Caltex Australia's estimates of its inventory holding gains/losses for the years 1997–1999.

First, compare the pattern of Caltex Australia's adjustments to replacement cost with the pattern of Sunoco's COGS on a FIFO and LIFO basis (Exhibit 6-3). For both companies, the effect of declining prices in 1997 and 1998 was that replacement cost income exceeded operating income ($COGS_L$ < $COGS_F$); in 1999, when prices rose, the situation reversed.

The data in Exhibit 6-4 speak for themselves. Historical cost profit experienced a sharp decline in 1997–1998 relative to 1995–1996 and then recovered slightly in 1999. When holding gains and losses are excluded, however, a different picture emerges: replacement cost profit rose steadily from 1995–1998 (20% increase) and experienced a dramatic 75% decrease in 1999 as prices rose. *Reported operating earnings over this time period were significantly affected by inventory holding gains or losses virtually every year.*

If we recall our discussion (Chapter 2) of the meaning of income, it seems clear that replacement cost profit is a better measure of earnings. Holding gains and losses are not predictable. Moreover, holding gains must be reinvested in inventory for the firm to remain in business; they are not available for distribution.

Although Caltex Australia, given wide swings in the price of oil, may be an extreme case, it illustrates the necessity of analyzing the inventory accounting of a firm to understand the impact of changing prices on its earnings and net worth. ■

FINANCIAL RATIOS: LIFO VERSUS FIFO

Exhibit 6-5, based on Dopuch and Pincus (1988), compares selected financial characteristics of FIFO and LIFO firms.[19] The comparison is made first on the basis of amounts reported in financial statements (part A) and again after adjusting to the alternative accounting method (part B).

Using reported financial data, part A shows that, based on median values, LIFO firms have higher turnover ratios, less inventory as a percentage of sales or total assets, and lower variation in inventory levels and pretax income.[20] However, for the most part, these differences are not real operating differences but rather are differences due to the accounting choice. In part B the FIFO firms are adjusted to LIFO and the LIFO firms are adjusted to FIFO. The appropriate comparison can now be made with all firms using the same accounting method; that is, the numbers in part B should be compared with those directly above them in part A.

Once the data are adjusted for accounting methods, the differences tend to disappear. For example, the inventory turnover ratio as reported is 4.97 for LIFO firms and 3.88 for FIFO firms—a difference of 28%. After we adjust to the same method, the turnover ratios are:

- With all firms on FIFO, 4.03 for LIFO-reporting firms and 3.88 for FIFO-reporting firms—a difference of only 4%
- With all firms on a LIFO basis, 4.97 versus 4.72, respectively—a difference of only 5%

Similar patterns exist for the other variables.

---

[19]Although the data used in their sample (1963–1981) may be outdated, (the direction and degree of) distortion resulting from inventory accounting differences remains relevant.

[20]The variation in inventory and pretax income is measured by the coefficient of variation—(standard deviation divided by the mean).

EXHIBIT 6-5
Analysis of FIFO/LIFO Firms Based on Median Data, 1963–1981

A. Data as Reported

	LIFO	FIFO
COGS/average Inventory	4.97	3.88
Inventory/sales	0.16	0.20
Inventory/assets	0.21	0.29
C.V. inventory*	0.42	0.63
C.V. pretax income	0.74	0.79

B. FIFO Firms Adjusted to LIFO and LIFO Firms to FIFO

	FIFO to LIFO	LIFO to FIFO
COGS/average inventory	4.72	4.03
Inventory/sales	0.17	0.22
Inventory/assets	0.25	0.24
C.V. inventory	0.52	0.67
C.V. pretax income	0.81	0.77

*C.V. is the coefficient of variation (standard deviation divided by the mean).
Source: Nicholas Dopuch and Morton Pincus, "Evidence of the Choice of Inventory Accounting Methods: LIFO Versus FIFO," *Journal of Accounting Research* (Spring 1988), pp. 28–59, Tables 4 and 5, p. 44 (adapted).

With Exhibit 6-5 as a prologue, we now focus on how the FIFO/LIFO choice distorts measures of financial performance.

The FIFO/LIFO choice impacts reported profitability, liquidity, activity, and leverage ratios. For some ratios, LIFO provides a better measure, whereas for others, FIFO does. The LIFO-to-FIFO and FIFO-to-LIFO adjustment procedures discussed earlier, however, allow the analyst to make the appropriate adjustments to arrive at the "correct" ratio regardless of the firm's choice of accounting method. *The general guideline is to use LIFO numbers for ratio components that are income related and FIFO-based data for components that are balance sheet related.*

Profitability: Gross Profit Margin

The argument that LIFO better measures current income can be made with reference to gross profit margins. When input prices increase, firms pass along the added costs to customers. Moreover, they try to mark up not only those items purchased at the higher price but also all goods previously purchased. (This policy is economically defensible using the argument made earlier that the real cost of an item sold is its replacement cost.)

Thus, if the pricing policy of the firm in our opening example is to mark up cost by 100% (implying gross profit margin of 50% of sales), the $10,000 of sales in our example would have been arrived at as follows:

Sales: 100 units per quarter for a total of 400 units

Sales Price: Assume 100% markup over current costs

	Unit		Sales	
Quarter	Cost	Price	Units	Dollars
1	$11	$22	100	$ 2,200
2	12	24	100	2,400
3	13	26	100	2,600
4	14	28	100	2,800
Total			400	$10,000

Gross profit margin under FIFO and LIFO would be

Method	Sales	−	COGS	=	Gross Profit	Percent Margin
FIFO	$10,000	−	$4,300	=	$5,700	$5,700/$10,000 = 57.0%
LIFO	$10,000	−	$5,150	=	$4,850	$4,850/$10,000 = 48.5%

The 48.5% gross profit margin reported when LIFO is used is clearly closer to the profit margin intended by the firm's pricing policy. FIFO accounting, in times of rising (falling) prices, will tend to overstate (understate) reported profit margins.

The gross profit margin, by measuring the profitability of current sales, also provides an indication of the future profitability of a firm. Clearly, FIFO net income (which includes holding gains resulting from rising prices) inflates expectations regarding future profitability as future holding gains may be smaller (or negative) if future price increases are lower (or prices fall). *LIFO gives a more accurate forecast of the firm's prospects by removing the impact of price changes.*

Liquidity: Working Capital

LIFO misstates working-capital-based ratios because, as discussed, the inventory component of working capital reports outdated costs. As the purpose of the current ratio is to compare a firm's cash or near-cash assets and liabilities, use of the current value of inventory (FIFO) results in the better measure.

For Sunoco, working capital and current ratios for 1996 to 1999 based on reported data are:

Sunoco
Current Position Based on Reported LIFO Inventory

	Years Ended December 31 (in $millions)			
	1996	1997	1998	1999
Current assets	$1,535	$1,248	$1,180	$1,456
Current liabilities	(1,817)	(1,464)	(1,384)	(1,766)
Working capital	**$ (282)**	**$ (216)**	**$ (204)**	**$ (310)**
Current ratio	**0.84**	**0.85**	**0.85**	**0.82**

Adjusting LIFO inventory (and hence current assets) to current cost (FIFO) by adding the LIFO reserves (see Exhibits 6-2 and 6-3) changes Sunoco's current position to:

Sunoco
Adjusted Current Position Based on Current Cost (FIFO) Inventory

	Years Ended December 31 (in $millions)			
	1996	1997	1998	1999
Current assets	$1,535	$1,248	$1,180	$1,456
LIFO reserve	780	492	205	763
Adjusted current assets	$2,315	$1,740	$1,385	$2,219
Current liabilities	(1,817)	(1,464)	(1,384)	(1,766)
Adjusted working capital	**$ 498**	**$ 276**	**$ 1**	**$ 453**
Adjusted current ratio	**1.27**	**1.19**	**1.00**	**1.26**

The adjustments convert negative working capital to a positive measure for each year. Similarly, adjusted current ratios are (approximately 20–50%) higher than the unadjusted measures. The adjusted current ratio is also more volatile than the original ratio, reflecting the volatility of the current cost of oil-based inventories.

Activity: Inventory Turnover

Inventory turnover, defined in Chapter 4 as COGS/average inventory, is often meaningless for LIFO firms due to the mismatching of costs. The numerator represents current costs, whereas the denominator reports outdated historical costs. Thus, the turnover ratio under LIFO will, when prices increase, trend higher irrespective of the trend of physical turnover.

This point is illustrated in Exhibit 6-6. We assume an actual physical turnover of four times per year; that is, the average inventory is sufficient for one quarter. Further, it is assumed that unit costs increase 10% per quarter.

The FIFO inventory ratio is unaffected by the change in price, and at 3.77 is a rough approximation of the actual physical turnover of 4. The LIFO-based ratios of 5.11 and 7.47 are, however, far from the actual measure of 4, and the discrepancy grows over time. *Thus, to arrive at a reasonable approximation of the inventory turnover ratio for a LIFO firm, we must first convert stated inventory to FIFO.*

The preferred measure of inventory turnover (labeled "current cost" in Exhibit 6-6), however, is based solely on current cost. It combines the two methods, using LIFO COGS in the numerator and the FIFO inventory balance in the denominator. This approach provides the best matching of costs, as current costs are used in both the numerator and denominator. The current cost ratio (4.14) comes closest to the actual measure (based on physical units) of 4.

Using data for Sunoco (Exhibit 6-3), the computed inventory turnover ratios for 1998 and 1999 are (in $millions)

Method	1998 Turnover	# Days	1999 Turnover	# Days
LIFO (reported)	$\dfrac{\$5,646}{(\$364 + \$403)/2} = 14.72$	25	$\dfrac{\$7,365}{(\$403 + \$321)/2} = 20.34$	18
FIFO (adjusted)	$\dfrac{\$5,933}{(\$856 + \$608)/2} = 8.10$	45	$\dfrac{\$6,807}{(\$608 + \$1,084)/2} = 8.04$	45
Current cost	$\dfrac{\$5,646}{(\$856 + \$608)/2} = 7.71$	47	$\dfrac{\$7,365}{(\$608 + \$1,084)/2} = 8.70$	42

EXHIBIT 6-6
Illustration of Turnover Ratio Under LIFO and FIFO

Year	Quarter	Purchases = Sales	Cost per Unit	Total		For Entire Year	
Opening inventory		100	$10.00	$1,000			
1	1	100	$11.00	$1,100	FIFO	COGS	$4,641
1	2	100	$12.10	$1,210		Avg. inv.	$1,232
1	3	100	$13.31	$1,331	LIFO	COGS	$5,105
1	4	100	$14.64	$1,464		Avg. inv.	$1,000
2	1	100	$16.11	$1,611	FIFO	COGS	$6,795
2	2	100	$17.72	$1,772		Avg. inv.	$1,804
2	3	100	$19.49	$1,949	LIFO	COGS	$7,474
2	4	100	$21.44	$2,144		Avg. inv.	$1,000

Turnover Ratios

	Year 1	Year 2
FIFO	3.77	3.77
LIFO	5.11	7.47
Current cost	4.14	4.14

Comparing the 1998 and 1999 inventory turnover ratios for Sunoco, we see the importance of making current cost adjustments. Based on reported data, it appears that Sunoco turns its inventory very rapidly and increased its efficiency (turnover ratio) by almost 50% in 1999. After adjustment to current cost, however, a different picture emerges as the adjusted ratios imply a six-week rather than a three-week supply of inventory on hand and a much smaller year-to-year improvement in turnover.

Note also the small differences between the FIFO turnover ratios and the more refined current cost ratios. The ratio levels are similar although the current cost ratio shows higher turnover in 1999 whereas the FIFO ratio does not. The similarity is empirically true in most situations and for all practical purposes these two ratio calculations are equivalent as long as prices are not rising too rapidly (as was the case for 1999 oil prices).

Our example illustrates the usefulness of the LIFO-to-current cost adjustment for the analysis of a given company's turnover ratio. The same methodology can be used to compare two companies in the same industry when one uses FIFO and the other LIFO. The first step would be to adjust the LIFO turnover ratio to current cost. *Having made the ratios comparable (by eliminating the effect of different accounting methods), the analyst can then look for other explanations for any difference in the current cost turnover ratio.*

Inventory Theory and Turnover Ratios

Computing the inventory turnover ratio implies that there is some standard against which to measure or that there is an optimal ratio. As for all turnover ratios, one's first instinct is to believe that higher is better, that more rapid inventory turnover indicates a more efficient use of capital. In practice, however, that assumption may be overly simplistic.

The management science literature has devoted much study to the design of optimal inventory ordering policies. The traditional literature in the United States has focused on the economic order quantity (EOQ). More recently, in line with developments in Japanese management practices, focus has turned to just-in-time inventory policies. It is worthwhile to note the implications of these theories for the interpretation of the turnover ratio.

Economic Order Quantity

The construction and use of ratios for cross-sectional and time-series comparisons implicitly assume (as discussed in Chapter 4) that the relationship between the numerator and denominator is linear. Applying this assumption to the inventory turnover ratio implies that, as demand increases, the quantity of inventory held should increase proportionately. The EOQ model, however, argues that the optimal level of inventory is proportionate to the *square root* of demand.

Thus, for example, if demand (COGS) increases by four times, one would expect average inventory to double (2 = the square root of 4). As a result, the turnover ratio would also double. Generally, under the EOQ model, turnover ratios should rise as sales increase and smaller firms should have lower turnover ratios. A high turnover ratio for a small firm might not be a sign of efficiency but, on the contrary, an indication that the firm was not managing its inventories in the most economic fashion.

Just in Time

Japanese management practices strive for the ideal that firms should not hold any inventory but rather should receive and ship orders "just in time" (JIT) as needed. Carried to its ultimate conclusion, this would argue for a turnover ratio approaching infinity with zero inventory held. Hence, we would expect the turnover ratios of Japanese firms to be considerably higher than those of American firms. To the extent that U.S. firms adopt these practices, they can be expected to have higher turnover ratios in the future.

One interesting byproduct of the trend toward JIT inventory is that it renders the LIFO/FIFO choice less meaningful. If a firm has no inventories (or relatively small quantities), then there is no significant difference between FIFO and LIFO.[21]

The FIFO/LIFO Choice and Inventory Holding Policy

Another important consideration is that the LIFO/FIFO choice may be related to a firm's actual inventory holding policy. Biddle (1980) found that LIFO firms tend to maintain higher inventory balances (in units) than comparably sized FIFO firms.[22] This finding is consistent with the following three factors:

1. Firms with higher inventory balances have larger potential tax savings from the use of LIFO. Thus, the higher inventory levels that result from the firm's production and operating environment may explain why the firm chose LIFO in the first place.

2. These higher balances may result from the LIFO choice, as LIFO firms attempt to get the most advantage from it by increasing their inventory levels.

3. To avoid LIFO liquidations and consequent higher income taxes, LIFO firms must buy (produce) at least as many items as they sell each year. For LIFO firms it is costly to reduce inventory levels, even when lower expected levels of demand might dictate lower levels.

Solvency: Debt-to-Equity Ratio

We have argued that, to compute liquidity ratios, understated LIFO inventory balances should be restated to current cost by adding the LIFO reserve. For the same reason, the firm's stockholders' equity should be increased by the same amount.[23] The rationale for this adjustment is that the reported equity of the firm is understated because the firm owns inventory whose current value exceeds its carrying value.[24]

For analytical purposes, the inventory choice should be treated like other accounting choices. The fact that the Internal Revenue Service does not permit any difference between financial reporting and tax accounting methods should not tie the hands of the analyst. The valuation of a LIFO firm should not be penalized because it takes advantage of the tax savings inherent in LIFO.

DECLINES IN LIFO RESERVE

LIFO reserves can decline for either of the following reasons:

- Liquidation of inventories
- Price declines

---

[21]However, suppliers may hold inventory and if a firm owns or controls its suppliers, it may indirectly bear the residual risk usually borne by the suppliers. To properly include the effect of captive suppliers, turnover ratios and other inventory measures should be based on consolidated financial statements, where consolidation reflects economic rather than legal or regulatory control. Admittedly, such consolidation is not always feasible given the paucity of disclosure regarding such relationships. Further discussion of consolidation appears in Chapter 13.

[22]Barlev et al. (1984) examined Canadian and Israeli firms that were not permitted to use LIFO but used an alternative method of tax adjustment for inflation. They found that inventory balances were higher for firms with large tax benefits from the inflation adjustment.

[23]Lasman and Weil (1978) suggest that the LIFO reserve should not be adjusted for taxes unless a liquidation of LIFO layers is assumed. Further, as liquidations are reported in reverse LIFO order (latest layers are liquidated first), the largest gains reside in the earliest layers. Thus, there is a low probability that the tax effect of "minor" liquidations will be significant and (if we assume that the firm remains in business) extensive liquidations are unlikely, also arguing against tax adjustment. Note that firms have strong incentives to avoid liquidations that would result in significant tax payments. See, however, Appendix 6-B and the discussion regarding the Dhaliwal, Trezevant and Wilkins (2000) paper.

[24]Using FIFO values for equity does not contradict our statement that the optimal choice for income presentation is LIFO. Recalling the example in footnote 6, the fact that your house doubled in value from $100,000 to $200,000 at a time when all houses doubled in value means that you do not benefit from selling the house as you will need the larger amount to buy a replacement house. The value of (your equity in) your house is, nevertheless, $200,000.

In either case, COGS will be smaller (and income larger) relative to what it would have been had the reserve not declined. *The response of the analyst should not be the same in both cases, however.* For LIFO liquidations, the analyst should exclude the effects of the LIFO liquidation to arrive at a better measure of the firm's operating performance. In the second case, no adjustment is required, as price decreases are a normal part of the firm's operating results (just as much as price increases).

LIFO Liquidations

The discussion of LIFO in this chapter thus far has assumed that inventory quantities are stable or increasing. When more goods are sold than are purchased (or manufactured), goods held in opening inventory are included in COGS. For LIFO companies, this results in the liquidation of LIFO layers established in prior years, and such *LIFO liquidations* can materially distort reported operating results.

The carrying cost of the old (in an accounting sense) inventories (which becomes the cost of goods sold associated with the inventory reduction) may be abnormally low and the gross profit margin abnormally high. Thus, LIFO cost no longer approximates current cost. For companies whose base inventory is very old, the distortion from these "paper profits" can be quite large;[25] for analysis, that distortion needs to be removed.

The higher income resulting from LIFO liquidations translates into increased income taxes and lower operating cash flows as taxes that were postponed through the use of LIFO must now be paid. To postpone taxes indefinitely, purchases (production) must always be greater than or equal to sales.[26]

LIFO liquidations may result from inventory reductions because of strikes, recession, or declining demand for a particular product line.[27] The paradoxical result is that companies may report surprisingly high profits during economic downturns, as production cuts result in the liquidation of low-cost LIFO inventories. Given the trend toward lower inventory levels in recent years as companies move toward just-in-time or other means of reducing their investment in inventories, LIFO liquidations have become common. Such liquidations are usually disclosed in the inventory footnote of the financial statements. *As profits from LIFO liquidations are nonoperating in nature, they should be excluded from earnings for purposes of analysis.*

■ Example: Oilgear

Exhibit 6-7 presents data from the inventory footnote for Oilgear, a manufacturer and distributor of systems and value-engineered components for a broad range of industrial machinery and industrial processes. The company uses the LIFO method of inventory for more than two-thirds of its inventory and reported inventory declines and LIFO liquidations in each of the years 1995–1999.[28] The motivation for the inventory declines (reported in the company's Management Discussion and Analysis) was to "align inventory levels with current (lower) customer demand."

LIFO liquidations added to Oilgear's reported earnings in each of the years 1995 to 1999. As the effect of LIFO liquidations is completely nonoperating in nature, operating

---

[25]Schiff (1983) showed that in the recession of 1980–1981, LIFO layers that were liquidated dated back as far as World War II.

[26]See Biddle (1980) for a discussion of the impact of LIFO/FIFO on inventory purchases and holding policy.

[27]A LIFO liquidation may not be a onetime, random occurrence but a signal that a company is entering an extended period of decline. Stober (1986) found that over 60% of his sample of firms had liquidations in more than one year and 33% experienced liquidations in three or more years. Similarly, Davis et al. (1984) found that liquidations were industry related, indicating a systematic effect, and Fried et al. (1989) found that writedowns and/or restructurings were often preceded by LIFO liquidations.

[28]Exhibit 6-7, from the *1999 Annual Report*, provides information only about 1997–1999 liquidations. Information as to prior-year liquidations was obtained from prior-year annual reports.

EXHIBIT 6-7. OILGEAR
LIFO Liquidations

From Notes to Financial Statements

INVENTORIES
Inventories at December 31, 1999 and 1998 consist of the following:

	1998	1999
Raw materials	$ 2,601.718	$ 2,447,402
Work in process	21,773,524	17,634,558
Finished goods	6,281,776	4,777,960
Total	$30,657,018	$24,859,920
LIFO reserve	(1,996,000)	(1,627,000)
Total (net of LIFO reserve)	$28,661,018	$23,232,920

During 1999, 1998, and 1997, LIFO inventory layers were reduced. These reductions resulted in charging lower inventory costs prevailing in previous years to cost of sales, thus reducing cost of sales by approximately $850,000, $740,000, and $750,000 below the amount that would have resulted from liquidating inventory recorded at December 31, 1999, 1998, and 1997 prices, respectively.

From Income Statement (in $millions)

	1997	1998	1999
Sales	$90,904	$96,455	$90,709
COGS	(62,507)	(70,634)	(65,521)
Gross margin	28,397	25,821	25,188
Pretax income	3,363	1,284	1,864

Source: Oilgear, 1999 *Annual Report.*

results (COGS) should be adjusted to exclude it. Adjustments for each year follow (data in $000):

	1995	1996	1997	1998	1999
Sales	$82,157	$89,621	$90,904	$96,455	$90,709
COGS	(55,858)	(60,184)	(62,507)	(70,634)	(65,521)
Gross margin (reported)	**$26,299**	**$29,437**	**$28,397**	**$25,821**	**$25,188**
LIFO liquidation	800	1,350	750	740	850
Adjusted gross margin	**$25,499**	**$28,087**	**$27,647**	**$25,081**	**$24,338**
Liquidation effect:					
Gross margin increases	**3%**	**5%**	**3%**	**3%**	**3%**
Pretax income (reported)	**$3,070**	**$3,620**	**$3,363**	**$1,284**	**$1,864**
LIFO liquidation	800	1,350	750	740	850
Adjusted pretax income	**$2,270**	**$2,270**	**$2,613**	**$ 544**	**$1,014**
Liquidation effect:					
Pretax income increases	**35%**	**59%**	**29%**	**136%**	**84%**

Removing the LIFO liquidation effectively adjusts reported LIFO COGS to a current cost basis. Although the effects on gross margin are relatively small (3% to 5%), the effects on income are significant. As a result of the liquidation, Oilgear's reported (pretax) income was 29% to 136% higher than without the liquidation! ■

Declining Prices

Our discussion thus far has assumed rising price levels. In the analysis of Sunoco, we saw that the LIFO reserve declines when prices fall. In some industries (notably those that are technology related), input prices decline steadily over time; in others (mainly commodity-based industries such as metals and petroleum), prices may fluctuate cyclically.

Declines in LIFO reserves occur whenever inventory costs fall as the lower-cost current purchases enter reported LIFO COGS, decreasing the cost difference between LIFO and FIFO ending inventories. Such declines are not considered LIFO liquidations, and disclosure of their impact is not required.

The theoretical arguments as to which accounting method provides better information still hold. LIFO provides more recent (or current) cost on the income statement and outdated costs on the balance sheet. The direction of the LIFO versus FIFO differences, however, reverses when prices decline. LIFO closing inventories are overstated, and FIFO COGS tends to be higher. Thus, although the pragmatic incentives to use LIFO for tax purposes are lost in an environment of declining prices[29] (LIFO results in higher taxes and lower cash flow), the nature of the information provided does not change. *The LIFO amounts on the balance sheet are not current and require adjustment, whereas the income statement amounts are current and do not need adjustment.*

■ **Example: Wyman-Gordon**

Exhibit 6-8 presents data from the inventory footnote for Wyman-Gordon,[30] a producer of components for the aerospace industry. Wyman-Gordon used the LIFO method for many years and had a large LIFO reserve on its balance sheet. Weak industry conditions led to inventory declines, resulting in significant LIFO liquidations; declining prices also reduced the LIFO reserve. The exhibit indicates that in 1992 and 1993 the LIFO reserve

EXHIBIT 6-8. WYMAN-GORDON
Inventories and Declines in LIFO Reserve

		in ($thousands)	
	1991	1992	1993
Inventory		$ 53,688	$42,388
LIFO reserve	64,203	41,365	33,448
Change in LIFO reserve (LIFO effect)		$(22,838)	$(7,917)

If all inventories valued at LIFO cost had been valued at FIFO cost or market, which approximates current replacement cost, inventories would have been $41,365,000 and $33,448,000 higher than reported at December 31, 1992 and 1993, respectively.

Inventory quantities were reduced in 1991, 1992, and 1993, resulting in the liquidation of LIFO inventories carried at lower costs prevailing in prior years as compared with the cost of current purchases. The effect of lower quantities decreased 1991 loss from operations by $1,529,000, increased 1992 income from operations by $18,388,000, and decreased 1993 loss from operations by $5,469,000, whereas the effect of deflation had no impact on 1991 loss from operations, increased 1992 income from operations by $4,450,000, and decreased 1993 loss from operations by $2,448,000.

Source: Wyman-Gordon, *1993 Annual Report.*

---

[29]In addition, companies whose inventories are subject to obsolescence often take advantage of the ability (not available, for tax purposes, under LIFO) to write down inventory to market value.

[30]Wyman-Gordon is no longer a public company.

declined $22.838 and $7.917 million, respectively. Wyman-Gordon separated the effects of liquidations and price declines:

	(in $thousands)	
	1992	1993
Effect of LIFO liquidation	$(18,388)	$(5,469)
Effect of lower prices	(4,450)	(2,448)
Total LIFO effect	$(22,838)	$(7,917)

When analyzing Wyman-Gordon, the LIFO liquidation effect and the declining price effect should be treated differently. If the analyst's objective is to obtain a more accurate estimate of current cost income, then (*just*) the LIFO liquidation effect should be removed; the effects of declining prices on current purchases and sales, which are operating in nature, should not be removed. However, *for purposes of comparison with firms using FIFO* (i.e., calculating COGS on a FIFO basis), adjustment should be made for the total LIFO effect (liquidations *and* declining prices).[31]   ∎

INITIAL ADOPTION OF LIFO AND CHANGES TO AND FROM LIFO

Changes in the inventory accounting method require examination for two reasons:

1. Reporting methods for these changes are not symmetric; changing from FIFO to LIFO is not accorded the same treatment as a LIFO to FIFO switch.
2. The implications and motivation behind the accounting change are equally important; the change itself may convey information about the company's operations.

Initial Adoption of LIFO

In the United States the change to LIFO is made only on a prospective basis: GAAP do not require either retroactive restatement or the disclosure of any cumulative effect of the adoption of LIFO. Records necessary for restatement or *pro forma* disclosures often do not exist. Opening inventory in the year of adoption is the base-period inventory for subsequent LIFO computations.

When LIFO is adopted, required footnote disclosures include the impact of the adoption on the period's income before extraordinary items, net income, and related earnings per share amounts. A brief explanation of the reasons for the change in method must be provided and the absence of any cumulative effect disclosures or retroactive adjustment must be noted.

Exhibit 6-9 provides an example of the required disclosures. Effective January 1, 1999, Amerada Hess adopted the LIFO method for its crude oil and refined petroleum products. As Amerada Hess reported earnings per share of $4.88 for that year, the LIFO adoption reduced reported earnings by 18% from the $5.96 that would have been reported without the change. On the other hand, the change to LIFO resulted in a substantial tax saving as calculated below:

From inventory note: LIFO adjustment (effect)	$149,309,000
From accounting change note: effect on net income	97,051,000
Tax saving	$ 52,258,000

Amerada Hess was the last major U.S. oil refiner to adopt LIFO. In its footnote the company states that it switched to LIFO because the "LIFO method more closely matches current costs

---

[31]See problem 6-18.

EXHIBIT 6-9. AMERADA HESS
Initial Adoption of LIFO

Accounting Changes

Effective January 1, 1999, the Corporation adopted the last-in, first-out (LIFO) inventory method for valuing its refining and marketing inventories. The corporation believes that the LIFO method more closely matches current costs and revenues and will improve comparability with other oil companies. The change to LIFO decreased net income by $97,051,000 for the year ended December 31, 1999 ($1.08 per share basic and diluted). There is no cumulative effect adjustment as of the beginning of the year for this type of accounting change.

Inventories

Inventories at December 31 are as follows:

	Thousands of Dollars	
	1998	1999
Crude oil and other charge stocks	$ 35,818	$ 67,539
Refined and other finished products	386,917	393,064
	$422,735	$460,603
Less: LIFO adjustment		(149,309)
		$311,294
Materials and supplies	59,447	61,419
Total	$482,182	$372,713

Source: Amerada Hess, *Annual Report 1999.*

and revenues and will improve comparability with other oil companies." That may be so but the $52.3 million tax saving may also have had something to do with the company's decision. Note that the company chose to adopt LIFO in 1999, a year in which oil prices rose significantly, justifying the cost of changing accounting methods.

Indeed, adoptions of LIFO are often made to take advantage of the tax benefits inherent in the LIFO method and the propensity to switch is often a function of inflationary conditions. For example, in the early 1970s, over 400 firms switched to LIFO, reflecting double-digit inflation. Interestingly, the stock market has not always regarded such switches favorably despite their (positive) cash flow implications. The empirical section of the chapter (and Appendix 6-B) examines the reasons for this market reaction more closely.

Change from LIFO Method

Unlike changes to LIFO, changes from LIFO to other methods require retroactive restatement of reported earnings to the new method for prior years. The cumulative effect of adopting the new inventory accounting method is credited to retained earnings at the beginning of the earliest restated year to avoid a misstatement of current period income.

SEC regulations require a preferability letter from the firm's independent auditor stating its concurrence with and the rationale for the change. Additionally, a change from LIFO requires Internal Revenue Service approval.[32] The IRS considers changes from LIFO as a loss of tax deferral privileges, and the previous LIFO reserve becomes immediately taxable. Thus, a change from LIFO may bring significant adverse tax and cash flow consequences and requires evaluation of the impact on operations as well as management incentives for the switch. These motivations are also discussed in the following section.

---

[32]Firms switching from LIFO to another method also agree not to switch back to LIFO for at least 10 years, except under "extraordinary circumstances."

LIFO: A HISTORICAL AND EMPIRICAL PERSPECTIVE

Overview of FIFO/LIFO Choice

Out of 600 (generally very large) firms sampled in *Accounting Trends and Techniques*,[33] about half use LIFO for at least part of their inventories. Few firms use LIFO for all inventories. Use by industry classification varies widely. LIFO is used by all rubber and plastic product firms (in this sample) and virtually all firms in the food and drug store, petroleum refining, furniture, and textile industries. None of the firms in the computer and data services, computer software, semiconductors, or telecommunications sectors do so.

Given the powerful incentives to use LIFO (tax savings and cash flow), two interrelated[34] questions arise:

1. Why do some firms continue to use FIFO?
2. Are firms that use LIFO perceived as being "better off" by the market despite lower reported earnings?

Many empirical studies have examined these issues; in this section we summarize their findings. Before doing so, we note that empirical research related to inventories is not confined to the FIFO/LIFO choice. Box 6-2 shows how analysts can use trends in inventory balances as an aid in forecasting future sales and profitability.

The large number of studies devoted to the FIFO/LIFO choice is due to its richness as the choice has opposite effects on reported income and cash flow. Moreover, the ability to adjust from one method to the other permits "as-if" comparisons in research design. The main empirical findings are relevant to the analyst as they provide evidence that the implications of the FIFO/LIFO choice (or any other accounting choice) are often complex and go beyond the simple trade-off of lower taxes (higher cash flow) versus higher reported income articulated in research designs.[35] We provide a synopsis of the findings in the next section, using the work of Cushing and LeClere (1992) to motivate the discussion.

Summary of FIFO/LIFO Choice

Cushing and LeClere (1992) asked 32 LIFO firms and 70 FIFO firms to rank their reasons for their choice of inventory method. For LIFO firms, the overwhelming primary reason was the favorable tax effect. This result is consistent with research findings that firms using LIFO are primarily motivated by its favorable tax effects and these firms stand to gain the most from using LIFO.

The market, however, does not always regard a switch to LIFO favorably. By switching to LIFO, the firm may be providing (unfavorable) information about its sensitivity to changing prices (or other firm characteristics). Thus, reaction to a change in accounting method may reflect this other information rather than the tax advantage alone.[36]

Reasons for choosing FIFO are complex. Based on the responses in Cushing and LeClere, no single reason emerges as most important for FIFO firms. Over half suggested economic reasons as their motivation. Twenty of the 70 firms (approximately 30%) indicated that LIFO did not provide them with any tax benefits (e.g., declining prices). Others claimed that the accounting and administrative costs to maintain LIFO records and/or ensure that there are no LIFO liquidations kept them from using LIFO. However, just as many firms stated that they chose FIFO because it was a "better accounting method" as it better reflected

---

[33]American Institute of Certified Public Accountants, 2000 edition.

[34]These questions are interrelated because if the market reacts (for whatever reason) negatively to a switch to LIFO, it may explain why some firms choose to remain on FIFO.

[35]Given the scope of this topic and the spectrum of research approaches covering it, a detailed discussion of the empirical studies is presented in Appendix 6-B. The objective of that appendix is to enable the reader to better appreciate the subtleties involved in the choice of, and the information provided by, alternative accounting reporting methods.

[36]A more detailed discussion of this issue and the factors that may influence the market reaction (time period, expected or unexpected inflation, and analysts' understanding of the effects of inflation) can be found in Appendix 6-B.

BOX 6-2
Using Inventory Balances to Aid in Forecasting*

Changes in inventory balances can provide ambiguous signals about a firm's future sales and earnings prospects. An unanticipated (from the analyst's perspective) increase in the inventory balance may signal either:†

1. An unexpected decrease in recent demand, causing an unplanned increase in inventory that signals lower future demand, or‡

2. A (planned) increase in inventory levels by management anticipating higher future demand.

These two arguments are, of course, mutually exclusive. Which condition prevails cannot be determined from changes in the inventory account itself. Rather, the change itself acts as a signal for the analyst to investigate (using other sources of information) which condition is most likely for the company in question.§

The previous dichotomy relates only to changes in finished goods inventory. In a manufacturing environment, changes in work-in-process inventory (and to some degree changes in raw materials inventory) may indicate that management is increasing production to meet an increase in actual or anticipated orders.

Consistent with the above, Bernard and Noel (1991) examined whether changes in inventory could be used to forecast future sales and earnings. They found that the implications of inventory changes are not homogeneous for all firms, but differ between retailers and manufacturers.

For retailers, inventory increases signal higher sales but lower earnings and profit margins. This may seem paradoxical but the explanation is straightforward; a drop in demand results in increased inventory. To eliminate "excess" inventory, retailers reduce prices to stimulate sales ("dumping" inventory). Therefore, sales increase but with lower earnings. These effects generally are short-lived as the effect on sales dissipates over time.

For manufacturers, increases in finished goods inventory again indicate lower future demand; higher sales and lower earnings in the short run follow these increases as manufacturers dump unwanted inventory. However, unlike retailers, in the long run (once the initial increase is worked down) the drop in demand persists and future sales and earnings decrease. For raw materials and work in process, on the other hand, increases in inventory levels are consistent with higher future demand and higher future sales.

The foregoing discussion provides a different analytical application of information contained in financial reports. The lessons of the chapter, however, must not be forgotten. Any changes in inventory balances must take into consideration the inventory method used. Thus, for a LIFO company, analysis of changes should be based on current cost inventory amounts. In addition, an effort should be made to ensure that the change in inventory balances is driven by quantity changes, not increased prices for the same inventory quantity.

---

*See Bernard and Noel (1991) for a more elaborate discussion of the issues discussed here.
†Unplanned inventory changes may also have a direct impact on future unit production costs. When excess inventory must be reduced, production levels decline and unit costs increase as fixed overhead is spread over fewer units. Conversely, inventory building reduces unit costs by spreading overhead over increased production.
‡Throughout this section, a distinction between demand and sales must be kept in mind. Lower current demand can be associated with higher future sales if a company, in response to lower demand, cuts prices, thus stimulating sales.
§The analyst must also be sure that the change is not (1) a result of a change in accounting method, (2) due to acquisitions of other companies, or (3) management's acquisition of more inventory in an attempt to beat an anticipated price increase.

---

the physical flow of goods. Close to 40% indicated, as one of their two primary reasons, their concern about the lower earnings resulting from LIFO.[37]

Consistent with the tax effects argument, Dopuch and Pincus (1988) found that FIFO firms were less likely (relative to LIFO firms) to have significant tax savings from LIFO. With respect to the income-enhancing arguments, Hunt (1985) did find some evidence that supported the bonus plan hypothesis.

Many of the inventory studies found the choice of inventory method closely related to industry and size factors, with larger firms opting for LIFO. The industry factor is a consequence of similar production, operating, and *inflation conditions* faced by firms in the same industry. The size factor has been explained in two ways. As noted, adoption of LIFO increases inventory management and control costs, which mitigate the benefit received from tax savings. For large firms, these costs are more readily absorbed and small relative to the potential tax benefits. Alternatively, the size effect reflects the fact that, for political reasons, larger firms tend to choose accounting methods that lower reported earnings.

Exhibit 6-10, based on Cushing and LeClere (1992), summarizes their findings; the variables and the rationale behind them are indicated in the table. Seven of the eight variables

---

[37]These percentages are considerably higher than those reported by Granof and Short (1984) in an earlier survey.

EXHIBIT 6-10
Variables Hypothesized to Affect FIFO-LIFO Choice

1. *Estimated tax savings* from use of LIFO expected to be larger for LIFO companies.

2. *Inventory materiality*: The larger a firm's inventory balance, the greater the incentive to use LIFO as the potential tax savings is larger.

3. *Tax loss carryforward*: The larger a firm's tax loss carryforward, the less incentive it has to use LIFO.

4. *Inventory variability*: The more variable a firm's inventory balance, the more likely it is to face inventory liquidations. This would tend to favor choosing FIFO over LIFO.

5. *Inventory obsolescence*: If a firm's inventory tends to become obsolete because of new product innovation, then the replacement of old products by new ones raises a difficult LIFO accounting question for which there is no authoritative answer. Such companies may prefer FIFO.

6. *Size as proxy for bookkeeping costs*: The larger the accounting costs required to use LIFO, the less likely a firm would choose LIFO. Larger firms would be able to absorb these costs more readily.

7. *Leverage*: Under the debt covenant hypothesis, firms with higher leverage would prefer FIFO as it would improve their debt/equity ratios.

8. *Current ratio*: Under the debt covenant hypothesis, firms with low current ratios would prefer FIFO, which improves their current ratio.

Source: Barry E. Cushing and Marc J. LeClere, "Evidence on the Determinants of Inventory Accounting Policy Choice," *Accounting Review* (April 1992), pp. 355–366, Table 4, p. 363.

that explain the FIFO/LIFO choice are significant in the predicted direction. The estimated tax savings are significantly greater for LIFO firms. Consistent with this, FIFO firms have higher average loss carryforwards. Inventory variability is higher for FIFO firms, increasing the chances of LIFO liquidations. FIFO firms tend to be smaller, more highly leveraged, and less liquid. Similarly, the likelihood of inventory obsolescence is also a significant factor. Only the materiality measure is not statistically significant.

These variables indicate possible motivations to stay on FIFO. For a given firm, the analyst should try to determine which of these motivations apply and, thus, whether the firm is justified in staying on FIFO or management is inefficient (or self-serving) by foregoing tax savings from the use of LIFO. Management that remains on FIFO for motives that are either selfish or based on the belief that the market can be fooled should not inspire confidence.

INTERNATIONAL ACCOUNTING AND REPORTING PRACTICES

FIFO and the weighted-average method are the most commonly used methods worldwide. Historically, the use of LIFO was essentially limited to companies in the United States, and the significant tax benefits this method can provide suggest that the method will continue to enjoy widespread acceptance. These benefits have resulted in gradual adoption of LIFO as a permitted alternative in countries such as Germany, Italy, and Japan.[38] In some countries, LIFO is allowed for financial reporting but not income taxes, which may account for its lack of popularity in these countries. In practice, LIFO is rarely used in these countries, perhaps because of the low inflation rates of recent years. Non-U.S. reporting standards do not require disclosure of LIFO reserves, reducing the analyst's ability to make the adjustments discussed in this chapter.

In the United Kingdom, Statement of Standard Accounting Practice (SSAP) 9 holds that LIFO may not result in a true and fair valuation and, in addition, the method is not allowed for tax purposes.

Average cost is the most widely used method in Germany, although LIFO has been allowed for tax purposes since 1990, and it may change reporting habits.

---

[38]As discussed in Chapter 1, financial reporting and tax reporting are identical in these countries.

IASB Standard 2

In 1993, the IASB issued revised International Accounting Standard (IAS) 2, designating FIFO and weighted-average costs as the benchmark treatments and LIFO as the allowed alternative. Firms using LIFO are required to provide FIFO/weighted-average or current cost disclosures, facilitating the adjustments discussed in this chapter.

Inventories are reported at the lower of cost or market value; cost depends on the method used. Market is generally defined as the net realizable value with specific limitations in the United States;[39] any writedown is determined on an item-by-item basis. Revised IAS 2 limits itself to net realizable value (NRV), and it does not specify whether the cost versus NRV comparison should be made on an item-by-item basis or by groups of similar items. This standard is similar to those of most other countries.

SUMMARY AND CONCLUDING COMMENTS

The choice of accounting method for inventories is one of the basic decisions made by nearly all companies engaged in the manufacturing and distribution of goods. Ideally, the method chosen should result in the best measure of income and financial condition. However, no single method accomplishes these objectives in most cases and, in an environment of changing prices, assumptions as to the flow of costs affect reported income, balance sheet amounts, and associated ratios.

For companies operating in the United States, under conditions of rising prices, the cash flow advantage of LIFO usually dictates the choice of that method. When LIFO is not chosen, therefore, the first question should be: Why not? As the empirical work indicates, managers offer a number of reasons for not using LIFO, only some of which appear valid. Thus, companies that should use LIFO but do not may appear unattractive to investors.

In many cases, the analytical techniques presented in this chapter enable the analyst to approximate the effect of LIFO on a company using FIFO or average cost. Such analysis can provide estimates of both the cash savings foregone (relevant to the discussion in the previous paragraph) and the holding gains included in reported income. Similarly, the chapter demonstrates how the analyst can adjust from LIFO to FIFO where appropriate. The chapter also explores the effects of liquidations and the incentives for the FIFO/LIFO choice, and concludes with a review of inventory accounting standards applied internationally.

Chapter 6

Problems

1. [Allocation of purchase costs under different inventory methods; CFA© adapted] Assume the following:

Quarter	Units Purchased	Per Unit Cost	Dollar Purchases	Unit Sales
I	200	$22	$ 4,400	200
II	300	24	7,200	200
III	300	26	7,800	200
IV	200	28	5,600	200
Year	1,000		$25,000	800

Inventory at beginning of Quarter I: 400 units at $20 per unit = $ 8,000
Inventory at end of Quarter IV: 600 units

a. Calculate reported inventory at the end of the year under *each* of the following inventory methods:

   (i) FIFO

   (ii) LIFO

   (iii) Average cost

b. Calculate the cost of goods sold for the year under each method listed in part a.

c. Discuss the effect of the differences among the three methods on:

   (i) Reported income for the year

   (ii) Stockholders' equity at the end of the year

2. [Effect of inventory methods on financial statements; CFA© adapted] Compare the effect of the use of the LIFO inventory

---

[39]Generally, these limitations ensure that inventories are written down to approximate current cost.

method with use of the FIFO method on each of the following, assuming rising prices and stable inventory quantities:

(i) Gross profit margin

(ii) Net income

(iii) Cash from operations

(iv) Inventories

(v) Inventory turnover ratio

(vi) Working capital

(vii) Total assets

(viii) Debt-to-equity ratio

3. [FIFO and LIFO—basic relationships] The Mogul Company, expecting that decreases in oil prices are only temporary, increases its monthly purchases as the price of oil decreases. Mogul's monthly oil purchases follow:

Period	Quantity (bbl)	Price/Barrel
First quarter		
January	100,000	$25
February	100,000	25
March	100,000	25
Second quarter		
April	125,000	20
May	125,000	20
June	125,000	20
Third quarter		
July	150,000	18
August	150,000	18
September	150,000	18
Fourth quarter		
October	200,000	15
November	200,000	15
December	200,000	15

Assumptions:

- The company has no opening inventory.
- Sales are 100,000 barrels per month for the period January through June and 150,000 per month for the period July through December.
- Mogul uses the LIFO inventory method.
- The company's tax rate is 40%.

a. Compute the difference in *each* of the following dollar amounts that Mogul would report under its present accounting method (LIFO), as compared with use of the FIFO method. (*Note*: The solution does not require long calculations; focus on the *differences* between FIFO and LIFO levels, not the actual amounts.)

(i) Inventory purchases

(ii) Closing inventory

(iii) COGS

(iv) Pretax income

(v) Income tax expense

(vi) Net income

(vii) Cash flow from operations

(viii) Working capital (year-end)

b. Assume that Mogul liquidates its entire inventory at year-end. Discuss how the answers to part a would differ.

4. [Inventory costing; basic relationships] During its first year of operations, Metro Retailers made the following inventory purchases:

February 1	1,000 units @ $2 each
April 1	2,800 units @ $3 each
August 1	1,000 units

For the year, it reported COGS of $10,500 and ending inventory of $3,500 using the weighted-average method.

a. Compute the price at which the August 1 purchase was made.

b. Compute COGS and ending inventory under *both* the LIFO and FIFO methods.

5. [Inventory methods; basic relationships; impact on turnover ratio] The Renemax Company begins operations on December 31, 20X0, with $500 of inventory, enough for one month's (January 20X1) sales. During 20X1, the company maintains its inventory at one month's sales. Monthly sales (in units) are constant, and the company replenishes inventory each month.

At the end of 20X1, Renemax must choose an inventory method. The following additional information is available:

- The cash flow difference between the FIFO and LIFO methods is $400. (*Note*: You do not know which is higher.)
- The COGS is $12,000 using the weighted-average method.
- The company's tax rate is 40%.
- Prices change only in one direction during the year.

a. Using the information provided, fill in the following blanks:

	FIFO	Weighted Average	LIFO
Opening inventory	___	___	___
Purchases	___	___	___
COGS	___	$12,000	___
Closing inventory	___	___	___
Inventory turnover (reported)	___	___	___
Inventory turnover (physical)	___	___	___

(*Hint*: The firm's physical inventory turnover is 12. Use this insight to complete the blanks for the weighted-average method. Then consider the effect of price changes on the amounts computed under the LIFO and FIFO methods.)

b. Compare the inventory turnover ratio reported under each method. Discuss which method provides the ratio that most accurately portrays the actual *physical* turnover.

c. Discuss the impact of the choice of accounting method on cash flow from operations and total cash flows.

6. [Inventory methods; basic relationships] The M&J Company begins operations on January 1, 20X0 with the following balance sheet:

Cash	$10,000	Common stock	$10,000

During the year, the company maintains its inventory accounts using the FIFO method. Before a provision for income tax, the balance sheet at December 31, 20X0, is:

Cash	$ 5,000	Common stock	$10,000
Inventory	10,000	Pretax income	5,000
	$15,000		$15,000

M&J has 20X0 sales of $25,000. The company sells half of the *units* purchased during the year. Operating expenses (excluding COGS) are $12,000.

Prior to issuing financial statements, the company considers its choice of inventory method. Assume a tax rate of 40% and a dividend payout ratio of 50%.

a. Using the information provided, complete the following table:

	FIFO	Weighted Average	LIFO
Sales	$25,000	$25,000	$25,000
COGS	_____	_____	_____
Other expenses	12,000	12,000	12,000
Pretax income	_____	_____	_____
Income tax expense	_____	_____	_____
Net income	_____	_____	_____
Dividends paid	_____	_____	_____
Retained earnings	_____	_____	_____
Cash from operations	_____	_____	_____
Closing cash balance	_____	_____	_____
Closing inventory	_____	_____	_____
Inventory purchases	_____	_____	_____

b. Prepare a balance sheet for M&J at December 31, 20X0, assuming use of the:

  (i) LIFO inventory method
  (ii) Weighted-average method
  (iii) FIFO inventory method

c. Discuss the advantages and disadvantages of each of the three possible choices of inventory method.

7. [Declining costs; LOCM] Prices for the ZB Company's products are falling due to lower production costs. On September 30, 20X2, the company had the following inventory balance:

  100 units @ $44 $4,400

Fourth-quarter purchases were

  200 units @ $43 $ 8,600
  300 units @ $40 $12,000

Fourth-quarter sales were

  125 units @ $50 $62,500

a. Compute the balance in the inventory account on December 31, 20X2 using the following accounting methods:
  (i) FIFO
  (ii) LIFO

b. State which method will result in lower income taxes. Compute the tax savings from the method producing the lower tax. Assume a 40% tax rate.

c. Now assume that, on December 31, 20X2, a competitor announces a new model and selling prices drop to $40. Describe the accounting (journal) entry necessary and state the effect of that entry on income taxes assuming the company uses:

  (i) FIFO
  (ii) LIFO

(Problems 6-8 and 6-9 are based on the following data, adapted from the actual financial statements of two firms in the automobile replacement parts industry.)

Zenab Distributors, Balance Sheets, at December 31

	20X1	20X2
Cash	$ 500	$ 100
Accounts receivable (net)	8,100	8,300
Inventory	24,900	25,200
Current assets	$33,500	$33,600
Current liabilities	11,600	12,700

Zenab Distributors uses the LIFO method of accounting for 70% of its inventories; it uses FIFO for the remainder. If all inventories were carried at FIFO, inventory would be higher by $3,600 and $5,100 in 20X1 and 20X2, respectively.

Faybech Parts, Balance Sheets, at December 31

	20X1	20X2
Cash	$ 1,000	$ 600
Accounts receivable (net)	11,400	13,900
Inventory	22,300	30,300
Current assets	$34,700	$44,800
Current liabilities	10,700	12,200

Faybech Parts uses FIFO accounting for all inventories.

Income Statements, Year Ended December 31, 20X2

	Zenab	Faybech
Sales	$92,700	$77,000
COGS	61,300	52,000
Gross profit	$31,400	$25,000
Selling and general expense	26,400	21,500
Pretax income	$ 5,000	$ 3,500
Income tax expense	2,000	1,400
Net income	$ 3,000	$ 2,100

8. [Adjusting LIFO to FIFO and FIFO to LIFO/current cost] Using the financial data provided:

a. Calculate Zenab's COGS and pretax income on a FIFO basis.

b. Calculate Faybech's COGS and pretax income on a LIFO/ current cost basis.

c. Discuss the circumstances under which income tax expense should be adjusted when computing net income in parts a and b.

9. [LIFO versus FIFO; effect on ratios; adjusting ratios]

a. Using *only reported* financial data, compute each of the following ratios for both Zenab and Faybech:

   (i) Current ratio (20X1 and 20X2)

   (ii) Inventory turnover (20X2)

   (iii) Gross profit margin (20X2)

   (iv) Pretax profit margin (EBT to sales) (20X2)

b. Briefly compare the performance of the two firms in 20X2 based on the ratios computed in part a.

c. Recalculate each of the ratios in part a with both companies:

   (i) On FIFO

   (ii) On LIFO

   (iii) Using the current cost method

d. Select the basis of comparison for *each* of the four ratios that you feel is most meaningful. Justify *each* choice.

10. [LIFO versus FIFO; effect on ratios; adjusting ratios; CFA© adapted] The Zeta Corp. uses LIFO inventory accounting. The footnotes to the 20X4 financial statements contain the following data as of December 31:

	20X3	20X4
Raw materials	$392,675	$369,725
Finished products	401,325	377,075
Inventory on FIFO basis	$794,000	$746,800
LIFO reserve	(46,000)	(50,000)
Inventory on LIFO basis	$748,000	$696,800

You are also provided with the following data:

- The company has a marginal tax rate of 35%.
- COGS for 20X4 is $3,800,000.
- Net income for 20X4 is $340,000.
- Return on equity for 20X4 is 4.6%.

a. Calculate 20X4 net income for Zeta, assuming that it uses the FIFO inventory method.

b. Calculate the company's inventory turnover ratio on both a FIFO and LIFO basis.

c. Calculate Zeta's return on equity on a FIFO basis. (Remember to adjust both the numerator and denominator.)

d. Discuss the usefulness of the adjustments made in parts a, b, and c to a financial analyst.

e. Describe alternative measures of inventory turnover and return on equity that would be more useful to assess Zeta's operating performance.

11. [Extension of Sunoco; FIFO vs. LIFO and effect on ratios] In its 2000 annual report, Sunoco reported a carrying value of $381 million for its crude oil and refined products inventories. The LIFO reserve at the 2000 year-end was $873 million. Sales and cost of sales data for 1998–2000 follow:

	Years Ended December 31 (in $millions)		
	1998	1999	2000
Sales	$8,413	$9,889	$14,062
Cost of sales	5,646	7,365	10,819

(*Note*: Solving certain parts of this problem may require the analysis of Sunoco in the text and data from Exhibits 6-2 and 6-3.)

a. Calculate the company's reported gross profit and gross profit margin (%) for 1998–2000.

b. Compute the price-level change of oil products in 2000. Compare that change to the 1998 and 1999 price-level changes.

c. Redo part a on the FIFO basis. State which measure of profitability more accurately reflects the real profitability of Sunoco for that period. Justify your choice.

d. Discuss the effects of price changes on the company's reported profitability.

e. Compare the company's 2000 inventory turnover to turnover in 1998 and 1999 based on:

   (i) Reported data

   (ii) FIFO data

   (iii) Current cost data

12. [LIFO versus FIFO; effect on inventory turnover ratio and cost of sales; adjusting turnover ratio] Sears uses the LIFO method to value its merchandise inventories. The following data (in $millions) were obtained from the company's annual reports:

Calendar Year	1997	1998	1999
Fiscal Year Ending	January 3, 1998	January 2, 1999	January 1, 2000
Cost of sales	$26,985	$27,444	$27,212
Merchandise inventories	5,044	4,816	5,069

a. Using the above data, calculate the following for 1998 and 1999:

- Inventory turnover ratio
- Number of days inventory

b. Sears states in its financial statements that if the FIFO method of inventory valuation had been used instead of the LIFO method, merchandise inventories would have been $595, $679, and $713 million higher at January 2, 2000, January 1, 1999, and January 3, 1998, respectively. Redo part a, using FIFO inventory balances.

c. State and justify which is the better measure of Sears inventory turnover ratio—the LIFO-based measure calculated in part a or the FIFO-based one in part b.

d. Sears states that

   the LIFO adjustment to cost of sales was a credit of $73, $34 and $17 million in 1999, 1998, and 1997, respectively.

Explain the meaning of "the LIFO adjustment to cost of sales." Based on the balance sheet data provided, estimate the 1998 and 1999 LIFO adjustments. Provide one explanation for the discrepancy.

(Problems 6-13 to 6-15 are based on the following data, taken from Westvaco's 2000 annual report.)

	Years Ended October 31 (in $millions)	
	1999	2000
Sales	$2,802	$3,663
Cost of sales	1,970	2,512
Net income	111	255
Shareholders' equity	2,171	2,333

The carrying value of Westvaco's 2000 inventories was $333 million (1999: $249 million). Westvaco uses LIFO accounting for certain inventories (including finished goods) and values other inventory at FIFO (or average cost). Westvaco's notes to its financial statements state:

> If inventories had been valued at current cost, they would have been $469 million in 2000 (1999: $368 million). Inventories valued on the LIFO basis were $202 million in 2000. (1999: $157 million).

(In solving Problems 6-13 to 6-15, assume that FIFO is the prevailing method for all of Westvaco's non-LIFO inventories and that its tax rate is 35%.)

13. [LIFO versus FIFO and effect on ratios]

a. Calculate Westvaco's inventory turnover, gross profit margin, and ROE for 2000 based on reported data.

b. Recompute the ratios in part a assuming Westvaco had used FIFO for all of its inventories.

c. Describe the impact of the LIFO method on Westvaco's ratios.

d. Explain how each of the three ratios should be calculated for maximum usefulness.

14. [Inflation rate and adjusting FIFO to LIFO]

a. Using the data provided and the adjustment method described in the chapter, calculate the rate of price change experienced by Westvaco in 2000.

b. Assume that all of Westvaco's inventories faced the same inflation rate. Adjust Westvaco's cost of sales to 100% LIFO and compute adjusted 2000 gross profit and net income.

c. Explain the usefulness of the adjusted data in part b.

d. Discuss briefly whether the assumption made in part b is a reasonable one.

15. [Estimating company-specific inflation rates] Paper and paperboard products account for 90% of Westvaco's business; the other 10% is devoted to (specialty) chemical products. Producer price index data relevant to these segments are presented below.

Producer Price Indices (1982 = 100)

		Pulp, Paper & Allied Products	Chemical & Allied Products
October	1999	177.0	147.0
November		177.7	147.1
December		177.9	147.3
January	2000	179.3	147.7
February		180.0	148.9
March		181.7	149.9
April		183.8	150.7
May		184.9	151.3
June		185.5	151.7
July		185.1	152.6
August		184.5	152.0
September		184.4	151.9
October		185.1	151.9

Source: Bureau of Labor Statistics.

a. Based on the Producer Price indices, estimate the rate of price change for Westvaco's products.

b. Compare these estimates with those that can be derived from Westvaco's inventory footnote disclosures.

c. Discuss the factors that may explain why the estimates derived in parts a and b differ.

16. [Inventory turnover ratio] General Electric [GE] reported that its inventory turnover ratio increased from 8.3 times in 1999 to 8.5 times in 2000. The following data appear in GE's annual report:

Years Ended December 31 (in $millions)

	1998	1999	2000
Sales of goods	$43,749	$47,785	$54,828
Sales of services	14,938	16,283	18,126
Total revenues	$58,687	$64,068	$72,954
Cost of goods sold	31,772	34,554	39,312
Cost of services sold	10,508	11,404	12,511
Cost of goods and services sold	$42,280	$45,958	$51,823
Year-end inventories at FIFO	6,316	6,725	7,991
Year-end inventories at LIFO	5,305	5,798	7,146

Note: All data exclude GE financial services.
Source: General Electric, 1998–2000 annual reports.

a. Compute GE's inventory turnover ratios for 1999 and 2000, using:
   (i) Cost of goods (and services sold) and LIFO inventory
   (ii) Cost of goods (and services sold) and FIFO inventory

b. Some firms calculate inventory turnover using sales rather than COGS in the numerator. Calculate GE's 1999 and 2000 turnover, using:
   (i) Sales and LIFO inventory
   (ii) Sales and FIFO inventory

c. Describe the method that GE appears to use.

d. State which method you would choose to evaluate GE's performance. Justify your choice.

17. [Adjusting for LIFO liquidations] The Jofen Company uses the LIFO inventory method. In 20X3, anticipating a downturn in demand, the company decides not to replenish inventory levels at year-end. The resulting LIFO liquidation increases pretax income by $300,000. Ending inventory on December 31, 20X3, is $2,000,000, a reduction of $700,000 from the level at January 1, 20X3.

a. Compute the LIFO cost of inventory at January 1, 20X3.

b. Compute the additional purchases that would have been required to fully replenish inventories, thus avoiding the LIFO liquidation during 20X3.

c. Describe the impact of the LIFO liquidation on cash flow from operations.

d. Describe how the foregoing data could be used to adjust reported income for 20X3.

e. Explain why net income as adjusted in part d is more useful for financial analysis.

18. [Adjusting for alternative accounting methods; effects of liquidation] The Noland Company [NOLD] reported the following operating results:

Years Ended December 31 in ($thousands)

	1997	1998	1999
Sales	$464,965	$465,479	$482,830
COGS	371,212	372,033	385,892
Gross margin	$ 93,753	$ 93,446	$ 96,938

In its 1999 annual report, the company states that

> 1999's gross profit margin suffered from the year-end LIFO adjustment which increased cost of goods sold by $1,391,000 compared to $381,000 a year ago.

Information from the company's inventory footnote is presented below:

December 31 (in $thousands)

	1997	1998	1999
Inventory, at approximate replacement cost	$98,965	$103,446	$104,106
Reduction to LIFO	32,495	32,876	34,267
LIFO inventory	$66,470	$ 70,570	$ 69,839

Liquidation of certain inventory layers carried at the higher/lower costs that prevailed in prior years as compared with the costs of 1999, 1998, and 1997 purchases had the effect of increasing 1999 and 1997 net income $47 thousand and $393 thousand, respectively, and decreasing 1998 net income $150 thousand.

a. Describe the "year-end LIFO adjustment" and show how the company calculated it for both 1998 and 1999.

b. Compute the company's 1998 and 1999 COGS using the FIFO method.

c. Explain how it is possible for a LIFO liquidation to decrease income as in 1998.

d. Excluding the effects of the LIFO liquidation, compute COGS for 1998 and 1999 using:

(i) The company's current accounting method

(ii) The FIFO method

e. State and justify which of the following measures of COGS is most appropriate to use to measure Noland's profitability:

(i) As reported

(ii) As computed in part b

(iii) As computed in part d

f. Describe how to use the inventory footnote data to adjust Noland's net worth (book value) to a current cost basis for 1998 and 1999.

19. [LIFO writedowns and liquidations] Caltex's 1999 net income of $390 million increased more than 100% from 1998 income of $193 million. A careful reading of the inventory footnote, however, reveals that:

- In 1998 and 1997, certain inventories were recorded at market, which was lower than the LIFO carrying value. Adjustments to market reduced net income $18 million in 1998 and $36 million in 1997. The market valuation adjustment reserves established in prior years were eliminated in 1999 as market prices improved and the physical units of inventory were sold. Elimination of these reserves increased net income in 1999 by $71 million.

- Inventory quantities valued on the LIFO basis were reduced at certain locations during the periods presented. Such inventory reductions increased net income in 1999 by $41 million, and decreased net income by $4 million and $5 million (net of related market valuation adjustments of $1 million and $14 million) in 1998 and 1997, respectively.

a. Explain how the market value adjustments reduced income by $18 and $36 million in 1998 and 1997, respectively.

b. Explain why the elimination of the market value adjustments in 1999 increased income by $71 million rather than ($18 + $36 =) $54 million.

c. Explain how it is possible for a LIFO liquidation to decrease net income as it did in 1998.

d. Recompute 1998 and 1999 net income on a replacement cost basis after eliminating the effects of the market value adjustments and the liquidations. Explain the effect on the trend in income over the two years.

20. [Decline in LIFO reserve] The following footnote appeared in the annual report of A. T. Cross [ATX], a pen manufacturer:

Note B—Inventories

Domestic writing instrument inventories, approximating $13,404,000 and $5,695,000 at December 30, 2000 and January 1, 2000, respectively, are priced at the lower of LIFO cost or market. The remaining inventories are priced at the lower of FIFO cost or market. If the FIFO method of inventory valuation had been used for those inventories priced using the LIFO method, inventories would have been approximately $9,614,000 and $11,227,000 higher than reported at December 30, 2000 and January 1, 2000, respectively. The Company believes the LIFO method of inventory valuation ordinarily results in a more appropriate matching of its revenues to their related costs, since current costs are included in cost of goods sold, and distortions in reported income due to the effect of changing prices are reduced.

a. Cross did not report any LIFO liquidation for 2000. Explain how its LIFO reserve could decline.

b. State two reasons why Cross might choose to continue to use the LIFO method despite the decline in the LIFO reserve.

21. [Effect of LIFO liquidations on gross margins] The following data were obtained from annual reports of Stride-Rite [SRR], a shoe manufacturer and retailer:

Years Ended December 31
(in $thousands)

	1997	1998	1999
Sales	$515,728	$539,413	$572,696
COGS	(328,172)	(348,587)	(362,108)
Gross profit	$187,556	$190,826	$210,588
LIFO liquidation (net of tax)	$ 3,379	$ 1,733	0

a. Compute the gross margin percentage for each year, 1997–1999.

b. Stride-Rite disclosed the effect of LIFO liquidations net of income tax. Assuming a tax rate of 35%, recompute Stride-Rite's gross margin for the years 1997–1999 after removing the effect of LIFO liquidations.

c. Explain why the trend in gross margins shown in part b is a better indictor of Stride-Rite's performance than the reported gross margins.

22. [Inventory costing for pricing purposes] The following paragraph was taken from the "Message to Stockholders" section of the Driver-Harris *1980 Annual Report*:

We would like to call your attention to a major effect caused by inflation. Our results are significantly affected by the use of LIFO accounting. We believe that this method better reflects the results of operations in inflationary times, even though, had the FIFO method been used for inventory valuation, our 1980 results before income taxes would have been approximately $1,800,000 better. Unfortunately, some of our competitors throughout the world are still using the FIFO method, and thus tend to offer unrealistically low prices, based on outdated costs.

Discuss the validity of this paragraph.

23. [Measuring operating performance in service economy] The inventory turnover ratio measures one aspect of a firm's operating efficiency. For companies that do not have significant inventories (i.e., service industries), this measure cannot be used. In some cases, even for firms that maintain inventory, the measure is inappropriate. Examples include:

- Airlines
- Car rental firms
- Private hospitals

a. Explain why the inventory turnover ratio is not a useful measure for firms in these industries.

b. Suggest and justify possible alternative measures of operating efficiency for such companies.

24. [Effect of inventory methods on contracts] The Sechne Company has entered into a number of agreements in the past year. These agreements contain provisions that depend on the firm's reported financial statements:

(i) *Management compensation plan*. Bonuses are based on a weighted average of reported net income and cash from operations.

(ii) *Bond indenture*. Specifies that the firm must maintain a minimum level of working capital, and dividend payments to shareholders require a minimum level of retained earnings.

(iii) *Labor contract*. Employees have a profit-sharing plan that pays them a share of reported net income in excess of a specified level.

Sechne's corporate controller, who is *both* a manager and a shareholder, must select the accounting methods used for financial reporting. Discuss how these agreements may affect the controller's choice of an inventory accounting method for Sechne.

7

ANALYSIS OF LONG-LIVED ASSETS: PART I—THE CAPITALIZATION DECISION

CHAPTER OUTLINE

INTRODUCTION

ACQUIRING THE ASSET: THE CAPITALIZATION DECISION

CAPITALIZATION VERSUS EXPENSING: CONCEPTUAL ISSUES
Financial Statement Effects of Capitalization
Income Variability
Profitability
Cash Flow from Operations
Leverage Ratios

CAPITALIZATION VERSUS EXPENSING: GENERAL ISSUES
Capitalization of Interest Costs
Interest Capitalization Outside the United States
Intangible Assets
Recognition and Measurement Issues
Research and Development
Patents and Copyrights
Franchises and Licenses
Brands and Trademarks
Advertising Costs

Goodwill
Asset Revaluation

CAPITALIZATION VERSUS EXPENSING: INDUSTRY ISSUES
Regulated Utilities
Computer Software Development Costs
Accounting for Oil and Gas Exploration

ANALYTICAL ADJUSTMENTS FOR CAPITALIZATION AND EXPENSING
Need for Analytical Adjustments
Valuation Implications
Other Economic Consequences
Additional Analysis of Fixed Asset Data
Capital Expenditures
Sale, Impairment, or Retirement of Assets

SUMMARY

APPENDIX 7-A
APPENDIX 7-B
CASE 7-1

CHAPTER OBJECTIVES

The objectives of Chapter 7 are to:

1. Discuss the effects of capitalization versus expensing on:
   - Income variability
   - Profitability
   - Cash from operations
   - Financial ratios used to measure leverage
2. Explain the rules governing the capitalization of interest and the effects of such capitalization on financial statements.
3. Review the circumstances under which intangible assets are capitalized.
4. Show how capitalization of expenditures for research and development and computer software affects

financial statements and how to restate to achieve comparability with firms that expense such expenditures.

5. Describe the two methods of accounting for oil and gas exploration and show their effects on the level and trend of reported income, cash flows, assets, and equity.
6. Examine the financial statement effects of revaluation of long-term assets.
7. Consider the accounting for industries with unusual capitalization practices and the effects of accounting choices on reported financial data.
8. Adjust reported financial statements for differences in capitalization policy.
9. Discuss the valuation implications of expenditures that may be either capitalized or expensed.

INTRODUCTION

The long-lived operating assets of a firm, unlike inventory, are not held for resale but are used in the firm's manufacturing, sales, and administrative operations. Such assets include tangible fixed assets (plant, machinery, and office facilities) as well as intangible assets such as computer software, patents, and trademarks.

This chapter examines financial reporting and analysis issues when these assets are originally acquired, with emphasis on:

- Which costs are included in the carrying amount of fixed assets
- The financial statement effects of capitalization versus expensing
- The capitalization of interest
- The circumstances under which research and development, computer software, and other intangible costs can be capitalized
- Analytical adjustments required to compare companies with different capitalization policies
- The analysis of fixed asset disclosures

Chapter 8 discusses the accounting for and analysis of the use, impairment, and disposal of these long-lived assets.

ACQUIRING THE ASSET: THE CAPITALIZATION DECISION

The costs of acquiring resources that provide services over more than one operating cycle are capitalized and carried as assets on the balance sheet. All costs incurred until the asset is ready for use must be capitalized, including the invoice price, applicable sales tax, freight and insurance costs incurred delivering the equipment, and any installation costs.[1]

However, considerable debate surrounds the application of these principles and significant differences remain (across countries and firms) with respect to three major issues:

1. Should some components of acquisition cost be included in the capitalized cost (e.g., interest during construction)?
2. Do some types of costs merit capitalization (e.g., software development and research and development costs)?
3. What accounting method should be used to determine the amount of costs capitalized (e.g., oil and gas properties)?

These choices affect the balance sheet, income and cash flow statements, and ratios both in the year the choice is made and over the life of the asset. Management discretion can result in smoothing or manipulation of reported income, cash flows, and other measures of financial performance. Moreover, unlike some accounting choices whose effects

---

[1]In June 2001, the Accounting Standards Executive Committee (AcSEC) of the AICPA issued an exposure draft of a proposed Statement of Position: Accounting for Certain Costs and Activities Related to Property, Plant, and Equipment. The SOP would require that:

- Costs incurred prior to asset acquisition must be expensed, with the exception of option payments and other costs directly related to specific PPE assets.
- All repair and maintenance costs during the life of PPE assets must be expensed.
- Overhead costs (including general and administrative and other support costs) must be expensed.

reverse over time, some effects of the decision to capitalize or expense may never reverse.

This chapter is devoted to the controversial issue of capitalization versus expensing of expenditures for long-lived assets. We start with an overview of the conceptual issues and a review of the implications of capitalization for financial statement analysis. The remaining sections then examine the specific components and categories of cost where capitalization practices vary.

CAPITALIZATION VERSUS EXPENSING: CONCEPTUAL ISSUES

The Financial Accounting Standards Board (FASB), in its Statement of Financial Accounting Concepts (SFAC) 6,[2] defines accounting assets as probable future economic benefits. Analytically, the concept of long-lived assets can also serve as:

1. An index of initial investment outlays, used as a base for measuring profitability (return on assets)
2. A measure of the firm's wealth, used for valuation and to measure solvency
3. Inputs in the firm's production function, used to measure capital intensity, leverage, and operating efficiency

Different analytical objectives require distinct definitions of what constitutes an asset. Although returns on research and development should be evaluated in the same way as returns on a purchased factory, measurement problems may preclude recognition of such expenditures as assets for assessment of shareholder wealth or collateral for bondholders.

For this reason, traditional, historical cost-based accounting rules cannot satisfy all contexts; analysts must evaluate asset definitions used for financial reporting and make necessary adjustments. The appropriate adjustment may require the capitalization of previously expensed costs, or the reverse. In some cases, particularly for intangible assets, there is no one "correct" choice that serves all analytical needs.

Financial Statement Effects of Capitalization

Box 7-1 (Figures 7-1 to 7-5) uses a simple illustration to demonstrate the financial statement effects of the capitalize-versus-expense choice on growing firms. That choice will have significant effects on reported cash flows, as well as on the balance sheet and income statement.

Income Variability

Firms that capitalize costs and depreciate them (systematically allocate them to income) over time show smoother patterns of reported income (Figure 7-2). Firms that expense costs as incurred have greater variance in reported income, as the variance in spending is transmitted directly to income. That variance declines as the firm matures and is lower for larger firms (or those with other sources of income).

Profitability

In the early years, expensing lowers profitability, both in absolute terms (as the cost of new assets exceeds depreciation of previously capitalized expenditures) and relative to assets, sales, etc. *Profitability remains lower for expensing firms as long as the level of expenditures is increasing* (positive growth). However, because they report lower assets (and equity), their

---

[2]See Chapter 1 for a discussion of SFAC 6.

BOX 7-1
Comparison of Financial Statement Effects: Capitalization versus Expensing

---

For our illustration we consider two hypothetical firms, each with an asset base of $1,000 on which it earns $150, which begin to grow. Growth requires the acquisition of an "asset," which has a three-year life. Each asset costs $100 and generates cash flows of $50 per year. The pattern of growth* (the number of assets acquired each year and the replacement of old assets) is illustrated in Figure 7-1.

Growth is assumed to continue for 15 years after which maturity is reached, and all subsequent acquisitions are for replacement only. We further assume that the asset cost may be capitalized or expensed at the discretion of management under the provisions of generally accepted accounting principles (GAAP). One firm capitalizes the acquisition cost; the other expenses it. The firms are otherwise operationally identical. Their reported income, cash flow from operations, and related ratios, however, will differ markedly.

Figure 7-2 compares the pattern of reported income. The "expensing" firm exhibits a fluctuating pattern of income growth through maturity. The "capitalizing" firm, on the other hand, ex-

hibits a smooth pattern of income growth. For firms that are initially larger,† the fluctuations are not as great throughout the growth and maturity cycle because of the larger base.

Figure 7-3 compares the return on assets (ROA) ratio for the two firms. The choice of accounting method affects both the numerator and denominator of the ROA. The expensing firm, having fewer recorded assets, will have a smaller denominator, increasing its reported ROA. The numerator (earnings) is volatile, so that sometimes ROA increases but at other times decreases. At the early stage of growth, the expensing firm's ROA gyrates about that of the capitalizing firm but will initially tend to be lower. As the expensing firm grows larger, the fluctuations persist, but its ROA is higher because the effect of lower reported assets on the denominator dominates.

Figure 7-4 compares reported cash from operations for the capitalizing and expensing firms. The capitalizing firm always shows higher cash from operations; the difference increases and does not reverse over the life of the asset (see Figure 7-5).

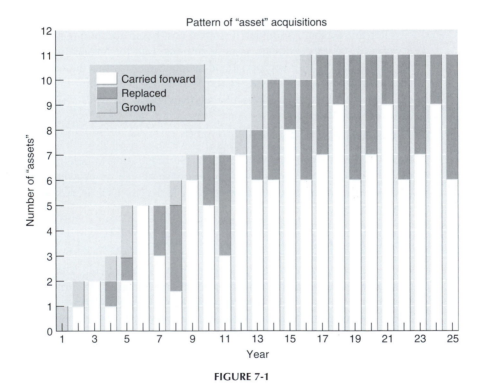

Pattern of "asset" acquisitions

FIGURE 7-1

---

*A variable growth rate is used in the illustration because it is more descriptive of reality (it has greater external validity). Any growth rate, other than a perfectly constant one, will create a similar pattern of differences between a capitalizing and expensing firm. At maturity or steady state, a constant growth rate generates identical (and constant) total expense for both firms. (ROA and cash flow from operations would still differ.)

†The term "larger" does not necessarily relate only to absolute size. It can also denote that the firm engages in other activities that offset the variability of the costs that are expensed.

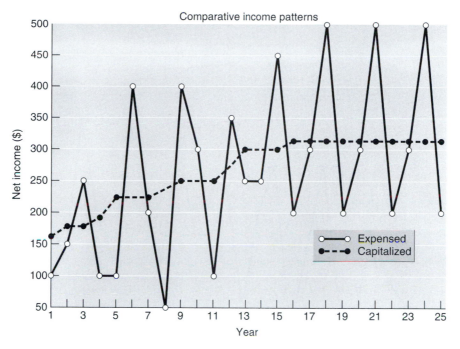

FIGURE 7-2

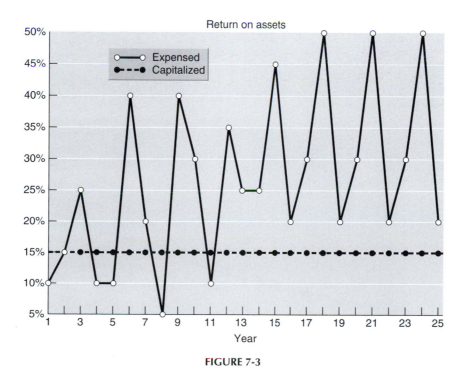

FIGURE 7-3

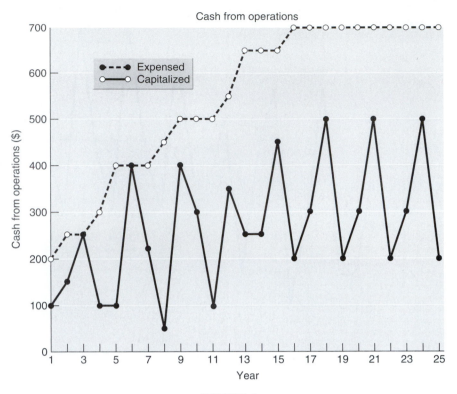

FIGURE 7-4

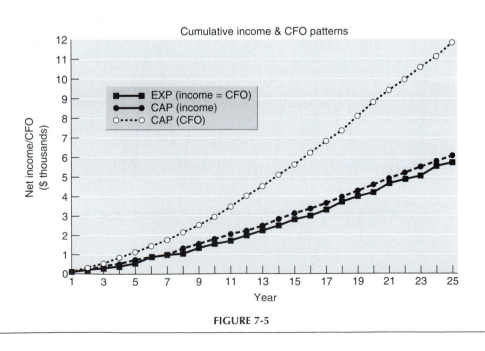

FIGURE 7-5

ROA/ROE measures can be higher than those of firms that capitalize costs (Figure 7-3). In general, whether ROA and ROE will be higher depends on the relationship between profitability and growth.[3]

Cash Flow from Operations

Reported *net cash flow*, unlike net income, is immune to accounting alternatives.[4] However, the capitalization decision has a significant impact on the components of cash flow, with a trade-off between *cash from operations (CFO) and cash from investment (CFI)*. As discussed in Chapter 3, cash expenditures for capitalized assets are included in investing cash flow and *never* flow through CFO. Firms that expense these outlays, however, include these expenditures in CFO. Thus, CFO will always be higher for the capitalizing firm (Figure 7-4),[5] and the cumulative difference (rather than reversing) increases over time (Figure 7-5). *Thus, the capitalization of long-lived assets results in a permanent shift of expenditures from CFO to CFI.*

Leverage Ratios

Expensing firms report lower assets and equity balances.[6] As a result, debt-to-equity and debt-to-assets solvency ratios will appear worse for expensing firms as compared with firms that capitalize the same costs.

Given management discretion as to capitalization, a great deal of care must be exercised when assessing financial performance. The remainder of this chapter considers particular areas where this problem occurs. Some issues are pervasive and cut across all industries; others are industry specific.

CAPITALIZATION VERSUS EXPENSING: GENERAL ISSUES

Capitalization of Interest Costs

Companies often construct long-lived assets, such as new operating facilities, for their own use and capitalize costs incurred during construction until the assets are ready to be placed in service. How should the firm measure the cost of these self-constructed assets? Should the interest cost on funds used for construction be capitalized or expensed? Should interest capitalization require specific borrowing to finance construction? Should the firm capitalize a return on equity when there is no debt or the firm has borrowed less than the total construction cost? The answers to these questions vary from country to country.

In the United States, SFAS 34 (1979) requires the capitalization of interest costs incurred during the construction period. When a specific borrowing is associated with the construction, the interest cost incurred on that borrowing is capitalized. If no specific borrowing is identifiable, the weighted-average interest rate on outstanding debt (up to the amount in-

---

[3]Sarath, Lev, and Sougiannis (2000) show that for a firm whose relevant expenditures are growing at a rate g, ROE on an expensing basis will be higher if that ROE $> g/(1+g/2)$. For growth rates (in the relevant range) below 30%, that relationship is equivalent to comparing ROE and g. As long as they are close, there is little difference between ROE on an expense basis and ROE on a capitalized basis. The greater the difference between ROE and g, the greater the difference between ROE on an expense basis and ROE on a capitalized basis. (A similar relationship holds for pretax ROA.)

For (after-tax) ROA, ROA will be higher for the expensing firm if its ROA $> (1 - \text{tax rate}) g/(1+g/2)$.

[4]Ignoring any income tax effects.

[5]This affects the cash from operations/capital expenditures ratio that measures the degree to which the firm's internally generated funds finance the replacement and expansion of productive capacity.

[6]These effects are not directly shown in Box 7-1. However, they can be deduced from the discussion of the return-on-investment (ROA/ROE) measures.

vested in the project) is capitalized. When the firm has no interest expense, no borrowing costs may be capitalized. Capitalization of the cost of equity is not permitted under any circumstances. SFAS 34 requires the disclosure of the amount of interest capitalized.

The argument for interest capitalization is that the cost of a self-constructed asset should equal the cost of one purchased after completion. In the latter case, the purchase price would presumably include the cost of capital of the seller. Capitalization of interest for self-constructed assets, it is argued, replicates this process. This argument should apply even when the firm has no debt; in that case, return on equity capital used for construction should be capitalized.

On the other hand, there are strong arguments against the capitalization of interest in general and SFAS 34 in particular. On a conceptual level, interest, as a financing cost, is different from the other costs of acquiring and getting the asset ready for service. It results from a financing decision rather than an operating decision.

Under SFAS 34, interest is capitalized only if the firm is leveraged. It seems illogical that two identical assets should be carried at different costs, depending on the firm's financing decisions. Further, the capitalization of interest creates differences between reported earnings and cash flow. Given these arguments, we believe that expensing of all interest is the preferable treatment.

For purposes of analysis, therefore, the income statement capitalization of interest should be reversed, resulting in the following effects:

1. *Capitalized interest should be added back to interest expense.* The adjusted interest expense provides a better representation of the level and trend of a firm's financing costs.

2. *Adding capitalized interest back to interest expense reduces net income.* Unfortunately, although the amount of interest capitalized in the current year must be disclosed, disclosure of the amortization of previously capitalized interest (included in the fixed asset account) is not required and is rarely provided.[7] This amortization must be deducted from depreciation expense to accurately determine the net effect of interest capitalization on net income. *However, if the amount of interest capitalization in previous years is not large and asset lives are long, the amortization (over the asset life) is likely to be immaterial and can be ignored.* If interest capitalization has been large, the analyst must estimate the amortization.[8]

3. *The capitalization of interest also distorts the classification of cash flows. Interest capitalized as part of the cost of fixed assets will never be reported as CFO, but as an investment outflow. To restore comparability with firms that do not capitalize interest, the amount of interest capitalized should be added back to cash for investment and subtracted from CFO.* The cash flows for capitalized interest are then included with other interest payments.[9]

4. *The interest coverage ratio should be calculated with interest expense adjusted to add back capitalized interest.* Otherwise, it is overstated.[10]

These adjustments tend to be small relative to cash flows but may be significant for interest expense and net income. The following example illustrates how adding back capitalized interest affects profitability and the interest coverage ratio.

---

[7]See Problem 7-1, based on Chevron, which does disclose the amortization of previously capitalized interest.

[8]The amortization of capitalized interest is included in depreciation expense. Thus, one can use the historical ratio of interest capitalized to total capital expenditures to estimate the portion of depreciation applicable to capitalized interest expense.

[9]These interest payments would be deducted from cash from operations, as required by SFAS 95. Alternatively, as we argue in Chapter 3, interest payments should be considered financing cash flows and thus excluded from both CFO and cash for investment regardless of capitalization.

[10]The SFAS 95 requirement for the disclosure of interest paid makes it possible to make this adjustment and compute interest coverage accurately (see Chapter 4) on a cash flow basis. On an accrual basis, the numerator, EBIT (and hence the coverage ratio), will be underestimated if the amortization of previous years' capitalized interest is not removed. However, as noted, this effect is relatively insignificant.

■ **Example: Westvaco**

Note F in Westvaco's fiscal 1999 financial statements reports capitalized interest, which can be used to adjust the interest coverage ratio:[11]

Westvaco, Years Ended October 31 (in $thousands)

	1997	1998	1999	*% Change* 1997–1999
As reported:				
EBIT	$339,872	$314,575	$271,514	(20%)
Interest expense	93,272	110,162	123,538	32%
Pretax income	$246,600	$204,413	$147,976	(40%)
Interest coverage	3.64X	2.86X	2.20X	(39%)
Interest capitalized	$ 25,962	$ 20,752	$ 8,890	(66%)
After adjustment:				
EBIT (unchanged)	$339,872	$314,575	$271,514	(20%)
Interest expense	119,234	130,914	132,428	11%
Pretax income	$220,638	$183,661	$139,086	(37%)
Interest coverage	2.85X	2.40X	2.05X	(28%)

Based on Westvaco's reported data, the interest coverage ratio fell 39% due to declining earnings before interest and taxes (EBIT) and rising interest expense. While adding back capitalized interest does not radically change the data, it does show that:

- Adjusted interest coverage, based on interest incurred before capitalization, is, as expected, below the (reported) ratio based on interest expense after capitalization.
- Interest expense over the period rose only 11% rather than 32% as reported.
- Interest coverage fell 28% based on interest incurred, a smaller decline than the 39% decline based on reported data.
- While pretax income is lower each year, the two-year decline in pretax income was slightly lower after adjustment.

Capitalization of interest provides additional information. Despite rising interest costs, capitalized interest declined 66%, apparently due to a lower level of qualifying assets. *A significant change in capitalized interest may signal a shift in the amount or nature of capital spending, and should be investigated by the analyst.* ■

Interest Capitalization Outside the United States

IAS 23, Borrowing Costs (revised 1993), makes expensing all borrowing costs the benchmark treatment. Alternatively, borrowing costs that are directly attributable to the acquisition, construction, or production of qualifying assets may be capitalized. Interest capitalization is also permitted in many jurisdictions worldwide. When comparing firms that capitalize interest with those do not, adjustment is required to achieve a base for proper valuation.

Intangible Assets

Growth of the computer, Internet, telecommunications, and service industries has led to significantly increased investment in and use of intangible assets. Licenses, computer software, patents, leasehold rights, brand names, and copyrights are among the more familiar examples of assets without tangible, physical substance. As a result of their increased use, the financial reporting and analysis of such intangible assets have gained importance; for some firms they are important on- or off-balance-sheet revenue-producing assets that account for a substantial portion of the value of a firm.

---

[11]Due to lack of disclosure, no adjustment has been made for the amortization of previously capitalized interest.

Intangible assets are identifiable, nonmonetary resources controlled by firms.[12] When acquired in an arm's-length transaction, recognition and measurement rules are similar to those for tangible assets. However, practice is diverse with respect to the recognition and measurement of such assets when they are internally developed. In addition, practices differ with respect to the revaluation, amortization, and impairment of intangible assets, regardless of their origin.

The decision whether to capitalize or expense the cost of asset acquisition is especially difficult when applied to intangible resources. The variations in legal protection available for intellectual property and other intangible assets in many countries also make the assessment of value more difficult than for tangible assets. We begin, therefore, with a review of the recognition and measurement issues associated with intangible assets.

Recognition and Measurement Issues

The cost of acquiring intangible assets from unrelated entities is capitalized at acquisition, measured by the amount paid to acquire them. Given an arm's-length transaction, the acquisition price is assumed to equal the market value of the assets acquired.

Intangible assets may also be received through government grants or generated internally by the firm. Few, if any, costs may be incurred in obtaining assets through government grants. Financial statement recognition of such assets would be informative, but in the absence of secondary markets it is difficult to defend any measurement basis other than cost. When active secondary markets do exist (such as for broadcast properties and cellular licenses), then market price can be a reliable measure of the value of these assets.

Internally generated intangible assets are the most troublesome category because:

- The costs incurred in developing these assets may not be easily separable.
- It is difficult to measure the amount and duration of benefits from such expenditures as advertising when they are made, or even later.
- There may be little relationship between the costs incurred and the value of the asset created.

For many internally generated intangible assets, discounted cash flow analysis may be the only way to measure their fair value. However, such measurement is subject to accurate forecasting of the amount and timing of cash flows and the choice of discount rates.

To illustrate these issues, we turn to a discussion of capitalization issues for specific intangible assets.

Research and Development

Companies invest in research and development (R&D) because they expect the investment to produce profitable future products. However, absent a resultant commercial product, these expenditures may have no value to the firm. Further, the value of the resulting product may be unrelated to the amount spent on R&D. Due to such valuation uncertainties, R&D is generally unacceptable to creditors as security for loans.

SFAS 2, Accounting for Research and Development Costs. SFAS 2 (1974) requires that virtually all R&D costs be expensed[13] in the period incurred and the amount disclosed. In effect, assets with uncertain future economic benefits are barred from the balance sheet. The impact of SFAS 2 on the financial statements of firms with significant R&D is substantial, and there is some evidence of a decrease in R&D expenditures when SFAS 2 was adopted. Accounting aside, R&D expenditures are clearly investments in the economic sense, albeit risky ones. Further, empirical evidence[14] suggests that benefits from R&D expenditures last, on average, seven to nine years (depending on the industry), supporting the argument that R&D is an economic asset. Pfizer, for example, spent nearly $2.8 billion (17.1% of revenue) on R&D in 1999.

---

[12]Goodwill is an intangible asset although it is not identifiable. See Chapter 14 for a discussion of acquisition goodwill.

[13]The main exception is contract R&D performed for unrelated entities. In this case, R&D is carried as an asset (similar to inventory) until completion of the contract.

[14]Research in this area can be found in both the accounting and economics literature. Lev and Sougiannis (1996) provide a brief review of the literature in this area. See also the discussion of valuation in Box 7-3.

Accounting for Research and Development Costs Outside the United States. IAS 9 (1993) requires the expensing of research costs but requires capitalization of development costs[15] when all of the following criteria are met:

1. The product (process) is clearly defined.
2. Costs can be clearly identified.
3. Technical feasibility has been established.
4. The firm intends to produce the product (use the process).
5. The market has been clearly defined.
6. The firm has sufficient resources to complete the project.

Capitalized costs must be reviewed periodically to ensure that these conditions are still operable and that capitalized costs do not exceed net realizable value.[16] The standard also requires disclosure of the accounting methods followed, amortization methods and lives, and a reconciliation of the carrying amount.

■ Example: Nokia

Nokia, an international telecommunications manufacturer, follows IASB GAAP and capitalized R&D costs in its 1998 and 1999 financial statements

As expensing research and development costs is the dominant accounting method worldwide, financial statements of companies such as Nokia that capitalize R&D must be restated (by expensing all such expenditures) to make them comparable with similar companies that expense these costs. Alternatively (or for other analytical purposes), it may be desirable to restate another firm's financial statements by capitalizing previously expensed R&D costs. Box 7-2 describes the procedures required to make the adjustments in both directions.[17] Below we illustrate the capitalization-to-expense adjustment, using Nokia as an example. Later (see Microsoft example) we adjust from expense to capitalization.

Nokia: Capitalized R&D Costs

	Years Ended December 31 (millions of euros)		
	1997	1998	1999
Opening balance	€426	€469	€650
Additions	156	182	271
Disposals	(113)	(1)	(110)
Closing balance	€469	€650	€811
Accumulated depreciation (year-end)*	(242)	(361)	(398)
Closing balance (net)	€227	€289	€413
Depreciation expense		119	110

*Note that the 1998 depreciation expense equals the change in accumulated depreciation; in 1999 accumulated depreciation has been reduced by the amount allocated to the disposal of R&D. We can deduce that reduction to equal €73 (361+110−398).

We can use these disclosures to compute the effect of capitalization compared to expense.

Adjustment to Pretax Income: Subtract the difference between R&D expenditure (additions) and depreciation/writedowns from reported income. This adjustment essen-

---

[15]IAS 9 defines development costs as expenditures incurred to translate research output into the production of materials, devices, products, processes, systems, and services.

[16]See Chapter 8 for a discussion of impairment.

[17]Appendix 7-A shows the difference between U.S. and Canadian GAAP (which allows capitalization) in the context of the acquisition of an R&D affiliate.

BOX 7-2
Adjusting Financing Statements for Capitalization versus Expensing

The capitalization-versus-expense decision has pervasive effects on firms' financial statements and ratios. In this box, we illustrate the adjustments from one method to the other. For convenience we use research and development (R&D) as the expenditure that can either be capitalized or expensed.

Adjusting from Capitalization to Expense		**Adjusting from Expense to Capitalization**	

Income Statement:

Pretax Income: Deduct difference between R&D additions (expenditures) and amount amortized (or written off). This adjustment is equivalent to the *change in the net (unamortized) R&D asset.*

Net Income: Deduct $(1 - \text{tax rate}) \times$ (change in the net (unamortized) R&D asset).

Balance Sheet:

Assets: Deduct net (unamortized) R&D asset from assets.

Liabilities: Deduct (tax rate) $\times$ (decrease in assets) from deferred tax liability.*

Equity: Deduct $(1 - \text{tax rate}) \times$ (decrease in assets) from equity.

Cash Flow Statement: Deduct R&D expenditures from CFO and add same amount to CFI.

To capitalize expenditures, we need an assumption as to the period of amortization. This illustration assumes amortization over three years beginning in the year of the expenditure (year t).

Income Statement:

Pretax Income:[†] In year t, increase pretax income by $R\&D_t - 1/3(R\&D_t + R\&D_{t-1} + R\&D_{t-2})$.

Net Income: Add $(1 - \text{tax rate}) \times$ (pretax income adjustment).

Balance Sheet:[‡]

Assets: Increase by $[2/3\ R\&D_t + 1/3\ R\&D_{t-1}]$.

Liabilities: Add (tax rate) $\times$ (increase in assets) to deferred tax liability.[§]

Equity: Increase by $(1 - \text{tax rate}) \times$ (increase in assets).

Cash Flow Statement: Add $R\&D_t$ to CFO and deduct same amount from CFI.

---

*Assumes that R&D was expensed for tax purposes, creating a deferred tax liability (see Chapter 9).
[†]General case, for amortization over n years: Increase pretax income by $[R\&D_t - 1/n (R\&D_t + R\&D_{t-1} + \ldots R\&D_{t-(n-1)})]$.
[‡]Increase assets by $[(n-1)/n\ R\&D_t + (n-2)/n\ R\&D_{t-1} + \ldots 1/n\ R\&D_{t-(n-2)}]$.
[§]Assumes that R&D is expensed for tax purposes, so that capitalization results in a deferred tax liability (see Chapter 9).

---

tially amounts to subtracting the change in net (unamortized) closing balance from reported income:

(Millions of Euros)	1998	1999
Pretax income (reported)	€2,456	€3,845
Less: change in net (unamortized) closing balance	62	124
Pretax income (adjusted)	€2,394	€3,721
% reduction	2.5%	3.2%

We can also adjust reported cash flows:

Adjustment to Cash Flows: Subtract R&D expenditure (additions) from CFO and add back to CFI:

(Millions of Euros)	1998	1999
Cash from operations	€1,687	€3,102
Cash flow from investing	(780)	(1,341)
Additions (R&D expenditures)	182	271
After adjustment		
Cash from operations	1,505	2,831
% reduction	10.8%	8.7%
Cash flow from investing	€(598)	€(1,070)

Finally, to make Nokia comparable to companies that expense all R&D, we must reduce equity[18] by the closing balance of unamortized R&D expense, net of tax effect:

(Millions of Euros)	1998	1999
Shareholders' equity (as reported)	€5,109	€7,378
Closing R&D balance (net of depreciation)	289	413
Less tax @ 28% (rate in Finland)	(81)	(116)
Net reduction in equity	€208	€297
Shareholders' equity (adjusted)	4,901	7,081
% reduction	4.1%	4.0%

These adjustments vary from 2% to 10% depending on the item being adjusted. Nokia is a very large company (1999 sales were nearly €20 billion). Depending on the size of the firm and the variability in expenditures, the effect on other firms may be more significant.[19]

One additional benefit of this analysis is that it highlights the actual expenditures on R&D activities. Changes in amount or trend (note the large 1999 increase for Nokia) should be examined for implications regarding the company's future sales and earnings. ∎

Research and Development Affiliates. Although SFAS 2 does not permit the capitalization of R&D costs, companies have found ways to defer the recognition of such costs. One method is the R&D partnership. Another involves the issuance of "callable common" shares to the public. These arrangements are discussed in Appendix 7-A.

Patents and Copyrights

All costs incurred in developing patents and copyrights are expensed in conformity with the treatment of R&D costs.[20] Only the legal fees incurred in registering internally developed patents and copyrights can be capitalized. However, the full acquisition cost is capitalized when such assets are purchased from other entities.

Patents have a legal life of 17 years under U.S. patent law; copyrights have a legal life of 50 years beyond the creator's life. However, these periods should be viewed as upper limits. Successful patented products invite competition and the development of comparable or improved products that can diminish the value of the patent or make it obsolete. In addition, there is often a gap between the time that a patent is registered and the time the product comes to market.

In the pharmaceutical industry, for example, even after a patent is registered, the product cannot be marketed in most countries until it obtains regulatory approval, which can take a number of years. The analysis of companies that are heavily dependent on patented or proprietary products must consider the remaining legal life of patents on existing products and the number of patents in the pipeline.

Franchises and Licenses

Companies may sell the right to use their name, products, processes, or management expertise to others for some negotiated time period or market. The franchisee or licensee capitalizes the cost of purchasing these rights.

---

[18]To adjust assets, we would deduct the closing balance of unamortized R&D expense.

[19]Nokia's 20-F report, in the required reconciliation between IASB and U.S. GAAP, shows somewhat different amounts for the income statement and balance sheet adjustments. These differences reflect the fact that, even under U.S. GAAP, Nokia could have capitalized a portion of these expenditures (computer software). The adjustments shown here eliminate the entire capitalized amount, facilitating comparison with firms that expense all R&D.

[20]However, publishers and motion picture producers capitalize all costs of creating their inventory.

Brands and Trademarks

The cost of acquiring brands and trademarks in arm's-length transactions is capitalized. However, as in the case of other intangibles, U.S. GAAP prohibit recognition of the value of *internally created* brands or trademarks. IAS 38 also prohibits recognition of internally generated brands, mastheads, publishing titles, customer lists, and similar items. Some national accounting standards do permit recognition of such assets. Problem 7-11 concerns News Corporation, an Australian company with substantial intangible assets.

Advertising Costs

Successful advertising campaigns can contribute to generating a customer base and establishing brand or firm loyalty for many years. However, as with R&D, these benefits are uncertain and difficult to measure, and hence advertising costs are expensed as incurred. Even though there may be economic benefits, no asset is recorded because of measurement problems.

In December 1994, the Accounting Standards Executive Committee (AcSEC) of the AICPA issued Practice Bulletin 13,[21] Direct-Response Advertising and Probable Future Benefits, requiring capitalization of the costs of direct-response advertising that result in probable future benefits.[22] These costs are amortized over the estimated life of the future benefits. Capitalization is not allowed when the advertising produces leads that require additional marketing efforts to convert into sales.[23]

Goodwill

The difference between the cost of an acquired firm and the fair market value of its net assets is accounted for as an intangible asset, goodwill. It represents the amount paid for the acquired firm's ability to earn excess profits, or value that cannot be assigned to tangible assets like property. The United States and most other GAAP limit the recognition of goodwill to cases where it is acquired in purchase method transactions. (See Chapter 14.)

Asset Revaluation

As discussed in Chapter 17, the balance sheet is more informative when assets and liabilities are stated at market value rather than historical cost. Although the recognition of changes in fixed asset value is not permitted under U.S. GAAP, IASB standards do permit such revaluations.

IAS 16 (revised 1998), Property, Plant, and Equipment, allows firms to report fixed assets at fair value less accumulated depreciation.[24] Revaluations must be made with sufficient regularity to keep them current. All items in an asset class must be revalued if any are. Revaluation decreases that place the asset value below historical cost must be included in reported earnings. Revaluations are credited directly to equity except when they reverse writedowns that were included in reported income. IAS 16 has extensive disclosure provisions regarding revaluations and requires a full reconciliation of fixed assets. Footnote 12 to the Roche 2000 financial statements is a typical reconciliation.

IAS 41 (2000), Agriculture, requires that agricultural produce (e.g. cotton, milk, and logs) and biological assets (plants and animals) be measured at fair value for financial reporting. This standard becomes effective in 2003.

Revaluation is permitted under some non-U.S. GAAP as well.[25] Unfortunately, revaluation is applied inconsistently as standards in most countries do not specify either the

---

[21]This bulletin provides an interpretation of AICPA SOP 93-7, Reporting on Advertising Costs.

[22]An example would be advertising that results in a telephone response with an order.

[23]America On Line (AOL) capitalized marketing costs prior to 1996 as "deferred subscriber acquisition costs." After pressure from the SEC and analysts, AOL took a $385 million write-off in 1997 to eliminate these assets from its financial statements. In March 2000, AOL paid a $3.5 million fine to the SEC to settle charges that it had inflated profits in the years prior to 1997.

[24]Although historical cost is the benchmark treatment, revaluation is an allowed alternative.

[25]Australian GAAP, for example, permits revaluations. Barth and Clinch (1998) examined a sample of revaluations in Australia and found that both tangible and intangible revaluations tended to be value relevant.

method(s) to be used for revaluations or the intervals at which they must be made. The resulting balance sheet accounts are not comparable and, in some cases, may be misleading.

■ Example: Holmen

Footnote 10 to Holmen's 1999 financial statements reports total revaluation surplus of SKr 4,372, almost all of which reflects the revaluation of forest land. No other data are provided although this item exceeds 27% of equity.

The revaluation of forest land has the following effects on Holmen compared with firms that do not revalue:

- Lower asset turnover due to the higher asset value for land
- Lower return on assets (ROA) due to higher assets
- Higher reported book value per share
- Lower return on equity (ROE) due to higher equity
- Lower debt ratios due to higher equity

As forestland is not depreciated, there is no effect on reported income. For assets that are depreciated, revaluation has the following additional effects:

- Lower earnings due to higher depreciation expense
- Lower interest coverage due to reduced EBIT

The earnings reduction further reduces ROA and ROE and dilutes the positive impact of the revaluation on book value per share.   ■

CAPITALIZATION VERSUS EXPENSING: INDUSTRY ISSUES

Regulated Utilities

Even prior to the issuance of SFAS 34, almost all U.S. regulated utilities capitalized interest on construction work in progress. In addition, utilities capitalize many cash outflows that unregulated companies cannot. The reason is that accounting rules have direct economic impact for utilities. Rates charged to customers are largely a function of accounting-generated numbers.[26]

Regulators allow utilities to earn profits equal to a specified allowable rate of return on assets (rate base). Adding expenses to this allowable profit yields the rates they can charge their customers. Revenues are derived as follows:

$$\textbf{Revenues} = \textbf{Expenses} + (\textbf{Rate of Return} \times \textbf{Rate Base})$$

Using interest for a self-constructed asset as an example, expensing increases revenue immediately as the interest expense is recovered in the year incurred. Capitalizing results in recovery of the expense over time as depreciation of the additional fixed asset. However, the total allowable profit is increased due to the fact that the asset base has been increased. Hence, although revenues are deferred, the total amount collected over the life of the asset is greater. As the average life of utility fixed assets (mainly generating plants) is quite long, the incentive to capitalize costs in fixed assets (increasing the rate base) is powerful.

Fairness to customers is often one argument for capitalization; as current customers do not (yet) benefit from investments in capacity growth, they should not bear the cost. Thus, the cost of financing new capacity is capitalized and spread over time, matching the costs with the benefits (service to ratepayers). This logic is also appealing to regulators who prefer

---

[26]For this reason, virtually all regulators that set prices also mandate the accounting principles followed by the companies that they regulate. This has given rise to so-called RAP (regulatory accounting principles), which may differ materially from GAAP.

(for political reasons) to defer rate increases to future time periods. Logic and fairness aside, utilities have a direct economic incentive to capitalize.[27]

Regulatory accounting results in the creation of *regulatory assets* and *regulatory liabilities*. Regulatory assets are expenditures that regulators will permit the utility to recover in future periods, even though these expenditures do not qualify as assets for unregulated companies under GAAP. Examples include:

- Capitalization (as part of fixed assets) of return on equity as well as interest. These are called the allowance for funds used during construction (AFUDC).
- Capitalization (as part of fixed assets) of employee costs and other overhead.
- Demand-side management costs (expenditures to reduce demand).
- Costs to buy out coal or gas purchase contracts.

Under SFAS 71, such expenditures can be recorded as regulatory assets (regulatory liabilities) as long as recovery (settlement) is expected. If an adverse regulatory ruling is made, such assets must be written off.

When deregulation occurs, the company must reassess the carrying value of its assets and liabilities under these new circumstances. In the United States, deregulation of the telephone industry resulted in significant write-offs by companies in that industry as they:

- Wrote down fixed assets to reflect shorter economic lives
- Wrote off regulatory assets that were no longer recoverable

The use of shorter asset lives as a result of the accounting change increases depreciation expense, somewhat offset by the elimination of depreciation on older assets that were fully written off as part of the change. The change also sharply reduces reported stockholders' equity, increasing the reported debt-to-equity ratio.

The deregulation of the electric utility industry in the United States is in its early stages. Such deregulation is likely to result in similar write-offs of regulatory assets and the use of shorter lives for fixed assets.[28]

Computer Software Development Costs

The growing importance of computer software led the FASB to issue SFAS 86 (1985), which applies to software intended for sale or lease to others. SFAS 86 requires that all costs incurred to establish the technological and/or economic feasibility of software be viewed as R&D costs and expensed as incurred. Once economic feasibility has been established, subsequent costs can be capitalized as part of product inventory and amortized based on product revenues or on a straight-line basis.

Although this provision allows software firms to increase reported assets and income, some software firms[29] (most notably, Microsoft[30]) have not taken advantage of the provisions

---

[27]This discussion assumes that the capitalized interest will, in fact, be recovered from future revenues. In practice, "regulatory lag" often results in actual rates of return below the "allowable" rate of return. In addition, by capitalizing interest, the recovery of that interest is delayed to a later period and thus current period cash flow is reduced. For these reasons, some utilities have successfully petitioned regulators to allow some portion of the interest on construction work in progress (CWIP) to be recovered currently (expensed) rather than capitalized.

[28]Deregulation also eliminates the incentives for investments in generating plants by eliminating the guaranteed recovery of the investment and a return on investment. Shortages of generating capacity started in appear in 1999.

[29]In 1996, the Software Publishers Association (SPA) petitioned the FASB to abolish SFAS 86 and make expensing the required method of accounting. The SPA argued that the uncertainty surrounding eventual product sales made capitalization both inappropriate and not beneficial to investors. As noted in Box 7-3, Aboody and Lev (1998) found, on the contrary, that software capitalization was indeed value relevant to investors. Aboody and Lev suggested (using recent trends in software development costs) that perhaps the SPA was motivated by the fact that software development expenditures had declined to a low level and that expensing would now show higher income than capitalization. By eliminating the previous years' capitalization overhang with a onetime accounting charge, software developers could (under the SPA's proposal) get the best of both worlds, using capitalization when costs were growing and expensing when costs declined.

[30]Microsoft's fiscal 2000 annual report states that it adopted SOP 98-1 (discussed shortly) in 2000 but provides no disclosure of the effects. On page 22 it states that SFAS 86 "does not materially affect the Company."

of SFAS 86. Disparate accounting for software hinders the comparison of computer software firms, requiring restatement to the same accounting method. SFAS 86 disclosures are sufficient to evaluate (and eliminate) the impact of capitalization. For some firms, the effect may be significant, as illustrated by the following example.

■ **Example: Lucent**

The following data were obtained from Lucent's annual report for fiscal 1999:

Capitalized Software

(in $millions)	1998	1999
Opening balance	$293	$298
Closing balance	298	470
Amortization	234	249

where the balances were obtained from Lucent's balance sheet and the amortization amount from the statement of cash flows. By adding the year-to-year increase in the balance to the amortization, we can deduce the amount invested during the year (which is included in capital expenditures under investing activities):

(in $millions)	1998	1999
New investment	$239	$421

If Lucent expensed this amount each year (as does Microsoft), its income would have been reduced by:

	(in $millions)	1998	1999
Income adjustment	Investment less amortization	$ 5	$ 172
	Tax offset (35%)	(2)	(60)
	Net adjustment	$ 3	$ 112
Net Income	Reported	$1,035	$3,458
	Adjusted	1,032	3,346
	% reduction	−0.3%	−3.2%

Note that the 1999 effect is much greater than the 1998 effect, reflecting the substantial increase in expenditures. Capitalization and amortization smoothes the effect of spending changes on reported income. It also obscures the large increase, which may suggest that Lucent hopes to expand its software sales.

Perhaps more important, however, is that amounts capitalized are included in cash for investing activities rather than cash from operations. By subtracting the new investment amount, we can adjust cash from operations:

Cash from Operations

(in $millions)	1998	1999
Reported	$1,860	$(276)
Adjusted	1,621	(697)
% reduction	−12.8%	−152.5%

While reported CFO turned negative in 1999, the effect is even greater when software expenditures are reclassified from investing to operating activities. ◼

SOP 98-1 governs accounting for the cost of developing computer software for internal use (rather than sale or lease).[31] This standard requires the capitalization and subsequent amortization of the cost of developing internal-use software once technical feasibility has been established. EITF Issue 00-2[32] extends SOP 98-1 to website development costs, allowing capitalization of costs to develop or add applications for websites. IBM, for example, capitalized $81 million of website development costs in 2000.

◼ Example: Lucent

The 10-Q report filed by Lucent for the first quarter of fiscal 2000 (ending December 31, 1999) states:

> Effective October 1, 1999, Lucent adopted Statement of Position 98-1, "Accounting for the Costs of Computer Software Developed or Obtained for Internal Use" ("SOP 98-1"). As a result, certain costs of computer software developed or obtained for internal use have been capitalized and will be amortized over a three-year period. The impact of adopting SOP 98-1 was a reduction of costs and operating expenses of $80 million during the three months ended December 31, 1999.

The impact of the new standard increased pretax income by $80 million, equal to nearly 5% of pretax income excluding "one-time items." If not for the accounting change, that adjusted pretax income would have declined by more than 28% instead of the reported decline of 25%. The effect of the accounting change was not reported in the January 20, 2000 press release announcing Lucent's first quarter earnings, providing an illustration of the importance of reviewing SEC filings. ◼

Case 7-1 uses International Business Machines to explore the financial statement effects and information content of capitalization of software costs in greater detail.

Accounting for Oil and Gas Exploration

Oil and gas exploration results in drilling both productive wells and dry holes.[33] As failure is an integral part of successful exploration, the cost of dry holes can be considered part of the cost of drilling productive ones. As in the case of R&D, the value of an oil discovery is frequently unrelated to the cost of drilling.

The FASB, in SFAS 19 (1977), required all firms to use the successful efforts (SE) accounting method that expenses all dry hole costs. Like the FASB's R&D reporting standard, this rule was conservative and eliminated assets with uncertain future benefits from the balance sheet. The Securities and Exchange Commission (SEC), fearing that the adoption of this rule would result in the curtailment of oil exploration (especially by smaller companies), forced the FASB to suspend SFAS 19 (SFAS 25, 1979). The SEC (ASR 253, 1978) permits public companies to use either SE or full cost (FC) methods of accounting. The latter permits the capitalization of dry hole costs.

Under current accounting practice, therefore, firms have the option of capitalizing the cost of dry holes (FC method) or expensing them as they occur (SE method). The choice between these two methods has a significant impact on the financial statements of oil and gas exploration companies and on many ratios as well. Exhibit 7-1 illustrates the difference between

---

[31]Issued by the Accounting Standards Executive Committee of the American Institute of Certified Public Accountants. For full discussion of SOP 98-1, see Daniel Noll, "Accounting for Internal Use Software," *Journal of Accountancy* (September 1998), pp. 95–98.

[32]Accounting for Web Site Development Costs, issued by the Emerging Issues Task Force based on discussions in January and March 2000. EITF 00-2 was effective for costs incurred after June 30, 2000.

[33]Dry holes are wells drilled that do not find commercial quantities of oil or gas.

EXHIBIT 7-1
Comparison of Successful Efforts and Full Cost Impact on Net Income and Cash from Operations

Assumptions:

1. $1,000 cost of drilling well (dry or productive).
2. Four wells are drilled: One is productive, the other three are dry.
3. The productive well has a four-year life, with revenues (net of cost of production) of $3,000 per year.

Successful Efforts Method

The $3,000 cost of dry holes is expensed immediately. Only the $1,000 cost of the productive well is capitalized and amortized over its four-year life.

Year	1	2	3	4	Total
Net revenues	$ 3,000	$3,000	$3,000	$3,000	$12,000
Dry hole expense	(3,000)	0	0	0	(3,000)
Amortization	(250)	(250)	(250)	(250)	(1,000)
Net income	$ (250)	$2,750	$2,750	$2,750	$ 8,000

Cash Flows

	1	2	3	4	Total
Operations*	$ 0	$3,000	$3,000	$3,000	$ 9,000
Investment	(1,000)	0	0	0	(1,000)
Total	$(1,000)	$3,000	$3,000	$3,000	$ 8,000

*Net revenues less dry hole expense.

Full Cost Method

The entire $4,000 drilling cost ($3,000 for dry holes and $1,000 for the productive well) is capitalized and amortized over the four-year life of the productive well.

Year	1	2	3	4	Total
Net revenues	$ 3,000	$3,000	$3,000	$3,000	$12,000
Amortization	(1,000)	(1,000)	(1,000)	(1,000)	(4,000)
Net income	$ 2,000	$2,000	$2,000	$2,000	$ 8,000

Cash Flows

	1	2	3	4	Total
Operations*	$ 3,000	$3,000	$3,000	$3,000	$12,000
Investment	(4,000)	0	0	0	(4,000)
Total	$(1,000)	$3,000	$3,000	$3,000	$ 8,000

*Net revenues.

the SE and FC methods of accounting for oil and gas exploration costs. The balance sheet carrying amount of reserves, $4,000, is higher under the FC method because of the inclusion of the cost of dry holes ($3,000). The SE firm carries its reserves at only $1,000.[34]

The reported profitability (both levels and trends over time) of production is also affected. The SE firm reports a net loss of $250 in year 1 but net income of $2,750 per year for years 2 through 4, for a total net income of $8,000. The FC firm shows constant net income of $2,000 per year, again for a total of $8,000 over the four years. The effect of the FC

---

[34]Using a sample of oil and gas companies, Harris and Ohlson (1987) found that the market distinguished between SE and FC companies in a rational fashion. Book values of full cost companies were given less weight than those of SE companies. Additionally, they found that FC book values had less explanatory power than those of SE companies. This finding is consistent with a survey that indicated analysts prefer SE.

method is to defer (capitalize) exploration costs and, therefore, accelerate the recognition of profit.

CFO may also differ. As previously discussed, although the income difference reverses over time, the difference in CFO does not. The cumulative CFO over the life of the well is higher for the FC firm by the cost of the capitalized dry holes ($12,000 − $9,000 = $3,000).

The differences between the methods cause SE firms to report:

* Lower carrying costs of oil and gas reserves than FC firms
* Lower stockholders' equity due to lower asset values
* Lower earnings than FC firms when exploration efforts are rising
* Lower cash from operations than FC firms

In practice, however, oil and gas firms using the SE method adjust their reported cash flow statements for this difference. They add exploration costs expensed back to net income (assuming use of the indirect method) and include those costs in capital expenditures. For example, Texaco's 1999 annual report states:

> We present cash flows from operating activities using the indirect method. We exclude exploratory expenses from cash flows of operating activities and apply them to cash flows of investing activities. On this basis, we reflect all capital and exploratory expenditures as investing activities.

However, Repsol, the large Spanish oil company, does not appear to make this adjustment. As a result, its reported cash flow components are not comparable with those of companies that make the adjustment.

Appendix 7-B discusses the motivation for firms to choose the SE or FC methods and the effects of changes between the two methods. The appendix also provides a detailed discussion of the disclosures provided by and the analysis of oil and gas companies.

ANALYTICAL ADJUSTMENTS FOR CAPITALIZATION AND EXPENSING

Need for Analytical Adjustments

Because the choices between capitalization and expensing discussed in this chapter affect reported corporate performance, analysts must sometimes adjust reported data to facilitate analysis and comparisons.

Software companies, as noted earlier, are allowed to capitalize software costs, and most do so. A notable exception is Microsoft. Comparisons with other (software) companies can be facilitated and insight as to Microsoft's motivations can be gained by comparing Microsoft's reported income with income had it capitalized R&D. In our analysis, we assume a three-year amortization period.

(in $millions)

	1996	1997	1998	1999	2000
Net income as reported			$4,490	$7,785	$9,421
Adjustment					
R&D as reported	$1,432	$1,925	2,601	2,970	3,775
Amortization of R&D*			(1,986)	(2,499)	(3,115)
Pretax adjustment			$ 615	$ 471	$ 660
After-tax @ 35% tax rate			400	306	429
Adjusted income			4,890	8,091	9,850
% increase in income			8.9%	3.9%	4.6%

*For example, for 2000: ($2,601 + $2,970 + $3,775)/3 = $3,115.

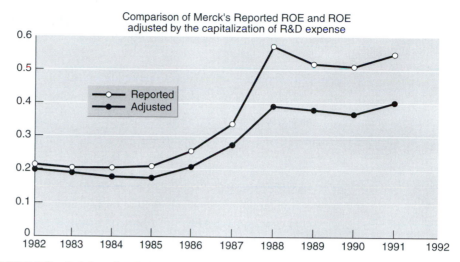

FIGURE 7-6 Recalculation of Profitability Ratios Assuming Capitalization of R&D Expenditures. *Source*: "The Capitalization, Amortization, and Value-Relevance of R&D," *Journal of Accounting and Economics*, Baruch Lev and Theodore Sougiannis, Table 6 (Feb. 1996), pp. 107–138.

Note that, as Microsoft's R&D is increasing, expensing R&D reduces reported income by 4% to 9%. Although one cannot be sure, it is possible that Microsoft opted not to capitalize costs in order to lessen pressure from antitrust authorities by reporting lower income.

In Microsoft's case, the adjustments to R&D do not significantly affect ROE and ROA.[35] However, that is a function of Microsoft's profitability and pattern of R&D expenditures. For other industries, the effects on ROE and ROA can be considerable.

The pharmaceutical industry, for example, reports ROE that is among the highest of all U.S. industries. Some suggest that this reflects a higher return for the risks inherent in R&D. Others contend that the industry simply earns excess profits, and drug prices have periodically become a political issue. To some extent, however, high drug-industry returns reflect the accounting method used for R&D. Expensing these costs understates equity, the denominator of the ROE ratio. Capitalizing R&D costs (treating them as an investment) would give a more accurate measure of ROE.

Figure 7-6 illustrates this point. Sougiannis (1994) and Lev and Sougiannis (1996) examined the effect on return on equity (ROE) of recalculating the financial results of Merck as if the company capitalized R&D expense and amortized the capitalized amounts over seven years.[36] Using the implied amortization schedule for Merck,[37] Figure 7-6 shows the effects of their conversion process graphically for the period 1982 to 1991. Adjusted ROE is significantly lower for all years, although the trend is unchanged.[38]

---

[35]In 2000, average equity was $34,903 million, yielding ROE of 27.0%. Capitalizing R&D would increase equity for

$$1999\left[.65x\left(\left(\frac{2}{3}\right)2,970 + \left(\frac{1}{3}\right)2,601\right)\right] = 1,851 \text{ and for } 2000\left[.65x\left(\left(\frac{2}{3}\right)3,775 + \left(\frac{1}{3}\right)2,970\right)\right] = 2,280$$

Average equity would increase by [.5 × ($1,851 + $2,280) = $2,065] to $36,968 and adjusted ROE would be ($9,850/$36,968=) 26.6%. The reason for the small adjustment is related to the discussion in footnote 3. Note the growth rate in Microsoft's R&D expenditures for 2000 is 27.1%. As that growth rate is almost identical to the ROE of 27.0%, the differences in reported and adjusted ROE (ROA) will be negligible.

[36]Their analysis suggests that R&D has (on average) a seven-year duration for the pharmaceutical industry.

[37]The amortization schedule is neither straight-line nor declining balance. Rather, it amortizes capitalized R&D in proportion to the benefits received. As there is a lag between the time of the expenditure and benefits received, amortization increases over the first three years and declines thereafter.

[38]In this case, Merck's profitability as measured by ROE was in the 40% range whereas growth in R&D expenditures was considerably smaller at 15%. As a result, there was a substantial adjustment to ROE on a capitalized

From the analyst's perspective, the problem is that accounting does not (and probably cannot) accurately measure the value of expenditures on research and development.[39] Thus the analyst must perform two tasks:

1. Adjust financial data to reflect differences in capitalization policy among firms.
2. Evaluate the flow of new products resulting from R&D expenditures.

The Merck example shows the effects of restating by capitalizing an expense. At times, it may be more appropriate to restate capitalized expenditures to expenses. West-vaco (capitalized interest) and Nokia (capitalized development costs) are examples of such restatements. The second task, far more difficult, is beyond the scope of financial statement analysis.

Similar adjustments are required for firms that differ in the extent to which they buy operating assets or lease them. Airlines, for example, may buy or lease airplanes. Similarly, retail store chains may own or lease stores. This choice has financial statement effects similar to those stemming from capitalizing or expensing. Reported ROA may be misleading; adjustments are required for comparability. Chapter 11 discusses leasing and other off-balance-sheet financing techniques in detail.

Valuation Implications

Expenditures for R&D and advertising are generally expensed because it is difficult, if not impossible, to reliably estimate their future benefits. That does not mean that these expenditures do not affect firm valuation. An outflow that is truly an expense reduces stockholder wealth; an outflow that generates future cash flows may actually increase it.

Chapter 19 discusses two types of valuation models: earnings based and asset based. Box 7-3 discusses how the capitalization decision affects these valuation models and presents empirical evidence that the market recognizes the asset characteristics of outflows in categories such as R&D, advertising, and oil and gas wells. These results suggest that the analyst cannot apply either capitalization or expensing mechanically, but must try to forecast the future benefits of these expenditures.

Other Economic Consequences

Although differences in accounting methods are cosmetic, they can have real consequences, as suggested by positive theory.[40]

First, a firm's borrowing ability may be limited by unfavorable profitability or leverage ratios resulting from, for example, expensing R&D expenditures. Second, because of these unfavorable ratios, a firm may curtail these expenditures, effectively scaling back operations. Finally, whether or not managers actually reduce R&D, the fact that the market perceives such a possibility can cause negative market reaction.

Mandated accounting changes is one area where such effects can be examined, as they provide a laboratory environment permitting before-and-after comparisons. Box 7-4 reviews empirical evidence regarding mandated accounting changes for R&D and oil and gas accounting.

The research confirms that, even if an accounting change has no direct economic impact, the effects of the change on reported income can have real indirect consequences, such as the curtailment of expenditures and negative market reaction. Indirect effects may also result from debt covenant constraints or the influence of management compensation contracts. Accounting choices may also be motivated by firm characteristics (see Appendix 7-B for a discussion of accounting choices by large and small oil companies).

---

[39]It is precisely this difficulty that prompted the FASB to require the expensing of R&D expenditures.

[40]See Chapter 5.

BOX 7-3
Capitalization and Valuation

Consider the following simplified valuation model:

Value = p × Net Inflows

The model can be used to represent a (constant) discounted earnings model, where net inflows represent revenue and expense flows and the coefficient p is simply the price/earnings (P/E) ratio. Disaggregating the net inflows into inflows and outflows yields

Value = p × Inflows − p × Expense Outflows + b × Asset Outflows

where asset outflows represent expenditures for such categories as R&D. If these outflows are actually expenses, then $b = -p$.

From a valuation perspective, the difference between asset and expense outflows should be whether the associated outflow has expected future benefits. The level and sign of the coefficient b measure whether the outflow should be considered an expense. An expense benefits only the period of occurrence, and the outlay reduces value by $-p$ times the outflow.[*] An asset outflow benefits future periods and, therefore, the coefficient b should be positive.[†]

Bublitz and Ettredge (1989) compared the market valuation of unexpected changes in advertising, R&D, and other expenses. Advertising was included because, like R&D, it is expected to provide benefits for more than one period, albeit for a shorter term than R&D. They expected the coefficient for R&D to be larger (more positive) than the coefficient for advertising, and both larger than the coefficient for other expenses. The results were mixed, but on balance they were consistent with a market assessment of advertising as short-lived and R&D as long-lived.[‡]

Their valuation model used a discounted earnings-based perspective. Shevlin (1991) used an asset-based valuation model for R&D partnerships. In such a model, the value of the firm is defined as

Value = Assets − Liabilities

Shevlin[§] found that when R&D expenditures were considered assets, they contributed to firm value. Moreover, the market weighting given these expenditures was larger than for other assets, indicating that the expected benefit from these expenditures exceeds their book value.

Lev and Sougiannis (1996) and Sougiannis (1994) estimated stock prices and returns as functions of *both* earnings and book values. They also found that the capitalized components of R&D have value relevance[**] and are associated with current-period stock returns. More important, Lev and Sougiannis found a significant association between capitalized R&D and *subsequent* stock returns. This implied either a (systematic) mispricing by the market of R&D-intensive companies or compensation for (extra-market) risk associated with R&D.

Aboody and Lev (1998) compared companies that capitalized software development costs with those that chose not to. They found software capitalization (as well as the subsequent amortization) to be value relevant. Amounts capitalized were strongly associated with (contemporaneous) market prices and returns and were also positively associated with subsequent earnings changes. Moreover, consistent with the reasoning underlying SFAS 86,

> the coefficient of capitalized software . . . is larger than the coefficient of the development costs expensed by "expensers" . . . which in turn is larger than the coefficient of the development costs expensed by "capitalizers". . . . *This order of coefficient sizes is consistent with the reasoning of SFAS No. 86 that capitalized software reflects the costs of projects close to fruition and should be strongly associated with near-term earnings, whereas the development costs of "expensers" reflect the costs of both feasible and prefeasibility projects, which should not be as strongly associated with near-term earnings. The development costs expensed by "capitalizers" reflect both prefeasibility costs and costs of failed projects, consistent with little or no association with subsequent earnings.*[††]

Lev, in a series of publications,[‡‡] attempts to arrive at capitalization values in an indirect manner. Rather than capitalizing intangible expenditures, he capitalizes *intangible-driven earnings*. More specifically, Lev argues that a firm's earnings are a function of its physical, financial, and intangible assets; i.e.,

Earnings = f (Physical Assets, Financial Assets, Intangible Assets)

Using a combination of past and forecasted earnings as well as "normal" returns on (known) physical and financial assets, he imputes *intangible-driven earnings* (i.e., earnings above those normally generated by a firm's physical and financial assets). Forecasted values of these intangible-driven earnings are then discounted to arrive at a capitalized value of intangible assets.

Such assets, known alternatively as "knowledge," "intellectual," or "intangible" capital, are not confined to technology companies. Lev shows that in addition to industries such as aerospace, telecommunications, computer hardware/software, and pharmaceuticals, the home products and food and beverage industries are also rich in intangible capital. This intangible capital he attributes to strong brand recognition.

Gu and Lev (2001) also test the valuation relevance of intangibles-driven earnings. They argue that their findings indicate that intangibles-driven earnings provide more relevant information to investors than conventional earnings and cash flows.

---

[*]The current benefits are reflected in the inflows.

[†]The asset outflows representing future benefits can be thought of as a growth component. In Chapter 19, we show that for a firm with growth, its value can be expressed as

$$\text{Value} = \frac{E}{r} + \left[\frac{1}{r}\left(\frac{r^* - r}{r - ar^*}\right)\right]aE$$

where E is earnings, r the appropriate discount rate, r^* the amount the firm earns on its investment, and aE the amount the firm reinvests. In our example, $p = 1/r$ and b is the coefficient of the asset investment aE. That is, b is equal to the term in brackets. On the margin, it may be zero (if $r^* = r$) as the firm undertakes zero or break-even net present value investments.

‡Their R&D results are consistent with those of Hirschey and Weygandt (1985), who found that the market valuation of R&D implies it is an asset outflow. Hirschey and Weygandt also found that advertising had characteristics similar to a long-lived asset.

§As noted in Appendix 7-A, Shevlin applied option-pricing models to the valuation of R&D partnerships.

**Sougiannis, for example, shows that (on average) a one-dollar increase in R&D expenditures produces a five-dollar increase in market value.

††David Aboody and Baruch Lev, "The Value Relevance of Intangibles: The Case of Software Capitalization, *Journal of Accounting Research* (Supplement 1998), p. 178, emphasis added.

‡‡See, for example, Lev (2001), Gu and Lev (2001), and articles published in *Fortune* ("Accounting Gets Radical," by Thomas A. Stewart, April 16, 2001) and *CFO* ("Knowledge Capital Scorecard: Treasures Revealed," by Andrew Osterland, April 2001) for a general description of the methodology and results. The exact methodology is proprietary.

Additional Analysis of Fixed Asset Data

Changes in the balance sheet cost of fixed assets result from four types of events:

1. Capital spending (acquisition of fixed assets)
2. Sale, impairment, or retirement (no longer in use) of fixed assets
3. Increases (decreases) in fixed assets due to acquisitions (disposals)
4. Changes due to the effects of foreign currency translation

The effects of acquisitions and foreign currency translation are considered in Chapters 14 and 15, respectively. The following sections discuss capital expenditures and the sale/retirement of assets.

Capital Expenditures

The capital expenditure decision provides information to the investor as to a firm's future profitability and growth prospects. Management often announces major capital expenditure plans separately. McConnell and Muscarella (1986) and Kerstein and Kim (1995) provide evidence that there is positive (negative) market reaction to unexpected increases (decreases) in capital expenditures. Similarly, Lev and Thiagarajan (1993) show that firms with higher (lower) changes in capital expenditures than their industry average experience positive (negative) market reaction. Thus, it is important to monitor (changes in) the level of a firm's capital expenditures.

In doing so, note that capital expenditures tend to be seasonal, with the majority of such expenditures being carried out in the fourth quarter. Different theories exist as to whether this phenomenon is tied to a firm's budgetary cycle [Callen et al. (1996)] or the timing is tax related [Kinney and Trezevant (1993)].

Sale, Impairment, or Retirement of Assets

The sale or retirement of fixed assets removes these assets from the balance sheet. For most firms, sale or retirement also generates gains or losses, included in reported income.

In the case of Westvaco, gains on asset sales are included in other income (see financial statement Note B). In 1999, such gains accounted for 12% of pretax income. Some companies report gains or losses on a separate line in the income statement, whereas others include them elsewhere.[41] The analyst should examine such gains or losses for several reasons.

First, gains and losses resulting from asset sales are considered nonrecurring and the inclusion of such gains in reported income lowers the quality of earnings. However, if such gains or losses occur in most years, it is difficult to consider them "nonrecurring." As asset

[41]Undisclosed gains and losses can sometimes be deduced from the statement of cash flows. Gains and losses from asset sales are non-operating in nature, and must be subtracted from cash from operations. The proceeds from asset sales must be reported in cash from investment.

BOX 7-4
Mandated Accounting Changes: Economic Consequences and Market Reaction

The capitalization-versus-expense issue has proved a fruitful area of empirical research. The issues examined provide interesting parallels between R&D (SFAS 2) and oil and gas accounting (SFAS 19). In both cases, mandated accounting changes favored expensing over capitalization (albeit in the case of SFAS 19, the standard was suspended).

Economic Consequences

Proponents of capitalization argued that the accounting change would lead to a reduction of risk-taking activities such as expenditures for R&D and exploration activities, as the cost of risk taking would increase. These fears were generally expressed for smaller companies* who feared that markets (at least private lenders) would focus on the effects on reported income (both amounts and variability). The change would thus impair their ability to raise capital.

As SFAS 19 was never implemented, the validity of these claims could not be verified. However, for SFAS 2, a number of studies attempted to verify whether the new standard curtailed R&D.

Horwitz and Kolodny (1980) reported that a majority of firms (58% to 67%) believed that small firms reduced planned R&D expenditures as a consequence of SFAS 2. Using a sample of small high-technology firms, they found evidence that the actual levels of R&D expenditures dropped following the introduction of SFAS 2.

In contrast, Dukes et al. (1980) found no evidence of curtailment of R&D subsequent to the adoption of SFAS 2. Their sample, however, consisted of larger companies, and in a subsequent study Elliott et al. (1984) confirmed the finding that small companies that had previously capitalized R&D curtailed R&D expenditures after the issuance of SFAS 2. However, they noted that the downward trend in R&D expenditures for these companies had already begun years prior to the issuance of SFAS 2. Comparing the operating performance of the "capitalizers" with a control sample of firms that had always expensed R&D, they found that the operating performance of the capitalizers was worse. They conjectured that financial difficulties, rather than the accounting change, may have caused the curtailment of R&D. In fact, it could be argued that the original decision to capitalize R&D by these firms may have been motivated by an effort to improve reported financial performance in the face of financial stress.

Selto and Clouse (1985) argued that firms would be likely to anticipate the effects of an accounting change such as SFAS 2 and adapt to it. Thus, if divisional managers would be motivated to reduce R&D expenditures because of the effect on their compensation (through earnings-based compensation plans), firms would adjust their compensation plans accordingly or, alternatively, take steps to centralize the R&D decision-making process. They found that although not all firms made such changes, those that did were the ones most likely to be affected by the provisions of SFAS 2. Thus, to the extent accounting changes have economic consequences, they may be manifested internally rather than externally.

Market Reaction

Vigeland (1981) found no market reaction to the mandated accounting change for R&D expenditures. There is little controversy with respect to this mandated accounting change. This is not true with respect to the mandated change(s) affecting accounting for oil and gas exploration. This issue spawned a cottage industry of research with studies examining the reaction to the announcement of (the exposure draft of) SFAS 19 and Accounting Series Release (ASR) 253, issued by the SEC, that suspended SFAS 19.

The research examined whether firms using the full cost method (FC) had negative (positive) returns when SFAS 19 (ASR 253) was announced. Generally negative reaction was found around the time of the announcement of the SFAS 19 exposure draft. Not everyone, however, agreed with its significance† and the results were found to be sensitive to the time period examined and (at the time of the exposure draft announcement) "confounding" news affecting the oil industry. Thus, even though negative market reaction was found, its cause was not clear.

With respect to the ASR 253 announcement, Collins et al. (1982) compared the market reaction at the time the SFAS 19 exposure draft was announced with the reaction experienced when ASR 253 was announced. They found that there was a significant negative correlation for the FC firms; that is, negative reaction to the first announcement was followed by positive reaction to the subsequent (suspension) announcement.

These studies tested market reaction without considering any factors that might cause differential market reactions across firms due to differential impacts on income and equity. Such factors might include firm size, the relative importance of exploration, firm leverage, and the existence of debt covenants and accounting-based management compensation schemes. Collins et al. (1981) and Lys (1984) tested for such factors with some success, finding, for example, that the degree of market reaction was related to (1) the size of the reduction in owner's equity that would result from SFAS 19, (2) the existence of debt covenants, and (3) management compensation schemes based on reported income.

---

*The standards primarily affected smaller firms, as for both R&D and exploration costs, larger firms generally used the expensing method. See Box 7-1 for further discussion of the differential impact of the capitalize-versus-expense decision on larger and small firms.
†Collins and Dent (1979) and Lev (1979) claimed that the results were statistically significant, whereas Dyckman and Smith (1979) argued that the market reaction was not statistically different from that experienced by firms using successful efforts (SE).

sales are to a great extent subject to management discretion, their timing and variation from year to year must be closely monitored as they can be used to distort operating trends. Bartov (1993) reported that firms use gains or losses from asset sales to smooth reported income.[42] Additionally, highly leveraged firms sell more long-lived assets than less leveraged firms in an effort to improve their reported debt-to-equity ratios.

A second reason for looking at asset sales is more fundamental. Sale of a significant portion of fixed assets is an indicator of change—in product line or production location. The examination of trends in capital spending and fixed asset sales can help the analyst ask perceptive questions regarding changes in future operations.

Finally, a pattern of gains suggests that the company's depreciation method is conservative, understating reported income and the net carrying amounts of fixed assets. A pattern of losses suggests that depreciation expense is understated (income is overstated) and fixed assets are overvalued on the balance sheet. In extreme cases, such losses are recognized as "impairments." Issues relating to depreciation and impairments are discussed in Chapter 8.

SUMMARY

This chapter considers the financial statement effects of the capitalize-versus-expense decision for long-lived assets. This decision is significant not only for firms with large investments in buildings and machinery, but also for those who have large expenditures on research, development, and computer software. The chapter reviews the analytical techniques that can be used to restore comparability despite the use of differing accounting methods for similar transactions.

Once the capitalized amount is determined, the firm must choose an appropriate pattern of depreciation or amortization. Analysts must also contend with financial reporting for impairments and disposal of these assets. We discuss these issues in the next chapter.

Chapter 7

Problems

1. [Capitalization of interest] The following data were obtained from the annual reports of Chevron, a multinational oil company (all data in $millions):

	1995	1996	1997	1998	1999
Interest expense	$ 401	$ 364	$ 312	$ 405	$ 472
Pretax income	1,789	4,740	5,502	1,834	3,648
Net income	930	2,607	3,256	1,339	2,070
Capitalized interest	141	108	82	39	59
Amortization of capitalized interest	47	24	28	35	9

a. Using reported interest expense, compute the earnings coverage ratio (times interest earned) for each year, 1995 to 1999.

b. Assuming that Chevron had always expensed interest as incurred:

   (i) Recompute the earnings coverage ratio for each year.

   (ii) Compare the two ratios (based on reported versus restated data).

   (iii) Recompute income (assume a 35% tax rate each year).

   (iv) Discuss the effect on net income of restatement to expense all interest.

c. Discuss the effect of restatement on the five-year trend of Chevron's:

   (i) Interest expense

   (ii) Interest coverage ratio

   (iii) Pretax and net income

d. State which calculation of the interest coverage ratio is better for financial analysis and justify your choice.

2. [Capitalization as property, plant, and equipment; CFA© adapted]

a. Discuss, for *each* of the following, the conditions (under U.S. GAAP) under which they may be included in the carrying amount of property, plant, and equipment:

   (i) Interest cost during the period of construction

   (ii) Cost of starting up a new production facility

---

[42]Whether this constitutes "good" or "bad" behavior depends on whether one views income smoothing (see Chapter 2) as "variance reducing" (providing information to investors as to a firm's expected performance) or manipulative behavior that hides a firm's actual performance.

(iii) Shipping costs incurred on machinery purchased

(iv) Increases in the market value of land and buildings during the period of construction

b. Repeat part a under IASC GAAP.

3. [Capitalization of computer software; CFA© adapted]

a. Discuss the conditions, under U.S. GAAP, under which computer software development costs may be capitalized, *before and after* a product is proven economically feasible.

b. How would your answer differ for IASB GAAP?

4. [Capitalization of computer software expenditures] Ericsson [ERICA], a multinational producer of wireless telephone equipment, produces its financial statements in accordance with Swedish GAAP but reconciles net income and shareholders' equity to U.S. GAAP. Swedish GAAP does not permit the capitalization of the cost of software development cost for either:

* Software to be sold externally

* Software developed for internal use

Ericsson's 1999 reconciliation, however, shows the effect of applying SFAS 86 (capitalization of software to be sold) for all years and SOP 98-1 (capitalization of software for internal use) starting in 1999 as shown in the following data.

Ericsson: 1999 Financial Data (SEK millions)

Under U.S. GAAP	1997	1998	1999
Development costs for software to be sold:			
Opening balance	6,100	7,398	10,744
Capitalization	5,232	7,170	7,898
Amortization	(3,934)	(3,824)	(4,460)
Writedown			(989)
Year-end balance	7,398	10,744	13,193
Development costs for software for internal use:			
Opening balance			
Capitalization			1,463
Amortization			(152)
Year-end balance			1,311
Under Swedish GAAP:			
Net sales	167,740	184,438	215,403
Pretax income	17,218	18,210	16,386
Total assets	147,440	167,456	202,628
Stockholders' equity	52,624	63,112	69,176

a. Compute each of the following ratios under Swedish GAAP for 1998 and 1999:

(i) Asset turnover (on average assets)

(ii) Pretax return on average equity

b. Using the data provided, adjust the 1997–1999 Swedish GAAP amounts assuming the capitalization of software development costs to be sold and for internal use. Using the ad-

justed data, compute the percentage change from the amounts originally reported for:

(i) Pretax income

(ii) Total assets

(iii) Shareholders' equity

(Assume a 35% tax rate.)

c. Recompute each of the following ratios using the adjusted data for 1998 and 1999:

(i) Asset turnover (on average assets)

(ii) Pretax return on average equity

d. Discuss the implications of your analysis for the comparison of firms that capitalize software development costs with those that do not.

e. Discuss whether the capitalization and amortization of software development costs under U.S. GAAP has any usefulness for investment analysis.

5. [Capitalization versus expensing] American Woodmark [AMWD] is a manufacturer of kitchen cabinets and similar items. Its fiscal year 2000 annual report contains the following footnote under Significant Accounting Policies:

> *Promotional Displays:* The Company's investment in promotional displays is carried at cost less applicable amortization. Amortization is provided by the straight-line method on an individual display basis over the estimated period of benefit (approximately 30 months).

Financial data at April 30 (in $thousands)

	1999	2000
Promotional displays	$ 8,451	$ 10,099
Total assets	140,609	166,656
Shareholders' equity	78,337	92,612
Sales	327,013	387,301
Net income	17,509	14,467

a. Explain why American Woodmark may have chosen to capitalize the cost of promotional displays rather than expense them.

b. Calculate the effect of that accounting choice on the following reported amounts for fiscal year 2000:

(i) Net income

(ii) Shareholders' equity

(iii) Return on assets

(Assume a 35% tax rate.)

6. [Brand names] "Buildings age and become dilapidated. Machines wear out. Cars rust. But what lives on are brands," argues Sir Hector Laing of Britain's United Biscuits (*The Economist*, December 24, 1988, p. 100).

a. Using this quotation as a point of departure, discuss the advantages and disadvantages (from the point of view of financial analysis) of the balance sheet recognition of brand names.

b. Discuss the advantages and disadvantages (also from the point of view of financial analysis) of the amortization of brand name intangible assets through charges to income.

7. [Capitalization versus expensing] Norsk Hydro [NHY], a multinational energy company, produces its financial statements in accordance with Norwegian GAAP but reconciles net income and shareholders' equity to U.S. GAAP. The reconciliation states that three major differences between Norwegian GAAP and U.S. GAAP are that under Norwegian GAAP:

- All exploration costs must be expensed, including some that must be capitalized under U.S. GAAP.

- Environmental expenditures incurred prior to 1992 were expensed, including some that were required to be capitalized under U.S. GAAP.

- All interest is expensed as incurred.

Data from the 1998 annual report follow:

Reconciliation from Norwegian GAAP to U.S. GAAP (NOK millions)

Pretax Income		Shareholders' Equity	
Norwegian GAAP	6,292	Norwegian GAAP	43,532
Exploration costs	(107)	Property, plant, equipment	7,999
Depreciation	(729)	Other differences (net)	(3,290)
Capitalized interest	614	U.S. GAAP	48,241
Other differences (net)	(239)		
U.S. GAAP	5,831	Total debt	30,842

(Assume that other differences in equity include income taxes at a 35% tax rate on the difference between Norwegian and U.S. GAAP amounts.)

a. Using the Norwegian GAAP amounts, compute each of the following ratios for 1998:

  (i) Pretax return on (ending) equity

  (ii) Total debt to equity

b. Using the U.S. GAAP amounts, compute each of the following ratios for 1998:

  (i) Pretax return on (ending) equity

  (ii) Total debt to equity

c. Adjust the Norwegian GAAP amounts *only* for the differences due to capitalization policy. Using the adjusted data, compute *each* of the following ratios for 1998:

  (i) Pretax return on (ending) equity

  (ii) Total debt to equity

d. Compare the ratios computed in parts a, b, and c and discuss the implications of the comparison of companies using U.S. GAAP with those using accounting systems with different capitalization rules.

e. Explain the inference that can be drawn from the negative adjustment in 1998 for exploration costs. (*Hint:* The 1996 and 1997 adjustments were positive.)

8. [Capitalization of development costs] Ericsson [ERICA] is a major producer of wireless telephone equipment, and reports according to Swedish GAAP. Its financial statements report that: "Research and development costs are expensed as incurred."

a. Discuss the effect of the differences between the accounting methods used by Ericsson and Nokia (see text) for development costs on reported:

  (i) Net income (assume that expenditures are rising rapidly)

  (ii) Cash from operations

  (iii) Stockholders' equity

b. Describe the effect of those differences on each of the following ratios:

  (i) Interest coverage ratio (times interest earned)

  (ii) Debt-to-equity ratio

c. Describe the analytical steps required to eliminate the effect of the accounting difference on the comparison of these two competitors.

9. [Capitalization of research and development] Pfizer's 1999 annual report contains a financial summary (p. 62) with 11 years of data including research and development expense.

a. Compute R&D expense as a % of sales for the five years ending in 1999. Discuss what this trend tells you about the importance of R&D to Pfizer's business. Describe the effect of that trend on Pfizer's reported earnings.

b. Pfizer expenses all R&D. Assuming Pfizer had capitalized and amortized R&D costs, compute the following adjusted amounts for 1997–1999:

  (i) Net

  (ii) Return on equity

  Your calculations should assume a tax rate of 35% and three-year amortization starting in the year of the R&D expenditure.

c. Compare the adjusted results in part b with those reported by Pfizer.

d. Discuss how the change in accounting method would affect the trend of Pfizer's:

  (i) Asset turnover

  (ii) Cash from operations

10. [Capitalization of research and development] SmithKline Beecham [SB], a multinational drug company, announced on August 31, 2000 that it had signed agreements to divest itself of drugs to other pharmaceutical firms for a total of £1,529 million. The sale resulted in a pretax gain of £1,416 million.

a. SB expenses the cost of developing new drugs, rather than capitalizing and amortizing the cost. Discuss the effect of SB's choice of accounting method on the income resulting from the announced sales.

b. The income resulting from the announced sales was reported in 2000, the year of their completion. Discuss whether this income was earned in that year or when the drugs were developed.

c. Discuss whether the income resulting from the announced sales should be included in earnings used for valuing the company.

11. [Effect of asset revaluations] The News Corporation [NCP] prepares its financial statements using Australian GAAP. Its annual report for the year ended June 30, 2000 includes the following accounting policy footnote:

1 (g) Publishing Rights, Titles and Television Licenses

As a creator and distributor of branded information and entertainment copyrights, the Group has significant and growing intangible assets, including free and cable television networks and stations, television licenses, sports franchises, entertainment franchises, newspaper mastheads, publishing rights and other copyright products and trademarks. These assets are stated at cost or valuation. While television licenses in the United States are renewable every five years, the Directors have no reason to believe that they will not be renewed.

The Group regularly assesses the carrying amount of intangible assets to ensure that they are not carried at a value greater than their recoverable amount. This assessment is primarily based on the Group's estimate of maintainable earnings before interest and tax ("EBIT") and an appropriate market-based EBIT multiple.

No amortization is provided against these assets since, in the opinion of the Directors, the life of the publishing rights, titles and television licenses is of such duration, and the residual value would be such that the amortization charge, if any, would not be material.

The News Corp. balance sheet at June 30, 2000 reports the following amounts ($A millions):

Publishing rights, titles, and television licenses*	$26,884
Total assets	65,585
Total borrowings	15,431
Stockholders' equity	32,660

*Includes $4,529 revaluation increment

a. Compute the debt-to-total assets and debt-to-equity ratio of NCP based on the data shown.

b. Compute the debt-to-total assets and debt-to-equity ratio of NCP after removing the revaluation increment. (*Note:* Assume there are no income tax effects.)

c. Describe the effect of the revaluation increment on the following:

   (i) Return on equity

   (ii) Asset turnover

   (iii) Earnings per share

   (iv) Cash from operations

d. Assuming that NCP were required to amortize publishing rights, titles, and television licenses, describe *both* the initial and long-term effects on the following:

   (i) Return on equity

   (ii) Asset turnover

   (iii) Earnings per share

   (iv) Cash from operations

e. If one of NCP's major media properties suffered from increased competition, describe the likely effect and the time of that effect on:

   • NCP's stock price

   • NCP's financial statements

f. Considering your answers to parts a through e, discuss the advantages and disadvantages of NCP's accounting for publishing rights, titles, and television licenses from the perspective of a financial analyst.

12. [Capitalization of research and development] Data from the financial statements of SUA (which follows U.S. GAAP) and MAY (a non-U.S. company following GAAP of its own country) follows (all data in $U.S.).

	SUA		
	2000	2001	2002
A. Income Statement			
R&D expense	15,200	16,500	18,100
Net income	27,000	29,000	32,000
B. Balance Sheet			
R&D assets			
Total assets	200,000	210,000	225,000
C. Statement of Cash Flows			
Cash from operations	13,000	14,000	16,000

	MAY		
	2000	2001	2002
A. Income Statement			
R&D expense	29,500	32,400	35,600
Net income	48,600	52,200	57,600
B. Balance Sheet			
R&D assets	28,800	31,500	34,600
Total assets	330,000	346,000	370,000
C. Statement of Cash Flows			
Cash from operations	25,000	27,000	31,000

Assumptions:

• Both companies pay zero income tax and have no interest expense.

• SUA follows U.S. GAAP and expenses R&D expenditures as they occur.

• GAAP in the country MAY operates in permit the capitalization of R&D. MAY's R&D expense equals the amortization of capitalized R&D expenditures. (*Note:* The amortization period is three years beginning in the year of the expenditure.)

a. Calculate ROA as reported for both companies for 2002.

b. To compare the two companies, adjust the 2002 financial data of MAY for the difference in accounting method for research and development.

c. Using the result of part b, calculate ROA for MAY in 2002 and discuss how the adjustment affects the comparison with SUA.

d. To compare the two companies under the GAAP used by MAY, adjust the 2002 financial data of SUA to capitalize research and development expense.

e. Using the result of part d, calculate ROA for SUA in 2002 and discuss how the adjustment affects the comparison with MAY.

13. [Capitalization of startup costs] Repsol [REP], a multinational oil and gas company headquartered in Spain, prepares its financial statements using Spanish GAAP. Under Spanish GAAP, Repsol is permitted to capitalize startup expenses, which must be expensed as incurred under U.S. GAAP. Footnote 3 to Repsol's financial statements for the year ended December 31, 1999 reports the following (in € millions):

Balance of capitalized cost at 12/31/98	€187
Amortization	(15)
Balance at 12/31/99	€172

a. Describe the effect of Repsol's policy of capitalizing startup expenses on 1999:
   (i) Reported income
   (ii) Cash from operations
   (iii) Return on equity
   (iv) Asset turnover ratio

b. Describe the effect of Repsol's policy in the year of initial startup cost capitalization on:
   (i) Reported income
   (ii) Cash from operations
   (iii) Return on equity
   (iv) Asset turnover ratio

c. Explain the advantages and disadvantages for a company that capitalizes startup costs, drawing on your answers to parts a and b.

8

ANALYSIS OF LONG-LIVED ASSETS: PART II—ANALYSIS OF DEPRECIATION AND IMPAIRMENT

CHAPTER OUTLINE

INTRODUCTION

THE DEPRECIATION CONCEPT
Depreciation Methods
Annuity or Sinking Fund Depreciation
Straight-Line Depreciation
Accelerated Depreciation Methods
Units-of-Production and Service Hours Methods
Group and Composite Depreciation Methods
Depletion
Amortization
Depreciation Method Disclosures
Depreciation Lives and Salvage Values
Impact of Depreciation Methods on Financial Statements
Accelerated Depreciation and Taxes
Impact of Inflation on Depreciation
Changes in Depreciation Method

ANALYSIS OF FIXED ASSET DISCLOSURES
Estimating Relative Age and Useful Lives
Estimating the Age of Assets

IMPAIRMENT OF LONG-LIVED ASSETS
Financial Reporting of Impaired Assets
Impairment of Assets Held for Sale
Impairment of Assets Remaining in Use
Financial Statement Impact of Impairments
Effect of SFAS 121 on Analysis of Impairment
Empirical Findings

LIABILITIES FOR ASSET RETIREMENT OBLIGATIONS
Provisions of SFAS 143
Effects of SFAS 143

SUMMARY

 APPENDIX 8-A

CHAPTER OBJECTIVES

Chapter 8 has the following objectives:

1. Define the characteristics of different depreciation methods.
2. Explain the role of depreciable lives and salvage values in the computation of depreciation expense.
3. Show the effects of different depreciation methods on the financial statements.
4. Discuss how inflation impacts the measurement of economic depreciation.
5. Illustrate the impact of changes from one depreciation method to another.

6. Define the measurement of relative age, useful life, and average age of fixed assets, and the use of these measures.
7. Illustrate the financial reporting of asset impairment and its financial statement effects.
8. Discuss the financial statement effects of recognizing obligations associated with disposal activities.
9. Discuss the liability for closure, removal, and environmental effects of long-lived operating assets and the financial statement impacts of recognizing that liability.

INTRODUCTION

This chapter continues the analysis of long-lived assets begun in the previous chapter where we examined financial reporting and analysis issues arising at acquisition. We now consider the reporting and analysis of long-lived assets:

1. Over their useful lives, with emphasis on
   - Depreciation methods
   - Depreciable lives and salvage values
   - Impact of choices on financial statements
2. When they are disposed of, or written off when impaired, or at the end of their useful lives, with particular attention to the effects of impairment writedowns on financial statements and ratios

Amortization, depletion, and depreciation are all terms used for the systematic allocation of the capitalized cost of an asset to income over its useful life. Depreciation, the most frequently used of these terms, is often used generically in discussions of the concept. Strictly speaking, *depreciation* represents the allocation of the cost of tangible fixed assets, *amortization* refers to the cost of intangible assets, and *depletion* applies to natural resource assets.

THE DEPRECIATION CONCEPT

For accountants, depreciation is an allocation process, not a valuation process. It is important, therefore, for analysts to differentiate between accounting depreciation and economic depreciation. Although the accounting process may be purely allocative, the concept of depreciation also has economic meaning.

In Chapter 2, income was defined as the amount that can be distributed during the period without impairing the productive capacity of the firm. The cash flows generated by an asset over its life, therefore, cannot be considered income until a provision is made for its replacement. These cash flows must be reduced by the amount required to replace the asset to determine the earnings generated by that asset.

This is the underlying principle of economic depreciation; profits are overstated if no allowance is made for the replacement of the asset. The periodic depreciation expense, therefore, segregates a portion of cash flows for reinvestment, preserving that sum from distribution as dividends and taxes.[1]

Continuing this conceptual argument, suppose an asset costs $240 and is expected to generate net cash flows of $100 per year over its three-year life. Over the life of the asset, income equals $60 ($300 − $240) as $240 is required to replace the asset (if we assume that the asset is worthless at the end of the three-year period and price levels do not change). As financial statements report income annually, it is necessary to determine how much income (how much depreciation) to report each year. This requires the allocation of a portion of the multiperiod return to each period.

The next section describes the depreciation methods used in financial reporting, followed by a discussion of the impact of depreciation methods on financial statements. A separate analysis of accelerated depreciation methods used for income taxes is followed by a discussion of the interaction of inflation and depreciation methods. Analysis of financial statement depreciation disclosures, changes in depreciation methods, and a comprehensive examination of fixed asset disclosures round out the discussion.

---

[1] This does not mean that cash equal to depreciation expense is set aside for reinvestment but, rather, that the definition of income requires a subtraction for asset replacement.

EXHIBIT 8-1
Sinking Fund Depreciation

Year	(1) Opening Balance Asset	(2) Cash Flow	(3) Depreciation Expense	(4) = (2) − (3) Net Income	(5) = (4)/(1) Rate of Return
1	$240	$100	$ 71	$29	12%
2	169	100	80	20	12
3	89	100	89	11	12
Totals		$300	$240	$60	

Depreciation Methods

Annuity or Sinking Fund Depreciation

From an economic perspective, the income reported each year should reflect the rate of return earned by the asset. For example, the asset just described generates a return of 12% over its three-year life.[2] To report a 12% return for each year requires the pattern of depreciation shown in Exhibit 8-1.

This pattern, with the amount of depreciation increasing every year, is known as *annuity or sinking fund depreciation*. U.S. GAAP, however, do not permit this form of depreciation. In Canada, increasing charge methods are used for income-producing properties in the real estate industry and by a few utilities, but they are not generally acceptable depreciation methods.

Straight-line and accelerated depreciation (discussed shortly) can also produce a constant rate of return when cash flows generated by the asset decline over time. Exhibit 8-2 illustrates this case; the rate of return is constant and reflects the true return earned by the asset.

Instead of depreciation patterns that generate a constant rate of return, accountants generally use depreciation patterns that result in constant or declining expense. These patterns are sometimes justified by the matching principle. Generally, however, they are arbitrary, their sole purpose being a systematic allocation of the asset cost over time.

Straight-Line Depreciation

Given the same asset and the pattern of constant cash flows shown in Exhibit 8-1, accountants (using the matching principle) argue that since the revenues (cash flows of

EXHIBIT 8-2
Straight-Line Depreciation with Declining Cash Flows

Year	(1) Opening Balance Asset	(2) Cash Flow	(3) Depreciation Expense	(4) = (2) − (3) Net Income	(5) = (4)/(1) Rate of Return
1	$240	$109	$ 80	$29	12%
2	160	99	80	19	12
3	80	90	80	10	12
Totals		$298	$240	$58	

[2]The present value of a three-year annuity of $100 per year discounted at 12% is (approximately) equal to $240.

EXHIBIT 8-3
Straight-Line Depreciation with Constant Cash Flows

Year	(1) Opening Balance Asset	(2) Cash Flow	(3) Depreciation Expense	(4) = (2) − (3) Net Income	(5) = (4)/(1) Rate of Return
1	$240	$100	$ 80	$20	8.3%
2	160	100	80	20	12.5
3	80	100	80	20	25.0
Totals		$300	$240	$60	

$100) generated by the asset are the same each year, the income shown each year should also be the same. The result of this line of reasoning is the *straight-line method*, the pattern of depreciation expense exhibited in Exhibit 8-3. *Straight-line depreciation is the dominant method in the United States and most countries worldwide*. Westvaco, for example, states in the summary of significant accounting policies in its fiscal 1999 annual report:

> The cost of plant and equipment is depreciated, generally by the straight-line method, over the estimated useful lives of the respective assets. . . .

Note that the use of this method results in an *increasing* rate of return rather than the actual rate of return earned over the life of the asset.

Accelerated Depreciation Methods

The matching principle can also justify accelerated depreciation patterns, with higher depreciation charges in early years and smaller amounts in later years. There are two arguments:

1. Benefits (revenues) from an asset may be higher in early years, declining in later years as efficiency falls (the asset wears out). The matching process suggests that depreciation should decline with benefits.

2. Even if revenues are constant over time, an asset requires maintenance and repairs over time, costs that tend to increase as the asset ages. Accelerated depreciation methods compensate for the rising trend of maintenance and repair costs so that total asset costs are level over the asset's life.

However, both the efficiency and maintenance of an asset are difficult to forecast, and, in any case, accelerated depreciation methods are (like straight-line) arbitrary procedures designed to yield the desired pattern of higher depreciation amounts in earlier years. Accelerated methods have historically been used for tax reporting, where they are justified by the desire to promote capital investment, rather than accounting theory.

The two most common accelerated methods are the *sum-of-years' digits* (SYD) method and the family of *declining-balance* methods. A comparison of these methods (using the double-declining-balance method) with straight-line (SL) depreciation is presented in Exhibit 8-4. In the example used, the concept of *salvage value*, the estimated amount for which the asset can be sold at the end of its useful life, is introduced into the calculations.

While U.S. firms rarely use accelerated methods, they are more widely used outside of the United States. Takeda, for example, states in its summary of significant accounting policies (Note 2 in fiscal 1999 annual report) that:

> Depreciation is primarily computed by the declining balance method. . . .

EXHIBIT 8-4
Comparison of Straight-Line and Accelerated Depreciation Methods

Original Cost = $18,000
Salvage Value = $3,000
Depreciable Life $n = 5$

A. Straight-Line Depreciation

Depreciation in Year $i = \dfrac{1}{n} \times$ (Original Cost − Salvage Value)

Depreciation expense is constant each year; at the end of the five-year period, the net book value of the asset equals its salvage value of $3,000.

Year	Rate	(Original Cost— Salvage Value)	Depreciation Expense	Accumulated Depreciation	Net Book Value
0					$18,000
1	1/5	$15,000	$ 3,000	$3,000	15,000
2	1/5	15,000	3,000	6,000	12,000
3	1/5	15,000	3,000	9,000	9,000
4	1/5	15,000	3,000	12,000	6,000
5	1/5	15,000	3,000	15,000	3,000
Total			$15,000		

B and C. Accelerated Depreciation Methods

B. Sum-of-Years' Digits (SYD) Method

Depreciation in Year $i = \dfrac{(n - i + 1)}{\text{SYD}} \times$ (Original Cost − Salvage Value)

where SYD $= 1 + 2 + 3 + \cdots + n$ the summation over the depreciable life of n years or simply SYD $= n(n + 1)/2$. For our example, $n = 5$.

$$\text{SYD} = 1 + 2 + 3 + 4 + 5 = 15$$

or, alternatively,

$$\text{SYD} = \frac{(5)(5 + 1)}{2} = 15$$

The rate of depreciation thus varies from year to year (as i varies) in reverse counting order of the years; that is, the pattern is 5/15, 4/15, 3/15, 2/15, and 1/15 and is depicted as follows:

Year	Rate	(Original Cost— Salvage Value)	Depreciation Expense	Accumulated Depreciation	Net Book Value
0					$18,000
1	5/15	$15,000	$ 5,000	$5,000	13,000
2	4/15	15,000	4,000	9,000	9,000
3	3/15	15,000	3,000	12,000	6,000
4	2/15	15,000	2,000	14,000	4,000
5	1/15	15,000	1,000	15,000	3,000
Total			$15,000		

EXHIBIT 8-4 (*continued*)

C. Double-Declining-Balance

Depreciation in Year $i = \frac{2}{n} \times$ (Original Cost $-$ Accumulated Depreciation)

or

$\frac{2}{n} \times$ (Net Book Value)

The rate of $(2/n)$ is what gives the double-declining-balance (DDB) method its name. The depreciation rate is double* the straight-line rate. The declining pattern occurs because the fixed rate is applied to an ever-decreasing asset balance (net book value),[†] and in our example it is calculated as

Year	Rate	Net Book Value	Depreciation Expense	Accumulated Depreciation	Net Book Value
0					$18,000
1	2/5	$18,000	$ 7,200	$ 7,200	10,800
2	2/5	10,800	4,320	11,520	6,480
3	2/5	6,480	2,592	14,112	3,888
4	NA	NA	888	15,000	3,000
5	NA	NA	0	15,000	3,000
Total			$15,000		

Note that in year 4 the DDB procedure is discontinued. This is because depreciation can be taken only until the salvage value is reached. Following DDB in year 4 and beyond would have reduced net book value below salvage. When the DDB method is applied to longer-lived assets, a switch to the straight-line method often occurs in later years, when the latter method results in higher depreciation expense.

NA = not applicable.

*The DDB method is actually only one case of the family of declining-balance methods. The same principle can be applied to other multiples of the straight-line rate (e.g., 150% declining balance). Higher multiples result in more accelerated patterns of depreciation expense.

[†]Note that salvage value is not used to calculate depreciation under declining-balance methods but acts as a floor for net book value.

Units-of-Production and Service Hours Method

These methods depreciate assets in proportion to their actual use rather than as a function of the passage of time. Thus, more depreciation is recognized in years of higher production. Measurement requires an initial estimate of the total number of units of output or service hours expected over the life of the machine. The methods differ in whether asset usage is measured by output or hours used.

Assume that the asset described in Exhibit 8-4 is expected to produce 60,000 units of output over its life and have a service life of 150,000 hours. The actual hours of service and output, and the resultant depreciation schedules, are presented in Exhibit 8-5.

These methods make depreciation expense a variable rather than a fixed cost, decreasing the volatility of reported earnings as compared to straight-line or accelerated methods. Some companies use a mix of depreciation methods.

International Paper, for example, reports on its depreciation methods as follows:

Plants, Properties and Equipment

Plants, properties and equipment are stated at cost, less accumulated depreciation. For financial reporting purposes, we use the units-of-production method of depreciation for our major pulp and paper mills and certain wood products facilities and the straight-line method for other plants and equipment.[3]

---

[3]*Source:* International Paper, 10-K report, year ended December 31, 1999.

EXHIBIT 8-5
Service Hours and Units-of-Production Methods

Original Cost = $18,000
Salvage Value = $3,000

	Service Hours Method Expected Service Hours = 150,000 Cost/Service Hour = $0.10*			Units-of-Production Method Expected Output = 60,000 Cost/Unit of Output = $0.25†		
Year	Hours Worked	Depreciation	Net Book Value	Units of Output	Depreciation	Net Book Value
0			$18,000			$18,000
1	40,000	$ 4,000	14,000	15,000	$ 3,750	14,250
2	35,000	3,500	10,500	16,000	4,000	10,250
3	45,000	4,500	6,000	20,000	5,000	5,250
4	20,000	2,000	4,000	10,000	2,250‡	3,000
5	40,000	1,000‡	3,000	12,500	0‡	3,000
Total		$15,000			$15,000	

*($18,000 − $3,000)/150,000.

†($18,000 − $3,000)/60,000.

‡Note that in both cases, the asset is never depreciated below the salvage value even when actual use exceeds estimated use.

A significant drawback of these two methods occurs when the firm's productive capacity becomes obsolete as it loses business to more efficient competitors. The units-of-production and service hours methods decrease depreciation expense during periods of low production. The result is to overstate reported income and asset values at the same time as the asset's economic value declines. This danger is particularly acute for mature industries facing increased competition from new entrants or imports. Competition frequently increases the rate of economic depreciation of fixed assets. However, the corporate response is often to relieve the pressure on earnings by decreasing depreciation expense by changing to a method such as units-of-production. Alternatively, firms may get the same effect by lengthening lives.

Sooner or later, however, the firm will recognize the impairment (see the discussion later in this chapter) of its productive capacity. Once impairment exists, companies report "restructuring" or similar charges to correct the overvaluation of fixed assets. Analysts often exclude such "nonrecurring" charges when evaluating corporate earnings. But to the extent that these charges represent an adjustment for past underdepreciation of assets, they correct a systematic overstatement of past earnings. As past earnings are used to forecast the future, this issue should not be ignored.

The following footnote from the 1992 financial statements of Brown & Sharpe, a machine tool manufacturer, illustrates this phenomenon:

> In 1992, the Company extended the estimated useful lives of machinery and equipment at its Swiss subsidiary, based upon the current low rate of utilization. The effect of this change was to reduce 1992 depreciation expense and net loss by $921,000 or $.19 per share.

Total depreciation expense for Brown & Sharpe fell from $8 million in 1992 to $6.8 million in 1993; the change in accounting estimate was apparently the major factor in that decline. In 1994, however, Brown & Sharpe reported restructuring charges that included: "costs . . . for . . . property, plant, and equipment . . . writeoffs . . . due to a plant closing in Switzerland."

Although the corporate temptation to change accounting methods when business is weak is understandable, that change can mislead investors. Furthermore, on occasion, a company recognizes the impairment of fixed assets gradually, by accelerating depreciation on a group of assets in danger of becoming obsolete. From an analytical point of view, it is preferable to recognize the impairment immediately. Because accounting depreciation is a systematic allocation of cost, its acceleration when the asset is impaired (and its use has declined or it has been temporarily idled) fails to match costs and revenues and misstates the earning power of the company.

Group and Composite Depreciation Methods

Depreciation methods described in the preceding sections apply to single assets; they may be impractical when firms use large numbers of similar assets in their operations. Group (composite) depreciation methods allocate the costs of similar (dissimilar) assets using depreciation rates based on a weighted average of the service lives of the assets.

Gains or losses on the disposal of assets depreciated using group or composite methods are either:

- Recognized in reported income, or
- Reported instead as a component of accumulated depreciation[4]

Example. Texaco uses group methods for most assets (see the Description of Significant Accounting Policies). Gains and losses are recognized only when a complete unit is disposed of.

Depletion

Financial reporting requirements for natural resources are similar to those for tangible assets. The carrying costs of natural resources include the costs of acquiring the land or mines and the costs of exploration and development of the resources. These costs may be capitalized or expensed as a function of the firm's accounting policies (such as successful efforts or full cost for oil and gas exploration).

The carrying costs of natural resources (excluding costs of machinery and equipment used in extraction or production) are allocated to accounting periods using the units-of-production method. This method requires an initial estimate of the units (of oil, coal, gold, or timber) in the resource base to compute a unit cost, which is then applied to the actual units produced, extracted, or harvested.

Amortization

Amortization of intangible assets may be based on useful lives as defined by law (e.g., patents) or regulation, or such assets may be depreciated over the period during which the firm expects to receive benefits from them (computer software). Companies use either straight-line or units-of-production methods. Goodwill and indefinite-term franchises and licenses may be amortized over periods not exceeding 40 years.[5] Note that SFAS 142 (2001) eliminated the amortization of goodwill and certain intangible assets.

Example. In Chapter 7, we examined Lucent's capitalization of software development costs; now we discuss amortization. The accounting policies footnote is vague about amortization periods.

Lucent's financial statements show the following (in $millions):

Years Ended September 30

	1997	1998	1999
Capitalized software costs (net)	293	298	470
Amortization	380	234	249

---

[4]At the time of the sale, the proceeds are added to cash, the original asset cost is removed from gross PPE, and the accumulated depreciation for the asset is removed from that account. The difference between the cash proceeds and the net book value of the assets sold is then credited-debited to the accumulated depreciation account; no gain or loss is recorded.

[5]See Chapter 14 for an extensive discussion of goodwill.

Amortization of capitalized software declined sharply in fiscal 1998. Amortization rose only slightly in fiscal 1999 despite the large increase in capitalized cost. There is no discussion of amortization in Lucent's Management Discussion and Analysis.

Depreciation Method Disclosures

As we have shown, the choice of the depreciation method can greatly affect the pattern of reported income. Disclosure of the depreciation method used is required and can usually be found in the footnote listing accounting policies. Most (more than 90%) American firms use straight-line depreciation, but accelerated methods are more widely used in other countries. The use of accelerated methods in the United States has declined in recent years as firms have changed to straight-line depreciation.

Depreciation Lives and Salvage Values

Even when the same depreciation method is used, comparability for a firm over time and among companies at a given point in time may be lacking. The *useful life* (the period over which the asset is depreciated) can vary from firm to firm, and excessively long lives understate reported depreciation expense. Although companies are required to disclose depreciation lives, in practice such disclosures are often vague, providing ranges rather than precise data. In such cases, the analyst must use available data to compute approximate depreciation lives (see the analysis of fixed asset disclosures later in the chapter).

■ Example: Westvaco

Westvaco's summary of significant accounting policies states that:

> The cost of plant and equipment is depreciated . . . over the estimated useful lives . . . which range from 20 to 40 years for buildings and 5 to 30 years for machinery and equipment.

Although usually a less significant factor, *salvage values* also affect comparisons; they (like asset lives) are also management estimates. High estimates reduce the depreciation base (cost less salvage value) and, therefore, reduce depreciation expense. (Note that salvage values are not employed in declining-balance depreciation methods.) In practice, companies rarely disclose data regarding salvage values, except when estimates are changed.[6]   ■

Impact of Depreciation Methods on Financial Statements

The choice of depreciation method impacts both the income statement and balance sheet; for capital-intensive companies, the impact can be significant. As depreciation is an allocation of past cash flows, the method chosen for financial reporting purposes has no impact on the statement of cash flows.[7]

Accelerated depreciation methods, with higher depreciation expense in the early years of asset life, tend to depress both net income and stockholders' equity when compared with the straight-line method. As the percentage effect on net income is usually greater than the effect on net assets, return ratios tend to be lower when accelerated depreciation methods are used. Consequently, these methods are considered more conservative.

Toward the end of an asset's life, however, the effect on net income reverses. In Exhibit 8-4, depreciation expense in years 4 and 5 is lower using accelerated methods than under the straight-line method. This is true for individual assets. However, for companies with stable

---

[6]As discussed in Chapter 1, changes in accounting estimates receive less disclosure than changes in method. APB 20 (para. 33) requires disclosure of the effect of a change that affects future periods, such as changes in depreciable lives.

[7]This assumes that the method chosen for tax purposes is independent of the method chosen for financial statement purposes.

or rising capital expenditures, the early-year impact of new assets acquired dominates, and depreciation expense on a total firm basis is higher under an accelerated method. When capital expenditures decline, however, accelerated depreciation decreases depreciation expense as the later-year effect on older assets dominates.

Depreciable lives and salvage values impact both depreciation expense and stated asset values. Shorter lives and lower salvage values are considered conservative in that they lead to higher depreciation expense. These factors interact with the depreciation method to determine the expense; for example, use of the straight-line method with short depreciation lives may result in depreciation expense similar to that obtained from the use of an accelerated method with longer lives. Conservative depreciation practices also increase asset turnover ratios by decreasing the denominator of that ratio. As noted in Chapter 4, fixed-asset turnover ratios should be computed using gross fixed-asset investment in the denominator, although that is not done in practice.

Accelerated Depreciation and Taxes

Notwithstanding the theoretical arguments and the financial statement effects discussed, the primary reason for accelerated depreciation methods is their beneficial effect on the firm's tax burden. At the onset of an asset's life, the total amount of depreciable cost available is fixed. Depreciation acts as a tax shield by reducing the amount of taxes paid in any given year. Given a positive interest rate, firms are better off using accelerated depreciation methods to obtain the benefit of increased cash flows (from reduced taxes) in the earlier years.

Governments have long used the tax code to encourage investment, and this was the intent of the U.S. government when it first allowed accelerated depreciation methods for tax purposes in 1954. Many foreign governments also permit the use of accelerated depreciation methods. Since 1954, the U.S. government has frequently changed tax depreciation regulations to increase or decrease investment incentives in certain types of fixed assets or simply to raise revenues. The present system is known as MACRS—modified accelerated cost recovery system—which consists of specified depreciation patterns and depreciable lives (generally shorter than actual useful service lives) for different property classes.

MACRS uses the double-declining-balance and 150% declining-balance methods, which few companies use for financial reporting purposes. Thus, in the United States the depreciation method and lives used for financial statements almost always differ from those used for tax purposes. The implications of these differences are discussed in Chapter 9, which also illustrates the use of tax disclosures to obtain insights into the depreciation practices used for financial reporting.

Impact of Inflation on Depreciation

Historical cost-based depreciation expense may be used to define income as long as the total expense over the asset's life is enough to replace the asset after it has been fully utilized. If, however, the replacement cost of the asset increases, then depreciation expense based on the original cost will be insufficient.

Returning to the example in Exhibit 8-1, assume that after three years the firm requires $300 to replace the asset. Now the total economic income earned by the firm is $0, as total cash flows equal the cost to replace. If we use the historical cost basis, however, total depreciation is limited to the original $240 cost, and reported income is overstated. In addition, because firms are only allowed to use historical cost basis depreciation for tax reporting, the resultant taxes are too high. Income taxes become, in effect, a tax on capital rather than a tax on income. Box 8-1 illustrates the resulting disincentives for investment in the context of a simple capital budgeting model.

Accelerated depreciation methods partially compensate for this inflation effect by shortening the (tax) recovery period. Depreciating the asset over a shorter life serves a similar purpose. A number of studies have examined whether accelerated methods compensate for inflation and/or reflect economic depreciation (variously defined).

BOX 8-1

Disincentives for Investment Arising from Historical Cost Depreciation

---

We begin by assuming that the inflation rate p is equal to zero. A project is profitable if the net present value (NPV) of the cash flows of the investment:

$$\text{NPV}_{(p=0)} = -I + (1-t)\sum \frac{C_i}{(1+r)^i} + t\sum \frac{d_i I}{(1+r)^i}$$

is greater than zero (i.e., NPV > 0), where C_i is the pretax (real) cash flow in period i, t is the marginal tax rate, d_i is the rate of depreciation in period i, I is the cost of the original investment, and r is the appropriate real discount rate.* The summation on the right reflects the depreciation tax shelter, and the NPV can be disaggregated into

NPV = −investment + present value (after-tax cash flows)

+ present value (depreciation tax shelter)

If we introduce an annual inflation rate of $p > 0$, then the expected (nominal) cash flows in any period will increase. In addition, the discount rate will change to reflect inflation. The depreciation deduction based on historical costs will not change. The expression for net present value now becomes

$$\text{NPV}_{(p>0)} = -I + (1-t)\sum \frac{(1+p)^i C_i}{(1+p)^i(1+r)^i} + t\sum \frac{d_i I}{(1+p)^i(1+r)^i}$$

As the $(1+p)^i$ terms in the first summation cancel, inflation (when it is expected) will not affect the after-tax cash flows. However, the depreciation tax shelter will now be worth less as

$$t\sum \frac{d_i I}{(1+r)^i} > t\sum \frac{d_i I}{(1+p)^i(1+r)^i}$$

The decline in the depreciation tax shelter will reduce the profitability of the project:

$$\text{NPV}_{(p>0)} < \text{NPV}_{(p=0)}$$

and *ceteris paribus*, there is less likelihood that the project will be undertaken.

---

*Generally, the depreciation tax shelter would be discounted at a rate lower than the cash flows themselves as the tax deduction is "riskless." We do not make the distinction here for the sake of simplification. Alternatively, one can view this problem in the context of certainty, and r is the risk-free rate.

Kim and Moore (1988), for example, report that, for the Canadian trucking industry, tax depreciation exceeded economic depreciation, resulting in a tax subsidy. Most (1984), focusing on reported income, found that in the United States the useful life (used for financial reporting) is generally longer than the economic life of the asset, understating reported depreciation and overstating reported income. Skinner (1982), on the other hand, reported the opposite phenomenon in the United Kingdom.

Beaver and Dukes (1973) examined firm price/earnings ratios and found that market prices, on average

assign a more accelerated form of depreciation than is implied by reported earnings.[8]

They did not attempt to discern the reasons for this result but recognized that it was consistent with either a constant rate of return depreciation model (with declining cash flows) or depreciation based on current costs rather than a historical cost system.

Generalizing these results to other time periods, particularly for studies that examined whether depreciation practices (whether for tax or book purposes) compensated for the actual economic or physical depreciation of assets, requires a great deal of caution, given changing economic environments. These comparisons are a function of the provisions of the

---

[8]William H. Beaver and Roland E. Dukes, "Interperiod Tax Allocation and δ-Depreciation Methods: Some Empirical Results," *Accounting Review* (July 1973), pp. 549–559.

tax code, the inflation rate, and varying degrees of technological obsolescence across industries during the comparison period. During the 1980s, the depreciation provisions of the U.S. tax code were changed three times, inflation declined to approximately 4% from double-digit rates, and technological change was rapid in many industries. International differences are an additional difficulty.

The benchmark issue emerging from these studies is: How does one determine the "correct" useful life and economic depreciation rate? This is an important question for analytical purposes. Estimates of economic lives on an aggregate industry basis can be derived from Department of Commerce data.

In 1982, the FASB issued SFAS 33 (Changing Prices), which required very large firms[9] to disclose supplementary, unaudited data on the effects of changing prices. Among the required disclosures were:

- The current cost of fixed assets
- Depreciation expense on a current cost basis

These disclosures were intended to help financial statement users adjust for the shortcomings of historical cost depreciation discussed earlier. However, studies that examined the informational content of the replacement cost data found that, although historical cost earnings had informational content above and beyond that of current cost data provided by SFAS 33, the reverse did not hold.[10] Inflation-adjusted data did not appear to have any marginal information content above that provided by historical cost data. The reasons offered for this surprising result were that the data were:

- Too difficult to comprehend, and the market had not yet learned how to use them
- Not new, as the market knew how to adjust historical costs for inflation without SFAS 33 disclosures[11]
- Irrelevant, either from a conceptual point of view or in the manner in which they were prepared and reported

Whatever the reason, in practice the data were difficult to prepare and use. Facing intense complaints regarding the cost of the disclosures and empirical research that seemed to belie the usefulness of the data, the FASB subsequently made the disclosures voluntary. A detailed discussion of the effects of inflation on fixed assets and depreciation appears in Appendix 8-A.

That appendix also includes a discussion of IAS 29, whose methodology for showing the impact of inflation differs in some important respects from SFAS 33. Foreign registrants with operations in hyperinflationary economies are permitted to use IAS 29 for reports filed with the SEC.

Changes in Depreciation Method

Companies may change the reported depreciation of fixed assets in different ways:

- Change in method applicable only to newly acquired assets
- Change in method applicable to all assets
- Changes in asset lives or salvage value

---

[9]SFAS 33 applied to firms with inventories and gross (before deducting depreciation) property exceeding $125 million (in the aggregate) or with total assets exceeding $1 billion.

[10]Some studies [e.g., Beaver et al. (1980, 1982)] found little information content, focusing on ASR 190 disclosures (see Appendix 8-A). Others [Beaver and Landsman (1983)] examined the SFAS 33 data with similar results. Although the consensus was that these data did not have information content, the conclusions were by no means unanimous [see, e.g., Easman et al. (1979) and Murdoch (1986)].

[11]One example is the work of Angela Falkenstein and Roman L. Weil, "Replacement Cost Accounting: What Will Income Statements Based on the SEC Disclosures Show?—Part I," *Financial Analysts Journal* (January–February 1977), pp. 46–57 and "Replacement Cost Accounting: What Will Income Statements Based on the SEC Disclosures Show?—Part II," *Financial Analysts Journal* (March–April 1977), pp. 48–57.

Change in Method Applicable Only to Newly Acquired Assets. A company can change its depreciation method only for newly acquired assets and continue to depreciate previously acquired similar assets using the same method(s) as in the past. The impact of the new method will be gradual, increasing as fixed assets acquired after the change grow in relative importance.

DuPont, for example, changed from the sum-of-the-years' digits method (for nonpetroleum properties) to the straight-line method for properties placed in service in 1995, with the following footnote disclosure:

> Property, plant and equipment (PP&E) is carried at cost and, except for petroleum PP&E, PP&E placed in service prior to 1995 is depreciated under the sum-of-the-years' digits method and other substantially similar methods. PP&E placed in service after 1994 is depreciated using the straight-line method. This change in accounting was made to reflect management's belief that the productivity of such PP&E will not appreciably diminish in the early years of its useful life, and it will not be subject to significant additional maintenance in the later years of its useful life. In these circumstances, straight-line depreciation is preferable in that it provides a better matching of costs with revenues. Additionally, the change to the straight-line method conforms to predominant industry practice. The effect of this change on net income will be dependent on the level of future capital spending; it did not have a material effect in 1995.[12]

This is a common method of changing accounting principles, as it does not require the restatement of past earnings.

The company made the uninformative statement that "the change is not expected to have a material effect on 1995 results." Nonetheless, *the change increased subsequent reported income* as depreciation charges for new PPE were lower (depreciation charges on old PPE continued to be computed using the SYD method).

Exhibit 8-6 contains an extract from duPont's segment disclosures for the years 1994 to 1996. As petroleum assets are depreciated by the units of production method, we must remove the capital spending and depreciation for that segment:

	1994	1995	1996
Capital spending	$3,151	$3,394	$3,317
Petroleum segment	(1,635)	(1,714)	(1,616)
All nonpetroleum	$1,516	$1,680	$1,701
% change		10.8%	1.3%
Total depreciation	$3,106	$2,823	$2,719
Petroleum segment	(1,266)	(1,111)	(1,128)
All nonpetroleum	$1,840	$1,712	$1,591
% change		−7.0%	−7.1%

Although nonpetroleum capital spending rose in both 1995 and 1996, depreciation expense fell 7% in both years. The decline is clearly due to the combined effect of straight-line (lower than SYD) depreciation expense relating to new assets and declining SYD depreciation on old assets.

Change in Method Applicable to All Assets. Instead of being implemented prospectively, the new method can be applied retroactively so that all fixed assets are depreciated using the new method. In this case, the effect is greater and can be significant in the year of the switch as well as in future years. For a sample of 38 companies that switched to straight-line depreciation, Healy et al. (1987) estimated that the median increase in income was 8% to

---

[12]*Source:* duPont 10-K report, 1995.

EXHIBIT 8-6
DuPont Segment Disclosures ($millions)

	Chemicals	Fibers	Polymers	Petroleum	Life Sciences	Diversified Businesses	Consolidated
1996:							
Depreciation, etc.	$330	$609	$350	$1,128	$70	$232	$2,719
Capital expenditures	338	611	446	1,616	93	213	3,317
1995:							
Depreciation, etc.	352	626	362	1,111	78	294	2,823
Capital expenditures	417	593	399	1,714	73	198	3,394
1994:							
Depreciation, etc.	405	686	386	1,266	79	284	3,106
Capital expenditures	258	640	356	1,635	47	215	3,151

Source: duPont 10-K report, December 31, 1996.

10% in the 10-year period following the change. In addition to the effect on current and future depreciation expense (and net income), there is a cumulative effect, given the retroactive nature of the change: the cumulative difference between originally reported depreciation and the restated depreciation for all past periods. When the new method is applied retroactively, companies must also disclose the pro forma impact of the new method on prior periods.

EXHIBIT 8-7. AMR CORPORATION
Change in Depreciation Lives of Flight Equipment

A. Extract from Depreciation Footnote

Effective January 1, 1999, in order to more accurately reflect the expected useful life of its aircraft, the Company changed its estimate of the depreciable lives of certain aircraft types from 20 to 25 years and increased the residual value from five to 10 percent. It also established a 30-year life for its new Boeing 777 aircraft, first delivered in the first quarter of 1999. As a result of this change, depreciation and amortization expense was reduced by approximately $158 million and net earnings were increased by approximately $99 million, or $0.63 per common share diluted, for the year ended December 31, 1999.

B. Extract from Income Statement

	Years Ended December 31 (in $millions)		
	1999	1998	1997
Revenues	$17,730	$17,516	$16,957
Expenses:			
Depreciation and amortization	1,092	1,040	1,040
Total operating expenses	16,574	15,528	15,362
Operating Income	1,156	1,988	1,595

C. Extract from Management Discussion and Analysis

Depreciation and amortization expense increased $52 million, or 5.0 percent, due primarily to the addition of new aircraft, partially offset by the change in depreciable lives and residual values for certain types of aircraft in 1999 (see Note 1 to the consolidated financial statements).

Source: AMR Corp. 10-K Report, December 31, 1999.

A change in depreciation method for all assets is considered a change in accounting principle under APB 20, Accounting Changes. *The cumulative effect of the change must be reported separately and net of taxes.*

Changes in Asset Lives or Salvage Value. Changes in asset lives and salvage values are changes in accounting estimates and are not considered changes in accounting principle. Their impact is only prospective, and no retroactive or cumulative effects are recognized. Estimate changes attract much less notice than do changes in depreciation methods (see footnote 6). They are not, for example, referred to in the auditor's opinion. Thus, it is important to read financial statement footnotes carefully to be sure that no changes in accounting estimates have been made.

■ Example: AMR

Exhibit 8-7 contains extracts from the *1999 Annual Report* of AMR, the parent of American Airlines, which changed the estimated useful lives *and* the salvage values used to compute depreciation on its flight equipment, effective January 1, 1999. Given the asset intensity of airlines, this change had a significant impact on reported earnings, as shown in the following table:

AMR (in $millions)

	Years Ended December 31		
	1997	1998	1999
As Reported (with Depreciation Changes)			
Depreciation expense	$1,040	$1,040	$1,092
% Change from previous year		0.0%	5.0%
Operating income	$1,595	$1,988	$1,156
% Change from previous year		24.6%	−41.9%
After Adjustment for Depreciation Change			
Depreciation expense	$1,040	$1,040	$1,250
% Change from previous year		0.0%	20.2%
Operating income	$1,595	$1,988	$ 998
% Change from previous year		24.6%	−49.8%

Despite the accounting change, depreciation expense rose 5% in 1991 due to new equipment. If not for the change, depreciation expense would have been more than 20% higher. Without the accounting change, the 1999 decline in operating income would have been steeper, 50% instead of 42%. This may have been the motivation for the change. *When analyzing firms that change depreciation methods or assumptions, it is important to remember that the effect of such changes persists, as depreciation on both old and new fixed assets is stretched out, increasing reported income.* ■

Increases in asset lives have been common in recent years. The effect of such increases is, of course, to increase reported earnings. Such changes are often made by more than one firm in an industry, as firms compete to show higher reported earnings and ROE. For example, in the airline industry, Delta Airlines changed both the estimated lives and the salvage values used to compute depreciation on flight equipment in 1993. Both Southwest Airlines and UAL (United Airlines) extended aircraft depreciable lives in 1999.

Box 8-2 examines the motivation for and reaction to depreciation changes. Whenever a change in depreciation method or lives is reported, the effect of the change on current year reported earnings should be removed to evaluate operating performance on a comparable basis. The change should also be factored into estimates of future reported income.

BOX 8-2
Changes in Depreciation Methods: Motivation and Reaction

When the Internal Revenue Code of 1954 permitted the use of accelerated depreciation for tax purposes, many firms also adopted these methods for financial statement purposes. Subsequently, many of these firms "switched back" to straight-line depreciation for financial reporting purposes. The effect of the switch-back was to increase the firm's reported net income, (tangible) assets, and retained earnings.

Unlike the FIFO-LIFO switch discussed in Chapter 6, the depreciation switch-back was a "pure accounting" change without any direct cash flow consequences as accelerated depreciation was retained for tax purposes. The phenomenon was originally studied by Archibald (1972) and Kaplan and Roll (1972) as a test of whether the efficient market hypothesis (EMH) or the functional fixation hypothesis prevailed with respect to financial statements; that is, was the market "fooled" by the numbers, or did it see through the accounting change, realizing that it had no economic consequence? As detailed in Chapter 5, the results of these studies (using weekly and monthly data) were consistent with the EMH, finding no market reaction to the switch.

With the advent of positive accounting research, the assumption of no economic consequences to a "pure accounting" change was reexamined. Management compensation contracts as well as debt covenants based on accounting numbers are affected by accounting changes. Holthausen (1981) examined the accounting switch-backs in this framework. He argued that an accounting change that increases reported income, given earnings-based management contracts, should result in negative market reaction, as there would be a wealth transfer from the owners of the firm to the managers. Conversely, the presence of debt covenants should result in a positive market reaction, as the increase in reported earnings and as-

sets would generally increase the slack associated with any leverage constraints. Empirical results did not confirm these hypotheses.

As noted in Chapter 5, studies of market reaction to voluntary accounting changes have generally not found results consistent with the positive accounting framework, as (it is argued that) by the time the change is made, it has been generally anticipated that the firm (or its managers) will make the change to improve reported performance. Thus, although the motivation for the change (compensation, debt covenants) is as specified, the market has already taken it into account.

Evidence consistent with the compensation motivation for depreciation switch-backs is reported by Dhaliwal et al. (1982), who found that management-controlled firms are more likely to adopt straight-line depreciation methods. Furthermore, Healy et al. (1987) found that when firms changed reporting methods to straight-line depreciation,

> the CEO's bonus and salary awards are based on reported earnings both before and after the accounting changes. We find no evidence that subsequent to either the inventory change or the depreciation change, reported earnings are transformed to earnings under the original accounting method for computing compensation awards.*

Generally, however, they note that the percentage of the CEO's compensation attributable to the accounting change is small relative to their overall compensation package. On average, these results do not find a debt covenant or (significant) management compensation motivation for the change in depreciation method. For a given company, however, an analyst would be wise to check these factors whenever an income-increasing accounting change is implemented.

---

*Paul H. Healy, Sok-Hyon Kang, and Krishna Palepu, "The Effect of Accounting Procedure Changes on CEO's Cash Salary and Bonus Compensation," *Journal of Accounting and Economics* (1987), pp. 7–34.

ANALYSIS OF FIXED ASSET DISCLOSURES

In practice, firms use varying accounting methods, lives, and residual value assumptions for fixed assets, hampering comparisons between firms. To improve comparability, the analyst must use financial statement disclosures to gain insight into a company's depreciation accounting. Unfortunately, in 1994 the SEC deleted the requirement for firms to disclose details of their property accounts.[13] However, the Commission has proposed restoring the requirement following complaints from financial analysts regarding the loss of these useful data. As a result, for American firms, only a broad analysis is possible except when detailed data are made available by the company. However, IAS 16 and many foreign GAAP require detailed disclosures about fixed assets, permitting detailed analysis as shown below.

---

[13]Financial Reporting Release (FRR) 44 (December 13, 1994) amended Rule 5-04 of Regulation S-X to eliminate Schedule V, Property, Plant and Equipment, and Schedule VI, Accumulated Depreciation, Depletion and Amortization of Property, Plant and Equipment. See FRR 44 for a listing of other schedules eliminated.

Estimating Relative Age and Useful Lives

Fixed-asset data can be used to estimate the relative age of companies' property, plant, and equipment. The relative age as a percentage of depreciable ("useful") life is calculated as

$$\text{Relative Age (\%)} = \text{Accumulated Depreciation/Ending Gross Investment}$$

As long as straight-line depreciation is used,[14] this is an accurate estimate of asset age as a percentage of depreciable life. Neither changes in asset mix (additions with longer or shorter lives than existing assets) nor the timing of purchases affect the calculation. The relative age is a useful measure of whether the firm's fixed-asset base is old or new. Newer assets are likely to be more efficient; when relative age is high, the firm has not been adding to (or modernizing) its capital stock and may find it difficult to compete with firms that have more modern facilities. Remember, however, that this calculation is affected by the firm's accounting methods in the following areas:

- Depreciation lives[15]
- Salvage values

Another useful calculation is the average depreciable life of fixed assets:

$$\text{Average Depreciable Life} = \text{Ending Gross Investment/Depreciation Expense}$$

This calculation is only a rough approximation as it can be affected by changes in asset mix. During periods of rapid growth in fixed assets, the time (within the year) when assets are placed into service can also affect the ratio. Over longer time periods, however, this ratio is a useful measure of a firm's depreciation policy and can be used for comparisons with competitors.

Estimating the Age of Assets

We can also calculate the approximate age (in years) of a firm's fixed assets by comparing accumulated depreciation with depreciation expense:[16]

$$\text{Average Age} = \text{Accumulated Depreciation/Depreciation Expense}$$

As in the case of depreciable life, average age calculations may be distorted by changes in asset mix and by acquisitions. Nonetheless, these data are useful for comparison purposes and can suggest a useful line of questioning when meeting with management.

Average age data, either as a percentage of gross cost or in absolute terms, are useful for two reasons. First, older assets tend to be less efficient; inefficient or obsolete fixed assets may make the firm uncompetitive. Second, knowing past patterns of capital replacement helps the analyst estimate when major capital expenditures will be required. The financing implications of capital expenditure requirements may be significant. Furthermore, when forecasting capital expenditures, the data should be compared with benchmark data on the useful (economic) life of fixed assets for that industry.

---

[14]The use of accelerated depreciation methods invalidates this analysis. However, since more than 90% of companies use straight-line depreciation, the method has general application.

[15]As noted earlier, depreciable lives and economic lives for reporting purposes are not equivalent. See the earlier reference to Most (1984).

[16]Average age can also be computed as relative age multiplied by average depreciable life.

EXHIBIT 8-8
Analysis of Fixed Assets for Scandinavian Forest Products Industry

1999	Assidoman	Holmen	SCA	Stora Enso
Buildings				
Average age %	41.6	49.1	29.4	35.1
Average depreciable life years	27.3	21.0	24.4	27.6
Average age years	11.3	10.3	7.2	9.7
Machinery and Equipment				
Average age %	55.7	50.0	42.7	48.3
Average depreciable life years	16.3	13.4	15.2	17.4
Average age years	9.1	6.7	6.5	8.4

Source: Data from 1999 annual reports.

■ **Example: Forest Products Industry Comparison**

Exhibit 8-8 contains average age and average depreciable life statistics for four Scandinavian companies in the forest products industry for 1999. Statistics for buildings and for machinery and equipment are shown separately, as required by Swedish GAAP.[17]

The statistics show significant differences among these four companies:

• SCA's fixed assets appear youngest and Assidoman's appear oldest.

• Holmen appears to use the shortest depreciable lives, followed by SCA.

These statistics are, however, only the starting point for analysis. They assume that all four firms have comparable assets when in fact they may have differing mixes of assets with different depreciable lives. Differences in product mix (requiring different fixed-asset mixes) and acquisitions and divestitures also affect the comparison. These statistics should be used to ask questions of management rather than to make decisions.

Several of these firms had major acquisitions or divestitures over the 1997–1999 period, making three-year comparisons meaningless. However data for SCA follow:

SCA: Analysis of Fixed Asset Disclosures by Property Class (SEK millions)

	1997	1998	1999
Buildings et al.			
Gross investment	12,566	13,986	12,513
Accumulated depreciation	(3,299)	(3,909)	(3,680)
Net investment	9,267	10,077	8,833
Depreciation expense	519	515	513
Average age %	26.3%	27.9%	29.4%
Average depreciable life years	24.2	27.2	24.4
Average age years	6.4	7.6	7.2
Machinery and Equipment			
Gross investment	42,404	47,256	47,487
Accumulated depreciation	(17,488)	(20,729)	(20,289)
Net investment	24,916	26,527	27,198
Depreciation expense	3,117	2,912	3,117
Average age %	41.2%	43.9%	42.7%
Average depreciable life years	13.6	16.2	15.2
Average age years	5.6	7.1	6.5

---

[17]IAS 16 requirements are similar.

Even within one company, the fixed asset statistics can show significant change over short periods. The apparent increase in average depreciable life in 1998 and the 1999 decline may be due to significant asset acquisitions and dispositions in those years (note the changes in gross investment and accumulated depreciation). As in the case of comparisons with other companies, these statistics are a means rather than an end. ∎

IMPAIRMENT OF LONG-LIVED ASSETS

Fixed assets used in continuing operations are carried at acquisition cost less accumulated depreciation. The carrying amount of fixed assets may also be affected by changes in market conditions and technology. These changes may increase or decrease the fair value of fixed assets. Unlike some foreign countries (and the IASB), U.S. GAAP do not allow firms to recognize increases in value.

This section is concerned with the recognition, measurement, and disclosure problems associated with decreases in fair value, often called impairment, of long-lived assets. Impairment means that some or all of the carrying cost cannot be recovered from expected levels of operations. Due to unfavorable economic conditions, technological developments, or declines in market demand, firms may temporarily idle, continue to operate at a significantly reduced level, sell, or abandon impaired assets. These economic conditions may also call for fewer employees or those with different skills.

Financial Reporting of Impaired Assets

Impairments are sometimes reported as part of "restructuring" provisions. Such provisions (see Chapter 2 for further discussion) contain elements that fall into two general categories. Some elements, including impairment writedowns, write off past cash flows.[18] Others reflect a major restructuring of the firm and may result in current and expected future cash outflows for such items as employee severance and lease payments. Restructuring provisions must, therefore, be separated into impairment (noncash writedowns of past cash outflows) and those with cash flow implications.

In October 2001, the FASB issued SFAS 144, Accounting for the Impairment or Disposal of Long-Lived Assets. The new standard superseded SFAS 121 (Accounting for Impairment) and APB 30,[19] and also nullified most of the guidance (EITF 94-3) on obligations associated with disposal activities.

SFAS 144 broadened the application of "discontinued operation" accounting[20] and changed the treatment of assets intended for disposal. SFAS 121 (1995) had distinguished between assets held for sale and those remaining in use.

Impairment of Assets Held for Sale

The new standard requires that long-lived assets held for sale:

- Be written down to fair value less cost to sell when lower than the carrying amount. In most cases estimated fair value would be the present value of expected cash flows, discounted at the credit-adjusted risk-free rate.[21] Costs to sell exclude costs associated with the ongoing operations of assets held for sale.
- Cease to be depreciated after reclassification as held for sale.

Subsequent increases in fair value less cost to sell would be recognized as gains only to the extent of previously recognized writedowns.

---

[18]However, they may signal departure from a business segment or the need for significant capital expenditures for investments in new and improved technologies.

[19]APB 30 deals with disposal of a segment and the classification of items as extraordinary.

[20]See Chapter 2 for discussion of discontinued operations accounting.

[21]See discussion of SFAC 7 in Box 1-1.

Impairment of Assets Remaining in Use

The standard requires the recognition of impairment when there is evidence that the carrying amount of an asset or a group of assets still in use can no longer be recovered. One or more of the following indicators may signal lack of recoverability:

- A significant decrease in the market value, physical change, or use of the assets
- Adverse changes in the legal or business climate
- Significant cost overruns
- Current period operating or cash flow losses combined with a history of operating or cash flow losses and a forecast of a significant decline in the long-term profitability of the asset

SFAS 144 provides a two-step process. First is the recoverability test: Impairment must be recognized when the carrying value of the assets exceeds the *undiscounted* expected future cash flows from their use and disposal. The second stage is loss measurement: the excess of the carrying amount over the fair value of the assets. When fair value cannot be determined, the *discounted* present value of future cash flows (discounted at the firm's incremental borrowing rate) must be used.[22]

For assets to be held and used, the new standard permits either a probability-weighted or a best-estimate approach when applying the undiscounted cash flows recoverability test. Estimates of future cash flows used in these tests would be based on the remaining useful life of the primary asset of the group, which may be recognized identifiable intangible assets that are being amortized. The standard includes guidance on the present value methods described in SFAC 7.

The recoverability test and loss measurement are based on assets grouped at the lowest level for which cash flows can be identified independently of cash flows of other asset groups. The impairment loss is reported pretax as a component of income from continuing operations.

The standard prohibits restoration of previous impairments. It requires disclosure of the amount of the loss, segments affected, events and circumstances surrounding the impairment, and how fair value was determined.

SFAS 144 does not require firms to disclose cash flows and discount rates used to measure impairment. Firms do not have to disclose impaired assets (even though one or more impairment indicators are present) as long as their gross *undiscounted* cash flows exceed their carrying amount (even when the discounted cash flows are below the carrying amount). Thus, there is no disclosure of early-warning signals.

SFAS 144 was effective in fiscal years beginning after December 15, 2001. The new standard applied prospectively to new disposal activities. Retroactive application was prohibited except for restatement for comparative purposes.

Analysts must develop supplementary techniques to counter inadequate disclosure requirements and the absence of early-warning signals. Significant declines in market value, abnormal technological changes, and overcapacity are good indicators of possible asset impairments. Research indicates that managers are slow to report impairments.

The telecommunications industry provides a good example; the three indicators mentioned earlier in the preceding paragraph were present during 2001. A June 25, 2001 article in the *Wall Street Journal* asked whether companies had delayed impairment announcements because asset writedowns would violate bond covenants based on minimum levels of fixed assets relative to debt. Impairment recognition would have reduced access to capital markets and risked technical insolvency.

---

[22]When the recoverability test is applied to assets acquired in purchase method business combinations, the standard requires the elimination of goodwill before recording writedowns of related impaired tangible and identifiable intangible assets. When only some of the acquired assets are subject to the recoverability test, goodwill must be allocated to the affected assets on a pro-rata basis using the relative fair values of all assets acquired. SFAS 142 (2001) made significant changes in accounting for the impairment of goodwill. See the discussion in Chapter 14.

The need to evaluate recoverability periodically may result in the review of depreciation methods, lives, and salvage values. Changes in depreciation may precede or accompany a firm's reporting of asset impairment. Problem 8-16 is based on a company that recognized impairment and shortened depreciable lives simultaneously.

■ Example: Texaco

Note 6 of Texaco's 1999 financial statements provides an example of impairment recognition and disclosure. Texaco, a multinational oil company, reported asset impairments (included in unusual items) in 1997, 1998, and 1999. While the impairment amounts are small compared to Texaco's net income, the disclosures illustrate the poor quality of disclosures in this area. Texaco's disclosures are very broad and uninformative. The statement that "fair value was determined by discounting expected future cash flows" provides no detail regarding the assumptions used. ■

Financial Statement Impact of Impairments

Impairment writedowns of long-lived assets have pervasive and significant effects on financial statements and financial ratios.

The principal balance sheet impacts of the writedowns are reductions in the:

- Carrying value of plant, equipment, and other production assets
- Deferred tax liabilities
- Stockholders' equity

The lower level of fixed assets is a direct consequence of the impairment writedown. As a result, the firm's fixed-asset and total-asset turnover increases, affecting any comparison with firms that have not recognized impairments.

The reduction in deferred tax liabilities reflects the fact that the impairment loss is not recognized for tax purposes until the property is disposed of. However, because virtually all firms depreciate fixed assets more quickly for tax purposes than for financial reporting, the impairment has the effect of reducing the difference between the tax basis and reporting basis of these assets. Thus, previously established deferred tax liabilities are reduced (see Chapter 9 for further discussion of deferred taxes).

The reduction in equity is the net effect of the impairment provision. This reduction increases the firm's debt-to-equity ratio and decreases reported book value per share. The price-to-book value ratio is increased.

Future financial statements are also affected by the writedown. Depreciation expense declines as a direct result of the reduction in the carrying value of fixed assets; reported earnings are higher than if no impairment were recognized. With higher earnings and lower assets and equity, return ratios (ROA and ROE) also increase.

The ratios used to evaluate fixed assets and depreciation policy earlier in this chapter are also distorted by the impairment writedown. For example, the apparent average age of fixed assets increases, and fixed assets appear older than they really are.

Effect of SFAS 121 on Analysis of Impairment

The lack of reporting guidelines for impairments prior to SFAS 121 resulted in widely divergent timing, measurement, and reporting practices. Fried, Schiff, and Sondhi (FSS) (1989) and two Financial Executives Institute surveys[23] found that a majority of companies used net realizable values (NRV) to measure impairments. However, NRV meant different things to different firms, and the definition used was rarely disclosed.[24] The use of undiscounted cash flows under SFAS 121 reduces the probability of recognition of impairments and overstates asset values because of the failure to recognize the time value of money.

---

[23]Financial Executives Institute, Committee on Corporate Reporting, "Survey on Unusual Charges," 1986 and 1991.

[24]The problem is compounded by SFAC 5, in which NRV is defined as a short-term, gross, undiscounted cash flow.

It is difficult to forecast impairment writedowns because managements have so much discretion as to timing. Substandard profitability, especially when persistent, is probably the surest sign of impaired assets. LIFO liquidations and changes in depreciation methods, estimated useful lives, and salvage values provide useful but very imprecise signals. Segment data (see Chapter 13) can help the analyst spot underperforming operations.

The cash flow and tax implications of write-offs are also unclear in some cases. Generally, impairments recognized for financial reporting are not deductible for tax purposes until the affected assets are disposed of. Recognition of the impairment, therefore, leads to a deferred tax asset (a probable future tax benefit), not a current refund. Beneficial cash flow impacts may occur only in the future, when tax deductions are realized. Close attention to the income tax footnote (see Chapter 9) should be helpful, but a complete understanding may require posing questions to management.

Timely recognition of impairments may correct understated past depreciation or permit recognition of the effect of changes in markets or technology on operating assets. Higher frequency of impairment announcements and the absence of reporting guidelines resulted in diverse accounting practices that were not comparable across companies and inconsistently applied within firms over time. The FASB recognized this problem when it placed asset impairment on its agenda. SFAS 144, and SEC efforts to improve disclosures regarding "restructuring" provisions have improved disclosure.

Empirical Findings

The frequency and dollar amount of writedowns have increased considerably in the last 25 years.[25] Elliott and Hanna (1996) report that fewer than 200 (5%) firms in the Compustat database reported write-offs in 1975, almost 800 (14%) did so in 1985, and over 1,200 (21%) in 1993. Moreover, in a phenomenon dubbed by Bleakley (1995) as a "recurring nonrecurring item," firms that report write-offs in one year tend to report write-offs again in subsequent years.[26]

The analysis of write-offs has been confounded by the existence of conflicting beliefs as to the nature and motivations behind such actions. Some view managers as manipulating earnings[27] by recognizing impairments only when it is to their benefit rather than as they occur. Others view impairment announcements as information provided by managers as to declines in asset values due to poor performance, technological shifts, and/or changes in the firm's objectives.

Articles in the financial and popular press as well as in academic journals often talk about the "big bath"—a tendency to take large write-offs during adverse times—and about "house cleaning"—large write-offs assumed to accompany changes in senior management. Consequently, write-off announcements often are viewed as a signal of improvement in future reported performance. However, debate lingers as to whether the subsequent improvement (should it materialize) is evidence that the upturn is real or merely a consequence of earnings management.

A number of studies have examined the write-off phenomenon. These studies document a number of recurring characteristics of write-offs.

1. *Poor financial as well as stock market performance usually precede write-offs.*

    Francis, Hanna, and Vincent (1996), Rees, Gill, and Gore (1996), and Elliott and Shaw (1988) all report poor stock market performance of write-off firms from three to five years prior to the write-off. Consistent with the foregoing, within their respec-

---

[25]The majority of write-offs (55%–60%) are taken in the fourth quarter. Given the detailed review (both by management and auditors) during preparation of the annual report, it is likely that the fourth quarter will always contain the largest number of write-offs.

[26]Elliott and Hanna found that 27% of the companies that take a write-off report a subsequent one the next year and approximately 60% do so within three years. Fried et al. (1990) also document multiple write-offs. Their probabilities, however, are higher (45% within one year and approximately 70% within three years).

[27]Earnings management can operate in both directions. Zucca and Campbell (1992) argue that firms may engage in big-bath behavior, taking write-offs when earnings are severely depressed, as well as smoothing behavior by taking write-offs when earnings are "too high."

tive industries, firms with write-offs had lower operating performance as measured by ROA (Rees et al.), earnings, and ROE (Elliott and Shaw). These results hold for the year of the write-off[28] as well as the three-year period preceding the write-off.[29] Francis et al. showed similar results (with respect to ROA) but only for firms classifying their write-offs as restructurings.

2. *Overall, negative returns occur around the time of the write-off and for up to 18 months following the write-off. These results, however, depend on the nature of the write-off.*

Elliott and Shaw reported that the negative return experienced around the time of the write-off was directly related to the size of the write-off; the larger the write-off, the more negative the reaction. On the other hand, Francis et al., as well as Lindhal and Ricks (1990), indicate that although, in general, market reaction to write-offs was negative, the results depend on whether the event is

a. A *writedown* comprising purely accounting decisions to reduce the carrying value of assets with no (apparent) change in operations; or

b. A *restructuring* that consists of decisions to modify operations (e.g., asset sales, employee layoffs, plant closings)

For the latter type of event, they report positive market reaction. Francis et al. argue that restructurings are associated with positive returns because they indicate decisions taken to modify and improve future operations and corporate strategy.[30]

3. *Problems leading to write-offs are rarely short-lived and generally persist after the write-off.*

This persistence is especially true for firms taking multiple write-offs. Rees et al. show that such firms had market-adjusted returns that were significantly negative for up to two years after the initial write-off. Furthermore, (industry-adjusted) ROA for these firms did not recover after the write-off. These results are consistent with Elliott and Hanna, who found that bond ratings were lower and default probability higher for firms with sequential write-offs.

Taken together, the evidence seems to indicate that firms write down assets during periods of poor performance. However, the assumption of big-bath behavior may not be well founded. The writedown may also be a response to the (negative) change in the firm's economic situation. The prevalence of multiple write-offs and their increasing size is inconsistent with big-bath behavior, usually associated with a once-and-for-all write-off.[31] Similarly, the persistent negative financial performance and market returns following writedowns are consistent not with an expected reversal following a big-bath but rather with a permanent deterioration in the firm's prospects. Furthermore, positive returns following write-offs are generally confined to those situations where the firm has made explicit operating decisions (restructurings) to modify operations.

Given the significance and frequency of impairments, it is unfortunate that indicators of initial write-offs other than poor financial condition are hard to find.[32] Better disclosure in financial statements (or the Management Discussion and Analysis) of problems with particular segments would make it easier to predict write-offs. However, the evidence indicates that care must be taken to distinguish whether the write-off is purely an accounting decision or is coupled with corrective operating decisions.

---

[28]These conditions hold even without taking the write-off into consideration.

[29]FSS (1989), using a control group of firms matched by industry and size, found similar results. Strong and Meyer (1987), however, reported that although the write-off firms were not the best performers in their industry, they were not the worst either, but tended to cluster in the middle quintiles.

[30]Bartov, Lindhal, and Ricks (1996) similarly partitioned their write-off sample into a *writedown category* and an *operating decision category*. Although they found negative returns for both categories, the stock performance of the writedown category was much worse than that of the operating decision category.

[31]In effect, if anything, firms seem to warehouse bad news and report it through multiple write-offs.

[32]FSS (1989) do report that LIFO liquidations are leading indicators of writedowns.

LIABILITIES FOR ASSET RETIREMENT OBLIGATIONS

Governments often require that owners of operating assets remedy the environmental damage caused by operating those assets or restore land to its preexisting condition. Common examples include:

- Restoration of strip mines after mining is completed
- Dismantlement of an offshore oil platform after the end of its useful life
- Removal of toxic wastes caused by production
- Decontamination of site when a nuclear power plant is decommissioned

Prior to SFAS 143, current period costs of these activities were often expensed except for capital expenditures that were capitalized.[33] As no standards have existed for the accrual of future expenditures, practice has been inconsistent with respect to:

- Whether (or when) accrual takes place
- Whether accruals increase the carrying amount of the related asset (and whether they must be depreciated)
- Whether accruals are included in depreciation expense
- Measurement of the liability (whether or not discounted, and at what rate)
- Disclosure

Because of inconsistent accounting practice, the FASB issued SFAS 143, Accounting for Asset Retirement Obligations (AROs), in June 2001.

Provisions of SFAS 143

The requirements of SFAS 143 become effective for fiscal years starting after June 15, 2002 (calendar 2003 for most companies). However some companies will apply the standard earlier. This standard changes accounting standards for ARO in the following ways:

- It applies to all entities[34] and to all legal obligations (including contractual obligations[35]) connected with the retirement of tangible fixed assets.
- Affected firms must recognize the fair value of an ARO liability in the period in which it is incurred (normally at acquisition).
- Absent a market value, fair value is the present value of the expected cash flows required to extinguish the liability.[36]
- As the liability is carried at its present value, the firm must recognize accretion expense in its income statement each period.
- An amount equal to the initial liability must be added to the carrying value of the asset, and depreciated over its useful life.
- Changes in the estimated liability are accounted for prospectively; prior period amounts are not restated.
- Required disclosures include:
  - Description of the ARO and associated asset
  - Reconciliation of the ARO liability, showing the effect of:
    - New liabilities incurred
    - Liabilities extinguished

---

[33]SFAS 19 required the accrual of an asset retirement obligation in some cases. Under SFAS 19, ARO was recognized over the life of the asset and measured using a cost-accumulation approach; it was not discounted, and was often recorded as a contra asset with no recognition of a separate liability. In addition, many electricity producers accrued for the decontamination of nuclear facilities.

[34]Paragraph 17 of SFAS 143 governs its application to leased assets.

[35]The standard also applies to legally enforceable contracts arising from promises made. One example would be a company's publicly stated promise to restore a site it is not required to restore by existing laws.

[36]See Box 8-3 for details.

BOX 8-3
SFAS 143 (2001): Accounting for Asset Retirement Obligations

Explanation of Accounting Method

Initial Recognition and Measurement

SFAS 143 requires the recognition of the fair value of the ARO liability in the period it is incurred if a reasonable estimate of fair value can be made. The fair value of the liability is defined as the amount at which the liability can be settled in a current transaction between willing parties. Quoted market prices are presumed to be the best evidence of fair value. In their absence, firms must estimate fair value using the best available information on prices of similar liabilities and present value (or other valuation) methods.

For present value techniques, SFAS 143 applies the provisions of SFAC 7 (see Box 1-1) to the measurement of ARO liabilities:

A. Estimate the expected (gross) cash flows required to extinguish the obligation, assuming an outside contractor is hired. Given uncertainty regarding future costs, the firm uses the expected value. Other assumptions (such as inflation rates) may be required.

B. The present value of the expected cash flows is computed using an interest rate based on the risk-free rate, but increased to reflect the credit risk of the firm (credit-adjusted risk-free rate).

C. The resulting measure of the ARO is recognized on the balance sheet, with periodic accretion (using the interest method) so that the liability equals the expected gross cash flows at the expected payment date. Use of the interest method means that accretion increases each year.

D. An equal amount is added to the carrying basis of the related asset and depreciated over that asset's useful life, using the same method used to depreciate the cost of the asset.

Subsequent Recognition and Measurement

E. If the timing or the amount of estimated gross cash flows change after the initial recognition, the ARO (and the related asset) is increased or decreased accordingly. Any increase is discounted using interest rates at the date of change; any decrease is discounted at the original interest rate. Accretion and depreciation charges change prospectively; there is no restatement of prior periods.

F. When the liability is extinguished (the cash flows occur), any difference between the amount paid and the carrying amount of the ARO liability is recognized as a gain or loss in the income statement.

Transition Method

The provisions of SFAS 143 were effective in fiscal years beginning after June 15, 2001, with earlier application encouraged. The new standard required use of the cumulative change method to recognize existing AROs. Such recognition was accomplished as follows:

1. Estimate gross obligation based on information available at the (current) transition date.

2. Discount to present value using current interest rates.

3. Replace any previous accrual with the following:

   a. Asset equal to ARO at date of asset acquisition

   b. Accumulated depreciation to transition date, assuming SFAS 143 implemented at asset acquisition date

   c. ARO liability at transition date

4. Record the difference between any previous accruals and those listed in the previous paragraph as the *cumulative effect* of implementing the new standard, shown in the income statement on a separate line.

5. Provide pro forma disclosure of the ARO liability for each year presented in the financial statement.

- Accretion expense
- Revisions of the estimated AROs
- Fair value of any restricted assets (such as funds) set aside for ARO obligations.

Further detail regarding SFAS 143 is contained in Box 8-3.

Effects of SFAS 143

Implementation of the new standard will result in the following financial statement effects for most firms:[37]

- Increase in the carrying value of fixed assets.
- Increase in liabilities due to recognition of the ARO.
- Lower net income due to recognition of additional depreciation (higher fixed assets) and accretion expense (on the ARO). Due to the nature of the accretion process, this expense will increase every year.

---

[37]For firms that have already recognized ARO liabilities (based on expected gross cash outflows), it is possible that the ARO liability will decrease under SFAS 143 because that standard measures the ARO at its present value.

The following ratio effects will also occur:

- Lower asset turnover (higher asset levels)
- Lower debt-to-equity ratio as equity is depressed by lower net income[38]
- Lower return on assets (lower income, higher assets)
- Lower interest coverage (lower income due to higher depreciation, higher interest expense)

Bond covenants that rely on these ratios will also be affected, unless rewritten to ignore the accounting change. Disclosures will be improved in almost all cases. Cash flows will be unaffected.

IAS 16 (1998) requires firms that recognize the liability for remediation costs to include such cost in the carrying amount of fixed assets and depreciate it. The liability recognition is governed by IAS 37 (1998), which (similar to SFAS 143) requires that companies recognize the present value of asset retirement obligations.

■   **Example: Texaco**

In the Management Discussion and Analysis section of its 1999 annual report, Texaco reports (p. 29):

> **Restoration and Abandonment Costs and Liabilities**
>
> Expenditures in 1999 for restoration and abandonment of our oil and gas producing properties amounted to $26 million. At year-end 1999, accruals to cover the cost of restoration and abandonment were $911 million.

Further, in its accounting policy section (p. 30), Texaco states that:

> We include estimated future restoration and abandonment costs in determining amortization and depreciation rates of productive properties.

These minimal disclosures are representative of practice prior to SFAS 143. The December 31, 1999 total accrual equals 7.6% of stockholders' equity. Note that the accrual is undiscounted and may be offset by expected recoveries from state funds. While it appears that accruals are made through depreciation charges, Texaco does not write up fixed assets. The accounting effect of the proposed accounting standard cannot be estimated due to the complexity of the transition requirements.   ■

SUMMARY

The capitalization decision is only the start of the accounting cycle for long-lived assets. Depreciation expense depends on the choice of accounting method and asset life and salvage value assumptions. Thus, the same asset can produce different amounts of depreciation expense, limiting the comparability of reported income. Economic depreciation may be entirely different from accounting depreciation.

Economic changes often result in asset lives that differ from those anticipated by accounting conventions. In such cases, asset impairment may require accounting recognition. Although SFAS 144 provides standards for impairment writedowns in the United States, management retains considerable discretion over their timing and amounts. The accrual (if any) for future environmental costs related to long-lived assets is another area where practice is highly inconsistent.

---

[38]The debt-to-equity ratio is also affected by whether AROs are considered debt or operating liabilities.

Chapter 8

Problems

1. [Depreciation methods; CFA© adapted] An analyst gathered the following information about a fixed asset purchased by a company:

- Purchase price: $12,000,000
- Estimated useful life: 5 years
- Estimated salvage value: $2,000,000

Compute the depreciation expense for this asset over its useful life using *each* of the following methods:

    (i) Straight-line

    (ii) Sum-of-years' digits (SYD)

    (iii) Double-declining balance

2. [Effect of depreciation methods; CFA© adapted] Compare the straight-line method of depreciation with accelerated methods with respect to their impact on:

    (i) Trend of depreciation expense

    (ii) Trend of net income

    (iii) Reported return on equity

    (iv) Reported return on assets

    (v) Reported cash from operations

    (vi) Asset turnover

3. [Impairment; CFA© adapted] Baxter Company owns machinery that, due to changes in industry conditions, may now be impaired.

a. Discuss the procedure that Baxter must follow, under SFAS 144, to decide whether impairment has occurred.

b. Discuss the alternatives available to Baxter to measure the impairment.

c. Discuss the effect of the impairment recognition on each of the following in the year of recognition and the year following recognition:

    (i) Reported net income

    (ii) Income from continuing operations

    (iii) Cash from operations

    (iv) Shareholders' equity

    (v) Return on equity

    (vi) Asset turnover

d. Assuming that (1) Baxter decides to sell the machine, and (2) it meets the plan of sale criteria of SAFS 144, discuss the effect of the loss recognition on each of the following in the year of recognition and the year following recognition:

    (i) Reported net income

    (ii) Income from continuing operations

    (iii) Cash from operations

    (iv) Shareholders' equity

    (v) Return on equity

    (vi) Asset turnover

4. [Effect of depreciation methods] The Jonathan Corp. acquires a machine with an original cost of $9,000 on January 1, 2000. The machine has a five-year life and estimated salvage value of $1,000.

a. Compute depreciation for 2000 and 2001 under each of the following methods:

    (i) Sum-of-years' digits

    (ii) Double-declining-balance

    (iii) Straight-line

b. Compare the impact of the straight-line method and the double-declining-balance method on each of the following:

    (i) Trend of depreciation expense over the five-year life

    (ii) Trend of net income over the five-year life

    (iii) Cash from operations over the five-year life

    (iv) Debt-to-equity ratio in year 2000

    (v) Fixed-asset turnover ratio in year 2000

5. [Effect of useful life and salvage value assumptions on depreciation] The Juliet Company acquires a machine with an original cost of $10,000 on January 1, 2000. Juliet uses the straight-line method of computing depreciation.

a. Compute depreciation expense for 2000 under the following assumptions:

    (i) Ten-year life, $1,000 salvage value

    (ii) Fifteen-year life, $1,000 salvage value

    (iii) Ten-year life, $2,500 salvage value

    (iv) Fifteen-year life, $2,500 salvage value

b. Assuming Juliet adopted choice (iv) rather than choice (i), describe the effect on Juliet's quality of earnings.

6. [Depreciation methods and cash flows, courtesy of Professor Stephen Ryan] The Capital Company considers investing in either of two assets. Cash flows of these assets are:

Year	Asset A	Asset B
1	$36	$26
2	23	24
3	11	22

a. At an interest rate of 10%, how much should Capital be willing to pay for each asset?

b. Assuming that the amount calculated in part a is paid for each asset, calculate the depreciation schedule for each asset that results in a constant rate of return.

c. What type of historical cost depreciation is equal to present value depreciation for Asset A? Asset B?

EXHIBIT 8P-1. BOEING
Extracts from 1999 Financial Statements ($millions)

Note 1. Summary of Significant Accounting Policies

Property, plant and equipment

Property, plant and equipment are recorded at cost, including applicable construction-period interest, and depreciated principally over the following estimated useful lives: new buildings and land improvements, from 20 to 45 years; and machinery and equipment, from 3 to 13 years. The principal methods of depreciation are as follows: buildings and land improvements, 150% declining balance; and machinery and equipment, sum-of-the-years' digits. The Company periodically evaluates the appropriateness of remaining depreciable lives assigned to long-lived assets subject to management's plan for use and disposition.

Note 11. Property, Plant and Equipment

Property, plant and equipment at December 31 consisted of the following:

	1999	1998
Land	$ 430	$ 499
Buildings	8,148	8,244
Machinery and equipment	10,411	10,521
Construction in progress	1,130	977
	$ 20,119	$ 20,241
Less accumulated depreciation	(11,874)	(11,652)
	$ 8,245	$ 8,589

Balances are net of impairment asset valuation reserve adjustments for real property available for sale of $76 and $64 for December 31, 1999 and 1998.

Depreciation expense was $1,330, $1,386 and $1,266 for 1999, 1998 and 1997, respectively. Interest capitalized as construction-period property, plant and equipment costs amounted to $64, $45 and $28 in 1999, 1998 and 1997, respectively.

Five-Year Summary

	1999	1998	1997	1996	1995
Total sales	$57,993	$56,154	$45,800	$35,453	$32,960
Net earnings (loss)	2,309	1,120	(178)	1,818	(36)
Additions to plant and equipment, net	1,236	1,665	1,391	971	747
Depreciation of plant and equipment	1,330	1,386	1,266	1,132	1,172
Net plant and equipment at year-end	8,245	8,589	8,391	8,266	7,927

Source: Boeing, 10-K report, December 31, 1999.

7. [Effects of accelerated depreciation] Exhibit 8P-1 contains data from the 1999 annual report of Boeing [BA], a leading manufacturer of aviation equipment.

a. Despite more than $5 billion of capital expenditures over the four years 1996–1999, Boeing's net plant and equipment rose by barely 4%. One explanation is the sale of fixed assets in 1999 (proceeds $359 million). Discuss *two* other reasons for the slow growth in net plant and equipment.

b. Boeing reported gains on the disposition of fixed assets of $100 million over the 1998–99 period. Discuss how that gain was affected by Boeing's depreciation method.

c. Assume that in 1999 Boeing adopted the straight-line depreciation method retroactively, with no change in depre-

ciable lives. Describe the expected effect of that change on Boeing's:

(i) Net income for 1998 and 1999. (*Hint:* Consider the trend of capital expenditures for those two years.)

(ii) Stockholders' equity at December 31, 1999.

(iii) Cash from operations for 1998 and 1999.

(iv) Fixed-asset turnover for 1999.

d. Assume that Boeing adopted the straight-line depreciation method prospectively as of January 1, 2000, with no change in depreciable lives. Describe the expected effect of that change on Boeing's:

(i) Net income for 2000 compared with net income assuming no accounting change

(ii) Trend of depreciation expense over the 1999 to 2004 period

e. As a financial analyst, what conclusions might you draw from either change (part c or d)?

8. [Change in depreciation method; effect and motivation] Pope and Talbot [POP] changed the method of depreciation for its U.S. pulp production assets from straight-line to units-of-production in 1998 in order to bring the accounting methods of the Company's pulp mills into conformity with its Canadian operations. The company stated:

> The Company believes this method, common within the industry, more appropriately matches production costs with pulp sales revenues. The impact to the 1998 loss from continuing operations was a reduction of depreciation expense before tax of $.8 million. The cumulative effect of this accounting change on years prior to 1998 was income of $.7 million, net of tax, or $.06 per share.

The company's 1998 net income was $342,000.

a. Compute POP's net income before the cumulative effect of the accounting change.

b. Compute POP's net income before the change in depreciation method. (Assume a 35% tax rate.)

c. Present another reason, other than conformity, that might explain why the firm made the accounting change in 1998.

9. [Comparison of firms with different depreciable lives] Delta Airlines [DAL], a competitor of AMR, reported the following information regarding its depreciation of flight equipment:

> Property and Equipment—Property and equipment is recorded at cost and depreciated on a straight-line basis to estimated residual values over their estimated useful lives. The estimated useful lives for major asset classifications are as follows:

Asset Classification	Estimated Useful Life
Owned flight equipment	15–25 years
Flight equipment under capital lease	Lease Term
Ground property and equipment	3–30 years
Leasehold rights and landing slots	Lease Term

> Residual values for flight equipment range from 5%–25% of cost.

(*Source:* Delta Airlines 10-K Report, June 30, 2000.)

a. Comparing the data above with the disclosures by AMR (Exhibit 8-7), discuss any difference between Delta and AMR with respect to each of the following *prior* to the AMR change in 1999:

(i) Depreciation expense

(ii) Shareholders' equity

(iii) Cash from operations

(iv) Quality of earnings

b. Discuss any effect of the AMR change in 1999 on your answer to part a.

10. [Change in depreciable lives] Teekay Shipping [TK], a major owner of oil tankers, merged with Bona Shipholding in June 1999. Effective April 1, 1999 Teekay:

> revised the estimated useful life of its vessels from 20 years to 25 years. . . . This change in accounting estimate resulted in a reduction of depreciation expense of $22.5 million or 62 cents per share for the nine-month period ended December 31, 1999. [Source: Annual Report]

Teekay Shipping: Selected Financial Data ($thousands)

	Years Ended December 31	
	1998	1999
Net voyage revenues	$327,016	$318,348
Income from vessel operations	103,660	34,189

a. Compute Teekay's 1999 income from vessel operations assuming that the company had not changed the estimated useful life of its ships.

b. Compare the percentage change in income from vessel operations assuming no accounting change with the percentage change reported.

c. Describe the effect of the accounting change on Teekay's:

(i) Shareholders' equity at December 31, 1999

(ii) Cash from operations for the period ended December 31, 1999

(iii) Asset turnover for the period ended December 31, 1999

(iv) Quality of earnings

d. Describe the effect of the accounting change on Teekay's income from vessel operations for the year ended December 31, 2000.

11. [Change in depreciation for regulated company] Laclede Group [LG] is a distributor of natural gas in St. Louis and nearby areas of Missouri. Its rates and accounting methods are regulated by the Missouri Public Service Commission (MoPSC). Laclede's 1999 annual report includes the following accounting policy:

> Utility plant (excluding insignificant exploration and development property held during 1997) is depreciated on the straight-line basis at rates based on estimated service lives of the various classes of property. Annual depreciation in 1999, 1998, and 1997 averaged approximately 2.6%, 3.1%, and 3.4%, respectively, of the original cost of depreciable property. In the Company's 1998 rate case, the MoPSC approved a settlement agreement that authorized a decrease in depreciation rates for the Company, which was instituted July 1, 1998.

Financial data for Laclede follow:

Years Ended September 30 ($thousands)

	1997	1998	1999
Operating revenues	$615,730	$561,987	$491,588
Depreciation expense	25,890	25,310	21,490
All other expense	520,896	473,213	408,609
Total operating expense	$546,786	$498,523	$430,099
Operating income	68,944	63,464	61,489
Other income/(expense)	964	1,139	(473)
Earnings before interest and tax	$ 69,908	$ 64,603	$ 61,016
Interest expense	(19,088)	(21,270)	(20,593)
Pretax income	$ 50,820	$ 43,333	$ 40,423
Income tax expense	(18,354)	(15,441)	(14,361)
Net income	$ 32,466	$ 27,892	$ 26,062
Utility plant: gross	$792,661	$835,923	$876,431
Accumulated depreciation	(325,088)	(345,241)	(357,053)
Net	$467,573	$490,682	$519,378

a. Based on reported data, compute each of the following ratios for 1997 through 1999:

  (i) Interest coverage

  (ii) Operating margin

b. Assume that Laclede's depreciation expense had remained at 3.4% of gross plant and equipment for all years. Compute the effect of that assumption on Laclede's

  (i) Earnings before interest and tax (EBIT)

  (ii) Operating income

c. Using the result of part b, compute each of the ratios in part a.

d. Discuss the differences between the ratios computed in part c and those computed in part a.

e. From the perspective of the Missouri Public Service Commission (representing the public), discuss one advantage and one disadvantage of the accounting change.

f. From the perspective of the financial analyst, discuss whether the accounting change is beneficial to stockholders and bondholders.

g. Assume that Laclede's business becomes deregulated over the next 10 years. As a financial analyst, evaluate the likely effect of deregulation on Laclede's accounting for its utility plant.

12. [Change in depreciation lives] On March 6, 2000, Pepsi Bottling Group [PBG] issued a press release containing the following:

> In recognition of its long-standing success in preventive maintenance programs, The Pepsi Bottling Group, Inc. (NYSE: PBG) today announced a change in the depreciation lives of certain categories of assets. This change will result in a reduction of about $58 million in depreciation expense, an increase in earnings per share of $0.22 and an increase in return on invested capital of 0.6% in the year 2000.

Exhibit 8P-2 contains extracts from the first-quarter 10-Q issued by PBG.

a. Compute each of the following ratios for the first quarter of 1999 and 2000, using reported data:

  (i) Gross profit margin

  (ii) Operating margin

b. Compute each of the following ratios for the first quarter of 1999 and 2000, after adjusting reported data for the depreciation change:

  (i) Gross profit margin

  (ii) Operating margin

c. Compute how much of the apparent improvement of each of these two ratios was due to the depreciation change.

d. Discuss the effect of the depreciation change on PBG's:

  (i) Fixed-asset turnover ratio

  (ii) Trend of reported earnings, 1999–2004

  (iii) Quality of earnings

  (iv) Cash from operations

The March 6 press release also contained the following statement:

> "We maintain that cash profits remain the best method of tracking our performance. However, since some investors look at us and other bottlers in terms of reported earnings, we thought it was important to reflect our depreciation expenses and reported profit more accurately," said John Cahill, Executive Vice President and Chief Financial Officer for PBG. "Even with these changes, the new policies still present our financial results conservatively."

e. Evaluate the benefits to PBG of making the depreciation change.

13. [Change in depreciation lives and residual values; follow-up to Problem 8-12] In 2000, Coca-Cola Enterprises [CCE] changed the estimated useful lives and residual values of certain fixed assets. Exhibit 8P-3 contains extracts from the CCE's 10-K report for 2000.

a. Compute the gross margin and operating margin for 1999 and 2000, using:

  (i) Reported data

  (ii) Data adjusted for the accounting change. *Allocate depreciation between cost of sales and selling expense using the PBG % allocation in Exhibit 8P-2.*

b. Compute how much of the improvement in the operating margin was due to the depreciation change.

c. Based on the disclosures in Exhibits 8P-2 and 8P-3, discuss:

  (i) Which company's disclosures regarding its depreciation lives is more useful for financial analysis

  (ii) Which company has the better quality of earnings (based only on the depreciation of fixed assets)

EXHIBIT 8P-2. PEPSI BOTTLING GROUP

The Pepsi Bottling Group, Inc.
Condensed Consolidated Statements of Operations
(in millions, unaudited)

	12 Weeks Ended	
	March 20, 1999	March 18, 2000
Net revenues	$1,452	$1,545
Cost of sales	(835)	(845)
Gross profit	$ 617	$ 700
Selling, delivery and administrative expenses	(575)	(625)
Operating income	$ 42	$ 75

Note 6. Comparability of Results

Asset Lives

At the beginning of fiscal year 2000, we changed the estimated useful lives of certain categories of assets to reflect the success of our preventive maintenance programs in extending the useful lives of these assets. The changes, which are detailed in the table below, lowered total depreciation cost for the quarter by $14 million ($8 million after tax and minority interest, or $0.05 per share) reducing cost of sales by $8 million and selling, delivery and administrative expenses by $6 million.

Estimated Useful Lives

	1999	2000
Manufacturing equipment	10	15
Heavy fleet	8	10
Fountain dispensing equipment	5	7
Small specialty coolers and marketing equipment	5 to 7	3

Source: Pepsi Bottling Group, 10-Q Report, March 18, 2000.

EXHIBIT 8P-3. COCA-COLA ENTERPRISES INC.

	($millions)	
	Years Ended December 31,	
Income Statement	**2000**	1999
Net operating revenues	**$14,750**	$14,406
Cost of sales	**9,083**	9,015
Selling, delivery, and administrative expenses	**4,541**	4,552
Operating income	**1,126**	839
Depreciation	**810**	899

Property, Plant, and Equipment: Property, plant, and equipment are stated at cost. Depreciation expense is computed using the straight-line method over the estimated useful lives of 20 to 40 years for buildings and improvements and three to 20 years for machinery and equipment. Leasehold improvements are amortized over the shorter of the asset's life or the remaining contractual lease term.

Effective January 1, 2000, the Company prospectively revised the estimated useful lives and residual values of certain fixed assets based on the results of a comprehensive analysis completed in late 1999 of the Company's historical fixed asset experience. . . . The study confirmed that these programs have extended the useful lives of certain fixed assets, principally vehicles and cold drink equipment, and increased the value of certain assets upon disposition. These changes in accounting estimates generally result in certain of the Company's operating assets being depreciated over longer useful lives, although the Company's asset life ranges generally did not change. The changes in estimates decreased depreciation expense in 2000 by approximately $161 million. . . .

Source: Coca-Cola Enterprises, 2000 10-K.

d. Discuss the possible information content of the fact that both PBG and CCE changed estimated depreciation lives in the same year.

14. [Analysis of fixed assets] Roche's summary of significant accounting policies states:

> Property, plant and equipment are initially recorded at cost of purchase or construction and are depreciated on a straight-line basis, except for land, which is not depreciated. Estimated useful lives of major classes of depreciable assets are as follows:

Buildings and land improvements	40 years
Machinery and equipment	5–15 years
Office equipment	3 years
Motor vehicles	5 years

The following data were obtained from Roche's annual reports (the 1999 data are located in Note 12 of its 2000 annual report):

Property, plant, and equipment (CHF millions)

	1997	1998	1999
Buildings and land improvements:			
Gross investment	$ 7,576	$ 7,947	$ 8,578
Accumulated depreciation	(2,580)	(2,695)	(2,944)
Net investment	$ 4,996	$ 5,252	$ 5,634
Depreciation expense	233	195	210
Machinery and equipment:			
Gross investment	$10,529	$11,350	$13,174
Accumulated depreciation	(5,755)	(6,079)	(7,015)
Net investment	$ 4,774	$ 5,271	$ 6,159
Depreciation expense	692	948	1,036

a. Using the above data, compute each of the following ratios for all three years:

  (i) Average depreciable life (years)

  (ii) Average age (years)

  (iii) Average age (%)

b. Compare the result of part a (i) with the accounting policy statement above.

c. Discuss the three-year trend of the three ratios in part a for both fixed-asset classes.

d. State the questions you would ask management after reviewing parts a through c above.

15. [Impairment] Roche, in its report for the half-year ended June 30, 2000, adopted IAS 36 (Impairment), with the following disclosure:

> **'Impairment of assets'.** When the recoverable amount of an asset, being the higher of its net selling price and its value in use, is less than its carrying amount, then the carrying amount is reduced to its recoverable value. This re-

duction is reported as an impairment loss. Value in use is calculated using estimated cash flows, generally over a five-year period, with extrapolating projections for subsequent years. These are discounted using an appropriate long-term interest rate. Previously the permitted alternative method for calculating value in use was applied, whereby it was calculated using cash flow projections on an undiscounted basis.

As a result, the Group recognized impairment charges of 1,161 million Swiss francs relating to acquired intangible assets. A reduction in deferred tax liabilities of 348 million Swiss francs was also recorded, giving a net charge of 813 million Swiss francs in the consolidated results. Also included within this is a minor amount relating to impairment on a small number of products acquired in an earlier acquisition as a consequence of reduced market expectations. Under the Group's previous accounting policy, no impairment would have arisen. As a result of the impairment, the net book value of intangible assets was reduced by the amount of the impairment charge, and consequently amortization in the first half of 2000 was 64 million Swiss francs lower than it would have been under the previous policy.

a. Describe the effect of the accounting change on the year 2000:

  (i) Income before the effect of accounting changes

  (ii) Net income

  (iii) Stockholders' equity

  (iv) Cash from operations

b. Describe the effect of the accounting change on the year 2001:

  (i) Net income

  (ii) Return on equity

  (iii) Cash from operations

16. [Impairment and depreciation lives]. IEC Electronics [IECE], a provider of electronics manufacturing services, reported impairment charges in 1998 and 1999 and a change in asset lives in 1999. Exhibit 8P-4 contains extracts from IEC's 1999 annual report.

a. Discuss whether the 1999 impairment charge and depreciation change should have been a surprise when they were announced on September 30, 1999.

b. Discuss the effects of the 1998 and 1999 impairment charges on IEC's 1999:

  (i) Cash from operations

  (ii) Fixed-asset turnover

  (iii) Debt-to-equity ratio

c. Discuss the effects of the accounting change on IEC's 2000:

  (i) Net income

  (ii) Cash from operations

  (iii) Fixed-asset turnover

  (iv) Debt-to-equity ratio

EXHIBIT 8P-4. IEC ELECTRONICS
Financial Statement Extracts (year ended September 30, 1999)

Note 1. Business and Summary of Significant Accounting Policies:

Property, Plant, and Equipment

Property, plant, and equipment are stated at cost and are depreciated over various estimated useful lives using the straight-line method.

During the fourth quarter of 1999, the Company completed a review of its fixed asset lives and, in turn, shortened the estimated lives of certain categories of equipment, effective July 1, 1999. The change in estimate was based on the following: the downsizing of the business; the loss of certain "large run" customers which have forced the Company to utilize a quick change-over mentality; and changing technology, therefore obsoleting production equipment more quickly. The effect of this change in estimate increased depreciation for the year ended September 30, 1999 by approximately $4.7 million.

Long-Lived Assets

The Company reviews its long-lived assets and certain identifiable intangibles to be held and used for impairment whenever events or changes in circumstances indicate that the carrying amount of an asset may not be recoverable. If such events or changes in circumstances are present, a loss is recognized to the extent the carrying value of the asset is in excess of the sum of the undiscounted cash flows expected to result from the use of the asset and its eventual disposition.

During the fourth quarter of 1999, certain fixed assets were no longer in use and identified as impaired. The equipment has been marketed for sale, and as such, the carrying value of these assets was written down to the estimated recoverable sales value, net of commissions obtained from appraisals and used equipment quotations. The effect of this impairment recognition totaled approximately $400,000 and was included with depreciation expense for the year ended September 30, 1999.

Selected Consolidated Financial Data

| | *($thousands)* | | |
| | *Years Ended September 30,* | | |
	1999	1998	1997
Income Statement Data:			
Net sales	$157,488	$248,159	$260,686
Gross (loss) profit	(5,766)	13,640	28,094
Operating (loss) income	(22,051)	(7,554)	12,321
Net (loss) income	(20,565)	(6,160)	6,958
Balance Sheet Data:			
Long-term debt, less current maturities	$ 16,547	$ 7,138	$ 6,988
Shareholders' equity	48,845	69,568	75,461

Source: IEC Electronics, *Annual Report*, September 30, 1999.

9

ANALYSIS OF INCOME TAXES

CHAPTER OBJECTIVES

All business enterprises are subject to income tax. Its analysis, therefore, is an essential part of an overall firm analysis. In this chapter, we:

1. Examine the liability method used to account for income tax under U.S. and IAS GAAP.

2. Explain how the tax effects of operating losses are accounted for under the liability method.

3. Discuss how the valuation allowance affects the income statement and balance sheet.

4. Discuss the factors governing the level and trend of deferred tax assets and liabilities.

5. Evaluate the relevance of deferred tax assets and liabilities to firm valuation.

6. Describe the three different measures of the effective tax rate.

7. Differentiate between temporary and permanent differences between taxable income and pretax income.

8. Show how financial statement disclosures can be used to analyze and forecast the firm's effective tax rate.

9. Examine the relationship between deferred taxes and cash outflows for tax payments.

10. Discuss international differences in the accounting for income taxes.

INTRODUCTION

Differences in the objectives of financial and tax reporting make income taxes a troublesome issue in financial reporting. The objective of financial reporting is to provide users with information needed to evaluate a firm's financial position, performance, and cash flows. The accrual basis of financial reporting allows management to select revenue and expense recognition methods that best reflect performance and smooth or otherwise manage (maximize or minimize) reported net income. As discussed throughout the text, management incentives to manage reported income result from management compensation contracts, bond covenants, political considerations, and the (presumed) effect of those factors on financial markets.

Tax reporting, in contrast, is the product of political and social objectives. Current-period *taxable income* is measured using the modified cash basis; revenue and expense recognition methods used in tax reporting often differ from those used for financial reporting as the firm has strong incentives to select methods allowing it to minimize taxable income and, therefore, taxes paid, maximizing cash from operations.[1]

Thus, differences between *taxes payable* for the period and reported *income tax expense* result from:

- The difference between accrual and modified cash bases of accounting
- Differences in reporting methods and estimates

These differences create *deferred tax liabilities* (credits) and prepaid taxes or *deferred tax assets* (debits) that are difficult to interpret. There are disagreements as to (1) whether they are true assets or liabilities and (2) their usefulness as indicators of future cash flows. When these deferrals become very large, their interpretation can have a significant effect on the financial analysis of a firm or group of firms.

Note: Terminology related to income tax accounting can be confusing because two terms that seem similar can have very different meanings. A glossary of terms used in this chapter is therefore provided in Box 9-1. Each term in the glossary is shown in italics when first used in the chapter.

BASIC INCOME TAX ACCOUNTING ISSUES

Basic accounting issues are discussed in Box 9-2. There we provide a discussion and an illustration of how temporary differences between tax and financial reporting affect the balance sheet and the income statement. The box also contains a review of the impact of tax law and rate changes on deferred tax assets and liabilities. This permits us to focus on analytical issues in the chapter.

THE LIABILITY METHOD: SFAS 109 AND IAS 12

The central accounting issue is whether the tax effects of transactions for which GAAP-based and tax-based accounting rules differ should be recognized in the period(s) in which they affect taxable income (in which case no deferred taxes would be recognized) or in the period(s) in which they are recognized in the financial statements (giving rise to deferred taxes). These alternatives produce different measures of operating and financial performance, affecting the evaluation of a firm's operating performance and earning power. Cash flows for taxes are not affected by financial reporting choices except when conformity between tax and financial reporting is required.

---

[1]In countries such as Japan, Germany, and Switzerland, statutory financial reporting is required to conform to tax reporting. In these countries, the problems discussed in this chapter do not occur for statutory (usually, parent company only) statements. However, consolidated financial statements, for example, those prepared under IAS GAAP, do not conform to tax reporting and deferred tax issues must be dealt with. See the discussion of financial reporting practices outside the United States later in this chapter.

BOX 9-1
Glossary: Income Tax Accounting

Amounts in Tax Return:

Taxable income	Income subject to tax.
Taxes payable (current tax expense)	Tax return liability resulting from current period taxable income. SFAS 109 calls this "current tax expense or benefit"
Income tax paid	Actual cash outflow for income taxes, including payments (refunds) for other years.
Tax loss carryforward	Tax return loss that can be used to reduce taxable income in future years.

Amounts in Financial Statements:

Pretax income	Income before income tax expense.
Income tax expense	Expense based on current period pre-tax income; includes taxes payable and deferred income tax expense.
Deferred income tax expense	Accrued income tax expense expected to be paid (or recovered) in future years; difference between taxes payable and income tax expense. Under SFAS 109, the amount depends on changes in deferred tax assets and liabilities.
Deferred tax asset (debit)	Balance sheet amounts; expected to be recovered from future operations.
Deferred tax liability (credit)	Balance sheet amounts; expected to result in future cash outflows.
Valuation allowance	Reserve against deferred tax assets (debits) based on likelihood that those assets will not be realized.
Timing difference	The difference between tax return and financial statement treatment (timing or amount) of a transaction.
Temporary difference	Difference between tax and financial statement reporting, which will affect taxable income when those differences reverse; similar to but broader than timing differences (see footnote 3).

Note: SFAS 109 contains a more technical glossary of terms used in that standard.

Both U.S. and IAS standards are based on the liability method, which is consistent with the second alternative.[2] This method measures the balance sheet deferred tax assets and liabilities first, under the assumption that temporary differences will reverse. Income tax expense reflects both the effect of any current period pretax income and future changes in the tax rate used to measure the tax effect of tax expense resulting from those reversals.

Accounting for taxes in the United States is based on SFAS 109 (1992), whose two objectives are to recognize:

1. Taxes payable or refundable for the current year
2. The deferred tax liabilities and assets (adjusted for recoverability) measured as the future tax consequences of events that have been recognized in financial statements or tax returns

SFAS 109 recognizes the deferred tax consequences of *temporary differences*.[3] Deferred tax assets (adjusted for recoverability) and liabilities are calculated directly and reported on the balance sheet; *deferred income tax expense* used to determine reported income is a consequence of the resulting balance sheet amounts.

---

[2]The deferral method (also consistent with the second alternative) measures income tax expense first. Changes in deferred tax assets and liabilities result *only* from current year deferred tax expense. These assets and liabilities are based on tax rates when they originated; the effect of tax rate changes is recognized only when timing differences actually reverse.

[3]This concept extends beyond chronological (timing) differences (e.g., earlier recognition of revenues and expenses on either the financial statements or tax returns), and also includes certain other events that result in differences between the tax bases of assets and liabilities and their carrying amounts in financial statements. Such differences arise when

1. The tax basis of an asset is reduced by tax credits.
2. Investment tax credits are deferred and amortized.
3. The tax basis of a foreign subsidiary's assets is increased as a result of indexing.
4. The carrying amounts and tax bases of assets differ in purchase method acquisitions.

BOX 9-2
Basic Income Tax Accounting Issues

We use a simple example to illustrate the issues faced when tax accounting differs from accounting for financial statements. We begin this example assuming that depreciation is the only item of expense. Part A of Exhibit B9-1 depicts income tax reporting where the company depreciates a $6,000 asset over two years, giving rise to *taxes payable* of $800, $800, and $2,000 over the three-year period.

For financial reporting (Part B), the firm depreciates the asset over three years. *Pretax income* exceeds taxable income in the first two years; taxable income is higher in year 3.* What *tax expense* should the company report in its financial statements?

Part B1 displays one approach (not permitted under U.S. GAAP) where the tax expense equals taxes payable. Pretax income is the same for all three years, but tax expense differs as the tax deferred in earlier years is paid in year 3. As a result, tax expense, as a percentage of pretax income, does not reflect the prevailing statutory tax rate, 40%. The reported tax rate is 26.7% for the first two years and 66.7% for year 3.

Timing Differences: Deferred Tax Liabilities

Part B2 illustrates the U.S. GAAP treatment, SFAS 109, which requires the recognition of deferred tax liabilities when future taxable income is expected to exceed pretax income. IAS 12 has the same requirement. In our example, pretax income exceeds taxable income in years 1 and 2, but year 3 taxable income is expected to exceed pretax income by $2,000. At the end of years 1 and 2, a deferred tax liability of $400 (timing difference of $1,000 × 40% tax rate) is recognized to reflect the tax on the $1,000 *timing difference* that will be paid in year 3. This liability is reported each year as a portion of that year's tax expense. Thus, income tax expense is $1,200 in both years 1 and 2: tax payable or current tax expense ($800) plus *deferred income tax expense* ($400). The matching principle is satisfied as the relationship between revenues and expenses (40% tax rate) is maintained. At the end of year 2, the cumulative timing difference is $2,000 and the aggregate deferred tax liability is $800.

No tax depreciation remains to be recorded in year 3, but book depreciation expense equals $2,000. At the end of year 3, the machine has been fully depreciated for both tax and financial reporting purposes. The effect of the year 1 and 2 timing differences must be reversed; year 3 income tax expense equals $1,200 or taxes payable ($2,000) *less* the reversal of the deferred tax liability of $800 accumulated over the first two years.

Timing Differences: Deferred Tax Assets

Differences between financial accounting and tax accounting can also give rise to *deferred tax assets* (debits) when future pretax income is expected to exceed taxable income. Part B3 introduces another timing difference, warranty expense, which gives rise to a deferred tax asset in years 1 and 2. As warranty payments are tax-deductible when paid rather than when accrued, larger amounts are charged to warranty expense earlier for financial statement purposes; tax deductions occur in later periods when the repairs or replacement services are provided.

As shown in part B3,[†] the firm recognizes a warranty expense of $500 in each of years 1 and 2, but receives no tax deduction because no expenditures are incurred in those years. The higher taxable income results in a prepayment of taxes; tax expense in the financial statements reflects lower pretax income. The difference of $500 in each of the first two years generates a deferred tax debit of $200 ($500 × 0.40) each year and decreases tax expense by that amount each year. At the end of year 2, there is a deferred tax asset of $400.

In year 3, tax-deductible expenditures of $1,500 are incurred for repairs, reducing taxable income and tax payments. These expenditures exceed the $500 of financial statement warranty expense of year 3 by $1,000; equal to the total additional expense accrued in the first two years. The temporary difference reverses, deferred income tax expense is reduced by $400 ($1,000 × 0.40), and the deferred tax debit generated during the first two years is eliminated.[‡]

Comprehensive Example: Deferred Tax Liabilities and Deferred Tax Assets

Exhibit B9-1 separately illustrates the treatment of timing differences that gave rise to a deferred tax liability and a deferred tax asset. In practice, firms report both deferred tax assets and liabilities, resulting from multiple timing differences. Exhibit B9-2 shows the accounting when a firm has both types of timing differences.

Taxes payable equal the tax rate multiplied by taxable income and reflect the effects of tax depreciation and allowable warranty deductions on the tax return. Income tax expense is based on pretax income, which reflects financial statement depreciation and estimated warranty expense for products sold. Over the three-year period, total revenues are $15,000, total depreciation expense is $6,000, and total warranty expense is $1,500 for both financial and tax reporting. The timing of expense recognition differs, but the total amount is the same.[§]

---

*Of the $3,000 pretax income reported in years 1 and 2, $1,000 (the excess tax depreciation) is not subject to taxes in those years. The $2,000 (2 × $1,000) deferred in the first two years is subject to taxation in the third as taxable income ($5,000) exceeds pretax income ($3,000) by $2,000.

[†]In part B3, we ignore depreciation expense to illustrate the accounting treatment of timing differences that generate deferred tax assets.

[‡]In these examples, income tax expense could also have been computed by applying the income tax rate of 40% directly to pretax income in each year. However, in more complex situations, discussed later, this approach would produce a different result.

[§]Warranty expense and actual repair costs are assumed to be identical for illustration only; it is difficult to predict the frequency and level of repair costs perfectly. Bad debt expenses and litigation losses are other examples of timing differences where predictions are uncertain.

Note: Box 9-2 continues through page 298 and includes Exhibits B9-1 through B9-3.

EXHIBIT B9-1
Alternative Approaches to Reported Income Tax Expense

Assumptions:

- The firm purchases a machine costing $6,000 with a three-year estimated service life and no salvage value.
- For financial reporting purposes, the firm uses straight-line depreciation over the three-year life.
- For income tax reporting, the machine is depreciated over two years using the straight-line depreciation method.
- Products manufactured using the machine generate annual revenues of $5,000 for three years.
- The statutory tax rate is 40% in all three years.

Part A. Income Tax Reporting: Straight-line Depreciation over Two Years

	Year 1	Year 2	Year 3	Total
Revenues	$5,000	$5,000	$5,000	$15,000
Depreciation expense	(3,000)	(3,000)	0	(6,000)
Taxable income	$2,000	$2,000	$5,000	$ 9,000
Taxes payable @ 40%	(800)	(800)	(2,000)	(3,600)
Net income	$1,200	$1,200	$3,000	$ 5,400

Part B. Financial Statements: Straight-line Depreciation over Three Years

B1: Flow-Through Method—Not Permitted by GAAP

- No recognition of deferred taxes.
- Tax expense defined as taxes payable.

	Year 1	Year 2	Year 3	Total
Revenues	$5,000	$5,000	$5,000	$15,000
Depreciation expense	(2,000)	(2,000)	(2,000)	(6,000)
Pretax income	$3,000	$3,000	$3,000	$ 9,000
Tax expense = taxes payable	(800)	(800)	(2,000)	(3,600)
Net income	$2,200	$2,200	$1,000	$ 5,400

B2: SFAS 109 and IAS 12—Deferred Tax Liabilities

- Recognition of deferred taxes.
- Tax expense differs from taxes payable.

	Year 1	Year 2	Year 3	Total
Revenues	$5,000	$5,000	$5,000	$15,000
Depreciation expense	(2,000)	(2,000)	(2,000)	(6,000)
Pretax income	$3,000	$3,000	$3,000	$ 9,000
Tax expense @ 40%	(1,200)	(1,200)	(1,200)	(3,600)
Net income	$1,800	$1,800	$1,800	$ 5,400
Taxes payable (from part A)	800	800	2,000	3,600
Deferred tax expense	400	400	(800)	0
Balance sheet deferred tax liability	400	800	0	N. A.

EXHIBIT B9-1 *(continued)*

Journal Entries

Years 1 and 2: Origination of the deferred tax liability

Tax expense	$1,200	
Deferred tax liability		$ 400
Taxes payable		800

Year 3: Reversal of the deferred tax liability

Tax expense	$1,200	
Deferred tax liability	800	
Taxes payable		$2,000

B3: SFAS 109 and IAS 12—Deferred Tax Assets

Assumption: Warranty expenses estimated at 10% of revenues each year; all repairs provided in year 3

Income Tax Reporting	Year 1	Year 2	Year 3	Total
Revenues	$5,000	$5,000	$5,000	$15,000
Warranty expense	0	0	(1,500)	(1,500)
Taxable income	$5,000	$5,000	$3,500	$13,500
Tax payable @ 40%	(2,000)	(2,000)	(1,400)	(5,400)
Net income	$3,000	$3,000	$2,100	$ 8,100

Financial Statements				
Revenues	$5,000	$5,000	$5,000	$15,000
Warranty expense	(500)	(500)	(500)	(1,500)
Pretax income	$4,500	$4,500	$4,500	$13,500
Tax expense @ 40%	(1,800)	(1,800)	(1,800)	(5,400)
Net income	$2,700	$2,700	$2,700	$ 8,100
Prepaid (deferred) tax	200	200	(400)	0
Balance sheet deferred tax asset	200	400	(400)	N. A.

Journal Entries

Years 1 and 2: Origination of deferred tax assets

Tax expense	$1,800	
Deferred tax asset	200	
Taxes payable		$2,000

Year 3: Reversal of deferred tax asset

Tax expense	$1,800	
Deferred tax asset		$ 400
Taxes payable		1,400

EXHIBIT B9-2
Financial Reporting Under SFAS 109

Income Tax Reporting	Year 1	Year 2	Year 3	Total
Revenues	$5,000	$5,000	$5,000	$15,000
Depreciation expense	(3,000)	(3,000)	0	(6,000)
Warranty expense	0	0	(1,500)	(1,500)
Taxable income	$2,000	$2,000	$3,500	$ 7,500
Tax payable @ 40%	(800)	(800)	(1,400)	(3,000)
Net Income	$1,200	$1,200	$2,100	$ 4,500
Financial Statements				
Revenues	$5,000	$5,000	$5,000	$15,000
Depreciation expense	(2,000)	(2,000)	(2,000)	(6,000)
Warranty expense	(500)	(500)	(500)	(1,500)
Pretax income	$2,500	$2,500	$2,500	$ 7,500
Tax expense @ 40%	(1,000)	(1,000)	(1,000)	(3,000)
Net Income	$1,500	$1,500	$1,500	$ 4,500
Deferred tax expense	400	400	(800)	0
Balance sheet deferred tax liability	400	800	0	N. A.
Prepaid tax	200	200	(400)	0
Balance sheet deferred tax asset	200	400	0	N. A.

Journal Entries

Years 1 and 2: Origination of deferred tax liabilities and deferred tax assets

Tax expense	$1,000	
Deferred tax asset	200	
Deferred tax liability		$ 400
Taxes payable		800

Year 3: Reversal of deferred tax liabilities and deferred tax assets

Tax expense	$1,000	
Deferred tax liability	800	
Deferred tax asset		$ 400
Taxes payable		1,400

Do the deferred tax liabilities at the end of years 1 and 2 actually represent a liability for tax payments due in year 3? Similarly, does the deferred tax asset qualify as an asset? In this simple case, they do, as the forecast reversals occurred as expected and the firm did not engage in any other transactions with timing differences. In the real world, the answer is not so clear; these are important issues from an analytical perspective and the chapter provides a comprehensive discussion of those issues.

Effect of Tax Rate and Tax Law Changes

The balance sheet orientation of SFAS 109 requires adjustments to deferred tax assets and liabilities to reflect the impact of a change in tax rates or tax laws. Using the example in Exhibit B9-2, Exhibit B9-3 depicts the impact of a tax rate decrease from 40% to 35% at the beginning of year 2. In panel A, we assume that the future tax decrease *was enacted before* the year 1 financial statements were prepared. Panel B illustrates the accounting under

the assumption that the year 2 tax decrease *was enacted after* year 1 financial statements were prepared.

Panel A: Future Tax Rate Change Enacted in Current Year.

Taxes payable for year 1 are based on the current tax rate of 40%, and the deferred tax assets and liabilities are based on the tax rate expected to be in effect when the differences reverse, 35%.

Note that year 1 tax expense as a percentage of pretax income (the effective tax rate) is 39% ($975/$2,500): a weighted average of the current tax rate of 40% and the 35% rate that will be in effect when the timing differences that gave rise to the deferred taxes reverse. There is no attempt to match income tax expense directly with pretax income, and one cannot calculate tax expense directly by multiplying pretax income by the current tax rate. For years 2 and 3, the calculations are similar to those in Exhibit B9-2 except that the new tax rate of 35% (rather than 40%) is used for all calculations.

EXHIBIT B9-3
Impact of Tax Rate Change: The Liability Method

Assumptions

Identical to Exhibit B9-2

- A firm purchases a machine costing $6,000 with a three-year estimated service life and no salvage value.
- For financial reporting purposes, the firm uses straight-line depreciation with a three-year life.
- For income tax reporting, the machine is depreciated straight-line over two years.
- The machine is used to manufacture a product that will generate annual revenue of $5,000 for three years.
- Warranty expenses are estimated at 10% of revenues each year; all repairs are provided in year 3.

A. Year 2 Tax Rate Change Enacted in Year 1

Year 1: Tax Rate = 40%

Year 2 Tax Rate Will Be 35%

Selected T-Accounts

			Deferred Tax Asset	Deferred Tax Liability
Income tax expense	975			
Deferred tax asset	175			
Deferred tax liability		350	$175	$350
Taxes payable		800	$175	$350

Year 2: Tax Rate = 35%

			Deferred Tax Asset	Deferred Tax Liability
			$175	$350
Income tax expense	875			
Deferred tax asset	175		175	
Deferred tax liability		350		350
Taxes payable		700	$350	$700

Year 3: Tax Rate = 35%

			Deferred Tax Asset	Deferred Tax Liability
			$350	$700
Income tax expense	875			
Deferred tax liability	700			700
Deferred tax asset		350	350	
Taxes payable		1,225	$ 0	$ 0

Calculations

	Temporary Differences			
	Depreciation (Liability)	Warranty (Asset)	Taxes Payable	Income Tax Expense
Year 1	35% × $1,000	35% × $(500)	40% × $2,000	$350 − $175 + $ 800
Year 2	35% × 1,000	35% × (500)	35% × 2,000	350 − 175 + 700
Year 3	35% × (2,000)	35% × 1,000	35% × 3,500	− 700 + 350 + 1,225

B. Year 2 Tax Rate Change Enacted in Year 2

Year 1: Tax Rate = 40%

Selected T-Accounts

			Deferred Tax Asset	Deferred Tax Liability
Income tax expense	1,000			
Deferred tax asset	200			
Deferred tax liability		400	$200	$400
Taxes payable		800	$200	$400

EXHIBIT B9-3 *(continued)*

Year 2: Tax Rate Reduced to 35%

(i) Adjustment of Prior-Year Deferrals

			Deferred Tax Asset		Deferred Tax Liability	
Deferred tax liability	50		$200			$400
Deferred tax asset		25		25	50	
Income tax expense		25	$175			$350

(ii) Current Year Operations

			Deferred Tax Asset		Deferred Tax Liability	
Income tax expense	875		$175			$350
Deferred tax asset	175		175			
Deferred tax liability		350				350
Taxes payable		700	$350			$700

Year 3: Tax Rate = 35%

			Deferred Tax Asset		Deferred Tax Liability	
Income tax expense	875		$350			$700
Deferred tax liability	700				700	
Deferred tax asset		350		350		
Taxes payable		1,225	$ 0			$ 0

Calculations

	Temporary Differences			
	Depreciation (Liability)	Warranty (Asset)	Taxes Payable	Income Tax Expense
Year 1	40% × $1,000	40% × $(500)	40% × $2,000	$400 − $200 + $800
Year 2	(5%) × 1,000	(5%) × (500)		−50 + 25
	35% × 1,000	35% × (500)	35% × 2,000	350 − 175 + 700
Year 3	35% × (2,000)	35% × 1,000	35% × 3,500	−700 + 350 + 1,225

Panel B: Future Tax Rate Change Enacted after Year 1 Statements Have Been Prepared.

Calculations for year 1 tax expense, taxes payable, and deferred taxes are based on the year 1 tax rate of 40% and are identical to those in Exhibit B9-2. A deferred tax asset of $200 and a deferred tax liability of $400 are created.

In year 2, when the rate decrease is effective, two steps are necessary to calculate the current year's tax expense:

1. Exhibit B9-3B illustrates the restatement of end of year 1 deferred tax asset and liability balances to the new (lower) tax rate of 35% (assumed to be in effect when the deferred taxes will be paid). Year 2 tax expense is reduced (income is increased) since the lower rate reduces the expected tax payment when the depreciation difference reverses, partially offset by a lower expected tax benefit when the warranty expense difference reverses. The adjustment results in a deferred tax asset of $175 and liability of $350.**

2. The taxes payable and deferred taxes arising from current year operations are calculated using the new rate of 35%.

Tax expense for year 2 is calculated as follows:

Adjustment of Year 1 Balances to New Rate:

Deferred tax asset of $200 restated to $175	$ 25
Deferred tax liability of $400 restated to $350	(50)

Year 2 Taxes Payable and New Temporary Differences:

Taxes payable = $2,000 taxable income × 35%	700
Deferred tax asset = $500 temporary difference × 35%	(175)
Deferred tax liability = $1,000 temporary difference × 35%	350
Income tax expense	$850

Note that, as in panel A, the income tax expense of $850 is affected by changes in the deferred tax liability and asset accounts and there is no attempt to directly match the relationship of tax expense to pretax income.

**These balances are now identical to those shown in panel A of the exhibit when the tax law change was known prior to the issuance of the year 1 financial statements. The only difference between the two panels is the timing of the restatement at the lower rate.

IAS 12 (2000) is also based on the liability method, with minor differences. Those differences are explained in the "Financial Reporting Outside the United States" section of this chapter.

Deferred Tax Liabilities

SFAS 109 emphasizes tax liabilities, focusing on the balance sheet. *The standard mandates the recognition of deferred tax liabilities for all temporary differences expected to generate net taxable amounts in future years.*

The FASB argued that deferred tax consequences of temporary differences that will result in net taxable amounts in future years meet the SFAC 6 definition of liabilities.[4] The board contended that deferred taxes are legal obligations imposed by tax laws and temporary differences will affect taxable income in future years as they reverse.

Treatment of Operating Losses

Operating losses are due to an excess of tax deductions over taxable revenues. Tax losses can be carried back to prior years to obtain refunds of taxes paid; the impact of the carryback on income tax expense is recognized in the loss period because it can be measured and is recoverable.

Tax losses may also be carried forward to future periods if insufficient taxes were paid during the carryback period or the firm would lose valuable tax credits if losses were carried back to that period. Because the realization of *tax loss carryforwards* depends on future taxable income, the expected benefits are recognized as deferred tax assets. Under SFAS 109, such assets are recognized in full but a *valuation allowance* may be required if recoverability is unlikely.

Deferred Tax Assets and the Valuation Allowance

SFAS 109 is permissive regarding the recognition of deferred tax assets whenever deductible temporary differences generate an operating loss or tax credit carryforward. However, management (and its auditors) must defend recognition of all deferred tax assets. A valuation allowance reducing the deferred tax asset is required if an analysis of the sources of future taxable income suggests that it is more likely than not that some portion or all of the deferred tax asset will not be realized.[5]

■ Example

Bethlehem Steel [BS] reported a net deferred tax asset at December 31, 2000 of about $985 million ($1,325 million less a valuation allowance of $340 million). This asset equaled 88% of stockholders' equity on that date. The company provided a valuation allowance equal to 50% of the deferred tax asset related to operating loss carryforwards and some temporary differences. BS stated,

> Based on our current outlook for 2001 and beyond, we believe that our net deferred tax asset will be realized by future operating results, asset sales, and tax planning opportunities.[6]

In the quarter ended June 30, 2001, however, BS recognized a 100% valuation allowance for its deferred tax assets, increasing income tax expense and net loss for the

---

[4]A common temporary difference is a firm's use of longer depreciation lives for financial reporting than for tax return reporting, creating a difference between the carrying amount of the asset and its tax basis. Use of the asset in operations results in taxable income in the year(s) no depreciation can be recorded on the tax return. The board acknowledged that other events may offset the net taxable amounts that would be generated when temporary differences reverse, but because those events have not yet occurred, and they are not assumed in the financial statements, their tax consequences should not be recognized. See SFAS 109 (paras. 75–79) for more discussion of this issue.

[5]Sources of future taxable income include existing taxable temporary differences, future taxable income net of reversing temporary differences, taxable income recognized during qualifying carryback periods, and applicable tax-planning strategies.

[6]*Source:* Note D to 2000 financial statements.

quarter by $1,009 million ($7.77 per diluted share) and for the first half of 2001 by $984 million ($7.58 per diluted share). Mainly due to the increased valuation allowance, Bethlehem's equity at June 30, 2001 became negative. The company stated that it now expected a financial accounting and tax loss in 2001 and that the outlook for the balance of 2001 was worse than earlier anticipated. Given its record of cumulative financial accounting losses, excluding unusual items, SFAS 109 required the increased valuation allowance. This is an excellent example of how management discretion with respect to the amount and timing of recognition of the valuation allowance affords management significant opportunity to manage earnings.

Tax-planning strategies can be used to reduce required valuation allowances, but they must be disclosed. SFAS 109 provides examples of positive and negative evidence that must be weighed to determine the need for a valuation allowance and to measure the amount of the allowance.[7] *Changes in the valuation allowance are included in income from continuing operations except when they are generated by unrecognized changes in the carrying amount of assets or liabilities.*[8]

Bethlehem reported that it expected to realize the deferred tax assets from future operating results and tax planning opportunities. The company included choices of depreciation methods and lives, sales of assets, and the timing of contributions to the pension trust fund as examples of tax-planning opportunities.

When there are significant deferred tax assets, the analyst should review the company's financial performance and its accounting choices to assess the likelihood of realization of those assets. ■

Financial Statement Presentation and Disclosure Requirements

Large multinational companies operate in dozens of tax jurisdictions and their financial reports must summarize their tax position for all consolidated entities. Such firms often generate deferred tax assets and liabilities in different tax jurisdictions. *SFAS 109 permits offsets of deferred tax effects only within each tax-paying component and tax jurisdiction of the firm.*

■ **Example**

Texaco reported (Note 8) a valuation allowance of $800 million at December 31, 1999, mostly related to foreign tax loss carryforwards and related book versus tax asset differences stemming from operations in Denmark. The company notes that the valuation allowance was required because these loss carryforwards are based on individual (oil and gas) fields and cannot be netted against taxable income from other fields. ■

Deferred tax assets and liabilities must be separated into current and noncurrent components based on the types of the assets and liabilities generating the deferral. However, deferred tax assets due to carryforwards are classified by reference to expected reversal dates. SFAS 109 specifically requires:

1. Separate disclosure of all deferred tax assets and liabilities, any valuation allowance, and the net change in that allowance for each reporting period.

2. Disclosure of any unrecognized deferred tax liability for the undistributed earnings of domestic or foreign subsidiaries and joint ventures. These disclosures should facilitate the comparison of the operating results of firms that have different policies with respect to deferred tax recognition or the remission of income from such affiliates.

---

[7]Existing contracts or backlogs expected to be profitable, appreciated assets, earnings over the past few years, and the nature (nonrecurring) of the loss would suggest that a valuation allowance is not needed. Examples of negative evidence include cumulative losses in recent years and the past inability to use loss or tax credit carryforwards.

[8]The most common example is the deferred tax assets that arise when the market value of "available-for-sale" securities is less than cost; the unrealized loss is included in equity, under SFAS 115, net of the related deferred income tax assets. See Chapter 13 for further discussion.

3. Disclosure of the current-year tax effect of each type of temporary difference.
4. Disclosure of the components of income tax expense.
5. Reconciliation of reported income tax expense with the amount based on the statutory income tax rate (the reconciliation can use either amounts or percentages of pretax income).
6. Disclosure of tax loss carryforwards and credits.

These six requirements determine income tax disclosures in financial statements, the raw material for the analysis provided later in this chapter.

DEFERRED TAXES: ANALYTICAL ISSUES

Estimates of the firm's future cash flows and earning power and the analysis of financial leverage must consider changes in deferred tax assets and liabilities, deferred tax expense, and any changes in the valuation allowance. *The key analytic issue is whether the deferred tax assets and liabilities will reverse in the future. If they will not, then it is highly debatable whether deferred taxes are assets or liabilities (that is, have cash flow consequences); it may be more appropriate to consider them as decreases or increases to equity.*

To resolve that issue, we need to understand the factors that determine the level of and trends in reported deferred taxes, to decide whether they are assets (or liabilities) and to evaluate their expected cash consequences.

Factors Influencing the Level and Trend of Deferred Taxes

In general, temporary differences originated by individual transactions will reverse and offset future taxable income and tax payments. However, *these reversals may be offset by other transactions, for example, newly originating temporary differences*. The cash consequences of deferred tax debits and credits depend on the following factors:

- Future tax rates and tax laws
- Changes in accounting methods
- The firm's growth rate (real or nominal)
- Nonrecurring items and equity adjustments

We discuss these factors next.

Effects of Changes in Tax Laws and Accounting Methods

Management incentives for choosing revenue and expense recognition methods on the tax return and financial statements differ, as mentioned previously. Choices (and subsequent changes) of tax and/or accounting methods determine taxes payable, income tax expense, and both the amounts and rate of change of reported deferred tax balances.

Under the liability method,[9] when a new tax law is enacted its effects must be recognized immediately. Thus, lower tax rates will reduce deferred tax liabilities and assets, and the adjustment is included in current-period income tax expense. Assuming a net deferred tax liability, equity will increase. The larger the net deferred tax liability, the greater the impact of the tax cut, as previous-year deferrals are adjusted to the lower rate. For analytical purposes, one need not wait for the actual tax change to be enacted; estimates can be made when legislation is proposed.

Changes in GAAP can also significantly impact deferred taxes. For example, in 1992, many companies adopted SFAS 106, Accounting for Postretirement Benefits Other Than Pensions. That standard (see Chapter 12) required accrual accounting for postretirement costs (mainly medical benefits for current employees after retirement) rather than cash-basis

---

[9]See the illustration in Exhibit B9-3 of Box 9-1.

accounting. As cash-basis accounting was used for income tax purposes, there was no temporary difference associated with these benefits prior to the adoption of SFAS 106.

■ **Example**

Upon adoption of SFAS 106 in 1992, duPont recognized a postretirement benefit liability of $5.9 billion and deferred tax asset of $2.1 billion. Was this $2.1 billion an asset? Would it reduce future taxes? The answers depend on the $5.9 billion liability associated with it. Eight years later, at December 31, 2000, duPont's postretirement benefit liability was $5.76 billion. Benefits paid exceeded cost recognized in both 1999 and 2000, reducing the liability. Assuming this trend continues, duPont will realize the deferred tax asset, but over a very long time period. A fair-value balance sheet should recognize the discounted present value of the deferred tax asset rather than its gross amount.

Thus, *realization of a deferred tax asset or liability depends on the realization of the temporary difference that created it.* ■

Effect of the Growth Rate of the Firm

For most firms, the deferred tax liability grows over time; temporary differences do not reverse on balance.[10] For growing firms, increased or higher-cost investments in fixed assets result in ever-increasing deferred tax liabilities due to the use of accelerated depreciation methods for tax reporting.

Exhibit 9-1 illustrates this effect by focusing on the deferred tax consequences of depreciation differences. Assume that a firm purchases one machine each year for $6,000 and uses the straight-line depreciation method over two years on its tax return and over three years in its financial statements. If we assume a 40% tax rate and zero residual value on both the tax return and the financial statements, the depreciation differences will produce a deferred tax expense (a deferred tax liability) of $400 in each year during the first two years of each machine's operation, with a reversal of $800 in its third year to eliminate the deferred tax liability generated over the first two years.

The acquisition of a second machine in year 2 generates another difference of $400; the deferred tax liability increases to $1,200 at the end of year 2. In year 3, the firm acquires and uses the third machine, originating its first-year temporary difference, and the asset acquired in year 2 originates its second-year difference. However, these originating differences are offset by the reversal of the accumulated temporary differences on the machine acquired in year 1 as it is depreciated in the financial statements, but no depreciation remains to be recorded for the asset on the tax return.

The deferred tax liability remains $1,200 and *stabilizes at that level* if asset acquisitions, depreciation methods, and tax rates and tax laws remain unchanged. Increased asset purchases above present levels (either in physical quantity or due to higher prices) would result in a growing deferred tax liability as originations exceeded reversals. Thus, as a result of growth, either in real or nominal terms, the net deferred tax liability will increase over time; *in effect, it will never be paid*.

If the firm reduces its acquisition of fixed assets and reversals exceed originations, the related deferred tax liability will decline. The cash consequences of this scenario, however, are uncertain. If the decrease in asset acquisitions results from declining product demand, then lower asset acquisitions may be accompanied by poor profitability. Without taxable in-

---

[10]This statement may not apply to deferred tax assets. Deferred tax assets (more precisely, prepaid taxes) stem from both recurring transactions (such as deferred revenues, warranty expenses, management compensation, employee benefits, and bad-debt reserves), and from more irregular events (such as restructuring costs, impairments, environmental remediation obligations, and provisions for litigation losses) that are accrued on the financial statements prior to their deduction on the tax return.

Management often has substantial discretion over the amount and timing of the origination of these debit balances as it controls the recognition of these expenses. However, the amount and timing of their reversal may not be as discretionary or predictable as the temporary differences (such as depreciation differences) that generate deferred tax liabilities.

EXHIBIT 9-1
Impact of Growth on Deferred Tax Liability

Assumptions

A firm purchases one machine during each year of operation. All other assumptions are identical to those used in Exhibit B9-1. Most important, temporary differences are originated and reversed as in Exhibit B9-1 and at the same tax rate, which is assumed to remain constant over time.

Deferred Tax Liability

Year 1	$ 400	Machine 1 (origination)
Year 2	400	Beginning balance
	400	Machine 1 (origination)
	400	Machine 2 (origination)
Year 3	$1,200	Beginning balance
	(800)	Machine 1 (reversal)
	400	Machine 2 (origination)
	400	Machine 3 (origination)
Year 4	$1,200	Beginning balance
	(800)	Machine 2 (reversal)
	400	Machine 3 (origination)
	400	Machine 4 (origination)
Year 5	$1,200	Beginning balance

Note: The balance stabilizes at $1,200 in this example at the end of year 3, with the originations exactly offset by the reversals. This result assumes constant levels of asset acquisitions, price levels, tax rates, and regulations. Increases in either price levels or acquisitions would result in rising balances of deferred tax liabilities.

come, the deferred taxes will never be paid. Alternatively, the firm may originate other temporary differences that offset depreciation reversals; in the aggregate, deferred tax liabilities may not decline.

The cash consequences of reversing temporary differences, therefore, depend on both future profitability and other activities of the firm that affect future taxable income.

Effects of Nonrecurring Items and Equity Adjustments

The following may also affect income tax expense, taxes paid, and deferred tax assets and liabilities:

- Nonrecurring items
- Extraordinary items
- Accounting changes
- Equity adjustments

Nonrecurring items (such as restructuring charges) may have future as well as current-period tax consequences, and complicate the analysis of the firm's tax position. Texaco, for example, reported restructuring changes in 1999, as detailed throughout its MD&A. These charges generated deferred tax assets.

Extraordinary items, such as a loss from the early retirement of debt, are reported after tax; the tax effect is often shown separately in the tax footnote. Transition effects of accounting changes often generate deferred tax effects, especially when the new method is not a permitted method of tax reporting. The large deferred tax asset resulting from the adoption of SFAS 106 (as discussed using duPont) is a typical example.

Finally, equity adjustments that bypass the income statement may have current and deferred tax consequences. Common examples include:

- Unrealized gains or losses on marketable securities (see Chapter 13)
- Currency translation adjustments (see Chapter 15)

The items discussed above may obscure the cash and deferred tax effects of continuing operations. Although firms generally disclose their associated tax effect, discerning their cash and deferred tax impact may require careful reading of the tax footnote supplemented by discussions with management.

Liability or Equity?

How should analysts treat deferred tax liabilities in the analysis of a firm's solvency?

As indicated above, changes in a firm's operations or tax laws may result in deferred taxes that are never paid (or recovered). Moreover, a firm's growth may continually generate deferred tax liabilities. Even if temporary differences do reverse, future losses may forestall tax payments. These factors suggest that, in many cases, deferred taxes are unlikely to be paid.

Even if deferred taxes are eventually paid, the present value of those payments is considerably lower than the stated amounts. Thus, the deferred tax liability should be discounted at an appropriate interest rate.[11]

These arguments suggest that the components of the deferred tax liability should be analyzed to evaluate the likelihood of reversal or continued growth. Only those components that are likely to reverse should be considered a liability.[12] In addition, the liability should be discounted to its present value based on an estimate of the year(s) of reversal. If the temporary differences giving rise to deferred tax liabilities are not expected to reverse, those amounts should not be considered liabilities.

SFAS 109 requires disclosure of the components of the deferred tax liability at each year-end. These components should be examined over time to see which tend to reverse and which do not. For example, the effect of using accelerated depreciation methods for tax reporting tends not to reverse.[13] If reversal is expected, as capital expenditures decline, the liability should be discounted to present value. Similar analysis can be applied to other major differences, keeping in mind any expected tax law changes.

To the extent that deferred taxes are not a liability, then they are stockholders' equity. Had they not been recorded, prior-period tax expense would have been lower and both net income and equity higher. This adjustment reduces the debt-to-equity ratio, in some cases considerably.[14]

In some cases, however, deferred taxes are neither liability nor equity. For example, if tax depreciation is a better measure of economic depreciation than financial statement depreciation, adding the deferred tax liability to equity overstates the value of the firm. However, if the deferred tax liability is unlikely to result in a cash outflow, it is not a liability either. Ultimately, the financial analyst must decide on the appropriate treatment of deferred taxes on a case-by-case basis.

In practice, the analytical treatment of deferred tax liabilities varies. Some creditors, notably banks, do not consider them to be liabilities (but neither do they include them as part of equity). In calculating solvency and other ratios, many analysts ignore deferred taxes altogether.

---

[11]Discounting of deferred taxes is not allowed under either U.S. or IAS GAAP and is rare elsewhere. It is currently allowed in the Netherlands; however, few firms discount. The UK accounting standard FRS 19, Deferred Tax, permits but does not require discounting of deferred tax liabilities (only for the time value of money) that are not expected to settle for some time.

[12]Prior to the issuance of FRS 19, Deferred Tax, the United Kingdom allowed partial allocation and deferred taxes were recognized only when reversal was expected within the foreseeable future.

[13]However, the recognition of fixed asset impairment (see the discussion in Chapter 8) may instantaneously offset many years of accelerated depreciation. Such writedowns do not affect tax reporting unless the affected assets are sold. As a result, previously established deferred tax liabilities relating to these assets reverse. If the carrying value of the impaired assets is reduced below their tax basis, deferred tax assets must be established. But this reversal has no effect on taxable income or, therefore, taxes payable. This is another case where the reversal of temporary differences may not generate income tax cash outflows.

[14]Some creditors treat deferred tax liabilities as debt. In this case, there is a double effect; debt is decreased and equity increased by the same amount, with an even greater decrease in the debt-to-equity ratio.

BOX 9-3
Valuation of Deferred Taxes

Surprisingly, not many empirical studies have examined whether the market as a whole treats deferred taxes as debt. However, the results of those few studies that examined this issue are consistent with our view that the extent to which deferred tax liabilities should be treated as debt is a function of the probability that the deferrals will be reversed and the debt (if considered) should be discounted to its present value.

Amir, Kirschenheiter, and Willard (1997) found that, overall, deferred taxes are value relevant in explaining the cross-sectional variation in market values of equity. However, the degree of value relevance was related to the probability of future reversal. For example, the valuation coefficient on deferred tax liabilities arising from depreciation was close to zero, reflecting investors' expectations that firms would continue to invest in depreciable assets, increasing the likelihood that tax deferrals would not reverse in the future. On the other hand, deferred tax components related to restructurings had the highest valuation coefficients, consistent with an expectation that they would reverse in the short run (as written-down plants are sold at a loss and/or severance payments are made to employees).

Givoly and Hayn (1992) examined these issues in the context of the Tax Reform Act (TRA) of 1986. The TRA cut the statutory tax rate for U.S. corporations from 46% to 34%. This rate reduction reduced both the current tax obligation and the amount that would have to be repaid if and when future reversals of temporary differences occurred.

The TRA was debated for over two years in Congress. Givoly and Hayn examined the effects on stock prices of events that increased (decreased) the chance of the measure passing. After controlling for the effects on current tax payments, they argued that if the market treated the deferred tax liability as debt, then:

1. The larger the deferred tax liability, the more positive the impact of the TRA on the firm's market price.
2. If temporary differences will not be reversed, or future tax losses will result in nonpayment of the tax at reversal, the effects of the TRA should be minimal regardless of the liability amount. Thus, they argued that the larger the growth rate in

the deferred tax account and the greater the probability of tax losses; the less likely there would be a positive impact on stock prices.

If the market ignored the deferred tax liability, none of these factors would have any impact. Overall, their results confirmed that the market incorporated the deferred tax liability into valuation.

When chances of the TRA adoption increased (decreased), then:

1. The larger the deferred tax liability, the more positive (negative) the market reaction.
2. A high liability growth rate and increased probability of losses decreased (increased) the abnormal return.

Givoly and Hayn also found that the market incorporated a discount factor in valuing the deferred tax liability. The deferred tax accounts of high-risk* firms tended to affect market valuation less than low-risk firms. This result is consistent with a higher discount rate being applied to the higher-risk firms.

Sansing (1998), and Guenther and Sansing (2000), however, using a theortical model, demonstrate analytically that deferred taxes should have value-relevance[†] *irrespective of the probability of eventual reversal.* However, the valuation coefficient on deferred taxes (which in their model is a function of the tax depreciation rate and the (market) rate of interest) is *considerably less than one.* Thus, they argue that the findings of Amir et al. and Givoly and Hayn should not be interpreted as reflecting the effects of the expected timing of the reversal of deferred taxes.

The above studies took a balance sheet perspective and found that deferred taxes are incorporated in valuation. Beaver and Dukes (1972), with an income statement perspective, had also found that market prices reflect the deferral method. They found that market reaction was more closely associated with income that incorporated deferred income taxes than with current tax expense.[‡] Rayburn (1986), however, found that the association between deferred tax accruals and security returns was dependent on the expectations model assumed.

---

*Based on the firm's market beta.

[†]Their reasoning is that, according to their model, the market (resale) value of the asset includes the tax basis of the asset. Deferred taxes reflect this factor, although not on a dollar-for-dollar basis.

[‡]The authors found this result surprising as they expected the measure closer to cash flow (earnings without deferral) to be more closely associated with security prices. In a subsequent paper (Beaver and Dukes, 1973) the authors offered a different explanation. They demonstrated (see the discussion in Chapter 8) that the market generally imputes accelerated depreciation rather than straight-line depreciation. As deferred taxes increase total expense for firms using straight-line depreciation, they argued that the observed results may be due to deferred taxes masking as a form of accelerated depreciation.

Standard and Poor's, a major U.S. rating agency, includes noncurrent deferred taxes in permanent capital for its computation of pretax return on permanent capital. However, it does not consider deferred tax liabilities as debt.[15]

Box 9-3 discusses evidence provided by market research regarding the relevance of deferred taxes to securities valuation. The evidence indicates that the market incorporates the

---

[15]See Standard and Poor's "Formulas for Key Ratios," *Corporate Ratings Criteria* (New York: McGraw-Hill, 2000), p. 55.

growth rate of an entity, the probability of reversal of deferred taxes, and the time value of money in its assessment of deferred taxes as liability or equity.

Analysis of Deferred Tax Assets and the Valuation Allowance

Deferred tax assets may be indicators of future cash flow, reported income, or both. Therefore, as with liabilities, one should examine the source of those assets and evaluate the likelihood and timing of reversal. Any valuation allowance should also be reviewed. To the extent that deferred tax assets have been offset by a valuation allowance, realization of those assets will increase reported income (and stockholders' equity) as well as generate cash flow. If no valuation allowance has been provided, then realization will have no effect on reported income or equity, although cash flow will still benefit.

Conversely, when deferred tax assets are no longer realizable, if no valuation allowance had been provided, then the establishment of such an allowance reduces reported income and equity (see the Bethlehem Steel example earlier in the chapter).

Given management discretion, the valuation allowance has become another factor used to evaluate the quality of earnings. Some firms are conservative, offsetting most or all deferred tax assets with valuation allowances. Other firms are more optimistic and assume that no valuation allowance is necessary.

The important point is that changes in the valuation allowance often affect reported earnings and can be used to manage them.

■   **Example**

Apple Computer had recorded a significant valuation allowance against its deferred tax assets due to losses in the mid-1990s. With its return to profitability, it realized its loss carryforwards, reducing both deferred tax assets and the valuation allowance. The result was to lower the effective tax rate, as seen below:

Apple Computer

	Years Ended September 30			Percent Change	
Amounts in $millions	1998	1999	2000	1999	2000
As reported:					
Pretax income	$329	$ 676	$1,092	105%	62%
Income tax expense	(20)	(75)	(306)		
Net income	$309	$ 601	$ 786	94%	31%
Tax rate	6.1%	11.1%	28.0%		
Change in valuation allowance	$ (97)	$(153)	$ (27)		
Excluding valuation allowance:					
Pretax income	$329	$ 676	$1,092	105%	62%
Income tax expense	(117)	(228)	(333)		
Net income	$212	$ 448	$ 759	111%	69%
Tax rate	35.6%	33.7%	30.5%		

Apple's pretax income increased by 105% in 1999 and 62% in 2000. The growth rate of net income was lower due to the diminishing effect of the valuation allowance. However, net income was inflated by the valuation allowance reductions. To eliminate these distortions, analysis should be based on net income excluding changes in the valuation allowance.   ■

Effective Tax Rates

Valuation models that forecast future income or cash flows use the firm's effective tax rate as one input. Moreover, trends in effective tax rates over time for a firm and the relative effective tax rates for comparable firms within an industry can help assess operating performance and the income available for stockholders. Several alternative measures can be used to assess the firm's effective tax rate. The *reported* effective tax rate is measured as:

$$\frac{\text{Income tax expense}}{\text{Pretax income}}$$

However, both reported tax expense and pretax income are affected by management choices of revenue and expense recognition methods. Although pretax income is a key indicator of financial performance and is an appropriate denominator, other numerators generate tax rates that provide additional information.[16]

The first alternative tax rate uses taxes payable (current tax expense) for the period, based on the revenue and the expense recognition methods used on the tax return:

$$\frac{\text{Taxes payable}}{\text{Pretax income}}$$

This ratio may also be used with cash taxes paid instead of taxes payable. The resulting ratio focuses more on cash flows:

$$\frac{\text{Income tax paid}}{\text{Pretax income}}$$

The amount of cash taxes paid can be easily obtained as both SFAS 95 (Statement of Cash Flows) and IAS 7 (Cash Flow Statements) require separate disclosure of this amount. Due to interim tax payments and refunds, cash taxes paid may be quite different from taxes payable.

Exhibit 9-2 calculates these differing measures of the effective tax rate for Pfizer.

Pfizer's reported effective tax rate (income tax expense/pretax income) rose from 27.0% in 1997 to 28% in 1999; the three-year average rate is 26.9%. All these rates are below the U.S. statutory rate for the period.[17]

Two questions are suggested by these data:

1. Why is Pfizer's effective tax rate below the statutory rate?
2. What is Pfizer's effective tax rate likely to be in the future?

We seek answers to these questions shortly.

The second effective tax rate (taxes payable/pretax income) calculated in Exhibit 9-2 was 35.4% in 1998 and 28.4% in both 1997 and 1999. The average rate is 30.3% over the three-year period, above the first effective rate and below the statutory rate. Again, we will try to understand the factors causing these differences and the likelihood that they will persist in the future.

The third measure of the effective tax rate, which compares income tax paid with pretax income, is also variable over the three-year period. The average rate of 32.0% is

---

[16]Some empirical evidence (see Zimmerman, 1983) indicates that effective tax rates calculated using income tax paid and/or current tax expense tend to be higher for large firms. This is cited as evidence of the political cost hypothesis as large firms, being more politically sensitive, are required to make (relatively) larger wealth transfers than smaller firms. As the research results are largely due to the oil and gas industry, it is difficult to tell whether political costs result from size or industrial classification. Wang (1991) notes that because smaller firms are more likely to have operating losses than larger firms, their effective tax rate is more likely to be zero. Ignoring these losses may bias Zimmerman's research results.

[17]The average statutory rate for a multiyear period should be a weighted average, with pretax income providing the weights.

EXHIBIT 9-2. PFIZER
Effective Tax Rates

	1997	1998	1999	Total
Taxes payable	$ 815	$ 918	$1,265	$2,998
Deferred tax expense	(40)	(276)	(21)	(337)
Income tax expense	$ 775	$ 642	$1,244	$2,661
Income taxes paid	809	1,073	1,293	3,175
Pretax income	2,867	2,594	4,448	9,909
Statutory tax rate	35.0%	35.0%	35.0%	35.0%
Income tax expense/pretax income	27.0%	24.7%	28.0%	26.9%
Taxes payable/pretax income	28.4%	35.4%	28.4%	30.3%
Taxes paid/pretax income	28.2%	41.4%	29.1%	32.0%

Source: Data from Pfizer annual reports.

close to the average rate for taxes payable. This congruence should be expected as the timing of taxes paid is affected by technical payment requirements and by errors in management's forecast of tax liability in each jurisdiction. Over time, these factors should cancel out.

We return to the analysis of Pfizer's income tax position shortly. To provide additional background for that analysis, we must first discuss the effect of temporary versus permanent differences on effective tax rates and other specialized issues that highlight differences between tax and financial reporting.

ACCOUNTING FOR TAXES: SPECIALIZED ISSUES

Temporary versus Permanent Differences

The different objectives of financial and tax reporting generate temporary differences between pretax financial income and taxable income. In addition, *permanent differences* result from revenues and expenses that are reportable either on tax returns or in financial statements but not both. In the United States, for example, interest income on tax-exempt bonds, premiums paid on officers' life insurance, and amortization of goodwill (in some cases) are included in financial statements but are never reported on the tax return. Similarly, certain dividends are not fully taxed, and tax or statutory depletion may exceed cost-based depletion reported in the financial statements.

Tax credits are another type of permanent difference. Such credits directly reduce taxes payable and are different from tax deductions that reduce taxable income. The Puerto Rico operations credit reported by Pfizer is one example. It partially exempts Pfizer from income, property, and municipal taxes.

No deferred tax consequences are recognized for permanent differences; however, they result in a difference between the effective tax rate and the statutory tax rate that should be considered in the analysis of effective tax rates.

Indefinite Reversals

The amount and timing of the reversal of some temporary differences are subject to management influence or control. Some differences may never reverse. The accounting for these differences is especially troublesome. The uncertainty as to the amount and timing of their cash consequences affects the estimation of cash flows and firm valuation.

The undistributed earnings of unconsolidated subsidiaries and joint ventures are the most common example of this problem. The U.S. tax code requires 80% ownership to consolidate for tax purposes, excluding joint ventures and many subsidiaries that are consolidated for accounting purposes. In addition, foreign subsidiaries are not consolidated in the U.S. tax return.[18]

As a result, the income of these affiliates is taxable on the parent's (U.S.) tax return only when dividends are received or the affiliate is sold, not when earnings are recognized. There is a difference between (tax return) taxable income and (financial reporting) pretax income. If the affiliate earnings are permanently reinvested, then affiliate earnings may never be taxable on the parent company's tax return.

SFAS 109 requires the recognition of deferred tax liabilities for temporary differences due to the undistributed earnings of essentially permanent domestic subsidiaries and joint ventures for fiscal years beginning on or after December 15, 1992.[19] SFAS 109 does not, however, require deferred tax provisions in the following cases:

- Undistributed earnings of a foreign subsidiary or joint venture that are considered to be permanently reinvested.
- Undistributed earnings of a domestic subsidiary or joint venture for fiscal years prior to December 15, 1992.

In its income tax note (Note 9), Pfizer reports that the firm has not recorded a U.S. tax provision of $1.9 billion on $8.2 billion of undistributed earnings of foreign affiliates at December 31, 1999. If the indefinite reversal assumption had not been applicable, the firm would have reported $1.9 billion of additional deferred tax liabilities, reducing equity by 21%. Earnings would also have been reduced in the years during which those provisions were not made.

Accounting for Acquisitions

SFAS 109 requires separate recognition of the deferred tax effects of any differences between the financial statement carrying amounts and tax bases of assets and liabilities recognized in purchase method acquisitions (see Chapter 14).

In some cases, a valuation allowance must be recorded for deferred tax assets due to the acquired firm's temporary differences or its operating loss or tax credit carryforwards. The tax benefits of subsequent reversals of the valuation allowance must be used, first, to reduce all related goodwill, second, to eliminate all other related noncurrent intangible assets, and third, to reduce reported income tax expense.

ANALYSIS OF INCOME TAX DISCLOSURES: PFIZER

Accounting for income taxes is complex; a large company may have many permanent and temporary differences between financial statement income and taxable income. A large multinational pays taxes in a number of jurisdictions, further complicating the process. From an analyst's perspective, unraveling these layers can seem daunting indeed.

Some analysts respond to this complexity by ignoring the issues. They analyze corporate performance on a pretax basis and simply accept that variations in the reported tax rate occur. We agree that analysis on a pretax basis is sound, but also believe that a firm's income tax accounting is too important to ignore.

The goals of income tax analysis are to:

1. Understand why the firm's effective tax rate differs (or does not differ) from the statutory rate in its home country.
2. Forecast changes in the effective tax rate, improving forecasts of earnings.
3. Review the historical differences between income tax expense and income taxes paid.

---

[18]In some cases, even wholly owned U.S. subsidiaries may not be consolidated for tax purposes. Insurance subsidiaries, which are governed by special tax regulations, are one example.

[19]But if the parent has the statutory ability to realize those earnings tax free, no deferred tax provision is required (para. 33, SFAS 109).

4. Forecast the future relationship between income tax expense and income tax payments.
5. Examine deferred tax liabilities and assets, including any valuation allowance, for
   - Possible effects on future earnings and cash flows
   - Their relevance to firm valuation
   - Their relevance in assessing a firm's capital structure

We pursue these five goals, using Pfizer as an example, and illustrate the insights regarding a firm that can be derived from its income tax disclosures.

Analysis of the Effective Tax Rate

The first step is an examination of the firm's tax rate, the trend in that rate, and the rate relative to similar companies. Variations are generally the consequence of:

- Different statutory tax rates in different jurisdictions; analysis can offer important clues as to the sources of income.
- Tax holidays that some countries offer; earnings from such operations usually cannot be remitted without payment of tax. Be alert to possible changes in the operations in such countries or the need to remit the accumulated earnings.
- Permanent differences between financial and taxable income: tax-exempt income, tax credits, and nondeductible expenses.
- The effect of tax rate and other tax law changes which, under SFAS 109, are included in income tax expense (a separate disclosure of this effect is required).
- Deferred taxes provided on the reinvested earnings of foreign affiliates and unconsolidated domestic affiliates.

As noted earlier, Pfizer's effective tax rate averaged 26.9% over the 1997 to 1999 period. Pfizer's tax footnote provides the required reconciliation between its statutory rate and effective rate for each year.[20] Because of the significance of some of these differences and variation in pretax income over the period, the rate-based disclosures are difficult to analyze. For that reason, Exhibit 9-3 converts them to dollar-based disclosures.

Starting with the three-year totals, the lower tax rate on non-U.S. earnings is the largest single factor in Pfizer's low effective tax rate, deducting nearly $500 million or 5 percentage points over the three-year period. Pfizer's international operations accounted for 39% of revenues and 42.5% of income from continuing operations in 1999, as shown in Pfizer's segment data. Thus, Pfizer's low effective tax rate is largely a function of its non-U.S. operations. Forecasting future effective tax rates, therefore, requires explicit forecasts of the earnings of these operations.

Pfizer's effective tax rate also benefits from lower tax rates paid by partially tax-exempt operations in Puerto Rico. This factor reduced the composite three-year tax rate by nearly two percentage points, adding $175 million to net income. Pfizer provides additional data regarding these operations, permitting a determination of the remaining benefits. Unexplained "other" benefits averaging 1.5 percentage points per year (but with considerable variability) further reduce the effective tax rate. Discussion with management should result in a better understanding of the source and likelihood of continuation of these benefits. The Belgian tax assessment[21] and the limited term of the Puerto Rican tax exemption suggest that significant contributors to Pfizer's lower effective tax rate may not be available in the future.

---

[20]The reconciliation can be done in either percentages (relative to the statutory tax rate) or monetary amounts (relative to "statutory" income tax expense equal to pretax income multiplied by the statutory rate).

[21]However, Pfizer may have benefited from the allocation and transfers of property to selected foreign operations. In 1994, Belgian tax authorities assessed additional taxes ($432 million) and interest ($97 million), claiming jurisdiction on certain income related to property transferred from non-Belgian subsidiaries to Pfizer's operations in Ireland.

EXHIBIT 9-3. PFIZER
Reconciliation of Effective and Statutory Tax Rates

	1997	1998	1999	1997 to 1999	
				Total	Rate
Pretax income	$2,867	$2,594	$4,448	$9,909	
Statutory rate	35.0%	35.0%	35.0%		35.0%
Variations from Statutory Rate (in percent)					
Partially tax-exempt operations in Puerto Rico	−1.8%	−2.2%	−1.5%		
International operations	−5.0%	−5.5%	−4.8%		
Other-net	−1.2%	−2.5%	−0.7%		
Net difference	−8.0%	−10.2%	−7.0%		
Effective tax rate (Income tax expense/ pretax income)	27.0%	24.7%	28.0%		
Tax in millions of dollars = Rate × Pretax Income					
At statutory rate	$1,003.5	$ 907.9	$1,556.8	$3,468.1	
Effect of					
Partially tax-exempt operations in Puerto Rico	$ (51.6)	$ (57.1)	$ (66.7)	$ (175.4)	−1.8%
International operations	(143.4)	(142.7)	(213.5)	(499.5)	−5.0%
Other-net	(34.4)	(64.9)	(31.1)	(130.4)	−1.3%
Net effect	$ (229.4)	$(264.6)	$ (311.4)	$ (805.3)	−8.1%
Income tax expense	$ 774.1	$ 643.3	$1,245.4	$2,662.8	26.9%

Source: Adapted from Pfizer, Note 9, 1999 annual report.

Now that we understand the reasons for Pfizer's low effective tax rate in the past, we turn to the future. A forecast of future income tax expense should start with estimated pretax income and apply the statutory rate of 35%. The analyst should then adjust for:

- Effects of the lower tax rate on foreign income
- Effects of the lower tax rate on U.S. possession operations
- "Other" effects

These adjustments may require input from Pfizer management or trade publications. Some firms provide periodic forecasts of their tax rate because of the difficulty of making such forecasts externally.

Analysis of Deferred Income Tax Expense

We now examine the effects of temporary differences on income tax expense. Companies are required to provide details of these differences, although formats vary. Pfizer's disclosure is typical, showing a breakdown in dollars for each year.

Temporary differences are generally the result of the use of different accounting policies or estimates for tax purposes than for financial reporting differences. Some of these differences are systematic; others are transaction specific. Frequent examples include:

- *Depreciation.* Different methods and/or lives result in different measures of depreciation expense.
- *Impairment.* Financial reporting writedowns do not generate tax deductions unless assets are sold.
- *Restructuring costs.* Usually tax-deductible when paid rather than when accrued.

- *Inventories.* Companies using last-in, first-out (LIFO) accounting for tax purposes in the United States must also use LIFO for reporting purposes; but when other methods are used, differences may occur.
- *Postemployment benefits.* The accruals required by SFAS 87 (pensions), SFAS 106 (other retiree benefits), and SFAS 112 (other post-employment benefits) are discussed in Chapter 12. Tax treatment of these costs is generally cash based, generating deferred tax effects.
- *Deferred compensation.* Tax-deductible only when payments are made.

On a cumulative basis, Pfizer generated negative deferred tax expense (taxes payable > income tax expense) over the 1997 to 1999 period.[22] Depreciation generated positive deferred tax expense over this period, reflected in a rising level of deferred tax liabilities for property, plant, and equipment (PP&E). Pfizer used accelerated depreciation methods for most property on its tax return and the straight-line method on its financial statements.

Pfizer also reports deferred tax debits from PP&E, likely due to its asset impairments in both 1997 and 1998. Pfizer reports that, in 1999, it had substantially completed the restructuring announced in 1998; the deferred tax debits due to restructuring and PP&E declined in 1999 after increasing in 1998. *When a restructuring charge is taken, the tax effects generally occur as expenditures are made, with significant effects on deferred tax expense both in the year of the charge and the year(s) of payment.*

Pfizer's Note 9 also shows numerous other sources of deferred tax assets and liabilities, some of them poorly explained. Significant year-to-changes in deferred tax balances reflect differences between the tax and financial reporting treatment of transactions, and should be examined for their implications for cash flow and quality of earnings. The most significant deferred tax assets relate to inventories and employee benefits. There is a significant deferred tax liability for "unremitted earnings." These items are discussed below as part of the analysis of deferred tax assets and liabilities.

Because Pfizer's deferred tax expense was negative over the 1997 to 1999 period, taxes payable (and income tax paid) exceeded income tax expense. Given increasing deferred tax debits for inventories, employee benefits, foreign tax credit, and other carryforwards, deferred tax expense may remain negative in the future.

Using Deferred Taxes to Estimate Taxable Income

Deferred tax expense reflects the difference between taxable income reported to tax authorities and pretax income reported to shareholders. This relationship can be used to estimate components of taxable income. The difference between taxable income and pretax income equals

$$\frac{\text{Deferred tax expense}}{\text{Statutory tax rate}}$$

For example, Pfizer's 1999 financial statement depreciation expense was $499 million (depreciation and amortization expense of $542 reported in the statement of cash flows less amortization of $43 million for goodwill and other intangibles in Note 8). The deferred tax liability related to depreciation was $514 million in 1999, an increase of $81 million over the amount reported in 1998 (Note 9). Using that amount and the statutory tax rate of 35%, we estimate that the additional depreciation expense under tax reporting was $231 million ($81 million divided by 0.35) and tax basis depreciation was $730 million ($499 + $231).

These calculations should be viewed as estimates. They are most reliable when they relate to a single tax jurisdiction as the appropriate tax rate and the difference between tax and financial reporting rules are clear. Although this method can, in theory, be used to calculate taxable income for the entire firm, such calculations for large multinationals are less reliable.

---

[22]See Note 9 in Pfizer's financial statements and data in Exhibit 9-2.

Similar calculations can be made for the cumulative financial reporting-tax differences using deferred tax asset and liability data. The calculation for Pfizer's fixed assets is shown in the next section of this chapter.

Deferred tax disclosures can also be used, in some cases, to estimate the taxes paid associated with components of income and expense.

Analysis of Deferred Tax Assets and Liabilities

Our final step is an examination of the balance sheet consequences of Pfizer's income tax accounting. As required by SFAS 109, Note 9 contains a table of significant deferred tax assets and liabilities, as well as the valuation allowance, at each balance sheet date.

The most significant deferred tax asset relates to accrued employee benefits. Financial reporting rules for pension and postretirement benefits (see Chapter 12) often result in large deferred tax assets. The second-largest deferred tax asset is associated with inventories, probably due to the 1999 Trovan write-off. Other contributors include prepaid/deferred items, restructuring charges, and various carryforwards. Pfizer reports a valuation allowance of $27 million at December 31, 1999 ($30 million at December 31, 1998). Note 9 says that tax credit carryforwards are the source of that allowance.

Pfizer's largest single source of deferred tax liabilities, as for most firms, is depreciation. If we assume a 35% tax rate for all depreciation-related deferred tax credits, the reporting difference can be estimated as $1.47 billion ($514/0.35) or 55% of accumulated depreciation of $2.7 billion. This is due to Pfizer's use of accelerated depreciation for tax purposes compared with straight-line for financial reporting.

Another source of large deferred tax credits is unremitted earnings of subsidiaries and joint venture affiliates that are included in financial statement income; the tax return only reflects dividends received.

Pfizer's net balance sheet debit (asset) for income tax is:

Deferred tax debits	$2,109
Less: valuation allowance	(27)
Less: deferred tax credits	(1,456)
Net debits	$ 626

Where do these debits and credits appear on Pfizer's balance sheet? The answer is: *in several places*. As required by SFAS 109, Note 9 discloses their location (in $millions):

Assets		*Liabilities*	
Prepaid expenses and taxes	$744		
Other assets, deferred taxes, and deferred charges	183	Deferred taxes on income	$301
Totals	$927		$301
		Net debit	$626

Is this $626 million a real asset? Or, to rephrase the question, What are the likely future cash flow effects of Pfizer's deferred tax assets and liabilities?

We begin with the largest deferred tax liability associated with accumulated depreciation. Capital expenditures have been rising (79% since 1997); unless there are decreases in capital spending, it seems unlikely that the deferred tax liability from depreciation will decline over the next few years. The trend in capital spending must, however, be monitored. Based on data available in the annual report, deferred tax credits due to unremitted earnings and other sources seem unlikely to reverse.

Pfizer's largest deferred tax asset, related to accrued employee benefits, might start to reverse at some point if employee levels stabilize or decrease. As retiree benefit payments increase, they may exceed the accrual for additional benefits earned (as in the case of duPont, discussed earlier). Trends in these amounts can be monitored using the techniques in Chapter

12. The deferred tax debit from restructuring charges will reduce tax payments as severance payments are made and impaired PP&E is sold.

In total, therefore, it appears unlikely that Pfizer's deferred tax accruals will generate any significant cash flows over the next few years. In addition, given the unlikelihood of near-term reversal, the deferred tax credit should be discounted for the time value of money. The combination of these factors suggests that neither an asset nor a liability should be recognized for valuation purposes.

Other Issues in Income Tax Analysis

The following issues, although not relevant to an analysis of Pfizer, occur frequently enough to warrant brief mention:

- Watch for companies that report substantial income for financial reporting purposes but little or no taxes payable (implying little or no taxable income). Such differences often reflect aggressive revenue and expense recognition methods used for financial reporting, and low quality of earnings. In such cases, caution is indicated as the methods used for financial reporting purposes may be based on optimistic assumptions.[23]

- Look for current or pending reversals of past temporary differences. For example, a decline in capital spending may result in a greater proportion of depreciation coming from old assets that have already been heavily depreciated for tax purposes. Thus, financial reporting depreciation may exceed tax depreciation, generating a tax liability.

- Remember that deferred tax assets and liabilities may point to near-term cash consequences. Restructuring provisions often generate little cash or tax effect in the year they occur, but substantial effects in following years.

- Tax law changes may also result in the reversal of past temporary differences. In the United States, tax law changes in recent years have curtailed the use of the completed contract and installment methods for tax purposes, generating substantial tax liabilities for affected companies.

FINANCIAL REPORTING OUTSIDE THE UNITED STATES

As already noted, many foreign jurisdictions require conformity between financial reporting and tax reporting in separate (parent company) financial statements. In such cases, the issues discussed in this chapter do not occur. That statement is no longer true, however, once consolidated statements include subsidiaries that are not consolidated for tax purposes. Given the worldwide tendency toward consolidated reporting, even firms in tax-conformity countries must grapple with the question of deferred tax accounting.

IASB Standards

IAS 12 (revised 2000) requires use of the liability method but *permits* companies to use "indefinite reversal" criteria to avoid recognizing deferred taxes on the reinvested earnings of subsidiaries, associates, and joint ventures, when both of the following conditions are met:

1. The parent, investor, or venturer can control the manner and timing of the reversal of the temporary difference.

2. It is probable that the temporary difference will not reverse in the foreseeable future.

As a result, there are significant differences in the recognition of deferred tax liabilities among firms using IAS and U.S. GAAP; the latter group must record deferred taxes for the

---

[23]Empirical evidence also suggests that firms cannot costlessly increase financial reporting income and at the same time keep taxable income very low. Mills (1998) shows that IRS audit adjustments increase as book–tax differences increase; that is, "The more book income (or tax expense) exceeds taxable income (or tax payable), the greater the proposed IRS audit adjustments."

reinvested earnings of domestic affiliates. In addition, deferred taxes are based on enacted laws and rates whereas IAS 12 uses substantially enacted rates (tax rate changes that have been announced by the government but not yet enacted).

Other National Standards

Virtually all countries require the recognition of deferred taxes on temporary differences. Germany and the United Kingdom use the liability method, whereas France and Japan allow either the deferral (see footnote 2) or liability method. Most countries limit the recognition of deferred tax liabilities and few address the issue of deferred tax assets. In Switzerland, deferred taxes not expected to reverse need not be recognized and the recognition of certain deferred tax assets is discretionary.

German GAAP permits the recognition of deferred tax assets for the elimination of intercompany profits. In general, deferred taxes are computed under the liability method, but the amounts recognized are limited to the excess of consolidated deferred tax liabilities over consolidated deferred tax assets.

The accounting differences among U.S., IAS, and foreign GAAP affect reported net income and stockholders' equity (lower when deferred tax assets are unrecognized or offset by a valuation allowance). Another difficulty when comparing firms using different GAAP is the paucity of disclosure requirements in many cases. Both SFAS 109 and IAS 12 have substantial disclosure requirements; similar information is rarely available in the financial statements of most foreign countries.

Form 20-F reconciliations of reported net income and stockholders' equity show the adjustments due to differences in deferred tax accounting. These differences can be used to restore comparability between U.S. firms and foreign firms that file Form 20-F. In some cases, these adjustments can be used to approximate adjustments for firms not providing Form 20-F reconciliations, when they are similar to firms that do provide them.

Exhibit 9-4 contains disclosures provided by Cadbury Schweppes in its 2000 Form 20-F. Applying UK GAAP, the company calculated deferred tax liabilities of £105 million (1999: £93) using the partial allocation method.[24] Had it used comprehensive allocation (U.S. GAAP), it would have recorded an additional deferred tax liability of £58 million in 2000 (1999: £62 million); most of the difference is attributed to the accelerated depreciation method. No deferred tax is recorded for the effect of accelerated depreciation because it is not expected to reverse.

Although we have recommended this approach in the section "Liability or Equity" and agree that partial allocation is a logical alternative to the comprehensive allocation method, it presents two analytical problems. First, it makes Cadbury's financial statements not comparable to its U.S. competitors, Coca-Cola and PepsiCo, who use comprehensive allocation. Comparability can be restored either by adjusting Cadbury's income statement provision, its deferred taxes (and equity), or by converting its competitors' financial statements to the partial allocation method.

The second problem with partial allocation is management discretion that can be used to manage earnings. This discretion is comparable to that available in the application of valuation allowances under SFAS 109 and IAS 12.

In December 2000, the UK Accounting Standards Board issued FRS 19, Deferred Tax, requiring comprehensive allocation. Cadbury will most likely adopt this standard in 2002 and the resulting financial statements will be more comparable to its U.S. competitors. The UK–U.S. GAAP reconciliation in the form 20-F as it relates to deferred taxes is reproduced in Panel B of Exhibit 9-4. On December 31, 2000, the U.S. GAAP–based deferred tax liability is £163 million (1999: £152 million). This information can be used to make Cadbury's financial statements comparable to those of its U.S. competitors.

---

[24]The partial allocation method in UK GAAP limits the recognition of net deferred tax assets to amounts expected to be recovered without the assumption of future taxable income. The standard is permissive regarding deferred tax consequences of pension and postretirement benefits; firms may use either comprehensive or partial allocation with disclosure of the method selected.

EXHIBIT 9-4. CADBURY SCHWEPPES

Panel A—Deferred Taxes: Partial Allocation

The analysis of the deferred tax liabilities/(assets) included in the financial statements at the end of the year is as follows:

in £millions	1999	2000
Accelerated capital allowances	£ 2	£ 3
Other timing differences	91	102
Deferred taxation liability	£93	£105

The deferred taxation liability is included in provisions for liabilities and charges. Gross deferred tax assets at year-end are £15 million (1999: £18 million). The potential liability for deferred taxation not provided comprised:

in £millions	1999	2000
UK accelerated capital allowances	£48	£77
UK property values	5	5
Other timing differences	9	(30)
	£62	£52

To the extent that dividends from overseas undertakings are expected to result in additional taxes, appropriate amounts have been provided. No taxes have been provided for other unremitted earnings since these amounts are considered permanently reinvested by subsidiary undertakings and in the case of associated undertakings the taxes would not be material. Distributable earnings retained by overseas subsidiary undertakings and the principal associated undertakings totaled approximately £846 million at 31 December 2000. The remittance of these amounts would incur tax at varying rates depending on available foreign tax credits.

    Tax losses carried forward as at 31 December 2000 for offset against future earnings of overseas companies were approximately £103 million (1999: £103 million). The utilization of losses is dependent upon the level of future earnings and other limiting factors within the countries concerned. Tax losses totaling £22 million have expiration periods in 2001 and 2002, tax losses of £25 million expire in 2003 to 2012 and tax losses totaling £56 million have no expiry date.

Panel B—US GAAP

The US GAAP analysis of deferred tax liability is as follows:

in £millions	1999	2000
Liabilities		
Fixed asset timing differences	£ 84	£ 84
Other timing differences	71	79
	£155	£163
Assets		
Operating loss carryforwards	(37)	(37)
Less: Valuation allowance	37	37
Net deferred tax liability	£155	£163

Source: Cadbury *20-F,* December 31, 2000

SUMMARY

In this chapter, we have seen how income tax expense and deferred tax assets and liabilities are affected by the accounting method used and by management choices and assumptions. As all business enterprises are subject to income tax, no financial analysis is complete until the issues raised in this chapter have been examined. Analysts must examine, in particular, the effective tax rate, the cash flow effects of deferred tax accruals, and the relevance of such accruals for valuation.

Chapter **9**

Problems

1. [Deferred tax classification; CFA© adapted] Explain in which of the following categories deferred taxes can be found. Provide an example for each category in your answer.

   (i) Current liabilities

   (ii) Long-term liabilities

   (iii) Stockholders' equity

   (iv) Current assets

   (v) Long-term assets

2. [Deferred taxes; CFA© adapted] State which of the following statements are correct under SFAS 109. Explain why.

   (i) The deferred tax liability account must be adjusted for the effect of enacted changes in tax laws or rates in the period of enactment.

   (ii) The deferred tax asset account must be adjusted for the effect of enacted changes in tax laws or rates in the period of enactment

   (iii) The tax consequences of an event must not be recognized until that event is recognized in the financial statements.

   (iv) Both deferred tax liabilities and deferred tax assets must be accounted for based on the tax laws and rates in effect at their origin.

   (v) Changes in deferred tax assets and liabilities are classified as extraordinary items in the income statement.

3. [Permanent versus temporary differences; CFA© adapted]

a. Define *permanent differences* and describe two events or transactions that generate such differences.

b. Describe the impact of permanent differences on a firm's effective tax rate.

4. [Treatment of deferred tax liability; CFA© adapted]

a. When computing a firm's debt-to-equity ratio, describe the conditions for treating the deferred tax liability:

   (i) As equity

   (ii) As debt

b. Provide arguments for excluding deferred tax liabilities from both the numerator and the denominator of the debt-to-equity ratio.

c. Describe the arguments for including a portion of the deferred taxes as equity and a portion as debt.

5. [Depreciation methods and deferred taxes] The Incurious George Company acquires assets K, L, and M at the beginning of year 1. Each asset has the same cost, a five-year life, and an expected salvage value of $3,000. For financial reporting, the firm uses the straight-line, sum-of-the-years' digits, and double-declining-balance depreciation methods for assets K, L, and M, respectively. It uses the double-declining-balance method for all assets on its tax return; its tax rate is 34%. Depreciation expense of $12,000 was reported for asset L for financial reporting purposes in year 2. Using this information:

a. Calculate the tax return depreciation expense for each asset in year 2.

b. Calculate the financial statement depreciation expense for assets K and M in year 2.

c. Calculate the deferred tax credit (liability) or debit (asset) for each asset at the end of:

   (i) Year 2

   (ii) Year 5

6. [Analysis of deferred tax; CFA© adapted] On December 29, 2000, Mother Prewitt's Handmade Cookies Corp. acquires a numerically controlled chocolate chip-milling machine. Due to differences in tax and financial accounting, depreciation for tax purposes is $150,000 more than depreciation in the financial statements, adding $52,500 to deferred taxes. At the same time, Mother Prewitt's sells $200,000 worth of cookies on an installment contract, recognizing the $100,000 profit immediately. For tax purposes, however, $80,000 of the profit will be recognized in 2001, requiring $27,200 of deferred taxes.

a. Compare the expected cash consequences of the two deferred tax items just described.

b. Explain your treatment of deferred taxes when calculating Mother Prewitt's solvency and leverage ratios.

c. In 2001, Mother Prewitt's tax rate will be 40%. Discuss the adjustments to *each* of the two deferred tax items in 2001 because of the change in the tax rate, assuming the use of SFAS 109.

d. Discuss the conditions under which Mother Prewitt would need to recognize a valuation allowance for any deferred tax assets.

7. [Tax effect of restructuring] Silicon Graphics [SGI] made the following announcements:

   • 1998: restructuring charges of $144 million, including a $47 million write-down of operating assets; additional $47 million impairment of long-lived assets.

   • 1999: $4.2 million of operating asset write-downs and a $16 million write-down of capitalized internal use software.

   • 2000: operating asset write-downs of $26.6 million.

The company reported the following deferred tax assets ($ thousands):

Years ended June 30	1997	1998	1999	2000
Depreciation	$57,675	$40,435	$49,226	$37,659

a. Using the U.S. statutory tax rates of 34% for 1998 and 35% for 1999 and 2000, estimate the changes in 1998, 1999, and 2000 deferred tax asset balances resulting from the write-downs of operating assets.

b. Explain why your answer to part a differs from the actual changes in the deferred tax asset during those three years.

8. [Tax effect of permanently reinvested earnings] Silicon Graphics reports, in the tax footnote to its fiscal 1999 *Annual Report*, that

> We have not provided U.S. federal taxes on approximately $242 million of accumulated undistributed earnings of certain of our foreign subsidiaries, since it is our intention to permanently invest such earnings in foreign operations.

a. Explain how Silicon Graphics' treatment of the undistributed earnings of its foreign subsidiaries has affected its reported:

  (i) Income tax expense

  (ii) Income tax paid

  (iii) Effective tax rate

  (iv) Earnings per share

  (v) Book value per share

b. If the subsidiaries remitted the previously undistributed earnings to the United States parent company, describe the effect on the following reported amounts in that year:

  (i) Pretax income

  (ii) Income tax expense

  (iii) Income tax paid

  (iv) Effective tax rate

  (v) Earnings per share

  (vi) Book value per share

c. State whether an analyst should adjust Silicon Graphics' reported financial data for the tax effect of the undistributed earnings. Justify your answer.

d. In the fourth quarter of fiscal 2000, Silicon Graphics recognized a provision for deferred U.S. and foreign tax income taxes on undistributed foreign earnings of approximately $93 million. Suggest why this liability was established given the statement quoted at the beginning of this question.

9. [Basis for and change in valuation allowance] Silicon Graphics reported the following components of (loss) income before income taxes:

Years ended June 30

$ in thousands	1998	1999	2000
United States	$(601,962)	$ 10,699	$(367,033)
Foreign	5,043	115,022	(14,851)
Total pretax income	$(596,919)	$125,721	$(381,884)
Provision for (benefit from) income taxes	(137,292)	71,892	447,660
Net income	$(459,627)	$ 53,829	$(829,544)

1999 income includes $272 million of pretax gain on the partial sale of its interest in MIPS Technologies. At June 30, 1999, the company retained a 65% interest in MIPS.

The company reported the following deferred tax assets and liabilities:

Years ended June 30

($ in thousands)	1998	1999	2000
Deferred tax assets:			
Net operating loss carryforwards	$103,705	$191,145	$423,047
General business credit carryforwards	53,449	63,000	63,000
All others combined	486,153	339,820	257,869
Subtotal	$643,307	$593,965	$743,916
Valuation allowance	(90,705)	(105,364)	(632,324)
Net deferred tax assets	$552,602	$488,601	$111,592
Total deferred tax liabilities	(23,665)	(38,191)	(129,622)
Net deferred tax	$528,937	$450,410	$(18,030)

At June 30, 1999 Silicon Graphics stated that the realization of net deferred tax assets depended on its ability to generate approximately $900 million of future taxable income. Silicon Graphics believed that it was more likely than not that the deferred tax asset will be realized based on forecasted income, including income from its planned divestiture of MIPS.

a. Given facts as of June 30, 1999, discuss whether the valuation allowance of $105.3 million was adequate.

b. Assume that SGI maintained a valuation allowance sufficient to offset all of its deferred tax asset in every year. Compute the effect of this assumption on *each* of the following for all three years:

  (i) Income tax expense

  (ii) Income tax paid

  (iii) Effective tax rate

  (iv) Net income

During the fourth quarter of fiscal 2000, Silicon Graphics made a tax-free distribution of its remaining shares of MIPS to shareholders, eliminating the sale of MIPS as an element of forecasted income.

c. Discuss the impact of that distribution on the fiscal 2000 change in SGI's valuation allowance.

10. [Effect of foreign operations on income tax rate and future effective tax rates] PepsiCo [PEP] reported the following tax rate reconciliation in its *2000 Annual Report*:

	1998	1999	2000
Statutory rate	35.0%	35.0%	35.0%
Effect of lower foreign tax rate	(3.0)	(2.7)	(3.0)
Settlement − prior years' audit issues	(5.7)	0.0	0.0
Puerto Rico settlement	(21.8)	0.0	0.0
Bottling transactions	0.0	10.6	0.0
Asset impairments and restructuring	3.4	0.0	0.0
Other effects (net)	4.0	1.0	0.0
Effective tax rate	11.9%	43.9%	32.0%

PepsiCo's pretax earnings were ($ in millions):

	1998	1999	2000
United States	$1,629	$2,771	$2,126
Foreign	634	885	1,084

Selected Additional Data:

The company reported beneficial effects of two settlements, one related to prior years' tax audits and the second to a tax case in Puerto Rico. The bottling transactions refer to:

- $1.0 billion ($476 million after tax) gain on issuance of stock by a subsidiary, Pepsi Bottling Group (PBG). The majority of the taxes are expected to be deferred indefinitely, and

- An after-tax loss of $206 million on a similar transaction with another group.

a. Using these data, calculate the following:

(i) U.S. dollar reduction in income tax expense in 1998 to 2000 due to lower foreign tax rates

(ii) Effective tax rate on foreign income for each year

(iii) Net foreign income (after tax) for each year

(iv) Effective tax rate on U.S. income for each year

(v) Net U.S. income (after tax) for each year

b. Using your answers to part a, calculate the percentage changes in foreign and U.S. income for 1999 and 2000:

(i) Pretax

(ii) After tax

c. Discuss the differences in the pretax and after-tax growth of income calculated in part b.

d. List and justify the questions you would want to ask PepsiCo management about their tax position based on your answers to parts a through c.

e. Explain why the asset impairment and restructuring charges increased PepsiCo's effective tax rate in 1998.

f. Using the data provided, predict the 2001 effective tax rate for PepsiCo.

g. In the Management's Discussion and Analysis section of its annual report, PepsiCo says that its effective tax rate on comparable operations was 31% in 1998, 32.2% in 1999, and 32% in 2000. Determine the tax effects the company must have deemed noncomparable.

h. Discuss whether earnings used to value PepsiCo should include or exclude the tax effects of the 1998 Puerto Rico settlement and the 1999 bottling transactions.

11. [Tax effect of zero coupon debt] PepsiCo [PEP] reported a deferred tax liability of $73 million at December 31, 2000 ($76 and $79 million at December 31, 1999 and 1998, respectively) resulting from outstanding zero coupon debt.

a. Explain why zero coupon debt might generate deferred tax liabilities.

b. Describe the expected trend of these deferred tax liabilities over the life of the debt. *Note:* Do not forget to consider what happens when the debt matures.

c. Without prejudice to your answer to part b, explain why the deferred tax liability related to the zero coupon debt has declined each year.

12. [Analysis of income tax footnote data] Exhibit 9P-1 contains the income tax footnote from the *2001 Annual Report* of Honda [7267], a multinational automobile manufacturer based in Japan. *Note that these data are prepared under U.S. GAAP.*

a. Calculate the differences (in yen) between Honda's income tax expense and that expense based on the statutory rate.

b. Using your answer to part a, compute the impact on Honda's income tax expense over the 1999 to 2001 period of:

(i) Changes in the valuation allowance

(ii) Tax law changes

(iii) Undistributed earnings of subsidiaries

c. Lower non-Japanese tax rates reduced Honda's tax expense in each year, 1999 to 2001.

(i) Discuss the trend in that reduction.

(ii) Discuss the likely explanation for that trend.

d. Discuss the factors that an analyst must consider when forecasting Honda's effective tax rate for 2002.

13. [Deferred taxes and interim reports] State Auto Financial [STFC] reported the following operating results for the first three quarters of 1991 and 1992 ($ in thousands):

	1991		
	Q1	Q2	Q3
Pretax income	$4,797	$2,600	$3,244
Income tax expense	(1,224)	(624)	(848)
Net income	$3,573	$1,976	$2,396

	1992		
	Q1	Q2	Q3
Pretax income	$1,123	$3,723	$ 98
Income tax expense	(232)	(934)	583
Net income	$ 891	$2,789	$681

State Auto's 1992 third-quarter 10-Q reported that

> the estimated annual effective tax rate was revised during the third quarter of 1992 from 25% to 17% to reflect the estimated tax impact of a decrease in taxable earnings, as prescribed by generally accepted accounting principles. The effect of this adjustment in the current quarter was a benefit of approximately $600,000.

a. Compute the tax rate used to compute net income for each quarter.

b. Using the data given, show how the change in the estimated tax rate increased third-quarter 1992 income by approximately $600,000.

c. Describe how the changed tax rate assumption distorted the comparison of third-quarter net income for 1991 and 1992.

d. Suggest two ways by which analysis can offset the distortion discussed in part c.

e. Assume that State Auto had estimated a tax rate of 17% for the first two quarters of 1992.

(i) Compute the effect of that assumption on reported net income for those quarters.

(ii) Discuss how that assumption would have affected the year-to-year comparison of operating results for the first two quarters.

EXHIBIT 9P-1. HONDA MOTOR
Income Tax Disclosures

The income before income taxes and equity in income of affiliates ("Income before income taxes") and income tax expense (benefit) for each of the years in the three-year period ended March 31, 2001 consist of the following

	Income before income taxes	Income taxes Current	Deferred	Total
1999:				
Japanese	¥199,848	¥125,423	¥ 15,144	¥140,567
Foreign (a)	320,663	107,875	(18,818)	89,057
	¥520,511	¥233,298	¥ (3,674)	¥229,624
2000:				
Japanese	¥127,562	¥ 76,015	¥(22,160)	¥ 53,855
Foreign (a)	288,501	136,963	(20,384)	116,579
	¥416,063	¥212,978	¥(42,544)	¥170,434
2001:				
Japanese	**¥133,166**	**¥ 65,444**	**¥ (4,697)**	**¥ 60,747**
Foreign (a)	**251,810**	**131,419**	**(13,727)**	**117,692**
	¥384,976	**¥196,863**	**¥(18,424)**	**¥178,439**

Yen (millions)

(a) Foreign includes income taxes provided on undistributed earnings of foreign subsidiaries and affiliates.

The effective tax rate of Honda for each of the years in the three-year period ended March 31, 2001 differs from the normal Japanese income tax rate for the following reasons.

	1999	2000	2001
Normal income tax rate	48.0%	41.0%	**41.0%**
Valuation allowance provided for current year operating losses of subsidiaries	1.2	2.8	**5.2**
Difference in normal tax rates of foreign subsidiaries	(3.0)	(1.3)	**(1.0)**
Adjustments to deferred tax assets and liabilities for enacted changes in tax laws and rates	(4.2)	—	—
Reversal of valuation allowance due to utilization of operating loss carryforwards	(0.1)	(0.1)	**(0.1)**
Other	2.2	(1.4)	**1.3**
Effective tax rate	44.1%	41.0%	**46.4%**

At March 31, 2001, certain of the company's subsidiaries have operating loss carryforwards for income tax purposes of approximately ¥112,857 million ($910,872 thousand), which are available to offset future taxable income, if any. Periods available to offset future taxable income vary in each tax jurisdiction and range from one year to an indefinite period as follows

	Yen (millions)
Within 1 year	¥ 510
1 to 5 years	11,528
5 to 15 years	4,147
Indefinite periods	96,672
	¥112,857

At March 31, 2000 and 2001, Honda did not recognize deferred tax liabilities of ¥5,131 million and ¥5,987 million ($48,321 thousand) respectively, for certain portions of the undistributed earnings of the company's subsidiaries because such portions were reinvested or were determined to be reinvested. At March 31, 2000 and 2001, the undistributed earnings not subject to deferred tax liabilities were ¥649,929 million and ¥663,540 million ($5,355,448 thousand), respectively. Honda has recognized deferred tax liabilities for undistributed earnings for which decisions of reinvestment have not been made.

14. [Effective tax rates] For the year ended December 31, 2000, in its Management's Financial Review, Coca Cola Enterprises [CCE] made the following comments on income taxes:

The Company's effective tax rate for 2000 was 29%, including the impact of a $14 million nonrecurring reduction of income tax expense in the fourth quarter of 2000. The reduction was due to a revaluation of income tax liabilities and an income tax rate reduction in France. Excluding the impact of this reduction, the Company's effective tax rate would have been 33%.

For the year ended December 31, 1999, the Company reported an effective tax rate of 33%, approximately equal to the 1998 effective tax rate and lower than the 1997 rate of 37%, excluding the impact of a United Kingdom tax rate change in both 1997 and 1998. The Company stated that its 1999 effective tax rate reflected a combination of actual 1999 pretax earnings and the beneficial tax impact of international operations including the favorable tax treatment granted to certain international operations under a tax holiday that expired in 1999.

Income tax expense reconciliation

(in $millions)	1997	1998	1999	2000
U.S. federal statutory expense	$ 62	$ 59	$31	$117
State expense, net of federal benefit	2	—	4	2
European and Canadian operations, net	(21)	(21)	(17)	(22)
Rate change benefit	(58)	(29)	—	(8)
Valuation allowance provision	15	8	3	7
Nondeductible items	5	6	7	7
Other (net)	2	4	1	(6)
Total provision for income taxes	$ 7	$ 27	$29	$ 97

Coca Cola Enterprise's pretax earnings were:

(in $millions)	1997	1998	1999	2000
Total	$178	$169	$88	$333
Foreign	162	151	49	141

a. List and justify the questions you would want to ask CCE management after comparing the management comments with the income tax expense reconciliation.

b. Using the data and management comments, estimate the effective tax rate on the company's foreign operations and U.S. operations separately for each year, 1997 to 2000. State any assumptions made.

c. Redo part b, excluding components of tax expense that you would consider to be nonrecurring in nature.

d. Compute net income for each year, 1997–2000, based on:

   (i) Actual income tax expense

   (ii) Income tax expense excluding the components identified in part c.

e. Forecast the 2001 effective tax rate for Coca Cola Enterprises. List any assumptions made and the additional information, if any, that would improve your forecast.

f. As noted above, Management's Financial Review suggests a long-term rate of 33%. Explain the difference, if any, between the effective tax rate calculated in part c and the long-term rate of 33%.

g. Discuss the relationship between the changing earnings mix (U.S. versus foreign) reported by Coca Cola Enterprises and the expected effective tax rate.

15. [Valuation of tax adjustments] On August 1, 2001 Holmen issued a press release reporting that a court ruling would permit the company to receive a tax deduction for a 1997 loss. The effect on 2001 earnings was estimated at MSEK 350, to be recognized in the third quarter.

Discuss the amount and timing of the expected effect of this announcement on Holmen's common shares.

16. [Adjustment of non-U.S. GAAP] Repsol, a major oil producer headquartered in Spain, prepares its financial statements in accordance with Spanish GAAP. Data from Repsol's financial statements for the year ended December 31, 1999 follow. The large 1999 increases reflect a major acquisition in that year.

(in €millions)	1998	1999
Deferred tax assets	€ 168	€ 464
Total assets	17,351	42,050
Deferred tax liabilities	325	919
Total liabilities	11,308	29,524
Stockholders' equity	6,043	12,526
Net sales	18,573	25,633
Pretax income	1,411	1,743
Income tax expense	(397)	(557)

The company's 20-F report reconciles its reported financial data with data adjusted to conform to U.S. GAAP. Two adjustments relate to income tax expense, as under Spanish GAAP:

- deferred tax assets arising from tax loss carryforwards are recognized only when realization is assured "beyond any reasonable doubt" as opposed to the "more likely than not" test under U.S. GAAP.

- Temporary differences expected to reverse in more than 10 years are not recorded as deferred tax assets

These and other differences between Spanish and U.S. GAAP result in the following amounts under U.S. GAAP:

(in €millions)	1998	1999
Deferred tax assets	€ 395	€ 754
Stockholders' equity	5,653	12,140
Pretax income	1,277	1,622
Income tax expense	(402)	(488)

a. Compute each of the following using the Spanish GAAP data for 1998 and 1999:

   (i) Effective tax rate

   (ii) Net profit margin

   (iii) Return on ending equity

b. Compute each of the ratios in part a using the U.S. GAAP data for 1998 and 1999.

c. Discuss the differences between the results in parts a and b and how they might affect valuation of Repsol shares.

d. Compare the 1999 increase in pretax and after tax income under Spanish and U.S. GAAP.

10

ANALYSIS OF FINANCING LIABILITIES

CHAPTER OUTLINE

INTRODUCTION

BALANCE SHEET DEBT
Current Liabilities
Long-Term Debt
Financial Statement Effects
Zero-Coupon Debt
Variable-Rate Debt
Fixed- versus Variable-Rate Debt and Interest Rate Swaps
Debt Denominated in a Foreign Currency
Project Debt
Debt with Equity Features
Convertible Bonds and Warrants
Commodity Bonds
Perpetual Debt
Preferred Stock

Effects of Changes in Interest Rates
Debt: Market or Book Value?
Debt of Firms in Distress
Accounting for Restructured and Impaired Debt
Retirement of Debt Prior to Maturity
Accounting for Debt Retirement
Callable Bonds
Defeasance

BOND COVENANTS
Nature of Covenants

SUMMARY

 CASE 10-1

CHAPTER OBJECTIVES

This chapter concerns debt obligations that are recognized on the firm's balance sheet. The objectives of Chapter 10 are to:

1. Discuss the difference between operating and financing liabilities.
2. Describe the effect on reported financial statements, including the carrying amount, the pattern of expense recognition, and reported cash flows, of:
   - Debt issued at a premium or discount
   - Zero-coupon debt
   - Fixed- and variable-rate debt
   - Debt denominated in foreign currencies
   - Debt with equity features, such as convertible and exchangeable debt
3. Compare the effects of changes in interest rates on both the interest payments and market value of fixed- and variable-rate debt.

4. Estimate the market value of debt and discuss its usefulness.
5. Explain how interest rate swaps change the firm's risk exposure to changing interest rates
6. Describe the circumstances under which preferred stock should be treated as debt, or debt as equity for financial analysis.
7. Differentiate between the economic and accounting effects (often different) of debt retirement or refinancing.
8. Explain the role of debt covenants in protecting creditors by limiting the firm's freedom to invest, pay dividends, or make other operating and strategic decisions.

INTRODUCTION

The assessment of a firm's liabilities is crucial to the analysis of its long-run viability and growth. A firm can incur obligations in myriad ways; some are a consequence of the firm's operating activities, whereas others result from its financing decisions. The former are characterized by exchanges of goods and services for the later payment of cash (or vice versa), whereas debt arising from financing decisions generally involves current receipts of cash in exchange for later payments of cash. Both forms of debt are generally reported "on balance sheet," and our focus in this chapter is on their measurement, interpretation, and analysis.

More complex arrangements, often based on contracts rather than immediate cash exchanges, involve promises to purchase (or use) products, services, or distribution systems in return for specified future payments of cash or equivalent resources. Such contractual arrangements are usually not recorded on the firm's balance sheet but may receive footnote disclosure. A thorough analysis of the firm's financial structure requires recognition of these liabilities as well. Such "off-balance-sheet" debt must first be identified, then measured, interpreted, and analyzed.

The analysis of a firm's short-term liquidity and long-term solvency position requires evaluation of both on- and off-balance-sheet debt. Debt-to-equity and interest coverage ratios based on reported financial data, for example, are affected by the form of transactions (rather than their substance), which determines whether they are recognized and how they are accounted for. This analysis must also consider incentives for management decisions regarding the proportion of on- versus off-balance-sheet debt.

An additional focus of analysis is debt covenants, used by creditors to protect themselves. These restrictions limit the firm's operations, its distributions to shareholders, and the amount of additional debt or leverage the firm can assume. Firms may alter their operating and financing activities and change accounting policies in an effort to operate within the confines of these covenants.

This chapter is the first of a series of chapters that deal with these issues. It primarily examines liabilities resulting from financing activities, the nature of various debt instruments, the impact of market rate (and credit) changes on reported and economic liabilities, and the nature and effect of covenants imposed by creditors. Liabilities arising from contractual obligations such as leases (a combined financing and investment activity) and other off-balance-sheet debt, debt guarantees, and obligations of the firm's affiliates are the subject of Chapter 11. Chapter 12 covers pensions and other postemployment benefits that arise from dealings between a firm and its employees. The effects of hedging or speculative activities in options, futures, and other derivatives on a firm's liability position are included in Chapter 16.

BALANCE SHEET DEBT

The liability amount reported on the balance sheet does not equal the total cash outflow required to satisfy the debt. Only the principal portion, that is, the present value of the future cash flow, is recorded. For example, if a firm borrows $100 at an interest rate of 10%, the actual amount payable at year-end is $110. The balance sheet liability equals the present value of the future payment or $100.

Current Liabilities

Current liabilities are defined as those due within one year or one operating cycle; they result from both operating and financing activities. Analysis must distinguish among different types of current operating and financing liabilities:

Consequences of Operating Activities
1. *Operating and trade liabilities*, the most frequent type, are the result of credit granted to the company by its suppliers and employees.

2. *Advances from customers* arise when customers pay in advance for services to be rendered by the company. The firm is obligated to render the service and/or deliver a product to the customer in the near future.

Consequences of Financing Activities

3. *Short-term debt* represents amounts borrowed from banks or the credit markets that are expected to be repaid within one year or less.

4. *Current portion of long-term debt* identifies the portion of long-term debt that is payable within the next year; it is excluded from the long-term liability section of the balance sheet.

Operating and trade debt is reported at the expected (undiscounted) cash flow and is an important exception to the rule that liabilities are recorded at present value. A purchase of goods for $100 on credit, to be paid for within the normal operating cycle of the firm, is recorded at $100 even though its present value is lower. This treatment is justified by the short period between the incurrence of the debt and its payment, rendering the adjustment to present value immaterial.

When analyzing a firm's liquidity, advances from customers should be distinguished from other payables. Payables require a future outlay of cash. Advances from customers, on the other hand, are satisfied by delivery of goods or services,[1] requiring a cash outlay lower[2] than the advances recorded; otherwise, the firm would be selling below cost. Increases in advances should be viewed favorably as *advances are a prediction of future revenues rather than of cash outflows*.

Short-term debt and the current portion of long-term debt are the result of prior financing cash inflows. They indicate the firm's need for either cash or a means of refinancing the debt. The inability to repay short-term credit is a sign of financial distress.

It is important to monitor the relative levels of debt from operating as compared to financing activities. The former arise from the normal course of business activities and represent the required operating capital for a given level of production and sales: *A shift from operating to financing liabilities may signal the beginning of a liquidity crisis, as reduced access to trade credit results in increased reliance on borrowings.*

■ **Example: Warnaco**

The following data for Warnaco Group, a major clothing manufacturer, illustrates this point:

Warnaco Group

Amounts in $000

	1/1/00	12/30/00	Change
Accounts payable	$599,768	$413,786	$(185,982)
Total debt	1,332,755	1,493,483	160,728

Over one year Warnaco's trade credit fell 31%, requiring borrowing that increased the company's already-large debt burden. The company filed for bankruptcy on June 11, 2001. ■

---

[1]The firm will have a cash obligation only if the goods and services are not delivered. Thus, the primary liability does not require cash.

[2]This is especially true in industries with high fixed/low variable cost structures (e.g., airlines). The marginal cost for any individual customer is low relative to the selling cost. Problem 10-3 is based on airline customer advances.

Long-Term Debt

Firms obtain long-term debt financing from public issuance; from private placements with insurance companies, pension plans, and other institutional investors; or from long-term bank credit agreements. Creditors may receive a claim on specific assets pledged as security for the debt (e.g., mortgages), or they may have only general claims on the assets of the firm. Some debt, known as *project financing*, is repaid solely from the operations of a particular activity (e.g., a coal mine or office building). Some creditor claims are *subordinated*, in that they rank below those of *senior* creditors, whose claims have priority.

Long-term liabilities are interest-bearing in nature, but the structure of interest and principal payments varies widely. The different payment terms are, however, conceptually identical. As the subtleties of the financing equation(s) can be overwhelming and obscure the sight of the forest for the trees, *we suggest that the reader keep two basic principles in mind:*

1. Debt equals the present value of the remaining future stream of (interest and principal) payments. The book value reported in the financial statements uses the discount rate (market interest rate) in effect when the debt was incurred. Market value measurements use the current market interest rate.

2. Interest expense is the amount paid by the debtor to the creditor in excess of the amount borrowed. Even when the *total* amount of interest paid over time is known, its allocation to individual time periods (both cash outflows and accrual of expense in periodic income statements) may vary with the form of the debt.

These points seem simplistic but reference to them from time to time may help focus the discussions that follow.

Although bonds are only part of the debt universe, they are used for convenience to illustrate the accounting and analysis issues.

A bond is a "contract" or written agreement that obligates the borrower (bond issuer) to make certain payments to the lender (bondholder) over the life of the bond. A typical bond promises two types of payments: periodic interest payments (usually semiannual in the United States but annual in other countries) and a lump-sum payment when the bond matures.

The *face value* of the bond is the lump-sum payment due at maturity. The *coupon rate* is the stated cash interest rate (but not necessarily the actual rate of return).

$$\text{Periodic Payment} = \text{``Coupon Rate''} \times \text{Face Value}$$

The coupon rate is in quotation marks because it is stated on an annual basis, whereas payments are made semiannually. The coupon rate (CR) used for the payment calculation is therefore equal to one-half the stated coupon rate.

The example in Exhibit 10-1 is based on a three-year bond[3] with the following terms:

Face Value (FV):	**$100,000**
Coupon:	**10%**
Interest Payment:	**Semiannual**

The purchaser of the bond expects six payments of interest (each payment is $5,000) and a final principal payment of $100,000 for a total of $130,000. Note that this stream of payments does not uniquely determine the principal amount borrowed by the bond issuer. *The amount borrowed (the proceeds received on issuance) depends on the market rate of interest for bonds of a similar maturity and risk as well as the payment stream.*

The market rate may be less than, equal to, or greater than the coupon rate. *It is the current market interest rate that allocates payments between interest and principal.*

---

[3]Bonds issued for periods of 10 years or less are usually called *notes*. There is no analytical distinction, and we call all debt issues *bonds* for convenience.

EXHIBIT 10-1
Comparison of Bond Issued at Par, Premium, and Discount

Face Value (FV) of bond = $100,000
Coupon (CR) = 5% (semiannual payment; 10% annual rate)
Maturity = 3 years
Semiannual payments of $5,000 (0.5 × 10% × $100,000)

A. Bond Issued at Par: Market Rate = 10% (MR = 5%)

	(1)	(2)	(3)	(4)	(5)	(6)
		(1) × MR	FV × CR	(2) − (3)	(1) + (4)	FV
Period	Liability	Interest	Coupon	Change in	Liability	Face Value
Ending	Opening	Expense	Payment	Liability	Closing	of Bond
01/01/01	Proceeds (see below)				$100,000	$100,000
06/30/01	$100,000	$ 5,000	$ 5,000	$0	100,000	100,000
12/31/01	100,000	5,000	5,000	0	100,000	100,000
06/30/02	100,000	5,000	5,000	0	100,000	100,000
12/31/02	100,000	5,000	5,000	0	100,000	100,000
06/30/03	100,000	5,000	5,000	0	100,000	100,000
12/31/03	100,000	5,000	5,000	0	100,000	100,000
Totals		$30,000	$30,000			

Calculation of Proceeds

Present value of annuity of $5,000 for 6 periods, discounted at 5%:
　$5,000 × 5.0756 = 　　　　　　　　　　　　　　$ 25,378
Present value of $100,000 in 6 periods, discounted at 5%:
　$100,000 × 0.74622 = 　　　　　　　　　　　　　74,622
Total 　　　　　　　　　　　　　　　　　　　　$100,000

B. Bond Issued at Premium: Market Rate = 8% (MR = 4%)

	(1)	(2)	(3)	(4)	(5)	(6)	(7)
		(1) × MR	FV × CR	(2) − (3)	(1) + (4)	FV	(5) − (6)
Period	Liability	Interest	Coupon	Change in	Liability	Face Value	Closing
Ending	Opening	Expense	Payment	Liability	Closing	of Bond	Premium
01/01/01	Proceeds (see below)				$105,242	$100,000	$5,242
06/30/01	$105,242	$ 4,210	$ 5,000	$ (790)	104,452	100,000	4,452
12/31/01	104,452	4,178	5,000	(822)	103,630	100,000	3,630
06/30/02	103,630	4,145	5,000	(855)	102,775	100,000	2,775
12/31/02	102,775	4,111	5,000	(889)	101,886	100,000	1,886
06/30/03	101,886	4,075	5,000	(925)	100,961	100,000	961
12/31/03	100,961	4,039	5,000	(961)	100,000	100,000	0
Totals		$24,758	$30,000	$(5,242)			

Calculation of Proceeds

Present value of annuity of $5,000 for 6 periods, discounted at 4%:
　$5,000 × 5.2421 = 　　　　　　　　　　　　　　$ 26,211
Present value of $100,000 in 6 periods, discounted at 4%:
　$100,000 × 0.79031 = 　　　　　　　　　　　　　79,031
Total 　　　　　　　　　　　　　　　　　　　　$105,242

EXHIBIT 10-1 (continued)

C. Bond Issued at Discount: Market Rate = 12% (MR = 6%)

Period Ending	(1) Liability Opening	(2) (1) × MR Interest Expense	(3) FV × CR Coupon Payment	(4) (2) − (3) Change in Liability	(5) (1) + (4) Liability Closing	(6) FV Face Value of Bond	(7) (5) − (6) Discount
01/01/01	Proceeds (see below)				$95,083	$100,000	$(4,917)
06/30/01	$95,083	$ 5,705	$ 5,000	$ 705	95,788	100,000	(4,212)
12/31/01	95,788	5,747	5,000	747	96,535	100,000	(3,465)
06/30/02	96,535	5,792	5,000	792	97,327	100,000	(2,673)
12/31/02	97,327	5,840	5,000	840	98,167	100,000	(1,833)
06/30/03	98,167	5,890	5,000	890	99,057	100,000	(943)
12/31/03	99,057	5,943	5,000	943	100,000	100,000	0
Totals		$34,917	$30,000	$4,917			

Calculation of Proceeds

Present value of annuity of $5,000 for 6 periods, discounted at 6%:
$5,000 × 4.9173 = $24,587
Present value of $100,000 in 6 periods, discounted at 6%:
$100,000 × 0.70496 =   70,496
Total $95,083

Exhibit 10-1, parts A through C, shows how the economics of the bond and the accounting treatment of the payments are affected by the relationship between the market and coupon rates. The following points should be noted:

1. The initial liability is the amount paid to the issuer by the creditor (present value of the stream of payments discounted at the market rate), not necessarily the face value of the debt.

2. The *effective interest rate* on the bond is the market (not the coupon) rate at the time of issuance, and interest expense is that market rate times the bond liability.

3. The coupon rate and face value determine the actual cash flows (stream of payments from the issuer).

4. Total interest expense is equal to the payments by the issuer to the creditor in excess of the amount received. (Thus, total interest expense = $130,000 − initial liability.)

5. The balance sheet liability over time is a function of (a) the initial liability and the relationship of (b) periodic interest expense to (c) the actual cash payments.

6. The balance sheet liability at any point in time is equal to the present value of the remaining payments, discounted at the market rate in effect at the time of the issuance of the bonds.

Exhibit 10-1A: Market Rate = Coupon Rate. When the market rate equals the coupon rate of 10% (compounded semiannually), the bond is issued at par; that is, the proceeds equal the face value.[4] The creditor is willing to pay $100,000, the present value of the stream of payments and the face value of the bond. In this case, the initial liability equals the face value.

Since the debt has been issued at a market rate of 10% (equal to the coupon rate), periodic interest expense (Exhibit 10-1A, column 2) equals the periodic cash payments (column 3). The liability remains $100,000 (column 5) throughout the life of the bond.

Exhibit 10-1B: Market Rate < Coupon Rate. When the market rate is less than the coupon rate, the creditor is willing to pay (and the bond issuer will demand) a premium

---

[4]We ignore, for simplicity, the underwriting costs and expenses associated with the bond issuance. These costs are generally capitalized and amortized over the life of the bond issue.

above the face value of $100,000.[5] If we assume a market rate of 8%, the proceeds and initial liability (Exhibit 10-1B) equal $105,242 (face value of $100,000 plus premium of $5,242).

After six months, the bondholder earns interest of $4,210 (4% × $105,242) but receives a payment of $5,000 (coupon rate times face value). This $5,000 payment includes interest expense of $4,210 and a $790 principal payment, reducing the liability to $104,452. For the second period, interest expense is $4,178 (4% × $104,452), lower than the first period expense since the liability has been reduced. After the second payment of $5,000, the liability is further reduced. This process is continued until the bond matures. At that time, as shown in Exhibit 10-1B, the liability is reduced to $100,000, the face value of the bond, which is repaid at maturity.

The process by which a bond premium (or discount) is amortized over the life of the bond is known as the *effective interest method*. This process, which results in a constant rate of interest over the life of the obligation, is widely used in financial reporting.

Exhibit 10-1C: Market Rate > Coupon Rate. When the market rate exceeds the coupon rate, the bond buyer is unwilling to pay the full face value of the bond.[6] At a market rate of 12%, the bond would be issued at a discount of $4,917, and the proceeds and initial liability equal $95,083.

Interest expense for the first six months is $5,705 (6% x $95,083), but cash interest paid is only $5,000; the shortfall of $705 is added to the balance sheet liability. As a result, a higher liability is used to calculate interest expense for the second period, increasing interest expense, increasing the shortfall, and further increasing the liability. This cycle is repeated for all remaining periods until the bond matures. At that point, the initial principal of $95,083 plus the accumulated (unpaid) interest of $4,917 equals $100,000, the face value payment that retires the debt. The zero-coupon bond, discussed shortly, is the extreme case; all interest is unpaid until the bond matures.

Financial Statement Effects

Interest expense reported in the income statement (column 2 of Exhibit 10-1) is the effective interest on the loan based on the market rate in effect at issuance times the balance sheet liability at the beginning of the period. The actual cash payments (column 3) may not equal interest expense, but do equal the reduction in cash from operations (CFO). The balance sheet liability is shown in column 5. The initial cash received and the final face value payment of $100,000 are both treated as cash from financing (CFF). The financial statement effects on an annual basis (if we assume a December fiscal year-end) are summarized in Exhibit 10-2. Note that for bonds issued at a premium (discount), the interest expense decreases (increases) over time. This is a direct function of the declining (rising) balance sheet liability; for each period, interest expense is the product of the beginning liability and the effective interest rate. At any point in time, the balance sheet liability equals the present value of the remaining payments discounted at the effective interest rate at the issuance date.[7,8]

The reported cash flows for each period over the life of the bond (Exhibit 10-2) are identical across all three scenarios; the $100,000 face value payment is treated as cash from fi-

---

[5]Assuming a market interest rate of 8%, the bond issuer could find an investor willing to lend $100,000 in exchange for a semiannual annuity stream of $4,000 (4% × $100,000) in addition to the lump-sum payment at maturity. For the borrower to obligate itself to pay the higher annuity of $5,000 requires additional proceeds above the face value.

[6]The bondholder can purchase a 12% bond and receive periodic payments of $6,000. The periodic payments from this bond are only $5,000. Thus, an investor would only purchase this bond at a *discount*.

[7]To illustrate this property, compute the balance sheet liability of $96,535 at December 31, 2001, for the bond issued at a discount. The present value of the remaining four periodic payments and lump-sum payment equals:

Present value of annuity of $5,000
   for 4 periods discounted at 6%: $5,000 × 3.46511 = $17,326
Present value of $100,000
   for 4 periods discounted at 6%: $100,000 × 0.79209 =   79,209
                                                            $96,535

[8]The *market* value of the debt, however, is equal to the present value of all remaining payments discounted at the *current market* interest rate.

EXHIBIT 10-2
Comparison of Financial Statement Effects of Bonds Issued at Par, Premium, and Discount

Bond Face Value = $100,000
Maturity = 3 years
Coupon Rate = 10% (semiannual payments)

Premium Case: Market Rate = 8%
Discount Case: Market Rate = 12%

| Year | Interest Expense Bond Issued at | | | Balance Sheet Liability Bond Issued at | | | Cash Flow from | |
	Par	Premium	Discount	Par	Premium	Discount	Operations	Financing (for all cases)
2001	$10,000	$ 8,388	$11,452	$100,000	$103,630	$ 96,535	$10,000	
2002*	10,000	8,256	11,632	100,000	101,886	98,167	10,000	
2003*	10,000	8,114	11,833	100,000	100,000	100,000	10,000	$100,000
Totals	$30,000	$24,758	$34,917				$30,000	$100,000

*Interest expense and cash flow total of June 30 and December 31 amounts for each year. All data from Exhibit 10-1.

nancing, and the periodic cash payments of $5,000 are reported as reductions in CFO.[9] For bonds issued at a premium or discount, however, these cash flows *incorrectly* describe the economics of the bond transaction.

The misclassification of cash flows results from reporting the coupon payments rather than interest expense as CFO. For bonds sold at a premium, part of the coupon payment is a reduction of principal and should be treated as a financing cash (out)flow. CFO is understated and financing cash flow is overstated by an equal amount. Similarly, when bonds are issued at a discount, part of the discount amortization represents additional interest expense. Consequently, CFO is overstated and financing cash flow is understated by that amount.

In summary, the cash flow classification of the debt payments depends on the coupon rates, not the effective interest rate. When these differ, CFO is misstated.

Exhibit 10-3 presents two cash flow reclassifications. The first correctly allocates cash outflows based on interest expense. After reallocation, the cash flows reflect the economics of the debt rather than the coupon payments alone.

The second reclassification, however, goes much further. In Chapter 3, we argue that all debt-related cash flows should be separated from operating cash flows. The "functional" reclassification in Exhibit 10-3 makes that separation so CFO is unaffected by borrowing. All debt-related cash flows are included in financing cash flow regardless of the coupon or effective interest rates.

Most debt is issued at or close to par (face value), making the distortion from bond premium or discount immaterial. However, when the discount is large, for example, with zero-coupon bonds, the difference between coupon and effective interest rates leads to the significant distortion of reported cash flows.

Zero-Coupon Debt

A zero-coupon bond has no periodic payments (coupon = 0).[10] For that reason, it must be issued at a deep discount to face value. The lump-sum payment at maturity includes all unpaid interest (equal to the face value minus the proceeds) from the time of issuance.

---

[9]Under the indirect method, net income is adjusted by the change in bond discount/premium (the periodic amortization of the bond/discount premium) to derive CFO. Thus for the first year, the cash flow statement will show an addback of $1,612 in the premium case and a deduction of $1,452 in the discount case.

[10]The following discussion also applies to bonds sold at deep discounts, that is, with coupons that are far below market interest rates, and to bonds issued with attached warrants that generate debt discount (discussed later in the chapter).

EXHIBIT 10-3
Reclassification of Cash Flows for Bonds in Exhibits 10-1 and 10-2

| | | SFAS 95 | | Reclassification Based on Interest Expense | | | | Functional Reclassification For All Bonds | |
| | Actual Cash Flow | Cash Flow for All Bonds | | Premium Bond | | Discount Bond | | | |
Year		Operations	Financing	Operations	Financing	Operations	Financing	Operations	Financing
2001	$ 10,000	$10,000	0	$ 8,388	$ 1,612	$11,452	$(1,452)	0	$ 10,000
2002	10,000	10,000	0	8,256	1,744	11,632	(1,632)	0	10,000
2003	110,000	10,000	100,000	8,114	101,886	11,833	98,167	0	110,000
Totals	$130,000	$30,000	$100,000	$24,758	$105,242	$34,917	$95,083	0	$130,000

SFAS 95 requires that cash flows be allocated between operations and financing based on the coupon interest rate.

The first reclassification allocates cash outflows based on interest expense. In 2001, for the premium case, $8,388 is shown as operating cash flow and the balance of $1,612 ($10,000 − $8,388) as financing. The interest expense reported for the discount issue, $11,452, is shown as operating cash flow and the excess over interest paid $1,452 ($11,452 − $10,000) is reported as a financing cash inflow. The 2003 financing cash flow for the discount issue, therefore, equals the outflow of $100,000 to repay the debt less $1,833 (interest expense in excess of interest paid).

The second reclassification is based on the authors' view that financing cash flow should include both principal and interest paid. Regardless of whether debt is issued at par, premium, or discount, financing cash flow reflects all payments made in the year of the actual payments.

The proceeds at issuance equal the present value of the face amount, discounted at the market interest rate. Thus, at a market rate of 10%, a $100,000 face value zero-coupon bond payable in three years will be issued at $74,622.

Exhibit 10-4 shows the income statement, cash flow, and balance sheet effects for this bond. Note that the repayment of $100,000 includes $25,378 of interest that is *never* reported

EXHIBIT 10-4
Zero-Coupon Bond Analysis

Bond: Face Value (FV) = $100,000 Coupon 0%
Maturity = 3 years
Market Rate = 10% (MR = 5%)

	(1) Liability Opening	(2) (1) × MR Interest Expense	(3) FV × CR Coupon Payment	(4) (2) − (3) Change in Liability	(5) (1) + (4) Liability Closing	(6) FV Face Value of Bond	(7) (5) − (6) Discount
01/01/01	Proceeds (see below)				$ 74,622	$100,000	$(25,378)
06/30/01	$74,622	$ 3,731	$0	$ 3,731	78,353	100,000	(21,647)
12/31/01	78,353	3,917	0	3,917	82,270	100,000	(17,730)
06/30/02	82,270	4,114	0	4,114	86,384	100,000	(13,616)
12/31/02	86,384	4,319	0	4,319	90,703	100,000	(9,297)
06/30/03	90,703	4,535	0	4,535	95,238	100,000	(4,762)
12/31/03	95,238	4,762	0	4,762	100,000	100,000	(0)
Totals		$25,378	$0	$25,378			

Calculation of Proceeds

Present value of $100,000 in 6 periods, discounted at 5%: $100,000 × 0.74622 = $74,622
Cash flow from operations: Zero in all periods
Cash flow from financing: $74,622 inflow at 1/1/01; $100,000 outflow at 12/31/03

EXHIBIT 10-5. EQK REALTY
Zero Coupon Financing, Financial Statement Excerpts

Balance Sheet

Year Ended December 31	1991	1992
Liabilities		
Mortgage note payable, net of debt discount of $392	—	$ 75,324
Zero-coupon mortgage notes, net of unamortized discount of $9,574	$89,410	—

Statement of Cash Flows

Year Ended December 31	1992
Cash flows from operating activities	
Net loss	$ (8,850)
Adjustments to reconcile net loss to net cash provided by operating activities	
Amortization of discount on zero-coupon mortgage notes	9,344
Other adjustments	7,574
Net cash provided by operating activities	$ 8,068
Cash flows from financing activities	
Prepayment of zero-coupon note	$(23,038)
Other adjustments	1,572
Net cash provided by (used in) financing activities	$(21,466)

Note 2: Debt Restructuring

In December 1992, the Company refinanced $75,689,000 representing the balance of its zero-coupon mortgage note that remained after reducing this indebtedness with the proceeds from the sale of properties. . . . The new financing, which is collateralized by first mortgage liens . . . matures in December 1995.

Source: EQK Realty Investors, *1992 Annual Report.*

as CFO; the full $100,000 payment is treated as cash from financing. The contrast with the bond issued at par (Exhibit 10-1A) is striking.

The interest on a zero-coupon bond never reduces operating cash flow. This surprising result has important analytic consequences. *One is that reported CFO is systematically overstated when a zero-coupon (or deep discount) bond is issued.* Furthermore, solvency ratios, such as cash-basis interest coverage, are improved relative to the issuance of par bonds. Finally, the cash eventually required to repay the obligation may become a significant burden.[11]

EQK Realty Investors (EQK), a real estate investment trust, illustrates this phenomenon. The company issued zero-coupon mortgage notes in 1985 and 1988. Adjustment of reported cash flow for the effect of interest on these zero-coupon bonds results in a quite different CFO trend.

Exhibit 10-5 presents excerpts from EQK's 1992 Balance Sheet, Cash Flow Statement, and Financial Statement Notes. The zero-coupon notes were retired in December 1992, using cash and a new (conventional) mortgage bond.

---

[11]In fact, interest expense increases cash flow by generating income tax deductions. (Zero-coupon bond interest expense is tax-deductible even though it is not paid.) This result can have real-world consequences. When valuing a company for leveraged buyout (LBO) purposes, the use of zero-coupon or low-coupon debt (issued at a discount) can result in the following anomaly: The higher the interest rate, the higher the cash flow, mistakenly resulting in a higher price for the company. An investment banker commented to one of the authors that this factor contributed to overbidding in the late 1980s. Of course, when the zero-coupon bond comes due, the cash must be found to repay the (much higher) face amount.

Given the opening (January 1, 1992) balance of $89,410 on the zero-coupon bond and the issuance of a mortgage bond having a face value of $75,716 ($75,324 + $392 debt discount), the cash required to retire the bond should have been $13,694 ($89,410 − $75,716). Why then did EQK report a cash payment of $23,038, an excess of $9,344, as cash from financing?

The answer can be found in the cash flows from operating activities section of the statement of cash flows. "Amortization of discount on zero-coupon mortgage notes" of $9,344 appears as an addback to net income, thereby *removing it from CFO*; $9,344 is the amount of interest that accrued on the zero-coupon bond from January 1992 through its retirement in December 1992. This interest, paid in 1992, was treated as a financing rather than an operating cash outflow. The impact of this misclassification on CFO is significant. Reclassifying the interest expense as CFO turns a positive cash flow of over $8 million into a negative $1.276 million:

Reported CFO	$8,068
Reclassify 1992 interest portion	(9,344)
Adjusted CFO	($1,276)

Similar reclassification can be extended to previous years, when the company accrued (but did not pay) interest cost (amortization of discount) on these notes. Reported CFO obscured the fact that at some point the accrued interest must be repaid. As the maturity of the debt approached, the company faced a liquidity crisis.[12]

The table below presents reported and adjusted CFO for the period 1989 to 1994. The treatment of the interest on the zero-coupon bond causes significant distortions both prior to and following the 1992 refinancing.[13]

EQK Realty Investors
Adjustment of Operating Cash Flow (CFO),
Years Ending December 31, 1989 to 1994
(in $thousands)

	1989	1990	1991	1992	1993	1994
Reported CFO	$10,458	$9,795	$ 5,728	$ 8,068	$4,087	$2,184
Less: zero-coupon interest	7,486	8,318	9,229	9,344	0	0
Adjusted CFO	$ 2,972	$1,477	$(3,501)	$(1,276)	$4,087	$2,184

After adjustment, the 1989 to 1991 deterioration in CFO is even more striking as 1991 CFO is negative.[14] The 1992 recovery is less impressive as adjusted CFO remains negative. In 1993, CFO rises despite the burden of full-coupon debt; the unadjusted data obscure this improvement. The adjusted CFO data provide better information regarding the operating cash flow trend.

Variable-Rate Debt

Some debt issues do not have a fixed coupon payment; the periodic interest payment varies with the level of interest rates. Such debt instruments are generally designed to trade at their face value. To achieve this objective, the interest rate "floats" above the rate on a specified-maturity U.S. Treasury obligation or some other benchmark rate such as the prime rate or LIBOR (London InterBank Offered Rate). The "spread" above the benchmark depends on the credit rating of the issuer.

---

[12]In 1991 EQK's auditors issued a "going concern qualification" due to the impending maturity of the zero-coupon bond.

[13]The adjustment ignores small amounts of amortization of other discount notes.

[14]Note the increasing trend of interest expense on the zero-coupon debt, similar to the trend in Exhibit 10-4.

Fixed- versus Variable-Rate Debt and Interest Rate Swaps

Borrowers can issue fixed-rate or variable-rate debt directly; alternatively, they can enter into interest rate swap agreements that convert a fixed-rate obligation to a floating-rate obligation or vice versa.

Whether a firm prefers to incur fixed-rate or variable-rate debt depends on a number of factors. Variable-rate debt exposes the firm's interest expense, cash flows, and related ratios to higher volatility due to interest rate changes.[15] On the other hand, when the firm's operating cash flows are correlated with movements in interest rates, variable-rate debt minimizes risk. The common notion that fixed rates minimize risk by reducing the volatility of a firm's income and cash flows is, thus, only a half-truth.[16]

Financial intermediaries (banks, finance companies) generally issue a high proportion of variable-rate debt, as their assets tend to be variable-rate in nature. Thus, they match the variability of their assets and liabilities (see the detailed discussion of hedging in Chapter 16).

However, a nonfinancial firm may also view variable-rate debt as hedging variable operating cash flows. For example, the 1996 financial statements of AMR (American Airlines) state:

> Because American's operating results tend to be better in economic cycles with relatively high interest rates and its capital instruments tend to be financed with long-term fixed-rate instruments, interest rate swaps in which American pays the floating rate and receives the fixed rate are used to reduce the impact of economic cycles on American's net income.[17]

Alternatively, a firm may prefer to issue variable-rate debt because management believes that interest rates will fall or short-term rates (the usual basis for variable debt) will remain below long-term rates charged on fixed-rate loans. The analysis of a firm's debt should include a consideration of whether management's choice of financing alternatives is based on the inherent economics of the business or management speculation on future interest rate changes.

Debtors use interest rate swaps to manage the fixed- and variable-rate mix of total borrowings. Box 10-1 presents the mechanics of interest rate swaps.

■ Example: Nash-Finch

Nash-Finch [NAFC] is a food wholesaler with annual sales exceeding $4 billion. The company's debt at December 31, 1998 and 1999 was $300 million and $315 million, respectively. For both years, the variable-rate debt was approximately 42% of the total debt ($128 million in 1998 and $132 million in 1999).

The company engaged in interest rate swaps, converting variable-rate to fixed-rate debt. The company disclosed the following information regarding interest rate swaps outstanding at the 1998 and 1999 year-ends (amounts in $thousands):

	Years Ended December 31	
	1998	1999
Receive variable/pay fixed	$90,000	$30,000
Average receive rate	5.5%	5.3%
Average pay rate	6.5%	6.5%

Note that Nash remains liable for the original principal and interest payments on the fixed-rate debt (see Box 10-1). *At the inception of the swap, no accounting recognition*

---

[15]The impact of interest rate changes can, of course, be either positive or negative.

[16]The investor point of view, however, is different. Variable-rate debt has low price risk; interest rate changes should have minimal impact on its market price. Significant market fluctuation should result only from perceived changes in credit quality. However, the variability of income is higher than for fixed-rate debt.

[17]AMR Corporation, 1996 Financial Statements, Note 6.

BOX 10-1
Interest Rate Swaps

Firms use interest rate swaps* to exchange variable- (floating-) rate debt for obligations with fixed interest rates or, alternatively, to exchange fixed-rate debt for obligations with variable rates.

Swaps are contractual obligations that supplement existing debt agreements. Each firm remains liable for its original debt, makes all payments on that debt, and carries that debt on its books. The firm with variable-rate debt agrees to pay, at specified intervals, amounts equal to a fixed rate times the *notional principal amount*. In return, the counterparty pays variable amounts equal to the variable interest rate (pegged to a specified rate or index) times that same notional principal amount.

Because firms wish to minimize credit risk, they do not engage in swaps with other industrial firms, even when a swap would meet the objectives of both parties. The counterparty is normally a bank or other financial institution with a high credit rating. Money center banks, as a result, have large portfolios of swaps.[†]

Given that some firms prefer variable-rate debt and others fixed-rate debt, why do they not arrange their preferred form of financing directly with their creditors? Why incur the additional costs and/or risks of swaps? Frictions in the credit markets and/or the institutional setting of the firm may result in differential borrowing costs that make it cheaper to borrow in the nonpreferred mode and swap into the preferred mode of borrowing rather than borrowing directly in the preferred mode. For example, some "household name" American firms can borrow at very low rates in certain foreign markets. A second factor leading to swaps is that preferences change over time. This is especially true of firms that use swaps to "match" assets and liabilities (see Chapter 16 for a discussion of hedging activities).

Illustration

The Triple A and Triple B companies each want to borrow $100 million. Assume that the Triple A company prefers variable-rate debt, whereas the Triple B company prefers fixed-rate debt. The companies' respective borrowing rates and preferences are:

Company	Fixed-Rate	Variable-Rate	Preferred Mode
Triple A	8%	Prime	Variable
Triple B	10%	Prime + 1%	Fixed

The Triple-A company is considered to be more creditworthy than the Triple B company and, hence, is offered more favorable borrowing terms. Note that the rate differential on fixed-rate debt (2%) is greater than the differential (1%) on floating-rate debt. This discrepancy makes it profitable for firms to enter into swaps.

Based on these rates, we demonstrate that the combined borrowing cost for the two firms is 1% lower when each company *borrows in its nonpreferred mode*. This 1% difference is independent of changes in the prime rate.

Company	Borrow Preferred Mode	Borrow Nonpreferred Mode
Triple A	Prime	8%
Triple B	10%	Prime + 1%
Total cost	Prime + 10%	Prime + 9%

The two firms are both better off borrowing in their nonpreferred mode, "swapping" the debt and splitting the 1% savings. The swap agreement requires the following payments:

- The Triple A company pays the Triple B company the prime rate (times the notional amount of $100 million).
- The Triple B company pays the Triple A company 8.5% (times the notional amount of $100 million).

The cost of the original borrowing and the swap for each company is

	Original Loan	+ To Swap Counterparty	− From Swap Counterparty	= Net Cost
Triple A	8%	Prime	(8.5%)	Prime − 0.5%
Triple B	Prime + 1%	8.5%	(Prime)	9.5%

Each company has obtained debt in its preferred mode at a rate one-half percent below the rate available on its preferred mode of borrowing.

Economic Effects of the Swap

Assume that the swap illustrated has a five-year term, the prime rate is 6% at inception, payments are made semiannually, and adjustments for changes in the prime rate are also semiannual. The first semiannual assessment results in a net payment of $1.25 million [$0.5 \times (8.5\% - 6\%) \times \$100$ million] from Triple B to Triple A. If, for the second semiannual period, the prime rate increases to 7%, then the second scheduled payment will be $0.75 million [$0.5 \times (8.5\% - 7\%) \times \$100$ million]. *Although Triple B has borrowed at a variable rate, increases in that rate are passed on to Triple A as Triple B's payments decline. Thus, Triple B's economic cost is the fixed rate of 9.5%. Conversely, Triple A is exposed to rising interest rates although it has incurred only fixed-rate debt. The swap has changed the economic position of both firms.*

Economic Effects of Termination

Now assume that Triple A, expecting increases in interest rates, wishes to terminate the swap agreement after the first payment. How much should Triple A pay to do so? The required payment

---

*For a further elaboration of these issues, see James Bicksler and Andrew Chen, "An Economic Analysis of Interest Rate Swaps," *Journal of Finance*, July 1986 and John Hull, *Introduction to Futures and Options Markets* (Englewood Cliffs, NJ: Prentice-Hall, 1995), Chapter 6.
[†]See Chapter 16 for further discussion of derivatives held by financial institutions.

should equal the fair value of the swap agreement, calculated as follows.[‡]

Triple B is liable for 9 semiannual payments of $4.25 million (0.5 × 8.5% × $100 million). If Triple B enters into another swap agreement, it would be based on current interest rates. If the fixed rate has increased by 0.5% (while the prime rate has increased by 1%), Triple B would have to make 9 payments of $4.5 million (0.5 × 9% × $100 million), an increase of $250 thousand. The present value of the increase discounted at the *new* rate of 9% is equal to approximately $1.8 million. Thus, to terminate the swap, Triple A must pay Triple B that amount.

[‡]In our simplified example, we assume that the swap is terminated at the same time when the floating rate is reset. Were this not the case, then a similar calculation would have to be made for the variable-rate bond to compensate for the fact that if Triple B entered into a new swap agreement, while it is true that it would pay a higher fixed rate, it would receive immediately floating-rate payments based on the higher floating rate and not have to wait for the next adjustment date. This calculation, however, is usually not very material; it is for only one payment and the discounting period is less than six months (from the termination date to the interest rate adjustment date).

is required although Nash has altered its debt obligation. Presumably at that time, the swap was "fair," that is, the net present value of the swap payments was zero. The transaction is an *off-balance-sheet contract.*

The effect of the swap was to reduce the sensitivity of Nash to changes in interest rates:

Effect of Swap on Debt Structure (amounts in $thousands)

	1998		1999	
	Before Swap	After Swap	Before Swap	After Swap
Fixed	$172,125	$262,125	$183,609	$213,609
Variable	127,665	37,665	131,990	101,990
Total	$299,790	$299,790	$315,599	$315,599
% Variable	42.6%	12.6%	41.8%	32.3%

The swap has also affected Nash's interest expense as the required payments (fixed) exceeded the amounts received (based on variable rates):

	Years Ended December 31	
	1998	1999
Swap	$90,000	$30,000
Interest received	4,950	1,590
Interest paid	(5,850)	(1,950)
Net payment	$ (900)	$ (360)
Interest expense:		
Reported	$29,034	$31,213
Ex-swap	28,134	30,853
Increase due to swap	3.2%	1.2%

What conclusions can we draw from these data?

1. Nash entered into the swaps to reduce its vulnerability to higher interest rates. It did not replace swaps expiring in 1999, thus increasing its exposure. Yet total debt (and variable debt) increased from 1998 to 1999.

2. The swaps increased Nash's interest expense as the fixed-rate payments exceeded the variable rate payments. The net payments can be viewed as the cost of insurance against the effect of higher interest rates.

3. While the fair value of the swaps at inception (net present value) can be assumed to be zero, the fair value will fluctuate over the swap term. If the changes are favorable, Nash-Finch will have an unrealized gain; if unfavorable there will be an unrealized loss.[18]

4. Nash also assumed *counterparty risk*, the risk that the other party will default. When Nash must make net payments (as in 1998 and 1999) there is no risk. If variable rates rose sharply, resulting in payments to Nash, then default risk would be present. [19] *When a company enters into swaps that are material to its financial position, the analyst should ensure that the counterparties are sufficiently strong so that the likelihood of default is insignificant.*[20]

These conclusions result in questions that the analyst may want to pursue by discussing them with management. Especially in the first case, the answer might yield useful insights regarding management's strategy regarding interest rate risk. ■

Debt Denominated in a Foreign Currency

Companies sometimes issue debt for which all interest and principal payments are made in a foreign currency. There are three motivations for such issuance:

1. More favorable terms in foreign markets than domestic ones.[21]

2. Assets denominated in the foreign currency and debt denominated in that currency can hedge[22] against exchange rate movements.

3. Need for foreign currency for a particular investment or other transaction.

The carrying value of foreign currency debt is adjusted for changes in exchange rates.

For example, Note 24 of the 2000 financial statements of Roche reports debt in Japanese yen and U.S. dollars as well as Roche's parent currency of Swiss francs. Note that the carrying amounts for the yen and U.S. dollar bonds[23] rose in 2000 due to appreciation of those currencies against the Swiss franc.[24]

This adjustment for exchange rate changes is distinct from any adjustment to current market value. Market value adjustments are based on changes in interest rates.[25] The market value of this debt in local currencies may have increased if interest rates declined since the debt was issued; this change is *not* reflected on the balance sheet. *Thus, the balance sheet liability has been adjusted for exchange rate changes but not interest rate changes.*

Project Debt

Some debt is issued to finance a single project, such as a factory, pipeline, or real estate. In these cases, the debt terms are tailored to the expected cash flows generated by the project. Project debt may be *nonrecourse*, meaning that the lender will be paid only from project cash

---

[18]See Chapter 16 for discussion of when and how gains and losses from derivatives must be recognized in the financial statements.

[19]When the fair value of the swap changes so that Nash-Finch has an unrealized gain, realization of that gain depends on the creditworthiness of the counterparty.

[20]If we assume that the counterparty is a highly rated financial institution, it would not provide collateral to protect Nash against default.

[21]For example, in July 1998, Pepsico issued one-year notes in Japan (to retail investors) and swapped the fixed-rate obligation for floating rate U.S. dollar payments. The company stated that its net borrowing cost was *comfortably below one-month LIBOR*.

[22]If the parent currency strengthens relative to the foreign currency, then the carrying amount of assets denominated in foreign currencies decreases. This decrease is offset by the decrease (in the parent currency) of the debt to be repaid.

[23]The rise in the carrying amount of the zero coupon U.S. dollar obligations is due to accretion of discount as well as the appreciation of the U.S. dollar.

[24]See the financial review (p. 51 of the Roche annual report) for foreign currency data.

[25]In theory, exchange rates are also affected by interest rates. However, that influence is based on the *difference* in interest rate levels between the two countries, *not the level* of interest rates.

flows and cannot demand payment from the debtor if the project is unsuccessful. Mortgages on real estate are the major example of nonrecourse debt. Even though such debt is shown on the debtor's balance sheet, the debt is a claim only against the project cash flows and assets. Some project debt is incurred by joint ventures, discussed in Chapter 11.

■ Example: Forest City Enterprises

Forest City [FCE], a U.S. developer of commercial and residential real estate, finances most of its projects with nonrecourse mortgage debt. The company's capital structure at January 31, 2000 was (in $millions):

Mortgage debt, nonrecourse	$2,382.4	74.5%
Recourse debt	429.9	13.4%
Shareholders' equity	386.5	12.1%
Total capital	$3,198.8	100.0%

The large proportion of nonrecourse debt protects the company from adversity. The effects of one poorly performing project cannot jeopardize others, as the company cannot lose more than its total investment in that project.   ■

Debt with Equity Features

Convertible Bonds and Warrants

To reduce borrowing costs, many companies issue debt convertible into their common shares or issue a combination of bonds and warrants to purchase common shares. Although conceptually these two types of "equity-linked" debt are identical, their accounting consequences may differ.[26]

Convertible Bonds. Under APB 14 (1969), the conversion feature of a bond is completely ignored when the bond is issued. Thus, the entire proceeds of the bond are recorded as a liability, and interest expense is recorded as if the bond were nonconvertible. However, the conversion feature lowers interest expense. When the bondholder converts the convertible bond into common stock, the entire proceeds are reclassified from debt to equity. As discussed in Box 10-2, however, the FASB issued an exposure draft that would change the accounting for convertible debt.

From an analytic perspective, however, recognition should be given to the equity feature prior to the conversion. When the stock price is (significantly) greater than the conversion price, it is likely that the debt will not have to be repaid, and the convertible bond should be treated as equity rather than debt when calculating solvency ratios such as debt-to-equity. When the stock price is significantly below the conversion price, the bond should be treated as debt. At levels close to the conversion price, the instrument has both debt and equity features, and its treatment becomes a more difficult issue.

One possibility is to separate the debt and equity values of the convertible bond, using option pricing models. This analysis is complex, however, and beyond the scope of this book. IAS 32 (2000) requires issuers to split compound instruments into their component parts. The FASB ED would require such separation. Alternatively, the analyst can examine the sensitivity of key ratios to bond classification, first treating the bond as debt and then as

---

[26]A convertible bond can be disaggregated into a bond plus an option to convert the bond into common shares. An important difference between a convertible and a debt-plus-warrant issue is that, in the former case, the bond must be surrendered to exercise the option, whereas in the latter case, the bond and warrant are not linked. Thus, the issuer can use the proceeds of exercised warrants for purposes other than the retirement of the associated debt. Another difference is their impact on earnings-per-share calculations. The interest expense on the convertible issue is eliminated when diluted earnings per share are computed (Chapter 4), whereas the interest on the debt component of the bond-plus-option alternative will never affect earnings-per-share calculations (however, there is an adjustment for the exercise of dilutive warrants).

BOX 10-2
FASB Exposure Draft: Accounting for Financial Instruments with Characteristics of Liabilities, Equity, or Both

---

On October 27, 2000, the Board issued an exposure draft (ED) that would change the accounting for:

- Convertible debt
- Redeemable preferred shares

In general, the ED would classify as equity all financial instruments components that establish an ownership relationship with the issuer. A component establishes an ownership relationship if it

1. Is an outstanding equity share not subject to redemption, or
2. Is an obligation that can or must be settled by the issuance of equity shares, and all changes in the monetary value of the obligation are attributable to, equal to, and in the same direction as the change in the fair value of the issuer's equity shares.

The new standard would require that proceeds of issuance of securities with both liability and equity components be allocated between the value of the liability component and that of the equity component. The most important example is the issuance of convertible debt, which would be accounted for as if the company sold a combination of debt and warrants.

When a company issued convertible debt, it would be required to allocate the proceeds (net of underwriting fees and other direct costs of issuance) between the debt (liability) component and the warrant (equity) component using their relative fair values. If the warrant could not be valued, the issuer would estimate the fair value of the debt component, and allocate the remaining proceeds to the equity component.*

Further, if the debt is repurchased or converted, the issuer must recognize gain or loss† equal to the difference between the fair value of the debt component and the carrying amount of the liability.

There would also be a gain or loss on the equity component at the date of repurchase or conversion. This gain or loss would be excluded from income but would affect stockholders' equity.

The accounting change would have the following effects:

1. The difference between the fair value of the debt component and its face value would be amortized over the life of the debt, using the effective interest method. This would result in higher interest expense and lower income than under current accounting.
2. Only the debt component would be shown as a liability; the equity component would be recorded in stockholders' equity. As a result, the debt-to-equity ratio would be lower than under the current accounting method.
3. At redemption or conversion, the company would recognize a gain or loss on the liability component. In general, companies would recognize a loss when interest rates were lower at the time of repurchase or conversion than when the debt was issued. In the case of conversion, the fair value of the liability component would be added to equity, rather than the carrying amount under current accounting.
4. At redemption or conversion, stockholders' equity would reflect the change in value of the equity component. When the underlying shares have risen in value, equity would rise, reducing the debt-to-equity ratio. Under current accounting, the market value at redemption or conversion date has no effect on the balance sheet.

The ED would also change the classification of redeemable preferred shares (and similar instruments such as Trust Preferreds) by requiring that they be recorded as debt in the issuer's balance sheet. Similarly, the "dividends" paid on such shares would be included in interest expense.

The effect of this change would be to increase the reported debt-equity ratio and reduce the interest coverage ratio of affected firms.

A final standard was expected to be issued prior to the end of 2002. It is likely that affected companies would be required to restate their financial statements for the accounting change.

---

*This method is styled the "with-and-without method" in the ED.

†Under SFAS 145 (2002), gains and losses from the extinguishment of debt are treated as extraordinary items only when they meet the APB 30 criteria for classification as an extraordinary item (see page 54 of chapter 2).

---

equity to see whether the differences are significant. If they are, then the question of whether the debt will be ultimately converted becomes a key issue, which may depend on the purpose of the analysis.[27]

■ Example: Holmen

Note 18 of Holmen's annual report shows that in 1998, the company issued debt of SKr 361 million, convertible into class B common shares in 2004 at a price of SKr 148.10. As the market price of Holmen's class B shares was SKr 307 at December 31, 1999,

---

[27]For example, in takeover analysis, the intended purchase price will determine whether convertible bonds will be converted to common or remain outstanding debt.

these bonds should be considered equity. The reclassification decreases the debt/total capital ratio:

Holmen Capital Structure

December 31, 1999

	Reported	Reclassification	Adjusted
SKr millions			
Financial liabilities	6,845	(361)	6,484
Equity	15,883	361	16,244
Total capital	22,728		22,728
Financial liabilities	30.1%		28.5%
Equity	69.9%		71.5%

Exchangeable Bonds. Some bond issues are convertible into shares of another firm rather than those of the issuing firm. The analysis of such issues is more complex than the analysis of convertible debt. Exercise of the conversion privilege results in:

- Extinguishment of the debt
- Elimination of the investment in the underlying shares
- Recognition of gain or loss from the "sale" (via debt conversion) of the underlying shares

The motivation for such debt issues may include:

1. The desire to obtain cash while retaining the underlying shares for strategic reasons.
2. Minimizing the market effect of sales; the underlying shares are sold over time as bonds are exchanged.
3. Financial benefits: The interest rate on the exchangeable bonds will be lower (because of the exchange feature) than on straight debt, and the exercise price will contain a premium over the current market price.
4. Delayed recognition of a large unrealized gain; recognition is postponed until the exchange privilege is exercised. This delays the income tax recognition of the gain and may permit management some control over the timing of the gain (it can call the bonds, forcing exchange, when it wishes to report the gain).
5. Hedging the investment. As discussed in Chapter 16, SFAS 133 changed the accounting for such hedges.

■ Example: Times Mirror

In March 1996, Times Mirror [TMC] sold 1.3 million shares of Premium Equity Participating Securities (PEPS) redeemable for shares of Netscape. TMC had purchased Netscape shares less than one year earlier, before Netscape's initial public offering, at a price of $2.25 per share. TMC's Netscape shares were restricted from public sale. The PEPS were sold at a price of $39.25 with a 4.25% coupon and a March 15, 2001 maturity. At that date, each PEPS was redeemable for the cash equivalent of:

- One Netscape share if that share's price was below $39.25
- .87 Netscape share if its price was $45.15 or higher
- $39.25 cash if Netscape's share price was between $45.15 and $39.25

The advantages to TMC of offering PEPS were that TMC:

1. Received the fair market value of its Netscape shares, at a low interest rate of 4.25%, despite the fact that the shares could not be legally sold.
2. Hedged its investment; if Netscape shares declined, the PEPS holders would receive smaller payments at maturity.

3. Maintained part of the upside potential given the reduced conversion rate if Netscape shares exceeded $45.15 in price at maturity.

4. Postponed capital gains tax until the actual sale of Netscape shares was effected through conversion of the PEPS.

5. Enabled TMC to control the timing of its realization of the large gain on the Netscape investment.

The last two advantages are illustrated by events in 1998 and 1999:

- In 1998, TMC sold part of its Netscape holding, redeemed a corresponding portion of the PEPS, and realized a pretax gain of $16 million.[28]
- In 1999, TMC sold shares of AOL (which had acquired Netscape) and redeemed additional PEPS, reporting a pretax gain of nearly $17 million. ■

Bonds with Warrants. When warrants and bonds are issued together, the accounting treatment differs from that of convertible bonds. The proceeds must be allocated between the two financial instruments.[29] The fair value of the bond portion is the recorded liability. As a result, the bond is issued at a discount, and interest expense includes amortization of that discount. The fair value of the warrants is included in equity and has no income statement impact. When warrants are exercised, the additional cash increases equity capital.

Roche has made extensive use of bonds with equity features (see Note 24 and pages 99–101 of the Roche annual report). Problem 10-11 describes one of these issues and explores its accounting and analytical consequences.

Comparison of Convertible Bonds and Bonds with Warrants. As bonds with warrants are accounted for as if they were issued at a discount, the reported liability is lower (but increases as the discount is amortized) as compared to that of a convertible bond. However, reported interest expense is higher.[30] As discussed earlier in this chapter, reported cash flow from operations is the same, equal to the coupon interest.

These differences are summarized in the list below, which also includes a comparison with a conventional bond. Note that issuing debt with equity features:

- Lowers interest expense
- Increases operating cash flows
- Results in a balance sheet liability equal to or below that of a conventional bond

In all respects, such debt appears less costly.

Interest Expense	Balance Sheet Liability	Operating Cash Flow
Conventional bond	Conventional bond	Conventional bond
greater than	*equal to*	*less than*
Bond with warrants	Convertible bond	Convertible bond
greater than	*greater than*	*equal to*
Convertible bond	Bond with warrants	Bond with warrants

However, the financial statement effects are misleading as the cost of the equity feature is ignored. When convertible debt is issued, there is a systematic understatement of interest expense.[31]

---

[28]This gain was previously reflected in equity as TMC carried its investment in Netscape at market value (see Chapter 13 for effects of such accounting).

[29]As discussed in Box 10-2, the FASB has proposed extending this accounting treatment to convertible bonds as well.

[30]Because of the accounting difference, American companies rarely issue debt/warrant combinations. However, such issues are common outside of the United States.

[31]Moreover, the impact of equity-linked bonds on earnings per share must always be taken into consideration (see Chapter 4).

Commodity Bonds

The interest and principal payments on bond issues are sometimes tied to the price of a commodity, such as gold, silver, or oil. Firms producing the commodity, as part of a hedge strategy, may issue such bonds. A higher commodity price increases the payments to bondholders but is offset by higher operating profitability. These bonds, therefore, convert interest from a fixed to a variable cost. Such bonds were issued during time periods when commodity prices were rising, making the bonds attractive to purchasers. A recent variation on this theme is the issuance of bonds whose payoff depends on losses due to insurance losses resulting from natural catastrophes. Problem 10-15 is based on one such "catastrophe bond."

Perpetual Debt

Some debt issues have no stated maturity. When debt does not have a maturity date, it may be considered preferred equity rather than a liability for analytic purposes. An exception would be cases where debt covenants are likely to force repayment or refinancing of the debt.

■ **Example: SAS**

In 1986, SAS (Scandinavian Airlines) issued a perpetual 200 million Swiss franc–denominated subordinated loan, with the interest rate fixed for 10 years and reset every 10 years. While there is no set maturity date, SAS has the exclusive right to terminate the loan once every five years.

In 1994, SAS repurchased SFR 55.35 million at a price of 72. This repurchase shows that perpetual notes are not the same as equity, as changes in market conditions may lead the issuer to refinance them. However, given management control over the refinancing decision, treatment as preferred equity is appropriate absent evidence of refinancing intent. ■

When long-term interest rates were at low levels, some firms issued debt with a maturity of 100 years. Although such issues are technically debt, their long maturity suggests that, for all practical purposes, they represent permanent capital and should be treated as equity when computing the debt-to-equity ratio. For example, Walt Disney issued 100-year bonds in 1993.[32]

Preferred Stock

Many companies issue more than one class of shares. Preferred (or preference) shares have priority over common shares with respect to dividends and entitlement to the proceeds of sale or liquidation. In exchange for this privileged position, preferred shareholders usually give up their right to participate fully in the success of the company.

Preferred shares generally have a fixed dividend payment and a fixed preference on liquidation. Dividend payments are almost always *cumulative*; if not paid when due, they remain a liability (but one that is not recorded). Dividend arrears must be paid before any dividend can be paid to common shareholders. When calculating the net worth of a company with preferred shares outstanding, the analyst should:

1. Subtract the liquidating value of the preferred, not the par or stated value, which may be lower.
2. Subtract any cumulative dividends that are in arrears.

Some preferred shares have a variable interest rate. "Auction rate" preferred shares have interest rates that change frequently, making them attractive to buyers seeking "money-market"-type investments.[33] From an analytical perspective, these preferred shares function as

---

[32]These bonds have a fixed interest rate of 7.55%, protecting Disney against future interest rate increases. As the bonds are not callable until 2023, the buyers were protected against lower interest rates for 30 years.

[33]For U.S. corporate buyers, preferred dividends are 70% tax-free when ownership is below 20%, making these issues more attractive on an after-tax basis than many other short-term investments. The exclusion is 80% for ownership of 20% but below 80%.

short-term liabilities and should be treated as such. They are often called when market conditions change, making them a less permanent source of funds.

Preferred shares are almost always callable by the issuer. Many issues are, however, redeemable by the preferred shareholder, often over a period of years.[34] Because of these "sinking fund" provisions, redeemable preferreds should be treated as debt for analysis; they should be included as debt in solvency ratios, and dividend payments should be treated as interest. The FASB has issued an exposure draft (see Box 10-2) that would require redeemable preferred shares to be reported as debt, and the "dividends" on such shares included in interest expense, as required by IAS 32 (2000).

Consistent with this view, the SEC requires that redeemable preferred shares be excluded from stockholders' equity. However, at the same time, the SEC does not require their classification as debt. The argument against debt classification is that, ultimately, *firms cannot be forced to pay the dividends or redeem the preferred shares. Unlike creditors, preferred shareholders do not have the power to force the firm into bankruptcy for noncompliance* with the terms of the agreement.[35] Often, when dividends are in arrears, they do gain representation on the board of directors.

The ambiguity as to whether these shares are debt or equity was shown in two studies by Kimmel and Warfield (1993, 1995). They found that only 60% of redeemable preferred shares are actually redeemed; the other 40% are eventually converted to common shares, arguing against treating these hybrids as debt. Furthermore, as a firm's systematic risk (its beta) is related to a firm's debt-to-equity ratio (as discussed in Chapter 18), they tested whether the relationship had a better "fit" with the redeemables treated as debt or equity. They found that they *did not fit into either category unless the redeemables had voting rights and were convertible*. Only when these attributes were present did the securities exhibit equitylike qualities. Thus, on average, one cannot generalize as to the nature of these hybrid securities.

The line between debt and equity has become increasingly blurred in recent years. Companies prefer to issue securities that minimize the after-tax cost of financing yet provide maximum flexibility.[36] Some issues are designated preferreds but are really debt; others are called debt but are functionally equity. Although help from accounting standards setters is on the way, analysts must evaluate such instruments on a case-by-case basis and decide whether to treat them as debt or equity.

Effects of Changes in Interest Rates

Debt reported on the balance sheet is equal to the present value of future cash payments discounted at the *market rate on the date of issuance*. Increases (decreases) in the *current market rate* decrease (increase) the *market value* of the debt. A company that issues fixed-rate debt prior to an increase (decrease) in market rates experiences an economic gain (loss) as a result of the rate change. This economic gain or loss is not reflected in either the income statement or balance sheet.

For some analytical purposes, however, the market value of a company's debt may be more relevant than its book value. It better reflects the firm's economic position and is as important as the current market values of a firm's assets. Analysis of a firm's absolute and relative level of debt and borrowing capacity should be based on current market conditions. Consider two firms reporting the same book value of debt. One firm issued the debt

---

[34]These provisions provide preferred shareholders with a guaranteed future value for the shares.

[35]In many states, a firm cannot pay dividends or redeem shares if such payments will jeopardize the company's survival.

[36]Trust Preferred Securities (TPS) are an example of such securities. For tax purposes, they are treated as debt. While they cannot be classified as equity, they are not reported as debt but rather as preferred shares or minority interest. Similarly, "dividend" payments are reported as preferred dividends or minority interest. Frischmann, Kimmel, and Warfield (1999) refer to TPSs as the "Holy Grail" of financial instruments and report that, since their introduction in 1993, they have become the primary mode of new issues of preferred shares.

when interest rates were low; the other at higher current interest rates. Debt-to-equity ratios based on book values may be the same. However, the firm that issued the bonds at the lower interest rate has higher borrowing capacity as the economic value of its debt is lower.[37] Ratios calculated using the market value of debt would reflect the stronger solvency position.

Furthermore, in valuation models that deduct the value of debt from the value of the firm (or of its assets), that debt should be measured at market value rather than book value.[38] Firms that issued debt at lower rates are relatively better off when interest rates increase, and this advantage should increase the equity value of the firm.

In the United States, SFAS 107, Disclosures about Fair Value of Financial Instruments, requires that firms report the fair value of outstanding debt. IAS 32 (1998) has similar requirements. Box 10-3 restates the debt of Westvaco from book to market value. This exercise is useful for several reasons.

First, financial statement disclosures are based on year-end (or quarter) prices. When interest rates have changed significantly since the last report date, the analyst may need to recalculate the market value of the firm's debt. Second, most non-U.S. firms, and firms in the United States that are not subject to FASB disclosure requirements, do not provide market value disclosures; analysts must know how to estimate the market value of debt for such firms. Finally, market valuation requires assumptions and (especially for firms with complex financial instruments) often there are competing valuation methods. In some cases, analysts may want to perform their own market value calculations. To do so, they must disaggregate management's aggregate fair value disclosure; this requires an understanding of how market values are estimated.

■ **Example: Westvaco**

The book value of Westvaco's long-term debt was $1,477 million at October 31, 1999; its market value was $1,494 million, or 1% higher. The October 31, 1998 book value was $1,557 million; its market value was $1,636 million, or 5% higher. Thus, during the 1999 fiscal year, market value relative to book value declined 4%. This decline reflected the rise in interest rates (see Box 10-3), which reduced the fair value. The decline reflects the structure of Westvaco's debt, which is mostly fixed-rate debt with long maturities. ■

The Westvaco example above is not unique. The market value of the long-term debt of Mead [MEA] was 6.6% higher than book value at December 31, 1998 (Mead was on a calendar year). One year later, the market value was 2.9% below the book value; during calendar 1999, therefore, market value relative to book value declined by 9.5% as interest rates rose. Mead, which merged with Westvaco early in 2002, had a similar debt structure, mostly fixed rate debt with long maturities.

These factors (confirmed by empirical results discussed in Box 10-4) suggest the conditions to be considered before deciding whether the restatement of debt to market value is a useful exercise. All of the following factors should be considered.

Debt: Market or Book Value?

Given the effort and assumptions required to estimate market values when they are not provided, we now turn to a discussion of the factors that determine whether the adjustment from book value to market value is a useful exercise. Empirical results with respect to these factors are discussed in Box 10-4.

---

[37]Theoretically, it could refinance its current debt at the same interest rate as the other firm, lowering the book value of debt.

[38]Similarly (as discussed in Chapter 19), in discounted cash flow valuation analysis, the calculation of a firm's (weighted-average) cost of capital is based on market rather than book values of debt (and equity).

BOX 10-3
Estimating the Market Value of Debt

In many cases, the replacement of book value with market value is simple. For publicly traded debt, market values are readily available.* If the debt is not publicly traded, its present value can be calculated by applying the current market rate to the original debt terms. The maturity, coupon rate, and other terms of long-term debt are generally disclosed for each debt security issued.

The appropriate current market rate can be obtained from:

1. Other publicly traded debt of the company having approximately the same maturity; estimate the rate used by the market to discount that debt.

2. Publicly traded debt of equivalent companies in the same industry; estimate the rate used to discount that debt.

3. Estimating the risk premium over the rate on government debt of the same maturity. The risk premium depends on the bond-rating "risk" class of the company's bonds.

Calculating the Market Value of Debt

Footnote J in Westvaco's financial statements shows notes payable and long-term obligations at October 31, 1999. The company reports the fair value as required by SFAS 107.[†] The book and fair values for the three years ended October 31, 2000 are (in $thousands):

October 31	1998	1999	2000
Book value	$1,557,477	$1,477,162	$2,716,772
Fair value	1,636,093	1,494,290	2,627,696
Difference	$ 78,616	$ 17,128	$ (89,076)

Source: Westvaco *Annual Reports, 1999 and 2000.*

The maturities, coupon rates, and carrying amounts for most obligations are listed in footnote J. Some obligations are publicly traded while others are not.

As Westvaco discloses the fair (market) value of its debt, we forgo the laborious task of calculating the estimated market value for each issue. The following comments are intended as a guide for use when such calculations are required.

Most of Westvaco's debt at October 31, 1999 consists of fixed-rate long-term debentures, some of which have sinking funds. Because the rate is fixed and the duration is long, the fair value of these bonds fluctuates with interest rates.

Example:

In 1990 Westvaco, which was A rated, issued $100 million of 9.75% bonds due June 15, 2020. At the issue date, the yield[‡] was 130 basis points (1.3%) above the yield on the U.S. Treasury 8.75% bonds due in May, 2020. The price and yield to maturity of the U.S. Treasury 8.75% issue at October 31, 1998–2001 was reported by Bloomberg as follows:

October 31	1998	1999	2000	2001
Price	142-11*	124-30	131-4	145-11
Yield-to-maturity	5.40%	6.53%	6.02%	4.98%

*US government securities with maturities longer than one year are quoted as a % of face value in 32nds. Thus 142-11 means 142 11/32% of face value or $1,423.44 per $1,000 bond.
Source: Price and yield data from Bloomberg.

Estimation of the fair value of the Westvaco 9¾% bonds requires an estimate of the spread over the U.S. Treasury bond. That spread is a function of the rating of the corporate issuer (Westvaco) and the spread between bonds of different ratings classes.[§] Bond quality spreads are variable over time, tending to compress when the economy is strong (and concerns about credit quality are low) and to widen when economic conditions weaken.

Westvaco was A rated by Standard & Poor's at October 31, 1997 and A rated at October 31, 1998. Standard & Poor's data show little change in quality spreads in 1998 and 1999. Thus, our calculations assume that the Westvaco bonds had a yield to maturity of 130 basis points for both years.

Extending this analysis to 2000 and 2001, we find two changes:

1. Westvaco's S&P rating was reduced from A− to BBB+ in May 2000 and further reduced to BBB in June 2001. These rating reductions reflected Westvaco's higher leverage.

2. Quality spreads started to widen in 2000 and 2001 as concerns grew about the economic outlook and the possible effect of recession on corporate credit quality. The September 11, 2001 terrorist attacks accelerated this trend.

Thus our estimated yield spread for the Westvaco bonds is 180 basis points at October 31, 2000 and 220 basis points at October 31, 2001.

The following table shows the results of these assumptions and the calculated fair value of the Westvaco bonds. These fair value estimates differ from the actual market value reported in Bloomberg by less than 2% each year.

---

*Sources include rating service publications (such as Standard & Poor's *Bond Guide*), newspapers, and electronic quotation services.
[†]The book value does not match the total of current and noncurrent obligations in footnote J. The company has apparently excluded some long-term obligations that it considers not to be financial instruments.
[‡]Throughout this box, yield means yield-to-maturity.
[§]See Chapter 18 for discussion of bond ratings.

October 31	1998	1999	2000	2001
Yield on U.S. 8.75% bond	5.40%	6.53%	6.02%	4.98%
Assumed spread	1.30%	1.30%	1.80%	2.20%
Assumed yield on Westvaco 9.75% bond	6.70%	7.83%	7.82%	7.18%
Calculated value of Westvaco bond	$1,344.85	$1,194.43	$1,191.50	$1,260.88
Bloomberg value of Westvaco bond	1,369.80	1,217.40	1,169.30	1,245.60
Difference	−1.8%	−1.9%	1.9%	1.2%

Source: Price and yield data from Bloomberg.

Complexities in Market Value Estimation

Because of the conventional nature of Westvaco's debt, the calculation of its market value is straightforward. Westvaco's debt is virtually all fixed rate and dollar denominated. Simple debt structures, however, are becoming the exception rather than the rule for large companies, given globalization and the increased sophistication of financial markets.

Some complexities make the calculation of market values almost impossible as the requisite information is lacking. A few of the complexities summarized below have been discussed earlier, others will be addressed in later sections of the text, and some remain beyond the scope of our book.

Convertible Bonds

Market prices are readily available for most convertible debt issues. However, these prices incorporate both the debt and equity features of the security. Only the debt component of the market value should be included as part of debt.

Variable-Rate Debt

Variable-rate debt usually requires no market value adjustment. Because of the continuous adjustment of the interest rate on the debt, market value approximates book value.**

Debt Denominated in a Foreign Currency

For debt denominated in a foreign currency, the present value calculations should be based on current interest rates for the currency in which the debt is denominated.

Hedges and Derivatives

Firms can protect themselves against changes in interest rates and/or currency exchange rates using instruments such as options or forward contracts (including swap agreements). We defer a discussion of the accounting treatment and economic impact of these instruments on the value of a firm's debt, for the most part, to Chapter 16. In this chapter we confine ourselves to a discussion of *interest rate swaps*.

As previously discussed, *the original debt instrument with its original parameters remains in effect and is reported in the firm's financial statements; if publicly traded, market prices are available.* However, the estimated market value of the underlying debt instrument must reflect any interest rate swap.

When fixed-rate debt has been converted to floating-rate debt with an interest rate swap covering its full term, no adjustment to market value is required. If a swap does not cover the full term of fixed-rate debt, changes in interest rates after the end of the swap term will affect market values. Thus, it is important to discern the terms of any swaps by careful reading of footnotes.

When a swap converts floating-rate debt to fixed-rate debt, however, the market value is exposed to changes in interest rates. Even though the market value of the original obligation does not change, the fair value of the effective (because of the swap) obligation does and should be calculated.

**This is not precisely accurate. The variable-rate adjustment may lag the interest rate change. Nevertheless, given the short period until adjustment, the effect of any lag on present value is usually immaterial. Because of this, SFAS 107 states that, for variable-rate debt, the book value can be used to approximate the market or fair value.

Debt Maturities. The effect of interest rate changes on the market value of debt increases with the maturity of the debt. If a firm's debt is mostly short-term, changes in interest rates will not appreciably affect its market value.[39]

Interest Rates on Debt. For adjustable-rate debt, whose interest rate varies with the market rate of interest, book value approximates market value and no adjustment is required. On the other hand, the market value of fixed-rate debt issues does change with interest rates. This is especially true of zero-coupon and other discount debt, due to their longer duration relative to debt of the same maturity issued at par.

---

[39]Thus, even if its long-term debt is adjusted by 10%, total debt will only be affected by 10% times the percentage of long-term debt. The lower the percentage of long-term debt, the smaller the overall adjustment.

BOX 10-4
Market or Book Values: Empirical Evidence

Bowman (1980) examined the relationship between firms' market betas and the debt-to-equity ratio. Finance theory predicts (see Chapter 18) that the higher a firm's debt-to-equity ratio (using market values), the higher the firm's beta.

Letting the superscripts M and B refer to the market and book value, respectively, Bowman examined which of the following four measures of the debt-to-equity ratio, D^M/E^M, D^M/E^B, D^B/E^M, and D^B/E^B, were more closely associated with the firm's beta.

Bowman obtained the best results when he used the market value of equity in the denominator. Whether debt was measured on a market basis or book basis made little difference as the ratios D^B/E^M and D^M/E^M yielded similar results. The pure book value ratio D^B/E^B did not perform as well; the measure of the market value of the debt-to-book value of equity (D^M/E^B) performed the poorest.

These results can be partly attributable to the fact that for close to 60% of the debt in Bowman's sample, book value and market value were equivalent. Furthermore, the correlation between the market value of debt and the book value of debt was close to 100%. As the study ranked debtors by relative rather than absolute levels of debt, changes in the market rates of interest shifted debt valuations without changing ranks.

Mulford (1986) replicated Bowman's study by using a later time period. Bowman's analysis was based on 1973 data, predating the dramatic rise in market interest rates of the late 1970s. Mulford, referring to Bowman's study, noted:

> His failure to find evidence of superior performance for a debt-to-equity ratio based on market values of debt may have been due to small differences between the book and market values of debt which accompanied the general level of interest rates at that time.*

To remedy this deficiency, Mulford focused on 1980, when market rates of interest were historically high. In addition, to alleviate potential measurement problems arising from the conversion of book to market values, he examined the performance of portfolios of firms in addition to individual firms. Mulford's results were more in line with theory, but only on a portfolio basis. No matter which variation was used to measure the relationship between beta and debt-to-equity, the market-based debt-to-equity ratio was always the most closely associated with beta on a portfolio basis. On an individual basis, D^M/E^M did not always perform as well, but the differences between it and the best performing ratio were minimal.

These results suggest, not surprisingly, that the market value of debt is not superior to book value when the difference between the stated and market rates of interest is small; the additional cost of obtaining market values is not worthwhile.† Adjustment is necessary only when the gap between the historic and market rates of interest is large. Even then, potential measurement problems‡ in estimating market values may offset any benefits from the adjustment process.

---

*Charles W. Mulford, "The Importance of a Market Value Measurement of Debt in Leverage Ratios: Replications and Extensions," *Journal of Accounting Research*, Autumn 1984, pp. 897–906.

†Given the high correlation between market and book values of debt, this is especially true for analyses that focus on relative rather than absolute debt burdens.

‡The issue of a measurement problem also calls into question the results of both Bowman and Mulford from a different perspective. They adjusted only on-balance-sheet debt, ignoring any "off-balance-sheet" debt. As Chapter 11 will make clear, the latter can be significant.

When a firm has swapped its fixed debt for floating-rate debt, there should be no adjustment, as the value of that debt is no longer exposed to interest rate changes. Conversely, when a firm swaps variable rates for fixed rates, the market value of that portion of its debt will vary with interest rates and adjustment is required.

Changes in Market Interest Rates. The adjustment to market value depends on changes in the market rate of interest. As long as there is no long-term trend, fluctuations in market value tend to offset, leaving the difference between book and market values small. However, when rates rise or fall greatly over several years, the differences between book and market value can be significant.

Embedded Interest Rate. Westvaco issued debt at various times and its (weighted) average outstanding coupon rate (*embedded rate*) was approximately 8.39%,[40] within the range of interest rates over the late 1990s. The adjustment from book value does not depend

[40]Calculated as interest incurred (from Westvaco footnote F) divided by the average debt level. For 1999, the calculation is

$$\frac{\$132,428}{(\$1,552,377 + \$1,605,415)/2} = 8.39\%$$

on the change in interest rates itself, but rate changes relative to the imbedded rate. As interest rates were below the embedded rate for both 1998 and 1999, the fair value exceeds book value.

Unless there are limits on the firm's ability to refinance (noncallable debt or deterioration in credit quality), the embedded rate should decline (with some lag) as interest rates fall. The reverse is not true; firms with long-term fixed-rate debt can enjoy low interest costs for many years even though interest rates in general have risen.

Debt of Firms in Distress

When the credit quality of a firm changes significantly (in either direction), the market price of debt will follow, independent of interest rate trends. When credit quality and the market value of debt decline, there appears to be a gain to the firm, yet it is difficult to argue that shareholders are better off. This apparent paradox reflects simultaneous changes in the value of assets as credit quality changes. It is reasonable to assume that some assets of such troubled companies are impaired (see the discussion in Chapter 8). Case 10-1 discusses the convertible debt of Read-Rite, a troubled debtor, the exchange of that debt for a new debt issue, and the ultimate conversion of that new issue into equity.

Accounting for Restructured and Impaired Debt

When a debtor is in financial difficulty, creditors may agree to accept assets in payment of the debt or to "restructure" the obligation by modifying its terms (e.g., reducing the interest rate or deferring principal payments). When debt is extinguished, both the debtor and creditor will recognize gain or loss measured as the difference between the fair value of the assets (cash or other assets) used to repay the debt and its carrying amount. This accounting treatment raises neither accounting nor analysis issues.

When the obligation is restructured, however, different accounting rules apply to creditors and debtors. Creditors adhere to SFAS 114 (1993), as amended by SFAS 118 (1994), whereas debtors use SFAS 15 (1977) to account for these transactions.

Under SFAS 114, the creditor must recognize a loss equal to the difference between the carrying value of the loan and the present value of the restructured payment stream *discounted at the original discount rate* (effective interest rate). Thus, if a 12% coupon loan with a face value of $100,000 and three years remaining to maturity is restructured by reducing the interest rate to 8%, the creditor recognizes a loss of $9,610 as the new carrying value of the loan is $90,390.[41] The loan impairment may also be measured using the observable market price of the loan or the fair value of collateral when the loan is collateral dependent.[42]

The FASB was reluctant, however, to allow debtors to record gains resulting from financial distress. SFAS 15 provides that the debtor's carrying amount of the debt be compared with the *undiscounted gross cash flows* (principal and interest) due after restructuring. As long as the gross cash flows exceed the carrying amount, the debtor recognizes no gain. In our example, the future payments are ($100,000 + 3 × $8,000) = $124,000. No gain is recognized.[43]

However, the present value of the cash flows has been reduced; in economic terms, the debtor has gained at the expense of the creditor. The accounting mandated by SFAS 15 recognizes this transfer only over the life of the loan as payments are made; the debtor

---

[41]If we assume annual payments, the present value of a three-year annuity of $8,000 discounted at 12% + present value of $100,000 in three years discounted at 12% equals $90,390.

[42]SFAS 118 amended SFAS 114 to allow creditors to continue income-recognition methods for impaired loans that had been used prior to the adoption of SFAS 114. For example, cost-recovery or cash-basis methods report investments in impaired loans at less than the present value of expected future cash flows. In these cases, no additional impairment needs to be recognized under SFAS 118. SFAS 114 was also amended to require additional disclosures regarding the investment in certain impaired loans and the recognition of interest income on those loans.

[43]If the payments do not exceed the carrying value, then the gain is limited to the difference between those amounts; the debt is discounted at an implicit interest rate of zero.

will show lower interest expense as the loan is amortized at the implicit interest rate of the loan. In our example, interest expense is now calculated at an interest rate of 8% rather than 12%.

A similar approach is mandated by the FASB for loans considered to be "impaired." Creditors are required to recognize the probable loss, but recognition of gains by debtors is not allowed. Under SFAS 114, creditors are required to carry impaired loans at the present value of cash flows expected after modification of the loan terms, *discounted at the original effective interest rate*. For the debtor, however, no gain recognition is permitted.

For purposes of analysis, however, both impaired and restructured debt should be restated to fair market value using a *current market interest rate* to discount the cash flows required by the (actual or expected) restructured obligation. However, as noted earlier, debtor "gains" should be viewed warily; gains resulting from an inability to repay loans are almost certainly offset by asset impairment.

Retirement of Debt Prior to Maturity

Firms generally choose the initial debt maturity of their obligations based on such considerations as cost and investment horizon (when projects funded with debt are expected to generate cash flows). Subsequently, conditions may change and a firm may wish to refinance or retire debt prior to the original maturity. Examples include:

- Declining interest rates permit the reduction of interest cost.
- Increasing cash from operations permits debt retirement earlier than expected.
- Sale of assets or additional equity generates funds and the firm decides to reduce financial leverage.

In such cases, the firm can reduce bank debt, commercial paper, and other short-term debt quickly and at small expense. For longer-maturity debt, the firm may exercise call provisions, tender offers, or in-substance defeasance. We examine the economic and accounting effects of these choices shortly.

Accounting for Debt Retirement

When firms retire debt prior to maturity, the gain or loss (difference between the book value of the liability and the amount paid at retirement) is treated as a component of continuing operations.[44]

Using the par bond example in Exhibit 10-1A (see p. 326), assume that on December 31, 2001, the market interest rate for the firm is 12%. As a result, the market price of the bonds should be $96,535.[45] If the firm paid $96,535 to retire the bond, the resulting gain on the bond retirement is $3,465 since the book value is $100,000.[46] While this gain must be included in income from continuing operations, there are two reasons why an analyst should consider treating it as a nonoperating item:

- In reality, the firm is no better off as a result of the refinancing. To finance the retirement of the bond, it must issue new debt[47] bearing at least the same effective interest rate (and must incur transaction costs). Effectively, over the remaining life of the original bond, the net borrowing cost would be identical; the company has simply replaced 10%

---

[44]SFAS 145 (2002) rescinded both SFAS 4 (1975), which mandated extraordinary item treatment for these gains and losses, and SFAS 64 (1982), which provided an exemption from extraordinary item reporting for gains and losses on normal sinking fund repurchases. Under SFAS 145, gains and losses on retirement of debt are reported as extraordinary items only if they meet APB 30 criteria (see page 54 of text).

[45]This can be seen from Exhibit 10-1C as the carrying amount of the discount bond is the present value at the (original) 12% interest rate.

[46]We have ignored unamortized debt issuance costs. When bonds are retired, the firm must write off these costs that were capitalized when the bonds were issued. This write-off becomes a component of the gain or loss on retirement.

[47]Even if it did not issue new debt to retire the bond but rather used internal funds, the firm would experience an opportunity cost equal to the forgone interest revenue.

coupon debt with 12% coupon debt. In economic terms, the gain took place as interest rates rose, not when the refinancing took place. Because of the use of historical cost as a measure of the bond liability, however, only refinancing results in a recognized gain.[48]

- The decision to refinance is a function of the change in market interest rates. The analyst should evaluate the transaction to determine whether the gain or loss should be considered as part of normal operations or treated analytically as an extraordinary item.

In the early 1970s, interest rates rose sharply at the same time the U.S. economy entered recession. Firms found their outstanding low-coupon bonds selling at deep discounts. Many of these firms had poor operating profitability, but were able to increase reported income by retiring bonds. The issuance of SFAS 4 in 1975 was partially a response to this income manipulation activity.

In the late 1990s, lower interest rates resulted in the refinancing of higher coupon debt, resulting in a recognized loss. That loss should be viewed, however, as a signal of lower future interest expense, as high-coupon debt is replaced by lower-coupon debt (also see the following discussion of callable bonds).

■ Example: DaimlerChrysler

In 1990, predecessor Chrysler had issued $1.1 billion of 12% debt, due in 2020. The high interest rate was due to the higher level of interest rates and Chrysler's poor debt rating. As a result of lower interest rates and improved financial condition, the bonds sold at a large premium in the late 1990s. Late in 1996, Chrysler repurchased half of the issue, recording an extraordinary pretax loss of $309 million. In 1998, DaimlerChrysler repurchased an additional $300 million of the bonds, recording an extraordinary pretax loss of $230 million (€203 million). The company replaced this high-cost debt with lower coupon debt, reducing interest expense significantly. The combined effect of the extraordinary loss from debt retirement (decreasing equity) and reduced future interest expense (increasing earnings) is a higher reported future return on equity. ■

Our discussion of discretionary debt retirements indicates that the amounts and timing of the accounting gain and the economic gain from debt retirement are quite different. This especially applies to callable bonds, whose retirement may give rise to economic profit but may generate a loss for accounting purposes.

Callable Bonds

When a bond is callable, the issuer has the option to buy back (call) the bond from bondholders at predetermined dates and prices. This differs from the case in which the issuer retires the old bond at a market price equal to the present value of the future payment stream. The call price is usually set at a premium over the face value of the bond, but is independent of the present value of the payment stream at the time the call is made. However, the actual exercise does depend on the relationship of the call price to that present value.

Exhibit 10-6 contains an analysis of a callable bond. The decline in interest rates constitutes an economic loss at the time of the rate change, as the market value of the bond rises. In the absence of the call provision, a decision to refinance would not impact Cole, which would incur new debt equal to $106,624 to refinance the debt at market rates. However, the call provision permits the firm to retire the bonds for only $102,000; the economic gain is the difference.[49]

---

[48]If the gain or loss is recognized at all, it should be in the period in which interest rates change, not in the year in which the refinancing takes place. In our example, the year is the same, but that coincidence is rare in practice.

[49]When bonds are issued, the call provisions are often an important ingredient in the market reception. As call provisions benefit only the issuer, bond buyers will bargain against them. Option-adjusted bond analysis is now routine. See, for example, Frank J. Fabozzi, *Fixed Income Analysis for the Chartered Financial Analyst Program*, New Hope, Pennsylvania; Frank J. Fabozzi Associates, 2000 (pp. 347ff). Many shorter-term issues are noncallable.

EXHIBIT 10-6
Analysis of Callable Bond

On January 1, 2001, Cole issues the following bond:

Face value:	$100,000
Coupon:	10% (annual payments assumed for simplicity)
Maturity:	5 years
Call provision:	Callable at any time after one year at 102

If the market interest rate applicable to Cole is 10%, then the bonds will be issued at par.

Reported Liability = $100,000
Annual Interest Expense = $10,000 (10% × $100,000)

Assume that, on December 31, 2001, the market rate applicable to Cole has declined to 8%. The rate change has no accounting impact on the company. However, the present value of the cash flows associated with the debt rises to $106,624 (discounted at 8%). Absent the call provision, the expected market price of the bonds is 106.624.

By calling the bonds at a price of 102, Cole realizes an economic gain of $4,624 [(106.624 − 102) × ($100,000)].

However, the call results in an accounting loss of $2,000 [(100 − 102) × ($100,000)].

Economically, it is beneficial to refinance the debt, but the income statement reports a loss. One can only speculate as to how many firms have not refinanced under such conditions because of the financial statement impact. This is yet another reason why analysts should ignore gains and losses from the retirement of debt.

Defeasance

In some cases, the firm wishes to retire debt but is unable to do so because the debt is non-callable. *In-substance defeasance* involves setting aside riskless securities sufficient to pay all remaining installments of principal and interest. The cash flow characteristics of the securities used must match those of the debt being defeased and must be placed in a trust fund restricted for that purpose.

Although the original debt remained outstanding, U.S. GAAP permitted debtor firms to derecognize the defeased obligations through December 31, 1996.[50] However, SFAS 125 (1996)[51] disallows in-substance defeasance and debt may be extinguished only on repayment or when the debtor is legally released from being the primary obligor. IAS 32 (2000) disallowed defeasance for firms following IAS GAAP.

BOND COVENANTS

Creditors use debt covenants in lending agreements to protect their interests by restricting activities of the debtor that could jeopardize the creditor's position. Auditors and management must certify that the firm has not violated the covenants. If any covenant is violated, the firm is in *technical default* of its lending agreement, and the creditor can demand repayment of the debt after the stated grace period. Generally, however, as we shall see, the terms are renegotiated but at a cost to the debtor as the lender demands concessions. The analysis of a firm's debt position must therefore take into consideration the nature of these covenants and the risk that the firm may violate them.

Information on debt covenants is important both to evaluate the firm's credit risk as well as to understand the implications of such restrictions for the firm's dividend and growth (in-

---

[50]See SFAS 76 (1983) and FASB Technical Bulletin 84-4 for accounting and disclosure requirements related to defeasance.

[51]See SFAS 125, Accounting for the Transfers and Servicing of Financial Assets and Extinguishments of Liabilities.

vestment) prospects. In addition, to the extent these covenants are accounting-based, they may affect the choice of accounting policies.

Nature of Covenants

Smith and Warner (1979) characterize debt covenants as placing limits on one or more of the following activities:

1. Payment of dividends (includes share repurchases)
2. Production and investment (includes mergers and acquisitions, sale and leaseback, or outright disposal of certain assets)
3. Issuance of new debt (or incurrence of other liabilities)
4. Payoff patterns (includes sinking fund requirements and the priorities of claims on assets)

In addition to direct restrictions on activities, covenants may require maintenance of certain levels of such accounting-based financial variables as stockholders' equity (or retained earnings), working capital, interest coverage, and debt-to-equity ratios. These levels are often related to the four types of activities listed above by restricting a certain activity if the accounting variable violates the specified target level. In some cases, the violation itself may signal a breach of the covenant even without any subsequent firm activity.

Bond covenants may also require that interest rates depend on certain financial ratios.

■ Example: Luby's

Based in Texas, Luby's [LUB] operates cafeterias. It entered into a credit agreement with a group of banks early in 1996. That agreement was subsequently amended four times:

1. January 24, 1997
2. July 3, 1997
3. October 27, 2000
4. June 29, 2001

The second and third amendments are of particular interest. The second amendment increased the credit line from $100 million to $125 million but added the following provision with respect to the spread over the LIBOR rate ("applicable margin"):

Applicable margin means the following per-annum percentages, applicable in the following situations:

Applicability If the leverage is:	LIBOR Basis for Advances of One, Two, Three, or Six Months	LIBOR Basis for Advances of Seven to Fourteen Days
not less than 2 to 1	0.225	0.325
less than 2 to 1	0.200	0.300
Difference	0.025	0.025

This provision gives the lender an additional margin over LIBOR of 2.5 basis points (.025%) if the leverage ratio (debt-to-equity ratio as defined in the original credit agreement) exceeds 2.0. This additional margin was presumably intended to compensate the lender for the additional risk.

The third amendment, adopted when Luby's earnings had fallen sharply, changed the *applicable margin* as follows:

Applicability If the Leverage Is:	LIBOR Basis for Advances of One, Two, Three, or Six Months	LIBOR Basis for Advances of Seven to Fourteen Days
greater than or equal to 2.75 to 1	0.500	2.500
greater than or equal to 2.50 to 1 but less than 2.75 to 1	0.375	2.125
greater than or equal to 2.25 to 1 but less than 2.50 to 1	0.000	1.750
less than 2.25 to 1	0.000	1.250

This amendment increased the lending spread to reflect the higher leverage ratio, and provided a sliding scale under which the spread increases and decreases with the leverage ratio (a measure of risk).

Additionally, as detailed in Exhibit 10-7, the third amendment introduced a covenant based on the fixed-charge coverage ratio as well as imposing restrictions on net worth (stockholders' equity) and the leverage ratio. Note the extent to which the ratios as well as their components are defined by the agreement.

These provisions had several effects:

1. To restrict the ability of Luby's to incur additional debt that would dilute the interest of the creditors.

2. To require Luby's to maintain stockholders' equity, limiting its ability to pay dividends (it eliminated its dividend in October 2000) or buy back stock, either of which would reduce cash and the equity cushion.

3. To reward creditors for the level of risk by increasing the interest rate margin as the leverage ratio increases.

Luby's provides an example of bond covenants. Additional discussion regarding the nature of accounting-based debt covenants can be found in Box 10-5. ■

EXHIBIT 10-7
Excerpts from Luby's Bond Covenants

Fixed Charge Coverage Provision

"Earnings Available for Fixed Charges" means, for any period, calculated for the Borrower and its Subsidiaries on a consolidated basis in accordance with GAAP, the sum of (a) EBITDA, plus (b) all lease and rental expense pursuant to Operating Leases, minus (c) cash taxes paid, minus (d) Capital Expenditures.

"Fixed Charges" means, for any period, calculated for the Borrower and its Subsidiaries on a consolidated basis in accordance with GAAP, the sum of (a) all interest, premium payments, fees, charges and related expenses (including, but not limited to, interest expense pursuant to Capitalized Lease Obligations) in connection with borrowed money or in connection with the deferred purchase price of assets, in each case to the extent treated as interest in accordance with GAAP, (b) all dividends and distributions paid in respect of Capital Stock and (c) all lease and rental expenses pursuant to Operating Leases.

"Fixed Charges Coverage Ratio" means, for any date of determination, the ratio of (a) Earnings Available for Fixed Charges for the period of four consecutive fiscal quarters ending on such date to (b) Fixed Charges for the period of four consecutive fiscal quarters ending on such date.

The Borrower covenants and agrees that it will not allow the Fixed Charges Coverage Ratio to be less than 1.20 to 1 at the fiscal

quarter ending November 30, 2000 or at the end of any fiscal quarter thereafter.

Net Worth Provision

The Borrower covenants and agrees that it will not allow its Net Worth at any time to be less than the sum of (i) $190,000,000 plus (ii) 50% of Consolidated Net Income (excluding Consolidated Net Income for any fiscal quarter in which Consolidated Net Income was a negative number) earned on or after September 1, 2000, plus (iii) 75% of the Net Cash Proceeds of any equity issues of the Borrower's Capital Stock in an underwritten public offering pursuant to an effective registration statement under the Securities Act of 1933, as amended, after September 1, 2000.

Leverage Ratio Provision

The Borrower covenants and agrees that it will not allow the Leverage Ratio to be greater than (a) 3.00 to 1 at the fiscal quarters ending November 30, 2000, February 28, 2001 and May 31, 2001, (b) 2.60 to 1 at the fiscal quarter ending August 31, 2001 and (c) 2.50 to 1 at the fiscal quarter ending November 30, 2001 and each fiscal quarter thereafter.

Source: Third Amendment to Credit Agreement, dated October 27, 2000, Exhibit 4(j) to Luby's Form 10-K for year ended August 31, 2000.

BOX 10-5
Accounting-Based Debt Covenants

Exhibit 10-8 contains a summary of the nature of accounting-based debt covenant restrictions, adapted from Duke and Hunt (1990). *Restricted retained earnings* as a constraint on dividend payments, one of the most common forms used, is outlined in Exhibit 10-9. The Luby's covenants discussed in the text are examples of these restrictions.

Information regarding these covenants was obtained by Smith and Warner (1979) and Duke and Hunt (1990) from the American Bar Foundation's *Commentaries on Debentures*, which summarizes typical covenants found in lending agreements. A cursory examination of these restrictions makes it clear that creditors seek to limit the firm's level of risk (investment and debt restrictions) and preserve the assets of the firm to ensure that debts are repaid (payment restrictions). Thus, covenants attempt to limit shareholders' ability to transfer assets to themselves (dividend restrictions), new shareholders (merger and acquisition restrictions), or new creditors (debt restrictions).

The best source of information on specific covenants (and other terms of the bond issue) for publicly issued bonds is the bond indenture, the legal document created when the bond is issued and filed with the registration statement filed with the SEC. The trustee (normally a bank) will have a copy of the indenture and is responsible for the enforcement of its terms. The bond prospectus should contain a good summary of these terms. Bank credit agreements entered into by public companies are filed with SEC annual (10-K) or quarterly (10-Q) reports.

For all debt issues, summarized data can be found in:

- Services such as Moody's Industrial Manual
- Annual reports
- SEC filings by debtors

Press and Weintrop (1990 and 1991) contend that information obtained from annual reports and Moody's is not comprehensive, especially with respect to covenants relating to privately placed debt, and that in these cases, it is necessary to access the original SEC filings.

Calculation of Accounting-Based Constraints

Each type of constraint is defined in the covenants. In addition, the covenants specify:

- Whether GAAP definitions are to be used or GAAP is to be modified. Leftwich (1983) noted that such modifications are most often associated with private rather than public debt indentures.
- Whether GAAP in effect at the time of the debt issuance are maintained throughout the life of the bond ("frozen" GAAP), or calculations in subsequent years are to be based on GAAP in effect at the date of the calculation ("rolling" GAAP). This is important when important new accounting standards are adopted.

Mohrman (1996) examined a sample of 174 lending agreements that contained covenants based on financial statement information. She found that over half (90) the covenants were based on *fixed* GAAP specified in the agreements. That is, the covenants were not affected by voluntary or FASB-mandated accounting changes, nor were they originally designed to mimic GAAP in effect at the time the contract was signed. Additionally, she found that contracts that contained more accounting-based covenants were more likely to specify fixed GAAP provisions and the use of such provisions in contracts was increasing over time.

EXHIBIT 10-8
Common Accounting-Based Debt Covenant Restrictions

Attribute:	Retained earnings
Measured as:	Restricted retained earnings
Limits:	Payments of dividends or stock repurchase below minimum level of restricted retained earnings
Attribute:	Net assets
Measured as:	Net tangible assets or net assets
Limits:	Investments, dividend payments, and new debt issues if net assets fall below a certain level
Attribute:	Working capital
Measured as:	Minimum working capital or current ratio
Limits:	Mergers and acquisitions, dividend payments, and new debt issues if the working capital or the current ratio fall below a certain level
Attribute:	Debt-to-equity
Measured as:	Debt divided by net tangible assets or debt divided by net assets
Limits:	Issuance of additional debt

Source: Joanne C. Duke and Herbert G. Hunt III, "An Empirical Examination of Debt Covenant Restrictions and Accounting-Related Debt Proxies," *Journal of Accounting and Economics*, Jan. 1990, adapted from Table 1, p. 52.

EXHIBIT 10-9
Unrestricted Retained Earnings: Inventory of Payable Funds

The most frequent accounting-based restriction specified is the dividend constraint. Dividends cannot be paid out of restricted retained earnings. Only unrestricted retained earnings, often referred to as the inventory of payable funds (IPF), are available for dividends. The general formulation of IPF is defined (see Smith and Warner, 1979) as the sum of:

1. A specified percentage k of earnings E from the date of the debt issuance to the present period, plus

2. Proceeds from the sale of common shares CS from the date of the debt issuance to the present period, plus

3. A prespecified constant F, less

4. The sum of dividends DV and stock repurchases from the date of the debt issuance to the present period

Algebraically, this is equal to

$$\text{IPF}_t = k \sum_{i=0}^{t} E_i + \sum_{i=0}^{t} CS_i + F - \sum_{i=0}^{t} DV_i$$

where period 0 represents the date of the debt issuance and period t refers to the current date. The prespecified constant F is usually set at approximately one year's earnings.* This builds some slack into the system in the event the firm has a loss.

---

*See Smith and Warner (1979), Note 36.

Costs and Effects of Covenant Violations

Although creditors have a right to demand immediate payment when an accounting-based debt covenant is violated, they do not usually do so. This does not mean that violating such covenants is costless. Waivers of such violations often come with strings attached. Creditors may renegotiate the terms of the debt to demand:

- Accelerated principal payments
- An increased interest rate
- Liens on assets (such as accounts receivable)
- New covenants increasing restrictions on the firm's investing, borrowing, and dividend-paying ability

Chen and Wei (1993) examined a sample of 128 companies that disclosed violations of their accounting-based debt covenants. For 71 of these firms, the creditors did not waive the violation but demanded accelerated payments or higher interest rates. Beneish and Press (1993) found the median interest rate increase to be 80 basis points; they estimated that the overall cost of such renegotiations averaged from 1 to 2% of the market value of the firm's equity or 4 to 7% of the balance on the loan.

When waivers were granted, not surprisingly, they were more often granted for secured debt and for smaller-size loans. Similarly, waivers were more likely to be granted to "healthier" firms considered less likely to become bankrupt. When waivers were granted, they were often (24 of the 57 companies) given only for limited time periods.

Successful renegotiation of the debt terms or receipt of a waiver may not be the last word. Chen and Wei found that by the following year creditors demanded payment of the debt for 39 companies (30% of the sample), forcing 13 companies into bankruptcy.

Beneish and Press found that accounting-based covenants were often relaxed as a result of renegotiation. However, they were supplanted with more direct covenants restricting capital expenditures, mergers, assets sales, stock repurchases, and future borrowings.

These results indicate the importance of monitoring debt covenants to ensure that the firm is not close to violating them. Such violations can expose the firm to direct out-of-pocket costs in the form of higher borrowing costs and/or limit the scope of a firm's investing and financing choices.*

---

*Given these costs, one can understand why DeFond and Jiambalvo (1994) reported that managements engage in (accounting) manipulations in an effort to satisfy the covenants.

SUMMARY

In this chapter, we have examined the different forms that debt financing can take. The choice of debt issue can have significant effects on the pattern of reported income, cash flows, and financial position. In addition, different debt instruments respond differently to changes in interest rates. The reader should now have an understanding of the following issues:

1. The effects of zero-coupon or low-coupon debt, variable rate debt, and foreign currency debt on the firm's financial statements.

2. The economic and financial statement effects of interest rate swaps.

3. The implications for financial analysis of variable-rate debt versus fixed-rate debt.

4. The economic and accounting effects of debt with equity features.

5. The analyst's need to classify between debt and equity based on the essence of the financial instrument rather than its form.

6. The effect of changes in interest rates on the market value of debt and when the market value should be used instead of carrying value.

7. The accounting effects of debt retirement and analytical adjustments required.

8. The importance of debt covenants to the analysis of the firm.

Debt can also take forms that do not require recognition on the balance sheet. Such off-balance-sheet debt is the subject of the next chapter.

Chapter 10

Problems

1. [Zero-coupon debt; CFA© adapted] Compare the effect of issuing zero-coupon debt with that of issuing full-coupon debt with the same effective interest rate on a company's:

a. Cash flow from operations over the life of the debt

b. Cash flow from financing in the year of issuance, the year of maturity, and over the life of the debt.

c. Cash flow from investing over the life of the debt

d. Trend of net income over the life of the debt

2. [Variable- vs. fixed-rate debt; CFA© adapted] Assuming that a firm has variable-rate debt and interest rates rise, describe the effect of the rise on:

   (i) Net income

  (ii) The market value of the firm's debt

3. [Current liabilities; customer advances] Exhibit 10P-1 contains selected balance sheet data for AMR (American Airlines) and U.S. Airways [U] for 1998 and 1999.

a. Calculate AMR's reported working capital and its current, quick, and cash ratios for both years.

b. The air traffic liability primarily reflects tickets sold in advance. Discuss any differences between the air traffic liability and other liabilities.

c. Eliminate the air traffic liability and recompute the ratios in part a. Discuss any differences from the ratios calculated in part a.

d. Compare US Airways short-term liquidity position with that of AMR at December 31, 1999 both as reported and after elimination of the air traffic liability.

e. The chapter states that accounts such as the air traffic liability may be better viewed as indicators of future profitability than as liabilities. Discuss that view using the data in Exhibit 10P-1.

4. [Zero-coupon bonds] The Null Company issued a zero-coupon bond on January 1, 2000, due December 31, 2004. The face value of the bond was $100,000. The bond was issued at an effective rate of 12% (compounded annually).

a. Calculate the cash proceeds of the bond issue.

b. Complete the following table on a *pretax* basis, assuming that all interest is paid in the year it is due:

EXHIBIT 10P-1
Selected Balance Sheet Data, December 31, 1998 and 1999 (in $millions)

	AMR Corp		US Airways	
	1998	1999	1998	1999
Cash and short-term investments	$2,073	$1,791	$1,210	$ 870
Net receivables	1,543	1,134	355	387
Inventories	596	708	228	226
Other current assets	663	791	571	613
Current assets	$4,875	$4,424	$2,364	$2,096
Accounts payable	1,152	1,115	430	474
Accrued liabilities	2,122	1,956	1,016	1,276
Air traffic liability	2,163	2,255	752	635
Notes payable and current portion long-term debt	202	538	71	116
Current liabilities	$5,639	$5,864	$2,269	$2,501

Source: AMR Corp. and US Airways, 1999 annual reports.

	2000	2001	2002	2003	2004
Earnings before interest and taxes	$50,000	$50,000	$50,000	$50,000	$50,000
Cash flow from operations before interest and taxes	60,000	60,000	60,000	60,000	60,000
Cash flow from operations					
Times interest earned					
Times interest earned (cash basis)					

c. Assume that Null had raised the same cash proceeds with a conventional bond issued at par, paying interest annually and the principal at maturity. Complete the following table, under the assumptions in part b:

	2000	2001	2002	2003	2004
Earnings before interest and taxes	$50,000	$50,000	$50,000	$50,000	$50,000
Cash flow from operations before interest and taxes	60,000	60,000	60,000	60,000	60,000
Cash flow from operations					
Times interest earned					
Times interest earned (cash basis)					

d. Using the results of parts b and c, discuss the impact on reported cash flow from operations and interest coverage of Null's choice of bond.

e. Explain how consideration of income taxes would change your answers to parts b through d.

5. [Zero-coupon bond; foreign currency debt] Roche has outstanding zero-coupon U.S. dollar notes, with a $2.15 billion face value due 2010, that were issued with a 7% yield to maturity. They are carried at the following amounts:

	12-31-98	12-31-99
Carrying amount (CHF millions)	1,282	1,618
Exchange rate (CHF/dollar)	1.37	1.60

a. Compute the carrying amount of the bonds in $U.S. at December 31, 1998.

b. Explain the difference between your answer to part a and the $2.15 billion face amounts of the notes.

c. Estimate the interest expense (in CHF) for these notes for 1999.

d. Using your answer for part c and the December 31, 1998 carrying value, estimate the carrying amount of the notes (in CHF) at December 31, 1999.

e. Provide two possible explanations for the difference between your answer to part d and the actual carrying amount in Swiss francs at December 31, 1999.

f. Describe the effect of issuing these notes, instead of full coupon notes, on Roche's:
  (i) Cash from operations
  (ii) Trend of interest expense

g. Describe the effect of the change in the value of the dollar during 1999 on Roche's interest expense on these notes.

6. [Understanding bond relationships; coupon versus effective interest] The Walk & Field Co. has outstanding bonds originally issued at a discount. During 2000, the unamortized bond discount decreased from $8,652 to $7,290. Annual interest paid was $7,200. The market rate of interest was 12% when the bond was issued.

Using the data provided, calculate:
  (i) Interest expense for 2000
  (ii) The face value of the bond
  (iii) The coupon rate of the bond

(*Note:* You do not need present value calculations or tables to solve this problem.)

7. [Fixed-rate versus variable-rate debt; effect of interest rate swap] Financial Federal [FIF] finances industrial and commercial equipment through installment sales and leasing programs. FIF obtains funds from bank loans and bonds, which have the following interest rate characteristics (amounts in $thousands):

	Bank Loans		Bonds	
July 31	1999	2000	1999	2000
Fixed rate	$513,447	$673,791	$352,790	$440,490
Variable rate	117,362	111,019	392,652	444,348
Totals	$630,809	$784,810	$745,442	$884,838
Fixed rate % of total	81.4%	85.9%	47.3%	49.8%
Direct financing leases	$317,918	$352,325		
Total finance receivables	948,727	1,137,135		

(*Note:* Assume that the direct financing leases have fixed interest rates.)

a. Discuss the effect of a rise in interest rates on the market value of FIF bonds (using the July 31, 2000 amounts).

b. Discuss the effect of a rise in interest rates on FIF's interest expense.

c. Considering your answers to parts a and b, discuss why FIF has increased its fixed-rate debt from 17% at the end of fiscal 1996 to nearly 50% at the end of fiscal 2000.

d. FIF states that, because of the variety and complexity of its finance receivables, it is not practical to estimate fair value. Given this statement, discuss the usefulness of the disclosure of the fair value of FIF debt.

8. [Interest rate swaps—extension of Problem 10-7] FIF's fiscal 2000 annual report also discloses the following information regarding interest rate swaps:

	1999	2000
Notional amount	$25,000	$25,000
Weighted-average receive rate	5.5%	7.0%
Weighted-average pay rate	5.2%	5.2%
Weighted-average remaining term (in months)	17	5

a. From the data shown, describe the swaps.

b. Compute the effect of the swaps on FIF's interest expense each year.

c. Explain how the swaps altered FIF's sensitivity to changes in interest rates.

9. [Foreign currency debt] Bristol-Myers [BMY] reported the following components of its long-term debt (in $millions):

December 31	1998	1999
2.14% yen notes, due 2005	$55	$62
1.73% yen notes, due 2003	54	62

The $U.S. equaled 113.60 Japanese yen at December 31, 1998 and 102.51 at December 31, 1999.

a. Compute the outstanding debt in Japanese yen at December 31, 1998 and 1999 for both issues.

b. Compute the percentage change in the outstanding debt in yen during 1999 for both issues.

c. Assuming that no new bonds were issued, state one conclusion that can be drawn from your answers to parts a and b.

d. State two possible motivations for Bristol-Myers, an American company, to issue debt in Japanese yen.

10. [Convertible debt] Note 5 of Takeda's annual report states that the company had convertible bonds outstanding at March 31, 1998 but none outstanding at March 31, 1999. From the statement of stockholders' equity and cash flow statement we can deduce that most of the bonds (more than 22 billion yen) were converted into approximately 11 million shares, implying a conversion price of approximately 2,000 yen per share. The market price of Takeda shares exceeded 3,000 yen during all of calendar 1998.

Years Ended March 31	1998	1999
As reported in millions yen		
Bank loans	9,509	9,361
Current debt	24,077	2,119
Long-term debt	10,896	9,858
Total debt	44,482	21,338
Equity	829,381	907,373
Total capital	873,863	928,711

a. Describe the advantages to Takeda of having issued these convertible notes rather than nonconvertible notes. State one disadvantage.

b. Compute Takeda's debt-to-total capital ratio at March 31, 1998 and March 31, 1999. State the factor that accounted for most of the change in that ratio.

c. State the appropriate classification for the convertible notes at March 31, 1998 (debt or equity) and justify your choice.

11. [Foreign currency convertible debt] In April 2000, Roche issued nearly ¥105 billion of debt, convertible into Roche shares.

The coupon was .25% with a maturity of 2005. The issue price was 96.4% of par value (face amount). The conversion price was set at a premium of 25% above the market price of Roche shares at the issue date.

a. Describe the benefits to Roche of issuing these bonds rather than full-coupon nonconvertible debt.

b. Describe how you would compute the interest expense for 2000 and the carrying amount of the bond (in yen) at December 31, 2000.

c. Describe the effect of changes in the exchange rate between the Japanese yen and Swiss franc on:

(i) The carrying amount of the debt at each balance sheet date

(ii) Interest expense on the debt

d. Discuss whether the bonds should be considered debt or equity at the issue date.

12. [Zero-coupon convertible debt with put option] In February 1998, Network Associates (NET) issued $885 million principal amount of zero-coupon bonds, with a maturity of 2018. The bonds were issued at a price of 39.106 (percent of par) to yield 4.75% to maturity. The holders of the bonds have the right to "put" the bonds to the company at the original purchase price plus accrued original issue discount at five-year intervals after the date of issue. Additionally, the bonds were convertible (valued at their principal amount) into NET shares at $45.80 per share, a 20% premium over the market price of NET at the issue date.

a. Discuss the advantages to NET of issuing these bonds rather than full-coupon nonconvertible bonds.

b. NET's cash flow statement shows a component of cash flows from operating activities of $17.332 million for 1999 as a result of the zero-coupon bond. Explain what this amount represents.

c. At December 31, 1998, NET shares closed at a price of $66.25. State whether these bonds should be considered debt or equity on that date and justify your choice.

d. At December 31, 2000, NET shares closed at a price of $4. State whether these bonds should be considered debt or equity on that date and justify your choice.

e. State the advantage and disadvantage to NET of issuing bonds with the embedded put option.

13. [Exchangeable debt] In May 2000, Munich Re [MUV2] issued €1.15 billion of exchangeable notes due in 2005. Investors received an interest rate of 1% and the right to receive shares of Allianz instead of cash at maturity. The initial conversion premium was 28%. The *Financial Times* reported that:

> Last month, the German re-insurer Munich Re divested itself of part of its holding of . . . Allianz. . . . But it did not do so by selling its shares in Allianz. Instead, it issued €1.15 billion of convertible bonds that investors will later be able to exchange for Allianz shares.
>
> The issue could save Munich Re millions. If it had simply sold the Allianz shares now it would have attracted capital gains tax of as much as 50%.

This way the issuer will not be taxed until the bonds are exchanged, by which time things may have changed. German companies are hoping that new legislation will slash capital gains tax to zero by the end of next year.[52]

Describe the advantages and disadvantages to Munich Re of issuing these notes rather than

(i) Selling shares of Allianz

(ii) Issuing bonds without the exchange feature

Your answer should address the effect on interest expense as well as the capital gains tax considerations.

14. [Perpetual debt] In 1986, PepsiCo [PEP] issued 400 million Swiss franc bonds with no maturity date. At the end of each 10-year period, PepsiCo and the bondholders each have the right to cause redemption of the bonds. If not redeemed, the coupon rate is adjusted based on the yield of 10-year U.S. Treasury securities. Interest payments are made in U.S. dollars.

a. Discuss the conditions under which the bonds are likely to be redeemed. Be sure to consider both the PepsiCo and investor points of view.

In 1996, CHF 327.3 million of these bonds were put to the company, reducing the outstanding amount to CHF 72.7 million.

b. Discuss whether the remaining bonds should be classified as debt or equity when analyzing PepsiCo's capital structure.

15. [Catastrophe bonds] In March 2000, Atlas Re, an affiliate of the French insurance company SCOR [SCO] issued three classes of three-year "catastrophe bonds." The three classes have coupon rates ranging from 270 to 1400 basis points (2.7% to 14%) in excess of the LIBOR rate. However, in the event of certain defined insurance losses in Europe, Japan, and the United States, interest and the redemption amounts would be reduced.

a. Explain why an investor might find these bonds to be a worthwhile investment.

b. Describe the impact of these bonds on SCOR's reported income and interest coverage ratio in a time period with no insurance losses covered by these bonds.

c. Describe the impact of these bonds on SCOR's reported income and interest coverage ratio in a time period with large insurance losses covered by these bonds.

d. Explain the effect of these bonds on the variability of SCOR's reported income.

16. [Preferred shares] Texaco's December 31, 1999 balance sheet shows $300 million of preferred shares outstanding. The characteristics of these shares are reported in Note 13.

a. State the appropriate classification for the preferred shares (debt or equity) and justify your choice.

b. On page 26 of its 1999 annual report, Texaco reports "key financial indicators," including:

Total debt/total capital   37.5%

Show how this ratio was arrived at and recalculate the ratio after making any appropriate adjustments.

17. [Interest rate sensitivity] Wal-Mart [WMT] is the largest retailer in the world. Its annual report for the year ended January 31, 2000 contains the following information about its debt.

Amounts in $millions

	1-31-99	1-31-00
Long-term, fixed-rate debt	$7,808	$15,636
Fair value of long-term debt	8,323	14,992
Average interest rate	7.2%	6.9%

a. Describe the inference about the change in interest rates during fiscal 2000 that you can draw from the comparison between the book value and fair (market) value of Wal-Mart debt at the two balance sheet dates.

b. Wal-Mart doubled its long-term debt during fiscal 2000 but reduced the average interest rate. Explain how this was possible given your answer to part a.

18. [Interest rate swaps; extension of Problem 10-17] Wal-Mart also entered into interest rate swaps under which it received fixed rates and paid variable rates.

a. Discuss the likely motivation for entering into these swaps.

b. Describe two risks that Wal-Mart assumed by entering into these swaps.

c. Under one of the interest rate swaps Wal-Mart receives a fixed rate of 5.7% and pays a variable rate on $500 million. The fair value of the swap was $10 million at January 31, 1999 and $(1) million at January 31, 2000. Explain the change in fair value. No calculations are required.

19. [Market value of debt versus book value; interest rate sensitivity] AMR [AMR] is the parent company of American Airlines. Exhibit 10P-2 contains extracts from Note 6 of AMR's 1999 annual report.

a. Based on the fair value data, state whether the long-term rates used to determine fair value rose or fell in 1999. Justify your choice.

b. State whether the interest rate used to determine the fair value of the $437 million "9.0%–10.20% debentures" (due through 2021) at December 31, 1999 was

(i) Below 10.20%

(ii) Above 10.20%

Justify your choice.

c. Explain why the fair value of the $86 million variable-rate indebtedness equals the carrying value for both years.

20. [Interest rate swaps; extension of Problem 10-19] Exhibit 10P-2 also describes interest rate swaps that AMR entered into.

a. Describe the effect of the interest rate swaps on AMR's interest expense for both 1998 and 1999.

b. Explain why the fair value of the swaps was positive in 1998 but negative in 1999. Elsewhere in its 1999 financial report, AMR states that:

Market risk for fixed-rate long-term debt is estimated as the potential increase in fair value resulting from a hypothetical

EXHIBIT 10P-2. AMR CORP.
Amounts in $millions

6. Financial Instruments and Risk Management Fair Values of Financial Instruments

The fair values of the Company's long-term debt were estimated using quoted market prices where available. For long-term debt not actively traded, fair values were estimated using discounted cash flow analyses, based on the Company's current incremental borrowing rates for similar types of borrowing arrangements. The carrying amounts and estimated fair values of the Company's long-term debt, including current maturities, were (in millions):

| | December 31, | | | |
| | 1999 | | 1998 | |
	Carrying Value	Fair Value	Carrying Value	Fair Value
Secured variable and fixed-rate indebtedness	$2,651	$2,613	$ 890	$1,013
7.875% − 10.62% notes	1,014	1,024	875	973
9.0% − 10.20% debentures	437	469	437	531
6.0% − 7.10% bonds	176	174	176	189
Variable rate indebtedness	86	86	86	86
Other	16	16	20	20
	$4,380	$4,382	$2,484	$2,812

Interest Rate Risk Management

American enters into interest rate swap contracts to effectively convert a portion of its fixed-rate obligations to floating-rate obligations. These agreements involve the exchange of amounts based on a floating interest rate for amounts based on fixed interest rates over the life of the agreement without an exchange of the notional amount upon which the payments are based. The differential to be paid or received as interest rates change is accrued and recognized as an adjustment of interest expense related to the obligation. The related amount payable to or receivable from counterparties is included in current liabilities or assets. The fair values of the swap agreements are not recognized in the financial statements. Gains and losses on terminations of interest rate swap agreements are deferred as an adjustment to the carrying amount of the outstanding obligation and amortized as an adjustment to interest expense related to the obligation over the remaining term of the original contract life of the terminated swap agreement. In the event of the early extinguishment of a designated obligation, any realized or unrealized gain or loss from the swap would be recognized in income coincident with the extinguishment.

The following table indicates the notional amounts and fair values of the Company's interest rate swap agreements (in millions):

| | December 31, | | | |
| | 1999 | | 1998 | |
	Notional Amount	Fair Value	Notional Amount	Fair Value
Interest rate swap agreements	$696	$(9)	$1,054	$38

The fair values represent the amount the Company would pay or receive if the agreements were terminated at December 31, 1999 and 1998, respectively.

At December 31, 1999, the weighted-average remaining life of the interest rate swap agreements in effect was 5.1 years. The weighted-average floating rates and fixed rates on the contracts outstanding were:

| | December 31, | |
	1999	1998
Average floating rate	5.855%	5.599%
Average fixed rate	6.593%	6.277%

Floating rates are based primarily on LIBOR and may change significantly, affecting future cash flows.

Source: AMR 10-K Report, December 31, 1999.

EXHIBIT 10P-3. ARCO CORP.

ARCO ANNOUNCES INTENTION TO SETTLE ITS EXCHANGEABLE NOTES
3/24/97 17:13 (New York)

LOS ANGELES, March 24 /PRNewswire/—ARCO (NYSE: ARC) today announced its present intention to settle all its 9% Exchangeable Notes due September 15, 1997 with Lyondell Petrochemical Company stock currently owned by ARCO.

"Our current intention to exchange out ARCO's equity interest in Lyondell is consistent with ARCO's priorities," said ARCO Chairman and Chief Executive Officer Mike R. Bowlin. "While ARCO has enjoyed a successful relationship with Lyondell, we no longer consider Lyondell central to ARCO's core business or part of our strategic growth objectives."

If market conditions remained unchanged, ARCO would expect to realize a gain in excess of $300 million upon the exchange of its shares of Lyondell stock. The decision to settle the Notes with Lyondell shares can still be affected by a material change in market conditions.

ARCO currently owns 39.9 million shares, or 49.9% of the total outstanding shares, of Houston-based Lyondell (NYSE: LYO), a leading manufacturer and marketer of petrochemicals and, through its interest in LYONDELL-CITGO Refining Company, a manufacturer of refined petroleum products.

In a 1994 offering, ARCO sold $988 million of 3-year Exchangeable Notes carrying a 9.0% annual coupon. At maturity on September 15, 1997, the Notes are payable, at ARCO's option, in shares of Lyondell Common Stock at a price determined in accordance with the terms of the Notes, or cash with an equal value.

Source: ARCO Press Release, March 24, 1997.

10% decrease in interest rates, and amounts to approximately $156 million and $96 million as of December 31, 1999 and 1998, respectively.

c. Relate the increased market risk in 1999 to changes in both AMR's debt and its interest rate swaps.

21. [Debt refinancing] On July 14, 2000, the *Wall Street Journal* reported on the earnings report by Fannie Mae [FNM], the largest mortgage lender in the United States. Fannie Mae has substantial outstanding debt and uses hedging techniques to manage its exposure to changing interest rates. Excerpts from that article follow:

Fannie Mae Posts 15% Earnings Gain for the Quarter
By Patrick Barta

Fannie Mae overcame a cooling housing market to report double-digit earnings growth for the second quarter. . . .

However, some pointed out that the company's results included a one-time after-tax gain of $32.7 million from the retirement of debt that helped compensate for a one-time trading loss. Typically, such gains are omitted when a company calculates its earnings-per-share results.

"In our mind, [the gain] should be excluded," says Charles L. Hill, First Call's director of research.

Fannie Mae says the company has long included retirement of debt in its earnings-per-share calculations, because it considers retirement of debt to be part of its continuing operations. The company notes that it reported gains and losses from debt retirement in its earnings-per-share calculations in 27 of the last 40 quarters. "It's something we do on a regular basis," says Mary Lou Christy, vice-president of investor relations.

At the heart of the debate was a one-time loss of about $60 million, attributed to a hedging strategy that lost money after interest rates for Fannie Mae debt rose unexpectedly.

The company was able to offset much of the loss by repurchasing debt at favorable rates, which produced the $32.7 million gain.[53]

a. Present one reason why the gain from debt retirement should be considered part of Fannie Mae's operating earnings and one reason why it should not.

[53] *Wall Street Journal*, July 14, 2000, p. A2.

b. Present one reason why the loss from the hedging strategy should be considered part of Fannie Mae's operating earnings and one reason why it should not.

c. Recommend the proper treatment for both items, from an analyst viewpoint, and justify your recommendation.

22. [Debt refinancing and exchangeable debt] In March 1997, ARCO (Atlantic Richfield) issued the press release shown in Exhibit 10P-3. Use only this information to answer the following questions.

a. Discuss whether you would consider the $300 million gain part of ARCO's operating earnings for 1997.

b. Discuss two reasons why ARCO chose to issue the notes in 1994 rather than sell shares of Lyondell.

c. Describe the effects of the redemption of the notes on ARCO's balance sheet, income statement, and cash flow statement for 1997.

23. [Issue and repurchase of debt] On January 1, 2000, Derek Corporation issues $20 million (face value) bonds due January 1, 2010. Interest is payable semiannually on January 1 and July 1 at a coupon rate of 10%. The market (effective interest) rate on the date of issuance is 8%.

a. Compute the impact of the bond issuance on Derek's balance sheet, income statement, and statement of cash flows for 2000 and 2001.

b. Calculate the gain or loss recorded by Derek if it repurchases the entire bond issue on July 1, 2003 at an effective interest rate of 10%.

c. Discuss whether this gain (loss) should be considered a component of continuing operating income.

d. Discuss two reasons why Derek might choose to refinance its 8% debt at a higher interest rate.

24. [Bond covenants and financing options] The Sleepman Company wishes to acquire plant and equipment worth $1 million. The purchase must be financed by issuing preferred shares or debt (in any combination, including zero-coupon). The only constraint is that the company not violate *any* of the following bond covenants:

(i) Times interest earned (cash basis) calculated as

$$\frac{\text{Cash from operations before interest}}{\text{Interest payments}} \text{ must be at least } 1.8$$

(ii) Fixed charge coverage ratio (cash basis) calculated as

$$\frac{\text{Cash from operations before interest}}{\text{Interest payments + preferred dividends}} \text{ must be at least } 1.4$$

(iii) Debt to gross tangible assets calculated as

$$\frac{\text{Long-term debt}}{\text{Gross tangible fixed assets}} \text{ must not exceed } 0.50$$

Sleepman has made the following financial projections for the coming year:

Interest expense (= interest paid)	$200,000
Preferred dividends	0
Cash flow from operations before interest	390,000
Long-term debt	2,000,000
Tangible fixed assets (gross)	5,000,000

These amounts include the operating results generated by the new plant and equipment. They exclude, however, the accounting impacts of the purchase (depreciation and interest expense) as well as the assets and liabilities arising from the purchase.

For simplicity, assume that all financing is available at an interest rate of 10% with a maturity of 10 years. Similarly, any required depreciation or amortization should assume an asset life of 10 years using the straight-line method and zero residual value. Ignore income taxes.

a. Assume that there are three alternatives to finance the asset purchase:

(i) Issue preferred shares

(ii) Issue conventional (full-coupon) bonds

(iii) Issue zero-coupon bonds

Calculate the three ratios in the bond covenants for *each* alternative for the *first year*. Discuss which of the alternatives would permit Sleepman to acquire the assets without violating at least one of the covenants.

b. Assume that the assets are divisible (you can acquire any amount using any financing mode). Calculate a combination of financing modes that enables Sleepman to acquire the assets without violating any of the covenants.

25. [Debt covenants] Exhibit 10P-4 contains information from NorAm Energy's 1994 Annual Report regarding debt covenants

EXHIBIT 10P-4. NORAM ENERGY CORP.
Stockholders' Equity and Debt Covenants

Condensed Shareholders' Equity		
	1994	1993
Capital Stock		
Preferred	$ 130,000	$ 130,000
Common stock including paid-in capital	944,870	944,118
	$1,074,870	$1,074,118
Retained Deficit		
Balance at beginning of year	(366,080)	(360,121)
Net income (loss)	48,066	36,087
Cash dividends		
Preferred stock, $3.00 per share	(7,800)	(7,800)
Common stock, $0.28 per share in 1994 and $0.28 per share in 1993	(34,265)	(34,246)
Balance at end of year	$ (360,079)	$ (366,080)
Unrealized gain on Itron investment, net of tax	2,586	
Total stockholders' equity	$ 717,377	$ 708,037

Note 5: Restrictions on Stockholders' Equity and Debt

Under the provisions of the Company's revolving credit facility as described in Note 3, and under similar provisions in certain of the Company's other financial arrangements, the Company's total debt capacity is limited and it is required to maintain a minimum level of stockholders' equity. The required minimum level of stockholders' equity was initially set at $650 million at December 31, 1993, increasing annually thereafter by (1) 50% of positive consolidated net income and (2) 50% of the proceeds (in excess of the first $50 million) of any incremental equity offering made after June 30, 1994. The Company's total debt is limited to $2,055 million. Based on these restrictions, the Company had incremental debt issuance and dividend capacity of $321.2 million and $43.3 million, respectively, at December 31, 1994. The Company's revolving credit facility also contains a provision which limits the Company's ability to reacquire, retire or otherwise prepay its long-term debt prior to its maturity to a total of $100 million.

Source: NorAm Energy, *1994 Annual Report.*

imposed by its creditors. The covenants restrict new borrowings and dividend payments. The exhibit states that as of December 31, 1994 the company has dividend capacity equal to $43.3 million. This amount was computed after reflecting the annual dividend of $42 million declared in 1994.

a. Show how the dividend capacity of $43.3 million as of December 31, 1994 was computed.

b. State whether the debt covenants restrict NorAm's ability to maintain its annual dividend through 1998. Justify your answer by preparing a schedule for the years 1995–1998 showing NorAm's expected and minimum shareholders' equity given current income and dividend levels.

c. Compute the level of income that would be required to maintain current dividend levels through 1998.

d. In 1995, NorAm approached its shareholders with a proposal to issue new shares. Suggest why the company was motivated to make this proposal and whether you, as a shareholder, would have supported the proposal.

11

LEASES AND OFF-BALANCE-SHEET DEBT

CHAPTER OUTLINE

INTRODUCTION

LEASES
Incentives for Leasing
Lease Classification: Lessees
Capital Leases
Operating Leases
Financial Reporting by Lessees: Capital versus Operating Leases
Comparative Analysis of Capitalized and Operating Leases
Analysis of Lease Disclosures
Lease Disclosure Requirements
Financial Reporting by Lessees: An Example
Impact of Operating Lease Adjustments
Other Lease-Related Issues

OFF-BALANCE-SHEET FINANCING ACTIVITIES
Take-or-Pay and Throughput Arrangements
Sale of Receivables

Other Securitizations
Joint Ventures, Finance Subsidiaries, and Investment in Affiliates

ANALYSIS OF OBS ACTIVITIES: TEXACO
Adjustments to 1999 Debt

FINANCIAL REPORTING BY LESSORS
Lease Classification: Lessors
Sales-Type Leases
Direct Financing Leases
Financial Reporting by Lessors: An Example
IAS Standards for Lessors

SUMMARY

 **APPENDIX 11-A**
CASE 11-1

CHAPTER OBJECTIVES

In this chapter, we:

1. Discuss the motivations for leasing assets as opposed to buying them and the incentives for reporting the leases as *operating leases* rather than *capital leases*.

2. Compare the financial statement effects of *operating leases* and *capital leases* from both a lessee and lessor perspective.

3. Demonstrate how operating leases keep substantial portions of a firm's operating capacity and debt off the balance sheet.

4. Adjust reported leverage, profitability, and cash flows for off-balance-sheet (OBS) leases.

5. Discuss the similarity between OBS leases and other OBS activities such as *take-or-pay and throughput arrangements* and adjust reported financial statements and ratios for these activities.

6. Explain the impact of *transfers of receivables* on reported cash flow from operations and short-term debt and how to undo those effects.

7. Illustrate the adjustments required to reflect the OBS debt of the subsidiaries and affiliates of a firm.

8. Compare lessor financial reporting for sales-type leases and direct financing leases.

INTRODUCTION

Rapid changes in manufacturing and information technology and expanding international trade and capital markets have resulted in the growth of multinational corporations that must cope with increasingly mobile capital, labor, and product markets. Volatile commodity and other factor price levels, fluctuating interest and foreign currency exchange rates, and continuous tax and regulatory changes have accompanied these changes. In addition, general inflation and industry-specific price changes have raised many asset prices and have increased the risks of operations and investments.

This economic climate has required increasing amounts of capital as firms acquire operating capacity (both for expansion and replacement purposes) at ever-higher prices. Because of the volatility of prices and cash flows, the risks of owning operating assets have also increased. These trends have driven firms to seek methods of:

1. Acquiring the rights to assets through methods other than traditional direct purchases (financed by debt)
2. Controlling the risks of operation through derivative and hedging transactions

Executory contracts are the primary alternative form of transactions used by firms to acquire operating capacity, supplies of raw materials, and other inputs. Such contracts or arrangements are the subject of this chapter. Hedging transactions will be discussed in Chapter 16.

The increased use of these financing techniques and hedging transactions has been encouraged by drawbacks in the historical cost-based financial reporting system, in which recognition and measurement depend primarily on actual transactions. As contracts are considered legal promises, and neither cash nor goods may be exchanged at the inception of these contracts, accounting recognition is not required in many cases. The emphasis on accounting assets and liabilities rather than the recognition of economic resources and obligations further encourages firms to keep resources and obligations off the balance sheet.

Firms may engage in these transactions to avoid reporting high debt levels and leverage ratios and to reduce the probability of technical default under restrictive covenants in debt indentures. Off-balance-sheet transactions may also keep assets and potential gains out of the financial statements but under the control of management, which can orchestrate the timing of gain recognition to offset periods of poor operating performance.

Footnote disclosures constitute the best source of information about off-balance-sheet activities. Additional information may be available from disclosures in 10-K filings and from other company publications. In some cases, the economic meaning behind the disclosures requires explanation from management. Thus, a complete analysis of the firm must include a review of all financial statement disclosures to obtain data on off-balance-sheet activities. In many cases, straightforward adjustments can be used to reflect off-balance-sheet assets and liabilities on the balance sheet. Such adjustments result in a balance sheet that presents a more complete portrait of the firm's resources and obligations and financial ratios that are more comparable to those of competitors whose use of off-balance-sheet techniques is different.

The chapter begins with a discussion of leases, the most common form of executory contract entered into by firms. The methods used to analyze and adjust for leases serve as a model for the analysis of other off-balance-sheet activities that comprise the second part of the chapter.

LEASES

Accounting policy makers have grappled with leases for years to develop reporting requirements that emphasize the economic substance rather than the legal form of the leasing transaction. We begin our discussion of leases with a review of incentives for leases. A discussion of reporting requirements and the analysis of leases complete this section of the chapter.

Incentives for Leasing

Firms generally acquire rights to use property, plant, and equipment by outright purchase, partially or fully funded by internal resources or externally borrowed funds. In a purchase transaction, the buyer acquires (and the seller surrenders) ownership, which includes all the benefits and risks embodied in the asset. Alternatively, firms may also acquire the use of property, including some or all of the benefits and risks of ownership, for specific periods of time and stipulated rental payments through contractual arrangements called *leases*.

Short-term, or *operating*, leases allow the lessee to use leased property for only a portion of its economic life. The lessee accounts for such leases as contracts, reporting (as rental expense) only the required rental payments as they are made. Because the lessor retains substantially all the risks of ownership of leased property, the leased assets remain on its balance sheet and are depreciated over their estimated economic lives; rental payments are recognized as revenues over time according to the terms of the lease.

However, longer-term leases may effectively transfer all (or substantially all) the risks and rewards of the leased property to the lessee. Such leases are the economic equivalent of sales with financing arrangements designed to effect the purchase (by the lessee) and sale (by the lessor) of the leased property. *Such leases, referred to as finance or capital leases, are treated for accounting purposes as sales.* The asset and associated debt are carried on the books of the lessee, and the lessor records a gain on "sale" at the inception of the lease. The lessee depreciates the asset over its life, and treats lease payments as payments of principal and interest.[1] The lessor records a financing profit over the lease term. The financial reporting differences between accounting for a lease as an operating or capital lease are far-reaching and affect the balance sheet, income statement, cash flow statement, and associated ratios.

One motivation for leasing rather than borrowing and buying an asset is to avoid recognition of the debt and asset on the lessee's financial statements.[2] Lease capitalization eliminates this advantage. Whether a lease is reported as operating or capitalized depends, as we shall see, on the terms of the lease and their relationship to criteria specified by SFAS 13 and IAS 17.

Notwithstanding these financial reporting requirements, leases may be structured to qualify as operating leases to achieve desired financial reporting effects and capital structure benefits. Operating leases allow lessees to avoid recognition of the asset and report higher profitability ratios and indicators of operating efficiency. Reported leverage is also lower because the related liability for contractual payments is not recognized.

Extensive use of operating leases needs careful evaluation and the analyst must adjust financial statements (to reflect unrecognized assets and liabilities) and the leverage, coverage, and profitability ratios for the effects of operating leases.

Box 11-1 reviews the finance literature on the competing incentives of the lease-versus-purchase decision. The impact of the financial reporting alternatives (operating vs. capitalization) on this decision is also discussed.

Lease Classification: Lessees

The preceding discussion suggests that lessees prefer to structure and report leases as operating leases. Their counterparts, lessors, however, prefer to structure leases as capital leases. This allows earlier recognition of revenue and income by reporting transactions that are in substance installment sales or financing arrangements as completed sales. The resulting higher profitability and turnover ratios are powerful incentives for lessors. The final section

---

[1] The lease payments made by the lessee to the lessor are recorded by the latter as receipts of principal and interest.

[2] Firms may believe that investors, lenders, and rating services do not adjust for leases. However, debt covenants sometimes explicitly include operating leases. Ratings services also incorporate leases when setting debt ratings (see, for example, Moody's Investors Service, *Off-Balance-Sheet Leases: Capitalization and Ratings Implications*, October 1999).

BOX 11-1
Incentives for Leasing and Their Effect on the Capital versus Operating Lease Choice

Management may have a number of reasons to prefer leasing compared to outright asset purchases. The choice may be a function of strategic investment and capital structure objectives, the comparative costs* of leasing versus equity or debt financing, the availability of tax benefits, and perceived financial reporting advantages. Some of these factors influence whether the lease will be treated as an operating or capital lease; others are unrelated to reporting methods.

Tax Incentives

The tax benefits of owning assets are exploited best by transferring them to the party in the higher marginal tax bracket. Firms with low effective tax rates more readily engage in leasing than firms in high tax brackets as the tax benefits can be passed on to the lessor. El-Gazzar et al. (1986) found that, consistent with this hypothesis, firms with lower effective tax rates had a higher proportion of lease debt to total assets than did firms with higher effective tax rates. Moreover, lessees with high effective tax rates tended to capitalize their leases for financial statement purposes. El-Gazzar et al. argue that tax effects also influence the choice of accounting method as the lessee attempts to influence the tax interpretation (by the IRS) of lease contracts. That is, it is more difficult to argue for capital lease treatment for tax purposes if the lease is treated as an operating lease for book purposes.

Nontax Incentives

Smith and Wakeman (1985) analyzed nontax incentives related to the lease-versus-purchase decision. Their list of eight nontax factors that make leasing more likely than purchase is presented here. Some of these factors are not directly related to the lessee's choice, but are motivated by the manufacturer or lessor and/or the type of asset involved. We have sorted these conditions by their potential impact on the operating-versus-capitalization accounting choice.

Nontax Incentives for Leasing versus Purchase: Incentives Classified by Potential Impact on Operating versus Capital Lease Choice

Favors Operating Lease per SFAS 13

1. Period of use is short relative to the overall life of the asset.
2. Lessor has comparative advantage in reselling the asset.

Favors Structuring Lease as Operating Lease

3. Corporate bond covenants contain specific covenants relating to financial policies that the firm must follow.
4. Management compensation contracts contain provisions expressing compensation as a function of returns on invested capital.

Not Relevant to Operating versus Capital Lease Decision

5. Lessee ownership is closely held so that risk reduction is important.
6. Lessor (manufacturer) has market power and can thus generate higher profits by leasing the asset (and controlling the terms of the lease) rather than selling it.
7. Asset is not specialized to the firm.
8. Asset's value is not sensitive to use or abuse (owner takes better care of asset than lessee).

Short periods of use and the resale factor favor the use of operating leases, and under GAAP, these conditions would lead to lease agreements consistent with operating leases. The bond covenant and management compensation incentives also favor the negotiated structuring of the agreement as an operating lease.

Consistent with the foregoing, both Abdel-Khalik (1981) and Nakayama et al. (1981) note that the expected covenant violations resulting from SFAS 13 influenced firms to lobby against its adoption. Furthermore, Abdel-Khalik notes that firms renegotiated the terms of their leases during SFAS 13's transition period to make them eligible for treatment as operating leases. Imhoff and Thomas (1988) found that subsequent to SFAS 13, there was a general decline in leases as a form of financing.[†] Taken together, these results confirm that debt covenant and compensation factors affect both the choice of leasing as a form of financing as well as the choice of accounting treatment of the lease.

Based on Smith and Wakeman (1985).

*Related to these costs are the risks related to residual values and obsolescence.

[†]Further evidence is provided by El-Gazzar et al., who note that in the pre-SFAS 13 period, firms that had high debt-to-equity ratios and/or had incentive-based contracts based on income after interest expense were more likely to have leases classified as operating leases.

of the chapter is devoted to a discussion of lease accounting from the perspective of the lessor. The discussion that follows retains the lessee perspective.

Lease classifications are not intended to be alternative reporting methods. However, management actively negotiates the provisions of lease agreements and the preferred accounting treatment is an important element of these contractual negotiations.

SFAS 13 (1976) and IAS 17 (revised 1997) attempt to promulgate "objective" and "reliable" criteria to facilitate the evaluation of the economic substance of lease agreements. One goal was to discourage off-balance-sheet financing by lessees and front-end loading of income by lessors. The criteria are designed to ensure that either the lessee or lessor recognize the leased assets on their books.

Capital Leases

A lease that, in economic substance, transfers to the lessee substantially all the risks and rewards inherent in the leased property is a financing or capital lease and should be capitalized. Under U.S. GAAP, the lessee must classify a lease meeting any one of the following SFAS 13 criteria at the inception of the lease as a capital lease:

1. The lease transfers ownership of the property to the lessee at the end of the lease term.
2. The lease contains a bargain purchase option.
3. The lease term is equal to 75% or more of the estimated economic life of the leased property (not applicable to land or when the lease term begins within the final 25% of the economic life of the asset).
4. The present value[3] of the minimum lease payments[4] (MLPs) equals or exceeds 90% of the fair value of leased property to the lessor.

The ownership and bargain purchase criteria imply a transfer of all the risks and benefits of the leased property to the lessee; in economic substance, such leases are financing arrangements. Lease terms extending to at least 75% of the economic life of the leased asset are also considered to achieve such a transfer; there is an implicit assumption that most of the value of an asset accrues to the user within that period. Finally, a lease must be capitalized when the present value of the minimum lease payments is equal to or exceeds 90% of the fair value of the leased property at the inception of the lease. In effect, the lessee has contractually agreed to payments ensuring that the lessor will recover its investment along with a reasonable return. The transaction is, therefore, an installment purchase for the lessee financed by the lessor, and capitalization reflects this economic interpretation of the leasing transaction.[5]

The provisions of IAS 17 are less precise. That standard defines a finance lease (the IAS term for a capital lease) as one:

> that transfers substantially all of the risks and rewards incident to ownership of an asset. Title may or may not eventually be transferred.[6]

As IAS 17 lacks the quantitative criteria of SFAS 13, it is easier for a lease to be classified as an operating lease under IAS standards than under U.S. GAAP.

Operating Leases

Under U.S. GAAP, leases not meeting any of the four SFAS 13 criteria listed above are not capitalized and no asset or obligation is reported in the financial statements of the lessee since no purchase is deemed to have occurred. Such leases are classified as operating leases,

---

[3]The discount rate used to compute the present values should be the lessee's incremental borrowing rate or the implicit interest rate of the lessor, whichever is *lower*. The use of the lower rate generates the higher of two present values, increasing the probability that this criterion will be met and the lease capitalized. Under IAS 17, there is a similar (but less precise) requirement.

[4]MLPs include residual values when they are guaranteed by lessees since the guarantee results in a contractually fixed residual value and effectively transfers the risk of changes in residual values to the lessee.

[5]Leases are classified at the inception of the lease; the classification is not changed when the lessee or lessor is acquired unless the provisions of the lease agreement are changed. See FASB Interpretation 21 (1978).

[6]IAS 17, para. 3. An operating lease is defined as a "lease other than a finance lease."

and payments are reported as rental expense. SFAS 13 mandates the use of the straight-line method of recognizing periodic rental payments unless another, systematic basis provides a better representation of the use of leased property. As a result, for leases with rising rental payments, lease expense and cash flow will not be identical.

Financial Reporting by Lessees: Capital versus Operating Leases

Financial reporting by lessees will be illustrated using a noncancellable lease beginning December 31, 2000, with annual MLPs of $10,000 made at the end of each year for four years. Ten percent is assumed to be the appropriate discount rate.

Operating Lease. If the lease does not meet any criteria requiring capitalization:

- No entry is made at the inception of the lease.
- Over the life of the lease, only the annual rental expense of $10,000 will be charged to income and CFO.

Capital Lease. If the lease meets any one of the four criteria of a capital lease:

- At the inception of the lease, an asset (leasehold asset) and liability (leasehold liability) equal to the present value of the lease payments, $31,700, is recognized.
- Over the life of the lease:
  1. The annual rental expense of $10,000 will be allocated between interest and principal payments on the $31,700 leasehold liability according to the following amortization schedule:

Allocation of Payment of $10,000

Year	Opening Liability	Interest*	Principal	Closing Liability[†]
2000				$31,700
2001	$31,700	$3,170	$6,830	24,870
2002	24,870	2,487	7,513	17,357
2003	17,357	1,735	8,265	9,092
2004	9,092	909	9,092	0

*10% of the opening liability.
[†]Equals the opening liability less the periodic amortization of the lease obligation. Also equals the present value of the remaining MLPs discounted at the interest rate in effect at the inception of the lease.

  2. The cost of the leasehold asset of $31,700 is charged to operations (annual depreciation is $7,925) using the straight-line method over the term of the lease.[7]

Comparative Analysis of Capitalized and Operating Leases

Balance Sheet Effects. No assets or liabilities are recognized if the lease is treated as an operating lease. When leases are capitalized, there is a major impact on a firm's balance sheet at inception and throughout the life of the lease. At the inception of the lease, an asset and a liability equal to the present value of the lease payments are recognized.

---

[7]Generally, depreciation methods used for similar purchased property are applied to leased assets over their estimated economic lives when one of the transfer of ownership criteria (1 or 2) is met and over the lease term when one of the other capitalization criteria (3 or 4) is satisfied.

Balance Sheet Effects of Lease Capitalization

	2000	2001	2002	2003	2004
Assets					
Leased assets	$31,700	$31,700	$31,700	$31,700	$31,700
Accumulated depreciation	0	7,925	15,850	23,775	31,700
Leased assets, net	$31,700	$23,775	$15,850	$ 7,925	$ 0
Liabilities					
Current portion of lease obligation	6,830	7,513	8,265	9,092	0
Long-term debt: lease obligation	24,870	17,357	9,092	0	0
	$31,700	$24,870	$17,357	$ 9,092	$ 0

The gross and net (of accumulated depreciation) amounts are reported at each balance sheet date. The current and noncurrent components of the lease obligation are reported as liabilities under capitalization. The current component is the principal portion of the lease payment to be made in the following year. Note that, at the inception of the lease, the leased asset and liability are equal at $31,700. Since the asset and liability are amortized using different methods, this equality is not again observed until the end of the lease term when both asset and liability are equal to zero.

Effect on Financial Ratios. Lease capitalization increases asset balances, resulting in lower asset turnover and return on asset ratios, as compared with the operating lease method, which does not record leased assets.

The most important effect of lease capitalization, however, is its impact on leverage ratios. As lease obligations are not recognized for operating leases, leverage ratios are understated. Lease capitalization adds both current and noncurrent liabilities to debt, resulting in a corresponding decrease in working capital and increases in the debt-to-equity and other leverage ratios.

Income Statement Effects. The income statement effects of lease reporting are also significant and impact operating income as well as net income. The operating lease method charges the periodic rental payments to expense as accrued, whereas capitalization recognizes depreciation and interest expense over the lease term.

Income Effects of Lease Classification

	Operating Lease	Capital Lease		
	Operating = Total Expense	Operating Expense	Nonoperating Expense	
Year	Rent	Depreciation	Interest	Total Expense
2001	$10,000	$ 7,925	$3,170	$11,095
2002	10,000	7,925	2,487	10,412
2003	10,000	7,925	1,735	9,660
2004	10,000	7,925	909	8,834
Totals	$40,000	$31,700	$8,300	$40,000

Operating Income. Capitalization results in higher operating income (earnings before interest and taxes, or EBIT) since the annual straight-line depreciation expense of $7,925 is lower than the annual rental expense of $10,000 reported under the operating lease method. For an individual lease, this difference is never reversed and remains constant over the lease term given use of the straight-line depreciation method. Accelerated depreciation methods would generate smaller differences in early years, with an increasing difference as depreciation declines, increasing both the level and trend of EBIT.

Total Expense and Net Income. Under capitalization, lease expense includes interest expense and depreciation of the leased asset. Initially, total expense for a capital lease exceeds rental expense reported for an operating lease, but declines over the lease term as interest expense falls.[8] In later years, total lease expense will be less than rental expense reported for an operating lease.

Note that total expense (interest plus depreciation) for a capital lease must equal total rental expense for an operating lease over the life of the lease.[9] Consequently, although total net income over the lease term is not affected by capitalization, the timing of income recognition is changed; lower net income is reported in the early years, followed by higher income in later years. This relationship holds for individual leases, but the effect on a firm depends on any additional leases entered into in subsequent periods. When asset prices (and lease rentals) are rising, the impact of old leases nearing expiration may be swamped by the impact of new leases. If a firm enters into new leases at the same or increasing rate over time, reported net income will remain lower under capitalization.

Effect on Financial Ratios. In general, firms with operating leases report higher profitability, interest coverage (as interest expense is lower), return on equity, and return on assets ratios. The higher ROE ratios are due to the higher profitability (numerator effect), whereas the higher ROA is due primarily to the lower assets (denominator effect).

Cash Flow Effects of Lease Classification. Lease classification provides another example where accounting methods affect the classification of cash flows.[10] Under the operating lease method, all cash flows are operating and there is an operating cash outflow of $10,000 per year. However, lease capitalization results in both operating and financing cash flows as the rental payments of $10,000 are allocated between interest expense (treated as CFO) and amortization of the lease obligation (reported as cash from financing).

Cash Flow Effects of Lease Classification

Year	Operating Lease	Capital Lease	
	Operations	Operations	Financing
2001	$10,000	$3,170	$6,830
2002	10,000	2,487	7,513
2003	10,000	1,735	8,265
2004	10,000	909	9,091

In 2001, for example, CFO differs between the two methods by $6,830, the amortization of the lease obligation. Because interest expense declines over the lease term and an increasing proportion of the annual payment is allocated to the lease obligation, the difference in CFO increases over the lease term. Thus, lease capitalization systematically decreases the operating cash outflow while increasing the financing cash outflow.

Therefore, although the capital lease method adversely affects some financial statement ratios, it allows firms to report higher operating cash flows compared to those reported using the operating lease method.

---

[8]If the company uses accelerated depreciation, then the difference in earlier years will be greater but the subsequent decline will also be rapid.

[9]This equality does not hold when the residual value is not zero.

[10]We discuss only the classification of cash flows. After-tax cash flows are not affected by lease classification as *generally* firms that use the capital lease method for financial reporting purposes use the operating lease method for tax purposes. Tax payments and actual cash flows are therefore identical. Under the capital lease method, the lease expense under financial reporting exceeds the lease expense reported for tax purposes, resulting in a deferred tax asset.

Before proceeding, it is important to point out that *at the inception of the lease (year 2000), no cash flows are reported*. This is true even though a capital lease implies the purchase of an asset (cash outflow for investment) financed by the issuance of new debt (cash inflow from financing). Disclosure of the event is reported as part of the "significant noncash financing and investing activities." Analysts attempting to estimate a firm's cash flow requirements for operating capacity should, however, include the present value of such leases as a cash requirement. *Moreover, free cash flow calculations for valuation purposes should incorporate the present value of leases as a cash outflow for investment at the inception of the lease* (see Chapter 19).

Analysis of Lease Disclosures

A noncancellable lease, whether reported as a capital or operating lease, in effect, constitutes debt and the right to use an asset. If the lease is reported as a capital lease, this information is on-balance-sheet. If it is reported as an operating lease, then the debt and asset are off-balance-sheet and the analyst must adjust accordingly.

This is especially true in industries such as airlines and retailers where some firms own operating assets (i.e., airplanes or stores), other firms lease them and report the leases as capital leases, and still other lessees account for them as operating leases. Given the same conditions, the firms using operating leases may report the "best" results as they will show minimal debt and their higher profits will appear to be generated by a relatively smaller investment in assets.

However, the disclosure requirements of firms with leases, capital or operating, are sufficiently detailed to provide the information required for adjustments.

Lease Disclosure Requirements

SFAS 13 requires the disclosure of gross amounts of capitalized lease assets as of each balance sheet date, by major classes or grouped by their nature or function; they may be combined with owned assets.

Lessees must also disclose future MLPs for each of the five succeeding fiscal years and the aggregate thereafter as well as the net present value of the capitalized leases.

Lessees reporting operating leases must also disclose future MLPs for each of the five succeeding fiscal years and in the aggregate thereafter (see Exhibit 11-1 for an example). The present value of the MLPs is not required but is occasionally provided. The rental expense under operating leases (classified as to minimum, contingent, and sublease rentals) for each period for which an income statement is presented must be disclosed as of the balance sheet date.

For both operating and capital leases, lessees must also disclose aggregate minimum rentals receivable under noncancellable subleases. Information regarding renewal terms, purchase options, contingent rentals, any escalation clauses, and restrictions on dividends, additional debt, and leasing is also required. However, rather than being informative, such disclosure is usually vague and general in nature.

IAS 17 disclosure requirements are far less extensive:

- MLPs due within one year
- MLPs due in more than one but less than five years
- MLPs due after five years

 This abbreviated disclosure (for an example, see Note 12 of the Roche 2000 annual report) makes the analysis that follows less precise, but does permit approximations.

Financial Reporting by Lessees: An Example

Exhibit 11-1 contains balance sheet information and the lease footnote of AMR Corp. [AMR], the parent of American Airlines. From the balance sheet alone, it would seem that AMR primarily purchases rather than leases its equipment. The carrying value of purchased equipment is over seven times that of leased equipment.

The footnote paints an entirely different picture. AMR has substantial leases that are mostly structured as operating leases. As required by GAAP, capital lease obligations and

EXHIBIT 11-1. AMR
Excerpts from Balance Sheet and Lease Footnote, December 31, 1999 (in $millions)

Assets

Equipment and property (net of accumulated depreciation of 7,403)		$14,338
Equipment and property under capital leases (net of accumulated amortization of 1,347)		1,949
Total assets		24,374

Liabilities

Long-term debt		
Current maturity	$ 302	
Noncurrent	4,078	4,380
Capital lease obligations		
Current	$ 236	
Noncurrent	1,611	1,847
Total long-term debt and capital lease obligations		$ 6,227

Shareholders' equity 6,858

Leases

AMR's subsidiaries lease various types of equipment and property, including aircraft and airport and off-airport facilities. The future minimum lease payments required under capital leases, together with the present value of net minimum lease payments, and future minimum lease payments required under operating leases that have initial or remaining noncancellable lease terms in excess of one year as of December 31, 1999, were (in millions):

Years Ending December 31	Capital Leases	Operating Leases
2000	$ 347	$ 1,015
2001	329	1,006
2002	280	952
2003	198	965
2004	249	954
2005 and subsequent	1,081	12,169
	$2,484	$17,061
Less amount representing interest	(637)	
Present value of net minimum lease payments	$1,847	

At December 31, 1999, the Company had 205 jet aircraft and 71 turboprop aircraft under operating leases, and 79 jet aircraft and 61 turboprop aircraft under capital leases.

Source: AMR, *1999 Annual Report.*

operating leases are shown separately. Future MLPs for the next five years, and the aggregate thereafter, are disclosed for both capital and operating leases. For capital leases, interest has been deducted to report their present value of $1,847 million ($236 million is reported as current and $1,611 million as long-term debt).

Note that the (aggregate) operating lease payments of $17,061 million are almost seven times the capital lease payments ($2,484 million). Moreover, the data suggest that the operating leases are of longer term than the capital leases!

Aggregate MLPs of the capital leases for the next five years are about 56% of total future MLPs, or $1,403 million. Total MLPs for the remaining years are $1,081 million, or 44% of the total MLPs of $2,484 million over the lease terms. The average lease term of the capitalized leases can be estimated by computing the number of payments included in the "later years" amount of $1,081 million; that is, ($1,081 million/$249 million) if we assume that annual payments remain at the 2004 level. This suggests a lease term of approximately 9 (initial five plus the estimated remaining four) years.

For operating leases, the proportion of payments after the first five years is ($12,169/$17,061) 71% of total payments. This suggests a longer term than for the capital leases. Dividing the remaining payments of $12,169 by the 2004 payment of $954 yields 13, suggesting a lease term of 18 years (5 plus 13) or *twice as long as the term of the capital leases.*

The note indicates that 205 jet aircraft and 71 turboprops are under operating leases. *Neither these assets nor the debt associated with them appear on the balance sheet.*

Investors and analysts can use the lease disclosures to adjust the balance sheet appropriately. The present value of the operating leases can be estimated by discounting the future minimum lease payments. This estimate requires assumptions about the pattern of MLPs after the first five years and the discount rate. The estimation procedure (described below) is "robust," with the calculated present value relatively invariant to the assumptions.

Assumed Pattern of MLPs. Footnote disclosures reflect the payments to be made over each of the next five years and the total payments thereafter. The present value computation requires an estimate of the number of payments implicit in the latter lump sum. Either the rate of decline suggested by the cash outflows for the next five years or a constant amount over the remaining term may be used to derive the present value of the operating lease payments.

Discount Rate. The discount rate should reflect the risk class of the leased assets as well as the company being analyzed. The interest rate implicit in the reported capital leases is a good approximation of that rate.[11]

Box 11-2 uses AMR to illustrate the estimation method(s). The procedure yields a rate of between 6.0% and 6.5% depending on the assumptions made; we use 6.4%. The two assumptions regarding pattern of cash flows over the lease term generate present value estimates of $10.1 and $9.9 billion, a difference of only 2%.

Impact of Operating Lease Adjustments

Liabilities. The impact of the adjustment is highly significant. AMR's reported long-term debt and capital leases total $6.2 billion. Adding approximately $10 billion for off-balance-sheet operating leases increases debt by more than 160% to approximately $16.2 billion. *AMR has more debt off the balance sheet than on the balance sheet.* With equity of $6.9 billion, the debt-to-equity ratio of 0.9 mushrooms to 2.3.

AMR: Effects of Operating Lease Adjustments (in $billions)

	Reported	+ Operating Leases	= Adjusted
Debt	$6.2	$10.0	$16.2
Equity	6.9		6.9
Debt/equity ratio	0.9X		2.3X
Assets	$24.4	$10.0	$34.4

Assets. Exhibit 11-1 reports total assets of $24.4 billion. Capitalization of the operating leases increases total assets by $10 billion. AMR is operating 41% more assets than reported on its balance sheet. *Efficiency measures such as turnover or ROA use total assets in the denominator and are highly overstated; adjusted ratios more accurately portray AMR's asset efficiency.*

Income and Cash Flow Effects. Adjustments for operating leases also affect the income and cash flow statements (as well as related ratios). These effects can be illustrated

---

[11]Because the implicit rate is an average rate based on terms at inception, it may be significantly different from either the reported or marginal long-term borrowing rate the company faces in the capital markets. The analyst may use a long-term borrowing rate estimated from the debt footnote or based on current market conditions.

BOX 11-2
Estimation of the Present Value of Operating Leases

A. The Implicit Discount Rate of a Firm's Capital Leases

Two approaches may be employed to estimate the average discount rate used to capitalize a firm's capital leases. The first uses only the next period's MLP; the second incorporates all future MLPs in the estimation procedure.

1. Using Next Period's MLP

The 2000 MLP for AMR's capital leases is $347 million. That payment includes interest and principal. The principal portion is shown in AMR's current liabilities section as $236 million. The difference, $111 million, represents the interest component of the MLP. As the present value of AMR's capital leases equals $1,847, the interest rate on the capitalized leases can be estimated as ($111/$1,847) 6.01%.

This calculation assumes that the principal payment of $236 million will be made at the end of the year. If it is made early in the year, then the interest expense is based on the principal outstanding after payment of the current portion. The results can be biased if the current portion is a significant portion of the overall liability. An alternative estimate of the implicit interest rate may be derived using the average liability balance; that is, $111/[0.5 × ($1,847 + $1,611)] = 6.42%.

2. Using All Future MLPs

The interest rate can also be estimated by solving for the implicit interest rate (internal rate of return) that equates the MLPs and their present value. This calculation requires an assumption about the pattern of MLPs after the first five years as the MLPs for the first five years (2000 to 2004) are given. From 2004 and on, two assumptions are possible:

1. Constant rate, or
2. Declining rate

Constant Rate

Under the simpler constant rate assumption, it is assumed that the payment level ($249 million) in the fifth year (2004) continues into the future, implying the following payment stream:

Year	2000	2001	2002	2003	2004	2005
MLP	$347	$329	$280	$198	$249	$249

Year	2006	2007	2008	2009[r]	Total
MLP	$249	$249	$249	$85	$2,484

[r]Residual.

The internal rate of return that equates this stream to the present value of $1,847 is 6.55%.

Declining Rate

Alternatively, and more realistically, one would expect the payments to decline over time. The rate of decline implicit in the MLPs reported individually for the first five years may be used

to estimate the payment pattern after the initial five years. In AMR's case, payments decrease initially and then jump in 2004. On average, the payments are approximately 94% of the previous year.* Using this rate we obtain the following pattern of payments:

Year	2000	2001	2002	2003	2004	2005
MLP	$347	$329	$280	$198	$249	$234

Year	2006	2007	2008	2009	2010[r]	Total
MLP	$220	$207	$194	$183	$43	$2,484

[r]Residual.

The internal rate of return that equates this stream to the present value of $1,847 is 6.40%; a rate close to the 6.55% based on the constant rate assumption. Generally, the differences are not significant and unless the rate of decline is very steep, the constant rate assumption simplifies the computation. The first procedure yields an estimate of 6.0 to 6.4%; the second yields estimates of 6.40 to 6.55%. Based on these estimates, we use 6.4% for our analysis of AMR's operating leases.

B. Finding the Present Value of the Operating Leases

For operating leases the MLPs for the first five years (2000 to 2004) are given. Again we can make two assumptions as to the pattern of payments for 2005 and on.

Under the constant rate assumption, it is assumed that MLPs from the year 2005 and on equal the 2004 payment of $954. Alternatively, based on the payment pattern of the operating lease MLPs over the first five years, one would expect the payments to decline at a rate of 1.5% a year. The assumed patterns and the resultant present values using the discount rate of 6.4% are presented below.

Constant Rate

Year	2000	2001	2002	2003	2004
MLP	$1,015	$1,006	$952	$965	$954

Year	2005–2016	2017[r]	Total	Present Value
MLP	$954	$721	$17,061	$10,060

[r]Residual.

Declining Rate

Year	2000	2001	2002	2003	2004	2005
MLP	$1,015	$1,006	$952	$965	$954	$940

Year	2006	...	2018	2019[r]	Total	Present Value
MLP	$926	...	$772	$221	$17,061	$9,911

[r]Residual.

Note that the two present value estimates of $10.1 and $9.9 billion are within 2% of each other.

C. Executory Costs

Reported MLPs at times include such executory costs as maintenance, taxes, and insurance on the leased assets. These costs are not financing costs and should be excluded from the calculation of the lease present value. However, because footnote disclosures generally do not reduce MLPs by executory costs, the present value calculation described above is biased.

In most cases that bias is small and can be ignored. However, the estimation method can be modified to adjust for this bias. When the firm discloses the total of the executory costs, we can

assume that the pattern of the executory costs follows that of the MLPs. If we define p as the proportion of total executory costs to total MLPs,

$$p = \frac{\text{Total executory costs}}{\text{Total MLPs}}$$

then the procedures described above can be applied[†] to a pattern of *adjusted MLPs*, where the

Adjusted MLP (for any year) $= (1 - p) \times$ unadjusted MLP (for that year)

---

*We have used the arithmetic mean. The geometric mean is 92%.

[†]Alternatively, one can use the unadjusted MLPs and make the following two adjustments:

1. In calculating the implicit interest rate of the capital leases, gross up the present value of the capital leases by *dividing* by $(1 - p)$.
2. Using the interest rate calculated in step 1, find the present value of the unadjusted MLPs. *Multiply* that present value by $(1 - p)$.

---

using the 2000 MLP of $1,015 million as an example. Under the operating lease method, both rent expense and the CFO outflow equal $1,015 million. Capitalization results in allocation of that $1,015 million between interest expense and principal payments; in addition, the leased asset must be depreciated. These changes reduce reported income but increase CFO.

AMR: Effects of Operating Lease Adjustment, 2000 (in $millions)

	As Reported	Adjusted
Income Statement		
Rent expense	$1,015	
Interest expense		$640*
Amortization expense		555[†]
Total expense	$1,015	$1,195
Cash Flow Statement		
If interest payments are treated as CFO (per SFAS 95)		
CFO outflow	$1,015	$640
CFF outflow	0	$375
If interest payments are treated as CFF (per Chapter 3)		
CFO outflow	$1,015	0
CFF outflow	0	$1,015

*Interest expense = interest rate × PV of leases = 0.064 × $10 billion = $640 million.
[†]Amortization expense = PV of leases divided by lease term = $10 billion/18 = $555 million.

Other Lease-Related Issues

While lease classification affects how leases are reported in financial statements, it is not the only issue that affects financial analysis. The following may also be significant for some companies:

1. *Lease impairment.* Because of changes in market conditions, leased assets can become uneconomic to the firm. In such cases, the firm may recognize an impairment charge similar to the impairment charges for fixed assets discussed in Chapter 8. For example, OMI [OMM], an operator of oil tankers, recorded a loss of $6.3 million in

June 1999 when it "determined that its current lease obligations for vessels exceeded its undiscounted forecasted future net cash flows."

2. *Sale and leaseback of assets.* Such sales can be a cost-effective source of funds, especially for firms with low credit ratings. Because the assets sold secure the obligation, lenders charge a lower interest rate than for unsecured borrowings. Both SFAS 13 and IAS 17 require the lessee to defer any gain on the asset sale, and recognize it over the lease term, when the lease is a capital (finance) lease. Amortization over the lease term is also required for sale/leasebacks classified as operating leases under SFAS 13. However, under IAS 17, gains on sale/leasebacks classified as operating leases are recognized immediately.[12]

3. *Lease guarantees.* Firms may guarantee leases for affiliates (see discussion of Texaco later in the chapter). Companies may also remain obligated for leases when operating units are sold. For example, Kmart [KM] sold its Builders Square subsidiary in 1997 to Hechinger, another chain of home improvement stores. When Hechinger filed for bankruptcy in June 1999, Kmart recognized a pretax charge of $350 million for its guarantees of long-term leases with a net present value of $711 million.

4. *Straight-line recognition.* Both SFAS 13 and IAS 17 require both lessors and lessees to recognize operating lease payments over the life of the lease on a straight-line basis (equal amounts in each year). However, the lease payments may take a different form, resulting in either prepaid rent or rent receivable.

   For example, in the first quarter of 2001, Cisco [CSCO] paid Catellus [CDX] $68 million in connection with a California ground lease. Catellus reported that this sum would be amortized over the 34-year lease term.

5. *Synthetic leases.* Such leases use a special purpose entity to finance an asset purchase. The asset is then leased to the user. While the user receives the tax benefits of ownership, the transaction is accounted for as an operating lease, keeping it off-balance-sheet.

   For example, AOL Time Warner [AOL] used a synthetic lease to finance the construction of its New York headquarters, keeping a reported one billion dollars of debt off its balance sheet.

OFF-BALANCE-SHEET FINANCING ACTIVITIES

Leases are but one example of contractual arrangements that give rise to off-balance-sheet debt. In this section, we discuss other such arrangements and show how financial statements should be adjusted to reflect the underlying economic consequences. Like leases, some of these off-balance-sheet activities are commonplace and can be found in many firms and industries. Others tend to be industry specific or are the product of specific market conditions.

Take-or-Pay and Throughput Arrangements

Firms use take-or-pay contracts to ensure the long-term availability of raw materials and other inputs necessary for operations.[13] These agreements are common in the energy, chemical, paper, and metal industries. Under these arrangements, the purchasing firm commits to buy a minimum quantity of an input over a specified time period. Input prices may be fixed by contract or may be related to market prices. Energy companies use throughput arrangements with pipelines or processors (such as refiners) to ensure future distribution or processing requirements.

These contracts are often used as collateral for bank or other financing by unrelated suppliers or by investors in joint ventures. The contract serves as an indirect guarantee of the re-

---

[12]The accounting for sale/leasebacks can be quite complex, with numerous variations and exceptions under both U.S. and IAS GAAP. See Box 11-4 for further discussion.

[13]Inventories can also be financed through product financing arrangements under which inventories are sold and later repurchased. SFAS 49 (1981) requires that such arrangements that do not effectively transfer the risk of ownership to the buyer must be accounted for as debt financing rather than sale of inventory. In such cases, the cost of holding inventories (storage and insurance) and interest cost on the imputed debt must be recognized as incurred. Prior to SFAS 49, companies sometimes used these arrangements to defer these costs and accelerate the recognition of profit. Product financing arrangements may still be accounted for as sales outside of the United States.

lated debt. However, neither the assets nor the debt incurred to obtain (or guarantee availability of) operating capacity are reflected on the balance sheet of the purchaser. SFAS 47 (1981) requires that, when a long-term commitment is used to obtain financing, the purchaser must disclose the nature of the commitment and the minimum required payments in its financial statement footnotes.

As take-or-pay contracts and throughput agreements effectively keep some operating assets and liabilities off the balance sheet, the analyst should add the present value of minimum future commitments to both property and debt.

Exhibit 11-2 contains the commitments and contingencies footnote from the 1999 annual report of Alcoa [AA], disclosing a take-or-pay obligation of Alcoa of Australia, a consolidated subsidiary. Note that the disclosure is similar to that required for (capital and operating) leases. We can apply the method used earlier to compute the present value of the debt. The calculation is shown in panel B of the exhibit.

The take-or-pay contracts reported by Alcoa represent $1,780 million of off-balance-sheet assets and debt. The impact of this adjustment on the leverage ratio is as follows:

Alcoa Balance Sheet, at December 31, 1999 (in $millions)

	Reported	Adjusted	Increase
Total debt	$3,067	$4,847	58%
Stockholders' equity	6,318	6,318	None
Debt-to-equity ratio	0.49X	0.77X	58%

EXHIBIT 11-2. ALCOA
Analysis of Take-or-Pay Contracts

A: Footnote: Contingent Liabilities

Alcoa of Australia (AofA) is party to a number of natural gas and electricity contracts that expire between 2001 and 2022. Under these take-or-pay contracts, AofA is obligated to pay for a minimum amount of natural gas or electricity even if these commodities are not required for operations. Commitments related to these contracts total $190 in 2000, $182 in 2001, $179 in 2002, $176 in 2003, $176 in 2004, and $2,222 thereafter.

Source: Alcoa, *1999 Annual Report.*

B. Analysis: Take-or-pay Contracts, 2000 to 2004 and Beyond (in $millions)

Year	Take-or-Pay Obligation
2000	$ 190
2001	182
2002	179
2003	176
2004	176
Thereafter	2,222

Using the technique for capitalizing operating leases discussed earlier in the chapter, the above payment stream can be discounted to its present value. Estimated payments continue after 2004 (using, for simplifying purposes, the constant rate assumption) for

$$\frac{\$2,222 \text{ million}}{\$176 \text{ million}} = 12.63 \text{ years}$$

Given this payment stream, the present value can be arrived at using an estimated cost of debt (based on capitalized lease disclosures or other long-term debt). For Alcoa, we estimate an interest rate of 7%. When applied to the minimum payments shown above, the resulting present value equals $1,780 million for take-or-pay obligations. Thus approximately $1.8 billion should be added as an adjustment to Alcoa's consolidated property and total debt.

Sale of Receivables

Receivables are sometimes financed by their sale (or securitization) to unrelated parties. That is, the firm sells the receivables to a buyer (normally a financial institution or investor group). Depending on the interest (if any) paid by customers and the effective interest rate on the sale transaction, the seller may recognize a gain or loss on the receivables sold. The seller uses the proceeds from the sale for operations or to reduce existing or planned debt. The firm continues to service the original receivables; customer payments are transferred to the new owner of the receivables. Some arrangements are revolving in nature as collected receivables are periodically replaced by new ones.

Such transactions are recorded as sales under SFAS 140, Accounting for Transfers and Servicing of Financial Assets and Extinguishments of Liabilities (2000), as long as there has been a *legal* transfer of ownership from the seller to the buyer.[14] To effect such transactions, firms often set up distinct (nonconsolidated) trusts or subsidiaries (often referred to as a *qualifying special-purpose entity, QSPE*) that the firm's creditors cannot access in the event of bankruptcy.[15] By selling the receivables through such entities, the firm has adhered to the strict legal definition of ownership transfer. Exhibit 11-3 provides examples of such arrangements from the financial statements of Lucent Technologies [LU]. Note that in 2000, Lucent's receivables and loans were sold through a "bankruptcy-remote subsidiary," as required by GAAP for sale recognition.

By reporting such transactions as sales, the company decreases accounts receivable and increases cash from operations in the period of sale. However, most such receivable sales and/or securitizations provide that the seller retains the effective credit risk by either:

- Retaining a portion of the receivables and receiving payment only after the securitized amount has been repaid. If the retained percentage exceeds the historic loss ratio, the seller has retained the effective risk.
- Providing other collateral, or agreeing to replace delinquent receivables with current receivables.

As shown in Exhibit 11-3, Lucent provided the second form of implicit guarantee. *When the seller retains the entire expected loss experience, these transactions are effectively collater-*

EXHIBIT 11-3. LUCENT TECHNOLOGIES
Receivable Securitization Activities (years ended September 30)

1999

- Subsidiary of Lucent sold approximately $625 million of accounts receivable to a nonconsolidated qualified special-purpose entity (QSPE).
- The QSPE resold the receivables to an unaffiliated financial institution.
- Lucent transferred $700 million of other receivables to the QSPE as collateral.

2000

- Lucent and a third-party financial institution arranged for the creation of a nonconsolidated Special Purpose Trust.
- Trust purchases, from a wholly owned (bankruptcy-remote) subsidiary of Lucent, customer finance loans, and receivables on a limited-recourse basis.
- Balance of receivables sold but uncollected was $1,329 million.

Source: Information from Lucent Technologies, *2000 Annual Report.*

---

[14]SFAS 140 states that the transferor (seller) accounts for the transfer as a sale when it surrenders effective control over those assets (see SFAS 140 for details).

[15]LTV, a steel company, filed for bankruptcy late in 2000. LTV argued that the transfer of receivables (and a similar transfer of inventories) to a QSPE was a "disguised finance transaction" and that it still had an interest in the transferred assets. However, the bankruptcy court ruled against the company in March 2001.

alized borrowings with the receivables serving as collateral. Sales of receivables are another form of off-balance-sheet financing and should be adjusted as follows:

1. *Balance Sheet.* Both accounts receivable and current liabilities should be increased by the amount of receivables sold that have not yet been collected.

2. *Cash Flow Statement.* CFO must be adjusted; the change in the uncollected amount should be classified as cash from financing rather than CFO.

These two adjustments usually capture the analytical effects of receivable sales. However, as sales/securitizations of receivables transactions can be quite complex, other aspects of the financial statements may also be affected. Moreover, to the extent amounts received from receivable sales are not equal to the "face value" of receivables sold, the (cash flow) adjustment is only an approximation, albeit a reasonably accurate one.

Box 11-3 illustrates the effects of sales/securitizations on the income statement. Treating the transaction as a sale results in earlier income recognition as compared to treating it as a

---

BOX 11-3
Income Statement Effects of Receivable Sales and Securitizations

Our illustration assumes that the company is selling (credit) receivables that it carries on its books at $1,000,000. Depending on the interest rate structure of the credit receivables and the risk, the buyer may pay more or less than $1,000,000.

Buyer Pays Less: $900,000

Transaction qualifies as a sale: The seller will *immediately* recognize a $100,000 loss on the sale.*

Transaction does not qualify as a sale and is treated as a financing: The $100,000 is treated as a "discount" on the loan payable taken by the seller.[†] The income statement is not affected at the time of the sale. Over time (as the receivables are collected) the discount is amortized as additional interest expense.[‡]

Buyer Pays More: $1,100,000

Transaction qualifies as a sale: The mirror image of the previous transaction occurs (i.e., the seller will *immediately* recognize a $100,000 gain on the sale).

Transaction does not qualify as a sale and is treated as a financing: The $100,000 is treated as a "premium" on the loan payable taken by the seller.[§] The income statement is not affected at the time of the sale. Over time (as the receivables are collected) the premium is amortized and interest expense is reduced.**

Analytical procedures: From an analytical perspective, the two approaches result in different timing of income or loss recognition. Thus, if a company recognized a securitization as a sale and the analyst felt that it would be more appropriate to view the transaction as a financing event, then the financial statement adjustments would be as follows:

- Remove gain/loss from current period income.
- Add the securitized receivables to the balance sheet amount.
- Classify the securitization proceeds as debt.

---

*The entry would be

Cash	$900,000	
Loss on sale	100,000	
Accounts receivable		$1,000,000

[†]The entry would be

Cash	$900,000	
Loan payable (net of discount)		$900,000

[‡]For example, when $200,000 of the receivables are collected, the entry for the "passthrough" would be

Amortization of discount	$ 20,000	
Loan payable	180,000	
Cash		200,000

Note, if the transaction were treated as a sale, there would be no entry at the time of collection.

[§]The entry would be

Cash	$1,100,000	
Loan payable (includes premium)		$1,100,000

**For example, when $200,000 of the receivables are collected, the entry would be

Loan payable	220,000	
Amortization of premium		20,000
Cash		200,000

Note, if the transaction were treated as a sale, there would be no entry at the time of collection.

collateralized borrowing. The disclosure requirements of SFAS 140 (2000) are illustrated in Appendix 11-A using Sears' annual report as an illustration.

■ Example: Lucent Technologies

Exhibit 11-4 continues with our Lucent example. Panel A summarizes data from the financial statements. As indicated in Exhibit 11-3, Lucent engaged in receivables securitization and reported balances of $625 and $1,329 million of outstanding uncollected receivables in 1999 and 2000, respectively. In both years, the receivables were sold through an entity established specifically for this purpose.

Balance Sheet. Lucent recorded the securitizations as sales as they were structured to satisfy the (legalistic) requirements of SFAS 125 and 140. Lucent, however, transferred other (not sold) receivables to the subsidiary as collateral for the receivables sold and therefore ultimately bears the credit risk.

The sale proceeds should therefore not be viewed as a reduction of accounts receivable, but rather as an increase in (short-term) borrowing. As Panel B of Exhibit 11-4 indicates, Lucent's 1999 (2000) accounts receivable, current assets, and current liabilities should be increased by $625 ($1,329) million.[16]

EXHIBIT 11-4. LUCENT TECHNOLOGIES
Analysis of Receivables Securitization

		A. Reported Data			B. Adjusted Data	
	1998	1999	2000		1999	2000
From Footnotes						
Balance of uncollected receivables	$ 0	$625	$1,329			
From Balance Sheet				*Adjustment:*	*Add $625*	*Add $1,329*
Accounts receivable	7,821	9,097	10,059		9,722	11,388
Current assets		19,240	21,490		19,865	22,819
Current liabilities		9,150	10,877		9,775	12,206
From Cash Flow Statement				*Adjustment:*	*Deduct $625*	*Deduct $704*
CFO	1,452	(962)	304		(1,587)	(400)
From Income Statement						
Sales	24,367	30,617	33,813			
Selected Trends and Ratios						
% Change in sales from 1998		26%	39%		26%	39%
% Change in A/R from 1998		16%	26%		24%	46%
# of days A/R outstanding	117	101	103		105	114
Current ratio	1.45	2.10	1.98		2.03	1.87
CFO/Current liabilities	0.13	(0.11)	0.03		(0.16)	(0.03)

Source: Data from Lucent Technologies, *1998–2000 Annual Reports.*

---

[16]The manner in which Lucent set up its QSPE in 1999 results in another, more subtle "off-balance-sheet activity." (See subsequent section entitled "Joint Ventures, Finance Subsidiaries, and Investment in Affiliates.") By transferring $700 million of its receivables to the subsidiary as collateral, Lucent effectively removed this amount from its receivables balances (where they belong) and buried it within the investment in subsidiary accounts. Total assets are not affected but the composition of those assets is. To keep the exposition for sale of receivables straightforward, we have ignored this factor in our presentation. However, this issue is addressed in Problem 11-17 as an extension of the Lucent example.

Cash Flow Classification. Accounting for these transactions as sales distorts the amount and timing of CFO as the firm received cash earlier than if the receivables had been collected in the normal course of business. An adjustment is required to reclassify *the change in the uncollected receivables sold*[17] from CFO to cash from financing.

Since 1999 was the first year Lucent engaged in sales securitization, the full $625 million should be deducted from CFO (and classified as CFF). For 2000, the adjustment should be the change in sold but uncollected receivables; that is, ($1,329 − $625 =) $704 million. These adjustments are made in Exhibit 11-4, Panel B.

Effects of Adjustments. The effects of these adjustments are also demonstrated in Exhibit 11-4. Relative to 1998, sales in 1999 and 2000 increased 26% and 39%, respectively. *Reported* accounts receivable, however, increased only 16% and 26% over that same period; an apparent improvement in receivables management. This improvement is reflected in the receivable turnover with days receivables outstanding improving by 14 days from 117 to 103 days over the 1998–2000 period.

However, after adjustment for receivables sold, the improvement disappears. Restoring the $625 million of receivables sold in 1999 results in an (adjusted) increase of 24% in receivables relative to 1998, similar to the 26% sales increase over the same period. For 2000, we find that, after adjustment, receivables increased 46%, greater than the 39% increase in sales. After adjustment, the number of days of outstanding receivables, which declined on a reported basis, rose to 114 in 2000, similar to the 1998 level.[18]

Moving to Lucent's liquidity ratios, we note that both the adjusted current ratio and the CFO/current liabilities ratio are below the reported amounts. For these ratios, there is an adjustment to both the numerator and denominator. For the current ratio, the same amount is added to both; the numerator adjustment improves the ratio whereas the denominator adjustment reduces the ratio. It is only because the (reported) ratio is greater than 1 that the net effect is a lower ratio. Were the ratio less than 1 to begin with, the effect of the adjustment would be to improve the ratio. Both adjustments to the CFO/current liabilities ratio, on the other hand, reduce the ratio as CFO is decreased and current liabilities are increased.

Turning to CFO, we find that the receivables sales masked the deterioration of the company's operating cash flow: 1998 CFO was $1,452 million; 1999 reported CFO plunged to ($962) million, recovering to $304 million in 2000.

After adjustment for receivables sold, CFO was considerably below the amounts reported. For 1999, adjusted CFO was ($1,587) million, an outflow two-thirds greater than the reported amount of ($962) million. Although 2000 CFO improved, on an adjusted basis it remained negative at ($400) million.

The cash flow trend may have been the motivation for Lucent beginning a program of receivable securitization in 1999; as CFO deteriorated, the company needed another source of cash. ∎

Other Securitizations

While the securitization of accounts receivable remains a major source of financing, other forms of securitization have emerged. A few examples follow:

1. PolyGram, the Dutch film producer, issued bonds in 1998 backed by expected revenues from films.
2. Marne et Champagne issued bonds in 2000 backed by its champagne inventories.

---

[17]In Chapter 3, it was shown that the change in accounts receivable is an adjustment to net income when deriving CFO. Because the uncollected balance of the receivables sold must be added to the reported balance of accounts receivable, calculation of the adjusted CFO requires exclusion of any change in the balance of uncollected receivables sold.

[18]As discussed in Chapter 2 (using Lucent as an example), sales of receivables should be added back when assessing the provision for bad debts.

3. Toys "R" Us [TOY] issued bonds in 2000 secured by license-fee income from its Japanese affiliate.

4. Yasuda Fire & Marine Insurance [8755] used auto and mortgage loans and leasing credits to back bonds issued in 2000.

Such issues are a growing form of off-balance-sheet financing, used worldwide, with significant implications for current and future period cash flows. The financial analyst must be alert to such transactions and make the appropriate analytical adjustments.[19]

Joint Ventures, Finance Subsidiaries, and Investment in Affiliates

Firms may acquire manufacturing and distribution capacity through investments in affiliated firms, including suppliers and end users. Joint ventures with other firms may offer economies of scale and provide opportunities to share operating, technological, and financial risks. To obtain financing, the venture may enter into take-or-pay or throughput contracts with minimum payments designed to meet the venture's debt service requirements. Direct or indirect guarantees of the joint venture debt may also be present. Generally, firms account for their investments in joint ventures and affiliates (where they have 20 to 50% ownership) using the equity method (discussed in Chapter 13) whereby the balance sheet reports the firm's *net investment* in the affiliate. The net investment reflects the parent's proportionate share of the assets minus the liabilities of the subsidiary (*i.e., the parent's financial statements do not report its share of the debt of these affiliates*).

For example, Micron [MU] stated in its August 31, 2000 10-K report that it participated in two joint ventures (in Singapore and Japan). Micron entered into take-or-pay contracts requiring it to purchase all of the output of the joint ventures and to provide technology, systems support, and other services. These joint ventures are not consolidated although they are clearly part of Micron operationally. They supplied more than one-third of all memory produced by Micron in fiscal 2001 and Micron reported all transactions with the venture as part of cost of goods sold.

Similarly, many firms have long used legally separate finance subsidiaries to borrow funds to finance parent-company receivables. Such debt is often lower-cost than general-purpose borrowings because of the well-defined collateral. Finance subsidiaries enable the parent to generate sales by granting credit to dealers and customers for purchases of its goods and services. Until 1987, most firms used the equity method to account for finance subsidiaries.[20] The FASB eliminated the nonconsolidation option (SFAS 94) and firms must now consolidate the assets and liabilities of controlled financial subsidiaries. As a result, some parent firms reduced their ownership of finance subsidiaries below 50% to gain the benefit of "debt suppression" afforded by the equity method.

From an overall economic entity (parent firm plus share in the affiliate) perspective, however, affiliate debt should be considered explicitly because it is clearly required to maintain the parent's operations. Additionally, the parent firm generally supports affiliate borrowings through extensive income maintenance agreements and direct or indirect guarantees of debt.

The information required for these adjustments to debt and related interest coverage and leverage ratios can be obtained from the footnotes, which may disclose the assets, liabilities, and results of operations of finance subsidiaries in a summarized format.[21]

---

[19]Bond ratings services recognize the effect of securitizations on a company's debt structure. For example, Moody's March 2000 analysis of Federal-Mogul [FMO] included $450 million of securitized receivables in its calculation of Federal Mogul's total debt.

[20]Livnat and Sondhi (1986) showed that the exclusion of finance subsidiary debt allowed firms to report higher coverage and lower leverage ratios, stabilized reported debt ratios over time, and reduced the probability of a technical violation of bond covenants. Heian and Thies (1989) identified 182 companies (in 35 industry groups) reporting unconsolidated finance subsidiaries in 1985. Supplementary disclosures provided by 140 of these companies indicated a total of $205 billion in subsidiary debt that had not been reported on the parent's balance sheet. The authors also computed debt-to-capital ratios on the basis of pro forma consolidation and compared them to the preconsolidation ratios; the average increase in the ratio for the sample was 34%, but nearly 90% for the firms with the 21 largest finance units.

[21]When the subsidiary or joint venture issues publicly traded debt, then full financial statements are available and can be used for more accurate adjustments.

EXHIBIT 11-5. GEORGIA-PACIFIC
Joint Venture Financing

Note 13: Related Party Transactions

The Corporation is a 50% partner in a joint venture (GA-MET) with Metropolitan Life Insurance Company (Metropolitan). GA-MET owns and operates the Corporation's main office building in Atlanta, Georgia. The Corporation accounts for its investment in GA-MET under the equity method.

At January 1, 2000, GA-MET had an outstanding mortgage loan payable to Metropolitan in the amount of $144 million. The note bears interest at $9\frac{1}{2}$%, requires monthly payments of principal and interest through 2011, and is secured by the land and building owned by the joint venture. In the event of foreclosure, each partner has severally guaranteed payment of one-half of any shortfall of collateral value to the outstanding secured indebtedness. Based on the present market conditions and building occupancy, the likelihood of any obligation to the Corporation with respect to this guarantee is considered remote.

Source: Georgia-Pacific, *1999 Annual Report.*

Exhibit 11-5 contains an excerpt from the footnote on commitments and contingencies in the *1999 Annual Report* issued by Georgia Pacific [GP]. It discloses a joint venture with Metropolitan Life [MET]. GP is clearly liable for one-half of this off-balance-sheet debt, and $72 million should be added to GP's (property and) debt. In the GP example, the parent explicitly guaranteed the debt of the affiliate. Even in the absence of such guarantees, the proportionate share of the affiliate's debt should be added to the reported debt of the investor and the financial statements should be adjusted accordingly. These adjustments will be illustrated shortly in the analysis of Texaco and Exhibits 11-6 and 11-7. Case 11-1 carries this analysis further and examines Texaco and its 50%-owned affiliate, Caltex, to explore the use of off-balance-sheet activities in a more complex setting.

ANALYSIS OF OBS ACTIVITIES: TEXACO

Texaco is a major worldwide refiner, marketer, and distributor of oil products. Exhibit 11-6 contains excerpts from footnotes to Texaco's 1999 financial statements relating to its unconsolidated subsidiaries, leases, and commitments and contingencies. *A complete assessment of a company's off-balance-sheet activities requires a review of all financial statement disclosures.*

Exhibit 11-7 illustrates the adjustments for off-balance-sheet financing activities discussed in this chapter. Panel A presents Texaco's reported and adjusted debt, total liabilities, and equity. Panel B shows each adjustment to the reported amounts, based on the information provided in Exhibit 11-6. The result is a more comprehensive measure of the firm's leverage.

Adjustments to 1999 Debt

Share of Affiliate Debt. Texaco has entered into a number of joint ventures with other major oil companies. The three primary ones are:

Joint Venture	Partners	Texaco's Share
Equilon	Shell Oil	44.0%
Motiva	Shell Oil, Saudi Refining	32.5%
Caltex	Chevron	50.0%

As Texaco is not the majority owner of any of these ventures, their financial results are not consolidated with Texaco's financial statements and (Texaco's portion of) the debt and liabilities of these joint ventures remains off-balance-sheet. Texaco, however, reports its proportionate share of its joint ventures' assets and liabilities in the final column of Note 5. The adjustment to

EXHIBIT 11-6. TEXACO
Off-Balance-Sheet Activities

Excerpts from 1999 Notes to Financial Statements

Note 5: Investments and Advances

We account for our investments in affiliates, including corporate joint ventures and partnerships owned 50% or less, on the equity method. . . . The following table provides summarized financial information on a 100% basis for the Caltex Group, Equilon, Motiva, Star and all other affiliates that we account for on the equity method, as well as Texaco's total share of the information.

As of December 31, 1999

(Millions of dollars)

	Equilon	Motiva	Caltex Group	Other Affiliates	Texaco's Total Share
Current assets	$ 4,209	$ 1,271	$ 2,705	$ 801	$ 3,796
Noncurrent assets	7,208	5,307	7,604	2,230	9,321
Current liabilities	(5,636)	(1,278)	(3,395)	(736)	(4,916)
Noncurrent liabilities	(735)	(2,095)	(2,639)	(792)	(2,638)
Net equity	$ 5,046	$ 3,205	$ 4,275	$1,503	$ 5,563

Note 10: Lease Commitments and Rental Expense

We have leasing arrangements involving service stations, tanker charters, crude oil production and processing equipment and other facilities. We reflect amounts due under capital leases in our balance sheet as obligations, while we reflect our interest in the related assets as properties, plant and equipment. The remaining lease commitments are operating leases, and we record payments on such leases as rental expense.

As of December 31, 1999, we had estimated minimum commitments for payment of rentals (net of noncancelable sublease rentals) under leases which, at inception, had a noncancellable term of more than one year, as follows:

(millions of dollars)

	Operating Leases	Capital Leases
2000	$ 134	$ 9
2001	93	9
2002	416	8
2003	50	7
2004	54	7
After 2004	315	14
Total lease commitments	$1,062	$54
Less interest		(8)
Present value of total capital lease obligations		$46

Note 15: Other Financial Information, Commitments and Contingencies

Preferred Shares of Subsidiaries

Minority holders own $602 million of preferred shares of our subsidiary companies, which is reflected as minority interest in subsidiary companies in the Consolidated Balance Sheet.

The above preferred stock issues currently require annual dividend payments of approximately $34 million. We are required to redeem $75 million of this preferred stock in 2003, $65 million (plus accreted dividends of $59 million) in 2005, $112 million in 2024 and $350 million in 2043. We have the ability to extend the required redemption dates for the $112 million and $350 million of preferred stock beyond 2024 and 2043.

EXHIBIT 11-6 *(continued)*

Financial Guarantees

We have guaranteed the payment of certain debt, lease commitments and other obligations of third parties and affiliate companies. These guarantees totaled $716 million and $797 million at December 31, 1999 and 1998. The year-end 1999 and 1998 amounts include $336 million and $387 million of operating lease commitments of Equilon, our affiliate.

Throughput Agreements

Texaco Inc. and certain of its subsidiary companies previously entered into certain long-term agreements wherein we committed to ship through affiliated pipeline companies and an offshore oil port sufficient volume of crude oil or petroleum products to enable these affiliated companies to meet a specified portion of their individual debt obligations, or, in lieu thereof, to advance sufficient funds to enable these affiliated companies to meet these obligations. In 1998, we assigned the shipping obligations to Equilon, our affiliate, but Texaco remains responsible for deficiency payments on virtually all of these agreements. Additionally, Texaco has entered into long-term purchase commitments with third parties for take or pay gas transportation. At December 31, 1999 and 1998, our maximum exposure to loss was estimated to be $445 million and $500 million.

However, based on our right of counterclaim against Equilon and unaffiliated third parties in the event of non-performance, our net exposure was estimated to be $173 million and $195 million at December 31, 1999 and 1998.

No significant losses are anticipated as a result of these obligations.

Litigation

Texaco and approximately 50 other oil companies are defendants in 17 purported class actions. The actions are pending in Texas, New Mexico, Oklahoma, Louisiana, Utah, Mississippi, and Alabama. . . . Plaintiffs seek to recover royalty underpayments and interest. In some cases plaintiffs also seek to recover severance taxes and treble and punitive damages. Texaco and 24 other defendants have executed a settlement agreement with most of the plaintiffs that will resolve many of these disputes. The federal court in Texas gave final approval to the settlement in April 1999 and the matter is now pending before the U.S. Fifth Circuit Court of Appeal.

Texaco has reached an agreement with the federal government to resolve similar claims. The claims of various state governments remain unresolved.

It is impossible for us to ascertain the ultimate legal and financial liability with respect to contingencies and commitments. However, we do not anticipate that the aggregate amount of such liability in excess of accrued liabilities will be materially important in relation to our consolidated financial position or results of operations.

Source: Texaco, *1999 Annual Report.*

---

debt equals Texaco's share in the noncurrent[22] liabilities of its joint ventures; Texaco's liabilities are increased by its share of total (current plus noncurrent) liabilities of its joint ventures.

Capitalization of Operating Leases. Note 10 (in Exhibit 11-6) provides information on Texaco's operating and capital leases. The interest rate implicit in the 1999 capital leases is 4.5%, relatively low even considering the low interest rate levels prevalent in the late 1990s. Texaco's long-term debt footnote (not shown) indicated a cost of debt of about 5.5% for new 10-year debt issued in 1999. We used a discount rate of 5% (and a straight-line assumption for payments after 2004), resulting in a present value adjustment of $864 million.

Redeemable Preferred Shares. As discussed in Chapter 10, redeemable preferred shares should be treated as debt. Note 15 (in Exhibit 11-6) states that Texaco includes $602 million of such preferred shares as part of minority interest. As minority interest is included

---

[22]Current liabilities may include financing obligations, but they are excluded in calculating the debt adjustment as no disclosures were provided. This "undercounting" may be partially offset by the "overcount" implied in including all noncurrent liabilities as certain noncurrent liabilities (e.g., deferred taxes) may not constitute debt.

EXHIBIT 11-7. TEXACO
Adjusted Long-Term Debt, Liabilities, and Solvency Analysis (amounts in $millions)

A. Reported and Adjusted Debt, Liabilities, and Capitalization Ratios

	Reported	Adjustments (Panel B below)	Adjusted	% increase
Debt	$ 7,647	$4,613	$12,260	60%
Total liabilities	16,930	8,927	25,857	53%
Shareholders' equity	12,042		12,042	
Capitalization Ratios				
Debt to equity	0.64		1.02	60%
Total liabilities to equity	1.41		2.15	53%

B. Adjustments for Off-Balance-Sheet Data

	Debt	Liabilities
Share of affiliate debt	$2,638	$7,554
Capitalization of operating leases	864	864
Redeemable preferred shares	602	—
Guarantees	336	336
Throughput agreements	173	173
Total Adjustments to Debt and Liabilities	**$4,613**	**$8,927**

in total liabilities, no adjustment is required there. However, debt must be increased by $602 million.

Financial Guarantees. As a portion of the $716 million of guarantees relates to affiliate debt, including it would result in double counting as we have already adjusted for Texaco's share of affiliate debt. Thus, we adjust only for $336 million of guarantees of Equilon's operating leases, as that amount is off-balance-sheet for Equilon as well. Note that Texaco's guarantee includes a guarantee of lease residual values.

Throughput Agreements. We have used the net exposure of $173 million, although a conservative approach would use the gross exposure of $445 million.

Litigation. We note only that potential liabilities related to litigation exist. However, a numeric adjustment is not possible based on the information provided.

The effect of these adjustments is summarized in Exhibit 11-7, panel A. Adjusted debt is 60% higher than reported debt in 1999 and total liabilities increase by 53%. The adjusted debt-to-equity and liabilities-to-equity ratios are significantly higher than the reported ratios.

FINANCIAL REPORTING BY LESSORS

Many manufacturers and dealers offer customers leases to market their products. Such *sales-type leases* include both a manufacturing or merchandising profit (the difference between the fair value at the inception of the lease and the cost or carrying value of the leased property) and interest income due to the financing nature of the transaction. Financial institutions and leasing intermediaries offer direct financing leases that generate interest income only. Either class of lessors may create operating leases.

BOX 11-4
Financial Reporting for Sales with Leasebacks

Sale leaseback transactions are sales of property by the owner who then leases it back from the buyer-lessor. Financial reporting for these transactions is governed by SFAS 28, Accounting for Sales with Leasebacks (1979), as amended by SFAS 66, Accounting for Sales of Real Estate (1982).

The amount and timing of profit (or loss) recognized on a sale leaseback transaction are determined by the proportion of the rights to use the leased property retained by the owner-lessee after the sale. If all or substantially all the use rights are retained by the owner-lessee, it is a financing transaction, and no profit or loss on the transaction should be recognized.

The extent of continuing use is determined by the proportion of the present value of reasonable rentals relative to the fair value of assets sold and leased back. This proportion is used to assign sale leaseback transactions to the following financial reporting categories.

Minor Leasebacks. Present value of reasonable rentals is less than 10% of the fair value of the leased property; the buyer-lessor obtains substantially all the rights to use the leased property. Any gain (or loss) on the transaction is recognized in full at the inception of the lease.

More than Minor but Less than "Substantially All" Leasebacks. Present value of reasonable rentals exceeds 10% but is less than 90% of the fair value of the asset sold; depending on specific criteria, some or all of the gain or loss must be deferred and amortized over the lease term.

Substantially All Leasebacks. Present value of MLPs equals or exceeds 90% of the fair value of property sold; the total gain (loss) must be deferred and amortized over the lease term. The leaseback is a financing transaction, and the gain (loss) is recognized as the leased property is used.

Example

OMI [OMM], an oil tanker operator, sold a vessel in May 1997 for $39.9 million and leased it back for five years. The $15.7 million gain was deferred and recognized as an adjustment to lease expense over the five-year lease term. Had the gain been recognized immediately, 1997 pretax income would have been more than twice the reported level.

IAS Standards for Sales with Leasebacks

IAS 17, the accounting standard for these transactions, is significantly different from U.S. GAAP as it requires that:

- When a sale/leaseback results in a finance lease, any profit on the sale must be deferred and recognized over the lease term.
- When a sale/leaseback results in an operating lease, and the sales price equals the asset's fair value, the seller recognizes any gain or loss.
- When a sale/leaseback results in an operating lease, and the sales price is below fair value, the seller recognizes any gain or loss. The exception is that any loss is deferred and amortized when the lease provides for payments that are below market.
- When a sale/leaseback results in an operating lease, and the sales price exceeds fair value, the seller defers any gain and amortizes it over the lease term.

The remainder of the chapter discusses the accounting by lessors for sales-type and direct financing leases. Leveraged leases are beyond the scope of this text and sales with leasebacks are discussed in Box 11-4.

Lessor financial reporting is illustrated using the lessee example of the beginning of the chapter with the additional assumptions that the leased equipment cost $20,000 to manufacture and the expected residual value (not guaranteed by the lessee) is $2,500 after four years.

Lease Classification: Lessors

Lease capitalization by lessors is required when the lease meets *any one* of the four criteria specified for capitalization by lessees and *both* of the following revenue-recognition criteria:

1. Collectibility of the MLPs is reasonably predictable.
2. There are no significant uncertainties regarding the amount of unreimbursable costs yet to be incurred by the lessor under the provisions of the lease agreement.

Leases not meeting these criteria must be reported as operating leases since either the risks and benefits of leased assets have not been transferred, or the earnings process is not complete.

Sales-Type Leases

Exhibit 11-8 presents financial reporting by a lessor for a sales-type lease using the lessee example. Part A illustrates the accounting recognition at inception and the determination of gross and net investment in the lease; part B provides the lessor's amortization schedule for the sales-type lease.

EXHIBIT 11-8
Lessor Financial Reporting

A. Sales-Type Lease

Lessor's Gross Investment in Leased Equipment

MLPs: $10,000 × 4	$40,000
Unguaranteed residual value	2,500
	$42,500

Lessor's Net Investment in Leased Equipment

Present value at 10% of an annuity of 4 payments of $10,000	$31,700
Present value at 10% of $2,500, 4 periods hence	1,707
	$33,407

Unearned Income

Gross investment in lease	$42,500
Less: Net investment	33,407
	$ 9,093

Accounting Recognition at Lease Inception

Sales revenue*	$ 31,700	
Cost of goods sold[†]	(18,293)	
Gross profit on sale		$13,407

Gross investment in lease	$ 42,500	
Unearned income	(9,093)	
Net investment in lease		$33,407

*Present value of lease payments, excluding residual value.

[†]Cost to manufacture (assumed to be $20,000) less PV of residual value.

B. Lessor Amortization Schedule: Sales-Type Lease

Year	Annual Payment Received (A)	Interest Income (B)	Reduction in Investment (C) = (A) − (B)	Net Investment (D)
2000				$33,407
2001	$10,000	$3,340	$ 6,660	26,747
2002	10,000	2,675	7,325	19,422
2003	10,000	1,942	8,058	11,364
2004	10,000	1,136	8,864	2,500
Totals	$40,000	$9,093	$30,907	

C. Balance Sheet Effects

	Capital (Sales-Type) Lease				Operating Lease	
	Net Investment in Leases			Assets Under	Accumulated	
Year	Current	Long-Term	Total	Lease	Depreciation	Net
---	---:	---:	---:	---:	---:	---:
2000	$6,660	$26,747	$33,407	$20,000	$ 0	$20,000
2001	7,325	19,422	26,747	20,000	4,375	15,625
2002	8,058	11,364	19,422	20,000	8,750	11,250
2003	8,864	2,500	11,364	20,000	13,125	6,875
2004	2,500	0	2,500	20,000	17,500	2,500

EXHIBIT 11-8 (continued)

D. Income Statement Effects

| | Capital (Sales-Type) Lease | | | Operating Lease | |
| | | | | | |
Year		Income	Rental Revenue	Depreciation	Income
2000	Gain on Sale	$13,407			
2001	Interest	3,340	$10,000	$ 4,375	$ 5,625
2002	Interest	2,675	10,000	4,375	5,625
2003	Interest	1,942	10,000	4,375	5,625
2004	Interest	1,136	10,000	4,375	5,625
Totals		$22,500	$40,000	$17,500	$22,500

E. Cash Flow Statement Effects

| | Capital (Sales-Type) Lease | | | Operating Lease |
| | | | | |
Year	CFO	Cash from Investment	Total	CFO
2000	$13,407	$(13,407)	$ 0	$ 0
2001	3,340	6,660	10,000	10,000
2002	2,675	7,325	10,000	10,000
2003	1,942	8,058	10,000	10,000
2004	1,136	8,864	10,000	10,000
Totals	$22,500	$ 17,500	$40,000	$40,000

The lessor recognizes sales revenue of $31,700, the present value of the MLPs. The cost of goods sold is the carrying amount of the leased property. The present value of the unguaranteed residual value of the leased property constitutes continuing investment by the lessor and is not included in costs charged against income; that is, it is deducted from cost to manufacture.

The lessor's gross investment in the lease is $42,500, the sum of the MLPs and the unguaranteed residual value. Net investment in the lease is $33,407, determined by discounting the MLPs and the unguaranteed residual value at the interest rate implicit in the lease (10%), as shown in part A.

The difference between the gross and net investment represents unearned income, the interest component of the transaction. Unearned income is systematically amortized to income over the lease term, using the interest method that reports a constant rate of return of 10% on the net investment in the lease. The lessor reports its net investment in the lease on the balance sheet (see the next section). Contingent rentals, if any, are reported as they are earned. SFAS 13 requires an annual review of the estimated residual value. Nontemporary declines must be recognized; however, increases in value or subsequent reversals of declines cannot be reported.

Balance Sheet Effects (Exhibit 11-8C). The lessor reports the current and noncurrent components of its net investment in sales-type leases. Lessors using the operating lease method do not report any investment in leases, but they continue to report the assets on the balance sheet as long-term assets, net of accumulated depreciation. These amounts assume straight-line depreciation over four years of the original cost of the asset less estimated residual value ($20,000 − $2,500). Note that the operating lease method reports lower net assets each year and, ignoring income effects, tends to increase return on assets relative to the sales-type lease method.

Income Statement Effects (Exhibit 11-8D). For the sales-type lease, the lessor records profit at inception of $13,407. The annual rental of $10,000 is allocated to interest income and return of principal. Reported interest income reflects a constant 10% return on the declining net investment in the lease. The balance of the rental payment is applied to amortize (reduce principal) the net investment systematically over the lease term.

The operating lease method reports constant income over the lease term as straight-line depreciation is charged against the constant annual rental. The use of accelerated depreciation would result in a pattern of increasing income over the lease term as depreciation declines.

The sales-type lease reports substantially higher income in the first year of the lease due to recognition of manufacturing profit at the inception of the lease. However, reported income declines thereafter due to declining interest income over the remainder of the lease term, relative to constant or increasing income under the operating lease method. In our example, reported net income is higher under the operating lease method after the initial year. *Over the lease term, the total net income is the same under both methods.*

Cash Flow Effects (Exhibit 11-8E). At the inception of the lease, no cash changes hands. The operating lease method reports no cash flow effects on the statement of cash flows. In contrast, the sales-type lease method reports 2000 operating cash flow of $13,407, equal to the sales profit at the inception of the lease. This cash inflow is offset by a net cash outflow for investment equal to $13,407 (the investment of $33,407 less the $20,000 prior carrying amount of the leased property). Net cash flow remains zero.

In subsequent years, under the operating lease method, CFO is equal to the rental payment of $10,000/year. Under the sale-type lease method, the $10,000 payment is allocated between CFO and cash from investment; CFO is equal to interest income and cash from investment is equal to the reduction in the net investment. Thus, after inception, the operating lease method reports higher CFO and, since interest income declines over the lease term, this difference in CFO increases. Simultaneously, a correspondingly larger reduction in net investment is reported in investment cash flow.

Note that total cash flow (operating plus investing) is unaffected by the method of lease accounting. The actual cash flow in each year is $10,000, the lease payment received. Only under the operating lease method does CFO equal the cash flows associated with the lease. Capitalization of the lease by the lessor reclassifies reported cash flows between operating and investing activities.

The use of sales-type lease accounting allows firms to recognize income earlier than the operating lease method. Lease capitalization also allows firms to report higher CFO at the inception of the lease. This aggressive recognition of income and cash flows ("front-end loading") improves financial ratios; it accurately reflects the firm's operations only if the risks and benefits of leased property have been fully transferred to the lessee and the lessor has no further performance obligation.

Footnote Disclosures. Footnote disclosure for lessors under U.S. GAAP is similar to that of lessees. The sales-type lease method requires the disclosure of gross MLPs receivable, unearned income, and the current and noncurrent components of the net investment in leases. Lessors must also provide information on lease terms, future MLPs receivable over the next five years, and the aggregate thereafter. Disclosure for operating leases is limited to MLPs receivable over the next five years and the aggregate thereafter.

Direct Financing Leases

In a direct financing lease, the lessor's original cost or carrying value (prior to the lease) of the asset approximates the market value of the leased asset (the present value of the MLPs). Such leases are pure financing transactions and financial reporting for direct financing leases reflects this fact. *No sale is recognized at the inception of the lease, and there is no manufacturing or dealer profit. Only financing income is reported.*

Unearned income is the difference between the gross investment in the lease and the cost or carrying amount of the leased property. It is amortized to report a constant periodic return (effective interest method) on the net investment in the lease (gross investment plus initial direct costs less unearned income). Thus, in our example, the lessor would report (interest) income and cash flows similar to those reported for the sales-type lease over the period 2001–2004. There are no income or cash flow consequences at the inception of the lease in 2000.

Disclosure requirements for financing leases are similar to those for sales-type leases. Lessors must disclose MLPs receivable over the next five fiscal years and the aggregate thereafter. Any allowance for uncollectibles, executory costs, unguaranteed residual value, and unearned income must also be reported.

The income reported on financing leases depends on assumptions made, particularly those regarding uncollectible payments and residual values. When uncollectibles are underestimated, or residual values overestimated, income is overstated. For example, the *New York Times* reported[23] that automobile lessors would lose more than $10 billion in 2000 because they overestimated the residual values of cars and trucks that they had leased to customers.

Financial Reporting by Lessors: An Example

Exhibit 11-9 contains IBM Credit Corp.'s footnote on its activities as lessor. The company finances customer purchases of information-handling equipment through direct financing leases; shorter-term leases of such equipment are treated as operating leases.

IBM discloses aggregate MLPs receivable and reports the periodic payments in each of the next five years and in the aggregate thereafter as a percentage of this total. The terms of both the direct financing leases and operating leases range from two to three years.[24] However, the operating leases generally have shorter terms: 57% of the operating leases are due within one year, higher than the 50% of direct financing leases due within 12 months of the financial statement date.

Additional disclosures are required for the capitalized direct financing leases: current and noncurrent components, allowance for uncollectibles, estimated unguaranteed residual values, and unearned interest. IBM Credit provides most applicable disclosures. No contingent rentals are reported; they may not be significant. However, the current and noncurrent components have not been reported separately. Computation of the implicit interest rate requires additional assumptions.

The footnote disclosure includes the securitization of direct financing lease receivables and reference to a reconciliation of the allowance for losses.

Going beyond the financial effects of IBM's lessor activities, the footnote data indicate that the company is experiencing minimal lease growth. Direct financing leases increased by 1% (using MLPs) during 1999 while operating leases grew at a rate less than 2%. These patterns may represent stable volume and prices, or higher volume offset by lower lease prices, or a shift from leases to sales (reflecting changes in relative prices or customer preferences). This is another example of how attention to footnote detail can suggest worthwhile questions about changes in operations to ask management.

IAS Standards for Lessors

IAS 17 provides accounting standards for lessors that are broadly similar to those of U.S. GAAP. The most significant differences are:

- Lease classification as a finance lease depends on broad principles (see discussion for lessees earlier in the chapter) rather than the SFAS 13 rules.
- Disclosure requirements are the same as for lessees, with MLPs disclosed for amounts due
  1. Within one year
  2. One to five years
  3. In more than five years

---

[23]December 15, 2000, p. F1.

[24]In its 1994 annual report, IBM Credit reported financing lease terms ranging three to five years and operating leases that spanned two to four years. The shortening of lease terms is consistent with the rapid technological changes in the computer industry.

EXHIBIT 11-9. IBM CREDIT CORP.
Net Investment in Capital Leases

The Company's capital lease portfolio includes direct financing and leveraged leases. The Company originates financing for customers in a variety of industries and throughout the United States. The Company has a diversified portfolio of capital equipment financing for end users.

Direct financing leases consist principally of IBM advanced information processing products with terms generally from two to three years. The components of the net investment in direct financing leases at December 31, 1999 and 1998 are as follows:

(dollars in thousands)

	1999	1998
Gross lease payments receivable	$5,335,352	$5,278,060
Estimated unguaranteed residual values	442,288	397,529
Deferred initial direct costs	18,339	30,634
Unearned income	(604,035)	(571,168)
Allowance for receivable losses	(47,220)	(65,644)
Total	$5,144,724	$5,069,411

The scheduled maturities of minimum lease payments outstanding at December 31, 1999, expressed as a percentage of the total, are due approximately as follows:

Within 12 months	50%
13 to 24 months	33
25 to 36 months	13
37 to 48 months	3
After 48 months	1
	100%

Included in the net investment in capital leases is $17.7 million of seller interest at December 31, 1998, relating to the securitization of such leases. These securitizations were terminated and settled in 1999.

Refer to the note on page 31, Allowance for Receivable Losses, for a reconciliation of the direct financing leases and leveraged leases allowances for receivable losses.

Equipment On Operating Leases:

Operating leases consist principally of IBM advanced information processing products with terms generally from two to three years. The components of equipment on operating leases at December 31, 1999 and 1998 are as follows:

(dollars in thousands)

	1999	1998
Cost	$ 7,166,892	$ 7,046,757
Accumulated depreciation	(3,780,206)	(3,427,172)
Total	$ 3,386,686	$ 3,619,585

Minimum future rentals were approximately $3,094.2 million at December 31, 1999. The scheduled maturities of the minimum future rentals at December 31, 1999, expressed as a percentage of the total, are due approximately as follows:

Within 12 months	57%
13 to 24 months	30
25 to 36 months	10
37 to 48 months	2
After 48 months	1
	100%

Source: IBM Credit Corp., *1999 Annual Report.*

SUMMARY

Financial liabilities can take many forms, from simple, full-coupon debt to leasing and other more esoteric forms of off-balance-sheet activities. This chapter and the previous one illustrated the far-reaching effects of such transactions on a firm's income, cash flow, and capital structure. The principal points made in this chapter are:

1. Operating leases are the most common form of off-balance-sheet financing. Such leases should be capitalized and adjustments made to reported financial data.

2. In addition to leases, there are other means of acquiring the use of assets without reflecting them on the balance sheet, such as
   - Joint ventures
   - Take-or-pay and throughput agreements
   - Sales of receivables

   The chapter illustrates techniques that can be used to adjust financial statements for these activities as well.

The discussion and analysis of OBS activities is not yet complete. Chapter 12 contains an analysis of employee benefit plans, an important off-balance-sheet activity. Hedging activities are covered in Chapter 16. These strands are brought together in Chapter 17, which shows how to prepare balance sheets and income statements that incorporate all of the analytical adjustments presented in the text.

Chapter **11**

Problems

1. [Lease classification and financial statement effects; CFA© adapted] On January 1, 2001, a company entered into a capital lease, recording a balance sheet obligation of $10,000, using an interest rate of 12%. The lease payment for 2001 was $1,300. Compute each of the following:

   (i) Interest expense for 2001

   (ii) The lease obligation at the end of 2001

   (iii) The effect of the lease payments on each of the three components of cash flow for 2001

   (iv) Each of items (i) through (iii) if the lease had been recorded as an operating lease

2. [Off-balance-sheet financing techniques; CFA© adapted] Describe each of the following and explain why they are considered off-balance-sheet financing techniques:

   (i) Take-or-pay arrangements

   (ii) Sales of receivables

   (iii) Joint ventures

3. [Leases; effect of interest rate] For assets under capital leases, lease expense has two components: interest and amortization (depreciation). Assume that a lease can be capitalized at either 9% or 10%. Compare the effects of this choice on the lessee in the first year and over the life of the lease on:

   (i) Interest expense

   (ii) Amortization expense

   (iii) Total lease expense

   (iv) Cash flow from operations

   (v) Average assets

   (vi) Average liabilities

4. [Analysis of lease terms] The Pallavi Company leases equipment (fair market value of $125,000) from Priyanka Corp. The lease contains a bargain purchase option and requires 14 annual minimum lease payments of $15,500 payable at the end of each year. The economic life of the equipment is 20 years. The lessee's borrowing rate is 10%, and the lessor's implicit rate is 8%.

a. Explain why Pallavi must capitalize this lease under U.S. GAAP.

b. Explain whether Pallavi must capitalize this lease under U.S. GAAP in the absence of the bargain purchase option.

c. Compute the amount at which Pallavi should capitalize the lease.

d. Select the number of years over which Pallavi should depreciate the leased equipment.

e. Discuss whether the absence of a bargain purchase option would change your answer to part d.

5. [Analysis of lessee] The Tolrem Company has decided to lease an airplane on January 1, 2002. The firm and its lessor have not yet decided the terms of the lease. Assume that the terms can be adjusted to permit Tolrem to either capitalize the lease or record it as an operating lease.

a. State the effect (higher, lower, or equal) of the choice of capitalizing the lease on the following for 2002 (the initial year of the lease):

(i) Cash flow from operations

(ii) Financing cash flow

(iii) Investing cash flow

(iv) Net cash flow

(v) Debt-to-equity ratio

(vi) Interest coverage ratio

(vii) Operating income

(viii) Net income

(ix) Deferred tax asset or liability

(x) Taxes paid

(xi) Pre- and posttax return on assets

(xii) Pre- and posttax return on equity

b. Recall that the difference between net income under the two methods changes direction at some point during the lease term. State which answers to part a will change in the year after the switch occurs and describe the change.

c. Assume that Tolrem enters into new aircraft leases at a constant annual rate. Describe the effect of the choice of accounting method on the items in part a.

6. [Leases, tax effects, cash flows and deferred taxes] On January 1, 2002, two identical companies, Caramino Corp. and Aglianico, Inc., lease similar assets with the following characteristics:

(i) Economic life is eight years.

(ii) Lease term is five years.

(iii) Lease payments of $10,000 per year are payable at the beginning of each year, with the first payment due on January 1, 2002.

(iv) Fair market value is $48,000.

(v) Each firm has an incremental borrowing rate of 8% and a tax rate of 40%.

Caramino capitalizes the lease, whereas Aglianico uses the operating lease method. Both firms use straight-line depreciation for all assets on their financial statements. Assume that both firms treat the lease as an operating lease on their tax returns. Assume that each firm generates income before lease-related expense and income taxes of $20,000 in 2002.

a. Compute earnings before interest and taxes and earnings before taxes for 2002 for each firm. Identify the sources of the difference.

b. Compute the deferred taxes resulting from the lease for each firm in the first year of the lease.

c. Compute the effect of the lease on the 2002 reported cash flow from operations for both firms. Explain the difference.

d. Compute the impact of the lease on the 2002 reported financing cash flows of both firms. Explain the difference.

e. Compute the impact of the lease on the 2002 reported cash flow for investing of both firms. Explain the difference.

f. Using your answers to parts c through e, compute the effect of the lease on the 2002 reported net cash flow of both firms. Explain why they are identical.

g. Using your answers to parts a through f, discuss the reasons why Caramino and Aglianico opted to use different accounting methods for the same transaction.

7. [Lease capitalization] In 1999, Liberty Bancorp [LIBB] leased new property and accounted for the lease as a capital lease. Until 1999, it had reported all of its leased assets as operating leases. The following information with respect to the capital lease was obtained from the company's 1999 annual report:

Capital lease assets (net of amortization)	$2,479,570
Capitalized lease obligations	2,596,031
Interest on capitalized leases	223,733
Repayment of capital lease obligations	3,969

Minimum lease payments over the next five years and thereafter (in $thousands):

	2000	2001	2002	2003
Capital Lease MLPs	$272	$280	$288	$297

	2004	Thereafter	Total
Capital Lease MLPs	$305	$4,596	$6,038

a. Determine the amount of the capital lease at its inception.

b. The company states that it amortizes its capital leases over the term of the lease. Determine the amortization expense for 1999 and the term of the lease. Compute the total expense for 1999 as a result of the capital lease.

c. Explain how the capital lease affected the 1999 cash flow statement.

d. Describe the adjustment to the company's 1999 free cash flows that should be made for the capital lease.

e. Assuming that the lease was reported as an operating lease, determine:

(i) Lease expense for 1999

(ii) The effect on the cash flow statement

f. Estimate the interest rate that Liberty used for its capital lease using both methods described in the chapter. Compare your results. (*Note:* Your estimate using the MLPs should use the lease term calculated in part b.)

8. [Effect of lease capitalization on ratios] Exhibit 11P-1 presents selected 1999 financial data provided by The Limited [LTD]. (*Note:* Use 6% as the appropriate interest rate for present-value calculations.)

a. In its 10-K filing, The Limited provides an adjusted "earnings to fixed charge coverage" ratio.

(i) Calculate the ratio without the adjustment.

(ii) Explain why the adjusted ratio is a better measure of the company's interest coverage.

EXHIBIT 11P-1. THE LIMITED INC.
Selected Financial Data

Liquidity and Capital Resources (MD&A)

A summary of the Company's working capital position and capitalization follows (in $thousands):

Year Ended January 30, 1999	
Cash provided by operating activities	$ 571,014
Working capital	1,070,249
Capitalization:	
Long-term debt	550,000
Shareholders' equity	2,233,303
Total capitalization	$2,783,303

Leased Facilities and Commitments (Notes to Financial Statements)

Minimum Rent Commitments Under Noncancellable Operating Leases

Year	2000	2001	2002	2003	2004	Thereafter
MLP	$643,828	$632,785	$602,868	$563,468	$502,880	$1,427,862

Ratio of Earnings to Fixed Charges (10-K)

Year Ended January 30, 1999		
Adjusted Earnings		
Pretax earnings		$2,363,646
Fixed Charges		
Portion of minimum rent of $689,240 representative of interest	$229,747	
Interest on indebtedness	68,528	298,275
Minority interest		64,564
Total earnings as adjusted		$2,726,485
Ratio of earnings to fixed charges	9.1X	

Source: The Limited, *1999 Annual Report* and 10-K.

b. Compute the debt-to-equity ratio for the Limited based on reported data.

c. In its MD&A, the company provides a summary of its working capital position and capitalization. Adjust each of the following for the effect of (capitalization of) the firm's operating leases:

  (i) Working capital
  (ii) Long-term debt
  (iii) Debt-to-equity ratio

9. [Effect of lease capitalization on interindustry comparison] Delta Airlines [DAL] leases many of its aircraft. Information taken from its June 30, 2000 annual report is presented below (in $millions):

Long-term debt (including current portion of $660)	$2,416
Capital leases (including current portion of $39)	235
Shareholders' equity	4,448

Minimum Lease Payments for Capital and Operating Leases

	2001	2002	2003	2004
Capital lease MLPs	$63	$57	$57	$48
Operating lease MLPs	$1,020	$1,030	$1,040	$1,020

	2005	Thereafter	Total
Capital lease MLPs	$32	$40	$297
Operating lease MLPs	$980	9,440	$14,530

a. Compute Delta's reported debt-to-equity ratio.

b. Calculate the interest rate used by Delta to discount its capital leases using
  (i) The first year's MLP
  (ii) All future MLPs

c. Using the *higher* of the two rates (calculated in part b), estimate the present value of Delta's operating leases.

d. Adjust Delta's debt-to-equity ratio for the effects of the operating lease.

e. Compare Delta's reported and adjusted debt-to-equity ratios with those computed for AMR in the text (p. 373). Describe how the comparison would be affected if you used the lower discount rate.

f. Explain how the comparison justifies the need to adjust for operating leases.

10. [Lease capitalization effects; non-U.S. GAAP] BASF [BAS] is a chemicals company based in Germany. Its 1999 annual report (German GAAP) shows the following lease commitments (in €millions):

Due within:	1 Year	2–5 years	>5 years	Total
Payments	€166.5	€275.2	€212.2	€653.8

a. Compute the present value of the BASF lease commitments, using an interest rate of 7% and the assumption that the years 2 through 5 payments occur evenly over the four years.

The 12/31/99 BASF balance sheet reports (in €millions):

Total debt	€1,294
Stockholders' equity	14,145

b. Compute the debt-to-equity ratio for BASF:

  (i) Using reported data

  (ii) After capitalization of the lease commitment in part a

c. Your answers to parts a and b were based on the assumption of even payments in years 2–5. State another assumption that might be appropriate and explain how that assumption would affect the adjustment for operating leases.

11. [Take-or-pay agreement; follow-up to Problem 11-10] BASF also reports long-term purchase agreements for raw materials, with the following required payments (in €millions):

	2000	2001	2002
Purchase Commitments	€1,718	€1,740	€1,433

	2003	2004	Thereafter
Purchase Commitments	€1,292	€1,370	€12,128

a. Compute the present value of the required payments, using an interest rate of 7%.

b. Using the debt and equity data from Problem 11-10, compute an adjusted debt-to-equity ratio for BASF at December 31, 1999:

  (i) Using the result of part a only

  (ii) Using the result of Problem 11-10 (part b) as well as part a

12. [Sale of receivables; cash flow effects] The following footnote appeared in Arkla Inc.'s March 31, 1995 10-Q interim report:

Under a March 1994 agreement (the "Agreement"), the Company sells an undivided interest (currently limited to a maximum of $235 million) in a designated pool of accounts receivable with limited recourse. The Company has retained servicing responsibility under the program, for which it is paid a fee which does not differ materially from a normal servicing fee. Total receivables sold under the Agreement but not yet collected were approximately $167.2 million, $192.8 million and $118.7 million, respectively, at March 31, 1995, December 31, 1994 and March 31, 1994, which amounts have been deducted from "Accounts and notes receivable" in the accompanying Consolidated Balance Sheet and, at March 31, 1995, $42.9 million of the Company's remaining receivables were collateral for receivables which had been sold. During the three months ended March 31, 1995 and 1994, the Company experienced cash outflows of $25.6 million and $107.7 million, respectively, under the program. In accordance with authoritative accounting guidelines, cash flows related to these sales of accounts receivable are included in the accompanying Statement of Consolidated Cash Flows within the category, "Cash flows from operating activities."

a. Explain Arkla's statement that it experienced a *cash outflow* of $25.6 million during the three months ended March 31, 1995.

b. State the amount of receivables sold but uncollected at December 31, 1993.

c. Compute the appropriate adjustments (for receivables sold) to Arkla's CFO for the quarters ended:

  (i) March 31, 1995

  (ii) March 31, 1994

13. [Sale of receivables; ratio effects] Pennzoil-Quaker State [PZL] sells certain of its accounts receivable through its wholly owned subsidiary, Pennzoil Receivables Company, a special limited-purpose corporation. The company's net accounts receivables sold under this facility totaled $153.1, $115.0, and $103.3 millions at December 31, 1999, 1998, and 1997, respectively. Selected reported financial data follow:

Years Ended December 31 (in $millions)

	1999	1998
Sales	$2,951	$1,802
Accounts receivable	312	546
Current assets	686	2,078
Current liabilities	369	1,993
Total debt	1,096	533
Stockholders' equity	950	1,518
Cash flow from operations	58	(96)

a. Compute the impact of the sale of receivables on Pennzoil's 1999:

  (i) Current ratio

  (ii) Cash cycle

  (iii) Receivable turnover ratio

b. Compute the reported and adjusted (for the sale of receivables) debt-to-equity ratio for 1999.

c. Discuss the impact of the sales on the trend in the firm's cash flow 1998–1999.

14. [Sale of receivables; ratio and cash flow effects] Foster Wheeler [FWC] entered into arrangements to sell receivables in 1998 and 1999. The accounts receivable footnote in the firm's *1999 Annual Report* noted that

> As of December 31, 1999 and December 25, 1998, $50 million and $38.4 million, respectively, in receivables were sold under the agreement and are therefore not reflected in the accounts receivable–trade balance in the Consolidated Balance Sheet.

Selected reported financial data for the company follow:

Years Ended December (in $millions)

	1997	1998	1999
Sales	$4,060	$4,537	$3,867
Trade accounts receivable	664	720	739
Current assets		1,673	1,615
Current liabilities		1,492	1,472
Total short- and long-term debt		963	961
Stockholders' equity		572	376
Cash flow from operations	(113)	(59)	(6)

a. Compute the impact of the sale of receivables on FWC's receivable turnover ratio and cash cycle for 1998 and 1999.

b. Compute the reported and adjusted (for the sale of receivables) current and debt-to-equity ratios for 1998 and 1999.

c. Discuss the impact of the sale on (the trend of) the firm's cash flow from operations over the period 1997 to 1999.

15. [Sale of receivables] Nash-Finch [NAFC] began selling receivables through its subsidiary, Nash-Finch Funding (Funding), in 1997. Funding sells most of these receivables to an outside purchaser. Nash-Finch reported the following year-end balances ($thousands):

	1997	1998	1999
Receivables (balance sheet)	$174.0	$169.7	$154.1
Receivables sold to Funding	44.6	45.7	50.5
Receivables sold by Funding to purchaser	37.0	36.8	41.8

Nash-Finch reported the following amounts in its cash flow statement ($thousands):

	1997	1998	1999
Cash from Investments			
Sale (repurchase) of receivables	$37.0	$(0.2)	$5.0

a. Relate the cash flow statement amounts to the receivables transactions.

b. Compute the effect of the receivables transactions on the amount of receivables shown on the Nash-Finch balance sheet at each year-end.

c. State and justify the cash flow category that, for financial analysis, should include the proceeds from receivables sales.

16. [Take-or-pay agreements] The following paragraphs were extracted from an article in the *Financial Times* on March 4, 1993:

> *Brazilians Cannot Afford to Cut Aluminum Losses*
>
> Any hopes that Brazil will this year relieve the pressure of oversupply on the languishing aluminum market by cutting its output seem destined to be disappointed. Despite a combination of low international prices and what local industry considers high domestic energy costs, the country registered record production of aluminum in 1992, and output is expected to remain at a similar level this year.
>
> Many energy contracts are "take-or-pay" agreements. . . . Some bauxite supply contracts run on a "take-or-pay" basis, meaning that [aluminum] producers must withdraw their share of raw material whether or not they intend to use it.

Explain the relationship between these two paragraphs. (*Note:* Aluminum is refined from bauxite using large amounts of energy.)

17. [Sales of receivables and investment in affiliates; extension of Lucent example] As noted in chapter footnote 16 and Exhibit 11-3, in creating the QSPE to sell its receivables, Lucent transferred $700 million in receivables to the QSPE as collateral for the receivables sold. These receivables are now reported as (part of) Lucent's investment in affiliates (a long-term asset).

a. Explain why this transfer requires analytical adjustment.

b. Redo Exhibit 11-4 for 1999 to adjust for this transfer.

18. [Off-balance-sheet obligations; CFA© adapted] Extracts from The Bowie Company's December 31, 2001, balance sheet and income statement are presented in the following schedule, along with its interest coverage ratio:

Debt	$12 million
Equity	20
Interest expense	1
Times interest earned	5.0X

The Bowie Corporation's financial statement footnotes include the following:

(i) At the beginning of 2001, Bowie entered into an operating lease with future payments of $40 million ($5 million/year) with a discounted present value of $20 million.

(ii) Bowie has guaranteed a $5 million, 10% bond issue, due in 2007, issued by Crockett, a nonconsolidated 30%-owned affiliate.

(iii) Bowie has committed itself (starting in 2002) to purchase a total of $12 million of phosphorous from PEPE, Inc., its major supplier, over the next five years. The estimated present value of these payments is $7 million.

a. Adjust Bowie's debt and equity and recompute the debt-to-equity ratio, using the information in footnotes (i) to (iii).

b. Adjust the times-interest-earned ratio for 2001 for these commitments.

c. Discuss the reasons (both financial and operating) why Bowie may have entered into these arrangements.

d. Describe the additional information required to fully evaluate the impact of these commitments on Bowie's current financial condition and future operating trends.

 (Problems 11-19 to 11-22 are based on Sears Roebuck. Problems 11-20 to 11-22 require data from the company's 1999 annual report.)

19. [Capitalization of operating leases] Leasing is prevalent among department stores. The following information with respect to operating and capital leases was taken from the 1999 annual reports of Sears Roebuck and J.C. Penney [JCP]. Note that JCP discloses the present value (and interest rate) of its *operating* as well as capital leases.

Minimum Lease Payments ($millions)

| | Sears Roebuck | | JC Penney | |
	Capital Leases	Operating Leases	Capital Leases	Operating Leases
2000	$ 66	$ 352	$10	$ 620
2001	60	303	10	568
2002	56	253	6	521
2003	56	224	1	492
2004	54	195	—	454
Thereafter	714	1,092	—	3,099
Total	$1,006	$2,419	$27	$5,754
Present value	417		24	3,302
Less current portion	(16)			
Long-term portion	$ 401			
Interest rate			10.0%	9.7%

Source: Sears Roebuck and JC Penney 1999 annual reports.

a. Using the interest rate provided by JC Penney, replicate the company's present-value calculation for its operating leases.

b. Estimate the interest rate that Sears Roebuck uses to discount its capital leases.

c. Compare the rate estimated in part b with the rate used by JC Penney.

d. Use the rate determined in part b to estimate the present value of Sears's operating leases.

20. [Effect of leases; extension of Problem 11-19] Using information from the Sears financial statements and your answers to Problem 11-19, adjust the company's assets and debt for its operating lease obligations and recompute its 1999:

  (i) Current ratio

  (ii) Debt-to-equity ratio

  (iii) Pretax return on assets

  (iv) Times-interest-earned ratio

21. [Securitization of receivables] Sears engages in securitization of its credit card receivables. (See MDA "Analysis of Consolidated Financial Position") Calculate the effect of its securitization program on its 1999:

  (i) Current ratio

  (ii) Ratio of CFO to current liabilities

  (iii) Debt-to-equity ratio

22. [Off-balance-sheet adjustments; extension of Problems 11-19 to 11-21] Use your answers to Problems 11-19 to 11-21 to calculate the combined effects of Sear's credit card securitizations and operating leases on its current and debt-to-equity ratios.

23. [Capitalization of operating leases] Texaco reports a guarantee of $336 million in its "Commitments and Contingencies" footnote (see Exhibit 11-6) relating to the 1999 operating leases of its 44%-owned affiliate, Equilon. Equilon's minimum lease payments as of December 31, 1999 for its operating leases are listed below (in $millions):

2000	$	76
2001		63
2002		62
2003		61
2004		59
After 2004		775
Total MLPs		$1,096
Less sublease rental income		(75)
Net MLPs		$1,021

a. Compute the implicit interest rate used by Texaco to estimate its share of Equilon's lease obligation.

b. Compare this rate to the rates calculated for Texaco in the chapter.

c. Explain why these rates would differ.

24. [Analysis of lessor] Carignane Corp., a manufacturer/lessor, enters into a sales-type lease agreement with Mourvedre, Inc., as lessee. The lessor capitalizes the lease rather than reporting it as an operating lease.

  Describe the effect (lower, higher, or none) of this choice on the following accounts and ratios of Carignane (the lessor) in the first and ninth years of a 10-year lease:

  (i) Total assets

  (ii) Revenues

  (iii) Expenses

  (iv) Asset turnover ratio

  (v) Interest income

  (vi) Cost of goods sold

  (vii) Net income

  (viii) Retained earnings

  (ix) Income taxes paid

  (x) Posttax return on assets

  (xi) Cash flow from operations

  (xii) Investment cash flow

25. [Analysis of lessor and lessee] On January 1, 2001, the Malbec Company leases a Willmess winepress to the Baldes Group under the following conditions:

    (i) Annual lease payments are $20,000 for 20 years.

    (ii) At the end of the lease term, the press is expected to have a value of $5,500.

    (iii) The fair market value of the press is $185,250.

    (iv) The estimated economic life of the press is 30 years.

    (v) Malbec's implicit interest rate is 12%; Baldes' incremental borrowing rate is 10%.

    (vi) Malbec reports similar presses at $150,000 in finished-goods inventory.

a. Based on the data given, state whether Baldes should treat this lease as an operating or a capital lease. Justify your answer. What additional information would help to answer the question?

b. Assume that Baldes capitalizes the lease. List the financial statement accounts affected (at January 1, 2001) by that decision and calculate each effect.

c. Assume that Baldes uses straight-line depreciation for financial reporting purposes. Compute the income statement, balance sheet, and statement of cash flows effects of the lease for 2001 and 2002 under each lease accounting method.

d. Based on the data given, state whether Malbec should treat this lease as an operating or a sales-type lease. Justify your answer. What additional information would help to answer the question?

e. Assume that Malbec treats the lease as an operating lease. List the financial statement accounts affected (at January 1, 2001) by that decision and calculate each effect.

f. Assume that Malbec treats the lease as a sales-type lease and the lessee does not guarantee the residual value of the winepress. List the financial statement accounts affected (at January 1, 2001) by that decision and calculate each effect.

g. Assume that Malbec uses straight-line depreciation for financial reporting purposes. Compute the income statement, balance sheet, and statement of cash flows effects of the lease for 2001 and 2002 under each lease accounting method.

12

PENSIONS AND OTHER EMPLOYEE BENEFITS

CHAPTER OUTLINE

CHAPTER OBJECTIVES

Companies motivate employees by supplementing cash compensation with other benefits that may be received:

- During the period of employee service
- After service ceases but before retirement
- After retirement

The objectives of this chapter are to examine the accounting methods used to record the obligation and expense resulting from these benefits. The chapter shows how to:

1. Differentiate between defined benefit and defined contribution pension plans.

2. Examine the components of pension cost, determine their significance, and forecast their trend.

3. Compute the funded status of a defined benefit pension plan and explain why the balance sheet does not fully report that status.

4. Compute the balance sheet adjustments required to reflect the actual plan status.

5. Explain how the provisions of SFAS 87 and IAS 19 smooth the financial reporting of defined benefit pension plans.

6. Define the key assumptions used in the accounting for defined benefit plans and explain how the choice of assumptions affects the reported plan status, pension cost, and the accrued benefit liability.

7. Explain how pension plans are affected by curtailments and settlements and how these effects are reported in the financial statements.

8. Explain how acquisitions and divestitures affect pension plans.

9. Discuss the significant differences between IAS 19 and SFAS 87.

10. Explain the similarities and differences between defined benefit pension plans and postretirement medical and life insurance plans.

11. Discuss the importance of the health care cost trend rate to the accounting for and analysis of postretirement health care plans.

12. Discuss the accounting for stock compensation plans and how the pro forma data required by SFAS 123 can be used for analysis.

INTRODUCTION

This chapter discusses the analysis of pension, profit sharing, and other employee benefit plans including postemployment life and health insurance benefit and stock compensation plans. Financial reporting and analysis of employee benefit plans is especially important for large (often unionized) companies with generous benefits, as the accounting for these plans defers and smoothes economic changes. Due to the size of benefit plans, they often constitute an important off-balance-sheet activity.

Stock option and other compensation plans using employer securities are almost always excluded from financial statement recognition. Yet for some firms the excluded expense is highly significant, distorting income measurement and interfirm comparisons.

Box 12-1 contains a glossary of concepts and specialized terms used in this chapter.

PENSION PLANS

A pension plan is an agreement under which an employer agrees to pay monetary benefits to employees on their retirement from active service. Employee benefits are based on predetermined factors such as average or final compensation, years of service, and age. The deferred compensation characteristic of pension plans may motivate employees to stay with a firm for a longer period of time, or at least until benefits are vested. Some labor economists therefore consider pensions as implicit contracts between the firm and its employees.[1]

---

[1]Although not unanimously accepted [see Bulow (1982)], the implicit contract concept is further supported by evidence that, given an equal level of deferred compensation, the present value of that compensation is lower for younger workers than older workers. Thus, defined benefit plans generally undercompensate employees during the earlier years of service and overcompensate them during later years. Employees therefore need to work until retirement to make up for early years of undercompensation.

The implicit contract argument has implications (discussed in later sections) for pension liability measurement and may help explain plan terminations.

BOX 12-1
Glossary

Accumulated benefit obligation (ABO)	The actuarial present value of pension benefits earned to date based on employee service and compensation to that date
Accumulated postretirement benefit obligation (APBO)	The actuarial present value of postretirement benefits earned to date based on employee service and compensation to that date
Assumed per-capita cost claims (by age)	Estimated costs of health care benefits at specific ages based on current costs adjusted using the assumed health care cost trend rates
Corridor method	Deferral of actuarial gains and losses that do not exceed 10% of the larger of the PBO and plan assets
Contractual termination benefits	Payments to terminated employees required by a plan
Curtailment	Change in plan that freezes benefits of affected employees at current levels
Discount rate	The interest rate used to compute the present value of the benefit obligation
Expected long-term rate of return on plan assets	The assumed rate of return on pension and other postretirement benefit funds
Fair value of plan assets	Current market value of plan assets
Gain or loss	Changes in the value of the PBO (due to changes in assumptions or experience different from that incorporated in the assumptions) or the fair value of plan assets (difference between actual and expected rates of return)
Health care cost trend rate	Assumed inflation rate for health care costs due to cost increases as well as changes in utilization and technology
Market-related value of plan assets	A smoothed measure of plan assets incorporating changes in market value over not more than five years; can be used to compute the expected return on plan assets
Medicare reimbursement rates	Currently legislated payments due to retirees from Medicare
Prior service cost	A retroactive change in the benefit obligation due to plan amendment
Projected benefit obligation (PBO)	The actuarial present value of pension benefits earned to date based on employee service to date and estimated future compensation levels for pay-related plans
Rate of compensation increase	The expected growth rate of employee compensation used to compute the PBO as well as the APBO
Service cost	The actuarial present value of benefits earned during the current period
Settlement	Transfer of benefit obligation to an unrelated party
Special termination benefits	Payments made to terminated employees; offered for a limited period of time
Vested benefit obligation (VBO)	The portion of the pension benefit obligation that does not depend on future employee service

Box 12-2 discusses incentives for the creation and funding of pension plans. It provides a framework for the analyses discussed in this chapter.

In the United States, pension plans are virtually always funded because of the requirements of the Employee Retirement Income Security Act of 1974 (ERISA), tax deductibility of the employer's contribution, and the tax-exempt status of earnings on plan investments. Outside the United States, pension obligations are often unfunded.

A pension fund is often used as an intermediary to satisfy the employer's pension obligations. Employer contributions to the fund[2] are invested; the principal and earnings on those investments are used to pay pension benefits. The following diagram depicts the relationship among employer, employees, and the pension fund:

Employer
(Makes contributions to)
↓
Pension Fund
(Invests contributions and pays benefits to)
↓
Eligible Retired Employees

---

[2]Firms are permitted to contribute (subject to certain limitations) their own securities to the pension fund. Texaco, for example, reports that on December 31, 1999 a benefit plan trust held 9.2 million common shares (Note 11). This issue has become very controversial in recent years because of some high-profile bankruptcies.

BOX 12-2
Incentives for Creating and Funding Pension Plans

Tax incentives are a powerful motivation for firms both to create pension plans and to overfund them. Contributions to pension plans are tax-deductible (subject to IRS limits) and the income earned by the funds is tax-exempt. This enables funds in pension plans to grow at a faster rate (compounded tax-free) than if they were held by firms or their employees. Employees pay taxes on benefits after retirement, when their marginal tax rate is expected to be lower than during their working years. *Ceteris paribus*, firms with higher tax rates should have greater incentives to fund pension plans than those with lower tax rates or tax loss carryforwards.

Firms facing a temporary decline in cash flows must reduce capital spending, cut dividends, or obtain external financing. Myers and Majluf (1984) argued that managements prefer to use internal resources to fund investments rather than to cut dividends or obtain costly external financing. When management has better information than potential investors or creditors as to the desirability of investment projects, any new securities issued would be underpriced. Therefore, managers build up financial slack, that is, an inventory of internal resources to avoid diluting the value of extant shareholders' claims. Pension plans (with the added benefits of favorable tax treatment) can be used to store this slack.* When needed, the firm can draw on it by reducing future contributions (by changing actuarial methods or assumptions) or by terminating the pension plan.

In addition to the bonding mechanism implied by the implicit contract view of pensions, employees become creditors of the firm when their pension plans are underfunded. This relationship may be an effective control mechanism with respect to both management (also beneficiaries of the pension plans) as well as lower-level employees.

When managers are also creditors, they have additional incentives to avoid actions that might hurt the firm in the long run. External bondholders are also less fearful of actions that might benefit shareholders at the expense of creditors, reducing their monitoring costs and thereby lowering the cost of debt to the firm. Underfunding may also constrain employees who might otherwise make greater economic demands at the expense of shareholders.

Francis and Reiter (1987) found that a plan's funded status was directly related to the firm's tax status and capital availability; the higher the taxes[†] and the greater the available financial slack, the higher the funded status. In addition, separate pension plans for unions and higher benefits per employee were significantly related to the level of underfunding of plans. This result is consistent with the use of underfunding as a control mechanism.

The support for labor underfunding incentives suggests that for some firms a long-term or implicit contract is evidenced. Other firms may choose, as a policy matter, to adopt the view that pension plans could be terminated at any time and overfund them. Tax and financial slack motivations are consistent with this point of view. Therefore it is not possible to reach an unambiguous conclusion as to which view of the pension contract is "correct." Both views of pensions appear to co-exist in our sample and this is one of the choices or tradeoffs firms can make.[‡]

Thus, the role of a pension plan and its funded status depend on the specific situation of the firm and its relationship with its employees.[§]

---

*Evidence that pension plans are used by firms to store financial slack is provided by Ballester, Fried, and Livnat (2002).
[†]Tax status in their study was based on whether or not the firm reported tax-loss carryforwards. Presence (absence) of a carryforward was deemed consistent with under- (over-) funding. Interestingly, when tax status was based on the firm's actual average tax rate, higher tax rates were associated with underfunding! Francis and Reiter argued that the explanation for this apparent inconsistency lay in the fact that highly profitable firms face higher average tax rates. *For those firms, it may be more profitable to earn higher (after-tax) returns on internal investments rather than investing (tax-free) in pension plans.* The tax incentive to invest in pension plans is overshadowed by the incentives provided by expansion within the company.
[‡]Jere R. Francis and Sara Ann Reiter, "Determinants of Corporate Pension Funding Strategy," *Journal of Accounting and Economics* (April 1987), p. 35.
[§]In addition to the pension-specific variables examined, they also found that firms with higher debt-to-equity ratios tend to underfund their plans, consistent with the debt covenant hypothesis that firms are reluctant to lower income and net worth if it could affect the status of their debt covenants.

Pension plans differ across industries and countries. Companies may offer different plans to unionized and nonunion employees; salaried employees may receive yet other plans. In addition, firms provide (typically unfunded) plans for senior management. However, two general types of pension plans exist: defined contribution and defined benefit.[3] A brief discussion of the critical features of these plans follows.

---

[3]A recent innovation and variation on defined benefit plans, cash-balance pension plans, is discussed in Box 12-3.

Defined Contribution Plans

Employer payments to defined contribution plans (e.g., 401(k) plans) may be contractually fixed or variable (e.g., profit-sharing plans). The employer does not promise a specific level of retirement benefits. The employee bears the risk in defined contribution plans because benefits received on retirement depend on the investment performance of the pension fund.

The accounting for a defined contribution plan is quite simple. The pension cost is determined by the required contribution. The employer's balance sheet asset or liability for pensions reflects the excess or shortfall in payments relative to the specified contribution. Because of their simple nature, defined contribution plans do not present significant analytical issues. The remaining discussions of pension plan accounting and analysis will deal solely with defined benefit plans.

However, the postbankruptcy problems faced by the employees of failed firms (such as Enron[4]) highlight the need for a careful evaluation (by employees) of:

- The form and method of employer contributions to these plans
- Proportion of employer stock in the plan assets
- Restrictions on investment choices
- Restrictions on the employees' ability to change investments
- Onerous vesting requirements

Defined Benefit Plans

Unlike defined contribution plans, defined benefit plans specify the benefit to be received on retirement. Employee benefit payments under "flat benefit" plans are fixed (e.g., $50 per month for each year worked). "Pay-related" plans are more common and tie the benefit to the level of employee earnings, either final salary (e.g., final year or the highest three of the last five years' compensation) or "career average" earnings. The accounting for pay-related plans is more complex than that for flat benefit plans due to the difficulty of predicting benefit levels that depend on future employee earnings.

The employer (plan sponsor) bears the investment risk in all defined benefit pension plans because it has promised a specific benefit amount. The employer needs to estimate future benefit payments to determine required contributions.

Defined benefit plans present difficult accounting and analysis issues. SFAS 87 governs the accounting for defined benefit plans.[5] However, to understand the accounting, the reader must first have an understanding of the mechanics and the underlying economics of pension plans. We review these mechanics using the Texaco pension footnote.[6]

The footnote disclosures are those mandated by SFAS 132. The standard requires explicit reporting of benefits paid and contributions made by employers and employees. The disclosure requirements of SFAS 132 also include a reconciliation of the beginning and ending balances of benefit obligations and plan assets including explicit disclosure of the effects of divestitures, business combinations, foreign currency exchange rates, settlement, curtailment, and termination benefits.

Following the discussion of the economic status of the pension plan we turn to a review of the accounting rules used in reporting pension plans. This will then allow us to develop the framework for analysis of the footnote disclosures to discern the economic status, pension costs, investment performance, and cash flows of the plan.

---

[4]Enron filed for bankruptcy late in 2001.

[5]Exhibit 12-1 provides a simple illustration of a defined benefit plan that the reader may choose to refer to prior to or concurrently with reading the next section.

[6]Our discussion will cover virtually the entire Texaco footnote, albeit for pedagogical reasons the sequence followed will not mirror the presentation by Texaco. Although not required, it is suggested that the reader download the Texaco footnote from the CD for reference purposes.

DEFINED BENEFIT PENSION PLANS

The principal elements of a defined benefit pension plan are:

- The obligation for benefits to be paid to retirees
- The plan assets that will be used to meet that obligation

Figure 12-1 illustrates the relationship between these two elements and the ongoing[7] factors that affect them. The link between these two elements is the use of plan assets to pay benefits.

Estimating Benefit Obligations

Employers must forecast the cash outflows required by the plan by developing complex actuarial estimates of future benefits. These estimates are based on employee variables such as expected turnover and quit rates, mortality, and retirement dates. Estimates of future salary increases are required in pay-related plans. Another complicating factor is that some plans reduce benefits to adjust for government-provided benefits (such as Social Security)[8] or the benefits provided by other company plans (such as a 401(k) plan). These assumptions are combined with the terms of the plan to develop decades-long forecasts of required future cash flows (benefit payments). *The pension obligation is the actuarial present value of these forecasted benefits.*

Identical assumptions and the same discount rate are used to develop three different measures of the pension obligation: The *vested benefit obligation (VBO)* is the amount of the benefit obligation that does not depend on future employee service. The *accumulated benefit obligation (ABO)* reflects the present value of pension benefits earned at the balance sheet date based on compensation to date.[9]

For career average or final pay plans, the *projected benefit obligation (PBO)* differs from the ABO in that its computation includes projected salary increases. The two

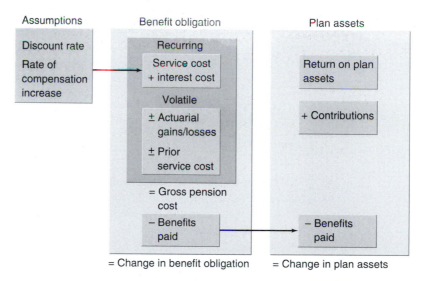

FIGURE 12-1 Components of benefit obligation and plan assets.

---

[7]Figure 12-1 (as well as subsequent Figures 12-2 and 12-3) includes only those principal factors that are ongoing. Factors such as curtailments and/or settlements that reflect pension plan discontinuities are excluded.

[8]In 1999, BP Amoco announced that it would no longer reduce plan benefits by government-provided benefits in the United Kingdom, thereby increasing the benefit obligation by £600 million.

[9]SFAS 132 eliminated the SFAS 87 requirement for separate disclosure of the VBO and the ABO.

measures are identical for flat-benefit (non-pay-related) plans. Unlike the VBO, employees will receive the benefits indicated by the ABO and PBO only if they provide future service.

SFAS 87 mandates use of the PBO to measure the pension obligation and SFAS 132 disclosures are based on the PBO as well. These requirements are consistent with the going-concern assumption as the PBO is the actuarial present value of the benefits that will be paid if the pension plan and the firm continue. However, the (vested) ABO is the employer's pension obligation to its employees in the event the plan is discontinued.

The benefit obligation is highly sensitive to the assumptions (see Figure 12-1) used to estimate future benefits. The most significant assumption, the *discount rate*, is used to compute the present value of the benefit obligation. It is intended to be a current interest rate (such as the rate at which the pension obligation could be settled).[10] Companies change the discount rate as market conditions change; financial statement users must be alert as such changes may significantly affect the benefit obligation and the pension cost, as discussed shortly.

The *rate of compensation increase* is another key assumption. Firms are expected to choose a rate of compensation increase that is economically consistent with other assumptions used. For example, a high-inflation scenario is not compatible with a very low compensation growth rate. Except for the general guidance indicated, SFAS 87 does not limit an employer's choice of compensation growth rate and discount rate.

In an AICPA survey[11] as of December 31, 2000, the 439 firms (of 600 surveyed) with defined benefit plans reported discount rates ranging from 4.5% or less to 11% or greater, with 404 (92%) reporting discount rates ranging from 7% to 8%. More than half (223 firms) used a rate of 7.5%. Compensation rates ranged from 4.5% or less (247 or nearly 57%) to 11% with 81% of respondents reporting rates at or below 5%.

■   **Example: Texaco**

As required by SFAS 132, Texaco discloses the following assumptions:

Texaco Table 1: Assumptions as of December 31

	1998		1999	
	U.S.	Int'l	U.S.	Int'l
Discount rate	6.75%	9.5%	8.0%	8.1%
Expected return on plan assets	10.0%	8.4%	10.0%	8.8%
Rate of compensation increase	4.0%	6.1%	4.0%	5.2%

Notice that the assumptions used for international plans are quite different than those used for U.S. plans, reflecting different economic conditions. Although Texaco increased the discount rate for U.S. plans, it decreased the rate for foreign plans as it did for the international plans' assumed rate of compensation increase.

Texaco also provides information about the expected return on plan assets, a term we will define later. At this point, we note only that the expected return of those plans remains quite high, with the expected rate of return increased slightly in 1999 for international plans.   ■

---

[10]Pension plans may be settled by transferring the obligation to another entity (e.g., an insurance company) in return for a cash payment from the employer (or plan).

[11]American Institute of Certified Public Accountants (AICPA), *Accounting Trends and Techniques* (New York: AICPA, 2001), p. 322

Factors Affecting Benefit Obligations

SFAS 132 requires a reconciliation of the opening and closing balances of the PBO, reporting separately *each* of the following pension cost components, cash flows (participant contributions and benefits paid), and other factors that affect the PBO.

Texaco Table 2: Reconciliation of PBO (in $millions)

		1999		
		U.S.	Int'l	Total
	Opening Balance (December 31, 1998)	$(1,884)	$(979)	$(2,863)
	Cost Components			
+	Service cost	(46)	(25)	(71)
+	Interest cost	(113)	(82)	(195)
+/−	Actuarial gains and losses	(16)	(26)	(42)
+/−	Prior service cost from plan amendments	(29)	(23)	(52)
	Other Factors			
+/−	Effects of foreign currency exchange rate changes	—	96	96
+/−	Effects of business combinations and divestitures	0	0	0
+/−	Curtailments, settlements, and special termination benefits	364	(2)	362
	Cash Flows			
+	Contributions by plan participants that increase plan benefits	(3)	(1)	(4)
−	Benefits paid	63	62	125
=	Closing Balance (December 31, 1999)	$(1,664)	$(980)	$(2,644)

Texaco provides information about its U.S. and international plans separately. For discussion purposes, we provide a total column.

The elements reconciling the PBO are defined below. For illustrative purposes, some simple examples are also provided in Exhibit 12-1.

Cost Components

Service Cost. The principal component of pension cost under SFAS 87, *the service cost*, is the actuarial present value of benefits earned during the current period. Although the discount rate has the most significant impact on the service cost, it is sensitive to all the assumptions used to compute the pension obligation. Service cost trends should generally track the number of employees, their age, and compensation trends. Changes in assumptions, acquisitions, divestitures, curtailments, settlements, and early terminations are among the factors that may have a significant impact on service cost trends.

Interest Cost. The increase in future pension payments (the benefit obligation) for a given period, or the interest cost, is measured as the product of the beginning balance of the PBO and the discount rate in effect at the previous period. For mature firms, such as Texaco, interest cost can be the most significant component of the pension cost.

Actuarial Gains and Losses. Changes in one or more actuarial assumptions, such as quit rates, retirement dates, mortality, and the discount and compensation increase rates are recorded as actuarial gains (decreases in PBO) or actuarial losses (increases in PBO).

EXHIBIT 12-1
Components of Pension Cost and Benefit Obligation

For illustrative purposes, we assume that a firm's pension plan promises to pay an employee at retirement one week's salary for each year of service.

Assumptions

Employee's age = 30 years	Retirement age = 65
Current salary = $1,500/week	Life expectancy after retirement = 15 years
Projected salary at retirement = $2,000/week	Discount rate = 10%

Computation of Projected Benefit Obligation

Projected benefit obligation (PBO)* after year 1 is equal to the present value of a 15-year annuity of $2,000 discounted for the 35 years until retirement begins.

Using Present Value Tables 4 and 2 for an interest rate of 10% yields

PBO = ($2,000 × 7.606) × .03558 = $15,212 × .03558 = $541

Service Cost

The $541 calculated above is the year 1 **service cost**, the PBO increase that results only from current-year service.

Interest Cost

In year 2 the PBO increases[†] (ignoring compensation for the second year's service) as retirement is one year closer. That increase is:

Interest cost = Discount rate × opening PBO =
10% × $541 = $54

Actuarial Gains and Losses

Now assume that at the end of year 2, the projected salary at retirement increases by 10% to $2,200 per week due to a higher expected rate of compensation increase. The annuity to be paid is now $4,400; $2,200 as a result of the first year's service and $2,200 as a result of the second year's service.

The PBO[‡] for *each of these $2,200* annuities is the present value of a 15-year annuity of $2,200 discounted for 34 years:

$2,200 × 7.606 × 0.03914 = $655

Before the estimate revision, the PBO resulting from the first year's service was $595. The revision in actuarial assumptions results in an

Actuarial loss = $60

the amount required to bring the PBO to the correct level.

Prior Service Cost

Now assume that there was no revision in the projected salary at retirement, which remains $2,000. Instead, assume that the plan is amended by a new union contract and the annuity payable is now equal to 110% of one week's salary for each year of service. Because of the revised benefit formula, the PBO resulting from the first year's service increases by $60.[§] This increase is referred to as

Prior service cost = $60

---

*In contrast, the accumulated benefit obligation (ABO) is based on the current salary level of $1,500 (not the projected level of $2,000) and equals

ABO = ($1,500 × 7.606) × .03558 = $11,409 × .03558 = $406

[†]Note that after the second year, the annuity amount is now $4,000; $2,000 from the first year's service and $2,000 due to the second year's service. The total PBO at the end of year 2 is the present value of a 15-year annuity of $4,000 discounted for 34 years:

$4,000 × 7.606 × .03914 = $1,190

This is an increase of $649 from the previous year ($1,190 − $541). This is the sum of:

Service cost for year 2 (present value of $2,000 benefit earned that year)	$595
Interest cost for year 2	54
Total increase	$649

[‡]The revised PBO at the end of year 2 is $1,310 (2 × $655), an increase of $769 from the previous year. This increase is the sum of:

Service cost for year 2 (present value of $2,200 benefit earned that year)	$655
Interest cost for year 2	54
Actuarial loss	60
Total increase	$769

[§]The calculations are identical as for the actuarial loss. Parenthetically, we note that the plan amendment affects the ABO; the revision in the rate of compensation increase does not.

Prior Service Cost. Plan amendments may increase (or decrease) previously specified pension obligations. Retroactive changes, *prior service cost*, that increase the PBO are allocated to (recognized as expense over) the future service periods of those employees active at the amendment date who are expected to benefit from the changes. PBO decreases resulting from plan changes must be used to reduce unrecognized prior service cost; any remaining excess is amortized to pension cost using the method applied to increases.

Other Factors

Effects of Foreign Currency Exchange Rate Changes. When plan benefits are denominated in another currency, exchange rate changes result in a change in the benefit amounts measured in the reporting currency.

Effects of Business Combinations and Divestitures. When a firm acquires another business with a defined benefit plan, the benefit obligation for the acquired employees must be added to the acquirer's PBO. Sales or other divestitures may remove the affected employees from the benefit plan (see discussion later in the chapter).

Curtailments, Settlements, and Special Termination Benefit. SFAS 88(1985) contains accounting standards for curtailments and settlements.[12] A plan *curtailment* due to plan termination in total or as a result of closing a division effectively freezes the benefits of the affected employees, changing the pension obligation. Any gain or loss due to plan termination must be recognized in current-period income.

A plan settlement shifts the obligation to an unrelated entity; for example, an employer may pay an insurance company to assume the pension obligation for a group of employees.[13] Any difference between the amount paid and the PBO "sold" is recognized as a gain or loss from settlement of the plan.

Employers may provide *special termination benefits* (for a short period of time) or *contractual termination benefits* triggered by specified events such as plant closings. Termination benefits may be paid in a lump sum or over several months and may be paid out of pension plan assets.

Cash Flows

Contributions by Plan Participants. Contributory defined benefit pension plans may permit or require contributions by plan participants that increase the obligation.

Benefits Paid. Payments to retirees reduce the PBO as a portion of the obligation has been extinguished.

■ Example: Texaco

In 1999, Texaco's PBO decreased $219 million from $2,863 to $2,644 million. The pension cost elements increased PBO by $360 million as below.

Service cost	$ 71 million
Interest cost	195
Actuarial gains and losses	42
Prior service cost from plan amendments	52
Total	$360 million

---

[12]SFAS 106 prescribes similar principles for settlements and curtailments of other postemployment benefits.

[13]Settlements usually cover employees that are retired or whose benefits are frozen, making estimates of future compensation increase unnecessary.

The relatively high interest cost of $195 million (almost 55% of the total cost) is reflective of a mature plan. That amount can be approximated as the product of the opening PBO balance(s) and the *1998* discount rates.[14]

The increase resulting from these cost elements was offset by

1. A curtailment/settlement related to a restructuring carried out in late 1998 of $362 million

2. Additionally, the strong dollar in 1999 reduced the PBO (of international plans) by   96 million

3. Finally, Texaco satisfied pension obligations by paying its retirees   125 million

     Total $583 million

The $223 net effect ($360 − $583) offset by a $4 million adjustment related to participant contributions reduced the PBO by $219 million.   ■

Factors Affecting Plan Assets

SFAS 132 requires the reconciliation of the beginning and ending balances of the fair value of plan assets, separately reporting the effect of each of the following factors:

Texaco Table 3: Reconciliation of Plan Assets (in $millions)

		1999		
		U.S.	Int'l	Total
	Opening Balance (December 31, 1998)	$1,826	$1,028	$2,854
+	Employer contributions	15	26	41
+	Contributions by plan participants	3	1	4
+	Return on assets	236	151	387
−	Expenses	(7)	—	(7)
+/−	Effects of foreign currency exchange rate changes	—	(74)	(74)
+/−	Effects of business combinations and divestitures			
+/−	Settlements	(364)	—	(364)
−	Benefits paid	(63)	(62)	(125)
=	Closing Balance (December 31, 1999)	$1,646	$1,070	$2,716

Employer Contributions

Employers make periodic contributions to pension funds to fund their benefit obligations. Funding policy is a function of income tax and ERISA rules, as well as employer cash flow considerations. Although some firms use the same actuarial cost methods to determine both pension cost and contributions, there is no requirement to do so.

Contributions by Plan Participants

Voluntary or required contributions by plan participants (described in the pension obligations section) increase the plan assets.

---

[14]The 1998 discount rate (see Texaco Table 1) is used since that is the rate that was in effect when the (opening) PBO was determined. The calculation follows:

U.S. plans:	$1,884 million × 6.75% = $127.2 million
International plans:	$979 million × 9.5% = 93.0 million
Total:	$220.2 million

The difference between the reported ($195 million) and estimated ($220 million) interest cost is due to the plan curtailments and settlements, the aggregation of data from multiple plans, and the fact that actual computations are made quarterly rather than annually. Other estimates in this chapter are affected by the same factors.

Return on Assets

Pension funds are (usually) managed by an independent trustee or investment advisor. The return on assets (ROA) is measured as the actual return (capital gains and losses plus dividends and interest) earned during the year. Given volatile capital markets, the ROA will fluctuate from year to year.[15]

Plan Expenses. Texaco also discloses the expenses (such as investment management fees) incurred by the plan. This item is generally not disclosed separately by most firms and is most likely deducted from the ROA.

Other Factors

Effects of Foreign Currency Exchange Rate Changes. For pension funds denominated in another currency, plan assets measured in the reporting currency are affected by exchange rate changes, just as the PBO is affected.

Effects of Business Combinations and Divestitures. When a firm acquires another business with a defined benefit plan, the plan assets are generally transferred to the acquirer's pension fund. Sales or other divestitures may remove plan assets supporting the benefits of the affected employees from the pension fund.

Settlements. Plan assets are decreased by amounts paid to unrelated entities to settle pension obligations.

Benefits Paid

The benefits paid from plan assets are, of course, the same amounts discussed in the section on pension obligations.[16] This amount often includes special termination benefits paid.

■ **Example: Texaco**

In 1999 Texaco's plan assets decreased by $138 million from $2,854 to $2,716 million. Investment performance increased plan assets by $387 million while (employer plus employee) contributions increased assets $45 million. These increases (totaling $432 million) were offset by plan assets being used to pay retirees of $125 million, $74 million resulting from exchange rate effects, and $364 million to pay for the settlement of the pension obligations to employees terminated by the restructuring discussed earlier. ■

Funded Status of Pension Plan

The difference between the PBO and the fair value of plan assets represents the funded status of the plan. When plan assets exceed (are less than) the PBO, the plan is overfunded (underfunded) and the firm has a net asset (liability) position with respect to its pension plan. Texaco's worldwide pension plans (U.S. and international plans combined) show a surplus of $72 million at the end of 1999, an improvement from 1998's slightly underfunded status of $9 million. For both years, overfunded international plans offset slightly underfunded U.S. plans.

---

[15]Because of this volatility, the expected long-term rate of return on plan assets is used to measure the periodic pension cost. See following section.

[16]The benefits paid reported in the asset reconciliation sometimes differs from the amount shown in the PBO reconciliation. We believe that this difference is due to benefit payments made directly by the employer rather than from plan assets.

Texaco Table 4: Plan Status (in $millions)

	1998			1999		
	U.S.	Int'l	**Total**	U.S.	Int'l	**Total**
Plan assets*	$1,826	$1,028	**$2,854**	$1,646	$1,070	**$2,716**
PBO**	(1,884)	(979)	**(2,863)**	(1,664)	(980)	**(2,644)**
Over- (under-) funded	$ (58)	$ 49	**$ (9)**	$ (18)	$ 90	**$72**

*From Texaco Table 3 (for 1999).
**From Texaco Table 2 (for 1999).

These data permit the analyst to see the plan status at a glance. However, a plan may appear to be overfunded (assets exceeding the benefit obligation) if an unrealistically high discount rate is used or appear underfunded (benefit obligation exceeding the assets) if a very low discount rate is employed.

SFAS 87 requires that all pension plan assets (other than operating assets such as office furniture) be carried at fair value with current appraisals used in lieu of market value for assets without market quotations (such as nonpublic investments, real estate, and venture capital).[17]

The funded status of the plan represents the pension plan's *economic position. It does not, however, reflect the carrying value or cost reported by companies on their financial statements.* To understand these we turn to a discussion of pension plan accounting.

FINANCIAL REPORTING FOR PENSIONS: SFAS 87 AND SFAS 132

SFAS 87 (1985) governs the recognition and measurement of pension obligations and cost. It requires all companies to use the same actuarial cost method and mandates disclosure of the key assumptions used to compute the pension obligation and cost. Under SFAS 87, however, *the accounting effects of (some) economic events are smoothed to avoid volatility in the reporting of pension costs.* As a result of this smoothing, accounting measures of periodic pension cost and pension plan status are often not reflective of economic reality. To evaluate the underlying cash flows and consequences of operating events, the analyst must unravel the smoothing and aggregating process.

This task was somewhat facilitated by SFAS 132 (1998), which amended the disclosure requirements of existing pension standards.[18] The new standard did not change the measurement or recognition requirements of the previous standards. SFAS 132 was designed to provide information enabling users of financial statements to:

- Evaluate the current and potential future cash flow consequences of an employer's pension and other postretirement benefit plans.
- Forecast benefit costs, facilitating the estimation of the impact of benefit costs on future reported net income.
- Assess the effect of accounting choices on reported benefit costs and the quality of reported earnings.

The disclosure requirements of SFAS 132 also include explicit reporting of benefits paid and contributions made by employers and employees and the reconciliation of the beginning and ending balances of benefit obligations and plan assets as described above. These disclosures significantly improved users' ability to analyze trends in benefit costs and payment and their impact on the enterprises' earnings and cash flows.

---

[17]We believe that, in practice, some employers smooth the recognition of value changes for assets with no clearly defined market value.

[18]SFAS 132 amended the disclosure requirements of SFAS 87, SFAS 88, Employers' Accounting for Settlements and Curtailments of Defined Benefit Pension Plans and for Termination Benefits, and SFAS 106, Employers' Accounting for Postretirement Benefits Other than Pensions.

Pension Cost: Components and Measurement

Under SFAS 87, reported pension cost[19] includes the following components. As noted, some report actual events, others smooth the effects of actual events:

Texaco Table 5: Components of Reported Pension Cost (in $millions)

	1999		
	U.S.	Int'l	Total
Actual Events			
Service cost	$46	$25	$71
Interest cost	113	82	195
Smoothed Events			
Expected return on plan assets	(140)	(81)	(221)
Amortization of gains and losses	4	(2)	2
Amortization of prior service costs	11	13	24
Amortization of transition asset or liability	(6)	(12)	(18)
Other Events			
Curtailments, settlements, and termination benefits	(15)	2	(13)
Reported pension cost (credit)	$13	$27	$40

Figures 12-2 and 12-3 illustrate the relationship among these elements.

Actual Events: Service Cost and Interest Cost

These components of pension cost are (as defined in the section "Factors Affecting Benefit Obligation") the actual amounts realized during the period. They correspond to the amounts used to reconcile the opening and closing PBO.

Smoothed Events

Expected Return on Plan Assets. Firms must use the expected long-term rate of return on plan assets (see Texaco Table 1) to compute this component of pension cost, which thus reflects the expected rather than the actual return on plan assets. A long-term expected rate is used to mitigate the effect of the volatility of capital markets. Although employers are permitted to change their assumption, this rate is intended to be a more stable assumption than the discount rate. Companies in the 2001 AICPA survey[20] reported expected rates of return ranging from 4.5% or less to 11% or greater with 300 (68%) reporting rates between 9% and 10%.

The expected return on plan assets (expected ROA), equal to the expected long-term rate of return times the opening fair value or market-related value of plan assets, offsets other components of pension cost. The difference between the actual and the expected return on plan assets is deferred and accumulated on the assumption that the unexpected returns will balance out over time.

Amortization of Gains or Losses. Actuarial gains and losses from reestimates of the PBO and the deferred return on assets are accumulated; they must be amortized to pension cost over the average remaining employee service life when total deferrals exceed 10% of

---

[19]For many companies, pension cost equals the expense reported on the income statement. In some cases, part of pension cost may be capitalized.

[20]AICPA, *Accounting Trends & Techniques* (2001), p. 322.

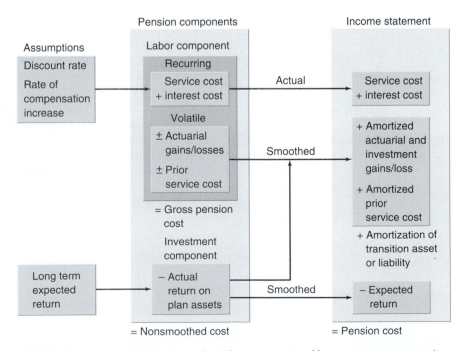

Pension fund

Opening balance Contributions Return on assets	Benefits paid
Closing balance	

Pension liability

	Opening balance Service cost Interest cost Actuarial gains or losses Prior service cost
Benefits paid	
	Closing balance

**Net economic position
(fund—liability)**

	Opening balance Service cost Interest cost Actuarial gains or losses Prior service cost
Contributions Return on assets	
	Closing balance

(a) Economic position

Balance sheet

	Opening balance Service cost Interest cost *Actuarial gains or* *losses* *Prior service cost*
Contributions *Return on* *assets*	
	Closing balance

(b) Financial statements
[Smoothed items in italics]

FIGURE 12-2 Comparison of economic position and accounting for pension plans.

FIGURE 12-3 Relationship between actual pension components and income statement presentation.

the *larger* of the PBO and the fair value of plan assets.[21] Amortization of the deferred amounts begins in the year following the year in which the deferrals originate.

Amortization of Prior Service Cost. When plan amendments create prior service cost, that amount must be amortized over the average remaining employee service life. As noted earlier, if plan amendments reduce benefits, the negative prior service cost must first be applied to any remaining unamortized prior service cost; the excess, if any, is amortized to pension cost. This allocation will lower pension cost.

Amortization of Transition Asset or Liability. The initial adoption of SFAS 87 generated either a transition asset or liability that was measured at the adoption date as the difference between the preadoption balance sheet accrual and the economic (funded) status. This unrecognized off-balance sheet asset or liability must be amortized to pension cost over the remaining employee service life.[22] Given the many years that have passed since passage of SFAS 87, some firms have fully amortized their transition asset or liability. See Problem 12-10 for an example.

Other Events: Curtailments, Settlements, and Termination Benefits

Although not components of ongoing operating activities, curtailments, settlements, and termination benefits appear frequently in reported financial statements, often in conjunction with restructuring activities. The analysis of these elements is discussed in a subsequent section of this chapter.

■ Example: Texaco

Texaco reported worldwide net pension cost for 1999 of $40 million including a net gain on settlements and curtailments of $13 million. Service cost ($71 million) and interest cost ($195 million) represent the primary sources of pension cost.

The remaining components of pension cost are smoothed rather than actual amounts originating during the year. SFAS 132 requires separate disclosure of the amortization of each of the smoothed components of pension cost: unrecognized prior service costs, transition asset, and net gain or loss (actuarial and deferred investment gains/losses). Generally, the largest of the smoothed items is the expected return on plan assets. Although the actual return on plan assets (as reported in the section "Factors Affecting Plan Assets") was a gain of $387 million, Texaco reported an expected return on plan assets of $221 million, calculated using the assumed long-term rate of return on plan assets for 1999.[23] The expected return serves to offset the service and interest cost components (lowering pension cost) even in years when the actual return on assets is small or negative.   ■

Balance Sheet Carrying Amounts and Reconciliation to Funded Status

The smoothing of certain pension components results in differences between the balance sheet carrying amounts and the funded status of the plan. Consequently, employers must reconcile the plan status with their balance sheet accruals.[24]

---

[21]SFAS 87 permits the use of this approach, called the *corridor method*, an arbitrary means of deferring the recognition of gains and losses expected to be temporary and to equalize over time unless they become so large that there is reason to question their eventual reversal. Note that the amount to be amortized is recomputed each year.

[22]An amortization period of 15 years must be used when this average is less than 15 years.

[23]This amount can be estimated as follows (see Texaco Table 1 for rates used):

U.S. plans:	$1,826 million × 10% =	$182.6 million
International plans:	$1,028 million × 8.8% =	90.5 million
Total		$273.1 million

See footnote 14 for discussion of the difference between the estimated and actual amounts.

[24]Balance sheet accruals represent the difference between the reported pension cost (credit) and employer contributions.

SFAS 132 requires reconciliation of the funded status of defined benefit pension plans and disclosure of both the amounts recognized and those not recognized in the statement of financial position, including the amount of any unrecognized prior service cost, net gain or loss (including asset gains and losses not yet reflected in market-related value), and unamortized transition asset or liability.

**Texaco Table 6: Reconciliation of Plan Status
with Balance Sheet Accrual (in $millions)**

	1998			1999		
	U.S.	Int'l	Total	U.S.	Int'l	Total
Over- (under-) funded*	$(58)	$49	$(9)	$ (18)	$ 90	$72
Unrecognized						
Net transition asset	(14)	(14)	(28)	(7)	(1)	(8)
Prior Service Cost	68	52	120	85	63	148
Actuarial (gain) loss	(93)	4	(89)	(161)	(17)	(177)
Net (liability) asset recorded in balance sheet	$(97)	$91	$(6)	$(101)	$135	$34

*See Texaco Table 4.

Texaco's worldwide pension plans (U.S. and international plans combined) show (as discussed earlier) a surplus of $72 million at the end of 1999 (overfunded international plans more than offset slightly underfunded U.S. plans) given plan assets of $2,716 million and PBO of $2,644 on December 31, 1999. The balance sheet reports net pension assets of $34 million, *understating* the economic status of the plan by $38 million ($72 − $34). For Texaco, the difference between the plan status and the balance sheet accrual is small (barely 1%) relative to the size of the pension obligation. For many firms, however, the difference is much greater.

The reconciliation between the funded status and the balance sheet amounts shows that this difference is due to three unrecognized components (prior service cost, transition asset, and net gain or loss) that arise out of the smoothing provisions of SFAS 87.[25]

---

[25]Texaco Table 6 also shows the balances in these three components as at December 31, 1998. The unrecognized transition asset was reduced from $28 to $8, reflecting the amortization (see Texaco Table 5) of $18 charged to pension cost. (The remaining differential of $2 may be due to rounding or to the effect of curtailments and settlements).

Similarly, the increase in the unrecognized prior service cost of $28 ($148 − $120) is a result of:

- Nonrecognition of (prior service cost) amendments (Texaco Table 2) $52 million
- Amortization of prior service cost (Texaco Table 5)   (24)
                                                                                                                         $28 million

Finally, we reconcile the $88 ($177 − $89) change in the unrecognized actuarial gains:

- Nonrecognition of actuarial losses (Texaco Table 2)   ($42)
- Nonrecognition of difference between the actual ROA of $387
  and expected ROA of $221 (Texaco Tables 3 and 5)   166
- Amortization of actuarial gains and losses (Texaco Table 5)   (2)
                                                                                                                      $122 million

That leaves a $34 discrepancy in the reconciliation. The $7 pension plan expense (Texaco Table 2) reduces the discrepancy to $27. The remaining differential is most likely due to the effects of curtailments and settlements as well as foreign currency effects as most of the discrepancy arises from the reconciliation of the international plans.

Texaco also discloses where the $34 million is recognized on the balance sheet. The four elements that receive balance sheet recognition are as follows:

Texaco Table 7: Balance Sheet Recognition (in $millions)

	Texaco 1999		
	U.S.	Int'l	Total
1. Prepaid benefit asset	$ 84	$373	$457
2. Accrued benefit liability	(231)	(246)	(477)
Net benefit asset (liability)	$(147)	$127	$ (20)
3. Intangible pension assets	23	8	31
4. Minimum pension liability adjustment reported in the accumulated other comprehensive income section of stockholders' equity	23	—	23
	$(101)	$135	$ 34

Texaco has a number of pension plans and does not net those that have asset balances against those that have liability balances. Texaco shows separately a prepaid asset of $457 million and an accrued liability of $477 million.[26]

The above presentation is incomplete as (in Texaco's case) there is an additional factor. Texaco Table 6 notes that Texaco's net benefit accrual recorded on the balance sheet is *an asset of $34 million*. However, in Texaco Table 7 we show a *net liability of $20 million*. The $54 million difference is a result of the *minimum liability adjustment (MLA)*. That adjustment also accounts for the recognition of the intangible asset as well as the charge to equity.

Minimum Liability Adjustment (MLA)

For plans where the balance sheet liability does not at least equal the accumulated benefit obligation less the (fair value of the) plan assets, the shortfall must be recognized on the balance sheet as a minimum liability. When that adjustment is taken, the firm *does not fully report it either in net income or stockholders' equity*. As required by SFAS 87, a portion[27] of the minimum liability adjustment is recorded as an intangible asset with the remainder charged directly to shareholder's equity (as part of comprehensive income).[28] The adjustment

- Increases the balance sheet liability and offsets it by
- Decreasing equity and/or increasing an intangible asset

Texaco (see Note 11) has unfunded plans for which it reported an MLA of $54 million. Of that adjustment, only $23 million was deducted from equity (as part of comprehensive

---

[26]We have shown the net liability subtotal of $20 in order to explain the remaining balance sheet disclosures.

[27]Per SFAS 87, the portion up to the sum of the unamortized prior service cost and unamortized transition liability is reported as an intangible asset.

[28]The amounts shown in the pension footnote (and in our tables) are pretax. The actual charge to shareholders' equity is taken on an after-tax basis with the difference charged to deferred taxes.

income). Another $31 million was recorded as an intangible asset rather than being charged to equity. The effects of the adjustment are presented here:

**Effects of Minimum Liability Adjustment (MLA) on Texaco's
1999 Balance Sheet (in $millions)**

	Balance Sheet prior to MLA	MLA	Balance Sheet after MLA (Texaco Table 7)
Prepaid benefit asset	$457		$457
Accrued benefit liability	(423)	$(54)	(477)
Net asset (liability)	$ 34	$(54)	$ (20)
Intangible asset	—	31	31
Equity	—	23	23
	$ 34	$ 0	$ 34

Texaco's recording of the MLA results in a balance sheet accrual ($20 million liability) that is even further from the $72 million funded status of the plan (see Texaco Table 4). Additionally, the MLA creates a dubious intangible asset.

In the next section we analyze the required adjustments to the reported data and how these data can be used to analyze pension plans.

ANALYSIS OF PENSION PLAN DISCLOSURES

As already discussed, pension plan accounting defers and smoothes some of the underlying plan economics. Analysis of reported pension costs and liabilities requires focus on the:

- Effects of the assumptions used
- Underlying status of the pension plan
- Calculation of the nonsmoothed pension cost and cash flows of the pension plan

Importance of Assumptions

The SFAS 87 requirement that all enterprises use the same actuarial method to calculate benefit obligations and pension costs enhances interfirm comparability. However, companies are free to choose actuarial assumptions, resulting in a wide range.

The choice of assumptions affects the reported pension plan status and pension cost in a number of ways. The most immediate impact of assumptions is on the benefit obligation and, hence, the reported plan status. There is an indirect impact on the balance sheet as assumptions affect pension cost. However, because pension obligations may remain largely off balance sheet, the full impact of changes (by one firm) and variations (across firms within an industry) in pension assumptions may not be fully reflected in balance sheet ratios based on reported data.

Assumptions about the employee population are undisclosed; we must assume that the company's estimates of such factors as mortality, quit rates, and retirement ages are realistic. However, three key assumptions—the discount rate, rate of compensation increase, and expected long-term rate of return on plan assets—are disclosed (see Texaco Table 1).

Impact of Assumptions on the Benefit Obligation

The discount rate assumption used to compute the present value has the greatest impact on the reported benefit obligation. A higher (lower) discount rate decreases (increases) the PBO. As companies are required to disclose the discount rate, the effect of the choice can be examined and compared to rates used by competitors and other employers. Because of the mathematics of present value, adjustments for different rates are difficult. For example, a 10% increase from 10% to 11% does not change the calculated PBO by 10%.

Blankley and Swanson (1995) show that firms do not change discount rates as often as would be warranted by movements in general interest rate levels. Furthermore, they note that this lack of conformity is greatest when rates are declining, as firms want to avoid increases in the PBO and pension costs.

The assumed rate of compensation increase also affects the PBO, but less than the discount rate. A higher (lower) rate increases (decreases) the PBO. The assumed rate is zero for non-pay-related plans. An increase (decrease) in the rate of compensation increase will increase (decrease) the difference between the PBO and the ABO because the latter excludes the impact of pay increases.

Comparisons of the PBO with the market value of plan assets require consideration of the choice of both the discount rate and the rate of compensation growth. Aggressive assumptions (high discount rate and low rate of compensation growth) improve the reported status of the plan, whereas conservative assumptions (low discount rate and high rate of compensation growth) make the plan appear less well funded.

Impact of Assumptions on Pension Cost

The discount rate has a direct effect on the calculation of service cost as it is used to compute the present value of benefits earned in the current year. The impact is similar to the effect on the pension obligation. A higher (lower) rate reduces (increases) service cost.

Calculation of the interest component of pension cost (PBO $\times$ the discount rate) is also affected by the discount rate because both elements of the formula change. Although the effects are opposite (a higher discount rate reduces the PBO), the net result of increasing the discount rate is an increase in the interest cost.[29] Although the effect on the service cost is offset in part by the interest cost effect, the effect on service cost is normally much greater. Thus, in most cases, a higher discount rate reduces reported pension cost.[30]

The effect of a change in the rate of compensation increase is easier to predict. A higher rate increases both the service cost and interest cost (by increasing the PBO). Conversely, a lower rate of compensation increase decreases all present value calculations and, therefore, pension cost.

Finally, a higher assumed rate of return on plan assets lowers pension cost, since the expected return on assets is an offset to other components of that cost.[31]

Summing up, we note that both a low rate of compensation growth and a high expected rate of return on plan assets decrease pension cost and, therefore, increase reported earnings. A higher discount rate lowers the obligation and pension cost. From a quality of earnings perspective, these choices are aggressive and result in higher income but lower-quality earnings. Ultimately, however, overly aggressive choices are likely to result in experience (actuarial) losses that will have to be amortized and will increase future pension cost. While the financial statements will reflect the economic pension plan status, recognition is deferred.

Intercompany Comparison of Assumptions

Assumptions made by a company should be compared with those of its domestic and foreign competitors. One might expect companies in the same industry, dealing with the same unions or employment market conditions, to have assumed similar rates of compensation increases. In practice, companies use different rates just as they use different depreciation methods and lives for similar assets. These differences reduce comparability of reported financial data and ratios derived from such data.

---

[29]This is analogous to the effect of rising interest rates on bond prices; prices fall but the interest cost of subsequent borrowings increases.

[30]In a very mature plan, with very high interest cost relative to service cost, the effect of the discount rate on interest cost may dominate the analysis.

[31]When a company uses the market-related value of plan assets rather than the actual asset value, the return on assets calculation is slower to reflect changes in market value. Therefore, when asset values are rising, use of the market-related value will result in higher pension cost.

EXHIBIT 12-2
Comparison of Pension Plan Assumptions for the Auto Industry

Weighted Average Assumptions	General Motors			Ford			DaimlerChrysler			Honda[1]		
	1998	1999	2000	1998	1999	2000	1998	1999	2000	1999	2000	2001
Discount Rate												
Domestic Plans[2]	6.80%	7.80%	7.30%	6.75%	6.25%	7.75%	6.00%	6.00%	6.50%	3.00%	3.00%	3.00%
International Plans	6.40%	7.10%	7.10%	6.50%	5.70%	6.10%	6.50%	7.50%	7.70%	5.5-7.5%	5.5-8.0%	5.5-8.0%
Rate of Compensation Increase												
Domestic Plans	5.00%	5.00%	5.00%	5.20%	5.20%	5.20%	3.00%	2.80%	3.00%	3.00%	2.70%	2.80%
International Plans	3.50%	4.00%	4.00%	5.10%	4.90%	4.20%	6.00%	5.90%	5.50%	3.5-6.0%	3.8-6.0%	4.0-6.0%
Expected Return on Plan Assets												
Domestic Plans	10.00%	10.00%	10.00%	9.00%	9.00%	9.00%	7.70%	7.70%	7.90%	4.00%	4.00%	4.00%
International Plans	9.20%	9.00%	9.00%	9.20%	9.30%	9.40%	9.80%	9.80%	10.20%	6.0-9.0%	6.3-9.0%	6.5-9.0%

[1]Honda data for years ending March 31.
[2]United States for GM and Ford, Germany for DaimlerChrysler, and Japan for Honda.

Exhibit 12-2 illustrates the use of different pension assumptions within a single industry. It compares the three key assumptions—the discount rate, rate of compensation increase, and expected long-term rate of return on plan assets—for four automakers: General Motors [GM], Ford [F], DaimlerChrysler [DCX], and Honda [7267]. The first two companies show assumptions separately for their U.S. and non-U.S. operations. DaimlerChrysler and Honda show German versus non-German and Japanese versus non-Japanese assumptions respectively.

Conceptually, the discount rate assumption, which drives the PBO and hence the funded status of the plan, should be identical for all U.S. companies. However, as Exhibit 12-2 demonstrates, in practice, discount rates vary across companies within the same industry. The discount rates used for U.S. operations by the two U.S. companies in 2000 are very similar, ranging from 7.75% (Ford) to 7.30% (GM). The spread for 1999, however, was much wider, with GM at 7.8% and Ford at 6.25%. Ford decreased the discount rate in 1999 and increased it in 2000; GM increased its discount rate in 1999 but decreased it in 2000. These rate changes affect both pension plan status and pension cost, as discussed above. Because Daimler and Honda aggregate their U.S. operations with other nondomestic operations, it is difficult to make comparisons. If we assume that Honda's highest rate shown (8% in 2000) pertains to its U.S. operations, then its discount rate is slightly above its U.S. competitors, resulting in a lower PBO (and improved plan status).

The discount rates used for non-U.S. plans also vary. Some differences may reflect operations in different countries. Honda uses a discount rate of 3% for its Japanese plans, reflecting that country's low interest rate environment.

The differences may be a function of either corporate personality (some companies are more conservative than others) or the plan status itself—companies with underfunded plans may be tempted to use a higher discount rate to minimize the reported underfunding.

Similarly, the assumed rate of compensation increase varies among the companies. GM uses the lowest assumed rate for its U.S. operations, reducing its PBO and service cost. Daimler uses the highest assumed rate for its international operations but the lowest rate for its German workforce. Ford's higher rate for foreign plans may reflect the locations of its foreign workforce. Note that the lower end of Honda's non-Japanese range has risen steadily from 3.5% to 4.0%.

DaimlerChrysler reports the highest (most aggressive) expected return on assets (10.2%) for nondomestic plans in 2000, increased from the 1998–1999 assumed rate of 9.8%. GM is not far behind at 10% while Ford uses 9.0%, resulting in higher pension cost than if it had used its competitors' higher rate. Honda assumes a 4% return for its Japanese plans, perhaps reflecting lower fixed-income returns in Japan. These differences should be compared with the actual returns earned by the plans over time. Theory says that all companies should have the same long-term expected ROA in each jurisdiction. In practice, the assumed rate varies. Companies have an incentive to choose a higher expected ROA to report lower pension costs. Unrealistically high assumed rates will create deferred losses that, over time, must be amortized as a component of future pension costs.

Analysis of Pension Plan: Status, Costs, and Cash Flows

Both pension cost and the balance sheet liability reflect the smoothing provisions of SFAS 87 as well as the choice of assumptions. This section addresses the following issues:

- What is the economic liability associated with the pension plan?
- What are the most significant components of pension cost?
- What is the impact of smoothing on reported pension cost?
- How can analysts separate the employee service components of pension cost from those related to the investment performance of plan assets?
- What alternative measures of pension cost can be computed?
- Which economic events have not been recognized for accounting purposes?
- What are the past and future cash flows (contributions and benefit payments) and what do trends in these cash flows mean?

Balance Sheet Adjustments. Reported balance sheet assets and liabilities should be replaced by the actual plan status: the PBO less the fair value of plan assets. Depending on the objective of the analysis and the firm's tax status, the measurements may be made either pre- or post-tax.

For liquidation analysis, the ABO (or VBO) should be used as that is the more accurate measure once the going-concern assumption is dropped. Unfortunately, SFAS 132 has eliminated the requirement that firms disclose information about the ABO except in rare cases.[32] Thus, the analyst must attempt to adjust the PBO (downward) to arrive at an estimate of the ABO. This is not an easy task, as the data are not readily available and the analyst may have to obtain such information directly from the company.

Analysis of the Components of Pension Cost and Cash Flows. The following alternative analytical pension cost measures should be computed and their trends analyzed. These measures eliminate the smoothing required by SFAS 87 and reflect the underlying economics of the plan.

- *Service cost* measures the benefits earned in the current period. It ignores interest cost and other adjustments (actuarial or experience) to previously earned benefits. The trend in service costs reflects changes in payroll cost and the number of employees and their age. Significant restructuring charges, acquisitions, divestitures, and other changes in employees may result in sharp declines or increases in service cost.[33]
- *Recurring cost* is the sum of service and interest cost. It excludes actuarial gains and losses and adjustments for prior service.
- *Gross pension cost* is measured as the change in the PBO excluding curtailments, settlements, special termination benefits, effects of exchange rate changes, and contractual benefits paid to retirees, but including all workforce-related factors (including the gross actuarial gains and losses and prior service cost).
- *Nonsmoothed pension cost*, calculated as gross pension cost less actual investment return, is volatile because it includes actual investment performance rather than expected returns and the gross actuarial gains and losses and prior service costs rather than only the net amortization of these amounts.

None of these measures reflects the actual cash flow from the employer. A comprehensive analysis of the plan must include an evaluation of employer contributons and benefits paid to employees.

- *Benefits paid* represent the actual payments made by the plan to retirees.
- *Employer contributions* constitute the actual cash flow from the company to the plan. The plan status can help forecast required cash flows. A growing plan deficit (PBO less plan assets) suggests that higher contributions will be required in the future; a surplus suggests that future contributions may be lower. As the plan status depends on changes in both the PBO and plan assets, economic events can cause rapid changes.

We illustrate the analysis of the pension plan using the Texaco example after a brief discussion of the merits of the alternative measures of pension liability and cost.

---

[32]The ABO need only be disclosed for those companies whose pension plan assets fall below the ABO (i.e., those companies that are required to report the minimum liability adjustment). However, even for those cases *the ABO need be disclosed only for the plans where the plan assets < ABO, and not the ABO for all of the company's plans.*

[33]Trends in service cost should be evaluated carefully following a firm's announcement of significant layoffs or early terminations. For example, service costs reported by Lucent Technologies rose from $312 million in 1997 to $509 million in 1999, an increase of 63%. For the year ended September 30, 2001, the company reported service cost of $316 million, a decline of 38% from 1999. In 2001, the number of employees had fallen from 106,000 to 77,000, excluding another planned divestiture. The company has recorded significant termination, settlement, and curtailment charges during this period.

Motivation for Adjustments to Liability and Cost

The research discussed in Box 12-3 indicates that the market incorporates the off-balance-sheet pension liability in its assessment of a firm's debt position. The market appears to ignore the smoothed cost measure, focusing instead on nonsmoothed cost. Specific adjustments depend on the following issues relating the firm to its pension plan:

- Measurement of the firm's liability to its employees
- Whether the pension plan is an integral part of the company or an independent entity

The finance and labor economics literature discusses both issues in great detail. We limit ourselves to a general discussion.

Measurement of the Pension Liability. Is the appropriate measure of the liability the PBO, the ABO, or the VBO? In theory, firms can terminate the plan or individual employees at any time. Upon termination, either the ABO or the VBO would measure the firm's obligation.

Under SFAS 87, pension cost must be measured using the PBO, making the implicit assumption that the firm will *not*:

- Terminate employees before they are vested (other than normal turnover, one of the actuarial assumptions).
- Terminate employees in their intermediate or later work years (excluding normal turnover) when the projections underlying the PBO come to fruition.
- Fail to grant pay raises.
- Curtail or terminate the plan.

These assumptions stem from the going-concern assumption underlying the preparation of financial statements. That is why, in most cases, PBO-based data should be used to analyze a company's pension plan.

The ABO would be the appropriate measure of pension obligations assuming plan termination or in the case of bankruptcy.[34] However, as noted earlier, SFAS 132 limited the availability of information related to the ABO.

Pension Plans: Separate Entity or Integral to Firm? The analyst must also decide whether the pension plan should be considered an integral part of the employer or treated as an independent entity. Under defined benefit plans, employers bear the risk of investment performance of the pension plan. When the pension fund is insufficient to meet the obligations of the pension plan, the employer must cover the shortfall. Conversely, the firm can capture any surplus or excess assets by either lowering future contributions or terminating the plan. There are some restrictions (in the U.S., mainly ERISA) affecting the level of contributions and the ability of the firm to gain control over the assets of the plan.[35]

If the pension plan is considered an integral part of the firm, plan assets and liabilities should be added to the firm's balance sheet. The plan surplus or deficit should be recorded in stockholders' equity. Gross pension cost (defined earlier) should be reported in the income statement. The actual return on plan investments should be reported as investment income within the income statement. The only cash flow consequence would be the benefits paid; contributions to the plan would be transfers of cash from one "subsidiary" of the firm to another.

However, if we see the pension plan as independent of the firm, only the net difference between the plan assets and the PBO should be added to the firm's balance sheet. The offset to this adjustment would again be a component of stockholders' equity. This approach recognizes

---

[34]In the event of a bankruptcy analysis or filing, all assets and liabilities must be reevaluated.

[35]For companies in regulated industries, such as public utilities, any surplus may belong to the consumers or ratepayers rather than the employer. Similarly, there is some question as to the "ownership" or control of surplus pension assets of defense contractors, whose profits are regulated by the U.S. government. For example, the pension footnote from the *1990 Annual Report* of McDonnell Douglas states that the U.S. government indicates that it is "entitled to its equitable share of pension fund reversions to the extent that the Government participated in pension costs through their contracts." Yet McDonnell Douglas recognized a substantial settlement gain in 1990.

BOX 12-3
Market Valuation of Pension Obligation and Costs

Market Valuation of Liability

Research on the market's view of corporate pension plans has focused on a number of issues:

- Does the market value pension (assets) liabilities in the same manner as it values other (assets) liabilities of a firm?

- What is the most appropriate measure of the benefit liability: the PBO, ABO, or VBO?

- Does the market evaluate the pension liability (however measured) as an integral part of the firm or as a separate entity?

The overall evidence indicates that market prices incorporate the (disclosed but unrecorded) pension plan assets and obligation. Feldstein and Morck (1983), Daley (1984), and Landsman (1986) found that pension plan assets and obligations were a significant element in asset-based valuation models. Dhaliwal (1986) found that including pension obligations enhanced the explanatory power of a model that related a firm's debt/equity ratio to its systematic risk (β). Market participants viewed pension liabilities in much the same way as they viewed other debt in assessing a firm's systematic risk.

As the above studies were based on pre–SFAS 87 data, they were confined to using the ABO (or VBO)—the only required disclosure at the time. Subsequent work by Barth (1991), Barth et al. (1992), and Gopalakrishnan and Sugrue (1993), using post–SFAS 87 data, confirmed that the market viewed pension plan assets and the PBO as assets and liabilities of the firm.

Barth (1991) examined the ABO and PBO, as well as the balance sheet liability, to determine which best reflects the liability measure (implicitly) used by investors. Barth found that the ABO exhibits less measurement error than the other alternatives, and although investors appear to include expectations about future salary progression (PBO) in assessing the pension obligation, they view the PBO measure as noisy. The balance sheet liability fared the worst.

The above studies did not distinguish between over- and underfunded plans. Some have argued [see Carroll and Niehaus (1998)] that underfunded pension plans should augment firm liabilities to a greater extent than overfunded plans augment firm assets. The reasoning behind this asymmetric approach is that a firm cannot escape the liability inherent in unfunded pension liabilities, but it may be difficult for the firm to capture the excess assets in overfunded plans.

In contrast, Ballester, Fried, and Livnat (2000) found that the market seemed to follow a symmetric approach. The treatment of pension plan assets and liabilities as an integral part of the firm was not affected by the plan's funded status.*

Overall, the empirical evidence shows that market prices recognize pension assets and obligations as assets and liabilities of the company. This conclusion reinforces our view that financial statements adjusted for pension plan status are more useful for financial analysis.

Market Valuation of Pension Cost Components

Some of the above studies also included measures of pension and nonpension income in their valuation models. Barth et al. (1992), using SFAS 87–based data, compared the market valuation of various components of pension expense with the valuation of nonpension expense items. They found that the income components (as well as the balance sheet elements) of the pension costs were incrementally informative when included in a firm's valuation model, and that the market seemed to treat pension costs as being less "risky" than other expense elements.[†]

With respect to the individual components of pension expense, they found the interest component as well as the expected and actual return on plan assets to have the highest valuation. The three amortization components had a "zero" valuation; this is to be expected as these items contain no new information. The most surprising result was that the service cost component seemed to be valued "incorrectly" by the market (i.e., the higher the component, the higher the firm's value). The authors attribute this result to correlations among the various components. Notwithstanding this anomalous finding, the study found that both income and balance sheet data about pension plans were incrementally informative when included in a firm's valuation model.

Similar results were reported by Ballester et al., who, using post–SFAS 132 data, incorporated pension plan cash flows as well as pension cost components in their model. These results again confirm that detailed analysis of a firm's pension plan contributes to better investment and credit decisions.

---

*Ballester et al. used SFAS 132 disclosures and thus were limited to examining the PBO. On the other hand, the enhanced disclosures with respect to the elements comprising the changes in the PBO and plan assets (which they included in their model) served to make the data less "noisy."

[†]Market valuation of a revenue or expense item reflects the extent to which the market discounts the future stream of this component. Therefore, a higher valuation means that the market uses a lower discount rate for that item. They found that pension expense was more heavily valued than other nonpension items. The reason for this higher valuation may be that the market views pension expense as less risky; hence, a lower discount rate is appropriate. The fact that pension expense includes the return on plan assets (mostly invested in lower-risk assets such as bonds) is consistent with this result. Moreover, the interest component of pension expense is also relatively predictable and hence less risky.

---

the priority of the retirees' claim on plan assets; only the residual is an asset or liability of the employer. Pension cost would be measured as the "nonsmoothed" amount net of the actual return on plan assets. The firm would report the cash outflow for contributions to the plan.

SFAS 87 treats the pension plan as a separate entity. Assets and liabilities are selectively recognized on the balance sheet and the smoothed pension cost or credit is reported on the income statement. Based on the going-concern principle, we believe that the PBO less plan assets should be used to measure the firm's asset or liability for the plan.

Analysis of Texaco Pension Plan Disclosures

 We now apply our analysis to Texaco's pension plan disclosures in Note 11, Employee Benefit Plans.

Balance Sheet Adjustments. On a going-concern basis, the economic status of Texaco's plan is the difference between plan assets and its PBO. On December 31, 1999, Texaco's plans (U.S. and international combined) were overfunded by $72 million (plan assets of $2,716 million less PBO of $2,644 million). Because its balance sheet reports a net pension liability of $20 million, Texaco's net pension assets and equity should be increased by $92 million [$72 − (−$20)].

An additional adjustment is required because Texaco reports a minimum liability adjustment of $54 million, of which $31 million was recorded as an intangible asset. This second adjustment to Texaco's balance sheet is, therefore, to decrease equity and intangible assets by $31 million.

For Texaco, overall, the adjustments that need to be made to the balance sheet are relatively insignificant:

Increase net pension asset	$92 million
Decrease (intangible) assets	$31 million
Increase equity ($92 − $31)	$61 million

For other companies, with larger differences between the economic status of the plan and the balance sheet accrual, the required adjustments may be more significant.

Cash Flow and Income Analysis. SFAS 132 footnote disclosures[36] give us the cash flows associated with the pension plan and include data necessary to compute nonsmoothed measures of pension cost. These data are presented below along with the pension cost reported by Texaco in its financial statements.

Analysis of Texaco's Pension Cost and Cash Flows (in $millions)

		1998	1999
	Service cost [Table 2 or 5]	$ 81	$ 71
+	Interest cost [Table 2 or 5]	203	195
=	**Recurring cost**	**$284**	**$266**
	Nonrecurring costs:		
+	Actuarial losses [Table 2]	308	42
+	Plan amendments [Table 2]	3	52
=	**Gross pension cost**	**$595**	**$360**
+	Actual ROA (gain) [Table 3]	(435)	(387)
=	**Nonsmoothed cost (credit)**	**$160**	**$ (27)**
	Compare to		
	Pension cost in reported income [Table 5]	**$ 91**	**$ 40**
	Compare to pension plan cash flows		
	Employer contributions [Table 3]	**$122**	**$ 41**
	Benefits paid [Table 2 or 3]	**310**	**125**

Note: Texaco table references in brackets indicate source of item.

[36]See disclosures discussed earlier with respect to the reconciliation of the PBO as well as plan assets.

Texaco reported pension expense of $91 million and $40 million in 1998 and 1999, respectively. However, our analysis shows significantly higher recurring and gross pension costs for those years. High actual return on plan assets generated a nonsmoothed credit of $27 million in 1999 after a 1998 cost of $160 million. The pension costs reported on the income statement reflect the beneficial effects of the deferral of actuarial losses and plan amendments.

Benefits paid declined sharply in 1999, surprising for a mature plan. The decline may be due to unusually large 1998 payouts due to employee terminations. The drop in contributions may be also related to these terminations but is more likely due to the high (actual) ROA enjoyed by Texaco, mitigating the need for employer contributions.

Analysis of Funding Status. These data can be also used to gain insight into changes in the firm's funded status:

Changes in Texaco's Funded Status
(in $millions)

	1998	1999
Over- (under-) funded status	$(9)	$72
Change in funded status		81
Components of change in funded status		
Nonsmoothed (cost) credit		27
Employer contributions		41
Other nonrecurring changes*		13
Total change		$81

*Net currency effect, less net curtailment/settlement cost and plan expenses (see Texaco Table 5).

The funded status of the firm improved by $81 million. The (economic) nonsmoothed pension credit and employee contributions improved the status by $27 million and $41 million respectively. The last item is the effect of curtailments, settlements, and termination benefits etc.

Analysis of Texaco's Pension Trends

Exhibit 12-3 summarizes Texaco's pension plan disclosures over the 1997–2000 period. Data for all periods presented has been obtained from the annual report for each year, with some pre-1997 data estimated. The pension status data for 1998 and 1999 can be found in Note 11 of Texaco's 1999 annual report.

With the exception of 1999, the plans have been underfunded (PBO exceeds plan assets) for all years. The degree of underfunding declined from $394 million at the end of 1995 to $204 million on December 31, 2000. One plan is completely unfunded, with a PBO equal to $410 million at December 31, 1999 (see Note 11).

The change in plan status can be explained by separately examining the components of the PBO and plan assets. The PBO grew from $2,468 million at year-end 1995 to $2,653 on December 31, 2000. During this period, plan assets rose to $2,449 million from $2,074 million at year-end 1995.

The PBO increase was partly due to large actuarial losses, especially in 1997 and 1998. A decreasing discount rate for international plans, partly offset by lower assumed rates of compensation increase for those plans, increased the PBO. On the other hand, the large curtailments and settlements in 1998 and 1999 reduced the PBO from 1999 on.

Plan assets rose through 1998 due to excellent investment performance. The 1998–1999 settlements and negative 2000 ROA reduced plan assets.

Service costs declined in 2000, showing the effect of employee terminations in 1999 and 2000. Reported interest costs remained around $200 million due, at least in part, to a decline in discount rates for foreign plans (from 12.0% in 1996 to 7.8% in 2000). Prior service costs have not been a major factor; actuarial losses were significant only in 1997 and 1998.

EXHIBIT 12-3. TEXACO
Analysis of Pension Plans, 1996–2000 (in $millions)

	December 31						
	1995	1996	1997	1998	1999	2000	
Pension Plan Status							
Plan assets	$2,074	$2,312	$2,602	$2,854	$2,716	$2,449	
Projected benefit obligation	2,468	2,458	2,604	2,863	2,644	2,653	
Surplus (deficit)	**$ (394)**	**$ (146)**	**$ (2)**	**$ (9)**	**$ 72**	**$ (204)**	
Prepaid pension cost (liability)	**(161)**	**(127)**	**(68)**	**(6)**	**34**	**68**	
		Years Ending December 31					5 Year
Pension Cost		1996	1997	1998	1999	2000	Totals
Service cost		$ 73	$ 71	$ 81	$ 71	$ 59	$ 355
Interest cost		198	202	203	195	195	993
Recurring Cost		**$ 271**	**$ 273**	**$ 284**	**$ 266**	**$ 254**	**$ 1,348**
Prior service cost		—	18	3	52	5	78
Actuarial loss (gain)		74	159	308	42	31	614
Gross Pension Cost		**$ 345**	**$ 450**	**$ 595**	**$ 360**	**$ 290**	**$ 2,040**
Actual investment return on plan assets (gain)		(328)	(473)	(435)	(387)	22	(1,601)
Nonsmoothed Pension Cost (credit)		**$ 17**	**$ (23)**	**$ 160**	**$ (27)**	**$ 312**	**$ 439**
Service cost		73	71	81	71	59	355
Interest cost		198	202	203	195	195	993
Expected ROA		(185)	(198)	(215)	(221)	(232)	(1,051)
Amortization of transition asset		(10)	(13)	(14)	(18)	(6)	(61)
Amortization of prior service cost		9	16	18	24	23	90
Amortization of (gain)/loss		—	3	4	2	(2)	7
Curtailments and settlements		—	—	6	(13)	1	(6)
Special termination benefits		—	—	8	—	—	8
Reported Pension Cost (credit)		**$ 85**	**$ 81**	**$ 91**	**$ 40**	**$ 38**	**$ 335**
Cash Flows							
Contributions		**$ 51**	**$ 87**	**$ 122**	**$ 41**	**$ 40**	**$ 341**
Benefits paid		**141**	**241**	**310**	**125**	**130**	**947**
Assumptions							
Discount rate							
U.S. plans	7.0%	7.5%	7.0%	6.8%	8.0%	7.5%	
Foreign plans	11.5%	12.0%	10.9%	9.5%	8.1%	7.8%	
Rate of compensation increase							
U.S. plans	4.0%	4.0%	4.0%	4.0%	4.0%	4.0%	
Foreign plans	7.9%	7.4%	6.2%	6.1%	5.2%	4.5%	
Expected ROA							
U.S. plans	10.0%	10.0%	10.0%	10.0%	10.0%	10.0%	
Foreign plans	8.7%	8.7%	8.5%	8.4%	8.8%	8.8%	
Actual ROA		**15.0%**	**19.3%**	**15.9%**	**13.9%**	**−0.9%**	**12.6%**

Investment Performance Trends. Texaco's actual return on plan assets ranged from a high of 19.3% in 1997 to a loss of 0.9% in 2000 with an arithmetic average of 12.6% over the five-year period. Texaco assumed a 10% expected ROA on domestic plans for the period and a lower (average of 8.6%) rate for its foreign plans. These rates are certainly reasonable given actual performance. However, 1996 to 1999 were unusually good years for stock market returns and the analyst must evaluate market conditions to assess the company's ability to sustain the expected ROA.

Analysis of Trends in Pension Costs. Texaco's reported pension cost declined over the 1996–2000 period, from $85 million in 1996 to $38 million in 2000. The major factors in the decline were declining service cost and increasing expected ROA, which offset higher amortization of prior service cost.

Recurring cost, however, remained far higher than pension cost and showed a lower rate of decline. Gross pension costs tell a similar tale. Nonsmoothed pension cost was highly volatile, with the 2000 level far higher than reported pension cost.

Over the five-year period, reported pension cost of $335 million was below the total nonsmoothed pension cost of $439 million. The delayed reporting of the poor investment performance in 2000 was a major factor in the difference between these two measures. The differences in individual years also result from the smoothing provisions of SFAS 87.

Cash Flow Trends. Texaco substantially reduced contributions to its plans in 1999 and 2000 to a third of the 1998 level. Texaco's plan contributions appear to be closely related to pension cost. The company reported significant curtailments and settlements in 1999 and 2000 and benefit payments declined to $130 million from a high of $310 million in 1998.

Summary and Conclusions. For the five years ended 2000, Texaco's pension plan status improved by $190 million. During this period the balance sheet liability of $161 million turned into a $68 million asset, an improvement of $229 million. While the income-smoothing provisions of SFAS 87 delay the financial statement recognition of pension plan changes, over longer time periods the balance sheet must reflect changes in plan status.

Over the five-year period, reported pension cost was $335 million, and total contributions were $341 million. While reported income benefited from smoothing of pension cost, Texaco has neither underreported its plan status nor underfunded its pension funds in the aggregate. However, the one unfunded plan may require funding in the future.

Estimating Future Pension Cost

We now use Texaco's 1999 pension plan disclosures and the preceding analyses to forecast Texaco's 2000 pension cost.[37]

Given recent employee terminations, service cost is difficult to forecast. Assuming that the company plans no further restructuring of its workforce, the major changes should be:

- Lower service cost due to the 1999 employee reductions.
- Lower service cost due to the net effect of the higher discount rate for the U.S. plan and the lower rate for international plans. As the U.S. plans are larger, the net result should be lower service cost.

Based on these two factors we forecast a 10% reduction in 2000 service cost to $64 million.

Interest cost is easier to forecast as the 1999 year-end PBO times the discount rate on that date or a total of $212 million calculated separately for domestic ($1,664 million × 8.0% = $133 million) and foreign plans ($980 million × 8.1% = $79 million).

The expected ROA is estimated at $259 million as year-end 1999 plan assets times the assumed expected return (assuming no change). Again, we calculate the expected ROA separately for the domestic ($1,646 million × 10% = $165 million) and foreign ($1,070 million × 8.8% = $94 million) plans.

We assume net amortization of $22 million for the following reasons:

- Amortization of gains (losses) equal to 0 as the unamortized gains are below the 10% threshold for amortization under the corridor method.
- The increase in unamortized prior service cost from $120 million to $148 million should result in increased amortization from $24 million in 1999 to $30 million in 2000.
- Amortization of the transition asset falls to the remaining $8 million.

---

[37]These forecasts were produced without reference to the year-2000 data.

These assumptions result in the following forecast of Texaco's 2000 pension cost:

Service cost	$ 64 million
Interest cost	212
Expected ROA	(259)
Net amortization	22
Net pension cost	$ 39 million

This forecast implies a small 2000 decline in pension cost. The actual 2000 pension cost was $38 million, very close to our forecast, as small errors in forecasts of cost components offset each other.

OTHER PENSION FUND ISSUES

The preceding sections have considered pension plans without focusing on significant changes in the firm or the plan. This section discusses the effects of departures from these assumptions.

Acquisitions and Divestitures

Acquisitions and divestitures often create discontinuities in data, hampering analysis (see Chapter 14). The acquisition or divestiture of an entity with a defined benefit plan impacts the balance sheet and related footnote disclosures, and, therefore, the analysis of the merged or surviving entity. This effect is a function of the accounting method used to report the acquisition.[38]

Under the purchase method of accounting for acquisitions,[39] lack of separate data for the benefit obligations and plan assets of the acquired firms would make reconciliations of footnote data and meaningful analysis difficult or impossible. SFAS 132 requires explicit disclosure of the impact of acquisitions and divestitures on both the PBO and the plan assets.

SFAS 87 requires explicit recognition of the funded status of an acquired firm's pension plan as part of the accounting for a purchase method acquisition. The excess of plan assets over the PBO at the acquisition date is treated as a purchased asset; a deficit must be reported as a liability. This asset or liability must be recognized on the balance sheet of the acquiring entity although the plan status of the acquiring entity remains off the balance sheet.

Divestitures of subsidiaries with benefit plans create similar discontinuities. The assets and obligations of divested plans removed must be explicitly disclosed in the reconciliations of the PBO and the plan assets. In some cases, benefit obligations may remain on the books of the divesting entity. For example, the divesting entity and the acquirer may not agree on the measurement of the liability for pensions and other postretirement benefits of employees of the divested entity.

Curtailments and Settlements

SFAS 88 established the accounting standards for curtailments and settlements.[40] A *plan curtailment* results from a plan termination in total or from the closure of a plant or a division. Either action effectively freezes the benefits of the affected employees for a

---

[38]Under the pooling of interests method, the financial statements of the merged entities are simply combined. Past statements must be restated so that all postacquisition pension and postretirement benefit footnotes include all plan data of the merged entities. When plan data for prior years are restated, the analyses discussed in this chapter are possible for the latest year. However, the data are no longer consistent with those of earlier nonrestated years. As discussed in Chapter 14, SFAS 141 prohibits the use of the pooling method for acquisitions initiated after July 1, 2001. However, the pooling method is still permitted under IASB and many non-U.S. GAAPs.

[39]The financial statements of the acquired entity are added to those of the acquiring entity as of the acquisition date. (See Chapter 14 for a comprehensive explanation of the purchase method.)

[40]SFAS 106 prescribes similar principles for settlements of other postemployment benefits.

pay-related plan, changing the pension obligation. The PBO is reduced as future pay increases no longer increase benefits, but is increased due to faster vesting that may accompany the curtailment. Any net gain or loss on plan curtailment must be recognized in current-period income.

A *plan settlement* shifts the obligation to an unrelated entity; for example, an employer may pay an insurance company to assume the pension obligation for a group of employees. Any difference between the amount paid and the PBO "sold" is recognized as a gain or loss from settlement of the plan.

When a plan curtailment or settlement occurs as part of a plan to dispose of a segment or a line of business, the effect must be included in the gain or loss from discontinued operations. For example, in August 2001, Lucent Technologies transferred certain of its manufacturing operations to Celestica Corporation. As a result of its plan to reduce and/or transfer the workforce of those operations to Celestica, Lucent recorded termination and curtailment charges of $378 million, and reported them as a component of employee separation restructuring costs.

Cash Balance Plans

In recent years, a number of U.S. companies have adopted cash balance plans in an effort to reduce costs. Such plans change the benefit accrual provisions of defined benefit plans, as described in Box 12-4. Adoption of a cash balance plan is accounted for as a plan amendment, but disclosure and discussion of the effects of the change are usually obscure. When a company adopts a cash balance plan, the analyst should try to obtain additional information from management about the effects on the benefit obligation and future pension cost and funding requirements.

BOX 12-4
Cash-Balance Pension Plans

Since 1998, many employers have offered employees cash-balance pension (CBP) plans* in lieu of traditional defined benefit pension plans (DBP). The most significant difference in these two types of plans is the timing of benefit accruals. In DBP, benefits are based primarily on years of service and final pay. Employees earn the most significant portion of their benefits during the final years of service when their salaries are near their peak and they have provided many years of service. By contrast, in CBP, benefits are earned evenly over the entire period of employment. Generally, older employees receive significantly lower pension benefits if they must switch to CBP from DBP. Although younger employees benefit the most from CBP, their higher turnover rate means that they may see little or no benefit from a conversion to such plans.

Employers reap several important benefits of the conversion:

- Lower future benefits under CBP mean lower PBO and declining underfunding; therefore, lower risk.

- Enhanced predictability of future benefit payments because CBP require contributions of a specified percentage of employee salaries and a promised annual increase in benefits that is often tied to a specified measure of interest rates.

- Because of the higher turnover among younger employees, fewer employees may vest, leading to lower final payments.

- Lower contributions to pension funds.

When a cash balance plan reduces the projected benefit obligation, it creates negative prior service cost (i.e., a prior service credit). SFAS 87 requires that any PBO reduction be accounted for as a negative plan amendment, reducing unamortized prior service cost. The result is that pension cost declines as prior service cost amortization is reduced. When the PBO reduction exceeds unamortized prior service cost, the excess becomes negative prior service cost and its amortization reduces pension cost directly.

In some cases, employers may also capture the surplus in overfunded plans and enjoy a higher credit rating because of the decreased uncertainty in pension plans.

Employers may be limited in their ability to use CBP due to agreements with unionized employees and concerns over age discrimination. IBM, for example, unsuccessfully tried to switch to CBP, estimating savings as high as $200 million per year. Some employers have tried to deflect objections to the conversions by augmenting 401(k) plans. However, those plans, which companies fund with their own shares, may carry significant risk for employees.[†]

---

*For a more complete discussion see Alex T. Arcady and Francine Mellors, "Cash Balance Conversions," *Journal of Accountancy* (February 2000), pp. 22–28.

[†]The 2001 bankruptcy of Enron resulted in a nearly total loss of 401(k) assets consisting largely of Enron shares. For highly successful companies, such plans can provide much higher benefits than a DBP. The risk (as in all defined contribution plans) is borne by the employee.

IASB AND NON-U.S. REPORTING REQUIREMENTS

IAS 19 (1998), Employee Benefits, became effective in 1999, with minor 2000 amendments effective in 2001. Its accounting provisions are quite similar to SFAS 87, with the following significant differences:

- IAS 19 has no minimum liability recognition requirement. Thus the financial statements may understate the liability for underfunded plans even more under IAS GAAP than under U.S. GAAP

- IAS 19 limits the recognition of accrued pension assets. Overfunding is, therefore, less likely to receive balance sheet recognition under IAS GAAP than under U.S. GAAP.

- Under U.S. GAAP, companies contributing to multiemployer plans can record an expense equal to their contribution even if the plan is a defined benefit plan. IAS 19 requires use of defined benefit plan accounting for such plans.

However, the most significant difference between IAS and U.S. GAAP is that IAS 19's disclosure provisions are similar to (but reduced from) those of SFAS 87 rather than the improved disclosure provisions of SFAS 132. As a result, companies reporting under IAS GAAP are not required to:

- Reconcile plan assets.
- Reconcile the projected benefit obligation.
- Provide separate data for domestic and foreign plans.
- Provide separate data for pension and other postretirement benefit plans.

As a result of limited disclosures, much of the analysis that has been illustrated using Texaco cannot be done for companies reporting under IAS GAAP. This is especially true when there are discontinuities as described in the previous chapter section.

■ **Example: Roche**

Note 8 to Roche's *2000 Annual Report* contains the benefit plan disclosures required by IAS 19. We comment briefly on these disclosures:[41]

- Roche reports the components of pension cost in a manner similar to the disclosures of U.S. GAAP companies. Note that the 2000 decline in pension cost was due to the higher expected return on assets.

- While Roche discloses assumptions, there is a wide range that reflects Roche's worldwide scope.

- The reconciliation of the balance sheet liability reveals that in 2000:
  - The spinoff of Givaudan reduced the liability by CHF84 million.[42]
  - Roche contributed CHF174 million to the funded plans and paid an additional CHF135 million in benefits for unfunded plans.
  - Exchange rate effects reduced the liability.[43]

- Roche's balance sheet liability is due to its unfunded plans.

- The funded plans have assets that exceed the PBO by CHF1,414 million, of which CHF574 million is recorded as an asset. The difference is almost all due to unrecognized actuarial gains.

- The funded plans own a small amount of Roche shares; that investment was greatly reduced during 2000. ■

---

[41]Problem 12-14 concerns the analysis of these disclosures and data from Note 8 is provided in Exhibit 12P-6.

[42]The financial statement effects of the spinoff are reviewed in Chapter 14.

[43]The Swiss franc declined against the U.S. dollar in 2000, and rose against the Euro and British pound. We can deduce that plans in the latter two currencies accounted for the reduced liability, more than offsetting the higher CHF value of plan liabilities in U.S. dollars.

BOX 12-5
Non-U.S. Employee Benefit Plan Accounting Standards

U.S. financial reporting requirements for employee benefit plans remain the most comprehensive and detailed of all international standards. IAS standards (discussed in this chapter) are the closest, followed by Canada, the United Kingdom, and Japan. Rules under other GAAP often do not include specific recognition and measurement rules for employee benefit obligations and lack recognition requirements for postemployment benefits.

Despite the similarity of the Canadian, UK, Japanese, IAS, and U.S. pension standards, significant differences remain. The interest rate used in the non-U.S. standards is usually a more stable, long-term rate, adjusted for actual experience, compared with the more volatile short-term rate, the settlement rate, used in the United States. The new UK standard (FRS 17, discussed below) and IAS 19 require the use of the AA corporate bond rate (for maturities comparable to the benefit obligation) as the discount rate.

Actuarial methods are not limited to the projected unit credit method as in the United States; vested prior service costs must be expensed, not amortized, and there are no requirements to recognize liabilities due to a plan's underfunded status (minimum liability required by SFAS 87). Most foreign standards mandate significantly less disclosure than SFAS 132.

Health care and life insurance benefits are rarely provided in other countries, accounting for the absence of related reporting standards. IAS 19, Employee Benefits, makes the accounting for postretirement benefits similar to that required by SFAS 106.

United Kingdom (FRS 17)

In the United Kingdom, FRS 17, Retirement Benefits, will be fully effective for accounting periods ending on or after June 22, 2003. FRS 17 requires recognition of the pension plan surplus (to the extent that it can be recovered) or deficit in full on the balance sheet. Changes in the pension plan surplus or deficit are reported as follows:

• Current service cost and any prior service costs are reported as components of operating income.

• Interest cost and the expected return on plan assets must be reported as other financing costs.

• Actuarial gains and losses are recorded as components of total recognized gains and losses, that is, as components of other comprehensive income.

Pension cost is the sum of regular cost (defined as the consistent ongoing cost recognized under the actuarial method used) and variations (including experience gains and losses) to regular costs. In practice, service cost, as defined in the United States, may differ from regular costs in the UK, even when the same ac-

tuarial method is used. Experience gains and losses are amortized over the remaining employee service life. Their impact on pension cost is greater and earlier than under SFAS 87 as the corridor method cannot be used.

Under UK GAAP, a change in accounting policy for postretirement benefits other than pensions may be treated as a prior-period adjustment requiring restatement of all financial statements presented.

Japanese Standards

Prior to 2000, Japanese accounting standards did not include any recognition and measurement rules for employee benefit obligations. Lump sum or severance payments on retirements are the norm in Japan, and these were recognized on the balance sheet assuming that all employees eligible to retire did so. The obligations generally are not funded, as contributions are not deductible for taxes.

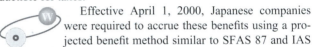 Effective April 1, 2000, Japanese companies were required to accrue these benefits using a projected benefit method similar to SFAS 87 and IAS 19. For Takeda, the transitional obligation of Yen4.2 billion was charged to income for fiscal 2000. Total pension cost under the new standards was Yen16.9 billion.

Following adoption of the new standard, Takeda's footnote reports:

• The PBO, plan assets, and the unrecognized actuarial loss

• Pension cost equal to service cost, interest cost, and the expected return on plan assets

• The range of assumptions for the discount rate and expected return on plan assets

• That actuarial gains and losses are amortized over five years

These disclosures, while better than the nondisclosure and nonrecognition that characterized Japanese standards in prior years, are less informative than U.S. or IAS requirements and therefore have only limited analytical usefulness.

Conclusion

In summary, accounting standards for employee benefit plans outside the United States are often different from U.S. GAAP, with less disclosure. Careful attention to disclosures, supplemented by discussions with management, may permit the analyst to obtain a better understanding of the extent to which the balance sheet reflects the true plan status. Adjustments to make pension cost more comparable may also be possible in some cases.

Box 12-5 contains a discussion of accounting standards for pensions under other non-U.S. GAAP.

OTHER POSTEMPLOYMENT BENEFITS

Many employers, especially large companies with unionized workforces, have historically provided other benefits to retirees in addition to pension benefits. Most significant of these benefits are health care and life insurance, often provided for dependents as well as retirees.

In the past, almost all companies accounted for such benefits on a pay-as-you-go basis, expensing actual payments when made.

The rapid growth in the cost of medical care resulted in increasing concern that employers providing these benefits were systematically overstating reported earnings and net worth by not accruing the costs of these benefits as they were earned during employees' periods of active service. Advances in medical technology, increased use of health care, and general inflation drove benefit costs to increasingly high levels. For example, General Motors' 2000 cost of providing such benefits to retirees was more than $2.8 billion!

Postemployment benefits other than pensions remain substantially unfunded as well. Unlike pension plans, contributions to retiree medical plans are generally not deductible for U.S. income tax purposes. Employers have no incentive to fund these plans because only payments for actual benefits are deductible. In addition, the earnings of such plans are not tax-exempt.

SFAS 106 (1990) governs the accounting for postemployment benefits other than pensions. SFAS 132 (1998) amended SFAS 106 disclosure requirements. We discuss the provisions of SFAS 106 and SFAS 132 mainly with reference to health care benefits, as these benefits are generally the most significant.

Estimating Health Care Benefits

Health care benefits differ from pension benefits in one important respect: Pension benefits are monetary amounts whereas health care benefits entitle employees (and, in many cases, their dependents) to coverage under which the cost may range from zero to a very large sum. Entitlement benefits are, therefore, much harder to estimate. As a result, the cash flow consequences (for employers) of these plans are much more difficult to predict.

A significant portion of the estimation process is identical to that for pensions: The employer must forecast how many employees will become eligible for benefits and the time period over which the retirees (and, when applicable, their dependents) will be eligible to receive them. Such variables as employee turnover, mortality, and retirement ages have to be predicted to forecast health care benefits.

Estimation of the *accumulated postretirement benefit obligation (APBO)*, however, requires additional assumptions not needed to forecast pension benefits. Among the most significant of these are the *health care cost trend rate*, the *assumed per-capita claims cost* (by age), and (in the U.S.) *Medicare reimbursement rates*. Also required are estimates of any required employee contributions (or cost sharing) and the effect of any cost limitations (caps) that are part of the benefit plan.

Forecasting health care cost is the most difficult aspect of estimating postretirement benefits. Health care costs (both direct reimbursement and insurance) have grown rapidly in recent years, often outstripping the rate of inflation. SFAS 106 gives employers some latitude in making these estimates. Companies whose plans have cost-sharing provisions (employer contributions, coinsurance provisions, deductibles, etc.) are permitted to incorporate such provisions when forecasting benefits.

The APBO is the actuarial present value of expected postretirement benefits earned to date. As in the case of pension benefits, the discount rate is an important determinant of the present value and may be changed by the employer from time to time. However, in contrast to SFAS 87, the discount rate is defined as a current, rather than as a settlement, rate. It is not possible, in practice, to settle (sell to another entity, such as an insurance company) obligations to provide health care benefits.

Computing Postretirement Benefit Cost

Net postretirement benefit cost contains the same elements identified earlier for net pension cost:

- Service cost
- Interest cost
- Return on plan assets
- Amortization of gains and losses

- Amortization of unrecognized prior service cost
- Amortization of transition asset or liability
- Curtailments and settlements

The computation of these elements is, for the most part, the same as for the corresponding elements of net pension cost. Service cost is the portion of the expected postretirement benefit obligation resulting from employee service during the period.

Interest cost reflects the passage of time. The discount rate used to compute both service cost and interest cost is, as in SFAS 87, almost always the rate used to compute the benefit obligation at the previous year-end.

The other elements are also analogous to the elements of net pension cost. Once again, the difference between the actual return on assets and the expected return is deferred. When a postretirement benefit health care plan is unfunded, however, there is no return-on-assets component, and the net cost does not depend on an assumed rate of return on assets.[44]

Because of the absence of plan funding, the transition liability was large for most employers when they adopted SFAS 106. As a result, the amortization of this liability (for the few companies that adopted the standard prospectively) was usually more significant for postretirement health care plans than pension plans. SFAS 106 allowed amortization of the transition liability over 20 years rather than the average remaining service period of active employees. This extended amortization mitigated the impact of this element on reported earnings. Almost all companies, however, adopted the standard using the cumulative adjustment method, reporting a large onetime reduction of net income. Box 12-6 discusses the empirical research and analytical implications of the choice between immediate and prospective recognition.

Disclosure of Plan Status

Employers with nonpension postretirement benefit plans are required to disclose the plan status in a manner similar to the disclosures required for pension plans by SFAS 132.

The fair value of plan assets and any accrual on the employer's balance sheet must be disclosed for funded plans. The difference between the plan status (APBO less plan assets) and the accrual consists of the following:

- Unrecognized prior service cost
- Unrecognized net gain or loss
- Unrecognized transition obligation (if the standard was adopted prospectively)

These unrecognized amounts have the same origin and meaning as those arising for pension plans discussed earlier.

Importance of Assumptions

SFAS 132 requires disclosure of the assumptions used to compute the APBO. These assumptions significantly affect both the stated obligation and the net postretirement benefit cost.

A higher discount rate reduces the present value of the APBO and improves the reported plan status (APBO compared to plan assets). A higher rate also reduces the benefit cost by decreasing the service cost, but it increases the interest cost.

The health care cost trend rate also directly affects the APBO: A lower rate reduces the estimated benefit obligation, improves the reported plan status, and reduces benefit costs by decreasing both the service cost and interest cost.

Because of the importance of the assumed health care cost trend rate, companies with postretirement health care plans are required to disclose the rate used for the next year as well as the pattern of rates assumed thereafter. This disclosure is intended to help financial

---

[44]When a postretirement benefit plan is funded but the earnings of the fund are taxable, fund earnings must be recognized on an after-tax basis.

BOX 12-6
Choice of SFAS 106 Transition Methods

Companies adopting SFAS 106 could either:

- Recognize the transition obligation immediately as a charge against net income in the year of the adoption, that is, recognize the cumulative effect of the accounting change, or
- Delay recognition by amortizing it over the greater of the average remaining service life of active plan participants or 20 years (prospective adoption).

The choice between immediate and prospective recognition involved consideration of the following issues:

- The ability to minimize the effect of the transition obligation by recording it on an after-tax basis; for this reason, some companies delayed adoption of SFAS 106 until SFAS 109 was adopted.*
- The effect on debt agreements.[†]
- Management's ability to amend postretirement plans and reduce the size of the liability prior to adoption.

Amir and Livnat (1996) found evidence supporting the third factor: firms adopting SFAS 106 in 1992 and 1993 were more likely to amend postretirement benefit plans to reduce benefits compared to 1991 adopters. They also found that 1991 adopters reported postretirement benefit obligations that were smaller than those expected by the market. In addition, firms generally announced the adoption of SFAS 106 in the period (year and quarter) with the lowest pre–SFAS 106 earnings, suggesting a big-bath effect.

Mittelstaedt et al. (1995) reported that firms with larger APBO tended to reduce postretirement benefits. However, they concluded that SFAS 106 was not the primary cause of these reductions; firm-specific increases in retiree health care costs as well as the financial condition of the firm were additional important factors.

In practice, virtually all companies with postretirement benefits used the cumulative effect method in adopting SFAS 106. Immediate recognition of a significant liability for postretirement benefits had the added advantage of a onetime impact on earnings[‡] rather than an adverse effect under the alternative method of amortization of the obligation over 20 years.

International Business Machines [IBM], for example, adopted SFAS 106 in the first quarter of 1991. It reported a cumulative effect of $2,263 million after a tax effect of $350 mil-

lion. This charge reduced stockholders' equity by 5%. Prior to adoption, like all other companies, IBM accrued health care and similar benefits at retirement. In 1990, the company reported postretirement benefits accruals of $96 million; under SFAS 106, IBM recorded $394 million in 1991.

Under the alternative prospective approach, IBM would have amortized the liability over 20 years and reported pretax earnings would have been reduced by $113 million ($2,263/20) in each future year. In 1991, total cost of postretirement benefits would have been $524 million ($394 for benefits accrued in 1991 and the amortization charge of $113 million). The cumulative approach, that is, immediate write-off, results in higher reported return on equity because earnings reported in future years are not burdened by annual amortization charges for the postretirement liability and the equity is significantly lower.

General Electric [GE] also adopted SFAS 106 in the first quarter of 1991. Like IBM, GE charged its transition liability to earnings. The amount charged was $2.7 billion pretax and $1.8 billion or $2.07 per share after tax. Stockholders' equity was reduced by 8.3%.

GE paid $374 million in benefits during 1991; the cost of benefits under SFAS 106 was 25% lower, or $279 million. However, if GE had chosen the prospective approach, it would have reported postretirement benefit charges of $415 million in 1991 (adding $2,710/20 or $136 million to $279 million accrued in 1991). Its choice of transition method continues to provide benefits to GE through 2000; GE has reported total health care and life insurance costs of $313, $318, and $478 million in 1998, 1999, and 2000, respectively.[§] The company paid $363, $499, and $578 million in benefits in 1998, 1999, and 2000 respectively.

In contrast to IBM and GE, other companies used the prospective method, electing to amortize the transition postretirement obligation over 20 years. For that entire period, financial analysts need to remember that a significant element of reported postretirement benefit costs is completely unrelated to current operations as it represents a charge for previously unrecorded costs.

One example is Noland [NOLD], a wholesale distributor of mechanical equipment and supplies to contractors and manufacturers. Noland adopted SFAS 106, prospectively, effective January 1, 1993. The transition APBO is being amortized over 20 years. Noland has reported an unrecognized transition obligation and annual amortization as follows (in $thousands):

	12/31/1998	12/31/1999	12/31/2000
As Reported—Prospective Method			
Unrecognized transition obligation	$2,848	$2,645	$2,442
Annual amortization	203	203	203
Cost (includes amortization)	594	593	581
Net income	5,870	8,147	9,308
Stockholders' equity	125,233	132,162	138,224
Return on year-end equity	4.69%	6.16%	6.73%
Adjusted—Cumulative Method			
Adjusted pretax cost	*$391*	*$390*	*$378*
Adjusted net income	*5,992*	*8,269*	*9,430*
Adjusted stockholders' equity	*123,524*	*130,575*	*136,759*
Adjusted return on year-end equity	*4.85%*	*6.33%*	*6.90%*

The preceding table indicates that Noland's annual postretirement benefit costs would have been one-third lower each year had it used the cumulative method. Had it done so, stockholders' equity at December 31, 2000 would be reduced by $1,465,000 [$2,442,000 × (1 − 0.40)], using Noland's tax rate of 40%. The adjusted panel in the table reports net income, equity, and return on equity had the company chosen the cumulative method. While adjusted equity is lower, both adjusted net income and adjusted ROE are higher each year. The comparison makes clear why the overwhelming majority of firms chose to immediately recognize the transition obligation. It also shows why financial analysts need to adjust the financial statements of companies using different methods to recognize the transition obligation.

---

*For example, Westinghouse Electric adopted both standards in the first quarter of 1992. It used the cumulative method to record an after-tax charge of $742 million for postretirement benefits and a $404 million deferred tax asset under SFAS 109. The net effect of this simultaneous adoption was $338 million. If SFAS 109 had not been adopted (and assuming that Westinghouse would not have been able to tax-effect the cumulative effect of SFAS 106), the pretax cumulative effect of adopting SFAS 106 would have exceeded $1 billion.

†In September 1991, Westinghouse Electric announced that it had asked bank lenders to change the terms of its loan agreement in anticipation of adopting SFAS 106.

‡In addition, many companies and most analysts emphasized the onetime nature of the charge.

§Under the prospective method, GE would have reported an additional $136 million each year.

---

statement users understand the assumptions used by employers to measure the APBO. For example, Westvaco discloses (Note M in the 1999 annual report) that

> The annual rate of increase of health care costs was assumed at 6% for 1998, 5% for 1999, and remaining at that level thereafter.

Just as for pension plans, assumptions vary among companies, reducing comparability. More conservative assumptions (lower discount rate and higher health cost trend rate) increase the quality of earnings.

Employers are also required to disclose the impact of *both* a one-percentage-point increase *and* an identical decrease in the assumed health care trend rate for each future year on:

- The APBO
- The combined service and interest cost components of the net postretirement health care benefit cost

These disclosures help analysts to compare the cost and benefit obligations of employers when they are computed under different assumptions. They also reveal the sensitivity of the measured benefit obligation to the trend rate assumption. Plans with a high degree of cost sharing can be expected to have a lower degree of sensitivity to the trend rate of health care costs because retirees will bear a portion of any cost increases.

Effect of Assumptions

Westvaco, for example, discloses that a one-percentage-point increase (decrease) would increase (decrease) the APBO by $288,000 or 1.4% ($252,000 or 1.3%) and the combined service and interest cost would increase (decrease) by $70,000 or 2.9% ($63,000 or 2.6%).

The low sensitivity of the Westvaco plans reflects lifetime benefit caps (see Note M) that limit the impact of unexpected inflation in health care costs.

In contrast, Ohio Casualty [OCAS] reports in its 2000 annual report that a 1% increase (decrease) in the assumed health care cost trend rate would increase (decrease) the APBO by 12% (10%) and benefit cost by 16% (13%). Companies like Ohio Casualty with higher sensitivity are much more at risk should health care costs exceed those assumed.

Assumptions about the effectiveness of the cost-sharing provisions of the employer plans thus have an important impact on the benefit obligation and costs. Some employers will be tempted to be overly optimistic about the effect of such provisions on their benefit costs. Overoptimism with respect to any assumptions will, however, result in actuarial losses that will eventually require amortization and increase the benefit cost.

Analysis of Westvaco's Postretirement Health Care Costs

Westvaco's plan is unfunded (see Note M) and, as of October 31, 1999, the company had recorded a liability of $27.1 million for postretirement benefits. The economic liability, as measured by the APBO, is $19.9 million. The difference represents primarily unrecognized net actuarial gain.[45]

Westvaco recognized postretirement health care expense of $1.3 million in 1999 compared with $2.1 million in 1998 and $1.3 million in 1997. Service cost declined, reflecting 1999 workforce reductions. Interest cost also fell, surprising as the 1998 increase in the APBO and decline in the discount rate should approximately offset.[46]

Calculation of Nonsmoothed Costs and Comparison to Cash Flows

The gross benefit (nonsmoothed) cost can be calculated from the data provided in the reconciliation of the APBO. Because the plan is unfunded there is no ROA, making gross pension cost and nonsmoothed cost identical. The cash outflow equals the actual benefit payments rather than plan contributions.

Analysis of Westvaco's Postretirement Health Care Costs
(in $thousands)

	1998	1999
Opening APBO	$21,700	$23,200
+ Gross benefit cost		
Service cost	1,400	1,200
+ Interest cost	1,500	1,200
= Recurring cost	**$ 2,900**	**$ 2,400**
Nonrecurring costs:		
Actuarial loss (gain)	1,100	(2,800)
= Gross benefit costs		
= Nonsmoothed costs	**$ 4,000**	**$ (400)**
** − Benefits paid:**	**2,500**	**2,900**
= Closing APBO	$23,200	$19,900

Note: The 1998 actuarial loss reflects the lower discount rate, increasing the APBO. The 1999 actuarial gain is probably due to the workforce reduction as well as the reduced rate of increase in health care costs.

Using SFAS 106 and SFAS 132 Disclosures

As the accounting for postretirement benefits other than pensions parallels that for pension benefits, the analytical adjustments are the same. Replace balance sheet accruals by the excess of the APBO over the plan assets (if any). For Westvaco, the 1999 liability should be decreased and equity increased by $7.2 million pretax ($27.1 million − $19.9 million).

Companies with postretirement benefits have argued that they can reduce or eliminate benefits, although this argument is more difficult to accept when benefits are mandated under union contract. The results of recent litigation suggest that benefits for retirees cannot be summarily discontinued, even in cases of severe financial distress.[47] Companies continue to

---

[45]As the plan is unfunded, all gains and losses are actuarial; there are no deferred investment gains or losses. As there is no transition liability, we know that Westvaco used the cumulative method when it adopted SFAS 106.

[46]The interest cost for 1999 can be estimated as 6.75% × $23.2 million = $1.57 million and the 1998 amount as 7.25% × $21.7 million = $1.57 million. When reported amounts differ from estimated amounts and the amounts are material, management should be asked for an explanation.

[47]Sears, for example, was sued by retired employees after it reduced life insurance coverage. The suit was settled in 2002 when the company restored most of the reduced benefits.

work hard to limit their exposure to health care costs. Westvaco's benefit limitation discussed above is a typical response to rising health care costs.

Nonetheless, like pensions, these benefits must be treated as corporate liabilities. In the absence of evidence that benefits will be curtailed or discontinued, financial analysis must include the evaluation of any unrecognized benefit assets or liabilities. Although SFAS 106 did not change cash flow, the APBO does represent a forecast of future cash outflows that will require the use of corporate resources.[48]

Adjustment of the income statement may also be necessary. Companies that adopted SFAS 106 prospectively include amortization of the transition liability in postretirement benefit expense. However, this liability represents prior-period costs. Current-period earnings, we believe, should not be burdened with costs incurred in prior periods. The matching principle suggests that amortization of the transition liability should, therefore, be excluded from postretirement benefit costs when evaluating a firm's earnings power and future cash flow needs. This adjustment is also necessary when comparing such a firm with one that fully recognized the transition obligation upon adoption of SFAS 106.

Postretirement Benefits Outside the United States

Health care and life insurance benefits are rarely provided outside of the United States. IAS 19 has requirements that are similar to those of SFAS 106. When national standards do not exist, companies expense benefit payments when made. This pay-as-you-go method overstates reported income and equity, and understates liabilities relative to the accrual method required by SFAS 106 and IAS 19.

PRERETIREMENT BENEFITS

Some employee benefits apply to periods of active service or periods following active service but prior to retirement. Such benefits include:

1. Insurance benefits (mainly health and life)
2. Vacations, holidays, and sick days
3. Severance benefits
4. Supplemental unemployment, disability, and similar benefits

The first class of benefits listed is accounted for on a pay-as-you-go basis; these life and health insurance benefits are period costs. SFAS 43 (1980), Accounting for Compensated Absences, covers the second category, requiring employers to accrue benefit costs when they can be reasonably estimated and employees have earned the right to receive them.

SFAS 112 (1992) extended the reasoning of SFAS 43 to the third and the fourth benefit groups listed above, unifying practice with respect to the accounting for these benefits.

STOCK COMPENSATION PLANS

In addition to salary and such traditional employee benefits as retirement and medical plans, some firms offer employees the opportunity to benefit from increases in the value of the firm. Such plans may take the form of restricted stock (phantom stock), under which the employee receives an amount that depends on the performance of a specified number of shares. Increasingly, however, companies have used stock options.

Under APB 25, the issuance of stock options to employees receives no accounting recognition when (1) the exercise price is fixed and is equal to or higher than the market price of the underlying common stock on the date the options are granted and (2) the number of shares to be received on exercise is fixed. The rationale is that such options have no intrinsic value at grant date. However, the increasing familiarity with and the ease of use of sophisticated option pric-

---

[48]Thus satisfying the FASB definition of a liability (see Chapter 1).

ing models[49] has made it more difficult to argue that fixed stock option awards have no value. APB 25 does require recognition of compensation expense for variable stock option awards (where either the exercise price of the number of shares to be issued on exercise are not fixed).

SFAS 123 (1995) was issued by the FASB after a long battle over whether the issuance of stock options to employees should result in income statement recognition of employee compensation expense. Strong protests from the corporate community and ill-considered objections from politicians resulted in a standard that permits either expense recognition on the income statement or *pro forma* disclosures. Most companies chose the latter option. *SFAS 123 does require recognition of expense* (measured as the fair value of options granted) *for all options issued to nonemployees such as suppliers and consultants.*

During the 1999–2002 period, significant declines in the share prices of many technology companies left many employees with worthless options. In order to retain employees and offer incentives to management, many of those companies modified one or more features of fixed options. These modifications raised the question whether the nonrecognition provisions of APB 25 still applied. On March 31, 2000, the FASB issued Interpretation 44 (FIN 44), Accounting for Certain Transactions Involving Stock Compensation, an Interpretation of APB Opinion 25, to provide accounting guidance. FIN 44 identifies three types of modifications that result in accounting recognition of the option as compensation expense:[50]

1. A reduction in the exercise price
2. A renewal or extension of the life of the award or renewal or extension contingent on the occurrence of a specified future separation from employment
3. An increase in the number of shares to be issued including the addition of a reload feature[51]

However, the interpretation permits continued fixed option accounting (no recognition of compensation expense in the income statement) when the exercise price is changed by canceling an existing fixed option award and replacing it with a new option at least six months and one day before or after cancellation of the existing option.[52]

FIN 44 also allows companies to not recognize compensation expense for options granted to independent members of the board of directors. This is justified by claiming that independent directors are hired by the shareholders and they are not employees of the company.

SFAS 123 Pro Forma Disclosures. Companies adopting the pro forma disclosure method of applying SFAS 123 must provide:

- Effect on income and EPS.
- Detailed data regarding the number of options outstanding, their exercise prices, and whether or not they are exercisable.
- The grant-date fair value of options granted during the year, with separate disclosure of options issued with exercise prices at, above, or below market price.
- A description of the method and significant assumptions used to determine the grant-date fair value. Specific assumptions that must be disclosed include the:
  - Risk-free interest rate
  - Expected option life
  - Expected stock volatility
  - Expected dividends

---

[49]The Black-Scholes model is widely used to value stock options.

[50]The compensation expense will equal the change in intrinsic value, i.e.

$$[(\text{Stock price} - \text{Original exercise price}) - (\text{Stock price} - \text{New exercise price})].$$

Use of this equation will result in recognition of compensation expense not only when the options are initially repriced *but each subsequent accounting period as the market value of the stock changes.* This would serve to increase the volatility of the company's reported income.

[51]A reload feature grants one or more new options upon the exercise of an existing option.

[52]Problem 12-22 examines an example of such a plan implemented by Eastman Kodak.

- Any compensation cost recognized during the period.
- Data regarding the modification of outstanding stock options (e.g., repricing of options after a significant decline in stock price).
- Data regarding other equity instruments (such as restricted stock) issued to employees.

■ **Example**

Exhibit 12-4 summarizes the footnote disclosures provided by Microsoft Corporation, IBM, and Novell. These companies use the pro forma method of SFAS 123 to disclose information about stock-based compensation. For the most recent year, the exhibit shows that if Microsoft had recognized stock compensation expense, its operating (net) income would have been reduced by 30% (31%). The operating margin adjusted for stock compensation expense would have been 32.78% compared to the reported margin of 46.33%. Finally, diluted EPS would have been 31% lower.

For the three years shown, the three companies would have reported lower net income, lower diluted earnings per share, and lower operating margins due to stock-based compensation. Novell would have reported the largest percentage dilution (200% in 2000) in earnings per share. The stock-based compensation plans at these companies also resulted in significant increases in shares outstanding.

The exhibit also shows that:

- The number of options granted by these companies has risen steadily. In Microsoft's case, options granted rose from 766 million on June 30, 1999 to 898 million on June 30, 2001, or an increase of 17%. If exercised, these options will increase diluted shares outstanding by more than 16%.

EXHIBIT 12-4
Stock Option Disclosures

	MICROSOFT Year Ended June 30			IBM Year Ended December 31			NOVELL Year Ended October 31		
	1999	2000	2001	1998	1999	2000	1998	1999	2000
Valuation Assumptions: Black-Scholes Model									
Volatility	32.00%	33.00%	39.00%	26.40%	27.30%	32.00%	51.00%	58.00%	75.00%
Aggregate expected life (in years)	5	6.2	6.4	*	*	*	5	5	5
Risk-free interest rate	4.90%	6.20%	5.30%	5.10%	6.60%	5.10%	5.43%	5.50%	6.30%
Dividend yield	0.00%	0.00%	0.00%	0.80%	0.40%	0.50%	0.00%	0.00%	0.00%
Weighted-average price—all options	$23.87	$41.23	$49.54	$36.00	$60.00	$73.00	$8.89	$14.22	$15.38
Weighted-average fair value of options granted during year	20.90	36.67	29.31	18.00	46.00	36.00	10.14	23.04	16.99
Options exercisable at year-end	406	341	331	46.2	51.6	66.6	15.5	17.5	21.7
Options outstanding at year-end	766	832	898	131.4	146.1	160.6	48.4	55.3	67.1
Weighted-average shares outstanding	5,482.0	5,536.0	5,574.0	1,920.1	1,871.1	1,812.1	356.4	349.4	335.0
% increase in shares outstanding	**14.0%**	**15.0%**	**16.1%**	**6.8%**	**7.8%**	**8.9%**	**13.6%**	**15.8%**	**20.0%**
Net income (loss): Reported	$7,785	$9,421	$7,346	$6,308	$7,692	$8,073	$102	$191	$49
Pro forma	7,109	8,172	5,084	5,985	7,044	7,183	62	118	(50)
Net income (loss) per share: Reported	1.42	1.70	1.32	3.29	4.12	4.44	0.29	0.55	0.15
Pro forma	1.30	1.48	0.91	3.12	3.78	3.99	0.18	0.34	(0.15)
Percentage reduction	**8.5%**	**12.9%**	**31.1%**	**5.2%**	**8.3%**	**10.1%**	**37.9%**	**38.2%**	**200.0%**
Adjustment to operating margin									
Net sales	$19,747	$22,956	$25,296	$81,667	$87,548	$88,396	$1,084	$1,273	$1,162
Operating income	10,010	11,006	11,720	9,040	11,757	11,534	98	223	(32)
Adjusted operating income	8,986	9,114	8,293	8,551	10,775	10,186	38	113	(182)
Reported operating margin	50.7%	47.9%	46.3%	11.1%	13.4%	13.0%	9.1%	17.5%	(2.7%)
Adjusted operating margin	45.5%	39.7%	32.8%	10.5%	12.3%	11.5%	3.5%	8.9%	(15.7%)

*IBM discloses the expected life assumption for options with and without tax incentives.
Note: All financial data in millions except for per-share data. Shares outstanding and per-share calculations are on diluted basis.

- Options exercisable rose for both IBM and Novell, but fell for Microsoft over the period shown. 41% of IBM's outstanding options were exercisable at year-end 2000; the percentage exercisable was lower for both Microsoft and Novell at the latest dates shown.
- The decrease in operating margins is significant (in Novell's case: from a reported operating margin of 9.08% in 1998 to an adjusted margin of 3.49% and from a reported −2.72% to an adjusted −15.67% in fiscal 2000) when the cost of stock compensation is included in the analysis. ■

Using SFAS 123 Disclosures

Based on our view that stock compensation should be recognized as part of employee compensation, the following analytical adjustments should be made for all firms choosing the disclosure-only option.[53]

1. Use the pro forma net income to compute such critical ratios as operating margins and such valuation measures as the price-earnings ratio. When computing normalized income from continuing operations or net income (see Chapter 17), the pro forma adjustment for stock compensation expense should be part of recurring income. Support for this adjustment comes from the finding by Aboody, Barth, and Kasznik (2001) that investors view stock-based compensation as an expense of the firm.

2. The balance sheet can be left unchanged. Although recognition of stock compensation expense has some effect on assets (creation of deferred tax assets), its major impact is a reclassification between retained earnings and paid-in capital. Such effects will be insignificant for most companies. However, the analyst should adjust the number of shares outstanding used to compute earnings per share by assuming exercise of all stock options whose strike price is below the market price.[54]

3. Although the grant of stock options has no direct cash flow effect, their exercise provides cash (included in financing cash flow) and sometimes (under U.S. tax law) a tax deduction (often included in cash from operations). These effects are illustrated in the next section of this chapter.

Effect on the Statement of Cash Flows

When an employee exercises a nonqualified[55] stock option, the exercise results in a tax liability for the employee (employee tax rate times the difference between the exercise price and the market price) and an equal tax benefit for the employer. As companies applying the disclosure-only provisions of SFAS 123 do not recognize compensation expense for fixed option awards, they credit the income tax benefit directly to equity. Emerging Issues Task Force Consensus No. 00-15 requires classification of the cash effects of the income tax benefit as a component of operating cash flows.

The income tax benefits of stock options can be highly significant. Exhibit 12-5 depicts this benefit as a percentage of reported net cash flow from operations for four large technology companies. The ratio ranged from 3% for Oracle and Hewlett-Packard in fiscal 1999 to

---

[53]An insignificant number of companies historically recognized the value of stock options as compensation expense. However, that trend may change. In mid 2002 (in reaction to the climate caused by accounting scandals), a number of firms announced that they would begin to record compensation expense for stock options. In August, 2002 the FASB proposed that SFAS 123 pro forma disclosures be required quarterly. Additionally, the IASB proposed a new standard that would require the expensing of stock options.

[54]The easiest way to make this adjustment is by the Treasury stock method described in the "Earnings Per Share" section of Chapter 4. For alternative adjustment methods, see Chapter 7 of Aswath Damodaron, *The Dark Side of Valuation* (New York: Wiley, 2001).

[55]Under U.S. tax laws, stock options may be either qualified (incentive stock options) or unqualified. The exercise of qualified options has no tax effect for either the employer or the employee.

EXHIBIT 12-5
Stock Option Income Tax Benefits as a Percentage of Reported CFO

	Year-End	Income Tax Benefits			As % of Reported CFO		
		1998	1999	2000	1998	1999	2000
Cisco	July	$ 837	$2,495	$1,397	19.4%	40.6%	21.9%
Hewlett-Packard	October	158	289	495	3.3%	9.3%	14.3%
Microsoft	June	3,107	5,535	2,066	25.6%	48.4%	15.4%
Oracle	May	56	493	1,149	3.1%	16.9%	52.7%

Source: Data from annual reports.

nearly 53% of reported CFO for Oracle in fiscal 2000. There are two important analytical considerations:

1. While the cash flows are real, they depend on highly profitable option exercises and are highly volatile. For valuation purposes they should receive little or no weight.
2. If companies report the tax benefits as part of cash from operations, they ought to deduct the value of stock option grants from income, but very few do so. Fortunately, the disclosure requirements of SFAS 123 enable analysts to adjust reported earnings.

Stock Repurchase Programs and Sales of Put Warrants

Companies using stock options often repurchase their own common stock to obtain shares required for option and employee stock ownership plans. Some companies use derivatives as part of their repurchase programs.

Companies sometimes sell put warrants in conjunction with stock repurchase programs. Generally, the put warrants entitle the holders to sell the company's common stock to the company at specified prices at certain dates. When the company's shares rise, the warrants expire unexercised and the premium received is included in income. Microsoft, for example, received more than $1.8 billion in the three years ended June 30, 2000 from the sale of put warrants. On June 30, 2000, warrants to put 157 million shares were outstanding. In fiscal 2001, however, the company paid cash of nearly $1.4 billion and issued 2.8 million shares to retire outstanding put warrants.

As the Microsoft example shows, stock repurchase programs and put warrants can be very expensive when share prices decline. Some technology companies have had to borrow funds to settle these contracts. Analysts should jointly evaluate stock-based compensation and the cash flow consequences of these contracts. When combined with stock repurchase programs and put warrants, the use of the disclosure-only method of SFAS 123 permits companies to keep all or a significant portion of their compensation costs off the income statement and minimize the cash flow consequences of stock-based compensation.

SUMMARY

Current accounting practices for pensions and other postretirement benefits result in an amalgam of smoothed and unsmoothed costs in net income; the actual obligations are sometimes disguised and reported either partly or wholly off balance sheet. In this chapter we have demonstrated the use of footnote disclosures to unravel the underlying events. This permits the calculation of the actual components of benefit costs, the analysis of the risks and cash flows of benefit plans, and the examination of trends in obligations, plan assets, and benefit costs. This chapter also suggests alternative measures of benefit costs and obligations.

The value of stock options granted to employees is rarely recognized, understating employee compensation and overstating net income. In addition, stock-based compensation may affect the statement of cash flows. Both the income statement and cash flow implications of stock option plans are discussed in the chapter.

Chapter 12

Problems

1. [Effect of pension plan assumptions; CFA© adapted] Chalker Industries maintains a defined benefit pension plan covering all its U.S. employees.

a. Discuss the effect of an increase in the discount rate on:

    (i) The projected benefit obligation in the year of the change

    (ii) Pension cost in the year of the change

    (iii) Pension cost in the year following the change

b. Discuss the effect of an increase in the assumed rate of compensation growth on:

    (i) The projected benefit obligation in the year of the change

    (ii) Pension cost in the year of the change

    (iii) Pension cost in the year following the change

c. Discuss the effect of an increase in the expected rate of return on plan assets on:

    (i) The projected benefit obligation in the year of the change

    (ii) Pension cost in the year of the change

    (iii) Pension cost in the year following the change

 2. [Analysis of pension plan disclosures; Westvaco] Use Note M of Westvaco's 1999 financial statements to answer the following questions:

a. State the most likely reason for the actuarial loss (gain) in 1998 (1999).

b. Explain why the amortization of prior service cost rose from 1997 to 1999.

c. Explain the change in the unrecognized actuarial gain during 1999, calculating each component.

d. Compute the actual rate (%) of return on assets for 1998 and 1999 and compare it to the expected return.

e. Explain why service cost rose in 1998 although the number of employees declined.

f. Estimate the effect on 1999 pension cost of the changes in the expected return on plan assets in 1998 and 1999.

g. Discuss Westvaco's possible motivation for changing the expected return on plan assets in light of the actual returns for those years.

h. Forecast the amortization of the transition asset for the three years ending 2002.

i. Forecast fiscal 2000 pension cost, stating any assumptions.

j. Calculate each of the following for 1998 and 1999:

    (i) Recurring pension cost

    (ii) Gross pension cost

    (iii) Nonsmoothed pension cost

k. Compare the measures of pension cost calculated in part j with

    (i) Pension cost reported by Westvaco

    (ii) The pension plan cash flows

l. Calculate and justify the adjustments you would make to Westvaco's balance sheet at October 31, 1999 to reflect the economic position of its pension plan.

m. State the principal reason for the difference between the adjustment in part l and the adjustment required at October 31, 1998.

 3. [Analysis of pension plan disclosures; Pfizer] Use Note 10 of Pfizer's 1999 financial statements to answer the following questions:

a. State the most likely reason for the 1998 actuarial loss.

b. Pfizer had an actuarial loss in 1999. State two reasons why a loss would be expected and one reason to expect a gain.

c. Explain why the reconciliation of both the projected benefit obligation and plan assets have foreign exchange impacts and state the information conveyed by the direction of those changes.

d. State why Pfizer's balance sheet contains an accrued benefit liability despite the excess of plan assets over the benefit obligation.

e. Explain what is represented by the amount ($317 million for 1999) shown in accumulated other comprehensive income.

f. Compute the actual rate of return on assets for 1997–1999.

g. Evaluate Pfizer's expected return on plan assets in light of the results in part f.

h. Pfizer's discount rate and assumed rate of compensation increase for its international plans are both below the assumptions for its U.S. plans. State the inference that can be made about the relative rates of inflation.

i. Calculate each of the following for 1997–1999:

    (i) Recurring pension cost

    (ii) Gross pension cost

    (iii) Nonsmoothed pension cost

j. Compare the measures of pension cost calculated in part i with

    (i) Pension cost reported by Pfizer

    (ii) The pension plan cash flows

k. Calculate and justify the adjustments you would make to Pfizer's balance sheet at December 31, 1999 to reflect the economic position of its pension plans.

l. Forecast Pfizer's 2000 pension cost, stating any assumptions.

Exhibit 12P-1 provides information regarding the Ford Motor [F] pension plans for U.S. employees. Problems 12-4 through 12-6 require the analysis of those disclosures.

4. [Effect of actuarial assumptions]

a. For 2000, Ford *decreased* (from 7.75% to 7.50%) the discount rate used to calculate its pension obligation, but *increased* (from 6.25% to 7.75%) the discount rate used to calculate pension expense. Explain how this is possible.

EXHIBIT 12P-1. FORD
Pension Plan Disclosures for U.S. Plans

(in $millions)

		Years Ending December 31	
	1998	1999	2000
Pension Cost Components			
Service cost*	$ 475	$ 522	$ 495
Interest cost*	1,609	1,714	2,345
Expected return	(2,208)	(2,475)	(3,281)
Amortization of: transition (asset)	(23)	(22)	(13)
Plan amendments	565	471	742
Losses (gains)	53	(20)	(405)
Less: allocation to Visteon	—	—	(71)
Net pension cost (income)	**$ 471**	**$ 190**	**$ (188)**

*Note that these components differ from the amounts shown in the PBO and asset reconciliations; use these amounts to answer questions.

Discount rate used for expense	6.75%	6.25%	7.75%
Expected return on assets	9.00%	9.00%	9.50%
Reconciliation of PBO			
Opening balance		$33,003	$31,846
Service cost		650	535
Interest cost		2,099	2,388
Plan amendments		3,113	—
Actuarial loss (gain)		(5,298)	689
Benefits paid		(1,950)	(2,273)
Other changes (net)		229	97
Closing balance		**$31,846**	**$33,282**
Discount rate		7.75%	7.50%
Expected rate of compensation increase		5.20%	5.20%
Reconciliation of Plan Assets			
Opening balance		$38,417	$40,845
Return on plan assets		4,239	979
Contributions by Ford		6	8
Benefits paid		(1,950)	(2,273)
Other changes (net)		133	271
Closing balance		**$40,845**	**$39,830**
Funded Status			
Excess of plan assets over PBO		**$ 8,999**	**$ 6,548**
Unamortized: transition (asset)		(36)	(17)
Prior service cost		4,548	3,912
Actuarial losses (gains)		(12,037)	(8,540)
Accrued pension cost (liability)		**$ 1,474**	**$ 1,903**

Source: Ford Motor 2000 annual report.

b. Describe the effect of the 2000 discount rate changes on 2000 and 2001:

   (i) Service cost

   (ii) Interest cost

   (iii) Net pension cost

   (iv) PBO

c. Estimate how Ford arrived at its reported interest cost for 1999 and 2000 using the reported PBO.

d. Calculate the actual rate of return on Ford's U.S. plan assets for 1999 and 2000.

e. In 2000, Ford increased the expected return on plan assets used to calculate pension expense for its U.S. plans. Estimate the effect of this change on Ford's 2000

   (i) Pension cost

   (ii) Year-end plan status

   (iii) Year-end balance sheet

f. State the most likely explanation for the actuarial loss in 2000 and the actuarial gain in 1999.

5. [Analysis of Ford's U.S. pension plan disclosures] Use the data from Exhibit 12P-1 to answer the following questions.

a. Calculate each of the following for 1999 and 2000:

　(i) Recurring pension cost

　(ii) Gross pension cost

　(iii) Nonsmoothed pension cost

b. Forecast Ford's 2001 pension cost (U.S. plans), stating any assumptions.

c. Calculate and justify the adjustments you would make to Ford's balance sheet at December 31, 1999 and 2000 to reflect the economic position of its U.S. pension plans.

d. State the principal reason for the difference between the adjustments in part c for 1999 and 2000.

6. [Significance of plan amendments] The plan amendment in 1999 reflects increased benefits under Ford's union contracts covering U.S. employees whose benefits are flat (not pay-related).

a. Describe the effect of the amendment on

　(i) The funded status of the U.S. plans at December 31, 1999

　(ii) 2000 service cost

　(iii) 2000 interest cost

b. Discuss the implication of this amendment for the evaluation of the funded status and future cost associated with these plans.

7. [Analysis of pension plan disclosures] Exhibit 12P-2 provides information taken from Electronic Data Systems' [EDS] pension plan footnotes.

EXHIBIT 12P-2. ELECTRONIC DATA SYSTEMS
Pension Plan Disclosures

(in $millions)

	Years Ending December 31		
	1999	2000	2001
Pension Cost Components			
Service cost	$ 256	$ 251	$ 283
Interest cost	183	232	263
Expected return	(252)	(320)	(382)
Amortization of: transition liability	1	1	1
Plan amendments	(33)	(30)	(31)
Losses	16	1	8
Net curtailment and settlement loss (gain)	(11)	8	10
Net pension cost	**$ 160**	**$ 143**	**$ 152**
Expected return on assets	9.90%	9.90%	9.70%
Reconciliation of PBO			
Opening balance	**$2,569**	**$3,200**	**$3,538**
Service cost	256	251	283
Interest cost	183	232	263
Plan amendments	30	(12)	(35)
Actuarial loss (gain)	62	192	(98)
Benefits paid	(83)	(258)	(94)
Exchange rate effects	(64)	(106)	(53)
Curtailments, settlements, terminations	190	8	10
Other changes (net)	57	31	129
Closing balance	**$3,200**	**$3,538**	**$3,943**
Discount rate	7.00%	7.20%	7.00%
Expected rate of compensation increase	5.20%	5.20%	4.30%
Reconciliation of Plan Assets			
Opening balance	**$2,563**	**$3,224**	**$3,849**
Return on plan assets	588	752	(421)
EDS contributions	141	199	176
Benefits paid	(83)	(258)	(94)
Exchange rate effects	(34)	(98)	(46)
Other changes (net)	49	30	121
Closing balance	**$3,224**	**$3,849**	**$3,585**
Funded Status			
Excess of plan assets over PBO	**$ 24**	**$ 311**	**$ (358)**
Unamortized: transition liability	17	15	13
Prior service cost	(328)	(313)	(296)
Actuarial losses (gains)	152	(88)	598
Accrued pension cost (liability)	**$ (135)**	**$ (75)**	**$ (43)**

Source: Electronic Data Systems 2000 and 2001 annual reports.

a. The reconciliation of the PBO shows an actuarial loss in 2000 and an actuarial gain in 2001. Discuss the likely reasons for these changes.

b. Explain why the reconciliations of both the projected benefit obligation and plan assets have foreign exchange impacts and state the information conveyed by the direction of those changes.

c. Calculate each of the following for 1999–2001:

   (i) Recurring pension cost

   (ii) Gross pension cost

   (iii) Nonsmoothed pension cost

d. Compare the measures of pension cost calculated in part c with

   (i) Pension cost reported by EDS

   (ii) The pension plan cash flows

e. In 1999, EDS reported a change for special termination benefits as part of a large restructuring charge. Discuss whether this reporting decision should affect the computation of gross and nonsmoothed pension cost.

f. Discuss the trend in benefits paid over the 1999–2001 period and possible reasons for that trend.

g. Calculate the rate of return on assets for each year, 1999–2001.

h. Forecast the 2002 pension cost for EDS, stating any assumptions made.

i. Calculate and justify the adjustments you would make to EDS's balance sheet at December 31, 2000 and 2001 to reflect the economic position of its pension plans.

j. State the principal reason for the difference between the adjustments in part i for 2000 and 2001.

EXHIBIT 12P-3. AMR
Pension Plan Disclosures

(in $millions)

	Years Ending December 31		
	1998	1999	2000
Pension Cost Components			
Service cost	$ 213	$ 236	$ 213
Interest cost	418	433	467
Expected return	(478)	(514)	(490)
Amortization of: transition (asset)	(11)	(4)	(1)
Plan amendments	4	5	10
Losses (gains)	22	21	17
Settlement loss	6	—	—
Net pension cost	**$ 174**	**$ 177**	**$ 216**
Expected return on assets	9.50%	9.50%	9.50%
Reconciliation of PBO			
Opening balance	**$5,666**	**$6,117**	**$5,628**
Service cost	213	236	213
Interest cost	418	433	467
Plan amendments	—	75	—
Actuarial loss (gain)	300	(849)	499
Benefits paid	(464)	(388)	(373)
Other changes (net)	(16)	4	—
Closing balance	**$6,117**	**$5,628**	**$6,434**
Discount rate	7.00%	8.25%	7.75%
Expected rate of compensation increase	4.26%	4.26%	4.26%
Reconciliation of Plan Assets			
Opening Balance	**$5,127**	**$5,564**	**$5,282**
Return on plan assets	850	7	735
AMR contributions	70	100	85
Benefits paid	(464)	(388)	(373)
Other changes (net)	(19)	(1)	2
Closing balance	**$5,564**	**$5,282**	**$5,731**
Funded Status			
Excess of plan assets over PBO	**$ (553)**	**$ (346)**	**$ (703)**
Unamortized: transition (asset)	(11)	(7)	(6)
Prior service cost	68	139	129
Actuarial losses	651	288	523
Accrued pension cost (liability)	**$ 155**	**$ 74**	**$ (57)**

Source: AMR 1999 and 2000 annual reports.

8. [Analysis of pension plan disclosures] Exhibit 12P-3 contains pension plan data from the financial statement footnotes of AMR Corporation [AMR].

a. The PBO reconciliation shows a large actuarial gain (loss) in 1999 (2000). Explain why.

b. Calculate the following measures of pension cost for 1998–2000:
   (i) Recurring cost
   (ii) Gross pension cost
   (iii) Nonsmoothed pension cost

c. Calculate the rate of return on plan assets for 1999 and 2000 and discuss the effect of variations in that return on pension cost.

d. Forecast the 2001 pension cost for AMR, stating any assumptions.

e. Calculate and justify the adjustments you would make to AMR's balance sheet at December 31, 1999 and 2000 to reflect the economic position of its pension plans.

f. State the principal reason for the difference between the adjustments in part e for 1999 and 2000.

9. [Effect of investment performance on pension cost] Exhibit 12P-4 contains pension plan data from the 2001 financial statement footnotes of General Electric [GE]. GE reported that the expected return on assets assumption for 2002 would be 8.5%, compared with 9.5% for 2001.

a. Estimate the expected return on assets component of GE's 2002 pension cost and compare that amount with the 2001 component.

b. Compute the effect on the expected return on assets component of GE's 2002 pension cost of each of the following:
   (i) Change in ROA assumption
   (ii) Negative return on assets in 2001 (assume that GE had earned its expected ROA in that year)

10. [Effect of transition asset on pension cost] Exhibit 12P-4 contains pension plan data from the 2001 financial statement footnotes of General Electric [GE].

a. Describe the origin of the "amortization of transition asset" component of 2000 pension cost.

b. Explain why that component does not appear in 2001.

11. [Taxable pension plans] Principal Financial [PFG] reported in its 2000 annual report that the expected return on plan assets was 5% for taxable plans and 8.1% for nontaxable plans.

a. Explain why a different return on assets assumption is required for taxable plans.

b. Compute the implied income tax rate on taxable plans, assuming no other difference between taxable and nontaxable plans.

c. Discuss why Principal may have chosen to fund these plans despite their taxable status.

12. [Analysis of pension plan disclosures] Exhibit 12P-5 contains pension plan data for Lucent [LU] for the five years ended September 30, 2001.

a. Compute the four-year totals for the following:
   (i) Recurring cost
   (ii) Gross pension cost
   (iii) Nonsmoothed pension cost
   (iv) Benefits paid
   (v) Pension plan contributions
   (vi) Reported pension cost

b. Select the four-year total computed in part a that best describes the economic cost of Lucent's pension plans and explain why the four-year total reported cost is different.

c. Explain why Lucent was able to make minimal contributions to its pension plans over the period despite large benefit payments.

d. State and justify the conditions (if any) under which the low level of contributions is likely to continue over the four-year period ending in 2005.

EXHIBIT 12P-4. GENERAL ELECTRIC
Pension Plan Disclosures

(in $millions)

	Years Ending December 31			Years Ending December 31	
	2000	2001		2000	2001
Pension Cost Components			*Reconciliation of Plan Assets*		
Service cost	$ 780	$ 884	**Opening balance**	**$50,243**	**$49,757**
Interest cost	1,966	2,065	Return on plan assets	1,287	(2,876)
Expected return	(3,754)	(4,327)	GE contributions	85	75
Amortization of transition asset	(154)	—	Benefits paid	(1,998)	(2,091)
All other components (net)	(582)	(717)	Other changes (net)	140	141
Net pension cost income	**$(1,744)**	**$(2,095)**	**Closing balance**	**$49,757**	**$45,006**
Expected return on assets	9.50%	9.50%			

Source: General Electric 2001 annual report.

EXHIBIT 12P-5. LUCENT
Pension Plan Disclosures

(in $millions)

		Years Ending September 30			
	1997	1998	1999	2000	2001
Pension Cost Components					
Service cost	$ 312	$ 331	$ 509	$ 478	$ 316
Interest cost	1,604	1,631	1,671	1,915	1,926
Expected return	(2,150)	(2,384)	(2,957)	(3,229)	(3,373)
Amortization of: transition asset	(300)	(300)	(300)	(300)	(222)
Plan amendments	149	164	461	362	326
Losses	—	—	2	(197)	(387)
Net curtailment and settlement loss (gain)	56	—	—	—	2,504
Net pension cost (income)	**$ (329)**	**$ (558)**	**$ (614)**	**$ (971)**	**$ 1,090**
Expected return on assets	9.00%	9.00%	9.00%	9.00%	9.00%
Reconciliation of PBO					
Opening balance		$23,187	$27,846	$27,401	$26,113
Service cost		331	509	478	316
Interest cost		1,631	1,671	1,915	1,926
Plan amendments		626	1,534	(1)	9
Actuarial loss (gain)		3,811	(2,182)	370	1,434
Benefits paid		(1,740)	(1,977)	(2,294)	(2,788)
Avaya spinoff		—	—	(1,756)	174
Curtailments, settlements, terminations		—	—	—	2,666
Closing balance	**$23,187**	**$27,846**	**$27,401**	**$26,113**	**$29,850**
Discount rate	7.25%	6.00%	7.25%	7.50%	7.00%
Expected rate of compensation increase	4.50%	4.50%	4.50%	4.50%	4.50%
Reconciliation of Plan Assets					
Opening balance		$36,204	$36,191	$41,067	$45,262
Return on plan assets		1,914	7,114	9,791	(6,830)
Lucent contributions		12	14	19	25
Benefits paid		(1,740)	(1,977)	(2,294)	(2,788)
Avaya spinoff				(2,984)	259
Other changes (net)		(199)	(275)	(337)	(389)
Closing balance	**$36,204**	**$36,191**	**$41,067**	**$45,262**	**$35,539**
Funded Status					
Excess of plan assets over PBO	**$13,017**	**$ 8,345**	**$13,666**	**$19,149**	**$ 5,689**
Unamortized: transition asset	(1,244)	(944)	(645)	(322)	(103)
Prior service cost	1,048	1,509	2,583	2,086	1,228
Actuarial losses (gains)	(9,669)	(5,175)	(9,466)	(14,499)	(1,790)
Accrued pension cost (liability)	**$ 3,152**	**$ 3,735**	**$ 6,138**	**$ 6,414**	**$ 5,024**

Source: Lucent annual reports, 1999 to 2001.

13. [Effect of change in accounting method] Effective the year ending October 1, 1999, Lucent [LU] changed its method of calculating the expected return on assets component of pension cost from the market-related method (valuation changes recognized over a five-year period) to use of the full market value of plan assets.

a. State one advantage and one disadvantage of using the market-related value of assets to compute the expected return.

b. Explain why making the accounting change in 1999 resulted in a greater effect than if the change had been made in 1998.

c. Describe how the accounting change affected pension cost in fiscal years after 1999.

d. In addition to the $427 million effect of the accounting change in fiscal 1999, there was a cumulative effect of $2,150 million. Discuss whether the cumulative effect should be included in operating income for 1998.

14. [Analysis of disclosures under IAS standards] Exhibit 12P-6 contains benefit plan data from the 2000 and 2001 financial statement footnotes of Roche.

a. Compute the actual rate of return on plan assets for 2000 and 2001 and compare those rates to the expected rates.

b. Discuss the most likely reason for the change in the unrecognized actuarial (gains) losses from 1999 to 2001.

EXHIBIT 12P-6. ROCHE
Benefit Plan Disclosures

(in CHFmillions)

	Years Ending December 31		
	1999	2000	2001
Benefit Cost Components			
Service cost	311	333	362
Interest cost	677	675	685
Expected return	(645)	(714)	(761)
Plan amendments	7	3	5
Amortization of losses (gains)	—	2	(12)
Curtailment (gains)	(28)	(1)	(15)
Net benefit cost	322	298	264
Discount rates	3% to 8%	3% to 8%	3% to 8%
Expected return on assets	3.5% to 10%	3% to 10%	3% to 10%
Compensation growth rate	2.5% to 9%	2% to 9%	2% to 9%
Healthcare cost trend rate	4% to 9%	4% to 10%	5% to 10%
Actual return on assets	932	1,175	(1,334)
Unfunded Plans			
Recognized liability	**(2,648)**	**(2,423)**	**(2,440)**
Funded Plans			
Actuarial present value	(9,028)	(9,034)	(9,575)
Plan assets	10,046	10,448	9,401
Excess of plan assets over PBO	**1,018**	**1,414**	**(174)**
Unrecognized actuarial (gains) losses	(467)	(862)	731
Unamortized prior service cost	19	22	46
Accrued pension cost	**570**	**574**	**603**
Liability for postemployment benefits	(2,764)	(2,502)	(2,610)
Included in long-term assets	686	653	773
Total net liability recognized	**(2,078)**	**(1,849)**	**(1,837)**
Value of Roche shares in plan assets	**32**	**149**	**77**
Reconciliation of Recognized Liability			
Net liability at January 1	(2,068)	(2,078)	(1,849)
Consolidation effects	(4)	84	—
Benefit cost	(322)	(298)	(264)
Roche contributions	165	174	177
Benefits paid—unfunded plans	125	135	116
Exchange rate and other effects	26	134	(17)
Net liability at December 31	**(2,078)**	**(1,849)**	**(1,837)**
Nonpension Plans Included in Above			
Actuarial present value	703	690	737
Plan assets	576	649	530
Net liability recognized	190	147	257
Unrecognized actuarial gains	63	106	50

Source: Roche 2000 and 2001 annual reports.

c. Compute the overall (pension and nonpension) funded status of Roche plans for 1999–2001 and the adjustment(s) to Roche's financial statements required to reflect the economic status of its benefit plans. [*Note:* Assume that for the unfunded pension plans, the PBO equals the Recognized Liability.]

d. The adjustments in part c were for Roche's pension and nonpension plans. Disaggregate that adjustment into the portion attributable to Roche's
  (i) Pension plans
  (ii) Nonpension plans

e. Discuss the benefits and drawbacks of having plan investments that include Roche shares.

f. Discuss the differences between Roche's disclosures and the requirements of SFAS 132.

g. List the questions that you would like to ask Roche management about its benefit plans.

15. [Effect of postretirement plan assumptions; CFA© adapted] A security analyst concludes that a company has increased reported earnings by changing assumptions for its postretirement health care plans. Explain the change in *each* of the following assumptions that would increase reported earnings. [*Note:* State any additional assumptions required for this effect.]

    (i) Discount rate

    (ii) Rate of compensation increase

    (iii) Estimated return on plan assets

    (iv) Estimated future health care inflation rate

16. [Analysis of postretirement benefit plans; Westvaco] Use Note M of Westvaco's 1999 financial statements to answer the following questions:

    a. The number of Westvaco employees fell from 1997 to 1999. Explain why this reduction would have decreased service cost and resulted in actuarial gains for the company's postretirement benefit plans.

b. Explain why there is no expected return on assets component in postretirement benefit cost.

c. Calculate each of the following for 1998 and 1999:

    (i) Recurring postretirement cost

    (ii) Gross postretirement cost

    (iii) Nonsmoothed postretirement cost

d. Compare the measures of postretirement benefit costs calculated in part c with

    (i) Postretirement benefit cost reported by Westvaco

    (ii) Cash flows associated with the postretirement benefits

e. Forecast fiscal 2000 postretirement benefit cost, stating any assumptions.

f. Calculate and justify the adjustments you would make to Westvaco's balance sheet at October 31, 1999 to reflect the economic position of its pension plan.

g. State the principal reason for the difference between the adjustment in part f and the adjustment required at October 31, 1998.

EXHIBIT 12P-7: AMR
Postretirement Health and Life Benefit Plan Disclosures

(in $millions)

	Years Ending December 31		
	1998	1999	2000
Benefit Cost Components			
Service cost	$ 52	$ 56	$ 43
Interest cost	99	108	108
Expected return	(5)	(6)	(7)
Amortization of:			
Prior service cost	(5)	(5)	(5)
Unrecognized loss (gain)	(2)	—	(14)
Net benefit cost	**$ 139**	**$ 153**	**$ 125**
Expected return on assets	9.50%	9.50%	9.50%
Reconciliation of APBO			
Opening balance	**$ 1,356**	**$ 1,526**	**$ 1,306**
Service cost	52	56	43
Interest cost	99	108	108
Actuarial loss (gain)	84	(311)	328
Benefits paid	(65)	(70)	(77)
Curtailments/settlements/termination benefits	—	(3)	—
Closing balance	**$ 1,526**	**$ 1,306**	**$ 1,708**
Discount rate	7.00%	8.25%	7.75%
Reconciliation of Plan Assets			
Opening balance	**$ 49**	**$ 62**	**$ 72**
Return on plan assets	4	1	.5
AMR contributions	74	79	88
Benefits paid	(65)	(70)	(77)
Closing balance	**$ 62**	**$ 72**	**$ 88**
Funded Status			
Excess of plan assets over APBO	**$(1,464)**	**$(1,234)**	**$(1,620)**
Unamortized:			
Prior service cost	(45)	(40)	(35)
Actuarial loss (gain)	(89)	(395)	(51)
Accrued benefit cost (liability)	**$(1,598)**	**$(1,669)**	**$(1,706)**

Source: AMR 1999 and 2000 annual reports.

17. [Analysis of OPEB disclosures] Exhibit 12P-7 contains health care and life insurance benefit plan data from the 1999 and 2000 financial statement footnotes of AMR.

a. Effective December 31, 2000 AMR increased its assumed health care cost trend to 7% (declining to 4% by 2004) from 5% (declining to 4% by 2001) in 1999. Describe the effect of this change on:

  (i) The benefit obligation at year-end 2000.

  (ii) Net benefit cost for 2001.

b. Explain the origin of the actuarial gain in 1999 and loss in 2000.

c. State two possible reasons why 2000 service cost declined.

d. Explain why interest cost in 2000 equaled the 1999 amount despite the lower benefit obligation.

e. Calculate each of the following for 1999 and 2000:

  (i) Recurring postretirement cost

  (ii) Gross postretirement cost

  (iii) Nonsmoothed postretirement cost

f. Explain the origin and likely future trend of the amortization of prior service cost component of the net benefit cost.

g. Explain why net benefit cost included the amortization of unrecognized gain in 2000 but not in 1999. Explain how the amount amortized was computed.

h. Forecast 2001 postretirement benefit cost, stating any assumptions.

i. Calculate and justify the adjustments you would make to AMR's balance sheet at December 31, 2000 to reflect the economic position of its postretirement benefit plans.

j. State the principal reason for the difference between the adjustment in part i and the adjustment required at December 31, 1999.

k. Explain why the accrued benefit liability increased over the two years ended December 31, 2000 despite the decline in the net benefit cost.

18. [Sensitivity to changes in the assumed health care cost rate] AMR reported that a 1% change in the assumed health care cost rate would have the following effects (in $millions):

	December 31, 1999		December 31, 2000	
	1% Increase	1% Decrease	1% Increase	1% Decrease
Service and interest cost	$24	$(22)	$20	$(19)
Benefit obligation	115	(105)	137	(131)

Using this table and Exhibit 12P-7, compare the sensitivity of AMR's postretirement plan obligations to changes in the health care cost trend rate for 1999 and 2000.

 19. [Analysis of postretirement benefit plan disclosures] Note 5 of Sears's 1999 annual report contains disclosures regarding postretirement benefits.

a. Explain the origin and likely future trend of the unrecognized prior service benefit.

b. Explain the origin of the actuarial gain in 1999.

c. Forecast 2000 postretirement benefit cost, stating any assumptions.

d. Calculate and justify the adjustments you would make to Sears's balance sheet at December 31, 1999 to reflect the economic position of its postretirement benefit plans.

e. Explain why Sears's plan contribution is exactly equal to benefits paid.

20. [Analysis of postretirement benefit plan disclosures] Exhibit 12P-8 contains health care and life insurance benefit plan data from the 2000 and 2001 financial statement footnotes of General Electric [GE].

a. Describe the impact of the 2000 plan amendments on:

  (i) 2000 plan status

  (ii) The trend of service cost

  (iii) The trend of prior service cost amortization

b. Discuss the size and direction of actuarial gains and losses in reference to the assumed discount rate. State the information conveyed by the gains and losses not explained by discount rate changes.

c. Compare the level and trend of postretirement benefit cost (on an economic basis and as reported), GE contributions, and benefits paid, and discuss any differences.

d. Explain why the expected return component of benefit cost increased in 1999–2001 despite a steady decline in plan assets.

e. Forecast 2002 postretirement benefit cost, stating any assumptions. GE states that the expected return on assets for 2002 will be 8.5%.

f. Redo part e assuming no change in the expected return on assets from 2001.

g. Calculate and justify the adjustments you would make to GE's balance sheet at December 31, 2001 to reflect the economic position of its postretirement benefit plans.

h. State the *two* principal reasons for the difference between the adjustment amount in part g and the adjustment required at December 31, 1999.

EXHIBIT 12P-8. GENERAL ELECTRIC
Postretirement Health and Life Benefit Plan Disclosures

(in $millions)

		Years Ending December 31		
	1998	1999	2000	2001
Benefit Cost Components				
Service cost		$ 107	$ 165	$ 191
Interest cost		323	402	459
Expected return		(165)	(178)	(185)
Amortization of:				
Prior service cost		8	49	90
Unrecognized loss (gain)		45	40	60
Net benefit cost		**$ 318**	**$ 478**	**$ 615**
Expected return on assets	9.50%	9.50%	9.50%	9.50%
Reconciliation of APBO				
Opening balance		**$ 5,007**	**$ 4,926**	**$ 6,422**
Service cost		107	165	191
Interest cost		323	402	459
Plan amendments		—	948	—
Actuarial loss (gain)		(62)	534	287
Benefits paid		(499)	(578)	(593)
Participant contributions		24	25	30
Other		26	—	—
Closing balance		**$ 4,926**	**$ 6,422**	**$ 6,796**
Discount rate	7.50%	7.75%	7.50%	7.25%
Rate of compensation increase	5.00%	5.00%	5.00%	5.00%
Reconciliation of Plan Assets				
Opening balance		**$ 2,121**	**$ 2,369**	**$ 2,031**
Return on plan assets		355	(85)	(163)
GE contributions		368	300	466
Participant contributions		24	25	30
Benefits paid		(499)	(578)	(593)
Closing balance		**$ 2,369**	**$ 2,031**	**$ 1,771**
Funded Status				
Excess of plan assets over APBO		**$(2,557)**	**$(4,391)**	**$(5,025)**
Unamortized:				
Prior service cost		100	999	909
Actuarial loss (gain)		61	818	1,393
Accrued benefit cost (liability)		**$(2,396)**	**$(2,574)**	**$(2,723)**

Source: General Electric 2000 and 2001 annual reports.

21. [Stock options plans] Note 16 of Pfizer's 1999 annual report contains data on its stock option plans.

a. State and justify whether valuation of Pfizer shares should be based on *as reported* or *pro forma* diluted earnings per share.

b. Explain the principal factor accounting for the increase in the fair value of options issued in 1999 compared with options issued in 1997 and 1998.

c. State and justify the effect of an increase in each of the following on the fair value of options:

  (i) Expected dividend yield

  (ii) Risk-free interest rate

  (iii) Expected stock price volatility

  (iv) Expected years until exercise

d. Calculate the effect on Pfizer's book value per share at December 31, 1999 of the exercise of all options outstanding with an exercise price below Pfizer's stock price at December 31, 1999 of $32.4375. Explain the usefulness of this calculation.

e. Pfizer reports substantial tax benefits related to stock option transactions. State and justify whether these benefits should be considered part of cash from operations.

f. State and justify whether these benefits should be considered part of cash from operations if Pfizer recognized the cost of stock option grants in reported income.

22. [Stock option repricing program] At a special meeting on January 25, 2002, the stockholders of Eastman Kodak [EK] approved a stock option exchange program, under which employees were permitted to exchange existing options for fewer options at a new (lower) exercise price. New options would be issued six months and one day following cancellation of the old ones. Because of declines in the market price of EK shares, most existing options had exercise prices well above the current market price.

a. Discuss the motivation for the exchange program.

b. The company stated that "the program has been designed so that we will avoid any variable accounting compensation charges against our earnings"[56] State and justify any analytical adjustments that should be made to EK's financial statements as a result of the exchange program.

[56]Proxy statement dated December 31, 2001, p. 9.

13

ANALYSIS OF INTERCORPORATE INVESTMENTS

CHAPTER OUTLINE

CHAPTER OBJECTIVES

The goal of this chapter is to enhance the understanding of the accounting and analysis issues related to intercorporate investments. Specific objectives include:

1. Differentiate between the return earned on investments in marketable securities and the recognition of that return in financial statements.

2. Compute the mark-to market return on portfolios of marketable securities.

3. Discuss the conditions under which the equity method is required.

4. Compare the financial statement effects of the equity method of accounting with the accounting for marketable securities.

5. Discuss the conditions under which consolidation is required.

6. Compare the financial statement effects of the equity method of accounting with the effects of consolidation.

7. Discuss the use of proportionate consolidation as an accounting method and tool for analysis.

8. Compare the financial statement effects of proportionate consolidation with the equity method of accounting.

9. Define minority interest and discuss its significance in financial analysis.

10. Compare the disclosure requirements for segment data under U.S. and IAS GAAP.

11. Show how segment data can be used to enhance the understanding of firms with operations in more than one industry.

INTRODUCTION

The modern company rarely consists of a single corporate entity. The larger the enterprise, the more likely that it will contain more than one unit; large multinationals may have hundreds of subsidiaries in dozens of jurisdictions. In addition, large enterprises frequently invest in other entities, including joint ventures and partnerships. In this chapter, we examine the accounting principles applicable to intercorporate investments, evaluate the impact of the reporting choice on the financial statements, and discuss applicable analytical techniques.

Enterprises invest in the securities of other companies for various reasons. Intercorporate investments may involve temporary purchases of equity or debt securities to capture dividends, interest income, or capital gains. Risk sharing or participation in new markets of technologies may also motivate investments. Finally, the investment may be a precursor to an acquisition.

Financial reporting of intercorporate investments depends primarily on the degree of investor influence or control over the investee. Percentage of ownership[1] in the investee firm is often used as a practical guideline to measure significant influence or control:

Ownership Level	Degree of Influence	Reporting Method
<20%	No significant influence	Cost or market
20–50%	Significant influence	Equity method
>50%	Control	Consolidation

These ownership percentages, however, are merely guidelines. If significant influence exists with ownership below 20%, the equity method may be used. Similarly, if control does not exist even with ownership of above 50%, consolidation is not appropriate.

The FASB has proposed[2] a modified definition of control, *effective rather than legal control*, paving the way for consolidation even when the investor owns less than 50% of the investee. However, that proposal is still a matter of fierce debate and has yet to be adopted.

The primary conceptual distinction among the different reporting requirements is the extent to which the investee (affiliate) constitutes an integral part of the investor (parent) company. Under the cost and market methods, the two firms are treated as separate entities and the parent's income from its investment is based on actual dividends received and any changes in market value of the investment.[3]

The parent's ability to exercise significant influence over the operating and strategic activities of the affiliate provides the rationale for the equity method: Income reported by the

---

[1]Percentage ownership may be defined by either ownership or voting control of investee common stock.

[2]See FASB exposure draft, Consolidated Financial Statements: Policy and Procedures (1999), a revision of an earlier (1995) exposure draft. Details of the ED are provided in Box 13-3.

[3]Under the cost method, changes in market value are recognized only on sale or impairment.

parent includes its share (in proportion to ownership) of the income reported by the affiliate. The parent's proportionate shares of dividends declared by the affiliate is reported as a reduction in the carrying amount of the investment to reflect the corresponding decline in the net assets of the affiliate. Reported income under the equity method is not affected by changes in market prices, unless the price decline is considered permanent or the investment is sold.

Finally, consolidated reporting views the two companies as a unified economic entity even when they are legally separate. The entire income of the affiliate (net of intercompany transactions) is added to that of the parent, adjusted for income attributable to the noncontrolling shareholders' minority interest.

INVESTMENTS IN SECURITIES

Enterprises often invest in the common and preferred shares, bonds, or other securities of other entities. Generally, when such investments are small relative to the capital of the investee (measured by the amount of outstanding voting common stock held), the investor is unlikely to have the ability to influence the activities of the investee.

Over the life of the investment, the total return earned on the investment equals

Dividends and Interest Received + Capital Gain or Loss

The following accounting methods used to report the investments in securities of other entities recognize dividends and interest as part of income in the year they are earned; they differ as to when changes in the market value of the asset are recognized:

- The *cost* method recognizes changes in market value only in the period the securities are sold.
- The *market* method mirrors the actual economic performance of the security and recognizes changes in market prices in the period they occur.
- *Lower of cost or market* (LOCOM) recognizes price changes prior to sale only when the market value *declines below original cost*.

These three methods are illustrated using the following data:

- Company P purchases 1 share (out of 100 shares outstanding) of Company S for $100.
- Company S reports net income of $25 per share for period 1 and declares dividends of $10 per share on its common stock.
- The market value of Company S's shares rises to $135 per share at the end of period 1.
- Company P sells its share of Company S for $120 during period 2.

Cost Method

Under the cost method, assets are reported at their amortized cost.[4] Market value changes are not recognized until there is an actual transaction (sale). Only dividends and interest received from the investee and realized gains and losses are recognized.

At acquisition, Company P reports the purchased asset on its balance sheet at the acquisition cost as follows:[5]

Investment in Company S $100

For period 1, Company P's income statement would include (as other income) the following:

Dividend received $10

---

[4]Premiums or discounts from the face amount of fixed income investments are amortized over the life of the debt issue using the interest method (see Chapter 10 for a discussion from the point of view of the debt issuer).

[5]The account title may not identify a specific company but may use a more general term such as marketable securities or investments in affiliate(s).

At the end of period 1, Company P does not record the increase in market price of the shares of Company S. When the security is sold, Company P recognizes the realized gain or loss equal to the difference between the proceeds of the sale and the original cost, $120 − $100, or $20 in our example, yielding a total two-period return (dividend + capital gain) of $30 on the investment.

In the absence of a dividend, sale, or writedown of the investment, the operating, financing, and investing activities of Company S have no impact on the financial statements of Company P. The carrying value of the investment remains $100 until the investment is sold. A writedown of the investment to its estimated market value is required only when Company P determines that it has been permanently impaired (e.g., due to financial problems of Company S). In that case, the writedown is recognized in current period income. The estimated market value becomes the new carrying amount. Upon subsequent sale of the investment, gain or loss would be determined by comparing the proceeds of sale with this new carrying amount, not the original cost. Writedowns cannot be restored under U.S. GAAP, regardless of future circumstances.

Market Method

Under the market method, securities with a *public market* are carried at their current market value. Unrealized changes in market value (from period to period) are included in net income[6] along with dividends, interest, and realized gains and losses.

In our example, the carrying value on Company P's books increases to $135 and an (unrealized) capital gain of $35 is reported to recognize the increase in the market value of Company S shares to $135 at the end of period 1. Total return (dividend + capital gain) in period 1 is $45. When the investment is sold for $120 in period 2, a loss of $15 is recognized. The total (two-period) return remains $30 as under the cost method. However, the returns recognized each period differ considerably. *The market method reflects the actual economic return earned on the investment in each time period.*

Lower of Cost or Market Method

LOCOM takes a conservative approach and recognizes unrealized losses (but not gains) and recoveries of previously recognized unrealized losses. In our example, market value is higher than cost at the end of period 1; therefore, no market value change is recognized. When market value is below cost, LOCOM produces the same result as the market method.

The methods can be summarized as follows:

Method	Balance Sheet (Carrying Value)	Income Statement (Recognized as Income)
Cost	Cost	Dividends and interest Realized gains and losses
Market	Market value	Dividends and interest Realized and unrealized gains and losses
LOCOM	LOCOM	Dividends and interest Realized gains and losses Unrealized losses and recoveries[7]

U.S. Accounting Standards for Investments in Securities

In the United States, the provisions of SFAS 115 (1993) require a hybrid of the cost and market methods.

The cost method is used for securities with no readily available market price (i.e., they are not publicly traded). Securities that have a public market or readily determined fair value must be classified into three categories:

1. *Held-to-maturity.* The cost method is used to report holdings of debt securities at amortized cost. Interest income and realized gains and losses are reported in income.

---

[6]As discussed in a subsequent section, unrealized changes in market values are reported in stockholders' equity when securities are classified as available-for-sale.

[7]. . . of previously recognized losses.

2. *Available-for-sale.* The market method is applied to record these debt and equity securities as assets at fair market value. Although dividends, interest income, and realized gains and losses are reported in income, unrealized gains and losses are reported (net of deferred income tax) as a separate component of other comprehensive income in stockholders' equity.

3. *Trading securities.* The market method is used to report these debt and equity securities as current assets at fair market value. Dividends, interest income, and all gains and losses (realized and unrealized) are reported in income.

The financial statement effects of classification are summarized below:

Portfolio	Balance Sheet (Carrying Value)	Income Statement (Recognized as Income)
Held-to-maturity	Cost	Interest Realized gains and losses
Available-for-sale	Market value	Dividends and interest Realized gains and losses
Trading	Market value	Dividends and interest Realized gains and losses Unrealized gains and losses

Classification Criteria

The classification decision depends on management intent, an inherently subjective standard. However, it is not a completely free choice. SFAS 115 establishes criteria governing the designation of securities among the three portfolio categories. These criteria are intended to ensure that portfolio holdings conform to the conceptual basis for the accounting principles used and to preclude arbitrary transfers among portfolios intended to circumvent those accounting principles.

To classify debt securities as held-to-maturity, the firm must have *both the intent and the ability* to do so. The intent requirement means that held-to-maturity securities cannot be sold prior to maturity except in exceptional circumstances.[8] Actively managed portfolios, therefore, must be classified as available-for-sale.

Transfers between portfolios are subject to special rules:

- Securities are transferred to the trading portfolio at fair market value; any unrealized gain or loss must be included in income.
- Debt securities from the held-to-maturity category are transferred to the available-for-sale portfolio at fair market value; any unrealized gain or loss is included in equity.
- Available-for-sale debt securities are transferred to held-for-maturity at fair market value; any unrealized gain or loss remains in equity but must be amortized over the remaining life of the bond.

The intent of the transfer rules is to prevent selective recognition of gains or losses merely by reclassifying securities among portfolios.[9] As discussed shortly, some scope for manipulation remains.

Exhibit 13-1 compares the accounting for marketable securities (trading and available-for-sale) to that of securities carried at cost.[10] Note the dichotomy in the accounting for available-for-sale securities. Market value is used on the balance sheet, as it is for the trading portfolio; both differ markedly from the cost method used for held-to-maturity investments. However, changes in market value of available-for-sale securities are excluded from reported

---

[8]SFAS 115 (para. 8) identifies the following *exceptional* changes in circumstances: significant deterioration in credit rating, change in tax law or regulatory requirements, or a major acquisition or disposition.

[9]However, the FASB has permitted companies to reclassify investment portfolios in conjunction with new accounting standards.

[10]The exhibit also shows results for the "equity method," covered later in the chapter.

EXHIBIT 13-1
Comparison of Accounting Methods for Intercorporate Investments

Assumptions

Year	Shares Purchased (Sold)	Price/Share
20X1	100	$80
20X2	(30)	60
20X3	40	70

Note: All sales and purchases assumed to occur on January 1. Price may vary from price on previous day (December 31).

	20X1	20X2	20X3
Investee earnings per share	$7	$8	$7
Investee dividend per share	2	2	2

Year-End Holdings Valued at Cost and Market

	No. of Shares	Cost/Share	Total Cost	Price/Share	Market Value
20X1	100	$80	$8,000	$70	$7,000
20X2	70	80	5,600	80	5,600
20X3	70	80	5,600	90	6,300
	40	70	2,800	90	3,600
			$8,400		$9,900

Accounting Methods

		Balance Sheet Carrying Amount		
Classification	Carried at	20X1	20X2	20X3
Held-to-maturity	Amortized cost	$8,000	$5,600	$8,400
Trading	Market value	7,000	5,600	9,900
Available-for-sale	Market value	7,000	5,600	9,900
Equity method	Cost plus equity in reinvested earnings	8,500	6,370	9,720

Total Investment Income

Classification	Measurement	20X1	20X2	20X3
Held-to-maturity	Dividends + realized G/L	$200	$(460)	$220
Trading	Dividends + all G/L	(800)	540	1,720
Available-for-sale	Dividends + realized G/L	200	(460)	220
Equity method	Share of investee earnings + realized G/L	700	(190)	770

Components of Investment Income

	20X1	20X2	20X3
Dividend income			
All methods except equity method	$200	$140	$220
Equity method		Not Relevant	
Equity in earnings of investee			
Equity method only	$700	$560	$770
(EPS × number of shares held)			
Recognized gains and losses			
Held-to-maturity Realized only	$ 0	$(600)	$ 0
Trading Realized and unrealized	(1,000)	400*	1,500
Available-for-sale Realized only	0	(600)	0
Equity method Realized only	0	(750)†	0

*30 × ($60 − $70) = $(300) Loss on sale
70 × ($80 − $70) = $700 Unrealized gain
                    $ 400

†Loss on shares sold = 30 × ($80 + $5 − $60) as sales proceeds must be compared with carrying value at date of sale.

income, although included in comprehensive income. Only the trading portfolio is marked to market for both reported income and balance sheet purposes. Finally, the reported operating performance of the investee (earnings or cash flow) does not affect the accounting in any of these cases.

IAS GAAP

The requirements of IAS 39 (1998) are quite similar to those of U.S. GAAP. The most significant differences related to the accounting for marketable securities are:

1. Securities that are not considered held-to-maturity are remeasured at market value at each balance sheet date. Under IAS 39, the firm may:
   - Recognize all gains and losses in income, or
   - Recognize gains or losses only on securities designated as trading (as under U.S. GAAP).

   The difference is that, under IAS GAAP, gains and losses recognized in income may include those on investments whose gains and losses are recorded in other comprehensive income under U.S. GAAP.

2. Under both U.S. and IAS GAAP, firms that violate the conditions for maintaining a held-to-maturity portfolio must reclassify such holdings as available-for-sale. Under IAS 39, such tainting expires after two years, permitting companies to reestablish a held-to-maturity portfolio.

Non-U.S. Accounting Standards

Outside of U.S. and IAS GAAP, cost and LOCOM are widely used. For example, AXA [AXA], a French insurance company that reports under French GAAP, uses the cost method:

> **Valuation of Investments[11]**
> FIXED MATURITY SECURITIES are stated at amortized cost, less valuation allowances. Purchase premium or discount is amortized over the life of the security. Generally, valuation allowances are recorded for declines in the value of a specific fixed maturity security that are deemed to be permanent. In the case of AXA's non-European subsidiaries, the amortized cost of fixed maturity securities is written down for impairments in value deemed to be other than temporary.
>
> EQUITY SECURITIES are stated at cost. For a decline in the estimated fair value of a specific equity investment that is deemed to be other than temporary, AXA's European subsidiaries record a valuation allowance and AXA's non-European subsidiaries directly write down the equity investments. Investments in mutual funds are included in equity securities.

Use of the cost method results in balance sheet carrying amounts that understate (overstate) assets and stockholders' equity when fair values exceed (are below) cost. As AXA discloses the fair value of its investments, the analyst should adjust AXA's balance sheet to achieve comparability with companies using U.S. or IAS GAAP. The fair value data disclosures also permit computation of the mark-to-market return, using the method described in the next section.

Japan, on, the other hand, changed from LOCOM to standards very similar to SFAS 115 in 2000. Takeda Chemical adopted the new standard in fiscal 2001, showing unrealized gains of ¥122 billion in the stockholders' equity section of its March 31, 2001 balance sheet. Reported equity (and book value per share) was increased 11% compared with amounts excluding the unrealized gains. These gains related to available-for-sale equity securities with total market values exceeding six times their historical cost.

---

[11]Source: AXA 2000 annual report.

ANALYSIS OF MARKETABLE SECURITIES

The following issues are important to the analysis of marketable securities:

1. The need to segregate the operating results of the firm from its investment results[12]
2. The differential effects of portfolio classification
3. The assessment of investment results

Separation of Operating from Investment Results

Although the success of corporate investments enhances the value of the enterprise, investment results and operating results must be clearly segregated and analyzed separately. Reported income from investments can distort operating trends. It is important to know how the firm's core business performs apart from investment results.

Helmerich & Payne [HP], an oil and gas company, has extensive holdings (approximately 20% of total assets) of marketable securities. HP's condensed income statements for the years 1996 to 1998 are shown in Exhibit 13-2. The company's aggregate pretax income increased in 1997 and 1998. However, when we separate operating results from investment income, we find that in 1998 operating income *decreased*. The overall increase for the year was due to investment performance.

EXHIBIT 13-2. HELMERICH & PAYNE
Marketable Securities: Disaggregation of Operating and Investment Results
1996 to 1998 (in $millions)

Condensed Income Statements			
	1996	1997	1998
Sales and operating revenues	$387.5	$506.4	$592.0
Investment income	5.8	11.4	44.6
Total revenues	$393.3	$517.8	$636.6
Operating costs	(323.7)	(390.4)	(484.4)
Pretax income	$ 69.6	$127.4	$152.2
Year-to-year change		57.8	24.8
Percentage change		83.0%	19.5%

Disaggregation of Operating and Investment Results			
	1996	1997	1998
Operating income	$ 63.8	$116.0	$107.6
Year-to-year change		52.2	(8.4)
Percentage change		81.8%	(7.2%)
Investment income	$ 5.8	$ 11.4	$ 44.6
Year-to-year change		5.6	33.2
Percentage change		96.6%	291.2%

Source: Helmerich & Payne, *1997–1998 Annual Reports.*

---

[12]See chapter footnote 46 reference to Foster (1975).

Segregation of operating from investment performance facilitates the analysis of HP's:

1. *Operating performance* relative to other firms in its industry (oil and gas)
2. *Investment performance* compared to investment benchmarks

However, *reported* data should *not* be used to analyze investment performance. Reported results are a function of accounting classifications and a hybrid of cost/market measurement bases that may distort the reported portfolio performance. This issue is explored further shortly.

Effects of Classification of Marketable Securities Under SFAS 115

The classification choice under SFAS 115 can affect *both*:

1. The firm's *reported* financial performance
2. The firm's financing and investment decisions

Effect on Reported Performance

Unrealized market value changes do not affect reported income for securities in the available-for-sale and held-to-maturity portfolios. On the other hand, such changes are components of reported income for trading securities, regardless of whether they are sold. SFAS 115 requires that transfers from trading to other categories take place at current market prices. This provision is designed to ensure that firms cannot avoid reporting unrealized losses by reclassification.

Notwithstanding that provision, it is still possible for managers to manipulate reported earnings through reclassification. Consider the case of unrealized gains in the available-for-sale portfolio. Reclassifying securities from available-for-sale to trading results in reporting the (still unrealized) gain as part of income.

Effect on Investment and Financing Decisions

Balance sheet carrying values of debt securities can be insulated from market value changes by classifying these securities as held-to-maturity. The FASB guarded against abuse of this provision by restricting sales (and reclassifications) of held-to-maturity debt. SFAS 115 states that held-to-maturity securities cannot be sold prior to maturity except under unusual circumstances (see footnote 8). Such sales "taint" the whole portfolio and force the firm to carry the remaining securities at market rather than cost.

As a result, classification of debt securities as held-to-maturity may affect a firm's performance in a more subtle way. A firm that wants to sell debt securities in anticipation of a rise in interest rates or to increase liquidity must weigh the accounting effects (i.e., increased reported balance sheet volatility.)[13] These accounting effects may cause the firm to curtail financing and investing activities related to its held-to-maturity debt.[14]

Analysis of Investment Performance

Exhibit 13-3 (panel A) presents balance sheet and income statement information related to the marketable securities of the Chubb Corporation [CB], a major insurance company. Panel B of the exhibit summarizes Chubb's reported investment income and ROA in total and portfolio-by-portfolio. The reported data suggest that Chubb's overall 1999 investment performance declined marginally from the 1998 level. Although overall returns were higher ($935 million versus $928 million), ROA declined from 7.0% to 6.5%. The reduced ROA was due to lower realized gains in the equity portfolio.

---

[13]The held-to-maturity classification hides the balance sheet volatility because it does not recognize unrealized changes in market values.

[14]The effects of these restrictions could be seen at the time firms adopted SFAS 115. On December 31, 1993, Chubb Corporation had over $8 billion (79%) of its debt securities classified as held-to-maturity. At December 31, 1994, after adoption of SFAS 115, that amount dropped to approximately $3.8 billion (35%) with the available-for-sale portfolio increasing accordingly.

EXHIBIT 13-3. THE CHUBB CORPORATION
Analysis of Investment Portfolio

A. Selected Balance Sheet and Income Statement Information (in $millions)

Balance Sheet, December 31

	1997	1998	1999
Fixed maturities			
Held-to-maturity (at amortized cost)*	$ 2,201	$ 2,002	$ 1,742
Available-for-sale (at market)†	10,253	11,317	12,777
Subtotal	$12,454	$13,319	$14,519
Equity securities			
Available-for-sale (at market)‡	871	1,092	769
Total investments	$13,325	$14,411	$15,288

Income Statement, Years Ended December 31

	1998	1999
Fixed maturities		
Interest income	$761	$817
Realized gains (losses)	42	24
Subtotal	$803	$841
Equity securities		
Dividend income	$ 25	$ 31
Realized gains (losses)	100	63
Subtotal	$125	$ 94
Total investment income	$928	$935

*Market values: $2,347, $2,140, and $1,801.
†Cost: $9,774, $10,768, and $12,944.
‡Cost: $734, $1,003, and $715.

B. Reported Investment Income and ROA, 1998 to 1999 (in $millions)

	1998	1999
Fixed maturities		
Investments (opening balance)	$12,454	$13,319
Investment income	803	841
Return on assets	6.4%	6.3%
Equity securities		
Investments (opening balance)	$871	$1,092
Investment income	125	94
Return on assets	14.4%	8.6%
Total		
Investments (opening balance)	$13,325	$14,411
Investment income	928	935
Return on assets	7.0%	6.5%

C. Mark-to-Market Income and ROA, 1998 to 1999 (in $millions)

	1998	1999
Fixed maturities		
Investments (opening balance)	$12,600	$13,457
Investment income	864	46
Return on assets	6.9%	0.3%
Equity securities		
Investments (opening balance)	$871	$1,092
Investment income	77	59
Return on assets	8.8%	5.4%
Total		
Investments (opening balance)	$13,471	$14,549
Investment income	941	105
Return on assets	7.0%	0.7%

Source: Based on data from Chubb, *1998–1999 Annual Reports.*

The reported results are, however, misleading, as the portfolio classifications and the accounting thereof are meaningless from an analytical standpoint. The results are misleading because unrealized changes in market value are recognized for some investments but not for others.

Chubb's balance sheet contains carrying values that are a mix of cost and market values. This blend limits the comparability of ROA measures between years and portfolios, as the carrying value of the assets is the ROA denominator.

Furthermore, due to classification effects, reported volatility and returns differ from actual volatility and portfolio returns. For the available-for-sale portfolio, only realized gains and losses are included in income. As long as the portfolio contains some unrealized gains, management has the ability to determine the amount and select the timing of (capital) gains recognized in income regardless of the performance of the total portfolio. Management can smooth reported income (and lower reported volatility) by realizing some gains each year regardless of market performance. This selective recognition process can be abused by "cherry picking" gains for recognition while allowing losses to remain in the portfolio, unrecognized in income.[15] In Chubb's case, as we show, the reported performance is misleading as it resulted from selective recognition rather than actual investment performance.

To analyze actual investment returns, the analyst must go beyond the reported results. *All securities should be shown at current market value and all gains and losses should be attributed to the period earned rather than the period realized.*[16] The periods in which market values change and those in which they are recognized (by sale) may be completely different. *The analyst should track investment performance on a mark-to-market basis, measuring the actual investment performance for each period.*

Mark-to-Market Accounting

The total return on a firm's portfolio equals the sum of:

- Dividends and interest income
- Realized gains and losses
- Unrealized (holding) gains and losses

Dividends and interest income, as well as realized gains and losses, are always reported in the period they occur. *Thus, calculation of the mark-to-market return requires measurement of the unrealized (holding) gains and losses.* This amount can be calculated easily as long as both cost and market values are reported.[17]

Calculation of Mark-to-Market Return. If we define the *market valuation adjustment (MVA)* as the difference between market value and cost at each balance sheet date, then for each time period,

Unrealized Holding Gains and Losses = Change in MVA

This holds true whether or not new securities are added to the portfolio during the year.

Thus, the actual portfolio performance (mark-to-market return) equals the sum of:

- Dividends and interest income
- Realized gains and losses
- Change in the market valuation adjustment

---

[15]The abuse of selective recognition by troubled financial institutions contributed to pressure from some regulators and politicians to use market value accounting for all investments.

[16]Provision should be made, however, for any income tax payable upon sale of the securities.

[17]Under the provisions of SFAS 115 the cost (market) basis must be disclosed for the available-for-sale (held-to-maturity) portfolio in addition to the market value (cost) carrying value. Thus, the required information is readily available.

Applying this procedure to Chubb, we use the data in panel A of Exhibit 13-3 to compute the 1999 change in the MVA:

1999 Change in MVA (in $millions)

	Held-to-Maturity	Available-for-Sale	Total	Equity Securities
		Fixed Maturity Portfolios		
1999				
Market value	$1,801	$12,777	$14,578	$ 769
Cost	1,742	12,944	14,686	715
MVA	$ 59	$ (167)	$ (108)	$ 54
1998				
Market value	$2,140	$11,317	$13,457	$1,092
Cost	2,002	10,768	12,770	1,003
MVA	$ 138	$ 549	$ 687	$ 89
Change in MVA				
Fixed maturities			($108) − $687 =	$(795)
Equity portfolio			$54 − $89 =	(35)
Total				$(830)

The change in the MVA must now be combined with the reported (realized) returns to calculate the mark-to-market return for 1999:

Calculation of 1999 Mark-to-Market Return

	Fixed Maturities	Equities	Total
Dividend and interest income	$ 817	$ 31	$ 848
Realized gains and losses	24	63	87
Reported income	**$ 841**	**$ 94**	**$ 935**
Change in MVA	(795)	(35)	(830)
Mark-to-market return	**$ 46**	**$ 59**	**$ 105**

Both the fixed and equity portfolios have unrealized losses (change in MVA) in 1999. These losses depress the mark-to-market returns considerably. The effect is much greater for the fixed portfolio as the reported return is reduced by 95%. Panel C of Exhibit 13-3 summarizes these marked-to-market performance data as well as those for 1998. Note that the computation of the marked-to-market ROA uses market values in the denominator as well.

As reported results only include realized gains and losses, 1999 reported results are greatly overstated (but are slightly understated for 1998). The failure to recognize losses overstates the 1999 performance. On a mark-to-market basis, the actual ROA is less than 1%. Chubb reported positive capital gains as it was able to select which securities it would sell and consequently recognize as income. Chubb appears to be smoothing reported earnings, a common practice among firms with large securities portfolios.[18]

---

[18]When there is a significant difference between the cost and market value of securities designated held-to-maturity, further adjustment should be made to the balance sheet. The unrealized gain (loss) (less a deferred tax offset) should be added to (subtracted from) stockholders' equity.

For Chubb, at December 31, 1999, market value exceeds cost by ($1,801 million − $1,742 million) $59 million. Assuming a 34% tax rate, the net of tax adjustment is ($59 × .66) $39 million. Compared with Chubb's equity of $6,272 million at December 31, 1999, the effect is immaterial.

Summary of Analytical Procedures

The following steps should be followed to:

- Segregate operating and investment results.
- Eliminate the effects of selective classification and inconsistent accounting rules on the measurement of investment results.

1. Identify the existence of marketable securities portfolios from financial statement data and footnote disclosures. Obtain information regarding the risk and income characteristics of each portfolio.

2. Identify the valuation method used in the financial statements. When investments are not valued at market, obtain actual or estimated market values. When adjusting stockholders' equity and equity-based ratios such as debt-to-equity and turnover ratios, substitute market value for cost or other carrying value whenever possible. Provision for capital gains tax on unrealized gains and losses should be made where applicable.

3. Remove realized gains and losses and any valuation adjustments from reported earnings. The result should be an earnings trend that represents the actual operating results, unaffected by selective recognition decisions by management.

4. If dividend and interest income are significant, remove them (after-tax) from reported earnings and operating cash flows as well. These adjustments will leave only the results of operating activities and enable the computation of return on equity excluding the impact of investments. This separation generally makes sense for firms whose investment activities are incidental to their operations. However, the investment activities of banks, insurance companies, and other financial intermediaries must be examined on an enterprise basis; investment income must be analyzed relative to the cost of funds.

5. Examine the actual mark-to-market returns on the investment portfolio over an appropriate time period—at least one market cycle. Compare the results with the risk level of the portfolio and with benchmark returns for portfolios of the same type.

6. When using earnings to value a company, normalize investment returns by including in earnings the average return over the cycle rather than returns only for that time period.

7. For companies with large investment portfolios, management should be held accountable, as would any investment manager, for returns on the portfolio.

EQUITY METHOD OF ACCOUNTING

Conditions for Use

The equity method must be used when the investor can exercise significant influence on the management, operations, and investing and financing decisions of the investee. The investor must report its proportionate share of the investee's net assets and recognize a proportionate share of the income of the investee, regardless of whether it is received as a dividend or is reinvested.

APB 18 (1971), which governs the use of the equity method under U.S. GAAP,[19] requires the investor to have significant influence over the operations of the investee; ownership of 20% is presumed to meet that test. FASB Interpretation 35 (1981) of APB 18 prohibits the use of the equity method, despite 20% (or greater) ownership, if *any* of the following conditions is present:

- Litigation between the investor and investee prevents the investor from exercising influence.
- A "standstill agreement" or similar restriction precludes the investor from voting its shares or influencing management of the investee.

---

[19] IAS 28 (2000) has very similar provisions.

- The investee has a majority holder that controls its operations.
- There are other indicators of a lack of ability to influence the investee such as lack of seats on the board of directors or lack of ability to obtain financial and operating data.

In practice, the equity method has been applied to holdings as low as 10% when "significant influence" has been demonstrated. On the other hand, holdings of well over 20% may be insufficient. The user of financial statements cannot take for granted that the equity method will be used if and only if the voting interest is in the range of 20 to 50%.

Illustration of the Equity Method

The following events are used to illustrate the application of the equity method:

1. On December 31, 2000, Company P invests $300 in Company S and receives 30% of the shares of Company S in return. For illustrative purposes, we assume that Company S's equity (book value) at the time of the purchase was $1,000 (i.e., P paid book value; 30% of $1,000 = $300).[20]

2. During the year ended December 31, 2001, Company S earns $100 and pays cash dividends of $20.

3. Company S earns $150 and pays dividends of $60 in 2002.

The Equity Method: At Acquisition and the First Year of Investment. On its balance sheet at December 31, 2000, Company P reports the purchased asset at its acquisition cost:

Investment in Company S   **$300**

To account for its investment in Company S for the year ended December 31, 2001, Company P must consider *both* the income earned and the dividends paid by Company S. The equity of Company S (or, equivalently, its net assets) increases by $100 as a result of the income earned during the year. Company P's share of that income (alternatively, its share in the increased equity of Company S) is $30 (30% of $100).

Using the equity method of accounting, Company P will report this $30 in its income statement and increase its "Investment in Company S" account by $30, thereby reflecting its 30% share of the earnings (and increase in the net assets) of Company S:[21]

Investment in Company S	$30
Equity in net income of Company S	$30

Company P receives $6 in cash dividends (30% of $20). In contrast to the cost and market methods, these dividends are not included directly as part of its income. Under the equity method, investment income is a function of the earnings of the investee and is independent of dividends received. Company P records dividends received as a reduction in the "Investment in Company S" account.

Cash	$6
Investment in Company S	$6

The rationale for this reporting method is that Company S's equity and net assets decline due to the declaration of dividends. The dividend of $20 reduces Company S's equity by $20; Company P's share of that decrease in equity is $6.

---

[20]If the amount paid is greater than the proportionate share of the investee's book value, as is generally the case, then *goodwill* is created. Accounting for goodwill is discussed further in Chapter 14.

[21]When the subsidiary has losses, the equity method requires a writedown of the carrying value of the investment. However, the carrying value cannot be written down below zero, unless the investor has economic exposure in addition to its investment (such as a loan guarantee). Subsequent profits cannot be recognized until any unrecognized losses have been made up.

The net effect is that Company P's share of the undistributed (reinvested) earnings of Company S ($100 − $20 = $80) is added to the investment in Company S's account on Company P's balance sheet. That is, the account is increased by $24 ($30 − $6, or 30% of $80). Company P will report the following asset on December 31, 2001:

Investment in Company S $324

The investment account, therefore, contains the original cost of the investment *plus the equity in the undistributed earnings of the investee.* When the investment is sold, any realized gain or loss (for financial reporting only, the tax basis is unaffected by the accounting method applied) is based on a comparison of the proceeds with the adjusted cost basis of $324, not the original cost of $300.

The Second Year of Investment. Company P receives cash of $18 (30% of $60) but recognizes earnings of $45 (30% of $150). The excess of income recognized over dividends received ($45 − $18 = $27) increases the investment account to $351, at December 31, 2002. The balance in the investment account reflects the following events:

Original investment in Company S	$300
Equity in reinvested 2001 income	24
Equity in reinvested 2002 income	27
Investment in Company S	$351

Note that over the period 12/31/00 to 12/31/02, the equity of S increased by (100 − 20 + 150 − 60 =) $170. Of that increase, 30% or $51 is company P's share, equivalent to the increase in the investment in S account. Hence, the terminology *equity* method reflects that the parent's investment account mirrors (changes in) the investee's equity.

Comparison of the Equity Method and SFAS 115

The differences between SFAS 115[22] and the equity method for the previous example follow:

	Income Reported		Cash Received	
Year	SFAS 115	Equity	SFAS 115	Equity
2001	$6	$30	$6	$6
2002	18	45	18	18

Under SFAS 115, Company P's income includes only dividends received. Use of the equity method results in higher earnings for Company P as it reports its proportionate share of the reinvested earnings of Company S. *Whenever the investee has earnings and a dividend payout ratio of less than 100%, use of the equity method will increase the earnings of the investor relative to those reported under SFAS 115.*

Cash flows, however, are unchanged. Although under SFAS 115, income and cash flow are identical, they differ under the equity method. In the indirect method cash flow statement, there is an adjustment to (subtraction from) net income for the difference between the equity income recognized and the dividends received.

When the equity method recognizes income in excess of dividends received, interest coverage and return on investment ratios for Company P improve. Its total assets and stockholders' equity rise due to recognition of its share of the reinvested earnings of Company S. This higher base may, in time, reduce the return-on-investment and return-on-equity ratios if

---

[22]As investments in affiliates are not made for "trading" purposes, in the absence of the equity method this security would be classified available-for-sale and (unrealized) market value changes would be ignored in the income statement. Thus, income and cash flow effects under SFAS 115 would be equivalent to the cost method.

the profitability of Company S declines. The increase in stockholders' equity also increases Company P's book value per share. *Moreover, as only assets and equity are affected, without any recognition of the investee's debt, the investor's debt-to-equity and debt-to-total capital ratios improve and may be significantly misstated.*

The preceding discussion assumes that the investee is profitable. When it reports losses, the equity method will report less favorable results.

Box 13-1 suggests that, as the criterion of "significant influence" is subject to some discretion, firms select the side of the 20% line that obtains the desired accounting treatment. If the investee is not profitable, a firm may avoid the adverse effect (recognizing its share of investee losses) of the equity method by purchasing less than 20%; if the investee is profitable, the firm prefers the equity method and it purchases just over 20%. For comparative purposes, it may be appropriate to adjust reported earnings to the equity method. This adjustment should be made when companies, although they have "significant influence" over their affiliates, account for them as marketable securities using SFAS 115.

Equity Method of Accounting and Analysis

The differences between accounting for an investment under the equity method and as a marketable security under SFAS 115, illustrated in Exhibit 13-1, are striking. Given a profitable investee and a low dividend payout ratio, the equity in reinvested earnings is a significant factor in the carrying amount under the equity method. In years when the market value of the investee changes significantly, reported investor earnings and carrying values can differ considerably depending on the choice of accounting method.

Carrying Value. Even when an investee's shares are publicly traded, changes in market price are not recognized by the equity method (unless there is a permanent impairment). *For financial analysis, however, the value placed by the securities markets on the investee should be considered a better indicator of value than the carrying amount in the financial statements of the investor.*

Earnings. Only under the equity method do the earnings of the investee directly affect the reported performance of the parent. The underlying premise is that the parent has or will have access to the earnings, *directly* or *indirectly*. This is a basic principle of accrual accounting, the assumption that the accrual measure is a better indicator of the cash-generating ability of the firm.[23]

In some cases, however, the parent does not have access to permanently reinvested (i.e., undistributed) earnings (or cash flows). It is questionable whether the reinvested earnings should be considered income. In such cases, analysts should adjust equity earnings by including as income of the parent only actual dividends received from the investee.

Box 13-2 discusses the impact of equity method earnings on deferred taxes; management's assumptions regarding realization of the (undistributed) earnings affect the rate used to calculate deferred taxes. This information can be used to assess whether the parent will have access to the undistributed earnings.

This line of reasoning can be extended further. If the parent does not have access to the earnings of the subsidiary, then the subsidiary should be treated as any other investment in marketable securities. The carrying value and earnings from the subsidiary should be evaluated on a mark-to-market basis.

---

[23]Ricks and Hughes (1985) offer evidence consistent with the assumption that the equity method provides data used for valuation purposes by the market. They found positive market reaction when financial statements using the equity method were first issued. The positive reaction was positively correlated to both the size of the equity earnings as well as the degree to which analysts underestimated earnings in their forecasts. Ricks and Hughes concluded the market found the information useful, as "the equity method provided information concerning affiliate earnings not previously available from other sources." [William E. Ricks and John S. Hughes, "Market Reactions to a Non-Discretionary Accounting Change: The Case of Long-Term Investments," *Accounting Review* (January 1985), p. 50.]

BOX 13-1
Equity Accounting and Its Impact on Ownership Position

Comiskey and Mulford (1986) tested whether "the inclusion in APB 18 of the 20 percent ownership criterion for application of the equity method (hereafter the 20 percent standard) influences the ownership position taken by investing firms."* Figure 13-1, from their study, shows the distribution of ownership positions taken by investing firms in 1982. The solid line indicates the actual percentage positions taken, and the dashed line depicts the predicted "fitted" distribution.[†]

As indicated in Figure 13-1, the actual concentration of firms in the 16 to 24% range is significantly greater than expected. Comiskey and Mulford argue that the 20% standard mandated by APB 18 may be responsible for the abnormal concentration. Different firms may have different motivations with respect to

whether they want to report on the cost or equity basis and stake out positions accordingly.

In further support of this contention, they found that affiliates in the 19 to 19.99% ownership range had reported (on average) a net loss 30.4% of the time in the previous four years. Firms in the 20 to 20.99% range reported losses only 16.1% of the time. As the equity method is increasingly preferable as the subsidiary's income (or more precisely, the undistributed income) increases, these results make sense. Owners of affiliates that are less likely to report losses are more likely to choose an ownership interest permitting use of the equity method. Alternatively, firms facing losses and holding over 20% may decide to sell some of their holdings to bring them below the 20% level.[‡]

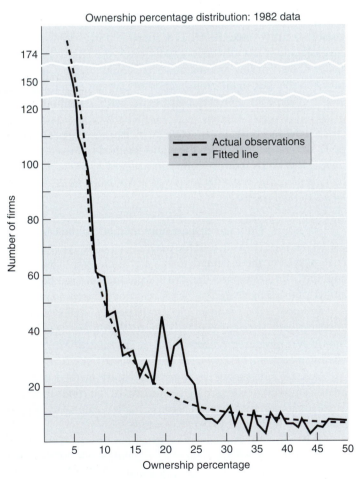

FIGURE 13-1 Ownership percentage distribution, 1982 data. *Source:* Eugene Comiskey and Charles W. Mulford, "Investment Decisions and the Equity Accounting Standard," *Accounting Review* (July 1986), pp. 519–525 (Fig. 1, p. 521).

---

*Eugene Comiskey and Charles W. Mulford, "Investment Decisions and the Equity Accounting Standard," *Accounting Review* (July 1986), p. 519.
[†]The "fitted" line was determined on the basis of extrapolation of the patterns existing below 16% and above 24%.
[‡]As discussed later, similar possibilities exist for firms that want to avoid consolidation (i.e., they acquire only 49% of the subsidiary).

BOX 13-2
The Equity Method and Deferred Taxes

The equity method of accounting is used only for financial reporting. Because it cannot be used on corporate tax returns, it creates temporary differences between financial income and taxable income.* In the United States, dividends received by corporations from qualifying domestic corporations are taxed at a low effective tax rate due to the dividends received exclusion available to eligible corporate investors.† Thus, the income tax payable on the dividend component of equity method income can be computed quite precisely. However, estimating the deferred tax expense related to undistributed income (income recognized under the equity method less that portion received as dividends) is difficult because any tax paid depends on future events.

Two different assumptions can be made about reinvested income:

1. It will be received in the form of future dividends in excess of future earnings; the deferred component of tax expense is computed using the effective tax rate on dividends (currently 7% if ownership exceeds 20%).

2. It will be realized via sale of the investment, requiring the use of the corporate capital gains rate (currently 35%) to compute deferred taxes.

If the proportion of reinvested (undistributed) income is significant, then the choice of tax rate applied to reinvested income can materially affect reported income. Unfortunately, explicit disclosure of the choice is almost never made. In some cases, analysis of the income tax footnote (see Chapter 9) will provide the information needed to evaluate the impact of the choice made on reported income.

For example, Corning's income tax footnote for 1999 disclosed deferred taxes of $16.2 million on $118.5 million of equity in earnings of associated companies. This disclosure suggests that Corning assumed that (the majority of) reinvested earnings would be received as future dividends ($16.2 million/$118.5 million = 13.7%).

A second issue arises upon sale of the investment. As the equity method is not applied for income tax purposes, the tax basis (cost) of the investment remains unchanged. In the financial statements, however, cost is augmented by reinvested income recognized under the equity method (net of dividends received and deferred tax expense). When the investment is sold, the capital gain for income tax purposes will, in all likelihood, be far greater than the capital gain for financial accounting purposes. In some cases, there is an accounting loss despite the income tax gain.

If the corporate investor has accrued deferred taxes based on the dividend assumption and later sells the investment, the deferred tax provision is inadequate. Thus, even if there is a pretax capital gain (sales price exceeds the sum of original cost and the recorded reinvested earnings), there may be an after-tax loss.‡

Thus, if it appears that a major investment accounted for under the equity method may be sold, the tax issue must be considered. The analyst should try to estimate the tax basis (cost for income tax purposes) of the investment; footnotes sometimes disclose the original cost. Look for information regarding the company's tax rate and the existence of any capital loss carryforwards that might shelter the gain from taxation. Most important, be aware that the accounting gain and taxable gain might be quite different.

---

*See Chapter 9 for a detailed discussion of temporary differences and deferred taxes.

†The exclusion is 70% if the investee is less than 20% owned, 80% if ownership exceeds 20%. If ownership exceeds 80%, the investee must be consolidated and dividends to the parent are tax-free. These rules have changed from time to time in recent years. Thus, at the current tax rate of 35%, the effective tax rate is 10.5% (35% × 30%) on less than 20%-owned investees and 7% (35% × 20%) when ownership exceeds 20%.

‡If the investee is a foreign corporation, the issues and analysis are slightly different. The preferential tax treatment for dividends does not apply to foreign investees. On the other hand, credits for foreign income taxes paid may be available to offset the U.S. tax liability when reinvested income is received as dividends. More significantly, no deferred tax provision is required for reinvested foreign earnings because of the "permanent reinvestment" option of SFAS 109. Thus, for foreign investees, no deferred tax provision may be made.

The appropriateness of mark-to-market analyses of equity investments depends, therefore, on the relationship between the two firms. When investee operations are related to the parent's core business (supplier, distributor, or customer), the investee is arguably an extension of the parent. The equity method is applicable but it may not be adequate because the assets, liabilities, and components of income of the investee are included in summary form only. We return to this issue after first examining consolidation accounting.

CONSOLIDATION

The financial statements of Pfizer, Takeda, Roche, or any other huge enterprise, are a consolidated set of statements that includes a large number of individual corporate entities. Each account in a set of consolidated financial statements consists of the sum (less any intercompany

BOX 13-3
February 1999, FASB Exposure Draft (ED): Consolidated Financial Statements:

Purpose and Policy

The ED would change the criterion for consolidation from majority ownership to control:

> Control of an entity is a present exclusionary power over its assets—power to use or direct the use of the individual assets of another entity in essentially the same ways as the controlling entity can use its own assets. Control enables a parent to use or direct the use of the assets of a subsidiary by:
>
> a. Establishing the controlled entity's policies as well as its capital and operating budgets
>
> b. Selecting, determining the compensation of, and terminating personnel responsible for implementing its policies and decisions*

Conditions for Assessing the Existence of Control

The ED states that control is a factual determination and goes beyond legal control. It discusses factors that lead to the presumption of control:

1. Ownership of the dominant, even when not a majority, voting interest (such as 40%) when no other stockholder (or group) has a significant interest.

2. The ability to dominate the selection of the board of directors.

3. The ability to achieve majority ownership, through rights or convertible securities.

4. For an entity that it has established but has no owners (e.g., a trust), provisions in its charter, bylaws, or trust instrument effectively convey control and cannot be changed without approval of the creator.

5. The unilateral ability to dissolve an entity and assume control of its assets.

6. An entity is the sole general partner in a limited partnership.

The ED also points out that control need not be absolute. There may be "protective" restrictions due to regulatory authorities or debt covenants, just as in the case of wholly owned subsidiaries. Such protective rights do not affect the presumption of control. However, certain "participative" approval or veto rights relating to operating, financing, and investing rights may suggest an absence of control.[†] Current guidance does not adequately distinguish between protective and participative rights; practice remains inconsistent, and comparability suffers.

The proposed standard remains controversial. Significant concerns include:

- Whether control (in terms of nonshared decision-making ability) can be assumed based on anticipated nonaction by other holders of voting rights

- Effectiveness and operationality of the proposed treatment of convertible and option securities that comprise "latent" control through to the ability to obtain voting rights

- Lack of effective guidance for (1) "straw man" or special-purpose entities lacking sufficient economic substance where control may exist but is unclear based on the form of the arrangement and (2) partnership and other noncorporate structures

The FASB is working on a "modified approach" to consolidation policy for entities with limited powers. Separately, the Board intends to develop consolidation policy for discrete activities isolated within an entity ("entity-within-an-entity").

Early in 2002, responding to pressures resulting from the Enron collapse, the FASB initiated a project intended to result in the consolidation of special purpose entities.

Effects on Financial Reporting

The proposed consolidation policy standard and the FASB ED, Accounting for Financial Instruments with Characteristics of Liabilities, Equity, or Both (see Box 10-2), would change current financial reporting in a number of ways, including:

- Minority interest is called "noncontrolling interest," which would be included in stockholders' equity on the balance sheet and shown as an allocation of net income on the face of the income statement.

- When less than 100% is purchased, goodwill would be inferred for and allocated to the noncontrolling interest.

- Once an affiliate is consolidated, changes in ownership that do not result in a loss of control would be equity transactions, with no effect on reported income.

- Transactions or events resulting in a loss of control or the sale of subsidiaries would require a reversal of the paid-in capital recorded for transactions in shares of subsidiaries. These amounts are components of the gain or loss on sale or disposal.

- Presentation of earnings-per-share by entities with one or more less-than-wholly-owned subsidiaries would be amended to require display in the income statement of the total adjustments to net income attributable to the controlling interest to derive the numerator for the calculation of basic earnings per share.

- Accounting policies of consolidated affiliates would have to be conformed to those of the parent, except when differences within a consolidated group are permitted (e.g., inventory).

---

*Para. 10 (continuation of part a omitted).

[†]See EITF 96-16, Investor's Accounting for an Investee When the Investor Has a Majority of the Voting Interest but the Minority Shareholder or Shareholders Have Certain Approval or Voting Rights.

eliminations) of the corresponding amounts for each included entity.[24] The inventories shown, for example, are the inventories of each corporate entity, added together, and adjusted for any intercompany transactions.

The "parent-only" statement reports its investment in each subsidiary on the equity basis, in which the assets and liabilities of the subsidiary are netted in a single investment account. When the firms are consolidated, it is implicitly assumed that the assets and liabilities of the subsidiary are controlled by the parent company. As we shall see, there are times when that assumption must be questioned.

Conditions for Use

Under SFAS 94 (1986), all entities in which the parent controls (directly or indirectly) more than 50% of the voting shares of the subsidiary must be consolidated.[25] There are two exceptions to this rule:

- Temporary control.
- Subsidiaries that are not considered controlled, despite majority ownership, due to governmental action, a nonconvertible currency, or civil disorder. The legal status of the subsidiary, such as bankruptcy or reorganization, may also preclude consolidation.

Exceptions are made because under these circumstance, the parent company does not have unrestricted use of the subsidiary's assets or cannot be considered to exercise control.

IAS 27 (2000) has provisions that are similar to SFAS 94. However, because of concern that the mechanistic 50% rule enabled firms to avoid consolidation despite effective control, the FASB has reconsidered its criteria for consolidation. Box 13-3 summarizes the FASB exposure draft, Consolidated Financial Statements: Policy and Procedures (1999), which defines control by whether the parent has *effective control of the assets* of the subsidiary. Box 13-3 also explains the consequences of the proposed new standard.

Illustration of Consolidation

In Exhibit 13-4, Company P, the parent, purchases an 80% interest in Company S, the subsidiary. To simplify matters, we assume that the amount paid ($2,000) equals the proportionate share of the book value of the subsidiary (80% of $2,500) purchased. When this is not the case, the subsidiary accounts are restated at their fair market values, and goodwill may be recorded.[26] The exhibit shows both the equity method and full consolidation, allowing for a comparison of the two methods.

COMPARISON OF CONSOLIDATION WITH THE EQUITY METHOD

The first part of Exhibit 13-4 shows the balance sheet under both the equity method and consolidation immediately following the acquisition. The second part shows the income statement, cash flows, and balance sheets after one year.

The equity method incorporates the investor's share of the net income and net assets of the investee in investor company results, reporting them as equity in the earnings of the subsidiary and investment in the subsidiary, respectively. Under consolidation, all the assets, liabilities, revenues, expense, and cash flows of the subsidiary are included in the corresponding accounts of the parent. When ownership is less than 100%, a "minority (noncontrolling) interest" (discussed shortly) results.

---

[24]See Chapter 15 for an analysis of requirements when some of those entities keep their records in a currency other than that of the parent.

[25]SFAS 144 (2001), Accounting for the Impairment of Disposal of Long-Lived Assets, eliminated the exemption to consolidation for a temporarily controlled subsidiary. Assets and liabilities held for sale must be presented separately in the asset and liability sections of the statement of financial position.

[26]A discussion of goodwill is contained in Chapter 14.

EXHIBIT 13-4
Comparison of Equity Method and Consolidation

Balance Sheet at Acquisition Date

	Preacquisition		After Acquisition of 80% of Company S for $2,000 Company P	
	Company P	Company S	Equity Method	Consolidated
Current assets	$12,000	$4,000	$10,000	$14,000
Investment in Company S	—	—	2,000	—
Other assets	8,000	2,000	8,000	10,000
	$20,000	$6,000	$20,000	$24,000
Current liabilities	$10,000	$3,500	$10,000	$13,500
Minority interest	—	—	—	500
Common stock	7,000	1,500	7,000	7,000
Retained earnings	3,000	1,000	3,000	3,000
	$20,000	$6,000	$20,000	$24,000

Results of First Year After Acquisition

Additional information:
  Dividends paid by Company S equal $250.
  There are no changes in noncash working capital.
  There are no noncash expenses.
  Company P loaned Company S $350.

		Company P	
	Company S	Equity Method	Consolidated
Revenue	$5,000	$15,000	$20,000
Expense	4,000	10,000	14,000
Operating income	$1,000	$ 5,000	$ 6,000
Equity in income of Company S	—	800	—
Minority interest	—	—	(200)
Net income	$1,000	$ 5,800	$ 5,800
Noncash adjustment	0	(600)*	200[†]
Cash from operations	1,000	$ 5,200	$ 6,000
Cash from affiliates	350	(350)	—
Dividends paid/received	(250)	—	(50)[‡]
Change in cash	$1,100	$ 4,850	$ 5,950

*Reinvested earnings of Company S ($800 earned − $200 dividends received).
[†]Minority interest.
[‡]Paid to minority investors.

Balance Sheet, End of First Year

		Company P	
	Company S	Equity Method	Consolidated
Current assets	$5,100	$14,850	$19,950
Investment in Company S	—	2,600	—
Receivable from Company S	—	350	
Other assets	2,000	8,000	10,000
	$7,100	$25,800	$29,950
Current liabilities	$3,500	$10,000	$13,500
Payable to Company P	350	—	
Minority interest	—	—	650
Common stock	1,500	7,000	7,000
Retained earnings	1,750	8,800	8,800
	$7,100	$25,800	$29,950

Note that only the assets and liabilities are changed by consolidation; *the common equity of the consolidated firm remains equal to the equity of the parent*. Similarly, while consolidation results in inclusion of the revenues and expenses of Company S in the income statement of Company P, *net income is unchanged*.

Under the equity method, only the investor's investment account and net income are affected by investee results. In consolidated statements, virtually every account and the accompanying footnotes include the subsidiary's operating, investing, and financing activities.

Reported cash flows also differ. Under the equity method, the investor's cash flow statement only reports capital flows between investor and investee (dividends, additional investments, and redemptions). When the investee is consolidated, the investor's cash flow statement includes all cash flows of the investee *except* those between investor and investee. Consolidated operating cash flow is $800 higher, equal to the operating cash flow of Company S less the dividends received by Company P. Thus, consolidation includes all the subsidiary's cash flows, not just payments to the investor. In some cases, such inclusion may result in misleading measures of the resources available to the investor.

The addition of a subsidiary to (or subtraction from) the consolidated group also changes financial statement ratios. Less obviously, financial statement footnote data now include subsidiary data. Although the investor owns only 80% of the subsidiary, 100% of the subsidiary's accounts are included, reflecting the control perspective in consolidated financial reporting.[27]

As the investor owns less than 100% of the subsidiary, however, it does not derive all the benefit from the subsidiary's assets and earnings (and it is not at risk for all subsidiary liabilities). Consolidated financial statements reflect this fact through accounts known as *minority or noncontrolling interest*. On the consolidated balance sheet, the share of the subsidiary's equity that does not accrue to the parent is shown as a liability (strictly speaking, it is a credit balance rather than a liability), normally just above stockholders' equity. However, the FASB ED would require characterization of the minority interest as equity since consolidated financial statements report the assets and liabilities of the consolidated entity (the assets and liabilities owned by the controlling *and* the noncontrolling interests). In Exhibit 13-4, minority interest is $500 (20% of $2,500) at acquisition. After one year, it is $650 (20% of $3,250). On the income statement, minority interest of $200 (20% of $1,000) is shown as a deduction.[28] We consider minority interest further later in this chapter.

Depending on the financial characteristics of the subsidiary, consolidation may result in financial statements that look either better or worse than those resulting from use of the equity method. Parent ownership levels just below 50% may signal a desire to avoid consolidation;[29] ownership of 50% or more may indicate a preference for consolidation. Changes from consolidation to the equity method (or vice versa) and the issuance of equity by a subsidiary also raise reporting issues, presented in Box 13-4.

Consolidation versus the Equity Method: Analytical Considerations

Consolidation combines different operating segments, obscuring their individual characteristics. The equity method, on the other hand, can result in oversummarization as significant operating and financial characteristics are reported off-balance-sheet.

Footnotes and other data may permit restatement of financial statements to a form better suited to the desired analysis. At times, the analyst may want to restate from the equity method to pro rata or full consolidation. At other times, deconsolidation is desirable. In subsequent sections of this chapter, we discuss and provide several examples of do-it-yourself restatement. The nature of the restatement often depends on the degree to which the sub-

---

[27]In some cases, however, proportionate consolidation may be more appropriate; that method is discussed later in this chapter.

[28]Generally, minority interest is shown as a separate line item in both balance sheet and income statement; some firms include it in other accounts. The FASB exposure draft would require that it be shown as part of equity in the balance sheet and as an allocation of net income in the income statement.

[29]After the issuance of SFAS 94, which required the consolidation of finance subsidiaries, some companies reduced ownership of their finance subsidiaries to 49% and did not consolidate them. In these cases, the analyst should apply the proportionate consolidation method, discussed shortly.

BOX 13-4
Equity Method and Consolidation: Effects of Changes in Ownership

Increases or decreases in a company's ownership of an affiliate can trigger significant accounting effects. In this box we discuss three examples:

1. Change from consolidation to equity method
2. Change from equity method to consolidation
3. Issuance of stock by subsidiary

Part 1: Change from Consolidation to Equity Method

 When a company enters into a joint venture with another firm, contributes existing operations, and accounts for the venture using the equity method, financial statement effects may be significant. Assets (and liabilities) that were included in the parent balance sheet are deconsolidated, replaced by its share of the venture's stockholders' equity.

Example: Texaco, effective January 1, 1998, formed a joint venture, Equilon, to which it contributed $2.8 billion of net properties from its U.S. refining and marketing segment.* Texaco accounts for its 44% interest in Equilon using the equity method. As a result, Texaco's assets were reduced. Note that U.S. assets for the U.S. refining, marketing, and distribution segment (Note 1) declined from $5,668 million at December 31, 1997 to $4,066 million at December 31, 1998 and capital expenditures for that segment fell from $262 million in 1997 to $1 million in 1998.

Texaco reports its equity in the earnings of the venture, rather than the sales and expenses of the contributed operations (note the 1999 decline in sales of the U.S. refining, marketing, and distribution segment). As a result, many of Texaco's ratios are affected, although disclosure is insufficient to adjust for the deconsolidation. The most significant likely effect is an increased return on assets.

Part 2: Change from Equity Method to Consolidation

Texaco owns 50% of Caltex, a joint venture with Chevron (see Note 5 to Texaco's 1999 financial statements). Following the merger with Chevron in October 2000, the Caltex group of companies became wholly owned, with consolidation required. The combined company reported all of the sales, expenses, assets, liabilities, and cash flows rather than only the net income, net assets, and cash flows between Caltex and its owners.

Part 3: Issuance of Stock by Subsidiary

Companies are not supposed to record a profit as a result of capital transactions (i.e., when they issue their own shares). Accounting standards, however, do allow companies to record profits when *their subsidiaries issue shares*. Consider the following hypothetical example:

Assume that a subsidiary begins business by issuing 5,000 shares in a private placement at $10/share and the parent pays $30,000 for 60% (3,000 shares) of the subsidiary. The subsidiary then goes public, issuing another 5,000 shares at the higher price of $50/share. The shareholders' equity of the subsidiary is now [(5,000 × $10) + (5,000 × $50)=] $300,000.

The parent now owns 30% of the outstanding shares of the subsidiary and accounts for the subsidiary using the equity method. How should it value its investment?

- At the historical cost of $30,000; or
- At 30% of current shareholders' equity; that is, $90,000 (reporting a gain of $60,000)?

The rationale for the second option[†] is that the equity method is supposed to reflect the parent's share of the subsidiary's stockholders' equity. As a result of the public offering, that share has increased and the parent investment account should reflect the increase.

Internet Capital Group [ICGE] is a B2B Internet incubator holding company. The following footnote from its 1999 annual report shows that the company reported $68 ($44) million of such pretax (after-tax) profits that year:

> As a result of VerticalNet completing its initial public offering in February 1999 and issuing additional shares for acquisitions in 1999, our share of VerticalNet's net equity increased by $50.7 million. This increase adjusted our carrying value in VerticalNet and resulted in a non-operating gain of $50.7 million, before deferred taxes of $17.7 million, in the year ended December 31, 1999. As a result of Breakaway Solutions completing its initial public offering in October 1999, our share of Breakaway Solutions' net equity increased by $17.3 million. This increase adjusts our carrying value in Breakaway Solutions and resulted in a non-operating gain of $17.3 million, before deferred taxes of $6.1 million, in the year ended December 31, 1999. These gains were recorded in accordance with SEC Staff Accounting Bulletin No. 84 and our accounting policy with respect to such transactions. We believe there is a high likelihood that transactions similar to these, in which a partner company we account for under the consolidation or equity method of accounting issues shares of its common stock, will occur in the future and we expect to record gains or losses related to such transactions provided they meet the requirements of SEC Staff Accounting Bulletin No. 84 and our accounting policy. In some cases, as described in SEC Staff Accounting Bulletin No. 84, the occurrence of similar transactions may not result in a non-operating gain or loss but would result in a direct increase or decrease to our shareholders' equity.

Overall the company reported a $30 million net loss for the year, which would have been 150% higher ($74 million) were it not for the gains resulting from their subsidiaries' IPOs. Note that the company states that it expects to record further profits of this nature in the future as more of its subsidiaries go public.

Notwithstanding SEC Staff Accounting Bulletin no. 84, which permits the recognition of profits on the sales of shares of a subsidiary under some conditions, the nature of these "profits" needs to be carefully examined. Are they paper profits or are they real?

In October 2000, the FASB issued Exposure Draft (ED) no. 213-B, Accounting for Financial Instruments with Characteristics of Liabilities, Equity, or Both. This ED would prohibit the recognition of gains or losses (as the difference between the carrying amount and the proceeds on sale) on sales of shares of a subsidiary unless deconsolidation of the subsidiary is required as a result of that sale of shares.

---

*See Note 5 to Texaco's 1999 annual report for details.
†Note that this is not equivalent to carrying the investment at market. Under the market method, the carrying value would be $150,000 (3,000 × $50) assuming the market price remained at $50.

sidiary's operations are integrated with those of a parent. Two contrasting types of subsidiaries are representative:

1. Nonhomogeneous subsidiaries
2. Joint ventures

Nonhomogeneous Subsidiaries

One drawback of consolidation is that nonhomogeneous (dissimilar) subsidiaries may be combined, masking the characteristics of individual segments of the firm. In these cases, fully disaggregated information is preferable (or necessary) for analysis. This is especially true when the subsidiary is in an unrelated line of business whose financial and operating characteristics differ from those of the remaining lines, for example, an oil company owned by a chemical or steel company or an insurance company owned by a manufacturer or retailer. In addition, the existence of subsidiary debt or other restrictions (e.g., regulatory) on the ability of the enterprise to draw on the assets of the subsidiary may further strengthen the case for separate analysis.

Prior to the adoption of SFAS 94, which became effective in 1988, credit, insurance, leasing, and other nonhomogeneous subsidiaries were excluded from the consolidated financial statements. This exclusion was the subject of much debate. Proponents of exclusion argued that the operating activities and capital structure of financial subsidiaries differ significantly from those of their manufacturing or retailing parents. Even the form of financial statements is different: Financial companies, for example, have unclassified balance sheets with no distinction between current and noncurrent assets or liabilities. Bond covenants and the degree of control over and claims on assets and cash flows may also differ. Consolidation of such dissimilar entities, it was argued, would confuse financial statement users.

On the other hand, proponents of full consolidation argued that it is illogical to segregate some subsidiaries from the consolidated group, especially when the operations of the subsidiary are integral to the business of the parent. For example, when a finance subsidiary provides credit to the dealers and customers of the parent, its assets are, in effect, the parent's accounts receivable. Financing those receivables through a separate subsidiary may facilitate the parent's borrowing activities, but it does not justify exclusion of the subsidiary from the consolidated financial statements.

The most serious limitation of consolidation is the loss of detailed operating results for the firm's different lines of business. Aggregation often disguises disparate trends and profitability among business segments. Some of this problem is alleviated by the requirement that firms operating in more than one business must provide segment data, albeit with considerably less detail. The analysis of segment data is discussed in a later section of this chapter.

Joint Ventures

Joint ventures are frequently found in the business world and are often extensions of the firm's core businesses. They offer advantages of economies of scale and allow companies to share technological, operating, and financial risk. They may also facilitate access to developing markets in Eastern Europe and emerging economies. The legal forms of these ventures vary due to tax, legal, and operational requirements. As a result, accounting sometimes follows form rather than substance, and the financial statements may need adjustment to reflect the economic nature of the joint venture and its impact on the venturers more appropriately.

Some joint ventures are primarily contractual arrangements whereby the venturers agree to cooperate toward a common goal but no new entity is created. Each venturer maintains its own assets and liabilities and recognizes revenues and expenses separately. This type of joint venture creates neither accounting nor analysis difficulties as each venturer already reflects the results of the venture in its financial statements. However, disclosure of the impact of the venture is highly variable across firms given the absence of specific reporting requirements.

Other joint ventures result in common ownership of assets, without the formation of a separate legal entity. Each venturer recognizes its proportionate share of common assets, liabilities, revenues, and expenses. Here again, because each venturer already reflects its share of the operations in its financial statements, neither accounting nor analysis is required to go further. Pipelines (oil and gas) and electric utility plants are common applications of this form of joint venture.

Jointly Controlled Entities. In many cases, however, the joint venture is a separate entity, either a corporation or partnership. The entity is created by capital contributions (cash and/or operating assets) from two or more venturers and is governed by a contract. The contract will generally specify how operating, investing, and financing decisions are to be made by the venturers.

Because the joint venture is a separate legal entity, it prepares its own financial statements; these may be available if it has issued publicly traded debt. However, if the venture is financed with bank debt, the statements are not public documents. The venturers, in most cases, account for their interests in such jointly controlled entities using the equity method of accounting, reporting their proportionate share of both net income and net investment in the venture.

Use of the equity method means that the gross assets and liabilities, as well as revenues and expenses, are excluded from the financial statements of the venturers. Footnotes of the venturers will also exclude data relating to the joint venture in such areas as leases, retirement plans, and contingent obligations (including off-balance-sheet financing).[30]

However, the operations of the joint venture may be as much a part of the integrated operations of the parent companies as those of other, wholly owned subsidiaries. For example, Micron Technology [MU], whose joint ventures are discussed in Chapter 11, includes the earnings of its joint ventures (primarily suppliers of memory for MU's chips) as adjustments to cost of goods sold, in recognition of the integrated nature of these operations. In such cases, the "one-line consolidation" resulting from use of the equity method understates the importance of the operations of the joint venture to the parent company and analysts must evaluate the appropriateness of the equity method.

In addition, the venture's often-significant debt is excluded because the equity method includes only the net assets of the investee in the investor's balance sheet; this debt may have been an important incentive to use the equity method rather than consolidate. In such cases, proportionate consolidation depicts the higher risk level, as we shall shortly see.

Thus, the equity method can distort firm performance in several ways:

1. *Profitability measures.* Although net income includes investee income, (most of) the assets that generate them are excluded. Thus, *the investor's ROA is overstated.* (Note that ROE is not affected.)

    As investee revenues and expenses are excluded, *investor return on sales measures are overstated.*

    Similarly, *interest coverage ratios are overstated* as the numerator includes investee income, while the denominator excludes investee interest expense.

2. *Solvency measures.* Investee assets and liabilities are excluded from the balance sheet. This has important implications for credit analysis as:

    • Liabilities are hidden in investees.

    • The nature of the investee's assets is unknown; are they tangible or intangible?

3. *Information loss.* The investor's footnotes exclude information relating to the investee in such areas as leases, derivatives, debt covenants, and employee benefit plans.[31]

Proportionate Consolidation

Because the equity method inadequately conveys the risk-and-return characteristics of investments in unconsolidated affiliates, alternative accounting methods have been developed for such ventures. These alternatives can provide better information to financial statement

---

[30]Any debt guarantees by co-venturers must be disclosed separately in their footnotes.

[31]See Case 11-1, regarding the Caltex joint venture between Chevron and Texaco, for an example.

users whether they are used by the reporting entity or produced by the financial analyst. Two alternatives to the equity method are:

- Proportionate consolidation (sometimes called pro rata consolidation)
- The expanded equity method

These alternatives gained support from IAS 31 (1990), which states that proportionate consolidation is the preferred method of accounting for jointly controlled entities:

> Proportionate consolidation better reflects the substance and economic reality of a venturer's interest in a jointly controlled entity, that is control over the venturer's share of the future economic benefits.[32]

Under the expanded equity method, the proportionate shares of assets, liabilities, revenues, and expenses are separated from those of the consolidated group. IAS 31, which became effective in 1992, considers the expanded equity method to be a reporting variant of proportionate consolidation and allows companies to use either method. Although use of the equity method is an allowed alternative under IAS 31, the strong endorsement of proportionate consolidation is likely to lead to greater use of the method. We illustrate proportionate consolidation in the next section.

Comparison of Proportionate Consolidation and the Equity Method

Exhibit 13-5 illustrates proportionate consolidation and compares it with the equity method. Although both net income and equity of Petroleum Corp. are the same under these two methods, virtually all other financial statement amounts are different.

Under proportionate consolidation, the parent company includes its share of *each* asset and liability account of the affiliate in the corresponding account of the parent. For example (if we assume 40% ownership of the joint venture), the parent includes 40% of the cash, inventories, receivables, and debt of the joint venture in the parent's cash, inventories, receivables, and debt. Only stockholders' equity is unaffected as the investment in the affiliate account is eliminated against the parent's share of the affiliate's equity. To some extent, this procedure is similar to the adjustments made for debt of an unconsolidated subsidiary in the off-balance-sheet analysis in Chapter 11. Here, however, adjustments are made for *all* financial statement accounts.

Similarly, the parent includes 40% of *each* affiliate revenue and expense category in its income statement. There is no impact on parent company net income, as the parent's share of affiliate income is eliminated in consolidation.

Impact of Proportionate Consolidation. As a result of the differences between the two methods, most financial ratios are changed, as shown in the following examples derived from Exhibit 13-5.

2001 Ratio Comparison

	PETROLEUM	SUPPLY	**PETROLEUM**
	Equity Method		Proportionate Consolidation (After Eliminations)
Current ratio	**3.00**	1.50	**2.82**
Long-term debt to equity	**0.40**	3.40	**0.50**
Interest coverage*	**6.20**	2.00	**4.96**
Return on sales (net income/sales)	**6.4%**	5.0%	**6.1%**
Return on assets (EBIT/assets)	**13.8%**	11.3%	**13.5%**

*EBIT (earnings before interest and taxes)/interest expense.

[32]IAS 31, Financial Reporting of Interests in Joint Ventures (1990), para. 24.

EXHIBIT 13-5
Illustration of Proportionate Consolidation

Assume that Petroleum Corp. owns 40% of a joint venture (Supply Corp.). The investment in Supply Corp., exactly equal to 40% of Supply Corp.'s net worth, is $16 on December 31, 2000. Columns (1) and (2) in the tables below present the condensed income statements and balance sheets for the Petroleum and Supply Corporations with the Petroleum Corp. carrying the Supply Corp. using the equity method.

Income Statements, Year Ended December 31, 2001

	(1) PETROLEUM	(2) SUPPLY	(3) PETROLEUM	(4) PETROLEUM
	Equity Method		Proportionate Consolidation	Proportionate Consolidation (after adjustment for intercompany transactions)
Revenue	$1,000	$200	$1,080	$1,056
Cost of goods sold	(800)	(140)	(856)	(832)
SG&A	(80)	(26)	(90)	(90)
Interest expense	(20)	(17)	(27)	(27)
Equity in earnings of Supply*	4	—	—	—
Pretax income	$ 104	$ 17	$ 107	$ 107
Income tax	(40)	(7)	(43)	(43)
Net income	$ 64	$ 10	$ 64	$ 64

*As Petroleum owns 40% of Supply, its equity in the 2001 earnings of Supply equals $4 (40% of $10).

Balance Sheets, at December 31, 2001

	(1) PETROLEUM	(2) SUPPLY	(3) PETROLEUM	(4) PETROLEUM
Assets	Equity Method		Proportionate Consolidation	Proportionate Consolidation (after adjustment for intercompany transactions)
Cash	$100	$ 20	$ 108	$108
Accounts receivable	300	50	320	316
Inventory	200	50	220	220
Property	280	180	352	352
Investment	20		—	—
Total	$900	$300	$1,000	$996
Liabilities and Equity				
Accounts payable	200	80	232	228
Long-term debt	200	170	268	268
Equity	500	50	500	500
Total	$900	$300	$1,000	$996

Column (3): Proportionate Consolidation

In Column (3) we apply the proportionate consolidation method to Petroleum's accounting for its investment in Supply. Under proportionate consolidation, 40% of the assets and liabilities of Supply are added to the corresponding assets and liabilities of Petroleum. For example, consolidated cash equals $100 + (0.40 × $20) = $108.

The investment in Supply is replaced by Petroleum's proportionate share of each asset and liability account of the affiliate. In the income statement, the equity in earnings of Supply has been replaced by a proportionate share of each revenue and expense line of Supply. These changes are identical to those made for a full consolidation except that only 40% of the accounts of the affiliate have been included.

EXHIBIT 13-5 *(continued)*

Column (4): Adjusting for Intercompany Transactions

This example assumes, thus far, that there are no intercompany transactions. If the venture is either a supplier to or a customer of the investor company, there are intercompany payables/receivables and intercompany sales. To complete the proportionate consolidation, we must eliminate these items from the consolidated statements. To make these eliminations, assume that:

- Petroleum purchases 30% of Supply's output.
- Supply has accounts receivable from Petroleum of $10 at December 31, 2001.

As intercompany sales are $60 (0.3 × $200), we must eliminate that amount from the consolidated revenues. Consolidated revenues are, therefore, $1,000 + (0.4 × $200) − [0.4 × (0.3 × $200)] = $1,056. The third item is the subtraction of intercompany sales.

Similarly, consolidated cost of goods sold are computed as $800 + (0.4 × $140) − [0.4 × (0.3 × $200)] = $832. The third item, which represents (the proportionate share of) sales from Supply to Petroleum, must also have been included in Petroleum's cost of goods sold. Whenever there are intercompany sales, we must eliminate them from the sales of the seller and the COGS of the buyer.

The second elimination, of intercompany payables, is simpler. We simply reduce the accounts receivable of Supply by 0.4 × $10 and, at the same time, reduce the accounts payable of Petroleum by the same amount. Consolidated accounts receivable are $300 + [0.4 × ($50 − $10)] = $316; accounts payable are $200 + [0.4 × ($80 − $10)] = $228.

For each case, the ratios for Supply are weaker than Petroleum's (using the equity method). As result, by including Supply's assets, debt, revenues, expenses, and interest on a pro rata basis, Petroleum's (Proportionate Consolidation) ratios declined. Note, however, that return on equity (not shown) is the same ($64/$500 = 12.8%) under both methods, as net income and equity are unchanged.

Use of Proportionate Consolidation in Practice

Neither proportionate consolidation nor the expanded equity method is widely used; in the United States, it is unclear whether these methods are permitted under GAAP. *This, of course, should not deter the analyst from making analytical adjustments.*

Within the construction industry, however, where joint ventures are the dominant form of doing business, proportionate consolidation is frequently used. Morrison Knudsen, for example, used proportionate consolidation in its income statement for its construction (and mining) joint ventures. As a result, revenues of $551 million (nearly 25% of total corporate revenues) and costs of $511 million were included in its 1999 income statement rather than just net operating income of $40 million. On its balance sheet, however, Morrison Knudsen reported its net equity in these joint ventures of $152 million, using the equity method rather than its share of gross assets and liabilities.

Significance of Consolidation: Summary

The preceding sections discussed types of intercorporate investments, different methods of accounting for them, and the analysis of the resulting (significantly different) reported financial data. We now summarize the process and the most significant insights for the financial analyst.

First, when examining a set of financial statements, it is essential to determine the accounting methods used for investments in affiliates. This is especially true of non-U.S. companies, as consolidation practices vary widely.

The second step should be to consider whether adjustments are needed to make the financial data more useful. When evaluating several different companies, the most overriding concern is likely to be comparability of basic data. You cannot compare, for example, Pfizer, Roche, and Takeda Chemical without comparable financial data.

An important aspect of this second step is to ask what form of presentation accords most closely with the objectives of the analysis. For example, current and prospective lenders to financial subsidiaries need separate financial statements for those entities; consolidated statements that include the manufacturing operations of the parent company are less useful.

As we have seen, accounting conventions do not always reflect economic reality. The analyst should determine, for example, which unconsolidated affiliates are integral to the enterprise and should, therefore, be consolidated. Analysts should also be aware of the potential use of off-balance-sheet unconsolidated affiliates to obtain financing.

The third step should be to make any required adjustments to the reported financial statements. For U.S. companies, the needed data are often available in 10-K reports or supplemental data (such as "fact books") that companies prepare for financial analysts. Even condensed statements are useful; it is better to be approximately right than precisely wrong!

Adjustments should not be made mechanically. They should be appropriate in the context of the company's operations and the objectives of the analysis. Finally, and most important, adjusted financial statements and ratios should be carefully examined for insights regarding the company's past results, current operations, and future performance. Analysts should concentrate on the differences between adjusted and unadjusted data.

ANALYSIS OF MINORITY INTEREST

Minority interest is the amount of the consolidated net assets and income that does not belong to the parent. The FASB exposure draft on consolidation (see Box 13-3), in keeping with its emphasis on effective control, refers to this as *noncontrolling interest*. We continue to use the term *minority interest* in our discussion as it is more widely understood.

The balance in the minority interest account shown on the balance sheet and the minority interest in net income are necessarily related. If the subsidiary pays no cash dividends, then the change in the balance sheet account equals the minority interest in net income. If a dividend is paid, then the balance sheet change equals the minority interest in net income less the dividends paid to minority owners; that is, the amount of undistributed earnings for the period. Capital contributions or withdrawals also affect the minority interest shown on the parent company balance sheet.

For example, Texaco's 1999 minority interest can be reconciled as follows:

Texaco: Analysis of Minority Interest ($millions)

Opening balance sheet liability: minority interest	$679
Income statement: minority interest	83
Financing cash flow: dividends paid to minority shareholders	(55)
Closing balance sheet liability: minority interest[33]	$707

Note that the accounting for minority interest is the mirror image of the equity method. It reflects the minority shareholders' investment in the consolidated subsidiary. Assets of a less-than-wholly owned subsidiary are not as freely available to the parent as those of a 100%-owned subsidiary because of the minority investor.

Minority interest can be quite significant. For Texaco, it was less than 6% of stockholders' equity. Alcoa [AA] in contrast, has large majority-owned subsidiaries, and the numbers are far more significant. At December 31, 1999, Alcoa's minority interest was $1.46 billion or more than 23% of equity of $6.31 billion. Minority interest in 1999 earnings was $242 million and reduced net income by 19%. Finally, dividends to the minority shareholders of the majority-owned subsidiaries were $122 million, 41% of the $298 million paid to Alcoa's own stockholders.

In some respects, minority interest can be considered equity for purposes of analysis. Minority shareholders have only a residual claim on the assets of the subsidiary.[34] From the point of view of both creditors and stockholders of the parent, however, minority interest has

---

[33]The actual closing balance is $710, a difference of $3 that may be due to foreign currency effects or other minor adjustments.

[34]The minority interest is also a residual claim on the assets of the consolidated entity. It is therefore appropriately reported as a component of equity in the consolidated financial statements.

the characteristics of a preferred shareholder. Generally, the creditors and shareholders of the parent cannot benefit from the assets of the subsidiary without respecting the claims of its creditors and minority holders. Thus, minority interest occupies a special position and should not be mechanically aggregated with either liabilities or equity.

CONSOLIDATION PRACTICES OUTSIDE THE UNITED STATES

IAS 27 requires that all controlled subsidiaries be consolidated.[35] While non-U.S. standards have been moving toward consolidation for many years, differences from U.S. practice persist.

In Japan and parts of Western Europe, parent company reporting was the norm until quite recently. "Parent-only" financial statements are still considered to be the primary set of statements in some countries where financial reporting is based on tax reporting. Parent-only statements may exclude significant operating subsidiaries, limiting the value of these statements for analysis.

In Germany, consolidated financial statements normally include only domestic subsidiaries; investments in foreign subsidiaries and affiliates are carried at acquisition cost. In the United Kingdom and Canada, firms may exclude nonhomogeneous subsidiaries from consolidated financial statements. However, current trends indicate that excluded affiliates are limited to those operating in the banking and insurance industries.

The Netherlands, Germany, Belgium, Italy, and France allow or require firms to exclude nonhomogeneous subsidiaries from consolidated financial statements. There are either no requirements or restrictions on consolidation of special-purpose entities (variously defined) in these countries. Germany and France permit the use of proportionate consolidation.

Where consolidation is required by local standards, the rules may differ from U.S./IAS GAAP. For example, AXA uses the following rules required by French GAAP:

Basis of Consolidation[36]

1. Companies in which AXA exercises controlling influence are fully consolidated. Controlling influence is generally presumed when AXA directly or indirectly holds at least 40% of the voting rights and no other shareholder directly or indirectly holds a percentage greater than AXA.
2. Companies in which AXA directly or indirectly holds at least 20% of the voting rights and for which AXA and other shareholders have agreed to exercise joint controlling influence are proportionately consolidated.
3. Companies in which AXA exercises significant long-term influence are accounted for by the equity method. Significant influence is presumed when AXA directly or indirectly holds at least 20% of the voting rights or when significant influence is exercised through an agreement with other shareholders.

Paragraph 1 means that some companies are consolidated under French GAAP that might not be consolidated under U.S./IAS GAAP because ownership is under 50%. Paragraph 2 requires proportionate consolidation for some affiliates; this method is not used under U.S. GAAP. While proportionate consolidation is preferred under IAS 31, it is not mandatory.

Japanese standards also vary somewhat from U.S./IAS GAAP. New (1999) standards require the consolidation of companies that are directly or indirectly controlled, even if ownership is less than 50%. As a result of the new standards, Takeda Chemical consolidated 15 affiliates in fiscal 2000 that were previously accounted for by the equity method. The change increased retained earnings by ¥11 billion (slightly over 1%). No information is provided about the effects of consolidation on debt or other balance sheet accounts. These affiliates probably would not be consolidated under U.S. or IAS rules.

[35]The standard allows only rare exceptions to this rule.
[36]Source: AXA 2000 annual report.

ANALYSIS OF SEGMENT DATA

The analysis of companies with more than one line of business has inherent difficulties as compared with the analysis of companies engaged in a single business. The aggregation of financial data for businesses with differing financial structures, risk attributes, and indicators of performance obscures the characteristics of each segment. The rise of the conglomerate corporation in the 1960s aggravated the problem as multidivisional corporations proliferated.

With strong encouragement from the financial analyst community, the Financial Accounting Standards Board placed segment reporting on its agenda soon after it was established in 1973. The key to segment disclosure naturally centers on the definition of the segments of the enterprise.

The FASB decided that a precise definition could not be written into an accounting standard. Hence, its original pronouncement, SFAS 14, Financial Reporting for Segments of a Business Enterprise (1974), provided for management judgment guided by factors such as the similarity of

- Products
- Production processes
- Markets or marketing methods

These guidelines invariably led to a "line-of-business approach" to segment disclosures. However, the line-of-business orientation meant that some firms reported data based on segmentation different from the firm's organizational structure. In addition, analysts lobbied for additional segment disclosures in a format consistent with how firms operate internally.[37]

In June 1997, the FASB issued SFAS 131, Disclosures about Segments of an Enterprise and Related Information, which revised SFAS 14. A major change from SFAS 14 was the adoption of the "management approach" in determining reportable segments (*i.e., operating segments of a company were to be determined on the basis of how the company was managed and organized internally*).

The IASB also revised its segment disclosure rules, IAS 14 (revised) in 1997. The IASB did not follow the FASB's management approach but rather followed the more traditional line-of-business approach. IAS 14 (para. 9) defines *business segment* as an enterprise component

> that is engaged in providing an individual product or service or a group of related products or services and that is *subject to risks and returns that are different from those of other business segments*. [emphasis added]

Unlike IAS 14 (revised), SFAS 131 does not require segment reporting on a secondary basis, although minimal geographic disclosures are required. IAS 14 permits management to select, as the primary "segmentation" approach, either the line-of-business method or geographic segmentation. Significant disclosures are required for the secondary segmentation method.

The differences in approaches will be illustrated below by comparing Lucent's segment disclosures (SFAS 131) with those of Roche (IAS 14). First, however, we describe the segment disclosures required by these standards.

Disclosure Requirements of SFAS 131 and IAS 14

Reportable segments are defined by SFAS 131 as components of the enterprise that account for at least 10% of *any one* of the following:

- Total revenues (before elimination of intersegment sales).
- Combined operating profit (of profitable segments); or its operating loss must exceed 10% of the combined operating loss of segments with losses.
- Combined identifiable assets of all segments.

---

[37]See "Financial Reporting in the 1990s and Beyond," *Association for Investment Management and Research*, Charlottesville, Virginia, 1993.

For each reportable segment, disclosure requirements include:

1. Operating profit or some other measure of profitability
2. Identifiable assets
3. Sales to unaffiliated customers and intersegment sales
4. Interest revenue and expense[38]
5. Depreciation, depletion, and amortization expense
6. Any unusual income component and/or extraordinary items
7. Income tax expense
8. Capital expenditures
9. Investment in and income from equity income investees

Items three to nine are required only if these items were included in the measure of profit and/or segment assets reported to the chief operating decision maker. Many of these items (e.g., income taxes, interest, equity income) are disclosures not required by SFAS 14.

Geographical Disclosures. SFAS 131 also requires that companies disclose the following geographical data: revenues from external customers and long-lived assets for

- The firm's home country
- All foreign countries
- Any material[39] single foreign country

Firms must also report sales to any customer accounting for more than 10% of sales. Disclosure is also required if 10% of sales comes from domestic government agencies as a group or foreign governments as a group. Note that the name of the major customer need not be disclosed, only the amount of sales.

The disclosures required by IAS 14 are similar to those of SFAS 131 with two major additions. IAS 14 requires the reporting of

- *Liabilities by (operating) segment, permitting the calculation of ROE.*
- *Profitability measures by geographical segment.*

Geographical segment profitability data were required by SFAS 14, but are not required by SFAS 131.

One important difference between U.S. and IAS standards concerns the accounting methods used to report segment data. IAS 14 requires segment data to be computed using the same accounting methods used to prepare consolidated statements (i.e., IAS GAAP). SFAS 131, in contrast, permits firms to disclose segment data based on different accounting methods (for example, regulatory or non-U.S. standards) as long as there is a reconciliation shown (in the aggregate) to U.S. GAAP.

Example. Quanex [NX] is a producer of metal products based in the United States. Its 10-K report for the year ended October 31, 2000 reports that:

> At the start of fiscal 1999, Quanex changed its inventory valuation method for measuring segment results from LIFO to FIFO. This change has no impact on consolidated results, which remain LIFO based.

When segment data use accounting principles that differ from those used by the parent, extra care is needed in interpreting such data. You should not assume that the differences impact all segments equally, or even in the same direction (prices may be rising in one segment, declining in another).

Early studies of the impact of SFAS 131 [Street, Nichols, and Gray (2000); Herrmann and Thomas (2000)] documented that, in general, more disaggregated information was being provided by firms as the number of operating segments reported increased. Moreover, the

---

[38]These may be netted if so reported to the segment's chief operating decision maker.

[39]As SFAS 131 does not define *materiality*, disclosures vary widely among firms.

"management approach" resulted in more consistency between the information provided in the segment report and other annual report disclosures, especially the MD&A section. This consistency allows for further in-depth analysis of the segment information. However, the number of items per segment being reported did not increase materially (although extra items were required by SFAS 131), and on a geographic basis there was a decrease in the number of segments and detail provided therein. With respect to analysts' (consolidated) earnings forecasts, preliminary evidence by Venkataraman (2001) indicated that, on average, forecast accuracy improved with the introduction of SFAS 131. This result, in some sense, validates the analyst community's request for the change in definition of reportable segments.

Illustration of Industry Segments: Lucent and Roche

The different approaches to segment classification and reporting are illustrated in Exhibit 13-6, which compares segments reported by Lucent Technologies (following SFAS 131 guidelines) and those used by Roche (following IAS 14). Both companies disclose sales to unaffiliated customers, intersegment sales, operating income, identifiable assets, depreciation, and capital expenditures for each segment for each year, although the Roche presentation is more detailed. Additionally, Roche, but not Lucent, provides information on segment liabilities.

Computations of sales and operating income concentration, as well as two profitability ratios, are presented below. The first ratio measures profitability relative to sales. The second, return on average assets (operating income divided by average identifiable assets), is the only available return-on-investment measure by segment.

Comparison of 1999 Segment Data

	Lucent Technologies			Roche			
Segment	SPN	Enterprise	MCT	Pharma-ceuticals	Diag-nostics	Vitamins & Fine Chemicals	Fragrances & Flavors
% of Sales*	*62%*	*22%*	*14%*	*60%*	*19%*	*13%*	*8%*
% of Operating Income*	*84%*	*11%*	*17%*	*69%*	*15%*	*12%*	*8%*
Operating Margin	**19%**	**7%**	**17%**	**21%**	**15%**	**16%**	**18%**
Return on Assets	**27%**	**16%**	**23%**	**14%**	**8%**	**13%**	**13%**

*Totals do not add to 100%; see footnote to Exhibit 13-6

Roche's segment reporting is more oriented toward a line-of-business approach. The four segments reflect different businesses, product lines, and customers. The segments are naturally delineated and are essentially four different companies operating under one umbrella corporation. The low level of intersegment transfers between divisions provides further evidence that Roche's industry segments are not significantly integrated. (The Vitamins & Fine Chemicals division has the highest proportion of intersegment sales—less than 5% of its total segment sales.) This low level of integration suggests that Roche's acquisitions were not undertaken to achieve synergies through vertical integration.

Lucent's segments are described in Exhibit 13-6. Note that all three divisions operate in the "telecommunications networking industry." The segmentation is based on Lucent's internal organization, primarily focused on customer base and market segments rather than product type or technology. Consistent with this, we find that Lucent's intersegment sales are significant. For the MCT division, they equal 20% of total divisional sales.[40]

---

[40]The exhibit notes that "intellectual capital" is a product of the MCT segment, indicating that the company's R&D efforts for all its operations may be focused there.

EXHIBIT 13-6
Segment Disclosures: Lucent and Roche

For 1999 Fiscal Years	Lucent (in $millions)				Roche (CHF in millions)				
Segment	SPN[1]	Enterprise[2]	MCT[3]	Total*	Pharmaceuticals	Diagnostics	Vitamins & Fine Chemicals	Fragrances & Flavors	Total*
Revenue	23,745	8,754	6,742	39,999	16,684	5,283	3,832	2,231	28,030
Less interdivisional sales	(183)	(195)	(1,318)	(1,696)	(197)	(1)	(183)	(82)	(463)
Divisional sales to third parties	23,562	8,559	5,424	38,303	16,487	5,282	3,649	2,149	27,567
EBITDA					4,759	1,430	799	524	7,324
Depreciation & amortization	(690)	(134)	(489)	(1,806)	(1,255)	(659)	(215)	(127)	(2,260)
Operating profit	4,563	616	944	5,406	3,504	771	584	397	5,064
Divisional operating assets					25,138	10,142	4,440	2,977	42,753
Other segment assets					534	35	100	17	686
Segment assets	16,939	3,884	4,095	24,918	25,672	10,177	4,540	2,994	43,439
Nonsegment assets				13,857					26,992
Total assets				38,775					70,431
Divisional operating liabilities					(674)	(346)	(149)	(72)	(1,242)
Other segment liabilities					(2,033)	(1,660)	(1,384)	(141)	(5,218)
Segment liabilities					(2,707)	(2,006)	(1,533)	(213)	(6,460)
Nonsegment liabilities									(33,970)
Total liabilities									(40,430)
Property additions	675	266	707	2,215	963	568	450	165	2,150
Other capital expenditures					5,544	65	27	(34)	5,604
Research and development					3,048	516	130	50	3,782

*Total may include other smaller divisions and corporate operations and is not necessarily sum of segments reported.

[1]Service Provider Networks (SPN) provides public networking systems and software to telecommunications service providers and public network operators around the world.

[2]Enterprise develops, manufactures, markets, and services advanced communications products and data networking systems for business customers.

[3]Microelectronics and Communications Technologies (MCT) designs and manufactures high-performance integrated circuits, power systems, and optoelectronic components for applications in the communications and computing industries. MCT also includes network products, new ventures, and intellectual property.

Using the 1999 data, we note that each company has a dominant segment measured by sales and operating income. For Lucent it is SPN (62% of sales; 84% of operating income); for Roche it is pharmaceuticals (60% and 69%). These dominant segments are also the most profitable. Each has the highest operating margin and ROA in their respective companies.

These patterns change when we move to the "secondary" segments. In Roche's case, Fragrances & Flavors, the smallest "contributor" to sales and operating income has the second highest operating margin and ROA.

For Lucent, the differences are more striking. Although MCT segment sales were one-third below the Enterprise segment (14% versus 22%), its contribution to Lucent's operating income was 50% higher (17% versus 11% of total operating income). Consistent with the above, MCT's profitability ratios (operating margin and ROA) are significantly higher than those of Enterprise.

These differences should be viewed in conjunction with the three-year growth in sales, operating income, and assets of these segments:

Lucent Segment Growth Rates, 1997 to 1999

Change in	SPN (%)	Enterprise (%)	MCT (%)
Sales	51	37	28
Operating income	201	(8)	72
Identifiable assets	87	56	40

The three-year trend in sales and operating income mirrors the 1999 levels of these variables. Again SPN is the best performer; operating income increased 201% on a sales increase of 51%. This indicates leveraging of operating efficiencies and increased returns to scale, "justifying" the increased investment in that segment as reflected by the growth in (identifiable) assets. A similar pattern emerges in the MCT segment; a 28% increase in sales translates into a 72% increase in operating profit.

On the other hand, as indicated earlier by its operating ratios, the Enterprise segment seems to be troubled. Although sales grew by 37%, operating income fell 8%! These data raise questions about the viability of the market in which Enterprise operates as well as whether the increased investment (56% asset growth) in that segment was justified.

The problems with the segment were obviously not lost to Lucent's management. *On September 30, 2000 (the last day of its fiscal year-end), Lucent spun off the Enterprises division (as Avaya Inc.) and reported a $462 million loss for that division as part of discontinued operations.*

The additional disclosures made by Roche provide useful insights into segment characteristics. The segment liabilities are not proportional to segment assets; they are relatively highest for Vitamins (1/3 of assets) and lowest for Pharmaceuticals and Fragrances. Thus returns on net investment are highest for Vitamins [(584/(4,540 − 1,533)] = 19.4%.

The R&D data show the highest investment for Pharmaceuticals (18.3% of revenue). While not surprising given the characteristics of that business, this ratio is a more useful comparison with other (pure drug) companies than the ratio (13.5%) based on consolidated data.

Illustration of Geographic Segments: Honda

SFAS 131 also requires disclosures regarding geographic areas. Such disclosures often augment insights obtained from industry segment data and point to further areas of consideration. Unfortunately, profitability data by geographical segments is no longer required, although sometimes provided.

Honda [7267], a leading automotive company based in Japan, issues financial statements prepared under U.S. GAAP. Geographic segment data are shown below, along with the same two profitability ratios used to examine industry segment data in the previous section.

Honda Geographic Segments

Years Ended March 31 (Yen billions)

2000	Japan	North America	Europe	Other	Total
External sales	1,806.9	3,197.4	664.5	430.1	6,098.9
Operating income	116.3	273.1	(14.5)	51.3	426.2
Assets	1,843.0	2,061.9	418.5	575.0	4,898.4
Operating margin	6.4%	8.5%	−2.2%	11.9%	7.0%
Return on assets	6.3%	13.2%	−3.5%	8.9%	8.7%
2001					
Sales	1,951.0	3,488.3	526.9	497.6	6,463.8
Operating income	146.1	276.5	(55.5)	39.9	407.0
Assets	2,022.0	2,713.5	457.6	474.2	5,667.3
Operating margin	7.5%	7.9%	−10.5%	8.0%	6.3%
Return on assets	7.2%	10.2%	−12.1%	8.4%	7.2%
% of total sales—2000	29.6%	52.4%	10.9%	7.1%	100.0%
% of total sales—2001	30.2%	54.0%	8.2%	7.7%	100.0%
% of total income—2000	27.3%	64.1%	−3.4%	12.0%	100.0%
% of total income—2001	35.9%	67.9%	−13.6%	9.8%	100.0%

Source: Data from Honda, *2001 annual report.*

The geographic segment data provide the following insights into Honda's operating performance:

1. North America is the dominant geographic segment, accounting for more than one-half of external sales and approximately two-thirds of operating income.
2. North America is the most profitable geographical segment measured by return on assets.
3. The small "other" segment has the highest operating margin, followed by North America.
4. The European segment has been the poorest performer, with sales declining in 2001 and with negative operating income for both years.

These insights are only the starting point for analysis. Factors such as exchange rate effects (see Chapter 15), cyclical trends, and nonrecurring items can distort segment data. For example, Honda states that the strong Yen depressed sales in both the North American and European segments. This factor helps explain the poor European performance but makes the North American performance even more impressive.

Management Discussion and Analysis

An additional source of information about segments may be found in the required management discussion and analysis (MD&A). Most companies use industry segments as the base for the MD&A discussion. Sears and Westvaco are two good examples.

Uses and Limitations of Segment Data

One limitation of segment data is the lack of information on liabilities under U.S. GAAP. Funded debt is, however, not the main issue, unless debt is allocated to segments. As operating income is computed before interest expense, return on total capital by segment should be comparable. The more significant issue is noninterest-bearing liabilities such as payables, accruals, and off-balance-sheet obligations. These liabilities reduce the net investment; segment return on assets understates the actual return on capital.

A second limitation is the computation of segment profit, which may be affected by intersegment pricing and any allocation of corporate overhead. It may also reflect different accounting principles (e.g., FIFO instead of LIFO for inventories) than are used by the firm for external reporting.

A third problem is the lack of segment cash flow data. Change in assets alone is a poor measure of changes in resources allocated to different segments. Without disclosure of liabilities or cash flow data, it is difficult to assess capital allocation among segments.

These limitations do not mean that segment data are useless; far from it. They do mean that segment data must be used with some care rather than in a simplistic manner.

Segment data are best used for the examination of trends. We can assume that the computation of segment profitability is consistent from year to year, as is the ratio of liabilities to assets. Therefore, although disclosed levels of profitability may have limited comparability and utility,[41] the trend of profitability is useful and may be more reliable. This is especially true when segment data are presented on a quarterly basis.

Segment trends can, and should, be compared to trends in the sales and operating income of companies in similar businesses and similar segments of multidivisional companies. Again, levels are less-reliable indicators than changes over time. It is also important to adjust for any differences in accounting methods (especially for inventories) and for any unusual items included in reported earnings. Many companies report the allocation of unusual items to individual segments. For example, see the Sears 1999 segment data (Note 15) with its disclosures of "noncomparable items."

Perhaps most important, segment data enable the analyst to obtain a better understanding of a company's operations. Segment disclosures can be used to ask questions that will better illuminate the determinants of sales growth and profitability. This understanding can then be applied to expected future business conditions, resulting in better forecasts of sales and earnings.

Thus, segment data are not an end in themselves but a means to better understanding of a firm's sources of profitability and growth.

Using Segment Data to Estimate Consolidated Earnings and Risk

Segment data can be used to assess both the expected return (profitability) and risk characteristics of a multidivisional firm. After elimination of intercompany transactions, the expected earnings of the total firm equals the sum of the expected earnings of the individual segments. Similarly, the overall risk of the entity is a weighted average of the risk of the individual segments.

Forecasting Sales and Income. A number of studies have compared the forecasting accuracy of models that predict consolidated earnings directly with those that predict individual segment earnings first and then combine those results to forecast firm earnings. Although intuitively one would expect segment data to improve forecast accuracy, results were often mixed.[42]

---

[41]Empirical results discussed later in the chapter suggest that segment data are most useful for forecasting sales. The aggregated sales forecast can then be used to forecast consolidated earnings.

[42]See, for example, Kinney (1971) and Collins (1976).

Hopwood et al. (1982) note that no gains in forecasting ability result from the use of segment data if either:

1. The time-series models of the component segments are identical, or
2. None of the component series leads or lags the consolidated series.

If the various industries that make up the segments are influenced by similar factors (e.g., they tend to move together during the business cycle), then a forecast based on consolidated data should be just as good as a forecast based on segment data. The more dissimilar the series or the greater the lag effects among segments, the greater the benefits of forecasting with segment data. Thus, the degree of improvement in forecasting ability should depend on the interrelationships of the firm's segments.

However, even under the best of conditions (disparate segments), knowledge of the parameters of the forecasting model is needed. As segment-based models require the estimation of more parameters (a set for each segment) than do consolidated-based models, measurement error may affect the results. Measurement error in estimating the parameters dilutes the benefits of segment data.

Chapter 19 discusses the time-series models used to forecast accounting earnings. Many (extrapolative models) are based on the previous time-series history of the variables being predicted. Thus, forecast earnings are a function of past earnings. As will be seen, there has been very little success in distinguishing firm-specific models for this class of models. That is, a firm-specific model does not forecast any better than a single model applied to all firms. Measurement error has been suggested as one reason for this finding. Thus, given the first condition specified by Hopwood et al., for extrapolative models, it is unlikely that forecasts would be improved by segment data.[43]

Improvement would be more likely for models that exploit the economic or fundamental differences between segments. For example, Collins (1976) combined segment-based information with industrywide data [44] to forecast sales and earnings and compared them to those based on consolidated numbers and economywide GNP data. The segment-based earnings forecasts had the lowest prediction errors. The results, however, suggested that improvement was due mainly to better sales forecasts and there was little marginal benefit in segment data beyond that of sales.

Baldwin (1984) provided other evidence that segment data can be used to improve forecasts by comparing analyst forecast accuracy before and after the disclosure of segment-based data was first required in 1971. He found that overall forecast accuracy improved. However, the most significant improvement was for those firms that had not provided segment data previously. The results indicate that analysts were able to use the segment data to improve their forecasting ability. Similarly, Swaminathan (1991) noted a reduction in the dispersion of analysts' forecasts.

The introduction of SFAS 131 also seems to have provided a similar outcome. As noted earlier, Venkataraman (2001) found that analysts' forecasting ability improved subsequent to the introduction of SFAS 131.

Balakrishnan et al. (1990) examined whether geographic segment disclosures could be used to enhance predictions of sales and income. Specifically, they forecast sales and income by geographic region and compared the aggregated regional forecasts with a forecast based on consolidated sales and income data alone. The regional forecasts considered macroeconomic factors characteristic of each region, such as exchange rates, regional GNP growth, and region-specific inflation rates.

They found that using geographical segment data improved forecasts, but that the improvement, not surprisingly, depended on the ability to forecast the macroeconomic factors.

---

[43]This is consistent with Silhan (1982), who simulated "mergers" of existing companies and tested (using extrapolative models) whether the individual series or the aggregated series better forecast the aggregated series. His results indicated no difference between the two approaches.

[44]Specifically, the estimated percentage change in shipments (sales) for industrial sectors corresponding to the individual segments of the consolidated firm was used.

Income forecasts were best when perfect foreknowledge of the macroeconomic factors was assumed; when this assumption was relaxed, they found reduced improvement.

Surprisingly, they found that sales forecasts were better when expectations (rather than perfect foreknowledge) were used for macroeconomic factors. They surmised that

> sales policies (e.g., prices) may be based on predicted exchange rates, and these cannot be adjusted quickly for unexpected exchange rate changes. Thus, the sales forecasts using exchange rate predictions do quite well.[45]

Estimating Risk. Segment information can also be used to assess a firm's risk. A firm's overall market beta is the weighted average of the beta of the individual segments. These, in turn, are a function of the industries in which they operate. Knowledge of the importance of each segment should provide information as to the relative risk class or beta of the overall firm.[46]

Collins and Simonds (1979) found that when segment data were first provided in 1971, there was a significant downward shift in the betas of firms reporting segment data for the first time.[47] Similarly, Greenstein and Sami (1994) found that bid-ask spreads decreased significantly for those firms reporting segment data for the first time and that the magnitude of the decrease was positively related to the number of segments reported.

These results should be viewed in the context of Swaminathan's finding of a reduction in the dispersion of analysts' forecasts, and Cragg and Malkiel (1982), who showed that firms' overall risk levels are highly correlated with the dispersion of analysts' forecasts.

Empirical evidence on the usefulness of segment data for forecasting purposes is mixed. In practice, analyst forecasts use segment data. Particularly in the case of firms operating in different industries, sales and earnings forecasts are based on segment-by-segment analysis. Segment data provide information regarding the source of revenue and earnings growth and indications of the future direction of the firm.

SUMMARY

Intercorporate investments can be accounted for in different ways, depending on ownership structure. In some cases, accounting choices are available within a given structure (e.g., the classification of marketable securities).

The analyst must examine accounting and structural choices to understand how they impact reported financial statements. As accounting standards often set arbitrary boundaries between accounting methods, transactions may be structured to achieve the desired accounting objective.

The principal issues examined in this chapter have been:

1. *Marketable securities.* Selective recognition of gains and losses can distort reported earnings. We show how to measure investment performance and separate it from operating performance.

2. *Consolidation.* The financial statement effects of consolidation (or proportionate consolidation) versus the equity method are considerable. In some cases, good analysis requires that the firm's financial statements be recast using a different accounting method.

3. *Segment data.* These disclosures allow considerable insight into the sources of sales and earnings growth and the performance of different operating divisions.

---

[45]R. Balakrishnan, T. Harris, and P. Sen, "The Predictive Ability of Geographic Segment Disclosures," *Journal of Accounting Research* (Autumn 1990), p. 316.

[46]In a related study of insurance companies, Foster (1975) found that the market discriminated between them on the basis of the performance of their three primary subearnings series: underwriting results, investment results, and capital gains results.

[47]Horwitz and Kolodny (1977) did not find any beta shifts. However, Collins and Simonds (1979) criticized their methodology.

Chapter 13

Problems

1. [Marketable securities—accounting versus mark-to-market returns; CFA© adapted] Bart, a U.S. company, owns the following marketable securities on December 31, 2001:

| | | | | Investee Data (per share except earnings) | | | |
| | | | | Market Value | | 2001 | 2001 |
Firm	Shares Owned	Ownership Percentage	Carrying Value*	12/31/00	12/31/01	Dividend	Earnings
X	100,000	15%	$50.00	$46.00	$49.00	$0.10	$100,000
Y	800,000	40	35.00	30.00	32.00	0.09	900,000
Z	150,000	10	25.00	27.00	30.00	0.00	100,000

*Per share at 1/1/00.

(*Note:* Assume that none of the securities are held for trading purposes.)

a. Compute the following effects of Bart's investment in marketable securities for 2001 on reported:

  (i) Dividend income

  (ii) Unrealized gains and losses (in shareholders' equity)

  (iii) Equity in income of affiliates

b. Describe the U.S. GAAP accounting method applicable to each investment.

c. Compute Bart's 2001 reported income from its marketable securities.

d. Compute where possible the balance sheet carrying amount of each security at December 31, 2001.

e. Calculate Bart's total investment return (mark-to-market basis) on each investment for 2001.

f. Discuss how your answers to parts c, d, and e would change if consolidation were required for ownership of 40% or higher.

2. [Analysis of investment portfolio] The 2000 financial statements of Chubb [CB] report the following data regarding its investment portfolio:

At December 31, 2000 (in $millions)

	Cost	Market
Fixed maturities		
Held-to-maturity	$ 1,496	$ 1,565
Available-for-sale	13,720	14,068
Equity securities	840	830

Investment Income

Year Ended December 31, 2000 (in $millions)

Interest income	$895
Dividend income	24
Realized gains	
Fixed maturities	8
Equity securities	(1)
Total	$926

(The following questions should be answered using the data in Exhibit 13-3 as well as that given above.)

a. Describe how each of the three portfolio components listed above is measured (cost or market value) on Chubb's balance sheet.

b. Compute the reported 2000 ROA for each portfolio component (as in Exhibit 13-3B) and compare the results to the reported 1999 ROA.

c. Compute the mark-to-market 2000 ROA for each portfolio component (as in Exhibit 13-3C) and compare the results to the mark-to-market 1999 ROA and the reported 2000 ROA.

d. During 2000, U.S. stock prices fell and bond prices rose sharply. Discuss whether the reported ROA or mark-to-market ROA provides a better means to evaluate the 2000 performance of Chubb's portfolio. Describe the additional data required to properly evaluate that performance relative to appropriate benchmarks.

3. [Analysis of investment portfolio and effect on financial statements] Exhibit 13P-1 contains data regarding the marketable securities portfolios of Safeco [SAFC], a large U.S. insurance company. Use these data to answer the following questions.

EXHIBIT 13P-1. SAFECO
Investment in Marketable Securities (in $millions)

Marketable Securities

December 31	1998	1999	2000
Fixed maturities			
Held-to-maturity (at amortized cost)*	$ 2,721	$ 2,733	$ —
Available-for-sale (at market)†	17,855	16,831	20,830
Subtotal	**$20,576**	**$19,564**	**$20,830**
Equity securities			
Available-for-sale (at market)‡	2,037	2,005	1,815
Total	**$22,613**	**$21,569**	**$22,645**

*Market values: $3,259, $2,772, and $0.
†Cost: $16,680, $17,259, and $20,388.
‡Cost: $953, $973, and $876.

Gross Investment Income

Years Ended December 31	1999	2000
Fixed maturities		
Interest income	$1,429	$1,477
Realized gains (losses)	—	(51)
Subtotal	**$1,429**	**$1,426**
Equity securities		
Dividend income	52	31
Realized gains (losses)	83	63
Subtotal	**$ 135**	**$ 94**
Total investment income	**$1,564**	**$1,520**

Source: Safeco, *1999–2000 Annual Reports.*

a. Compute the reported ROA for each portfolio component (as in Exhibit 13-3B) for 1999 and 2000. Explain what these data suggest about investment performance for 2000 compared with 1999.

b. Compute the mark-to-market ROA for each portfolio component (as in Exhibit 13-3C) for 1999 and 2000. Explain what these data suggest about investment performance for 2000 compared with 1999.

c. U.S. stock prices fell and bond prices rose sharply in 2000. Discuss which measure of investment performance (reported ROA or mark-to-market ROA) provides a better measure of the performance of Safeco's portfolios.

d. Discuss how you would evaluate the performance of Safeco's portfolio relative to the markets in which it is invested.

e. Safeco reported pretax income (including securities gains) of $332 million in 1999 and $159 million in 2000.

   (i) Compute the effect on pretax income for both years if Safeco reported its actual return on assets (mark-to-market basis) rather than the returns actually reported.

   (ii) Discuss why managements generally oppose mark-to-market accounting for marketable securities.

   (iii) Discuss how the recognition of only realized gains and losses permits managements to manage reported income.

f. In 1996, Safeco management suggested at a meeting with financial analysts that its corporate return on equity should be evaluated with all investments measured at historical cost. Discuss whether you agree with that statement.

4. [Comparison of SFAS 115 and equity method] Company P acquires 100 shares of Company S on January 1, 2001 at $40 per share. Relevant data of Company S for 2001 are:

Earnings per share	$ 3.00
Dividend per share	1.00
Market price at 12-31-01	37.00

Company P sells all its shares of Company S on January 2, 2002 at $39 per share.

a. Compute the carrying amount on December 31, 2001, assuming that P accounts for its investment in S as each of the following:

   (i) Trading security

   (ii) Available-for-sale investment

   (iii) Equity investment

b. Compute the investment income reported by P for 2001, assuming that P accounts for its investment in S as each of the following:

   (i) Trading security

   (ii) Available-for-sale investment

   (iii) Equity investment

c. Compute the total income reported by P on its investment in S over the entire holding period. Discuss the effect of the choice of accounting method on this amount.

5. [Comparison of cost and equity methods; CFA© adapted] Burry acquired 19% of Bowman for $10 million on January 1, 2000. Bowman's securities are not publicly traded. On January 1, 2001, Burry purchased an additional 1% share in Bowman for $500,000.

For the years ended December 31, 2000, and December 31, 2001, Bowman reported earnings and paid dividends as follows:

	Net Income (Loss)	Dividends Paid
2000	$ (600,000)	$800,000
2001	2,000,000	1,000,000

a. Under a strict reading of U.S. GAAP, state which method Burry should use to account for its investment in Bowman in 2000 and in 2001.

b. Based on the accounting choices made in part a, how would Burry's financial statements be affected by Bowman's operating results for 2000 and 2001?

c. Repeat part b, assuming that Burry applied SFAS 115 in both 2000 and 2001.

d. Repeat part b, assuming that Burry used the equity method in both 2000 and 2001.

e. State and justify which of the three answers (parts b, c, or d) provides the most useful information in Burry's financial statements regarding its investment in Bowman.

6. [Marketable securities—comparison of cost, equity method, and consolidation; CFA© adapted] The following data are derived from the annual report of the San Francisco Company, a manufacturer of cardboard boxes:

	2001	2002	2003
Sales	$25,000	$30,000	$35,000
Net income	2,000	2,200	2,500
Dividends paid	1,000	1,200	1,500
Book value per share (year-end)	$11.00	$12.00	$13.00

San Francisco had 1,000 common shares outstanding during the entire period. There is no public market for San Francisco shares.

Potter Company, a manufacturer of glassware, made the following acquisitions of San Francisco common shares:

January 1, 2001	10 shares at $10 per share
January 1, 2002	290 shares at $11 per share, increasing ownership to 300 shares
January 1, 2003	700 shares at $15 per share, resulting in 100% ownership of San Francisco

(When answering the following questions, ignore income tax effects and the effect of lost income on funds used to make these investments.)

a. Calculate the effect of these investments on Potter's reported sales, net income, and cash flow for each of the years 2001 and 2002.

b. Calculate the carrying amount of Potter's investment in San Francisco as of December 31, 2001, and December 31, 2002.

c. Briefly discuss how Potter would account for its investment in San Francisco during 2003. State the additional information needed to calculate the effect on Potter's 2003 financial statements.

(Problems 13-7 and 13-8 are extensions of the Helmerich & Payne [HP] example in the chapter. Exhibit 13P-2 contains information about HP taken from its 1998 through 2000 financial statements.)

7. [Marketable securities; assessing investment performance]

a. HP's "investment in marketable securities" consists of an available-for-sale portfolio and an affiliate carried on the equity basis. Show how the (balance sheet) carrying value for the total investment portfolio was determined.

b. Disaggregate HP's reported income for 1999 and 2000 into the following components:

(i) Income from operations

(ii) Income from marketable securities

(iii) Income from affiliates carried on equity basis

c. Calculate the reported ROA for each component of income calculated in part b (for each year) as well as HP's overall ROA.

d. Discuss the usefulness of the results of parts a and b in explaining HP's operating results for the two years.

e. Calculate each of the following for HP's available-for-sale portfolio for 1999 and 2000:

(i) Dividends and interest earned

(ii) Realized gains and losses

(iii) Unrealized gains and losses

f. Calculate the mark-to-market return and ROA for HP's available-for-sale portfolio for 1999 and 2000.

g. Calculate the mark-to-market return and ROA for HP's investments reported on the equity basis for 1999 and 2000. (*Note:* HP did not purchase or sell any of these securities, nor did it receive any dividends from these investments in the period 1998–2000.)

h. Compare HP's overall mark-to-market returns on its investments (capital appreciation plus dividends and interest) and ROA with those reported for 1999 and 2000.

i. Discuss whether the equity method or mark-to-market return provides a better measure of the performance of equity-based investments over the 1998 to 2000 period.

EXHIBIT 13P-2. HELMERICH & PAYNE
Financial Data (in $millions)

Condensed Balance Sheets

September 30

	1998	1999	2000
Current assets	$ 184,345	$160,624	$ 265,144
Investment in marketable securities	200,400	238,475	304,326
Property plant, and equipment*	705,685	710,600	690,022
Total assets	$1,090,430	$1,109,699	$1,259,492
Current liabilities	125,484	71,904	78,894
Noncurrent liabilities	171,798	189,686	224,895
Stockholders' equity	793,148	848,109	955,703
Total liabilities and equity	$1,090,430	$1,109,699	$1,259,492

*Includes other assets

Condensed Income Statements

Years Ended September 30

	1999	2000
Sales and other operating revenues	$556,562	$599,122
Income from investments	7,757	31,973
Subtotal	$564,319	$631,095
Operating costs	492,900	491,256
Interest	6,481	3,076
Subtotal	$499,381	$494,332
Income before income taxes and equity in income of affiliate	64,938	136,763
Income tax expense	(25,706)	(57,684)
Income before equity in income of affiliate	$ 39,232	$ 79,079
Equity in income of affiliate (net of income taxes)	3,556	3,221
Net income	$ 42,788	$ 82,300

Investment in Marketable Securities

September 30

	1998		1999		2000	
	Cost/ Equity	Market	Cost/ Equity	Market	Cost/ Equity	Market
Available-for-sale portfolio	$76,770	$164,978	$76,057	$197,318	$86,901	$257,973
Affiliate on equity method	35,422	62,437	41,157	91,687	46,353	125,063
Realized capital gains (Pretax)	**$38,421**		**$2,547**		**$13,295**	

Source: Helmerich & Payne, *1998–2000 Annual Reports.*

8. [Equity method; tax rate assumption] HP has one affiliate, Atwood [ATW], which is 24% owned and for which it uses the equity method. In the period 1998–2000, HP did not change its investment in ATW and did not receive any dividends from ATW. Equity income from ATW is reported net of income tax.

a. Calculate Atwood's pretax income for 1999 and 2000. (*Hint:* Consider the change in HP's carrying amount.)

b. Determine HP's assumption as to how it would eventually receive income earned by Atwood. (*Hint:* Compute the effective tax rate used for equity income.)

c. Suggest why HP reported its net-of-tax equity in Atwood's income separately, below after-tax income from other operations.

(Problems 13-9 and 13-10 are based on Moore Motors and Exhibit 13P-3.)

Exhibit 13P-3 presents the consolidated financial statements of Moore Motors Company (Moore). Its 100%-owned finance subsidiary, MM Finance (MMF), provides financing for the dealers and customers of Moore. MMF's separate balance sheet and income statement are also included.

9. [Finance subsidiaries] Moore's consolidated statements aggregate Moore's manufacturing and its financing operations. The consolidated statements are more useful for some purposes, but have drawbacks for other types of analysis, and it may be more useful to treat the subsidiary on an equity basis.

a. Prepare a balance sheet for Moore Motors at December 31, 2001 and 2002 using the equity method of accounting for MMF.

b. Prepare an income statement for Moore Motors for 2002 using the equity method of accounting.

c. Compute each of the following ratios for Moore on a fully consolidated basis, and for Moore (with MMF on an equity basis):

  (i) Gross profit margin

  (ii) Return on assets

  (iii) Return on equity

  (iv) Receivables turnover

  (v) Times-interest-earned

  (vi) Debt-to-equity

EXHIBIT 13P-3. MOORE MOTORS

Balance Sheets, at December 31, 2001 and 2002 (in $thousands)

	Moore Motors Consolidated Balance Sheet		MM Finance	
	2001	2002	2001	2002
Cash and equivalents	$ 10,181	$ 10,213	$ 3,272	$ 3,143
Accounts receivable				
Trade	4,541	5,447		
Parent			14,840	14,460
Finance receivables	87,477	92,355	74,231	79,120
Inventories	10,020	10,065		
Fixed assets (net)	36,936	39,125	6,698	6,839
Miscellaneous assets	14,908	16,092		
Total assets	$164,063	$173,297	$99,041	$103,562
Accounts payable				
Trade	$ 7,897	$ 7,708		
Parent			$ 3,515	$ 2,898
Bank debt	88,130	93,425	81,875	86,868
Accrued liabilities	27,434	29,861	6,380	6,014
Accrued income tax	4,930	5,671		
Total liabilities	$128,391	$136,665	$91,770	$ 95,780
Common stock	6,702	5,401	500	500
Retained earnings	28,970	31,231	6,771	7,282
Total equity	$ 35,672	$ 36,632	$ 7,271	$ 7,782
Total liabilities and equity	$164,063	$173,297	$99,041	$103,562

Income Statements, for Year Ended December 31, 2002 (in $thousands)

	Moore Motors Consolidated	MM Finance
Sales	$110,448	—
Finance revenues	14,504	$14,504
Interest income	1,980	—
Total revenues	$126,932	$14,504
Cost of goods sold	94,683	—
Selling and administrative expense	9,926	3,540
Interest	8,757	7,908
Depreciation and amortization	7,168	1,504
Total expenses	$120,534	$12,952
Pretax income	6,398	1,552
Income tax expense	(2,174)	(441)
Net income	$ 4,224	$ 1,111

(continued)

EXHIBIT 13P-3. *(continued)*

Statement of Cash Flows, for Year Ended December 31, 2002 (in $thousands)

	Moore Motors Consolidated
Net income	$ 4,224
Depreciation and amortization	7,168
Change in accounts receivable	(906)
Change in inventory	(45)
Change in accrued liabilities	2,427
Change in accrued income tax	741
Change in accounts payable	(189)
Other	(414)
Operating cash flow	$ 13,006
Investment in fixed assets	(9,938)
Sale of fixed assets	228
Investment in finance receivables	(100,689)
Liquidation of finance receivables	95,394
Investing cash flow	$ (15,005)
Increase in bank debt	15,267
Decrease in bank debt	(9,972)
Repurchase of shares	(1,474)
New shares issued	173
Dividends paid	(1,963)
Financing cash flow	$ 2,031
Net change in cash and equivalents	$ 32

d. For each of the six ratios in part c, discuss which of the two reporting methods results in ratios that are most useful for analytical purposes. Justify your choices.

10. [Finance subsidiaries; cash flow analysis] MMF's finance (credit) receivables arise from long-term financing provided by MMF to Moore's customers. MMF "pays" Moore, and the customer repays the loan plus interest to MMF.

a. Discuss Moore's classification of the cash received from such transactions in its cash flow statement. Discuss an adjustment to Moore's cash flow statement that would make that statement a more useful indicator of Moore's ability to generate cash from operations.

b. In Chapter 3, we argue that interest payments should be included in financing cash flows rather than operating cash flows. Evaluate this argument as applied to Moore's (consolidated) interest payments.

c. Moore's consolidated cash flow statement combines cash flows from Moore's manufacturing and MMF's financing activities. Using the data in Exhibit 13P-3 and your answers to parts a and b, prepare 2002 statements of cash flows (using the direct method) for:

(i) MMF

(ii) Moore's manufacturing operations

d. Using the cash flow statements prepared in part c, compute the cash flow from MMF to Moore's manufacturing operations (from all sources) during 2002.

e. Discuss how the segmentation of Moore's financial statements aids your understanding of the company's financial condition.

11. [Control requirement for consolidation] On April 12, 1996, Ford Motor Company [F] announced an increase in its ownership of Mazda Motor [7261], a Japanese company, from 25 to 33.4%. The infusion of $481 million of additional equity was required by Mazda's weak financial condition. The announcement also stated that:

- Henry Wallace, a Ford executive, would be President of Mazda.

- Additional Ford personnel would be added to Mazda management.

- Mazda's board contains seven Ford-nominated directors, four of whom hold executive positions in Mazda.

The Economist (April 20, 1996, p. 57) stated that these changes give Ford "de facto control" over Mazda. Ford accounts for its investment in Mazda using the equity method of accounting.

a. Discuss the effect of the increase of ownership on Ford's accounting for the Mazda investment under current U.S. GAAP.

b. Discuss whether the new definition of control in the FASB exposure draft (Box 13-3) would change the answer to part a. Your answer should include a discussion of any additional information required.

c. Regardless of GAAP requirements, discuss whether the analysis of Ford would be improved by:

   (i) Applying proportionate consolidation to the investment in Mazda

   (ii) Fully consolidating Mazda

 12. [Consolidation versus equity method]. On October 1, 1999 Holmen merged its fine paper operations with those of SCA [SCAB] to form Modo Paper, a joint venture owned 50% by each company.

a. Explain how this transaction affected Holmen's financial statements, citing the financial statements and footnotes that show the effects.

b. Describe the effect of the Modo transaction on the following Holmen ratios:

   (i) Current ratio

   (ii) Fixed-asset turnover

   (iii) Return on equity

13. [Proportionate consolidation] ExxonMobil [XOM] uses the equity method to account for its investments in affiliates owned 50% or less. Exhibit 13P-4 contains condensed financial statements for ExxonMobil and summarized financial information for its unconsolidated equity affiliates.

a. Prepare a pro forma 2000 balance sheet and income statement for ExxonMobil with its affiliates:

   (i) Fully consolidated

   (ii) Proportionately consolidated

b. Compute the following ratios for ExxonMobil (as reported) and, using the pro forma statements prepared in parts a(i) and a(ii):

   (i) Current ratio

   (ii) Long-term debt-to-equity

   (iii) Pretax income to sales

   (iv) Effective tax rate

   (v) Pretax return on assets

c. Summarize the impact on ExxonMobil of the pro forma adjustments, using the results of part b.

14. [Minority interest] The following data were obtained from the *1999 Annual Report* of Nucor Corporation [NUE], which has a 51%-owned consolidated subsidiary:

Minority interest at December 31, 1998	$282,396,469
Minority interest at December 31, 1999	280,871,235
Distribution to minority interest	(87,176,880)
(1999 financing cash flow)	

a. Nucor's operating cash flow reported minority interest for 1999. From the data given, compute that amount and explain its significance.

b. Using the data provided and the result of part a, compute the net profit and return on average equity of the subsidiary for 1999.

c. Discuss the conditions under which the proportionate consolidation method would be more appropriate for this subsidiary.

d. Discuss the advantages and disadvantages of the proportionate consolidation method in this case from the point of view of:

   (i) Nucor's management

   (ii) A financial analyst

15. [Analysis of segment data] Exhibit 13P-5 contains industry segment data reported by Lumex (now Cybex [CYB]) in its *1994 Annual Report*. Use these data to answer the following questions.

a. Compute the following ratios for each segment for the years 1992 to 1994:

   (i) Operating profit margin

   (ii) Return on assets

   (iii) Asset turnover

   (iv) Capital expenditures-to-depreciation

b. For each ratio calculated in part a, discuss what information the level and trend of that ratio convey about the business segment.

c. Discuss the limitations of segment data, both in terms of trends within the company over time and comparisons with similar segments of other companies.

d. Discuss what additional information you would require to improve your analysis of segment operations.

e. In 1996, Lumex sold its Lumex segment for cash and restated its financial statements to show the Lumex segment as a discontinued operation. Discuss whether the segment data shown in Exhibit 13P-5 permitted financial statement users to anticipate the effect of that divestiture on the company.

16. [Analysis of geographic segment data] Exhibit 13P-6 contains geographic segment data from the *2000 Annual Report* of Coca-Cola [KO]. Use the exhibit data to answer the following questions.

a. Compute the following ratios for each segment for the years 1998 to 2000:

   (i) Operating profit margin

   (ii) Return on assets

   (iii) Asset turnover

   (iv) Capital expenditures-to-depreciation

b. For each ratio calculated in part a, discuss what information the level and trend of that ratio convey about the business segment.

c. Use footnotes (a) through (e) in Exhibit 13P-6 to compute adjusted operating profit and pretax income for the affected segments.

d. Use the results of part c to recompute the following ratios for the affected segments:

   (i) Operating profit margin

   (ii) Return on assets

e. Discuss the limitations of segment data, both in terms of trends within the company over time and comparisons with similar segments of other companies.

f. Discuss what additional information you would require to improve your analysis of segment operations.

EXHIBIT 13P-4. EXXON-MOBIL CORPORATION
Condensed Financial Statements (in $millions)

Consolidated Balance Sheet, December 31, 2000

Current assets	$ 40,399
Investments and advances	12,618
Other assets	95,983
Total assets	$149,000
Current liabilities	$ 38,191
Long-term debt	7,280
Other long-term liabilities	32,772
Total liabilities	$ 78,243
Shareholders' equity	70,757
Total liabilities and equity	$149,000

Consolidated Income Statement, Year Ended December 31, 2000

Sales and other operating revenue*	$228,439
Earnings from equity interests and other revenue	4,309
Total revenue	$232,748
Operating expenses	150,603
Taxes other than income taxes*	55,064
Income taxes	11,091
Total costs and deductions	$216,758
Income before extraordinary item	15,990
Extraordinary gain	1,730
Net income	$ 17,720

*Includes excise taxes of $22,356

Equity Company Information

The summarized financial information below includes amounts related to certain less than majority owned companies and majority owned subsidiaries where minority shareholders possess the right to participate in significant management decisions. These companies are primarily engaged in crude production, natural gas marketing and refining operations in North America; natural gas production, natural gas distribution, and downstream operations in Europe and crude production in Kazakhstan and the Middle East. Also included are several power generation, petrochemical/lubes manufacturing and chemical ventures.

Equity Company Financial Summary	Total	ExxonMobil Share
Total revenues*	$ 81,371	$ 32,452
Income before income taxes	7,632	3,092
Less: related income taxes	(1,382)	(658)
Net income	$ 6,250	$ 2,434
Current assets	$ 28,784	$ 11,479
Property, plant, and equipment (net)	36,553	13,733
Other long-term assets	6,656	2,979
Total assets	$ 71,993	$ 28,191
Short-term debt	(2,636)	(1,093)
Other current liabilities	(25,377)	(10,357)
Long-term debt	(11,116)	(4,094)
Other long-term liabilities	(7,054)	(3,273)
Advances from shareholders	(8,485)	(2,510)
Net assets	$ 17,325	$ 6,864

*11% from ExxonMobil consolidated companies.
Source: Exxon-Mobil, *2000 Annual Report.*

EXHIBIT 13P-5. LUMEX
Segment Data

Note H—Business Segment Information

The Company conducts manufacturing operations principally in two industries, the medical equipment industry through its Lumex division ("Lumex") and the exercise equipment industry through its Cybex division ("Cybex"). In addition, the Company's wholly-owned captive finance subsidiary, Cybex Financial Corp. ("CFC"), provides capital equipment financing to customers of both Lumex and Cybex.

Operating results and other financial data are presented for each business segment of the Company for the three years ended December 31, 1994, 1993 and 1992:

Year Ended December 31,

(in thousands)	1994	1993	1992
Net sales:			
Lumex	$ 60,764	$ 54,187	$ 50,038
Cybex	70,420	54,781	53,850
Consolidated	$131,184	$108,968	$103,888
Operating profit (loss):			
Lumex	4,012	3,881	3,445
Cybex	2,218	(692)	3,690
CFC	543	215	9
Corporate & other	(2,194)	(1,446)	(1,119)
Nonrecurring charges	—	(3,160)	—
Consolidated	$ 4,579	$ (1,202)	$ 6,025
Identifiable assets:			
Lumex	28,659	24,756	24,297
Cybex	37,087	32,117	31,452
CFC	12,128	13,223	2,868
Corporate & other	16,294	15,670	10,420
Consolidated	$ 94,168	$ 85,766	$ 69,037
Capital expenditures:			
Lumex	1,532	1,481	603
Cybex	2,047	1,736	1,550
Corporate & other	35	46	10
Consolidated	$ 3,614	$ 3,263	$ 2,163
Depreciation & amortization:			
Lumex	1,568	1,283	1,142
Cybex	1,671	1,523	1,382
Corporate & other	(15)	22	19
Consolidated	$ 3,224	$ 2,828	$ 2,543

Intersegment sales are immaterial. CFC provides financing for certain capital equipment sales as further described in Note G. CFC treats these lease transactions as direct finance leases whereby the equipment sales and cost of sales are reflected on the books of the respective manufacturing segment while CFC retains all financing revenue.

Operating profit (loss) by segment represents, for Lumex and Cybex, net sales less operating expenses including certain administrative costs allocated on a reasonable basis consistently applied. The operating profit of CFC reflects financing revenue.

Source: Lumex, *1994 Annual Report.*

EXHIBIT 13P-6. THE COCA-COLA COMPANY AND SUBSIDIARIES
Geographic Segment Data (in $millions)

	North America	Africa & Middle East	Europe & Eurasia	Latin America	Asia Pacific	Corporate	Consolidated
2000							
Net operating revenues	$7,870	$729	$4,377	$2,174	$5,159	$ 149	$20,458
Operating income (a)	1,406	80	1,415	916	956	(1,082) (b)	3,691
Interest income						345	345
Interest expense						447	447
Equity income (loss) (c)	3	(73)	35	(75)	(290)	111	(289)
Identifiable operating assets	4,271	622	1,408	1,545	1,953	5,270	15,069
Investments	141	338	1,757	1,767	993	769	5,765
Capital expenditures	259	11	194	16	132	121	733
Depreciation and amortization	244	54	64	96	211	104	773
Income before income taxes	1,410	(6)	1,568 (d)	866	651	(1,090)	3,399
1999							
Net operating revenues	$7,519	$792	$4,540	$1,961	$4,828	$ 165	$19,805
Operating income (e)	1,436	67	1,068	840	1,194	(623)	3,982
Interest income						260	260
Interest expense						337	337
Equity income (loss)	(5)	(29)	(73)	(5)	(37)	(35)	(184)
Identifiable operating assets	3,591	672	1,624	1,653	2,439	4,852	14,831
Investments	139	333	1,870	1,833	1,837	780	6,792
Capital expenditures	269	22	218	67	317	176	1,069
Depreciation and amortization	263	47	80	96	184	122	792
Income before income taxes	1,432	24	984	846	1,143	(610)	3,819
1998							
Net operating revenues	$6,934	$780	$4,827	$2,240	$3,856	$ 176	$18,813
Operating income	1,383	223	1,655	1,056	1,343	(693)	4,967
Interest income						219	219
Interest expense						277	277
Equity income (loss)	(1)	(21)	(47)	68	(38)	71	32
Identifiable operating assets	3,467	541	1,711	1,364	1,595	3,781	12,459
Investments	141	312	2,010	1,629	1,979	615	6,686
Capital expenditures	274	22	216	72	104	175	863
Depreciation and amortization	231	40	92	93	101	88	645
Income before income taxes	1,392	192	1,577	1,132	1,289	(384)	5,198

Intercompany transfers between operating segments are not material. Certain prior year amounts have been reclassified to conform to the current year presentation.

(a) Operating income was reduced by $3 million for North America, $397 million for Asia Pacific, and $5 million for Corporate related to the other operating charges recorded for asset impairments in the first quarter of 2000. Operating income was also reduced by $128 million for North America, $64 million for Africa and the Middle East, $174 million for Europe and Eurasia, $63 million for Latin America, $127 million for Asia Pacific and $294 million for Corporate as a result of other operating charges associated with the Realignment.

(b) Operating income was reduced by $188 million for Corporate related to the settlement terms of a discrimination lawsuit and a donation to the Coca-Cola Foundation.

(c) Equity income (loss) was reduced by $9 million for Africa and the Middle East, $26 million for Europe and Eurasia, $124 million for Latin America and $306 million for Asia Pacific, as a result of our Company's portion of nonrecurring charges recorded by equity investees.

(d) Income before taxes was increased by $118 million for Europe and Eurasia as a result of a gain related to the merger of Coca-Cola Beverages plc and Hellenic Bottling Company S.A.

(e) Operating income was reduced by $34 million for North America, $79 million for Africa and Middle East, $430 million for Europe and Eurasia, $35 million for Latin America, $176 million for Asia Pacific and $59 million for Corporate related to the other operating charges recorded in the fourth quarter of 1999.

Source: Coca-Cola, 2000 Annual Report.

14

ANALYSIS OF BUSINESS COMBINATIONS

CHAPTER OUTLINE

CHAPTER OBJECTIVES

Chapter 14 examines the accounting and analysis issues related to business combinations, spinoffs, and other forms of corporate reorganization. In this chapter, we:

1. Explain the mechanics of the pooling of interests and purchase methods of accounting for business combinations, including the differences between U.S. and IASB GAAP.

2. Consider the conditions that determine which method is used.

3. Compare the effects of pooling and the two variants of the purchase method on postacquisition balance sheet, income, and cash flow statements.

4. Describe the effects of the three methods on financial ratios.

503

5. Consider the analytical significance of acquisition goodwill.

6. Discuss international differences in acquisition accounting and the treatment of goodwill.

7. Review factors that affect management motivations when choosing an acquisition accounting method.

8. Explain how push-down accounting affects financial statements and ratios.

9. Describe the effects of a spinoff on a firm's financial statements.

INTRODUCTION

Corporate reorganizations have become an increasingly important aspect of the international financial landscape in recent years. Acquisitions and divestitures of portions of operating segments or entire lines of business are used to modify existing levels of horizontal and vertical integration, diversify, increase market share, improve operating efficiency, and increase the market value of the firm.

Financial restructuring, on the other hand, only alters the capital structure of a firm, changing its debt burden. Capital structure may also be changed through reorganizations in bankruptcy, quasireorganizations, recapitalizations, and initial public offerings or secondary issues of stock in subsidiaries.

In the case of mergers or acquisitions, the use of a new accounting basis (purchase method) or continuation of the historical carrying amounts of the acquired company (pooling method) affects the preparation of subsequent financial statements for the combined operations of the two entities. For financial analysts the choice of accounting method is significant as it affects the comparability of reported results before and after acquisitions. Since sales, income, and return measures of the combined entity following the combination differ from those of the acquirer alone, the question is whether and how to restate reported results to facilitate comparisons of pre- and postmerger operations.

When a subsidiary acquired using the purchase method provides separate financial statements, another issue arises. Should the new basis be "pushed down" into those separate statements? This issue is important because these transactions often generate substantial goodwill and the implications for equity and liability valuation can be quite complex.

Many economic and financial reporting considerations affect the accounting method chosen to report acquisitions; it is important to understand management incentives for these choices. Much has been written in recent years regarding the comparative merits of the different methods of accounting for business combinations, their differential ability to obscure the "true" operating results, and their impact on international competition because of international tax and reporting differences. Although this chapter shows how each of these methods may have these effects, its objectives are to enable the financial analyst to interpret postacquisition financial statements prepared using either method and to provide some insights into management decisions.

The chapter begins with an explanation and simplified illustration of the purchase and pooling methods of accounting for mergers and acquisitions, followed by a comparison of their impact on financial statements and ratios. The adoption of SFAS 141 (2001) by the FASB eliminated use of the pooling method in the United States but that method is still permitted by IASB standards and those of many other countries. Next, we provide a discussion of the issue of acquisition goodwill followed by a review of empirical research into market reaction and management incentives to engage in acquisition activities.

The final sections examine push-down accounting and the significant accounting and analysis issues raised by spinoffs.

ACCOUNTING FOR ACQUISITIONS

Financial reporting rules for acquisitions in the United States were radically changed by SFAS 141. That standard requires that all acquisitions be accounted for using the *purchase method* of accounting, which treats such acquisitions as a purchase of the assets and assumption of the liabilities of the acquired or target firm, by the buyer.

The purchase method requires the allocation of the purchase price to all of the acquired company's identifiable tangible and intangible assets and liabilities, some of which may have been previously unrecognized. *The assets and liabilities of the acquired company are received into the financial statements of the acquirer at their fair market values at the acquisition date.* Due to the acquisition, and the mix of historical and market values, post-merger balance sheets are not comparable to the preacquisition balance sheet of the acquirer.

The income and cash flow statements include the operating results of the acquired company effective with the date of acquisition. Operating results prior to the merger are not restated, although pro forma data on a combined basis may be disclosed. Like the balance sheet, pre- and postmerger income and cash flow statements are not comparable.

Under IASB standards and those of many non-U.S. jurisdictions, some business combinations are assumed to merge the ownership interests of two firms rather than transfer control from the stockholders of one entity to those of the surviving firm. When such transactions meet certain restrictive conditions, they are reported using the *pooling of interests method (uniting of interests under IASB GAAP).* IAS 22 (revised 1998) defines such a business combination as one:

> In which the shareholders of the combining enterprises combine control over the whole of their net assets and operations, to achieve a continuing mutual sharing in the risks and benefits attaching to the combined entity such that neither party can be identified as the acquirer.

Pooling differs from the purchase method in the following respects:

- The two parties are treated identically; there is no acquirer or acquired firm.

- The financial statements are consolidated without adjustment; fair market values are not recognized for either company.

- Operating results for the combined firm are restated (combined) for all periods prior to the merger date.

Conditions Necessary for Use of the Pooling of Interests Method

IAS 22 sets three conditions under which the pooling method can be used to account for an acquisition:

1. The substantial majority of the voting common shares of the combining enterprises are exchanged or pooled.
2. The fair value of one enterprise is not significantly different from that of the other enterprise.
3. The shareholders of each enterprise maintain substantially the same voting rights and interests in the combined entity, relative to each other, after the combination as before.

These criteria state that the pooling of interests method of accounting is intended only for combinations of companies of roughly equal market value, when both groups of shareholders retain their ownership interest in the new company. Thus purchases for cash or nonvoting shares do not qualify as poolings. Strictly speaking, the accounting method is determined by the transaction terms.

In practice, however, transaction terms are usually designed to achieve specific reporting objectives. Companies planning an acquisition prepare pro forma financial statements to estimate the impact of a proposed transaction and evaluate different terms and their different accounting consequences. In the United States, prior to the adoption of SFAS 141, the pooling method was frequently used, even in the case of unfriendly acquisitions, by restructuring the terms after the surrender.

ILLUSTRATION OF THE PURCHASE AND POOLING METHODS

The application of the purchase and pooling methods of accounting is illustrated by the Acquire Corporation's acquisition of the Target Company for $750 million on June 30, 2001. Scenario A assumes that Acquire issues shares with a market value of $750 million in exchange for all the common shares of Target. Scenario B, discussed in Box 14-1 at the end of the next section, assumes that Acquire pays $750 million cash for all the common shares of Target.

Exhibit 14-1 presents the preacquisition balance sheets of both companies and the fair market values of Target's assets and liabilities on the acquisition date. Prior to the acquisition, Target has common equity of $250 million ($500 million assets less $250 million liabilities). The adjustments of Target's assets and liabilities to fair market value are typical of those found in real companies with significant technological activities.

The Purchase Method

Application of the purchase method requires that all assets and liabilities of the target entity be revalued to fair market value. In addition, previously unrecognized contingencies and off-balance-sheet items must also be recognized. Examples include lawsuits and environmental contingencies as well as employee benefit plans.

Inventories carried at the lower of cost or market value are frequently reported at amounts below fair value, especially when the last-in, first-out (LIFO) inventory method is employed. Property is another common area of adjustment; in an inflationary world, fair

EXHIBIT 14-1. ACQUIRE AND TARGET
Comparative Balance Sheets, at June 30, 2001 (in $millions)

| | Historical | | | | Fair Value | |
	Acquire		Target		Target	
Cash	$100		$ 75		$ 75	
Inventories	200		100		150	
Receivables	200		75		75	
Current assets		$ 500		$250		$ 300
Property		500		250		350
In-process R&D						100
Software cost						120
Licenses						60
Goodwill*		—		—		80
Total assets		$1,000		$500		$1,010
Payables	150		50		50	
Accrued liabilities	100		50		50	
Current liabilities		$ 250		$100		$ 100
Long-term debt		250		150		160
Common stock	350		225			
Retained earnings	150		25			
Common equities		500		250		750[†]
Total equities		$1,000		$500		$1,010
Shares outstanding (millions)		80.00		25.00		

*See discussion in the text of the purchase method for allocation rules.
[†]Acquire has agreed to pay $750 million for Target's net assets; the $750 million presented for common equity reflects that purchase price.

value usually exceeds historical cost. The use of accelerated depreciation methods by the acquired firm may also result in understated asset values.

The adjustment to long-term debt depends on the current level of interest rates as compared with the interest rate embedded in the company's long-term debt. In the case of Target, we assume that the interest rate on the company's long-term debt is above current rates. The fair market value of this debt is the present value, at the current interest rate, of the cash flows (both principal and interest) required by the company's debt, or $160 million in this case, which is above the face amount ($150 million) of the debt. When the current interest rate is below the historic rate, then the present value exceeds the face amount.[1]

SFAS 141 (2001) requires that identifiable intangible assets be valued and reported separately. Exhibit 14-1 shows the following identifiable intangibles for Target:

- $100 million of research and development in-process
- $120 million of software
- $60 million of licenses

However, the first of these acquired intangibles is not recorded as an asset under U.S. GAAP.[2] The acquisition price of computer, biotechnology, and other firms with high technological content recognizes that such firms have significant assets in the form of *in-process research and development (IPRD)*. U.S. GAAP require that IPRD be expensed immediately when the purchase method of accounting is used. Thus Target's IPRD of $100 is immediately recorded as an expense at the acquisition date under U.S. GAAP but recorded as an asset under IASB GAAP.

Having determined the fair values of assets and liabilities, we now compare the purchase price with the fair value of all assets (excluding goodwill):

Assets at fair market value (includes IPRD)	$ 930 million
Liabilities at fair market value	(260)
Net assets at fair market value	$ 670 million

The purchase price of $750 million is $80 million higher than the fair value of net assets. Once all tangible assets and liabilities are restated at fair market value, any excess, residual purchase price must be allocated to goodwill.[3]

Alternatively, the fair value of the net assets acquired may exceed the purchase price of the entire company.[4] In this case, U.S. GAAP requires that the fair value of assets other than:

- Cash and cash equivalents,
- Trade receivables,
- Inventories,
- Financial instruments carried at fair value, and
- Assets held-for-sale

be reduced pro rata to the extent necessary to equate the net fair value of assets to the purchase price.[5] In such cases, the new carrying amount of these assets may be less than their fair market value.[6]

---

[1]Note that SFAS 107, Disclosures About Fair Value of Financial Instruments, requires footnote disclosures of the fair value of debt and other financial assets and liabilities.

[2]The reason is that SFAS 2 does not permit the capitalization of research and development, as discussed in Chapter 7.

[3]Goodwill is the excess purchase price over the fair market value of all identifiable assets net of all identifiable liabilities. It is one of the most controversial subjects in the accounting literature, as discussed in a later section of this chapter. SFAS 142 radically changed the accounting for goodwill under U.S. GAAP.

[4]This may be due to unrecognized obligations or a low rate of return on assets.

[5]The IASB treatment of "negative goodwill" is somewhat different (see Exhibit 14-8 below).

[6]In the rare case when negative goodwill remains after reducing all affected assets to zero, the excess must be recognized as an extraordinary gain.

Exhibit 14-2A shows the postmerger consolidated balance sheet under the

- Pooling method (column 3)
- Purchase method under U.S. GAAP (column 5)
- Purchase method under IASB GAAP (column 7)

Notice that, under the purchase method, Target's common equity has not been carried forward; it has been eliminated as a result of the merger. The combined common equity equals the sum of Acquire's preacquisition equity and the market value of newly issued equity, reduced (under U.S. GAAP only) by the write-off of in-process R&D.

The combined balance sheet carries forward the assets and liabilities of Acquire without any change; adjustments are made only to the assets and liabilities of Target. If Target had purchased Acquire, the results would be quite different. Acquire's assets and liabilities would be restated, and Target's would remain unchanged.

EXHIBIT 14-2A
Comparison of Purchase and Pooling Methods: Scenario A (All Equity)
Consolidated Balance Sheets at June 30, 2001 (in $millions)

	(1)	(2)	(3)	(4)	(5)	(6)	(7)
	Historical Cost		Pooling	Purchase Method			
			IASB GAAP	U.S. GAAP (SFAS 141)		IASB GAAP (IAS 22)	
	Acquire	Target	Consolidated	Adjustments	Consolidated	Adjustments	Consolidated
Cash	$ 100	$ 75	$ 175	—	$ 175	—	$ 175
Inventories	200	100	300	50	350	50	350
Receivables	200	75	275	—	275	—	275
Current assets	$ 500	$250	$ 750	$ 50	$ 800	$ 50	$ 800
Property	500	250	750	100	850	100	850
In-process R&D				100		100	100
R&D writeoff				(100)			—
Software cost				120	120	120	120
Licenses				60	60	60	60
Goodwill*	—	—	—	80	80	80	80
Total assets	$1,000	$500	$1,500	$410	$1,910	$510	$2,010
Payables	150	50	200	—	200	—	200
Accrued liabilities	100	50	150	—	150	—	150
Current liabilities	$ 250	$100	$ 350	—	$ 350	—	$ 350
Long-term debt	250	150	400	10	410	10	410
Common stock	350	225	575	525	1,100	525	1,100
Retained earnings	150	25	175	(125)	50	(25)	$ 150
Common equity	500	250	750	400†	1,150	500‡	1,250
Total equities	$1,000	$500	$1,500	$410	$1,910	$510	$2,010
Current ratio	2.00×	2.50×	2.14×		2.29×		2.29×
Debt/equity ratio	50.00%	60.00%	53.30%		35.65%		32.80%

*See text discussion of the purchase method for allocation rules.
†The net adjustment of $400 million reflects the issuance of Acquire common stock with a market value of $750 million, less the purchase and retirement of all of Target's equity ($225 million common stock + $25 million retained earnings), and the immediate writeoff of $100 million of acquired in-process R&D: $750 million − $250 million − $100 million = $400 million.
‡Under IAS GAAP, there is no R&D write-off; total assets and equity are both $100 million higher than under U.S. GAAP.

The application of the purchase method of accounting to the balance sheet can be summarized as follows:

1. The purchase price is allocated to the assets and liabilities of the acquired firm; all assets (including intangible assets) and liabilities are restated to their fair market value.

2. The restated net fair value is compared with the purchase price; any excess purchase price over net fair value is attributed to goodwill.

3. If the restated net fair value exceeds the purchase price, then the write-up of property is reduced until equality is achieved. See chapter note 6.

4. The common equity of the acquired firm is eliminated, replaced with the market value of Acquire shares issued.

Column 4 (U.S. GAAP) and column 6 (IASB GAAP) show the adjustments to the assets and liabilities of Target; there is one important difference. Under U.S. GAAP the $100 million value of purchased R&D must be charged against the earnings of Acquire at the acquisition date. This reduces the postacquisition equity of Acquire by the identical $100 million amount.[7] Under IASB GAAP, the $100 million is not written off immediately but is amortized over time.

The Pooling of Interests Method

The pooling method is illustrated using the same transaction. The postmerger balance sheet is also shown in Exhibit 14-2A (column 3) and is simply the summation of Target and Acquire's balance sheets.

Notice that the pooling method is similar to consolidation of a previously unconsolidated subsidiary, as discussed in Chapter 13. All assets and liabilities of the two firms are combined (and intercompany accounts eliminated), without any adjustment for fair values. When the pooling method is used, fair market values are irrelevant to recording the combination. *The actual market price and premium paid for the acquired firm are suppressed from both the balance sheet and income statement.*

Unlike the purchase method, the pooling method is symmetrical. The accounting result is identical whether Target is being acquired or is the firm making the acquisition. Note that the common equity of the two firms is simply combined. Neither company's share price has any bearing on the accounting result.[8]

EFFECTS OF ACCOUNTING METHODS

Comparison of Balance Sheets

Scenario A: All Stock

Exhibit 14-2A shows that the pooling and purchase methods produce very different postmerger balance sheets. Yet the economic reality resulting from the transaction is identical (if we ignore, for the moment, income tax effects), regardless of the accounting method used.

The differences between the balance sheets under the purchase method (columns 5 and 7) and the pooling method (column 3) result from recognition of the market value of the transaction and the fair values of Target's assets and liabilities. As a result, a number of financial ratios are changed; we show two examples within the exhibit.

The current ratio is higher under the purchase method because of the adjustment of the acquired firm's inventories (part of current assets) to their higher fair market value. The debt-to-equity ratio is lower under the purchase method because the newly issued equity of Acquire is reported at market value rather than at the preacquisition equity of Target.

---

[7]For ease of exposition, we have ignored the deferred tax asset that might arise at the time of the in-process R&D write-off.

[8]Share prices have no effect on the accounting result once the terms of the deal have been set. They do, however, affect the basic terms of the transaction and the exchange ratio.

Comparison of Income Statements

The acquisition method also affects the income statement. Exhibit 14-3 contains condensed income statements for Target and Acquire for 2000, 2001, and 2002 as well as for the second half of 2001. Exhibit 14-4A contains the income statement effects of the purchase method adjustments for Scenario A under both U.S. and IASB GAAP. We have assumed that Acquire is in a steady state, reporting a constant gross margin (40%) and interest coverage ratio (11×). Target reports annual sales growth of 10%, constant gross margin of 50%, and interest coverage that increases from 16× in 2000 to 19.6× in 2002.

Exhibit 14-5 contains combined income statements for Scenario A under both the U.S. and IASB purchase methods. Under these methods, Acquire's income statement includes Target's operations only after the effective date of the merger. Thus, the 2001 combined income statement (see panel I of Exhibit 14-5) includes the operations of Acquire for the entire year, but the operations of Target only for the six months following the merger on June 30, 2001. The restatement of Target's assets and liabilities to their fair market values affects certain categories of expense as well. The balance sheet adjustments and their income statement effects under both U.S. and IASB GAAP are described in Exhibit 14-4A.

EXHIBIT 14-3. ACQUIRE AND TARGET
Income Statements, 2000–2002 (in $millions)

| | Years Ended December 31 | | | |
	2000	2001	2001*	2002
Target				
Sales	$600	$660	$340	$726
Cost of goods sold	(300)	(330)	(170)	(363)
Gross margin	$300	$330	$170	$363
Selling expense	(115)	(125)	(65)	(135)
Depreciation expense	(25)	(28)	(14)	(32)
Interest expense	(10)	(10)	(5)	(10)
Pretax income	$150	$167	$86	$186
Income tax expense	(50)	(56)	(29)	(62)
Net income	$100	$111	$57	$124
Shares outstanding (millions)	25	25	25	25
Earnings per share	$4.00	$4.44	$2.28	$4.96
Gross margin as a % of sales	50.00%	50.00%	50.00%	50.00%
Interest coverage ratio	16.00	17.70	18.20	19.60
Acquire				
Sales	$1,000	$1,000	$ 500	$1,000
Cost of goods sold	(600)	(600)	(300)	(600)
Gross margin	$ 400	$ 400	$ 200	$ 400
Selling expense	(130)	(130)	(65)	(130)
Depreciation expense	(50)	(50)	(25)	(50)
Interest expense	(20)	(20)	(10)	(20)
Pretax income	$ 200	$ 200	$ 100	$ 200
Income tax expense	(68)	(68)	(34)	(68)
Net income	$ 132	$ 132	$ 66	$ 132
Shares outstanding (millions)	80	80	80	80
Earnings per share	$1.65	$1.65	$0.83	$1.65
Gross margin as a % of sales	40.00%	40.00%	40.00%	40.00%
Interest coverage ratio	11.00	11.00	11.00	11.00

*Six months ended December 31.

EXHIBIT 14-4A
Income Statement Effects of Balance Sheet Adjustments Under Purchase Method: Scenario A (All Equity)

| | Balance Sheet Adjustment | | Income Statement Effect | | | |
| | Amount | | 2001 (6 months) | | 2002 | |
Description	U.S. GAAP	IASB GAAP	U.S. GAAP	IASB GAAP	U.S. GAAP	IASB GAAP
1. Inventories	$ 50	$ 50	$ (50)	$(50)	$ —	$ —
2. Property	100	100	(5)	(5)	(10)	(10)
3. In-process R&D	—	100	(100)	(12)		(25)
4. Software cost	120	120	(20)	(20)	(40)	(40)
5. Licenses	60	60				
6. Goodwill	80	80		(4)		(8)
Subtotals	$410	$510	$(175)	$(91)	$(50)	$(83)
7. Long-term debt	10	10	(1)	(1)	(2)	(2)
8. Net totals	$400	$500	$(174)	$(90)	$(48)	$(81)
9. Tax effect (35%)			61	31	17	28
10. Net effect			$(113)	$(59)	$(31)	$(53)

EXHIBIT 14-5
Purchase Method Consolidated Income Statements: Scenario A (All Equity) 2001 and 2002 (in $millions)

I. Year Ended December 31, 2001

| | | | U.S. GAAP | | IASB GAAP | |
	Acquire	Target	Adjustments	Consolidated	Adjustments	Consolidated
Sales	$1,000	$ 340	$ —	$1,340	$ —	$1,340
Cost of goods sold	(600)	(170)	(50)	(820)	(50)	(820)
Gross margin	$ 400	$ 170	$ (50)	$ 520	$(50)	$ 520
Selling expense	(130)	(65)	—	(195)		(195)
In-process R&D			(100)	(100)		
Depreciation expense	(50)	(14)	(5)	(69)	(5)	(69)
Amortization expense			(20)	(20)	(36)	(36)
Interest expense	(20)	(5)	1	(24)	1	(24)
Pretax income	$ 200	$ 86	$(174)	$ 112	$(90)	$ 196
Income tax expense	(68)	(29)	61	(36)	31	(66)
Net income	$ 132	$ 57	$(113)	$ 76	$(59)	$ 130
Gross margin (% of sales)	40.00%	50.00%	NA	38.81%	NA	38.81%
Interest coverage ratio	11.00	18.20	NA	5.67	NA	9.17

II. Year Ended December 31, 2002

| | | | U.S. GAAP | | IASB GAAP | |
	Acquire	Target	Adjustments	Consolidated	Adjustments	Consolidated
Sales	$1,000	$ 726	$ —	$1,726	$ —	$1,726
Cost of goods sold	(600)	(363)		(963)		(963)
Gross margin	$ 400	$ 363	$ —	$ 763		763
Selling expense	(130)	(135)	—	(265)		(265)
Depreciation expense	(50)	(32)	(10)	(92)	(10)	(92)
Amortization expense*			(40)	(40)	(73)	(73)
Interest expense	(20)	(10)	2	(28)	2	(28)
Pretax income	$ 200	$ 186	$(48)	$ 338	(81)	$ 305
Income tax expense	(68)	(62)	17	(113)	28	(102)
Net income	$ 132	$ 124	$(31)	$ 225	$(53)	$ 203
Gross margin (% of sales)	40.00%	50.00%	NA	44.21%	NA	44.21%
Interest coverage ratio	11.00	19.60	NA	13.07	NA	11.89

*See text discussion.

511

The following adjustments are identical under U.S. and IASB GAAP:

- Cost of goods sold (COGS), which increases as inventory that has been written up in value is sold. Given Target's inventory turnover ratio (sales/COGS) of 3.3, we assume that all inventory on hand at the acquisition date is sold prior to December 31, 2001.[9]
- Higher depreciation expense due to depreciation of the higher fair values of Target's property (assuming that Target's average depreciable life of 10 years does not change).[10]
- Amortization of software over its useful life (assumed to be 3 years).
- Lower interest expense due to amortization, over the remaining life of the debt, of the debt premium created by revaluing long-term debt.

But two adjustments differ between the two methods:

1. Under IASB GAAP only, goodwill must be amortized (we assume a 10-year life). Under U.S. GAAP, no amortization is permitted, as discussed later in the chapter.[11]
2. Under IASB GAAP only, acquired research and development must be amortized over its useful life (assumed to be 4 years). Under U.S. GAAP, as noted, it is written off immediately.

The purchase method income statement for the year ended December 31, 2001 includes Acquire's operations for the full year, Target's operations for the six months following the merger, and the effects of the purchase method adjustments (net of applicable tax savings). Panel II of Exhibit 14-5 shows the income statement for 2002 for the combined firm, also under Scenario A.

We see the full impact of purchase accounting from Acquire's income statements for the three years ended December 31, 2002, shown in Exhibit 14-6A for all three accounting methods under Scenario A. Under the purchase method (both variations), 2000 sales and expenses are those of Acquire only; 2001 and 2002 data include Target for the period following the merger on June 30, 2001.

When the pooling method is used, the operating results of Target are included for all three years, including the periods prior to the merger. The restatement of prior period results is one of the salient features of the pooling of interests method of accounting, and it facilitates comparability. These comparisons highlight the significant differences between the pooling and purchase methods.

Income Statement Distortion Under the Purchase Method

As shown in Exhibit 14-6A, the acquisition of Target significantly affects the income statement under the purchase method.

First, note the distortion of the sales trend that the purchase method creates. From 2000 to 2002, Acquire's purchase method income statements report a sales increase of 72.6%, none of which is due to its own internal growth. Most of the growth is due to the inclusion of Target's sales starting with the second half of 2001; part is due to the sales growth of Target following its acquisition.

---

[9]When inventory is accounted for by using either first-in, first-out (FIFO) or average cost, written-up inventory values flow into the cost of goods sold fairly quickly, depressing gross margins. Although reported income is reduced, some of the acquisition cost is recovered quickly as the higher costs reduce taxable income in a taxable purchase transaction. When last-in, first-out (LIFO) inventory accounting is used, the higher costs remain in inventory indefinitely unless a LIFO invasion (reduction of inventory quantities) takes place. We assume that Target uses the FIFO method.

[10]Note that this assumes all Target's property is written up by the same percentage. If the write-up is disproportionately high in a class of property with an average life significantly different from the company average, this assumption does not hold.

In addition, the depreciation expense may be affected as Acquire applies its depreciation methods and lives to Target's fixed assets.

[11]Under U.S. tax law, goodwill is tax-deductible only when the acquirer steps up the tax basis of the assets of the acquired company. Box 14-2 reviews the U.S. tax treatment of acquisitions.

EXHIBIT 14-6A. ACQUIRE CORP.
Consolidated Income Statements, 2000–2002: Scenario A (All Equity)

Year Ended December 31 (in $millions)

| | Pooling Method | | | Purchase Method | | | | | |
| | IASB GAAP | | | U.S. GAAP | | | IASB GAAP | | |
	2000	2001	2002	2000	2001	2002	2000	2001	2002
Sales	$1,600	$1,660	$1,726	$1,000	$1,340	$1,726	$1,000	$1,340	$1,726
Cost of goods sold	(900)	(930)	(963)	(600)	(820)	(963)	(600)	(820)	(963)
Gross margin	$ 700	$ 730	$ 763	$ 400	$ 520	$ 763	$ 400	$ 520	$ 763
Selling expense	(245)	(255)	(265)	(130)	(195)	(265)	(130)	(195)	(265)
Purchased R&D					(100)				
Depreciation expense	(75)	(78)	(82)	(50)	(69)	(92)	(50)	(69)	(92)
Amortization expense				0	(20)	(40)	0	(36)	(73)
Interest expense	(30)	(30)	(30)	(20)	(24)	(28)	(20)	(24)	(28)
Pretax income	$ 350	$ 367	$ 386	$ 200	$ 112	$ 338	$ 200	$ 196	$ 305
Income tax expense	(118)	(124)	(130)	(68)	(36)	(113)	(68)	(66)	(102)
Net income	$ 232	$ 243	$ 256	$ 132	$ 76	$ 225	$ 132	$ 130	$ 203
Shares outstanding (millions)	105.0	105.0	105.0	80.0	92.5	105.0	80.0	92.5	105.0
Earnings per share	$2.21	$2.31	$2.44	$1.65	$0.82	$2.14	$1.65	$1.41	$1.93
Gross margin (% of sales)	43.75%	43.98%	44.21%	40.00%	38.81%	44.21%	40.00%	38.81%	44.21%
Interest coverage ratio	12.67	13.23	13.87	11.00	5.67	13.07	11.00	9.17	11.89

Because, under pooling, the operating results of all three years include both Acquire and Target, the purchase method's "illusion of growth" is absent. Sales growth over the period 2000 to 2002 is 7.9%, reflecting only the internal sales growth of Target.

As there is no restatement, 2000 EPS remains the originally reported $1.65 under both U.S. and IASB GAAP; 2001 EPS declines, reflecting purchase method adjustments, notably the sale of written-up inventory. U.S. GAAP earnings are especially depressed by the write-off of purchased R&D; IASB earnings are impacted by the amortization of R&D and goodwill.

In 2002, EPS rises under both U.S. and IASB GAAP, exceeding the 2000 level but remaining below the pooling method EPS. *The effects of purchase method adjustments persist until all of these adjustments flow through reported income.*

Income Statement Distortion Under the Pooling of Interests Method

However, the pooling of interests method can also mislead. The first problem is that it creates a fictitious history. Results for 2000 have been restated as if the two companies were combined in that year. In reality, they were separate enterprises, with different managements. The pooling method permits the management of Acquire to take credit for the operating results of Target for the period prior to its acquisition.

The pooling method allows companies whose shares sell at high price/earnings ratios to improve earnings per share via acquisition. When a company uses its highly valued shares (i.e., high price/earnings multiple) to acquire a company whose shares sell at a low multiple of earnings under the pooling method, then earnings per share increase. This technique is sometimes known as "bootstrapping," as the acquired company can raise earnings per share through financial engineering rather than operating improvement.

This effect is illustrated in Exhibit 14-6A, using the Target acquisition by Acquire. As Target has 25 million shares outstanding (from Exhibit 14-3), the $750 million purchase price implies a stock price of $30 per share, a price/earnings ratio (PER) of 7.5 based on 2000 EPS of $4.00. For simplicity we set Acquire's share price at $30 as well, making the stock transaction one share of Acquire for each share of Target. Acquire's PER (using 2000 EPS of $1.65) is 18.2, more than twice Target's PER.

Under the pooling method Acquire's EPS for 2000 rises from $1.65 before the merger to $2.21 (see Exhibit 14-6) after restatement. *Whenever a company uses the pooling method to acquire another firm with a lower PER, EPS rises.* In theory, this technique should fail as the market assigns a lower price/earnings ratio to the postmerger firm to reflect the inclusion of "lower-quality" earnings.[12] In practice, the technique can be effective for many years.

In the extreme case, an acquisition can be made after the close of the fiscal year to meet sales and earnings objectives. Because of the restatement feature of the pooling method, a company can include in its reported results the operations of firms acquired after the end of the year but before release of the annual report.[13]

Another serious problem with the pooling method of accounting *is the suppression of the true cost of the acquisition.* Since the pooling method carries forward historical costs, *no recognition is given to the true value of the assets acquired or any securities used to pay for the acquired company.*

There are several consequences of this failure to recognize the fair values acquired and paid for. One is that the acquiring company may sell acquired assets whose carrying cost is well below fair or market value. As a result, reported income includes fictitious gains. Although the acquirer presumably paid the full value of the assets acquired, the price paid was not recognized by the pooling method. Similarly, depreciation and amortization reflect the historical cost of assets acquired rather than their market value. As a result, income is overstated.[14]

Ratio Effects

Profitability ratios are affected by both acquisition methods. Acquire alone (see Exhibit 14-3) has a constant gross margin (sales less COGS) of 40% of sales; Target has a constant gross margin of 50% of sales. The combined gross margin percentage (Exhibit 14-6) shows little variability under the pooling method. Under the purchase method, the 2001 gross margin is depressed by the sale of written-up inventory of Target following the merger. The gross margin in 2002 is much higher, reflecting the inclusion of Target sales (with their higher gross margin) in the total. The gross margin percentage under pooling shows small year-to-year increases, reflecting the growing importance of Target's higher-margin operations.

The reported interest coverage ratio, under pooling, gradually rises due to Target's lower leverage. Interest coverage under the purchase method declines in 2001 as purchase method adjustments depress operating income (EBIT), more so under U.S. GAAP due to the writeoff of purchased R&D. Interest coverage improves in 2002 (exceeding the 2000 ratio) but is still below the ratio reported under pooling. The IASB-based ratio is lower than the U.S.-based ratio due to the amortization of R&D and goodwill.

Without the underlying data (from Exhibits 14-3, 14-4A, and 14-5), it is impossible to determine whether the rising profitability of Acquire is due to improvement in its own operations, the higher profitability of Target, efficiencies from the merger, or the impact of purchase method adjustments. As these data are not provided, the analyst must search elsewhere to answer this question. In some cases, we can keep track of an acquired company through the use of segment data (see Chapter 13). However, as the frequency of acquisition rises, the ability to discern the impact of any single acquisition diminishes. When there are many small acquisitions or acquisitions within existing segments, their effect cannot be isolated.

Ratios using balance sheet data also differ under the two methods, reflecting recognition of the purchase price and the fair values of the assets and liabilities of Target by Acquire under the purchase method; the pooling method suppresses both the purchase price and fair values.

---

[12]The efficient markets hypothesis suggests that the market price of the acquirer should adjust instantaneously.

[13]National Student Marketing, a "high-flyer" in the late 1960s and early 1970s until its collapse, was reported to have made acquisitions *after the end of each fiscal year* to bring reported earnings up to the forecasted level.

[14]Abraham J. Briloff has written extensively over the years on the problems associated with the use of the pooling method. For example, see Briloff, "Distortions Arising from Pooling-of-Interests Accounting," *Financial Analysts Journal* (March–April 1968), pp. 71–80. Despite the venerable age of this article, it remains a superb illustration of the suppression of the fair value of the acquisition in the pooling method, permitting the reporting of "gains" on acquired assets. A more recent article in *Barron's* (October 21, 2000) uses Cisco Systems to illustrate how the pooling method can enhance the reported earnings of the acquiring firm.

Exhibit 14-2A shows that the purchase method reports higher asset values and higher common equity than the pooling of interests method when the purchase price exceeds the stated net worth of the acquired company. As a result, the base for activity and return ratios is higher. In addition, adjustments required by the purchase method usually reduce reported earnings. (Acquire's 2002 earnings are $256 million under the pooling method, but only $225 million under the purchase method under U.S. GAAP and $209 million under IASB GAAP.) The result is that profitability ratios are generally lower when the purchase method is used.

The purchase method makes financial ratios difficult to interpret in other ways. Acquire's assets and liabilities are carried forward at historical cost, whereas Target's are restated to fair market values, generating a mixture of historical costs and market values in the combined accounts. As a result, activity ratios are difficult to compare with those of other companies.

In addition, postacquisition ratios are not comparable with preacquisition ratios, because:

- Target may have had a different turnover ratio than Acquire (both the level and trend may differ), reflecting the nature of its business; the postmerger ratio is a blend of the ratios of the two companies.
- Turnover ratios are reduced solely because of the fair value adjustments required by the purchase method.

Comparison of a company that has made a purchase method acquisition with one that has made a pooling acquisition (or none at all) is also affected by these same problems.

A purchase method acquisition creates a discontinuity throughout the financial statements of the acquiring company. Comparison with preacquisition data for the same company and comparison with other companies are hampered by the inclusion of the acquired entity at the acquisition date (balance sheet effects), and by the subsequent purchase method adjustments (balance sheet and income statement effects).

Because the pooling method restates preacquisition financial statements, it produces comparable financial statements. However, this comparability is fictitious; the combined companies were not operated as one or by the same management prior to the combination. The restated levels and trends in ratios may not represent expected performance over time under different management.

The reader is cautioned that ratio effects described in this section are company and transaction specific. Depending on the purchase price relative to book value, the fair values of assets and liabilities acquired, the means of financing, and the earnings of the target firm, the effect on ratios of use of the purchase method or pooling method will vary in practice. Use of trend data for such companies can easily lead to misleading conclusions. *We can, however, make the general statement that the choice of method does affect the ratios of the combined enterprise, often significantly.*

Cash Flow Statement Effects

When the pooling method is used, the merger itself (an exchange of shares) is not reported in the cash flow statement as no cash flows are considered to take place. The postacquisition cash flow statement is the sum of the individual cash flow statements. As in the case of the income statement, previously issued cash flow statements are restated on a combined basis.

Under purchase method accounting, however, cash flows associated with the acquisition are reported on the cash flow statement, but in highly abbreviated form. The net assets acquired are reported as cash used for investment and the applicable financing sources as cash from financing.

When shares are used to make the acquisition, the cash flow statement effects are even more abbreviated. The only effect for Scenario A would be the cash acquired of $75, reported as an inflow in cash from investing activities.[15]

---

[15]For scenario B, where Target is acquired for cash, the statement of cash flows would report the $675 million paid for the acquisition (net of cash acquired) in cash from investing activities. See Box 14-1.

None of the individual assets and liabilities acquired are reported in the cash flow statement. SFAS 95 (see Chapter 3) specifically requires that reported cash flows exclude the effect of acquisitions (other than actual cash flows). The failure to report the individual asset and liability changes for purchase method acquisitions has two consequences:

1. Consecutive balance sheets and the cash flow statement must be used to deduce the assets and liabilities acquired.
2. Operating cash flow (CFO) can be distorted.

We consider each of these consequences in turn.

Deducing Assets and Liabilities Acquired

Because SFAS 95 requires the exclusion of acquisition balance sheet changes from the cash flow statement, balance sheet changes for any period have three components:

1. Operating changes for the period
2. Effect of acquisitions
3. Effect of foreign currency changes

For companies with no foreign operations, only the first two components exist. In that case, we can deduct the operating change component from the total change and deduce the acquisition effects.

Exhibit 14-7A illustrates this process in a simplified way; it shows the balance sheet of Acquire just before and just after its acquisition of Target. We assume that the time period is so short that there are no operations. In this case, therefore, the balance sheet changes are entirely due to the acquisition. If we did not have the consolidating balance sheet (Exhibit 14-2A) for Scenario A, we could deduce it.

For example, inventories rose by $150 million. As the operating change was zero, the acquired inventories of Acquire must have been $150 million (at fair value). This same analysis can be applied to all other assets and liabilities.

EXHIBIT 14-7A
Impact of the Acquisition of Target on Balance Sheet of Acquire
Purchase Method (U.S. GAAP): Scenario A (All Equity)

Acquire Corp. Pre- and Postacquisition Balance Sheets

in $millions

	Preacquisition*		Postacquisition[†]		Change
Cash		$ 100		$ 175	$ 75
Inventories		200		350	150
Receivables		200		275	75
Current assets		$ 500		$ 800	$300
Property		500		850	350
Software				120	120
Licenses				60	60
Goodwill		—		80	80
Total assets		$1,000		$1,910	$910
Payables		150		200	50
Accrued liabilities		100		150	50
Current liabilities		$ 250		$ 350	$100
Long-term debt		250		410	160
Common stock	$350		$1,100		$ 750
Retained earnings	150		50		(100)
Common equity		500		1,150	650
Total equity		$1,000		$1,910	$910

*Exhibit 14-2A, column 1.
[†]Exhibit 14-2A, column 5.

BOX 14-1
Comparison of Purchase Methods Under U.S. and IAS GAAP

Scenario B: Cash Transaction

The text illustrates the financial statement effects of differing accounting methods using an all-stock transaction. Many transactions are made for cash, or a combination of cash and securities. In this box we illustrate the accounting for such transactions under U.S. and international accounting standards.

Transactions that are not made entirely for stock cannot qualify as poolings under IAS GAAP. Therefore we compare the two variants of the purchase method. The starting point is the same set of financial statements shown in Exhibit 14-1. However, we now assume that Acquire pays $750 million in cash, which it obtains by borrowing an equal amount at an interest rate of 8%. The consolidated balance sheets at the acquisition date of June 30, 2001 are shown in Exhibit 14-2B.

The asset accounts are identical to those for the purchase method in Exhibit 14-2A. The differences on the liability side of the balance sheet are:

- Debt is increased by $750 million to reflect the funds borrowed for the acquisition of Target.
- Equity is reduced by the elimination of the common stock and retained earnings of Target and (under U.S. GAAP) by the write-off of in-process research and development (net of tax). In contrast to Scenario A, there is no additional equity issued by Acquire.

Because of the use of debt rather than equity, the debt-to-equity ratios are far higher than under Scenario A. Because of the R&D write-off under U.S. GAAP, the debt-to-equity ratio is higher than under IAS GAAP.

EXHIBIT 14-2B
Comparison of Purchase and Pooling Methods: Scenario B (All Cash)
Consolidated Balance Sheets at June 30, 2001 (in $millions)

	(1)	(2)	(3)	(4)	(5)	(6)
	Historical Cost		Purchase Method			
			U.S.GAAP (SFAS 141)		IASB GAAP (IAS 22)	
	Acquire	Target	Adjustments	Consolidated	Adjustments	Consolidated
Cash	$ 100	$ 75	—	$ 175	—	$ 175
Inventories	200	100	50	350	50	350
Receivables	200	75	—	275	—	275
Current assets	$ 500	$250	$ 50	$ 800	$ 50	$ 800
Property	500	250	100	850	100	850
In-process R&D			100		100	100
R&D writeoff			(100)			—
Software cost			120	120	120	120
Licenses			60	60	60	60
Goodwill*	—	—	80	80	80	80
Total assets	$1,000	$500	$ 410	$1,910	$ 510	$2,010
Payables	150	50	—	200	—	200
Accrued liabilities	100	50	—	150	—	150
Current liabilities	$ 250	$100	—	$ 350	—	$ 350
Long-term debt	250	150	760	1,160	760	1,160
Common stock	350	225	(225)	350	(225)	350
Retained earnings	150	25	(125)	50	(25)	150
Common equity	500	250	(350)†	400	(250)‡	500
Total equities	$1,000	$500	$ 410	$1,910	$ 510	$2,010
Current ratio	2.00×	2.50×		2.29×		2.29×
Debt/equity ratio	50.00%	60.00%		290.00%		232.00%

*See text discussion of the purchase method for allocation rules.
†The net reduction of $350 million reflects the purchase and retirement of all of Target's equity ($225 million common stock + $25 million retained earnings) and the immediate write-off of $100 million of acquired in-process R&D.
‡Under IAS 22 there is no R&D writeoff; total assets and equity are both $100 million higher than under U.S. GAAP.

The balance sheet differences from Scenario A have corresponding income statement effects, as shown in Exhibit 14-4B, which should be compared with Exhibit 14-4A in the text. The additional interest expense (net of tax) reduces net income by $20 million in 2001 and $39 million in 2002 and 2003.

Exhibit 14-6B shows the resulting income statements for Scenario B. Under both U.S. and IAS GAAP, 2002 earnings per share is higher when the acquisition is financed by debt. However, 2001 EPS is lower than the Scenario A level. These effects reflect the higher leverage. As the acquisition of Target reduces 2001 net income (especially under U.S. GAAP), EPS is lower despite the fewer shares outstanding. In 2002, however, when the earnings of Target exceed the additional interest

cost, the lower number of shares outstanding under Scenario B increases EPS.

The reported cash flow effects under Scenario B are similar to those under Scenario A in that the balance sheet changes are largely omitted. The only cash flows reported would be:

Cash for investment	(675)	Net assets of Target (net of cash acquired)
Cash from financing	750	Proceeds of debt issue

Exhibit 14-7B is the same as Exhibit 14-7A in the text except that it reflects the debt financing required to fund the acquisition rather than the stock issuance under Scenario A.

EXHIBIT 14-4B
Income Statement Effects of Balance Sheet Adjustments Under Purchase Method: Scenario B (All Cash)

	Balance Sheet Adjustment		Income Statement Effect					
	Amount		2001 (6 months)		2002		2003	
Description	U.S. GAAP	IASB GAAP	U.S. GAAP	IASB GAAP	U.S. GAAP	IASB GAAP	U.S.GAAP	IASB GAAP
1. Inventories	$ 50	$ 50	$ (50)	$ (50)	$ —	$ —	$ —	$ —
2. Property	100	100	(5)	(5)	(10)	(10)	(10)	(10)
3. In-process R&D	—	100	(100)	(12)		(25)		(25)
4. Software cost	120	120	(20)	(20)	(40)	(40)	(40)	(40)
5. Licenses	60	60						
6. Goodwill	80	80		(4)		(8)		(8)
Subtotals	$ 410	$ 510	$(175)	$ (91)	$ (50)	$ (83)	$ (50)	$ (83)
7. Long-term debt	760	760	29	29	58	58	58	58
8. Net totals	$(350)	$(250)	$(204)	$(120)	$(108)	$(141)	$(108)	$(141)
9. Tax effect (35%)			71	42	38	49	38	49
10. Net effect			$(133)	$ (78)	$ (70)	$ (92)	$ (70)	$ (92)

EXHIBIT 14-6B. ACQUIRE CORP.
Consolidated Income Statements, 2000–2002: Scenario B (All Cash)

Year Ended December 31 ($ millions)

	Purchase Method					
	U.S. GAAP			IASB GAAP		
	2000	2001	2002	2000	2001	2002
Sales	$1,000	$1,340	$1,726	$1,000	$1,340	$1,726
Cost of goods sold	(600)	(820)	(963)	(600)	(820)	(963)
Gross margin	$ 400	$ 520	$ 763	$ 400	$ 520	$ 763
Selling expense	(130)	(195)	(265)	(130)	(195)	(265)
Purchased R&D		(100)				
Depreciation expense	(50)	(69)	(92)	(50)	(69)	(92)
Amortization expense	0	(20)	(40)	0	(36)	(73)
Interest expense	(20)	(54)	(88)	(20)	(54)	(88)
Pretax income	$ 200	$ 82	$ 278	$ 200	$ 166	$ 245
Income tax expense	(68)	(26)	(92)	(68)	(55)	(81)
Net income	$ 132	$ 56	$ 186	$ 132	$ 111	$ 164
Shares outstanding (millions)	80.0	80.0	80.0	80.0	80.0	80.0
Earnings per share	$1.65	$0.70	$2.33	$1.65	$1.39	$2.05
Gross margin (% of sales)	40.00%	38.81%	44.21%	40.00%	38.81%	44.21%
Interest coverage ratio	11.00	2.52	4.16	11.00	4.07	3.78

EXHIBIT 14-7B

Impact of the Acquisition of Target on Balance Sheet of Acquire Purchase Method (U.S. GAAP), Scenario B (All Cash)

Acquire Corp. Pre- and Postacquisition Balance Sheets

in $millions

	Preacquisition*	Postacquisition[†]	Change
Cash	$ 100	$ 175	$ 75
Inventories	200	350	150
Receivables	200	275	75
Current assets	$ 500	$ 800	$300
Property	500	850	350
Software		120	120
Licenses		60	60
Goodwill	—	80	80
Total assets	$1,000	$1,910	$910
Payables	150	200	50
Accrued liabilities	100	150	50
Current liabilities	$ 250	$ 350	$100
Long-term debt	250	1,160	910
Common stock	$350	$350	$ —
Retained earnings	150	50	(100)
Common equity	500	400	(100)
Total equity	$1,000	$1,910	$910

*Exhibit 14-2B, column 1.
[†]Exhibit 14-2B, column 4.

> *This example illustrates the general procedure used to deduce acquisition assets and liabilities: Subtract the operating change shown in the cash flow statement from the actual balance sheet change for the period. The difference should be the effect of acquisitions or divestitures.*

Use of this procedure is illustrated in Problem 14-12. Its accuracy, however, depends on an absence of foreign currency effects; these are discussed in Chapter 15.[16]

Distortion of Cash from Operations

Although the acquisition increases operating assets and liabilities, that increase is not included in cash from operations (CFO). The cash flow change in operating accounts does not equal the actual balance sheet change. Because the additional inventories and receivables are acquired as part of an acquisition, the cash paid for their acquisition is included in cash for investment.

However, CFO reported in the year of the acquisition (and in subsequent years) still may be distorted. The degree of distortion depends on whether the levels of operating assets and liabilities immediately after the acquisition are maintained over time.

The potential distortion can be illustrated by considering the inventory acquired. Although the cash paid for the acquisition of the inventory does not flow through cash from operations, the cash received when the inventory is sold does. Thus, CFO is inflated as the proceeds of sale are included, whereas the cost of acquiring the inventory is not.

This distortion is minimal if inventory is continually replaced, as the cash outflows for new inventory offset cash inflows from sales. However, if there is a reduction in the acquired firm's net operating assets, CFO may be distorted, and careful analysis is required to understand the impact.

---

[16]When some assets and liabilities are denominated in other currencies, fluctuations in exchange rates affect year-to-year balance sheet comparisons, making it impossible to isolate the effect of acquisitions and divestitures.

COMPLICATING FACTORS IN PURCHASE METHOD ACQUISITIONS

Both Target–Acquire scenarios are simplistic. In actual transactions, there are three complicating factors that sometimes appear:

1. Contingent payments
2. Allocation of purchase price
3. Restructuring provisions

We discuss each issue briefly.

Contingent Payments

Some acquisition agreements provide that the acquisition price is dependent on future earnings of the acquired entity or other future events. Accounting principles require that the additional purchase price be recognized by the acquirer as soon as those conditions are met.

The purchase price increase must be allocated to the assets and liabilities acquired. If some assets (e.g., property) were not fully written up to fair value, then a further write-up would occur. The usual case, however, is that the contingent compensation increases goodwill.

For example, Boron LePore provides services to the healthcare industry. Boron paid $15.1 million plus performance incentives for three companies acquired in 1998. During 1999, contingent payments to the former owners of three of the companies totaled $11.4 million, increasing the acquisition cost by 75%. These additional payments were added to goodwill.

Allocation of Purchase Price

Under the purchase method, the acquisition cost must be allocated among the acquired assets and liabilities according to their fair (market) values.[17] However, the measurement of fair value for some asset and liability classes can be highly subjective. This is especially true for intangible assets such as computer software, patents, and acquired "in-process" research and development.

Acquirers may have strong incentives to allocate more of the purchase price to some assets than others. Allocating cost to depreciable fixed assets rather than goodwill reduces reported income, as goodwill (under U.S. GAAP) does not have to be amortized. On the other hand, depreciation is tax-deductible; allocation to fixed assets rather than goodwill increases cash flow when goodwill amortization is not tax-deductible.

■ Example: Lucent

When Lucent acquired Octel in 1997, $945 million (more than half of the $1,819 million purchase price) was expensed and virtually the entire price paid for Sahara in 1997 ($219 million) was expensed as IPRD. Similarly, more than half of the 1999 purchase of Yurie (for $1,056 million) was allocated to IPRD and expensed.

There are two important effects of such expensing:

1. Reported income of the acquirer is reduced in the period of the acquisition. As this effect is nonoperating, IPRD and other acquisition-related charges are routinely removed from reported earnings for valuation purposes.
2. The immediate write-off reduces the amount of goodwill or other intangible assets that would otherwise be recognized. When IPRD replaces an intangible asset that must be amortized, future reported income increases. If Lucent had capitalized the 1997 IPRD of $1,176 million, amortization would have reduced reported 1998 pretax income by nearly 12% (if amortized over four years). This may create an incentive

---

[17]Henning, Lewis, and Shaw (2000) report that (for their sample of over 1,500 acquisitions) target assets were written up on average $42 million. However, that amount represented less than 20% of the $218 million differential between the average acquisition price ($318 million) and book value ($100 million). Thus, over 80% of the price-book value differential remained unallocated as goodwill.

for firms to allocate as much of the purchase price as possible to in-process research and development.[18]

Under IASB standards for purchase method acquisitions, however, IPRD must be capitalized and the incentive for high allocation disappears. As technology-related intangibles are generally amortized over shorter time periods than goodwill, companies using IASB standards may prefer to allocate acquisition cost to goodwill, enhancing reported earnings. (If analysts add goodwill amortization back to earnings to make them "comparable" with those of U.S. companies, the incentive to allocate cost to goodwill is even higher.) ■

Restructuring Provisions

A frequent motivation for the combination of two firms is that cost savings can be achieved by eliminating duplicate facilities or shifting activities between the two firms. The costs associated with such activities are deemed "restructuring costs," which include both cash and noncash charges. Charges with cash flow consequences include employee severance costs and lease-related payments: Noncash charges are due to the write-off or writedown of inventories, property, and intangible assets.

The recognition of restructuring charges at the merger date has two advantages (note the similarity to purchased research and development):

1. The restructuring charge is considered nonoperating in nature and routinely ignored by analysts forecasting earnings and other performance measures (such as EBITDA) used for valuation.

2. Future earnings are increased because the "restructuring" costs will not be recognized in future periods.

Lucent, for example, reports that it recorded a pretax charge of $150 million in 1997 in connection with two acquisitions. That charge had the effect of shifting $150 million of expense from 1998 to 1997.[19] The 1997 charge would have been excluded from "operating earnings" by many analysts.

Restructuring provisions can be made regardless of whether the purchase or pooling method is used to account for the acquisition. Both U.S. and IASB GAAP require that the company have in place a formal plan that details the operating changes that justify the restructuring provision. This requirement is intended to preclude companies from recognizing overly broad contingency reserves.[20]

INCOME TAX EFFECTS OF BUSINESS COMBINATIONS

The income tax aspects of accounting for business combinations have always been complex. Changes in U.S. tax laws in recent years have only increased that complexity. A thorough discussion of this subject is well beyond the scope of this book. However, a few general comments may be helpful.

Most pooling of interests acquisitions are nontaxable events under the Internal Revenue Code (the Code) of the United States. Nontaxability has two consequences:

1. Shareholders of the acquired company do not recognize gain or loss as a result of the merger. They transfer the cost basis of their shares in the acquired company to the shares of the acquirer that they receive in exchange.

2. The cost basis of the assets and liabilities of the acquired company is not affected by the merger. There is no income tax recognition of the fair value of assets and liabilities and no change in tax benefits or deductibility as these assets are used or liabilities paid.

---

[18]The Securities and Exchange Commission, concerned that high allocations to IPRD could not be justified, forced some companies to restate their accounting for acquisitions, reducing the allocation to IPRD.

[19]In fact, $18 million of the reserve was not needed at all and later reversed.

[20]Due to abusive use of restructuring provisions, the Securities and Exchange Commission clamped down on overly broad provisions.

A purchase method acquisition, in contrast, is usually a taxable event under the Code. In a taxable exchange, selling shareholders must recognize gain or loss on the sale of their shares, even if they receive securities of the acquiring company. In some cases (see Box 14-2), the tax basis of assets and liabilities of the acquired firm is changed from original cost to fair value, reflecting the price paid for the company.

When the accounting treatment and the income tax treatment are identical, the post-merger accounting and tax basis of assets and liabilities are the same. However, accounting and tax rules differ, and the tax treatment of an acquisition is often different from the accounting treatment. In such cases, care must be taken to discern the impact of the difference on future earnings and cash flows. Careful reading of the income tax footnote (see Chapter 9) may reveal different tax and accounting bases for some assets and liabilities. Differential merger treatment is usually the cause of such differences.

When a merger is tax-free, but accounted for as a purchase, the tax basis of the assets is below the accounting basis (if we assume that the purchase price exceeds historical equity). As a result, the additional depreciation and other expenses resulting from purchase method adjustments are not tax-deductible. This increases the firm's effective tax rate.

Another effect is that recognized gains on the sale of assets are higher for tax purposes than for accounting purposes, reducing after-tax cash proceeds and adversely affecting the after-tax gain or loss from the sale.

Box 14-2 contains a summary of the tax treatment of mergers in the United States.

BOX 14-2
United States Tax Aspects of Mergers and Acquisitions*

With the elimination of pooling of interests under U.S. GAAP, the number of mergers for which the tax and accounting treatments differ has greatly increased.

The purpose of this box is to

- Provide a summary of the tax treatment of mergers and acquisitions in the United States, and

- Discuss the financial statement effects of purchase method acquisitions that are tax-free transactions.

Tax Treatment of Mergers and Acquisitions in the United States

Transactions fall into three categories under the Internal Revenue Code. We will discuss each in turn.

1. Purchase of assets

2. Purchase of corporation

3. Tax-free reorganization

1. *Purchase of assets.* When a buyer purchases assets (and assumes specified liabilities) from the target, it establishes a new basis of accounting for the acquired operations. The purchase price is allocated among the assets acquired, similar to the allocation required for accounting purposes under the purchase method. Goodwill is recognized only after the fair value of all other assets (including identifiable intangibles) has been recorded. Such Section 197 goodwill is amortized over a fifteen-year period.[†]

The advantage to the buyer of purchasing assets rather than the entire corporation is that the risk of contingent or unrecorded liabilities (including back taxes) remains with the seller. However the buyer loses the benefit of any tax loss carryforwards (see discussion of NOLs later in this box). In addition, asset purchases may require that counterparties to contractual agreements (such as leases and franchises) consent to the transaction.

As the tax and financial reporting bases of purchased assets should be identical, such transactions create few accounting or analytical difficulties. It is worth noting that goodwill amortized for tax purposes will not generate deferred tax liabilities, as no amortization is permitted under SFAS 142.

2. *Purchase of corporation.* The purchase of the entire corporation is more complicated. The buyer can make a Section 338 election, under which the transaction is treated as an asset purchase for tax purposes. That election allows the buyer to record the purchased assets at fair value for tax purposes, obtaining the same tax benefits (higher depreciation, for example) and retaining the tax benefits of NOL carryforwards. However that election triggers an immediate tax liability on the difference between the purchase price and the target's tax basis in its assets.[‡]

The advantage to the buyer is that it acquires all of the target company contracts and other rights (such as the right to conduct business). The disadvantage is that when the target company remains in existence, the buyer retains any unrecognized liabilities. When there is no Section 338 election, the tax basis of the acquired assets remains unchanged.

3. *Tax-free recognition.* The tax requirements are, in general:

(i) Continuity of business—the buyer must continue the target's business or continue to use its assets in the buyer's business

(ii) Continuity of shareholder interest—the shareholders of the target must receive voting shares of the buyer.

The tax laws permit some "boot" (cash or securities) that do not meet the "continuity of interest" rules. However, boot generates some tax liability for the target shareholders.

Tax-free reorganizations under the Internal Revenue Code, fall into four categories:

- Type A: statutory merger, where target company disappears
- Type B: stock swap, the easiest form to implement as all contracts and other rights and obligations of the seller (which remains in existence) remain; only control has changed.
- Type C: asset acquisition for voting stock, where the buyer acquires only the desired assets and liabilities.
- Type D: reverse acquisition, where the buyer merges into the target, which is the surviving entity. Type D acquisitions are used when the target has contracts or other rights that are difficult or impossible to transfer to the buyer.

Each form has detailed regulations governing its use.

In addition, there are triangular mergers, where the target merges with a subsidiary of the buyer. The advantage is that parent (and other subsidiaries of the parent) are insulated from liabilities of the target.

Target shareholders generally prefer tax-free reorganizations because they do not recognize any taxable gain. The buyer retains the tax basis of the acquired assets, any tax loss carryforwards, and any unrecorded liabilities.

When an acquisition is tax-free but is accounted for as a purchase, the tax and accounting bases of the acquired operations are different. These differences generate differences between pretax (financial reporting) income and taxable (tax return) income. We review the consequences of those differences shortly, after reviewing tax loss carryforwards.

Net operating loss (NOL) carryforwards

Tax loss carryforwards (the unused tax benefits of prior period losses) of the target company may be a significant element of the target's value to the buyer. NOLs can be used to offset future earnings of the acquired operations and (with limits) of the buyer.

The existence of NOLs may affect the form of the merger. IRS regulations require that the target remain in existence and that its operations continue.

However, when a merger results in a new controlling shareholder, regulations limit the amount of NOLs that can be used in each year. Additional restrictions apply to "built-in loss" (when the tax basis of acquired assets exceeds their fair market value at the acquisition date). On the other hand, NOL use can offset the realization of "built-in gain" (fair market value in excess of tax basis).

Financial Statement Effects

SFAS 109 (see Chapter 9) governs the accounting for income taxes. When purchase method acquisitions are taxable transactions, and the buyer either purchases assets or makes a Section 338 election to step up the basis of the target, there is no difference between the tax and financial reporting basis of assets and liabilities, and no accounting or analysis issues arise.

However, when the purchase method is used for tax-free reorganizations, or when a Section 338 election is not made, the asset and liability revaluations discussed in the chapter are not reflected for tax purposes. SFAS 109 requires that deferred tax assets and liabilities be established at the acquisition date for the differences between the tax and financial reporting bases (carrying amount) of the acquired assets and liabilities.

For example, for financial reporting, fixed assets are recorded at fair value, normally higher than historic cost. Depreciation of the higher carrying amount generates depreciation and amortization increases that are not tax deductible.

Example: Assume that the purchased company has fixed assets of $100 million, depreciated over ten years, with annual depreciation (10 year life) of $10 million. If the fair value of these assets is $200 million, the buyer will report annual deprecation of $20 million; the additional $10 million of depreciation is not tax deductible. If pretax income before depreciation is $40 million, pretax income is $20 million but taxable income is $30 million. With a 34% tax rate, taxes payable equal $10.2 million.

Under SFAS 109, a deferred tax liability of $34 million (34% of $100 million) must be created at the acquisition date. Each year, the $3.4 million difference between taxes payable ($10.2 million in prior paragraph) and income tax expense of $6.8 million (34% of $20 million) reduces the deferred tax liability. After ten years, the fixed assets are zero for both tax and financial reporting and the deferred tax liability has also been extinguished. The initial $34 million was equal to the total tax payments ($3.4 million × 10) due to the basis differences.

Deferred taxes are not, however, applied to non tax-deductible goodwill. The result is a permanent difference, increasing the reported income tax rate.

When unrecognized NOLs are used, SFAS 109 requires that they be recorded:

1. As reduction of acquisition goodwill, then
2. As reductions of other acquired intangible assets, then
3. As reduction of income tax expense of the period used.

Concluding Comments

When a company has made a purchase method acquisition, the analyst should determine its tax treatment. This information may be obtained from the merger proxy statement, SEC filings, and discussions with management. Review of the tax footnote for periods following the merger may also provide relevant information. The critical issues are whether:

1. There has been a step-up in basis for the acquired assets and liabilities.
2. There are any recognized deferred tax assets or liabilities, the period over which these will liquidate, and the cash flow implications of their liquidation.
3. Goodwill is tax-deductible.
4. There are unused NOL carryforwards, their size, the likelihood and expected period of utilization, and the accounting result of such use (goodwill or intangible writedown versus income recognition).

---

*Summarized from Vidas and Viens, Mergers and Acquisitions: Tax and Accounting Considerations, Controllers Handbook.
†This applies to goodwill from acquisitions after August 10, 1993.
‡Target company NOLs can be used to offset this gain, however.

INTERNATIONAL DIFFERENCES IN ACCOUNTING FOR BUSINESS COMBINATIONS

IAS 22 (revised 1998) generally requires the use of the purchase method to account for acquisitions. It allows pooling (merger or uniting of interests) accounting only in exceptional circumstances, when it is not possible to identify the acquirer. However, pooling continues to be used in practice as the criteria governing the identification of the acquirer are provided only as background material and implementation guidance. For example, in 1998 Swiss Bank and Union Bank of Switzerland formed UBS. The pooling method was used (under IASB GAAP) even though the combination was generally viewed as a takeover of Union Bank by Swiss Bank.[21] Pooling is also permitted by the accounting standards of most countries outside of the United States.

The major differences between U.S. and IASB standards are summarized in Exhibit 14-8. These differences were illustrated using the Target–Acquire transaction earlier in the chapter.

Differences in Historical Treatment of Goodwill

Accounting standards related to goodwill outside of the United States reflect differing views of financial reporting, cultural differences, and legal requirements.[22] Both the recognition and amortization of goodwill have varied widely.

While most discussions of goodwill focus on the amortization issue, historically some accounting systems have permitted the immediate write-off of goodwill to stockholders' equity.[23] The financial statement effects of immediate write-off are long lasting:

1. Reported earnings are not reduced by goodwill amortization.
2. As both assets and stockholders' equity are reduced by the write-off, financial statement ratios using those amounts are altered. Return on equity and return on assets rise; they are doubly affected as the numerator is higher and the denominator lower than they would have been if goodwill were recognized as assets and amortized. Asset and equity turnover also increase due to the lower denominator.

EXHIBIT 14-8
Differences Between U.S. and International Accounting Standards in Accounting for Mergers and Acquisitions

Issue	U.S. GAAP (SFAS 141 and SFAS 142)	IAS GAAP (IAS 22)
Method	Purchase method only	Pooling method permitted under restrictive conditions
Allocation of purchase price	All assets and liabilities measured at fair value	All assets and liabilities measured at fair value when purchase method required
Amortization of goodwill	Not permitted	Required with 20-year limit other than exceptional cases
Test goodwill for impairment	Required annually	Required annually
Restructuring cost provisions	Permitted	Permitted for acquired company only
Purchased R&D (IPRD)	Expensed immediately	Capitalized and amortized
Treatment of negative goodwill	(i) Allocated pro rata over defined assets acquired (see text) (ii) Excess recognized as extraordinary gain	(i) When related to expected losses, recognize when those losses occur (ii) Recognize over life of depreciable assets (iii) Excess recognized in income

[21]A story on Bloomberg (January 28, 1998) reported that Swiss Bank executives would have four of the top six jobs in the combined bank and that most job cuts would occur among Union Bank employees.

[22]See *Issues in Accounting Education* (Fall 1996), vol. 11, no. 2, for articles presenting the U.S., U.K., German, and Japanese perspective on goodwill accounting.

[23]France, Germany, and the United Kingdom are prominent examples.

■ **Example: Roche**

For purchase method acquisitions prior to 1995, Roche charged goodwill directly to stockholders' equity on the acquisition date. This practice was permitted by IASB standards at the time. However, IAS 22 required retroactive restatement to capitalize and amortize such goodwill. Therefore, in its 2000 financial statements, Roche reinstated (as of January 1, 2000) nearly CHF13 billion of previously unrecognized goodwill and CHF1.7 billion of previously unrecognized other intangible assets arising from pre-1995 acquisitions. Roche also recognized CHF11.8 billion of amortization that would have appeared in income in years subsequent to these acquisitions.[24] The net result of the restatement was an increase in Roche net assets of CHF1.5 billion (2% of total assets). Roche also disclosed that this accounting change

- Increased 2000 goodwill amortization by CHF104 million
- Would have increased 1999 expenses (which were not restated) by CHF187 million

The accounting change, therefore, had the effect of increasing assets and decreasing reported income. While these effects are small, they reduce Roche's return on assets (and ROE). ■

ANALYSIS OF GOODWILL

Goodwill is one of the most controversial subjects in all of accounting and has been so for at least three decades. In most cases, goodwill and other intangible assets arise in purchase method acquisitions; they are the residual portion of the purchase price that cannot be allocated to other tangible and intangible assets. Goodwill is the premium paid for the target's reputation, technology, brand names, or other attributes that enable it to earn an excess return on investment, justifying that premium price. Hence, the name goodwill.

Since goodwill arises as a residual, it cannot be measured directly. It can be independently appraised only by measuring the "excess" return earned by the business to which it is attributed; such measurements require many assumptions, making such appraisals controversial.

Proponents of goodwill recognition argue that goodwill is simply the capitalized present value of excess returns some companies are able to earn and no more subjective than the present value of future cash flows connected with tangible assets.

Opponents of the goodwill concept dislike the subjective nature and indirect measurement of this "asset." They argue that it often turns out to be ephemeral; write-offs of goodwill are common (see Chapter 8). Prices paid for acquisitions often turn out to be based on unrealistic expectations rather than true earnings prospects.

Empirical evidence is consistent with both approaches. Jennings et al. (1996), using an asset-based valuation framework, found that on average, the market views goodwill as an asset. Henning et al. (2000), however, disaggregated goodwill (excess of purchase price over fair-value of target assets) into a component recognized (valued) by the market at the time of the acquisition (excess of market value over fair-value) and a residual component (excess of acquisition cost over market value[25]). They found that Jennings et al.'s results held only for the former component. The residual component (approximately 30% of total goodwill) had a negative association with market price consistent with the market writing off the overpayment.

Both arguments, in our view, have merit both when stated in the abstract and when applied to specific companies. We believe that goodwill can, and should, be examined only with respect to a specific enterprise. There are many companies that are able to earn above-normal returns over long periods of time. The common shares of such companies usually sell at prices well above tangible book value, even after tangible assets are revalued to current cost.

---

[24]While not explicitly stated, we can infer that Roche assumed fairly short amortization periods for this newly recognized goodwill, so that most had been amortized prior to 2000.

[25]More precisely, they defined market value to be the pre-offer market price of the target plus the cumulative net increase in the acquirer and target's market values around the acquisition announcement date.

In such cases, investors are paying for intangible assets, such as reputation, brand names, patents, management expertise, or other factors. The allocation of the excess purchase price to these factors can only be arbitrary; accounting cannot measure every attribute of an enterprise.

In other cases, companies earn below-normal returns despite the intangible assets on their balance sheet. These assets may be overstated; share prices of such companies are often below stated book value. The fact that an intangible asset originated in an acquisition does not guarantee that it will have continuing value any more than if the intangible asset were self-generated.

To sum up, the existence of economic goodwill is largely independent of the existence of accounting goodwill. The former is a function of economic performance; the latter is a function of accounting standards. Investors and financial analysts are primarily interested in economic goodwill, yet accounting goodwill exists in abundant quantity in the financial statements of many companies.

For purposes of analysis, therefore, the analyst should remove goodwill from reported balance sheets. When a company clearly earns excess returns, this factor will enter into the valuation of the company's shares.

Goodwill Amortization

For companies whose statements are subject to IASB GAAP and for some others, the recognition of acquisition goodwill necessarily leads to its amortization. Standards are flexible; goodwill can be amortized over a period as long as 20 years under IAS 22 with the possibility of even longer amortization periods when justification can be provided. As companies choose the period of amortization and in practice make different choices, comparability is poor.

When present, goodwill amortization is a noncash charge; it is merely the amortization of a past expenditure.[26] In the United States, most classes of goodwill are not deductible expenses under the Internal Revenue Code so there is no income tax benefit. In short, the amortization of goodwill is a nonevent, with no real consequences.[27]

Goodwill amortization does, however, affect reported income. When goodwill is written off (such write-offs are often part of restructuring provisions), future reported income increases. Under both U.S. and IASB standards, goodwill must be reviewed whenever there are indications that it may have been impaired.

Goodwill Impairment

Impairment writedowns are noncash events, but have significant effects on reported financial statements. For example, in 1997 Eli Lilly [LLY] wrote down the goodwill associated with its 1994 acquisition of PCS Health Systems. Lilly's 10-K report included the following footnote:

Note 2: Asset Impairment

In November 1994, the company purchased PCS Health Systems, Inc. (PCS), McKesson Corporation's pharmaceutical-benefits-management business, for approximately $4.1 billion. Substantially all the purchase price was allocated to goodwill.

Subsequently, pursuant to SFAS No. 121, "Accounting for the Impairment of Long-Lived Assets and for Long-Lived Assets to Be Disposed Of," the company evaluated the recoverability of the long-lived assets, including intangibles, of its PCS health-care-management businesses. While revenues and profits are growing and new capabilities are being developed at PCS, the rapidly changing, competitive and highly regulated environ-

---

[26]Some believe that goodwill amortization should remain a deduction from net income, similar to depreciation expense (also an allocation of a past expenditure).

[27]Empirical studies are consistent with goodwill amortization being a nonevent. Moehrle, Reynolds-Mehrle, and Wallace (2001) find that the market ignores goodwill amortization, as there is little difference between the relative informativeness of earnings before and after goodwill amortization. Jennings, Leclere, and Thompson (2001) argue that goodwill amortization adds "noise" to the system, as they found earnings before goodwill amortization to explain significantly more of the distribution in share prices than earnings after amortization.

ment in which PCS operates has prevented the company from significantly increasing PCS' operating profits from levels that existed prior to the acquisition. In addition, since the acquisition, the health-care-industry trend toward highly managed care has been slower than originally expected and the possibility of selling a portion of PCS' equity to a strategic partner has not been realized. In the second quarter of 1997, concurrent with PCS' annual planning process, the company determined that PCS' estimated future undiscounted cash flows were below the carrying value of PCS' long-lived assets. Accordingly, during the second quarter of 1997, the company adjusted the carrying value of PCS' long-lived assets, primarily goodwill, to their estimated fair value of approximately $1.5 billion, resulting in a noncash impairment loss of approximately $2.4 billion ($2.21 per share). The estimated fair value was based on anticipated future cash flows discounted at a rate commensurate with the risk involved.

As a result of the impairment charge, Lilly reported a loss for 1997. However, earnings per share excluding the impairment charge (and excluding an unrelated capital gain) increased 21%. It appears that the writedown had no impact on Lilly's stock price.[28] Apparently investors treated the writedown, which followed well-known problems with the PCS acquisition, as a nonevent.

In addition to the immediate income statement impact, the writedown had significant financial statement effects, as can be seen from the following data

Years Ended December 31

	1996	1997
Intangible assets	$ 4,028.2	$ 1,550.5
Total assets	14,307.2	12,577.4
Total debt	3,729.4	2,553.7
Stockholders' equity	6,100.1	4,645.6
Debt/equity ratio	61%	55%

Despite the nearly one-third decline in total debt during 1997, Lilly's debt/equity ratio showed only a small decrease as much of the debt reduction was offset by lower equity. In years subsequent to 1997, Lilly's earnings increased due to the absence of goodwill amortization.[29] Return on equity and other return ratios were also increased.

This example illustrates the effect of goodwill impairment on financial statements. Under IAS, the reduction of amortization that follows an impairment charge makes these effects even greater.

Goodwill Impairment Under SFAS 142

SFAS 142, which became effective in 2002, eliminated the amortization of acquisition goodwill. However, companies are now required to test goodwill for possible impairment at least annually.[30] Such testing requires that the firm estimate the fair value of each reporting unit to which goodwill is attributed and compare that estimated fair value with the carrying amount of the reporting unit. Any excess of the carrying amount over the estimated fair value must be recognized as an impairment loss up to the amount of goodwill.

SFAS 142 became effective when the financial markets were suffering from the aftereffects of the technology-media-telecom (TMT) bubble of the late 1990s. Many firms had made acquisitions, recognizing large amounts of goodwill that could not be justified by operating results. As a consequence, many companies recognized substantial goodwill impairments in the

---

[28]While the writedown was announced in late June, Lilly stock outperformed the S&P drug index before and after the announcement date.

[29]Goodwill amortization was required by U.S. GAAP prior to the adoption of SFAS 142 in 2001.

[30]Interim testing is required when there has been an adverse change in the business (see para. 28 of SFAS 142 for more detail).

first quarter of 2002 when they adopted SFAS 142. These noncash impairment charges (which companies expected the financial markets to ignore) had the following effects:

- Reduced net assets, increasing return on asset and asset turnover ratios
- Reduced stockholders' equity (and book value per share), increasing return on equity and equity turnover ratios but increasing the debt-to-equity ratio.

Market reaction to these charges was limited. In most cases common share prices already reflected the reduced value of the affected acquisitions.

■ **Example**

AOL Time Warner [AOL] was formed in January 2001 when America Online purchased Time-Warner for $147 billion, of which $128 billion was allocated to goodwill; $54 billion of that goodwill was written off when the company adopted SFAS 142 in the first quarter of 2002.

AOL shares, however, had declined from a high of $58 per share in May 2001 to $32 at the end of 2001 and $24 when the 2001 10-K report was filed. That decline exceeded that of the Standard & Poor's Movies and Entertainment Index, which includes Viacom and Walt Disney as well as AOL. The poor relative performance of AOL shares may reflect investors' views that AOL overpaid for Time-Warner. ■

Summary of Goodwill Discussion. Goodwill recognition, amortization, and impairment can significantly affect the comparability of companies using different accounting principles (such as U.S. vs. IASB) and the trend of financial data for a single company. The following four adjustments can allow the analyst to remove any distortion that obscures true operating trends:

1. Examine operating trends using data that excludes goodwill amortization or impairment charges.
2. Compute measures of solvency and other ratios using balance sheet data that exclude goodwill.
3. Evaluate prospective acquisitions by considering the price paid relative to the assets and earnings prospects of the acquired firm, regardless of the accounting method used.
4. In subsequent years, compare the earnings of the acquired firm with the price paid, regardless of whether the purchase or pooling method was used.

CHOOSING THE ACQUISITION METHOD

The analysis of Acquire–Target may suggest that the purchase and pooling methods of acquisition accounting are optional alternatives. With the adoption of SFAS 141, that is no longer the case in the United States. For companies following IASB GAAP or the standards of other countries that allow pooling, use of that method must meet certain conditions. However, it is naive to believe that acquirers ignore the accounting consequences of planned acquisitions.

From the corporate viewpoint, the pooling method is usually preferred under the following three conditions:

1. Purchase price greatly exceeds stated equity or book value of target.
2. Target does not have significant depreciable assets that can be written up substantially for tax purposes, creating higher tax deductions.
3. Target has securities or other assets with market values above historic cost. Under pooling, the cost is unchanged; after the acquisition these assets can be sold, increasing reported income.

Under the purchase method, the first two conditions would generate a large amount of goodwill and subsequent amortization reducing reported earnings without a cash (tax reduction) benefit. In general, acquisitions of service companies and others with low asset intensity (few assets to write up) and targets with high returns on equity (implying purchase prices well above stated equity) lend themselves to pooling.

On the other hand, purchase accounting can be advantageous under various conditions:

- Target is "asset rich," allowing write-ups, consequent tax reduction, and quick recovery of the investment. Allocation of the purchase price to inventory is a good example.
- Purchase price is below stated book value, facilitating a writedown of assets, reducing depreciation, and increasing reported earnings.
- Purchase accounting includes the target's "off-balance-sheet" obligations (e.g., underfunded postretirement plans) in the allocation of the purchase price, reducing future charges to earnings.
- Shareholders of the acquirer do not wish to dilute their voting control or equity interest by issuing additional shares. They may prefer to use cash or securities with little or no voting power to effect the acquisition.

Thus, when pooling is permitted, the accounting method is a consequence of the acquisition terms and the specific circumstances of the acquirer, target company, and shareholders. Although not truly optional, it is subject to management control, and the terms of the merger can be fashioned to achieve the desired accounting alternative. Anecdotal evidence suggests that the accounting treatment can significantly affect the negotiated terms[31] and that certain mergers would not have been consummated if pooling could not be used.

Both the choice of accounting method and different market reactions to mergers accounted for as pooling or purchases must, therefore, be understood in the context of the overall motivation for mergers. These issues can be illustrated by examining the income maximization hypothesis often used to explain the accounting choice. While the research referenced below was derived from studies of transactions in the United States, there is no reason to believe that the conclusions would not apply to non-U.S. companies, especially as financial markets speedily globalize.

Income Maximization as Motivation for the Pooling/Purchase Choice

Many researchers have explored income maximization and price (P) to book value (BV) ratio as motivations for the pooling/purchase choice. Under this hypothesis, when the price paid exceeds the target's book value ($P > BV$), pooling is preferred as subsequent reported income, return on equity (ROE), and return on assets (ROA) will be higher. On the other hand, when $P < BV$, purchase accounting is preferred.

Empirical evidence (see Robinson and Shane (1990)) tends to be consistent with the income maximization hypothesis. The evidence indicates that when $P > BV$ there is a strong preference for the pooling method (84% overall). Furthermore, Davis (1990) documents that the price to book value differential is considerably larger for poolings.

For $P < BV$, although the purchase method does not dominate, there is clearly less of a preference for the pooling method. Thus the results are generally consistent with the overall hypothesis, albeit in an asymmetric fashion.

Market Reaction and the Pooling/Purchase Choice

For mergers in general, Morck et al. (1990) report that

> average returns to bidding shareholders are at best slightly positive and significantly negative in some studies.[32]

Hong et al. (1978) and Davis (1990) studied two separate time periods (1954 to 1964 and 1971 to 1982, respectively), and compared the abnormal returns of acquiring firms using the

---

[31]When pooling was permitted in the United States, it could be used even for unfriendly takeovers by changing the acquisition terms (from cash to stock) after the target had capitulated.

[32]Randall Morck, Andrei Shleifer, and Robert W. Vishny, "Do Managerial Objectives Drive Bad Acquisitions?" *Journal of Finance* (March 1990), pp. 31–48. These results contrast with those of target shareholders, who generally fare well as a result of the merger.

pooling method with those using the purchase method to evaluate the impact of the choice of accounting method.

Little or no market reaction was observed for pooling firms, either in the period leading up to the merger or around the first post-merger earnings announcement. However, for the purchase method firms, significant positive reaction was found in the period preceding the merger.

Given the results, the explanations offered for the market reaction were not directly related to the accounting choice of pooling versus purchase and/or their income consequences. Hong et al. explained the results by suggesting that firms that instigated purchase transactions were, *a priori*, better performing firms (hence the positive returns) and that

> firms who choose the purchase method can "afford" to report the lower earnings caused by the use of this method.[33]

An alternative explanation[34] suggests that the positive market reaction to the purchase acquisitions may be associated with the *bargain purchase* implied by the low bid premia[35] found for purchase acquisitions. Relatively higher payments for the pooling transactions, on the other hand, may indicate overpayment (or at least no bargain) and hence the muted market reaction.

Interpreting the Research Results

It is difficult to draw conclusions from the above research for two reasons. First, as cash or debt (taxable) transactions could not be accounted for by use of the pooling method, comparable purchase method transactions, used in the research, were confined to nontaxable acquisitions using shares of the acquirer. In many cases, however, factors that preclude the use of pooling are characteristic of higher bid premia. When cash is used, the bid premium tends to be higher.[36] Moreover, when the transaction is taxable to the target shareholders, a higher bid premium may be required to compensate them for the tax consequences.

Thus, these studies are limited to those transactions where the bid premia are a priori smaller. This self-selection bias may explain smaller price to book value differentials associated with purchase accounting and limit the generalizability of these results.

The second issue in interpreting research results is related to the question of *cause and effect*. Firms may be interested in income maximization because managers (with compensation plans based on earnings, ROA, or ROE) are motivated to choose pooling over purchase to enhance their compensation (see Dunne (1990) and Aboody et al. (2000)). This line of reasoning is consistent with theories of merger activity (see Roll (1986) and Morck et al. (1990)) that argue that managers initiate mergers for their own self-interest and consequently may overpay for the target. They enter into mergers to "buy" growth or to diversify their own risk even if this growth or diversification is not (necessarily) in the best interests of their shareholders.

This underlying motivation may explain (1) the merger, (2) the accounting choice, and (3) the degree of overpayment. If the accounting choice is deemed desirable, then it may be that the accounting choice itself was one of the terms of the negotiation. The acquirer may have paid more for the target to obtain a deal structure permitting it to use the pooling method.

Thus, the choice of accounting method cannot be viewed separately from the acquisition itself. In many ways it is endogenous to the overall terms of the merger.

[33]Hai Hong, Robert S. Kaplan, and Gershon Mandelker, "Pooling vs. Purchase: The Effects of Accounting for Mergers on Stock Prices," *The Accounting Review* (January 1978), pp. 31–47.

[34]This explanation assumes that the market reacts to mergers that had been anticipated because of leaks in the weeks leading up to the merger announcement. As most of the reaction in the Davis (1990) study was in the 11-week period leading up to the merger announcement, this is a plausible explanation.

[35]Bid premium refers to the difference between P and the premerger price of the Target. Higher *P* to *BV* differentials are associated with higher bid premia.

[36]See Robinson and Shane (1990), p. 81.

EXHIBIT 14-9
Merger Characteristics, Bid Premia, and Choice of Accounting Method

Characteristics of Transaction	Accounting Choice	Bid Premia	Explanation
Cash payment	Purchase	High	Per APB 16, pooling permitted only for noncash transactions and for acquisitions exceeding 90% of target's shares. Pooling transactions tend to be nontaxable. Higher bid premia are associated with mergers that (1) involve cash payments, (2) are taxable, and (3) acquire larger percentage of target.
Taxable	Purchase	High	
Large percentage acquired	Pooling	High	
Acquirer			
Management compensation plan	Pooling	—	When $P > BV$, compensation plans can induce managers to increase their compensation by choosing the pooling method.
Bond covenant with debt constraint	Purchase	—	When $P > BV$, the purchase method reports higher assets and equity, improving liquidity and leverage ratios.
Bond covenant with dividend constraint	Pooling	—	On the other hand, although pooling reports lower total equity, retained earnings are higher.* Thus pooling may be preferred, if the dividend constraints are related to levels of retained earnings.
Type of management ("managers")	Purchase	Low	Better managers make better acquisitions [Servaes (1991)]. Such managers tend not to overpay thus lowering bid premia, and such managers do not need or use artificial income-increasing methods such as pooling.
Target			
High liquidity/low leverage	—	High	Firms with excess cash are attractive acquisition targets and would receive higher bid premia.
Relative size of target	Purchase	Low	Acquiring shareholder's fear of losing control if target is relatively large. Thus, full voting rights may not be granted to target shareholders, precluding (per APB 16) the pooling method. At the same time, Robinson and Shane cite empirical evidence that bid premia tend to be lower when the target is relatively large.
Type of management ("poor managers")	—	Low	Firms run by poor managers are often viewed as prime takeover targets as the new managers feel they can do a better job of running the firm. A low price-to-book ratio is often viewed as an indicator of poor management, as the firm is not favorably valued by the market. Such firms can be typically bought with low bid premia.
Low P/E ratios	Pooling	—	It is hypothesized that a firm with a high P/E ratio can increase its own market price by acquiring companies with low P/E ratios. The newly acquired earnings will be valued by the market at the acquirer's higher P/E ratio. For this to work, the market has to be naive. When companies using this technique make many insignificant mergers (with little disclosure), however, it may be hard for analysts to see through the technique.†

*Under pooling, the retained earnings of the acquirer and target are combined. Under purchase accounting, only the acquirer's retained earnings are carried forward.

†This phenomenon is discussed in "After the Party," *The Economist* (May 18, 1996), p. 65. It argues that Softbank, a Japanese computer software firm, has successfully taken advantage of the fact that price-earnings ratios are higher in Japan than in the United States. By making acquisitions (using the purchase method) in the United States, it increases reported earnings and its stock price, allowing it to sell shares to fund further acquisitions.

This is true not only for the effects implied by the income maximization theory and the differential market reactions discussed above. Similar patterns can also be shown in the context of other merger characteristics as illustrated in Exhibit 14-9.

The exhibit lists a number of factors that can impact the pooling/purchase choice either directly or indirectly (through its influence on the bid premium). In addition, (some of) these factors have been found in other studies to be associated with positive market reaction to mergers. These categories and the explanations provided serve to illustrate the complexities involved in analyzing the relationship of accounting choice and economic characteristics of mergers. Note the many combinations of bid premia and accounting choices independent of any income/asset manipulation motivation. One should, therefore, not draw immediate conclusions as to managers' motivations and/or potential market reaction. The effects and implications of the accounting method cannot be understood without a thorough examination of the merger's economic characteristics.

PUSH-DOWN ACCOUNTING

Firms that have been acquired in purchase method acquisitions (in effect, subsidiaries of new parents) often continue to issue their own financial statements, due to such factors as:

- Statutory or regulatory reporting requirements
- Minority equity interest, including preferred shareholders
- Need to provide information to creditors

The issuance of such financial statements raises an important accounting issue. Should they reflect the operations of the firm, as if it had not been acquired, or should the financial statements be adjusted to reflect the purchase method adjustments shown in its (new) parent company statements? In other words, should the parent company's purchase method adjustments be "pushed down" into the financial statements of the subsidiary?

Push-down accounting has a controversial history. The SEC requires its use when all the equity of a company is sold to the public, thus marking a complete change in ownership.[37] The SEC also requires push-down accounting:

- When separate financial statements of a company are included in its parent's SEC filings, or
- The subsidiary is registering stock or debt offerings.

The discussion that follows focuses on the impact of the use of push-down accounting rather than the theoretical concerns with the new basis of accounting.

Example: Genentech

As explained in Note 3 to its 2000 annual report, Roche purchased all of the publicly held shares of Genentech in June 1999. Later in 1999, Genentech again became a public company. When Genentech issued its 1999 annual report, it was required to "push down" the purchase method adjustments into its own financial statements. The note explaining the accounting entries is shown in Exhibit 14-10.[38]

Because Roche had already owned a majority of Genentech shares, the purchase method adjustments consist of one portion relating to the 1990–1997 Roche investment and a second portion resulting from the 1999 purchase. The excess of purchase price over book value of assets acquired totals $5.2 billion. That excess was allocated based on the fair value of assets acquired, with the largest adjustments applied to in-process research and development and technology. The residual amount was applied to goodwill. The important items to note are:

- One-quarter of the excess value was allocated to IPRD, which was immediately expensed.[39]
- Adjustments relating to Roche's pre-1998 ownership of Genentech were charged directly to retained earnings.
- Half of the inventory write-up flowed through cost of sales in 1999.

---

[37]The SEC requires push-down accounting when the change in ownership is greater than 95% (unless public debt, preferred stock, or significant minority interests affects control), permits it for changes between 80% and 95%, and objects to it for changes below 80%. See SEC Staff Accounting Bulletins No. 54 (1983) and No. 73 (1987).

[38]Exhibit 14-10 excludes portions of the footnote that detail adjustments relating to Roche's pre-1999 investment in Genentech.

[39]Note that, while Roche reports under IASB standards, Genentech reports under U.S. GAAP.

EXHIBIT 14-10
Illustration of Push-Down Accounting: Genentech

Redemption of Our Special Common Stock

Basis of Presentation

Roche accounted for the Redemption as a purchase of a business. As a result, we were required to push down the effect of the Redemption and Roche's 1990 through 1997 purchases of our Common and Special Common Stock into our consolidated financial statements at the date of the Redemption. Under this method of accounting, our assets and liabilities, including other intangible assets, were recorded at their fair values not to exceed the aggregate purchase price plus Roche's transaction costs at June 30, 1999. Management of Genentech determined the values of tangible and intangible assets, including in-process research and development, used in allocating the purchase prices.

The following table shows details of the excess of purchase price over net book value (in $millions):

	Purchase Period		
	1990–1997	1999	Total
Total purchase price	$2,843.5	$3,761.4	$6,604.9
Less portion of net book value purchased	(566.6)	(836.4)	(1,403.0)
Excess of purchase price over net book value	$2,276.9	$2,925.0	$5,201.9

The following table shows the allocation of the excess of the purchase price over net book value (in $millions):

	Purchase Period		
	1990–1997	1999	Total
Inventories	$ 102.0	$ 186.2	$ 288.2
Land	—	16.6	16.6
In-process research and development	500.5	752.5	1,253.0
Developed product technology [10]	429.0	765.0	1,194.0
Core technology [10]	240.5	203.0	443.5
Developed license technology [6]	292.5	175.0	467.5
Trained and assembled workforce [7]	32.5	49.0	81.5
Tradenames [15]	39.0	105.0	144.0
Key distributor relationships [6]	6.5	73.5	80.0
Goodwill	1,091.2	1,228.4	2,319.6
Deferred tax liability	(456.8)	(629.2)	(1,086.0)
Total	$2,276.9	$2,925.0	$5,201.9

Note: Numbers in square brackets [ ] represent the amortization period in years for the given item.
Source: Genentech 10-K Report, Year Ended December 31, 1999.

- The newly created goodwill and other intangible assets resulted in amortization expense of more than $190 million in 1999.
- The different categories of intangible assets were assigned varying estimated lives. While under SFAS 142 goodwill amortization has ceased, the amortization of other intangible assets continues.

Impact on the Balance Sheet

The impact of push-down accounting can be seen in Exhibit 14-11. The adjusted column removes the push-down adjustments from the 1999 reported financial statement. Push-down accounting doubled the assets and stockholders' equity of Genentech. Because the adjustments cover only the 1999 portion of the transaction, and ignores the (much smaller) residual effects of the 1990–1997 portion, Exhibit 14-11 understates the effect of push-down on Genentech's balance sheet.

EXHIBIT 14-11. GENENTECH
Financial Statement Effects of Push-Down Accounting Adjustments

Years Ended December 31 (in $millions)

	Reported		Adjustments	Adjusted	% Change from 1998	
Balance Sheet	1998	1999	1999	1999	Reported	Adjusted
Inventories	$ 149	$ 275	$ (93)	$ 182		
Total current assets	1,242	1,326	(93)	1,233		
Long-term assets	1,613	5,228	(3,170)	2,058		
Total assets	$2,855	$ 6,554	$(3,263)	$3,291	130%	15%
Current liabilities	291	484		484		
Long-term liabilities	220	787	(629)	158		
Total liabilities	$ 511	$ 1,271	$ (629)	$ 642	149%	26%
Stockholders' equity	2,344	5,283	(2,634)	2,649	125%	13%
Liabilities and equity	$2,855	$ 6,554	$(3,263)	$3,291		
Income Statement						
Total revenues	$1,151	$ 1,421	$ —	$1,421		
Cost of sales	(139)	(286)	93	(193)		
Research & development	(396)	(367)		(367)		
Marketing, etc.	(358)	(468)		(468)		
Special charges		(1,438)	1,438	—		
Amortization		(198)	198	—		
Interest expense	(5)	(5)		(5)		
Pretax income	$ 253	$(1,341)	$ 1,729	$ 388	−630%	53%
Income tax expense	(71)	196	(318)	(122)		
Net income	$ 182	$(1,145)	$ 1,411	$ 266	−729%	46%
Ratios						
Gross profit margin %	88%	80%		86%		
Pretax margin %	22%	−94%		27%		
Net profit margin %	16%	−81%		19%		
ROE %	8%	−22%		10%		
Assets to equity %	122%	124%		124%		
Asset turnover ×	0.40	0.22		0.43		
Equity turnover ×	0.49	0.27		0.54		
Inventory turnover ×	0.93	1.04		1.06		

Impact on the Income Statement

Genentech's 1999 income was affected by:

1. The chargeoff of $1,208 million relating to the Roche transaction, which includes the write-off of IPRD of $752 million.
2. A legal settlement of $230 million unrelated to the takeover. (Items 1 and 2 are combined in Exhibit 14-11.)
3. $198 million of amortization of purchase method adjustments (mostly amortization of goodwill and other intangible assets).
4. The $93 million effect of writing inventories up to fair value.

Removing these amounts, and the related deferred tax effect, the 1999 reported loss becomes a substantial profit. The effects of the push-down adjustments have obscured the 1999 improvement in operating results.

Effect on Cash Flows

As the 1999 redemption-related charges and amortization of the purchase method adjustments that are pushed down into the financial statements of Genentech are noncash charges, they have no impact on the company's cash flow. There would be an indirect impact if capital spending decisions were based on reported earnings, but that is unlikely.

Effect on Financial Ratios

The effects of push-down accounting on financial ratios are similar to those of the purchase method from whence it derives. Activity ratios decline. Return ratios are affected by the change in both numerator (income) and denominator (total capital). Exhibit 14-11 shows selected ratios for 1998, for 1999 using reported data, and for 1999 after adjustment. The adjusted ratios for 1999 provide a much better comparison with 1998 as the distortion resulting from the push-down process is removed. Despite lower gross margins, pretax, net profit margins, and ROE rose. Leverage (assets to equity) and turnover ratios also show small improvement from the 1998 ratios.

Push-Down Summed Up

Although push-down accounting is no more than an application of the purchase method to the separate statements of the acquired firm, it remains a controversial topic. From the analyst's perspective, push-down accounting replaces historical cost with current values, which may be more useful for making investment decisions.

It is important to understand the effects of push-down because it radically changes the financial statements (and ratios) of affected companies. Consistency over time and comparability with other companies are destroyed by push-down; if the impact of push-down adjustments is not understood, financial data may be misinterpreted.

SPINOFFS

A spinoff occurs when a company separates a portion of its business into a newly created subsidiary and distributes shares of that subsidiary to its shareholders pro rata. The accounting for such spinoffs is quite simple and can be characterized as a "reverse pooling." The assets and liabilities of the subsidiary to be spun off are removed from the balance sheet of the parent company at their historical amounts, that is, without adjustment. The spinoff's balance sheet "inherits" the historical cost of the assets and liabilities transferred. The stockholders' equity of the parent company is reduced by the stockholders' equity (net assets) of the spinoff. The only adjustment will be for any capital transactions (debt repayment, equity infusion, or dividend) with the parent that are part of the spinoff transaction.

The income statement of the spinoff is little changed from what it would have been if it had remained part of its former parent. The only differences are the effects of any capital transactions (e.g., reduced interest expense on debt forgiven by the parent) and the additional administrative expenses borne by the subsidiary as a public company. The pro forma income statements issued in connection with the spinoff disclose these impacts.

From the parent company perspective, spinoffs offer some advantages. First, a spinoff can be an easy way to dispose of a "problem" subsidiary without recognizing any gain or loss. Sometimes, the spinoff will have a higher market value as a public company than could have been realized via sale, for reasons discussed in the paragraphs that follow. Thus, stockholders are better off receiving the spinoff shares than if the subsidiary had been sold, especially if its sale would have resulted in capital gains tax payable by the parent.

Second, spinoffs often pay special dividends to their parent as part of the spinoff transaction. In addition, the debt of the spinoff is removed from the parent company's balance sheet. The result is lower parent company debt and, possibly, reduced financial leverage.

Third, if the spinoff was losing money (or had very low profitability), the parent company reports either higher net income or, at least, higher profit margins. Fixed income coverage may also improve.

Analysis of Spinoffs

When analyzing a spinoff, it is important to look for the following information, usually found in the financial statement footnotes:

1. Has the spinoff company paid a special dividend to the parent or, alternatively, has the parent forgiven debt or contributed capital? Such transactions alter the financial structure of the spinoff and its profitability going forward.

2. How have postretirement benefits been dealt with? If the parent company retains responsibility for all benefits for retirees, for example, the spinoff company will have a reduced burden. Also evaluate the allocation of pension plan assets and liabilities.

3. Examine income tax sharing agreements, which detail the impact of additional tax assessments or refunds covering periods prior to the spinoff. Also consider that the spinoff company inherits the tax basis as well as the accounting basis of assets and liabilities. If tax depreciation of fixed assets has exceeded depreciation expense, then future tax deductions will be below depreciation expense. Although the deferred tax liability in the balance sheet should provide for the reversal of this and other timing differences, there may still be a cash flow consequence if income taxes paid exceed future income tax expense.

4. Look for other transactions between parent and spinoff that may affect future profitability or cash flow. Possible problem areas include:

   - Contingent liability for debt or other obligations of the parent company.
   - Guarantees of spinoff obligations by the parent, but with the spinoff company paying a fee for the guarantee.
   - Parent company charges for administrative or other services.
   - Higher rental costs due to spinoff company occupancy of parent company office space or operating facilities.
   - Intercompany supply agreements, which can be either positive or negative for the spinoff, depending on their terms. Such agreements often have "sunset" provisions providing for termination or diminishment over time.

5. Read the footnotes of the spinoff carefully, even if you are familiar with the operations of the parent. Some data (e.g., off-balance-sheet financing) may not have been significant for the parent, but are significant to the spinoff company because of its smaller size.

Example: Lucent

Lucent was created in 1996 as a spinoff from AT&T. It subsequently spun off Avaya [AV] in 2000 and Agere Systems [AGRA] in 2001. Both of the spinoffs from Lucent had significant impacts on its financial statements.

The spinoff of Avaya on September 30, 2000 was accounted for as a discontinued operation (see Chapter 2). The September 30, 1999 balance sheet was restated to remove nearly $5 billion of assets (nearly 13% of Lucent's total assets) and $4 billion (16%) of liabilities. Avaya's sales and operating results for all years, which were removed from Lucent's income statement (prior periods were restated), follow in $millions:

	Years Ended September 30		
	1998	1999	2000
Revenues	$7,741	$8,157	$7,607
Income from operations	296	455	303
Loss on disposal			(765)
Net income	$296	$455	$ (462)

Both income from operations and the loss on disposal (which includes a "restructuring" writedown of $545 million pretax) are reported net of income tax.

Lucent's fiscal 2000 income statement shows the following:[40]

	1998	1999	2000
Revenues	$24,367	$30,617	$33,813
Income from continuing operations	769	3,026	1,681

If we add back the "discontinued" Avaya, we can see what Lucent's reported revenue and income would have been if the spinoff had not taken place:

Revenues	$32,108	$38,774	$41,420
Net income	1,065	3,481	1,219

By removing the slow growth and unprofitable operations of Avaya, Lucent improved its reported growth rates for both sales and income:

	% Change	
	1999	2000
Revenue		
Avaya	5.4%	−6.7%
Lucent as reported after restatement	25.6%	10.4%
Combined	20.8%	6.8%
Income		
Avaya	53.7%	−201.5%
Lucent as reported after restatement	293.5%	−44.4%
Combined	226.9%	−65.0%

Lucent's fiscal 2000 sales grew 10.4% after the Avaya sales were removed as opposed to the 6.8% growth rate with Avaya. While earnings fell under either measure, the decline was lower without Avaya's large loss. The fiscal 1999 growth rates of both revenue and income were improved as well.

An additional positive factor was that $780 million of Lucent debt was assumed by Avaya prior to the spinoff. The debt transfer may explain why Avaya reduced Lucent's liabilities by a greater percentage than Lucent's assets. Additional debt was transferred to Agere when it was spun off in fiscal 2001. The Agere spinoff is the subject of Problem 14-13.

Reasons for Investment in Spinoffs

Although some investors immediately sell the shares of spinoffs they receive, others find spinoffs to be attractive investment opportunities. The following factors may make spinoffs profitable investments:

- Operations that are "lost" in a large corporation may benefit from the focus of a management undistracted by other activities. Spinoff firms frequently provide stock options and other incentives for managers to improve profitability.
- The smaller size of a spinoff may increase the flexibility of managers no longer bound by the bureaucracy of the former parent.
- The spinoff may attract investors who wish to invest in its industry, but were deterred by the other operations of the former parent. The spinoff may also attract customers not previously accessible because they are competitors of the parent.
- Even if the spinoff company has poor current profitability, investors may be attracted by high book value, cash flow, or other attributes.

[40]Lucent also made several acquisitions during fiscal 2000 that were accounted for under the pooling method. Thus, the 1999 restatement reflects those acquisitions as well as the spinoff of Avaya.

As a result, a spinoff may increase shareholder wealth as the combined market value of the spinoff and parent company shares exceeds the pre-spinoff market value of the parent. Although financial theory says that should not happen, in practice it often does.[41] Operations that contributed little or nothing to the parent company's market value (because of low profitability, or lack of visibility) may have substantial market value as a standalone company.

SUMMARY

This chapter reviews the accounting and financial analysis issues posed by business combinations and other types of corporate reorganizations. The two reporting methods for mergers, purchase and pooling, are not strictly speaking alternatives. However, their financial statement and ratio effects are so significantly different that they are clearly important variables in any acquisition decision. The differences between these two methods are illustrated using the simplified Target–Acquire example.

The chapter goes on to review the effect of push-down accounting on the financial statements of firms acquired in transactions requiring use of the purchase method. Genentech illustrates the significant effect of these adjustments on reported income, book value, and financial ratios. Spinoffs, which appear to create shareholder value from unwanted subsidiaries, are examined next.

The transactions discussed in this chapter are particularly troublesome for financial analysts as they create a discontinuity. The firm's business and financial statements may be radically changed overnight. The goal of the chapter was to present analytical tools to help financial statement users separate the effects of these transactions from ongoing operating results.

Chapter 15 deals with another source of discontinuity, changes in exchange rates. Our goal in that chapter is to separate changes in operating activities from the effects of changing exchange rates.

Chapter 14

Problems

1. [Purchase versus pooling; CFA© adapted] Martin Manufacturing, Inc., and Green Precision Machinery are two small metal casting and milling companies serving the aerospace and defense industry. On June 30, 2001, Martin acquired Green at a price per share equal to two times Green's book value per share. Martin can structure the acquisition to either:

- Pay cash, in which case Martin will sell new Martin shares to obtain the cash required and use the purchase method to account for the acquisition, or
- Issue new Martin shares for shares of Green and use the pooling-of-interests method of accounting.

Martin uses International Accounting Standards to prepare its financial statements.

Sales data for Martin and Green and additional financial data on Green are provided in Exhibit 14P-1. Assume that sales are generated evenly throughout the year for both companies.

a. Calculate the sales reported by Martin Manufacturing in its 2001 and 2002 financial statements for 2000, 2001, and 2002 using *both* the purchase and pooling-of-interests methods of accounting. Show all calculations.

b. State the effect (higher, lower, or no difference) the purchase method of accounting (IASB GAAP) has on the following fi-

nancial measures for Martin when compared with the pooling-of-interests method of accounting. Justify your response.

  (i) Sales growth from 2000 through 2002

  (ii) Return on year-end 2001 equity

  (iii) Long-term debt-to-equity ratio as of June 30, 2001

c. Now assume that Martin prepares its financial statements under U.S. GAAP. State the effect (higher, lower, or no difference) that using the purchase method under U.S. GAAP has on the following financial measures for Martin when compared with the purchase method under IASB GAAP. Justify your response.

  (i) Sales growth from 2000 through 2002

  (ii) Return on year-end 2001 equity

  (iii) Long-term debt-to-equity ratio as of June 30, 2001

2. [Pooling versus purchase] Ace Co. and Tar Co. merged on January 1 of year 2, forming the Acetar Co. Ace issued stock worth $1,500 to effect the merger. The merger was accounted for as a pooling of interests.

Balance sheets for the individual companies at the end of year 1 and for the combined entity at the end of year 2 are presented below. Estimates of the fair value of inventory and fixed assets of the two companies at the end of Year 1 are also provided.

---

[41]For example, see Schipper and Smith (1983).

EXHIBIT 14P-1
Sales Data, Years Ended December 31, (in $millions)

	Martin			Green		
	2000	2001	2002	2000	2001	2002
Sales	$435	$550	$970	$90	$120	$150

Additional Financial Data as of June 30, 2001:
- Green has property whose appraised value at June 30, 2001 exceeds the carrying amount.
- The present value of Green's long-term debt is lower than its carrying amount because market interest rates are currently higher than when the debt was issued.
- Green has no goodwill or deferred income taxes on its balance sheet.

	Ace (Year 1)		Tar (Year 1)		Acetar
	Historical Cost	Fair Value	Historical Cost	Fair Value	(Year 2)
Cash	$ 100		$ 50		$ 200
Inventory	1,000	1,200	300	330	1,400
Fixed assets (net)	3,000	3,500	1,000	1,050	4,100
Total assets	$4,100		$1,350		$5,700
Current liabilities	1,000		250		1,300
Equity	3,100		1,100		4,400
Liabilities and equity	$4,100		$1,350		$5,700

Acetar reported the following cash flows for year 2:

Acetar Cash Flow Statement: Year 2

Net income	$ 200
Depreciation expense	400
Change in inventory	(100)
Change in accounts payable	50
Cash from operations	$ 550
Cash for investing	
Capital expenditures	(500)
Change in cash	$ 50

Additional Information:
- Acetar reports using IASB GAAP.
- Acetar uses the FIFO inventory method.
- Acetar depreciates its assets using the straight-line method with an average life of 10 years.
- Year 2 dividends paid = 0.

a. Prepare Acetar's pooling method balance sheet at the merger date.

For parts b through e, assume that the merger was accounted for as a purchase with Ace acquiring Tar.

b. Prepare the balance sheet of the merged company at the merger date.

c. Calculate reported net income for year 2. Explain all differences from the $200 reported net income under the pooling method. (*Note:* Ignore any tax effects.)

d. Prepare the balance sheet of the merged company at the end of year 2.

e. Prepare the statement of cash flows for year 2.

f. Discuss how your answers to parts b through e would differ if Acetar used U.S. GAAP.

3. [Pooling versus purchase] On January 1, 2001, Hawk Company acquired Dove Company. The acquisition was treated as a purchase. The historical cost balance sheets of Hawk and Dove at the acquisition date follow, along with the consolidated balance sheet at December 31, 2001, consolidated cash flow statement for 2001, and relevant information about the company's accounting policies.

Balance Sheet Data

	Hawk Historical 1/1/01	Dove Historical 1/1/01	Fair Value 1/1/01	Consolidated 12/31/01
Cash	$1,000			$ 1,800
Accounts receivable	300	$ 200	?	550
Inventory	1,200	300	?	1,600
Fixed assets (net)	5,000	500	?	6,400
Goodwill	0	0	?	380
Total assets	$7,500	$1,000	?	$10,730
Accounts payable	1,000	500	?	1,700
Long-term debt	2,000	700	?	2,750
Equity	4,500	(200)	?	6,280
Liabilities and equity	$7,500	$1,000	?	$10,730

2001 Consolidated Statement of Cash Flows

Net income	$ 1,230
Depreciation and amortization	610
Increase in accounts payable	200
Increase in accounts receivable	(50)
Cash from operations	$ 1,990
Cash for investments: January 1 purchase of plant, property, and equipment	(1,290)
Cash from financing: debt issued	100
Change in cash	$ 800

Significant noncash financing and investment activities: The company acquired Dove Company on January 1, 2001 by issuing shares whose market value was $550.

Additional Information:

- Hawk Company uses the LIFO inventory method.
- Goodwill is amortized over 20 years on a straight-line basis but is not deductible for tax purposes.
- 2001 combined depreciation expense equals $580.
- Dove's long-term debt is due in five years.
- Hawk prepares its financial statements using IASB GAAP.
- The tax rate is 35%.

a. Calculate the fair value of Dove's assets and liabilities at the acquisition date.

b. Determine the goodwill recorded at the acquisition date.

c. Assuming that the acquisition of Dove had been treated as a pooling of interest, calculate Hawk's 2001 net income. *Explain all assumptions and adjustments made.*

d. Prepare the 2001 cash flow statement under the pooling assumption.

e. Assuming that Hawk used U.S. GAAP, calculate Hawk's

  (i) 2001 net income

  (ii) December 31, 2001 stockholders' equity

4. [Recast pooling to purchase] On April 4, 2001, Microsoft [MSFT] acquired Great Plains Software [GPSI], a supplier of business applications software. The merger was accounted for as a pooling in accordance with U.S. GAAP in effect at that time.

This problem assumes that Microsoft used the purchase method to account for the acquisition of Great Plains.

Exhibit 14P-2 shows the summarized balance sheet of Great Plains at November 30, 2000, the last balance sheet published prior to the merger. The fair values of some assets and liabilities are also shown. Use this balance sheet to solve this problem assuming that any changes between November 30, 2000 and April 4, 2001 were not material.

a. Using the additional information and assumptions provided, complete Exhibit 14P-2.

b. Using the completed exhibit, calculate the effect of the purchase method adjustments on income for fiscal 2001 and fiscal 2002, assuming:

  (i) Use of U.S. GAAP

  (ii) Use of IAS GAAP

For simplicity, assume that the merger was completed on March 31, 2001 so that purchase method adjustments for the three months following the merger equal one-quarter of the annual adjustment.

c. Explain why Microsoft preferred to use the pooling method to account for the acquisition of Great Plains.

d. State which purchase method (U.S. or IASB) Microsoft would prefer to use to account for the acquisition of Great Plains. Justify your choice.

EXHIBIT 14P-2. GREAT PLAINS SOFTWARE
Balance Sheet, November 30, 2002 (in $thousands)

	Reported	Fair Value
Cash and equivalents	$ 40,764	$ 40,764
Other current assets	79,794	79,794
Current assets	$120,558	$120,558
Property	55,814	75,814
Goodwill and other intangibles	234,550	
Other assets	6,123	6,123
Total assets	$417,045	
Current liabilities	115,507	115,507
Long-term liabilities	11,028	11,028
Stockholders' equity	290,510	
Total liabilities and equity	$417,045	

Additional Information:

- Great Plains had 20,226,146 shares outstanding on November 30, 2000.
- Microsoft issued 1.1 shares for each Great Plains share.
- Microsoft shares closed at $51.938 on April 4, 2001.
- Microsoft fiscal years end June 30.

Assumptions Regarding Great Plains for Application of Purchase Method:

- In-process R&D equals $200 million.
- Identifiable intangibles equal $100 million, amortized over five years.
- Under IAS GAAP, Microsoft would amortize goodwill over 10 years and capitalized R&D over four years.

5. [Accounting versus Economics] On December 4, 2000, PepsiCo [PEP] announced plans to merge with Quaker Oats [OAT], with the combination to be accounted for using the pooling method. The press release stated:

> The acquisition will immediately improve PepsiCo's return on invested capital by 200 basis points.

Exhibit 14P-3 contains data extracted from the merger proxy statement dated March 15, 2001. In order to qualify for the pooling method under APB 16, PepsiCo was required to reissue 20 million shares that had been repurchased.

a. Using the data in Exhibit 14P-3, compute each of the following ratios for PepsiCo, Quaker Oats, and the combined firms:

  (i) Return on total capital (operating income to long-term debt plus equity)

  (ii) Pretax return on equity

  (iii) After-tax return on equity

  (iv) After-tax return on equity excluding adjustments

b. Based on your answer to part a, critique the statement in the press release regarding the effect of the acquisition.

c. Describe how the pro forma statements would differ if PepsiCo were required to use the purchase method of accounting for the merger with Quaker Oats. Assume the value of PepsiCo stock issued equals $13.5 billion.

d. Describe the effect of use of the purchase method on the return ratios in part a.

e. Assume that the press release statement was correct based on use of the pooling method. Discuss whether that statement reflects the economics of the transaction.

6. [Purchase Method Effect on Sales Trend] Boron LePore [BLPG], which provides marketing, educational, and sales services to pharmaceutical firms, reported the following financial data (in $millions)

	Years Ended December 31		
	1998	1999	2000
Net revenues	$164.7	$149.4	$167.9
Net income	10.4	(0.6)	5.4
Earnings per share (diluted)	.84	(.05)	.45

BLPG made four acquisitions in 1998 and two in 2000, using the purchase method to account for all six. In the year of the acquisitions, the company reported the following pro forma data as if the acquisitions had occurred at the beginning of the respective periods:

	Years Ended December 31		
	1998	1999	2000
Includes	1998 acquisitions	All six acquisitions	
Net revenues	$177.4	$170.0	$178.2
Net income	10.6	2.0	6.3
Earnings per share (diluted)	.85	.16	.51

a. Using the data provided, describe the likely trend of BLPG sales from 1998 to 2000 *excluding* the six acquired companies.

b. Using the data provided, describe the likely trend of BLPG earnings per share from 1998 to 2000 *excluding* the six acquired companies.

EXHIBIT 14P-3
PepsiCo/Quaker Oats Pro Forma

Year Ended December 30, 2000 (in $millions)

Balance Sheet:	PEP	OAT	Adjustments*	Combined
Current assets	$ 4,604	$1,014	$847	$ 6,465
Net property	5,438	1,120		6,558
Intangible assets	4,485	229		4,714
Other assets	3,812	56		3,868
Total assets	$18,339	$2,419	$847	$21,605
Current liabilities	3,935	860	100	4,895
Long-term debt	2,346	664		3,010
Other liabilities	4,809	540		5,349
Common equity	7,249	355	747	8,351
Total liabilities and equity	$18,339	$2,419	$847	$21,605
Income Statement:				
Operating profit	3,225	601	(5)	3,821
Pretax income	3,210	551	—	3,761
Net income for common	2,183	356	—	2,539

*Estimated proceeds ($847 million) of issuing PepsiCo shares to qualify for pooling less $10 million transaction costs.

7. [Effect of amortization periods] The following news story appeared on April 26, 2001:

SEC Wireless License Move May Raise Charges for Verizon, Others

Washington, April 26 (Bloomberg)—The wireless units of AT&T Corp., Sprint Corp. and Verizon Communications Inc. face increased accounting charges under a push by the Securities and Exchange Commission for faster write-offs of new airwave licenses.

The agency is telling companies they should write down the purchase price of wireless licenses in 20 years or less, rather than the 40 years most businesses currently use. That would double the non-cash earnings charges companies must take each quarter under U.S. accounting standards, though it would also slash the duration of such write-offs.

The change reflects the SEC's belief that companies cannot guarantee they will retain the multibillion dollar licenses indefinitely, even though communications regulations allow holders to seek renewal of the spectrum rights every 10 years. The SEC position contrasts with efforts by the Federal Communications Commission to stress the long-term availability of licenses it awards.

"The FCC has alluded to the need to create certainty for licenses in order (for recipients) to attract investment capital," said Louis Gurman, a partner at Morrison & Foerster LLP who has spent 25 years practicing telecommunications law. "It's somewhat strange that the SEC is taking this position at this particular time."

a. Compare the effect of 20-year amortization with 40-year amortization on each of the following:

  (i) Return on equity

  (ii) Interest coverage ratio

  (iii) Cash from operations

b. Compare the effect of 20-year amortization with 40-year amortization on the three items listed in part a after 20 years.

c. Discuss whether the shorter amortization period should affect the securities prices of companies such as Verizon.

d. Evaluate Mr. Gurman's statement about the "need to create certainty . . . to attract investors."

8. [Effect of purchase method on inventory and gross margin] Beringer Wine [BERW] made a series of acquisitions, using the purchase method of accounting. The company disclosed the inventory stepup (from cost to fair value at the acquisition date) that was included in cost of goods sold for each accounting period, as shown below (in $thousands):

	Years Ended June 30		
	1998	1999	2000
Net revenues	$ 318,448	$ 376,154	$ 438,805
Cost of goods sold	(182,557)	(198,030)	(224,565)
Gross profit	$ 137,889	$ 180,123	$ 216,240
Inventory stepup	27,845	16,448	5,687
Adjusted gross profit	$ 165,734	$ 196,571	$ 221,927

Source: Beringer Wine 10-K, June 30, 2000.

a. Compute the gross profit percentage (relative to sales) for each year based on both the unadjusted and adjusted gross profit.

b. Compare the trends in gross profit percentage over the three-year period.

c. State which computation (unadjusted or adjusted) provides a better measure of operating performance. Justify your choice.

9. [Immediate write-off of goodwill] On October 11, 2000, China Mobile [941] announced that it would write off HK$242 billion of goodwill resulting from the acquisition of seven wireless networks. The total purchase price of the acquisitions was HK$256 billion.

a. Compare the impact of the immediate write-off of goodwill with the treatment under both U.S. GAAP and IASB GAAP. Your answer should include the impact on each of the following in the periods following the acquisitions:

  (i) Shareholders' equity

  (ii) Asset turnover

  (iii) Return on equity

  (iv) Earnings per share

  (v) Cash from operations

b. Based on your answers to part a, discuss the advantages of immediate write-off from the perspective of China Mobile.

c. Describe the adjustments to China Mobile's financial statements that you would make when comparing the company with another firm that uses

  (i) U.S. GAAP

  (ii) IASB GAAP

10. [Goodwill impairment] Safeco [SAFC] is a large U.S.-based insurance company whose earnings were depressed by heavy competition and disappointing results from a major acquisition. Effective March 31, 2001, Safeco elected to change its accounting policy for assessing goodwill from one based on undiscounted cash flows to one based on a market-value method. As a result, Safeco recorded a one-time write-off of $916.9 million after tax.

a. Explain why the change in accounting policy would be likely to result in a goodwill write-off.

b. Describe the effect of the write-off on the following subsequent to the write-off:

  (i) Return on equity

  (ii) Debt-to-equity ratio

  (iii) Cash from operations

11. [Acquisitions and stock prices] The following extracts are taken from a story in the *Financial Times* on March 29, 2001, page 15:

Cisco Puts New Acquisitions on Hold

Cisco Systems, the largest networking equipment company, has put an informal hold on making any more acquisitions as a result of the drop in the high-tech market and Cisco's own share price.

The decision is expected to last until the high-tech market starts to recover, according to executives.

Cisco's share price has fallen by more than 40 per cent this year partly because of a steep decline in the order book. Cisco typically acquires companies by issuing new shares.

a. Explain why a drop in Cisco's share price would be expected to deter it from using shares for acquisitions.

b. Explain why poor industry conditions would be expected to deter Cisco from making acquisitions, whether for cash or stock.

12. [Derivation of acquisition data from cash flow statement] On June 24, 1992, Roadway Services [ROAD], a large U.S. motor carrier, acquired Cole Enterprises, a regional carrier. Exhibit 14P-4 contains the financial statement footnote describing

the transaction. Elsewhere, Roadway states that 1991 revenues of Cole were approximately $19 million. Roadway's 1991 revenues were $3,177 million.

Exhibit 14P-4 also contains Roadway's statement of cash flows (1992) and balance sheets (1991 to 1992).

a. Using the data in Exhibit 14P-4, derive the balance sheet of Cole at the date of its acquisition. (*Hint:* You must compare each balance sheet change with the corresponding cash flow; some aggregation is required. Remember that noncash transactions are excluded from the cash flow statement.)

EXHIBIT 14P-4. ROADWAY SERVICES, INC. AND SUBSIDIARIES
Financial Statements and Selected Financial Data

Note B—Acquisitions

On June 24, 1992, the company acquired Cole Enterprises, Inc., the parent company of Coles Express, Inc., a New England regional motor common carrier based in Bangor, Maine, for $4,617,000 in cash and 235,892 shares of the company's common stock valued at $15,127,000. The acquisition was accounted for as a purchase and the cost in excess of net assets acquired was $3,441,000. Earnings of Coles since its acquisition are included in the accompanying statement of consolidated income, and are not material in relation to consolidated operations.

A. Statement of Consolidated Cash Flows

	Year Ended December 31 1992
CASH FLOWS FROM OPERATING ACTIVITIES	
Net income	$147,407
Adjustments to reconcile net income to net cash provided by operating activities:	
Depreciation and amortization	172,695
(Gain) loss on sale of carrier operating property	23
Issuance of treasury shares for stock plans	18,507
Changes in assets and liabilities, net of effects from the purchase of Cole Enterprises, Inc.:	
(Increase) in accounts receivable	(39,999)
(Increase) decrease in prepaid expenses and supplies	7,925
Increase in accounts payable and accrued items	34,269
Increase (decrease) in current income taxes payable	3,022
Increase (decrease) in other liabilities	(4,984)
Total adjustments	191,458
NET CASH PROVIDED BY OPERATING ACTIVITIES	338,865
CASH FLOWS FROM INVESTING ACTIVITIES	
Purchases of carrier operating property	(211,073)
Sales of carrier operating property	10,062
Purchases of marketable securities	(197,263)
Sales of marketable securities	124,787
Purchase of Cole Enterprises, Inc., net of cash acquired	(866)
NET CASH USED IN INVESTING ACTIVITIES	(274,353)
CASH FLOWS FROM FINANCING ACTIVITIES	
Dividends paid	(48,984)
Purchases of common stock for treasury	—
Proceeds from exercise of stock options	186
NET CASH USED IN FINANCING ACTIVITIES	(49,798)
NET INCREASE (DECREASE) IN CASH	15,714
CASH AT BEGINNING OF YEAR	25,322
CASH AT END OF YEAR	$ 41,036

(continued)

EXHIBIT 14P-4. *(continued)*

B. Consolidated Balance Sheet (dollars in thousands)

ASSETS

	December 31	
	1992	1991
Cash	$ 41,036	$ 25,322
Marketable securities	274,898	201,917
Accounts receivable, net	304,645	261,252
Prepaid expenses and supplies	55,954	61,650
	$ 676,533	$ 550,141
Property, plant and equipment		
Original cost	2,044,451	1,850,411
(allowances for depreciation)	(1,148,791)	(998,217)
	$ 895,660	$ 852,194
Goodwill	87,330	86,297
Total assets	$1,659,523	$1,488,632

LIABILITIES AND SHAREHOLDERS' EQUITY

Current liabilities		
Accounts payable	$ 225,361	$ 186,496
Salaries and wages	149,501	154,514
Income taxes payable	25,792	22,712
Freight and casualty claims payable within one year	81,395	78,747
Dividend payable	12,803	11,664
	$ 494,852	$ 454,133
Noncurrent liabilities		
Deferred taxes	41,096	49,507
Future equipment repairs	21,321	18,572
Casualty claims payable after one year	80,894	76,164
	$ 143,311	$ 144,243
Shareholders' equity		
Common stock	39,898	39,898
Additional capital	50,392	31,271
Retained earnings	966,061	868,777
Treasury stock	(34,991)	(49,690)
	$1,021,360	$ 890,256
Total liabilities and equity	$1,659,523	$1,488,632

Source: Roadway Services, Inc., 1992 Annual Report.

b. Using the data in Exhibit 14P-4 and the results of part a, compute the following ratios for Cole (postacquisition) and Roadway (at December 31, 1991):

    (i) Fixed asset turnover

  (ii) Accounts receivable turnover

 (iii) Equity-to-assets

c. Discuss the possible reasons for the ratio differences in part b. Describe the possible implications of the ratio differences for future cash flows.

d. Roadway has insignificant non-U.S. operations. Discuss how this impacts the accuracy of your answer to part a.

e. Discuss how you would measure the future return on Roadway's acquisition of Cole.

13. [Spinoff] In February 2001 Lucent [LU] set up Agere Systems [AGR] as a separate company. On April 2, 2001, the following took place:

- Agere sold 600 million shares in an initial public offering at a net price of $5.77 per share.
- Lucent sold 90 million shares of Agere at a net price of $5.77 per share.
- Agere assumed $2.5 billion of Lucent debt.
- Lucent announced plans to distribute its remaining shares of Agere to Lucent stockholders prior to the end of 2001.

Exhibit 14P-5 contains extracts from the financial statements of Lucent and Agere for the period ending March 31, 2001. Use that data and the information provided to answer the following questions.

a. Compute the percentage change in each of the following for the six months ended March 31, 2001 (compared with the six months ended March 31, 2000) for Lucent, Agere, and the two companies combined:

   (i) Revenue

   (ii) Income from continuing operations

   (iii) Cash from operating activities

   (iv) Capital expenditures

b. Discuss the effect of the spinoff of Agere on each of the percentage changes computed in part a.

c. Compute *each* of the following ratios at March 31, 2001 for Lucent, Agere, and the two companies combined:

   (i) Current ratio (based on continuing operations)

   (ii) Debt-to-equity ratio

d. Compute the total debt of Lucent and the debt-to-equity ratio after the April 2, 2001 transactions.

e. Using the results of parts a through d, explain the advantages and disadvantages to Lucent of the spinoff and IPO of Agere. State which factor most likely influenced the decision and justify your choice.

EXHIBIT 14P-5
Financial Statement Data: Lucent and Agere (in $millions)

	Lucent		Agere	
	2000	2001	2000	2001
Income statement, six months ended March 31				
Revenues	$14,320	$10,269	$2,033	$2,553
Income from continuing operations	1,441	(4,954)	159	(148)
Income from discontinued operations	563	(313)		
Statement of cash flows, six months ended March 31				
Cash from operating activities (continuing operations)	(338)	(2,825)	279	369
Capital expenditures	(740)	(752)	(333)	(485)
Disposition of businesses	210	2,494		
Balance sheet at March 31				
Current assets		18,819		1,553
Noncurrent assets		19,947		5,746
Net long-term assets of discontinued operations		5,361		
Total assets		$44,127		$7,299
Debt maturing within one year		2,314		16
Other current liabilities		7,629		1,166
Net current liabilities of discontinued operations		2,101		
Long-term debt		3,056		42
Other long-term liabilities		6,967		298
Stockholders' equity		22,060		5,777
Total liabilities and equity		$44,127		$7,299

15

ANALYSIS OF MULTINATIONAL OPERATIONS

CHAPTER OUTLINE

CHAPTER OBJECTIVES

Changes in exchange rates have pervasive effects on the financial statements of multinational enterprises. The objectives of Chapter 15 are to:

1. Describe the difference between the two reporting methods used to account for exchange rate changes with respect to the:

- Exchange rates used to translate financial statement data

- Measurement of firm exposure to exchange rate changes

- Disposition of translation gains and losses

2. Compare the impact of the two reporting methods on the income statement, especially the trend of reported revenue and income.

3. Describe the differential impact of the two methods on the balance sheet, including the role of the currency translation adjustment under the all-current rate method.

4. Describe the effects of exchange rate changes on reported cash flow.

5. Show how financial statement ratios are affected by the choice of accounting method, with emphasis on the differences between ratios based on translated data and those based on local currency data.

6. Explain how hyperinflation affects financial statement data and compare the two different methods used to account for subsidiaries in hyperinflationary economies.

7. Describe the importance of the choice of functional currency and the effects of changes in the functional currency.

8. Show how financial statement disclosures can be used to analyze the firm's exposure to exchange rate changes and the effect of such changes on reported financial statements.

9. Explain how reported data can give false signals about the economic effect of exchange rate changes on the firm.

10. Describe the differences between U.S. GAAP, IASB GAAP, and foreign accounting methods dealing with recognition of the effect of rate changes and the effect of those differences on financial statements.

INTRODUCTION

The globalization of the economic world is almost a cliché. International trade has expanded significantly in recent years, aided by such factors as the entry of the Eastern European bloc into world markets, the growth of the Pacific Rim countries, and the expansion of the European Economic Community.

Trade has led to investment, as multinational companies (MNCs) add manufacturing capacity in foreign countries. Trade frictions and political considerations join economic factors such as access to low-cost labor or raw materials as incentives for international expansion. Expanding international capital markets facilitate this growth by allowing MNCs to borrow and lend in foreign currencies and markets and to hedge foreign operations with an array of complex instruments, including options, forward contracts (futures), and currency swaps.

MNCs conduct operations in countries where local financial reporting regulations may be quite different from those governing parent company financial statements. Foreign operations are carried out under varied economic conditions and in currencies whose relative prices (exchange rates) fluctuate widely, with significant effects on both actual and reported operating performance, financial position, and cash flows. Hedging operations often involve innovative instruments for which the financial reporting requirements are new and untested, making it difficult for investors to evaluate the risk/return trade-offs.

MNCs prepare financial statements that consolidate their domestic and foreign operations that are based on different sets of accounting principles (with varying methods and estimates) and different measurement units (currencies) with fluctuating exchange rates. The foreign currency–dominated financial statements of foreign subsidiaries must be translated into their parent's reporting currency to permit consolidation.

This chapter considers the impact of the translation of operations denominated in foreign currencies on the consolidated financial statements of MNCs. We discuss U.S. standards and IASB requirements for foreign currency transactions and translation.

EFFECTS OF EXCHANGE RATE CHANGES

Exchange rate changes result in two effects on a firm's actual and reported performance:

1. "Flow" effects
2. Holding gain/loss effects

These effects can be illustrated by the following example.

■ **Example**

Assume that a foreign subsidiary generates revenues in its local currency (LC) of LC 10,000 in year 1 and LC 11,000 in year 2. On the subsidiary's income statement, this will appear as:

Year	1	2	Total
Revenues (LC)	10,000	11,000	21,000

The subsidiary reports a revenue growth rate of 10%. If the exchange rate between the LC and dollar is constant at LC 1 = $1, then when the U.S. parent consolidates the foreign subsidiary, the same 10% growth will be shown with revenues of $10,000 in year 1 and $11,000 in year 2.

Flow Effect. If the exchange rate, however, fluctuates, the parent will show a corresponding variation in its (consolidated) results. Thus, if we assume average exchange rates of:

Year 1	LC 1 = $1.00
Year 2	LC 1 = $1.30

the subsidiary's results will be reflected in the parent's statements as:

Year	1	2	Total
Revenues ($)	10,000	14,300	24,300

The parent now reports revenue growth of 43%, although the subsidiary's revenues only grew by 10%. The "additional" 33% is the *flow effect* on the income statement, the result of changes in the exchange rate. *The analyst should unbundle the effects of the exchange rate changes from the results of the subsidiary's operations.* In this example, the $4,300 revenue growth is the sum of the:

• $1,000 increase in local currency revenue
• $3,300 (LC 11,000 × .30 change in exchange rate) exchange rate effect

Holding Gain/Loss Effect. The effect on revenue, however, is not the only consequence of the change in exchange rates. If we assume that the subsidiary retains all cash receipts, then the cash balance in LC (on the subsidiary's statements) and in dollars (on the parent's statements) at the end of the year is:

Year	0	1	2
Subsidiary			
Cash (LC)	0	LC 10,000	LC 21,000
Exchange rate		LC 1 = $1	LC 1 = $1.30
Parent—Consolidated			
Cash ($)		$10,000	$27,300

For the subsidiary, the increase in cash in year 2 is equal to the revenue (net income assuming there are no expenses) of LC 11,000 earned that year and the cash balance at the end of the second year equals the cumulative two-year revenue/income of LC 21,000.

This relationship does not hold, however, for the dollar cash balances. At the end of year 2, the dollar cash balance equals $27,300. Cumulative revenues (income), however, equal only $24,300. The difference of $3,000 is the *holding gain*. As the LC strengthened relative to the LC, the LC 10,000 *earned in year 1* and *held* to the end of year 2 appreciated in value. Specifically:

	Dollar Value at Year-End		
	1	2	Holding Gain
LC 10,000 earned in year 1	$10,000	$13,000	$3,000

The two effects of exchange rate changes can be summarized as follows:

Amount in dollars if we assume exchange rate stayed constant		$21,000
Exchange Rate Effects		
Flow effect on *year 2* income	$3,300	
Holding gain on amount earned in year 1	3,000	
Total effect		6,300
Amount including exchange rate effect		$27,300

Accounting standards and public discussion largely focus on the treatment of holding gains and losses. *For analytical purposes, however, although the holding gain/loss effect is relevant, the income statement "flow" effect may have the most direct effect on reported income.* ■

BASIC ACCOUNTING ISSUES

Given fluctuating exchange rates, the accounting for operations conducted in foreign currencies creates issues not present in single-currency statements. Accounting for foreign operations raises three basic issues.

The first issue is the choice of exchange rate used to translate foreign currency transactions and financial statements into the parent company currency, the *reporting currency*. For convenience, we use the U.S. dollar as the parent currency in the examples that follow. However, the principles apply equally whether the reporting currency is U.S. dollars, Euros, Swiss francs, or Japanese yen.

All transactions denominated in currencies other than the parent currency must be translated into the parent or reporting currency as part of the process of preparing consolidated financial statements. There are two possible choices of exchange rate.

1. The *historical rate*, the exchange rate at the time the transaction (sale of output, purchase of inventory, borrowing, etc.) took place
2. The *current rate*, the exchange rate at the balance sheet date or for the income statement period

Further, the rate chosen may be used for all transactions not denominated in the reporting currency, or different rates may be used for different types of transactions. We discuss the implications of these choices shortly.

The other two issues are:

1. The definition of exposure to exchange rate changes (i.e., which assets or liabilities should be adjusted for exchange rate changes)
2. The treatment of translation gains and losses

Both are a consequence of fluctuating exchange rates. When exchange rates change, financial data recorded in the parent currency (after translation) change, even when the local currency data have not. The translated financial statements of the subsidiary commingle the effects of exchange rate changes with the results of operating, investment, and financing activities on the consolidated financial statements. Further, these exchange rate effects, *translation gains and losses*, must be accounted for. They can be recognized immediately as a component of net income in the period of change, deferred (and possibly amortized) or accounted for as adjustments to stockholders' equity.

Ideally, the translation gain or loss should capture the impact of changing exchange rates on the parent's economic exposure related to its foreign operations. In practice, however, the reported translation gain or loss depends on two characteristics of the reporting method:

1. The transactions selected for translation
2. The exchanges rate(s) chosen for translation

In other words, the reported translation gain or loss reflects the impact of changing exchange rates on the parent's "accounting" rather than its "economic" exposure.

The interaction of the choice of exchange rate, the definition of exposure, and the disposition of the resulting translation adjustments can significantly affect the reported earnings and financial condition of MNCs.

FOREIGN CURRENCY TRANSLATION UNDER SFAS 52

SFAS 52 (1981), Foreign Currency Translation, prescribes reporting requirements for the translation of the financial statements of foreign operations. The primary objectives of SFAS 52 are set out in paragraph 4:

a. Provide information that is generally compatible with the expected economic effects of a rate change on an enterprise's cash flows and equity.

b. Reflect in consolidated statements the financial results and relationships of the individual consolidated entities as measured in their functional currencies in conformity with U.S. GAAP.[1]

We discuss whether the standard achieves both objectives later in the chapter.

SFAS 52 provides two translation methods:

1. The *temporal* method or the *remeasurement* process
2. The *all-current* method or the *translation* process

and delineates the conditions when each method is appropriate. Generally, the choice of method follows from the choice of *functional currency* for each subsidiary. The functional currency reflects the primary currency in which the foreign subsidiary operates. The choice depends on the operating characteristics of that subsidiary and (in some cases) the economy in which it operates.

Role of the Functional Currency

Management must determine the functional currency (primary currency) of each foreign subsidiary based on an evaluation of the unit's operating environment. The functional currency may be the foreign subsidiary's local currency, the parent's reporting currency, or a third currency. Factors to be considered in the choice of functional currency includes sales markets, input sources, and financing sources.[2] Ultimately, however, the choice of functional currency is based on management judgment and may not be completely objective.[3]

---

[1]Statement of Financial Accounting Standards 52, Foreign Currency Translation, Financial Accounting Standards Board, December 1981.

[2]Appendix A of SFAS 52 lists the following indicators to be used when choosing the functional currency: cash flows, output markets and prices, inputs, financing, and intercompany transactions. The general principle is that the functional currency should be the primary currency for most of these indicators.

   The functional currency designated for a foreign operation must be used consistently unless changing economic circumstances require change to a different functional currency. No restatement of prior financial statements is required, since a change in functional currency reflects new economic circumstances and, as such, does not qualify as a change in accounting principle. However, the change should be disclosed in the financial statement footnotes. See the later discussion of Westvaco's investment in Rigesa, a Brazilian subsidiary.

[3]At times, management may be able to justify the choice of either one of two functional currencies. In such cases, the functional currency that produces the better reported operating result is likely to be chosen. For example, in the early 1980s, companies with operations in Mexico could justify either the Mexican peso or the U.S. dollar as the functional currency for those operations. Employees of major drug companies told one of the authors that "we looked at the numbers both ways and chose the better result."

SFAS 52 defines three categories of foreign operations:

1. Relatively self-contained, independent entities operating primarily in local markets. Operating, financing, and investing activities are primarily local, although there may be reliance on the parent's patents and managerial or technological expertise and there may be some exports. *The functional currency for such an "autonomous" affiliate is generally the local currency. The all-current method is used.*

2. Foreign subsidiaries may be significantly integrated operations serving as sales outlets for the parent's products and services with substantially all the operating, financing, and investing decisions based on the reporting (parent) currency. *In such cases, the functional currency should be the parent (reporting) currency and the temporal method is used.*

3. *Finally, SFAS 52 mandates the use of the parent (reporting) currency as the functional currency for foreign operations in highly inflationary economies* (an economy with cumulative inflation of 100% or more over three years).

Management's choice of functional currency determines which accounting method is used.

Remeasurement: The Temporal Method

The temporal method or remeasurement is used when the functional currency of the foreign subsidiary is the reporting (parent) currency. In this situation, the operations of the subsidiary are deemed to be an integral part of those of the parent and the accounting method is designed to reflect that relationship. To understand this method, first consider a situation where a (U.S.) firm (without a subsidiary) carries out transactions denominated in a foreign currency:

Acquisition of Inventory or Fixed Assets. If a U.S. firm purchases inventory or fixed assets and pays for the transaction in a foreign currency, it carries the asset on its balance sheet in U.S. dollars, converting the foreign currency amount paid at the exchange rate *in effect at the time of the transaction.* Under the historical cost principle, that carrying cost remains unchanged (no matter what happens to the exchange rate subsequently) and is the amount used to compute COGS or depreciation expense.

Acquisition of Monetary Assets or Liabilities. If a U.S. firm incurs debt denominated in a foreign currency, the debt is reported on the balance sheet in dollars using the exchange rate *in effect at the time of the balance sheet date.* Any gains or losses since the previous balance sheet date as a result of changes in the exchange rate are reported in the income statement. Similarly, the carrying value of any monetary assets denominated in a foreign currency will be measured at the current exchange rate.

The temporal method extends this approach to a foreign subsidiary deemed to be an integral part of the parent's operations and deals with the three basic accounting issues as follows:

1. Nonmonetary assets (mainly inventories and fixed assets) are translated using the historical rate,[4] whereas almost all other (monetary) assets and liabilities are translated using the current rate.[5]

2. The standard defines the accounting exposure as the net monetary asset of liability position since nonmonetary assets (inventories and fixed assets) are translated at historical rates and therefore are not affected by changing exchange rates.[6]

3. The resulting translation gains and losses are included in net income as they are considered to be part of the parent's income. Thus, the effects of volatile exchange rates are transmitted directly to reported earnings quarterly.

---

[4]This results in these assets being carried at the same (historical) cost as they would have been had they been purchased directly by the parent company.

[5]Para. 48 (Appendix B) of SFAS 52 contains detail on the distinction between monetary and nonmonetary assets when applying the temporal method.

[6]As noted in the next section, this is true only for unrealized gains and losses on nonmonetary assets. Realized gains and losses on nonmonetary assets are recognized and commingled with operating income.

These concepts can be illustrated with a simple example.

Assume that a U.S. parent acquires a foreign subsidiary for $500 on December 31, 2000, when the exchange rate between the local currency (LC) and the U.S. dollar is LC 1 = $1. The subsidiary has cash = LC 400 and inventory = LC 100. The inventory is sold, during 2001, when the exchange rate is LC 1 = $1.50, for LC 200 ($300). At year-end 2001, the exchange rate is LC 1 = $2. The subsidiary now has cash of LC 600 ($1,200) and the parent reports total profit of $700 ($1,200 − $500) during the year, which includes both operating and translation gains.

Under the temporal method, only the cash has any accounting exposure to exchange rate changes. The actual translation gain on the cash is $500. (The original LC 400 increased in dollar terms from $400 to $800 for a gain of $400. The LC 200 received from the sale of inventory increased from $300 to $400 for an additional translation gain of $100.) The remaining $200 profit is from operations. (Revenues from the sale are $300 and COGS equals $100, the original cost of the inventory, since under the temporal method inventories are not adjusted for exchange rate changes.)

Prior to SFAS 52, the prevailing accounting standard was SFAS 8 (1975), Accounting for the Translation of Foreign Currency Transactions and Foreign Currency Financial Statements. Under this standard, the temporal method was the only method permitted. Because of the resulting earnings volatility, SFAS 8 was one of the most unpopular standards issued by the FASB. Because the accounting exposure and economic exposure to a currency are frequently quite different, companies wishing to hedge were forced to choose between hedging their accounting exposure and hedging their "real" exposure. As a result, within a few years, the FASB reexamined the accounting for foreign operations and issued SFAS 52.

Translation: The All-Current Method

SFAS 52 requires use of the all-current rate method to translate foreign currency financial data into the parent currency when the functional currency is the local currency. In this case, the subsidiary in its entirety (its operations and assets) is deemed "independent" of the parent's operations and viewed as an "investment" of the parent. As such:

- The exchange rate as of the balance sheet date is employed for *all* assets and liabilities.
- Since all assets and liabilities are translated at the current rate, the accounting exposure becomes the parent's net investment in the foreign operations.
- Gains and losses arising from the translation process are reported separately as a component of stockholders' equity and excluded from reported net income.

Continuing our example, under the all-current rate method, both cash and inventory are exposed to exchange rate changes. The total translation gain is $550. (Translation gain on cash is $500 as previously calculated. The translation gain on inventory is $50 as its dollar value increases from $100 to $150 between the date of purchase and the date of sale.) Operating profit is $150. Revenues from the sale are $300, and COGS equals $150, the cost of the inventory in dollars at the time of sale (under the all-current method, all assets and liabilities are adjusted for exchange rate changes).

Only the operating profit of $150 is included in reported income; the $550 translation gain is added to the cumulative translation adjustment in the stockholders' equity section.

As we shall see shortly, the differences between the two methods have significant implications for the financial statements of MNCs. Before proceeding, however, it is important to note where the two methods differ (and where they do not) in the recognition of the effects of changes in exchange rates.

Treatment of Exchange Rate Gains and Losses

Exchange rate holding gains and losses result from the net asset or liability position (the exposure) of the foreign subsidiary. However, as shown in our example (on p. 548), even if the foreign subsidiary liquidated its asset and liability positions each day, leaving no foreign subsidiary assets or liabilities, the parent's reported performance would still be affected by changes in exchange rates as a result of the flow effect. *This effect would remain, regardless of accounting method.*

EXHIBIT 15-1
Summary of Differences Between Temporal and All-Current Methods in Treatment of Exchange Rate Holding Gains and Losses

Asset/ Liability	Nature of Gain/Loss	Treatment	
		Temporal Method	All-Current Method
Monetary	Realized and unrealized	Income statement, explicit disclosure of translation gain/loss	Equity, cumulative translation adjustment
Nonmonetary	Realized	Income statement, implicit within operating income	Equity, cumulative translation adjustment
	Unrealized	Ignored	Equity, cumulative translation adjustment
Summary		All gains and losses except unrealized nonmonetary in income statement	All gains and losses in cumulative translation adjustment

The crux of the difference between the temporal and all-current method lies in the treatment of the effect of exchange rate changes on assets held—the holding gains/losses. Exhibit 15-1 summarizes these differences.

Under the all-current method, all exchange rate holding gains and losses, whether realized or not, are recognized. However, they are not reported in the income statement but flow into the cumulative translation adjustment account in stockholders' equity.

Under the temporal method, only some exchange rate holding gains and losses are recognized. Gains and losses on monetary assets, both realized and unrealized, are given separate disclosure. Unrealized gains and losses on nonmonetary assets are ignored. Realized gains and losses on nonmonetary assets are recognized, but "buried" within reported operating profits. This important distinction is often overlooked, and it is incorrectly assumed that only gains and losses derived from monetary assets are explicitly recognized in the income statement under the temporal method.[7]

Returning to our previous example, under the temporal method the amount of operating profit is $200. Under the all-current method, operating profit is $150. The difference of $50 is the realized exchange rate gain on the inventory held from the beginning of the year to the time of sale. Under the temporal method, this $50 is part of operating income; under the current rate method, it is calculated separately, removed from operating income, and added to the cumulative translation adjustment.

Note that the gains and losses on monetary items and the realized gains and losses on nonmonetary items are identical under both methods. *Thus, in terms of which holding gains/losses are recognized, the one difference between the two methods is the treatment of unrealized gains and losses on nonmonetary assets and liabilities.* As these include inventories and fixed assets, the difference may be highly significant; we return to this subject later.

Remeasurement versus Translation

Much of the confusion that surrounds the accounting for foreign operations under SFAS 52 concerns the two terms, *remeasurement* and *translation*. *Remeasurement refers to the process of converting local currency transactions into the functional currency either by a firm with transactions in a foreign currency or with a foreign subsidiary. Translation refers to conversion of the functional currency data of a subsidiary into the reporting currency.*

---

[7]The accounting is analogous to LIFO and FIFO. FIFO includes holding gains due to inflation as part of operating income, whereas LIFO removes them.

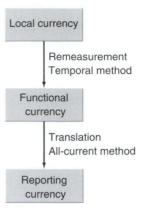

FIGURE 15-1 Accounting for foreign operations.

As Figure 15-1 implies, accounting for foreign operations can be a two-step process. The first step is the remeasurement of the subsidiary's financial data into its functional currency. For example, a subsidiary located in Germany, whose functional currency is the Euro (€), may have transactions denominated in other currencies. If it sells its output in other (non-Euro) countries, it will have cash and accounts receivable in the currency of each market. If it purchases inputs outside Germany, it will have accounts payable in other currencies.

At year-end, a balance sheet in the functional currency (Euros) must be prepared, and each non-Euro (e.g., Swiss francs) asset and liability must be converted into the functional currency. This is the process of remeasurement under SFAS 52, and it is carried out using the temporal method with all translation gains and losses recognized in reported income. The second step is the translation of all functional currency statements into the parent (reporting) currency. Translation gains and losses arising at the translation stage do not appear in the income statement but flow directly to stockholders' equity. However, translation gains or losses that result from remeasurement remain in the income statement even after the translation stage.

Figure 15-2 shows that, in many cases, only one step is needed. If the foreign subsidiary conducted business only in Euros and the local currency is the functional currency, the remeasurement step is not required. Only translation is required.

Similarly, Figure 15-3 shows that, if the functional currency for a subsidiary is the parent currency (e.g., a subsidiary operating in a highly inflationary economy), then it is necessary only to remeasure its accounts into the parent (reporting) currency and no further translation is required.

There is an important consequence of this two-step process of remeasurement and translation. The accounting for a particular transaction may depend on geography—its location within the consolidated group. For example, if the German subsidiary (whose functional currency is the Euro) has €-denominated debt, changes in the exchange rate between the euro and the dollar do not impact reported earnings. The gains or losses arising from translation of the euro debt into dollars flow directly into stockholders' equity.

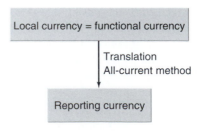

FIGURE 15-2 Translation.

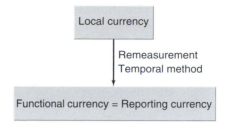

FIGURE 15-3 Remeasurement.

If the €-denominated debt is incurred by the parent company [or by another subsidiary whose functional currency is the dollar (or another currency)] then fluctuations in the exchange rate between the dollar and the euro will affect reported earnings. Gains and losses arising from remeasurement of the €debt into the functional currency are included in net income.

Thus, consolidated financial statements may incorporate various types of foreign operations with different functional currencies remeasured and/or translated into the reporting currency The processes and effects of remeasurement and translation on consolidated financial statements are described next.

ILLUSTRATION OF TRANSLATION AND REMEASUREMENT

Exhibit 15-2 provides balance sheets and exchange rates for the three years ended December 31, 2002 for Foreign Subsidiary, Inc. (FSI), a hypothetical foreign subsidiary of a U.S. multinational. It is assumed that FSI was acquired on December 31, 2000. Exhibit 15-3 contains the subsidiary's income statements for 2001 and 2002. These statements are used to illustrate remeasurement and translation. The different effects of these methods are presented in Ex-

EXHIBIT 15-2. FOREIGN SUBSIDIARY, INC.
Comparative Balance Sheets, at December 31, 2000 to 2002 (LC in millions)

	2000		2001		2002	
Cash	LC 34		LC 170		LC 333	
Accounts receivable	300		410		475	
Inventory	175		220		310	
Current assets		509		800		1,118
Fixed assets	860		1,260		1,690	
Accumulated depreciation	(150)		(360)		(610)	
Fixed assets—net		710		900		1,080
Total assets		LC 1,219		LC 1,700		LC 2,198
Operating payables	LC 255		LC 290		LC 240	
Current debt	110		130		180	
Long-term debt	140		440		790	
Total liabilities		505		860		1,210
Common stock		230		230		230
Retained earnings		484		610		758
Total equities		LC 1,219		LC 1,700		LC 2,198

Exchange Rates

Fixed assets and stockholders' equity	LC 1.06 = $U.S. 1.00		
Inventory	LC 1.06 = $U.S. 1.00		
Year-end	LC 1.06 = $U.S. 1.00	LC 0.95 = $U.S. 1.00	LC 0.85 = $U.S. 1.00
Average	N/A	LC 1.02 = $U.S. 1.00	LC 0.90 = $U.S. 1.00

N/A = not applicable.

EXHIBIT 15-3. FOREIGN SUBSIDIARY, INC.
Income Statements, for Years Ended December 31, 2001 to 2002 (LC in millions)

	2001	2002	% Change
Revenues	LC 1,290	LC 1,430	10.9%
Less: Cost of goods sold	(540)	(611)	
Gross margin	750	819	
Other expenses	(414)	(421)	
Depreciation expense	(210)	(250)	
Net income	LC 126	LC 148	17.5%

hibits 15-4 through 15-7 under the heading of all-current for translation and temporal for re-measurement.

Translation: The All-Current Method

If management designates the local currency (LC) as the functional currency of Foreign Subsidiary, Inc. (FSI), then the all-current rate method is used to translate the LC-based financial statements into U.S. dollars (the reporting currency). All assets and liabilities are translated using the exchange rate in effect at the balance sheet date. This process is illustrated in Exhibit 15-4 in the columns headed all-current. All assets and liabilities are translated at LC0.95 = $1.00 (LC0.85 = $1.00) at December 31, 2001 (2002). For example:

- Accounts receivable at December 31, 2001, equal LC410 (Exhibit 15-2). With the exchange rate of LC0.95 = $1.00 on that date, the U.S. dollar equivalent is LC410/0.95 = $431. This result is shown as accounts receivable in dollars on December 31, 2001 in the all-current column in Exhibit 15-4.
- Inventory at December 31, 2002, equals LC310 (Exhibit 15-2). If we use the exchange rate of LC0.85 = $1.00 on that date, the U.S. dollar equivalent is LC310/0.85 = $364. This result is shown as inventory in dollars in the all-current column in Exhibit 15-4.

EXHIBIT 15-4. FOREIGN SUBSIDIARY, INC.
Translated Balance Sheets, at December 31, 2000 to 2002 ($U.S. in millions)

	2000		2001		2002	
	Temporal	All-Current	Temporal	All-Current	Temporal	All-Current
Cash	$U.S. 32	$U.S. 32	$U.S. 179	$U.S. 179	$U.S. 392	$U.S. 392
Accounts receivable	283	283	431	431	559	559
Inventory	165	165	216	232	344	364
Current assets	480	480	826	842	1,295	1,315
Fixed assets	811	811	1,203	1,327	1,680	1,988
Accumulated depreciation	(141)	(141)	(341)	(379)	(590)	(717)
Fixed assets—net	670	670	862	948	1,090	1,271
Total assets	$U.S. 1,150	$U.S. 1,150	$U.S. 1,688	$U.S. 1,790	$U.S. 2,385	$U.S. 2,586
Operating liabilities	$U.S. 241	$U.S. 241	$U.S. 305	$U.S. 305	$U.S. 282	$U.S. 282
Current debt	103	103	137	137	212	212
Long-term debt	132	132	463	463	929	929
Total liabilities	476	476	905	905	1,423	1,423
Common stock	217	217	217	217	217	217
Retained earnings	457	457	566	581	745	745
Cumulative transaction adjustment	—	—	—	87	—	201
Total equities	$U.S. 1,150	$U.S. 1,150	$U.S. 1,688	$U.S. 1,790	$U.S. 2,385	$U.S. 2,586

EXHIBIT 15-4. FOREIGN SUBSIDIARY, INC. *(continued)*

Computation of Translation Adjustment Under Temporal Method

	2000	2001	2002
Net monetary liability (year end)	LC 171	LC 280	LC 402
Increase during year	—	109	122

2001:	Loss on December 31, 2000, liability		2002:	Loss on December 31, 2001, liability	
	LC 171 [(1/1.06) − (1/0.95)] =	19		LC 280 [(1/0.95) − (1/0.85)] =	35
	Loss on 2001 increase in liability			Loss on 2002 increase in liability	
	LC 109 [(1/1.02) − (1/0.95)] =	8		LC 122 [(1/0.90) − (1/0.85)] =	8
	Total translation loss	27		Total translation loss	43

Note: The translation loss appears in the income statement. See Exhibit 15-5.

Computation of Translation Adjustment Under All-Current Method

Net assets	December 31, 2001	LC 840		December 31, 2002	LC 988
	December 31, 2000	714		December 31, 2001	840
Increase for the year		LC 126			LC 148

2001:	Gain on December 31, 2000, net assets		2002:	Gain on December 31, 2001, net assets	
	LC 714 [(1/1.06) − (1/0.95)] =	78		LC 840 [(1/0.95) − (1/0.85)] =	104
	Gain on 2001 increase in net assets			Gain on 2002 increase in net assets	
	LC 126 [(1/1.02) − (1/0.95)] =	9		LC 148 [(1/0.90) − (1/0.85)] =	10
	Total translation gain	87		Total translation gain	114

In 2001, the subsidiary begins operations with net assets (stockholders' equity) of LC 714 and ends the year with net assets of LC 840. The beginning balance of net assets translates to $U.S. 674, as the exchange rate is LC 1.06 = $U.S. 1.00 on December 31, 2000. These assets are held for the year, at the end of which they translate to $U.S. 752 (LC 0.95 = $U.S. 1.00), for a gain of $U.S. 78.

However, net assets have increased during the year by LC 126, the net income for the year (if we assume no dividend payout). We assume this income is generated evenly throughout the year, at the average exchange rate of LC 1.02 = $U.S. 1.00, or $U.S. 124. At the end of the year, the net income translates to $U.S. 133 (LC 126/0.95), an increase of $U.S. 9. Thus, the change in the local currency/dollar exchange rate has increased the net assets expressed in dollars by a total of $U.S. 87 ($U.S. 78 + $U.S. 9); this amount is reported as the translation gain in the equity section of the translated balance sheet.

The 2002 translation gain of $U.S. 114 is computed using the procedures just described. This translation gain is added to the 2001 gain of $U.S. 87, and the aggregate translation gain of $U.S. 201 ($U.S. 87 + $U.S. 114) is reported as the cumulative translation adjustment (CTA) in the equity section of the 2002 balance sheet.

EXHIBIT 15-5. FOREIGN SUBSIDIARY INC.
Translated Income Statements, for Years Ended December 31, 2001 to 2002 ($U.S. in millions)

	2001		2002	
	Temporal	All-Current	Temporal	All-Current
Revenues	$U.S. 1,265	$U.S. 1,265	$U.S. 1,589	$U.S. 1,589
COGS	(523)	(529)	(650)	(679)
	742	736	939	910
Depreciation expense	(200)	(206)	(249)	(278)
	542	530	690	632
Other expenses	(406)	(406)	(468)	(468)
Net income before translation	136	124	222	164
Translation loss	(27)	—	(43)	—
Net income	$U.S. 109	$U.S. 124	$U.S. 179	$U.S. 164

Rate of Increase, 2001 to 2002

Sales	= 25.6%
Net Income	
Temporal method	= 64.0
All-current method	= 32.3

Components of the income statement (Exhibit 15-3) should, in theory, be translated at the exchange rates in effect at the dates of the underlying transactions. However, the weighted-average exchange rate for the period is more practical and has been used instead in our example, as it is in practice. All revenues and expenses are translated at the average rate for each year, as listed in Exhibit 15-2. For example:

- Revenue for 2001 is LC 1,290 (Exhibit 15-3). If we use the average exchange rate of LC 1.02 = $1.00 for 2001 (Exhibit 15-2), the U.S. dollar revenue for that year is LC 1,290/1.02 = $1,265. That result is shown in Exhibit 15-5.
- Other expenses for 2002 equal LC 421 (Exhibit 15-3). If we use the average exchange rate of LC 0.90 = $1.00 (Exhibit 15-2), the U.S. dollar equivalent is LC 421/0.90 = $468, shown in Exhibit 15-5.

Note that for these two items, the temporal and all-current results are identical.

For the columns headed all-current in Exhibit 15-5, all the U.S. dollar equivalents can be easily computed by dividing the LC amounts by the appropriate exchange rate. Note that some of the amounts in the temporal method columns are different; we will see why shortly.

The translation process generates gains or losses since assets and liabilities are translated at different exchange rates at the beginning and end of the period. In addition, income statement components are translated at average rates, but their contribution to equity (change in retained earnings) is translated at the year-end rate.

Cumulative Translation Adjustment

The cumulative translation adjustment (CTA) is a separate component of stockholders' equity[8] used by the all-current method to accumulate translation gains and losses, excluded from net income. Thus, volatility due to fluctuating exchange rates does not affect reported income but is permanently accumulated in the CTA. When the foreign operation is sold, liquidated, or considered impaired, the translation adjustment is recognized as a component of the resulting gain or loss.

For some firms, accumulated gains and losses balance out over time. If the CTA account consistently reports significant translation losses, this may signal a failure to manage currency exposure. As accumulated losses must be recognized in income if the foreign operations are sold or liquidated, a negative CTA also represents a potential loss.

Computation of the translation gain or loss under the all-current method is shown in Exhibit 15-4. Note that under this method, the accounting exposure is defined as the net asset position (the financial statement–based measure of the parent's reported net investment in the subsidiary). However, this accounting definition of exposure may not reflect the economic exposure. We discuss the effects of this lack of congruence later in this chapter.

The more immediate question is what analysts should do with the CTA. The prevailing practice is simply to accept it, to use the financial statement data without any adjustment. Few analysts argue that the change in the CTA should be added to net income.

We concur with the latter practice for two reasons. First, it is not clear that the change in the CTA represents economic gain or loss. Neither theory nor evidence suggests that adding the change to reported earnings produces a better measure of corporate performance.

Second, analysis that considers the CTA alone is incomplete. The CTA is nothing more than an accounting "plug," accumulating the effect of exchange rate changes on assets and liabilities denominated in foreign currencies. It is the effect of rate changes on those assets and liabilities (and on reported sales and net income) that distorts financial statements. Our emphasis, therefore, is on understanding how that distortion occurs and how adjustments can be made to offset it.

---

[8]The cumulative translation adjustment is included in comprehensive income, as discussed in Chapter 2.

Notwithstanding the above, the next section shows how changes in the CTA can provide useful information as to the exchange rate effects facing a firm.

Using the CTA to Estimate Exchange Rate Changes

In 2001, the LC appreciated by 11.6% relative to the dollar.[9] Similarly, in 2002, the LC appreciated by 11.8%. Unless the firm has only one foreign subsidiary, the information as to the (average) change in the "basket" of LCs used by the firm's foreign subsidiaries is usually not known.

The change in the CTA, however, can be used to estimate the (average) change in the exchange rate of the local currencies used by the firm's subsidiaries.[10]

$$\text{Change in exchange rate} = \frac{\text{Change in CTA}}{\text{Net assets of foreign subsidiary}}$$

Applying this formula to the example of Exhibit 15-4 yields[11]

	2000	2001	2002
Change in CTA		$87 − 0 = $87	$201 − 87 = $114
Net assets	$1,150 − 476 = $674	$1,790 − 905 = $885	$2,586 − 1,423 = $1,163
Average net assets		$780	$1,024
Change in exchange rate:			
Estimated		$87/$780 = 11.2%	$114/$1,024 = 11.1%
Actual		11.6%	11.8%

This procedure provides a good approximation of the average change in the exchange rate. We make use of it later in the chapter and in our cases. However, the procedure may not be appropriate if:

- The direction of the change in the exchange rate shifts dramatically during the year.
- The firm radically shifts the composition of the subsidiary's net assets prior to the shift in the direction of the exchange rate changes.

Remeasurement: The Temporal Method

The principles of remeasurement apply under *each* of the following three conditions:

1. The reporting currency (the U.S. dollar in our examples) is the functional currency of Foreign Subsidiary, Inc.
2. The unit operates in a hyperinflationary economy.
3. The foreign operation's records are kept in a currency other than its functional currency.

SFAS 52 mandates remeasurement into the reporting currency (also the functional currency in the first two cases) or the designated functional currency (in the third case) using the temporal method.

Unlike the current rate method, the temporal method applies the current rate only to monetary assets and liabilities, such as accounts receivable, marketable securities carried at

---

[9]At the end of 2000, LC1 was equivalent to $0.943 (1/1.06). At the end of 2001, LC1 = $1.053 (1/.95), an 11.6% increase. At the end of 2002, LC1 = 1.176 (1/.85), for an 11.8% increase.

[10]This computation should use the CTA change before any tax effects. While few companies report the tax effect included in the CTA, such disclosure is now required by SFAS 130 (1997).

[11]We use average net assets. If net assets have not changed dramatically, then using opening net assets provides a reasonable estimate.

EXHIBIT 15-6. FOREIGN SUBSIDIARY, INC.
Analysis of Inventory and Fixed Assets: Temporal Method ($millions)

	LC	Rate	$U.S.		LC	Rate	$U.S.
			Analysis of Inventory				
December 31, 2000	175	1.06	165	COGS (FIFO):	175	1.06 =	165
2001 purchases	585	1.02	574		365	1.02 =	358
2001 COGS (at right)	(540)		(523)	Total	540		523
December 31, 2001	220	1.02	216				
2002 purchases	701	0.90	779	COGS (FIFO):	220	1.02 =	216
2002 COGS (at right)	(611)		(650)		391	0.90 =	434
December 31, 2002	310		345	Total	611		650
			Analysis of Fixed Assets				
December 31, 2000	860	1.06	811				
2001 investment	400	1.02	392				
December 31, 2001	1,260		1,203				
2002 investment	430	0.90	477				
December 31, 2002	1,690		1,680				
			Analysis of Accumulated Depreciation				
December 31, 2000	150	1.06	141				
2001 expense	210	1.047*	200				
December 31, 2001	360		341				
2002 expense	250	1.005†	249				
December 31, 2002	610		590				

*December 31, 2001, blended rate for fixed assets.
†December 31, 2002, blended rate.
Note: The exchange rate used to translate depreciation expense is a blend of the historical rates at the time fixed assets were acquired. Under the temporal method, depreciation expense is determined in U.S. dollars; the blended rate is derived by dividing U.S. dollar depreciation expense by LC depreciation expense.

market, current liabilities, and long-term debt.[12] Exhibit 15-4 depicts this translation process for the FSI balance sheet, if we assume that the U.S. dollar is the functional currency and remeasurement is therefore required.

Note that the process for monetary assets and liabilities is the same as under the all-current method. However, nonmonetary accounts are translated at the rates in effect when the transaction occurred. As a result, inventories and fixed assets have been translated at their historical rates. The derivation of U.S. dollar inventories and fixed assets is shown in Exhibit 15-6.

Similarly, cost of goods sold and depreciation expense are translated at historical rates (also shown in Exhibit 15-6), whereas all other revenues and expenses are translated at the weighted-average exchange rate for the period.

The translation adjustment resulting from remeasurement is based on the net monetary assets or liabilities (the accounting exposure under the temporal method) rather than the net assets of the foreign operation. The reported translation adjustment, therefore, ignores the impact of changing exchange rates on inventories and fixed assets even though they may be effective hedges for major components of the net monetary position, that is, accounts payable and long-term liabilities.[13]

---

[12]See footnote 5.

[13]As inventories are sold for cash, it can be argued that a change in the exchange rate changes the expected amount of cash to be received when inventories are sold. In that sense, inventories can be considered monetary assets, hedging accounts payable, which will be repaid from the sale proceeds of the inventories. A similar argument can be made for fixed assets, which are used to produce inventories.

Under the temporal method, remeasured income statements also include the translation gain or loss on net monetary assets and liabilities, thereby adding significant volatility to reported income. Moreover, where the translation gain or loss does not reflect the economic exposure, the accounting-induced volatility reduces the utility of financial statements.

These calculations for FSI are shown in Exhibit 15-4. *As the local currency has appreciated against the dollar during the period, the net monetary liability has increased in U.S. dollar terms, resulting in a translation loss.* Like the SFAS 52 calculation, the adjustment occurs in two parts. There is a loss from the increase in the beginning balance of the net monetary liability (due to the appreciating local currency). There is an additional loss from the impact of the rising local currency on the *increase* in the net monetary liability during the year. The first portion of the loss is based on the change in the local currency/dollar exchange rate during the year. The second part results from the difference between the *average rate* during the year (the rate at which the incremental liability is assumed to have been incurred) and the *year-end rate*.

The resulting translation losses are included in net income under remeasurement rather than as part of equity under translation. *Note that under the current rate method there is a translation gain, whereas under the temporal method there is a translation loss. The choice of the functional currency defines the accounting exposure, thereby determining the amount of the reported translation gain or loss and its accounting treatment (income versus equity). The choice of functional currency matters!*

COMPARISON OF TRANSLATION AND REMEASUREMENT

Income Statement Effects

As shown in Exhibit 15-5, the current rate method translates all revenues, expenses, gains, and losses at the weighted-average rate. The temporal method also uses the weighted average for all the elements of the income statement *except* cost of goods sold and depreciation expense. Thus, these two expense lines differ, reflecting the choice of functional currency.

Effect on Gross Profit Margin

The temporal method, when combined with the use of first-in, first-out (FIFO) inventory accounting (the method generally used outside of the United States), can distort reported earnings. Use of the historical rate for inventories delays recognition of the effects of rate changes, just as FIFO delays the recognition of price level changes.[14] In the case of FSI, with an appreciating local currency, historical-cost-basis cost of goods sold is lower than the cost of goods sold translated at the average rate. If the local currency declined, cost of goods sold would be higher under the temporal method.

In either case, use of the temporal method distorts gross profit margins. We can see the distortion by comparing the gross profit margin under each method (shown in Exhibit 15-7) with the actual gross profit margin in local currency units.

The gross margin after remeasurement for 2002 is higher than the actual gross margin in local currency (59.1% compared to 57.3%). Equally important, it appears that the gross margin percentage in 2002 increased slightly from that in 2001, 59.1% versus 58.7%; in local currency units, the gross margin percentage declined to 57.3% in 2002 from 58.1% in 2001. The gross margin percentage after translation, however, preserves the trends and relationships of the functional currency of the subsidiary. This preservation of local currency trends and relationships is often viewed as an important advantage of the all-current rate method.

However, preservation of the local currency ratio may not be appropriate. Box 15-1 illustrates one situation for which the temporal method was designed; with the U.S. dollar as the functional currency, the remeasured dollar ratio rather than the local currency ratio reports the underlying economics with less distortion.

---

[14]Problem 15-4 further explores the relationship between the translation method and inventory method.

BOX 15-1
Parent versus Local Currency Relationships

The temporal method is often criticized for distorting local currency relationships. This box illustrates that, in situations the temporal method was designed for, it is the (remeasured) parent currency relationship that is relevant rather than the local currency relationship.

Assumptions:

- Company charges 50% markup over cost or 33% gross profit margin.
- When inventory is produced, the exchange rate is $1 = LC1.
- When inventory is sold, the exchange rate is $1.20 = LC1.
- Cost of inventory is $1.

If pricing decisions are made in dollars, when inventory is sold, its price will be $1.50. The local currency price will be LC1.25 ($1.50/1.20). The local currency income statement is:

Sales	LC1.25
COGS	LC1.00
Gross profit	LC0.25
Gross margin	20%

The local currency gross margin of 20% does not reflect the underlying economic relationship.*

Under the temporal method, the income statement is remeasured as

Sales	$1.50
COGS	$1.00
Gross profit	$0.50
Gross margin	33%

The gross margin reported in dollars (in the parent's income statement) differs from the local currency relationship. It does, however, better reflect the economics of the transaction!

---

*Essentially, the local currency relationship distorts the parent relationship rather than the other way around. Further examples of this nature are discussed in the section entitled, "Analytical Difficulties Related to Foreign Operations."

Effect on Net Income

The temporal method may also significantly affect depreciation expense. Again, an appreciating local currency results in depreciation expense that is lower as compared with that resulting from the current rate method (see Exhibit 15-5). Net income before the effect of translation is again inflated by this effect.

Once again, the all-current rate method faithfully reproduces the net profit margin (as shown in Exhibit 15-7) from the original local currency statements, whereas the temporal method results in higher profit margins and a larger increase in the net profit margin in 2002.

The inclusion of translation (holding) gains and losses in net income under the temporal method results in further distortion. Translation losses in both 2001 and 2002 reduce the positive impact of the temporal method. The fact that the operating effects and translation effects are opposite, it must be noted, is a function of the asset and liability composition of FSI and the direction of change in exchange rates. Specifically, FSI had a net monetary *liability* combined with an increase in the value of the local currency relative to the dollar.

If the local currency had declined, both cost of goods sold and depreciation expense would be higher under the temporal method. The resulting lower reported income would be offset by the inclusion of translation gains on the monetary liability in income. Although the situation described here is not unusual, some companies have operating effects and translation effects in the same direction.

Although the remeasurement net profit margin for 2001 (Exhibit 15-7) falls below the original local currency results, the exaggerated profit margin improvement in 2002 remains. Translation still does the better job of reflecting the local currency operating results in U.S. dollars.

These income effects relate to the *holding gains/losses* resulting from exchange rate changes. Additionally, the use of weighted-average rates to translate the income statement creates the *flow effect* (discussed at the beginning of the chapter) on reported sales and net income. A strengthening (declining) local currency creates the illusion of higher (lower) sales and earnings of foreign operations.

FSI's sales increased by 10.9% in 2002 in local currency units (Exhibit 15-3) but by 25.6% in U.S. dollars (Exhibit 15-5). Net income increased by 17.5% in local currency units but by 32.3% in dollars (all-current).[15] The 13% appreciation of the local currency against the dollar inflates both the sales and earnings comparisons. For companies with significant foreign operations, the effect of changing exchange rates can make it difficult to discern true operating trends.

Balance Sheet Effects

The choice of functional currency also affects the balance sheet of the foreign operation and, after consolidation, that of the parent company. Exhibit 15-4 shows the FSI balance sheets for 2000, 2001, and 2002 under both methods.

Since the subsidiary was acquired on December 31, 2000, the balance sheets as of December 31, 2000, are identical under both methods. For 2001 and 2002, many of the asset and liability accounts are still identical as both methods translate monetary assets and liabilities at the current (balance sheet date) exchange rate. There are, however, some significant differences.

When the reporting currency (here, the U.S. dollar) is the functional currency, the temporal method requires that inventories, fixed assets, and other nonmonetary accounts be translated at historic rates. Exhibit 15-6 provides detailed calculations for both the inventory and fixed asset accounts.

Because the local currency has appreciated against the dollar, the historical costs of both inventories and fixed assets are below the amounts reported under the current rate method. As a result, total assets are lower under the temporal method. The asset turnover ratio increases, as discussed in the next section.

Turning to the right side of the balance sheet, we see that stockholders' equity is also lower under the temporal method. Under the current rate method, equity includes the cumulative translation adjustment gains for 2001 and 2002. Retained earnings at December 31, 2001 are lower under the temporal method as earnings have been reduced by translation losses resulting from the impact of the appreciation of the local currency on the net monetary liability. However, retained earnings are, by coincidence, the same under both methods at December 31, 2002.

Impact on Financial Ratios

We have already seen how the choice of functional currency affects income statement ratios. Because the balance sheet and income statement are both affected, many financial ratios vary with the choice of the functional currency. Exhibit 15-7 includes a number of examples.

Reviewing this exhibit leads to two conclusions: First, the ratios are quite different under translation and remeasurement, and second, the ratios under translation are often different from those in the local currency. Although the first conclusion should not surprise us, the second is disturbing given the objectives of SFAS 52. Let us examine each conclusion in detail.

Comparison of Ratios Under Translation and Remeasurement

As can be seen by comparing the translation ratios with the remeasurement ratios, they give quite different indications of the performance of FSI. Note that:

- The distortion of ratios and financial statement relationships arises from the foreign subsidiary component of consolidated financial statements.
- When a firm uses more than one foreign currency, it is very difficult to predict the financial statement and ratio effects, especially when the currencies move in different directions relative to the parent (reporting) currency. Basket indices may or may not reflect the firm's exposure.

---

[15]Note that under remeasurement, the increase in net income (even after translation losses) was 64%: twice the growth rate under translation and close to four times the rate reported in local currency terms! This is partly due to the computation of cost of goods sold and depreciation expense at historical exchange rates.

EXHIBIT 15-7. FOREIGN SUBSIDIARY, INC.
Financial Ratios,* 2001 to 2002

	Year	LC Units	All-Current	Temporal
Gross margin percentage	2001	58.1%	58.1%	58.7%
	2002	57.3%	57.3%	59.1%
Net income as % of sales	2001	9.8%	9.8%	10.8%
(Before translation loss)	2002	10.3%	10.3%	14.0%
Net income as % of sales	2001	9.8%	9.8%	8.6%
	2002	10.3%	10.3%	11.3%
Debt as % of equity	2001	67.9%	67.9%	76.6%
	2002	98.2%	98.2%	118.6%
Inventory turnover	2001	2.73X	2.66X	2.75X
	2002	2.31X	2.27X	2.43X
Receivable turnover	2001	3.63X	3.54X	3.54X
	2002	3.23X	3.21X	3.21X
Fixed asset turnover	2001	1.60X	1.56X	1.65X
	2002	1.44X	1.43X	1.63X
Total asset turnover	2001	0.88X	0.86X	0.89X
	2002	0.73X	0.72X	0.78X
Return on average equity	2001	16.2%	15.9%	18.7%
(Before translation loss)	2002	16.2%	16.0%	25.4%
Return on average equity	2001	16.2%	15.9%	15.0%
	2002	16.2%	16.0%	20.5%
Return on average assets	2001	8.8%	8.4%	9.5%
(Before translation loss)	2002	7.6%	7.5%	10.5%
Return on average assets	2001	8.8%	8.4%	7.7%
	2002	7.6%	7.5%	8.8%

*See Chapter 4 for definitions of ratios.

We have already discussed the differences in the gross margin and net margin ratios. The debt/equity ratio (current and long-term debt) is significantly higher under remeasurement. Although the debt is the same, the lower level of equity results in a higher debt ratio.

The asset turnover ratios are also different, with one exception. The receivable turnover ratio is identical under both translation and remeasurement because both methods translate receivables and sales at the same rates (year-end rate and average rate, respectively).

For inventory turnover, however, that is not true. Under remeasurement, both cost of goods sold and average inventories are lower, reflecting the lagged effect of the higher value of the local currency against the dollar. The result is a higher turnover ratio for both years. This result, however, reflects the assumed turnover rate and exchange rate changes in this example. It does not hold in all cases.

The fixed asset turnover ratio is significantly higher under remeasurement, reflecting the lower historic cost of fixed assets under the temporal method (given the appreciating local currency). This is a universal result; a rising local currency always increases fixed asset turnover for remeasurement as compared with translation. A depreciating local currency would result in higher fixed assets under remeasurement and a lower turnover ratio.

Total asset turnover is also higher under remeasurement, reflecting the lower historic costs of inventory and fixed assets. As in the case of all turnover ratios except inventory, the numerator (sales) is the same under both methods. Thus, the denominator drives the difference in the turnover ratio. Given a rising local currency, assets are higher under translation, resulting in lower turnover ratios.

Return ratios are also different under the two methods, as both the numerator and denominator are different. Under translation, return on equity is virtually unchanged; under remeasurement, return on equity shows a sharp increase in 2002. Both the levels and trend are therefore affected by the choice of functional currency.

This is also true of the return-on-assets ratio. This ratio (before translation losses) is higher under remeasurement than under translation for both years. The trend is also different: Return on assets (ROA) rises in 2002 under translation but declines under remeasurement.

Comparison of Translated and Local Currency Ratios

Turning to our second (perhaps surprising) conclusion that ratios under the all-current method are often different from those in the local currency, compare the U.S. dollar ratios with the local currency ratios in Exhibit 15-7. In most cases, the all-current ratios differ from the local currency ratios. The exceptions are the pure income statement (e.g., gross margin) and pure balance sheet (e.g., debt-to-equity) ratios. As all income statement components are translated at the average rate and all balance sheet components are translated at the ending rate, it is mathematically true that the LC ratios and U.S. dollar ratios are identical.

When ratios combine income statement and balance sheet components, however, the equality is disturbed. That is because the numerator and denominator do not rise or fall by the same percentage. Thus, turnover and return ratios are changed by translation. The differences between the ratios under translation and the local currency ratios are not large, and the 2001 to 2002 trends are similar, but the ratios are different.

One more effect of changing exchange rates on ratios deserves comment. When foreign operations have different trends and ratio characteristics than domestic operations, then exchange rate changes can distort consolidated ratios by changing the weight of foreign data. For example, if the local currency appreciates, foreign data will constitute a larger percentage of the consolidated group, and consolidated ratios will be affected. We can see this from the following example.

Assume that a U.S. parent has a foreign subsidiary as well as U.S. operations, and that the exchange rate has changed from LC 0.95 = $1.00, at the end of 2001, to LC 0.85 = $1.00, at the end of 2002. The debt and equity of the subsidiaries as well as the consolidated entity (after translation) are presented below:

	Foreign Subsidiary		U.S. Operations		Consolidated	
	2001	2002	2001	2002	2001	2002
Debt	LC 570	LC 570	$ 200	$ 200	$ 800	$ 871
Equity	840	840	1,000	1,000	1,884	1,988
Ratio	0.679	0.679	0.200	0.200	0.425	0.438

There has been no real change in debt, equity, or the debt-to-equity ratio. However, the appreciation of the local currency increases the foreign subsidiary's U.S. dollar debt and equity. In consolidation, the debt-to-equity ratio increases *only* because of the change in exchange rates. *Whenever a financial ratio differs between the foreign subsidiary and the remainder of the consolidated group, a change in exchange rate will affect the consolidated ratio even if there has been no change in the underlying ratios.*

We therefore conclude our discussion of ratios with the following observations:

- For pure income statement and pure balance sheet ratios, translation using the all-current rate method maintains the local currency relationships.

- For ratios using both income statement and balance sheet components, the all-current method ratios do not exactly maintain the local currency relationships, but usually do not differ greatly.

- Ratios computed under the temporal method, in most cases, differ markedly from both the local currency ratios and those computed from translated data.
- Changes in exchange rates can affect consolidated ratios, even when there is no real change, by increasing or decreasing the "weighting" of the foreign subsidiary.

Impact on Reported Cash Flows

SFAS 95, Statement of Cash Flows (1987), affects the reporting of cash flows for foreign operations. SFAS 95 provides that cash flows in the parent (reporting) currency must replicate the cash flows in the local currency. To accomplish this objective, cash flows in the reporting currency must exclude the effects of exchange rate changes. This requirement means that the cash flow statement should be unaffected by whether the temporal or all-current rate method is used.

To understand the consequences of this requirement, compare the statement of cash flows with the balance sheet and income statement. Exhibit 15-8 contains FSI cash flow statements for 2001 and 2002, both in local currency units and U.S. dollars. First, look at the local currency statements.

The local currency cash flow statements were prepared from the balance sheet (Exhibit 15-2) and income statement (Exhibit 15-3) of FSI. The cash flows in Exhibit 15-8 consist of a mixture of income statement data and changes in balance sheet accounts. For example, the 2002 change in receivables is the difference between the balance of accounts receivable at December 31, 2002 and the balance at December 31, 2001 (LC 475 − LC 410 = LC 65).

Investing cash flow equals capital spending, or the change in fixed assets (before depreciation). Financing cash flow equals the increase in current and long-term debt. The net cash flow is necessarily equal to the change in cash for the year.

When local currency cash flows are translated into U.S. dollars, these relationships break down because of the impact of exchange rate changes. For example, the U.S. dollar cash flow statement for 2002 shows an increase of $72 in accounts receivable, whereas the year-to-year increase in accounts receivable on the U.S. dollar balance sheet (Exhibit 15-4) is $128 under either method of translation. How can we reconcile this difference?

Although the $56 difference between $72 and $128 can easily be reconciled,[16] it is important to understand why these two amounts are different. The year-to-year increase in accounts receivable in U.S. dollars is the result of two factors:

1. The change in accounts receivable in LC units
2. The impact of changing exchange rates on the balance.

Given the change in the value of the local currency against the dollar, this difference affects every balance sheet account. In each case, the reported U.S. dollar cash flow must exclude the impact of exchange rate changes; the cash flow in dollars is simply the cash flow in the local currency, translated at the average rate for the year (LC 0.90 = $1.00 for 2002). For accounts receivable, the change is

$$\frac{\text{LC } 65}{0.90} = \$72$$

As a result of SFAS 95, the U.S. dollar cash flow statement replicates the local currency statement, consistent with the objectives of SFAS 52. Prior to that standard, cash flow statements were distorted by the inclusion of exchange rate effects. Cash flow statements not prepared in accordance with standards containing rules similar to SFAS 95 (non-U.S. GAAP) retain the distortion resulting from exchange rate changes.[17]

---

[16]Effect of exchange rate change on December 31, 2001 balance = LC 410 (1/0.95 − 1/0.85) = $51. Effect on 2002 increase = LC 65 (1/0.90 − 1/0.85) = $4. Total effect is $51 + $4 = $55. Difference from $56 is rounding error. This computation is analogous to the translation adjustments computed in Exhibit 15-4.

[17]IAS 7 (1992) on cash flow is largely consistent with SFAS 95. Cash flow statements prepared using IASB GAAP should be similar to those prepared in the United States under SFAS 95.

EXHIBIT 15-8. FOREIGN SUBSIDIARY, INC.
Cash Flow Statements, 2001 to 2002 (in millions)

	LC		$U.S.	
	2001	2002	2001	2002
Revenues	LC 1,290	LC 1,430	$U.S. 1,265	$U.S. 1,589
Change in receivables	(110)	(65)	(108)	(72)
Collections	LC 1,180	LC 1,365	$U.S. 1,157	$U.S. 1,517
Cost of goods sold	(540)	(611)	(529)	(679)
Change in inventories	(45)	(90)	(44)	(100)
Change in payables	35	(50)	34	(56)
Inputs	LC (550)	LC (751)	$U.S. (539)	$U.S. (835)
Expenses	(414)	(421)	(406)	(468)
Operating cash flow	LC 216	LC 193	$U.S. 212	$U.S. 214
Investing cash flow	(400)	(430)	(392)	(478)
Financing cash flow	320	400	313	445
Effect of translation on cash*	—	—	14	32
Net cash flow	LC 136	LC 163	$U.S. 147	$U.S. 213

*2001:				
	Opening cash balance	LC 34/1.06 =	$U.S. 32	
	2001 increase in cash	136/1.02 =	133	
	Total	170	165	
	Actual cash balance	170/0.95 =	179	
	Effect of translation	—	14	
*2002:	Opening cash balance	LC 170/0.95 =	$U.S. 179	
	2002 increase in cash	163/0.90 =	181	
	Total	333	360	
	Actual cash balance	333/0.85 =	392	
	Effect of translation	—	32	

2002: Alternative Computation

Beginning cash balance	LC 170	
Effect of change in exchange rate*	$\dfrac{170}{0.95} - \dfrac{170}{0.85} =$	$U.S. 21
Cash flow from operations (CFO)	LC 193	
Effect of change in exchange rate[†]	$\dfrac{193}{0.90} - \dfrac{193}{0.85} =$	13
Cash flow from investing activities	LC (430)	
Effect of change in exchange rate[†]	$\dfrac{(430)}{0.90} - \dfrac{(430)}{0.85} =$	(28)
Cash flow from financing activities	LC 400	
Effect of change in exchange rate[†]	$\dfrac{400}{0.90} - \dfrac{400}{0.85} =$	26
Total effect of exchange rate changes on cash		$U.S. 32

*The revaluation of the LC cash balance to reflect the change in exchange rate during the year.
[†]The difference between the amount shown on the cash flow statement (translated at the average rate for the year) and the U.S. dollar equivalent of that cash flow at the year-end rate.

According to the provisions of SFAS 95, the consolidated cash flows of MNCs should represent the reporting currency equivalent of local currency cash flows of foreign operations, unaffected by the choice of functional currency.[18]

---

[18]Discussions with some preparers and a review of reported cash flow statements convince us that this is not true in all cases. We believe that, in some cases, consolidated cash flow statements are prepared from translated functional currency cash flow statements rather than local currency statements. We conclude that, in these cases, the choice of functional currency does affect reported cash flows!

The U.S. dollar cash flows all exclude the impact of exchange rate changes. The net cash flow, however, will not equal the year-to-year change in cash unless the effect of rate changes on cash is recognized. This effect is computed in Exhibit 15-8.[19]

The effect of exchange rate changes on cash ($32 for 2002) may also be broken down into its components, the effects on the opening cash balance and on cash flows for operating, investing, and financing activities. This breakdown is also shown in Exhibit 15-8.

Although we have stated that SFAS 95 mandates the removal of the effects of exchange rate changes on cash flows, that statement is not entirely true. Reported cash flows exclude only the impact of changing exchange rates on assets and liabilities (holding effect).

However, as local currency cash flows are translated at the average exchange rate for the year, changes in currency rates do affect reporting currency cash flows. This flow effect is similar to the impact on reported sales and earnings previously discussed. When a foreign currency rises in value, the parent currency equivalent of cash flows in that currency will also rise; when a currency falls, the translated cash flows decline. So although the provisions of SFAS 95 do provide us with a cash flow statement that replicates the local currency cash flow statement, the parent company cash flow statement is still affected by changes in currency rates.

ANALYSIS OF FOREIGN CURRENCY DISCLOSURES

We now turn to the analysis of disclosures typically found in the financial statements of multinational firms. Our goal is to use the disclosures and our understanding of the accounting for foreign operations to discern the effect of exchange rate changes on reported financial statements. The ultimate objective is to understand the firm's economic exposure to exchange rates, the effects of rate changes on this exposure, and whether or not the effects reported in financial statements reflect the economic effects appropriately.

Exchange Rate Changes: Exposure and Effects

The starting point for any analysis is the determination of exposure to currencies other than the parent (reporting) currency. The next step is to estimate the effects of exchange rate changes. These effects are the consequence of two factors, exposure and rate changes. What is most important, however, is not the precise measurement of the distortions resulting from exchange rate changes, but the recognition that they exist. Once you recognize the issues, you can usually estimate the financial statement effects. Given the imprecision of financial statements to begin with, even a general understanding of the effects of changing exchange rates should improve investment decisions.

Information about exposure can be obtained from:

- Financial statement references to exchange rate effects
- Footnote disclosures about translation gains and losses
- Geographic segment disclosures
- Management discussion and analysis
- Listings of subsidiaries or divisions
- Descriptive material about business operations

From such references, the analyst should seek to answer the following questions:

1. In which currencies is business conducted?
2. How much exposure does the company have to each currency?

---

[19]A simplified way to view the issue is to assume that all LC cash flows are received in the middle of the year; that is the implicit assumption of the cash flow statement. However, between the middle of the year and year-end, there is an exchange gain on the cash received as the LC rises. In addition, the opening balance of LC currency increases in dollar terms. These gains total $32. We can use the method shown in Exhibit 15-4 to confirm this answer.

The effect on December 31, 2001 cash is LC 170 (1/0.95 − 1/0.85) = $21. The effect on the 2002 increase in cash is LC 163 (1/0.90 − 1/0.85) = $11. The total effect for 2002 is $21 + $11 = $32.

3. What accounting method does the firm use for its foreign operations?

4. What functional currencies does the firm use?

5. How does the firm hedge its exposure to exchange rate effects?

Hedging is deferred to Chapter 16; we focus our discussion on the first four items. As exchange rate changes affect all three financial statements, we must examine the accounting exposure to rate changes for each in turn.

Balance Sheet

A company's balance sheet exposure depends on:[20]

- The choice of functional currency
- Composition of foreign subsidiaries' balance sheets

Choice of Functional Currency. When the parent currency is the functional currency, then exposure equals net monetary assets (the temporal method). When the local currency is the functional currency, exposure equals net assets by currency (the all-current rate method).

Some large U.S. multinationals use the U.S. dollar as functional currency for all foreign operations. In other cases, the functional currency choice is made for each foreign operation. For example, the following disclosure appears in footnote 1E of Pfizer's *1999 Annual Report*:

> For most international operations, local currencies are considered their functional currencies.

The choice of functional currency is a management decision. Despite the criteria laid down by SFAS 52, there is disparity even among companies with similar operations. Merck, one of Pfizer's principal competitors, uses the U.S. dollar as its functional currency worldwide. Among U.S.-based oil multinationals, Chevron and Texaco use the U.S. dollar as their functional currency worldwide; Exxon mostly uses local currencies.

Financial statement disclosures regarding exposure are typically poor, as neither SFAS 52 nor IAS 21 have meaningful disclosure requirements. DuPont [DD] is a notable exception, as it reports the company's principal exposures:

Currency	After-Tax Monetary Exposure			Open Contracts To Buy (Sell) Foreign Currency		Net After-Tax Exposure Asset/(Liability)
	Asset	Liability	Net	Pre-Tax	After-Tax	
Brazilian real	$324	$ (216)	$ 108	$(163)	$(101)	$ 7
British pound sterling	723	(1,060)	(337)	539	334	(3)
Canadian dollar	695	(181)	514	(822)	(509)	5
Japanese yen	722	(646)	76	(114)	(71)	5
Taiwan dollar	103	(239)	(136)	219	136	0

Source: DuPont10-K December 31, 1999.

As DuPont uses the U.S. dollar as functional currency for most of its operations, all exposures are measured by the net monetary assets of liabilities. DuPont has hedged all these exposures on an after-tax basis. Hedging is discussed in Chapter 16.

When the firm does not explicitly state its choice of functional currency, then the absence of a cumulative translation adjustment on the balance sheet indicates that the firm is using the temporal method and the functional currency for all its foreign subsidiaries is the

---

[20]Hedging activities can mitigate the effect of these factors.

parent currency. If a CTA appears on the balance sheet, then the analyst knows that for at least some of the subsidiaries the firm is using the all-current method and the local currency is the functional currency.

Balance Sheet Composition. Balance sheet exposure is also affected by the asset/liability structure of foreign operations. Subsidiaries with few liabilities are heavily exposed to exchange rate effects. Exposure can be reduced by borrowing in the local currency or through hedging activities.

Once exposures are known or estimated, the exchange effects can be computed, following the Foreign Subsidiary example earlier in the chapter. The effect has two parts, similar to those shown in Exhibit 15-4:

1. The opening balance (in local currency) multiplied by the rate change over the entire time period.
2. The change in balance (in local currency) multiplied by the rate change from the date of the change to the end of the period. Absent better information, assume that the local currency change occurred evenly and use the average rate for the period.

Translation adjustments for operations with nonparent functional currencies are accounted for in the cumulative translation adjustment section of equity; adjustments for operations with the parent currency as functional currency are included in reported income.

■ Example: PepsiCo Mexico

Part A of Exhibit 15-9 contains data regarding PepsiCo's Mexican operations from its *1995 Annual Report*; year-end and average peso–dollar exchange rates are given in part B. Exhibit 15-9 shows that identifiable assets declined from $995 to $637 in 1995. To ascertain how much of this change resulted from exchange rate changes rather than an actual asset decline in pesos, we use the year-end rates to translate identifiable assets into pesos:

	1994	1995	% Change
Assets (in $millions)	995	637	−36.0
× Year-end exchange rate	5.075	7.695	
= Assets (pesos in millions)	5,050	4,902	−2.9

The sharp decline in assets of PepsiCo's Mexican subsidiary was due almost entirely to the peso's decline. Although the (undisclosed) net investment in Mexico is undoubtedly smaller, PepsiCo states that the peso devaluation was the primary factor in the 1995 negative CTA of $337 million. We can compute the translation loss on the identifiable assets:

$$\text{Opening balance} \quad 5{,}050 \times \left[\frac{1}{7.695} - \frac{1}{5.075}\right] = \$(338)$$

$$\text{Change } (4{,}902 - 5{,}050) \quad (148) \times \left[\frac{1}{7.695} - \frac{1}{6.418}\right] = \underline{\quad 4 \quad}$$

$$\text{Translation loss on identifiable assets}[21] \qquad \$(334)$$

In this case, the currency and exposure are known. However, because most firms do not disclose exposures by currency, analysts must use the available data about foreign operations, supplemented by discussions with management, to estimate major exposures

---

[21]The closeness of this amount to the actual change in the CTA suggests that PepsiCo's peso liabilities were small and the CTA change for all other functional currencies balanced out. Due to nondisclosure, we ignore any possible tax effects (see footnote 10).

EXHIBIT 15-9. PEPSICO MEXICO
Effects of Devaluation

A. Selected Financial Data

Mexico is an important foreign market for PepsiCo and the 1995 decline in the value of the peso had a significant negative impact on operating profit. To explain that impact, PepsiCo's *1995 Annual Report* included the following data:

	1994	1995	% Change
$U.S. millions			
Net sales	$2,023	$1,228	−39.3%
Operating profit	261	80	−69.3
Identifiable assets	995	637	−36.0

PepsiCo's Management's Analysis states that:

- Operations were adversely impacted by the effects of the approximately 50% devaluation of the Mexican peso.

- Consumer demand shrank dramatically.

- [Management actions] resulted in only a modest decline in local currency segment operating profit for Mexico.

B. Peso-Dollar Exchange Rate

	1994	1995	% Change
Year-end rate, December 31	$1 = 5.075	7.695	−51.6%
Average rate during year*	$1 = 3.397	6.418	−88.9

*Average of month-end rates.
Source: PepsiCo, *1995 Annual Report.*

and their effects. For some multinationals, an index approach can be used. In other cases, the change in the CTA for the firm can be used to estimate the year-end to year-end change in foreign currency rates weighted by the operations of the firm itself. This firm-specific index can then be used to discern the effect of exchange rate changes on assets and liabilities. ∎

Income Statement

As in the case of the balance sheet, income statement exposure depends on the choice of functional currency. Generally, revenues and most expense categories are translated at the average rate for the period regardless of the choice of functional currency. When the local currency is the functional currency, then all revenue and expense categories are translated at the average rate. When the parent currency is the functional currency, then inventories and fixed assets and consequently COGS and depreciation expense are translated at historical rates (see Exhibits 15-5 and 15-6). In addition, translation gains and losses are included in reported income, as the temporal method is used.

Exchange rate changes affect reported income because the average rate used to translate the income statement is different each period. Analysis of the effect of exchange rate changes on the income statement requires an "average for the period" index. In some cases, a trade-weighted index will serve the purpose. For companies whose operations are concentrated in one or a few countries, it may be possible to construct a firm-specific index. Despite the difficulty of the approximations required, some effort must be made to gauge the income statement exposure to rate changes.

The most pervasive income statement effect of exchange rate changes is the flow effect of rate changes on revenue and expense. This effect must be disaggregated from the effect of operations:

1. *The exchange rate effect is estimated by multiplying the income statement component (in local currency) by the change in the average exchange rate.*

2. *The operational effect is estimated by multiplying the change in the income statement component (in local currency) by the previous period's average exchange rate.*

The exchange rate effect is always present, although management comments about operating results frequently provide little disclosure. Pfizer's Financial Review, for example, discloses the percentage effect of exchange rate changes on segment revenues:

Segment	1998 vs. 1997	1999 vs. 1998
Pharmaceutical	(3.3)	(0.1)
Animal Health	(4.1)	(3.7)
Total	(3.5)	(0.5)

We can see from these data that currency effects were significantly negative for both segments in 1998, but that, in 1999, only the animal health segment was materially affected. As the pharmaceutical segment is far larger, the total effect for 1999 was small.

Pfizer's Note 19 (segment data) indicates that Japan accounted for nearly 8% of total 1999 revenues. No other information is provided about the effect of currency rate changes on reported income.

When making international comparisons, it is important to remember that exchange rate effects on the income statement depend on the point of view. Roche, reporting in Swiss francs, reported that 2000 sales rose 2% in local currencies, but 8% in Swiss francs, implying a positive currency effect of 6%. Takeda is silent regarding the effect of currency changes. As the average value of the yen against the dollar was lower in fiscal 1999 than in fiscal 1998, there was some effect. Problem 15-5 considers the effect of currency changes on Takeda's financial statements.

When comparing the sales growth of firms with different reporting currencies, therefore, the analyst must consider differences in the impact of exchange rates. Differences in both the reporting currency and geographic business mix affect sales comparisons.

We illustrate the procedure using PepsiCo Mexico. The analysis will allow us to check the accuracy of management's statements quoted in Exhibit 15-9. Multiplying the PepsiCo Mexico data by the *average rate* produces income statement data in millions of pesos:

Pesos (in millions)	1994	1995	% Change
Net sales	6,872	7,881	14.7%
Operating profit	887	513	(42.1)%
Operating margin	12.9%	6.5%	

PepsiCo's statements (Exhibit 15-9) do not match the data:

- Consumer demand did not shrink. Peso sales actually rose 14.7%. The only way to reconcile these statements is to assume that peso prices rose sharply.
- The decline in local currency segment operating profit was not moderate. Peso operating profit fell 42%.

These observations can be confirmed when we disaggregate the decline in sales ($795) and operating income ($181) into the exchange rate flow effect and operational effect as follows:

Sales	Operating Income

Exchange Rate Flow Effect

$$7,881 \times \left[\frac{1}{6.418} - \frac{1}{3.397} \right] = \$(1,092) \qquad 513 \times \left[\frac{1}{6.418} - \frac{1}{3.397} \right] = \$(71)$$

Operational Effect

$$(7,881 - 6,872) \times \left[\frac{1}{3.397} \right] = \underline{\quad 297 \quad} \qquad (513 - 887) \times \left[\frac{1}{3.397} \right] = \underline{\quad (110) \quad}$$

$$\$(795) \qquad\qquad \$(181)$$

For sales we have a positive operational effect, whereas for operating income it is negative.

Cash Flow Statement

As all cash flows must be translated at the average rate for the period, the choice of functional currency does not matter. Period-to-period changes in average rates directly affect reported cash flows. However, seasonal cash flow patterns or other timing differences can result in cash flow effects that differ from income statement effects, even when the local currency is the functional currency.

For recurring transactions, the exchange rate effects on reported cash flows are quite simple. Cash flows are translated at the average rate for the period, regardless of the choice of functional currency. Almost all operating cash flows and many investing and financing cash flows occur relatively evenly over the year. However, such transactions as payments for acquisitions, and major debt issuance or retirements, are occasional and their timing is important. The timing of major investment and debt changes can significantly change currency exposure.

The index used to measure rate change effects on cash flows should be the same one used to measure the income statement effects. It is important to keep a clear distinction between period-end rates used for balance sheet analysis and period-average rates that affect income and cash flow data.

The devaluation's effect on PepsiCo's cash flows from its Mexican operations can only be guessed at, given the lack of disclosure. Given the decline in the average peso–dollar rate during 1995, we can assume that the Mexican subsidiary contributed little to corporate cash flow in 1995, although Management's Discussion and Analysis is silent on this point.

HYPERINFLATIONARY ECONOMIES

Countries experiencing very high rates of inflation present problems for both accountants and financial analysts. Because the currencies of high-inflation countries normally depreciate at a rapid rate (reflecting the diminishing purchasing power of the currency), translation of the financial statements of companies operating in such countries into "strong" currencies creates special difficulties.

If the current exchange rate is used to translate the assets and liabilities of subsidiaries located in high-inflation countries, their translated amounts quickly become insignificant. Such accounting would misrepresent the financial condition of the subsidiary, suggesting that its assets are disappearing.

In most cases, however, the real value of nonmonetary assets is not destroyed by the high rate of inflation. Inventories and fixed assets generally rise in value (in local currency), enough to offset the rate of inflation. This is to be expected as, otherwise, such assets could be transported to other countries where their value would be higher. This effect is usually explicitly recognized in the accounting system of such countries by indexing the carrying value of nonmonetary assets by the rate of inflation. (See the discussion of constant dollar accounting in Appendix 8-A.)

Alternative Accounting Methods for Hyperinflationary Subsidiaries

There are two solutions to the accounting problem:

1. The reporting (parent) currency can be the functional currency for all operations in highly inflationary economies. Nonmonetary assets and liabilities of the subsidiary, under this method, are effectively accounted for in the parent currency.

2. The indexed value of nonmonetary assets and liabilities can be translated at the current exchange rate. This method has the effect of approximately maintaining the carrying amount of subsidiary assets and liabilities in the reporting currency.

SFAS 52 takes the first approach. It defines hyperinflationary as cumulative three-year inflation exceeding 100%.

With the parent (reporting) currency as the functional currency, use of the temporal method maintains the historical cost of nonmonetary assets and liabilities (most significantly, inventory and fixed assets) in the parent currency. Neither exchange rates nor price changes affect that carrying value. Cost of goods sold and depreciation expense are also measured in the parent currency. The temporal method includes gains and losses resulting from the remeasurement process in reported earnings. Companies operating in high-inflation countries generally try to balance their exposure (net monetary position) to the local currency by borrowing locally if necessary. Because they are frequently unable to do so, or the interest cost is too high, companies with large operations in hyperinflationary economies frequently report translation losses.

IAS 21 takes the second approach to accounting for subsidiaries in hyperinflationary economies.[22] The IASB standard does not, however, explicitly state when a country is considered hyperinflationary.

The two methods are broadly similar as they eliminate the problem of disappearing assets and liabilities. However, the two approaches are different and produce different measures of equity and income. As the IASB method does produce different results and the U.S. Securities and Exchange Commission does not require reconciliation to U.S. GAAP for these differences, analysts must determine whether the effect on comparability is material on a case-by-case basis.

Effects of Debt Denominated in Hyperinflationary Currencies

Borrowing in a high-inflation currency creates another analysis problem. Such currencies normally have extremely high nominal interest rates, as the lender must be compensated for the loss of purchasing power (due to high inflation). The high interest rate is acceptable because the borrower invests in comparatively inflation-proof assets and reduces its net monetary asset exposure. The high interest expense, in reality, is mostly offset by the purchasing power gain from the diminishing real value of the debt.

Aracruz, for example, uses the U.S. dollar as its functional currency but has some of its debt in Brazilian reals. This debt reduces the company's exposure to reals, reducing the potential for translation gains or losses that, under remeasurement, are included in reported income. Case 15-2 explores this issue in greater detail.

CHANGES IN FUNCTIONAL CURRENCY

The choice of functional currencies for a firm's foreign operations has a pervasive effect on the accounting for exchange rate effects. Companies do, on occasion, alter their choice for one or more foreign affiliates. A change in functional currency is considered a change in accounting estimate and may not be clearly disclosed. Even when the change is disclosed, the financial statement effects of that change are generally not disclosed, except when considered highly material.

---

[22]While Roche adheres to IASB standards, it accounts for its subsidiaries in hyperinflationary countries using the SFAS 52 method; the U.S. dollar and Swiss franc are used as functional currencies for such units.

Changes in functional currency are generally the result of one of the following:

- Change in subsidiary operations, resulting in determination that the functional currency is no longer the same. (The factors that determine the choice of functional currency are discussed earlier in this chapter.) Caltex, for example, changed the functional currency for its affiliates in Korea and Japan from local currencies to the dollar, effective October 1, 1997, due to changes in the regulatory environment.[23]
- Change in inflation rates that either classify the subsidiary currency as hyperinflationary, or remove it from that category. In recent years, the major examples have been Mexico, which moved out of the hyperinflationary category in the early 1990s, and Brazil, which moved out of that category in the late 1990s.

■ Example: Westvaco–Rigesa

Westvaco owns Rigesa, a packaging company located in Brazil. Westvaco's summary of significant accounting policies reports that

Due to the decline in the rate of inflation in Brazil in recent years, effective November 1, 1997, the Brazilian real became the functional currency for the company's Brazilian operations.

We can see the change from the consolidated statement of shareholders' equity. Starting in fiscal 1998 (which began November 1, 1997) there is a foreign currency translation adjustment for each year. Problem 15-9 is based on Rigesa. ■

ANALYTICAL DIFFICULTIES RELATED TO FOREIGN OPERATIONS

The all-current method lowers the volatility of reported earnings and produces financial statements and ratios closer to those under the local currency than the temporal method. However, it also generates two types of problems:

1. The lack of consistency or symmetry in the accounting for equivalent transactions
2. The economic interpretation of the financial statements generated by SFAS 52

These problems can be illustrated using the highly stylized environment of perfect markets. The following exposition summarizes work by Beaver and Wolfson (1982, 1984). The analysis is used to demonstrate the relationships among inflation, interest rates, and exchange rates that form the basis for much of the discussion that follows.

Relationships Among Interest Rates, Inflation, and Exchange Rates

Consider two countries, A and B, where the ratio of exchange rates between their currencies is 1:1 (1 LC_A = 1 LC_B). Let i_A = 1% and i_B = 6.8% equal the inflation rates of countries A and B, respectively. If we assume a real interest rate of r (equal in both countries) of 3%, inflation will result in a higher nominal interest rate R. In equation form, the relationship among inflation and real and nominal interest rates is

$$R = [(1 + i)(1 + r)] - 1$$

The (nominal) interest rates in countries A and B, respectively, are

$$R_A = [(1 + 0.01)(1 + 0.03)] - 1 = 4\%$$
$$R_B = [(1 + 0.068)(1.03)] - 1 = 10\%$$

Given these conditions, Exhibit 15-10 demonstrates that, *ceteris paribus*, the exchange rate at the end of the year should be 1 LC_A = 1.058 LC_B. This illustration can now be used to discuss the two analytical problems presented above.

---

[23]Note 7 of Texaco's financial statements refers to the change in functional currency, but provides no explanation.

EXHIBIT 15-10
Relationship Between Interest Rates, Inflation, and Exchange Rates

Given interest and inflation rates described in the chapter:

Country	Inflation Rate	(Nominal) Interest Rate
A	1%	4%
B	6.8%	10%

the exchange rate between the two country's currencies will be $1 \text{ LC}_A = 1.058 \text{ LC}_B$. This can be demonstrated by examining the effects on either nonmonetary or monetary assets.

Nonmonetary Assets

A nonmonetary asset with a cost of $P(0)$ at the beginning of a year will cost

$$P(1) = P(0)(1 + i)$$

at the end of the year. An asset that cost 1 LC (in each country's currency) at the beginning of the year (when the exchange rate is $1 \text{ LC}_A = 1 \text{ LC}_B$) now costs 1.01 LC_A in Country A and 1.068 LC_B in Country B. Since in real terms the assets are identical, they should carry an equivalent real price. That is, $1.01 \text{ LC}_A = 1.068 \text{ LC}_B$ or, equivalently, $1 \text{ LC}_A = 1.058 \text{ LC}_B$, the year-end exchange rate.

Monetary Assets

Under perfect markets, investors are indifferent as to where they invest. At the year-end exchange rate of $1 \text{ LC}_A = 1.058 \text{ LC}_B$, as the following table indicates, investors would be indifferent about investing in country A or B.*

Comparison of Return on $100 Investment

	Country A	Country B
Interest rate	4%	10%
Return on LC 100 After 1 Year		
In local currencies	104 LC_A	110 LC_B
Converted to Common Currency at Exchange Rate $1 \text{ LC}_A = 1.058 \text{ LC}_B$		
To currency A	104 LC_A	$110/1.058 = 104 \text{ LC}_A$
To currency B	$104 \times 1.058 = 110 \text{ LC}_B$	110 LC_B

*Otherwise, arbitrage opportunities would exist with money flowing into one currency from the other until the equilibrium of $1 \text{ LC}_A: 1.058 \text{ LC}_B$ was reached.

Consistency in Reporting

When the local currency is the functional currency, local currency–denominated assets and liabilities are translated at the current exchange rate at each balance sheet date. For monetary assets and liabilities, the result is reasonable: The parent company balance sheet includes the assets and liabilities in the parent currency at amounts similar to their fair value. For non-monetary assets and liabilities, that is not the case.

If a nonmonetary asset is purchased at the beginning of year 1 by a subsidiary located in Country B, it will be carried at the end of the year on the subsidiary's books at either the historical cost of 1 LC_B, or the current cost (if permitted) of 1.068 LC_B. Similarly, if the parent (located in Country A) had purchased the asset, it would carry it at either the historical cost of 1 LC_A, or the current cost (if permitted) of 1.01 LC_A.

However, SFAS 52 requires the assets of the foreign subsidiary to be reported on the parent's books at the historical cost divided by the current exchange rate or ($1 \text{ LC}_B/1.058 =$

0.95 LC$_A$), which is neither the historical cost (in LC$_A$) nor the current cost. The accounting result conflicts with the expectation, just discussed, that the real price should be the same in both countries.

This point can be reinforced through another example. Assume that a company builds two identical factories, at identical initial cost, one in the United States and one in Country G, where it has a subsidiary. Assume also that the currency of Country G appreciates relative to the dollar, rising by 50% over the next five years. If the currency of Country G is the functional currency for that subsidiary, the "cost" of the factory in that country will be 50% higher than the cost of the U.S. plant.

Presumably, the rise in Country G's currency is due to a lower rate of inflation. But the inflation rate does not change the asset's historical cost. The higher carrying amount for the factory in Country G (and higher depreciation expense as well) is not logical. It is equally absurd for a factory in a country whose currency depreciates against the dollar to decline steadily in carrying amount. Yet this is the consequence of the application of the all-current rate method. Financial ratios are also affected, giving improper signals regarding the performance of operations in different countries.

Selling and Sorter (1983) make this argument as follows:

> The balance sheet (and income) numbers provided under Statement No. 52 may be difficult to interpret. Under Statement No. 8, a historical cost . . . would be multiplied by the exchange rate prevailing at the time of the transaction to yield a dollar-denominated amount that is easy to interpret: It is simply a description of the actual cash flow that occurred in order to acquire an asset, translated at the dollar equivalent of that time period. The same local-currency-denominated historical cost multiplied by the current exchange rate (per Statement No. 52) yields a number that defies description: It is not a meaningful description of past cash flows, nor is it a description of future flows.
>
> Statement No. 52 further confounds interpretation . . . by requiring that these meaningless balances be consolidated with the accounts of the parent company. The result is an aggregation of parent company figures representing a history of the cash flows with a number that is neither fish nor fowl.[24]

This problem results from the use of historical cost for nonmonetary assets. If current costs were used and assets and liabilities were translated at current exchange rates, then balance sheet carrying amounts would have more meaning. Until current cost accounting is adopted, analysts must simply be aware that the carrying amounts of nonmonetary assets in nondollar functional currencies (and the original or reporting currency) are not representative of fair value and are distorted by changes in price levels and exchange rates.

These issues are compounded by generally inadequate disclosure in the financial statements of companies with significant foreign operations. Some firms provide extensive data on exchange rates but provide no data on their exposures to change in those rates.

The second and more serious problem created by SFAS 52: The accounting data may provide false signals regarding the economic impact of currency changes on foreign operations.

Economic Interpretation of Results

We noted earlier that one of the stated objectives of SFAS 52 was to provide information "compatible with the expected economic effects of a rate change." The standard does not meet that objective in many cases.

---

[24]Thomas Selling and George Sorter, "FASB Statement No. 52 and Its Implications for Financial Statement Analysis," *Financial Analysts Journal* (May–June 1983), pp. 66–67.

Using our example in Exhibit 15-10 of a 100 LC investment in monetary assets, assume that the parent firm in Country A has a subsidiary in Country B, whose functional currency is LC_B. Then, if we use the temporal method, the investment would be reported as follows:

	Subsidiary	Parent
Interest income	LC_B 10	$\dfrac{10}{1.058} = LC_A\ 9.5$
Translation loss		$100 \times \left[\left(\dfrac{1}{1.058} \right) - 1 \right] = \underline{(5.5)}$
Net gain		$LC_A\ 4.0$

This accounting reflects the economics of the transaction as the parent has earned (and reported) LC_A 4 during the year. Under SFAS 52's all-current method, however, the translation loss is not reported in the income statement. Income reflects only the interest income of 9.5 LC_A. Since the (monetary) asset is restated to 95 LC_A, the 10% nominal return relationship is maintained. However, the accounting result no longer accord with the economic reality.

Although this example is constructed in the realm of perfect markets, an examination of spot and forward exchange rates, as well as prime rates, indicates [see Beaver and Wolfson (1984)] that markets generally anticipate currency weakening and compensate for it by requiring higher *nominal* interest rates.

Other plausible scenarios also lead to accounting that distorts economic reality. First, consider a foreign subsidiary operating within the local environment, with no exports and no import competition. Such an operation is well served by SFAS 52. The parent company data largely replicate (in the reporting currency) the performance of the subsidiary in its local currency. The net investment in the subsidiary, the measure of exposure under SFAS 52, rises or falls depending on the exchange rate. When the local currency rises, the net investment increases in the reporting currency. The net investment is a fair proxy for the value of the investment to the parent.

However, consider a Brazilian manufacturing subsidiary that exports all output. All revenues are in U.S. dollars, whereas costs are incurred entirely in Brazilian reals (BRL).

If the BRL declines against the U.S. dollar, the subsidiary's BRL revenues rise (if we assume that prices in foreign currencies remain the same) while costs remain unchanged. The effect of devaluation of the BRL is to increase profit margins. Yet with the BRL as the functional currency, the accounting consequences are quite different from the economic impact. The U.S. parent translates Brazilian assets and liabilities at the lower exchange rate, and the U.S. dollar equity decreases (despite higher earnings). However, the economic impact of the declining BRL is to increase the subsidiary's net income and cash flows (in either currency) and therefore its value to the parent company. Case 15-2 uses Aracruz, a Brazilian company that uses the $U.S. as its functional currency, to explore these issues further.

Consider a third case, a British manufacturing subsidiary whose output is sold entirely within Great Britain and whose costs are incurred entirely in pounds sterling. If the value of the pound sterling rises, imports will enter, taking market share from the British subsidiary. The result is likely to be lower sales, lower earnings (price cutting may be necessary to keep market share), and lower cash flows. Once again, with sterling as the functional currency, the U.S. dollar net assets will increase. Yet the value of the British subsidiary has almost certainly declined, despite the higher currency exchange rate.

A partial answer to these contradictions is that accounting net worth is not meant to represent the value of a business. The role of accounting is to provide data that help users to make better investment decisions. Analysis of that data, and conclusions regarding the value of investments, are not part of that role. Analysts must not fall into the trap of believing that preparers and auditors have done their job for them. Although the examples given are superficial, they should suggest the need for a thorough analysis of the economic impact of exchange rate changes.

Impact of SFAS 8 and SFAS 52 on Management and Investor Behavior

SFAS 8 was one of the most unpopular standards ever issued by the FASB. Much corporate criticism was due to the volatility introduced into net income. Ziebart and Kim (1987) note that a number of studies reported that, as a result of SFAS 8, MNCs increased their hedging activities in the currency markets to hedge their "paper" (accounting) gains and losses rather than their underlying economic exposure. Such hedging activities are costly and can actually add to the firm's economic exposure. One can speculate about the motivations underlying this "irrational" hedging in terms of the various theories concerning investor and management behavior discussed throughout this book:

1. Management believed (rightly or wrongly) that its investors or creditors were fooled by volatile reported income.

2. The added volatility adversely affected the firm's contractual arrangements such as management compensation and debt covenants. At the very least, the volatility adversely affected the monitoring role played by financial statements.

3. The volatility lowered the predictability of the firm's income and future cash flows as the reported exchange gains and losses masked the underlying economic events. This added to the firm's uncertainty and risk.

Empirical studies did not address these motivational issues.[25] Rather they examined market reaction, hypothesizing that SFAS 8 was viewed adversely by the market and that the introduction of SFAS 52, with its dampening of earnings volatility, would result in positive market reaction.

Early studies (e.g., Dukes, 1978) could not document a negative market reaction to the introduction of SFAS 8. Ziebart and Kim[26] extensively analyzed the major events surrounding the inception of SFAS 8 in 1974 and its eventual replacement by SFAS 52 in 1980. They found the expected market reaction to adoption of the accounting standards. For two of the three events associated with SFAS 8, there is significant negative market reaction. The market reaction to the SFAS 52 exposure draft was significantly positive (as expected). Ziebart and Kim's results were generally consistent with negative effects associated with SFAS 8 and positive effects with SFAS 52.

Bartov and Bodnar (1994) demonstrated that the market found it difficult to understand the effects of changes in foreign currencies. They examined a sample of MNCs for which weakness (strength) in the dollar should translate into higher (lower) income.[27] Market prices would be expected to react in the quarter when the (known) changes in exchange rates occur. They found no significant reaction until the following quarter, when financial results for the previous quarter were reported. This lagged reaction suggests that mispricing does occur and a trading strategy designed to take advantage of this phenomenon generated significant abnormal returns.

Financial analysts also did not seem to fully appreciate the effect of the exchange rate changes. Examining whether analysts incorporate these effects in their forecasts, the authors note that analysts could have improved

the accuracy of their estimates by using information contained in the past movements of the U.S. dollar. These results also give further credence to the view that investors fail to correctly characterize the contemporaneous relation between dollar fluctuations and firm value when they form future expectations of the value of the firm.[28]

Interestingly, the study found that the lagged reaction, although it still remained, was somewhat mitigated after the issuance of SFAS 52. In a subsequent paper, Bartov and Bod-

---

[25]Some of these studies were commissioned by the FASB in response to the criticism of SFAS 8.

[26]Their methodology differed from previous studies in their calculation of abnormal returns. In addition, and perhaps more important, they used a shorter test period. Although previous studies used time periods ranging from five months to two years, Ziebart and Kim used (for all event dates) a two-month test period. Use of a shorter test period increases the possibility of finding abnormal returns since, if they exist, they are not "swamped" by other events.

[27]This higher income effect, as noted earlier, is not necessarily a function of the accounting method used.

[28]Eli Bartov and Gordon M. Bodnar, "Firm Valuation, Earnings Expectations and the Exchange-Rate Exposure Effect," *Journal of Finance* (December 1994), p. 1782.

nar (1995) found that the results depend on the firm's choice of functional currency. For firms using the temporal method, the lagged reaction remained; for firms using the all-current method, the lagged reaction disappeared. They hypothesize that these results reflect lower income statement volatility (inherent in the all-current method), perhaps enabling investors to assess more accurately the impact of exchange rate changes on firm income.

FINANCIAL REPORTING OUTSIDE OF THE UNITED STATES

International Accounting Standards

IAS 21 (1993) is similar to SFAS 52. Although the IASC does not use the term *functional currency*, it does classify subsidiaries into operations that are *integral* and those that are *foreign entities*. The clear implication of this distinction is that parent companies should use the temporal method to account for integral operations and the all-current method for foreign entities. For the latter, exchange gains and losses flow directly into stockholders' equity, bypassing the income statement as in SFAS 52.

For foreign currency transactions and integral operations the temporal method is required, with gains and losses on monetary items included in income (except for those arising from hedges and some long-term intercompany items). Recognizing that revaluations (e.g., fixed assets) are permitted in some countries, the standard requires that any revalued assets and liabilities be translated at the exchange rate at the date of revaluation.

IAS 21, like SFAS 52, requires use of the average exchange rate to translate all income and cash flow statement accounts of "foreign entities." The same analytical techniques used to assess the effect of exchange rate changes on U.S. companies can be applied to foreign firms using IASC GAAP.

IAS 21 has several important differences from SFAS 52:

- Its treatment of foreign subsidiaries in hyperinflationary economies. That difference was discussed earlier in this chapter.
- When goodwill and other fair value adjustments under the purchase method of accounting are carried only on the parent company balance sheet,[29] they may be translated either at the current exchange rate or the rate at the acquisition date.
- Exchange losses resulting from acquisition of an asset invoiced in a foreign currency can either be charged to income (as required by SFAS 52) or added to the carrying value of the asset in exceptional circumstances; that is, the currency cannot be hedged.

SUMMARY

Changing exchange rates introduce an additional layer of complication to the analysis of financial statements. The most significant insights in this chapter follow:

- The choice of functional currency is an important determinant of the accounting for foreign operations.
- Translation and remeasurement are fundamentally different accounting processes—both the definition of exposure and the disposition of exchange adjustments differ.
- Exchange rate changes distort all financial data for operations in currencies other than the parent (reporting) currency.
- The analyst's goal is to separate the effects of currency changes from actual operating changes; analysis can often approximate the currency effects.
- Accounting effects of currency changes are frequently different from the economic effects; analysis of the business is required to discern the impact of exchange rate changes on the value of a business.

[29]In the United States, such adjustments must also be made on the subsidiary balance sheet. See discussion of push-down accounting in Chapter 14.

Chapter 15

Problems

1. [Effects of functional currency choice; CFA© adapted] MasterToy has a foreign subsidiary, Nippon MT, that makes and sells toys in Japan. All of Nippon MT's operations and sales take place in Japan, transactions are denominated in Japanese yen, and the books and records are maintained in yen. The functional currency is the yen. MasterToy, the parent company, reports its earnings in U.S. dollars.

Exchange Rates: Yen/$U.S.

December 31, 1998	150
December 31, 1997	130
1998 Average	140
1997 Average	120
Exchange rate on date 1998 dividends were paid to the parent company	145
Exchange rate on the date of stock issue and acquisition of fixed assets	100

The 1998 balance sheet and income statement for Nippon MT are shown in Exhibit 15P-1.

a. Identify the method that MasterToy should use to translate the Japanese yen results of Nippon MT into U.S. dollars.

b. Calculate the 1998 balance sheet and income statement in $U.S. (showing the cumulative translation adjustment).

c. Explain how the decline in the value of the yen relative to the U.S. dollar affected Nippon MT's earnings in the reported currency in 1998.

d. Identify the alternative method for translating the Japanese yen statements of Nippon MT into U.S. dollars. State two circumstances that would require use of this method of translation.

e. Describe how this method would differ from the method used in part b.

EXHIBIT 15P-1. NIPPON MT
Financial Statements for Year Ending December 31, 1998 (in thousands of yen)

Statement of Income and Retained Earnings	
Sales	700,000
Expenses	
Cost of sales	280,000
Depreciation	126,000
Selling, general, and administrative	77,000
Total expenses	483,000
Income before taxes	217,000
Income taxes	(98,000)
Net income	119,000
Retained earnings December 31, 1997	250,000
	369,000
Dividends	(58,000)
Retained earnings December 31, 1998	311,000

Balance Sheet	
Assets	
Cash and receivables	60,000
Inventory	180,000
Land	200,000
Fixed assets	346,000
Total assets	786,000
Liabilities and stockholders equity	
Liabilities	300,000
Capital stock	175,000
Retained earnings*	311,000
Total liabilities and stockholders' equity	786,000

*Retained earnings on December 31, 1997, were U.S.$2 million.

2. [Effects of functional currency choice; ratio effects; CFA© adapted] Telluride has a wholly owned foreign subsidiary, Fuente, Ltd., whose functional currency is the local currency (LC). The 1999 balance sheet and income statement for Fuente are shown in Exhibit 15P-2.

The relevant exchange rates for Fuente are shown below.

Exchange Rates

Date	LC/$U.S.
At purchase of fixed assets (historic rate)	1.10
January 1, 1999	1.03
Average for 1999	0.95
December 31, 1999	0.87

a. Calculate the reporting currency ($U.S.) amounts, using the appropriate translation method, for Fuente's 1999 balance sheet and income statement.

b. Indicate, based on the all-current method, whether the following four ratios are the same or different in the reporting currency compared to the local currency. No calculations are necessary.

  (i) Return on assets

 (ii) Debt to total assets

(iii) Net profit margin

 (iv) Accounts receivable turnover

c. Indicate whether the following five ratios are the same or different under the temporal method compared to the all-current method. No calculations are necessary.

  (i) Return on assets

 (ii) Debt to total assets

(iii) Net profit margin

 (iv) Accounting receivable turnover

  (v) Quick ratio

3. [Effects of functional currency choice; CFA© adapted] On December 31, 2000, U.S. Dental Supplies [USDS] created a wholly owned foreign subsidiary, Funimuni, Inc. [FI], located in the country of Lumbaria. The balance sheet of FI as of December 31, 2000, stated in local currency (the pont), follows:

Funimuni, Inc.
Balance Sheet, at December 31, 2000
(ponts in millions)

Cash	180
Fixed assets	420
Total assets	600
Capital stock	600

EXHIBIT 15P-2. FUENTE, LTD.
Financial Statements for Year Ending December 31, 1999 (in LC millions)

Balance Sheet at December 31, 1999

	LC
Cash	15.20
Accounts receivable	3.80
Inventories	7.70
Fixed assets (net)	35.60
Other	12.10
Total assets	74.40
Current liabilities	13.30
Long-term debt	19.60
Total liabilities	32.90
Stockholders' equity	41.50
Total liabilities and equity	74.40

Income Statement, for Year Ended December 31, 1999

	LC
Revenue	47.10
Cost of goods sold	(16.90)
Depreciation	(3.20)
Other operating costs	(14.80)
Operating profit	12.20
Interest expense	(3.40)
Pretax income	8.80
Income tax expense	(3.20)
Net income	5.60

EXHIBIT 15P-3. FUNIMUNI, INC.
2001 Financial Statements

	Ponts (millions)	Exchange Rate (ponts/$U.S.)	$U.S. (millions)
Balance Sheet, at December 31, 2001			
Cash	82	4.0	20.5
Accounts receivable	700	4.0	175.0
Inventory	455	3.5	130.0
Fixed assets (net)	360	3.0	120.0
Total assets	1,597		445.5
Accounts payable	532	4.0	133.0
Capital stock	600	3.0	200.0
Retained earnings	465		112.5
Total liabilities and shareholders' equity	1,597		445.5

	Ponts (millions)	Exchange Rate (ponts/$U.S.)	$U.S. (millions)
Income Statement, for Year Ended December 31, 2001			
Sales	3,500	3.5	1,000.0
Cost of sales	(2,345)	3.5	(670.0)
Depreciation expense	(60)	3.0	(20.0)
Selling expense	(630)	3.5	(180.0)
Translation gain (loss)	—		(17.5)
Net income	465		112.5

FI initially adopted the U.S. dollar as its functional currency and translated its 2001 balance sheet and income statement in accordance with SFAS 52 (shown in Exhibit 15P-3). USDS subsequently instructed FI to change its functional currency to the pont.
Assume the following exchange rates:

January 1, 2001	3.0 ponts/U.S. dollar
2001 average	3.5
December 31, 2001	4.0

a. Prepare a balance sheet as of December 31, 2001, and a 2001 income statement for FI, both in U.S. dollars, using the pont as the functional currency for FI.

b. Describe the impact of the change in FI's functional currency to the pont on FI's U.S. dollar:

   (i) Balance sheet as of December 31, 2000

   (ii) 2000 income statement

   (iii) Financial ratios for 2000

4. [Interaction of inflation, inventory valuation, and foreign exchange effects; CFA© adapted] The Emerald Company has a wholly owned subsidiary in Hibernia, whose currency is the hib. Emerald reports its financial results in U.S. dollars. The exchange rate between the dollar and the hib follows:

December 31, 2001	$1 = 4 hib
December 31, 2002	$1 = 6 hib
2002 average	$1 = 5 hib

On December 31, 2001, the subsidiary acquired 100 units of inventory at a cost of 60 hib per unit. During 2002, 100 additional units were purchased at a cost of 75 hib per unit. On December 31, 2002, 100 units were sold at a price of 150 hib per unit.

a. Assume that the hib is the subsidiary's functional currency. Calculate the cost of goods sold and closing inventory in U.S. dollars using both the first-in, first-out (FIFO) and the last-in, first-out (LIFO) inventory methods.

b. Assume that the U.S. dollar is the subsidiary functional currency. Calculate the cost of goods sold and closing inventory in U.S. dollars using both the FIFO and LIFO methods.

c. Briefly discuss how *both* the choice of inventory method and the choice of functional currency impact reported income *and* inventory valuation during periods of rising prices.

5. [Effect of exchange rates on foreign sales] Note 12 of Takeda's fiscal 1999 annual report shows geographic data for sales to customers outside of Japan. The sales in North America and average exchange rates for the fiscal years ended March 31 were:

	1998	1999
Sales (yen millions)	53,753	82,717
Exchange rate	128.53	123.61

Assume that all sales in North America were made in U.S. dollars.

a. Compute the percentage change in sales to North America in:

   (i) Japanese yen

   (ii) U.S. dollars

b. Describe the expected effect of the exchange rate change on Takeda's operating profit margin on export sales to North America.

6. [Currency effect on revenues and balance sheet accounts] Holmen reports net turnover (sales), operating profit, and capital expenditures by country. The 1999 annual report shows the following net turnover (in Skr millions):

	1998	1999
Sweden	17,612	16,387
Great Britain	2,622	2,066
France	2,284	1,839
Holland	834	700
All other net*	(676)	(484)
Total	22,676	20,508

*Includes intercompany eliminations.

Assume the following average exchange rates:

Skr/Sterling	13.24	13.39
Skr/French franc	1.36	1.35

a. Compute the percentage change in sales for Great Britain and France in Swedish krona.

b. Using the exchange rate data provided, compute sales for Great Britain and France in their local currencies and the percentage change from 1998 to 1999.

c. Compare the percentage changes in local currencies (part b) with those in Swedish krona and discuss the differences.

d. Discuss the pitfalls of using the "local currency" data to draw conclusions about relative growth rates. Consider that much of Holmen's output consists of commodity products that are easily transported from one market to another.

e. The Swedish krona declined 4% against the British pound sterling in 2000, but gained more than 1% against the Euro. Discuss how you would use this information to forecast 2000 sales in Great Britain, France, and Holland.

f. Holmen's footnote 10 shows the effect of exchange rates on its fixed assets. Based on those data, state whether the Swedish krona rose or fell against the currencies of countries in which Holmen's non-Swedish manufacturing takes place. Justify your answer.

7. [Balance sheet effects of currency changes] Lucent Technologies [LU] has substantial foreign operations. The company's annual report for the year ended September 30, 2001 includes the following data (in $millions):

Years Ending September 30

	1999	2000	2001
Change in currency translation adjustment	$(33)	$(185)	$(30)
Effect of exchange rate changes on cash	41	10	4
Gain (loss) on foreign currency translation	(8)	(18)	(58)

a. State the information that these disclosures provide about Lucent's choice of functional currency for its non-U.S. operations.

b. State the information that the change in the CTA amounts conveys about the change in the value of currencies to which Lucent was exposed relative to the U.S. dollar.

c. Compare the effect of exchange rate changes on cash for each year with the change in the CTA for the same year. State for which year(s) the effect on cash is surprising and explain why. Provide one possible explanation for the surprising result(s).

d. Describe *two* possible sources of the gain (loss) on foreign currency translation.

8. [Disaggregating operating and exchange rate effects] Roche, a drug multinational headquartered in Switzerland, is greatly affected by exchange rate changes, as can be seen from its 2000 financial statements.

Before answering the questions that follow, examine the "foreign exchange rate" information on page 54 of the Roche statements. These data are presented as they are quoted on foreign exchange markets. The year-end 2000 rates are: $1 = 1.64 SFr; €1 = 1.52 SFr; SFr 1 = 143 JPY, where SFr is the Swiss franc and JPY the Japanese yen.

a. Compute the percentage change versus the Swiss franc for each of the three currencies listed, from 1999 to 2000, using the

  (i) Average rate for the year

  (ii) Year-end rate

b. State which of the three currencies had the greatest percentage change in 2000.

c. Describe the expected effect of the change in part b on each of the following amounts originating in that currency:

  (i) Revenues

  (ii) Operating income

  (iii) Operating margin

  (iv) Assets

  (v) Capital expenditures

d. Compute the percentage change in 2000 in each of the following, using the *geographical information* in Roche's footnote 4. *Assume that North American operations are conducted entirely in U.S. dollars.*

  (i) European Union sales

  (ii) North America sales

  (iii) European Union segment assets

  (iv) North America segment assets

e. Compute the percentage change in 2000 in each of the amounts in part d in local currencies (European Union in €; North America in $U.S.).

f. Roche's consolidated statement of changes in equity show currency translation adjustments for both 1999 and 2000. State whether the direction of those adjustments is consistent with the "foreign exchange rate" information and justify your response.

g. Roche's footnotes 12 and 13 show currency translation effects for tangible and intangible fixed assets respectively. State whether the direction of those changes is consistent with the change in the currency translation adjustment for 2000 and justify your response.

h. Assume that Roche used the Swiss franc as its functional currency worldwide. Describe the expected effect of that change on Roche's financial statements, including *each* of the following:

 (i) Balance sheet assets and liabilities

 (ii) Currency translation adjustment

 (iii) Revenue

 (iv) Cost of goods sold

 (v) Depreciation expense

 (vi) Foreign currency translation gains and losses

9. [Disaggregating operating and exchange rate effects] West-vaco's consolidated subsidiary, Rigesa, operates in Brazil. As discussed in the text, Westvaco uses the Brazilian real (BRL) as the functional currency for Rigesa. Westvaco's segment data include Rigesa for the three fiscal years ended October 31, 1999. Exchange rates for the years ended October 31 were (BRL per $U.S.):

	1996	1997	1998	1999
Exchange rate (average)		1.06	1.15	1.70
Exchange rate (closing)	1.03	1.10	1.19	1.95

a. Compute the percent change in each of the following for fiscal years 1997, 1998, and 1999 using the reported ($U.S.) data:

 (i) Sales

 (ii) Operating profit

 (iii) Capital expenditures

 (iv) Segment assets

b. Using the exchange rate data, compute each of the four items in part a in BRL.

c. Compute the percent change in each of the four items in part a for fiscal years 1997, 1998, and 1999 using the BRL data from part b.

d. Compare the results of part c with those of part a.

e. Explain why the percent changes computed in part c provide more useful information about Rigesa's operations.

f. Compute Rigesa's operating profit margin in both $U.S. and BRL. Explain why your answers do (or do not) differ.

The BRL exchange rate at October 31, 2000 was 1.90BRL per $U.S. The average exchange rate for fiscal 2000 was 1.83BRL per $U.S.

g. Compare the expected percent change during fiscal 2000 in $U.S. with the percent change in BRL (higher/lower/same) in each of the following:

 (i) Sales

 (ii) Operating profit

 (iii) Operating profit margin

 (iv) Segment assets

10. [Disaggregating operating and exchange rate effects] Consolidated income statements for the E&O Corporation follow (in $millions):

	2000	2001	2002
Revenues	$100.0	$110.0	$120.0
Operating expenses	(70.0)	(72.0)	(74.0)
Income taxes	(9.0)	(11.4)	(13.8)
Net income	$ 21.0	$ 26.6	$ 32.2

These statements include the operations of E&O's foreign subsidiary, Erzi Limited, which operates in a country whose currency is the LC. Erzi has no inventory and no fixed assets. Excluding the effects of Erzi, E&O's income statement was constant in years 2000 to 2002 at:

Revenues	$ 50.0 million
Operating expenses	(45.0)
Income	(2.0)
Net income	$ 3.0 million

Average and year-end exchange rates for years 2000 through 2002 follow:

	2000	2001	2002
Average	LC1 = $1.00	LC1 = $1.50	LC1 = $0.75
Year-end	LC1 = $1.50	LC1 = $2.00	LC1 = $0.50

As E&O's (unconsolidated) revenues and income were constant over the three-year period, all variations must result from the operations of Erzi.

a. Calculate how much of the observed growth in consolidated revenues and income over the 2000 to 2002 period resulted from Erzi's operations and how much was due to exchange rate changes.

b. Discuss how the choice of functional currency affected the U.S. dollar income statement.

11. [Analysis of foreign operations] Exhibit 15P-4 contains extracts from the *1991 Annual Report* of Commercial Intertech regarding its foreign operations. The effect of exchange rate changes on cash for 1991 was $(2,075,000); inventories at October 31, 1990 and 1991 were $59,762,000 and $51,777,000, respectively.

The foreign currency translation footnote discusses a subsidiary in Switzerland.

a. What was the functional currency used to account for that subsidiary? Explain.

b. What economic events caused the $3,213,000 gain to appear in the company's financial statements?

c. Discuss whether the $3,213,000 gain:

 (i) Should be considered operating income

 (ii) Should be considered 1991 income

d. Using the change in the cumulative translation adjustment, compute the composite effect of exchange rate changes on the company's foreign assets in non-dollar functional currencies. (*Hint:* Don't forget about the Swiss subsidiary.)

e. Using the result of part d, estimate Commercial Intertech's cash balances in non-dollar functional currencies.

f. Using the result of part d, estimate the effect of exchange rate changes on the company's inventories during fiscal 1991. Compare your result with the estimate derived from cash flow data and explain any discrepancy.

g. Do you agree with the statement that Commercial Intertech reduced its investment in its foreign subsidiaries? Why or why not?

h. The company's foreign sales declined from $233.5 million (fiscal 1991) to $229.1 million (fiscal 1992).

 (i) Considering only exchange rate changes, does this result surprise you? Why or why not?

 (ii) What additional information would be required to determine the effect of exchange rate changes on the trend of sales?

 (iii) Briefly discuss the other factors that affect the sales trend.

EXHIBIT 15P-4. COMMERCIAL INTERTECH
Selected Footnotes

Foreign Currency Translation

The cumulative effects of foreign currency translation gains and losses are reflected in the translation adjustment account of the balance sheet. Translation adjustments decreased shareholders' equity by $6,405,000 and $3,607,000 in 1991 and 1989, respectively, and increased equity in 1990 by $13,246,000. The translation adjustment account was further reduced by $3,213,000 in the current year due to the liquidation of an inactive subsidiary located in Switzerland. The liquidation, which was completed during the first quarter, increased income from continuing operations by $3,213,000 ($.31 per share after related taxes) as a result of recognized deferred translation gains in income. The gain is recorded as nonoperating income in the income statement.

 Foreign currency transaction gains and losses, as well as U.S. dollar translation gains and losses in Brazil, are reflected in income. For the three-year period reported herein, foreign currency losses have decreased income from continuing operations before income taxes as follows:

(in thousands)	
1991	$1,790
1990	95
1989	2,154

Net assets of foreign subsidiaries at October 31, 1991 and 1990 were $94,709,000 and $100,146,000, respectively, of which net current assets were $47,320,000 and $56,795,000, also respectively.

12. [Change in functional currency] The aluminum company Alcoa's 10-Q report for the quarter ended June 30, 1999 contains the following disclosure:

> L. Foreign Currency—Effective July 1, 1999 the Brazilian Real became the functional currency for translating the financial statements of Alcoa's 59%-owned Brazilian subsidiary, Alcoa Aluminio. Economic factors and circumstances related to Aluminio's operations have changed significantly since the devaluation of the Real in the 1999 first quarter. Under SFAS 52, Foreign Currency Translation, the change in these facts and circumstances requires a change to Aluminio's functional currency.
>
> As a result of the change, at July 1, 1999, Alcoa's shareholders' equity and minority interests accounts were reduced by $156 and $108, respectively. These amounts were driven principally by a reduction in fixed assets.

a. Explain why the change in functional currency reduced Alcoa's fixed assets, shareholders' equity, and minority interest.

b. Describe how the change in functional currency affects each of the following, as reported in Alcoa's financial statements:

 (i) Sales

 (ii) Cost of goods sold

 (iii) Depreciation expense

13. [Interaction of accounting for intercorporate investments and effect of exchange rate changes] The Ace Company uses the *equity method* to account for its foreign subsidiary (FC). (Note that the same accounting principles that apply to a consolidated foreign subsidiary apply to a foreign subsidiary on the equity method.) The subsidiary's functional currency is determined to be the local foreign currency.

 Ace purchased shares of FC, whose shares are traded on a stock exchange, for $1,000 at the end of year 0. At that time, the exchange rate was $1 = LC1. Based on the subsidiary's past performance, Ace expected its equity in FC's income to be $100 per year.

 Ace reported the following amounts with respect to its investment in FC:

	Year 1	Year 2
Income Statement		
Equity in income of affiliate	$140	$225
Cash Flow Statement		
Dividends from subsidiary	28	150

The company did not make any additional purchases (or sales) of shares in FC in years 1 and 2.

 The applicable exchange rates were:

Year 1	$1.40 = LC1	
Year 2	$1.50 = LC1	

To simplify the problem, assume that the average and year-end rates are identical.

a. Ace's equity in the net income of FC exceeded original expectations. Calculate how much of that excess was due to operations and how much to exchange rate effects.

b. The market value of Ace's investment in FC at year-end was:

Year 1	LC1,200
Year 2	LC1,300

(i) Calculate Ace's mark-to-market return (capital gains plus dividends) *in LC* on its investment in FC for years 1 and 2. Calculate the mark-to-market rate of return earned in those years.

(ii) Calculate Ace's mark-to-market return (capital gains plus dividends) *in U.S. dollars* on its investment in FC for years 1 and 2. Calculate the mark-to-market rate of return earned in those years.

c. Ace's balance sheet reported the following investment in FC:

	Year 1	Year 2
Investment in affiliate	$1,512	$1,695

(i) Show how these amounts were calculated.

(ii) Calculate the balance in the cumulative translation adjustment account at the end of years 1 and 2.

(iii) In the problem description, you were given the exchange rates for each year. Explain how you could have derived the exchange rates from the other data provided (investment in affiliate, equity in income of affiliate, dividends from affiliate).

Note that part c (i), (ii), and (iii) are really the same question asked three different ways.

14. [Interaction of acquisition methods and foreign currency effects] The AMREK Company acquired its foreign subsidiary, the FX Company, on January 1, 2000. AMREK issued shares whose market value was $2,000. The acquisition was accounted for as a purchase. No goodwill was recorded and the only asset to be restated to fair value was net fixed assets. The balance sheets of AMREK (in U.S. dollars) and FX (in LCs) just prior to the merger follow:

	AMREK	FX
Cash	$ 2,000	LC500
Accounts receivable	3,000	2,000
Inventory	1,500	500
Net fixed assets	5,500	1,000
Total assets	$12,000	LC4,000
Long-term debt	7,000	500
Stockholders' equity	5,000	3,500
Total liabilities and equity	$12,000	LC4,000

At the time of the merger, $1 = LC2.

To simplify the problem, assume that any exchange rate changes occurred immediately following the merger and rates remained unchanged thereafter.

a. Prepare AMREK's balance sheet after the merger.

b. Explain how the acquisition will be reported on AMREK's cash flow statement in 2000.

c. Briefly discuss how future income statements would differ if the acquisition were treated as a pooling.

The AMREK balance sheet on December 31, 2000 (including the assets and liabilities of FX) follows:

Cash	$ 1,000
Accounts receivable	4,500
Inventory	1,500
Net fixed assets	6,700
Total assets	$13,700
Long-term debt	7,300
Stockholders' equity*	6,400
Total liabilities and equity	$13,700

*Includes cumulative translation adjustment of $200.

d. Estimate the LC versus U.S. dollar exchange rate as of December 31, 2000.

e. Calculate the following amounts shown on AMREK's 2000 cash flow statement:

(i) Change in accounts receivable

(ii) Change in inventory

15. [Pooling versus purchase of foreign subsidiary] The ASU Company acquired the COL Company, its first foreign subsidiary, on January 1, 2000. To effect the acquisition of COL, ASU issued shares whose market value was $3,500.

COL's net assets (before restatement to fair value) at the time of the merger were LC3,000 and the exchange rate at that time was LC1 = $1.

The December 31, 2000 financial statements of ASU contained the following:

From the balance sheet	
Cumulative translation adjustment	$300
From the income statement	
Sales revenue	$600,000
From the statement of cash flows	
Exchange rate effect on cash	$20
From the geographic segment information	
Sales revenue of foreign subsidiary	$33,000

To simplify the problem, assume that any exchange rate changes occurred immediately following the merger and that rates remained unchanged thereafter.

a. Calculate the effect on the shareholders' equity of the merged company (at the time of the acquisition) if the merger was accounted for as a pooling rather than a purchase.

b. Assuming that the acquisition was accounted for as a pooling:

    (i) Compute the amount of COL's cash when it was acquired.

    (ii) Explain how the acquisition affected the statement of cash flows at the acquisition date and for 2000.

c. Assuming that the acquisition was accounted for as a purchase:

    (i) Compute the amount of COL's cash when it was acquired.

    (ii) Explain how the acquisition affected the statement of cash flows at the acquisition date and for 2000.

d. Your economic forecasters predicted that:

    (i) Exchange rates would be LC1 = $1.65 for 2001 and LC1 = $1.32 for 2002.

    (ii) Sales in the U.S. market will remain stable for 2001 and 2002.

    (iii) Sales volume in the foreign market will decrease by one-third in 2001 and rebound 25% (from 2001 levels) in 2002.

Using these assumptions, estimate the reported sales of ASU in 2001 and 2002, assuming that the acquisition was accounted for as a:

- Pooling
- Purchase

16

DERIVATIVES AND HEDGING ACTIVITIES

CHAPTER OUTLINE

CHAPTER OBJECTIVES

This chapter is concerned with transactions that firms use to manage the effect of price changes on assets, liabilities, reported income, and future cash flows. Our goal is to:

1. Define and illustrate the primary risks that firms may hedge, including foreign currency risk, interest rate risk, commodity price risk, risk of changes in market value, and event risk.

2. Examine the hedging techniques used to manage these risks, including forward contracts, options, and economic hedges.

3. Define and illustrate the types of hedge transactions:
   • Fair value hedges
   • Cash flow hedges
   • Foreign currency hedges

4. Discuss the recognition and measurement issues connected with hedge accounting, including the treatment of both realized and unrealized gains and losses.

5. Define, illustrate, and explain the accounting for embedded derivatives.

6. Explain the significance of hedge effectiveness in the accounting and analysis of hedge transactions.

7. Explain how financial statement disclosures can be used to gain insight into risks faced by the firm, its risk management activities, and the impact of these activities on reported financial statements.

INTRODUCTION

Businesses, faced with myriad risks, seek to protect themselves from the consequences of adversity. The purchase of property (damage) and casualty (liability) insurance is the most common risk management technique, one that is used by virtually all firms.

Some risks relate to the effect of price changes on the value of assets and liabilities and the amounts of contractual and forecasted future cash flows. The management of these risks is often referred to as hedging; in this chapter, we use the terms *hedging* and *risk management* identically.

Hedging is designed to protect the firm against adverse movements in prices, interest rates, and foreign currency exchange rates. Hedging transactions include, but are not limited to, *futures contracts, options, forward contracts, interest rate swaps, currency swaps,* and *combined interest rate and currency swaps.*[1] Firms may hedge existing assets and liabilities, *firm commitments*, and *forecasted transactions*.

Corporate hedging activities have grown due to management efforts to counter the economic and accounting effects of volatility of prices, interest rates, and foreign currency exchange rates. As financial markets have developed and instruments suitable for hedging have become more available, firms have increasingly used such instruments to control their exposure to these risks.

Hedges are employed to control or reduce price, interest rate, or currency exchange rate risks associated with:

- Physical or tangible assets such as inventories of commodities
- Assets with interest rate and/or currency exposure
- Liabilities with interest rate and/or currency exposure
- Firm commitments to purchase or sell raw materials or financial instruments, borrow funds, or repay debt
- Forecasted transactions such as acquisitions and the repatriation of funds, in addition to items included above

The primary financial reporting issues are:

- When to give financial statement recognition to derivatives and other hedging instruments
- Whether to recognize the fair (market) value of these instruments
- The conditions under which gains and losses on the hedge transaction can be deferred and matched with gains and losses on the assets or liabilities, firm commitments, or anticipated transactions being hedged.

This chapter addresses the financial statement effects of hedging transactions. Our objective is the assessment of the:

- Risks inherent in the business
- Hedging strategies used
- Outcome of these hedging activities

DEFINING RISK

For purposes of this chapter, we define risk as potential variability of financial outcomes, or uncertainty. Future financial outcomes of firm activities are uncertain because they depend on unknown future prices. In some cases, this price risk is uncontrollable as it depends on factors such as technological change. For example, the continuous decline in the cost of semiconductor chips has rapidly driven down computer prices.

Some price risks, however, relate to standardized commodities, interest rates, and foreign currency exchange rates. These risks can be managed by using *derivatives* and other

[1]Derivatives and other terms used in this chapter are italicized when first used and defined in the glossary in Box 16-1.

BOX 16-1
Glossary

Combined interest rate and currency swap (CIRCUS)	Interest rate and currency swap may be combined to convert both the nature (fixed or floating rate) and the currency of a series of payments. For example, an obligation to make variable rate payments in Japanese yen may be swapped for the obligation to make fixed interest payments in U.S. dollars.
Collar	A derivative that limits the effects of (foreign currency or interest rate) fluctuations beyond a predetermined range.
Counterparty or credit risk	Potential for loss due to the failure of the other party to discharge its obligations under a contract, for example, the uncertainty that firm will collect unrealized gain on a derivative from the other party to the transaction.
Currency swap	Contract that requires one firm to make payments in one currency in exchange for the obligation to make payments in another currency. Counterparties exchange the underlying notional (principal) amounts. (See *interest rate swap*.)
Derivatives	Financial instruments deriving their value from changes in the value of an index, interest or exchange rates, or another financial instrument (the underlying).
Duration	Weighted-average maturity of cash flows associated with bond. The market value of bonds with high duration is more sensitive to fluctuations in interest rates. For bonds with similar maturity and yield-to-maturity, a zero coupon bond (duration is equal to maturity) has a higher duration than a coupon-paying bond.
Embedded derivative	A financial instrument meeting the definition of a derivative that is a component of a hybrid contract.
Financial instrument	Cash, a contract that requires the delivery or exchange of cash or another financial instrument with another entity, or an ownership interest in another entity.
Firm commitment	Generally, a legally enforceable contract under which performance is probable because of significant penalties for nonperformance.
Forecasted transaction	One that is expected to occur, but is not subject to a firm commitment or contract.
Forward contract	Contractual agreement between a buyer and a seller to deliver an asset in exchange for cash or another financial instrument at a specified future date. Price is fixed at the contract date for the life of the contract. Forwards may be customized to fit the needs of the counterparties. (See *counterparty risk*.)
Futures contract	Standardized *forward contract* normally traded on an organized exchange. The contract is marked to market daily, and margin is required. There is little or no default (counterparty) risk since the exchange guarantees the contracts.
Hedge	Financial instrument or transaction used to manage risk exposure.
Highly effective	The degree to which the hedging instrument offsets changes in fair value or cash flows of the hedged risk.
Host contract	The nonderivative component of a hybrid contract.
Hybrid contract	A contract (not meeting the definition of a derivative) containing a host contract and an embedded derivative.
Interest rate swap	Contractual agreement to exchange fixed for floating-rate interest payments to effectively convert fixed to floating-rate debt. Alternatively, to exchange floating for fixed-rate interest payments to effectively convert floating to fixed-rate debt. In effect, an interest rate swap is a series of forward contracts based on interest rates (net payments must be made at specified intervals). Counterparties do not exchange or deliver the notional (principal) amount of the underlying debt instrument. The counterparties exchange only the interest payments resulting in a payment (net cash flow reflecting the difference between the fixed and floating-rate interest on the notional amount) by one counterparty to the other.
Notional amount	The number of units (commodity, currency, or principal amount) specified in a derivative.
Option	An agreement that gives one party the unilateral right to buy (call option) or sell (put option) a specified quantity at a specified price (the exercise price) until a specified maturity date.
Premium	Amount paid by one party to the other in return for an option.
Risk exposure	Vulnerability to adverse consequences; uncertainty, potential for loss, or degree of variability of outcomes.
Spot contract	Contractual agreement between a buyer and a seller to deliver an asset in exchange for cash or another financial instrument. However, delivery may occur at a later (settlement) date. For example, U.S. equity securities purchased in spot contracts are settled three days after the trade date.
Swap	Contract that exchanges one series of payments for another. (See *interest rate swap*, and *combined currency and interest rate swap*.)
Swaption	An option that gives one party the right (upon exercise) to require the other party to enter into a swap contract.
Underlying	The specified risk (price, exchange rate, interest rate) that is being hedged.

hedging techniques. We say managed rather than reduced because *risk management often involves replacing one risk with another one rather than reducing risk in an absolute sense.*

In the sections that follow, we examine each of the following risk categories:

- Foreign currency risk
- Interest rate risk
- Commodity risk
- Risk of changes in market value
- Event risk

Thereafter, we turn to the hedging techniques used to manage these risks.

Foreign Currency Risk

Firms that operate across national borders are exposed to the risk of changes in currency exchange rates. Pfizer, for example, reported that 39% of 1999 sales (and 49% of long-lived assets) were outside the United States.

In Chapter 15, we examined the effects of exchange rate changes on reported sales, income, cash flows, assets, liabilities, and net worth. These effects also distort financial ratios based on these data. The accounting risks faced by multinationals can be summarized as follows:

- Reported sales and earnings denominated in foreign currencies vary after translation, depending on the *average* exchange rate for the period.
- Reported cash flows denominated in foreign currencies vary after translation, depending on the *average* exchange rate for the period.
- Reported assets and liabilities denominated in foreign currencies vary after translation, depending on the *closing* exchange rate for the period.
- Expected foreign currency cash flows (e.g., a dividend expected from a foreign subsidiary) depend on the *actual* exchange rate when the cash flow takes place.

In Chapter 15, we also discussed the economic effects of exchange rate changes, which may be different from their accounting effects. Firms with foreign currency risk must, therefore, first decide whether to hedge the accounting risk or the economic risk of foreign operations. Some critics of SFAS 8 stated that the temporal method encouraged firms to hedge accounting risk (the effect of exchange rate changes on reported income). As discussed in Chapter 15, SFAS 52 redefined accounting risk rather than eliminated it.

Interest Rate Risk

When businesses borrow funds, the interest rate may be either fixed or variable, as discussed in Chapter 10. When the interest rate is variable, future interest expense and interest paid are uncertain as they depend on the future level of the reference rate (often LIBOR or the bank's prime rate).[2] From the lender (investor) point of view, variable rate loans or investments make future interest income and interest received uncertain. When the interest rate is fixed, however, future interest expense (income) and interest paid (received) are known.

Commodity Risk

Oil and gas companies like Texaco are engaged in the exploration, production, refining, and marketing of crude oil and natural gas. The revenues, expenses, and cash flows of these activities depend on the price of oil and gas, commodities whose price is the same for all producers and consumers.[3] Texaco cannot control that price and the related uncertainty of future financial results.

---

[2]In some cases, the spread may also vary. For example, it may depend on specified financial ratios or the debtor's credit rating.

[3]We ignore, in this discussion, the fact that there are different grades of oil whose price varies (as does the spread among them). These differences do not change the fundamental issues.

Other commodities have similar effects on firms that either produce or use them, including:

- Other energy sources such as coal
- Industrial metals such as iron, steel, aluminum, and copper
- Precious metals such as gold, silver, and platinum
- Agricultural commodities such as cotton, wheat, coffee, and sugar

Risk of Changes in Market Value

Fluctuations in foreign currency exchange rates, interest rates, and commodity prices can also affect the market value of assets and liabilities. For example, when the coupon rate is fixed, the market value of a bond varies inversely with interest rate changes.

One consequence of the interrelationship of income/cash flow risk and market value risk is that managing one risk necessarily changes the other. The fixed-rate bond has certain future interest payments (ignoring currency, credit, and prepayment risk) but uncertain future market value. Transactions that eliminate the market value risk (such as interest rate swaps) increase the income/cash flow risk. That is why we discuss risk management rather than risk reduction.

A second issue is that the accounting risk is often different from the market risk. When the fixed-rate bond is carried at amortized cost, changes in its market value have no impact on the reported balance sheet. But the economic (market) risk remains.

Event Risk

Sales and earnings of a given company are affected by innumerable events beyond its control. Firms can protect themselves, however, against some adverse events. For example, firms buy insurance against losses due to fire or storms.

Hedging is another form of insurance. For example, a firm whose sales depend on weather conditions can buy a derivative contract that pays an agreed-upon amount when temperature or rainfall exceeds (or falls short of) a specified level. Such contracts (known as weather derivatives) reduce the risk to the firm of abnormal weather conditions. Credit risk, the risk that the firm will not receive payment, is another form of event risk.

Many firms have more than one of these risk factors. For example, Barrick Gold [ABK], discussed in the next section, reported in its 2001 annual report that it was exposed to commodity price, interest rate, foreign currency, and credit risk.

HEDGING TECHNIQUES

Having discussed the risks that firms face, we turn to the techniques available to hedge them. These techniques fall into two general categories: derivatives and natural hedges. We start with a discussion of derivatives.

Forward Contracts

One way to eliminate the price risk of future transactions is to fix the transaction price in advance. Forward contracts accomplish that goal by fixing the:

- Amount and nature of the transaction
- Maturity date
- Price

For example, Barrick Gold has an extensive program of selling gold for future delivery. At December 31, 2001 the company had contracted to sell 22% of total gold reserves, including 50% of planned 2002 production. It also had made forward sales of silver, a byproduct of gold mining.

Barrick's earnings and cash flows from operations depend on the difference between sales prices and the fixed and variable expenses of their gold production. Forward sales lock in the selling price. The company's strategy[4] is to

set a minimum floor price to ensure sufficient cash flow to cover cash requirements for the year, including capital expenditures.

That strategy gives the company "security and predictability."

Forward contracts can be used to fix input costs as well. For example, AMR, which owns American Airlines (for whom jet fuel is a significant cost), enters into forward contracts to buy fuel at a fixed price. If the fuel price rises, the airline will use the contracted fuel instead of buying more expensive fuel in the open market. Alternatively, the profit on the forward contract offsets the higher cost of fuel. The effect of AMR's hedging strategy is discussed in the analysis section later in this chapter.

Forward contracts can also be used to hedge forecasted transactions. For example, DTE [DTE] expected to issue debt to finance the acquisition of MCN Energy. To protect itself in the event interest rates rose, the company entered into a series of interest rate swaps and other derivative transactions during 2000, in an attempt to lock in current interest rate levels.

In the end, DTE did not complete all planned transactions related to the debt and interest rates did not rise. In retrospect, the hedge was not needed by DTE. By the time the debt was issued in May 2001 and the hedge was terminated, the cost of the hedge to the company was $88 million. *The $88 million can be viewed as the cost of insurance*; $83 million of that cost will be amortized into earnings (as a component of interest expense) over the next 30 years (the term of the debt).[5]

The benefit of forward contracts is that the company can fix the outcome. In the DTE example, had interest rates risen and the expected financing taken place, DTE would have locked in lower interest expense. But forward contracts reduce the benefit of favorable price changes. In the AMR example, if fuel prices decrease the airline is locked into the higher contracted price.

Counterparty Risk

Forward contracts are private contracts between the buyer and seller and are often customized to meet the needs of the buyer. Both the buyer and seller assume *counterparty risk*, the risk that the other party to the contract will default. This risk is significant only to the party that has a gain on the contract; the party with a loss is unconcerned about the ability of the counterparty to perform.

Counterparty risk requires firms to use credit policies to minimize credit risk. Therefore, parties to forward contracts must evaluate the credit risk of the other party; collateral is often required. Firms may also use standardized netting agreements that enable them to offset positive and negative exposures with a specific counterparty. Barrick, for example, states in its 2001 financial statement footnotes that:

The Company's policy is to use master netting agreements with all counterparties.

Futures contracts are standardized forward contracts normally traded on organized commodity exchanges. Since the exchange clearinghouse is interposed between the two parties, it bears the counterparty risk. For this reason, exchange-listed futures contracts are marked to market daily, requiring additional collateral (margin) from the party with a loss on the contract.

---

[4]Quotes that follow are from page 21 of Barrick's 2001 annual report.

[5]As discussed in the next section, hedges of forecasted transactions are treated as *cash flow hedges*. Therefore, $83 million of the cost was initially charged to accumulated other comprehensive income. The remaining $5 million, relating to transactions no longer expected to take place, was expensed in the first quarter of 2001.

Swaps are combination forward contracts. For example, one party may promise to pay the other a fixed interest rate on a specified (*notional*) amount in return for a variable rate on the same base amount.[6] This interest rate swap encompasses two contracts: one covering the fixed rate payment, the other the variable rate payment. Swaps are frequently used for foreign currencies as well as interest rates. Interest rate and currency swaps can also be used in tandem. When evaluating interest rate swaps, it is important to distinguish between the notional (principal) amount that underlies the swap and the interest payments that are at risk.

Sears, for example, reports (2001 annual report, Note 5) that it uses interest rate swaps

> as a cost-effective means to synthetically convert certain of the company's fixed rate debt to variable rate.

The same footnote shows the following interest rate swap agreements:

December 31, 2000:   Pay fixed rate, receive floating rate $1.382 billion notional amount

December 31, 2001:   Pay floating rate, receive fixed rate $10.642 billion notional amount

Note that:

- The notional amount of the 2001 swaps is much higher than the 2000 level.
- Sears has moved from a variable-to-fixed swap in 2000 to a fixed-to-variable swap in 2001. This change may reflect changes in the mix (fixed versus variable rate) of Sears debt.

Options

An option gives one party the right to buy (call) or sell (put) a specified (notional) amount at a fixed price until a fixed maturity date. In contrast to a forward contract that requires performance (even when the transaction is unfavorable), an option provides its holder with flexibility. If the option is favorable (there is a gain) at maturity, it can be exercised. If the call option (strike) price is above the market price at the maturity date, the option is allowed to lapse without exercise.

The option buyer pays a *premium* to the seller to induce it to accept the price risk. If the option is not exercised, the premium is lost; flexibility does have a cost.

Exchange-traded options, like futures, have no counterparty risk. However, when option agreements are private, the buyer must consider counterparty risk. The seller, which receives its premium at inception of the transaction, has no such risk.

Returning to our airline example, AMR also purchases call options to hedge its exposure to jet fuel prices. If prices rise, the options can be exercised (obtaining lower-cost fuel) or the profit on the call options will offset the higher fuel cost. If prices decline, however, the option is valueless but the airline benefits from lower market prices. In this case the option purchase can be viewed as an insurance premium. The benefit of options relative to forward contracts is that AMR is not locked into any particular price.

Economic Hedges

An alternative risk management device is the economic or natural hedge. Such hedges exist when the effects of a price change on a firm offset each other. For example, if a firm can immediately pass through input price changes to its customers, such changes increase or decrease revenue and expense equally, leaving income unchanged.[7] For example, many gas and electric utilities in the United States are permitted to pass through changes in fuel prices to customers automatically.

---

[6]Swaps can be variable rate to fixed rate, fixed rate to variable rate, or one variable rate to another variable rate. See Chapter 10 for a discussion and illustration of interest rate swaps.

[7]However, gross margin percentage and similar ratios are affected even when the amount of gross margin remains unchanged.

Such pure economic hedges are rare. More commonly, output prices may reflect changes in input prices, but with both a time lag and variable effect. For example, changes in the price of crude oil impact the retail price of gasoline, but the spread between the two can vary significantly, making the profits of oil refiners quite volatile.

Interest Rate Matching

Financial intermediaries (banks, insurance companies, finance companies) devote considerable attention to their vulnerability to interest rate changes. Such intermediaries usually seek to maintain a fixed spread between their return on assets and their cost of funds (interest). Management must be concerned with both:

* Fixed versus variable interest rates on both assets and liabilities
* *Duration* of assets and liabilities

In an ideal situation, creating a perfect economic hedge, a given change in interest rates would have the same effect on revenue (interest income) and interest expense, leaving income unchanged. But revenue is unpredictable and its sensitivity to interest rates may depend on customer decisions (e.g., preference for fixed-rate versus variable-rate mortgages). Similarly, the cost of funds may depend on whether bank depositors prefer fixed-rate certificates of deposit or variable rate money market accounts.

Duration is an important indicator of the sensitivity of the market value of assets and liabilities to interest rate changes. It reflects stated maturity as well as the coupon and call (prepayment) characteristics.

Financial intermediaries seek to match the interest rate sensitivity of their assets and liabilities through product pricing and financing decisions. Mismatches can be rectified by using derivative instruments.

Foreign Currency Matching

Multinational enterprises have assets and liabilities in many currencies. They can minimize the effect of exchange rate changes on foreign subsidiary equity by minimizing their exposure to specific currencies, especially those expected to decline. One way of accomplishing this is to borrow in the weak currency, reducing the net exposure.

Revenues and expenses can be similarly matched, although it is difficult to do so for subsidiaries with many cross-border transactions. When unusual cross-border cash flows are anticipated, derivatives can be used to fix the exchange rate.

ACCOUNTING STANDARDS FOR DERIVATIVE INSTRUMENTS AND HEDGING ACTIVITIES

SFAS 133 (1998), Accounting for Derivative Instruments and Hedging Activities, and SFAS 138 (2000), Accounting for Certain Derivative Instruments and Certain Hedging Activities, established financial reporting standards for derivatives and for hedging activities under U.S. GAAP. IAS 39 (revised 2000) governs hedge accounting under IASB GAAP. These accounting standards are a significant departure from previous reporting rules and implementation has been complex. The FASB established the derivatives implementation group (DIG) to address application issues and to ensure consistent practice in accounting for derivatives and hedging activities.

These standards made fundamental changes in financial reporting for derivatives and hedging transactions. The most significant provisions, common to both U.S. and IASB GAAP, are:

1. All derivatives must be recognized in the financial statements.
2. All derivatives must be measured at fair value.
3. For derivatives that are not considered to be part of a designated hedge, changes in the market value of derivatives must be recognized in net income.

4. Changes in market value of derivatives used to hedge risk exposures (i.e. designated hedges) may be included

   - In net income, or
   - As part of other comprehensive income in the equity section of that balance sheet

   depending on the hedge's classification (fair value, cash flow, or foreign currency hedge as described below).

   When included in other comprehensive income, accumulated gains and losses are recognized in income when the underlying risk exposure is sold (or otherwise terminated) and reported in income in that period.

5. The accounting for the "hedged item" in the designated hedge is affected by that of the derivative. Thus, if an asset, carried at cost, is hedged, changes in the market value of the derivative also change the carrying amount of the asset by an equal amount (assuming full effectiveness).

6. When a derivative is not fully effective as a hedge, the ineffective portion of changes in the derivative's market value must be included in net income.

7. Derivatives can be used to hedge the following risk exposures:

   a. Fair value hedges: changes in the fair (market) value of recognized assets and liabilities, or of *firm commitments*[8]

   b. Cash flow hedges: variations in future cash flows related to recognized assets and liabilities, or of *forecasted transactions*.

   c. Foreign currency hedges: the effect of exchange rate changes on the net investment in a foreign operation, a foreign-currency denominated forecasted transaction, a recognized foreign-currency denominated asset or liability including an available-for-sale security, or a firm commitment. Foreign currency hedges may be either fair value or cash flow hedges.

   (We discuss each of these hedging categories in the following section.)

8. *Embedded derivatives*, such as the conversion feature of a convertible bond, must be separated from the "host" contract and accounted for as if it were a standalone transaction.

Box 16-2 contains details of some of the accounting provisions governing derivatives and hedge accounting under both U.S. and IASB GAAP. The principal provisions of the accounting standards are discussed in the sections that follow.

Recognition of Derivatives and Measurement of Derivatives and Hedged Items

Both SFAS 133 and IAS 39 contain measurement rules for derivatives and hedges. We examine each category in turn.

Derivatives Held for Trading

The gain or loss on derivatives not designated as hedging instruments (speculative or trading hedges) must be recognized currently in earnings.

■ **Example**

U.S. Lime [USLM] reported in its financial statements at December 31, 2001 that

> the company had commitments to purchase, under two forward purchase contracts, a total of 15MM/BTU [million BTU of natural gas] per month for the months of January, February, and March 2002. The delivery prices in dollars for these volumes averaged $3.51 per M/BTU. The market prices in dollars for deliveries in these months as of December 31, 2001 were $2.60 per M/BTU for January deliveries and $2.65 per M/BTU for February and March deliveries. The company elected not to designate these instruments as hedges for accounting purposes, accordingly the company has recorded a mark-to-market adjustment of $39,000.[9] ■

---

[8] IAS 39 requires that hedges of firm commitments be accounted for as cash flow hedges. However, in June 2002, the IASB proposed that firm commitment hedges be accounted for as fair value hedges, conforming to SFAS 133.

[9] The $39,000 loss is calculated as [($3.51 − $2.60) + ($3.51 − $2.65) + ($3.51 − $2.65)] × 15,000.

BOX 16-2

Accounting Standards Governing Accounting for Derivatives and Hedging Activities

This box discusses the provisions of accounting standards on derivatives and hedging activities under both U.S. and IASB GAAP:

- U.S. GAAP: SFAS 133 (1998) and SFAS 138 (2000)
- IASB GAAP: IAS 32 (revised 1998) and IAS 39 (revised 2000)

As the dates of these standards suggest, they were developed in parallel and there are relatively few differences.

Definition of a Derivative

Derivatives are *financial instruments* or other contracts with three distinguishing characteristics:

1. One or more *underlyings*, and one or more *notional amounts* or a payment provision or both.
2. No initial investment or a relatively low initial investment compared with alternative contracts or instruments with similar response to changes in market factors.
3. Net settlement is required or permitted*. Net settlement can be achieved outside the contract (e.g., through an options exchange) or by delivery of cash or another asset equivalent to net settlement.

Example: In an interest rate swap, one entity with fixed-rate debt may swap interest payments with a counterparty that has variable-rate debt. The swap qualifies as a derivative because:

1. It has an underlying, the basis for the variable interest rate such as LIBOR or the federal funds rate, and it has a notional amount, which is the face amount of debt in the swap. The payment provision is the formula used to calculate the net payment, for example, the notional amount of the debt times the difference between the fixed rate and the variable rate.
2. At inception, the fair value of the swap is either zero or very small, and it is measured as the present value of the payment provision over the life of the swap.
3. Net settlement is normally accomplished by exchange of the payment provision in cash.

Among the contracts specifically excluded are the following:

- *Normal purchases and normal sales*, which are contracts for delivery of something other than a financial instrument or a derivative that is used, purchased, or sold in the operations of the reporting entity.

   Example: Barrick Gold enters into spot deferred sales contracts that qualify for the normal purchases and sales exemption. The contracts are not treated as derivatives and neither the fair value nor changes in the fair value of these contracts are reported on Barrick's balance sheet. The MD&A reports the notional value of these contracts as $5.5 billion.

   This exception encompasses virtually all contracts that firms enter into for the purchase of inputs and sale of outputs.

These contracts receive income statement recognition only when they result in transactions unless they are so burdensome that the firm chooses to recognize the loss.

   Example: Sunoco [SUN] had a take-or-pay contract† for a gasoline additive known as MTBE. However, in 1996, Sunoco recognized a pretax loss of $130 million, recognizing the expected loss as the contract price was expected to remain above the market price. The loss provision was increased by $40 million pretax in 1998.

- *Instruments indexed to an entity's own stock and reported in stockholders' equity, stock-based compensation contracts, and contingent consideration issued by the purchaser.*

   Example: Microsoft [MSFT] sold put options on its own common shares in connection with its stock purchase program. When Microsoft shares were rising, the put options expired, generating substantial cash flow to the company. However, when MSFT shares declined, the company was required to purchase shares at above-market prices. In fiscal 2001 the company issued 2.8 million shares to settle a portion of those options.

   Although the put options were derivatives, Microsoft did not have to account for them under SFAS 133 and recognize gains or losses because the underlying was the company's own shares. The cash flows from the program were reported in cash from financing activities (in $millions):

Years Ended June 30

	1999	2000	2001
Sales/(repurchases) of put warrants	$766	$472	$(1,367)

Identical amounts were reported as changes in stockholders' equity.

- *Financial guarantee and insurance contracts* that are not traded on an exchange or contract in which settlement depends on the occurrence of an insured event (theft, fire, or a hurricane) rather than a change in a variable such as price (specified amount of damages or financial loss). However, contracts that combine insurance and nonderivative contracts with derivative instruments (variable life insurance contracts and indexed annuities) are hybrid contracts, whose embedded derivative must be accounted for separately (see below).

- *Regular-way* securities trades, which call for delivery of securities within a time frame established by the market where the trades are executed. These contracts have no net settlement provisions or market mechanisms to permit net settlement.

- *Derivatives that preclude sales accounting,* such as when sales-type lease accounting cannot be used because of residual-value guarantees of leased assets.

Hedge Effectiveness

IAS 39 requires (para. 142b) that:

> The hedge is expected to be highly effective in achieving offsetting changes in fair values or cash flows attributable to the hedged risk, consistent with the originally documented risk management strategy for that particular hedging strategy.

SFAS 133 has similar language. What this means in practice is that:

1. The hedge is expected to be effective at hedge inception.
2. The firm must state (at inception) how hedge effectiveness will be measured.
3. Hedge effectiveness must be measured at each financial reporting date.[‡]

Accounting for Embedded Derivatives

Embedded derivatives must be separated from the host contract and accounted for as derivatives if and only if *all* of the following conditions are met:

- The embedded derivative has economic characteristics and risks that are unrelated to the economic characteristics and risks of the host contract.
- GAAP do not require reporting of the hybrid instrument at fair value with changes in fair value reported in earnings.
- A separate instrument with the same terms as the embedded derivative would meet the definition of a derivative.

Example: An investment in a convertible bond (hybrid instrument) reported as an available-for-sale security. The debt component is the host contract and the conversion feature (option on the underlying common stock) must be treated as an embedded derivative as it satisfies all three conditions:

1. Because the fair value of the debt component is a function of interest rates and the creditworthiness of the issuer, whereas the fair value of the conversion option depends entirely on the value of the underlying common stock, they have clearly different economic characteristics and risks.
2. Although available-for-sale securities must be reported at fair value, changes in that fair value are reported as a component of other comprehensive income in stockholders' equity.
3. The conversion feature meets the definition of a derivative because it has an underlying (the common stock), the investment in the option is generally significantly lower than that of the underlying common stock, and similar options can be net settled.

The separate host contract, debt in our example, must be accounted for under GAAP applicable to similar instruments. The qualifying embedded derivatives must be separated from the host contract and may be designated as hedges of identified exposures. See the Alliant Energy example in the chapter.

If an entity cannot reliably identify and measure the embedded derivative, the hybrid contract must be reported at fair value and changes in fair value must be reported in earnings and the contract is not eligible for hedge or offset accounting.

General Disclosure Requirements for All Designated and Qualifying Hedging Instruments

For each type of hedge, the entity must disclose its:

- Objectives for holding or issuing derivatives
- Risk management policy, including a description of the hedged items or transactions

Exhibits 16-3 (IBM) and 16-4 (AMR) are typical examples of these disclosures.

Disclosure Requirements Common to Fair Value and Cash Flow Hedges

- The net gain or loss recognized in earnings during the reporting period from
  - Hedge ineffectiveness
  - Any component of the derivative instruments' gain or loss excluded from the assessment of hedge effectiveness

Additional Disclosure Requirements for Fair Value Hedges

- Where the net gain or loss is reported
- The amount of net gain or loss recognized in earnings when a hedged firm commitment no longer qualifies as a firm commitment

Additional Disclosure Requirements for Cash Flow Hedges

- At the reporting date, a description of transactions or other events that will result in the reclassification into earnings of gains or losses reported in other comprehensive income, and the net amount of gains or losses expected to be reclassified into net income over the next twelve months
- The maximum time period over which the entity has hedged its exposure to the variability in future cash flows for forecasted transactions
- The amount of gains or losses reclassified into earnings due to the discontinued cash flow hedges because it is probable that the original forecasted transactions will not occur

---

[*]IAS 39 requires only future settlement.

[†]As discussed in Chapter 11, these contracts are a form of off-balance-sheet financing.

[‡]In practice, the dollar offset (comparison of historical changes in the fair value of the hedged item and the hedging mechanism) ratio is used to assess level of effectiveness:

$$0.8 < -1 \times \text{(Gain (loss) on the derivative/Gain (loss) on the hedged item)} < 1.25$$

Hedge accounting is not permitted when the 0.8–1.25 range is violated even if the dollar offset justifies hedge accounting. However, the entity can continue to apply hedge accounting if an alternative statistical analysis satisfies hedge accounting criteria even if the 0.8–1.25 range is violated. Continued application of hedge accounting requires new analysis of effectiveness in subsequent periods.

Hedge Qualification Criteria

To qualify for hedge accounting treatment, the firm must

- Formally document the hedge.
- Disclose its risk management objectives, and the strategies used to achieve those goals.
- Identify both the hedged item or transaction and the hedging instrument.
- Identify the nature of the risk being hedged.
- Demonstrate the effectiveness of the hedge, stating the methods used to assess that effectiveness.

In cases where the hedged item is subject to multiple risks, the firm may hedge only part of the risk. For example, an investment in a fixed-rate corporate obligation denominated in a foreign currency is subject to the following risks:

- Interest rate risk
- Credit risk
- Foreign currency risk

Any one (or more than one) of these risks can be hedged. However, partial hedging does not fully eliminate the investment risk.[10]

Types Of Hedges

There are two principal types of hedges under both U.S. and IAS GAAP: fair value and cash flow hedges. Foreign currency hedges can be of either type but the term encompasses other forms of hedges as well. We discuss each of these in turn.

Fair Value Hedges

Some transactions hedge the risk of changes in the fair value of a recognized asset or liability, or of a firm commitment.[11] The following are examples of risk exposures that can be mitigated by fair value hedges:

- The market value of a fixed-income investment (or a portfolio of similar fixed-income investments) that is not designated as "held-to-maturity"
- The market value of inventories
- The market value of a fixed-rate debt obligation
- The market value of a firm commitment
- The effect of exchange rate changes on an available-for-sale investment denominated in a foreign currency

Derivatives designated as fair value hedging instruments are marked to market and any gain or loss must be recognized in earnings. The change in market value of the hedged item due to the specified risk factor is also recognized in earnings; the carrying amount of the hedged item is adjusted by the same amount. As a result, the effect on reported income will be zero if the hedge is fully effective. If the hedge is not fully effective, the noneffective portion of the market value changes does affect income.

[10]Hedge effectiveness (discussed below) would be evaluated relative to the hedged risk alone.

[11]Note that a firm commitment, although similar to a forward contract, is not considered a derivative because it is generally not settled by a cash payment of the net settlement price difference (see Box 16-2). However, the firm commitment can be considered a "hedged item" when it is hedged by a forward contract in the other direction. See below for further discussion of this issue.

■ **Example**

Bellerose Oil reports the following on December 31, 2001:

Inventory (10,000 gallons of fuel oil) $10,000

On that date Bellerose sells a futures contract, maturing December 31, 2002, at a price of $1.20 per gallon (notional value = $12,000). No cash is paid or received. By entering into the hedge, Bellerose has ensured that it will earn a $2,000 profit on the inventory.

    On March 31, 2002, the futures price for that contract is $1.30 per gallon, giving the contract a fair value of $13,000.

- Bellerose will record the following items in net income (ignoring tax effects):

Recognized gain on inventory	**$ 1,000**
Loss on forward contract	**$(1,000)**

Because the hedge is fully effective, there is no net effect on reported income.

- At March 31, 2002, Bellerose will report the following on its balance sheet:

Inventory (10,000 gallons of fuel oil)	**$11,000**
Forward contract liability	**$1,000**

The $1,000 loss on the forward contract is shown as a liability;[12] the carrying value of inventory is increased by an equal amount.

    Now assume that the inventory and futures contract are sold on June 30, 2002 and that prices have not changed since March 31. The income statement entries follow:

Revenue [10,000 gallons at $1.30/gallon]	$13,000
Cost of goods sold	(11,000)
Gross margin	$ 2,000

Note that gross margin is 15.4% ($2,000/$13,000). If the hedge had not been entered into, profit would have been higher by $1,000 and the gross profit margin would have been 23.1% ($3,000/$13,000).

    If the price of fuel oil had fallen by $1,000, the gross profit would have been $1,000 less and the margin would have been 9.1% ($1,000/$11,000). The hedge protected Bellerose against a price decline at the cost of giving up the possible holding gain from price increases. ■

Hedging is a strategic decision, and can have a significant effect on profitability.

    Before proceeding to cash flow hedges, note that, as a result of the hedge, inventory (the hedged item), which is normally carried at cost, is now marked-to-market. Changes in its market value flow through earnings as an offset to the gains or losses on the derivative. Similarly, if derivatives were used to hedge a security carried as "available-for-sale," changes in the security's market value would no longer be charged to other comprehensive income but would flow directly to earnings. *Accounting for the hedged item follows that of the derivative.*

    Another effect of this principle occurs when firm commitments are hedged. Absent the hedge, the firm commitment is off balance sheet. No asset or liability is recognized at the

---

[12]The liability is removed when the $1,000 is paid upon settlement of the forward contract.

time of the commitment and any changes in its value are unrecognized in the financial statements. However, when the firm commitment is hedged by a derivative, the firm commitment is given balance sheet recognition[13] and changes in its fair value are charged to earnings as an offset to the derivative.

Cash Flow Hedges

Cash flow hedges are intended to mitigate the volatility of future cash inflows and outflows. The following are examples of hedged items under cash flow hedges:

- Interest income on variable-rate investments.
- Interest expense on variable-rate debt.
- Forecasted transactions or a group of transactions with the same risk characteristics. Forecasted transactions must be probable, for example, an issue of debt expected when a pending acquisition is completed.
- Expected receipt of a payment denominated in a foreign currency.

Derivatives designated as cash flow hedging instruments are marked to market and the effective portion of any gain or loss must be reported as a component of other comprehensive income. The accumulated gain or loss is recognized in earnings in the same period or periods in which the hedged item affects earnings. Any ineffective portion of the derivative gain or loss must be recognized currently in earnings.

■   **Example**

The Chelsea company expects to receive a payment of €1 million on June 30, 2002. On January 1, 2002, it sells a forward contract, maturing June 30, 2002 on €1 million at an exchange rate of $.89 per €1.00, locking in a dollar value for the receipt of $890,000.

On March 31, the exchange rate was $.87 per €1.00. As the euro has declined by $.02, there is a gain on the forward contract of $20,000 ($.02 × €1 million). That gain is excluded from net income but is recorded in the carrying value of the derivative and in comprehensive income as follows.

Forward Contract	**$20,000**	
Comprehensive income		**$20,000**

The exchange rate on June 30, 2002 was $.99 per €1.00. As the euro has gained $.12 since March, there has been a loss of $120,000 on the forward contract over this period requiring the following entries:

Comprehensive income	**$120,000**	
Forward contract		**$120,000**

The balance sheet now shows a loss of $100,000 in comprehensive income and a derivative liability equal to that amount.

When Chelsea receives payment, it realizes $.99 million by converting the euro payment at the current exchange rate. However, Chelsea must settle the forward contract at its current market value of $.99 million by paying $100,000[14] and recognizing a loss

---

[13]The balance sheet recognition equals *only* the change in fair value of the hedging derivative, not the entire fair value of the firm commitment.

[14]The payment removes the derivative liability of $100,000.

of $100,000 ($990,000 − $890,000). The result is that Chelsea's income statement for the three months ended June 30 reports the following:

Loss on settlement of forward contract	**$100,000**
Reclassification from comprehensive income	**$100,000**

The net result is that Chelsea receives $890,000, the amount of the receivable translated at the exchange rate ($0.89) implicit in the hedge. As long as the hedge is fully effective, exchange rate variations have no effect on net income. Chelsea has achieved its objective of creating certainty about the $ amount of the receivable. Had it not hedged, it would have received $990,000, based on the exchange rate at the payment date. Risk reduction has eliminated the potential for gain as well as loss. ■

The distinction between a cash flow hedge and a fair value hedge lies in the hedged item (what the derivative is hedging), not in the derivative itself. A fair value hedge is designed to hedge changes in market value whereas a cash flow hedge is intended for situations where market value is not at risk but the level of cash flows is.

An interest rate swap, where the company receives variable/pays fixed, would be part of a cash flow hedge if it was undertaken as a hedge of variable-rate debt. If, on the other hand, the hedged item was a fixed-rate mortgage receivable, the hedge would qualify for fair value accounting treatment.[15]

Foreign Currency Hedges

In addition to foreign currency hedges that are fair value or cash flow hedges, SFAS 133 and IAS 39 also permit companies to hedge the net investment in a foreign operation. This is an exception to the fundamental principle of limiting hedge accounting to specific rather than enterprisewide exposures and the limitation of hedge accounting to portfolios of similar exposures.[16]

The gain or loss on the derivative or nonderivative hedging instrument in a hedge of a net investment in a foreign operation must be reported in other comprehensive income as part of the cumulative translation adjustment (CTA). The CTA remains in comprehensive income until the foreign operation is sold, liquidated, or considered impaired. Any ineffective component of the gain or loss on the hedging instrument must be recognized currently in earnings.

■ **Example**

Applied Industrial Technologies [AIT] entered into two cross-currency swaps in November 2000 to hedge its investment in its Canadian subsidiary. The swaps effectively converted $25 million of debt from $U.S. to $Canadian obligations. The fair value of the $20 million swap accounted for as a foreign currency cash flow hedge was $504,000 on June 30, 2001. That amount was recorded as an asset, with a corresponding amount (the deferred gain) recorded in comprehensive income.[17] ■

Embedded Derivatives

Some transactions create derivatives that are included within assets or liabilities. Examples include convertible securities, structured notes, and other securities with embedded options. Both SFAS 133 and IAS 39 require that embedded derivatives included in *hybrid*

---

[15]See Problem 16-14.

[16]In another departure from the basic principles, SFAS 133 permits the use of nonderivatives as hedges of a net investment in a foreign operation.

[17]The remaining $5 million swap was not accorded hedge treatment; its $126,000 fair value at June 30, 2001 was included in net income.

contracts be separated from the *host contract* and accounted for as if they were stand alone derivatives.

■ Example

Alliant Energy [LNT] issued $402.5 million of notes in February 2000 that are exchangeable at maturity for the value of shares of McLeod [MCLD] held by Alliant as a held-for-trading investment.[18] The notes have a stated interest rate of 7.25% for three years, and 2.5% thereafter, with a maturity date of 2030. At maturity, the noteholders will receive the higher of the face amount of $402.5 million or the value of the underlying McLeod shares. The hybrid contract (exchangeable note) is separated into its two components:

1. *Host contract:* notes issued at a discount, which must be amortized over the life of the bond, using the interest method (see Chapter 10)
2. *Derivative:* bondholders' exchange option, reported at fair value

At December 31, 2001, the carrying amount of the notes (host contract) was $56.1 million.[19] Interest expense is recorded at the effective interest rate of 26.8%. The difference between interest expense and interest paid adjusts the carrying amount of the debt. At maturity the debt discount will be fully amortized.

The value of the underlying McLeod shares declined from $220.9 million at December 31, 2000 to $5.8 million at December 31, 2001. As the shares are trading securities, the decline reduced Alliant's pretax income by $215.1 million. However, the fair value of the derivative liability (the exchange option) also declined, by $181.6 million, due to the decline in the market price of McLeod shares. As this decline was also included in Alliant's pretax income, the net effect was a pretax income reduction of $33.5 million.[20]

By issuing the exchangeable notes, Alliant was able to hedge a portion of its McLeod investment at the high price of McLeod shares in February 2000.[21] Assuming that McLeod shares never recover to their former price level, Alliant will have borrowed $402.5 million at a low effective interest rate. However, due to the requirements of SFAS 133, Alliant's income is affected by significant price movements in McLeod shares.   ■

Hedge Effectiveness

Effectiveness is a measure of the hedging instrument's ability to offset changes in the fair value or cash flows of the hedged item or transaction.

In order to qualify for hedge accounting treatment, the hedge is expected to be *highly effective* both at the inception and during the hedge term. Effectiveness must be measured and reported at least every quarter and whenever earnings are reported.[22] When a hedge ceases to be highly effective, hedge accounting must be terminated.

---

[18]Prior to adoption of SFAS 133, Alliant held the McLeod shares as available-for-sale. Upon adoption, Alliant reclassified the McLeod shares underlying the exchangeable notes as trading securities, recognizing a gain of $321 million. Following this reclassification, changes in the fair value of the embedded derivative are offset by changes in the market value of the shares held-for-trading.

[19]Given the value of McLeod shares at February 2000, most of the $402.5 million proceeds from the hybrid contract were allocated to the conversion option.

[20]Alliant reports that amount in its statement of cash flow as "non-cash valuation changes from exchangeable senior notes and McLeod trading securities." In Alliant's income statement, the net loss is included in "miscellaneous, net."

[21]Alliant had agreements with McLeod that restricted share sales.

[22]Hedge ineffectiveness may be due to differences in

- Notional and principal amounts for the derivative and hedged item
- Maturity or repricing dates
- Underlying interest rate bases (e.g., variable-rate debt at the federal funds rate, swap at LIBOR)
- Currencies
- Credit quality

For some hedges, effectiveness is not an issue. The hedges described in the Bellerose and Chelsea examples above are effective because derivatives exactly match the underlying risk (price of fuel oil and €/$ exchange rate respectively). In such cases changes in market value of the derivatives will completely offset changes in market value of the underlying.

Some risks, however, cannot be hedged so precisely. When hedging instruments that match the risk of the hedged item are not available, the firm must consider using hedges that have high correlation. Examples would be:

- Using derivatives based on heating oil to hedge changes in the price of aircraft fuel. While the price of both products fluctuates with the price of crude oil, price movements are less than 100% correlated. AMR reported $72 million of expense due to hedge ineffectiveness in 2001.

- Using derivatives based on a commodity price in one location to hedge the price of the same commodity in another location. For example, crude oil is traded in London and New York but actual production and sale takes place in neither location.

- Using derivatives based on one interest rate index to hedge interest payments based on another index. The two indices may move together but the spread between them may change. However, companies are permitted to designate a benchmark interest rate as the hedged risk, even when the underlying cash flows are based on another rate.

When a hedge is not fully effective, the ineffective portion of changes in the market value of the hedging instrument must be recognized in net income.

Hedge Termination

Hedge accounting must be discontinued when

- The hedge is no longer effective.
- The hedge qualification criteria are no longer satisfied, for example, when a forecasted transaction is no longer probable.
- The derivative expires or is sold, terminated, or exercised.
- The hedge designation is removed.

However, hedge termination does not always result in recognition of gains and losses on derivatives:

- *Fair value hedges.* As accumulated gains and losses are included in the carrying amount of the hedged asset or liability, they remain on the balance sheet until that asset or liability is sold.

- *Cash flow hedges.* Accumulated gains and losses on forecasted transactions are recognized in income when that transaction affects reported income (e.g., through interest expense, depreciation expense, or cost of goods sold). However, when the hedge is terminated because the *forecasted transaction* takes place, accumulated gains and losses are recognized over the life of the forecasted transaction (see DTE example under "Forward Contracts" earlier in the chapter).

- *Foreign currency hedges.* Accumulated gains and losses remain in the currency translation adjustment until the foreign operations are sold, liquidated, or considered impaired.

Effect of Hedging on Impairment

Neither SFAS 133 nor IAS 39 exempt hedged assets and liabilities from impairment reviews even though the carrying amount of the hedged item includes changes in fair values. Because the hedging instrument is reported separately as an asset or liability, neither its fair value nor the expected cash flows should be considered in assessing impairment of the hedged item.

Disclosure Requirements

Both SFAS 133 and IAS 39 require extensive disclosures regarding derivatives and hedge activities:

- General disclosures with respect to objectives and strategies
- Specific disclosures for fair value, cash flow hedges, and for hedges of net investment in foreign operations, including gains and losses recognized in net income and included in comprehensive income.[23]

Details of the disclosure requirements are contained in Box 16-2. We will review the usefulness of these disclosures in the "Analysis of Hedging Disclosures" section of this chapter.

Related Financial Reporting Requirements

Fair Value Disclosures

SFAS 107 (1991) requires the disclosure of market values for all financial instruments (on and off balance sheet). It exempts insurance contracts, leases, equity investments, and trade receivables and payables. Firms must disclose assumptions and methods used to develop estimates of fair values. Additional narrative disclosures are required if it is not practicable to estimate fair values. In keeping with the exploratory nature of these standards, the board did not specify or limit estimation methods but instead asked for qualitative information. IAS 39 has similar requirements.

■ Example

American Express [AXP] reports carrying value and fair value for groups of assets and liabilities. Exhibit 16-1 shows the carrying value and fair value for asset and liability groups excluding those where carrying value and fair value are the same (such as cash and cash equivalents).

Short-term interest rates declined during 2001. As a result, the fair value of fixed-rate financial assets and liabilities should rise. Investments, most of which are carried at *market values*, showed little change in the difference between carrying value and fair value. The loan portfolio did not perform as expected, as the unrealized loss rose by more than $1 billion. As American Express made a large provision for loan losses during 2001, it is possible that loan quality deteriorated, reducing the fair value of the loan portfolio.

For financial liabilities, the difference between fair value and carrying value narrowed, as expected with declining interest rates. The improvement over all four liability groups was $563 million.

Financial intermediaries such as American Express make a serious effort to match the interest rate sensitivity of financial assets and liabilities. Thus it is surprising to see the net fair value deteriorate by $1.8 billion [$1,580 million less ($228) million] in one year. While these data do not tell the whole story,[24] they can be used to question management about both the strategy and results of its interest-rate-risk-matching activities.

The data in Exhibit 16-1 can be used for another purpose—to adjust the balance sheet to fair value. As discussed more fully in Chapter 17, a current cost balance sheet should replace carrying cost with market value whenever possible. For American Express the adjustment would be an equity *increase* of $1.58 billion at December 31, 2000 and an equity *decrease* of $228 million at December 31, 2001.   ■

---

[23]In June 2002, the IASB proposed amendments that move the disclosure requirements of IAS 39 to IAS 32. However, the disclosure requirements are not significantly changed.

[24]Changes in the fair value of assets and liabilities may be offset by changes in the fair values of derivatives that hedge them. The disclosures of American Express are insufficiently detailed to isolate these effects.

EXHIBIT 16-1. AMERICAN EXPRESS
Fair Value Disclosures (in $millions)

| | December 31 | | | |
| | 2000 | | 2001 | |
	Carrying Value	Fair Value	Carrying Value	Fair Value
Financial Assets				
Investments	$43,747	$43,910	$46,488	$46,659
Loans	26,213	26,118	26,789	25,441
Subtotal	$69,960	$70,028	$73,277	$72,100
Fair value less carrying value		68		(1,177)
Financial Liabilities				
Fixed annuity reserves	$18,021	$17,479	$18,139	$17,672
Investment certificate reserves	7,322	7,289	8,205	8,223
Long-term debt	4,711	4,743	7,788	7,851
Separate account liabilities	28,792	27,823	24,280	23,717
Subtotal	$58,846	$57,334	$58,412	$57,463
Fair value less carrying value		(1,512)		(949)
Net fair value less carrying value		1,580		(228)

Source: American Express annual report, year ended December 31, 2001, Note 12.

Disclosures of Concentration of Credit Risk

SFAS 133 amended SFAS 119 to require augmented disclosure of significant concentrations of credit risk from all financial instruments. Companies must provide information about the common economic characteristic of the group, maximum expected loss, collateral policies, and use of master netting arrangements.

Sears provides a simple example of the disclosure of credit risk. Note 9 in the 1999 annual report shows that California accounts for 10.4% of credit card balances due from Sears customers. Texas and Florida each account for more than 7%. These data can help the analyst anticipate the effect of regional economic trends on the loss rates for Sears credit card receivables.

Enron's risks were of a different nature. Exhibit 16-2 shows the counterparties for the company's assets from risk management activities. The concentrations of credit risk for six industries are divided between investment grade and other credits. For comparison, the exhibit shows the data two years earlier. These disclosures show that:

1. Enron's risk management activities multiplied by more than five times over the two-year period, an enormous growth rate by any measure.
2. Energy marketers (24% non–investment grade) showed the fastest growth rate over the two-year period. Oil and gas producers (more than 50% non–investment grade) also grew rapidly.
3. Non-investment-grade assets rose nearly seven times over the two-year period, while investment-grade assets increased by less than five times.
4. The proportion of non–investment-grade counterparties grew from 16.5% in 1998 to 22.1% in 2000, suggesting that Enron's counterparty risk rose substantially.
5. Despite these indicators of higher risk, credit and other reserves fell to 2.1% of gross assets from 7.8% two years earlier.

Assets from risk management activities include substantial unrealized gains that had been recognized in reported income. The Enron disclosures suggested that the company was taking on substantial balance sheet risk while using aggressive accounting methods, making reported earnings suspect.

EXHIBIT 16-2. ENRON
Credit Risk Disclosures

Assets from Price Risk Management Activities (amounts in $millions)	December 31, 2000			December 31, 1998		
	Total	Investment Grade		Total	Investment Grade	
	Amount	Amount	% of Total	Amount	Amount	% of Total
Gas and electric utilities	$ 5,327	$ 5,050	94.8%	$1,251	$1,181	94.4%
Energy marketers	6,124	4,677	76.4%	795	684	86.0%
Financial institutions	4,917	4,145	84.3%	505	505	100.0%
Independent power producers	791	672	85.0%	613	416	67.9%
Oil and gas producers	2,804	1,308	46.6%	549	365	66.5%
Industrials	1,138	607	53.3%	341	229	67.2%
Others	357	256	71.7%	116	101	87.1%
Total	$21,458	$16,715	77.9%	$4,170	$3,481	83.5%
Credit and other reserves	(452)		2.1%	(325)		7.8%
Net assets from price risk management activities	**$21,006**			**$3,845**		

Source: Enron annual reports, 1998 and 2000.

The SEC requires firms to provide specific contract data, sensitivity analysis, or value-at-risk disclosures, effective for fiscal years ending after June 30, 1997 (one year later for firms with market capitalizations below $2.5 billion).

ANALYSIS OF HEDGING DISCLOSURES

We now use our discussion of the financial reporting requirements for derivatives and hedging activities to improve our understanding of:

- The risks faced by the firm
- The activities, including the use of derivatives, undertaken to manage those risks
- The financial statement effects of risk management activities
- Differences between accounting and economic hedging

To illustrate these issues, we use two examples. The first is International Business Machines [IBM], whose disclosures are typical of those made by large multinational enterprises. Exhibit 16-3 contains extracts from IBM's 2001 financial statement footnote on derivatives and hedging.

Analysis of IBM's Risk Management Disclosures

Multinational enterprises such as IBM are subject to a number of financial risks that can be managed through hedging.[25] IBM operates in about 35 functional currencies and is both a significant lender *and* a borrower in global capital markets. As such, it must contend with many interest rate and foreign currency exposures. The company:

- Uses derivatives (primarily) swaps to convert fixed-rate to variable-rate debt (fair value hedges) and to fix the rates on variable debt and anticipated issues of commercial paper (cash flow hedges). The weighted-average maturity of debt-related swaps is four years.
- Designates a significant portion of its non-U.S.-dollar debt as a hedge of its net investment in foreign operations. It also uses currency swaps and forward contracts to hedge this exposure. The 2001 effect of these hedges was $506 million (net of tax) and is included in the cumulative translation adjustment section of stockholders' equity.

[25]The discussion that follows was summarized from various IBM disclosures not shown in Exhibit 16-3.

- Uses foreign currency forward and option contracts to hedge foreign-currency-denominated anticipated royalties and other cash flows. The average maturity of these contracts is less than two years.

- Manages the cash and exposures of its subsidiaries centrally, and uses currency swaps and forward contracts to hedge its exposure to exchange rate changes for both functional and nonfunctional currencies.

- Uses equity derivatives to economically hedge its exposure (due to employee compensation plans) to its own stock price and broad stock market indices. These transactions are not, however, accounted for as hedges, and derivative gains and losses are included in income.

EXHIBIT 16-3. INTERNATIONAL BUSINESS MACHINES
Derivatives and Hedging Disclosures

k Derivatives and Hedging Transactions

DERIVATIVES AND HEDGING

The company operates in approximately 35 functional currencies and is a significant lender and a borrower in the global markets. In the normal course of business, the company is exposed to the impact of interest rate changes and foreign currency fluctuations. The company limits these risks by following established risk management policies and procedures including use of derivatives and, where cost-effective, financing with debt in the currencies in which assets are denominated. For interest rate exposures, derivatives are used to align rate movements between the interest rates associated with the company's lease and other financial assets and the interest rates associated with its financing debt. Derivatives are also used to manage the related cost of debt. For currency exposures, derivatives are used to limit the effects of foreign exchange rate fluctuations on financial results.

The company does not use derivatives for trading or speculative purposes, nor is it a party to leveraged derivatives. Further, the company has a policy of only entering into contracts with carefully selected major financial institutions based upon their credit ratings and other factors and maintains strict dollar and term limits that correspond to the institution's credit rating. When viewed in conjunction with the underlying and offsetting exposure that the derivatives are designed to hedge, the company has not sustained a material loss from these instruments.

In its hedging programs, the company employs the use of forward contracts, interest rate and currency swaps, options, caps, floors or a combination thereof depending upon the underlying exposure.

RISK MANAGEMENT PROGRAM

($ in millions)	Hedge Designation			Non-Hedge/ Other
	Fair Value	Cash Flow	Net Investment	
Derivatives:				
Debt risk management	$301	$(26)	$ —	$(13)
Long-term investments in foreign subsidiaries ("net investments")			92	
Anticipated royalties and cost transactions		375		
Subsidiary cash and foreign currency asset/liability management				16
Equity risk management				22
All other				3
Total derivatives	$301[1]	$349[2]	$ 92[3]	$28[4]
Debt:				
Long-term investments in foreign subsidiaries ("net investments")	—	—	(5,519)[5]	—
Total	$301	$349	$(5,427)	$28

[1]Assets of $301 million.
[2]Assets of $383 million and liabilities of $34 million.
[3]Assets of 92 million.
[4]Assets of $60 million and liabilities of $32 million.
[5]Fair value of foreign-denominated debt designed as hedge of net investment.

ACCUMULATED DERIVATIVE GAINS OR LOSSES

. . . the company makes extensive use of cash flow hedges, principally in the anticipated royalties and cost transactions risk management program. In connection with the company's cash flow hedges, it has recorded approximately $296 million of net gains in accumulated gains and losses not affecting retained earnings as of December 31, 2001, net of tax, of which approximately $276 million is expected to be reclassified to net income within the next year to provide an economic offset to the impact of the underlying anticipated cash flows hedged.

Source: International Business Machines Form 10-K, December 31, 2001.

The Risk Management Program table in Exhibit 16-3 summarizes the net fair value of the company's derivatives at December 31, 2001. IBM reports elsewhere that the fair value of derivatives increased by $456 million during 2001, of which $379 million was reclassified into income during the year. However, the disclosure does not identify the income statement line items (functional categories) receiving these reclassifications.

The balance of net accumulated gains reported in other comprehensive income was $296 million at December 31, 2001, of which $276 million was expected to be reclassified into income during calendar 2002 as the hedged items affect reported income.

What can an analyst do with these disclosures? Given IBM's size and complexity, the answer is: very little. A large multinational company has so many exposures and so many hedge transactions that disclosures are highly summarized. The analyst can, however:

1. Read the disclosures and all other references (such as in the Management Discussion and Analysis) to obtain a general understanding of the company's risk exposures, hedging objectives, and hedging strategies. For example, IBM hedges much of its exposure to its investment in foreign affiliates but many multinationals do not.

2. Look for large changes in the amount of hedging activities (e.g., Enron) or in the risk profile (e.g., Sears). Such changes may be clues to significant underlying changes within the company.

3. Question management about its risk management activities, using the disclosures as a starting point. When management is unable or unwilling to discuss its risk management activities, that may signal poor or dishonest management.

For some companies, however, the effects of risk management are easier to understand. Our second example is AMR, the parent of American Airlines. Exhibit 16-4 contains extracts from AMR's financial statements and footnotes on derivatives and hedging.

Analysis of AMR's Risk Management Disclosures

AMR uses derivatives to manage risks relating to fuel cost, interest rates, and foreign exchange rates. This analysis concerns only fuel price risk management.

Panel A of Exhibit 16-4 contains extracts (edited to remove redundancies and extraneous language) from AMR's disclosures about its fuel risk management activities. Panel B contains financial statement data. AMR adopted SFAS 133 in 2001, perhaps explaining the more detailed disclosures for that year. The quantitative disclosures are compared in panel C. The disclosures reveal that:

1. Aircraft fuel is an important expense component, rising from 9.6% of revenues in 1999 to 15.2% in 2001.

2. Hedging mitigated the effect of rising fuel prices on AMR. Excluding hedge gains, fuel cost expense would have been 15.4% in both 2000 and 2001.

3. AMR hedged a substantial portion of its fuel requirements, about two-thirds of annual usage (combining hedges for all following years).

4. The number of gallons hedged increased in 2000, perhaps in expectation of higher use and/or higher prices. In addition, AMR extended the time horizon for hedging activities.

5. Ineffective hedges resulted in $72 million of expense in 2001. It is unclear whether prior-year ineffectiveness was insignificant or not reported. It is also possible that AMR's hedge strategy changed in 2001, or that unusual variability of the spreads between different oil-based products caused this loss.

6. Net hedging gains made a significant contribution to income in 1999 (9.6% of operating income) and 2000 (39.5% of operating income). As shown in panel C, net income excluding hedging gains declined 27% in 2000 in contrast to the 19% reported gain.

7. Unrecognized hedging gains at year-end are a poor predictor of gains for the following year, perhaps due to high fuel price volatility.

EXHIBIT 16-4. AMR CORP.
Fuel Price Risk Management

Panel A. Excerpts from Fuel Risk Management Footnotes

December 31, 1999:

American enters into fuel swap and option contracts to protect against increases in jet fuel prices. . . . The changes in market value of such agreements have a high correlation to the price changes of the fuel being hedged. Gains and losses on fuel hedging agreements are recognized as a component of fuel expense when the underlying fuel being hedged is used. . . . At December 31, 1999 American had fuel hedging agreements with broker-dealers on approximately 2 billion gallons of fuel products, which represents approximately 48% of its expected 2000 fuel needs and approximately 10% of its expected 2001 fuel needs. The fair value of the Company's fuel hedging agreements at December 31, 1999, representing the amount the Company would receive to terminate the agreements, totaled $232 million.

December 31, 2000:

At December 31, 2000 American had fuel hedging agreements with broker-dealers on approximately 2.3 billion gallons of fuel products, which represents approximately 40% of its expected 2001 fuel needs, approximately 15% of its expected 2002 fuel needs, and approximately seven percent of its expected 2003 fuel needs. . . . The fair value of the Company's fuel hedging agreements at December 31, 2000, representing the amount the Company would receive to terminate the agreements, totaled $223 million.

December 31, 2001:

American enters into jet fuel, heating oil and crude oil swap and option contracts to protect against increases in jet fuel prices. These instruments generally have maturities of up to 36 months. In accordance with SFAS 133, the Company accounts for its fuel swap and option contracts as cash flow hedges. . . . Effective gains and losses on fuel hedging agreements are deferred in Accumulated other comprehensive loss and are recognized in earnings as a component of fuel expense when the underlying fuel being hedged is used. The ineffective portion of the fuel hedge agreements is . . . recognized as a component of fuel expense.

The year ending December 31, 2001 and 2000, the Company recognized net gains of approximately $29 million and $545 million . . . relating to its fuel hedging agreements. The net gains recognized in 2001 included approximately $72 million of ineffectiveness expense. . . . At December 31, 2001 American had fuel hedging agreements with broker-dealers on approximately 2.3 billion gallons of fuel products, which represents approximately 40% of its expected 2001 fuel needs, approximately 21% of its expected 2003 fuel needs, and approximately five percent of its expected 2004 fuel needs. The fair value of the Company's fuel hedging agreements at December 31, 2001, representing the amount the Company would receive to terminate the agreements, totaled $39 million.

Panel B. AMR Financial Statement Data (in $millions)

	Years Ended December 31		
Condensed income statement	1999	2000	2001
Operating revenues	$ 17,730	$ 19,703	$ 18,963
Operating expenses*	(16,574)	(18,322)	(21,433)
Operating income (loss	$ 1,156	$ 1,381	$ (2,470)
Other income (expense)	(150)	(94)	(286)
Pretax income	$ 1,006	$ 1,287	$ (2,756)
Income tax expense	(350)	(508)	994
Income from continuing operations	$ 656	$ 779	$ (1,762)
*Includes aircraft fuel expense	$ (1,696)	$ (2,495)	$ (2,888)
*Includes net hedging gains	111	545	29
Unrecognized gain (loss) at year-end	232	223	39
Billions of gallons hedged at year-end	2.0	2.3	2.3
% expected fuel needs hedged:			
Next year	48%	40%	40%
Following year	19%	15%	21%
Following year	0%	7%	5%
Total	67%	62%	66%

Source: AMR annual reports, 1999–2001.

(continued)

EXHIBIT 16-4. AMR CORP. (*continued*)

Panel C. Analysis of Fuel Price Hedging Activities

	Years Ended December 31		
Condensed income statement	1999	2000	2001
Aircraft fuel expense			
As reported	$(1,696)	$ (2,495)	$ (2,888)
Excluding hedge gains	(1,807)	(3,040)	(2,917)
As a % of operating revenues:			
As reported	9.6%	12.7%	15.2%
Excluding hedge gains	10.2%	15.4%	15.4%
Net hedging gains	$ 111	$ 545	$ 29
As a % of operating income	9.6%	39.5%	−1.2%
Hedge gains net of 35% income tax	72	354	19
Income from continuing operations			
As reported	$ 656	$ 779	$(1,762)
% change from prior year	N.A.	18.8%	−326.2%
Excluding hedge gains	$ 584	$ 425	$(1,781)
% change from prior year	N.A.	−27.3%	−519.3%

The AMR disclosures help explain the effects of the company's fuel price hedging activities on the trends of fuel expense, total operating expense, and net income. Discussions with management about its hedging strategy (and any changes in that strategy) and careful monitoring of market prices should result in better earnings forecasts, especially when fuel price changes are significant.

Risk Factors in Derivatives and Hedging Activities

Our discussion of derivatives and hedging activities is not complete without a review of the risk factors that analysts must look for. They fall into three categories and we discuss each in turn.

Hedge Ineffectiveness

In the narrow sense, hedge ineffectiveness refers to the fact that derivatives may not precisely hedge the underlying risk. If the firm is unable to enter into derivative contracts on the commodity, currency, or interest rate to which it is exposed, it may use derivatives based on one that is believed to be highly correlated. In the analysis of AMR in the previous section, we saw that hedge ineffectiveness, presumably due to adverse changes in the price spread between jet fuel and the commodities (such as heating oil) hedged, resulted in 2001 losses of $72 million, offsetting most of the hedging gain for that year. Unexpected changes in the spread between various interest rates can also result in hedge ineffectiveness.

However, hedge ineffectiveness can also be used in a broader sense, as in the failure to hedge risk factors that can severely impact the firm. If a financial institution has assets exposed to long-term interest rates and liabilities exposed to short-term rates, short-term rate increases will compress net interest income. Therefore, careful analysis of the interest rate sensitivity of financial institutions is essential.

Counterparty Risk

Earlier in the chapter we defined counterparty risk as the risk that the other party to a derivative contract will be unable to meet its obligations. That risk is present whenever there is an unrealized gain on derivatives that are not exchange-traded.

There is another risk associated with derivatives—the risk that the firm's credit risk will be downgraded. A credit downgrade may result in:

- Additional collateral requirements
- Termination of the contract
- Inability to enter into future contracts

■ Example

General Electric's 2001 annual report contains the following disclosure about counterparty credit risk:

> All swaps are executed under master swap agreements containing mutual credit downgrade provisions that provide the ability to require assignment or termination in the event that either party is downgraded below A3 or A−. If the downgrade provisions had been triggered at December 31, 2001, GE and GECS [General Electric Credit] could have been required to disburse up to $2.9 billion and could have claimed $0.8 billion from counterparties. . . .

The risks associated with credit downgrades are highest when downgrades are sudden or cover more than one rating step. When credit deterioration is gradual, the firm may have enough time to change its derivative arrangements and avoid these trigger effects. ■

Derivative Pricing

For derivatives that are exchange-traded, pricing is not an issue. However, many derivatives are not traded on organized exchanges. The more complicated the derivative, and the longer its term, the more subjective pricing may be. For example, consider the following statement from the March 31, 2002 Form 10-Q report of Aquila [ILA]:

> When market prices are not readily available or determinable, certain contracts are valued at fair value using an alternative approach such as model pricing.

For long-term contracts, model pricing is based on management's future price and discount rate assumptions. Model pricing is inherently imprecise and, in some cases, has been proven to be fraudulent.

SUMMARY

In this chapter, we discussed the use of derivatives and other hedging activities to manage the firm's foreign currency, interest rate, and commodity risks. We have examined the risks that can be hedged, the instruments that can be used for hedging, and the related accounting requirements. Our emphasis has been on understanding both the accounting and economic effects of risk management activities and using disclosures to obtain a better understanding of the risks faced by the firm and its efforts to manage those risks.

This chapter was the last to examine specific subject areas. Having completed our survey of major topics in financial statement analysis, we turn to a synthesis of these topics in Chapter 17, which includes comprehensive adjustments to financial statements.

Chapter 16

Problems

1. [Interest rate swap] The following data were extracted from a table provided by American Express [AXP] showing the effect of interest rate swaps on its long-term debt:

At December 31, 2000

Description	Balance Outstanding	Notional Swap	Interest Rate	
			Stated	Effective
Notes due 8/12/02	$400	$400	6.50%	6.83%
Notes due 5/01/02	400	400	6.81%	6.90%

At December 31, 2001

Description	Balance Outstanding	Notional Swap	Interest Rate	
			Stated	Effective
Notes due 8/12/02	$411	$411	6.50%	6.43%
Notes due 5/01/02	400	400	1.88%	1.88%

Balance outstanding and notional swap amounts in $millions.
Effective interest rate reflects effect of swap.

a. State and justify which of the two note issues is fixed and which is floating rate.

b. Explain why there could be a difference between the stated and effective rate on the floating rate note. (*Hint:* The variable rate in a swap may differ from the variable rate on the underlying.)

c. Compute the effect of the interest rate swap on interest expense for both note issues for both 2000 and 2001.

d. Describe one possible motivation for each of the two swaps.

2. [Interest rate swap] PepsiCo [PEP] had long-term debt of $3,460 million at December 31, 2000 and $2,970 million at December 31, 2001. The company reports the following information regarding interest rate swaps:

Receive fixed-pay variable	2000	2001
Notional amount ($millions)	$1,335	$1,077
Weighted-average receive rate	4.4%	5.6%
Weighted-average pay rate	4.9%	1.7%
Fair value of swaps ($millions)	$12	$32

a. Explain the probable reason that PEP entered into these swaps.

b. State the likely reason why the notional amount of swaps declined in 2001.

c. Explain why the fair value of the swaps could be positive for both years.

d. Compute the effect of the swaps on PepsiCo's interest expense in 2000 and 2001.

e. State when, where, and how the fair value of these swaps is reported in PEP's financial statements.

f. Discuss whether these swaps met PepsiCo's likely objective(s) for entering into them.

3. [Hedging commodity price risk] PepsiCo [PEP][26] reports that it is

> subject to market risk with respect to the cost of commodities because our ability to recover increased costs through higher prices may be limited by the competitive environment in which we operate. We manage this risk primarily through the use of fixed-price purchase orders, pricing agreements, geographic diversity and derivative instruments. . . . Our use of derivative instruments is not significant to our commodity purchases.

PEP also reports that it has

> commitments for the purchase of goods and services used in the production of our products approximating $2 billion with terms up to 5 years.

a. Explain how PepsiCo would report the derivative contracts (and the hedged items) used to hedge commodity price risk in the company's financial statements at the time they are entered into and when the underlying commodities are purchased.

b. Explain how PepsiCo would report the commitments for the purchase of goods and services in the company's financial statements at the time they are entered into and when the goods and services are paid for.

c. State the information that you would need to evaluate the potential gains and losses from the firm commitments and purchase contracts.

4. [Hedging commodity price risk] Kemet [KMT] manufactures electronic products that use precious metals such as palladium and tantalum. The company reported that

> The increase in demand for tantalum capacitors during fiscal year 2001, along with the limited number of tantalum powder suppliers, led to increases in tantalum prices and impacted availability. Tight supplies . . . caused the price to increase from under $50 per pound early in calendar 2000 to over $300 per pound in calendar 2001. . . . The Company's contractual commitments for the supply of tantalum are at prices well above market prices.[27]

---

[26]Quotations from PepsiCo 2001 financial statements.

[27]Quotation from Kemet's 10-K report for the fiscal year ended March 31, 2002.

Kemet also reported that

> The Company has a contract to purchase tantalum . . . through 2003 . . . at fixed prices. The contracted amounts are estimated to be $77 million and $65 million for calendar 2002 and 2003 respectively.

a. Discuss Kemet's motivation for entering into the purchase contract.

b. State and justify whether the contract is considered a derivative for accounting purposes.

c. Describe Kemet's accounting for this contract.

d. State the additional information that you would need to evaluate the effect of this contract on KMT's earnings for fiscal 2002 and 2003.

e. Describe an alternative hedging strategy that Kemet might have used to protect itself against tantalum shortages and price increases. State one advantage and one disadvantage of this alternate strategy.

f. Kemet also

> enters into contracts for the purchase of its raw materials, primarily palladium, which are considered to be derivatives or embedded derivatives.

Contrast the accounting for these contracts with KMT's accounting for its purchase contract.

5. [Foreign currency hedges] Aracruz [ARA], a Brazilian company, maintains its accounting records in $U.S. The company's 2001 Form 20-F reports that

> At December 31, 2001, the Company had entered into five forward foreign-exchange contracts to protect its foreign currency denominated accounts receivable and bank balances against exchange rate movements in the aggregate amount of EUR 14,623 thousand (2000—EUR 3,103 thousand). . . . The contracts expire in January, February, March and April 2002.

The following table shows contract and receivables data for the four years ending in 2001.

| | Forwards at 12/31 | | € Receivables at |
	€000	$000	12/31 ($000)
1998	€ 8,905	$10,097	$ 2,932
1999	23,840	24,173	29,399
2000	3,103	2,885	1,766
2001	14,623	13,124	3,448

a. Explain the fluctuation in the amount of $/€ forward contracts over the four-year period.

b. Describe how Aracruz accounts for these forward contracts under U.S. GAAP.

c. Aracruz always shows losses from these contracts. State and justify one possible explanation for these losses.

6. [Economic hedge] On July 12, 2001, Tokio Marine and Fire Insurance (now Millea Holdings [8766]) and Swiss Reinsurance

[RUKN] announced a catastrophe risk exposure swap. Tokio Marine exchanged:

- $150 million of Japanese earthquake risk for an equal amount of California earthquake risk
- $150 million of Japanese typhoon risk for an equal amount of Florida hurricane risk
- $150 million of Japanese typhoon risk for an equal amount of French storm risk

Tokio Marine's risk exposures are primarily in Japan.

a. Explain why this agreement is an economic hedge for both companies.

b. Describe how these contracts would be accounted for at inception and over their life under U.S. and IASB GAAP. (*Note:* Insurance contracts are not derivatives under either GAAP.)

7. [Economic and accounting effects of hedges] American Express [AXP] describes the following economic hedges in its 2001 Form 10-K report:

1. Foreign currency forward sales . . . were contracted to manage a portion of anticipated cash flows from operations in major overseas markets for the subsequent year.
2. AEFA [subsidiary of AXP] uses interest rate caps, swaps, and floors to protect the margin between the interest rates earned on investments and the interest rates credited to holders of certain investment certificates and fixed annuities.
3. Certain of AEFA's investment and certificate products have returns tied to the performance of equity markets. These elements are considered derivatives under SFAS No. 133. AEFA manages this equity market risk by entering into options and futures with offsetting characteristics.

These derivatives are *not* designated as hedges.

a. For *each* of these *three* hedges, describe the company's motivation for hedging.

b. For each of these three hedges, describe how the hedging instrument is an economic hedge of the risk exposure.

c. For each of these three hedges, describe whether the hedging instrument is an accounting hedge of the risk exposure.

8. [Embedded derivatives] Holmen issued convertible bonds in 1998.

a. Describe how the proceeds from the bond issue would be accounted for under SFAS 133 and IAS 39.

b. Describe how income in the years following the bond issue would differ from the accounting treatment that ignores the conversion feature of the bond.

9. [Cash flow classification] Black & Decker [BDK] reports the cash effects of its derivative financial instruments as follows:

- Except as noted below, cash flow from operating activities includes the cash effects of the Corporation's interest rate swaps and caps, foreign currency transaction hedges, hedges of foreign currency firm commitments, and hedges of forecasted transactions.

- Cash flow from investing activities includes the cash effects of
  a. hedges of net investments in subsidiaries located outside of the United States, and
  b. the exchange of notional principal amounts on interest rate swaps that swap from fixed United States dollars to fixed or variable foreign currencies because such amounts have been designated as hedges of net investments in subsidiaries located outside of the United States.

a. Discuss whether you agree with:

(i) The company's classification of the cash flows from hedges of net investments in foreign subsidiaries as components of cash flows from investing activities

(ii) The company's classification of the cash flows from hedges of other hedging activities as components of cash flows from operations

Justify your response with reference to the requirements of SFAS No. 95.

b. As an analyst, state where you would classify cash flows from hedging activities related to net investments in foreign subsidiaries. Justify your answer.

10. [Hedging inputs] Exhibit 16P-1 contains extracts from the 2001 financial statements of Delta Airlines [DAL]. Exhibit 16-4

and the related discussion of AMR are also needed to answer portions of the problem.

a. Compare Delta's fuel price hedging strategy with that of AMR. Your answer should include the amount and duration of hedging.

b. Compare the information provided by AMR and Delta. State which data provided by Delta regarding its fuel price hedging activities you would wish to have for AMR. State which data provided by AMR regarding its fuel price hedging activities you would wish to have for Delta. Explain why.

c. Compute the effect of Delta's fuel hedging on each of the following for the years 1999–2001:

(i) Fuel expense

(ii) Operating income

(iii) Net income before accounting change

d. Compute the change in net income before accounting change for 2000 and 2001 using

(i) Reported income

(ii) Income excluding hedging gains

e. Compute Delta's average fuel price per gallon for 1999–2001

(i) As reported

(ii) Excluding hedging gains

EXHIBIT 16P-1. DELTA AIRLINES
Fuel Price Hedging Activities (in $millions)

	Years Ended December 31		
Condensed income statement	1999	2000	2001
Operating revenues	$ 14,883	$ 16,741	$ 13,879
Operating expenses*	(13,565)	(15,104)	(15,481)
Operating income (loss)	$ 1,318	$ 1,637	$ (1,602)
Other income (expense)	775	(88)	(262)
Pretax income	$ 2,093	$ 1,549	$ (1,864)
Income tax expense	(831)	(621)	648
Income before accounting change	$ 1,262	$ 928	$ (1,216)
*Includes aircraft fuel expense	$ (1,421)	$ (1,969)	$ (1,817)
*Includes net hedging gains	79	684	299
Unrecognized gain (loss) at year-end		449	64
Fuel consumed (millions of gallons)	2,779	2,922	2,649
Average price (cents per gallon)**	51.13	67.38	68.60
**Includes fuel hedge gains.			
% of fuel hedged during year	75%	67%	58%
% expected fuel needs hedged:			
Next year**	80%	51%	46%
Average hedge price (cents per gallon)			60.50

**1999 and 2000 disclosures are for fiscal years ended June 30.

f. Discuss whether Delta's fuel price hedging program has been more successful than AMR's program. State the additional information you need to provide a definitive answer, explaining how that additional data would help.

g. Discuss the trend in the percentage of fuel needs hedged by Delta and the possible explanations for that trend.

11. [Hedging output prices] Amerada Hess [AHC] reported in its 2001 financial statements (Note 14) that:

> The corporation produced 109 million barrels of crude oil and natural gas liquids and 296 million Mcf of natural gas in 2001. At December 31, 2001, the Corporation's crude oil and natural gas hedging activities included commodity futures, option and swap contracts. Crude oil hedges mature in 2002 and cover 29 million barrels of crude oil production (88 million barrels of crude oil in 2000). The corporation has natural gas hedges covering 143 million Mcf of natural gas production at December 31, 2001, which mature in 2002 and 2003 (20 million Mcf of natural gas at December 31, 2000).

a. Explain the likely motivation for Amerada's hedging activities.

b. Explain the likely reason for the change in hedge quantities from 2000 to 2001.

c. State the additional information you would need to evaluate the impact of these hedges on Amerada's earnings and explain how that information would be useful.

d. Describe the effect of Amerada's 2001 hedges on 2002 income assuming that oil and gas prices

  (i) Increase

  (ii) Decrease

e. State the additional information that you would need to evaluate the success of Amerada's hedging activities for oil and gas revenues and explain how that information would be useful.

12. [Foreign currency hedges] Amerada Hess [AHC] reports in its 2001 financial statements that

> The Corporation uses foreign exchange contracts to reduce its exposure to fluctuating foreign currency rates, principally the pound sterling. At December 31, 2001, the Corporation has $136 million of notional value foreign currency contracts ($438 million at December 31, 2000). Generally, the Corporation uses these foreign exchange contracts to fix the exchange rate on net monetary liabilities of its North Sea operations. [MD&A]

> The Corporation enters into foreign currency contracts, which are not designated as hedges, and the change in fair value is included in income currently. [Note 14]

a. State and justify whether Amerada's foreign currency contracts referred to in the first quotation above are likely to be

  (i) Long the pound sterling versus the dollar, or

  (ii) Short the pound sterling versus the dollar

b. Amerada uses the $U.S. as the functional currency for its North Sea operations. Explain why the choice of functional

currency is relevant to the accounting impact of AHC's hedging activities.

c. State two reasons that would explain the reduction in the notional value of foreign exchange contracts from 2000 to 2001. State which reason is most likely.

13. [Hedging foreign currency cash flows]. Holmen exports much of its paper, paperboard, and timber production to other European countries. Panel A of Exhibit 16P-2 contains data from Holmen's 2001 financial risk management discussion. Holmen reports in Swedish krona (SEK).

a. Discuss why Holmen might wish to hedge the foreign exchange risk associated with its transaction-related cash flows.

b. Holmen had hedged four to five months of currency flows in 1999 and 2000. Using the exchange rate data in panel B of Exhibit 16P-2, discuss what may have motivated Holmen to increase its hedge to the amounts shown in panel A.

c. Holmen translates foreign currency revenues using the hedged exchange rate. The SEK declined against both the euro and pound sterling during the first half of 2002. Explain how the company's exchange rate hedges affected reported sales and income during that period.

14. [Derivatives and hedges] The Resh Company borrows using variable-rate debt and invests the proceeds in fixed-rate mortgages. On January 1, 2000, the company entered into an interest rate swap maturing December 31, 2001 with a notional amount of $10 million. The company agreed to pay a fixed rate of 6% and receive a variable rate indexed to the U.S. prime rate. The fair value of the swap was zero at inception.

The variable rate paid was 7% in 2000. That rate dropped to 5% on December 31, 2000 and stayed at that level through

EXHIBIT 16P-2. HOLMEN
Currency Risk Management

Panel A: Transaction Exposure, December 31, 2001 (MSEK)

Currency	Annual Cash Flow	Hedged Amounts	
		2002	2003
€	5,500	4,350	2,250
£	1,450	1,250	700
Other	1,350	900	350
Total	8,300	6,500	3,300

Source: Holmen 2001 annual report.

Panel B: Currency Exchange Rates

Date	SEK/€	SEK/£
12/31/99	8.46	13.78
12/31/00	9.99	14.06
6/30/01	12.78	15.35
12/31/01	11.78	15.25

Source: Computed from Bloomberg data.

December 31, 2002, when the swap matured. The level of fixed rates remained at 6% throughout the two-year period.

a. Describe the risks faced by the company, in the absence of the swap, assuming that interest rates

   (i) Increased

   (ii) Declined

b. Describe the risks faced by the company, after entering into the swap, assuming that interest rates

   (i) Increased

   (ii) Declined

c. Assuming the company did not designate the swap as a hedge, describe the effect of the hedge on Resh's

   (i) 2000 income

   (ii) 2001 income

   (iii) December 31, 2000 balance sheet

   (iv) December 31, 2001 balance sheet

d. Assuming the company designated the swap as a hedge of its variable rate debt, describe the effect of the hedge on Resh's

   (i) 2000 income

   (ii) 2001 income

   (iii) December 31, 2000 balance sheet

   (iv) December 31, 2001 balance sheet

e. Assuming the company designated the swap as a hedge of its fixed-rate loans, describe the effect of the hedge on Resh's

   (i) 2000 income

   (ii) 2001 income

   (iii) December 31, 2000 balance sheet

   (iv) December 31, 2001 balance sheet

f. Discuss the differing accounting treatments accorded the swap in parts c through e in light of your answers to parts a and b.

17

ANALYSIS OF FINANCIAL STATEMENTS: A SYNTHESIS

CHAPTER OUTLINE

CHAPTER OBJECTIVES

This chapter addresses debt and equity analysis and provides a bridge between financial statement and security analysis. It shows how to:

1. Adjust the balance sheet for current values and off-balance-sheet activities.
2. Compute adjusted book value per common share.
3. Adjust the capital structure to reflect current values and off-balance-sheet activities.
4. Normalize reported income.
5. Estimate the earning power of the firm.
6. Assess the quality of earnings.
7. Adjust cash from operations for analytical purposes.
8. Compute free cash flow.
9. Adjust financial ratios for noncomparability.

INTRODUCTION

This chapter is both a review and synthesis of the concepts and techniques discussed in prior chapters. It shows how reported financial data can be adjusted to create more useful input for valuation models; those models are discussed in Chapter 19. The financial analysis in this chapter is illustrated using Westvaco, whose financial statements are provided on the CD and website.[1]

The objectives of equity and credit analysis are similar, with differences only in emphasis. Creditors are primarily concerned with evaluating the firm's ability to service and repay its debt, both when extending credit and while credit is outstanding. Credit analysis is an important factor in setting the interest rate and debt covenants.

Short-term creditors, such as banks, were historically more concerned with liquidity, as they expected to be repaid in a short time period. Insurance companies, pension plans, and other investors in long-term bonds focused on long-term profitability and asset protection, given their longer time horizon. As more bank credit consists of revolving credits and term loans, the required analysis encompasses both short- and long-term credit risk.

Equity investors bear the residual risk of the firm. Their investment return depends on the long-term profitability and growth of the firm, and equity analysts may be tempted to ignore credit risk. However, equity investors should also be concerned with the firm's credit risk since financial distress may result in the loss of some or all of their investment. Firms with excellent long-term prospects may not survive if they cannot manage their credit needs.

However, the ultimate objective of equity analysis is valuation. Such valuation techniques as price/book value, price/earnings, price/cash flow, and discounted cash flow all use financial statement data. Research cited in earlier chapters shows that adjusted financial data often have greater value relevance and predictive value than reported data. Our view is that all financial statement data used to make investment and credit decisions should be adjusted to reflect accounting differences, current values, and the use of off-balance-sheet financing techniques. These adjustments should be made regardless of whether the objective is credit or equity analysis. We start with the balance sheet.

ANALYSIS OF AND ADJUSTMENTS TO THE BALANCE SHEET

The balance sheet shows the recorded assets, liabilities, and equity of the firm. As illustrated throughout the text, the reported balance sheet suffers from two defects:

1. Some assets and liabilities are not recorded.
2. The amounts at which assets and liabilities are measured may differ significantly from their economic value.

For these reasons, the usefulness of the reported balance sheet for investment decisions is limited. Its utility can be enhanced by the following adjustments to address those deficiencies:

- Off-balance-sheet assets and liabilities are added to the balance sheet.
- All assets and liabilities are measured at current values.

The first part of this chapter is concerned with the adjustments required to prepare a current value balance sheet. One of the objectives of that exercise is a better estimate of book value per share.

Analysis of Book Value

Book value is the reported stockholders' equity of the company, less the liquidating value of any preferred shares. Although book value per common share is often displayed in corporate and investment reports, it is frequently misunderstood. *Except by coincidence, book value equals neither the market value of the firm nor the fair value of its net assets.* It is primarily

---

[1]The reader is advised to read this chapter in conjunction with the Westvaco financial statements, to which there are frequent references throughout the chapter.

the accumulation of accounting entries and adjustments over the lifetime of the company and contains the following three elements:

1. Original capital used to start the firm, plus proceeds from any additional shares issued, less the cost of shares repurchased.

2. Retained earnings accumulated over the firm's life.

3. Accounting adjustments. Certain accounting standards result in entries directly to equity, without flowing through the income statement. Examples include the minimum liability provision for pension plans, changes in the market value of long-term marketable securities, and foreign exchange rate effects.

Firms do not distinguish between original capital and subsequent share issuance. The *Treasury stock* account accumulates the cost of shares repurchased, although firms may, from time to time, retire treasury shares, eliminating this account. Such technical retirement has no analytical significance.

The direct-to-equity accounting adjustments reflect accounting standards that delay recognition of the income statement impact of economic events. As preparation of a current value balance sheet requires recognition of all such events, the accounting adjustments are replaced by direct adjustments to assets and liabilities. These adjustments replace arbitrary accounting adjustments, some based on management discretion, with recognition of all known economic effects.

Because of the accounting choices available and the selective recognition inherent in GAAP, book value after adjustment may be more useful for decision making. The balance sheet adjustments required to compute adjusted book value are discussed in the following sections.

Adjustments to Assets

The reported book values of assets should be adjusted to current market value to approximate their value as collateral for creditors and resources available to equityholders. The current market value also facilitates an assessment of the earning power and cash-generating potential of the assets. The assets must also be adjusted for the impact of accounting choices, for example, adjustment of last-in, first-out (LIFO) inventories to first-in, first-out (FIFO).

GAAP-required accruals and deferrals may impact reported asset amounts and must be evaluated for their relevance to value. Examples include the reserve for bad debts, asset impairment, the valuation reserve for deferred tax assets, and the impact of exchange rate changes.

In principle, market values should be used for all assets and liabilities that have a determinable market. Financial reporting standards increasingly require the recognition or disclosure of market value for such financial assets as marketable securities, bank loans, mortgages, and private placement debt.

Some nonfinancial assets, including real estate, timberland, and mineral properties should also be marked to market. These assets have alternative uses and their market values can be estimated with sufficient reliability. However, the estimated current value of an operating facility (such as a paper mill or computer manufacturing facility) is far more subjective as its value is derived primarily from its ability to produce. Even if precision of measurement is not a problem, it is not clear which measure of current value should be used (see Appendix 8-A for a discussion of this issue).

For other assets, notably such intangible assets as brand names, customer relationships, and technology, reliable valuation may be difficult if not virtually impossible. Valuing the intangible by valuing the firm and working backward (subtracting all tangible assets and liabilities) serves no useful purpose when performed by financial statement preparers or auditors. If the purpose is firm valuation, the process becomes circular. Applying models such as those discussed in Lev and Sougiannis (1996) (see Chapter 7) to *individual* firms may be feasible, albeit fraught with statistical difficulties.

Thus, somewhere a line must be drawn between those assets (and liabilities) that are revalued and those that are not. This line is easier to draw in practice than in theory. The right decision depends on the purpose of the analysis and a judgment of the reliability of the current value data.

Adjustments to Liabilities

Market value adjustments and recognition of the effect of accounting choices are equally applicable to liabilities for the same reasons given earlier for assets. The recognition of off-balance-sheet activities, including all off-balance-sheet debt, consolidation of unconsolidated affiliates deemed to be integral to the firm's operations, and replacement of the balance sheet accrual for pensions and other postemployment benefits with the actual status of the plan are especially important.

These adjustments recognize obligations that do not meet the accounting definition of debt or whose recognition is not required under current GAAP. Note that some of these adjustments affect both assets and liabilities; for example, the capitalization of operating leases increases both assets (property) and liabilities.

Finally, some reported liabilities must be eliminated or reclassified. Some liability balances are not debt, as they will not require cash repayment, but will be satisfied by the delivery of goods and services. They are indicators of a firm's future sales or profitability rather than cash outflow. Examples of liabilities that should be excluded from debt follow:

Advances from customers. Income from the sale of syndication rights for films to be shown on television or cable, for example, is recognized over the term of the contract, with the unearned amount shown as a liability. The cost of creating the film has already been incurred. The deferred amount is unearned income, not debt.

Investment tax credits. Credits recognized under the deferral method are another example; they are purely unrecognized income, not debt.

Deferred income taxes. This liability estimates future taxes payable if the tax basis of income measurement "catches up" to the accounting basis. The deferred tax liability balance may continuously grow, especially if arising from depreciation, and the net timing difference will not reverse in the near future. When the deferred tax liability (or asset) is significant, the analyst should examine its source and the likelihood of its reversal. Components that are likely to reverse should be included, but restated to present value.[2]

Balance Sheet Adjustments for Westvaco

Box 17-1 lists the most common balance sheet adjustments. Such adjustments generate measures of book value and debt that are more useful for analytical purposes. The adjusted measures, and ratios derived from them, should be better indicators of shareholder wealth and risk than measures based on unadjusted data. We now illustrate these adjustment techniques by applying them to Westvaco.

Exhibit 17-1 shows Westvaco's reported balance sheet at October 31, 1999, and applies a number of adjustments to derive a current cost balance sheet. All adjustments are based on data disclosed in Westvaco's financial statements and discussed in the appropriate chapter of this text.

Adjustments to Current Assets

Each asset account should be evaluated for possible adjustments ranging from recognition of market value to the effects of accrual accounting and management choices.

Cash and Marketable Securities. Cash and marketable securities require no adjustment as they represent current cash balances and highly liquid investments with maturities of no more than three months (foreign currency amounts are translated at current exchange rates). Note E reports the amount of marketable securities included in the total.

---

[2]Some analysts treat deferred taxes as equity. But deferred taxes result from the use of different accounting methods and estimates for financial reporting than for tax purposes. The deferred tax liability partially offsets the different amounts of income recognized for financial reporting and tax purposes. If income recognized in the financial statements is overstated (e.g., by using depreciation lives that are too long), retained earnings are overstated. Adding the deferred tax liability to equity would increase the overstatement. For that reason, the components of the deferred tax asset or liability must be analyzed, rather than blindly added to debt or equity.

BOX 17-1
Checklist of Balance Sheet Adjustments

Account Area of Analysis or Adjustment Required*	Adjustment Effects		
	Asset	Liability	Equity
Marketable securities			
Mark to market (13)	x		x
Accounts receivable			
Revenue recognition methods (2)	x		x
Analysis of bad debts (2)	x		x
Interest rate effects (10)	x		x
Sale of receivables (11)	x	x	x
Inventories			
Capitalization policy (6)	x		x
Addback of LIFO reserve (6)	x		x
Foreign currency effects (15)	x		x
Property, plant, and equipment			
Capitalization policy (7)	x		x
Capitalization of interest (7)	x		x
Foreign currency effects (15)	x		x
Effects of inflation (8)	x		x
Computer software (7)	x		x
Natural resource assets (7)	x		x
Depreciation methods and lives (8)	x		x
Impairment (8)	x		x
Long-term investments			
Proportionate consolidation (13)	x	x	
Mark to market (13)	x		x
Intangible assets			
Treatment of goodwill (14)	x		x
Brand names (7)	x		x
Research and development (7)	x		x
Deferred charges			
Expense recognition policy (2)	x		x
Advances from customers			
Deferred revenue (10)		x	x
Long-term debt			
Capitalization of leases (11)	x	x	x
Guarantees (11)	x	x	x
Take-or-pay contracts (11)	x	x	
Convertible debt (10)		x	x
Redeemable preferred stock (10)		x	x
Employee benefits			
Pension plans (12)	x	x	x
Health and life insurance (12)	x	x	x
Stock option plans (12)			x
Deferred income taxes			
Probability of reversal (9)	x	x	x
Valuation allowance (9)	x		x
Tax loss carryforwards (9)	x		x
Discount to present value (9)	x	x	x

*Required adjustment may be either pretax or aftertax.
Note: The chapter where the issue is discussed is shown in parentheses after each item.

EXHIBIT 17-1. WESTVACO
Current Cost Balance Sheet, October 31, 1999 (in $millions)

	Reported	Adjusted	Adjustment
Assets			
Cash and marketable securities	$ 109	$ 109	
Receivables	318	318	
Inventories	249	368	119
Other current assets	62	19	(43)
Current assets	$ 738	$ 814	$ 76
Gross property	5,994		
Less: accumulated depreciation	(2,779)		
Net property	$3,215	$3,297	$ 82
Timberlands—net	266	750	484
Construction in progress	100	100	
Total fixed assets (net)	$3,581	$4,147	$ 566
Other assets (excluding prepaid pension cost)	48	48	
Prepaid pension cost	529	1,491	962
Total assets	$4,896	$6,500	$1,604
Liabilities and Equity			
Accounts payable and accruals	$ 362	$ 362	
Notes payable and current maturities	50	50	
Income taxes payable	13	13	
Current liabilities	$ 425	$ 425	
Long-term debt	1,427	1,445	18
Capitalized operating leases		82	82
Other long-term liabilities (excluding those listed below)	24	24	—
Postretirement benefits	27	20	(7)
Pension benefits	24	—	(24)
Deferred income taxes (net)	798	—	(798)
Total liabilities	$2,725	$1,996	$ (729)
Stockholders' equity (reported)	2,171	2,171	
Adjustments to assets and liabilities	—	2,333	2,333
Adjusted stockholders' equity	$2,171	$4,504	$2,333
Total liabilities and equity	$4,896	$6,500	$1,604
Shares outstanding (millions)	100.293	100.745	
Book value per common share	$21.65	$44.71	
Current ratio	1.74	1.92	

Receivables. This total includes both trade (customer) receivables and those from other transactions (such as from asset sales). Both credit risk and interest rate risk must be considered.

The underlying credit risk (the probability that trade receivables will not be collected on time, or at all) is related to Westvaco's customer base. The allowance for uncollectable accounts is the company's estimate of that risk. Note E reports that:

- Receivables at October 31, 1999 include $12.4 million from nontrade sources (probably from asset sales)
- The allowance for discounts and doubtful accounts was $12.8 million at October 31, 1999.

Companies that sell to consumers or small businesses generally provide higher loss reserves. *When customers suffer from financial distress, such as during a recession, an additional loss provision may be required.*[3]

When a firm has sold receivables with partial or full recourse, the allowance for bad debts must include the expected recourse obligation. As a result, the allowance will be higher (as a percent of gross receivables) than if no receivables had been sold.[4]

Interest rate risk refers to the possibility that the interest rate on receivables is below the appropriate (risk-related) market rate, resulting in fair value below cost. This issue arises mainly in companies that sell to consumers or high-risk businesses.

Inventories. Westvaco's summary of significant accounting policies states that

> Cost is determined using the last-in, first-out (LIFO) method for raw materials, finished goods, and certain production materials

indicating that an adjustment to current cost is required. Note E discloses that the current cost of inventory is $368 million, shown in our current cost balance sheet. The LIFO reserve is $119 million, the difference between total inventories of $249 million and current cost. We note that the LIFO reserve at October 31, 1998 was $123 million. The decline during fiscal 1999 reflects lower prices for Westvaco's main products.

Should the adjustment be made on a pre- or post-tax basis? For tax purposes, the LIFO cost is still relevant; if all LIFO inventories were liquidated, the company would be forced to pay income tax on the realization of the current value of its inventories. As Westvaco has no history of LIFO invasions, we cannot assume that its inventories will be liquidated without violating the going-concern assumption. Thus, tax recognition of the LIFO reserve is an unrealistic assumption, and we do not make any adjustment for taxes.[5]

Deferred Income Taxes. We reduce other current assets by $43 million, the amount of current deferred tax assets disclosed in Note D, as explained in the discussion of Westvaco's income tax liability account below.

Adjustments to Long-Term Assets

The adjustments to Westvaco's long-term assets are more complex. We start with fixed assets.

Property, Plant, and Equipment. There are two issues to consider: off-balance-sheet financing and valuation. Because Westvaco has significant operating leases (Note I), some facilities and equipment are not shown on the balance sheet. The present value of these leases (calculated using the methodology shown in Box 11-2) of $82 million[6] has been added to property to reflect their omission.

The valuation issue is more difficult. As discussed in Chapters 7 and 8, the carrying value of property, plant, and equipment (PPE) is determined by accounting choices related to capitalization, depreciation method, and accounting estimates (lives and salvage values). Thus, comparability among companies is poor, reflecting various accounting choices. On the other hand, the current cost of PPE may have little relation to historical cost, regardless of accounting choices.

---

[3]Westvaco's reserve increased to $17.6 million at October 31, 2000. See the analysis of Lucent in Chapter 2 for a detailed example of the disclosure and analysis of bad-debt reserves.

[4]As discussed in Chapter 11, although book value is not affected, the accounts receivable and current liability balances should be adjusted to reflect the financing nature of the transaction.

[5]Any adjustment would equal the present value of estimated tax payments, as discussed in Chapter 9.

[6]The discount rate used is Westvaco's embedded interest rate calculated in footnote 40 of Chapter 10 of 8.39%. As discussed in Chapter 11, the present value is insensitive to small differences in the assumed interest rate.

Timberlands are an excellent example. Westvaco has substantial land holdings carried at historical cost. The recurring gains from land sales (see the normalization of income discussion later in the chapter) reflect the difference between cost and current market value. However, market value can vary considerably based on location and type of timber. We use a value of $750 million, approximately $500 per acre.[7]

The current value of Westvaco's other PPE is unknown. The company uses the straight-line depreciation method, and the disclosures regarding asset lives are typically vague. The large restructuring charge in fiscal 1999 included an impairment charge for some production facilities. Lacking any basis for an adjustment, none is made.[8]

Other Assets. Note M reports that other assets include $529 million of prepaid pension cost. Prepaid pension cost is the result of the smoothing devices of SFAS 87. We have removed this accrual and added a new asset equal to $1,491 million, the excess of pension assets over the projected benefit obligation.[9] This adjustment was computed in Problem 12-2.

A similar adjustment for Westvaco's postretirement medical benefits is shown as a liability adjustment in the "Adjustments to Liabilities" section.

The amount of intangible assets included in other assets was not disclosed in the fiscal 1999 financial statements.[10] As goodwill has no value separate from the business, any balance sheet goodwill should be eliminated from a current cost balance sheet. In Chapter 14 (page 528), many firms wrote off goodwill in 2002.[11]

Some firms show deferred charges that reflect unrecognized expenses, such as the deferral of financing fees, startup expenses, or major maintenance expenditures. When cash outlays have occurred but have yet to be recognized as expenses, they should not be considered assets for purposes of analysis and should be removed from the adjusted balance sheet. Westvaco is likely to have a small amount of deferred financing fees but no adjustment is made due to lack of disclosure.

The net effect of these adjustments has been to increase Westvaco's assets by $1,604 million (nearly 33%) from $4,896 million to $6,500 million. We now turn to adjustments applicable to the firm's liabilities.

Adjustments to Current Liabilities

Current liabilities are generally stated at the amount expected to be paid, making adjustment unnecessary. Given the short time period to liquidation, any interest rate adjustment is usually immaterial. Note G contains details of accounts payable and accrued expenses. None of these require any adjustment.

Adjustments to Long-Term Liabilities

As these liabilities are longer in duration and some reflect accounting choices rather than economic events, significant adjustments are required. We have separated Westvaco's long-term obligations into two portions: long-term debt and other long-term obligations.

Long-Term Debt and Capital Lease Obligations. Westvaco's Note J contains details of the company's notes payable and long-term obligation, including the fair value disclosure mandated by SFAS 107. The carrying amount of long-term debt in Exhibit 17-1 is increased

---

[7]The valuation is based on the prices obtained from Westvaco's sales of surplus timberlands.

[8]Appendix 8-A contains further discussion of the difficulty of estimating the current cost of PPE.

[9]When making this adjustment, the company's discount and compensation growth rate assumptions should be compared with similar companies. In some cases, analytical adjustment of the projected benefit obligation may be required. In addition, consideration should be given to the historical pattern of plan amendment, especially for flat benefit plans, to ensure that the PBO does not understate the company's obligation.

[10]The fiscal 2000 report states that goodwill was $5 million at October 31, 1999. Given the immaterial amount. we have made no adjustment in Exhibit 17-1.

[11]In the second quarter of 2002, Westvaco wrote off $352 million of goodwill relating to its 1999 and 2000 acquisitions.

by $18 million to reflect the higher fair value.[12] As discussed in Box 10-3, interest rates rose during fiscal 1999, reducing the fair value adjustment ($79 million at October 31, 1998).

The second adjustment is the recognition of the $82 million debt associated with the capitalization of Westvaco's operating leases. This adjustment was discussed under property, plant, and equipment above.

Other Long-Term Obligations. Note M shows that the $27 million accrual for postretirement medical benefits, accounted for under SFAS 106, is included under long-term obligations. In the current value balance sheet, we replace the accrued cost with the actual plan obligation of $20 million, shown in Note M.

The second adjustment to other long-term obligations is $24 million of accrued pension liability (also reported in Note M). As the entire pension net asset is shown on the asset side in Exhibit 17-1, this accrual must also be eliminated.

Deferred Income Taxes. Note D reports noncurrent deferred tax assets of $144 million and noncurrent deferred tax liabilities of $942 million, for a net noncurrent deferred tax liability of $798 million. This amount is shown on Westvaco's balance sheet.

Depreciation is the major factor in Westvaco's net deferred tax liability. Employee benefits are the second largest. Westvaco's deferred tax liability has increased in each of the last three years (see provision for income taxes in Note D), suggesting that timing differences are unlikely to reverse. For that reason we assume zero deferred taxes on the current value balance sheet. However, Note D states that

> Provision has not been made for income taxes which would become payable upon remittance of $167 million of the October 31, 1999 undistributed earnings of certain foreign subsidiaries representing that portion of such earnings which the company considers to have been indefinitely reinvested in the subsidiaries, principally in Brazil. Computation of the potential deferred tax liability associated with these undistributed earnings is not practicable.

If analysis of a firm assumes that such "permanently reinvested" earnings would have to be repatriated,[13] then long-term liabilities should be increased by an estimate of the required income tax payments.

Commitments and Contingent Liabilities. Every large firm has contracts and other commitments that are not recognized in the financial statements. We have already capitalized operating leases, a common example of such unrecognized "executory contracts."

Note N refers to "various legal proceedings and environmental actions" that are not further described. In the United States, much litigation is routine, and its outcome is rarely material to the firm. However, the analyst should look for footnote references to litigation that may be material, for example, related to:

- Firm patents that are challenged by competitors
- Patents of others that the firm may have violated
- Alleged illegal conduct, such as bribery
- Violations of contracts

Companies rarely disclose the details of such litigation, but court filings are often publicly available.

Environmental obligations are also hard to assess, even from inside the firm. Changing laws and technology hamper estimates of the cost of environmental remediation. Uncertainty as to insurance coverage complicates this issue further. As always, some firms are conserva-

---

[12]When fair value is not disclosed (such as for non-U.S. firms), it should be estimated using the method shown in Box 10-3.

[13]For example, liquidation or a leveraged buyout that would require repatriation of all earnings to service parent company debt.

tive in accruing such costs; others record these obligations only when they are virtually certain. Disclosures have improved in recent years, but analysts should seek additional information regarding the nature of such obligations and the range of possible cost. Environmental and other legal contingencies should be monitored as court decisions and legislation can turn immaterial liabilities into threats to the firm's existence.[14]

Westvaco describes its environmental liabilities in the summary of significant accounting policies. The company has accrued $15 million for these obligations. No adjustment is made in Exhibit 17-1 due to lack of information.

Adjustments to Stockholders' Equity

Westvaco's stockholders' equity section contains the following components:

1. Common stock (Westvaco has no preferred shares)
2. Retained income
3. Accumulated other comprehensive income
4. Common stock in treasury

The second component, often called *retained earnings*, reflects the reinvestment of more than $1.6 billion of earnings over Westvaco's lifetime.

Accumulated other comprehensive income (loss) contains the accumulated adjustments from the translation of the accounts of Westvaco's foreign subsidiaries into U.S. dollars. Such adjustments are discussed in Chapter 15. The following additional components are often present in accumulated other comprehensive income (but not in the case of Westvaco):

- Minimum pension liability (Chapter 12)
- Unrealized securities gains and losses (Chapter 13)
- Deferred hedging gains and losses (Chapter 16)

These and any other "smoothing" accounts must be removed from the current cost balance sheet when present. They are reclassified by restating the related assets and liabilities to their fair market value.

Common stock in treasury is the cost of shares repurchased by the company.

The final adjustment is the total of all adjustments to assets and liabilities. In order for the current value balance sheet to balance, this total must be added to stockholders' equity. The adjustment equals:

Net adjustments to assets	$1,604 million
Net adjustments to liabilities	(729)
Net adjustment to stockholders' equity	$2,333 million

Adjusted Book Value per Common Share

After all balance sheet components have been restated to current cost (and any preferred stock deducted), the resulting amount is divided by the number of common shares outstanding at the balance sheet date. The result is adjusted book value per common share, a far better measure of the resources of the firm.

The computation of adjusted equity is discussed in the previous section. The number of outstanding shares must also be adjusted to reflect outstanding stock options. Note L reports stock options, grouped by exercise price. As the price of Westvaco shares on October 31, 1999 was $29.69, we adjust only for the options with exercise prices below $26.88.

As shown in the table below, the exercise proceeds would total $68.747 million. Using the treasury stock method,[15] the proceeds could repurchase 2.315 million shares ($68.747 million/$29.69), leaving 452,000 additional shares outstanding. Thus the number of shares

---

[14]The number of companies forced into bankruptcy by asbestos-related lawsuits far surpassed initial expectations.

[15]Used to compute the dilutive effect of stock options on earnings per share (see Chapter 4).

used to compute adjusted book value per share in Exhibit 17-1 must be increased to 100.745 million.[16]

Option Strike Prices	Average Price	Shares (000)	Proceeds ($000)	Market ($000)
$18.29–$19.13	$18.52	128.32	$ 2,376.52	$ 3,809.88
$23.08–$26.88	25.15	2,639.00	66,370.93	78,351.90
Total		2,767.32	$68,747.45	$82,161.78
Shares repurchased		(2,315.51)		
Additional shares		451.82		

Westvaco's adjusted book value per share is computed as:

Adjusted stockholders' equity	$4,504 million
Adjusted number of common shares (100.293[17] + .452)	100.745 million
Adjusted common equity per share = $4,504/100.745 =	$44.71

Westvaco's reported book value per share is calculated as:

Reported stockholders' equity	$2,171 million
Number of common shares	100.293 million
Common equity per share = $2,171/100.293 =	$21.65

Westvaco's adjusted book value per share is more than two times the historical cost amount. Using the adjusted book value changes the price/book value ratio for Westvaco at October 31, 1999 from:

$$\$29.69/\$21.65 = 1.37 \text{ times}$$

to

$$\$29.69/\$44.71 = .66 \text{ times}$$

Westvaco shares appeared to sell at a significant premium to book value when, using the adjusted book value, they actually sold at a one-third discount to book value per share.

Although adjusted book value per share is more useful than historical book value per share, it is not an end in itself. This better estimate of the net assets available to the firm is important for current and potential creditors interested in the firm's solvency (see the next section) and for purposes of valuation (see Chapter 19).[18] Additionally, it measures the resources of the firm on which an adequate return must be earned. The next section turns to the analysis of Westvaco's capital structure to further our understanding of its obligations, liquidity, short- and long-term borrowing needs, and risk.

Analysis of Capital Structure

Exhibit 17-2 compares Westvaco's reported capitalization at October 31, 1999 with the adjusted amounts. The reported debt-to-equity ratio does not include the impact of off-balance-sheet financing techniques, does not reflect the real value of Westvaco's assets,

---

[16]The astute reader will note that the number of additional shares calculated exceeds the difference between the number of shares used by Westvaco to compute basic and diluted earnings per share. The EPS calculation uses the average price during the year; as the closing price was higher, the dilution is greater.

[17]Given in Westvaco's statement of shareholders' equity. Remember to use the number of shares outstanding at the period end, net of any treasury shares. The average number of shares outstanding during the period should be used only for earnings per share and cash flow per share calculations.

[18]We note that the extensive discussion in recent years of whether stock prices are "too high" compares market prices with *reported* book values per share. The analysis of Westvaco illustrates how wide the disparity between reported and adjusted amounts can be.

EXHIBIT 17-2. WESTVACO
Adjusted Long-Term Debt and Solvency Analysis

Capitalization Table (in $millions)	10/31/99	10/31/00
Short-term debt	$ 50	$ 30
Long-term debt	1,427	2,686
Total reported debt	**$1,477**	**$2,716**
Adjustments to total debt		
Capitalization of operating leases	82	140
Restatement of debt to market value	18	(89)
Adjusted total debt	***$1,577***	***$2,767***
Reported stockholders' equity	**2,171**	**2,333**
Adjustments to equity	2,333	1,891
Adjusted stockholders' equity	***$4,504***	***$4,224***
Reported total capital	**3,648**	**5,049**
Adjusted total capital	***6,081***	***6,991***
Ratios		
Debt-to-equity	**0.68**	**1.16**
Debt-to-total-capital	**0.40**	**0.54**
Adjusted ratios		
Debt-to-equity	***0.35***	***0.66***
Debt-to-total-capital	***0.26***	***0.40***

and is a product of management's reporting choices. It can be misleading if used for comparative analysis. The adjustments discussed in the preceding sections produce a more complete capital structure and ratios that facilitate comparisons with other firms (after similar adjustments).

Total adjusted stockholders' equity of $4.5 billion is more than twice the reported amount of $2.2 billion. The adjusted debt obligation is only slightly higher after adjustment, mainly for off-balance-sheet leases. As a result, the debt-to-equity and debt-to-total-capital ratios are much lower after adjustment. Westvaco's real financial leverage is considerably lower than the reported level.

The exhibit also extends the analysis to the year ended October 31, 2000. The adjustments (not shown) are similar to those for fiscal 1999 with one exception. Westvaco made four acquisitions in fiscal 2000 using the purchase method. As a result, the year-end 2000 balance sheet included $606 million of goodwill, removed from the current cost balance sheet. The result is that the difference between the reported and adjusted equity amounts is smaller than in 1999.

Balance Sheet Adjustments for Non-U.S. Companies

IASB GAAP

Adjustments to the balance sheet of an enterprise that follows IASB GAAP will be similar to those shown in Box 17-1 and illustrated using Westvaco in Exhibit 17-1. The major differences are that IASB GAAP permits the

- *Revaluation of fixed assets.* The advantage of such revaluation is the restatement of such assets to their current value, providing information generally not available for U.S. firms. The disadvantage is the loss of comparability, as assets, equity, and capital are increased relative to those of firms using historical cost for fixed assets. Either such revaluations must be reversed, or (our preference) estimates made of the current value of fixed assets for firms that do not revalue.

- *Pooling of interests method of accounting for acquisitions.* Restoring comparability requires restatement from one method to the other.[19]

Non-U.S. GAAP

When comparing firms that use other sets of accounting principles, special consideration is required for the following issues:

- Some local GAAP permit the revaluation of fixed assets (see comment above).
- In some foreign jurisdictions, the pooling method of acquisition accounting is permitted (see comment above). In others, acquisition goodwill is written off at the acquisition date rather than amortized over time. When intangibles are eliminated, this accounting difference disappears.
- Differences in the rules for capitalization of research and development costs distort comparisons using reported data. The removal of capitalized research or development costs places all firms on the same basis.
- Disclosures are generally less informative for non-U.S. firms, especially with respect to operating leases and other off-balance-sheet financing activities. The analyst must use any available data to make approximate adjustments; in some cases, management may provide additional disclosures on request.
- Other differences in accounting methods (e.g., deferred income taxes) reduce the comparability of balance sheets before adjustment. When possible, adjustment for those differences should be made, using reconciliations to U.S. or IASB standards that are sometimes provided.

ADJUSTMENTS TO REPORTED INCOME

As in the case of book value, reported net income should also be examined for possible adjustments. There are two objectives:

1. Remove nonoperating items from reported income to obtain a better measure of operating results for the period, and better interperiod comparisons.
2. Obtain a measure of the earning power of the firm. The concept of earning power represents the (permanent) net income of the firm, ignoring temporary, nonrecurring, or unusual factors. In theory, the earning power of the firm is stable but grows at a long-term growth rate. As discussed in Chapter 19, earning power (expected earnings) rather than reported income should be the input in valuation models.

Accounting standards setters have struggled to define such terms as "nonrecurring" and "extraordinary," with a notable lack of success. There is no reason for users of financial statements to be drawn into this semantic morass. Analysts must, however, identify the factors that affect reported operating performance. The objective is to estimate the earning power of the firm by removing nonrecurring factors.

Normalization of Reported Income

In practice, determining the earning power of the firm is difficult, requiring judgment to remove the "noise" that is always present. Part of the difficulty is that one analyst's definition of noise may differ from another's. Normalization is the term applied to the process of estimating normal operating earnings for each period.

---

[19]As we believe the purchase method provides better information, the first choice should be to restate pooling method mergers to the purchase method.

For noncyclical companies, the normalization of earnings consists mainly of removing nonrecurring items from reported income. Such items may include:

- Accounting changes
- Realized capital gains or losses
- Gains or losses on the repurchase of debt
- Catastrophes such as natural disasters, accidents, or terrorism
- Strikes
- Impairment or "restructuring" charges
- Litigation or government actions
- Discontinued operations

The impact of some of these items may be segregated as a line item in the income statement. Alternatively, in some cases, it may be disclosed in footnotes or in the Management Discussion and Analysis. Sometimes, the effect is given on a pretax basis only; other times, the after-tax impact on EPS is disclosed.

The analyst should search the financial statements and management discussion for such items and then remove the effect of those deemed to be nonrecurring from net income. Capital gains or losses, for example, should be segregated from operating earnings. Recurring losses from discontinued operations, impairments, or restructurings suggest that the company's depreciation or other accounting methods may overstate reported income. Because restructurings consist of past and future expenditures, they reflect on either past income or future income. Such write-offs should be segregated from operating earnings but not ignored. Rather, they should be allocated to past or future income (as the case may be) to more accurately reflect the *trend and level of income*.

Exhibit 17-3 normalizes Westvaco's reported earnings for the four years ended October 31, 2000. The adjustments for 1997 to 1999 use data from Westvaco's 1999 financial statement footnotes and the MD&A. We have extended the analysis to fiscal 2000 (data not provided) to illustrate several additional adjustments and to provide a longer time perspective. Some adjustments are related to the balance sheet adjustments already discussed; others apply only to reported income.

Accounting Changes. The effect of mandated and voluntary accounting changes is another frequent source of nonrecurring items. Most such effects are reported outside of income from continuing operations, making it easy to isolate them. However, the effect of changes in accounting estimates (such as changes in depreciation lives and pension assumptions) is rarely segregated. When material, all such effects should be removed from normalized income.

Westvaco's summary of significant accounting policies reports that it adopted SFAS 130 (comprehensive income) effective November 1, 1998 and SFAS 132 (pension disclosures) in fiscal 1999. As both standards concern disclosure rather than measurement (see Chapters 1 and 12 respectively), there were no income statement effects. Westvaco also reports that it expects an immaterial impact from the adoption of SFAS 133 (derivatives and hedging).[20]

Early Extinguishment of Debt. When interest rates change, firms may find it advantageous to refinance a portion of their debt. As discussed in Chapter 10, the accounting gains or losses from refinancing may be quite different from the economic effects; for that reason, these gains and losses should be considered nonrecurring, whether or not they are reported as extraordinary items. For that reason the $8.8 million loss from debt refinancing has been added back to fiscal 2000 income.[21]

---

[20]In fact there was no cumulative effect when SFAS 133 was adopted in fiscal 2001.

[21]Westvaco refinanced three sinking fund issues with interest rates exceeding 10% (see fiscal 1999 Note J). The new debt carries lower interest rates.

EXHIBIT 17-3. WESTVACO
Normalization of Reported Net Income, 1997–2000 (in $millions)

	Years Ending October 31				
	1997	1998	1999	2000	4-Year Total
Reported net income	**$162.7**	**$132.0**	**$111.2**	**$245.9**	**$651.8**
Items reported after tax					
Early debt retirement				8.8	8.8
State tax adjustment			(15.0)		(15.0)
Stock option grants	(3.6)	(4.5)	(3.3)	(5.1)	(16.5)
Subtotal	$ (3.6)	$ (4.5)	$(18.3)	$ 3.7	$(22.7)
Items reported pretax					
Restructuring charges			80.5	16.1	96.6
Loss (gain) on asset sales	(10.5)	0.9	(17.9)	(26.8)	(54.3)
Interest capitalization	(26.0)	(20.8)	(8.9)	(5.5)	(61.2)
Goodwill amortization				7.2	7.2
Subtotal	$(36.5)	$(19.9)	$ 53.7	$ (9.0)	$(11.7)
Income tax @ 35%	12.8	7.0	(18.8)	3.1	4.1
Subtotal	$(23.7)	$(12.9)	$ 34.9	$ (5.9)	$ (7.6)
Total after—tax adjustment	$(27.3)	$(17.4)	$ 16.6	$ (2.2)	$(30.3)
Operating net income	**135.4**	**114.6**	**127.8**	**243.7**	**621.5**
Percentage difference	(17%)	(13%)	15%	(1%)	(5%)
Amortization of nonrecurring items	$ (6.9)	$ (6.9)	$ (6.9)	$ (6.9)	$(27.5)
Normalized net income	**128.5**	**107.7**	**120.9**	**236.8**	**594.0**
Percentage difference	(21%)	(18%)	9%	(4%)	(9%)

Income Tax Adjustments. As explained in Note D, Westvaco reported a onetime $15 million state tax reduction due to a business reorganization. It is important to segregate such amounts because they do not relate to current-year operations and distort the relationship between pretax and after-tax income. The use of tax carryforwards and significant changes in the valuation allowance, although not an issue for Westvaco, are frequent causes of distortions in the reported tax rate.[22]

Stock Option Expense. SFAS 123 permits companies to disclose (without income statement recognition) the cost of stock options granted to employees. As we argue in Chapter 12, such cost should be recognized as an operating expense. The adjustments in Exhibit 17-3 use the data in Westvaco's Note L.

Restructuring Provisions. Westvaco reported an $80.5 million restructuring charge in 1999, detailed in Note A. Most of the charge reflected the writedown of impaired fixed assets. Fiscal 2000 income included another charge of $16.1 million. Such provisions have become increasingly common in the United States; non-U.S. firms may report them as well. Restructuring provisions represent costs either of prior periods (e.g., underdepreciation of assets) or of later periods (severance and postemployment benefits; lease costs). These accruals are estimates, subject to later revision.[23]

---

[22]See Chapter 9 for discussion of both tax loss carryforwards and the valuation allowance.

[23]Westvaco's 2000 annual report states that the gross restructuring charge was $27 million, reduced by an $11 million gain from sale of a packaging plant written down in fiscal 1999. Thus, the 1999 restructuring charge turned out to be too high, distorting comparisons using reported data. When restructuring charges are added back to income, operating comparability is restored.

Realized Capital Gains and Losses. Westvaco reports gains or losses on asset sales in every year. The significant gains in fiscal 1999 and 2000 were due to a program of selling timberlands not needed for operations. The gains from this source increased to $35 million in fiscal 2001, and were expected to remain significant for several future years. While these gains are reported in the year of sale, as required by GAAP, they originated over a number of years. As shown in Exhibit 17-1, Westvaco has substantial unrealized gains remaining.

Gains and losses on sales of fixed assets and intercorporate investments reflect management decisions rather than changes in economic value in that period. For that reason they should not be considered operating in nature, even when recurring.

Capitalized Interest. As disclosed in Note F, Westvaco capitalizes interest on fixed assets under construction. Operating earnings should be adjusted by deducting the capitalized amount (see Chapter 7 for discussion). Note the sharp decline in capitalized interest in fiscal 1999, due to lower capital spending.

Goodwill Amortization. As discussed in Chapter 14, U.S. GAAP (SFAS 142) no longer requires the amortization of acquisition goodwill. However, companies following IASB GAAP and some non-U.S. GAAP continue to include goodwill amortization in income. In Exhibit 17-3 we add back goodwill amortization in 2000[24] for the following reasons:

1. Comparability with fiscal 2002 and following years that do not report goodwill amortization.
2. Comparability with firms that have either written off goodwill or used the pooling method, which does not result in goodwill.
3. Concerns about the arbitrary nature of goodwill amortization.

LIFO Liquidations. LIFO invasions distort reported gross margins. For this reason, they must be identified so that the analyst can disentangle their impact on the level and trend of gross margins and operating earnings. Westvaco did not report any LIFO liquidations in the years included in Exhibit 17-3.

Litigation or Government Actions. While not present in Westvaco's financial statements, charges or recoveries due to legal or governmental actions are common. Such charges or recoveries are nonoperating in nature and should be removed and analyzed separately.

Operating Net Income

Subtracting all nonrecurring items from reported net income results in operating earnings. Note the importance of distinguishing items reported pretax from those whose impact is reported after tax. When the after-tax effect is not reported, the analyst should estimate that effect by applying the marginal tax rate to pretax amounts.

The pattern of operating earnings is still erratic (Westvaco's business is cyclical), but there are significant differences in both level and trend:

- Operating income exceeds reported income in only one of the four years.
- The four-year total of operating income was 5% lower than total reported income for the same time span.
- Operating income increased in fiscal 1999 but reported net income fell.

Analytical Treatment of Nonrecurring Items

Our analysis thus far has removed nonrecurring items from reported income to obtain the trend of operating earnings. However, if we ignore nonrecurring items, we permit companies to sweep their mistakes under the rug. The purpose of analysis is to understand, not to forgive. Nonrecurring items, in some cases, do change the wealth of the firm's stockholders.

---

[24]Goodwill amortization was immaterial in prior years.

The four-year total of Westvaco's nonrecurring items is $30.3 million or about $7.6 million per year. How should this amount be handled? One approach would allocate $7.6 million to each year. The reasoning is that, although a given event may be nonrecurring, on average, some such event does occur and must be accounted for.

The better method is to examine major nonrecurring charges on an individual basis. Consider whether each item provides any information regarding:

- Future cash flows
- Future reported income
- Valuation
- Management behavior

Nonrecurring items with none of these should be ignored.

Restructuring provisions require special scrutiny. Such provisions often contain both noncash write-offs and provisions for future expenditures. The former indicate that prior-year income was overstated; the latter increase future-year income (that will no longer include these costs) and forecast future cash flows. Repeated writedowns suggest that depreciation is inadequate and the firm's quality of earnings is low.

Westvaco reports capital gains every year, mainly due to timberland sales. Such sales generally result in gains because of the historical cost bias: Declines in value (impairment) must be recognized when evident, whereas gains can be reported only when the property is sold. Recurring losses from the sale of operating assets would suggest that depreciation rates are too low.

Capitalized interest is not a nonrecurring item, but an example of how the income statement can be adjusted to a preferred accounting method. Similar adjustments can be made for capitalized software or intangibles, as discussed in Chapter 7.

Nonrecurring items often have implications for securities valuation. Some have a "one-time effect" as they are not expected to recur. Others are recurring in nature; as they affect the estimate of earning power, they can impact both:

1. The base to which a price-earnings multiple is applied
2. The expected earnings growth rate that determines the multiple itself.

For Westvaco, the following nonrecurring items should be included in normalized income:

1. Restructuring provisions as adjustments to the firm's portfolio of businesses should be considered a normal operating activity
2. Gains on asset sales that are clearly recurring in nature and offset some of the losses included in restructuring charges

Over the four-year period, these two items equal a net expense of $42.3 million pretax, or $27.5 million after tax (using a 35% tax rate). Averaged over four years, there is a $6.9 million per year reduction. The result is labeled *normalized net income* in Exhibit 17-3. This measure reduces income (compared with operating net income) each year. Over the four-year period, normalized net income is 9% below reported income.

The ultimate goal is an estimate of earnings power, which can be defined as the expected earnings of the firm in a normal year. Normalized net income can be used with an appropriate statistical model (such as least squares) to estimate earnings power. Valuation methods such as the price/earnings ratio and discounted earnings models (discussed in Chapter 19) should use normalized earnings or earnings power as inputs.

Earnings Normalization for Interfirm Comparisons

Our discussion thus far has been concerned with adjusting reported earnings in order to discern the operating trend. This process is essential when comparing two or more alternative investments. However, in this case, an additional step is required. Because firms may use alternative accounting methods for similar transactions, the analyst must adjust for such differences as:

- Inventory methods
- Depreciation methods and assumptions
- Benefit plan assumptions

When the firms in the comparison use different accounting systems (e.g., U.S. vs. IASB or non-U.S. GAAP), these adjustments can be highly significant.

Income Normalization for Non-U.S. Firms

The normalization process applied to non-U.S. firms is complicated by differences in accounting methods. When the goal is comparison of firms from different reporting jurisdictions, an effort must be made to apply the same accounting principles to all firms. In international comparisons, major issues include:

- Differing classification rules for extraordinary and other nonrecurring items.
- Inventory methods, as LIFO is rare outside of the United States.
- Differences in capitalization of research and development.
- Depreciation; accelerated methods are more common outside of the United States, especially in tax conformity countries.
- Differing lease accounting rules.
- Differences in accounting for marketable securities.
- Acquisition accounting differences that affect the amortization of goodwill and other balance sheet accounts affected by the purchase method.

When data are available (e.g., from reconciliations to U.S. or IASB GAAP), adjustments to reported income should be made to improve comparability.

Normalization Over the Economic Cycle

For cyclical firms, there is another complicating factor. The analyst must consider current operating earnings relative to the business cycle. This is true whether earnings are sensitive to the general economy or industry-specific cycles (property and casualty insurance is but one example). Given the varying length of business cycles, the analysis of cyclical firms should encompass a substantial time period—at least one full business cycle. Once these data are assembled, then earning power can be estimated using one of several methods.

One simplistic method is to average operating earnings over the entire cycle and use that average for valuation purposes. A slightly more sophisticated method uses average profitability ratios (such as gross margin or operating margin) or return ratios (return on equity) applied to current period sales or equity to estimate earning power based on the current level of operation.

A better approach is to create an earnings model of the firm based on the economic factors that drive the firm's profitability. For example, industrial production might be an independent variable for Westvaco, a manufacturer of paper and packaging. Firm sales could then be forecast using regression analysis. That sales forecast, combined with an analysis of the firm's cost structure (see the discussion of fixed and variable costs in Chapter 4), could be used to forecast the firm's earnings.

For conglomerates or other multidivisional firms, analysis needs to be done separately for each segment. Segment data should be used to estimate the future sales and earnings of each line of business. Firm forecasts are arrived at by adding together the segment forecasts and adjusting for corporate overhead (such as debt). We return to these issues in Chapter 19 (see also Chapter 13).

Acquisition Effects

Acquisitions affect reported earnings as the results of the acquired firm are included. Both the earnings of the acquired firm and the accounting method used must be examined.

Under the pooling of interests method, the operating results of the two firms are combined retroactively and prospectively. Thus, previously reported earnings are restated. Depending on the profitability of the acquired firm, the growth rate of reported earnings will change in most cases. For example, a firm with a high growth rate (whose shares sell at a high price/earnings ratio) can merge with a low-growth firm (whose shares sell at a low price/earnings ratio). The result will be higher earnings but a lower growth rate.

When the purchase method is used to account for an acquisition, the results of the acquired firm are included only following the merger. Depending on the price paid, the means of payment (cash or stock), the earnings of the acquired firm, and the accounting adjustments required by the purchase method, the acquisition may either increase or dilute reported earnings per share. The trend of reported sales and earnings is always distorted.

Because the sales of the acquired firm are included only following the merger, reported sales and expenses of the acquiring firm appear to rise. Although pro forma statements (which are required disclosures) provide some basis of comparison, they are too limited to permit separation of internal growth from the effect of acquisitions. When there are many small acquisitions, it becomes impossible to segregate the impact of each one. Sometimes, segment data can help the analyst track significant acquisitions that are maintained as separate segments.

The earnings trend is also impacted, but not in any predictable fashion. The earnings of the acquired firm are included postmerger. However, these earnings are offset by the impact of purchase method adjustments and financing costs. If the acquisition is partly financed with common stock (directly, or indirectly by selling shares shortly thereafter), then the additional shares dilute reported EPS.

Exchange Rate Effects

When firms operate in foreign countries, changing exchange rates also affect reported earnings. Translation gains and losses may be included in reported income. More subtle, but no less real, is the impact of translating the operating results of foreign subsidiaries into the parent (reporting) currency. When foreign currencies appreciate, the sales and earnings of operations in those currencies translate into more dollars (or other reporting currency), increasing consolidated sales and earnings. This phenomenon is discussed in Chapter 15.

Effect of Accounting Changes

Last, but far from least, changes in accounting methods or estimates can significantly influence the trend of reported earnings. Frequently found examples of voluntary changes include:

- Inventory method
- Depreciation method or lives
- Assumptions used for benefit plans
- Accounting method for affiliates

Mandated accounting changes also have had significant effects on reported earnings in recent years. Examples include:

- Impairment
- Asset retirement obligations
- Hedging and derivatives

Quality of Earnings

The term *quality of earnings* usually refers to the degree of conservatism in a firm's reported earnings. Indicators of high earnings quality include:

- Conservative revenue and expense recognition methods
- Use of LIFO inventory accounting (assumes rising prices)
- Bad-debt reserves that are high relative to receivables and past credit losses
- Use of accelerated depreciation methods and short lives
- Rapid write-off of acquisition-related intangible assets
- Minimal capitalization of interest and overhead
- Minimal capitalization of computer software costs
- Expensing of startup costs of new operations
- Use of the completed contract method of accounting

- Conservative assumptions used for employee benefit plans
- Adequate provisions for lawsuits and other loss contingencies
- Minimal use of off-balance-sheet financing techniques
- Absence of nonrecurring gains
- Absence of noncash earnings
- Clear and adequate disclosures

These issues were discussed in earlier chapters. Indicators listed tend to result in the underreporting of income through a combination of delayed recognition of revenues and accelerated recognition of expenses and losses.

Why is the quality of earnings important? One reason is that companies with high earnings quality are considered less risky because these firms have "banked" earnings using conservative accounting policies.[25] Such firms frequently are risk averse in other ways, in their financial structures and business plans, for example. High-quality earnings should be accorded a higher price/earnings multiple (all other things being equal) than low-quality earnings. The higher multiple reflects the lower risk as well as the understatement of reported income.

Alternatively, firms with different degrees of earnings quality can be compared by making adjustments to reported earnings so that the earnings of all firms are based on the same accounting principles and estimates. Techniques for making such adjustments appear throughout the book.

The last indicator, clear and adequate disclosures, is the most important. Companies sometimes use opaque or hard-to-understand disclosures to discourage analysts from questioning the accounting methods and assumptions that underlie the financial statements. *If the company discourages questions that would clarify these issues, or is unable to provide satisfactory answers, the analyst should carefully consider whether there are enough data to form an opinion regarding the valuation of the firm's securities or the evaluation of the risk of those securities.*

It should be noted that the term *earnings quality* is sometimes used to denote the predictability of earnings. Firms with predictable earnings growth (such as drug and consumer product firms) are sometimes said to have "high-quality" earnings. This usage is, of course, quite different; in some cases, predictability is the result of income manipulation, creating low-quality earnings by our definition. Analysts should be careful to determine which meaning of the term "quality of earnings" is intended when it is used.

In our examination of Westvaco's quality of earnings, we consider the following issues:

1. There is no evidence of revenue recognition problems.
2. Acquisitions have been minimal, with little impact on reported growth.
3. Westvaco's summary of significant accounting policies reports that it uses the straight-line depreciation method but provides only broad ranges of useful lives (e.g., 5–30 years) for machinery and equipment. As discussed in Chapter 8, no analysis is possible without better data.
4. Note A discusses the 1999 restructuring charge, mainly for asset impairment. The impairment charge suggests that depreciation rates were too low, at least for some facilities.
5. Note B reports significant gains from asset sales in 1997 and 1999. There are foreign currency translation losses each year.
6. Note D shows that the 1999 tax rate was artificially lowered by the state tax refund. That note also reports that Westvaco does not provide deferred taxes on the reinvested earnings of its foreign subsidiaries.
7. Westvaco used the more conservative LIFO method for 63% of 1999 inventories[26] (Note E). There have been no reported LIFO liquidations.

---

[25]It has been suggested that firms with conservative accounting methods can increase reported income by changing to less conservative methods. Only when the firm has exhausted this source must it turn to accounting chicanery.

[26]The amount of inventories on LIFO was disclosed in the 2000 annual report. The 1999 disclosure suggests that the proportion is substantial but no quantification was provided.

8. The allowance for bad debts (Note E) equals approximately 4% of trade receivables. However, Westvaco does not provide Schedule II in its 10-K report and detailed analysis of changes in the reserve is impossible.

9. Note F reports significant capitalized interest, requiring adjustment when computing operating earnings.

10. Westvaco makes limited use of off-balance-sheet financing techniques. Westvaco's moderate leasing activities are disclosed in Note I.

11. Note L reports Westvaco's stock options. The number of shares subject to employee options is 5.6 million or less than 6% of shares outstanding. While the current level of dilution is small (as computed above), the dilution would be greater if the market value of Westvaco shares rose significantly.

12. Pension plan assumptions shown in Note M are conservative relative to those reported in Accounting Trends and Techniques (see Chapter 12, footnotes 11 and 20 and related text). The discount rate is low, increasing the pension obligation, and the expected return is low, increasing pension cost. Both pension and postretirement benefit plans are overfunded and that overfunding is not fully recognized on the balance sheet. The current cost balance sheet in Exhibit 17-1 shows significant adjustments for these plans.

13. Segment disclosures (see Note O) are appropriate but provide no more detail than required.

14. Westvaco's disclosures are generally understandable.

Our conclusion is that Westvaco has, on balance, accounting policies that are more conservative than the average large American public company. However, the income adjustments shown in Exhibit 17-3 do result in operating earnings below reported income, which is a negative indicator of earnings quality.

Comprehensive Income

In Chapter 1, we discussed the concept of comprehensive income and the requirements of SFAS 130. In this section, we consider the application of that concept to Westvaco. As seen in Westvaco's consolidated statement of shareholders' equity, there is only one component of other comprehensive income—foreign currency translation losses. Westvaco does not use derivative instruments for hedging purposes, generating gains and losses that would be included in comprehensive income under SFAS 133. Its marketable securities are all short-term, so that there are no unrealized gains or losses from that source. Finally, as its pension plans are overfunded, it does not report a minimum liability provision.

As discussed in Chapter 15, Westvaco changed the functional currency for its investment in Rigesa from the U.S. dollar to the Brazilian real effective November 1, 1997. Thus, translation gains and losses prior to that date were included in reported income while subsequent losses are shown as other comprehensive income (loss). That loss had grown to $130 million at October 31, 1999 due to depreciation of the real.

The theoretical justification of including translation gains in equity rather than net income was to remove the volatility caused by transient variations in exchange rates. However, the real has continuously depreciated against the dollar in recent years, raising the issue of whether the translation losses are permanent and therefore should be included in operating income. We have not made that adjustment, which would further reduce operating income relative to reported income, in Exhibit 17-3.[27]

We see comprehensive income, however, in broader terms, encompassing all changes in current-cost net worth other than transactions with shareholders. Under this definition, Westvaco has a number of qualifying elements, as seen in Exhibit 17-1. The largest are:

- LIFO reserve on inventory
- Adjustment of timberlands to estimated fair value

---

[27]Expensing the change in the foreign currency translation component of comprehensive income would reduce 1999 income by $.97 per diluted share and 1998 income by $.32 per diluted share.

- Adjustment of debt to fair value
- Adjustment for employee benefit plans: equal to the difference between nonsmoothed cost and reported cost.
- Elimination of deferred income taxes

By examining the changes in these items during 1999,[28] we can compute a more meaningful measure of comprehensive income:

	Years Ended October 31		
	1998	1999	Change
LIFO reserve	$123	$119	$ (4)
Fair value debt adjustment	(79)	(18)	61
Pension plan adjustment[29]			155
OPEB plan adjustment[29]			2
Total			$214

We use these computations to prepare a statement of current cost comprehensive income for 1999:

	In $millions	Per Share*
Net income	$111.2	$1.11
Plus: nonoperating items	16.6	
Equals: operating income	$127.8	1.27
Valuation changes	214.0	
Current cost comprehensive income	$341.8	3.41

*All calculations use 100.293 million average shares outstanding.

Westvaco's income, measured using the comprehensive income concept, was nearly four times reported net income for 1999. The major factor was the improved funded status of the employee pension plan (resulting from the high return on plan assets for that year). Although this income measure is far more volatile than reported net income, it captures economic changes that are excluded from income under current GAAP.

ANALYSIS OF CASH FLOW

The adjusted balance sheet reports the current or market value of the resources that are available for firm operations and generate cash flows. We now turn to an analysis of cash flows to evaluate Westvaco's ability to service debt and generate cash flows for investment or return of capital to the equityholders.

The analysis is based on Chapter 3, where we discuss the use of cash flow analysis to develop insights into a firm's financial position and performance. In other chapters, we show the cash flow implications of different reporting methods. We focus on both the level and trends in cash flow components. Our primary objectives are to:

1. Determine the firm's ability to generate cash flows to meet operating needs.
2. Evaluate the role of different sources of financing for current operations and growth.

[28]We assume no change in the fair value of timberlands. Given that the fair value is a rough estimate, it is not practical to look at value changes for any one year.

[29]These adjustments are computed in problems 12-2 (pensions) and 12-16 (OPEB).

Another goal of our analysis is to illustrate the extent to which cash flow classifications are affected by reporting choices. Examples include:

- Capitalization of fixed assets, such as the cost of finding natural resources or developing new products (Chapter 7)
- Exclusion of "off-balance-sheet" obligations from the firm's financial statements (Chapter 11)
- Accounting methods applied to investments in affiliates (Chapter 13)
- Accounting methods used for acquisitions (Chapter 14)

Adjustment for these effects is seldom easy. The first (and most important) step is to recognize that distortion is present. In many cases, the analyst may judge that the degree of distortion is too small to warrant adjustment. In other cases (e.g., accounting for affiliates), analytical techniques (proportionate consolidation) permit approximate adjustment.

As discussed in Chapter 3, the classification of cash flows among operating, investing, and financing activities is the starting point for cash flow analysis. Exhibit 17-4 shows these amounts, obtained from Westvaco's cash flow statement, for the four years 1997–2000. The 1997–1999 data are shown in Westvaco's 1999 annual report.

The net change in cash is essentially meaningless; a firm can sell assets or incur liabilities to improve its cash position at the end of an accounting period (often called "window dressing"). What is important is the trend in the components of cash flow and the relationship among them.

Analysis of Cash Flow Components

Cash flow from operations (CFO) reports the cash flows generated by the firm's operating activities. Westvaco's CFO is positive every year and increased in each year. There is little correlation with reported net income (before extraordinary items and the effect of accounting changes), which declined in 1998 and 1999 and then rose sharply in 2000.

Exhibit 17-4 recasts the cash flow statement to a format that provides better insight into cash from operations by:

1. Reclassifying interest paid from CFO to cash from financing (CFF)
2. Segregating capital expenditures from other investment cash flows
3. Estimating cash flows related to nonrecurring items
4. Reporting the free cash flow.

We discuss each of these issues in turn.

Reclassification of Interest Paid. In Chapter 3, we state that interest paid should be included in CFF rather than CFO because:

- Excluding interest paid from CFO makes that amount comparable among firms with different degrees of financial leverage.

The first adjustment in Exhibit 17-4 estimates after-tax interest paid by applying Westvaco's marginal income tax rate (assumed to be the U.S. statutory rate) to interest paid. The amount of interest paid reported in Note H is *net* of interest capitalized, which we have added back.[30] This adjustment increases aggregate CFO (4-year total) by more than $346 million (19.3%). The reclassification does not materially change the trend of CFO for those years.

Interest received should, under similar reasoning, be reclassified from CFO to CFI. We have not done so because the amount is small ($15 million interest income in 1999).[31]

---

[30]We have omitted as immaterial the adjustment of cash for investment to remove the capitalized interest ($8.9 million pretax) included in additions to plant and timberlands.

[31]There is no information regarding interest received on a cash basis. Lacking other evidence, we would assume that cash received equals the income statement amount.

EXHIBIT 17-4. WESTVACO
Analysis of Cash Flows, 1997–2000 (in $millions)

	Years Ending October 31				
	1997	1998	1999	2000	4-Year Total
Cash and marketable securities					
End of prior year	$ 115.4	$ 175.4	$105.1	$ 108.8	$ 115.4
End of current year	175.4	105.1	108.8	225.3	225.3
Change in cash and marketable securities	$ 60.0	$ (70.3)	$ 3.7	$ 116.5	$ 109.9
As reported					
Cash from operations (CFO)	390.7	406.7	412.7	583.1	1,793.2
Cash from investment (CFI)	(593.0)	(416.0)	(229.9)	(1,475.0)	(2,713.9)
Cash from financing (CFF)	262.9	(57.0)	(160.6)	1,006.2	1,051.5
Effect of exchange rates	(0.6)	(4.0)	(18.5)	2.2	(20.9)
Change in cash and marketable securities	$ 60.0	$ (70.3)	$ 3.7	$ 116.5	$ 109.9
Free cash flow (CFO + CFI)	(202.3)	(9.3)	182.8	(891.9)	(920.7)
Dividends paid	(89.8)	(89.3)	(88.2)	(88.5)	(355.8)
Free cash flow after dividends	$(292.1)	$ (98.6)	$ 94.6	$ (980.4)	$(1,276.5)
Classification adjustment					
Interest incurred	110.5	128.8	121.0	172.7	533.0
Less: income tax offset @ 35%	(38.7)	(45.1)	(42.3)	(60.4)	(186.5)
After-tax interest incurred	$ 71.8	$ 83.7	$ 78.7	$ 112.3	$ 346.5
Capital expenditures	(621.2)	(423.0)	(228.9)	(214.0)	(1,487.1)
Acquisitions	—	—	(22.7)	(1,342.9)	(1,365.6)
Proceeds from asset sales	22.3	6.9	22.8	81.6	133.6
Totals	$(598.9)	$(416.1)	$(228.8)	$(1,475.3)	$(2,719.1)
After classification adjustment					
Cash from operations (CFO)	462.5	490.4	491.4	695.4	2,139.7
Cash from investment (CFI)	(593.0)	(416.0)	(229.9)	(1,475.0)	(2,713.9)
Cash from financing (CFF)	191.1	(140.7)	(239.3)	893.9	705.0
Effect of exchange rates	(0.6)	(4.0)	(18.5)	2.2	(20.9)
Change in cash and marketable securities	$ 60.0	$ (70.3)	$ 3.7	$ 116.5	$ 109.9
Free cash flow (adjusted CFO—capex)	(158.7)	67.4	262.5	481.4	652.6
Dividends paid and stock purchases	(107.2)	(138.8)	(99.0)	(90.8)	(435.8)
Free cash flow after dividends and stock (re)purchases	$(265.9)	$ (71.4)	$163.5	$ 390.6	$ 216.8

Segregation of Capital Expenditures. Investing cash flow contains three major components, shown in Exhibit 17-4, that deserve separate analysis:

1. Purchases of property and equipment represent Westvaco's capital expenditures and are a principal factor in the estimation of free cash flow. Capital expenditures declined steadily, from $621 million in 1997 to $214 million in 2000. Westvaco's 1999 MD&A states that

   > This planned lower level of capital expenditures follows the completion of several important initiatives that added significant support to our long-term strategy.

2. Westvaco's acquisition activity, which had been minimal, accelerated in fiscal 2000, with payments of more than $1.3 billion. Westvaco has clearly shifted its emphasis from capital expenditures to growth by acquisition.[32]

[32]In its 2000 MD&A, Westvaco stated its intention to keep capital expenditures below the level of depreciation.

3. Westvaco has undertaken a long-term program to sell timberlands not needed for current operations. Such sales help to finance acquisition expenditures.

Taken together, these actions represent a major strategic change for Westvaco.

Estimating Nonrecurring Cash Flows. CFO can be distorted by unusual items. Examples include:

- *Changes in normal seasonal patterns.* For example, a royalty payment normally received in late December might be received early in January. As a result, current-year CFO would be understated, whereas following-year CFO is overstated.
- *Sales of receivables.* As shown in Chapter 11, changes in the amount of receivables sold (or securitized) distort the pattern of CFO.
- *Nonrecurring cash flows*, such as those related to lawsuits.

Nonrecurring income statement items often have no impact on CFO, because either they have no cash flow effect at all (most accounting changes and asset writedowns) or their cash effect is not included in CFO (gains and losses on asset sales).

Reviewing Westvaco's nonrecurring items in Exhibit 17-3, we see that there was little effect on CFO. Most are noncash items. Some items (gains on asset sales) are included in other cash flow components.

Restructuring provisions contain both cash and noncash components. Note A states that the restructuring charge consisted almost entirely of noncash asset writedowns. As the cash costs relate to "employee separation and other exit costs" no adjustment to CFO is required; such costs should be viewed as normal operating cash flows.

As Westvaco has no cash flows that would be considered nonrecurring, there is no adjustment to reported CFO other than for interest paid.

Free Cash Flow

Although widely used in the investment world, free cash flow (FCF) has no uniform definition. Using the conventional definition of free cash flow (reported CFO less cash from investment), Westvaco's free cash flow was negative by more than $920 million over the 1997–2000 period and was negative each year except 1999. The shortfall grows to $1,276 million when dividends paid are subtracted.

As discussed in Chapter 3, we believe that the most useful definition for financial analysis is CFO before interest less capital expenditures.[33] That definition is used in Exhibit 17-4. Adjusted (to that definition) FCF aggregated $652 million over the 1997–2000 period, and was positive in every year after 1997. FCF for the four-year period was $217 million after subtracting dividends and stock repurchases.[34]

These data provide a clearer understanding of Westvaco's cash flows over the four-year period. In short, the company cut back on capital expenditures, started a timberland asset sale program, and used its free cash flow and proceeds from asset sales to start an aggressive acquisition program.

International Cash Flow Comparisons

Because of accounting differences that limit the comparability of income statements, many analysts focus on cash flows. However, the international comparison of cash flows is also fraught with danger, as noncomparability results from:

- Consolidation differences that may exclude some operating affiliates.
- Various definitions of cash from operations. As discussed on page 98, CFO amounts may differ among companies using IAS and U.S. GAAP. Some non-U.S. firms still report funds from operations, which differs considerably from CFO. Reclassification adjustments or use of the transactional analysis method (see Chapter 3) can produce more comparable cash flow statements.

---

[33]That is true as long as acquisitions are not a replacement for "normal" growth (i.e., acquiring new facilities rather than constructing them).

[34]We have included stock repurchases as part of dividends as that is a better measure of dividends paid (see Chapter 19).

- Some accounting principle differences do affect reported CFO. Methods that result in more capitalization (interest and research costs are two examples) increase reported CFO. Lease accounting, which differs from GAAP to GAAP, also changes CFO.

Because of these factors, valid cross-border cash flow comparisons depend on adjustments that restore comparability.

FCF calculations may also be affected by these problems. When FCF is defined as CFO (properly adjusted) less *all* capitalized operating assets, it should be reasonably comparable.

ADJUSTED FINANCIAL RATIOS

The current cost balance sheet shown in Exhibit 17-1 should be used to compute financial ratios that incorporate these better measures of resources (assets) and obligations (liabilities). Exhibit 17-5 shows such computations for some key ratios, using definitions from Chapter 4.

Activity (turnover) ratios are reduced mainly due to the valuation adjustments that increase reported assets. Given the firm-to-firm differences in both valuation effects and the use of off-balance-sheet activities, activity ratios using adjusted data provide a better measure of the efficiency with which assets are used. Westvaco's inventory turnover ratio declines from 7.37 to 5.06 and its total asset turnover declines from .57 to .43 after adjustment.

Westvaco's 1999 current ratio increases as the LIFO reserve more than offsets the elimination of the current deferred tax asset.

Solvency ratios were recomputed in Exhibit 17-2. For 1999, the highly positive valuation adjustments offset the inclusion of off-balance-sheet financing. Despite elimination of acquisition goodwill from the 2000 current cost balance sheet, the adjusted ratios are still well above the unadjusted ratios. Westvaco's reported data overstate the company's debt burden.

However, current cost-based data are more volatile than reported data, as the latter ignore many valuation changes. This does not mean that analysts should avoid using adjusted data; such data tell us about real economic effects. It does mean that single-year valuation effects should be used with caution; such effects are best evaluated over longer time periods.

Profitability ratios are also very different after adjustment. Exhibit 17-5 shows three ratios, all computed after tax: return-on-assets, return-on-total capital, and return on equity. These ratios decline after adjustment because the denominators are higher, mainly reflecting

EXHIBIT 17-5. WESTVACO
Adjusted Financial Ratios, Year Ended October 31, 1999 (in $millions)

	Reported	Adjusted
Activity		
Inventory turnover	7.37	5.06
Number of days	49.56	72.16
Total asset turnover	0.57	0.43
Liquidity		
Current ratio	1.74	1.92
Solvency		
Debt-to-equity	0.68	0.35
Debt-to-total capital	0.40	0.26
Profitability		
Return on assets	3.91%	3.18%
Return on total capital	5.25%	3.40%
Return on equity	5.12%	2.84%

valuation adjustments. The adjusted numerators use operating income from Exhibit 17-3 and interest paid. Tax adjustments assume a 35% tax rate.

This analysis can be taken a step further by using current cost comprehensive income in the numerator of the return ratios. Using the 1999 amount computed above, the 1999 return on equity would be 7.59% ($341.8/$4,504). While current cost-based ratios are inherently more volatile, they are ultimately the best measure of management's stewardship of corporate assets. If the returns on corporate assets (stated at market value) are inadequate over time, stockholders would be better off if those assets were sold and the proceeds distributed.

International Ratio Comparisons

As ratios are constructed from reported financial data, ratio comparability depends on comparable underlying data. It should be evident from discussions throughout the chapter that ratios constructed from unadjusted financial data are unlikely to be useful measures of activity, liquidity, solvency, and profitability. Only when balance sheet, income statement, and cash flow data are adjusted for differences in accounting and reporting methods will the resultant ratios be comparable.

SUMMARY

Throughout the text, we emphasize the need to adjust reported financial data for the effects of accounting choice. In this chapter, we have brought all these adjustments together to produce a set of adjusted financial statements and ratios. Our adjustments include:

1. Preparation of a current cost balance sheet
2. Normalization of reported income
3. Adjustments to reported cash flows
4. Adjusted ratios using the adjusted balance sheet, income statement, and cash flow data

The rationale for this adjustment process is the production of data that are useful for investment and credit decisions, the subject of the next two chapters.

18

ACCOUNTING- AND FINANCE-BASED MEASURES OF RISK

CHAPTER OUTLINE

CHAPTER OBJECTIVES

INTRODUCTION

Earnings Variability and Its Components

Operating and Financial Risk

Measures of Financial and Operating Leverage

Accounting Beta

CREDIT RISK

Bankruptcy Prediction

Research Results

Univariate Models

Multivariate Models

Bankruptcy Prediction and Cash Flows

Bankruptcy and Financial Distress: Concluding Comments

The Prediction of Bond Ratings

Bond Rating Classifications

The Bond Ratings Process

Ratings: Risk and Returns

Impact of Ratings

Usefulness of Bond Ratings Predictions

Choice of Explanatory Variables

Model Results

The Z"-Score and Bond Ratings

The Significance of Ratings: Another Look

Measurement of Financial Variables

EQUITY RISK: MEASUREMENT AND PREDICTION

Risk and Return: Theoretical Models

The CAPM and Beta (β)

APT and Multifactor Models

Importance and Usefulness of Beta (β)

Review of Theoretical and Empirical Findings

Theoretical Framework

Empirical Studies

The Attack on the CAPM and β

Alternative Measures of Equity Risk or Market Inefficiency?

The Defense of β and the CAPM

Implications for Accounting Risk Measures

SUMMARY

APPENDIX 18-A

CHAPTER OBJECTIVES

This chapter is concerned with the evaluation of risk and it focuses on different measures of risk suggested by theory and used in practice. Our purpose is to:

1. Define measures of *earnings variability* and examine their use in the prediction and evaluation of risk.

2. Evaluate and review research on the prediction of bankruptcy. We also discuss the role of cash flows in the prediction of bankruptcy.

3. Describe the role of the debt rating process and the resulting debt classifications in the evaluation of default risk.

4. Examine the value of predictions of bond ratings and review empirical research.

5. Discuss equity risk in the context of the capital asset pricing model and the arbitrage pricing theory.

6. Review theoretical and empirical research related to the measurement and prediction of equity risk.

7. Discuss the controversy over the efficacy of CAPM and beta.

INTRODUCTION

An important objective of the analysis of financial statements in general and that of ratios in particular is an assessment of the risk inherent in a firm's operations. Although liquidity, solvency, and profitability analysis implicitly address the probability that a firm's cash will fall below some level, commonly used ratios do not directly measure this uncertainty. A large body of research[1] has examined the utility of accounting-based measures in *credit* and *equity* risk evaluation and prediction.

Credit risk refers to the risk of default and/or bankruptcy. Bondholders face uncertain returns. The level of uncertainty is not (directly) related to the firm's expected return; rather, it is related to a minimum level of return, that is, the return that is sufficient to avoid default on principal and interest payments. The risk of bankruptcy reflects the uncertainty about the ability of the firm to continue operations if its financial condition were to fall below some minimum level.

The equity investor takes on more risk than an investor in the debt securities of that same firm and expects a commensurably higher return. The equity investor's risk relates to the uncertainty of achieving the firm's expected return.

Research in these areas typically involves two phases. The first calibrates the association between the risk measure and a set of financial ratios. The second step uses this association to predict risk. A result of this research is often an equation of the form

$$Y = w_0 + w_1 X_1 + w_2 X_2 + \ldots + w_n X_n$$

which measures the relationship between the dependent variable Y (e.g., bankruptcy, bond rating, or beta) and the independent, explanatory variable X_I's (financial ratios or, more generally speaking, accounting-based measures of risk).

Such research is discussed throughout the chapter, which is divided into sections corresponding to each of the risk categories. Each section contains a brief discussion of the relevant financial risk measure(s) as well as the accounting-based measures of risk used to forecast those financial risk measures. Exhibits in Appendix 18-A summarize the explanatory independent variables (financial risk measures) used in key studies in each of the areas. Some of these measures and their classifications are familiar as they fall into the four ratio categories (activity, liquidity, solvency, and profitability) discussed in Chapter 4. Other indicators used in these models are primarily explicit measures of the firm's *earnings variability*. These measures and the theoretical justification for their use in the prediction and evaluation of risk are presented below.

Earnings Variability and Its Components

The variance of a firm's earnings is a direct measure of the uncertainty (risk) of its earnings stream. A smooth earnings stream is assumed to be desirable by firms, their creditors, and the financial markets. To the extent that accounting earnings mirror a firm's economic well-being, the variance in that measure would be expected to measure a firm's risk.

Box 18-1 presents the theoretical justification for a ratio that explicitly incorporates variance. That ratio, expressed in terms of CFO, is equal to

$$\frac{\text{Cash balance} + \text{E(CFO)}}{\text{Standard deviation of CFO}}$$

where E(CFO) equals expected CFO. The higher the ratio, the lower the likelihood that the firm's cash balance will fall below a certain level. As will be seen, variations of this ratio (using measures other than CFO) appear in a number of credit risk models. The intuitive meaning of this ratio is that cash flow analysis must consider the variance of the cash flows as well as levels.

---

[1]An important caveat with respect to this research is the timeliness issue. As Ryan (1997, p. 83) notes, "A particular limitation is that most risk research was performed in the 1970s and so employs models of the economic environment and data generated by the accounting system at that time."

BOX 18-1
A Probabilistic Measure of Liquidity

Emery and Cogger (1982) discuss liquidity in the following theoretical framework. If we let L equal the liquid reserves (e.g., cash)* at the beginning of the period and C equal operating cash flow during the period, insolvency or lack of liquidity is defined as occurring when additional financing is required, that is, when

$$L + C < 0$$

The analytical question becomes determining the probability that the foregoing will occur. If we assume that C is normally distributed, the probability[†] can be found by looking at the normal distribution table for the standardized value

$$-\frac{L + \mu_c}{\sigma_c}$$

where μ_C and σ_c are the mean and standard deviation of the operating cash flows. Since this measure is related to the probability of insolvency, Emery and Cogger suggest that it is a useful and relevant liquidity ratio. It combines the stock of cash with the flows and the variance of those flows.

---

*The analysis need not be confined to defining L as cash but can be extended to include other liquid reserves (such as working capital and accounts receivable) with appropriate definition of terms. See also Box 18-4, which describes a model utilizing the market value of the firm's assets as L.
[†]This measure will be an upwardly biased measure as it ignores the probability of falling below zero before the period ends. However, as Emery and Cogger point out, for short intervals the bias will be small.

Several factors contribute to the volatility of a firm's earnings. These components are presented schematically in Figure 18-1.

Earnings volatility is primarily related to the underlying uncertainty of demand for the firm's output, the *variability of its sales*. The effect of sales variability on earnings variability is a function of the firm's *operating and financial leverage*. In addition, earnings variability is affected by uncertainty regarding the prices of outputs and inputs.

If we use the argument usually made with respect to market returns, sales and earnings can be said to depend on general economic conditions as well as firm-specific policies. Thus, earnings variability has a systematic as well as an unsystematic component. The systematic component of earnings (sales) is referred to as the *accounting beta*,[2] $B_{earnings}$ (B_{sales}), defined as the relationship between the firm's operating results and general economic factors.

Many of the models use components of variability (operating and financial risk) instead of (or in addition to) overall earnings variability. These components are discussed in greater detail below.

Operating and Financial Risk

Operating (OLE) and financial (FLE) leverage measure the extent to which a firm's income varies as a result of variations in sales. *Operating leverage* is the percentage of fixed operating costs, and *financial leverage* the percentage of fixed financing costs in a firm's overall cost structure. The higher the percentage of fixed costs, the greater the variation in income as a result of variation in sales.[3]

FIGURE 18-1 Relationship of components of earnings variability.

[2]Throughout this chapter we use "B" to represent accounting betas and the Greek symbol β to represent market betas.
[3]These concepts are explained in greater detail in Chapter 4.

It is important to distinguish between the concepts of operating *leverage* and operating *risk*. Operating leverage does not, by itself, create risk. If a firm's sales are predictable, then leverage does not create uncertainty. However, when a firm's sales are uncertain, high leverage increases operating risk and the variance of income. Operating risk is, therefore, a function of operating leverage and sales variance:

$$\text{Operating risk} = f\{\text{OLE, Variance (Sales)}\}$$

Leverage and risk are directly associated only for two firms having the same level of uncertainty with respect to sales. The firm with the higher leverage will be the riskier of the two.

Operating risk is also referred to as *business risk* as it represents the underlying risk of the firm's operations in the absence of financing. When financial leverage is also considered, the total risk of the firm can be expressed[4] as

$$\text{Variance (income)} = \text{Total risk} = f\{\text{FLE, Operating risk}\}$$
$$= f\{\text{FLE, OLE, Variance (Sales)}\}$$

Measures of Financial and Operating Leverage

As fixed and variable costs are generally not disclosed, the measurement of leverage often requires the use of surrogate measures. This is less of a problem for financial leverage, where direct measures such as the ratio of interest expense to total expense or earnings before interest and taxes (EBIT) to earnings before taxes (EBT) can be computed from financial data. Nevertheless, some researchers use such ratios as debt/equity, debt/assets, or debt/capital as surrogate measures of financial leverage, where higher ratios imply greater financial leverage. The use of these surrogates seems reasonable, since higher debt would be expected to result in higher fixed interest charges.[5]

Measuring operating leverage is somewhat more difficult. Appendix 4-A shows how to estimate a firm's fixed and variable costs using regression analysis. A common measure used to estimate operating leverage is the coefficient v derived from the regression equation

$$TC_t = F + vS_t$$

where TC_t and S_t are the firm's total costs and sales, respectively, in period t, and F and v are regression estimates of the firm's fixed and variable costs (the latter as a percentage of sales), respectively. The lower the coefficient v, the greater the operating leverage, as fixed costs are relatively higher.

Another surrogate for operating leverage is the ratio of fixed assets to total assets. High capital intensity (high fixed depreciation cost) increases operating leverage.

An important issue is whether the two measures of risk, financial and operating leverage, are independent of each other. Watts and Zimmerman (1986) take the position that the two should be highly (positively) correlated. Consistent with Myers (1977), they posit that capital-intensive industries (and firms) have higher operating leverage. Such firms have more fixed assets (which determine capital intensity) and find it (relatively) easier to finance these assets by issuing debt, increasing financial leverage.[6]

Others argue (see Mandelker and Rhee, 1984) that the amount of total risk a firm should undertake is fixed, commensurate with its expected return. Therefore, if it increases operating risk, it should compensate by reducing financial leverage.[7] This would imply that these two

---

[4]There is a clear parallel between this expression and the definition in Chapter 4 of the *total leverage effect* (TLE):

$$\% \text{ Change in income} = \text{TLE} = \text{FLE} \times \text{OLE} \times \% \text{ Change in sales}$$

[5]It is, however, somewhat mystifying why some researchers use surrogate measures rather than direct measures of financial leverage.

[6]See also Bergman and Callen (1991), who provide another rationale why operating and financial leverage should be positively correlated.

[7]As noted in Chapter 4, in recent years a number of firms with high operating leverage assumed significantly greater debt. When the economy weakened, the combination of financial and operating leverage was too much for many of these firms. They were forced into default or major restructuring to survive.

risk measures are negatively correlated. Using regression estimates of both financial and operating leverage, Mandelker and Rhee report a significant negative correlation (approximately -0.3) between operating and financial leverage, indicating that firms tend to balance the two sources of risk. More interesting, perhaps, is their finding that the trade-off between the two risk sources is not uniform across all firms. Rather, riskier firms [as measured by their systematic beta (β) risk measure] "engage in trade-offs more actively than firms with low betas."[8]

Accounting Beta

Earlier it was noted that the variability in a firm's earnings has two components: one due to (systematic) industry and economywide factors and the other to (nonsystematic) firm-specific factors. The systematic factor reflects the degree to which the earnings of the firm vary with the earnings of other firms in the economy. Its empirical measure is the "accounting beta," $B_{earnings}$, the regression coefficient derived from the following equation:

$$E_t = a + B_{earnings} ME_t$$

where E_t is the firm's earnings for period t and ME_t an index of market earnings[9] for period t. When earnings are defined as operating income, then the corresponding $B_{earnings}$ measures the systematic component of operating or business risk. $B_{earnings}$ measures risk, or the degree to which a firm's earnings (co)vary with general economic conditions. The higher the $B_{earnings}$, the greater the level of systematic risk.

$B_{earnings}$ is, of course, affected by the variability of sales or, more precisely, the systematic portion of sales variability, B_{sales}. Thus, just as we have expressed a firm's earnings variability as a function of FLE, OLE, and variance (sales), we can also express its systematic component as a function of FLE, OLE, and the systematic portion of variance (sales):

$$B_{earnings} = f\{FLE, OLE, B_{sales}\}$$

We will return to these measures and their use in the prediction of risk during the discussions of credit and equity risk.

CREDIT RISK

The focus of credit risk is the risk of default, resulting in loss of principal and interest. The ultimate form of default is, of course, bankruptcy.

Bankruptcy Prediction

The ability to predict which firms will face insolvency in the near term is important to both potential creditors and investors. When a firm files for bankruptcy, creditors often lose a portion of principal and interest payments due; common stock investors may suffer substantial dilution or even a total loss of their equity interest. In addition, bankruptcy imposes significant legal costs and risks on its investors and creditors as well as the firm, even if it survives.

For these reasons, there has been considerable research into the use of ratios and cash flow data to predict bankruptcy. Before reviewing this research, however, we must discuss the appropriate measurement criterion to use in assessing the efficacy of bankruptcy prediction models.

The total percentage of correct predictions provided by a predictive model is not a sufficient criterion. The evaluation of any predictive model is not complete unless the relative

---

[8]Mandelker and Rhee (1984), p. 55.

[9]Different indices can be used to measure market earnings. One may be the average earnings of the Standard & Poor's 500; others include earnings of another broad stock market index, corporate earnings calculated by the Labor Department, or an index created by the researcher (e.g., the average earnings of a random sample of firms). Since the purpose of the index is to measure general economic conditions, measures of GNP may also be used. For statistical purposes, this model is often expressed in terms of changes in earnings ($E_t - E_{t-1}$), and changes in the earnings index ($ME_t - ME_{t-1}$).

EXHIBIT 18-1
Types of Misclassification Errors in Bankruptcy Prediction

Predicted Outcome	Actual Outcome	
	Bankrupt	Nonbankrupt
Bankrupt	Correct	Error: Type II Cost: Small 0–10%
Nonbankrupt	Error: Type I Cost: Large Up to 100%	Correct

costs and benefits of correct versus incorrect predictions are considered. As Exhibit 18-1 indicates, there are two types of misclassification errors:

1. *Type I error* refers to the misclassification of a firm by predicting nonbankruptcy when in reality the firm becomes bankrupt.
2. *Type II error* reflects the misclassification of a solvent firm as bankrupt.

The cost of the two types of error is very different. This is especially relevant for a bankruptcy prediction model, where the cost of incorrectly classifying a bankrupt firm as solvent (type I error) is much greater than the cost of incorrectly classifying a solvent firm as bankrupt (type II error). Altman et al. (1977) estimate type I errors to be 35 times as costly as type II errors.

In the first case, the creditor can lose 100% of its investment. In the second case, the loss is limited to the spread between the rate the (incorrectly) misclassified firm would have paid and the actual return on an alternative investment. This ranges from zero if an investment with the same return is found, to (worst case) the spread between the forgone rate and the risk-free rate.

To put these arguments in perspective, consider a strategy of forecasting nonbankruptcy for every firm. Since on average, for established firms, the rate of bankruptcy is only 5%, this strategy would have a 95% success rate. However, it misclassifies every bankrupt firm, and it is precisely this type of costly error one would like to avoid. At the other extreme, predicting bankruptcy for every firm avoids the potential losses associated with lending to a bankrupt firm, but is tantamount to ceasing business as a creditor.

Thus, given the relative magnitudes of the cost of the two error types, one should be willing to make the following trade-off: lower accuracy of correctly predicting solvent firms for higher accuracy in the prediction of bankrupt firms.[10] [Figure 18-3 from Ohlson (1980) illustrates this trade-off.] In evaluating (and designing) a bankruptcy prediction model, therefore, both the percentage correctly classified as bankrupt and the percentage correctly classified as nonbankrupt should be viewed separately.

Research Results

Univariate Models

The early studies of bankruptcy prediction date back more than 30 years. Beaver (1966) compared patterns of 29 ratios in the five years preceding bankruptcy for a sample of failed firms with a control group of firms that did not fail. The purpose was to see which

---

[10]Bankruptcy models have also been used in other contexts, where the relative costs of the different types of errors may be radically different. Antitrust laws forbid mergers of certain companies unless one of the companies is deemed to be "failing." Blum (1974) reports a case where a bankruptcy prediction model was used. The philosophy underlying the antitrust laws might argue that allowing the merger when the firm is not bankrupt (predicting bankruptcy when the firm is solvent, type II error) is more costly to society than stopping the merger even if the firm is failing (but the model incorrectly classified it as nonfailing, type I error).

ratios could forecast bankruptcy and how many years in advance such forecasts could be made.[11]

"Cash flow"/total liabilities proved to be the best predictor overall.[12] Overall, in the first year prior to bankruptcy, this model had a 13% misclassification rate. The distribution of errors between type I and type II errors, however, was not uniform. There was a greater frequency of type I errors (22%) relative to type II errors (5%) as it was more difficult to classify bankrupt firms correctly. This difficulty increased dramatically with the length of the prediction horizon. Given the greater costs associated with type I errors, these results underscore the importance of evaluating each type of error separately.

Beaver's approach was "univariate" in that each ratio was evaluated in terms of how it alone could predict bankruptcy without consideration of the other ratios. Most work in this area, however, is "multivariate," wherein predictive models use a combination of ratios to forecast bankruptcy.

Multivariate Models

A summary of 14 multivariate models by Gentry et al. (1984) finds that liquidity and solvency ratios are most frequently used followed by profitability and activity ratios. (See Apendix 18-A)

Altman's Z-Score. The best known of the bankruptcy prediction studies that have withstood the test of time is Altman's (1968) Z-score model. The Z-score is the value resulting from the following discriminant analysis equation:

$$\mathbf{Z} = \mathbf{1.2} \times \textbf{Working capital / Total assets}$$
$$+ \mathbf{1.4} \times \textbf{Retained earnings / Total assets}$$
$$+ \mathbf{3.3} \times \textbf{EBIT / Total assets}$$
$$+ \mathbf{0.6} \times \textbf{Market value of equity / Book value of debt}$$
$$+ \mathbf{1.0} \times \textbf{Sales / Total assets}$$

A Z-score below (above) the critical value of 2.675 signals bankruptcy (solvency). Analysis of the misclassifications resulting from use of this critical value resulted in a more intuitively appealing dichotomy:

> It is concluded that all firms having a Z score of greater than 2.99 clearly fall into the "non-bankrupt" sector, while those firms having a Z below 1.81 are all bankrupt. The area between 1.81 and 2.99 will be defined as the "zone of ignorance" or "gray area" because of the susceptibility to error classification.[13]

The original Z-model was designed for manufacturing firms. Additionally, the model was directly applicable only to publicly traded companies because one of its inputs was the market value of equity. To remedy these shortcomings, Altman developed two variations of the Z-model, Z′ and Z″. The Z′-model was developed for nonpublic companies and used the book value of equity in place of the market value of equity. The Z″-model (which omitted the sales turnover ratio) was designed to be applicable to nonmanufacturing (public or pri-

---

[11]The procedure involved ranking the ratios of the bankrupt and nonbankrupt firms and finding the optimal cutoff point that discriminated between the two groups. This cutoff point was then tested against a holdout sample of companies.

[12]We place "cash flow" in quotation marks as, consistent with the definition used at that time, the measure actually used was funds from operations (i.e., net income +/− noncash expenses/revenues).

[13]Edward I. Altman, "Financial Ratios, Discriminant Analysis and the Prediction of Corporate Bankruptcy," *Journal of Finance* (September 1968), pp. 589–609. Also see Edward I. Altman, *Corporate Financial Distress and Bankruptcy* (New York: Wiley, 1993) and Caouette, Altman, and Narayanan, *Managing Credit Risk* (New York: Wiley, 1998).

BOX 18-2
Z′ and Z″: Variations of Altman's Z-Score*

For Private Firms Z′ =	For Service Sector Z″ =

$$0.717 \times \frac{\text{Working capital}}{\text{Total assets}}$$

$$+ 0.847 \times \frac{\text{Retained earnings}}{\text{Total assets}}$$

$$+ 3.107 \times \frac{\text{EBIT}}{\text{Total assets}}$$

$$+ 0.420 \times \frac{\text{Book value of equity}}{\text{Book value of debt}}$$

$$+ 0.998 \times \frac{\text{Sales}}{\text{Total assets}}$$

$$6.56 \times \frac{\text{Working capital}}{\text{Total assets}}$$

$$+ 3.26 \times \frac{\text{Retained earnings}}{\text{Total assets}}$$

$$+ 6.72 \times \frac{\text{EBIT}}{\text{Total assets}}$$

$$+ 1.05 \times \frac{\text{Book value of equity}}{\text{Book value of debt}}$$

Appropriate cutoff points for bankruptcy/nonbankruptcy and the gray areas are:

Z′ score	Indication	Z″ score	Indication
<1.23	Bankruptcy	<1.10	Bankruptcy
1.23–2.90	Gray area	1.10–2.60	Gray area
>2.90	Nonbankruptcy	>2.60	Nonbankruptcy

*See Chapter 8 of Edward I. Altman, *Corporate Financial Distress and Bankruptcy* (New York: Wiley, 1993).

---

vate) companies as well.[14] These models and the relevant "cutoff" scores are described in Box 18-2.

The ZETA™ Model. A more refined bankruptcy prediction model, the ZETA™ model, was developed by Altman et al. (1977). The parameters and design of the model remain proprietary. The explanatory variables used were, however, disclosed:

- Liquidity ratios
  - Current ratio
- Solvency
  - Equity (market) / Capital
  - Times interest earned
- Profitability
  - ROA
  - Retained earnings / Assets
- Other
  - Size (total assets)
  - Variability (σ of ROA)

Although no theoretical bankruptcy model was envisioned in designing this model, Scott (1981) showed that the variables used by Altman's ZETA™ model are consistent with parameters relevant for a theoretical bankruptcy model along the lines of the ratio discussed in Box 18-1. Details of this relationship are presented in Box 18-3.

Figure 18-2 illustrates the pattern of ZETA™ scores for bankrupt and nonbankrupt firms for the five years prior to bankruptcy along with the bankrupt, nonbankrupt, and overlap (gray) zones.

---

[14]As discussed in the next section, this model also has applicability to the bond ratings decision.

BOX 18-3
ZETA™ and a Theoretical Bankruptcy Model

Scott (1981) compares a theoretical model of bankruptcy with the variables used in Altman et al.'s ZETA™ prediction model. In Scott's model, debt (interest) payments (R) can be made from current earnings before interest and taxes (EBIT) or from the firm's equity. This equity is defined as the present value of the firm's future dividends and is symbolized by S. Thus, bankruptcy* occurs when

$$R > \text{EBIT} + S$$

or, alternatively, bankruptcy is defined as

$$\text{EBIT} \leq R - S$$

If we let u_{EBIT} represent the expected (average) EBIT and s_{EBIT} the standard deviation of EBIT, the equation can be standardized, and (as in the Emery and Cogger model of Box 18-2) the probability of bankruptcy will be related to

$$\frac{\text{EBIT} - u_{\text{EBIT}}}{s_{\text{EBIT}}} \leq \frac{R - S - u_{\text{EBIT}}}{s_{\text{EBIT}}}$$

Dividing the numerator and denominator of the right-hand side of this equation by total assets (TA) and rearranging terms yield

$$\frac{\text{EBIT} - u_{\text{EBIT}}}{s_{\text{EBIT}}} \leq \frac{\left[\left(\dfrac{1}{u_{\text{EBIT}}/R} - 1 \right) \dfrac{u_{\text{EBIT}}}{TA} - \left(\dfrac{S}{TA} \right) \right]}{s_{\text{EBIT}}/TA}$$

Scott points out that although the functional form differs, all the ratios in the right-hand side are represented (exactly or in surrogate form) in ZETA™.

ZETA™ Variable	Bankruptcy Model Variable
Times interest earned	u_{EBIT}/R
ROA	u_{EBIT}/TA
Standard deviation of EBIT over TA	s_{EBIT}/TA
Common equity to total capital	S/TA

---

*To ease the already cumbersome notation, we have dropped the tax term. With a corporate tax rate equal to t, the model becomes

$$R \geq \text{EBIT} + \frac{S}{(1 - t)}$$

The classification errors for the two Altman models are:

	Original Z-Model Classification Errors (%)		**ZETA™ Model** Classification Errors (%)	
Years Prior to Bankruptcy	Bankrupt (Type I)	Nonbankrupt (Type II)	Bankrupt (Type I)	Nonbankrupt (Type II)
1	6	3	4	10
2	18	6	15	7
3	52	NA	25	9
4	71	NA	32	10
5	64	NA	30	18

NA = Not available.

Source: Edward I. Altman, Robert G. Haldeman, and P. Narayanan, "ZETA™ Analysis: A New Model to Identify Bankruptcy Risk of Corporations," *Journal of Banking and Finance* (June 1977), Table 5, p. 41 (adapted).

The predictive accuracy of both models is about equal in the year immediately preceding bankruptcy. Similar to Beaver, classifying bankrupt firms was more difficult than classifying nonbankrupt ones.[15] In addition, the longer the time period preceding bankruptcy, the

---

[15]Dambolena and Shulman (1988) found that, *for their sample,* the Z-model was more accurate in classifying *failed* firms. They attempted to improve on the Z-model by adding a variable, the net liquid balance (NLB), defined as

$$\text{NLB} = \text{Cash} + \text{Marketable securities} - (\text{Short-term debt} + \text{Current portion of long-term debt})$$

to the Z-model. By doing so, they increased the one- (two-) year-ahead prediction accuracy for *nonfailed* firms from 72% to 86% (76% to 80%).

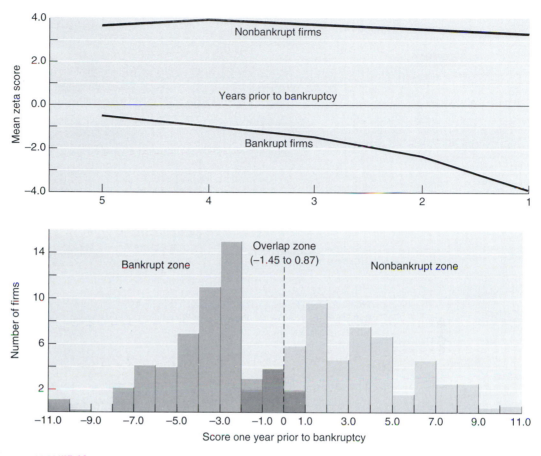

FIGURE 18-2 Zeta scores in years preceding bankruptcy. *Source:* Edward I. Altman, Robert G. Haldeman, and P. Narayanan, "ZETA™ Analysis: A New Model to Identify Bankruptcy Risk of Corporations," *Journal of Banking and Finance* (June 1977), Figures 1 and 2, p. 49.

less accurate the results. Notwithstanding the foregoing, the ZETA™ model is a major improvement over the original Z-model as it is far more accurate in years 2 through 5 preceding bankruptcy. The original model produced type I errors exceeding 50%, whereas the accuracy of the ZETA™ model is closer to 70%.

An interesting aspect of the ZETA™ model is its use of adjusted rather than reported accounting data. These adjustments, although not comprehensive, are certainly a step in the right direction.[16] Two of the adjustments are:

1. *Off-balance-sheet debt.* All noncancelable operating leases are added to firm assets and liabilities. In addition, finance and other nonconsolidated subsidiaries are consolidated with the parent company.[17]

2. *Intangible assets.* Capitalized items such as interest costs, goodwill, and other intangible assets are expensed.

The Probability of Bankruptcy. Ohlson (1980) approached the problem from a different perspective. He used probit analysis, which does not specify a cutoff point delineating a firm as bankrupt or nonbankrupt. Rather, it assigns a *probability of bankruptcy* to each firm. The user of the model can then decide how high a probability he or she is willing to tolerate.

---

[16]Dambolena and Khoury (1980), however, downplay the importance of these adjustments. They argue that Altman's results do not demonstrate that his adjustments caused improvement. What would constitute a proof is running a Zeta model without lease capitalization and observing whether the predictive power of the model decreases significantly. Also see Elam (1975), who found that lease capitalization did not enhance a model's predictive ability.

[17]Altman's work preceded SFAS 94 (1987), which requires consolidation of these subsidiaries.

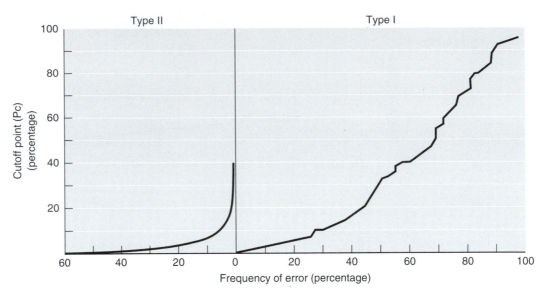

FIGURE 18-3 Trade-offs in classification errors in bankruptcy prediction. *Source:* James A. Ohlson, "Financial Ratios and the Probabilistic Prediction of Bankruptcy," *Journal of Accounting Research* (Spring 1980), Figure 5, p. 127. Reprinted with permission.

The higher (lower) the probability cutoff, the greater the chance of misclassifying a (non)bankrupt company. These trade-offs[18] are illustrated in Figure 18-3.

At a cutoff probability of approximately 1%, no type I error occurs, but type II errors equal 47%. At that low level, essentially all firms are classified as bankrupt. Raising the cutoff probability increases the chances of making a type I error (misclassifying a bankrupt company) but lowers the type II error. At a 3.8% cutoff, the overall classification errors are minimized with 12% type I errors and 17% type II errors.

Box 18-4 describes the KMV bankruptcy prediction model, which also provides a *probability of bankruptcy* as its output.[19] This model, similar to ZETA™, is proprietary and thus can be described only in general terms. Note the relationship between the metrics used in this model and the ratio described earlier in Box 18-1.

Bankruptcy Prediction and Cash Flows

Cash flow variables (or surrogates such as funds flows) are intuitively important factors in bankruptcy analysis. Although the evidence bears this out, both the selection of cash flow measures and interpretation of the results must be made carefully.

Beaver's original study found cash (defined as funds) flows/total debt to be the best *univariate* predictor. Subsequent studies examined whether the use of cash flow variables by themselves or together with a ratio-based model would improve the accuracy of bankruptcy prediction.

Gentry et al. (1985a) found that funds from operations and working capital changes (tested separately) did not aid bankruptcy prediction. Dividend flows were the most significant variable; capital expenditures and debt financing were among the variables that were not significant. However, as dividends are usually a function of cash available from operations after reinvestment (i.e., free cash flow), one measure may subsume the other. Gentry et al. (1985b) subsequently found that a model that combined cash flow vari-

---

[18]Ohlson reverses the nomenclature, calling type I errors type II and vice versa.

[19]Merton (1973, 1974) provides theoretical underpinnings for this model. Other proprietary models exist, many of which are modifications of those described. A comparison of the performance of some of these models (including the Z-score) is provided by J. Sobehart, S. Keenan, and R. Stein, "Benchmarking Quantitative Default Risk Models: A Validation Methodology," *Moody's Investment Services* (March 2000).

BOX 18-4
KMV Bankruptcy Model

The KMV model views bankruptcy as occurring when

Market value of assets < Payable liabilities

When the above condition holds, bankruptcy occurs as the firm cannot sell off assets and/or raise additional capital as existing assets are fully encumbered. The probability or likelihood of bankruptcy is a function of the firm's *distance to default ratio (DDR)* defined as*

$$DDR = \frac{\text{Market value of assets} - \text{Payable liabilities}}{\text{Standard deviation (Assets)}}$$

The larger the DDR, the smaller the probability of bankruptcy.[†] KMV maintains a large database that tracks

1. The total population of firms with equivalent DDRs
2. The number of firms with equivalent DDRs that defaulted

The database is utilized to arrive at the firm's *expected default frequency (EDF)*:

$$EDF = \frac{\text{Number of firms with equivalent DDRs that defaulted}}{\text{Total population of firms with equivalent DDR}}$$

Operationalizing this model requires measurement of the market value of the firm's assets and their standard deviation as well as defining the firm's payable liabilities. The exact process used by KMV in determining these values is proprietary but makes use of option pricing models in determining the expected value and variance of the market value of assets. In calculating payable liabilities, not all debt is included as consideration is given to the due date and maturity of the debt. Generally, payable liabilities are defined as an aggregation of a firm's interest payments, short-term debt, and (a portion of) the firm's long-term debt.

The model's strengths and weaknesses are related to one another. By using market value to measure assets, the firm uses forward-looking data that are responsive to changes in the environment. As a result, the model is adaptive and does not depend on periodic financial statements to update. At the same time, its sensitivity to stock market movements can result in market overreactions or bubbles yielding unreasonable values for the market value of assets. Similarly, with respect to liabilities, its sensitivity to the maturity dates of long-term assets can cause "blips" in the DDR as debt reaches maturity.

---

*Conceptually, of course, this model is similar to the one described in Box 18-1.

[†]A DDR of 2, for example, indicates that the market value of the firm's assets is two standard deviations greater than its liabilities.

---

ables[20] with financial ratios performed better than one based on cash flows or financial ratios alone.

Casey and Bartczak (1984, 1985) put the whole bankruptcy classification issue in sharp focus. They concluded that cash flow variables either by themselves or added to a model such as the Z-model did not improve the prediction of bankruptcy. The conclusion, however, was based on *overall* results. A careful examination of their results indicates that an approximation of CFO (which was not reported during the period studied) *clearly aids in the prediction of bankrupt companies*. In the five years prior to bankruptcy, CFO correctly classified bankrupt firms from 83% to 92% of the time (depending on the time period). In contrast, accrual accounting measures correctly classified bankrupt companies only 30% to 83% of the time. On the other hand, CFO did not do as well as accrual measures in predicting nonbankrupt firms as it classified too many of them as bankrupt (47% incorrectly classified one year prior).[21] Given the relative costs of these errors, however, it is the former type of error that must be avoided. The CFO measure, contrary to Casey and Bartczak's conclusions, does seem to be useful for bankruptcy prediction.

This ability of cash flow variables to improve the prediction of bankrupt companies (but without improving the ability to classify nonbankrupt companies) is borne out by other studies. Aziz and Lawson (1989) found that adding cash flow variables to Altman's Z-model and

---

[20]Their results may be due to the use of several cash flow variables, as opposed to Gombola et al. (1987), who did not find an improvement in the ability to predict bankruptcy when they added (*only*) CFO to a set of financial ratios.

[21]CFO classified as bankrupt many financially distressed firms that ultimately recovered, such as Chrysler and Massey Ferguson.

ZETA™ model did not improve the accuracy of the overall (failed and nonfailed) classifications. *However, the combined models did a better job of predicting failures one and two years before bankruptcy.* Thus, when the combined models erred, they did so in a conservative fashion and overpredicted the number of failed firms. As noted earlier, this type of error is less costly.

Bankruptcy and Financial Distress: Concluding Comments

One of the issues raised by Casey and Bartczak was that the misclassification of nonbankrupt companies results from ignoring companies' ability to stay alive. In spite of lengthy periods of negative CFO, companies can continue to operate by renegotiating credit terms with creditors or selling assets to raise cash. We do not dispute this point, but rather question the focus of these models on the event of bankruptcy alone.

Bankruptcy is a legal, not an economic phenomenon. It is fraught with political and other nonmarket considerations. Staying alive by selling assets or renegotiating (restructuring) debt is not a sign of success. Creditors and stockholders may suffer large losses even when bankruptcy does not occur. A better focus would be on whether the company is "healthy" or "sick," or on whether financial statement information and ratios allow users to forecast future investment performance.[22] Such a focus would move from a dichotomous bankruptcy/nonbankruptcy classification to one with differing gradients of financial health.

The Prediction of Bond Ratings

Bond ratings are issued by bond rating agencies, the most prominent of which are Moody's and Standard & Poor's. The ratings attest to the creditworthiness of the firm. The probability that adverse conditions will result in financial difficulties is used to assess the likelihood that the firm will default on its interest or principal payments. Bond indentures and the degree of protection afforded in the event of bankruptcy are among other important considerations in the ratings process.

Bond Rating Classifications

The ratings[23] used by Standard & Poor's along with a brief description of each are presented in Exhibit 18-2. A summary of these ratings along with their Moody's counterparts is presented below:

	Very High-Quality	High-Quality	Speculative	Very Poor
Standard & Poor's	AAA and AA	A and BBB	BB and B	CCC and D
Moody's	Aaa and Aa	A and Baa	Ba and B	Caa and C

The Bond Ratings Process

Ratings are sought by companies when they issue new debt. They pay a fee and the agency issues a rating following an examination of the creditworthiness of the company. The agency analyzes the company's operations and personnel, its financial statements, and its pro forma projections as well as other relevant financial and nonfinancial information.[24]

The rating agencies go to great lengths to discourage speculation that the rating process is mechanical and based only on mathematical formulas. Rather, they stress that ratings are

---

[22]In that sense, Ohlson's probabilistic model is useful as the predictive variable is not the ultimate event of bankruptcy, but rather a probability of going bankrupt. A higher probability can be used to assess corporate performance. Burgstahler et al. (1989), in fact, used Ohlson's model to assess how changes in the probability of bankruptcy affected firms' equity values.

[23]The ratings are further modified by + and − designations, permitting a finer gradation in the rating categories.

[24]For a more detailed discussion of the rating process, see Chapter 1 of Ahmed Belkaoui, *Industrial Bonds and the Rating Process* (Westport, CT: Quorum Books, an imprint of Greenwood Publishing Group, 1983).

EXHIBIT 18-2
Standard & Poor's Ratings Definition

Issue Credit Rating Definitions

A Standard & Poor's issue credit rating is a current opinion of the creditworthiness of an obligor with respect to a specific financial obligation, a specific class of financial obligations, or a specific financial program (including ratings on medium term note programs and commercial paper programs). It takes into consideration the creditworthiness of guarantors, insurers, or other forms of credit enhancement on the obligation and takes into account the currency in which the obligation is denominated. The issue credit rating is not a recommendation to purchase, sell, or hold a financial obligation, inasmuch as it does not comment as to market price or suitability for a particular investor.

Issue credit ratings are based on current information furnished by the obligors or obtained by Standard & Poor's from other sources it considers reliable. Standard & Poor's does not perform an audit in connection with any credit rating and may, on occasion, rely on unaudited financial information. Credit ratings may be changed, suspended, or withdrawn as a result of changes in, or unavailability of, such information, or based on other circumstances.

Issue credit ratings can be either long-term or short-term. Short-term ratings are generally assigned to those obligations considered short-term in the relevant market. In the U.S., for example, that means obligations with an original maturity of no more than 365 days—including commercial paper. Short-term ratings are also used to indicate the creditworthiness of an obligor with respect to put features on long-term obligations. The result is a dual rating, in which the short-term rating addresses the put feature, in addition to the usual long-term rating. Medium-term notes are assigned long-term ratings.

Long-Term Issue Credit Ratings

Issue credit ratings are based, in varying degrees, on the following considerations:

1. Likelihood of payment—capacity and willingness of the obligor to meet its financial commitment on an obligation in accordance with the terms of the obligation;
2. Nature of and provisions of the obligation;
3. Protection afforded by, and relative position of, the obligation in the event of bankruptcy, reorganization, or other arrangement under the laws of bankruptcy and other laws affecting creditors' rights.

The issue rating definitions are expressed in terms of default risk. As such, they pertain to senior obligations of an entity. Junior obligations are typically rated lower than senior obligations, to reflect the lower priority in bankruptcy, as noted above. (Such differentiation applies when an entity has both senior and subordinated obligations, secured and unsecured obligations, or operating company and holding company obligations.) Accordingly, in the case of junior debt, the rating may not conform exactly with the category definition.

'AAA' An obligation rated 'AAA' has the highest rating assigned by Standard & Poor's. The obligor's capacity to meet its financial commitment on the obligation is extremely strong.

'AA' An obligation rated 'AA' differs from the highest rated obligations only in small degree. The obligor's capacity to meet its financial commitment on the obligation is very strong.

'A' An obligation rated 'A' is somewhat more susceptible to the adverse effects of changes in circumstances and economic conditions than obligations in higher rated categories. However, the obligor's capacity to meet its financial commitment on the obligation is still strong.

'BBB' An obligation rated 'BBB' exhibits adequate protection parameters. However, adverse economic conditions or changing circumstances are more likely to lead to a weakened capacity of the obligor to meet its financial commitment on the obligation. Obligations rated 'BB', 'B', 'CCC', 'CC', and 'C' are regarded as having significant speculative characteristics. 'BB' indicates the least degree of speculation and 'C' the highest. While such obligations will likely have some quality and protective characteristics, these may be outweighed by large uncertainties or major exposures to adverse conditions.

'BB' An obligation rated 'BB' is less vulnerable to nonpayment than other speculative issues. However, it faces major ongoing uncertainties or exposure to adverse business, financial, or economic conditions which could lead to the obligor's inadequate capacity to meet its financial commitment on the obligation.

'B' An obligation rated 'B' is more vulnerable to nonpayment than obligations rated 'BB', but the obligor currently has the capacity to meet its financial commitment on the obligation. Adverse business, financial, or economic conditions will likely impair the obligor's capacity or willingness to meet its financial commitment on the obligation.

'CCC' An obligation rated 'CCC' is currently vulnerable to nonpayment, and is dependent upon favorable business, financial, and economic conditions for the obligor to meet its financial commitment on the obligation. In the event of adverse business, financial, or economic conditions, the obligor is not likely to have the capacity to meet its financial commitment on the obligation.

'CC' An obligation rated 'CC' is currently highly vulnerable to nonpayment.

'C' The 'C' rating may be used to cover a situation where a bankruptcy petition has been filed or similar action has been taken, but payments on this obligation are being continued.

'D' An obligation rated 'D' is in payment default. The 'D' rating category is used when payments on an obligation are not made on the date due even if the applicable grace period has not expired, unless Standard & Poor's believes that such payments will be made during such grace period. The 'D' rating also will be used upon the filing of a bankruptcy petition or the taking of a similar action if payments on an obligation are jeopardized.

Source: Standard & Poor's *Bond Guide*, June 2000. Used by permission of Standard & Poor's Corporation.

based on the judgment of their analysts who determine their ratings after assimilating quantitative as well as available qualitative data.

When the ratings are announced by the agency, the firm, if it is unhappy with the rating, may decide to drop the debt offering and search for alternative financing sources, or alternatively, it may decide to appeal the rating. The appeal may result in a series of negotiations,[25] whereby the terms of the offering (such as payment terms or the restrictive covenants) are changed.

Ratings: Risk and Returns

Exhibit 18-3 illustrates the relationship between bond ratings and measures of credit risk and return. Historical cumulative default rates in panel A show that bond ratings reflect default risk. The higher the rating, the lower the probability of default. For an AAA bond there is

EXHIBIT 18-3
Default Rates, Expected Loss, and Risk Premium

A. Cumulative Default Rates

	Years Since Issuance		
Rating	3 year	5 year	10 year
AAA	0.00%	0.06%	0.06%
AA	0.47%	0.74%	0.82%
A	0.05%	0.27%	0.79%
BBB	0.82%	1.88%	3.27%
BB	4.77%	9.09%	18.09%
B	12.51%	24.33%	34.99%
CCC	33.02%	43.82%	56.65%

B. Cumulative Expected Loss

	Years Since Issuance		
Rating	3 year	5 year	10 year
AAA	0.00%	0.01%	0.01%
AA	0.09%	0.19%	0.24%
A	0.03%	0.18%	0.49%
BBB	0.47%	0.95%	1.89%
BB	3.46%	6.15%	11.47%
B	9.11%	18.38%	25.89%
CCC	25.69%	33.03%	44.60%

C. Bond Yield Spread Over 30-Year Treasury Bond

Rating	1991	1997
AAA	0.82%	0.28%
AA	1.13%	0.39%
A	1.61%	0.57%
BBB	2.71%	0.83%
BB	3.92%	1.53%
B	8.93%	3.30%
CCC	12.95%	7.29%

Source: Adapted from J. Caouette, E. I. Altman, and P. Narayanan, *Managing Credit Risk: The Next Great Financial Challenge* (New York: Wiley, 1998), Tables 15-3 and 15-8, and Figure 6.3.

---

[25]The underwriter will play a major role in these negotiations.

zero-percent probability of default in the first three years and less than 1/1,000 chance of default in 10 years. A B-rated bond, on the other hand, has a 12.5% probability of default over the first three years and close to a 35% probability of default within 10 years of issuance.

Default does not necessarily mean that 100% of the investment is lost. Recovery rates of in excess of 40% of the original investment have been common in recent years. Panel B of Exhibit 18-3 shows that the *expected loss*[26] is also a function of bond rating—the lower the rating the greater the expected loss. The expected loss after 10 years is merely .01% of the original investment for AAA debt but 25.89% for B-rated debt.

To compensate for the higher default risk, lower-rated bonds are issued with higher yields. Panel C of Exhibit 18-3 shows the risk premium by bond rating for 1991 and 1997; the higher the rating, the smaller the risk premium. The AAA bond with an expected loss of .01% is virtually risk-free and thus its spread over the U.S. Treasury bond yield was merely 0.28% in 1997. On the other hand, the B-rated bond's cumulative expected loss of 25.89% over 10 years translates into an expected loss of approximately 2.5% per year. To compensate for this higher expected loss, the spread over the U.S. Treasury bond yield was 3.3% in 1997.[27]

Impact of Ratings

The ratings process affects a firm's liability position in at least three ways:

1. As Exhibit 18-3 indicates, the higher the rating, the lower the interest rate required. Ratings, therefore, affect real, ongoing costs to the issuing firm.

2. The covenants written into a bond offering are often designed to obtain favorable ratings. As these covenants protect creditors by putting restrictions on the equity shareholders, ratings influence the sharing of risk and reward between equity- and debtholders. Some covenants are specifically tied to ratings, and may require a higher interest rate or redemption if the rating falls below a specified level.

3. Many institutional investors are restricted (legally or by internal policy) to debt with a minimum rating. Thus, the success or failure of an offering (or whether the debt is even issued) is often determined by the rating.

Rating agencies argue that ratings do not cause differential borrowing costs, but that ratings and differential borrowing costs reflect the same set of economic conditions indicating the relative risk of the firm's debt. Others, however, contend that, as with any grading device originally designed to measure some attribute, the emphasis tends to shift to the measuring device itself rather than the underlying attribute.[28]

Thus, ratings themselves can influence bond yields beyond the effect warranted by the firm's economic position. This may be especially true for adjacent ratings such as, for example, AAA versus AA or Baa versus Ba. This argument is bolstered by point 3, which indicates that some investment policies are based on the ratings themselves. To the extent that these factors affect the demand for a debt issue, they clearly affect the yield required for its successful sale.

Notwithstanding the agencies' claims that ratings are not in any sense mechanically or mathematically derived, researchers have constructed mathematical models to predict bond ratings. Explanatory independent variables, methodology, and the success rates of some of these studies are discussed next. First, however, we discuss the purpose of such models.

---

[26]Expected loss is the probability of default times the loss resulting from default. Thus, for the B rating (from panel A) there is a 34.99% chance of default within 10 years of issuance. The 25.89% expected loss is derived as 34.99% $\times$ (1 − recovery rate) = 25.89%, implying a recovery rate of about 26% of the original investment. The actual calculation is somewhat more detailed and described in Caouette et al. (1998).

[27]As Exhibit 18-3 shows (compare 1997 spreads with 1991 spreads), quality yield spreads can vary considerably over time. Economic conditions and the market attitude toward risk are major variables that affect yield spreads.

[28]Accounting income is an obvious example of this phenomenon. Consistent with the behavior predicted by positive accounting theory as to the incentives to influence accounting data (artificially), there is also evidence that firms attempt to cultivate debt-rating agencies to obtain favorable ratings.

Usefulness of Bond Ratings Predictions

Bond investors are concerned with *the probability of default and the required bond yield*. Many of the bond-rating models developed do not forecast these attributes directly. Rather, they forecast bond ratings—another predictor of these attributes. This raises the following question: If the goal of the mathematical model is simply to duplicate the rating agencies' classification, why bother? Just use the ratings issued by the agency.[29] The responses to this question follow:

1. Most firms (including publicly traded ones) have unrated debt. A mathematical model would, therefore, be a useful surrogate for the ratings process in determining the appropriate yield and indentures for debt offerings of such firms (e.g., private placements).

2. Ratings are not continuously revised, and there is evidence of a considerable lag between the time conditions change and when ratings agencies respond by revising ratings. Furthermore, there is conflicting evidence[30] as to the extent to which the market anticipates a ratings change. These factors lead to the following interrelated benefits of a bond ratings model:

   a. The model can be used to monitor the debt after the original rating is made. This provides a more accurate prediction of the debt's current risk/return characteristics and whether it is over/undervalued.

   b. Given that the market may not fully anticipate a ratings change, the model can be used to forecast a ratings change.

3. Firms sometimes undertake large investment or acquisition programs. These programs usually affect the firm's financial (and operating) structure as a result of the differing characteristics of the acquired firm and/or any new debt required to finance these programs. To the extent that these changes mirror changes in the underlying characteristics of the firm's new and existing debt, the firm's cost of debt capital may change. A ratings model may help the firm (or its investment banker) anticipate these changes in the planning stages of the program.

4. The independent or explanatory variables in a predictive model can provide insight into the important factors that determine the (perceived) riskiness of debt. A firm seeking a favorable rating can take action ahead of time to improve those areas in which it is deficient. This is not to suggest that firms engage in "window dressing" (although some do) to improve key ratios, but rather that they remedy the underlying economic factors that drive these ratios.[31]

5. Finally, as discussed in this section, there is some evidence that ratings at the lower end of the spectrum, especially for subordinated debt, may be inconsistent and rigid. This evidence may provide some investment opportunities.

Choice of Explanatory Variables

The relationship between financial performance as measured by accounting ratios and bond rating classification is demonstrated in Exhibit 18-4. Stronger companies have better ratings and *an initial estimate of a firm's ratings can be derived by mapping the firm's ratios to those found in the table*. It must, however, be noted that the data in this table are based on a large sample. These relationships may not necessarily hold for firms on an individual or

---

[29]The prediction of bond ratings differs from the prediction of beta. The object there is to improve on the predictions of beta readily available. The prediction of bankruptcy is similar; the object is to forecast the event itself, not duplicate someone else's prediction.

[30]Holthausen and Leftwich (1986) found that an upgrading of a firm's rating is anticipated by the market, whereas downgrades are not fully anticipated. Companies' shares suffer (negative) abnormal returns following downgrades.

[31]This point is reinforced by recalling that ratios in such models are often used as a surrogate for an overall category or factor (see Chapter 4). Thus, the ratio may be masking the actual relationship contributing to the riskiness of the debt.

EXHIBIT 18-4
Relationship Between Ratings and Financial Ratios

U.S. Industrial Long-Term Debt
Three-year (1998–2000) medians

	AAA	AA	A	BBB	BB	B	CCC
EBIT interest coverage ($\times$)	21.4	10.1	6.1	3.7	2.1	0.8	0.1
EBITDA interest coverage ($\times$)	26.5	12.9	9.1	5.8	3.4	1.8	1.3
Free operating cash flow/total debt (%)	84.2	25.2	15.0	8.5	2.6	(3.2)	(12.9)
FFO/total debt (%)	128.8	55.4	43.2	30.8	18.8	7.8	1.6
Return on capital (%)	34.9	21.7	19.4	13.6	11.6	6.6	1
Operating income/sales (%)	27.0	22.1	18.6	15.4	15.9	11.9	11.9
Long-term debt/capital (%)	13.3	28.2	33.9	42.5	57.2	69.7	68.8
Total debt/capital (incl. STD) (%)	22.9	37.7	42.5	48.2	62.6	74.8	87.7

Note:
EBIT = Earnings before interest and taxes
EBITDA = Earnings before interest, taxes, depreciation, and amortization
FFO = Funds from operations
STD = Short-term debt
Source: Standard & Poor's *2002 Corporate Ratings Criteria Handbook.*

small-group basis. A firm, for example, may have profitability ratios in the AAA–A categories but leverage ratios that place it in the BBB–B categories.

Appendix 18-A describes models used to predict bond ratings and the variables in these models.[32] Similar to bankruptcy models, formal theoretical models do not exist. Not surprisingly, *liquidity, long-term solvency, and leverage* ratios feature prominently in these studies. In addition, as bondholders are primarily interested in receiving a (steady) stream of interest and principal payments, *variables related to the stability of the firm's earnings* are included. Similarly, the appearance of *size* variables is explained by the added protection for debtholders, as a result of the greater endurance of larger firms, in the event earnings decline.

Subordination, as seen in the next section, plays a very important role in bond classification. This issue has implications only in the event of financial distress when the claims of subordinated bondholders rank behind those of senior claimants. On a going-concern basis, it has no impact on a firm's interest and principal obligations to the subordinated bondholders.

Model Results

Generally, the models perform quite well; they average anywhere from 60% to 70% accuracy in duplicating the agency rating. Further, when they are in error, it is usually by misclassifying the rating into the immediately adjacent category. When adjacent categories are included, the "success" prediction rate is over 90%.

When we move from the overall rating to specific categories, the results are less positive. The Baa or BBB classifications are most difficult to predict. This category is important[33] because it is the generally accepted cutoff between investment- and noninvestment-grade bonds.

It should be noted that a number of studies have found *subordination* to be the most important variable in the classification model. The reason for this finding is that Aa- and A-rated bonds are typically nonsubordinated, while those rated Ba and B are often subordinated to more senior debt. Only at Baa are bonds generally found to be evenly distributed between subordinated and unsubordinated. Thus, *the subordination variable by itself is a good indicator of the bond rating.*

---

[32]Generally, the variables used are arrived at by first selecting a set of ratios/variables from the ratio classifications described in Chapter 4. The original set is then scaled down, using techniques such as factor analysis, to a subset of ratios capturing the information contained in the full set. The final set of variables then chosen is the subset that provides the best fit in the model's classification (whether regression, discriminant, or probit) equation. These best-fit results are explanatory in nature as they are based on the same sample companies that were used to develop the models. The model is then tested on a holdout sample to test its predictive ability.

[33]For this reason, firms may work harder to retain the higher rating.

Subordination, however, provides no discriminating power within the Baa category. Therefore, the poor classification within the Baa category, where subordination does not play a role, *implies that the other variables do not possess strong discriminating power.*

The relevance of this point from our perspective is reinforced when we examine the other variables and their relative significance in the classification models. A size measure (total assets or debt) typically ranks second or third. Depending on the study, the other measure in the top three is either debt/capital (Belkaoui) or a measure of earnings stability (years of consecutive dividends in Pinches and Mingo). *Conventional financial ratios thus contribute less than the size and subordination variables.*

The implication of this weak relationship depends on one's perspective. One argument is that financial variables measuring solvency and leverage are not related to the risk of a firm's debt. At face value, this seems contrary to the thrust of this book and the most fundamental tenets of financial analysis. We shall explore this point later. Ratings agencies would argue that financial variables are relevant, but in a more complex way than can be captured via a linear weighted summation with other selected variables. Others, however, argue that the lack of consistency, as firms with similar financial characteristics obtain different rankings, is a weakness in the ratings process itself and is precisely why the focus on the ratings process needs to be reevaluated.

The Z″-Score and Bond Ratings

In the previous section, we discussed bankruptcy models such as ZETA™ and the Z (′ and ″)-scores. As higher scores in these models indicate a more solvent firm, a natural extension of these models is to apply them to bond ratings. Exhibit 18-5 illustrates the relationship between bond ratings in the United States and the Z″-score (augmented by an intercept term of 3.25).

EXHIBIT 18-5
Relationship Between U.S. Bond Ratings and (Intercept-Adjusted) Z″-Score

The relationship between bond ratings and the Z″-score adjusted for an intercept of 3.25 is presented in the table below. The purpose of the adjustment was to set zero as the "base" score below which a default is signaled. The relevant Z″-score is:

$$Z'' = 6.56 \frac{\text{Working capital}}{\text{Total assets}}$$

$$+ 3.26 \frac{\text{Retained earnings}}{\text{Total assets}}$$

$$+ 6.72 \frac{\text{EBIT}}{\text{Total assets}}$$

$$+ 1.05 \frac{\text{Book value of equity}}{\text{Total liabilities}}$$

$$+ 3.25$$

U.S. Bond Rating	Average Z″-Score (with Intercept)	U.S. Bond Rating	Average Z″-Score (with Intercept)
AAA	8.15	BB+	5.25
AA+	7.60	BB	4.95
AA	7.30	BB−	4.75
AA−	7.00	B+	4.50
A+	6.85	B	4.15
A	6.65	B−	3.75
A−	6.40	CCC+	3.20
BBB+	6.25	CCC	2.50
BBB	5.85	CCC−	1.75
BBB−	5.65	D(efault)	0

Source: J. M. Hartzell, Matthew Peck, and E. I. Altman, "Emerging Market Corporate Bonds—A Scoring System," Salomon Brothers, New York, May 15, 1995, p. 9.

These relationships were determined on an *ex post* basis; that is, by calculating the Z''-score for a sample of 750 U.S. firms and finding the average Z''-score within each rating category.

Applications to Emerging Markets. This model was used by Salomon Brothers[34] as a *starting point* to determine ratings for corporate bonds issued in emerging markets. An initial rating was determined by the Z''-score and then adjusted up or down after considering specific firm and country factors (e.g., currency risk, inflation, political environment, and industry classification).

In a similar vein, Sondhi (1995) used the Form 20-F GAAP reconciliations published by foreign firms to compute ratios used by Standard & Poor's for U.S. firms. The adjusted ratios were used to develop initial estimates of ratings for a sample of emerging market debt securities. The study reported differences among the S&P ratings, ratings based on adjusted local GAAP, and U.S. GAAP-based ratings of emerging market debt.

The Significance of Ratings: Another Look

Qualitative factors (raters' judgment) may be one explanation for apparent inconsistencies in bond ratings. The rating agencies believe this to be a positive factor. However, from other perspectives it is not a very satisfactory answer unless there is an objective evaluation of the efficacy of these qualitative factors. That is, if the purpose of the ratings is to rank the probability of timely repayment of interest and principal, then there needs to be evidence that the differentially rated bonds actually do exhibit different risk characteristics.

The subordination issue mentioned earlier is a case in point. If ratings measure the probability of repayment, then

> *conventional wisdom suggests that the financial strength of the firm is a better measure of risk than subordination.* However, prior ratings prediction models . . . have identified subordination as an important predictor variable. Such results apparently reflect the actions of bond raters; when a firm has subordinated and unsubordinated bonds, the subordinated issue is invariably rated one grade lower than the nonsubordinated issue. *Apparently, raters automatically downgrade a subordinate bond by one rating.*[35]

Is this downgrading justified? That is, do the financial characteristics of the firm suggest that its two issues be rated differently?[36] If not, then the ratings process is at fault, and if the yield on the subordinated bond is higher as a result of the lower rating, an astute investor can take advantage of the higher return without adding any risk to the portfolio.

Our implicit conclusion is that the focus of the research is misguided. The focus should not be on the relationship of financial variables to bond ratings, but rather on their relationship with the actual probabilities of repayment and/or realized yields.[37] Such a model, specifically designed to examine the relationship between default risk and yield and a set of explanatory variables, would, of course, be an original ratings model. Unfortunately, most (academic) studies focus on the less-interesting case of models that duplicate existing ratings rather than attempting to design a better ratings model.

---

[34]See John M. Hartzell, Matthew B. Peck, and Edward I. Altman, *Emerging Markets Corporate Bonds—A Scoring System,* Salomon Brothers Inc., New York, May 15, 1995, and updates issued July 31, 1995 and December 14, 1995.

[35]L. G. Martin and G. V. Henderson, "On Bond Ratings and Pension Obligations: A Note," *Journal of Financial and Quantitative Analysis* (December 1983), pp. 463–470. Emphasis added.

[36]Remember, subordination is an issue only in the case of financial distress.

[37]This was an early focus of this line of research. Fisher (1959) examined the factors accounting for differences in corporate bonds' risk premia (i.e., excess yield over the risk-free rate). The explanatory variables used by Fisher were the same four used in West's study (Appendix 18-A). In fact, West's purpose was to examine whether Fisher's explanatory variables of bond yields could be also used to explain differences in bond ratings. See also Ang and Patel (1975), who compared Moody's ratings and ratings predicted by four statistical bond-rating models with actual measures of bond default and loss rate on investment yield (defined as the difference between realized and promised yield). They found insignificant differences between the performance of Moody's and the bond-rating models on an overall basis.

Measurement of Financial Variables

Earlier, we noted that clear-cut distinctions in financial variables do not exist across bond-rating categories. One possible explanation lies in how these ratios are measured. For the most part, no systematic[38] adjustments for differences in accounting policies, off-balance-sheet obligations, unusual items, and so forth (as suggested throughout this book and summarized in Chapter 17) are made to the ratios used in these statistical models. Bond-rating agencies may be presumed to consider all the available information that could be used to adjust these ratios. Hence, the ratios used may be misspecified and in that sense may have little or no discriminating value.

EQUITY RISK: MEASUREMENT AND PREDICTION

The last index of risk we examine is the measure of the firm's equity risk. Implicitly, this risk is related to a firm's valuation and expected return.

Exhibit 18-3 indicated that the greater the risk of default as measured by the lower rating, the greater the effective yield (return) paid by the bond. This accords with a cardinal principle of investment theory: The greater the expected risk, the greater the expected return. The question becomes how to define, measure, and quantify risk.

These issues are important. Theories of the relationship between equity risk and return have come under fire as the definitions of risk embodied by the CAPM and β have not held up empirically. On the other hand, empirical notions of risk that outperform β have tenuous theoretical underpinnings. In this section of the chapter, we:

1. Review the relationship between accounting variables and β.
2. Turn to a discussion of the controversy as to alternative measures of risk that outperform β and, some argue, may supplant β.

Risk and Return: Theoretical Models

In general, the uncertain investment return constitutes the risk borne by equityholders. This risk reflects uncertainty of demand, output prices, input costs, and so on. These factors themselves are impacted by global and national economic and political conditions, industrywide and competitive pressures, and conditions endemic to the firm itself. Thus, risk can be classified by its two sources:

1. *Unsystematic risk:* Factors specific to the firm.
2. *Systematic risk.* Factors common across a wide spectrum of firms.

Portfolio theory suggests that diversification enables investors to eliminate unsystematic risk. Moreover, in an efficient market, it argues that investors are compensated only for risk that cannot be eliminated by diversification. *Thus, the only risk measure that remains relevant is systematic risk.*

The CAPM and Beta (β)

As discussed in Chapter 5, both the capital asset pricing model (CAPM), which expresses expected returns as

$$E(R_t) = R_f + \beta_e E(R_m - R_f)$$

or (its empirical counterpart) the market model, which expresses expected returns as

$$E(R_t) = a + \beta_e E(R_m)$$

use beta (β_e), the (standardized) covariance (comovement) between the returns of a given firm and overall market returns, as a measure of systematic risk.

---

[38]We stress "systematic" as there have been some isolated adjustments. Belkaoui, for example, capitalized off-balance-sheet leases and included the resultant debt in his ratios. He did not report the effects of this procedure as this was not the thrust of his study.

These models predict that a firm's expected return should be positively related to β_e (i.e., the higher the risk, as measured by β_e, the higher the return) and β_e *is sufficient* to describe the cross-sectional variation of expected returns.

APT and Multifactor Models

The theoretical development of the CAPM relies on a number of restrictive assumptions. For example, the CAPM assumes that there exists a market portfolio consisting of *all* risky assets. This portfolio is, by definition, unobservable. Additionally, tests of the model that use different proxies (e.g., the S&P 500 index or the NYSE index) for the market portfolio may give different results depending on the proxy used.

The Arbitrage Pricing Theory (APT), an asset pricing model developed by Stephen Ross in the 1970s, does not require the CAPM assumptions. Its theoretical development is beyond the scope of this book.[39] The intuition behind it, however, is relatively straightforward (and in a sense similar to that of the CAPM). The APT depicts the return of a security as a function of N (macro) factors F and a (micro) firm-specific factor e:

$$R_i = E(R_i) + b_{i1}F_1 + b_{i2}F_2 + \ldots b_{iN}F_N + e_i$$

where

R_i and $E(R_i)$ = the actual and expected (see below) return of the ith asset for a given period.

F_j = a common factor that affects all securities. Examples of such factors are interest rates, inflation, the business cycle, and general economic conditions.

b_{ij} = the sensitivity of the ith security's return to movements of the jth factor.

e_i = the firm-specific portion of the return not explained by the N factors.

In a portfolio of sufficient size, the firm-specific component can be diversified away. The expected return is therefore the risk-free rate plus the sum of the risk premium associated with each of the factors times the sensitivity b_{ij} of the ith security to the jth factor:

$$E(R_i) = \text{Risk-free rate} + b_{i1}f_1 + b_{i2}f_2 + \ldots b_{iN}f_N$$

where f_j is the risk premium associated with the F_j factor.

In a single-index environment, the CAPM model

$$E(R_t) = R_f + \beta_e E(R_m - R_f)$$

is consistent with the APT relationship with the sensitivity b_1 equal to the β and the risk premium $f_1 = (R_m - R_f)$ *if we assume that the market index is the appropriate single factor.*

The identification of relevant factors is the greatest difficulty in application of the APT. They are not a priori specified in the development of the model; they are defined as generic "factors" that influence security returns. Empirical research is, therefore, more difficult. Chen, Roll, and Ross (1986) examined the APT with prespecified factors; this paper and others have used the following factors to study the APT:

- Level of industrial activity
- Inflation rate
- Spread between short- and long-term interest rates
- Yield spread between low- and high-risk corporate bonds

Another problem in specifying relevant factors is that the factors affecting returns need not persist and their role may change over time. Because of these difficulties in testing the APT, it has not proved to be a viable substitute for the CAPM and researchers have focused on tests of the CAPM and β_e. To this end, the studies discussed below (and listed in Appendix 18-A) were designed to determine accounting-based measures that could be used to explain and/or predict a firm's β_e. However, as we shall see, the recent controversy surrounding the CAPM has important implications for multifactor models such as the APT as well as for models that can be used to estimate β_e.

---

[39]The interested reader is referred to Chapters 10 and 11 of Z. Bodie, A. Kane, and A. Marcus, *Investments*, 4th ed. (Homewood, IL: Irwin, 1999).

Importance and Usefulness of Beta (β)

Knowledge of beta is important to analysts, investors, and management for a number of reasons:

1. To construct investment portfolios with the desired risk and return characteristics, you must know the beta of individual securities.

2. Discounted cash flow valuation models require an estimate of the firm's expected rate of return. With the CAPM formula, beta can be used to estimate that return (see Chapter 19).

3. Similarly, management, in making capital budgeting decisions, needs to know the firm's cost of capital or hurdle rate. The CAPM formula with beta provides an estimate of the firm's cost of equity capital.

In all three situations, the *ex ante*, or the next period's beta, is required. As this value is not directly observable, it must be estimated. One possibility is to estimate beta (using ordinary least-squares regression (OLS)) from the past history of firm and market returns. This estimate, the historical beta, has been found [e.g., Beaver and Manegold (1975)] to have a high *ex post* correlation (45%) with the next-period beta. Thus, the historical betas can be used to predict the next-period beta. Historical betas, however, are not perfect predictors of future betas,[40] as the regression estimates are subject to measurement error, and the firm's production, investment, and financing decisions change over time. Beta also may not be stable from period to period.

Estimating betas on a portfolio basis rather than individually is one remedy for these problems. Additionally, since investors are interested in the systematic risk of portfolios, the prediction of portfolio beta rather than individual beta is of primary importance.[41] On a portfolio basis the results improve dramatically. For a 5-security portfolio, the correlation is 82% (65% variation explained) and for 10-security portfolios, the correlation increases to 91% (82% variation explained).

Note that these correlations and percentage variation explained are derived ex post; that is, the predictive equations are developed with knowledge of the predicted period's values. In a sense, the equation is developed by asking the following question: "Given the second period beta, what is the best predictive model I can construct using the first period's beta?" The statistics that result define the degree of association between the two periods but not the degree of predictive power between one observation and the next. The latter should be measured with models that do not use data from the predicted period. Such models address the following question: "Given only the first period's beta, what is the best predictive model I can construct?"

The next section compares the performance of predictive models based on historical betas with those based on accounting-based risk measures. These latter models use accounting measures individually or in conjunction with historical betas in an attempt to improve the forecasting ability of models just using historical betas. As we shall see, there is an emphasis on the components of earnings variability discussed at the beginning of this chapter in many of these models.[42]

Review of Theoretical and Empirical Findings

The literature in this area is both theoretical and empirical. The theoretical papers attempt to link finance-based measures of risk with accounting measures of risk. Not all measures can be justified on a theoretical basis, and the literature indicates those areas where a theoretical

---

[40]The level of correlation of 45% implies that only about 20% of the (cross-sectional) variation in the second period's beta is explained by the first period's historical beta. (Percentage variation explained is equal to the correlation squared.)

[41]The problem of measurement error and the benefits of forecasting on a portfolio basis exist not only for forecasts based on historical betas, but also when accounting variables are used to forecast beta.

[42]Many of the studies find a more meaningful association between earnings and market returns when earnings are also expressed as a return measure. In the discussion that follows, therefore, the term "earnings" encompasses not only its traditional meaning of net income or EPS, but also return measures such as ROA, ROE, and the earnings/price ratio. When necessary, the exact definition used will be disclosed.

EXHIBIT 18-6
Market and Accounting Betas: Notation and Definitions

Market-based Betas

β_e = the "classical" beta used in finance to measure the systematic risk of an equity security. This is the beta we are attempting to forecast.

β_a = the beta of the equity of a firm that has no debt, the unlevered beta. This beta is a function solely of the underlying systematic risk of the firm's assets, that is, its operating risk. It is a theoretical, unobservable construct as few firms have no debt. It is used to demonstrate the contribution of a firm's operating risk to its overall beta.

β_d = the beta of a firm's debt. If debt is riskless, β_d equals zero.

Accounting-based Betas

$B_{earnings}$ = the accounting beta previously defined.
B_{sales} = the systematic component of the variability of a firm's sales.

---

relationship should not exist. Empirical studies test these relationships. We first discuss the theoretical underpinnings of the various risk measures and then provide a review of empirical work.

Theoretical Framework

In this section, beta is used in a number of contexts. The notation and a brief definition of each beta discussed are provided in Exhibit 18-6. Based on our discussion thus far, it should be expected that earnings volatility[43] is associated with the stock beta. Thus, operating leverage, financing leverage, the variance of sales or earnings, and the accounting beta should all be related to the stock beta. A number of theoretical papers, including those of Hamada (1972) and Bowman (1979), explicitly developed these relationships.

Relationship Among the Stock Beta, Operating Risk, Accounting Beta, and Earnings Variability. β_a, the unlevered beta, is related to operating risk. Clearly, for an unlevered firm, $B_{earnings}$ is also solely related to operating risk. Bowman (1979) has shown that for an unlevered firm, the relationship between the stock beta and the accounting beta is[44]

$$\beta_a = \beta_e = B_{earnings} \times \frac{1}{\text{Relative market value of debt}}$$

Earnings variability, from a theoretical perspective, is related to β_e only insofar as its systematic component ($B_{earnings}$) is related. *Empirical studies, however, find earnings variability to be the most significant accounting variable in explaining stock beta.* As Ryan (1997) notes:

> Earnings variability is the most significant of the accounting variables even though accounting beta is conceptually more analogous to beta. This is probably due to the fact that accounting beta is very noisy (it has four times the variance of beta) and it is highly positively correlated with earnings variability[45]

Thus, although earnings variability is not directly related to β_e, on an empirical level a relationship is found to the extent that earnings variability captures the systematic risk component of earnings.

---

[43]This, of course, is true as long as it is not solely due to unsystematic (firm-specific) factors.

[44]The relative market value of firm converts earnings into a return measure. It is the ratio of the firm's market value to the total market value of all firms in the economy.

[45]Stephen G. Ryan, "A Survey of Research Relating Accounting Numbers to Systematic Equity Risk, with Implications for Risk Disclosure Policy and Future Risk," *Accounting Horizons* (June 1997), p. 89.

Relationship Among Stock Beta, Financial Leverage, Operating Leverage, and Accounting Beta. Introducing (riskless) debt results in the following relationship:

$$\beta_e = \beta_a + \left[\frac{D}{E}\right]\beta_a$$

Thus, adding financial leverage (as measured by the debt-to-equity ratio) to the capital structure of a firm increases its systematic risk.

When debt is risky, the relationship can be expressed as

$$\beta_e = \beta_a + \left\{\left[\frac{D}{E}\right] \times (\beta_a - \beta_d)\right\}$$

An obvious parallel to this equation is the equation used in Chapter 4 for the disaggregation of ROE into ROA and the cost of debt:

$$ROE = ROA + \left\{\left[\frac{D}{E}\right] \times (ROA - \text{Cost of debt})\right\}$$

This similarity is not coincidental but is a direct outcome of the risk/return trade-off inherent in all investment opportunities. As higher risks require higher returns, the relationships that determine risk should be similar to those that determine returns.

The foregoing equations imply that equity risk (β_e) is a function of the risk of the underlying assets combined with the risk inherent in financing, that is, the operating and financial leverage. A more direct description of this relationship is given by Mandelker and Rhee (1984), who derive the following expression for systematic risk:

$$\beta_e = \text{FLE} \times \text{OLE} \times \left[\frac{B_{\text{sales}}}{\text{Price/earnings}}\right]$$

where B_{sales} measures the covariance of the *percentage change in sales* with the market return R_m. Again, note the similarity between the foregoing and the expression for total leverage effect derived in Chapter 4:

$$\text{TLE} = (\% \text{ Change in income}) = \text{FLE} \times \text{OLE} \times (\% \text{ Change in sales})$$

The expressions are parallel except for the price/earnings ratio factor that is needed to convert sales to market returns. In the latter expression, we deal with the returns themselves, whereas in the former we are concerned with the uncertainty of these returns. Hence, "% change in sales" is replaced in the former by its (systematic) risk term.

Relationship Between the Stock Beta and Other Risk Measures. Bowman demonstrates that size, growth, and dividend payout have no theoretical relationship to a stock's systematic risk. Hochman (1983), however, reviews studies with conflicting views of the theoretical relationship between β_e and various definitions of growth. Furthermore, Hochman argues that dividend yield (dividend/market value) should be low for companies with high growth[46] potential. Thus, if growth is positively associated with β_e, then (empirically) we expect a negative relationship between β_e and dividend yield.

Empirical Studies

Given these theoretical relationships, researchers have attempted to use accounting variables and ratios to either explain or predict differences in firm betas. Some studies examine the historical relationship between β_e and accounting measures of risk to see how much of the variation in β_e can be explained ex post by the accounting risk measures. The predictive studies, on the other hand, attempt to use the relationships derived to predict future-period β_e.

Some of the relationships tested had no theoretical underpinnings. Their inclusion in the models was based on a combination of researcher intuition and "conventional wisdom."

---

[46]Higher growth means that income is reinvested in the business and dividends are lower. The high growth would be reflected in higher market value and, therefore, a lower dividend yield.

Explanatory Studies. Ball and Brown (1968) found a high degree of association between the accounting beta and the market beta.[47] Depending on how the accounting beta was measured, its correlation with the market beta ranged from 39% to 46%. Lev (1973) examined the association of operating leverage with both the overall risk (total variance) of a firm's returns as well as the systematic risk component β_e. Using firms in three industries (electric utilities, steel manufacturers, and oil producers), he obtained regression estimates of each firm's variable cost percentage v from the equation

$$TC_t = F + vS_t$$

Lev then regressed the β_e of these companies against these estimates of v. The hypothesized relationship was negative: The lower the variable cost, the higher the total variance of returns and the higher the beta. Empirical results confirmed this negative relationship as the regression coefficient on v was negative (and statistically significant) for all industries and for both risk measures.[48]

Mandelker and Rhee examined the association of beta with the OLE and FLE. They found that (ex post) OLE and FLE explain anywhere between 38% and 48% of the variation in beta on a portfolio basis. On an individual basis, only 11% of the variation was explained.

Explanatory and Predictive Studies. The above tests measured association only, not predictive ability. Beaver et al. (1970) tested the association and predictive ability of seven accounting risk measures and beta over two separate subperiods. The seven variables examined were: dividend payout, financial leverage (debt/assets), earnings variability (standard deviation of the earnings/price ratio), accounting beta, asset size, current ratio, and asset growth. The relationship between each accounting risk measure and β_e was tested first individually and then in a multivariate context.

The univariate results, presented in Exhibit 18-7, indicate that for four of the listed measures, the correlations were significant on an individual and (five-security) portfolio

EXHIBIT 18-7
Predictive Ability of Accounting Risk Measures

	Predicted Association	Findings Confirmed
1. Payout Dividend/income	Negative	Yes
2. Growth Assets (year 5)/assets (year 1)	Positive	Only period 1
3. Leverage (financial) Debt/assets	Positive	Yes
4. Liquidity Current ratio	Negative	Only period 1
5. Size Average assets	Negative	Only period 2
6. Earnings variability Standard deviation of earnings/price ratio	Positive	Yes
7. Accounting beta Beta of firm's ratio of earnings/price with market index of earnings/price	Positive	Yes

Source: William Beaver, Paul Kettler, and Myron Scholes, "The Association Between Market Determined and Accounting Determined Risk Measures," *Accounting Review* (October 1970), Table 5, p. 669 (adapted).

[47]This result was not the main thrust of their study (see Chapter 5 for a detailed discussion of Ball and Brown), and they did not attempt to improve the predictive ability of the market beta by use of the accounting beta.

[48]The percentage variation explained (R^2), however, was meaningful only for the steel manufacturers' risk measures and the overall risk measure for oil producers. The low R^2 may be due to the fact that Lev (1973) examined firms only on an individual rather than a portfolio basis.

level over both subperiods examined and in the direction predicted, with earnings variability being the most significant in explaining risk. The findings for *financial leverage, accounting beta*, and *earnings variability* are consistent with arguments presented earlier in terms of the predicted association with β_e. The theoretical justification stated by Beaver et al. for the findings with respect to the *dividend payout ratio* is that, since firms are reluctant to cut dividends, those firms that face more uncertainty (i.e., have higher β_e's) pay lower dividends.[49]

These relationships are all univariate as they measure the correlation between β_e and each of the accounting-based measures individually. Beaver et al. then constructed a multivariate model to forecast the next period's β_e. The *benchmark* forecast to be compared against this forecast was period 1's historic (OLS) β_e.

Using only the accounting-based data from the first subperiod in conjunction with the period-1 (OLS) β_e, the following predictive equation resulted:[50]

$$\begin{aligned} \text{Period 2 } \beta_e &= \text{Fitted period 1 } \beta_e \\ &= 1.016 - (0.584 \times \text{Payout}) + (0.835 \times \text{Growth}) \\ &\quad + (3.027 \times \text{Earnings variability}) \end{aligned}$$

This model thus uses accounting-based data to modify a market-based measure.[51] The period-2 forecast developed with the foregoing model was compared with the benchmark forecast. The accounting-based forecast explained between 63% and 69% (depending on how the portfolios were constructed) of the variation, whereas the benchmark forecast explained only 37% to 42%. The benchmark forecast error was higher than the accounting-based forecast error 54% (57% to 66%) of the time on an individual (portfolio) basis.

Generally, it is more difficult to forecast variables that are outliers relative to the mean of the distribution. For market betas, this means it is easier to forecast stocks of average systematic risk (beta approximately equal to 1) than to forecast high-beta (extremely risky) or low-beta (low-risk) stocks. The accounting-based model did much better than the benchmark model at these extreme values,[52] with smaller forecast errors more than three-fourths of the time.

Rosenberg (by himself or in conjunction with others) undertook comprehensive attempts to forecast "fundamental" β_e's using a variety of accounting as well as nonaccounting variables. Exhibit 18-8 lists the 13 variables used by Rosenberg and McKibben (1973). Using the criterion of which (predicted) beta best forecast future returns, they tested the predictive power of their beta against a number of alternative (return-based) beta forecasts. They found their model to have the best predictive power. The results were statistically significant, although in some cases the additional predictive power was marginal (2% increase in R^2). Rosenberg and Guy (1976) found that the variance of earnings and cash flows, as well as firm size, earnings growth, dividend yield, and the debt-to-asset ratio were useful in predicting betas. It should be noted that these studies confirmed Beaver et al.'s original finding that earnings variability was the most significant in explaining beta.

As with models of credit risk discussed in the previous section, academic research efforts to predict equity risk also led to proprietary and commercial modeling efforts. The in-

---

[49]Watts and Zimmerman (1986) use another justification, based on the leverage ratio, to explain the finding. They argue that since it has been shown empirically that firms with more debt pay lower dividends relative to earnings, then the negative relationship between dividend payout and β is another manifestation of the positive relationship between β and leverage.

[50]The parameters of the model were developed as follows. First, for each firm in the sample, the historic OLS beta for the first period was found using the market model. This OLS beta was then regressed on the firm's accounting variables. The resultant regression equation was then used to determine the next period's market beta. Since only the first period's data were used, the predicted beta is identical to the first period's "fitted" beta, that is, the beta that falls on the regression line.

[51]Note that the multivariate model does not include the same variables that proved to be significant on an individual basis. This happens often in empirical work as interrelationships among independent variables can alter their significance on a univariate level.

[52]The extreme values were defined as the upper and lower deciles (quartiles) on an individual (portfolio) basis.

EXHIBIT 18-8
Variables Used by Rosenberg and McKibben

Accounting-based Descriptors

1. Standard deviation of a per share earnings growth measure
2. Latest annual proportional change in per share earnings
3. Standard & Poor's quality rating
4. Liquidity (the quick ratio)
5. Absolute magnitude of per share dividend cuts
6. Mean leverage (senior securities/total assets)
7. Growth measure for total net sales
8. Growth measure of per share earnings available for common
9. Gross plant per dollar of total assets

Market-based Descriptors

10. Historical beta, a regression of stock return on market return over preceding calendar years in the sample, if we assume alpha equals zero
11. Share turnover as a percentage of shares outstanding
12. Logarithm of unadjusted share price

Market Valuation Descriptors

13. Book value of common equity per share/price

Source: Barr Rosenberg and Walt McKibben, "The Prediction of Systematic and Specific Risk in Common Stocks," *Journal of Financial and Quantitative Analysis* (March 1973), p. 324.

vestment service company, Barr Rosenberg & Associates (BARRA) was formed to provide forecasts of betas based on models incorporating accounting-based and other fundamental factors. The actual models used, being proprietary, are not available. This service competes with other investment services that provide beta forecasts based on models that primarily use historical stock returns data.[53]

The Attack on the CAPM and β

There is a growing body of (empirical) literature that contradicts the implications of the CAPM and by extension the usefulness of β. Figure 18-4*a–d*, based on data from Fama and French (1992), illustrates these issues graphically.

Figure 18-4*a* plots the average monthly return earned by portfolios formed on the basis of beta. If beta reflects risk, then portfolios with higher (lower) betas should on average earn a higher (lower) return. *The figure, however, indicates very little difference in returns* earned by the various portfolios, with average monthly returns all hovering around 1.2%. On the other hand, there is a relationship between returns and portfolios formed on the basis of:[54]

- Size (Figure 18-4*b*),
- Earnings-to-price (E/P) ratio (Figure 18-4*c*), or
- Book-to-market value of equity (B/M) (Figure 18-4*d*)

---

[53]Harrington (1983) tested the forecasting ability of betas provided by such investment services. In all, 12 different predictors of beta were examined. Included in the test were two models based on firm-fundamental characteristics developed by BARRA. For the industrial companies, one fundamental BARRA model had the lowest mean-square prediction error over all four time horizons examined. Their other fundamental model finished second over two of the horizons. The results also showed that it is easier to forecast betas calculated over longer horizons. (In all cases, the longer horizons had lower mean-square prediction errors.)

[54]The ratios E/P and B/M are inverses of the more familiar P/E and market-to-book ratios. The inverses are used because of the computational problems that can occur when small or negative earnings or book values appear in ratio denominators.

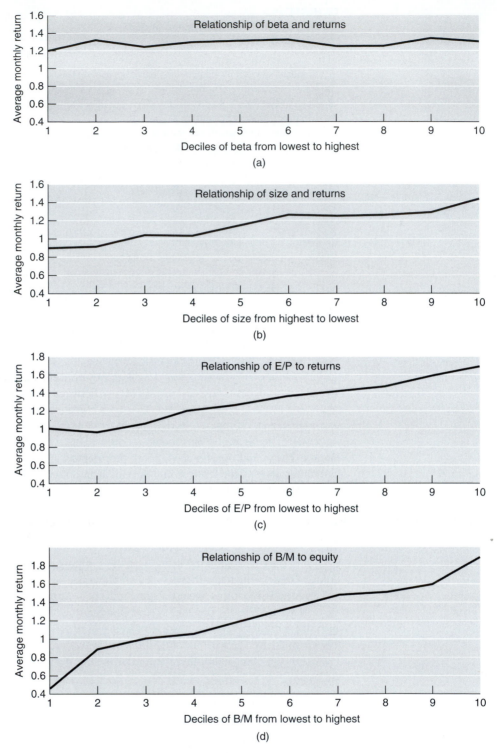

FIGURE 18-4 Relationship of returns and various measures of "risk." *Source:* Adapted from data presented in E. Fama and K. R. French, "The Cross-Section of Expected Stock Returns," *Journal of Finance* (June 1992), pp. 427–65.

These results pose problems for the CAPM (and β) from two perspectives:

1. The CAPM predicts that a firm's returns are determined *solely* by its systematic risk β. These results indicate *that alternative measures of "risk" tend to be (more) closely related to returns.*

2. The results indicate that *returns are not related to* β.

Alternative Measures of Equity Risk or Market Inefficiency?

Fama and French were not the first to examine the relationship between returns and these alternative "risk" measures. The size effect was first documented by Banz (1981). Banz found that market equity (ME—stock price multiplied by outstanding shares) can be used as an additional factor explaining average returns, with smaller firms earning excess returns (over those predicted by β_e) relative to large firms. Similarly, the P/E (the inverse of the E/P ratio) was found by Basu (1983) to explain average returns in tests that also included β_e and size. Rosenberg et al. (1985) documented the relationship of returns and the book-to-market value of equity ratio. In addition to the measures shown in Figure 18-4, financial leverage has also been shown to be positively related to returns. This is not surprising as β_e is a function of leverage. Thus, we should expect higher leverage to be associated with higher returns. Bhandari (1988), however, determined that leverage had (additional) explanatory power in tests that included β_e (as well as size).[55]

When discussing these alternative measures of "risk," we use quotation marks because, although these variables display empirical properties similar to those of risk (i.e., they are related to expected returns), for the most part, the literature struggles to find convincing explanations for the relationships.

In fact, two views of these findings have emerged. At one extreme, some do not view these measures as "risk." Rather, they view these relationships as evidence of market inefficiency. As discussed in Chapter 5, Lakonishok et al. (1994) and Haugen (1995) argue that the B/M effect is evidence of market *overreaction*. Similarly, the *neglected firm* argument is used to explain the size effect, and the P/E ratio effect is often cited as an example of a market anomaly.

Others argue that whereas the CAPM (and/or the importance of β) may be damaged, market efficiency is not. That is, although they concede that markets may not act in a manner consistent with the CAPM, the relationship between size and the B/M ratio and average returns, they argue, is based on risk and return considerations.

Amihud and Mendelson (1986, 1991), for example, argue that the size effect is related to liquidity. As small firms are not traded as often as larger firms, the bid-asked spread on these securities is wider. To compensate for this, a higher expected return (liquidity premium) is required.

Chan and Chen (1991) argue that the B/M effect is due to the fact that firms with high B/M ratios are intrinsically riskier. The market, therefore, discounts their price, accounting for the lower market price (and higher B/M).

Fama and French (1995) also take the position that the B/M and size effects are related to risk and not market inefficiency. As stock prices are discounted future earnings, they note that

> if the size and B/M risk factors in returns (unexpected changes in stock prices) are the result of rational pricing, they must be driven by common factors in shocks to expected earnings that are related to size and B/M.[56]

They proceed to demonstrate that firm profitability (as measured by ROE) is related to differences in size and E/M. However, they concede that

> size and B/M remain arbitrary indicator variables, that, for unexplained economic reasons, are related to risk factors in returns.[57]

The Defense of β and the CAPM

The defenders of β and the CAPM respond to Fama and French by taking a closer look at the data and methodology used in that study. They argue that those data suffer from measurement error in the following areas:

- How returns were measured
- How β was measured
- How the market index was measured

---

[55]Fama and French also examined leverage but argued that its effects were subsumed by the B/M effect.

[56]Eugene F. Fama and Kenneth R. French, "Size and Book-to-Market Factors in Earnings and Returns," *Journal of Finance* (March 1995), p. 132.

[57]Ibid., p. 131.

Kothari et al. (1995) found that when returns are measured annually rather than monthly there is a positive relationship between β and returns. Similarly, Amihud et al. (1992), using a different statistical methodology than Fama and French, also show a significant positive relationship between β and returns.

Kothari et al. also argue that the B/M results may be due to *survivorship bias*. That is, a high B/M ratio indicates a low market price and a potentially distressed firm. If such a firm fails, it (and its low return) will not appear in databases used by researchers such as Fama and French. Thus, only the high B/M firms that recovered and consequently had high returns were included in the sample examined by Fama and French. Omitting the high B/M firms that had low returns (by failing) biased the results in an upward direction.

Others noted that the CAPM is predicated on the use of a market index that includes *all* risky assets. With an index such as the NYSE or the S&P 500 index, the model used in the empirical tests may be misspecified as it ignores other assets, thus accounting for β's poor showing. Additionally, they argue that historical β's may not be the best estimates of the ex ante β as β may shift with changes in the economic environment.

Jagannathan and Wang (1993, 1995), for example, construct a CAPM[58] model that includes, in addition to the standard stock market index, an index to reflect human capital (thus broadening the set of risky assets) and an index to reflect potential changes in β due to shifts in the business cycle. This expanded model shows the expected relationship between β and returns.

Parenthetically, the criticism of the use of historical β's is especially interesting in the context of our earlier discussions. The evidence indicates that accounting variables can be used to estimate β more accurately than historical β's. Thus, the performance of β as a risk measure may be enhanced if one compared "fundamental" β's (rather than historical β's) with average returns.

In response to some of the criticisms levied against their work, Fama and French (1995) note that even if there were flaws in their tests (which they attempt to disprove[59]) and β is related to returns, at best *that would only save β but not the CAPM*. The fact that, in a three-factor model incorporating β, B/M, and size, the latter two measures are also related to returns contradicts the CAPM, which contends that β (however measured) is the *sole* risk measure.

Implications for Accounting Risk Measures

The need for more research in multifactor models is implicit in the arguments that β may not be the sole risk measure and findings that indicate that there are alternative measures of risk. These findings have important implications for accounting-based measures of risk:

1. Research findings indicate a strong explanatory as well as predictive relationship between accounting-based measures of risk and β_e. Although doubt has been cast on the relationship of returns to β_e, the use of improperly measured β's may account for the results. This point highlights the potential need (and benefits) of using accounting variables to improve the estimation of β_e.

2. The alternative (empirical) measures that have been suggested as risk proxies, such as the B/M, P/E, and leverage ratios, are accounting-based ratios.

3. Given the previous points, it is worth noting that the accounting ratios used in the empirical studies discussed, were, for the most part, computed without adjustment for differences in accounting policies, unusual items, and off-balance-sheet information. Such adjustments could potentially improve the models[60] and provide further insight into the nature of the alternative "risk" measures.

---

[58]One can debate whether this model should be considered a modified CAPM or a new asset pricing model [see Jagannathan and McGrattan (1995)].

[59]See, for example, Fama and French (1996) and Davis, Fama, and French (2000).

[60]Dhaliwal (discussed in Chapter 12), for example, found that better predictions of β_e could be obtained if the explanatory variable debt/equity was adjusted to reflect off-balance-sheet pension information.

SUMMARY

The classification studies demonstrated strong linkages between accounting-based measures of risk and various forms of risk facing a firm. It is, however, troublesome that the major effort in constructing the models has been devoted to the statistical analysis techniques rather than examination of the inputs going into the models.

Our criticism takes two forms. The first deals with the theoretical underpinnings for the models. It is one thing when there is no theory, as in the case of bankruptcy prediction. It is another when the theory exists but is ignored. The prediction of beta and bond ratings are examples of the latter. In the case of beta prediction, many of the models focus on only one or two variables when the theory specifies a larger set of explanatory variables. In the case of bond ratings, the research may be focused on the wrong variable of interest entirely.

The second criticism concerns the data used in these models. The research focus is on the tools that measure the data rather than the data themselves. It is true that there is no clear-cut evidence that adjustments (such as for off-balance-sheet financing) would improve the models. That is what should make it such an interesting area for research. Ignoring this issue reminds us of the suggestion by Oskar Morgenstern that working with sophisticated statistics and poor data was equivalent to calculating the circumference of a circle by pacing off the radius with one's feet and multiplying by pi taken to the tenth decimal place.

Chapter 18

Problems

Problems 1 to 3 relate to the takeover of Kraft by Philip Morris and are based on the data in Exhibit 18P-1.

1. [Ratios and bond ratings; CFA© adapted] Philip Morris [MO] is one of the world's largest cigarette manufacturers as well as a major producer and distributor of a broad line of food and beverage products. The company has compiled a steady record of growth in sales, earnings, and cash flow.

In October 1988, Philip Morris announced an unsolicited cash tender offer for all the 124 million outstanding shares of Kraft at $90 per share. Kraft subsequently accepted a $106-per-share all-cash offer from Philip Morris.

Kraft's major products include cheese, edible oils, nonfluid dairy products, and frozen foods. Exhibit 18P-1 provides projected financial data for Philip Morris and Kraft individually and on a consolidated basis.

Exhibit 18P-2 reports the median values, according to bond rating category, for the following three financial ratios:

(i) Pretax interest coverage

(ii) Long-term debt as a percentage of capitalization

(iii) Cash flow as a percentage of total debt (note the definition of cash flow in Exhibit 18P-2)

Using the information provided in Exhibits 18P-1 and 18P-2:

a. Calculate the three ratios listed for Philip Morris for 1989, first, using the figures prior to the Kraft acquisition and, second, using the consolidated figures after the acquisition.

b. Compare these two sets of ratios to the medians for each rating category.

c. Formulate and support an opinion as to the appropriate rating category for Philip Morris (before and after the Kraft acquisition).

2. [Ratios and bankruptcy prediction] Given the variables used in Altman's two bankruptcy models, discuss the impact of the Kraft acquisition on the probability that Philip Morris will become insolvent. (Use the data in Exhibit 18P-1 as part of your answer.)

3. [Effect of acquisition on beta] Describe the expected effect of the Kraft acquisition on Philip Morris's beta. (Your answer should consider the effects on the "unlevered" beta as well as the "levered" beta and should distinguish between operating and financial leverage effects.)

4. [Comprehensive financial analysis; CFA© adapted] The Investment Policy Committee of your firm has decided that the soft drink industry, specifically Coca-Cola Company [KO] and Coca-Cola Enterprises [CCE], qualifies as potential purchases for the firm's portfolios. As the firm's beverage industry expert, you must prepare an extensive financial analysis of these two soft drink producers.

KO owns the brands included in its broad product line. It plays almost no direct role in the domestic manufacturing and distribution beyond the output of soft drink extract.

The business of CCE is also dominated by soft drinks. CCE, however, purchases extract from KO and transforms it into completed products sold in a wide variety of retail outlets throughout the United States.

EXHIBIT 18P-1. PHILIP MORRIS COMPANIES, INC.
Projected Financial Data, 1988 to 1989 (in $millions)

	1988 Estimate Excluding Kraft	1989 Estimate Before Kraft	Kraft Only	Adjustments	Consolidated
A. Selected Income Statement Data					
Total sales	$30,450	$33,080	$11,610		$44,690
Total operating income	$ 4,875	$ 5,550	$ 1,050	$ (210)	$ 6,390
As a % of sales	16.0%	16.8%	9.0%		14.3%
Interest expense	(575)	(500)	(75)	(1,025)	(1,600)
Corporate expense	(200)	(225)	(100)	(40)	(365)
Other expense	(5)	(5)			(5)
Pretax income	$ 4,095	$ 4,820	$ 875	$(1,275)	$ 4,420
As a % of sales	13.4%	14.6%	7.5%		9.9%
Income taxes	(1,740)	$(2,000)	(349)	493	(1,856)
Tax rate	42.5%	41.5%	39.9%		42.0%
Net income	$ 2,355	$ 2,820	$ 526	$ (782)	$ 2,564
B. Selected Balance Sheet Data as of Year-End					
Short-term debt	$ 1,125	$ 1,100	$ 683		$ 1,783
Long-term debt	4,757	3,883	895	$11,000	15,778
Stockholders' equity	8,141	9,931	2,150	(2,406)	9,675
C. Other Selected Financial Data					
Depreciation and amortization	$ 720	$ 750	$ 190	$ 295	$ 1,235
Deferred taxes	100	100	10	280	390
Equity in undistributed earnings of unconsolidated subsidiaries	110	125			125

EXHIBIT 18P-2
Median Ratios According to Bond Rating Category

Ratio	AAA	AA	A	BBB	BB	B	CCC
Pretax interest coverage	14.10X	9.67X	5.40X	3.63X	2.25X	1.58X	(0.42X)
Long-term debt as a % of capitalization	11.5%	18.7%	28.3%	34.3%	48.4%	57.2%	73.2%
Cash flow* as a % of total debt	111.8%	86.0%	50.9%	34.2%	22.8%	14.1%	6.2%

*For the purpose of calculating this ratio, Standard & Poor's defines cash flow as "net income plus depreciation, amortization and deferred taxes, less equity in undistributed earnings of unconsolidated subsidiaries."
Source: Standard & Poor's.

Use the financial statements of KO and CCE provided in Case 13-1 to answer parts a, b, and c.

a. Your comparative analysis of these two soft drink companies requires calculations of various ratios. You have identified four key areas of comparison:

   (i) Short-term liquidity
   (ii) Capital structure and long-term solvency
   (iii) Asset utilization
   (iv) Operating profitability

   Compute the ratios required to make these comparisons. Discuss the differences between KO and CCE in these four areas based on the ratios and the financial statements.

b. Using the financial statement data below, identify at least three financial statement adjustments (for each firm) required to enhance their comparability and usefulness for financial analysis.

Data Extracted from Financial Statement Footnotes

Coca-Cola Company (KO)

(1) The market value of the Company's investments in publicly traded equity investees exceeded the Company's carrying value at December 31, 2001, by approximately $3.2 billion.

(2) The Company is contingently liable for guarantees of indebtedness owed by some of its licensees and others, totaling approximately $431 million at December 31, 2001.

(3) Had stock options been expensed, the after-tax compensation cost would have been (in $millions) $160, $182, $202 for 1999, 2000, and 2001 respectively.

Coca-Cola Enterprises (CCE)

(1) At December 31, 2001, the fair value of long-term debt was $12,587 million versus carrying value of $12,165 million.

(2) As of December 31, 2001, the company has entered into long-term purchase agreements with suppliers, aggregating approximately $1,621 million in 2002, $1,637 million in 2003, $861 million in 2004, $874 million in 2005, $887 million in 2006, and $1,777 thereafter.

(3) At December 31, 2001, the benefit obligation of the company's pension plans exceeded plan assets by $361 million. The company had recognized a net pension asset of $1 million on the same date.

c. For each of the adjustments identified in part b, discuss the effects of these adjustments on your answer to part a.

5. [Westvaco; fixed-income analysis] Exhibit 18-4 presents median values of financial ratios according to Standard & Poor's bond rating categories. Use this exhibit and the financial statements of Westvaco to:

a. Compute the corresponding ratios (where possible) for Westvaco for 1999.

b. Determine the "appropriate" bond rating for Westvaco.

c. Determine a bond rating for Westvaco based on its Z''-score (use the data provided in Exhibit 18-5).

d. Westvaco's actual bond rating was A− (as of December 1999). Compare the "ratings" calculated in parts b and c with the actual rating and discuss any differences.

6 [Extension of Problem 18-5]

a. Using the current cost balance sheet and normalized income statement developed in Chapter 17 for Westvaco, recalculate the ratios in Problem 18-5.

b. State and justify the bond rating implied by the adjusted ratios.

c. Notwithstanding your answer to part b, explain why these adjustments might not make a difference in Westvaco's bond rating.

d. Discuss whether these adjustments make a difference in assessing Westvaco's default risk.

e. Discuss whether these adjustments affect the assessment of Westvaco's bankruptcy risk.

7. [Bond ratings] Exhibit 18P-3 contains a comparison of Westvaco with two other paper companies.

a. Using only the data provided in Exhibits 18P-3 and 18-4, determine the appropriate debt rating for the three companies as of December 1999. If different from the actual rating, discuss briefly.

b. Evaluate the risk that the debt of the three companies listed will be downgraded in 2000.

c. The years 1999 and 2000 were prosperous for the paper industry. Discuss how that should affect the evaluation of debt ratings for the three companies.

8. [Forecasting bond rating changes] Standard & Poor's states that it places firms on its Creditwatch list when changes in operating profit trends, completed or planned mergers, capital structure changes, or regulatory actions suggest a need for reevaluation of the current credit rating. A listing with negative implications may result in the rating being lowered.

Steelcase [SCS] is a major manufacturer of office furniture. On April 17, 2002, Standard & Poor's revised its outlook on Steelcase from stable to negative. It cited challenging market conditions and Steelcase's deteriorating operating performance. The current debt rating of A− was affirmed with a warning that if "credit protection ratios continue to deteriorate, ratings could be lowered."

EXHIBIT 18P-3
Comparison of Paper Company Ratios and Debt Ratings

	Total Debt to Capital		Times Interest Earned	
Company (1999 Rating)	1999	2000	1999	2000
Westvaco (A−)	0.40	0.54	22.6	18.3
International Paper (BBB+)	0.45	0.55	1.8	2.1
Georgia-Pacific (BBB−)	0.63	0.73	4.7	2.3

Source: Ratios computed from 2000 annual reports.

EXHIBIT 18P-4. STEELCASE INC.
Selected Financial Data for Years Ended February 23, 2001 and February 22, 2002 (in $millions)

	Fiscal Years	
	2001	2002
Total debt	$ 537	$ 594
Total equity	1,637	1,556
Sales	4,049	3,090
Earnings before interest and taxes	322	19
Interest expense	(18)	(21)
Income before tax	$ 304	$ (2)
Cash from operations	210	295
Capital expenditures	(260)	123
Cash for investing activities	(220)	(250)
Discretionary cash flows*	(140)	82

*Computed using Standard & Poor's definitions.
Source: Steelcase fiscal 2002 annual report.

Exhibit 18P-4 provides selected balance sheet, income statement, and cash flow data.

a. Using the data in Exhibits 18P-4 and 18-4, evaluate Standard & Poor's decision to revise its outlook on Steelcase Inc.

b. State the additional information you would need to determine whether the firm's debt should be downgraded. Specify financial statement or footnote information and discuss how you would use it.

c. Discuss the factor(s) you believe may have led Standard & Poor's to reaffirm the A- rating of Steelcase.

d. Discuss the limitations of comparing Steelcase's ratios with those in Exhibit 18-4.

9. [Credit analysis and fixed-income investments; CFA© adapted] Margaret O'Flaherty, a portfolio manager for MCF Investments, is considering two fixed-income investment alternatives for her clients' portfolios. Neither bond is callable.

Issuer	Coupon	Maturity	Price
Alpine Chemical	7%	June 30, 2014	100
U.S. Treasury Note	6%	June 30, 2014	100

Currently the spreads between noncallable, 10-year industrial bonds and 10-year U.S. Treasury notes are as follows:

Treasuries to AAA-rated industrials	25 basis points
Treasuries to AA-rated industrials	50 basis points
Treasuries to A-rated industrials	75 basis points
Treasuries to BBB-rated industrials	100 basis points
Treasuries to BB-rated industrials	125 basis points
Treasuries to B-rated industrials	150 basis points

a. Selected financial ratios for the Alpine Chemical Company are presented below:

Alpine Chemical Company Credit Ratios

Credit Ratios	1999	2000	2001	2002	2003
EBIT/interest expense	3.46×	4.96×	4.79×	4.70×	5.65×
Long-term debt/total capitalization	28%	34%	34%	34%	44%
Funds from operations/total debt	84%	93%	56%	51%	59%
Operating income/sales	13%	13%	14%	12%	13%

Briefly explain the significance of each of the four ratios to the assessment of Alpine Chemical's creditworthiness.

b. Select an appropriate credit rating for Alpine Chemical by relating the level and trend of the four credit ratios to the medians for those ratios shown in Exhibit 18-4.

c. Given your assessment of Alpine Chemical's credit rating, state and justify which of the two bonds (Alpine Chemical or U.S. Treasury) O'Flaherty should recommend for purchase.

10. [Credit analysis and off-balance sheet debt; CFA© adapted] Michelle Smith, CFA, an analyst with Blue River Investments, is considering buying a Montrose Cable Company corporate bond. The bond is currently trading at a credit premium of 55 basis points.

Balance sheet and income statement information for Montrose is shown in Part A of Exhibit 18P-5. Part B of the exhibit provides information with respect to Blue River Investments' internal bond-rating criteria and the estimated credit premium over U.S. Treasuries associated with each rating category.

In carrying out her credit analysis, Smith has decided to consider some off-balance-sheet items. Specifically, Smith

EXHIBIT 18P-5. MONTROSE CABLE

A. Financial Statements, Year Ended March 31, 2001 (in $thousands)

Balance Sheet

Current assets	$ 4,735
Fixed assets	43,225
Total assets	$47,960
Current liabilities	$ 4,500
Long-term debt	10,000
Total liabilities	$14,500
Shareholders' equity	33,460
Total liabilities and shareholders' equity	$47,960

Income Statement

Revenue	$18,500
Operating and administrative expenses	(14,050)
Operating income	$ 4,450
Interest expense	(942)
Income before income taxes	$ 3,508
Income tax expense	(1,228)
Net income	$ 2,280

B. Blue River Investments: Internal Bond-Rating Criteria and Credit Yield Premium Data

Bond Rating	Interest Coverage (EBIT/interest expense)	Leverage (Long-term debt/equity)	Current Ratio (Current assets/ current liabilities)	Credit Yield Premium over U.S. Treasuries (in basis points)
AA	5.00 to 6.00	0.25 to 0.30	1.15 to 1.25	30 bps
A	4.00 to 5.00	0.30 to 0.40	1.00 to 1.15	50 bps
BBB	3.00 to 4.00	0.40 to 0.50	0.90 to 1.00	100 bps
BB	2.00 to 3.00	0.50 to 0.60	0.75 to 0.90	125 bps

wishes to evaluate the impact of the following off-balance-sheet items on Montrose's credit evaluation.

- Montrose has guaranteed the long-term debt (principal only) of an unconsolidated affiliate. This obligation has a present value of $995,000.

- Montrose has sold $500,000 of accounts receivable with recourse at a yield of 8%.

- Montrose is a lessee in a new noncancelable operating leasing agreement to finance transmission equipment. The discounted present value of the lease payments is $6,144,000 using an interest rate of 10%. The annual payment will be $1,000,000.

a. Using only the reported data, calculate the three ratios needed as inputs to Blue River Investments' internal bond-rating criteria.

b. State and justify the rating category implied by the ratios calculated in part a. Is the 55 bps credit premium the bond is trading at now appropriate for that rating category?

c. Calculate the combined effect of the *three* off-balance-sheet items on *each* of the *three* financial ratios calculated in part a.

d. State and justify whether the current credit yield premium compensates Smith for the credit risk of the bond after considering the effects of the off-balance-sheet items.

19

VALUATION AND FORECASTING

CHAPTER OUTLINE

FINANCIAL STATEMENT FORECASTS

SUMMARY

Alpha Growth

Analysis of Historical Data

Forecasting 2002 Data

Review

APPENDIX 19-A
APPENDIX 19-B

CHAPTER OBJECTIVES

Chapter 19 concludes the text with an examination of valuation models and forecasting. The chapter objectives are to:

1. Discuss the use of book value to measure value, and the effects on book value of:
   - Measurement problems
   - Transactions with stockholders
   - Acquisitions
   - Exchange rate changes
   - Financial reporting choices
2. Compare the valuation models (DCF models) based on discounting estimates of future dividends, earnings, and cash flows.
3. Show that these three valuation models are theoretically equivalent but that the choice of model depends on such factors as:
   - Definition of earnings and cash flows
   - Estimating the growth rate

   - Effect of transitory earnings components
   - Inability to reliably forecast far into the future

4. Describe the abnormal earnings or EBO model, explain how it avoids some of the limitations of DCF models, and explain its following advantages:
   - Short forecast horizon
   - Reliance on book value as a principal input
   - Limited impact of accounting choices
5. Review the research that compares analyst forecasts to those based on extrapolative or index models that use time-series models. Discuss the research findings that quarterly data, segment data, and financial statement components all improve forecast accuracy under some conditions.
6. Forecast a company's financial statements using historical data and appropriate assumptions regarding revenue growth and future financial statement ratios.

INTRODUCTION

This chapter provides an overview of valuation models. In a perfect world, the models based on assets, dividends, cash flows, and earnings are identical. However, in the real world, this highly stylized environment does not exist and model results can differ. In such settings, the data used in valuation models are estimates of expected future values and their measurement is as important as their predictive ability.

The primary focus of the chapter, therefore, is not the theoretical underpinnings of these models, but rather the relationship of their parameters to information obtainable from the accounting system. In addition, consistent with forecasting requirements of valuation models, the chapter includes a discussion of forecasting and the time-series properties of earnings.

The chapter concludes with an integrated forecast of financial statements, using historical and projected data and relationships for a fictional company.

VALUATION MODELS

OVERVIEW OF MODELS

The valuation models most commonly used by analysts and investors generally fall into two classes:

1. Asset-based valuation models
2. Discounted cash flow (DCF) models

Additionally, we explore a third class, which has characteristics of the first two:

3. The abnormal earnings or Edwards–Bell–Ohlson (EBO) model.

Asset-based valuation models assign a value to the firm based on the current market value of the individual component assets. Liabilities (also at market value) are deducted to arrive at the (market) value of the firm's equity:

$$\text{Value} = \text{Assets} - \text{Liabilities}$$

In DCF models, value at time t is determined as the present value of future cash flows:

$$\text{Value}_t = \sum_i \frac{\text{CF}_{t+i}}{(1 + r)^i} \tag{1}$$

where CF_{t+i} represents (expected[1]) cash flows i periods from time t and r is the discount factor (the firm's required rate of return). DCF models vary as to the appropriate measure of cash flow CF, defined variously as streams of future dividends, earnings, or free cash flows.

Conceptually, the DCF and asset-based approaches to valuation are related through the actual rate of return r^* earned by a firm on its equity investment. For an infinite (constant) cash flow stream, using the DCF model, we obtain

$$\text{Value} = \frac{\text{CF}}{r} \tag{2}$$

But the amount a firm earns, CF, is equal to

$$\text{CF} = r^*B$$

where B is the book value of the firm. If we assume that the firm earns the required rate of return r, $(r^* = r)$, then $\text{CF} = rB$ and

$$\text{Value} = \frac{\text{CF}}{r} = \frac{rB}{r} = B \tag{3}$$

This equation suggests that value can be equivalently defined as either a "stock" of assets or the flows those assets generate.

The EBO model, we shall see, determines value as a combination of the stock of assets representing the normal flow that assets generate and the discounted value of abnormal earnings generated by these assets.

The various approaches are equivalent in a highly stylized and perfect world. Such a world has no need for financial analysis as all is known. Analysis is challenging and rewarding, however, in real-world settings, with finite knowledge and horizons and costly information. In the real world, there is uncertainty with respect to both the definition and measurement of the model parameters and their actual outcomes. The equivalence of asset-based, DCF, and EBO models breaks down, and different valuations result. The uncertainties in these models include:

- Difficulties in forecasting over a finite horizon, let alone to infinity
- The random nature of cash flows and earnings and the difficulty in assessing whether reported amounts are *permanent* (will persist in the future) or *transitory* (nonrecurring)
- The measurement of assets, earnings, and cash flows, which can be influenced by the selection of accounting policies and by discretionary management policies

---

[1]Technically, we should use the expectation operator $E(*)$ when discussing future period (as yet unknown) cash flows/earnings to differentiate from current period (known) earnings. This would, however, only add needlessly to the notation. From the context, it should be clear that when we speak of future earnings or cash flows, we are talking about their expected rather than actual value.

Analysts must be able to circumvent the pitfalls introduced by uncertainty and measurement problems. This chapter will discuss these problems further in the context of the valuation models themselves.

ASSET-BASED VALUATION MODELS

Asset-based models assign a value to the firm by aggregating the current market value of its individual component assets and liabilities. Chapter 17 discussed the steps required to develop an asset-based valuation. As derived in Exhibit 17-1, Westvaco's adjusted book value on December 31, 1999, was $4.5 billion, or $44.71 per share, more than double the reported book value of $2.2 billion, or $21.65 per share. The closing market price (at December 31, 1999) of $29.69, although 37% higher than the reported book value, was considerably below the adjusted book value. How should these discrepancies be interpreted? Should we expect to see the market price equal (the adjusted) book value?

When market price exceeds book value, a reasonable explanation is that the value of the firm exceeds the sum of its parts. Asset-based valuation calculates that sum; synergistic effects could then result in a premium (economic goodwill) for the going concern. Whether or not this occurs depends on the firm's profitability. When profitability is below normal, (adjusted) book value may exceed market price. This latter phenomenon is often a precursor of a takeover or merger as the firm is considered a "bargain."

There may be other reasons for the discrepancy between market price and book value, including but not limited to the nature of the firm's assets, management's choice of financial reporting methods, mandatory and discretionary accounting changes, and other problems in the measurement of book value. We explore these causes to develop our understanding of the insights they provide and the pitfalls in the use of asset-based valuation models.

Market Price and Book Value: Theoretical Considerations

Earlier we showed that when the actual rate of return r^* equals the required rate of return r, then

$$\text{Value} = \frac{\text{CF}}{r} = \frac{rB}{r} = B$$

When r^* is not equal to r, then this equation can be transformed to

$$\text{CF} = r^*B = rB + (r^* - r)\,B$$

and, therefore, if

$$\text{Value} = \frac{\text{CF}}{r}$$

then

$$\begin{aligned}
\text{Value} &= \frac{rB + (r^* - r)\,B}{r} \\
&= \left[1 + \frac{(r^* - r)}{r}\right] B \\
&= B + \left[\frac{(r^* - r)}{r}\right] B
\end{aligned} \tag{4}$$

Whether or not a firm's stock price is above or below book value depends on the intuitively appealing factor of how high the firm's expected rate of return is. As we shall see, $r^* > r$ is characteristic of a firm with positive growth opportunities, leading to market values greater than book value. Thus, the shares of a firm whose expected $r*$ is higher (lower) than the required r should sell at a price above (below) book value. The component

$$\left[\frac{(r* - r)}{r}\right] B$$

is, in effect, a measure of the firm's economic goodwill, the excess of market over book value.[2]

Book Value: Measurement Issues

The calculation of Westvaco's adjusted book value in Chapter 17, although complex, was relatively straightforward for current assets and for all liabilities as much of the required information was available. The major difficulty was estimating the current cost (market value) of timberlands and fixed assets. For companies where technology is important, valuing technological assets (whether on or off the balance sheet) is even more difficult. Thus, while adjusted book value is better than reported book value as a proxy for firm value, it is subject to significant measurement error.

For some analysts, reported book value is an "index" against which to compare the stock price. Under the assumption that the differential between market price and book value should be similar for firms in the same industry, the analysis turns on whether the relationship for a given firm is "in line" with a comparable population of firms.

When book value is used as an indicator, it is common practice to rely on unadjusted data that are simpler to obtain. These amounts do not measure value directly, but rather are viewed as benchmarks against which market value is compared. The focus is on how close market value is to book value. If it is very close to book value or below book value, then the stock is a "buy," as the downside risk is viewed as negligible.[3]

This comparison is generally conducted under the implicit or explicit assumption that historical cost-based book value reflects the minimum value of the firm. This minimum value assumption is justified by the fact that, since book value is based on historical cost, it does not reflect increases in value caused by inflation. Moreover, when there are adjustments to historical cost, only markdowns (such as impairment) not markups are permitted. (In some cases, such as marketable securities, markups are allowed.) Thus, book value is viewed as a conservative estimate of the firm's value.

Notwithstanding the foregoing, stocks do trade below the firm's book value. On an economy-wide level, Stober (1996) found the average price-to-book ratio to be less than 1 for every year in the 1973 to 1979 period; since that period, it has been greater than 1. Feltham and Ohlson (1995) noted that close to one-third of companies on the COMPUSTAT tape traded below their book values at some time. The relationship between price and book value depends to a great extent on the nature of the firm's assets, its reporting methods, its profitability, and the overall economy.

Firms reporting intangible assets such as goodwill can trade below reported book value. Relating this to the theoretical model earlier, we see that if the economic goodwill component $[(r* - r)/r] B$ is less than the recorded goodwill, then a company can trade below its reported book value.[4] For a company that has no recorded goodwill, if its profitability is poor $(r* < r)$, then it is possible for the firm's shares to trade below even its (historical) book value. Such a firm may have greater value broken up than as a going concern.

Book value is also a function of management's financial reporting choices that affect the allocations of revenues and expenses across time periods and as a result determine reported

---

[2]As we shall see, this relationship is basic to the EBO model.

[3]The results of Fama and French (1992), discussed in Chapters 5 and 18, imply that one of the variables that best explain differential market returns is the book value/price ratio. They suggest that this ratio may serve as a surrogate risk measure.

[4]This is true even if $r* > r$.

asset and liability balances. In some cases, these choices result in nonrecognition of economic obligations. These choices affect reported book value over time for a given firm, and at any given point in time, they affect comparisons of book value across firms.

A final point relates to restructuring and write-offs. It was indicated in Chapter 8 that the decision to write down long-lived tangible assets is somewhat subjective. Management determines the amount and may accelerate or delay the recognition of write-offs and restructurings affecting reported book value and earnings. Thus, if the market anticipates a write-off, the firm's shares could trade below book value.

Tobin's Q Ratio

The relationship between a company's market and book values can be measured by Tobin's q ratio,[5] defined as the market value of the firm divided by its book value on a replacement cost basis.[6] Q values below 1 (price less than replacement book value) imply that the firm earns less than the required rate of return; a (marginal) dollar invested in the firm's assets results in future cash flows whose present value is less than \$1. Such firms are poor performers.

However (as discussed in Chapter 14), firms with low q ratios are often seen as prime takeover or merger targets. Firms that want to expand find it cheaper to grow by acquiring an existing firm rather than constructing new production or marketing facilities. Implicit in such takeovers is the assumption that the acquired assets will perform better within the new firm due to diversification, synergistic effects, or better management. As noted earlier, as of December 31, 1999, Westvaco's q ratio was below 1 (replacement cost book value per share of \$44.71 exceeded the market price of \$29.69). In 2002, the firm merged with Mead, another major firm in the paper industry.

The assumption of poor management can also motivate acquisitions even when the target firm is not in the same line of business. Low q ratios indicate poor firm performance. If this performance is due to poor management, bidders who believe they are better managers can buy the business at an attractive price.

Stability and Growth of Book Value

The growth of equity capital, the base on which shareholder returns are earned, is an important component of firm value. Even a constant return on equity, if applied to a growing capital base, will increase earnings. Thus, the trend of book value per share (BPS) is as important as its level; both are affected by operating, investing, and financing decisions, financial reporting choices, and discretionary or mandatory accounting changes. A brief discussion of factors which affect (and sometimes distort) BPS follows.

Earnings Retention

For most firms, retained earnings provide most of the growth in book value. That growth is affected by the firm's return on equity (ROE) and its dividend policy. If the payout ratio (dividends/net income) equals k, then the increase in book value B is

$$
\begin{aligned}
B_1 - B_0 &= \textbf{Income} - \textbf{Dividends} \\
&= (\textbf{ROE} \times B_0) - (k \times \textbf{ROE} \times B_0) \\
&= (1 - k) \times \textbf{ROE} \times B_0
\end{aligned} \tag{5}
$$

where B_0 is the book value at the beginning of the period and $(1 - k)$ is the *earnings retention rate*. Thus, $(1 - k) \times$ ROE is the growth rate of book value per share due to earnings retention.[7]

---

[5]The ratio was developed by the Nobel prize–winning economist James Tobin.

[6]See Chapter 7 and Appendix 8-A for a discussion of the concepts of current cost and replacement cost.

[7]As we shall see in our discussion of DCF models, this is also one way of estimating earnings growth. We shall also indicate the problems in using these parameters to estimate growth.

Effect of New Equity Financing

Sales of new shares at prices above BPS increase book value per share, whereas sales below BPS result in dilution.[8] Similarly, repurchases of outstanding shares at prices below BPS increase it, whereas repurchases of shares above BPS dilute it.

Effect of Acquisitions

Acquisitions that are made for stock affect book value per share under either the purchase or pooling methods of acquisition accounting (see Chapter 14), although the impact differs.

When the pooling method is used, the newly issued shares are reflected at the book value of the acquired company:

$$\frac{\text{Book value of acquired company}}{\text{Number of shares issued}}$$

If the BPS of the newly issued shares exceeds that of the acquirer, then BPS increases. If the BPS of the newly issued shares is lower, the acquirer's BPS is diluted.

Under the purchase method of accounting, the newly issued shares are recorded at market value. Thus, the effect on the acquirer's BPS depends on whether or not the market price of its shares is above or below its own BPS; it is as if the acquirer sold shares for cash and used that cash to purchase the acquired company.

Effect of Changing Exchange Rates

As discussed in Chapter 15, the equity of operations in functional currencies other than the reporting (parent) currency is translated at the exchange rate on the balance sheet date. As a result, when functional currencies appreciate, the firm's BPS rises. Similarly, the remeasurement of foreign operations and translation of foreign currency transactions affect the BPS and need careful evaluation.

Effect of Financial Reporting Choices and Accounting Changes

Much of this text has been devoted to analyses of the effects (including those on book value) of financial reporting choices such as inventory valuation, depreciation, employee benefits, leases, and other capitalization versus expensing decisions. Discretionary changes in these policies can also change the level and trend of growth (or decline) in BPS.

Finally, mandatory accounting changes can have a significant impact on reported book value. In recent years, new accounting standards have had significantly positive (income taxes and marketable securities) and negative (postemployment benefits and impairment) impacts on BPS. As noted in earlier chapters, long transition periods and alternative transition methods affect the level and trend of BPS of a given firm and comparisons across firms.

The adoption of SFAS 142 in 2001 (see Chapter 14) resulted in the writedown of goodwill by many firms in 2002. In some cases the effect on reported book value per share was highly significant. AOL Time Warner, for example, wrote down goodwill by $54 billion in the first quarter of 2002, reducing book value per share by one-third.

Thus, although the trend of BPS is an important indicator of potential earnings growth, the analyst must discern whether or not BPS growth comes from operations (increases in retained earnings)[9] or the other factors discussed. To the extent that BPS growth evolves from nonoperating factors, that growth may be artificial or nonrecurring. Failure to consider the sources of BPS growth can result in erroneous conclusions regarding future earnings trends.

---

[8]A mathematical formulation of this effect can be found in Cohen et al. (1987), p. 399.

[9]This source of growth in BPS may also stem from financial reporting choices and the impact of such changes is not necessarily the same as real operating improvements.

Restructuring Provisions and Write-offs

In recent years, many companies have reported large restructuring provisions and write-offs that significantly reduced reported BPS, as discussed in Chapter 8. Goodwill writedowns, such as the AOL Time Warner writedown cited, may also materially reduce BPS.

Although asset-based valuation can be a useful tool, because of the complexities and problems discussed above, analysts have sought to value companies using forecasts of future cash flows rather than the evaluation of the current stock of assets. We now turn to these models.

DISCOUNTED CASH FLOW VALUATION MODELS

The parameters that make up the DCF model

$$\textbf{Value} = \sum \frac{\textbf{CF}_{t+i}}{(1+r)^i}$$

are related to risk (the required rate of return) and the return itself (CF). Chapter 18 dealt with the elements of risk and their impact on the required rate of return. This chapter focuses primarily on measurement of the return or CF measure.

These models (originating in the finance literature) use three alternative CF measures: dividends, accounting earnings, and free cash flows. Just as DCF and asset-based valuation models are equivalent under the assumptions of perfect markets, dividends, earnings, and free cash flow measures can be shown (theoretically) to yield equivalent results. Their implementation, however, is not straightforward.

First, there is inherent difficulty in defining the cash flows used in these models. Which cash flows and to whom do they flow? Conceptually, cash flows are defined differently depending on whether the valuation objective is the firm's equity (denoted as P), or the value of the firm's debt plus equity (V).

Assuming that we can define CF, we are left with another issue. The models need future cash flows as inputs. How is the cash flow stream estimated from the present data? More important, are current and past dividends, earnings, or cash flows the best indicators of that stream? These (and other) pragmatic issues determine which model should be used. Before addressing these issues directly, we discuss various models based on these measures. Doing so will highlight some of the difficulties inherent in using them.

Dividend-based Models

The value of a firm's equity (P) equals the present value of all future dividends paid by the firm to its equity holders:

$$P_0 = \frac{D_1}{(1+r)} + \frac{D_2}{(1+r)^2} + \cdots$$

$$= \sum_{i=1}^{\infty} \frac{D_i}{(1+r)^i} \tag{6}$$

where

P_0 = the value of the firm's equity at the end of period 0
D_i = the dividend paid by the firm in period i
r = the firm's required rate of return based on the firm's risk class

This formulation requires forecasting dividends to infinity (see the discussion below), which is impossible. Thus, different patterns of future dividend payments must be assumed.

Growth Patterns

No-Growth–Constant Dividend Model. In its no-growth form, the dividend discount model assumes a constant dividend rate equal to the current dividend level, and Eq. (6) reduces to

$$P_0 = \frac{D_1}{r} \tag{7}$$

In effect, dividends are capitalized at r to derive the value of the firm.

Constant Growth Model. For a firm with an expected (constant) growth rate g, dividends in the next period are expected to equal $(1 + g)$ times current dividends, $D_1 = D_0(1 + g)$, and the valuation model becomes

$$P_0 = \frac{D_0(1 + g)}{r - g} = \frac{D_1}{r - g} \tag{8}$$

Explicit Forecasts with Terminal Value Assumptions. Equation (6) can be rewritten as

$$P_0 = \sum_{i=1}^{T} \frac{D_i}{(1 + r)^i} + \frac{P_T}{(1 + r)^T} \tag{9}$$

where

$$P_T = \sum_{j=1}^{\infty} \frac{D_{T+j}}{(1 + r)^{T+j}}$$

Equation (9) states that firm value in period 0 equals the discounted value of a stream of dividends for T periods plus the (discounted) value of the firm at the end of T periods. Using this form of the model requires *explicit* forecasts of dividends for T (usually three to five) years, plus a forecast of the terminal price (P_T) at the end of period T. This forecasted price usually incorporates (one of) the previously discussed growth assumptions.

Although the dividend model is easy to use, it presents a conceptual dilemma.[10] Finance theory[11] says that dividend policy does not matter; the pattern of dividends up to the terminal (liquidating) dividend is irrelevant. The model, however, requires forecasting dividends to infinity or making terminal value assumptions. Firms that presently do not pay any dividends are a case in point.[12] Such firms are not valueless. In fact, high-growth firms often pay no dividends, as they reinvest all funds available to them. When firm value is estimated using a dividend discount model, it depends on the dividend level of the firm after its growth stabilizes. *Future dividends depend on the earnings stream the firm will be able to generate.* Thus, the firm's expected future earnings are fundamental to such a valuation. Similarly, for a firm paying dividends, the level of dividends *may be* a discretionary choice of management that is restricted by available earnings.

When dividends are not paid out, value accumulates within the firm in the form of reinvested earnings. Alternatively, firms sometimes pay dividends right up to bankruptcy. Thus, dividends may say more about the allocation of earnings to different claimants than valuation.

Earnings-based Models

The implementation problems with dividend-based models highlight the crucial role of earnings in valuation. We now proceed to a discussion of earnings-based valuation models by showing the relationship between dividends and earnings models. However, one caveat must be noted: The concept of earnings used in these models and accounting income are the same

---

[10]Penman labels this paradox the dividend conundrum.

[11]Miller and Modigliani's proposition. We ignore the potentially signaling aspect of dividends. (See footnote 20.)

[12]See Appendix 19-A for a discussion of such firms.

only under specific simplified assumptions. The notion of earnings in these theoretic models is closer to CFO or free cash flows. For the present, the term "earnings" should be viewed broadly. We shall expand and clarify this issue as we proceed.

Relationship Between Earnings-based and Dividend-based Models

An earnings-based model can be derived from the dividend-based model using k, the dividend payout ratio. If $D_i = kE_i$, then, for the *growth case*,

$$P_0 = \frac{kE_0(1 + g)}{r - g} = \frac{kE_1}{r - g} \tag{10}$$

As discussed shortly, a firm with no growth in dividends and earnings is (generally) not making *new* investments. Thus, all earnings are paid out as dividends. The payout ratio k equals 1, and the valuation model becomes

$$P_0 = \frac{E_0}{r}$$

The Definition of Earnings and the Valuation Objective

Earnings-based models can be used to value either:

1. The equity of the firm (P), or
2. The firm as a whole (V), debt plus equity

The definition of earnings used depends on the valuation objective. To measure the value of the firm (V), earnings are defined *prior* to payment of interest, as net operating income. To value equity, earnings are measured *after* payment of interest, net income.[13] *The definition of such other parameters as the rate of return also differs for each case.*

No-Growth Model

For the no-growth case and a simplified income statement (Exhibit 19-1), the appropriate definitions for each case are:

Value	= Earnings	/ Rate of Return
Equity P = Net income	/ Rate of return on equity [e.g., $r = r_f + \beta(r_m - r_f)$]
Firm V = Net operating income	/ Rate of return on debt and equity (weighted-average cost of capital)

EXHIBIT 19-1
No-Growth Model

Income Statement	
	All Years
Operating revenue	$ 350
Operating expense	(150)
	$ 200
Depreciation expense	(50)
Operating income before tax	$ 150
Tax @ 20%	(30)
Net operating income	**$ 120**
Interest expense (net of taxes)	(20)
Net income	**$ 100**

[13]This discussion assumes that there is no preferred stock. When preferred stock exists, a third possibility exists, the valuation of total (common and preferred) equity.

(1) Equity Valuation. When the valuation objective is the firm's equity, earnings are defined as net income, the amount available for distribution to equity shareholders. Similarly, the required rate of return is the *equity rate of return.* This rate of return is similar to that used for the dividend-based model and its estimation is discussed in Chapter 18. By estimating the firm's beta,[14] the risk-free rate, and the (excess) market return, the CAPM can be used[15] to estimate *r*. If we assume *r* is 10%, the value of equity is

$$P = \frac{E}{r} = \frac{\$100}{0.10} = \$1,000$$

(2) Value of the Firm. Net operating income (before deducting interest), that is, the cash available to all providers of capital, is the appropriate measure of earnings when valuing the firm as a whole. Similarly, the rate of return is a weighted average of the required rates of return of all providers of capital: the weighted-average cost of capital (WACC). The weighting is based on the relative proportions of debt and equity.

In our example, if we assume that the firm has a debt-to-capital ratio of 20% (four-fifths equity and one-fifth debt) and further that the (after-tax) cost of debt is 8%, then the weighted-average cost of capital is

$$\text{WACC} = (0.8 \times 0.10) + (0.2 \times 0.08) = 0.096$$

and the value of the firm as a whole is

$$V = \frac{\text{Net operating income}}{\text{WACC}} = \frac{\$120}{0.096} = \$1,250$$

The value of the firm equals the value of its debt plus the value of its equity. The equity value *P* can be derived from the firm value *V* by deducting the value of debt. As we have assumed an (after-tax) cost of debt (interest rate) of 8% and the (after-tax) interest expense is $20, then the value of its debt must equal $250 ($20/8%). Thus, the equity value is $1,250 − $250 = $1,000, identical to the value for equity derived directly.[16]

Growth Model

For a growing firm, the relationships between earnings and the amounts flowing to the equity- and debtholders are somewhat more complex. We begin again with the valuation of equity followed by the valuation of the firm.

(1) Equity Valuation and Earnings. The firm's net income is assumed to be used either for (1) payment of dividends or (2) investment in new assets.

With *k* equal to the payout ratio, then $(1 - k)$ is the fraction of earnings reinvested in new assets. Exhibit 19-2A illustrates the allocation of net income between new investment and dividends given an assumed dividend payout ratio of 80%. If these new assets earn a rate of return $r^* = 20\%$, then the pattern of net income and its distribution between dividends and reinvestment, for $k = 0.80$, is:

Period	Earnings	= Dividend	+ New Investments
0	$E_0 = \$100$	$= 0.8E_0 = \$80$	$+ 0.2E_0 = \$20$
1	$E_1 = \$100 + (r^* \times \$20) = \$104$	$= 0.8E_1 = \$83.2$	$+ 0.2E_1 = \$20.8$
2	$E_2 = \$104 + (r^* \times \$20.8) = \$108.16$	$= 0.8E_2 = \$86.53$	$+ 0.2E_2 = \$21.63$

---

[14]In Chapter 18, we discuss alternative estimation procedures for beta.

[15]Additional adjustments may also be appropriate to control for such other risk factors as size.

[16]It should be noted that $1,000 equity and $250 debt are consistent with the debt-to-capital ratio of 20% based on the market values of the debt and equity.

EXHIBIT 19-2
Growth Model

A. Derivation of Amount Available for Equityholders for Valuation of Equity

	Year 0
Operating revenue	$ 350
Operating expense	(150)
	$ 200
Depreciation expense	(50)
Operating income before tax	$ 150
Tax @ 20%	(30)
Net operating income	**$ 120**
Interest expense (net of taxes)	(20)
Net income	**$ 100**
New investment (equity)	(20)
Available for equityholders (dividends)	**$ 80**

B. Derivation of Amount Available for Debt- and Equityholders for Valuation of Firm

	Year 0
Operating revenue	$ 350
Operating expense	(150)
	$ 200
Depreciation expense	(50)
Operating income before tax	$ 150
Tax @ 20%	(30)
Net operating income	**$ 120**
New investment	(30)
Available for debt- and equityholders	**$ 90**
Financing Distribution (Cash for Financing)	
Dividends	$ 80
Interest expense (net of taxes)	20
New debt	(10)
	$ 90

The firm's earnings, dividends, and investments all grow at a rate of 4%. As the next table indicates, this growth rate is the product of the fraction reinvested $(1 - k)$ times the rate of return the firm can earn on the reinvestment (r^*):

Period	Earnings	= Dividend	+ New Investments
0	E_0	$= kE_0$	$+ (1 - k) E_0$
1	$E_1 = E_0 + r^*(1 - k) E_0 = kE_1$		$+ (1 - k) E_1$
	$= E_0[1 + r^*(1 - k)] = kE_0[1 + r^*(1 - k)]$		$+ (1 - k) E_0[1 + r^*(1 - k)]$
2	$E_2 = E_1[1 + r^*(1 - k)] = kE_2$		$+ (1 - k) E_2$
	$= E_0[1 + r(1 - k)]^2 = kE_0[1 + r^*(1 - k)]^2$		$+ (1 - k) E_0[1 + r^*(1 - k)]^2$

Note that earnings, dividends, and new investment each grow at the rate $[r^*(1 - k)]$. The firm's growth rate g thus equals

$$g = r^*(1 - k) = 0.2 \times (1 - 0.8) = 0.04$$

This result is intuitively appealing: A firm's growth rate depends on the level of investment and the return on that investment. Thus, a no-growth company is one with no new investment: $k = 1$.

Using the growth formula to find the value of the firm's equity yields

$$P_0 = \frac{kE_0(1 + g)}{r - g} = \frac{kE_1}{r - r^*(1 - k)}$$

$$= \frac{0.8(\$104)}{0.10 - 0.04} = \$1,387$$

(2) Value of the Firm. We continue with our previous example. In the no-growth case, equity value was related to the earnings available to the equity shareholder, net income. To value the firm (total capital), we used the earnings available to the debt holders and shareholders, net operating income.

In the growth model, to value equity, net income is replaced by the amount available to the equity shareholder after new investment of equity (net income − reinvestment of equity). Similarly, to value the firm as a whole, we must determine the earnings available to all providers of capital: the debt- and equityholders. This amount equals net operating income minus *total* new investment. Total new investment is provided by both equity- and debtholders. Given the growth rate of 4% implied by the equity investment of $20, debt[17] must be increased[18] by $10 (4% of $250), making the total new investment equal to $30.

The two approaches are contrasted in Exhibit 19-2. We must carefully distinguish between total new investments and the reinvestment of equity referred to previously. The first is the actual investment in new assets made by the firm ($30, in the example). Financing for this investment is provided by debt ($10) and equity ($20). For equity valuation, reinvestment refers only to that amount (i.e., $20) provided by equityholders (net income − dividends).

With new debt of $10, total debt is now $260. The market value of equity, we have shown, is $1,387. Therefore, the firm's WACC equals 9.7%.[19]

Exhibit 19-2 provides year 0 data. All year 1 values are 4% higher. The value of the firm using this approach therefore equals

$$\frac{(\text{Net operating income} - \text{Total new investment}) (1 + g)}{\text{WACC} - g} = \frac{(\$120 - \$30)(1.04)}{(0.097 - 0.04)}$$

$$= \frac{93.6}{0.057} = \$1,647$$

The $1,647 value of the firm is the sum of the value of the equity ($1,387) plus the value of the debt ($260).

Estimating Growth

The firm's growth rate can be estimated in one of two ways:

1. Estimating the individual components, k and r^*, that contribute to growth as $g = (1 - k)r^*$
2. Extrapolating the historical growth rate to the future

Defining and Estimating r^*: Return on New (Equity) Investment. The terms r^* and r both represent rates of return for the equity investor. The former represents the actual return,

---

[17]The debt-to-capital ratio of 20% developed for the no-growth case can no longer be maintained. That ratio was based on relative market values. Growth opportunities, however, are "captured" by equity shareholders, thereby altering the relative proportions of debt and equity. The new debt-to-capital ratio is 15.8% [$260/($1,387 + $260)], based on equity of $1,387 and debt of $260. This ratio will now be maintained as both the market value of debt and equity grow at a rate of 4%.

[18]The $10 of new debt is consistent with an assumed 4% growth in net income. For interest expense to increase by 4%, debt must increase by 4% from $250 to $260.

[19]With debt of $260 and equity of $1,387, and the (after-tax) cost of debt and equity equal to 8% and 10%, respectively:

$$\text{WACC} = \frac{\$1,387}{\$1,387 + \$260} \times 10\% + \frac{\$260}{\$1,387 + \$260} \times 8\% = 9.7\%$$

whereas the latter refers to the required rate of return. *Growth opportunities exist only when expected returns r^* exceed the required rate of return r (i.e., $r^* > r$). When $r^* = r$, then the growth model reduces to the no-growth case:

$$P = \frac{kE}{[r - r^*(1 - k)]}$$

$$= \frac{kE}{[r - r^* + r^*k]}$$

But $r = r^*$:

$$P = \frac{kE}{(r - r + rk)}$$

$$= \frac{E}{r}$$

This result does not imply that firms cannot make new investments and grow even when $r^* = r$. It does show that it does not make any difference whether or not the firm decides to grow. The value of the firm's equity is not affected whether the firm reinvests its net income or pays dividends. Recall our earlier example for the no-growth model in which we found the value of the equity equal to $\$100/0.10 = \$1,000$. That example assumed all income is paid out as dividends. The following table indicates the effect of alternative dividend payout ratios, beginning in period 1, when the remainder is reinvested at the rate $r^* = r = 0.10$:

Payout Ratio k	Reinvested Income $(1 - k) E_1$	Growth Rate $g = (1 - k) r$	Share Value $P_0 = kE_1/(r - g)$
0.75	25	$0.025 = (1 - 0.75) \times 0.1$	$\$1,000 = 75/(0.1 - 0.025)$
0.50	50	$0.050 = (1 - 0.50) \times 0.1$	$\$1,000 = 50/(0.1 - 0.050)$
0.25	75	$0.075 = (1 - 0.25) \times 0.1$	$\$1,000 = 25/(0.1 - 0.075)$

Shareholder's wealth is not affected by the firm's dividend policy.[20]

As r^* measures the actual return earned on (reinvested) equity, it is conceptually equivalent to the familiar ROE measure. Using ROE to measure r^* is reasonable if (along with the other assumptions of our simplified world) the firm's new investment opportunities are similar to past ones.

Estimating k: The Dividend Payout Ratio. The current dividend payout ratio is often used to estimate k. This gives us an estimate of the firm's earnings growth rate (often called the sustainable or implicit growth rate) in terms of the same ratios previously used to estimate growth in book value:

$$g = (1 - k) \times r^* = (1 - \text{Dividend payout}) \times \text{ROE}$$

Using the dividend payout ratio and ROE to estimate future growth rates assumes constant levels for these parameters that can limit the usefulness of this technique. For

---

[20]We do not intend to review all the literature on dividend policy. Modigliani and Miller, in their famous proposition, note that, given a level of investment (growth opportunities), dividends are irrelevant as they are readily replaced by external financing. We address this issue in the next section by pointing out that dividend payout must be considered net of the raising of additional capital.

The issue of a firm's dividend policy remains controversial in the finance literature. There are those who argue that dividend policy is relevant because investors prefer the security of dividends; others view dividend policy in a "signaling" framework whereby management conveys its intentions and/or forecasts by its level of dividends. These issues are beyond the scope of our discussion. The foregoing argues only that in the context of this model, *ceteris paribus*, dividend policy is irrelevant.

EXHIBIT 19-3. PFIZER AND WESTVACO
Sustainable Growth Rate Estimates

	Pfizer			Westvaco		
Year	k	ROE	Growth Rate $(1 - k) \times$ ROE	k	ROE	Growth Rate $(1 - k) \times$ ROE
1995	0.42	0.320	**0.186**	0.28	0.142	**0.102**
1996	0.40	0.310	**0.186**	0.42	0.099	**0.057**
1997	0.40	0.297	**0.178**	0.55	0.073	**0.033**
1998	0.38	0.400	**0.248**	0.68	0.058	**0.019**
1999	0.35	0.359	**0.233**	0.79	0.043	**0.009**

Source: Based on data from Pfizer and Westvaco annual reports 1995–1999.

stable growth companies, k and ROE are relatively constant. For cyclical companies, they are not.

This difference is illustrated in Exhibit 19-3. Pfizer's ROE, k, and growth rate estimates are relatively stable over the 1995–1999 period. The estimated growth rate for Westvaco, on the other hand, declines dramatically as the company's earnings (and therefore ROE) go through a cyclical downturn. Westvaco did not change its dividend rate, maintaining the existing payout level despite the earnings decline. Consequently, as earnings and ROE decline, the dividend payout ratio k increases, reducing the estimated growth rate.

Given the volatility of these estimates, it is hard to use them with any confidence. Whenever dividends exceed EPS, the projected growth rate is negative. It should also be noted that it is theoretically incorrect to use the dividend payout ratio to estimate k. In the development of these models, no distinction is made among dividends paid out, stock repurchases, and issuance of new equity. That is,

$$kE = \textbf{Dividends + Share repurchases − New equity issued}$$

should reflect net cash flows to and from equity shareholders; not just dividends.

Dividend payout measures only one portion of the total flow; it ignores new issues and repurchases and can distort the valuation model. A firm's choice of the form (the mix of dividends and the sale or repurchase of shares) of equity financing should not affect valuation. Thus, the more appropriate definition of k is

$$k = \frac{\textbf{Dividends + Share repurchases − New equity issued}}{\textbf{Earnings}}$$

The potential instability of the individual growth rate components suggests that historical growth trends should not be used blindly to make growth projections. In a similar fashion, dividend policy affects the observed earnings trend.

Dividend Policy and EPS Growth. As stock values are expressed as price per share, many models that estimate earnings trends use earnings per share (EPS). The EPS growth rate can be distorted by a number of factors, not all of them value related.

Dividend policy has an important impact on earnings growth. A firm with a low payout ratio grows faster than if it paid out most of its earnings, since reinvested earnings generate future earnings. This effect of dividend policy is meaningful. However, by choosing the mode of equity financing, that is, trading off dividends and the sale and repurchase of equity securities, the growth rate in EPS can be distorted.

This phenomenon is illustrated in Box 19-1. Dividend policy, by modifying the firm's need for external financing, ultimately affects the number of shares outstanding and, as a result, reported earnings per share. Firms with low dividend payouts report faster EPS growth than firms with high payout policies, and using the EPS growth rate to estimate g will lead to erroneous results.

BOX 19-1

Effect of Dividend Policy on Per-Share Growth

The relevance of dividend policy to valuation has been the subject of much debate in the finance literature. It is clear, however, that a firm's payout ratio (combined with its financing policy) can lead to differing growth rates in EPS and book value per share.

Firms with low dividend payout ratios will show higher growth than those with high payout ratios. As a result, misleading conclusions can arise when firms with different dividend policies are compared. The following example illustrates these effects.

	2001	2002	2003	2004	2005
Firm A: Low Dividend Payout					
Net income ($000)	1,000	1,090	1,188	1,295	1,412
Average shares (000)	1,000	1,000	1,000	1,000	1,000
Earnings per share ($)	1.00	1.09	1.19	1.30	1.41
Dividends paid ($000)	100	109	119	130	141
Year-end book value ($000)	10,900	11,881	12,950	14,116	15,386
Book value/share ($)	10.90	11.88	12.95	14.12	15.39
Firm B: High Dividend Payout					
Net income ($000)	1,000	1,090	1,188	1,295	1,412
Average shares (000)	1,000	1,090	1,188	1,295	1,412
Earnings per share ($)	1.00	1.00	1.00	1.00	1.00
Dividends paid ($000)	1,000	1,090	1,188	1,295	1,412
Stock issued ($000)	900	981	1,069	1,166	1,270
Assumed price per share ($)	10.00	10.00	10.00	10.00	10.00
No. of shares issued (000)	90	98	107	117	127
Year-end book value ($000)	10,900	11,881	12,950	14,116	15,386
Book value/share ($)	10.00	10.00	10.00	10.00	10.00
Firm A Compared to Firm B					
Ratio of earnings per share	1.00	1.09	1.19	1.30	1.41
Ratio of book value per share	1.09	1.19	1.30	1.41	1.54

Note: Opening book value January 1, 2001 assumed to be $10 million.

Firm A has a low dividend payout ratio of 10%. The reinvestment of earnings produces steady growth in EPS given a constant ROE of 10% and no issuance of new stock. Firm B pays out all net income as dividends. To obtain capital for growth, it sells new shares at the price indicated (for simplicity, we assume a constant price-earnings ratio of 10). Although both firms show the same (9%) growth rate for net income, Firm B shows no growth in per-share earnings and book value. The growth in shares outstanding is as rapid as the growth in earnings and book value. The last part of the illustration shows the widening differential between the two firms over time.

Although this example may appear unrealistic, it is a reasonable description of the plight of public utility companies (gas, electric, water) in the United States. To attract investors, these firms historically paid out most of their earnings as dividends. To finance growth, they periodically sold additional common shares. As a result, EPS growth rates were low. These firms were trapped in a vicious cycle. If they reduced their dividend rates, their EPS growth rates would rise, and they might be considered growth companies rather than bond substitutes.*

Other U.S. industries with very high payout ratios also report low EPS growth rates. Real Estate Investment Trusts (REITs)

and companies organized as limited partnerships must pay out all of their taxable income as dividends. For most companies, however, the effects of dividend policy are more modest, although their cumulative effect over time may be significant.

Example: Pfizer's 1999 net income and dividends were

Net income	$ 3,179 million
Dividends	(1,222)
Increase in retained earnings	$ 1,957 million

If Pfizer distributed all its earnings as dividends, it would need to recover $1,957 million by selling new shares. Using the 1999 mean price of approximately $39/share, Pfizer would have sold approximately 50 million shares ($1,957/$39), increasing the number of shares outstanding by 1.3% and reducing EPS by 1.3%.

The analysis can be used another way. If Pfizer paid no dividends in 1999, it would have an additional $1,222 million of equity. If shares were repurchased (using the same price of $39), Pfizer would have repurchased 31 million shares ($1,222/$39), reducing the number of shares outstanding and increasing future EPS.

---

*In recent years, some utilities have reduced their dividends or restricted dividend growth to increase retained earnings available for new investment. Other utilities have long been successful in promoting themselves as growth companies by paying low dividends and/or stock dividends and retaining their earnings for growth.

Alternative and Finite Growth Assumptions

We have demonstrated that the benefits from growth depend on the availability of investment opportunities earning a high rate of return, specifically, $r^* > r$. The valuation formula

$$P_0 = \frac{kE_0(1 + g)}{r - g} = \frac{kE_1}{r - g} \tag{10}$$

can be disaggregated into two components:

$$P_i = \frac{E_{i+1}}{r} + \frac{(1 - k) E_{i+1}}{r} \left[\frac{r^* - r}{r - (1 - k) r^*} \right]$$

The first component is the value of the firm in the absence of growth, the second component is the value of the firm's growth opportunities. Although the models assume infinite growth opportunities, high-return investment opportunities ($r^* > r$) do not exist forever in the real world. Appendix 19-A presents variations of (some of) these models using alternative growth assumptions.

Additionally, as discussed earlier, valuation models may use the following relationship:

$$P_0 = \frac{kE_1}{(1 + r)} + \frac{kE_2}{(1 + r)^2} \cdots \frac{kE_n}{(1 + r)^n} + \frac{P_n}{(1 + r)^n} \tag{11}$$

Explicit short-term horizon forecasts of earnings ($E_1, \ldots, E_n$) for a three-to-five-year period are made and then a terminal value (P_n) at the end of the period is estimated. This terminal value often incorporates the more general growth assumptions discussed. This valuation technique is especially useful under the more realistic assumption of growth opportunities with a finite horizon. We return to this issue later in the chapter.

Earnings Valuation and the Price/Earnings Ratio

The price/earnings (P/E) ratio is often used to compare firm valuations. This ratio is the multiple of earnings used by the market to value the firm. Its relationship to our valuation models is straightforward.

For the no-growth case,

$$P = \frac{E}{r}$$

becomes

$$\frac{P}{E} = \frac{1}{r} \tag{12}$$

The P/E ratio in this case equals the inverse of the firm's capitalization rate. For the growth case,

$$P_i = \frac{kE_i(1 + g)}{r - g}$$

becomes

$$\frac{P_i}{E_i} = \frac{k(1 + g)}{r - g} \tag{13}$$

Price/Earnings cum Dividend. Dividend irrelevancy implies that dividends and price are equivalent, dollar for dollar. Thus, from a pure theoretical perspective, P/E should be expressed as the ratio of *price plus dividends* to earnings. In practice, as dividends are small relative to price, modification does not affect the calculation materially. For discussion, however, we include this modification when necessary to show the development of these models.

Adding k to both sides of Eqs. (11) and (12) yields the *price/earnings cum dividend ratio*. For the no-growth case [Eq. (12)],

$$\frac{P}{E} + k = \frac{1}{r} + k$$

Since in the no-growth case, $k = 1$ and $D = E$:

$$\frac{P + D}{E} = \frac{1 + r}{r} \tag{14}$$

In the growth case [Eq. (13)],

$$\frac{P_i}{E_i} + k = \frac{k(1 + g)}{r - g} + k$$

$$\frac{P_i + D_i}{E_i} = \frac{k(1 + r)}{r - g} \tag{15}$$

Earlier, we showed that, when a firm does not possess extraordinary growth opportunities (i.e., $r^* = r$), although it can still grow by reinvesting dividends, growth does not affect valuation. This can be illustrated with the price/earnings cum dividend ratio. When $r^* = r$, then $g = (1 - k)\,r$ and Eq. 15 reduces to

$$\frac{P_i + D_i}{E_i} = \frac{1 + r}{r} \tag{16}$$

which is identical to the no-growth relationship. *Thus, in the absence of (extraordinary) growth opportunities* $(1 + r)/r$ *is the normal price/earnings relationship.*

Growth, Risk, and Valuation

The preceding discussions imply that the relationship between price and earnings is a function of the firm's growth rate and risk (as captured by r). Beaver and Morse (1978) compared the price/earnings ratios of a sample of firms to see whether growth and/or risk could explain differentials among firms. For 25 portfolios of firms ranked by P/E ratios, they compared the average portfolio P/E ratios over 15 years. Parts A and B of Exhibit 19-4 show P/E ratios and average earnings growth rates for different portfolios. Extreme P/E ratios revert to the mean over the period. Note the trend in the ratio of portfolio 1's P/E to that of portfolio 25.

Initially, at least, some of the differences in P/E ratios are due to the earnings growth rate. Portfolios with high P/E ratios have higher earnings growth in the first few years. However, persistent differences in P/E ratios could not be explained by growth rate differentials (e.g., see year 10).

> Comparing the P/E analysis with the growth analysis, we conclude that some of the initial dissipation of the P/E ratio in the first three years after formation can be explained by differential growth in earnings. Beyond that, however, there clearly exists a P/E differential that cannot be explained by differential earnings growth.[21]

In addition to being unable to explain the long-run differentials using growth rates, Beaver and Morse could not explain variations in P/E ratios by differences in risk. They

---

[21]William H. Beaver and Dale Morse, "What Determines Price-Earnings Ratios?," *Financial Analysts Journal* (July–August 1978), pp. 65–76.

EXHIBIT 19-4
Results of Beaver and Morse: P/E Ratio Patterns

A. Price/Earnings Ratio of Portfolio

Number of Years After Portfolio Formation

Portfolio	0	1	2	3	5	10	14
1	50.0	22.7	16.4	13.8	13.2	13.0	8.3
5	20.8	17.5	16.9	15.9	13.7	11.9	8.4
10	14.3	11.9	11.5	10.3	10.1	9.9	8.3
15	11.1	10.8	10.4	10.0	10.0	8.6	7.1
20	8.9	9.1	9.6	9.4	9.3	9.0	7.7
25	5.8	6.9	8.0	7.9	7.9	7.8	8.9
Portfolio 1 / Portfolio 25	8.6	3.3	2.1	1.7	1.7	1.7	0.9

B. Cumulative Earnings Growth (%)

1	−4.1	9.5	37.2	28.2	18.9	15.3	11.8
5	10.7	14.9	12.1	13.1	10.9	8.0	18.1
10	9.6	12.9	11.5	12.3	9.2	12.9	29.6
15	10.0	8.8	8.5	8.1	14.3	11.0	33.4
20	10.8	5.2	9.3	12.6	6.0	11.1	18.0
25	26.4	−3.3	7.5	10.8	12.9	16.7	10.1

Source: William Beaver and Dale Morse, "What Determines Price-Earnings Ratios?," *Financial Analysts Journal* (July–August 1978), pp. 65–76. Adapted from Table 3 (p. 68) and Table 5 (p. 70).

hypothesized that the long-run differential in P/E ratios was probably due to the effects of different accounting policies.[22]

Zarowin (1990) reexamined Beaver and Morse's findings and came to a different conclusion. Using a database in which earnings had been "normalized" in an effort to remove the effect of accounting differences,[23] Zarowin found[24] that the P/E ratio differences could not be explained (solely) by differing accounting policies. Even with normalized earnings, persistent differences remained among firms' P/E ratios.

To explain these differences, Zarowin used forecasted growth as a growth proxy. This contrasts with Beaver and Morse who used (*ex post*) actual growth. For *ex ante* valuation purposes, forecasted growth is more appropriate. As the model predicted, the differences in P/E ratios were attributable to differences in expected growth. Zarowin argued that Beaver and Morse's nonfindings resulted from using actual growth rather than expected growth rates.

Effects of Permanent and Transitory Earnings and Measurement Error

Beaver and Morse's findings with respect to short-term growth rates provide valuable insight into differential P/E ratios: the filtering of transitory earnings components by the market. In Exhibit 19-4, the high (low) P/E portfolios had low (high) earnings changes in the years that the portfolios were formed. Portfolio 1's earnings change in year 0 was −4%, whereas portfolio 25's exceeded 25%. The following year (year 1), the high- (low-) growth experienced was the opposite of the previous year. These observations indicate that reported earnings when the initial P/E portfolios were formed were abnormally low (high) for the high (low) P/E categories. The following year, earnings returned to their normal level. The market ignored the transitory component of earnings; it multiplied normal earnings by a constant. As a

---

[22]They did not test this hypothesis.

[23]The database used was from Cragg and Malkiel (1982).

[24]In his actual testing procedure, Zarowin used the earnings-to-price (E/P) ratio as the relationship between this ratio and risk, and growth is hypothesized to be linear.

BOX 19-2
The Effects of Transitory Components and Measurement Error on Valuation

---

Permanent versus Transitory Earnings and Valuation

The effects of the permanent/transitory dichotomy on the P/E ratio are described below. The P/E ratio, as we have shown, is consistent with some simplified valuation models. Use of the P/E ratio is meant to be illustrative of the general class of models discussed. The effects are more readily shown on the P/E ratio due to its simplicity.

A firm's permanent earnings are defined as the portion of the earnings stream that is to be carried into the future. For example, if we assume a constant dividend model where a firm pays out all earnings as dividends, the firm's expected earnings (dividends) are $5 per share, and $r = 10\%$, the value of the firm would be $5/0.1 = $50. The P/E ratio would be 10.

At the beginning of period 1, suppose it is known that due to some windfall the firm will actually earn $6.10 but after that the EPS will revert to $5. The value of the firm will be equal to $51 derived as

$$P_0 = \frac{E_1}{1.1} + \frac{P_1}{1.1} = \frac{\$6.10}{1.1} + \frac{\$50}{1.1} = \$51$$

The extra $1.10 earned in period 1 was not capitalized (i.e., the value of the firm did not go to $6.10/0.1 = $61). Only the permanent portion of $5.00 was capitalized. The one-shot or transitory portion of earnings entered into valuation only as a one-period adjustment (adding $\frac{\$1.10}{1.1} = \$1$ to value) without any

carryover effects. The observed P/E ratio for this firm will be $51/$6.10 = 8.4 even though the firm's "true" capitalization rate is 10.

Would this low P/E ratio indicate that the firm is a buy?* It should not. The potential distortion in P/E ratios can be even greater if we consider measurement error inherent in accounting earnings.

Measurement Error and Its Effects on Valuation

Let E_a represent accounting earnings and E_e economic earnings. We will define the difference between them as measurement noise, $M = E_e - E_a$. Further, assume that economic earnings has a permanent and transitory component, that is,

$$E_e = E_{ep} + E_{et}$$

The true relationship between price and earnings will be $P = E_{ep}/r$, with an underlying "unobservable" P/E ratio of $1/r$. The market will fully capitalize only the permanent E_{ep}. Empirically, however, one observes P/E_a, which is equivalent to $P/(E_{ep} + E_{et} + M)$. This observable P/E ratio may be larger or smaller than the "true" P/E_{ep} capitalization rate, depending on the magnitudes and directions of the transitory component (E_{et}) and measurement error (M).

---

*In Chapter 5, we noted that one of the reported anomalies of efficient markets is the abnormal returns that seem to accrue to firms with low P/E ratios.

---

result, firms whose earnings were unusually low (high) appeared to have abnormally high (low) P/E ratios.

On a more general level, academic research has used the earnings response coefficient (ERC) to capture the relationship between prices and earnings. The ERC measures the price change that results from an earnings change. If the relationship between prices and earnings is exactly as the simple models suggest, then the ERC should equal (or approximate) the P/E ratio. Although Collins and Kothari (1989) show that risk and growth explain some of the cross-sectional differences in ERCs, the ERCs generated are typically much lower than expected.

Explanations for these differences include the points we raised earlier. Collins and Kothari note that "persistence" (the extent to which earnings changes carry into the future) also affects the ERCs. That is, prices will not react as much to changes in earnings caused by transitory components. More specifically (as Box 19-2 indicates), transitory earnings components increase value on a dollar-for-dollar basis,[25] whereas permanent changes increase value by a multiplier (the P/E ratio).

This is consistent with Kormendi and Lipe's (1987) finding that higher persistence increases the ERC. Ryan and Zarowin (1995) demonstrate that measurement error also contributes to low ERCs.[26] The relationship between earnings and price (as Box 19-2 shows) is

---

[25]An example of a transitory component is a holding gain such as an increase in the value of the firm's inventory. If such increases are not expected to be repeated in the future, then the effect on value should be dollar for dollar: A dollar increase in inventory value would result in a dollar increase in firm value.

[26]In the literature, the measurement error is referred to as the valuation-irrelevant component. See Ramakrishnan and Thomas (1998).

distorted by both transitory noise and measurement problems resulting from accounting choices. Thus, it is important, when using an earnings-based valuation model, to normalize earnings for nonrecurring items as well as to evaluate the impact of accounting choices, that is, the quality of earnings. Such an analysis and normalization of earnings for Westvaco are shown in Chapter 17.

Earnings or Cash Flows?

The concept of earnings used in these valuation models is closer to cash flow than GAAP net income. In the theoretical development of these models, earnings are generally defined as cash flow after the replacement of depreciated assets. Net income, as defined by GAAP, is not the appropriate input for these models. Only in a simplified world under stringent assumptions does net (operating) income under GAAP meet the foregoing definition of earnings.

The first assumption required is the equality of funds flow and cash flow. This holds only when working capital levels are kept (relatively) constant over time.[27] Generally, however, this assumption does not hold. Moreover, differences between cash flows and income are not due solely to working capital changes. The second required assumption is that depreciation expense approximates the replacement cost of depreciated assets. This also is generally true only by coincidence. Furthermore, the choice of accounting methods affects the calculation of income. Thus, as soon as we move away from a simplified world, the use of accounting income becomes problematic.

Using reported cash from operations (CFO) rather than income may solve some of the problems inherent in the first assumption. However, as has been shown throughout the book, reported CFO, cash for investments, and cash from financing are also affected by accounting choice. In addition, CFO does not provide for the replacement of depreciated assets. Finally, the classification of capital expenditures between investments made to maintain capacity and those made for growth is not directly available in most cases. Thus, the use of CFO in valuation models is also fraught with difficulties.

Free Cash Flow Approach to Valuation

The free cash flow (FCF) approach has been suggested by some as a potential solution to the problems just discussed. Free cash flow, *when the valuation objective is the firm*, is defined as the cash available to debt- and equityholders after investment.

Just as the dividend model is essentially equivalent to the earnings model, the FCF model that follows is equivalent to the earnings-based model of Exhibit 19-2B, where the valuation objective is the value of the firm. To illustrate the free cash flow approach, we return to that example. Free cash flow in that example is equal to $90, derived as follows:

Net operating income	$120
Total new investment	(30)
Free cash flow	$ 90

The problem with this definition in the general case is that, as previously noted, the breakdown between *new* and *replacement* investment is rarely provided. Only the total cash for investment is given in the statement of cash flows. Upon reflection, however, total investment is really the amount we want. There is no need to use depreciation expense, or any other surrogate for that matter, to estimate the cost of replacing depreciated assets. Our objective, in general, is the following calculation of free cash flow:

	Net operating income before replacement of depreciated assets
−	Replacement of depreciated assets
−	New investment
=	Free cash flow

---

[27]Under this assumption, cash from operations and funds (working capital) from operations converge.

This is equivalent to:

$$
\begin{aligned}
&\text{Adjusted CFO (net operating income plus adjustments)} \\
-\ &\underline{\text{Cash for investment (new + replacement)}} \\
=\ &\text{Free cash flow}
\end{aligned}
$$

Note that adjusted CFO is not the same CFO reported in the statement of cash flows. They differ with respect to the treatment of interest payments: CFO is reduced by interest payments as required by SFAS 95, whereas the adjusted measure is preinterest.

Exhibit 19-5 compares an SFAS 95 Statement of Cash Flows for our hypothetical company (column A) with free cash flow in the form used in this section (column B). The difference between them is the treatment of interest and the related income tax reduction. In column A, cash from operations is reduced by interest paid and income taxes include the related tax effect. In column B, interest paid and the associated tax deduction ($5 = 20% of $25) have been removed, increasing CFO by $20 ($25 − $5). After-tax interest paid is included in cash from financing.

Note that we have assumed no change in cash during the period. If a change had taken place, column B would include the change in cash from operations. By doing so, we explicitly assume that cash is an element of working capital, as is accounts receivable.

Column B calculates free cash flow, which, by definition, equals adjusted cash from financing (CFF). This definition of CFF differs from CFF under SFAS 95 as it includes (after-tax) interest paid.

The free cash flow approach yields an estimated value for the firm. The appropriate discount rate is the WACC. To derive the value of equity, subtract the value of debt from the firm value.

The advantage of the FCF approach is that many (but not all) of the issues relating to differences in accounting policies and of income versus cash flows disappear. Whether or not the accounting method defines something as CFO or cash from investment (e.g., capitalization versus expense issues) does not make any difference as the focus is on FCF (the net amount). Similarly, whether or not a cash flow is treated as principal or interest (see Chapter 10) also does not matter as all payments to creditors are excluded from free cash flow.

The remaining problems relate to whether or not to treat an item as operating/investment or financing. Some potential adjustments follow.

EXHIBIT 19-5
Comparison of Statement of Cash Flows and Free Cash Flow

	A	B
	Cash Flow Statement (SFAS 95)	Free Cash Flow For Firm Valuation
Cash from customers	$ 350	$ 350
Cash for operating expenses	(150)	(150)
Cash for interest (pretax)	(25)	NA
Cash for taxes	(25)	(30)
Cash from operations	**$ 150**	**$ 170**
Cash for investment*	**(80)**	**(80)**
Free cash flow	**$ 70**	**$ 90**
Interest (net of tax)	NA	(20)
Dividends	(80)	(80)
New debt	10	10
Cash for financing	**$ (70)**	**$ (90)**
Net change in cash	$ 0	$ 0

NA = not applicable

*Cash from investment is equal to the $30 of total new investment plus the $50 of depreciation that in this simplified example is assumed to be equivalent to the replacement cost of depreciated assets.

Adjustments to Reported Cash from Investment

- All leases should be capitalized and treated as a reduction in free cash flow at the time the lease is entered into even though no cash has yet changed hands.
- Capitalized interest expense should be removed from cash for investment and added to free cash flow.
- Assets acquired in exchange for debt or equity are presently not included in either cash from investment or financing. Such transactions are disclosed as "significant noncash investing and financing activities." The cost of these assets should be deducted from free cash flow.

The free cash flow approach, however, is not without problems. Valuation should not be affected by purely discretionary policies. The model assumes that any cash held within the firm is needed as operating working capital. But firms may decide to hold excess cash for other reasons.[28] Moreover, as shown, free cash flow is equal to financing cash flow. As Penman (1991) states:

> Thus the value increment under this accounting regime would represent (be manipulated by) stock and debt issues or repurchases, and, yes, dividends. This is venturing on the absurd. Free cash flow concerns *the distribution of wealth rather than the generation of wealth.*[29]

Dividends, Earnings, or Free Cash Flows?

All three DCF approaches rely on a measure of cash flows to the suppliers of capital (debt and equity) to the firm. They differ only in the choice of measurement, with the dividend approach measuring these cash flows directly and the others arriving at them in an indirect manner. The free cash flow approach arrives at the cash flow measure (if the firm is all-equity) by subtracting investment from operating cash flows, whereas the earnings approach expresses dividends indirectly as a fraction of earnings.

This begs the question: If the dividend approach can measure cash flows directly, why use a roundabout approach? The answer to this question brings us to the issues of uncertainty and forecasting.

Valuation depends on future CF, not current CF. The firm's future dividends depend on its future earnings. Thus, to forecast future dividends, it is first necessary to forecast future earnings. Similarly, the free cash flow model attempts to avoid the problem of estimating dividends from earnings, given the problems with earnings measurement. Nevertheless, free cash flow forecasts generally require[30] the analyst *to first forecast earnings and then adjust the forecasted earnings to generate free cash flow.* Additionally, in many applications of the free cash flow model, the following formulation is used:

$$V_0 = \sum_{i=1}^{n} \frac{\text{FCF}_i}{(1 + r)^i} + \frac{V_n}{(1 + r)^n} \qquad (17)$$

As with earnings, free cash flows are forecast over a short horizon of n years (usually 5), and then a terminal value V_n is estimated. This terminal value, which can contribute over 60% of the total value, is often earnings-based.

Regardless of which valuation model is used, it relies on the ability to forecast future earnings. Analysts, as well as academics, often use accounting earnings for valuation purposes. The price/earnings ratio is the most widely used valuation measure and is calculated on the basis of accounting earnings. To a great extent, this is because reported earnings are readily available.

---

[28]See, for example, the discussion of financial slack in Box 12-2.

[29]Stephen H. Penman, "Return to Fundamentals," working paper, University of California at Berkeley (November 1991), pp. 29–30 (emphasis added).

[30]See, for example, Tom Copeland, Tim Koller, and Jack Murrin, *Valuation: Measuring and Managing the Value of Companies* (New York: Wiley, 1996). They advocate the use of free cash flow for valuation, but arrive at that measure by first forecasting earnings.

Additionally, accounting earnings may yield better forecasts of future earnings power or cash flows than historical cash flows. This should not come as a shock. After all, the underlying premise of accrual accounting is just that; recording a credit sale (but one example) provides useful information about future cash flows.

Another factor may make net income a better input for forecasting purposes than cash flows. Period-to-period changes in income and cash flows are random, with some portion transitory and the remainder permanent. For valuation, only permanent earnings are fully capitalized. If cash flow is more subject to random fluctuations due, for example, to the timing of payments, then income may produce better forecasts of permanent earnings than cash flows.

One final point must be reiterated before leaving this section. DCF models are all predicated on the dividend discount model. Finance theory, however, argues that dividends up to the terminal and liquidating dividend are irrelevant to valuation. Thus, applying these models requires growth assumptions to forecast past a finite horizon. As we cannot assume that dividends, earnings, and cash flows will converge (to zero or some steady state-value), the infinite horizon remains a problem. The next section introduces a valuation model that, although derivable from the dividend discount model, has a number of unique characteristics that warrant its own classification.

THE ABNORMAL EARNINGS OR EBO MODEL

The residual or abnormal earnings model, also referred to as the Edwards–Bell–Ohlson (EBO) model, is based on work by Ohlson (1991 and 1995) and Edwards and Bell (1961).[31] This model transforms the dividend discount model into a model based on book values and (abnormal) earnings and defines the value of equity as

$$P_0 = B_0 + \sum_{j=1}^{\infty} \frac{E_j - rB_{j-1}}{(1 + r)^j} \tag{18}$$

As $\text{ROE}_t = E_t/B_{t-1}$ the above is often expressed in its ROE form as

$$P_0 = B_0 + \sum_{j=1}^{\infty} \frac{(\text{ROE}_j - r)\,B_{j-1}}{(1 + r)^j} \tag{19}$$

The model is derived in Box 19-3. The link between book value, earnings, and dividends is based on the accounting identity

$$B_t = B_{t-1} + E_t - d_t$$

known as the *clean surplus relation*. Changes in book value are the result of income and dividends.[32]

If we define rB_{t-1} as the required rate of return earned on the firm's (opening) book value in period t, residual or abnormal earnings can be defined as

$$E_t^a = E_t - rB_{t-1}$$

and we can express the valuation formulation as

$$P_0 = B_0 + \sum_{j=1}^{\infty} \frac{E_j^a}{(1 + r)^j} \tag{20}$$

[31]The origins of the residual income model can be traced to earlier work by Preinreich (1938), Edwards and Bell (1961), and Peasnell (1982). The model is also conceptually similar to the EVA model advocated by G. Bennett Stewart III, *The Quest for Value* (New York: Harper Business, 1991), Chapter 8. Stewart's EVA model is structured to value the firm; the model we discuss focuses on the value of equity. Feltham and Ohlson (1995) expand the EBO model to encompass the value of the firm.

[32]As in our previous discussion, dividends include share issues and repurchases.

BOX 19-3
Derivation of the EBO Model

Our derivation makes use of the following three relationships:

$$B_t = B_{t-1} + E_t - d_t \quad \text{or} \quad d_t = E_t - (B_t - B_{t-1}) \qquad (1)$$

$$E_t = \text{ROE}_t B_{t-1} \qquad (2)$$

$$\frac{B_t}{(1 + r)} = B_t - \frac{rB_t}{(1 + r)} \qquad (3)$$

Relationships (1) and (2) are definitions: (1) is the clean surplus relationship and (2) defines income as ROE times opening book value. The dividend discount model is

$$P_0 = \sum_{j=1}^{\infty} \frac{d_j}{(1 + r)^j}$$

Substituting the clean surplus relationship (1) yields

$$P_0 = \sum_{j=1}^{\infty} \frac{E_j - (B_j - B_{j-1})}{(1 + r)^j}$$

For demonstration purposes, we expand the above expression for $j = 1$ and $j = 2$ and find that

$$P_0 = \frac{E_1 - (B_1 - B_0)}{(1 + r)} + \frac{E_2 - (B_2 - B_0)}{(1 + r)^2} + \sum_{j=3}^{\infty} \frac{E_j - (B_j - B_{j-1})}{(1 + r)^j}$$

Using (3) yields

$$P_0 = \left[\frac{E_1}{(1 + r)} - \frac{B_1}{(1 + r)} + B_0 - \frac{rB_0}{(1 + r)} \right] + \left[\frac{E_2}{(1 + r)^2} - \frac{B_2}{(1 + r)^2} + \frac{B_1}{(1 + r)} - \frac{rB_1}{(1 + r)^2} \right] + \sum_{j=3}^{\infty} \frac{E_j - (B_j - B_{j-1})}{(1 + r)^j}$$

and

$$P_0 = B_0 + \left[\frac{E_1 - rB_0}{(1 + r)} \right] + \left[\frac{E_2 - rB_1}{(1 + r)^2} \right] - \frac{B_2}{(1 + r)^2} + \sum_{j=3}^{\infty} \frac{E_j - (B_j - B_{j-1})}{(1 + r)^j}$$

By similarly expanding the summation from $j = 3$ to ∞, we arrive at

$$P_0 = B_0 + \sum_{j=1}^{\infty} \frac{E_j - rB_{j-1}}{(1 + r)^j}$$

Now from (2), since earnings in any period $E_t = \text{ROE}_t B_{t-1}$,

$$P_0 = B_0 + \sum_{j=1}^{\infty} \frac{(\text{ROE}_j - r)B_{j-1}}{(1 + r)^j}$$

Thus, we have defined the value of the firm in terms of opening book value (B_0), ROE, and abnormal earnings [($\text{ROE}_j - r$) B_{j-1}].

The intuition behind the model is perhaps better understood if we consider a firm that only earns the required rate of return r (ROE $= r$) on its book value. Such a firm's shares will sell at a price equal to book value. If it earns more (less) than the required rate of return, the premium (discount) to book value is the present value of those abnormal earnings.[33]

The EBO valuation model can be applied to the example of Exhibits 19-1 and 19-2. Prior to the introduction of "growth," the firm earns a 10% return on its equity investment of

[33]This is, of course, equivalent to our earlier formulation [Eq. (4)] for economic goodwill, albeit in a more rigorous fashion.

$1,000. Using that as our starting point, we set the initial book value (B_{-1}) at the *beginning period zero* at $1,000. During period zero, the firm's net income is $100 (see Exhibit 19-1). Because it now has growth opportunities, it pays a dividend of $80, leaving book value at the end of period 0; $B_0 = $1,020. Recall that net income grows at 4%.

Period i	Book Value Beginning B_{i-1}	Net Income E_i	Abnormal Earnings $E_t^a = E_i - (r \times B_{i-1})$	Dividend kE_i	Book Value End $B_i = B_{i-1} + (1 - k) E_i$
0	$1,000	$100	0	$80	$1,020
1	1,020	104	$104 - (0.1)(1,020) = 2$	83.2	1,040.8
2	1,040.8	108.16	$108.16 - (0.1)(1,040.8) = 4.08$	86.528	1,062.432
3	1,062.432	112.4864	6.2432	. . .	. . .

Therefore, inserting the above into the EBO valuation (20), we obtain

$$P_0 = B_0 + \sum_{i=1}^{\infty} \frac{E_i^a}{(1 + r)^i}$$

$$P_0 = 1,020 + \left[\frac{2}{(1.1)^1} + \frac{4.08}{(1.1)^2} + \frac{6.2432}{(1.1)^3} \cdots \right]$$

The series in the right bracket converges to $367, yielding, as before, the value of equity:

$$P_0 = 1,020 + 367 = \$1,387$$

EBO versus DCF Models

As the EBO model is essentially a variation of the DCF model, its result is identical. What then are its advantages? We consider both pragmatic and conceptual answers to this question.

Finite Horizons

In a nondeterministic world, where the future is unknown, valuation depends on forecasts of future dividends, earnings, or cash flows. As discussed earlier, it is not possible to make reliable forecasts to infinity. In practice, therefore, analysts make explicit forecasts for a few (usually five) years and then estimate a terminal value, based on simplifying assumptions, to capture the remaining value. In DCF models, the assumptions made to estimate the terminal value may be crucial, as it may constitute 70% of total value.

Proponents of the EBO model argue that terminal value estimates in that model are less troublesome. If we consider a finite horizon T, the valuation model (19) becomes[34]

$$P_0 = B_0 + \sum_{j=1}^{T} \frac{(\text{ROE}_j - r) B_{j-1}}{(1 + r)^j} + \frac{(P_T - B_T)}{(1 + r)^T} \tag{21}$$

The last expression ($P_T - B_T$) represents the premium over book value at the end of the finite horizon T. This premium is based on the abnormal earnings earned following period T.

---

[34]This expression can be derived by expansion of (19) to

$$P_0 = B_0 + \sum_{j=1}^{T} \frac{(\text{ROE}_j - r) B_{j-1}}{(1 + r)^j} + \sum_{k=T+1}^{\infty} \frac{(\text{ROE}_k - r) B_{k-1}}{(1 + r)^k}$$

and by using

$$P_T = B_T + (1 + r)^T \sum_{k=T+1}^{\infty} \frac{(\text{ROE}_k - r) B_{T-1}}{(1 + r)^k}$$

Advocates of the EBO model argue that this premium should disappear as economic factors tend to drive abnormal earnings to zero within a relatively short time.[35] More formally, as long as T is sufficiently large, $(P_T - B_T) \rightarrow 0$.

Recall that Figure 4-3 provides empirical evidence that ROEs converge from extreme positions toward an overall mean within approximately five years. As abnormal earnings are a function of the difference between ROE and the required rate of return r, this convergence in ROE is equivalent to abnormal earnings approaching zero.

Competitive forces are one reason for this convergence, as competitors enter business segments with abnormal profits, eventually reducing those profits to zero. *Even if a company could protect a particular source of abnormal profits indefinitely (through patents or copyrights), it is unlikely that it could find additional sources of abnormal profits indefinitely. Thus, reinvested profits would only earn a normal rate of return.* As reinvested profits increase book value, ROE (a weighted average of normal and abnormal profits) declines and the firm's abnormal earnings converge to a steady-state level.[36] That level can be used to estimate the terminal premium $(P_T - B_T)$.

> Whatever the firm's current earnings, competitive forces are assumed to reduce the firm's abnormal earnings over time. At some point, the firm will have only zero net present value opportunities and zero abnormal earnings. Because of this convergence property, abnormal earnings play a central role in the valuation function . . .

> . . . Although the valuation formula, like the Dividend Discount Model, incorporates the sum of an infinite series, its power derives from the fact that estimating abnormal earnings over a finite horizon can generate reasonable firm valuations.[37]

Simplified Assumptions for ROE, Book Values, and Terminal Value. The convergence of ROE, along with assumptions about the level and growth of ROE, leads to reasonably accurate and simplified valuation calculations. For example, assume $T = 3$ and ROE $= r$ after three periods. Then the valuation model reduces to estimates of ROE for the next three years and book values for the next two:

$$P_0 = B_0 + \frac{(\text{ROE}_1 - r)\, B_0}{(1 + r)} + \frac{(\text{ROE}_2 - r)\, B_1}{(1 + r)^2} + \frac{(\text{ROE}_3 - r)\, B_2}{(1 + r)^3}$$

This model is sometimes expressed in the form of the price/book value ratio, yielding

$$\frac{P_0}{B_0} = 1 + \frac{(\text{ROE}_1 - r)}{(1 + r)} + \frac{(\text{ROE}_2 - r)(1 + g_1)}{(1 + r)^2} + \frac{(\text{ROE}_3 - r)(1 + g_1)(1 + g_2)}{(1 + r)^3}$$

where g_i is the growth in book value in period i. Value equals current book value (B_0) multiplied by the price/book (P/B) ratio. This model requires an estimate of growth in book value. As noted earlier, the growth rate of book value equals $(1 - k)$ ROE; the exercise thus boils down to estimating ROEs and dividend payout ratios.

If we assume that abnormal earnings do not disappear, but reach steady state *after* period 3, then the above can be modified to incorporate the terminal value as

$$\frac{P_0}{B_0} = 1 + \frac{(\text{ROE}_1 - r)}{(1 + r)} + \frac{(\text{ROE}_2 - r)(1 + g_1)}{(1 + r)^2} + \frac{(\text{ROE}_3 - r)(1 + g_1)(1 + g_2)}{(1 + r)^3}$$
$$+ \frac{(\text{ROE}_4 - r)(1 + g_1)(1 + g_2)(1 + g_3)}{r(1 + r)^3}$$

[35]Or, at the very least, their discounted values. Our example does not have this property as abnormal growth opportunities are considered to exist to infinity. However, (ROE $- r$) does reach steady state at 10% as ROE approaches 20%.

[36]See the section entitled, "Unbiased versus Conservative Accounting."

[37]Patricia M. Fairfield, "P/E, P/B and the Present Value of Future Dividends," *Financial Analysts Journal* (July–August 1994), p. 24.

where $(ROE_4 - r)$ is the terminal steady-state difference between the firm's ROE and its required rate of return r.

This formulation assumes that although the firm has abnormal earnings equal to $(ROE_4 - r) B_3$ after period 3, these abnormal earnings do not grow (although book value grows after period 3); similar reinvestment opportunities do not exist.

If, however, we assume that abnormal earnings do grow as book value grows at a rate equal to g_3, then the P/B ratio can be expressed as

$$\frac{P_0}{B_0} = 1 + \frac{(ROE_1 - r)}{(1 + r)} + \frac{(ROE_2 - r)(1 + g_1)}{(1 + r)^2} + \frac{(ROE_3 - r)(1 + g_1)(1 + g_2)}{(1 + r)^3}$$
$$+ \frac{(ROE_4 - r)(1 + g_1)(1 + g_2)(1 + g_3)}{(r - g_3)(1 + r)^3}$$

Additional formulae for estimates of terminal values under differing growth assumptions and steady-state values are provided in Appendix 19-B.

Relative Importance of Terminal Value Calculations

The relative importance of terminal value calculations is a significant issue. In our previous example, the book value of $1,020 approximates 75% of the $1,387 firm value. *Book value, which often represents a sizable portion of firm value, is given and does not have to be estimated.* Further, when we consider the value derived from forecasts of the first few periods' abnormal earnings, the proportion of the terminal value to total value is small.

In DCF models, as noted, terminal values frequently constitute 60 to 70% of total value. All parameters must be estimated, and those that are most difficult to estimate play a large role in valuation.

The reason for the difference in the relative importance of terminal value relates to the accrual system of accounting. That system essentially quantifies (net) assets in terms of future benefits; that is, will they generate future cash flows? Those future benefits are, therefore, already quantified within the book value of the firm. The EBO model makes use of this quantification; it focuses on the difference between firm value and book value: abnormal earnings.

The DCF model, on the other hand, undoes the accrual process, forecasts future cash flows, and then rebundles them in the present value calculations. Everything must be reestimated. Put differently, DCF models estimate *firm value* itself; the EBO model estimates the *differential between firm value and book value*, a more manageable problem.

To be sure, when the models are applied in a consistent manner, they obtain the same result. The errors in DCF terminal value calculations are expected to appear in the shorter horizons of the EBO model. Pragmatically, however, forecasting is simpler for EBO models.

Growth Companies

For growth companies that make large capital expenditures, reflecting their rapid growth, FCF tends to be negative. As it may take years for FCF to turn positive (as growth slows), using the FCF model to value growth companies may require a longer time horizon of explicit annual forecasts until the terminal value can be estimated.

The EBO model, on the other hand, based on accrual accounting, eliminates the distortion caused by high capital expenditures. Depreciation allocates the capital expenditures over time effectively, matching it to the revenue it generates. The time horizon needed to implement the model is correspondingly smaller, reducing the effects of forecasting errors.

Effect of Accounting Policies

Both the EBO model and the earnings version of the dividend DCF models use accounting earnings as an input. There is, however, an important distinction between the two. In the DCF model, earnings (together with the payout ratio k) are a surrogate for dividends, and the efficacy of the model depends on the validity of that relationship.

Although the EBO model can be derived (as shown in Box 19-3) from the dividend discount model, it is not dependent on any set of accounting standards. Consistent with its accounting definition, earnings in the EBO model measure the creation of wealth, not as a surrogate for another parameter such as cash flows, dividends, or even economic earnings. As long as the *clean surplus* relationship is maintained, the model is applicable to any set of accounting rules.

At first glance, this may seem illogical. How can value be determined by a number (earnings) that can be manipulated by accounting choices? The answer lies in the *self-correcting* nature of accounting. Value under the EBO model is a function of current book value and (discounted) future abnormal earnings. If a given accounting method recognizes earnings in the current period, *the book value portion of the EBO valuation increases as current book value is higher*. However, in following periods, the higher book value increases the normal (required) earnings (*rB*). Consequently, *future abnormal earnings are lower (or negative), offsetting the higher book value in the valuation formula*. Thus, *over time*, different accounting choices catch up with each other.[38]

The foregoing does not mean that accounting is irrelevant. On the contrary, it creates an objective measure of "better" accounting policies. Our earlier discussion notes that the strength of the EBO model is its use of finite horizons, as abnormal earnings converge to zero as long as *T* is *sufficiently* large. The self-correcting process of differing accounting policies is another manifestation of this convergence process. Thus, a better accounting system is one in which this convergence takes place over a shorter horizon *T*. More important, in terms of adjusting reported financial data:

> . . . the accounting-based valuation methods *provide a motive for adjusting book values and earnings*, *much as analysts do*; with "better" accounting, value can be summarized with forecasts over shorter horizons.[39]

The Clean Surplus Relationship

The clean surplus relationship requires a definition of income similar to comprehensive income, discussed in Chapters 2 and 17. All changes in book value (other than transactions with stockholders) flow through the income statement without any direct charges to stockholders' equity.

U.S. GAAP are generally consistent with clean surplus accounting. There are exceptions, all discussed in the book:

1. Adjustment for the minimum pension liability (Chapter 12)
2. Recognition of unrealized gains and losses on available-for-sale marketable securities (Chapter 13)
3. Exchange rate gains and losses under the all-current method (Chapter 15).
4. Deferred gains and losses on cash flow hedges under SFAS 133 (Chapter 16)

Thus, applying the EBO to U.S. firms requires adjustments to income for these items.

Unbiased versus Conservative Accounting

The self-correcting process that drives abnormal earnings to zero and ROE to *r* is characterized by Ohlson as *unbiased* accounting. Not all accounting methods, however, possess this property.

For example, Chapter 7 compares capitalization versus expense accounting policies. Figure 7-3 shows that for a company that grows and then reaches steady state, ROA for the expensing firm is *higher and remains higher* relative to that of the capitalizing firm. *Conservative* accounting that expenses current expenditures *leads to higher abnormal earnings* (ROE > *r*) *indefinitely*. Thus, firms with high R&D expenditures (that must be expensed) report positive

---

[38]Problem 19-11 illustrates this property.

[39]Victor L. Bernard, "Accounting-Based Valuation Methods, Determinants of Market-to-Book Ratios and Implications for Financial Statement Analysis," working paper, University of Michigan (June 1993), p. 8 (emphasis added).

abnormal earnings indefinitely.[40] *The level of these abnormal earnings, however, reach steady state and the analysis discussed earlier and in Appendix 19-B must be adopted.*

Value Drivers

The EBO model also has conceptual advantages. By focusing on earnings rather than dividends, *the model defines value in terms of wealth generation rather than wealth distribution.*

> Value is determined by the *creation* of wealth, measured by aggregate accounting earnings, rather than the *distribution* of wealth, measured as dividends.[41]

This argument can be extended to the valuation of firms that do not pay dividends. The valuation of these firms by EBO models is no different from that of any other firm, as value is determined by the generation of wealth (earnings), not its distribution as dividends.

The value drivers in the EBO model are precisely those attributes that analysts normally consider. Abnormal earnings depend on ROE, a ratio whose disaggregation and analysis are familiar (see Chapter 4). The various DCF models also use many of these drivers to estimate cash flows. However, as the EBO paradigm focuses on the attributes that are important for valuation, the impact of parameter and assumption changes can be seen *directly*. The valuation equation allows us to focus directly on price and its relationship to earnings, book value, ROE, and the growth and persistence of these components.

Price/Book Value and Price/Earnings Ratios Revisited

The EBO model provides a useful framework to revisit the questions addressed earlier: why companies sell at higher or lower price/book value and price/earnings ratios. The model allows us to reevaluate the parameters that are relevant to these ratios.

Price/Book Value Ratios. We begin with expression (19) evaluated at time t:

$$P_t = B_t + \sum_{j=1}^{\infty} \frac{(\text{ROE}_{j+t} - r)\, B_{j+t-1}}{(1 + r)^j}$$

Dividing by B_t yields

$$\frac{P_t}{B_t} = 1 + \sum_{j=1}^{\infty} \frac{(\text{ROE}_{j+t} - r)\, B_{j+t-1}}{(1 + r)^j}\, \frac{B_{j+t-1}}{B_t}$$

This equation implies that the P/B ratio is related to future abnormal earnings (the difference between ROE and r*) and the growth of book value.* If future abnormal earnings are zero, then the P/B ratio is "normal" (equal to 1). *Note that current profitability is not relevant.*

Price/Earnings Ratio. We begin with expression (20) evaluated at time t:

$$P_t = B_t + \sum_{j=1}^{\infty} \frac{E_{j+t}^a}{(1 + r)^j}$$

Adding D_t to both sides and dividing by E_t and using the clean surplus relationship, we obtain

$$\frac{P_t + D_t}{E_t} = 1 + \frac{B_{t-1}}{E_t} + \sum_{j=1}^{\infty} \frac{E_{j+t}^a}{(1 + r)^j\, E_t} \tag{22}$$

B_{t-1}/E_t measures current year profitability, (the inverse of) ROE_t. The summation term reflects future (abnormal) earnings relative to current earnings. *Expression (22) states that the*

---

[40]See, for example, Figure 7-6, and the analysis of Merck's ROE from Lev and Sougiannis.

[41]Bernard, op. cit.

P/E ratio is related to both current and future profitability and the extent to which current profitability will persist.

Since $E_t = E_t^a + rB_{t-1}$, after substituting for B_{t-1}, Eq. (22) reduces to

$$\frac{P_t + D_t}{E_t} = \left[\frac{1+r}{r}\right] + \frac{1}{E_t}\left[\sum_{j=1}^{\infty}\frac{E_{j+t}^a}{(1+r)^j} - \frac{E_t^a}{r}\right] \qquad (23)$$

The term in the left bracket is the same one derived for "normal" P/E ratios (cum dividend) in the earnings DCF model. The term in the right bracket is the difference between the present value of *future abnormal* earnings and *current abnormal* earnings in perpetuity. That difference determines whether or not P/E ratios are high or low.

We first consider a situation where future abnormal earnings are equivalent to current abnormal earnings for all j; that is, $E_{j+t}^a = E_t^a$. Then

$$\sum_{j=1}^{\infty}\frac{1}{(1+r)^j} = \frac{1}{r}$$

Equation (23) reduces to

$$\frac{P_t + D_t}{E_t} = \frac{1+r}{r} \qquad (24)$$

the expression for normal P/E ratios. *When future abnormal earnings are equivalent to current abnormal earnings, P/E ratios are normal.*[42]

High (low) P/E ratios are dependent on future abnormal earnings that are higher (lower) than current abnormal earnings. *The P/E ratio is a function of current abnormal earnings, their persistence, and the growth in future abnormal earnings.* Note that it is the *relative*, not absolute, levels of current and future abnormal earnings that matter. Growth affects P/E ratios only if future abnormal earnings exceed current abnormal earnings.

The relationship between P/B and P/E ratios and current and future (abnormal) earnings is illustrated in Figure 19-1.[43] The vertical axis plots future abnormal earnings (FE^a); the horizontal axis plots current abnormal earnings (CE^a).

Figure 19-1a shows that P/E ratios are a function of whether or not current levels of profitability persist in the future. The 45° line drawn in the graph represents $CE^a = FE^a$. Along this line, current abnormal earnings are a good indicator of future abnormal earnings (earnings are persistent). The P/E ratio is normal and equal to $(1 + r)/r$.

On either side of this line, current profitability is not a good indicator of future profitability and P/E ratios are high or low. To the right and below the line, current profitability exceeds future profitability. Either current earnings have a transitory positive component or the high abnormal earnings are not sustainable in the future. The result is a low P/E ratio. To the left and above the 45° line, future profitability exceeds current profitability. Current earnings may have a transitory negative component. The P/E ratio is high.

Figure 19-1b shows that the P/B ratio is purely a function of future abnormal earnings. The horizontal axis is equivalent to $FE^a = 0$. When $FE^a = 0$, the P/B ratio is normal (equivalent to 1). When FE^a is positive, P/B ratios are high (exceed 1). When future abnormal earnings are negative, the P/B ratio is below 1.

---

[42]In Eq. (16), we showed that P/E ratios are normal when there are no abnormal growth opportunities ($r^* = r$). Our EBO formulation shows that this restriction is too limiting. The important issue is the relative level of current and future abnormal earnings, not whether or not there are abnormal earnings at all.

[43]Figure 19-1 is similar to the analysis of Table 2 in Fairfield (1994) and the matrix of Penman (1996).

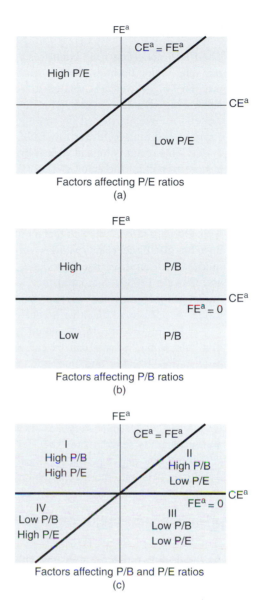

FIGURE 19-1 Factors affecting price/earnings and price/book value ratios.

Figure 19-1*c* combines Figures 19-1*a* and *b*, showing conditions for all possible combinations of (high or low) P/B and (high or low) P/E ratios. At the origin, the P/B and P/E ratios are normal.

- Region I represents companies with strong growth potential. FE^a is high and future profitability exceeds current levels. These companies have high P/E and P/B ratios.
- Region II contains mature companies in their harvesting years. Current and future E^a is positive; however, future profitability is below current profitability. These companies exhibit high P/B ratios and low P/E ratios.
- Region III represents poor performers. Future profitability is expected to be below normal ($FE^a < 0$) as well as below current levels. These companies exhibit low P/E and P/B ratios.
- Region IV shows distressed companies that are recovering. Future earnings are below normal ($FE^a < 0$); however, they are expected to rise from current levels. Companies that have had major restructurings (or a "big bath") would fall into this category, as current earnings are depressed. Although P/B ratios are low, P/E ratios are high.

The EBO Model: Concluding Comments

The EBO model has been empirically tested in a number of studies. Beaver (2002) summarizes the major findings. Both book value and earnings are significant in pricing but their (relative) significance is related to some extent to the financial health of the firm. Book value's significance is greater for "unhealthy" firms and is lower for healthier firms. Conversely, the weight placed on earnings in valuation is strongest for firms reporting positive earnings and high ROE; for low ROE, the weighting is smaller, and zero for firms reporting losses. This result is logical. When firms have low or zero profitability, book value becomes a more important indicator of firm value. Overall [see Frankel and Lee (1998)], valuations based on the EBO model were found to explain approximately 70% of the variance in stock prices.

When compared with the other models discussed in the chapter, the EBO has also fared well. Bernard (1995) showed that a model using book values and forecasts of abnormal earnings for just three years explains variations in market prices far better than a comparable model based on discounted dividends. Penman and Sougiannis (1998) and Francis, Olsson, and Oswald (2000) compared the EBO model to a free cash flow and dividend discount model using current stock price as the valuation benchmark. Both studies found that the EBO model outperformed the other models.

In Chapters 5 and 18, we noted that a number of studies have documented the anomaly that "abnormal" returns can be earned by constructing portfolios on the basis of price-to-book ratios. Frankel and Lee extended this analysis by constructing portfolios based on price-to-*value* ratios with value based on the EBO model and found that returns earned by the price-to-value strategies were twice those earned using price-to-book strategies.

The valuation models discussed above require forecasts of dividends, earnings, and/or cash flows. Other than Penman and Sougiannis (who used reported amounts), the studies above generally relied on analysts' forecasts of earnings. The next section of the chapter discusses the time-series properties of earnings and compares the relative merits of various forecasting models with those generated by analysts.

FORECASTING MODELS AND TIME SERIES PROPERTIES OF EARNINGS

As the discussion so far indicates, valuation depends to a great degree on the ability to forecast earnings and filter out its transitory and permanent components. A great deal of empirical research has focused on the time-series properties of earnings and the development of appropriate forecasting models. The research has generally been based on income rather than cash flow. Although unfortunate from a theoretical standpoint, from a practical point of view it may be that earnings work as well as or better than (free) cash flow, for reasons discussed earlier. Moreover, available evidence on the time-series properties of cash flows indicates little difference between the properties of income and cash flows. This section reviews some of these results.

FORECASTING MODELS

Generally, there are two classes of forecasting models in the literature: extrapolative models and index models. These are mechanical models in that forecasts use the statistical properties of these models without any further judgment on the part of the forecaster.

Extrapolative Models

Extrapolative models use the previous time series of earnings to forecast the future level of earnings. That is, the forecast of next period's income, defined as $E(Y_{t+1})$, is a function of the past history of earnings:

$$E(Y_{t+1}) = f(Y_t, Y_{t-1}, \ldots, Y_1)$$

Permanent versus Transitory Components

When using time series of a firm's earnings, it is important to separate the permanent and transitory components. The permanent component is expected to persist into the future. That permanent earnings stream itself can, however, be altered by random events affecting the firm or its environment. If these random occurrences have permanent effects, then they alter the permanent earnings stream.[44] The permanent earnings stream includes all prior permanent random events.

Nonpermanent (transitory) events do not affect the permanent earnings stream. These random shocks disguise the underlying (permanent) stream. Reported income is the sum of the permanent and transitory components. The goal of time-series analysis is to identify the firm's permanent earnings stream.

The following example shows the importance of the difference, for forecasting purposes, between permanent and transitory components. Assume that a company in a no-growth environment had expected earnings of $10 but actual (reported) earnings of $11 for the current period (a positive earnings surprise). What should the estimate of the next period's earnings be? Maintaining the original estimate of $10 assumes that next period the company's earnings will revert from its present level of $11 to the previous expectation of $10. The $1 deviation ($11 − $10) is treated as a one-time, transitory event that will not recur in the future; expectations are not affected by the reported earnings for a given period. Such a process is referred to as mean reverting, as the earnings revert to a constant level.

In general, for a mean-reverting process, the forecast of next period or, for that matter, any period earnings is a constant u. The estimate of u is the mean of all prior period earnings. That is,

$$E(Y_{t+1}) = u$$

where u is estimated as

$$u = \frac{1}{t}(Y_t + Y_{t-1} + \cdots + Y_2 + Y_1)$$

If, on the other hand, the $1 deviation from expected earnings is viewed as permanent, then the next period expectation becomes $11. Such a process is referred to as a *martingale* or *random walk*. For such processes, the only information needed to generate the next period forecast is the prior period result. All earlier information is irrelevant:

$$E(Y_{t+1}) = Y_t$$

In a martingale process, expectations change from period to period based on reported earnings.

The distinction between mean-reverting and martingale processes need not be confined to a no-growth environment. Assume that a company whose income is expected to grow by $2.00 each year had an expected income of $12.00 for this year. The actual earnings of $11.50 were $0.50 below expectation. If this negative earnings surprise is viewed as transitory, then the underlying income of the firm is still assumed to be $12.00. The forecast of next period's income is $12.00 + $2.00 = $14.00:

$$E(Y_{t+1}) = E(Y_t) + d$$

where d represents the growth term.

If the $0.50 deviation is viewed as permanent, then the starting point for the next period estimate is the reported $11.50 and the next period forecast is $11.50 + $2.00 = $13.50. This is an example of a *martingale with drift* or a *submartingale*, and can be expressed as

$$E(Y_{t+1}) = Y_t + d$$

[44]For example, an external event may raise oil prices, permanently increasing the earnings of oil producers.

BOX 19-4
Description of a Time-Series Process Having Transitory and Permanent Components

---

The process is described as

$$X_t = X_{t-1} + v_t$$
$$Y_t = X_t + e_t$$

Therefore,

$$Y_t = X_{t-1} + v_t + e_t$$

Let X_t represent the firm's permanent earnings stream. Then the v_t are the periodic random occurrences that become a perma-

nent part of the firm's earnings.* If there are transitory components, symbolized by e_t, the permanent stream X_t would be unobservable. Instead, one would observe Y_t, which is made up of the permanent and transitory components.[†] If there are no transitory components, the description of the process would stop at the first equation ($X_t = X_{t-1} + v_t$), and we would have a random walk process. If, on the other hand, there are no permanent random components, the underlying permanent earnings stream of the firm is a constant, as $X_t = X_{t-1} = X_{t-2}, \ldots$ and so on. This constant would be the mean, as by definition all random occurrences are represented by the transitory component e_t and the process is mean-reverting.

---

*Note that

$$X_t = X_0 + \Sigma v_i$$

That is, this period's permanent earnings is a summation of all previous permanent random occurrences since period 0.
[†]Note that

$$Y_t = X_0 + \Sigma v_i + e_t$$

That is, this period's reported earnings is a summation of all previous permanent random occurrences and this period's transitory component.

The martingale and mean-reverting processes are two extremes on a continuum. In the first case, the forecast of the next period is determined solely by current period results. For the mean-reverting process, current period results are only used to estimate the underlying mean. Choosing between the two extremes of random walk or mean-reverting processes, *the overwhelming empirical evidence indicates that, on average, earnings follow a submartingale process.*

It is, of course, possible that an earnings surprise has both transitory and permanent components. Such a process is described in Box 19-4. Forecasting such a time series places one within the two extremes. The forecast does not depend solely on current period results, but also on all previous results, as is the case for mean-reverting models. Typically, the forecast should be a weighted average of previous reported earnings. The *exponential smoothing* model is an example; it uses higher weights for more recent data and lower weights for earlier data. A more complex set of forecasting models used in the literature are the *Box–Jenkins models*.[45]

Diagnostic tests, using these models, indicate that, for many firms, the pure (sub)martingale model does not describe the underlying time series. Nevertheless, when forecasting models were designed for these firms individually, they did not, on average, outperform the (sub)martingale process. The best forecast *based solely on the previous time series* was a (sub)martingale forecast.

The only consistent results that belie this point occurred when the previous year deviation was abnormally large.[46] Brooks and Buckmaster (1976) found that such very large deviations are typically transitory and that forecasts based on the exponential smoothing model are better than martingale-based forecasts. These results confirm those of Beaver and Morse discussed earlier.

---

[45]This class of models is beyond the scope of this book. The interested reader is referred to Box and Jenkins (1976).

[46]There are a number of ways to define "abnormally large." Brooks and Buckmaster, for example, define the normalized first difference (nfd) as

$$\text{nfd} = (Y_t - Y_{t-1})/\textbf{Standard deviation of earnings}$$

For large absolute values of nfd, they found exponential smoothing parameters ranging from 0.2 to 0.9 (depending on the sign and magnitude of nfd) to be better predictors than a martingale model.

In a similar vein, Freeman et al. (1982) showed that earnings forecasts can be improved by considering the trend in the firm's ROE. ROE, *unlike earnings, is mean-reverting*. ROE measures the rate of return on the firm's book value; if the current ROE is considerably above (below) its recent mean,[47] that indicates current earnings are too high (low) and a reversal can be expected in the next period. This is, of course, consistent with our discussion of EBO models (and Figure 4-3), indicating that ROE reverts to a mean level.

Index Models

The second class of models does not rely on the previous earnings history, but rather uses independent variables or indices to forecast earnings. The earnings forecast is described as $E(Y_{t+1}) = f(Z_{1t}, Z_{2t}, \ldots, Z_{nt})$, where the Z's represent independent variables. The most commonly used model of this sort is described in Chapter 18 in the discussion of the accounting beta. This model, the market model of accounting income, expresses earnings as a function of some overall market index of earnings (ME) such as the S&P 500 earnings index, GNP, corporate earnings, or the average earnings of the sample of firms being examined. Operationally, the model is represented as

$$E(Y_{t+1}) = a + bME_{t+1}$$

where a and b are regression parameters derived from the previous history of earnings and the market index.[48]

Comparisons between this model and the submartingale show that they perform equally well. Fried and Givoly (1982), for example, found that, over an 11-year period (1969–1979), the index model had an average percentage forecast error of 20.3%, whereas the (modified[49]) submartingale's percentage forecast error was 19.3%.

Forecasting with Disaggregated Data

The models described here all use time series of annual earnings data to forecast annual earnings. The literature has also examined forecasts of annual income using data disaggregated along three dimensions:

1. By time, using quarterly data
2. By segment, using segment-based data
3. By component, using income statement components

Quarterly Forecasting Models

Forecasting models using quarterly data have been those most commonly examined. Although quarterly models have been used primarily to forecast quarterly earnings, they have also been utilized to forecast annual earnings; such forecasts usually sum the individual quarterly forecasts. These forecasts have been generally found to outperform forecasts based on annual models alone (see Hopwood et al., 1982). Moreover, as expected, the farther along in the year and the more interim periods that have gone by, the greater the accuracy of forecasts using quarterly reports.

Unlike annual earnings data, which seem to follow martingale or submartingale patterns, quarterly earnings are generally better described by more complex models. The seasonality of many businesses makes the task of designing quarterly models more challenging. Box–Jenkins forecasting techniques, mentioned earlier, are designed to detect seasonality components and have been used with some success in quarterly time-series models.

---

[47]This result assumes stable book values with no major new stock issues, repurchases, or acquisitions.

[48]As noted in Chapter 18, these models are generally expressed in terms of the relationship between the change in earnings and the change in the index.

[49]The model is referred to as modified because it applies the Brooks and Buckmaster criterion when appropriate.

Generally, the extrapolative models for quarterly series find that a quarter's income Q_t (e.g., second quarter of 2002) is related to the immediately preceding quarter Q_{t-1} (first quarter of 2002) and the same quarter of the preceding year Q_{t-4} (second quarter of 2001). Three competing models have been put forward to represent the average firm; individually fitted models were not able to improve on these models in a meaningful way. The models follow. Model 1 is based on Watts (1975) and Griffin (1977):

$$E(Q_t) = Q_{t-4} + (Q_{t-1} - Q_{t-5}) - be_{t-1} - ce_{t-4} + bce_{t-5}$$

Model 2 is based on Foster (1977):

$$E(Q_t) = Q_{t-4} + a(Q_{t-1} - Q_{t-5}) + d$$

Brown and Rozeff (1979) is the basis for Model 3:

$$E(Q_t) = Q_{t-4} + a(Q_{t-1} - Q_{t-5}) - ce_{t-4}$$

where a, b, and c are estimated parameters; d is a drift term (the average seasonal change); and e_t (times the respective parameter) represents the transitory portion of a period's Q_t.

It is interesting to note that an explanation of the post-announcement drift anomaly (see Chapter 5) would seem to lie in the market's (and analyst's) inability to correctly estimate the pattern of serial correlation between quarters. This phenomenon is documented by Bernard and Thomas (1989) as well as Bartov (1992). Ball and Bartov (1996) show that the market is cognizant of the serial correlation between quarters but underestimates its magnitude by up to 50%. Mendenhall (1991) and Abarbanell and Bernard (1992) show that forecasts by (Value Line) analysts do not fully incorporate the quarterly serial correlations.

Segment-based Forecasts

The merits of forecasting annual earnings using segment-based data are discussed at some length in Chapter 13. For time-series models, the potential improvement is highly dependent on the differences in the underlying time-series behavior of the individual segments. If segments, for example, are similarly affected by the business cycle, that reduces the advantage of using segment data. Moreover (again, for time-series models), the improvement of segment-based forecasts seems not to go beyond the prediction of sales.

Forecasts Using Income or Balance Sheet Components

Studies that use income statement (or balance sheet) components to help forecast income are few and far between. These models come in two forms. The first, similar to segment-based models, generates an earnings forecast from separate forecasts of sales, cost of goods sold, operating expenses, depreciation, and so forth, and then aggregating these components to forecast earnings. The results suggest that this method of forecasting *earnings* is not fruitful for the same reason as for segment-based models.[50] The time series of the individual components are interdependent, which precludes substantial gains in predictive power from disaggregated data. However, Fairfield et al. (1996) show that the use of disaggregated data can improve ROE predictions.

The second model form shows more potential. These explicitly model interrelationships among income and balance sheet components and construct a structural model of the firm. Such *econometric models* were designed by Elliott and Uphoff (1972) and Wild (1987). Unfortunately, it is difficult to generalize from these models. Although their results improved predictive ability, given the difficulty in constructing such models, studies were usually limited to small samples.[51]

---

[50]See, for example, Fried (1978).

[51]Wild, for example, is based on one firm.

EXHIBIT 19-6
Results of Ou and Penman

Summary of Prediction Performance of Earnings Prediction Models;
Earnings Changes are Predicted One Year Ahead on the Basis of $\overline{Pr}$. *

	Predictions Over 1973–1977		Predictions Over 1978–1983	
	$\overline{Pr}$ Cutoff		$\overline{Pr}$ Cutoff	
	(0.5, 0.5)	(0.6, 0.4)	(0.5, 0.5)	(0.6, 0.4)
Number of observations	9138	5791	9640	4779
% correct predictions	62%	67%	60%	67%
χ_1^2 from 2 × 2 table (and p value)	299.94	271.63	387.46	444.54
	(0.000)	(0.000)	(0.000)	(0.000)
% predicted EPS increases correct	62%	67%	59%	66%
% predicted EPS decreases correct	61%	66%	62%	67%

*$\overline{Pr}$ is the estimated probability of an earnings increase indicated by the prediction models.
Source: Jane A. Ou and Stephen Penman, "Financial Statement Analysis and the Prediction of Stock Returns," *Journal of Accounting and Economics*, Vol. 11 (1989), pp. 295–329, Table 4 (p. 308).

Ou and Penman (1989), in a variation of this approach, use common financial ratios to improve the forecasting ability of a random walk model. Their model forecasts the probability that a firm's earnings change would be higher or lower than that forecasted by a random walk (with drift) process. That is, they estimated the probability that a firm's earnings next year (Y_{t-1}) would exceed a random walk (with drift) forecast of earnings:

$$E(Y_{t+1}) = Y_t + d$$

where d represents the drift term calculated as the average change in earnings over the previous four years. More formally, the model generates the following probability (Pr):

$$Pr[Y_{t+1} > (Y_t + d)]$$

The results are presented in Exhibit 19-6. At a cutoff of $Pr = 60\%$, the model correctly predicted the direction of earnings change close to two-thirds of the time. Ou and Penman thus demonstrate that financial ratios can successfully improve predictive power. Their use of ratios, however, is mechanical in that they do not use any judgment in interpreting their variables. This method is driven in part by the nature of their research process and sample size.

Bernard and Noel (1991) approach forecasting in a less mechanical fashion by using trends in (finished goods and work in process) inventory levels to forecast sales and earnings.[52] As discussed in Chapter 6, they use these variables to aid prediction. However, they conclude that the nature of the analysis calls for a "contextual" approach. That is, changes in inventory may mean different things to different firms. Knowledge of the firm, the industry, and the overall state of the economy at that time is needed before such models can realize their fullest potential.

Lev and Thiagarajan (1993) allow for such a contextual approach in their forecasting model. That model, discussed in Chapter 5 (along with other forecasting models), however, was designed with a different objective. The original objective of Ou and Penman was valuation, but used forecasted earnings as an input. These other models were developed to forecast (abnormal) returns directly.

[52]Freeman et al., discussed earlier, also qualifies as nonmechanical as it combines the relationship of the firm's book value, ROE, and earnings.

COMPARISON WITH FINANCIAL ANALYST FORECASTS

Earnings forecasting is a prime activity of financial analysts. Such financial analyst forecasts (FAFs) are important inputs in valuation models and usually use a contextual approach. These forecasts possess two advantages over those generated by time-series models. First, analysts base their forecasts on a broader set of data. Extrapolative models use only historical earnings; index models are limited to the information in the chosen indices.

Analysts are not restricted in the information they can incorporate in their forecasts. Their broader set includes information that time-series models ignore, such as:

- The analysis of financial statements
- Assessment of the competitive environment
- Economic forecasts and company disclosures of current business conditions[53]

In addition, analysts possess a timing advantage in that they update their forecasts based on data available after publication of the annual (or quarterly) report. This information is not available for time-series forecasting until the publication of the next report.

Of course, FAFs are much costlier and time-consuming to generate than simple time-series forecasts. Bhushan (1989) analyzed analyst services as an economic good by examining the factors that affect the supply and demand for such services. His results are summarized in Exhibit 19-7. These results are only descriptive in the sense that they describe environments calling for more or fewer analyst services. Whether or not the services provided actually prove to be "useful" was not the focus of Bhushan's study.

A number of studies have compared analyst and time-series-based forecasts. These studies generally use publicly available analyst forecasts collected by services such as Zacks Investment Research and the Institutional Brokers Estimate System (IBES). These services collect data from a number of analysts. In addition, investor services such as Value Line, Moody's, and Standard & Poor's publish earnings forecasts.

EXHIBIT 19-7
Factors Influencing Degree of Analyst Coverage

Factors Leading to Increased Analyst Coverage

1. *Firm size.* The larger the firm, the greater the profit that can be earned on any piece of information. This would tend to increase analyst coverage. Additionally, to the extent (brokerage house) analysts are interested in increasing the volume of business for their firms, the larger the firm, the greater the potential for transactions business.
2. *Institutional holdings.* The number of analysts is positively related to both the number of institutions holding shares in a company and the percentage of shares held by institutions.
3. *Greater return variability.* The greater the uncertainty associated with a firm, the greater the need for analysts to provide information that may reduce that uncertainty.
4. *Correlation between firm and market return.* For information relating to macro variables, information acquisition costs are likely to be lower, and the more the firm's returns are correlated with the market. This lower cost would therefore increase analyst coverage.

Factors Leading to Decreased Analyst Coverage

5. *Insider holdings* (manager-controlled). The greater the percentage of shares held by insiders, the less demand there is for analysts as presumably the insiders have direct access to all the information they need.
6. *Degree of diversification.* The greater the number of segments, the more complex and costly it is to follow the company.

Source: Derived from Ravi Bhushan, "Firm Characteristics and Analyst Following," *Journal of Accounting and Economics* (July 1989), pp. 255–274.

---

[53]Few firms explicitly forecast earnings. Many do, however, provide "guidance" regarding future operating results to prevent surprises (especially negative ones) when actual earnings are released.

The results generally indicate that analyst forecasts are superior, but not dramatically. Givoly and Lakonishok (1984) surveyed comparisons of analyst forecasts with mechanical models and concluded that

> the common finding is that analysts predict earnings significantly more accurately than mechanical models.[54]

Similar results were reported by Brown, Hagerman, Griffin, and Zmijewski (1987), who found that forecasts generated by analysts outperformed the three quarterly earnings forecasting models described earlier. The superiority of the analyst forecasts is generally attributed to

- The richer information set available to analysts, as they are not limited to the past earnings series
- A timing advantage, as analyst forecasts are generated using information (such as interim reports and other announcements) closer to the actual earnings report

In a subsequent paper, Brown, Griffin, Hagerman, and Zmijewski (1987) noted that analyst expectations seem to be a better surrogate for market expectations than time-series forecasts. Market reaction to earnings announcements is more closely associated with errors in analyst forecasts than with errors emanating from time-series models. The predictive ability of analysts (or at the least the information utilized by them) seems to be recognized by the market in forming its aggregate expectations.[55]

Analyst Forecasts: Some Caveats

Not all the evidence as to the superiority of analysts' forecasting ability is clear cut. Dreman and Berry (1995) acknowledge that, although analyst forecasts may be superior to forecasts generated by alternative naïve extrapolative models, the magnitude of analyst forecast errors was "too large" to render them useful in any meaningful analysis. Their results indicated (for forecasts of quarterly earnings) mean percentage errors[56] equal to 44%. Furthermore, for their sample of over 66,000 (consensus) forecasts, more than 55% of them resulted in percentage errors greater than 10%; for 44%, the errors were greater than 15%. Additionally, their results confirmed earlier evidence [e.g., O'Brien (1988)] that analysts tend to be overly optimistic, resulting in forecasts that are upwards biased.

Improved Forecasting Ability or Earnings Management?

Brown (1997 and 2001) found that, although overall results were similar to those reported by Dreman and Berry, the characteristics of analyst forecast errors led to some intriguing findings. Figure 19-2, adapted from Brown (1997), is a histogram of the distribution of forecast

---

[54]Dan Givoly and Josef Lakonishok, "The Quality of Analysts' Forecasts of Earnings," *Financial Analysts Journal* (September–October 1984), pp. 40–47.

[55]Similar findings for annual earnings were reported by Dov Fried and Dan Givoly, "Financial Analysts' Forecasts of Earnings: A Better Surrogate for Market Expectations," *Journal of Accounting and Economics* (October 1982), pp. 85–108. They found that market expectations were more closely associated with analyst forecasts and financial analysts' forecasts of annual earnings were more accurate due to

> the existence of some timing advantage to forecasts that are made well after the end of the fiscal year and which presumably incorporate more recent information. However, the main contributor to the better performance of FAF is their ability to utilize a much broader set of information than that used by the univariate time-series models (p. 102).

[56]The percentage error is measured as

$$\frac{|\text{Actual quarterly EPS} - \text{Forcasted quarterly EPS}|}{\text{Actual quarterly EPS}}$$

where the numerator is the absolute value (ignoring the sign) of the error. Later we refer to earnings "surprise," which is identical to the above but without the absolute value sign (i.e., the actual positive or negative error).

Another measure, where the percentage error is divided by the forecasted quarterly EPS, yielded similar results.

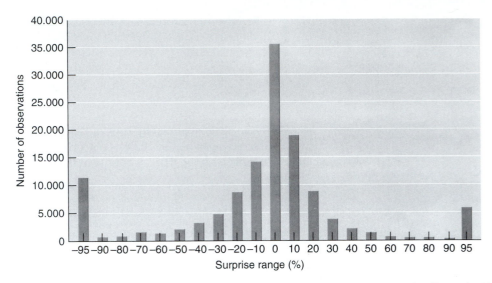

FIGURE 19-2 Frequency distribution of earnings surprises. *Source:* Lawrence D. Brown, "Analyst Forecasting Errors: Additional Evidence," *Financial Analysts Journal* (November–December 1997), Figure 1, p. 83.

"surprises."[57] The relative fat-tails[58] of the distribution are consistent with the high median forecast errors. Three characteristics of forecast surprises emerge from Figure 19-2:

1. The median (and modal) surprise is zero.
2. There are more small positive surprises than small negative surprises.
3. There are more large negative surprises than large positive surprises.

To some extent these results may reflect patterns of *earnings management* rather than *forecast accuracy.*

> These findings suggest that whereas analysts are more likely to be on target than anywhere else, managers may manipulate earnings in a way to generate a considerable number of small positive (relative to small negative) surprises and large negative (relative to large positive) surprises ("big baths").[59]

As discussed in Chapter 2, there is evidence that (managers perceive that) the market rewards firms whose earnings beat analyst forecasts. Hence, management may manage earnings to achieve that result (report small positive surprises). Similarly, when a firm is having an "off-year," and cannot report small positive surprises, there is evidence that managers engage in big-bath behavior (large negative surprises).

The increasing focus on meeting or beating analyst forecasts may also explain (to some extent) two other results documented by Brown. Brown shows that the magnitude of forecast errors has decreased over time as has the tendency for analysts to be optimistic.[60] Managers striving to "just beat" analyst forecasts can account for these phenomena.

Figure 19-3, adapted from Brown (2001), takes the analysis further by analyzing the pattern of median surprises separately for firms reporting profits as opposed to those reporting

---

[57]See previous footnote.

[58]The large number of observations at the two extreme ends of the distribution.

[59]Lawrence D. Brown, "Analyst Forecasting Errors: Additional Evidence," *Financial Analysts Journal* (November–December 1997), p. 82.

[60]These results predate the adoption of Regulation F-D by the SEC in 2000. There are some indications that the dispersion of analyst forecasts increased following that adoption. The Enron scandal, the end of the technology bubble, and the resulting scrutiny of the research practices of investment banking firms may also make these results period specific and therefore less likely to recur.

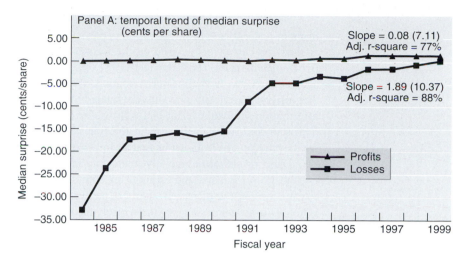

FIGURE 19-3 Temporal trend of median profit and loss surprises (cents per share). *Source:* Lawrence D. Brown, "A Temporal Analysis of Earnings Surprises: Profits versus Losses," *Journal of Accounting Research* (September 2001), Figure 2, Panel A, p. 231.

losses. For the 1984–1999 period, Brown reports that the median surprise (in cents/share) went from slightly negative to slightly positive for all firms as a whole. However, the

> shift from small negative to small positive describes neither profits nor losses. *For profits*, median surprise shifts temporally from zero to one cent per share, *indicating a shift from just meeting analyst estimates to beating them slightly. For losses*, median surprise shifts temporally from nearly −33 cents/share to zero *revealing a shift from failing to meet analyst estimates by a large amount to meeting them exactly.* (Emphasis added.)[61]

The situation thus seems to have reversed. Rather than analyst forecasts aiming to hit earnings—earnings are being aimed to hit (or beat) analyst forecasts.

Further evidence of this phenomenon relates to so-called growth versus value firms. Brown found that the former are more likely to report positive surprises and that these positive surprises tend to be reported as "little bits of good news."

Market Expectation and Anomalies

The fact that analyst forecasts tend to be a better surrogate for market expectations does not, however, mean that such forecasts (and market expectations conditioned on those forecasts) are "efficient." Earlier, we noted that the post-announcement drift phenomenon was consistent with analysts (and the market) not fully incorporating quarterly serial correlations when forming expectations, thereby underestimating the persistency of earnings [Abarbanell and Bernard (1992)]. Dechow and Sloan (1997) and Frankel and Lee (1998) both attribute (a significant portion of) the abnormal returns associated with the market-to-book anomaly to the market naïvely using analysts' forecasts in setting prices without adjusting for the shortcomings of those forecasts.

Large versus Small Firms

Brown, Griffin, Hagerman, and Zmijewski (1987) show that the superior performance of analyst forecasts as surrogates of market expectation is related to firm size. For smaller firms, pooling analyst forecasts with those of time-series models reduces the measurement error in unexpected earnings.

[61]Lawrence D. Brown, "A Temporal Analysis of Earnings Surprises: Profits versus Losses," *Journal of Accounting Research* (September 2001), p. 222.

These results are consistent with Brown (2001), who reported that earnings for larger firms in general, and S&P 500 firms in particular, were easier to forecast. The magnitude of analyst forecast errors as well as the forecast bias was smaller for larger firms. Similarly, Brown, Richardson, and Schwager (1987) examined factors accounting for the superiority of analyst forecasts over time-series models. After controlling for the timing effect, they find that analyst superiority is positively related to firm size, which they attribute to the broader information set available for larger firms. On the other hand, they find that the more difficult it was to forecast a given firm in the first place (as measured by forecast dispersion), the smaller the benefit from using analyst forecasts.

These results are especially interesting in light of Bhushan's (1989) findings, shown in Exhibit 19-7. Firm size and earnings uncertainty both contribute to increased analyst coverage. For the former, the increased supply of analyst services seems to be justified. For the latter, it is not. This is troublesome as, in precisely the environment (high uncertainty) where there is a need for analyst services, the analyst does not seem to outperform time-series models.

Individual versus Consensus Forecasts

The forecasting results discussed above generally were based on analysts' consensus (average or median) forecasts. However, some have argued in favor of using the most recent forecast, as more timely forecasts tend to be more accurate and more consistent with market expectations.[62]

The motivation for the use of consensus forecasts was to eliminate the idiosyncrasies of individual forecasters.[63] With respect to individual forecasters, Stickel (1989, 1990) notes that publicly available forecasts are often "stale." Forecasters may not continually update their forecasts, but rather wait for interim reports or other events (such as company meetings or press releases) to revise forecasts.[64] Using information from interim reports, Stickel demonstrates that it is possible to anticipate forecast revisions of individual analysts. Stickel does, however, note that those analysts with the best forecasting record were those whose forecasting behavior was the most difficult to predict. These analysts are able to add something to the simple extrapolation of interim results. More recently, Clement (1999) and Mikhail, Walther, and Wills (1999) show that analysts with better forecasting records tend to "survive" the longest.

FINANCIAL STATEMENT FORECASTS

Forecasting is an important aspect of financial analysis. Securities prices generally anticipate future earnings and cash flows. Analysis that ignores the future is incomplete.

In the previous section we discussed earnings forecasting models and the properties of analyst forecasts. Published analyst forecasts of earnings (per share) are common. We believe that such forecasts cannot be made in a vacuum; they must reflect expected cash flows and balance sheet changes. The objective of this section is to illustrate an integrated financial statement forecast.

Preparing projected financial statements[65] typically requires the following procedures:

1. *Analyze historical data.* Ratio analysis and the preparation of common size statements help the analyst determine the financial characteristics of the firm and its historical trends.

---

[62]See, for example, O'Brian (1988) and Brown and Kim (1991).

[63]Kirt C. Butler and Larry H. P. Lang, "The Forecast Accuracy of Individual Forecasts: Evidence of Systematic Optimism and Pessimism," *Journal of Accounting Research* (Spring 1991), pp. 150–156, for example, show that certain analysts tend to be "persistently optimistic or pessimistic relative to consensus forecasts."

[64]It is also possible that there is a time lag between when forecasts are revised and when those revisions are publicly reported.

[65]These projected financial statements are sometimes referred to as *pro forma* statements. We prefer to reserve the term *pro forma* for financial statements prepared following accounting procedures other than those required by GAAP. (See Chapters 2 and 14 for examples.)

2. *Project income statement.* The first step is to forecast sales. The elements of the income statement can then be projected from the company's cost structure and profitability ratios.

3. *Project the balance sheet.* The common size balance sheet as well as the firm's activity ratios can be used to project the level of assets (and liabilities) required to maintain the output levels projected by the income statement.

4. *Project the cash flow statement.* The cash flow statement can now be derived from the projected income statement and balance sheet.

These steps are generally not as sequential as laid out above. For example, some projected balance sheet elements (e.g., fixed assets and debt) are related to income statement components (e.g., depreciation and interest expense). To maintain consistency, such projections need to be done in tandem or through an iterative process.

These procedures are illustrated in the next section for a company we have created—Alpha Growth (Alpha).

Alpha Growth

Historical financial data of Alpha Growth are shown in Exhibit 19-8. Alpha is a growth company whose products are relatively insensitive to the business cycle. It has the following financial characteristics:

- Alpha operates entirely in the United States.
- Sales are expected to grow at 15% annually.
- High gross margin.
- The average depreciable life of fixed assets is nine years.
- Long-term debt has an interest rate of 7%.
- Tax rate is constant at 35%.

Analysis of Historical Data

We start by using the historical data in Exhibit 19-8 to do a common size and ratio analysis, shown in Exhibit 19-9. This analysis helps the analyst understand the financial characteristics of the company.

Exhibits 19-8, 19-9, and 19-10 lead to the following six observations about the income statement:

1. Sales increased 15% in 2000, in line with long-term expectations. Sales grew only 10% in 2001 as demand was lower than expected due to the U.S. recession.

2. Gross margins averaged nearly 70% over the 1999–2001 period, rising in 2000 but falling in 2001. The management discussion and analysis (MD&A) (not provided in the exhibit) stated that the 2000 rise reflected heavy 1999 expenditures to protect against year-2000 computer problems. The 2001 margin decline was due to disappointing sales growth.

3. Selling and administrative expense increased 12% in 2000 and 10% in 2001. The 2000 rate of increase was below that of sales as year-2000 expenses inflated the 1999 level. The 2001 increase reflected cost reductions as sales failed to meet expectations.

4. Depreciation expense rose each year as the company made new investments in productive capacity and software.

5. Interest expense declined in 2000 and in 2001 due to reduction of long-term debt. The interest coverage ratio rose as EBIT increased and interest expense fell.

6. As a result of all of the preceding items, operating and net margins increased significantly in 2000 but decline in 2001. Despite higher sales, net income declined in 2001.

EXHIBIT 19-8. ALPHA GROWTH
Historical Data (in $millions)

		Years Ending December 31	

Income Statement

	1999	2000	2001
Sales	$ 500.0	$ 575.0	$ 632.5
Cost of goods sold	(155.0)	(172.5)	(202.4)
Gross margin	$ 345.0	$ 402.5	$ 430.1
Selling and administrative	(165.0)	(181.5)	(203.3)
Depreciation expense	(60.0)	(72.2)	(82.8)
Operating income (EBIT)	$ 120.0	$ 148.8	$ 144.0
Interest expense	(11.0)	(10.5)	(8.8)
Pretax income	$ 109.0	$ 138.3	$ 135.3
Income tax expense	(38.2)	(48.4)	(47.4)
Net income	$ 70.9	$ 89.9	$ 87.9

Balance Sheet

Assets

Cash	$ 11.1	$ 23.0	$ 50.1
Accounts receivable	83.3	95.8	109.1
Inventories	12.9	14.4	18.4
Fixed assets (net)	500.0	527.8	535.0
Total assets	$ 607.3	$ 661.0	$ 712.5
Fixed assets gross	$ 600.0	$ 700.0	$ 790.0
Accumulated depreciation	(100.0)	(172.2)	(255.0)

Liabilities

Accounts payable	$ 25.8	$ 28.8	$ 33.7
Accrued liabilities	6.5	7.2	8.4
Long-term debt	150.0	125.0	100.0
Stockholders' equity	425.0	500.0	570.4
Total liabilities and equity	$ 607.3	$ 661.0	$ 712.5

Statement of Cash Flows

Net income	$ 70.9	$ 89.9	$ 87.9
Depreciation expense	60.0	72.2	82.8
Δ Accounts receivable	(10.0)	(12.5)	(13.2)
Δ Inventories	(5.0)	(1.5)	(4.0)
Δ Accounts payable	7.0	3.0	5.0
Δ Accrued liabilities	2.0	0.7	1.2
Cash from operations	$ 124.9	$ 151.8	$ 159.7
Capital expenditures	(80.0)	(100.0)	(90.0)
Cash for investment	$ (80.0)	$(100.0)	$ (90.0)
Repayment of debt	(10.0)	(25.0)	(25.0)
Dividends paid	(12.0)	(14.9)	(17.6)
Cash for financing	$ (22.0)	$ (39.9)	$ (42.6)
Net cash flow	22.9	11.9	27.1

Note: There are minor rounding errors in Exhibits 19-8, 19-9, and 19-10.

EXHIBIT 19-9. ALPHA GROWTH
Common Size and Ratio Analysis

	Years Ending December 31		
	1999	2000	2001

As % of Sales

Sales	100.0%	100.0%	100.0%
Cost of goods sold	−31.0%	−30.0%	−32.0%
Gross margin	69.0%	70.0%	68.0%
Selling and administrative	−33.0%	−31.6%	−32.1%
Depreciation expense	−12.0%	−12.6%	−13.1%
Operating income (EBIT)	24.0%	25.8%	22.8%
Interest expense	−2.2%	−1.8%	−1.4%
Pretax income	21.8%	24.0%	21.4%
Income tax expense	−7.6%	−8.4%	−7.5%
Net income	14.2%	15.6%	13.9%
Tax rate	35.0%	35.0%	35.0%
Interest coverage ratio	10.91	14.17	16.46

Balance Sheet

Accounts receivable/sales	0.167	0.167	0.172
Inventories/COGS	0.083	0.083	0.091
Accounts payable/COGS	0.167	0.167	0.167
Accrued liabilities/COGS	0.042	0.042	0.042
Sales-to-fixed assets ratio	0.840	0.885	0.849
Debt-to-equity ratio	35%	25%	18%
Return on total capital	20.9%	23.8%	21.5%
Return on equity	16.7%	18.0%	15.4%

Statement of Cash Flows

Free cash flow ($millions)	44.9	51.8	69.7
CFO to debt	0.83	1.21	1.60
Dividend payout ratio	0.17	0.17	0.20

Turning to the balance sheet and cash flow statement, we note the following:

- Accounts receivable equals .167 (2 months) of sales in 1999 and 2000, increasing slightly in 2001.
- Inventory equals .083 (1 month) of COGS in 1999 and 2000, increasing in 2001.
- Fixed assets grow due to high capital expenditures required by the high sales growth rate with an average fixed asset turnover ratio of approximately 0.85.
- Accounts payable equals .167 (2 months) of COGS for all years.
- Accrued liabilities equal .042 (½ month of COGS) for all years.
- Debt-to-equity ratio declines from 35% in 1999 to 18% in 2001.
- Return on total capital and return on equity rise in 2000 but fall in 2001 as shareholders' equity rises and income falls.
- Free cash flow rises each year. The CFO-to-debt ratio is high and rising.
- Dividend payout ratio rises from 17% in 1999 to approximately 20%.

Forecasting 2002 Data

We now turn to a forecast of 2002 financial statements. As the financial statements interconnect, we cannot forecast net income without forecasting the balance sheet and cash flow statement. We make the following assumptions about the income statement for 2002:

- Sales growth = 10% based on the U.S. recession and management expectations of a slow first half followed by a strong second half.
- Gross margin = 67%, below the 2001 level due to low sales growth.
- Selling and administrative expense falls to 31.6% of sales resulting in a rise of 8% as the cost-cutting efforts of management take effect.
- Depreciation expense depends on the level of capital spending. With projected sales of $695.8 million and a fixed asset turnover ratio of 0.85, $820 million of average fixed assets are required. As 2001 year-end fixed assets are $790 million, management has forecast capital expenditures of $60 million for 2002 (a decline of one-third from the 2001 level), as low growth postpones the need for new facilities. Capital spending of $60 million increases gross fixed assets to $850 million. Assuming that management has not provided a forecast of depreciation expense, we can estimate 2002 depreciation as follows:

$$\text{Average gross fixed assets}/9$$

where 9 is the average depreciable life of fixed assets.[66]

- *Interest expense:* Alpha's footnote (not shown) reports that its long-term debt bears a fixed interest rate of 7% and that debt payments of $25 million are required on December 31 of each year. Therefore interest expense for 2002 = .07 × $100 million = $7 million.
- *Income tax:* Alpha's normal tax rate is 35% and, unless management indicates a change, forecasts should use that rate.[67]

The forecast income statement for 2002 is shown in Exhibit 19-10. Lower gross margins are mostly offset by lower selling and interest expense relative to sales. The pretax margin is only marginally lower than the 2001 level. Pretax and net income rise as higher sales more than offset the slight margin decline.

Turning to the balance sheet, we must make assumptions about a number of ratios. For simplicity we assume that the following turnover ratios are unchanged from the 2001 level:[68]

- Accounts receivable turnover
- Inventory turnover
- Accounts payable turnover
- Accrued liabilities to COGS

These estimates should not be made lightly, especially when economic activity is accelerating or decelerating. Involuntary inventory accumulation is common when sales fail to meet expectations. Periods of recovery, on the other hand, are often accompanied by inventory reduction in the earliest stage as firms seek to restore their desired turnover ratio and to generate cash. Economic conditions can also affect the turnover of accounts receivable and payable as firms try to stretch out payments to conserve cash. Estimates of these ratios should be made only after considering historic trends, management comments, and quarterly data.

---

[66]We make the simplifying assumption that Alpha does not retire any fixed assets.

[67]See Chapter 9 for discussion of the factors affecting the effective tax rate.

[68]An alternative approach is to use the sales-to-total assets activity ratio to forecast total assets and then use (historical) common size statements to forecast the balance sheet components.

EXHIBIT 19-10. ALPHA GROWTH
Forecast (in $millions)

		Years Ending December 31		
	1999	2000	2001	Forecast 2002

Income Statement

Sales	$ 500.0	$ 575.0	$ 632.5	$ 695.8
Cost of goods sold	(155.0)	(172.5)	(202.4)	(229.6)
Gross margin	$ 345.0	$ 402.5	$ 430.1	$ 466.2
Selling and administrative	(165.0)	(181.5)	(203.3)	(219.5)
Depreciation expense	(60.0)	(72.2)	(82.8)	(91.1)
Operating income (EBIT)	$ 120.0	$ 148.8	$ 144.0	$ 155.5
Interest expense	(11.0)	(10.5)	(8.8)	(7.0)
Pretax income	$ 109.0	$ 138.3	$ 135.3	$ 148.5
Income tax expense	(38.2)	(48.4)	(47.4)	(52.0)
Net income	$ 70.9	$ 89.9	$ 87.9	$ 96.5

As % of Sales

Sales	100.0%	100.0%	100.0%	100.0%
Cost of goods sold	−31.0%	−30.0%	−32.0%	−33.0%
Gross margin	69.0%	70.0%	68.0%	67.0%
Selling and administrative	−33.0%	−31.6%	−32.1%	−31.6%
Depreciation expense	−12.0%	−12.6%	−13.1%	−13.1%
Operating income (EBIT)	24.0%	25.8%	22.8%	22.3%
Interest expense	−2.2%	−1.8%	−1.4%	−1.0%
Pretax income	21.8%	24.0%	21.4%	21.3%
Income tax expense	−7.6%	−8.4%	−7.5%	−7.5%
Net income	14.2%	15.6%	13.9%	13.9%

% Changes

Sales		15.0%	10.0%	10.0%
Cost of goods sold		11.3%	17.3%	13.4%
Gross margin		16.7%	6.9%	8.4%
Selling and administrative		10.0%	12.0%	8.0%
Depreciation expense		20.4%	14.6%	10.1%
Operating income (EBIT)		24.0%	−3.2%	8.0%
Interest expense		−4.5%	−16.7%	−20.0%
Pretax income		26.9%	−2.2%	9.8%
Net income		26.9%	−2.2%	9.8%

Tax rate	35.0%	35.0%	35.0%	35.0%
Interest coverage ratio	10.91	14.17	16.46	22.21

Balance Sheet

Assets

Cash	$ 11.1	$ 23.0	$ 50.1	$ 123.6
Accounts receivable	83.3	95.8	109.1	122.1
Inventories	12.9	14.4	18.4	20.9
Fixed assets (net)	500.0	527.8	535.0	503.9
Total assets	$ 607.3	$ 661.0	$ 712.5	$ 770.5
Fixed assets gross	$ 600.0	$ 700.0	$ 790.0	$ 850.0
Accumulated depreciation	(100.0)	(172.2)	(255.0)	(346.1)

(continued)

EXHIBIT 19-10 (continued)

Liabilities

Accounts payable	$ 25.8	$ 28.8	$ 33.7	$ 38.3
Accrued liabilities	6.5	7.2	8.4	9.6
Long-term debt	150.0	125.0	100.0	75.0
Stockholders' equity	425.0	500.0	570.4	647.6
Total liabilities and equity	$ 607.3	$ 661.0	$ 712.5	$ 770.5
Accounts receivables/sales	0.167	0.167	0.172	0.175
Inventories/COGS	0.083	0.083	0.091	0.091
Accounts payable/COGS	0.167	0.167	0.167	0.167
Accrued liabilities/COGS	0.042	0.042	0.042	0.042
Sales-to-fixed assets ratio	0.840	0.885	0.849	0.848
Debt-to-equity ratio	35%	25%	18%	12%
Return on total capital	20.9%	23.8%	21.5%	21.5%
Return on equity	16.7%	18.0%	15.4%	14.9%

Statement of Cash Flows

Net income	$ 70.9	$ 89.9	$ 87.9	$ 96.5
Depreciation expense	60.0	72.2	82.8	91.1
Δ Accounts receivable	(10.0)	(12.5)	(13.2)	(13.0)
Δ Inventories	(5.0)	(1.5)	(4.0)	(2.5)
Δ Accounts payable	7.0	3.0	5.0	4.6
Δ Accrued liabilities	2.0	0.7	1.2	1.1
Cash from operations	$ 124.9	$ 151.8	$ 159.7	$ 177.8
Capital expenditures	(80.0)	(100.0)	(90.0)	(60.0)
Cash for investment	$ (80.0)	$(100.0)	$ (90.0)	$ (60.0)
Δ Long-term debt	(10.0)	(25.0)	(25.0)	(25.0)
Dividends paid	(12.0)	(14.9)	(17.6)	(19.3)
Cash for financing	$ (22.0)	$ (39.9)	$ (42.6)	$ (44.3)
Net cash flow	22.9	11.9	27.1	73.5
Change in cash	22.9	11.9	27.1	73.5
Free cash flow	44.9	51.8	69.7	117.8
CFO to debt	0.83	1.21	1.60	2.37
Dividend payout ratio	0.17	0.17	0.20	0.20

The remaining balance sheet items are relatively easy to forecast:

- Gross fixed assets = 2001 level plus 2002 capital expenditures.
- Accumulated depreciation = 2001 level plus 2002 depreciation expense.[69]
- Long-term debt = 2001 level less $25 million payment (see interest expense above).
- Stockholders' equity = 2001 level plus 2002 net income, less dividends paid. We assume that Alpha continues to increase its dividend, but at a lower rate than in prior years due to the economic slowdown.

The resulting balance sheet at December 31, 2002 is shown in Exhibit 19-10 along with the forecast turnover ratios, the debt-to-equity ratio, and two return ratios.

---

[69]As stated in footnote 66, we assume no fixed asset retirement. In practice, both gross fixed assets and accumulated depreciation are reduced by asset sales and retirements. Asset impairment charges may also be present. See Chapter 8 for further discussion and analysis.

Finally, we forecast the cash flow statement. Due to the interrelationships among the three financial statements, no further assumptions are required. Cash from operations accelerates, and free cash flow grows even faster due to lower capital spending. Cash increases by $73.5 million.

The resulting forecasts can be summarized as follows:

1. On a sales increase of 10%, operating income increases 8% and net income 9.8%.
2. Return on total capital is flat while ROE decreases as equity increases faster than net income.
3. Higher earnings and depreciation expense result in higher cash from operations. Higher CFO combines with lower capital expenditures to generate a substantial increase in free cash flow. Given the low (and declining) debt-to-equity ratio, Alpha has substantial financial flexibility to fund internal growth, acquisitions, or share repurchases.

Annual forecasts should be adjusted as each interim period is reported. Quarterly results that are inconsistent with the assumptions made for the annual forecast should result in the review of those assumptions and other forecast parameters.

Review

Forecasting future results, while a key part of the analyst's job, is not an easy exercise. Even for the relatively simple example of Alpha, forecasts are greatly dependent on the assumptions made. Real companies are much more complex.

The Alpha example is intended as a template to show how to go about making forecasts. The key steps are:

1. Assemble the historical data and compute the related financial ratios.
2. Make the required assumptions about the forecast period, considering the economic environment, your understanding of the company's business, and management statements. Make sure that the assumptions are consistent and allow for any nonoperating items during the historical or forecast periods.
3. Use the historical data and assumptions to forecast all three financial statements. Be sure to consider the interrelationships among them (such as between capital spending and depreciation expense).
4. Test alternative assumptions to establish the sensitivity of key forecasts (such as earnings per share and cash from operations) to unexpected changes in economic conditions.

SUMMARY

Chapter 19 has two critical objectives.

1. First, together with Chapters 17 and 18, it provides both a summation and integration of the preceding chapters by presenting models that use the variables generated by the analysis in those chapters.
2. Equally important, it introduces the final phase in the use and analysis of financial statements: forecasts of the additional variables required for decision making.

These objectives are complementary in that the analyses in the earlier chapters are essential if the variables used in decision models are to reflect the economics of the firm rather than accounting choice. Forecasts based on reported data alone, which ignore the database inherent in financial statements, are mechanical exercises at best.

The first part of this chapter discusses valuation models based on discounted cash flows, earnings, net assets, and abnormal earnings. It is not surprising that these diverse models are conceptually equivalent. Although reported cash flows and earnings can diverge sharply in the short run (and, as we have shown, there may be some permanent differences as well), they tend toward equality over longer time periods. As net assets include the cumulative impact of earnings, changes in net assets reflect earnings (as well as capital transactions).

The discussion of asset-based valuation models includes a reexamination of the impact of dividend policy, equity transactions, acquisitions, exchange rate changes, and accounting methods on net assets. The discussion of discounted cash flow and earnings models provides a similar reevaluation. These reviews reinforce the view, presented throughout this text, that both economic and accounting factors must be considered when using financial data.

The second part of the chapter is quite unlike the preceding sections of the book in that it describes and evaluates statistical procedures useful in forecasting. However, it relies on the preceding chapters through reminders that financial data used in forecasting models may require adjustment. The discussion of forecasting, as always in this text, is primarily concerned with the rationale for the analytic techniques used rather than the mechanics of forecasting, which is left to technical statistics and econometrics texts.

The chapter concludes with an example of the use of historical financial data and relationships to forecast financial statements. The integrated nature of financial statements requires that the balance sheet and statement of cash flows be forecast simultaneously with the income statement, with compatible assumptions.

Chapter 19 closes the cycle that started with the framework for financial statement analysis presented in Chapter 1. Our goal has been to take the reader from the basics of financial reporting through the valuation models and forecasts that, ultimately, are the basis for investment decisions. The theme of this text has been that the financial analyst, armed with knowledge of the financial reporting system and analytical techniques that exploit the shortcomings of that system, can make better informed investment decisions.

Chapter 19

Problems

1. [Dividend- versus earnings-based models; CFA© adapted] The Director of Research has asked you to recommend whether the Green Fund should add shares of Emfil stock to its portfolio. Apply the following valuation data to Emfil and determine the attractiveness of its shares, using the:

   (i) Dividend discount model

   (ii) Earnings discount model

EMFIL COMPANY
Valuation Data, June 30, 2003

	Amount	Percentage Change from Prior Year
Current price per share	$115	
2002 earnings per share	10.03	28%
2002 dividends per share	4.05	29
Current annual dividends per share	4.50	11
2003 estimated earnings per share	11.40	14
Predicted long-term growth rates		
Dividends per share	15%	
Earnings per share	14	
Discount rate	20	

2. [Permanent versus transitory earnings and growth] The CF company, an all-equity company, has a policy of paying out all earnings as dividends. The company's earnings per share remain constant at $10 per share. CF stock sells at a price/earnings ratio of 12. The company has not issued any shares in recent years.

a. Calculate the firm's cost of (equity) capital.

b. For the most recent year, the firm reports earnings per share of $13. Consider three possible price/earnings ratios (on current-year earnings per share):

   (i) Below 12

   (ii) Equal to 12

   (iii) Greater than 12

Discuss what each ratio implies about whether the earnings increase is permanent or nonrecurring.

3. [Effect of dividend policy on valuation] The historical earnings per share and dividends per share for the Lo Company (Lo) and Hi Company (Hi) follow:

	2001	2002	2003	2004	2005
Lo Company					
Earnings per share	$1.00	$1.04	$1.08	$1.12	$1.17
Dividends per share	0.200	0.208	0.216	0.225	0.234
Hi Company					
Earnings per share	1.00	0.80	0.64	0.51	0.41
Dividends per share	1.00	0.80	0.64	0.51	0.41

A portfolio manager has just handed you these data with a perplexed look, stating: "Look at these numbers. Both companies are in the same industry. Neither has any debt. The EPS of one are obviously growing; the other's EPS are declining. The funny thing about it is that, although Hi's EPS are declining, its market value is identical to that of Lo, and it is constantly able to sell new shares in the equity market. Lo hasn't obtained external financing in years. I just don't get it!"

Preliminary investigation indicates that the capital expenditures of both companies are identical each year. Furthermore, you find that the appropriate discount rate for the industry in question is 10%.

a. Calculate the appropriate price/earnings (P/E) ratio for Lo, based on the above data.

b. Determine the appropriate price/earnings ratio for Hi. (*Hint:* Consider the P/E ratio of Lo.)

c. Complete the following table. To simplify, assume that 2001 net income was $1,000 for each company and any new financing by Hi was effected at the end of the year. Further, assume that depreciation expense is sufficient to cover the replacement of assets.

	2001	2002	2003	2004	2005
Lo Company					
Earnings per share	$1.00	$1.04	$1.08	$1.12	$1.17
Number of shares outstanding	1,000				
Net income	$1,000				
Dividends paid	200				
New investment	800				
Firm value at period end					
Price per share					
P/E ratio					

	2001	2002	2003	2004	2005
Hi Company					
Earnings per share	$1.00	$0.80	$0.64	$0.51	$0.41
Number of shares outstanding	1,000				
Net income	$1,000				
Dividends paid	1,000				
New investment	800				
New financing	800				
Firm value at period end					
P/E ratio					
Price per share before new issue					
P/E ratio					
Shares issued					
Price per share at new issue					

d. Calculate the growth rate of net income, dividends paid, and firm value for both companies. Explain why Hi's earnings

per share growth rate is not consistent with these growth rates.

e. The P/E ratio is relatively low for both companies. Explain why. Discuss the companies' returns on new investments.

4. [Extension of previous problem; application of EBO model] The previous problem suggests that when new investments are not profitable, companies are better off paying out all earnings as dividends.

a. Assuming an opening book value of $10,000, show how the EBO model demonstrates this point.

b. Redo part a, assuming an opening book value of:

(i) $9,000

(ii) $11,000

5. [Valuation with free cash flows; alternate financing modes] You are considering investing in a new joint venture. The investment is expected to have a two-year life. In addition to equity financing, the syndicate intends to borrow $10 million at the current market rate of 10%. There is some debate, however, as to whether the debt should be incurred by issuing:

(i) "Conventional" notes with annual interest payments

(ii) Zero-coupon notes

These funds would be borrowed January 1, 2003, and repaid January 1, 2005.

Projected income statements and cash flow from operations under both alternatives follow (in $millions):

	Conventional		Zero-Coupon	
	2003	2004	2003	2004
Earnings before interest and taxes	$20.00	$20.00	$20.00	$20.00
Interest expense*	(1.00)	(1.00)	(1.00)	(1.10)
Earnings before taxes	$19.00	$19.00	$19.00	$18.90
Income tax expense (30% rate)	(5.70)	(5.70)	(5.70)	(5.67)
Net income	$13.30	$13.30	$13.30	$13.23
Noncash charges*	0	0	1.00	1.10
Cash from operations	$13.30	$13.30	$14.30	$14.33

*Interest expense on the zero-coupon bond, although not paid currently, is tax-deductible.

Some investors support the zero-coupon alternative, given the higher cash from operations in both years.

a. Calculate free cash flow for each year under *both* alternatives.

b. Calculate the cash flows for debtholders and the firm for *each* of the years 2003–2004 under *both* alternatives.

c. Calculate funds available for dividend payments *each year under both alternatives.* (*Hint:* Consider where the funds required to repay debt will come from.)

d. Discuss whether the zero-coupon note is the better financing alternative from the investor point of view.

6. [Valuation models; calculation of free cash flows] The LZ Company income statement for the current year and the forecast for the coming year follow:

	Current	Forecast
Sales	$100,000	$112,000
Cost of goods sold	(40,000)	(44,800)
Selling expense	(25,000)	(28,000)
Operating income	$ 35,000	$ 39,200
Interest expense	(5,000)	(5,600)
Net income	$ 30,000	$ 33,600

The forecast is based on a projected growth rate of 12% arising from new investment opportunities. To simplify, assume that income taxes are zero and depreciation expense approximates replacement cost. Depreciation for the current year is $8,000 and is included in selling expense.

Assume that the cost of equity capital is 15%, the cost of debt 10%, and the rate of return on the firm's new investment opportunities 20%.

a. Based on the data provided, calculate the firm's implied dividend payout ratio.

b. Calculate the firm's total capital expenditures (for replacement and new investment) for the current year. Calculate how much of the new investment will come from debt and how much from equity.

c. Prepare a statement of cash flows for the current and forecast years.

d. Calculate the company's free cash flow for the current and forecast years.

e. Calculate, as of the end of the current year, the value of:
  (i) The firm
  (ii) Its equity
  (iii) Its debt

7. [Extension of Problem 19-6; application of EBO model] Estimate the value of the firm's equity using the EBO framework and the data in Problem 19-6. Assume that the current period's (closing) book value equals:
  (i) $168,000
  (ii) $212,000

8. [Extension of Problem 19-6; treatment of leases in free cash flow calculations] Use the same basic assumptions as in Problem 19-6. However, now assume that LZ has decided to lease assets instead of borrowing funds for capital expenditures. Assets exceeding those that the company can acquire using internally generated (equity) funds will be leased. The interest rate on leases is the same as for other debt, 10%.

Current income statements are unchanged from Problem 19-6. Two forecast statements are shown: One assumes that leases are operating leases; the second assumes that they are capital leases. Both statements assume a five-year lease term. The capital lease forecast assumes straight-line depreciation. (*Note:*

No longer assume that straight-line depreciation for leased assets approximates replacement cost.)

		Forecast	
	Current	Operating	Capital
Sales	$100,000	$112,000	$112,000
Cost of goods sold	(40,000)	(44,800)	(44,800)
Selling expense	(25,000)	(29,343)	(28,960)
Operating income	$ 35,000	$ 37,857	$ 38,240
Interest expense	(5,000)	(5,000)	(5,600)
Net income	$ 30,000	$ 32,857	$ 33,640

a. Calculate the annual lease payments.

b. Reconcile the forecast income statements under *both* the operating and capital lease methods with the forecast income statement in Problem 19-6.

c. Prepare a statement of cash flows for the current and forecast years, assuming that the leases are reported as *operating* leases. Describe how the "acquisition" of the leased assets is reported in the financial statements.

d. Prepare a statement of cash flows for the current and forecast years, assuming that the leases are reported as *capital* leases. Again, describe how the acquisition of the leased assets is reported in the financial statements.

e. Calculate the company's free cash flows for the current and forecast years, assuming that the leases are reported as:
  (i) Operating leases
  (ii) Capital leases

f. Redo Problem 19-6e. Discuss how lease financing affects the value of the firm, its equity, and its debt.

g. Discuss what this problem suggests regarding the treatment of leases in a valuation model.

9. [Projecting financial statements] Beta Manufacturing (Beta) manufactures and sells products whose demand is sensitive to the level of industrial output. Exhibit 19P-1 contains financial statement data for the three years ended December 31, 2001.

a. Prepare a common size income statement for the three years ended December 31, 2001.

b. Forecast the 2002 income statement, balance sheet, and statement of cash flows for Beta using the data in Exhibit 19P-1, your answer to part a, and the following assumptions:
  • Sales increase of 15%.
  • Gross margin of 60%.
  • Increase of 3% in selling and administrative expense.
  • Other financial statement relationships (ratios) are unchanged from 2001.

EXHIBIT 19P-1. BETA MANUFACTURING
Financial Data (in $millions)

Years Ending December 31

	1999	2000	2001
Income Statement			
Sales	$ 400.0	$ 440.0	$ 352.0
Cost of goods sold	(160.0)	(184.8)	(133.8)
Gross margin	$ 240.0	$ 255.2	$ 218.2
Selling and administrative	(60.0)	(64.7)	(64.1)
Depreciation expense	(45.0)	(53.8)	(59.3)
Operating income	$ 135.0	$ 136.7	$ 94.8
Interest expense	(40.0)	(45.6)	(46.4)
Pretax income	$ 95.0	$ 91.1	$ 48.4
Income tax expense	(33.2)	(31.9)	(16.9)
Net income	$ 61.8	$ 59.2	$ 31.5
Balance Sheet			
Assets			
Cash	$ 33.4	$ 30.0	$ 38.4
Accounts receivable	66.7	73.3	73.3
Inventories	26.7	30.8	27.9
Fixed assets (net)	900.0	996.3	1,008.0
Total assets	$1,026.7	$1,130.4	$1,147.6
Fixed assets (gross)	$1,000.0	$1,150.0	$1,221.0
Accumulated depreciation	(100.0)	(153.8)	(213.0)
Liabilities			
Accounts payable	$ 20.0	$ 23.1	$ 16.7
Accrued liabilities	6.7	7.7	5.6
Long-term debt	500.0	570.0	580.0
Stockholders' equity	500.0	529.6	545.3
Total liabilities and equity	$1,026.7	$1,130.4	$1,147.6
Statement of Cash Flows			
Net income	$ 61.8	$ 59.2	$ 31.5
Depreciation expense	45.0	53.8	59.3
Δ Accounts receivable	(7.0)	(6.7)	—
Δ Inventories	(6.0)	(4.1)	2.9
Δ Accounts payable	5.0	3.1	(6.4)
Δ Accrued liabilities	2.0	1.0	(2.1)
Cash from operations	$ 100.8	$ 106.3	$ 85.2
Capital expenditures	(100.0)	(150.0)	(71.0)
Cash for investment	$ (100.0)	$ (150.0)	$ (71.0)
Net borrowings	30.0	70.0	10.0
Dividends paid	(30.9)	(29.6)	(15.7)
Cash for financing	$ (0.9)	$ 40.4	$ (5.7)
Net cash flow	(0.1)	(3.3)	8.4

Note: There are minor rounding errors in Exhibit 19-P1.

c. Discuss the expected impact on your forecast if the 2002 sales increase is

 (i) 10%

 (ii) 20%

Your answer should include the impact on each of the following:

- Pretax margins
- Cash from operations
- Debt-to-equity ratio

State any assumptions made.

10. [Using ratios as forecasting tools; valuation with changing growth patterns] Exhibit 19P-2 presents comparative income statements (2001 and 2002) and comparative balance sheets (2000–2002) for the EFF Company.

At the end of 2002, the company forecast a dramatic increase in sales for 2003, 2004, and 2005:

Sales Forecast

2003	$150,000
2004	180,000
2005	200,000

After 2005, the company expects sales to stabilize at the 2005 level.

a. Prepare a statement of cash flows for 2002 and an estimate of free cash flow.

b. Using the relationships and ratios implied by the financial statements in Exhibit 19P-2, forecast the income statements and balance sheets for 2003–2005.

c. Use the forecast balance sheets and income statements to estimate free cash flow for 2003–2005.

d. Assuming a cost of equity of 15%, estimate the value of the EFF Company at the end of 2002.

11. [The EBO model; alternative accounting methods] Selected data for the Expac Company are:

1/1/2000	Stockholders' equity	$5,000
2000	Income before restructuring costs	1,000

At the end of 2000, the company considers a major restructuring. Given the nature of the restructuring, the company has the flexibility to recognize the $300 restructuring cost either:

 (i) As a $300 expense in 2000, or

 (ii) As expenses of $150 in 2001, $100 in 2002, and $50 in 2003

EXHIBIT 19P-2. EFF COMPANY
Selected Financial Data for Years Ended December 31

A. Income Statement

	2001	2002
Sales	$100,000	$110,000
Cost of goods sold	(50,000)	(53,000)
Selling and general expense	(20,000)	(22,000)
Operating income	$ 30,000	$ 35,000
Interest expense	(3,000)	(3,000)
Income before tax	$ 27,000	$ 32,000
Tax expense	(10,800)	(12,800)
Net income	$ 16,200	$ 19,200
Earnings per share	$ 16.20	$ 19.20

B. Balance Sheet

	2000	2001	2002
Cash	$ 7,000	$ 9,000	$ 11,000
Accounts receivable	8,000	8,500	9,000
Inventory	6,000	6,000	6,000
Current assets	$ 21,000	$ 23,500	$ 26,000
Fixed assets, gross	83,000	94,000	103,000
Accumulated depreciation	(24,000)	(32,500)	(41,000)
Fixed assets, net	$ 59,000	$ 61,500	$ 62,000
Total assets	$ 80,000	$ 85,000	$ 88,000
Accounts payable	$ 8,000	$ 8,500	$ 9,000
Long-term debt	30,000	30,000	30,000
Stockholders' equity	42,000	46,500	49,000
Total liabilities and stockholders' equity	$ 80,000	$ 85,000	$ 88,000

Under alternative i, 2000 net income will be $700, and closing book value B_{2000} will be $5,700. Under alternative ii, 2000 net income will be $1,000, and closing book value B_{2000} will be $6,000.

a. Using the template(s) provided below as a guide, show that the EBO valuation model is immune to the choice of accounting recognition methods. Assume that the valuation is made at the *end* of 2000 and:

- Income before restructuring costs will grow by $50 in each of the next three years.
- No dividends are paid.
- The discount rate is 10%.
- The recognition method chosen does not affect the actual cash flows associated with the restructuring.

$300 Restructuring Charge Taken in 2000

	Opening Book Value	Income Before Restructuring	Restructuring Charge	Net Income	0.10 × Opening Book Value	Abnormal Earnings
2001	$5,700	$1,050	0	$1,050	$570	$480
2002			0			
2003			0			

Book value at the end of 2003 _____.

B_{2000} + present value of abnormal earnings in years 2001, 2002, and 2003 _____.

Restructuring Charge Recognized over Next Three Years

	Opening Book Value	Income Before Restructuring	Restructuring Charge	Net Income	0.10 × Opening Book Value	Abnormal Earnings
2001	$6,000	$1,050	$150	$900	$600	$300
2002			100			
2003			50			

Book value at the end of 2003 _____.

B_{2000} + present value of abnormal earnings in years 2001, 2002, and 2003 _____.

b. Now assume that the valuation is made as of the *beginning* of 2000 and the firm is already aware of its restructuring choices. Opening book value is $5,000 in both cases. However, 2000 net income differs with the accounting choice.

(i) Discuss whether abnormal earnings differ for years 2001, 2002, and 2003.

(ii) Show that the EBO valuation as of the beginning of 2000 is also immune to the choice of recognition methods.

12. [Valuation; CFA© adapted] Following its October 1988 announcement that it was prepared to purchase all of Kraft's outstanding shares at $90.00 per share, Philip Morris's own shares dropped $4.50 to $95.50 per share. At the time of the announcement, it was assumed that Philip Morris would raise the funds required for the takeover by issuing 11% notes. Prior to the merger, Philip Morris's earnings growth rate approximated 20%; Kraft's earnings growth rate was 8%. Selected financial data follow (in $millions, except per-share data):

October 1988	Philip Morris	Kraft
Common shares outstanding (millions)	234	120
Price per share (preannouncement)	$100	$65
Long-term debt	4,700	800
Stockholders' equity	7,394	1,920
Earnings before interest and tax	$4,340	$796
Interest expense	(475)	(81)
Pretax income	$3,865	$715
Income tax expense	(1,623)	(279)
Net income	$2,242	$436
Cash flow from operations	$2,974	$607
Capital expenditures	850	260
Dividends paid	892	251
Earnings per share	$9.58	$3.63

a. Using an asset-based valuation approach and assuming that market prices prior to the merger were appropriate, predict the price change for Philip Morris shares that should have followed the merger announcement.

b. Suggest why the actual decline in Philip Morris shares following the merger announcement was significantly different from your forecast in part a.

c. The discussion of discounted cash flow (DCF) valuation models in the chapter suggests that the models are identical in theory and the main differences are in their ease of application. For *each* of the three DCF models discussed in the chapter:

(i) Dividend discount model

(ii) Earnings-based model

(iii) Free cash flow model

discuss the difficulties in using the model to predict the change in Philip Morris's stock price following the merger announcement. Describe the advantages that one model may have over the others. (*Hint:* Focus on the *change* in the value of Philip Morris rather than the value itself.)

13. [Cash flow and valuation] On March 1, 1993, the *New York Times* "Market Place" column featured an article by Robert Hurtado entitled "Analysts Urge Investors to Look Beyond Earnings at Cash Flow."

"Analyzing the cash flow, which is generally defined as net income plus depreciation and amortization costs, of a company enables an investor to see beyond the bottom line and unearth hidden values," said Allison Bisno, director of research for Stephens, Inc., a brokerage firm in Little Rock, Ark. "Cash flows often show a company's future earnings potential, which may be more dramatic than the current net income indicates."

To identify bargain stocks on this basis, an investor needs first to calculate the issue's price-to-cash-flow

EXHIBIT 19P-3
Standard and Poor's Defines Core Earnings

Widely Supported "Core Earnings" Approach to Be Applied to Earnings Analyses and Forecasts for U.S. Indices, Company Data, and Equity Research

New York, May 14, 2002—Standard & Poor's today published a set of new definitions it will use for equity analysis to evaluate corporate operating earnings of publicly held companies in the United States. Release of "Measures of Corporate Earnings" completes a process Standard & Poor's began in August 2001 when the firm began discussions with securities and accounting analysts, portfolio managers, academic research groups and others to build a consensus for changes that will reduce investor frustration and confusion over growing differences in the reporting of corporate earnings.

At the center of Standard & Poor's effort to return transparency and consistency to corporate reporting is a focus on what it refers to as Core Earnings, or the after-tax earnings generated from a corporation's principal business or businesses. Since Standard & Poor's believes that there is a general understanding of what is included in As Reported Earnings, its definition of Core Earnings begins with As Reported and then makes a series of adjustments. As Reported Earnings are earnings as defined by Generally Accepted Accounting Principles (GAAP), which excludes two items—discontinued operations and extraordinary items, both as defined by GAAP. . . .

Included in Standard & Poor's definition of Core Earnings are employee stock options grant expenses, restructuring charges from on-going operations, write-downs of depreciable or amortizable operating assets, pensions costs and purchased research and development. Excluded from this definition are impairment of goodwill charges, gains or losses from asset sales, pension gains, unrealized gains or losses from hedging activities, merger and acquisition related fees and litigation settlements.

Source: Standard & Poor's Press Release (May 14, 2002).

---

ratio. . . . Wall Street analysts say that stocks are now trading at about 11 times cash flow and investors should seek companies whose shares are trading below this multiple.

The best opportunities naturally lie in companies that have strong corporate earnings and good cash flow, along with a low stock price.

On February 15, 2002, a *New York Times* article by Floyd Norris was entitled "Can Investors Believe Cash Flow Numbers?"

"You can't fake cash flow."

Well, actually, you can.

As corporate America became better at managing earnings in the 1990s—normally using tactics that corporate officials regarded as proper but sometimes pushing on to methods that auditors knew would outrage the Securities and Exchange Commission if it found out about them—investors reassured themselves that if they only looked at cash flow, they would be safe.

Now we know that accountants rose to the challenge. If investors wanted to see operating cash flow, well, by jiggery, they would see it. Cash flow mirages are crucial parts of what went on at Enron and Global Crossing.

Enron found ways to borrow money and report the cash as if it were real operating cash flow. The S.E.C. will decide whether Enron found clever ways around accounting rules, or whether it flouted the rules. Either way, investors were misled.

At Global Crossing, the company traded capacity with other fiber optics companies. In reality, almost nothing happened, but both companies involved in a swap were able to report revenue without offsetting expenses. They treated their purchases as capital investments. So the companies reported profits and operating cash flows. . . .

Global Crossing's accounting appears to be within the rules—so long as the transactions were not shams. Whether or not they are viewed that way will probably be the major issue the S.E.C. will face in determining if fraud charges are warranted. But for investors, the big issue is that they did not know just how unreal the cash flow was.

a. Comment on the investment approach advocated by Hurtado in the 1993 article. Your answer should include a discussion of:

(i) Any theoretical basis for a price-to-cash-flow ratio

(ii) The advantages and disadvantages of using this ratio to select investments as compared with using the price/earnings ratio

b. Discuss the effect of the issues raised by Norris in the 2002 article on your answer to part a.

c. Discuss whether the price-to-free-cash-flow approach to valuation remedies the issues raised in parts a and b.

14. [Earnings and Valuation] Exhibit 19P-3 contains excerpts from a press release concerning Standard & Poor's decision to use "core earnings" to evaluate corporate performance.

a. Discuss how S&P's definition of *core earnings* is related to *each* of the following definitions of income: operating income, permanent income, sustainable income, and economic income.

b. Many believe that a single number cannot be used to measure the performance of a complex organization. Assuming this statement is correct, discuss the benefits of defining core earnings.

c. Discuss the significance for valuation of the differences between reported earnings and core earnings.

d. Prepare a letter, as a user of S&P's ratings that are based on core earnings, that states your views on their decision. (Be brief and to the point.)

TABLE 1
Amount of 1

$$a = (1 + i)^n$$

(n) PERIODS	2%	2.5%	3%	4%	5%	6%	8%	9%	10%	12%	15%	(n) PERIODS
1	1.02000	1.02500	1.03000	1.04000	1.05000	1.06000	1.08000	1.09000	1.10000	1.12000	1.15000	1
2	1.04040	1.05063	1.06090	1.08160	1.10250	1.12360	1.16640	1.18810	1.21000	1.25440	1.32250	2
3	1.06121	1.07689	1.09273	1.12486	1.15763	1.19102	1.25971	1.29503	1.33100	1.40493	1.52088	3
4	1.08243	1.10381	1.12551	1.16986	1.21551	1.26248	1.36049	1.41158	1.46410	1.57352	1.74901	4
5	1.10408	1.13141	1.15927	1.21665	1.27628	1.33823	1.46933	1.53862	1.61051	1.76234	2.01136	5
6	1.12616	1.15969	1.19405	1.26532	1.34010	1.41852	1.58687	1.67710	1.77156	1.97382	2.31306	6
7	1.14869	1.18869	1.22987	1.31593	1.40710	1.50363	1.71382	1.82804	1.94872	2.21068	2.66002	7
8	1.17166	1.21840	1.26677	1.36857	1.47746	1.59385	1.85093	1.99256	2.14359	2.47596	3.05902	8
9	1.19509	1.24886	1.30477	1.42331	1.55133	1.68948	1.99900	2.17189	2.35795	2.77308	3.51788	9
10	1.21899	1.28008	1.34392	1.48024	1.62889	1.79085	2.15892	2.36736	2.59374	3.10585	4.04556	10
11	1.24337	1.31209	1.38423	1.53945	1.71034	1.89830	2.33164	2.58043	2.85312	3.47855	4.65239	11
12	1.26824	1.34489	1.42576	1.60103	1.79586	2.01220	2.51817	2.81266	3.13843	3.89598	5.35025	12
13	1.29361	1.37851	1.46853	1.66507	1.88565	2.13293	2.71962	3.06580	3.45227	4.36349	6.15279	13
14	1.31948	1.41297	1.51259	1.73168	1.97993	2.26090	2.93719	3.34173	3.79750	4.88711	7.07571	14
15	1.34587	1.44830	1.55797	1.80094	2.07893	2.39656	3.17217	3.64248	4.17725	5.47357	8.13706	15
16	1.37279	1.48451	1.60471	1.87298	2.18287	2.54035	3.42594	3.97031	4.59497	6.13039	9.35762	16
17	1.40024	1.52162	1.65285	1.94790	2.29202	2.69277	3.70002	4.32763	5.05447	6.86604	10.76126	17
18	1.42825	1.55966	1.70243	2.02582	2.40662	2.85434	3.99602	4.71712	5.55992	7.68997	12.37545	18
19	1.45681	1.59865	1.75351	2.10685	2.52695	3.02560	4.31570	5.14166	6.11591	8.61276	14.23177	19
20	1.48595	1.63862	1.80611	2.19112	2.65330	3.20714	4.66096	5.60441	6.72750	9.64629	16.36654	20
21	1.51567	1.67958	1.86029	2.27877	2.78596	3.39956	5.03383	6.10881	7.40025	10.80385	18.82152	21
22	1.54598	1.72157	1.91610	2.36992	2.92526	3.60354	5.43654	6.65860	8.14027	12.10031	21.64475	22
23	1.57690	1.76461	1.97359	2.46472	3.07152	3.81975	5.87146	7.25787	8.95430	13.55235	24.89146	23
24	1.60844	1.80873	2.03279	2.56330	3.22510	4.04893	6.34118	7.91108	9.84973	15.17863	28.62518	24
25	1.64061	1.85394	2.09378	2.66584	3.38635	4.29187	6.84848	8.62308	10.83471	17.00006	32.91895	25
26	1.67342	1.90029	2.15659	2.77247	3.55567	4.54938	7.39635	9.39916	11.91818	19.04007	37.85680	26
27	1.70689	1.94780	2.22129	2.88337	3.73346	4.82235	7.98806	10.24508	13.10999	21.32488	43.53531	27
28	1.74102	1.99650	2.28793	2.99870	3.92013	5.11169	8.62711	11.16714	14.42099	23.88387	50.06561	28
29	1.77584	2.04641	2.35657	3.11865	4.11614	5.41839	9.31727	12.17218	15.86309	26.74993	57.57545	29
30	1.81136	2.09757	2.42726	3.24340	4.32194	5.74349	10.06266	13.26768	17.44940	29.95992	66.21177	30
31	1.84759	2.15001	2.50008	3.37313	4.53804	6.08810	10.86767	14.46177	19.19434	33.55511	76.14354	31
32	1.88454	2.20376	2.57508	3.50806	4.76494	6.45339	11.73708	15.76333	21.11378	37.58173	87.56507	32
33	1.92223	2.25885	2.65234	3.64838	5.00319	6.84059	12.67605	17.18203	23.22515	42.09153	100.69983	33
34	1.96068	2.31532	2.73191	3.79432	5.25335	7.25103	13.69013	18.72841	25.54767	47.14252	115.80480	34
35	1.99989	2.37321	2.81386	3.94609	5.51602	7.68609	14.78534	20.41397	28.10244	52.79962	133.17552	35
36	2.03989	2.43254	2.89828	4.10393	5.79182	8.14725	15.96817	22.25123	30.91268	59.13557	153.15185	36
37	2.08069	2.49335	2.98523	4.26809	6.08141	8.63609	17.24563	24.25384	34.00395	66.23184	176.12463	37
38	2.12230	2.55568	3.07478	4.43881	6.38548	9.15425	18.62528	26.43668	37.40434	74.17966	202.54332	38
39	2.16474	2.61957	3.16703	4.61637	6.70475	9.70351	20.11530	28.81598	41.14478	83.08122	232.92482	39
40	2.20804	2.68506	3.26204	4.80102	7.03999	10.28572	21.72452	31.40942	45.25926	93.05097	267.86355	40

TABLE 2
Present Value of 1

$$p^n = \frac{1}{(1+i)^n} = (1+i)^{-n}$$

(n) PERIODS	2%	2.5%	3%	4%	5%	6%	8%	9%	10%	12%	15%	(n) PERIODS
1	.98039	.97561	.97087	.96154	.95238	.94340	.92593	.91743	.90909	.89286	.86957	1
2	.96117	.95181	.94260	.92456	.90703	.89000	.85734	.84168	.82645	.79719	.75614	2
3	.94232	.92860	.91514	.88900	.86384	.83962	.79383	.77218	.75131	.71178	.65752	3
4	.92385	.90595	.88849	.85480	.82270	.79209	.73503	.70843	.68301	.63552	.57175	4
5	.90573	.88385	.86261	.82193	.78353	.74726	.68058	.64993	.62092	.56743	.49718	5
6	.88797	.86230	.83748	.79031	.74622	.70496	.63017	.59627	.56447	.50663	.43233	6
7	.87056	.84127	.81309	.75992	.71068	.66506	.58349	.54703	.51316	.45235	.37594	7
8	.85349	.82075	.78941	.73069	.67684	.62741	.54027	.50187	.46651	.40388	.32690	8
9	.83676	.80073	.76642	.70259	.64461	.59190	.50025	.46043	.42410	.36061	.28426	9
10	.82035	.78120	.74409	.67556	.61391	.55839	.46319	.42241	.38554	.32197	.24718	10
11	.80426	.76214	.72242	.64958	.58468	.52679	.42888	.38753	.35049	.28748	.21494	11
12	.78849	.74356	.70138	.62460	.55684	.49697	.39711	.35553	.31863	.25668	.18691	12
13	.77303	.72542	.68095	.60057	.53032	.46884	.36770	.32618	.28966	.22917	.16253	13
14	.75788	.70773	.66112	.57748	.50507	.44230	.34046	.29925	.26333	.20462	.14133	14
15	.74301	.69047	.64186	.55526	.48102	.41727	.31524	.27454	.23939	.18270	.12289	15
16	.72845	.67362	.62317	.53391	.45811	.39365	.29189	.25187	.21763	.16312	.10686	16
17	.71416	.65720	.60502	.51337	.43630	.37136	.27027	.23107	.19784	.14564	.09293	17
18	.70016	.64117	.58739	.49363	.41552	.35034	.25025	.21199	.17986	.13004	.08081	18
19	.68643	.62553	.57029	.47464	.39573	.33051	.23171	.19449	.16351	.11611	.07027	19
20	.67297	.61027	.55368	.45639	.37689	.31180	.21455	.17843	.14864	.10367	.06110	20
21	.65978	.59539	.53755	.43883	.35894	.29416	.19866	.16370	.13513	.09256	.05313	21
22	.64684	.58086	.52189	.42196	.34185	.27751	.18394	.15018	.12285	.08264	.04620	22
23	.63416	.56670	.50669	.40573	.32557	.26180	.17032	.13778	.11168	.07379	.04017	23
24	.62172	.55288	.49193	.39012	.31007	.24698	.15770	.12640	.10153	.06588	.03493	24
25	.60953	.53939	.47761	.37512	.29530	.23300	.14602	.11597	.09230	.05882	.03038	25
26	.59758	.52623	.46369	.36069	.28124	.21981	.13520	.10639	.08391	.05252	.02642	26
27	.58586	.51340	.45019	.34682	.26785	.20737	.12519	.09761	.07628	.04689	.02297	27
28	.57437	.50088	.43708	.33348	.25509	.19563	.11591	.08955	.06934	.04187	.01997	28
29	.56311	.48866	.42435	.32065	.24295	.18456	.10733	.08215	.06304	.03738	.01737	29
30	.55207	.47674	.41199	.30832	.23138	.17411	.09938	.07537	.05731	.03338	.01510	30
31	.54125	.46511	.39999	.29646	.22036	.16425	.09202	.06915	.05210	.02980	.01313	31
32	.53063	.45377	.38834	.28506	.20987	.15496	.08520	.06344	.04736	.02661	.01142	32
33	.52023	.44270	.37703	.27409	.19987	.14619	.07889	.05820	.04306	.02376	.00993	33
34	.51003	.43191	.36604	.26355	.19035	.13791	.07305	.05339	.03914	.02121	.00864	34
35	.50003	.42137	.35538	.25342	.18129	.13011	.06763	.04899	.03558	.01894	.00751	35
36	.49022	.41109	.34503	.24367	.17266	.12274	.06262	.04494	.03235	.01691	.00653	36
37	.48061	.40107	.33498	.23430	.16444	.11579	.05799	.04123	.02941	.01510	.00568	37
38	.47119	.39128	.32523	.22529	.15661	.10924	.05369	.03783	.02673	.01348	.00494	38
39	.46195	.38174	.31575	.21662	.14915	.10306	.04971	.03470	.02430	.01204	.00429	39
40	.45289	.37243	.30656	.20829	.14205	.09722	.04603	.03184	.02209	.01075	.00373	40

TABLE 3
Amount of an Ordinary Annuity of 1

$$A_{\overline{n}|i} = \frac{(1+i)^n - 1}{i}$$

(n) PERIODS	2%	2.5%	3%	4%	5%	6%	8%	9%	10%	12%	15%	(n) PERIODS
1	1.00000	1.00000	1.00000	1.00000	1.00000	1.00000	1.00000	1.00000	1.00000	1.00000	1.00000	1
2	2.02000	2.02500	2.03000	2.04000	2.05000	2.06000	2.08000	2.09000	2.10000	2.12000	2.15000	2
3	3.06040	3.07563	3.09090	3.12160	3.15250	3.18360	3.24640	3.27810	3.31000	3.37440	3.47250	3
4	4.12161	4.15252	4.18363	4.24646	4.31013	4.37462	4.50611	4.57313	4.64100	4.77933	4.99338	4
5	5.20404	5.25633	5.30914	5.41632	5.52563	5.63709	5.86660	5.98471	6.10510	6.35285	6.74238	5
6	6.30812	6.38774	6.46841	6.63298	6.80191	6.97532	7.33593	7.52333	7.71561	8.11519	8.75374	6
7	7.43428	7.54743	7.66246	7.89829	8.14201	8.39384	8.92280	9.20043	9.48717	10.08901	11.06680	7
8	8.58297	8.73612	8.89234	9.21423	9.54911	9.89747	10.63663	11.02847	11.43589	12.29969	13.72682	8
9	9.75463	9.95452	10.15911	10.58280	11.02656	11.49132	12.48756	13.02104	13.57948	14.77566	16.78584	9
10	10.94972	11.20338	11.46388	12.00611	12.57789	13.18079	14.48656	15.19293	15.93742	17.54874	20.30372	10
11	12.16872	12.48347	12.80780	13.48635	14.20679	14.97164	16.64549	17.56029	18.53117	20.65458	24.34928	11
12	13.41209	13.79555	14.19203	15.02581	15.91713	16.86994	18.97713	20.14072	21.38428	24.13313	29.00167	12
13	14.68033	15.14044	15.61779	16.62684	17.71298	18.88214	21.49530	22.95338	24.52271	28.02911	34.35192	13
14	15.97394	16.51895	17.08632	18.29191	19.59863	21.01507	24.21492	26.01919	27.97498	32.39260	40.50471	14
15	17.29342	17.93193	18.59891	20.02359	21.57856	23.27597	27.15211	29.36092	31.77248	37.27971	47.58041	15
16	18.63929	19.38022	20.15688	21.82453	23.65749	25.67253	30.32428	33.00340	35.94973	42.75328	55.71747	16
17	20.01207	20.86473	21.76159	23.69751	25.84037	28.21288	33.75023	36.97370	40.54470	48.88367	65.07509	17
18	21.41231	22.38635	23.41444	25.64541	28.13238	30.90565	37.45024	41.30134	45.59917	55.74971	75.83636	18
19	22.84056	23.94601	25.11687	27.67123	30.53900	33.75999	41.44626	46.01846	51.15909	63.43968	88.21181	19
20	24.29737	25.54466	26.87037	29.77808	33.06595	36.78559	45.76196	51.16012	57.27500	72.05244	102.44358	20
21	25.78332	27.18327	28.67649	31.96920	35.71925	39.99273	50.42292	56.76453	64.00250	81.69874	118.81012	21
22	27.29898	28.86286	30.53678	34.24797	38.50521	43.39229	55.45676	62.87334	71.40275	92.50258	137.63164	22
23	28.84496	30.58443	32.45288	36.61789	41.43048	46.99583	60.89330	69.53194	79.54302	104.60289	159.27638	23
24	30.42186	32.34904	34.42647	39.08260	44.50200	50.81558	66.76476	76.78981	88.49733	118.15524	184.16784	24
25	32.03030	34.15776	36.45926	41.64591	47.72710	54.86451	73.10594	84.70090	98.34706	133.33387	212.79302	25
26	33.67091	36.01171	38.55304	44.31174	51.11345	59.15638	79.95442	93.32398	109.18177	150.33393	245.71197	26
27	35.34432	37.91200	40.70963	47.08421	54.66913	63.70577	87.35077	102.72313	121.09994	169.37401	283.56877	27
28	37.05121	39.85980	42.93092	49.96758	58.40258	68.52811	95.33883	112.96822	134.20994	190.69889	327.10408	28
29	38.79223	41.85630	45.21885	52.96629	62.32271	73.63980	103.96594	124.13536	148.63093	214.58275	377.16969	29
30	40.56808	43.90270	47.57542	56.08494	66.43885	79.05819	113.28321	136.30754	164.49402	241.33268	434.74515	30
31	42.37944	46.00027	50.00268	59.32834	70.76079	84.80168	123.34587	149.57522	181.94342	271.29261	500.95692	31
32	44.22703	48.15028	52.50276	62.70147	75.29883	90.88978	134.21354	164.03699	201.13777	304.84772	577.10046	32
33	46.11157	50.35403	55.07784	66.20953	80.06377	97.34316	145.95062	179.80032	222.25154	342.42945	664.66552	33
34	48.03380	52.61289	57.73018	69.85791	85.06696	104.18375	158.62667	196.98234	245.47670	384.52098	765.36535	34
35	49.99448	54.92821	60.46208	73.65222	90.32031	111.43478	172.31680	215.71075	271.02437	431.66350	881.17016	35
36	51.99437	57.30141	63.27594	77.59831	95.83632	119.12087	187.10215	236.12472	299.12681	484.46312	1014.34568	36
37	54.03425	59.73395	66.17422	81.70225	101.62814	127.26812	203.07032	258.37595	330.03949	543.59869	1167.49753	37
38	56.11494	62.22730	69.15945	85.97034	107.70955	135.90421	220.31595	282.62978	364.04343	609.83053	1343.62216	38
39	58.23724	64.78298	72.23423	90.40915	114.09502	145.05846	238.94122	309.06646	401.44778	684.01020	1546.16549	39
40	60.40198	67.40255	75.40126	95.02552	120.79977	154.76197	259.05652	337.88245	442.59256	767.09142	1779.09031	40

TABLE 4
Present Value of an Ordinary Annuity of 1

$$P_{n,i} = \frac{1 - \frac{1}{(1+i)^n}}{i} = \frac{1 - p^n}{i}$$

(n) PERIODS	2%	2.5%	3%	4%	5%	6%	8%	9%	10%	12%	15%	(n) PERIODS
1	0.98039	0.97561	0.97087	0.96154	0.95238	0.94340	0.92593	0.91743	0.90909	0.89286	0.86957	1
2	1.94156	1.92742	1.91347	1.88609	1.85941	1.83339	1.78326	1.75911	1.73554	1.69005	1.62571	2
3	2.88388	2.85602	2.82861	2.77509	2.72325	2.67301	2.57710	2.53129	2.48685	2.40183	2.28323	3
4	3.80773	3.76197	3.71710	3.62990	3.54595	3.46511	3.31213	3.23972	3.16987	3.03735	2.85498	4
5	4.71346	4.64583	4.57971	4.45182	4.32948	4.21236	3.99271	3.88965	3.79079	3.60478	3.35216	5
6	5.60143	5.50813	5.41719	5.24214	5.07569	4.91732	4.62288	4.48592	4.35526	4.11141	3.78448	6
7	6.47199	6.34939	6.23028	6.00205	5.78637	5.58238	5.20637	5.03295	4.86842	4.56376	4.16042	7
8	7.32548	7.17014	7.01969	6.73274	6.46321	6.20979	5.74664	5.53482	5.33493	4.96764	4.48732	8
9	8.16224	7.97087	7.78611	7.43533	7.10782	6.80169	6.24689	5.99525	5.75902	5.32825	4.77158	9
10	8.98259	8.75206	8.53020	8.11090	7.72173	7.36009	6.71008	6.41766	6.14457	5.65022	5.01877	10
11	9.78685	9.51421	9.25262	8.76048	8.30641	7.88687	7.13896	6.80519	6.49506	5.93770	5.23371	11
12	10.57534	10.25776	9.95400	9.38507	8.86325	8.38384	7.53608	7.16073	6.81369	6.19437	5.42062	12
13	11.34837	10.98318	10.63496	9.98565	9.39357	8.85268	7.90378	7.48690	7.10336	6.42355	5.58315	13
14	12.10625	11.69091	11.29607	10.56312	9.89864	9.29498	8.24424	7.78615	7.36669	6.62817	5.72448	14
15	12.84926	12.38138	11.93794	11.11839	10.37966	9.71225	8.55948	8.06069	7.60608	6.81086	5.84737	15
16	13.57771	13.05500	12.56110	11.65230	10.83777	10.10590	8.85137	8.31256	7.82371	6.97399	5.95423	16
17	14.29187	13.71220	13.16612	12.16567	11.27407	10.47726	9.12164	8.54363	8.02155	7.11963	6.04716	17
18	14.99203	14.35336	13.75351	12.65930	11.68959	10.82760	9.37189	8.75563	8.20141	7.24967	6.12797	18
19	15.67846	14.97889	14.32380	13.13394	12.08532	11.15812	9.60360	8.95011	8.36492	7.36578	6.19823	19
20	16.35143	15.58916	14.87747	13.59033	12.46221	11.46992	9.81815	9.12855	8.51356	7.46944	6.25933	20
21	17.01121	16.18455	15.41502	14.02916	12.82115	11.76408	10.01680	9.29224	8.64869	7.56200	6.31246	21
22	17.65805	16.76541	15.93692	14.45112	13.16300	12.04158	10.20074	9.44243	8.77154	7.64465	6.35866	22
23	18.29220	17.33211	16.44361	14.85684	13.48857	12.30338	10.37106	9.58021	8.88322	7.71843	6.39884	23
24	18.91393	17.88499	16.93554	15.24696	13.79864	12.55036	10.52876	9.70661	8.98474	7.78432	6.43377	24
25	19.52346	18.42438	17.41315	15.62208	14.09394	12.78336	10.67478	9.82258	9.07704	7.84314	6.46415	25
26	20.12104	18.95061	17.87684	15.98277	14.37519	13.00317	10.80998	9.92897	9.16095	7.89566	6.49056	26
27	20.70690	19.46401	18.32703	16.32959	14.64303	13.21053	10.93516	10.02658	9.23722	7.94255	6.51353	27
28	21.28127	19.96489	18.76411	16.66306	14.89813	13.40616	11.05108	10.11613	9.30657	7.98442	6.53351	28
29	21.84438	20.45355	19.18845	16.98371	15.14107	13.59072	11.15841	10.19828	9.36961	8.02181	6.55088	29
30	22.39646	20.93029	19.60044	17.29203	15.37245	13.76483	11.25778	10.27365	9.42691	8.05518	6.56598	30
31	22.93770	21.39541	20.00043	17.58849	15.59281	13.92909	11.34980	10.34280	9.47901	8.08499	6.57911	31
32	23.46833	21.84918	20.38877	17.87355	15.80268	14.08404	11.43500	10.40624	9.52638	8.11159	6.59053	32
33	23.98856	22.29188	20.76579	18.14765	16.00255	14.23023	11.51389	10.46444	9.56943	8.13535	6.60046	33
34	24.49859	22.72379	21.13184	18.41120	16.19290	14.36814	11.58693	10.51784	9.60857	8.15656	6.60910	34
35	24.99862	23.14516	21.48722	18.66461	16.37419	14.49825	11.65457	10.56682	9.64416	8.17550	6.61661	35
36	25.48884	23.55625	21.83225	18.90828	16.54685	14.62099	11.71719	10.61176	9.67651	8.19241	6.62314	36
37	25.96945	23.95732	22.16724	19.14258	16.71129	14.73678	11.77518	10.65299	9.70592	8.20751	6.62881	37
38	26.44064	24.34860	22.49246	19.36786	16.86789	14.84602	11.82887	10.69082	9.73265	8.22099	6.63375	38
39	26.90259	24.73034	22.80822	19.58448	17.01704	14.94907	11.87858	10.72552	9.75696	8.23303	6.63805	39
40	27.35548	25.10278	23.11477	19.79277	17.15909	15.04630	11.92461	10.75736	9.77905	8.24378	6.64178	40

BIBLIOGRAPHY

A

Abarbanell, J., and B. Bushee, "Fundamental Analysis, Future Earnings, and Stock Prices," *Journal of Accounting Research* (Spring 1997), pp. 1–24.

Abarbanell, J., and B. Bushee, "Abnormal Returns to a Fundamental Analysis Strategy," *The Accounting Review* (January 1998), pp. 19–45.

Abarbanell, J., and V. L. Bernard, "Tests of Analysts' Overreaction/Underreaction to Earnings Information as an Explanation for Anomalous Stock Price Behavior," *Journal of Finance* (July 1992), pp. 1181–1208.

Abdel-khalik, A. Rashad, *Economic Effects on Leases of FASB Statement No. 13, Accounting for Leases*. Stamford, CT: Financial Accounting Standards Board, 1981.

Abdel-khalik, A. Rashad, "The Effect of LIFO-Switching and Firm Ownership on Executives' Pay," *Journal of Accounting Research* (Autumn 1985), pp. 427–447.

Abdel-khalik, A. Rashad, and James C. McKeown, "Disclosures of Estimates of Holding Gains and the Assessment of Systematic Risk," *Journal of Accounting Research* (Supplement 1978), pp. 46–92.

Abdel-khalik, A. Rashad, Philip R. Regier, and Sara Ann Reiter, "Some Thoughts on Empirical Research in Positive Accounting," in Thomas Frecka (ed.), *The State of Accounting Research as We Enter the 1990's*, pp. 153–189. Urbana-Champaign: University of Illinois, 1989.

Aboody, David, Mary E. Barth, and Ron Kasznik, "SFAS 123 Stock-based Compensation Expense and Equity Market Values," working paper, Stanford University, 2001.

Aboody, D., R. Kasznik, and M. Williams, "Purchase versus Pooling in Stock-for-Stock Acquisitions: Why Do Firms Care?" *Journal of Accounting and Economics* (June 2000), pp. 261–286.

Aboody, D., and Baruch Lev, "The Value-Relevance of Intangibles: The Case of Software Capitalization," *Journal of Accounting Research* (Supplement 1998), pp. 161–191.

Ahmed, A., "Accounting Earnings and Future Economic Rents: An Empirical Analysis," *Journal of Accounting & Economics* (May 1994), pp. 377–400.

Ali, Ashiq, L. Hwang, and M. A. Trombley, "Accruals and Future Stock Returns: Tests of the Naïve Investor Hypothesis," working paper, University of Arizona, 1999.

Altman, Edward I., "Financial Ratios, Discriminant Analysis and the Prediction of Corporate Bankruptcy," *Journal of Finance* (September 1968), pp. 578–609.

Altman, Edward I., *Corporate Bankruptcy in America*. Lexington, MA: Heath Lexington Books, 1971.

Altman, Edward I., *Corporate Financial Distress and Bankruptcy*, 2nd ed. New York: John Wiley & Sons, 1993.

Altman, Edward I., Robert G. Haldeman, and P. Narayanan, "Zeta[TM] Analysis: A New Model to Identify Bankruptcy Risk of Corporations," *Journal of Banking and Finance* (June 1977), pp. 29–54.

American Bar Foundation, *Commentaries on Indentures*. Chicago: American Bar Foundation, 1971.

Amihud, Y., and H. Mendelson, "Asset Pricing and the Bid-Ask Spread," *Journal of Financial Economics* (December 1986), pp. 223–249.

Amihud, Y., and H. Mendelson, "Liquidity, Asset Prices and Financial Policy," *The Financial Analysts Journal* (November/December 1991), pp. 56–66.

Amihud, Y., B. J. Christensen, and H. Mendelson, "Further Evidence on the Risk-Return Relationship," working paper, New York University, November 1992.

Amir, Eli, "The Effect of Accounting Aggregation on the Value-Relevance of Financial Disclosures: The Case of SFAS No. 106," *Accounting Review* (October 1996), pp. 573–590.

Amir, Eli, Michael Kirschenheiter and Kristen Willard, "The Valuation of Deferred Taxes," *Contemporary Accounting Research* (Winter 1997), pp. 597–622.

Amir, Eli, and Baruch Lev, "Value-relevance of Nonfinancial Information: The Wireless Communications Industry," *Journal of Accounting and Economics* (August/December 1996), pp. 3–30.

Amir, Eli, and Joshua Livnat, "Multiperiod Analysis of Adoption Motives: The Case of SFAS No. 106," *The Accounting Review* (October 1996), pp. 513–538.

Ang, James S., and Kiritkumar A. Patel, "Bond Rating Methods: Comparison and Validation," *Journal of Finance* (May 1975), pp. 631–640.

Anthony, J., and K. Ramesh, "Association between Accounting Performance Measures and Stock Prices: A Test of the Life Cycle Hypothesis," *Journal of Accounting & Economics* (June/September 1992), pp. 203–227.

Arcady, Alex T., and Francine Mellors, "Cash Balance Conversions," *Journal of Accountancy* (February 2000), pp. 22–28.

Archibald, T. Ross, "Stock Market Reaction to the Depreciation Switchback," *The Accounting Review* (January 1972), pp. 22–30.

Aziz, A., and G. H. Lawson, "Cash Flow Reporting and Financial Distress Models: Testing of Hypothesis," *Financial Management*, No. 1 (Spring 1989).

B

Balakrishnan R., T. Harris, and P. Sen, "The Predictive Ability of Geographic Segment Disclosures," *Journal of Accounting Research* (Autumn 1990), pp. 305–325.

Baldwin, Bruce A., "Segment Earnings Disclosure and the Ability of Security Analysts to Forecast Earnings per Share," *The Accounting Review* (July 1984), pp. 376–389.

Ball, Ray, "Changes in Accounting Techniques and Stock Prices," *Journal of Accounting Research* (Supplement 1972), pp. 1–38.

Ball, Ray, "Anomalies in Relationships Between Securities' Yields and Yield-Surrogates," *Journal of Financial Economics* (June/September 1978), pp. 103–126.

Ball, Ray, "The Earnings-Price Anomaly," *Journal of Accounting and Economics* (June/September 1992), pp. 319–346.

Ball, R., and E. Bartov, "How Naive Is the Stock Market's Use of Earnings Information?," *Journal of Accounting and Economics* (June 1996), pp. 319–338.

Ball, Ray, and Philip Brown, "An Empirical Evaluation of Accounting Income Numbers," *Journal of Accounting Research* (Autumn 1968), pp. 158–178.

Ballester, Marta, Dov Fried, and Joshua Livant, "Pension Plan Assets: Who Owns Them?," working paper, New York University, 2000.

Ballester, Marta, Dov Fried, and Joshua Livant, "Pension Plan Contributions, Free Cash Flows and Financial Slack," working paper, New York University, 2002.

Banz, Rolf W., "The Relationship Between Return and Market Value of Common Stocks," *Journal of Financial Economics*, Vol. 9, 1981, pp. 3–18.

Barlev, Benzion, Dov Fried, and Joshua Livnat, "Economic and Financial Reporting Effects of Inventory Tax Allowances," *Contemporary Accounting Review* (Spring 1986), pp. 288–310.

Barth, M. E., and M. F. McNichols, "Estimation and Valuation of Environmental Liabilities," *Journal of Accounting Research* (Supplement 1994), pp. 177–209.

Barth, Mary, "Relative Measurement Errors among Alternative Pension Asset and Liability Measures," *The Accounting Review* (July 1991), pp. 433–463.

Barth, Mary, William H. Beaver, and Wayne Landsman, "The Market Valuation Implications of Net Periodic Pension Cost Components," *Journal of Accounting and Economics* (March 1992), pp. 27–62.

Barth, Mary, William H. Beaver, and Wayne Landsman, "The Relevance of the Value Relevance Literature for Financial Accounting Standard Setting: Another View," *Journal of Accounting and Economics* (September 2001), pp. 77–104.

Barth, Mary, and Greg Clinch, "Revalued Financial, Tangible, and Intangible Assets: Associations with Share Prices and Non-Market-based Value Estimates," *Journal of Accounting Research* (Supplement 1998), pp. 199–233.

Barth, Mary, Donald P. Cram, and Karen Nelson, "Accruals and the Prediction of Future Cash Flows," *The Accounting Review* (January 2001), pp. 27–58.

Bartley, Jon W., and Al Y. S. Chen, "Material Changes in Financial Reporting Attributable to the Tax Reform Act of 1986," *Accounting Horizons* (March 1992), pp. 62–74.

Bartov, Eli, "Patterns in Unexpected Earnings as an Explanation for Post-Announcement Drift," *The Accounting Review* (July 1992), pp. 610–622.

Bartov, Eli, "The Timing of Asset Sales and Earnings Manipulation," *The Accounting Review* (October 1993), pp. 840–855.

Bartov, Eli, and G. M. Bodnar, "Firm Valuation, Earnings Expectations and the Exchange-Rate Exposure Effect," *Journal of Finance* (December 1994), pp. 1755–1785.

Bartov, Eli, and G. M. Bodnar, "Foreign Currency Translation Reporting and the Exchange-Rate Exposure Effect," *Journal of International Financial Management and Accounting* (Summer 1995), pp. 93–114.

Bartov, Eli, Frederick W. Lindahl, and William E. Ricks, "Stock Price Behavior around Announcements of Write-Offs," *Review of Accounting Studies* (December 1998), pp. 327–346.

Bartov, E., S. Radhakrishnan, and I. Krinsky, "Investor Sophistication and Patterns in Stock Returns after Earnings Announcements," *The Accounting Review* (January 2000), pp. 43–64.

Basu, Sanjoy, "The Relationship Between Earnings Yield, Market Value, and Return for NYSE Common Stocks: Further Evidence," *Journal of Finance* (June 1988), pp. 129–156.

Bathke, Allen W., Jr., and Kenneth S. Lorek, "The Relationship Between Time-Series Models and the Security Market's Expectations of Quarterly Earnings," *The Accounting Review* (April 1984), pp. 163–176.

Beatty, A., S. Chamberlain, and J. Magliolo, "Managing the Financial Reports of Commercial Banks: The Influence of Capital, Earnings and Taxes," *Journal of Accounting Research* (Autumn 1996), pp. 231–261.

Beaver, William H., "Financial Ratios as Predictors of Failure," *Journal of Accounting Research* (Supplement 1966), pp. 71–111.

Beaver, William H., "What Should Be the FASB's Objectives?" *Journal of Accountancy* (August 1973), pp. 49–56.

Beaver, William H., *Financial Reporting: An Accounting Revolution*, 3rd ed., Englewood Cliffs, NJ: Prentice Hall, 1998.

Beaver, William H., "Perspectives in Recent Capital Market Research," *The Accounting Review* (April 2002), pp. 453–474.

Beaver, William H., Andrew A. Christie, and Paul A. Griffin, "The Information Content of SEC Accounting Release No. 190," *Journal of Accounting and Economics* (August 1980), pp. 127–157.

Beaver, William H., R. Clarke, and W. F. Wright, "The Association Between Unsystematic Security Returns and the Magnitude of Earnings Forecast Errors," *Journal of Accounting Research* (Autumn 1979), pp. 316–340.

Beaver, William H., and Roland E. Dukes, "Interperiod Tax Allocation, Earnings Expectations, and the Behavior of Security Prices," *The Accounting Review* (April 1972), pp. 320–332.

Beaver, William H., and Roland E. Dukes, "Interperiod Tax Allocation and δ-Depreciation Methods: Some Empirical Results," *The Accounting Review* (July 1973), pp. 549–559.

Beaver, William H., Paul Griffin, and Wayne R. Landsman, "The Incremental Information Content of Replacement Cost Earnings," *Journal of Accounting and Economics* (July 1982), pp. 15–39.

Beaver, William H., Paul Kettler, and Myron Scholes, "The Association Between Market-Determined and Accounting-Determined Risk Measures," *The Accounting Review* (October 1970), pp. 654–682.

Beaver, William H., and Wayne R. Landsman, *Incremental Information Content of Statement 33 Disclosures* (Stamford CT: Financial Accounting Standards Board, 1983).

Beaver, William H., and James Manegold, "The Association Between Market-Determined and Accounting-Determined Measures of Systematic Risk: Some Further Evidence," *Journal of Financial and Quantitative Analysis* (June 1975), pp. 231–284.

Beaver, William H., and Dale Morse, "What Determines Price-Earnings Ratios?" *The Financial Analysts Journal* (July/August 1978), pp. 65–76.

Beaver, William H., and Mark Wolfson, "Foreign Currency Translation and Changing Prices in Perfect and Complete Markets," *Journal of Accounting Research* (Autumn 1982), pp. 528–550.

Beaver, William H., and Mark Wolfson, "Foreign Currency Translation Gains and Losses: What Effect Do They Have and What Do They Mean?" *The Financial Analysts Journal* (March/April 1984), pp. 28–36.

Beder, T. S., "VAR: Seductive but Dangerous," *Financial Analysts Journal* (September/October 1995), pp. 12–14.

Belkaoui, Ahmed, "Industrial Bonds Ratings: A New Look," *Financial Management* (Autumn 1980), pp. 44–51.

Belkaoui, Ahmed, *Industrial Bonds and the Rating Process*. Westport, CT: Quorum Books, an imprint of Greenwood Publishing Group, 1983.

Beneish, M., and E. Press, "Costs of Technical Violation of Accounting-Based Debt Covenants," *The Accounting Review* (April 1993), pp. 233–257.

Beneish, M., and E. Press, "The Resolution of Technical Default," *The Accounting Review* (April 1995), pp. 337–353.

Bergman Y., and J. Callen, "Opportunistic Underinvestment in Debt Renegotiation and Capital Structure," *Journal of Financial Economics* (March 1991), pp. 137–171.

Bernard, Victor L., "The Feltham-Ohlson Framework: Implications for Empiricists," *Contemporary Accounting Research* (Spring 1995), pp. 733–747.

Bernard, Victor L., "Capital Market Research During the 1980's: A Critical Review," in Thomas Frecka (ed.), *The State of Accounting Research as We Enter the 1990's*, pp. 72–120. Urbana-Champaign: University of Illinois, 1989.

Bernard, Victor L., "Accounting-Based Valuation Methods, Determinants of Market-to-Book Ratios, and Implications for Financial Statement Analysis," working paper, University of Michigan 1993.

Bernard, Victor L., and James Noel, "Do Inventory Disclosures Predict Sales and Earnings?," *Journal of Accounting, Auditing and Finance* (March 1991), pp. 145–182.

Bernard, Victor L., and Thomas Stober, "The Nature and Amount of Information in Cash Flows and Accruals," *The Accounting Review* (October 1989), pp. 624–652.

Bernard, V. L., and J. K. Thomas, "Evidence That Stock Prices Do Not Fully Reflect the Implications of Current Earnings for Future Earnings," *Journal of Accounting and Economics* (December 1990), pp. 305–340.

Bernstein, Leopold, *Financial Statement Analysis*, 5th ed. Homewood, IL: Richard D. Irwin 1993.

Bhandari, Laxmi Chand, "Debt/Equity Ratio and Expected Common Stock Returns: Empirical Evidence," *Journal of Finance* (June 1988), pp. 507–528.

Bhushan, Ravi, "Firm Characteristics and Analyst Following," *Journal of Accounting and Economics* (July 1989), pp. 255–274.

Bicksler, James, and Andrew Chen, "An Economic Analysis of Interest Rate Swaps," *Journal of Finance* (July 1986), pp. 645–656.

Biddle, Gary C., "Accounting Methods and Management Decisions: The Case of Inventory Costing and Inventory Policy," *Journal of Accounting Research* (Supplement 1980), pp. 235–280.

Biddle, G., R. Bowen, and J. Wallace, "Does EVA Beat Earnings? Evidence on Associations with Returns and Firm Values," *Journal of Accounting & Economics* (December 1997), pp. 301–336.

Biddle, Gary C., and Frederick W. Lindahl, "Stock Price Reactions to LIFO Adoptions: The Association Between Excess Returns and LIFO Tax Savings," *Journal of Accounting Research* (Autumn 1982, Part II), pp. 551–588.

Biddle, Gary C., and William E. Ricks, "Analyst Forecast Errors and Stock Price Behavior Near the Earnings Announcement Dates of LIFO Adopters," *Journal of Accounting Research* (Autumn 1988), pp. 169–194.

Bildersee, John S., "The Association Between a Market-Determined Measure of Risk and Alternative Measures of Risk," *Accounting Review* (January 1975), pp. 81–98.

Bishop, Marguerite L., "Managing Bank Regulation Through Accruals," Stern School of Business, working paper, New York University (1996).

Blankley, Alan I., and Edward P. Swanson, "A Longitudinal Study of SFAS 87 Pension Rate Assumptions," *Accounting Horizons* (December 1995), pp. 1–21.

Bleakley, Fred, "New Write-offs Mostly Please Investors," *The Wall Street Journal* (December 21, 1995), pp. C1–C2.

Blum, Marc, "Failing Company Discriminant Analysis," *Journal of Accounting Research* (Spring 1974), pp. 1–25.

Bodie, Zvi, Alex Kane, and Alan J. Marcus, *Investments*, 4th ed. Homewood, IL: Richard D. Irwin 1999.

Boer, Germaine, "Managing the Cash Gap," *Journal of Accountancy* (October 1999), p. 27.

Boone, Jeff P., "Revising the Reportedly Weak Value Relevance of Oil and Gas Asset Present Values: The Roles of Measurement Error, Model Misspecification and Time-Period Idiosyncrasy," *The Accounting Review* (January 2002), pp. 73–106.

Bowen, Robert M., "Valuation of Earnings Components in the Electric Utility Industry," *The Accounting Review* (January 1981), pp. 1–22.

Bowen, Robert M., David Burgstahler, and Lane A. Daley, "The Incremental Information Content of Accrual Versus Cash Flows," *The Accounting Review* (October 1987), pp. 723–747.

Bowman, Robert G., "The Theoretical Relationship Between Systematic Risk and Financial (Accounting) Variables," *Journal of Finance* (June 1979) pp. 617–630.

Bowman, Robert G., "The Importance of a Market-Value Measurement of Debt in Assessing Leverage," *Journal of Accounting Research* (Spring 1980), pp. 242–254.

Box, G. E. P., and G. M. Jenkins, *Time-Series Analysis: Forecasting and Control*, San Francisco: Holden Day, 1976.

Bradley, J., A. Desai, and E. H. Kim, "Synergistic Gains from Corporate Acquisitions and Their Division Between the Stockholders of Target and Acquiring Firms," *Journal of Financial Economics* (May 1988), pp. 3–40.

Bradshaw, Mark, and Richard Sloan, "GAAP versus The Street: An Empirical Assessment of Two Alternative Definitions of Earnings," *Journal of Accounting Research* (March 2002), pp. 41–67.

Briloff, Abraham J., "Distortions Arising from Pooling-of-Interests Accounting," *The Financial Analysts Journal* (March/April 1968), pp. 71–80.

Brooks, Leroy, and Dale Buckmaster, "Further Evidence of the Time Series Properties of Accounting Income," *Journal of Finance* (December 1976), pp. 1359–1373.

Brown, Lawrence D., "Analyst Forecasting Errors: Additional Evidence," *Financial Analysts Journal* (November/December 1997), pp. 81–88.

Brown, Lawrence D., "A Temporal Analysis of Earnings Surprises: Profits versus Losses," *Journal of Accounting Research* (September 2001), pp. 221–241.

Brown, Lawrence D., Paul A. Griffin, Robert L. Hagerman, and Mark E. Zmijewski, "An Evaluation of Alternative Proxies for the Market's Assessment of Unexpected Earnings" *Journal of Accounting and Economics* (July 1987), pp. 159–193.

Brown, Lawrence D., Robert L. Hagerman, Paul A. Griffin, and Mark E. Zmijewski, "Security Analyst Superiority Relative to Univariate Time-Series Models in Forecasting Quarterly Earnings," *Journal of Accounting and Economics* (April 1987), pp. 61–87.

Brown, Lawrence D. and K. J. Kim, "Timely Aggregate Analyst Forecasts as Better Proxies for Market Earnings Estimates," *Journal of Accounting Research* (Autumn 1991), pp. 382–385.

Brown, Lawrence D., Gordon D. Richardson, and Steven J. Schwager, "An Information Interpretation of Financial Analyst Superiority in Forecasting Earnings," *Journal of Accounting Research* (Spring 1987), pp. 49–67.

Brown, Lawrence D., and Michael S. Rozeff, "Univariate Time-Series Models of Quarterly Accounting Earnings per Share: A Proposed Model" *Journal of Accounting Research* (Spring 1979), pp. 179–189.

Brown, Philip, George Foster, and Eric Noreen, *Security Analyst Multi-Year Earnings Forecasts and the Capital Market*. Sarasota, FL: American Accounting Association, 1985.

Brown, Robert M., "Short-Range Market Reaction to Changes to LIFO Accounting Using Preliminary Announcement Dates," *Journal of Accounting Research* (Spring 1980), pp. 38–63.

Bublitz, Bruce, and Michael Ettredge, "The Information in Discretionary Outlays: Advertising, Research and Development," *The Accounting Review* (January 1989), pp. 108–124.

Bulow, Jeremy, "What Are Corporate Pension Liabilities?" *The Quarterly Journal of Economics* (August 1982), pp. 435–442.

Burgstahler, D., and M. Eames, "Management of Earnings and Analysts' Forecasts," working paper, University of Washington, 1999.

Burgstahler, David, James Jiambalvo, and Eric Noreen, "Changes in the Probability of Bankruptcy and Equity Value," *Journal of Accounting and Economics* (July 1989) pp. 207–224.

Butler, Kirt C., and Larry H. P. Lang, "The Forecast Accuracy of Individual Analysts: Evidence of Systematic Optimism and Pessimism," *Journal of Accounting Research* (Spring 1991), pp. 150–156.

C

Callen, J. L., J. Livnat, and S. Ryan, "Capital Expenditures: Value Relevance and Fourth Quarter Effects," *Journal of Financial Statement Analysis* (Spring 1996), pp. 13–24.

Canning, John B., *The Economics of Accountancy*. New York: The Ronald Press, 1929.

Caouette, J., E. I. Altman, and P. Narayanan, *Managing Credit Risk: The Next Great Financial Challenge*. New York: John Wiley & Sons, 1998.

Carcello, J. V., D. R. Hermanson, and F. F. Huss, "Temporal Changes in Bankruptcy-Related Reporting," *Auditing: A Journal of Practice and Theory* (Fall 1995), pp. 133–143.

Carroll, Thomas M., and Greg Niehaus, "Pension Plan Property Rights: Evidence from Debt Ratings and SFAS 87 Data," working paper, University of Nevada, 1998.

Casey, Cornelius J., and Norman J. Bartczak, "Cash Flow, It's Not the Bottom Line," *The Harvard Business Review* (July/August 1984), pp. 60–66.

Casey, Cornelius J., and Norman J. Bartczak, "Using Operating Cash Flow Data to Predict Financial Distress: Some Extensions," *Journal of Accounting Research* (Spring 1985), pp. 384–401.

Chambers, R. J., *Accounting Evaluation and Economic Behavior*. Englewood Cliffs, NJ: Prentice Hall, 1966.

Chan, K. C., and N. Chen, "Structural and Return Characteristics of Small and Large Firms," *Journal of Finance* (September 1991), pp. 1467–1484.

Chen, Kung H., and Thomas A. Shimerda, "An Empirical Analysis of Useful Financial Ratios," *Financial Management* (Spring 1981), pp. 51–60.

Chen, K., and J. Wei, "Creditors' Decisions to Waive Violations of Accounting-Based Debt Covenants," *The Accounting Review* (April 1993), pp. 218–232.

Christie, Andrew, "Aggregation of Test Statistics: An Evaluation of the Evidence on Contracting and Size Hypothesis," *Journal of Accounting and Economics* (January 1990), pp. 127–157.

Clement, M., "Analyst Forecast Accuracy: Do Ability, Resources and Portfolio Complexity Matter?," *Journal of Accounting and Economics* (June 1999), pp. 285–303.

Clinch, Greg J., and Joseph Magliolo, "Market Perceptions of Reserve Disclosures Under SFAS No. 69, *The Accounting Review* (October 1992), pp. 843–861.

Cloyd, C. B., J. Pratt and T. Stock, "The Use of Financial Accounting Choice to Support Aggressive Tax Positions: Public and Private Firms," *Journal of Accounting Research* (Spring 1996), pp. 23–43.

Cohen, Jerome B., Edward D. Zinbarg, and Arthur Zeikel, *Investment Analysis and Portfolio Management*, 5th ed., Homewood, IL: Richard D. Irwin, 1987.

Collins, Daniel W., "Predicting Earnings with Subentity Data: Some Further Evidence," *Journal of Accounting Research* (Spring 1976), pp. 163–177.

Collins, Daniel W., and Warren T. Dent, "The Proposed Elimination of Full Cost Accounting in the Extractive Petroleum Industry: An Empirical Assessment of the Market Consequences," *Journal of Accounting and Economics* (March 1979), pp. 3–44.

Collins, Daniel W., and S. P. Kothari, "An Analysis of Intertemporal and Cross-sectional Determinants of Earnings Response Coefficients," *Journal of Accounting and Economics* (July 1989), pp. 143–181.

Collins, Daniel W., Michael Rozeff, and Dan Dhaliwal, "The Economic Determinants of the Market Reaction to Proposed Mandatory Accounting Changes in the Oil and Gas Industry: A Cross-sectional Analysis," *Journal of Accounting and Economics* (March 1981), pp. 37–71.

Collins, Daniel W., Michael Rozeff, and William K. Salatka, "The SEC's Rejection of SFAS 19: Tests of Market Price Reversal," *The Accounting Review* (January 1982), pp. 1–17.

Collins, Daniel W., and Richard R. Simmonds, "SEC Line-of-Business Disclosure and Market Risk Adjustments," *Journal of Accounting Research* (Autumn 1979), pp. 352–383.

Collins, J., D. Shakelford, and J. Whalen, "Bank Differences in the Coordination of Regulatory Capital, Earnings and Taxes," *Journal of Accounting Research* (Autumn 1996), pp. 263–291.

Comiskey, Eugene, and Charles W. Mulford, "Investment Decisions and the Equity Accounting Standard," *The Accounting Review* (July 1986), pp. 519–525.

Copeland, R. M., and M. L. Moore, "The Financial Bath: Is It Common?" *MSU Business Topics* (Autumn 1972), pp. 63–69.

Copeland, T., T. Koller, and J. Murrin, *Valuation: Measuring and Managing the Value of Companies*, 2nd ed., New York: John Wiley and Sons, 1996.

Cragg, J. G., and B. G. Malkiel, *Expectations and the Structure of Share Prices*. Chicago: University of Chicago Press, 1982.

Cushing, Barry E., and Marc J. LeClere, "Evidence on the Determinants of Inventory Accounting Policy Choice," *The Accounting Review* (April 1992), pp. 355–366.

D

Daley, Lane A. "The Valuation of Reported Pension Measures for Firms Sponsoring Defined Benefit Plans," *The Accounting Review* (April 1984), pp. 177–198.

Dambolena, Ismael G., and Sarkis J. Khoury, "Ratio Stability and Corporate Failure," *Journal of Finance* (September 1980), pp. 1017–1026.

Damodaran, Aswath, *The Dark Side of Valuation*, New York: John Wiley & Sons, 2001.

Davis, H. Z., and Y. C. Peles, "Measuring Equilibrating Forces of Financial Ratios," *The Accounting Review* (October 1993), pp. 725–747.

Davis, Harry Z., Nathan Kahn, and Etzmun Rosen, "LIFO Inventory Liquidations: An Empirical Study," *Journal of Accounting Research* (Autumn 1984), pp. 480–496.

Davis, J. L., E. Fama, and K. French, "Characteristics, Covariances and Average Returns: 1929 to 1997," *Journal of Finance* (February 2000), pp. 389–406.

Davis, Michael L., "Differential Market Reaction to Pooling and Purchase Methods," *The Accounting Review* (July 1990), pp. 696–709.

Deakin, Edward B. III, "A Discriminant Analysis of Predictors of Business Failure," *Journal of Accounting Research* (Spring 1972), pp. 167–179.

Deakin, Edward B. III, "An Analysis of Differences Between Non-Major Oil Firms Using Successful Efforts and Full Cost Methods," *The Accounting Review* (October 1979), pp. 722–734.

Deakin, Edward B. III. "Rational Economic Behavior and Lobbying on Accounting Issues: Evidence from the Oil and Gas Industry," *The Accounting Review* (January 1989), pp. 137–151.

DeBondt, W., and R. Thaler, "Does the Stock Market Overreact?" *Journal of Finance* (March 1985), pp. 793–805.

Dechow, Patricia M., "Accounting Earnings and Cash Flows as Measures of Firm Performance: The Role of Accounting Accruals," *Journal of Accounting and Economics* (July 1994), pp. 3–42.

Dechow, Patricia., A. Hutton, and R. Sloan, "An Empirical Assessment of the Residual Income Valuation Model," *Journal of Accounting & Economics* (January 1999), pp. 1–34.

Dechow Patricia, S. P. Kothari, and R. Watts, "The Relation Between Earnings and Cash Flows," *Journal of Accounting and Economics* (May 1998), pp. 133–168.

Dechow, Patricia M., and Douglas J. Skinner, "Earnings Management: Reconciling the Views of Accounting Academics, Practitioners, and Regulators," *Accounting Horizons* (June 2000), pp. 235–250.

Dechow Patricia, and R.G. Sloan, "Returns to Contrarian Strategies: Tests of Naïve Expectations Hypotheses," *Journal of Financial Economics* (January 1997), pp. 3–37.

DeFond, M., and J. Jiambalvo, "Debt Covenant Violation and Manipulation of Accruals," *Journal of Accounting and Economics* (January 1994), pp. 145–176.

Devine, Michael, "Using Pro Forma Allocations to Evaluate Business Purchases," *The Financial Executive* (June 1981), pp. 15–18.

Dhaliwal, Dan S., "Measurement of Financial Leverage in the Presence of Unfunded Pension Liabilities," *The Accounting Review* (October 1986), pp. 651–661.

Dhaliwal, Dan, Gerald Saloman, and E. Dan Smith, "The Effect of Owner Versus Management Control on the Choice of Accounting Methods," *Journal of Accounting and Economics* (July 1982), pp. 89–96.

Dhaliwal, D., K. Subramanyam, and R. Trezevant, "Is Comprehensive Income Superior to Net Income as a Measure of Performance?" *Journal of Accounting & Economics* (January 1999), pp. 43–67.

Dhaliwal, D., R. Trezevant, and M. S. Wilkins, "Tests of a Deferred Tax Explanation of the Negative Association between the LIFO Reserve and Firm Value," *Contemporary Accounting Research* (Spring 2000), pp. 41–59.

Dieter, R., and J. A. Heyman, "Implications of SEC Staff Accounting Bulletin 88 for Foreign Registrants," *Journal of Accountancy* (August 1991), pp. 121–125.

Dopuch, Nicholas, and Morton Pincus, "Evidence on the Choice of Inventory Accounting Methods: LIFO Versus FIFO," *Journal of Accounting Research* (Spring 1988), pp. 28–59.

Dreman, David, "Value Will Out," *Forbes* (June 17, 1996), p. 146.

Dreman, D. N., and M. A. Berry, "Forecasting Errors and Their Implications for Security Analysis," *The Financial Analysts Journal* (May/June 1995), pp. 30–41.

Duke, Joanne C., and Herbert G. Hunt III, "An Empirical Examination of Debt Covenant Restrictions and Accounting-Related Debt Proxies," *Journal of Accounting and Economics* (January 1990), pp. 45–63.

Dukes, Roland E., *An Empirical Investigation of the Effects of Statement of Financial Accounting Standards No. 8 on Security Return Behavior*. Stamford, CT: Financial Accounting Standards Board, 1978.

Dukes, Roland E., Thomas R. Dyckman, and John A. Elliott, "Accounting for Research and Development Costs: The Impact on Research and Development Expenditures," *Journal of Accounting Research* (Supplement 1980), pp. 1–26.

Dumbolena, I. G., and J. M. Shulman, "A Primary Rule for Detecting Bankruptcy: Watch the Cash," *The Financial Analysts Journal* (September/October 1988), pp. 74–78.

Dunne, Kathleen M., "An Empirical Analysis of Management's Choice of Accounting Treatment for Business Combinations," *Journal of Accounting and Public Policy* (July 1990), pp. 111–133.

Dyckman, Thomas R., and Abbie J. Smith, "Financial Accounting and Reporting by Oil and Gas Producing Companies: A Study of Information Effects," *Journal of Accounting and Economics* (March 1979), pp. 45–75.

E

Easman, W., A. Falkenstein, and R. Weil, "The Correlation Between Sustainable Income and Stock Returns," *The Financial Analysts Journal* (September/October 1979), pp. 44–47.

Easton, Peter D., Trevor Harris, and James Ohlson, "Aggregate Accounting Earnings Can Explain Most of Security Returns: The Case of Long Run Intervals," *Journal of Accounting and Economics* (June/September 1992), pp. 119–142.

Easton, P., and M. Zmijewski, "Cross-Sectional Variation in the Stock Market Response to Accounting Earnings Announcements," *Journal of Accounting & Economics* (July 1989), pp. 117–141.

Eccher, Elizabeth A., "The Value Relevance of Capitalized Software Development Costs," working paper, Sloan School of Management, April 1996.

Edwards, E. O., and P. W. Bell, *The Theory and Measurement of Business Income*. University of California Press, 1961.

Eggleton, Ian R., Stephen H. Penman, and John R. Twombly, "Accounting Changes and Stock Prices: An Examination of Selected Uncontrolled Variables," *Journal of Accounting Research* (Spring 1976), pp. 66–88.

Elam, Rick, "The Effect of Lease Data on the Predictive Ability of Financial Ratios," *The Accounting Review* (January 1975), pp. 25–53.

Elliott, J. W., and H. L. Uphoff, "Predicting the Near Term Profit and Loss Statement with an Econometric Model: A Feasibility Study," *Journal of Accounting Research* (Autumn 1972), pp. 259–274.

Elliott, John A., and Douglas J. Hanna, "Repeated Accounting Write-Offs and the Information Content of Earnings," *Journal of Accounting Research* (Supplement 1996), pp. 135–55.

Elliott, John A., and Donna R. Philbrick, "Accounting Changes and Earnings Predictability," *The Accounting Review* (January 1990), pp. 157–174.

Elliott, John A., Gordon Richardson, Thomas R. Dyckman, and Roland E. Dukes, "The Impact of SFAS No. 2 on Firm Expenditures on Research and Development: Replications and Extensions," *Journal of Accounting Research* (Spring 1984), pp. 85–102.

Elliott, John A., and Wayne Shaw, "Write-offs as Accounting Procedures to Manage Perceptions," *Journal of Accounting Research* (Supplement 1988), pp. 91–119.

El-Gazzar, Samir M., Steven Lilien, and Victor Pastena, "Accounting for Leases by Lessees," *Journal of Accounting and Economics* (October 1986), pp. 217–237.

Emery, Gary W., and Kenneth O. Cogger, "The Measurement of Liquidity," *Journal of Accounting Research* (Autumn 1982), pp. 290–303.

F

Fairfield, Patricia, "P/E, P/B and the Present Value of Future Dividends," *Financial Analysts Journal* (July/August 1994), pp. 23–31.

Fairfield, Patricia, R. Sweeney, and T. L. Yohn, "Accounting Classification and the Predictive Content of Earnings," *Accounting Review* (July 1996), pp. 337–356.

Fairfield, Patricia, and Teri L. Yohn, "Changes in Asset Turnover Signal Changes in Profitability," working paper, Georgetown University, 1999.

Falkenstein, Angela, and Roman L. Weil, "Replacement Cost Accounting: What Will Income Statements Based on the SEC Disclosures Show? Part I," *The Financial Analysts Journal* (January/February 1977a), pp. 46–57.

Falkenstein, Angela, and Roman L. Weil, "Replacement Cost Accounting: What Will Income Statements Based on the SEC Disclosures Show? Part II," *The Financial Analysts Journal* (March/April 1977b), pp. 48–57.

Fama, Eugene, "Efficient Capital Markets: A Review of Theory and Empirical Work," *Journal of Finance* (May 1970), pp. 383–417.

Fama, Eugene, and Kenneth R. French, "The Cross-section of Expected Stock Returns," *Journal of Finance* (June 1992), pp. 427–466.

Fama, Eugene, and Kenneth French, "Common Risk Factors in the Returns on Stocks and Bonds," *Journal of Financial Economics* (February 1993), pp. 3–56.

Fama, Eugene, and Kenneth French, "Size and Book-to-Market Factors in Earnings and Returns," *Journal of Finance* (March 1995), pp. 131–155.

Fama, Eugene, and Kenneth French, "The CAPM Is Wanted, Dead or Alive," working paper, Graduate School of Business, University of Chicago, April 1995.

Fama, Eugene, and Kenneth French, "Multifactor Explanations of Asset Pricing Anomalies," *Journal of Finance* (March 1996), pp. 55–84.

Feldstein, Martin, and Randall Morck, "Pension Funding Decisions, Interest Rate Assumptions and Share Prices," in Zvi Bodie and John B. Shoven (eds.), *Financial Aspects of the United States Pension System*. Chicago: University of Chicago Press, 1983.

Feltham, Gerald, and James A. Ohlson, "Valuation and Clean Surplus Accounting for Operating and Financial Activities," *Contemporary Accounting Research* (Spring 1995), pp. 689–731.

Fields, Thomas, Thomas Lys, and Linda Vincent, "Empirical Research on Accounting Choice," *Journal of Accounting and Economics* (September 2001), pp. 255–308.

Financial Executives Institute, Committee on Corporate Reporting, "Survey on Unusual Charges" (1986 and 1991).

Foster, George, "Accounting Earnings and Stock Prices of Insurance Companies," *The Accounting Review* (October 1975), pp. 686–698.

Foster, George, "Quarterly Accounting Data: Time Series Properties and Predictive-Ability Results," *The Accounting Review* (January 1977), pp. 1–21.

Foster, George, "Briloff and the Capital Market," *Journal of Accounting Research* (Spring 1979), pp. 262–274.

Francis, Jennifer, J. Douglas Hanna, and Linda Vincent, "Causes and Effects of Discretionary Asset Writeoffs," *Journal of Accounting Research* (Supplement 1996), pp. 117–34.

Francis, J., P. Olsson, and D. Oswald, "Comparing the Accuracy and Explainability of Dividend, Free Cash Flow and Abnormal Earnings Equity Valuation Models," *Journal of Accounting Research* (Spring 2000), pp. 45–70.

Francis, Jere R., and Sara Ann Reiter, "Determinants of Corporate Pension Funding Strategy," *Journal of Accounting and Economics* (April 1987), pp. 35–59.

Frankel, Richard, and Charles M. C. Lee, "Accounting Diversity and International Valuation," working paper, University of Michigan, 1996.

Frankel, R., and C. Lee, "Accounting Valuation, Market Expectation, and Cross-Sectional Stock Returns," *Journal of Accounting & Economics* (June 1998), pp. 283–319.

Frecka, Thomas J., and Cheng F. Lee, "Generalized Financial Ratio Adjustment Processes and Their Implications," *Journal of Accounting Research* (Spring 1983), pp. 308–316.

Freeman, Robert N., James A. Ohlson, and Stephen H. Penman, "Book Rate-of-Return and Prediction of Earnings Changes: An Empirical Investigation," *Journal of Accounting Research* (Autumn 1982), pp. 639–653.

Fried, Dov, "Aggregation Versus Disaggregation and the Predictive Ability Criterion," unpublished dissertation, New York University, 1978.

Fried, Dov, and Dan Givoly, "Financial Analysts' Forecasts of Earnings: A Better Surrogate for Market Expectations," *Journal of Accounting and Economics* (October 1982), pp. 85–108.

Fried, Dov, Haim Mozes, Donna Rapaccioli, and Allen Schiff, "Earnings Manipulation and the Sale of a Business Segment," *Journal of Financial Statement Analysis* (Spring 1996), pp. 25–33.

Fried, Dov, Michael Schiff, and Ashwinpaul C. Sondhi, *Impairments and Writeoffs of Long-Lived Assets*. Montvale, NJ: National Association of Accountants, 1989.

Fried, Dov, Michael Schiff, and Ashwinpaul C. Sondhi, "Big Bath or Intermittent Showers? Another Look at Write-offs," working paper, New York University, 1990.

Frischmann, Peter Jr., Paul D. Kimmel, and Terry D. Warfield, "Innovation in Preferred Stock: Current Developments and Implications for Financial Reporting," *Accounting Horizons* (September 1999), pp. 201–218.

Fuller, Russell J., and Chi-Cheng Hsia, "A Simplified Common Stock Valuation Model," *The Financial Analysts Journal* (September/October 1984), pp. 49–56.

G

Gahlon, James M., and James A. Gentry, "On the Relationship Between Systematic Risk and the Degrees of Operating and Financial Leverage," *Financial Management* (Summer 1982), pp. 15–23.

Gaver, J. J., K. M. Gaver, and J. R. Austin, "Additional Evidence on the Association Between Income Management and Earnings-based Bonus Plans," *Journal of Accounting and Economics* (February 1995), pp. 3–28.

Gentry, James A., Paul Newbold, and David T. Whitford, "Bankruptcy, Working Capital, and Funds Flows," *Managerial Finance*. Vol. 10, No. 3/4, 1984.

Gentry, James A., Paul Newbold, and David T. Whitford, "Classifying Bankrupt Firms with Funds Flow Components," *Journal of Accounting Research* (Spring 1985), pp. 146–160.

Gentry, James A., Paul Newbold, and David T. Whitford, "Predicting Bankruptcy: If Cash Flow's Not the Bottom Line, What Is?," *Financial Analysts Journal* (September/October 1985), pp. 47–58.

Ghicas, Dimitrios C., "Determinants of Actuarial Cost Method Changes for Pension Accounting and Funding," *The Accounting Review* (April 1990), pp. 384–405.

Gibson, Charles H., "Financial Ratios in Annual Reports," *The CPA Journal* (September 1982), pp. 18–29.

Gibson, Charles H., "How Chartered Financial Analysts View Financial Ratios," *Financial Analysts Journal* (May/June 1987), pp. 74–76.

Givoly, Dan, and Carla Hayn, "The Valuation of the Deferred Tax Liability: Evidence from the Stock Market," *The Accounting Review* (April 1992), pp. 394–410.

Givoly, Dan, and Josef Lakonishok, "The Information Content of Financial Analysts' Forecasts of Earnings: Some Evidence of Semi-Strong Inefficiency," *Journal of Accounting and Economics* (December 1979), pp. 165–185.

Givoly, Dan, and Josef Lakonishok, "The Quality of Analysts' Forecasts of Earnings," *Financial Analysts Journal* (September/October 1984), pp. 40–47.

Gombola, M. F., M. E. Haskins, J. E. Katz, and D. D. Williams, "Cash Flow in Bankruptcy Prediction," *Financial Management* (Winter 1987).

Gombola, Michael J., and J. Edward Katz, "Financial Ratio Patterns in Retail and Manufacturing Organizations," *Financial Management* (Summer 1983), pp. 45–56.

Gonedes, Nicholas, J., "Risk, Information and the Effects of Special Accounting Items on Capital Market Equilibrium," *Journal of Accounting Research* (Autumn 1975), pp. 220–256.

Gonedes, Nicholas J., "Corporate Signalling, External Accounting and Capital Market Equilibrium: Evidence on Dividends, Income and Extraordinary Items," *Journal of Accounting Research* (Spring 1978), pp. 26–79.

Gonedes, Nicholas J., and Nicholas Dopuch, "Capital Market Equilibrium, Information Production and Selecting Accounting Techniques: Theoretical Framework and Review of Empirical Work," *Journal of Accounting Research* (Supplement 1974), pp. 48–129.

Gopalakrishnan, V., and T. F. Sugrue, "An Empirical Investigation of Stock Market Valuation of Corporate Projected Pension Liabilities," *Journal of Business Finance & Accounting* (September 1993), pp. 711–724.

Granof, Michael H., and Daniel G. Short, "Why Do Companies Reject LIFO?," *Journal of Accounting Auditing and Finance* (Summer 1984), pp. 323–333.

Greenstein, M. M., and H. Sami, "The Impact of the SEC's Segment Disclosure Requirement on Bid-Ask Spreads," *The Accounting Review* (January 1994), pp. 179–199.

Griffin, Paul A., "The Time-Series Behavior of Quarterly Earnings: Preliminary Evidence," *Journal of Accounting Research* (Spring 1977), pp. 71–83.

Gu, Feng, and Baruch Lev, "Intangible Assets: Measurement, Drivers, Usefulness," working paper, New York University, 2001.

Guenther, David, and Richard Sansing, "Valuation of the Firm in the Presence of Temporary Book-Tax Differences: The Role of Deferred Tax Assets and Liabilities," *The Accounting Review* (January 2000), pp. 1–12.

Guenther, David, and M. A. Trombley, "The 'LIFO Reserve' and the Value of the Firm: Theory and Empirical Evidence," *Contemporary Accounting Research* (Spring 1994), pp. 433–452.

H

Hackel, Kenneth S., and Joshua Livnat, "International Investments Based on Free Cash Flow: A Practical Approach," *Journal of Financial Statement Analysis* (Fall 1995), pp. 5–14.

Hackel, Kenneth S., and Joshua Livnat, *Cash Flow and Security Analysis*, 2nd ed. Homewood, IL: Business One-Irwin, 1995.

Hamada, Robert S., "The Effect of the Firm's Capital Structure on the Systematic Risk of Common Stocks," *Journal of Finance* (May 1972), pp. 435–452.

Hamilton, R., *An Introduction to Merchandize*. Edinburgh, 1777.

Han, Jerry C. Y., and Shiing-wu Wang, "Political Costs and Earnings Management of Oil Companies During the 1990 Persian Gulf Crisis," *The Accounting Review* (January 1998), pp. 103–117.

Hand, John R. M., "Did Firms Undertake Debt-Equity Swaps for Accounting Paper Profits or True Financial Gains?" *The Accounting Review* (October 1989), pp. 587–623.

Hand, John R. M., "A Test of the Extended Functional Fixation Hypothesis," *The Accounting Review* (October 1990), pp. 739–763.

Harrington, Diana R., "Whose Beta Is Best?" *Financial Analysts Journal* (July/August 1983), pp. 67–77.

Harris, Trevor S., and James A. Ohlson, "Accounting Disclosures and the Market's Valuation of Oil and Gas Properties" *The Accounting Review* (October 1987), pp. 651–670.

Harris, Trevor S., and James A. Ohlson, "Accounting Disclosures and the Market's Valuation of Oil and Gas Properties: Evaluation of Market Efficiency and Functional Fixation," *The Accounting Review* (October 1990), pp. 764–780.

Haugen, Robert A., *The New Finance: The Case Against Efficient Markets*, 2nd ed. Englewood Cliffs, NJ: Prentice Hall, 1999.

Hauworth, William P. II, and Lailani Moody, "An Accountant's Option Primer: Puts and Calls Demystified," *Journal of Accountancy* (January 1987), pp. 87–97.

Healy, Paul M., "The Effect of Bonus Schemes on Accounting Decisions," *Journal of Accounting and Economics* (April 1985), pp. 85–107.

Healy, Paul M., Sok-Hyon Kang, and Kirshna Palepu, "The Effect of Accounting Procedure Changes on CEO's Cash Salary and Bonus Compensation," *Journal of Accounting and Economics* (April 1987), pp. 7–34.

Healy, P., and J. Wahlen., "A Review of the Earnings Management Literature and Its Implications for Standard Setting," *Accounting Horizons* (December 1999), pp. 365–383.

Heian, James B., and James B. Thies, "Consolidation of Finance Subsidiaries: $230 Billion in Off-Balance-Sheet Financing Comes Home to Roost," *Accounting Horizons* (March 1989), pp. 1–9.

Henning, S. L., B. L. Lewis, and W. H. Shaw, "Valuation of Components of Purchased Goodwill," *Journal of Accounting Research* (Autumn 2000), pp. 375–386.

Herrmann, D., and W. Thomas, "An Analysis of Segment Disclosures under SFAS No. 131 and SFAS No. 14," *Accounting Horizons* (September 2000), pp. 287–302.

Hicks, J. R., *Value and Capital*, 2nd ed. Oxford: Chaundon Press, 1946.

Hirschey, Mark, and Jerry J. Weygandt, "Amortization Policy for Advertising and Research and Development," *Journal of Accounting Research* (Spring 1985), pp. 326–335.

Hochman, Shalom, "The Beta Coefficient: An Instrumental Variables Approach," in Haim Levy (ed.), *Research in Finance*, Vol. 4. Greenwich, CT: JAI Press, 1983.

Holthausen, Robert W., "Evidence on the Effect of Bond Covenants and Management Compensation Contracts on the Choice of Accounting Techniques: The Case of The Depreciation Switch-Back," *Journal of Accounting and Economics* (March 1981), pp. 73–109.

Holthausen, Robert W., and Richard E. Leftwich, "The Effect of Bond Ratings on Common Stock Prices," *Journal of Financial Economics* (September 1986), pp. 57–90.

Holthausen, Robert W., and D. F. Larcker, "The Prediction of Stock Return Using Financial Statement Information" *Journal of Accounting and Economics* (June/September 1992), pp. 373–411.

Holthausen, R., D. F. Larcker, and R. G. Sloan, "Annual Bonus Schemes and the Manipulation of Earnings," *Journal of Accounting and Economics* (February 1995), pp. 29–74.

Holthausen, Robert, and Ross Watts, "The Relevance of the Value Relevance Literature for Financial Accounting Standard Setting: Another View," *Journal of Accounting and Economics* (September 2001), pp. 3–76.

Holder-Webb, Lori M., and Michael Wilkins, "The Incremental Information Content of SFAS 59 Going-Concern Opinions," *Journal of Accounting Research* (Spring 2000), pp. 209–221.

Hong, Hai, Robert S. Kaplan, and Gershon Mandelker, "Pooling vs. Purchase: The Effects of Accounting for Mergers on Stock Prices," *The Accounting Review* (January 1978), pp. 31–47.

Hopwood, William, James C. McKeown, and Paul Newbold, "The Additional Information Content of Quarterly Earnings Reports," *Journal of Accounting Research* (Autumn 1982), pp. 343–349.

Hopwood, William, Paul Newbold, and Peter A. Silhan, "The Potential for Gains in Predictive Ability Through Disaggregation: Segmented Annual Earnings," *Journal of Accounting Research* (Autumn 1982), pp. 724–732.

Horrigan, James O., "Some Empirical Bases of Financial Ratio Analysis," *The Accounting Review* (July 1965), pp. 558–568.

Horrigan, James O., "The Determination of Long-Term Credit Standing with Financial Ratios," *Journal of Accounting Research* (Supplement 1966), pp. 44–62.

Horwitz, Bertrand, and Richard Kolodny, "Line of Business Reporting and Security Prices: An Analysis of an SEC Disclosure Rule," *Bell Journal of Economics* (Spring 1977), pp. 234–249.

Horwitz, Bertrand N., and Richard Kolodny, "The Economic Effects of Involuntary Uniformity in the Financial Reporting of R&D Expenditures," *Journal of Accounting Research* (Supplement 1980), pp. 38–74.

Hull, John, *Introduction to Futures and Options Markets*. Englewood Cliffs, NJ: Prentice Hall, 1995.

Hunt, Herbert G., III, "Potential Determinants of Corporate Inventory Accounting Decisions," *Journal of Accounting Research* (Autumn 1985), pp. 448–467.

I

Imhoff, Eugene A., Jr., and Jacob K. Thomas, "Economic Consequences of Accounting Changes: The Lease Disclosure Rule Change," *Journal of Accounting and Economics* (December 1988), pp. 277–310.

Ingberman, Monroe and George H. Sorter, "The Role of Financial Statements in an Efficient Market," *Journal of Accounting, Auditing, and Finance* (Fall 1978), pp. 58–62.

J

Jagannathan, Ravi, and Z. Wang, "The CAPM Is Alive and Well," *Staff Report 165, Federal Reserve Bank of Minneapolis*, 1993.

Jagannathan, Ravi, and Z. Wang, "The Conditional CAPM and the Cross-section of Expected Returns," *Journal of Finance* (March 1996), pp. 3–54.

Jagannathan, Ravi, and McGrattan, "The CAPM Debate," *Federal Reserve Bank of Minneapolis, Quarterly Report*, Vol. 19(4), 1995, pp. 2–17.

Jennings, Ross, M. LeClere, and Robert B. Thompson II., "Goodwill Amortization and the Usefulness of Earnings," *Financial Analysts Journal* (September/October 2001), pp. 20–28.

Jennings, Ross, David P. Mest, and Robert B. Thompson II, "Investor Reaction to Disclosures of 1974–75 LIFO Adoption Decisions," *The Accounting Review* (April 1992), pp. 337–354.

Jennings, R., J. Robinson, R. B. Thompson II, and L. Duvall, "The Relation Between Accounting Goodwill Numbers and Equity Values," *Journal of Business, Finance and Accounting* (June 1996), pp. 513–534.

Jennings, Ross, Paul J. Simko, and Robert B. Thompson II, "Does LIFO Inventory Accounting Improve the Income Statement at the Expense of the Balance Sheet?," *Journal of Accounting Research,* (Spring 1996), pp. 85–109.

Jensen, M. C., and W. H. Meckling, "Theory of the Firm: Managerial Behavior, Agency Costs, and Ownership Structure," *Journal of Financial Economics* (October 1976), pp. 305–360.

Johnson, W. Bruce, "The Cross Sectional Stability of Financial Ratio Patterns," *Journal of Financial and Quantitative Analysis* (December 1979), pp. 1035–1048.

Johnson, W. Bruce, and Dan S. Dhaliwal, "LIFO Abandonment," *Journal of Accounting Research* (Autumn 1988), pp. 236–272.

Jones, Jennifer J., "Earnings Management During Import Relief Investigations," *Journal of Accounting Research* (Autumn 1991), pp. 193–228.

Joy, O. M., and C. P. Jones, "Earnings Reports and Market Efficiencies: An Analysis of the Contrary Evidence," *Journal of Financial Research* (Spring 1979), pp. 51–63.

K

Kaplan, Robert S., and Richard Roll, "Investor Evaluation of Accounting Information: Some Empirical Evidence," *Journal of Business* (April 1972), pp. 225–257.

Kaplan, Robert S., and Gabriel Urwitz, "Statistical Models of Bond Ratings: A Methodological Inquiry," *Journal of Business* (April 1979), pp. 231–261.

Kasznik, Ron, "On the Association Between Voluntary Disclosure and Earnings Management," *Journal of Accounting Research* (Spring 1999), pp. 57–82.

Kerstein, Joseph, and Sungsoo Kim, "The Incremental Information Content of Capital Expenditures," *The Accounting Review* (July 1995), pp. 513–526.

Kim, Moshe, and Giora Moore, "Economic vs. Accounting Depreciation," *Journal of Accounting and Economics* (April 1988), pp. 111–125.

Kimmel, Paul, and Terry D. Warfield, "Variation in Attributes of Redeemable Preferred Stock: Implications for Accounting Standards," *Accounting Horizons* (June 1993), pp. 30–40.

Kimmel, Paul, and Terry D. Warfield, "The Usefulness of Hybrid Security Classifications—Evidence from Redeemable Preferred Stock," *The Accounting Review* (January 1995), pp. 151–167.

Kinney, M., and R. H. Trezevat, "Taxes and the Timing of Corporate Capital Expenditures," *Journal of the American Taxation Association* (1993), pp. 40–62.

Kinney, William R., Jr., "Predicting Earnings: Entity Versus Subentity Data," *Journal of Accounting Research* (Spring 1971), pp. 127–136.

Kormendi, Roger, and Robert Lipe, "Earnings Innovations, Earnings Persistence, and Stock Returns," *Journal of Business* (July 1987), pp. 323–345.

Kothari, S. P., "Capital Markets Research in Accounting," *Journal of Accounting and Economics* (September 2001), pp. 105–232.

Kothari, S. P., Jay Shanken, and Richard G. Sloan, "Another Look at the Cross-section of Expected Stock Returns," *Journal of Finance* (March 1995), pp. 185–224.

L

Lakonishok, Josef, Andrei Shleifer, and Robert W. Vishny, "Contrarian Investment, Extrapolation and Risk," *Journal of Finance* (December 1994), pp. 1541–1578.

Landsman, Wayne, "An Empirical Investigation of Pension and Property Rights," *The Accounting Review* (October 1986), pp. 662–691.

Largay, James A., III, and Clyde P. Stickney, "Cash Flows, Ratio Analysis and the W. T. Grant Bankruptcy," *Financial Analysts Journal* (July/August 1980), pp. 51–54.

Lasman, Daniel A., and Roman L. Weil, "Adjusting the Debt-Equity Ratio," *Financial Analysts Journal* (September/October 1978), pp. 49–58.

Lau, Amy Hing-Ling, "A Five-State Financial Distress Prediction Model," *Journal of Accounting Research* (Spring 1987), pp. 127–138.

Leftwich, Richard W., "Evidence of the Impact of Mandatory Changes in Accounting Principles on Corporate Loan Agreements, *Journal of Accounting and Economics* (March 1981), pp. 3–36.

Leftwich, Richard W., "Accounting Information in Private Markets: Evidence from Private Lending Agreements," *The Accounting Review* (January 1983), pp. 23–42.

Lev, Baruch, "Industry Averages as Targets for Financial Ratios," *Journal of Accounting Research* (Autumn 1969), pp. 290–299.

Lev, Baruch, *Intangibles: Management, Measurement, and Reporting.* Washington D.C.: Brookings Institution Press, 2001.

Lev, Baruch, "On the Association Between Operating Leverage and Risk," *Journal of Financial and Quantitative Analysis* (September 1974), pp. 627–640.

Lev, Baruch, "The Impact of Accounting Regulation on the Stock Market: The Case of Oil and Gas Companies," *The Accounting Review* (July 1979), pp. 485–503.

Lev, Baruch, "On the Usefulness of Earnings and Earnings Research: Lessons and Directions from Two Decades of Empirical Research," *Journal of Accounting Research* (Supplement 1989), pp. 153–192.

Lev, Baruch, and Theodore Sougiannis, "The Capitalization, Amortization and Value-Relevance of R&D," *Journal of Accounting and Economics* (February 1996), pp. 107–138.

Lev, Baruch, and S. Ramu Thiagarajan, "Fundamental Information Analysis," *Journal of Accounting Research* (Autumn 1993), pp. 190–215.

Lilien, Steven, and Victor Pastena, "Determinants of Intra-Method Choice in the Oil and Gas Industry," *Journal of Accounting and Economics* (December 1982), pp. 145–170.

Lindhal, F. W., and W. E. Ricks, "Market Reactions to Announcements of Writeoffs," working paper, Fuqua School of Business, Duke University, January 1990.

Lipe, Robert C., "The Information Contained in the Components of Earnings," *Journal of Accounting Research* (Supplement 1986), pp. 37–64.

Livnat, Joshua, and Ashwinpaul C. Sondhi, "Finance Subsidiaries: Their Formation and Consolidation," *Journal of Business Finance & Accounting* (Spring 1986), pp. 137–147.

Livnat, Joshua, and Paul Zarowin, "The Incremental Informational Content of Cash-flow Components," *Journal of Accounting and Economics* (May 1990), pp. 25–46.

Lys, Thomas, "Mandated Accounting Changes and Debt Covenants: The Case of Oil and Gas Accounting," *Journal of Accounting and Economics* (April 1984), pp. 39–65.

M

Malmquist, David H. "Efficient Contracting and the Choice of Accounting Method in the Oil and Gas Industry," *Journal of Accounting and Economics* (January 1990), pp. 173–205.

Mandelker, Gershon M., and S. Ghon Rhee, "The Impact of the Degrees of Operating and Financial Leverage on Systematic Risk of Common Stock," *Journal of Financial and Quantitative Analysis* (March 1984), pp. 45–57.

Marshall, A., *Principles of Economics*. London: MacMillan Press Ltd., 1890.

Martin, L. G., and G. V. Henderson, "On Bond Ratings and Pension Obligations: A Note," *Journal of Financial and Quantitative Analysis* (December 1983), pp. 463–470.

McConnell, J. J., and C. J. Muscarella, "Corporate Capital Expenditure Decisions and the Market Value of the Firm," *Journal of Financial Economics* (1985), pp. 399–422.

Mellman, Martin, and Leopold Bernstein, "Lease Capitalization Under APB Opinion No. 5," *The New York Certified Accountant* (February 1966), pp. 115–122.

Mendenhall, R., "Evidence on the Possible Under-weighting of Earnings Related Information," *Journal of Accounting Research* (Spring 1991), pp. 170–179.

Mikhail, M., B. Walther, and R. Willis, "Does Forecast Accuracy Matter to Security Analysts?," *The Accounting Review* (April 1999), pp. 185–200.

Mills, L., "Book-tax Differences and Internal Revenue Service Adjustments," *Journal of Accounting Research* (Autumn 1998), pp. 343–356.

Mittelstaedt, H. F., W. D. Nichols, and P. R. Regier. "SFAS No. 106 and Benefit Reduction in Employer-Sponsored Retiree Health Care Plans." *The Accounting Review* (October 1995), pp. 535–556.

Moehrle, S. R., J. A. Reynolds-Moehrle, and J. S. Wallace, "How Informative Are Earnings Numbers that Exclude Goodwill Amortization?," *Accounting Horizons* (September 2001), pp. 243–255.

Mohrman, Mary Beth, "The Use of Fixed GAAP Provisions in Debt Contracts," *Accounting Horizons* (September 1996), pp. 78–91.

Morck, Randall, Andrei Shleifer, and Robert W. Vishny, "Do Managerial Objectives Drive Bad Acquisitions?" *Journal of Finance* (March 1990), pp. 31–48.

Moses, Douglas, "Income Smoothing and Incentives: Empirical Tests Using Accounting Changes," *The Accounting Review* (April 1987), pp. 358–377.

Most, Kenneth S., "Depreciation Expense and the Effect of Inflation," *Journal of Accounting Research* (Autumn 1984), pp. 782–788.

Mulford, Charles W., "The Importance of a Market Value Measurement of Debt in Leverage Ratios: Replications and Extensions," *Journal of Accounting Research* (Autumn 1985), pp. 897–906.

Murdoch, Brock, "The Information Content of FAS 33 Returns on Equity," *The Accounting Review* (April 1986), pp. 273–287.

Myers, Stewart C., and Nicholas S. Majluf, "Corporate Financing and Investment Decisions When Firms Have Information That Investors Do Not Have," *Journal of Financial Economics* (June 1984), pp. 187–221.

N

Nakayama, Mie, Steven Lilien, and Martin Benis, "Due Process and FAS No. 13," *Management Accounting* (April 1981), pp. 49–53.

Nissim, D., and S. Penman, "Ratio Analysis and Equity Valuation," working paper, Columbia University, 1999.

Noll, Daniel, "Accounting for Internal Use Software," *Journal of Accountancy* (September 1998), pp. 95–98.

Nurnberg, Hugo, "Inconsistencies and Ambiguities in Cash Flow Statements Under FASB Statement No. 95," *Accounting Horizons* (June 1993), pp. 60–75.

O

O'Brien, Patricia, "Analysts' Forecasts as Earnings Expectations," *Journal of Accounting and Economics* (January 1988), pp. 53–83.

Ohlson, James A., "Financial Ratios and the Probabilistic Prediction of Bankruptcy," *Journal of Accounting Research* (Spring 1980), pp. 109–131.

Ohlson, James A., "Accounting Earnings, Book Value and Dividends: The Theory of the Clean Surplus Equation (Part I)," working paper, Columbia University, 1989.

Ohlson, James A., "Earnings, Book Values and Dividends in Equity Valuation," *Contemporary Accounting Research* (Spring 1995), pp. 661–687.

Osterland, Andrew, "Knowledge Capital Scorecard: Treasures Revealed," *CFO* (April 2001).

Ou, Jane A., "The Information Content of Nonearnings Accounting Numbers as Earnings Predictors," *Journal of Accounting Research* (Spring 1990), pp. 144–162.

Ou, Jane A., and Stephen Penman, "Financial Statement Analysis and the Evaluation of Market-to-Book Ratios," working paper, University of California at Berkeley, 1995.

Ou, Jane A., and Stephen H. Penman, "Financial Statement Analysis and the Prediction of Stock Returns," *Journal of Accounting and Economics* (November 1989), pp. 295–329.

P

Pariser, David B., and Pierre L. Titard, "Impairment of Oil and Gas Properties," *Journal of Accountancy* (December 1991), pp. 52–62.

Patell, James M., and Mark A. Wolfson, "Good News, Bad News, and the Intraday Timing of Corporate Disclosure," *The Accounting Review* (July 1982), pp. 509–527.

Patell, James M., and Mark A. Wolfson, "The Intraday Speed of Adjustment of Stock Prices to Earnings and Dividend Announcements," *Journal of Financial Economics* (June 1984), pp. 223–252.

Peasnell, K., "Some Formal Connections Between Economic Values and Yields and Accounting Numbers," *Journal of Business, Finance and Accounting* (October 1982), pp. 361–381.

Peles, Y. C., and M. Schneller, "The Duration of the Adjustment Process of Financial Ratios," *The Review of Economics and Statistics* (November 1989), pp. 527–532.

Penman, Stephen, "An Evaluation of Accounting Rate-of-Return," *Journal of Accounting, Auditing and Finance* (Spring 1991), pp. 233–255.

Penman, Stephen H., "Return to Fundamentals," *Journal of Accounting, Auditing and Finance* (Fall 1992), pp. 465–483.

Penman, Stephen, "The Articulation of Price-Earnings Ratios and Market-to-Book Ratios and the Evaluation of Growth," *Journal of Accounting Research* (Autumn 1996), pp. 235–259.

Penman, S., "Combining Earnings and Book Values in Equity Valuation," *Contemporary Accounting Research* 15, 291–324.

Penman, S., and T. Sougiannis, "A Comparison of Dividend, Cash Flow, and Earnings Approaches to Equity Valuation," *Contemporary Accounting Research* (Fall 1998), pp. 343–383.

Pinches, George E., and Kent A. Mingo, "A Multivariate Analysis of Industrial Bond Ratings," *Journal of Finance* (March 1973), pp. 1–18.

Pinches, George E., and Kent A. Mingo, "The Role of Subordination and Industrial Bond Ratings," *Journal of Finance* (March 1975), pp. 201–206.

Pinches, George E., Kent A. Mingo, and J. Kent Caruthers, "The Stability of Financial Ratio Patterns in Industrial Organizations," *Journal of Finance* (May 1973), pp. 384–396.

Pinches, George E., A. A. Eubank, Kent A. Mingo, and J. Kent Caruthers, "The Hierarchical Classification of Financial Ratios," *Journal of Business Research* (October 1975), pp. 295–310.

Piotroski, J., "Value Investing: The Use of Historical Financial Statement Information to Separate Winners from Losers," *Journal of Accounting Research* (Supplement 2000), pp. 15–41.

Pogue, T., and R. Soldovsky, "What's in a Bond Rating," *Journal of Financial and Quantitative Analysis* (June 1969), pp. 201–228.

Preinreich, G. A. D., "Annual Survey of Economic Theory: The Theory of Depreciation," *Econometrica* (July 1938), pp. 219–241.

Press, Eric G., and Joseph B. Weintrop, "Accounting-Based Constraints in Public and Private Debt Agreements," *Journal of Accounting and Economics* (January 1990), pp. 65–95.

R

Rama, D. V., K. Raghunandan, and M. A. Geiger, "Economic Conditions, Audit Reports and Bankruptcies," working paper, University of Massachusetts-Dartmouth, October 1995.

Ramakrishnan, Ram, and Jacob Thomas, "Valuation of Permanent, Transitory and Price-Irrelevant Components of Reported Earnings," *Journal of Accounting Auditing and Finance* (Summer 1998), pp. 301–336.

Rapaccioli, Donna, and Allen Schiff, "Reporting Segment Sales Under APB Opinion No. 30," *Accounting Horizons* (December 1991), pp. 53–59.

Rayburn, Judy, "The Association of Operating Cash Flow and Accruals with Security Returns," *Journal of Accounting Research* (Supplement 1986), pp. 112–133.

Rees, Lynn, Susan Gill, and Richard Gore, "An Investigation of Asset Writedowns and Concurrent Abnormal Accruals," *Journal of Accounting Research* (Supplement 1996), pp. 157–169.

Reeve, James H., and Keith G. Stanga, "The LIFO Pooling Decision: Some Empirical Results from Accounting Practice," *Accounting Horizons* (March 1987), pp. 25–34.

Reilly, Frank K., "Using Cash Flows and Financial Ratios to Predict Bankruptcies," *Analyzing Investment Opportunities in Distressed and Bankrupt Companies.* Charlottesville, VA: The Institute of Chartered Financial Analysts, 1991.

Rendelman, R. J., Jr., C. P. Jones, and H. A. Latane, "Empirical Anomalies Based on Unexpected Earnings and the Importance of Risk Adjustments," *Journal of Financial Economics* (November 1982), pp. 269–287.

Richards, Verlyn D., and Eugene J. Laughlin, "A Cash Conversion Cycle Approach to Liquidity Analysis," *Financial Management* (Spring 1980), pp. 32–38.

Ricks, William E., "The Market's Response to the 1974 LIFO Adoption," *Journal of Accounting Research* (Autumn 1982, Part I), pp. 367–387.

Ricks, William E., and John S. Hughes, "Market Reactions to a Non-Discretionary Accounting Change: The Case of Long-Term Investments," *The Accounting Review* (January 1985), pp. 33–52.

Robert Morris Associates, *Annual Statement Studies.* Philadelphia: RMA, 1999.

Robinson, John R., and Philip B. Shane, "Acquisition Accounting Method and Bid Premia for Target Firms," *The Accounting Review* (January 1990), pp. 25–48.

Roll, Richard, "The Hubris Hypothesis of Corporate Takeovers," *Journal of Business* (April 1986), pp. 197–216.

Ronen, Joshua, and Simcha Sadan, *Smoothing Income Numbers: Objectives, Means, and Implications.* Reading, MA: Addison-Wesley, 1981.

Rosenberg, Barr, and James Guy, "Beta and Investment Fundamentals," *The Financial Analysts Journal*, Vol. 32(3) 1976, pp. 60–72.

Rosenberg, Barr, and Walt McKibben, "The Prediction of Systematic and Specific Risk in Common Stocks," *Journal of Financial and Quantitative Analysis* (March 1973), pp. 317–333.

Rosenberg, Barr, Keith Reid, and Ronald Lansten, "Persuasive Evidence of Market Inefficiency," *Journal of Portfolio Management*, Vol. 11, 1984, pp. 9–17.

Roussey, R. S., E. L. Ten Eyck, and M. Blanco-Best, "Three New SASs: Closing the Communications Gap," *Journal of Accountancy* (December 1988), pp. 44–52.

Rue, Joseph C., David E. Tosh, and William B. Francis, "Accounting for Interest Rate Swaps," *Management Accounting* (January 1988), pp. 43–49.

Ryan, Stephen, "Structural Models of the Accounting Process and Earnings," unpublished dissertation, Stanford University, 1988.

Ryan, Steven, "A Survey of Research Relating Accounting Numbers to Systematic Equity Risk, with Implications for Risk Disclosure Policy and Future Research," *Accounting Horizons* (September 1997), pp. 82–95.

Ryan, Stephen G., and Paul Zarowin, "On the Ability of the Classical Errors in Variables Approach to Explain Earnings Response Coefficients and R^2s in Alternative Valuation Models," *Journal of Accounting, Auditing and Finance* (Fall 1995), pp. 767–786.

S

Sansing, Richard, "Valuing the Deferred Tax Liability," *Journal of Accounting Research* (Autumn 1998), pp. 357–363.

Sarath, B., B. Lev, and T. Sougiannis, "R&D Reporting Biases and their Consequences," working paper, Baruch College, 2000.

Saunders, Anthony, *Financial Institutions Management: A Modern Perspective*, 2nd ed. (Chicago, IL: Richard D. Irwin), 1997.

Savich, Richard S., and Laurence A. Thompson, "Resource Allocation Within the Product Life Cycle," *MSU Business Topics* (Autumn 1978), pp. 35–44.

Schiff, Allen I., "The Other Side of LIFO," *Journal of Accountancy* (May 1983), pp. 120–121.

Schiff, Michael, "A Closer Look at Variable Costing," *Management Accounting* (August 1987), pp. 36–39.

Schipper, Katherine, and Abbie J. Smith, "Effects of Recontracting on Shareholder Wealth: The Case of Voluntary Spin-offs," *Journal of Financial Economics* (December 1983), pp. 437–467.

Scott, James, "The Probability of Bankruptcy: A Comparison of Empirical Predictions and Theoretical Models," *Journal of Banking and Finance* (September 1981), pp. 317–344.

Selling, Thomas I., and George H. Sorter, "FASB Statement No. 52 and Its Implications for Financial Statement Analysis," *The Financial Analysts Journal* (May/June 1983), pp. 64–69.

Selling, Thomas I., and Clyde P. Stickney, "The Effects of Business Environment and Strategy on a Firm's Rate of Return on Assets," *The Financial Analysts Journal* (January/February 1989), pp. 43–52.

Selling, Thomas I., and Clyde P. Stickney, "Disaggregating the Rate of Return on Common Shareholders' Equity: A New Approach," *Accounting Horizons* (December 1990), pp. 9–17.

Selto, Frank H., and Maclyn L. Clouse, "An Investigation of Managers' Adaptations to SFAS No. 2: Accounting for Research and Development Costs," *Journal of Accounting Research* (Autumn 1985), pp. 700–717.

Servaes, Henri, "Tobin's Q and the Gains from Takeovers," *Journal of Finance* (March 1991), pp. 409–419.

Shaw, W. and H. Weir, "Organizational Form Choice and the Valuation of Oil and Gas Producers," *The Accounting Review* (October 1993), pp. 657–667.

Shevlin, Terry, "The Valuation of R&D Firms with R&D Limited Partnerships" *The Accounting Review* (January 1991), pp. 1–21.

Silhan, Peter A., "Simulated Mergers of Existent Autonomous Firms: A New Approach to Segmentation Research," *Journal of Accounting Research* (Spring 1982), pp. 255–262.

Skinner, R. C., "Fixed Asset Lives and Replacement Cost Accounting," *Journal of Accounting Research* (Spring 1982), pp. 210–226.

Sloan, Richard G., "Do Stock Prices Fully Reflect Information in Accruals and Cash Flows About Future Earnings?," *The Accounting Review* (July 1996), pp. 289–316.

Smith, Clifford, Jr., and L. Macdonald Wakeman, "Determinants of Corporate Leasing Policy," *Journal of Finance* (July 1985), pp. 895–908.

Smith, Clifford, Jr., and Jerold B. Warner, "On Financial Contracting: An Analysis of Bond Covenants," *Journal of Financial Economics* (June 1979), pp. 117–161.

Sobehart, J., S. Keenan, and R. Stein, "Benchmarking Quantitative Default Risk Models: A Validation Methodology," *Moody's Investment Services* (March 2000).

Solomons, David, "The FASB's Conceptual Framework: An Evaluation," *Journal of Accountancy* (June 1986), pp. 114–124.

Sondhi, Ashwinpaul C., "Analyzing the Credit Risk of Emerging Market Debt," *Credit Analysis of Nontraditional Debt Securities*, AIMR 1995.

Sondhi, Ashwinpaul C., George H. Sorter, and Gerald I. White, "Transactional Analysis," *Financial Analysts Journal* (September/October 1987), pp. 57–64.

Sondhi, Ashwinpaul C., George H. Sorter, and Gerald I. White, "Cash Flow Redefined: FAS 95 and Security Analysis," *The Financial Analysts Journal* (November/December 1988), pp. 19–20.

Sorter, George H., and George Benston, "Appraising the Defensive Position of a Firm: The Interval Measure," *The Accounting Review* (October 1960), pp. 633–640.

Sterling, Robert R, *Theory of the Measurement of Enterprise Income*. Lawrence, KS: University Press of Kansas, 1970.

Stewart, G. Bennet, III, *The Quest for Value*. New York: Harper Business, 1991.

Stewart, John E., "The Challenges of Hedge Accounting," *Journal of Accountancy* (November 1989), pp. 48–62.

Stewart, Thomas A., "Accounting Gets Radical," *Fortune* (April 16, 2001).

Stickel, Scott E., "The Timing of and Incentives for Annual Earnings Forecasts Near Interim Earnings Announcements," *Journal of Accounting and Economics* (July 1989), pp. 275–292.

Stickel, Scott E., "Predicting Individual Analysts Earnings Forecasts," *Journal of Accounting Research* (Autumn 1990), pp. 409–417.

Stickney, Clyde P., "Analyzing Effective Corporate Tax Rates," *The Financial Analysts Journal* (July/August 1979), pp. 45–54.

Stober, Thomas L., "The Incremental Information Content of Financial Statement Disclosures: The Case of LIFO Liquidations," *Journal of Accounting Research* (Supplement 1986), pp. 138–160.

Stober, Thomas L., "Do Prices Behave as if Accounting Is Conservative? Cross-sectional Evidence from the Feltham-Ohlson Valuation Model," working paper, University of Notre Dame, October 1996.

Street, Donna L., Nancy B. Nichols, and Sidney J. Gray, "Segment Disclosures under SFAS No. 131: Has Business Segment Reporting Improved?," *Accounting Horizons* (September 2000), pp. 259–285.

Strong, John S., and John R. Meyer, "Asset Writedowns: Managerial Incentives and Security Returns," *Journal of Finance* (July 1987), pp. 643–663.

Sunder, Shyam, "Relationship Between Accounting Changes and Stock Prices: Problems of Measurement and Some Empirical Evidence," *Journal of Accounting Research* (Supplement 1973), pp. 1–45.

Sunder, Shyam, "Properties of Accounting Numbers Under Full Costing and Successful-Efforts Costing in the Petroleum Industry," *The Accounting Review* (January 1976), pp. 1–18.

Swaminathan, Siva, "The Impact of SEC Mandated Segment Data on Price Variability and Divergence of Beliefs," *The Accounting Review* (January 1991), pp. 23–41.

T

Teets, W., and C. Wasley, "Estimating Earnings Response Coefficients: Pooled versus Firm-Specific Models," *Journal of Accounting & Economics* (June 1996), pp. 279–296.

Teoh, S., I. Welch, and T. Wong, "Earnings Management and the Long-Run Underperformance of Seasoned Equity Offerings," *Journal of Financial Economics* (October 1998a), pp. 63–100.

Teoh, S., I. Welch, and T. Wong, "Earnings Management and the Long-run Underperformance of Initial Public Offerings, *Journal of Finance* (December 1998b), pp. 1935–1974.

Todd, Kenneth R., Jr., "How One Financial Officer Uses Inflation-Adjusted Accounting Data," *The Financial Executive* (October 1982), pp. 13–19.

Train, John, *Money Masters*. New York: Harper & Row, 1987.

Tse, Senyo, "LIFO Liquidations," *Journal of Accounting Research* (Spring 1990), pp. 229–238.

V

Venkataraman, R., "The Impact of SFAS 131 on Financial Analysts' Information Environment," unpublished dissertation, Penn State University, 2001.

Vigeland, Robert L., "The Market Reaction to Statement of Financial Accounting Standards No. 2," *The Accounting Review* (April 1981), pp. 309–325.

W

Wang, Shiing-Wu, "The Relation Between Firm Size and Effective Tax Rates: A Test of Firms' Political Success," *The Accounting Review* (January 1991), pp. 158–169.

Watts, Ross, "The Time-Series Behavior of Quarterly Earnings," working paper, University of Newcastle, England, 1975.

Watts, Ross, and Richard W. Leftwich, "The Time Series of Annual Accounting Earnings," *Journal of Accounting Research* (Fall 1977), pp. 253–271.

Watts, Ross, and Jerold L. Zimmerman, *Positive Accounting Theory*. Englewood Cliffs, NJ: Prentice Hall. 1986.

Watts, Ross, and Jerold L. Zimmerman, "Positive Accounting Theory: A Ten Year Perspective," *The Accounting Review* (January 1990), pp. 131–156.

West, Richard R., "An Alternative Approach to Predicting Corporate Bond Ratings," *Journal of Accounting Research* (Spring 1970), pp. 118–127.

Wild, John, "The Prediction Performance of a Structural Model of Accounting Numbers," *Journal of Accounting Research* (Spring 1987), pp. 139–160.

Williamson, R. W. "Evidence on the Selective Reporting of Financial Ratios," *The Accounting Review* (April 1984), pp. 296–299.

Wilson, Peter G., "The Relative Information Content of Accruals and Cash Flows: Combined Evidence at the Earnings Announcement and Annual Report Release Date," *Journal of Accounting Research* (Supplement 1986), pp. 165–200.

Z

Zarowin, Paul, "What Determines Earnings-Price Ratios: Revisited," *Journal of Accounting, Auditing and Finance* (Summer 1990), pp. 439–454.

Zarowin, Paul, "Does the Stock Market Overreact to Corporate Earnings Information?" *Journal of Finance* (December 1989), pp. 1385–1399.

Zarowin, Paul, "Size, Seasonality and Stock Market Overreaction," *Journal of Financial and Quantitative Analysis* (March 1990), pp. 113–124.

Ziebart, David A., and David H. Kim, "An Examination of the Market Reactions Associated with SFAS No. 8 and SFAS No. 52," *The Accounting Review* (April 1987), pp. 343–357.

Zimmerman, Jerold L., "Taxes and Firm Size," *Journal of Accounting and Economics* (August 1983), pp. 119–149.

Zmijewski, Mark E., and Robert L. Hagerman, "An Income Strategy Approach to the Positive Theory of Accounting Standard Setting/Choice," *Journal of Accounting and Economics* (August 1981), pp. 129–149.

INDEX